McGraw-Hill
MEDICAL
DICTIONARY
for Allied Health

McGraw-Hill
MEDICAL DICTIONARY
for Allied Health

Myrna Breskin
Chestnut Hill Enterprises, Inc.

Kevin Dumith
Sanford Brown Institute

Enid Pearsons

Robert Seeman

18 19 DOC/DOC 17 16

ISBN-13: 978-0-07-758586-0
ISBN-10: 0-07-758586-0

Learning Solutions Manager: Melani Theis
Production Editor: Kathy Phelan

Contents

Anatomical Plates (Following page 264)

Appendices   397

Introduction

McGraw-Hill Medical Dictionary for Allied Health serves the needs of the allied health market—those people who work or will work alongside the medical practitioner in a wide variety of roles. Everyone from students in the many allied health career programs to workers in the field will find that this dictionary addresses their need to have a reference book written specifically for their understanding. You, the user, will find simple clear definitions with an easily understandable pronunciation system.

The front section of this dictionary describes the ways to most effectively use this reference tool. As you read through the next section, "How To Use This Dictionary," you will learn the pronunciation system, how to use the cross-references, style issues, and the word-building feature at the end of many entries. You will learn about the anatomy features included in this book and how they can help you understand the anatomy of the human body. This section also covers the extensive reference appendices which will serve you, the allied health user, as a comprehensive reference tool that you can go to whenever you have a question about specific areas of allied health.

While the *McGraw-Hill Medical Dictionary for Allied Health* can be used by itself as a reference tool, it is also geared to accompany many McGraw-Hill products in the allied health field. Go to www.mhhe.com for more information on the following Allied Health titles.

Computers in the Medical Office, 5/e (0-07-311213-5)
From Patient to Payment: Insurance Procedures for the Medical Office, 5/e (0-07-325479-7)
Insurance Coding and Electronic Claims for the Medical Office, (0-07-305307-4)
Introduction to Medical Terminology, (0-07-302261-6)
Law and Ethics for Medical Careers, 4/e (0-07-302263-2)
Medical Assisting: Administrative and Clinical Competencies, 2/e (0 07 297410 9)
Medical Insurance: An Integrated Claims Process Approach, 3/e (0-07-325645-5)
Medical Language for Modern Health Care, (0-07-327294-9)
Medical Terminology Word Builder and Communication Workbook, (0-07-331544-3)
Medical Terminology: A Programmed Approach, (0-07-333505-3)
Medical Terminology: Language for Health Care, 2/e, (0-07-327295-7)
Medical Terminology Essentials, (0-07-325644-7)

About the Authors

Myrna Breskin   The ad in the newspaper said, "Etymologist, if you know what it is, come in." Myrna Breskin had just graduated from the City College of New York with a major in linguistics and a minor in classics. She got the job, eventually becoming Chief Etymology Editor of the first edition of the American Heritage Dictionary and from there branched out into many other reference books including other dictionaries and encyclopedias. Next, she joined the staff at McGraw-Hill in the editing department of the postsecondary division. She left McGraw-Hill ten years later as a Senior Acquisitions Editor. She then went to work as a freelance writer and editor while raising her twin boys in Connecticut, with her husband Daniel. For the past 15 years, she has worked on allied health and other postsecondary products.

Kevin Dumith   Kevin Dumith is the Client Services Coordinator in Dallas, Texas for the Organ Procurement Organization (OPO) - Southwest Transplant Alliance (STA) and provides his hospital's healthcare professionals education on organ and tissue donation. Mr. Dumith has been in education for many years both as an administrator and classroom instructor. Prior to his present position he was an Interim Surgical Technology Program Director and Clinical Education Coordinator at Sanford Brown College in the Allied Health Fields. There, he also served as Community Relations Liaison between the college and the healthcare community. Mr. Dumith holds a B.S. degree in Health Kinesiology Education with a minor in Biology from Fort Hays State University, M.S. from Texas A & M-Commerce, and will earn his MBA from Texas Women's University in the Spring of 2007. He now enjoys a quite life with his family that consists of wife Bobbi, children Julia and Darren and bassett hound Breezy.

Enid Pearsons   Enid Pearsons began her lexicographic career as pronunciation editor for the first edition of *The Random House Dictionary of the English Language: The Unabridged Edition*. After she earned her Master's degree at Teachers College, Columbia University, and post-Masters academic work in linguistics, she returned to Random House as Senior Editor in charge of pronunciation and style for their entire line of dictionaries, including the second edition of the unabridged dictionary. At Random House, she edited thesauruses, spellers, and general dictionaries and served as in-house editor for specialized dictionaries in fields as diverse as computers, law, medicine, and sign language. Ms. Pearsons played a major role in the early adoption by Random House of dictionary computerization. Since retiring from that post in 2001, she has served as consultant on projects for various publishing houses—setting up, revising, and implementing pronunciation systems and pioneering the use of emerging computer software and Unicode fonts to enable diacritical symbols, such as the ones used in this book, as well as symbols from the International Phonetic Alphabet (IPA), to be inputted directly into manuscripts. Ms. Pearsons is a member of the American Dialect Society and the International Linguistics Association and was recently elected a Fellow of the Dictionary Society of North America. She lives with her husband in Brooklyn, New York, and visits her daughter, son-in-law, and new grandson in New England whenever possible.

Dr. Robert G. Seeman   Dr. Seeman graduated from Oberlin College, received his MD from Case Western Reserve, and participated in advanced studies at Harvard Medical School where he was an instructor in pediatric anesthesia. Dr. Seeman has practiced for nearly 40 years in the United States and Europe, during which time he has published many articles in medical journals and made numerous professional presentations. Currently, he divides his professional time between Paris, France, and San Diego, California. In addition to his medical credentials and practice, he is also an accomplished pianist, chorister, and *tanguista*.

Acknowledgments

For insightful reviews, criticisms, helpful suggestions, and information, we would like to acknowledge the following:

Laura Abbott, BS, MS, NCTMB, ACSM HFD
Georgia State University
Decatur, GA

Bernice Bicknase, AAS, BS
Ivy Tech Community College-Northeast
Fort Wayne, IN

Kathy Bode, RN, BS, MS
Flint Hills Technical College
Emporia, KS

Nia Bullock, Ph.D.
Miller-Motte Technical College
Cary, NC

Michelle L. Carfagna, CST, RMA, RHE
Brevard Community College-Surgical Technology
Cocoa, FL

Michael Gallucci, PT, MS
New York Medical College
Valhalla, NY

Donna E. Guisado, BS, RDA
North-West College
West Covina, CA

Shawnie Haas, RN/MBA
YVCC
Wapato, WA

Donna D. Kyle-Brown, Ph.D., RMA
Blue Cliff College of Gulfport
Gulfport, MS

Nelly Mangarova, MD
Heald College
Milpitas, CA

Gloria Pring, CPhT
National Institute of Technology
Cross Lanes, WV

Candace Schladenhauffen, MS, RRT-NPS, RPFT, RCP
Ivy Tech Community College of Indiana, Northeast
Fort Wayne, IN

David Sessoms, M.Ed., CMA
Miller-Motte Technical College
Morrisville, NC

Kelly Smith-Campbell, MA
Miller-Motte Technical College
Cary, NC

Nina Thierer, CMA, BS, CPC, CCAT
Ivy Tech
Fort Wayne, IN

Charlene Thiessen, M.Ed., CMT
GateWay Community College
Phoenix, AZ

Jim Wallace, MHSA
Marie College Los Angeles
Los Angeles, CA

How to Use This Dictionary

Alphabetical Pages

Each letter starts on a new page with a colored thumb index so you can find it easily as you flip through the book. At the top of each of these pages are a large colored letter also to guide you in finding the beginning of the letters easily.

The pages that follow the letter-opening page have a rule across the top above which sit the range of words that appear on that page. For example, the following page begins with **cardiorrhaphy** and ends with **cartilage.**

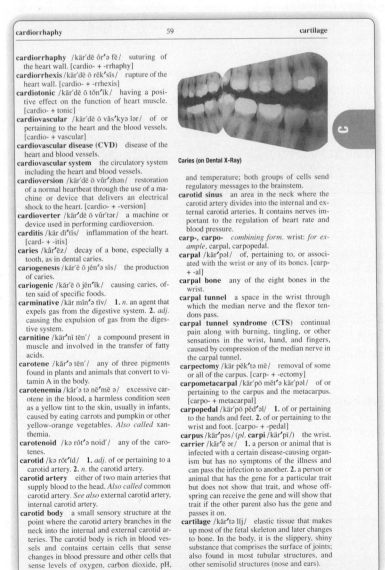

cardiorrhaphy /kär′dē ôr′ə fē/ suturing of the heart wall. [cardio- + -rrhaphy]

cardiorrhexis /kär′dē ō rĕk′sĭs/ rupture of the heart wall. [cardio- + -rrhexis]

cardiotonic /kär′dē ō tŏn′ĭk/ having a positive effect on the function of heart muscle. [cardio- + tonic]

cardiovascular /kär′dē ō văs′kyə lər/ of or pertaining to the heart and the blood vessels. [cardio- + vascular]

cardiovascular disease (CVD) disease of the heart and blood vessels.

cardiovascular system the circulatory system including the heart and blood vessels.

cardioversion /kär′dē ō vûr′zhən/ restoration of a normal heartbeat through the use of a machine or device that delivers an electrical shock to the heart. [cardio- + -version]

cardioverter /kär′dē ō vûr′tər/ a machine or device used in performing cardioversion.

carditis /kär dī′tĭs/ inflammation of the heart. [card- + -itis]

caries /kâr′ēz/ decay of a bone, especially a tooth, as in dental caries.

cariogenesis /kăr′ē ō jĕn′ə sĭs/ the production of caries.

cariogenic /kăr′ē ō jĕn′ĭk/ causing caries, often said of specific foods.

carminative /kär mĭn′ə tĭv/ **1.** *n.* an agent that expels gas from the digestive system. **2.** *adj.* causing the expulsion of gas from the digestive system.

carnitine /kär′nĭ tēn′/ a compound present in muscle and involved in the transfer of fatty acids.

carotene /kăr′ə tēn′/ any of three pigments found in plants and animals that convert to vitamin A in the body.

carotenemia /kăr′ə tə nē′mē ə/ excessive carotene in the blood, a harmless condition seen as a yellow tint to the skin, usually in infants, caused by eating carrots and pumpkin or other yellow-orange vegetables. *Also called* xanthemia.

carotenoid /kə rŏt′ə noid′/ any of the carotenes.

carotid /kə rŏt′ĭd/ **1.** *adj.* of or pertaining to a carotid artery. **2.** *n.* the carotid artery.

carotid artery either of two main arteries that supply blood to the head. *Also called* common carotid artery. *See also* external carotid artery, internal carotid artery.

carotid body a small sensory structure at the point where the carotid artery branches in the neck into the internal and external carotid arteries. The carotid body is rich in blood vessels and contains certain cells that sense changes in blood pressure and other cells that sense levels of oxygen, carbon dioxide, pH,

Caries (on Dental X-Ray)

and temperature; both groups of cells send regulatory messages to the brainstem.

carotid sinus an area in the neck where the carotid artery divides into the internal and external carotid arteries. It contains nerves important to the regulation of heart rate and blood pressure.

carp-, carpo- *combining form.* wrist: *for example,* carpal, carpopedal.

carpal /kär′pəl/ of, pertaining to, or associated with the wrist or any of its bones. [carp- + -al]

carpal bone any of the eight bones in the wrist.

carpal tunnel a space in the wrist through which the median nerve and the flexor tendons pass.

carpal tunnel syndrome (CTS) continual pain along with burning, tingling, or other sensations in the wrist, hand, and fingers, caused by compression of the median nerve in the carpal tunnel.

carpectomy /kär pĕk′tə mē/ removal of some or all of the carpus. [carp- + -ectomy]

carpometacarpal /kär′pō mĕt′ə kär′pəl/ of or pertaining to the carpus and the metacarpus. [carpo- + metacarpal]

carpopedal /kär′pō pĕd′əl/ **1.** of or pertaining to the hands and feet. **2.** of or pertaining to the wrist and foot. [carpo- + -pedal]

carpus /kär′pəs/ (*pl.* **carpi** /kär′pī/) the wrist.

carrier /kăr′ē ər/ **1.** a person or animal that is infected with a certain disease-causing organism but has no symptoms of the illness and can pass the infection to another. **2.** a person or animal that has the gene for a particular trait but does not show that trait, and whose offspring can receive the gene and will show that trait if the other parent also has the gene and passes it on.

cartilage /kär′tə lĭj/ elastic tissue that makes up most of the fetal skeleton and later changes to bone. In the body, it is the slippery, shiny substance that comprises the surface of joints; also found in most tubular structures, and other semisolid structures (nose and ears).

Main Entries

Each new main entry is in its place in alphabetical order and appears in boldface. Alphabetical order is based on the complete entry so a two-word phrase is alphabetized as though it was one word. In some medical dictionaries, you have to look for an entry out of alphabetical order. For example, in this dictionary, adducens nerve is in the A words, but in some dictionaries, you would look in the N words under nerve. For the allied health user, it is felt that pure alphabetical order is the most user-friendly option.

M

macerate /măs′ə rāt′/ to soften something, as tissue or an organ, by steeping or soaking.

Macewen('s) sign /mə kyōō′ən(z)/ a dull sound heard on percussion (tapping) of the skull, indicating hydrocephalus.

Machado-Joseph disease /mə chä′dō jō′zəf, -səf/ a degenerative disease of the central nervous system that tends to occur in families of Portuguese ancestry.

macro- *prefix.* large; long; *for example,* macrocephaly.

macroadenoma /măk′rō ăd′ə nō′mə/ a pituitary tumor larger than ten millimeters in diameter. [macro- + adenoma]

macrobiotic /măk′rō bī ŏt′ĭk/ **diet** a highly restricted diet consisting mostly of whole grains and beans thought to promote well-being and longevity.

macrocephalic /măk′rō sə făl′ĭk/ of or related to macrocephaly.

macrocephalus /măk′rō sĕf′ə ləs/ or **macrocephaly** /măk′rō sĕf′ə lē/ having an abnormally large skull, acquired either after or prior to birth. *See also* megacephaly. [macro- + -cephaly]

macrocheilia /măk′rō kī′lē ə/ having abnormally enlarged lips.

macrocranium /măk′rō krā′nē əm/ an overly large skull, especially the bones of the skull that contain the brain, often seen in hydrocephaly. [macro- + -cranium]

macrocyte /măk′rə sīt′/ an unusually large red blood cell, indicative of certain diseases, such as pernicious anemia (a disease with vitamin B12 deficiency). [macro- + -cyte]

macrocytic /măk′rə sĭt′ĭk/ of or pertaining to macrocytes.

macrocytosis /măk′rō sī tō′sĭs/ a condition marked by unusually large numbers of macrocytes in the blood. [macro- + -cytosis]

macrodactylia /măk′rō dăk tĭl′ē ə/ a condition with unusual enlargement of one or more digits (fingers or toes).

macrodontia /măk′rō dŏn′shē ə/ condition in which one or several teeth are enlarged.

macroglia /mă krŏg′lē ə/ a large star-shaped neuroglia (nerve cell) with many branches. *Also called* astrocyte.

macroglobulin /măk′rō glŏb′yə lĭn/ a globulin (a type of protein found in the body) of high molecular weight. [macro- + globulin]

macroglobulinemia /măk′rō glŏb′yə lĭ nē′mē ə/ increased levels of macroglobulins in the blood serum. [macro- + globulin + -emia]

macroglossia /măk′rō glŏs′ē ə/ having an abnormally large tongue, either by birth or as a result of a pathology.

macrognathia /măk′rō nă′thē ə/ having an unusually large or elongated jaw.

macrolides /măk′rō lĭdz/ any of several common antibiotics that are produced by a certain species of *Streptomyces*, such as erythromycin.

macromastia /măk′rō măs′tē ə/ having abnormally large breasts.

macrophage /măk′rə fāj′/ any of the large phagocytes (scavenger cells) that rid the body of unwanted microorganisms and cell debris by engulfing and devouring them (phagocytosis). [macro- + -phage]

macrorhinia /măk′rō rīn′ē ə/ having an unusually large nose, either by birth or resulting from a pathology.

macroscopic /măk′rə skŏp′ĭk/ large enough to be examined with the naked eye, i.e., without the use of a microscope. [macro- + -scopic]

macrosomia /măk′rə sō′mē ə/ having an abnormally large-sized body, as in gigantism.

macrovascular /măk′rō văs′kyə lər/ of or related to the large blood vessels. [macro- + vascular]

macula /măk′yə lə/ (*pl.* **maculae** /măk′yə lē′/) **1.** a small spot **2.** a discolored flat spot or patch on the skin; macule. **3.** the macula lutea of the eye.

macula lutea /lōō′tē ə/ (*pl.* **maculae luteae** /lōō′tē ē/) a small yellowish spot on the retina of the eye where vision is most acute.

macular /măk′yə lər/ of or related to the macula.

macular cyst /sĭst/ a hole in the macula lutea of the eye, usually caused by the shrinking of the vitreous humor (jellylike substance) in the eye.

macular degeneration /dĭ jĕn′ə rā′shən/ a disease in which the macula lutea of the eye degenerates, resulting in a progressive loss of sharp, central vision. *Also known as* age-related macular degeneration.

M

abdominocentesis /ăb dŏm′ə nō sĕn tē′sĭs/ the removal of fluid from the abdominal cavity, accomplished by using a needle or other catheter. [abdomino- + -centesis]

abdominohysterectomy /ăb dŏm′ə nō hĭs′tə rĕk′tə mē/ a hysterectomy performed through an incision into the abdominal wall. [abdomino- + hysterectomy]

abdominopelvic /ăb dŏm′ə nō pĕl′vĭk/ of or relating to the abdomen and pelvic area. [abdomino- + pelvic]

abdominopelvic cavity the area of the trunk below the chest, including the abdominal and pelvic cavities.

abdominopelvic quadrants any of four segments into which the abdominopelvic area can be divided by vertical and horizontal lines through its midpoint. *See also* abdominopelvic regions.

abdominopelvic regions areas of the abdominal and pelvic cavities identified by their relative positions: right upper quadrant, right lower quadrant, left upper quadrant, left lower quadrant.

abdominoperineal /ăb dŏm′ə nō pĕr′ə nē′əl/ relating to both the abdomen and the perineum (tissue between the anus and scrotum in men and between the anus and vaginal opening in women). [abdomino- + perineal]

Some main entries have variant forms that are pronounced the same. These words are separated by a slash. A word may have two or more variant spellings that are pronounced differently. These are separated by the word *or*. A phrasal entry may have several variants. These are also separated by the word *or*.

disc/disk /dĭsk/ a thick, round piece of cartilage (fibrous tissue) separating the vertebrae (bones of the spinal column).

akinesia /ā′kĭ nē′zhə/ or **akinesis** /ā′kĭ nē′sĭs/ the inability to move voluntarily caused by brain dysfunction. [a- + -kinesia]

advance directive or **advance medical directive** a legal document signed by the patient or patient's agent, specifying the acceptable kinds of medical measures that may be used to prolong life in a life-threatening situation. *Also called* durable power of attorney, living will.

Main entries were chosen based on the allied health market. Also included are informal familiar terms which are defined and cross-referenced to appropriate medical terms.

nosebleed /nōz′blēd′/ bleeding from the nose. *Also called* epistaxis, rhinorrhagia.

Combining forms, suffixes, and prefixes are entered throughout and examples given for each entry. The used of combining forms and the combining vowel is discussed in the word building part of this section starting on page xv.

bacteri-, bacterio- *combining form.* bacteria: *for example,* bactericide, bacteriology.

brachy- *prefix.* short: *for example,* brachytherapy.

-acusis, -acousis *suffix.* hearing: *for example,* anacusis, presbyacousis.

Common abbreviations as well as abbreviations commonly used for many of the main entries are entered. The definition of an abbreviation is either a cross-reference to the main entry or has an explanation at the abbreviation itself.

> **BUN** *abbreviation.* blood urea nitrogen.
> **blood urea nitrogen (BUN)** /yōō rē′ə nī′trə jən/ a determination of the amount of nitrogen (in the form of urea) present in the blood, providing a quick rough estimate of kidney function.

> **MASS syndrome** /măs/ an inherited disorder of the body's connective tissue that results in the following group of symptoms: *m*itral valve prolapse, *a*ortic anomalies, *s*keletal changes, and *s*kin changes (MASS); it closely resembles Marfan('s) syndrome.

Certain abbreviations are now on a "forbidden" list. This list was compiled by the Joint Commission on Accreditation of Healthcare Organizations (JCHAO) to help minimize medical errors. Such abbreviations can no longer be written and must be spelled out in full. To help the user be aware of these limitations, we have put a symbol as a warning and we have inserted Appendix B which covers this in detail.

> **q.i.d., qid** *abbreviation.* Latin *quatuor in die,* four times a day.

Abbreviations that are acronyms for common organizations include the appropriate websites in case you wish to get further information.

> **AHIMA** *abbreviation.* American Health Information Management Association (www. ahima.org)

There are some ongoing style issues in medical terminology. The use of eponyms (names that are derived from a person's name) is quite common in the naming of diseases. In the past and in some uses, such eponyms contained an apostrophe followed by the letter s as in Parkinson's disease. Lately, such names are being shown without the apostrophe s. In this dictionary, we present both options by putting the ('s) in parentheses. Appendix G, Medical Terminology Style, covers this subject in more detail.

> **Parkinson('s) disease** /pär′kĭn sən(z)/ a progressive neurologic disease occurring mostly in older adults, marked chiefly by tremors, muscle weakness and rigidity, and changes in posture and gait as a result of a deficiency of dopamine.

Pronunciations

Pronunciations are given for all single-word entries and for those parts of phrasal entries that do not appear elsewhere or are not commonly know words. The pronunciation key (shown on page xiv) tells you how to pronounce the sounds. Pronunciations are also available on the CD-ROM that accompanies this book.

Pronunciation Key

ă	cap	ôr	for
ā	cape		
âr	care	oi	poise
ä	car, father	o͝o	foot, put
		o͞o	food, rude
b	boy	ou	loud, crowd
ch	chip	p	peppy
d	dad	r	rear
ě	fed	s	soma, less
ē	feed	sh	shop
êr	fear	t	tip, matter
f	fun	th	thin
		_th_	this, other
g	good	ŭ	run, other
h	happy		
hw	what		[no ŭ; use yo͞o for few, fuse]
		ûr	fur, bird, dermatology, worse
ĭ	lit	v	vacuum
ī	lite		
j	joy, gentle	w	witty, bewitch [but not in an (ou) pron, like: however = (hou ěv′ər)
k	cat, kitten	y	young
l	less	z	zigzag, Xanax
m	make	zh	measure, dressage
n	number	ə	above, brother, animate, commit, fungus
ŏ	hot	′	secondary stress
ō	hope, coat	ˈ	primary stress
ô	law		

The following examples show pronunciations. Note that some plurals are given pronunciations where it is felt that they are needed.

> **macula** /măk′yə lə/ (*pl.* **maculae** /măk′yə lē′/) **1.** a small spot **2.** a discolored flat spot or patch on the skin; macule **3.** the macula lutea of the eye.
> **adenoma** /ăd′ə nō′mə/ (*pl.* **adenomas** or **adenomata** /ăd′ə nō′mə tə/) a usually benign growth of epithelial tissue. [aden- + -oma]

Definitions

Definitions are given as clearly as possible and, where necessary, further explanation is given. Also, if a word has more than one part of speech (i.e., it is both a noun and a verb, those things are marked separately.

> **mask** /măsk/ **1.** *n.* a covering for the mouth and nose used to protect against inhaling toxic substances, to administer oxygen or anesthesia, or to prevent the spread of infection. **2.** *v.* to cover something, as with a mask.

Cross-References

In order to avoid the back and forth required when cross-references are put in without definitions, this dictionary has attempted to give cross-referenced entries at every place they occur. So, if you look up phlebotomy, you will find a cross-reference to venotomy and at venotomy, you will find a cross-reference to phlebotomy.

> **phlebotomy** /flə bŏt′ə mē/ puncturing a vein to draw blood. *Also called* venotomy. [phlebo- + -tomy]

> **venotomy** /vē nŏt′ə mē/ incision into a vein. *Also called* phlebotomy. [veno- + -tomy]

Etymologies and Word Building

Etymologies are the history of how words are formed. Many medical terms actually have a long history dating back to Ancient Greece and Ancient Rome. Currently, medical terminology is taught to allied health students using word building because so many medical words are built up from word roots that appear in combining forms and from prefixes and suffixes. Word building is described here because it is such a useful tool for allied health students and workers to gain a larger medical vocabulary. Generally, built-up words are made up of some of the following four parts.

- A **word root** is the portion of the word that contains its basic meaning. For example, the word root cardi means "heart."

Some other examples of common medical word roots are

dent, tooth	*laryng, larynx*	*ven, vein*
gastr, stomach	*rhin, nose*	

- **Combining forms** are the word root that can be connected to another word part. In some cases, a combining vowel is needed to connect word parts. For example, the word root *cardi* + the combining vowel *o* can form words that relate to the basic meaning "heart," such as *cardiology,* the medical practice involved with studying, diagnosing, and treating disorders of the heart. In this dictionary, combining vowels are shown in parentheses: cardi(o)-.

    Some other examples of words form from combining forms are:

    dentalgia: dent-, tooth + -algia, pain = toothache
    gastrodynia: gastr-, stomach + combining vowel –o- + -dynia, pain = stomache
    laryngoplasty: laryng-, larynx + -o- + -plasty, plastic surgery + plastic surgery on the larynx
    rhinitis: rhin-, nose + -it is, inflammation = nose inflammation or runny nose
    venogram: ven-, vein + -o- + -gram, written record = x-ray image of a vein

- **Prefixes** are word parts attached to the beginning of a word or word root that modify its meaning. For example, the prefix *peri-*, meaning "around, near, surrounding," helps to form the word *pericardium*, meaning "around or surrounding the heart."

    Some other examples of words formed from prefixes are:

    disinfection: dis-, apart + infection
    retroperitoneum: retro-, behind + peritoneum, the space behind the peritoneum

- **Suffixes** are word parts attached to the end of a word or word root that modify its meaning. For example, the suffix –oid, meaning "like or resembling," helps to form the word fibroid, meaning "made of fibrous tissue."

    Some other examples of words formed from suffixes are:

    gastrectomy: gastr-, stomach + -ectomy, removal of = removal of the stomach
    laryngoscope: laryng-, larynx + -o- + -scope, tool for examining = device for examining the larynx

In this dictionary, there are no foreign etymologies. We only show the word building etymologies to reinforce the word building tools that are so valuable in allied health.

Illustrations

The illustrations that appear in this dictionary are used to illustrate concepts such as the difference between adduction and abduction.

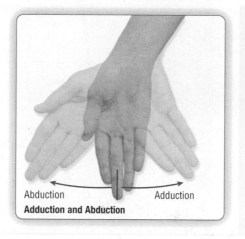

Abduction   Adduction
Adduction and Abduction

Other illustrations shown body parts and anatomical drawings to expand your anatomical knowledge.

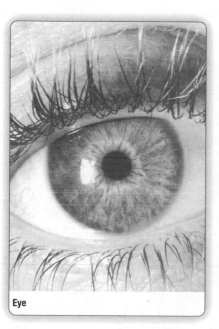

Eye

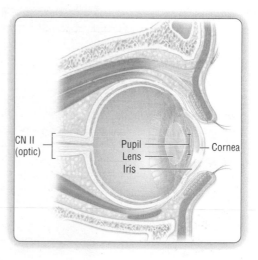

CN II
(optic)

Pupil
Lens
Iris

Cornea

Some illustrations show allied health professionals on the job.

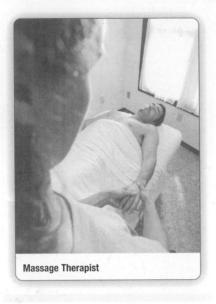

Massage Therapist

Still other illustrations show diseases or conditions.

Mumps

Many anatomical drawings and other illustrations help to illuminate the entries in the dictionary. In addition, there is a 48-page insert described in the next section.

Insert of Anatomical Plates

The 48 plates in the insert that follows page 264 cover many aspects of the human body. The first few plates show positioning, directions, and regions used in anatomy. The next group of plates cover the body's thirteen systems. For each system, a drawing of the whole system is given followed by drawings and photos of specific parts, tests, and or pathology of that system. Some written material on the plates covers aspects of allied health related to that system. After the body systems plates, there are plates that cover dentistry, pharmacology, and complementary and alternative medicine.

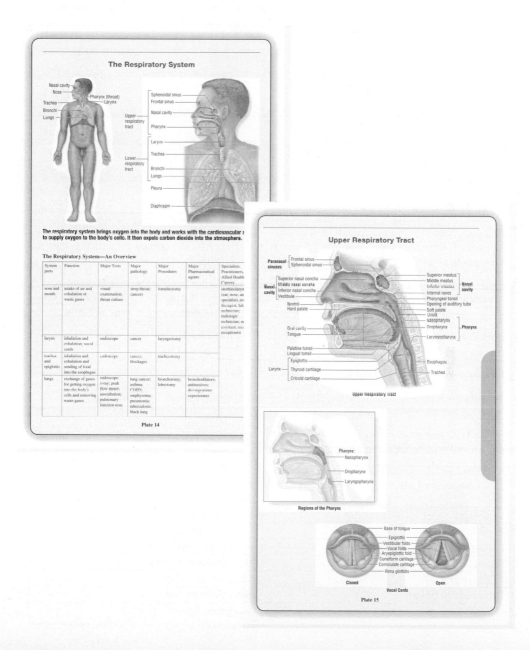

Appendices

The last part of the *McGraw-Hill Medical Dictionary for Allied Health* is an extensive collection of appendix material designed to be a comprehensive reference tool for you as an allied health student as well as a worker in any allied health profession. A description of each appendix follows.

Appendix A provides an extensive list of combining forms, prefixes, and suffixes to help you increase your vocabulary using word-building techniques.

circum- *prefix*. around.

-clasis *suffix*. breaking.

-clast *suffix*. breaking.

cleido- *combining form*. clavicle.

clino- *combining form*. sloping: curving.

co-, com-, con- *prefix*. with, together.

-coccus *suffix*. belonging to a group of bacteria having a spherical shape.

cochle-, cochleo- *combining form*. of or relating to the inner ear.

col-, colo- *combining form*. colon.

Appendix B is a discussion of medical errors caused by written abbreviations followed by a comprehensive list of medical abbreviations.

F

F Fahrenheit.

FAE fetal alcohol effects.

FAP **1.** familial adenomatous polyposis. **2.** functional ambulation profile (analysis of a patient's ability to walk).

FAS fetal alcohol syndrome.

Appendix C describes some common laboratory tests then lists the normal reference values for many medical tests.

Laboratory Test	Normal Range in US Units	Normal Range in SI Units	To Convert US to SI Units
Basophils	0-3% of lymphocytes	0.0-0.3 fraction of white blood cells	x 0.01
Bilirubin – Direct	0.0-0.4 mg/dl	0-7 mmol/liter	x 17.1
Bilirubin – Total	0.0-1.0 mg/dl	0-17 mmol/liter	x 17.1

Appendix D is a short list of those metric conversions that are most commonly used in everyday life and will be useful in allied health.

U.S. Customary Units	Metric Units or Standard International (SI) Units
1 inch (in)	25.4 millimeters (mm)
.6 cubic inch	1 cubic centimeter (cc)
1 foot (ft)	30.5 centimeters (cm)
1 yard (yd)	91.4 centimeters (cm)
1 mile (mi)	1.6 kilometers (km)
1 fluid ounce (fl oz)	29.6 milliliters (mL)
1 dry ounce (oz)	28.3 grams (g)

Appendix E includes the daily reference intake of vitamins as well as the nutritional recommendations set by the Food and Drug Administration (www.fda.gov). It also provides information on nutritional labeling.

Nutrient	RDA	UL	
Vitamin A	900	3,000	mcg/day
Vitamin C	90	2,000	mg/day
Vitamin D	5	50	mcg/day

Appendix F gives the BMI or body mass index chart and tells you how to calculate your BMI.

We Can! Watch Our Weight

BMI	Healthy Weight						Overweight					Obese					
	19	20	21	22	23	24	25	26	27	28	29	30	31	32	33	34	35
Height							Body Weight (pounds)										
4'10"	91	96	100	105	110	115	119	124	129	134	138	143	148	153	158	162	167
4'11"	94	99	104	109	114	119	124	128	133	138	143	148	153	158	163	168	173
5'0"	97	102	107	112	118	123	128	133	138	143	148	153	158	163	168	174	179
5'1"	100	106	111	116	122	127	132	137	143	148	153	158	164	169	174	180	185

Appendix G is a brief description of the medical terminology style of eponyms (diseases and tests named for a person).

U.S. Government	AMA and AAMT
Alzheimer's disease	Alzheimer disease
Babinski's reflex	Babinski reflex
Bartholin's glands	Bartholin glands
Bell's palsy	Bell palsy
Cooley's anemia	Cooley anemia
Cushing's syndrome	Cushing syndrome
Fontan's operation	Fontan operation

Appendix H is a list of all the bones in the human body.

Bones of the neck and spinal column:
   cervical vertebrae (7) including the atlas and axis
   lumbar vertebrae (5)
   thoracic vertebrae (12)
   sacrum
   coccyx

Appendix I is a list of some of the nerves of the human body.

Nerve	Name	Functions	Origin
Cranial Nerve I (CN I)	olfactory nerve	olfaction (sense of smell)	nasal cavity
Cranial Nerve II (CN II)	optic nerve	vision	retina
Cranial Nerve III	oculomotor nerve	eye muscles, eyelid muscles, contraction of pupil and shaping of eye lens	mesencephalon

Appendix J is a list of the major muscles of the human body.

Muscle Groups of the Arms and Hands

    Brachium
    Antebrachial Flexors
    Antebrachial Extensors
    Hand & Wrist

Appendix K is a list of the major joints of the human body.

Upper extremity:

    sternoclavicular
    acromioclavicular
    shoulder
    elbow/proximal radioulnar articulation
    wrist/distal radioulnar articulation
    carpometacarpal
    metacarpophalangeal
    interphalangeal

Appendix L is a list of the English terms that are translated into Spanish in Appendix M.

Appendix M is a Spanish-English glossary.

Appendix N is a list of organizations and websites related to allied health.

Appendix O is a list of diagnosis-related groups

DRG	MDC	TYPE	DRG TITLE
001	1	SURG	CRANIOTOMY AGE >17 W CC
002	1	SURG	CRANIOTOMY AGE >17 W/O CC
003	1	SURG	CRANIOTOMY AGE 0–17
004	1	SURG	NO LONGER VALID
005	1	SURG	NO LONGER VALID
006	1	SURG	CARPAL TUNNEL RELEASE

Appendix P gives the standard precautions important to safety.

Appendix Q covers complementary and alternative medicine.

Appendix R provides the signs used in American Sign Language.

Appendix S is an overview of HIPAA rules.

McGraw-Hill
MEDICAL DICTIONARY
for Allied Health

a *abbreviation.* **1.** ante. **2.** area. **3.** asymmetric. **4.** artery.

A *abbreviation.* **1.** adenine. **2.** alanine. **3.** as a subscript, used to refer to alveolar gas.

a-, an- *prefix.* not, without, lacking: *for example,* acranial, analgesia.

AA, aa *abbreviation.* **1.** amino acid. **2.** AA Alcoholics Anonymous (www.alcoholics-anonymous.org).

AAA *abbreviation.* abdominal aortic aneurysm.

AMA *abbreviation.* American Medical Association (www.ama-assn.org).

AAMA *abbreviation.* American Association of Medical Assistants (www.aama-ntl.org).

AAMT *abbreviation.* American Association for Medical Transcription (www.aamt.org).

A&P *abbreviation.* **1.** auscultation and percussion. **2.** anterior and posterior.

ab- *prefix.* from; away; off: *for example,* abaxial.

abandonment /ə bän′dən mənt/ premature termination of treatment by a health care provider without notice or the patient's consent.

abasia /ə bā′zhə/ inability to walk due to a disease or muscular problem.

abate /ə bāt′/ to lessen or decrease.

abatement /ə bāt′mənt/ decrease or lessening of pain or symptoms.

abaxial /ăb ăk′sē əl/ outside of, beyond, or at the opposite end of the axis of something such as the body. [ab- + axial]

ABC *abbreviation.* airway, breathing, and circulation, used in cardiac life support.

ABCD *abbreviation.* airway, breathing, circulation, and defibrillation, used in cardiac life support.

ABCDE *abbreviation.* airway, breathing, circulation and cervical spine, disability, and exposure, used in advanced trauma life support.

abdomen /ăb′də mən, ăb dō′mən/ the part of the trunk between the chest and pelvis. In some cases, it is understood to include the pelvic contents.

abdomin-, abdomino- *combining form.* abdomen: *for example,* abdominocentesis.

abdominal /ăb dŏm′ə nəl/ relating to the abdomen. [abdomin- + -al]

abdominal aneurysm /ăn′yə rĭz′əm/ an abnormally distended blood vessel in the abdomen, almost always referring to the aorta.

abdominal angina /ăn′jə nə, ăn jī′nə/ a dull pain in the abdomen that usually occurs shortly after a meal and is associated with a bowel disease.

abdominal aorta /ā ôr′tə/ the part of the descending aorta that supplies blood to parts lying below the diaphragm.

abdominal aortic aneurysm (AAA) /ā ôr′tĭk ăn′yə rĭz′əm/ an abnormally stretched or ballooned out abdominal aorta.

abdominal cavity the abdomen, sometimes including the pelvis.

abdominal guarding a reflex spasm of the abdominal muscles in response to pressure or touch, indicative of inflamed tissues.

abdominal hernia /hûr′ne ə/ a hernia protruding through the abdominal wall.

abdominal hysterectomy /hĭs′tə rĕk′tə mē/ surgical removal of the uterus by cutting through the abdominal wall. *Also called* abdominohysterectomy.

abdominal muscle any of the muscles in the abdomen. *See illustration at* muscles.

abdominal muscle deficiency syndrome partial or complete lack of tone in the abdominal muscles. *Also called* prune belly syndrome.

abdominal pain pain in the abdominal cavity.

abdominal pregnancy /prĕg′nən sē/ implantation of a fertilized ovum in the peritoneal cavity.

abdominal pressure pressure from the distension of the bladder, stomach, or intestines.

abdominal regions nine areas of the abdomen identified by their relative positions; for example, RUQ equals right upper quadrant, which contains the liver and hepatic flexure of the colon. The regions are also identified as epigastric, hypochondriac, hypogastric, iliac, lumbar, and umbilical. *See illustration* at anatomy plate 3 starting after page 264.

abdominal respiration /rĕs′pə rā′shən/ breathing affected by the contraction and expansion of the diaphragm.

abdominal sonogram /sŏn′ə grăm′, sō′nə-/ an examination of the abdominal area using ultrasound; abdominal ultrasonography.

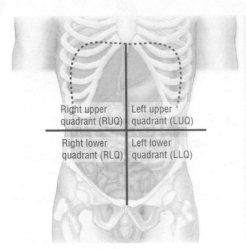

Abdominopelvic Quadrants

abdominal thrust maneuver   an emergency technique used to discharge an object from the trachea, using firm upwards thrusts below the rib cage of a choking person. *Also called* Heimlich maneuver.

abdominal ultrasonography /ŭl′trə sə nŏg′rə fē, -sō nŏg′-/   abdominal sonogram.

abdominocentesis   /ăb dŏm′ə nō sĕn tē′sĭs/ the removal of fluid from the abdominal cavity, accomplished by using a needle or other catheter. [abdomino- + -centesis]

abdominohysterectomy   /ăb dŏm′ə nō hĭs′tə rĕk′tə mē/   a   hysterectomy   performed through an incision into the abdominal wall. [abdomino- + hysterectomy]

abdominopelvic /ăb dŏm′ə nō pĕl′vĭk/   of or relating to the abdomen and pelvic area. [abdomino- + pelvic]

abdominopelvic cavity   the area of the trunk below the chest, including the abdominal and pelvic cavities.

abdominopelvic quadrants   any of four segments into which the abdominopelvic area can be divided by vertical and horizontal lines through its midpoint. *See also* abdominopelvic regions.

abdominopelvic regions   areas of the abdominal and pelvic cavities identified by their relative positions: right upper quadrant, right lower quadrant, left upper quadrant, left lower quadrant.

abdominoperineal   /ăb dŏm′ə nō pĕr′ə nē′əl/ relating to both the abdomen and the perineum (tissue between the anus and scrotum in men and between the anus and vaginal opening in women). [abdomino- + perineal]

abdominoplasty /ăb dŏm′ə nə plăs′tē/   plastic surgery performed on the abdominal wall unrelated to any abnormality or diseased condition. [abdomino- + -plasty]

abdominoscopy /ăb dŏm′ə nŏs′kə pē/   visual examination of the abdomen through a scope. *Also called* peritoneoscopy.

abdominovesical /ăb dŏm′ə nō vĕs′ĭ kəl/   of or relating to the abdomen and the bladder or gallbladder. [abdomino- + vesical]

abducens (nerve) /ăb doo′sənz/ or **abducent (nerve)** /ăb doo′sənt/   cranial nerve VI; either of a pair of motor nerves that innervate the muscles that rotate the eyeball away from the middle plane of the body and allow for lateral eye movement.

abduct /ăb dŭkt′/   to move away from the median plane of the body.

abduction /ăb dŭk′shən/   movement of an arm or a leg away from the median plane of the body, or the median plane of a hand or foot, in the case of fingers or toes. *Compare* adduction.

abductor (muscle) /ăb dŭk′tər/   a muscle that draws a part away from the median plane of the body or, in the case of fingers or toes, away from the axis of the second toe or middle finger.

aberrant /ə bĕr′ənt, ăb′ər-/   **1.** wandering, said of ducts, nerves, or blood vessels that deviate from their normal course or pattern. **2.** not normal.

aberration /ăb′ə rā′shən/   **1.** any deviation from the normal course or pattern. **2.** abnormal development.

ABG   *abbreviation.* arterial blood gas.

ablate /ăb lāt′/   to take out or to make nonfunctional.

ablation /ăb lā′shən/   surgical destruction of a body part and its ability to function.

abnormal /ăb nôr′məl/   not usual or normal; deviating from what is usually expected. [ab- + normal]

abnormality /ăb′nôr măl′ĭ tē/   **1.** a state or quality of not being average or normal. **2.** something that is not properly shaped or that fails to function properly.

ABO blood group   the major grouping used to determine blood type—A, B, AB, or O—based on the antigens found on the surface of the blood cell, in order to match potential blood donors and recipients.

aboral /ăb ôr′əl/   away from the mouth. [ab- + oral]

abort /ə bôrt′/   **1.** to deliver a fetus before it is capable of surviving. **2.** to stop a disease in its early stages. **3.** to halt growth.

aborted /ə bôr′tĭd/   **1.** delivered stillborn or prematurely. **2.** ended prematurely or before completion.

abortifacient /ə bôr′tə fā′shənt/   a drug that causes abortion; abortive.

abortion /ə bôr′shən/   ending a pregnancy before or after the death of a fetus; may occur spontaneously as in a miscarriage or may be induced.

abortive /ə bôr′tĭv/ **1.** *adj.* abnormally formed or developed; unsuccessful. **2.** *n.* an abortifacient.

abortus /ə bôr′təs/ the product of an abortion.

above-knee amputation (AKA) /ămp′yōō tā′shən/ surgical removal of a leg above the knee.

ABR *abbreviation.* auditory brainstem response.

abrachia /ā brā′kē ə, ā brăk′ē ə/ a congenital lack of arms.

abrachiocephaly /ā brā′kē ō sĕf′ə lē, ā brăk′ ē ō-/ a congenital lack of arms and a head. [a- + brachio- + -cephaly]

abrade /ə brād′/ to remove a surface layer by scraping.

abrasion /ə brā′zhən/ **1.** removal of the surface layers of skin or a mucous membrane by scraping. **2.** abnormal grinding away of tooth surfaces.

abrasive /ə brā′sĭv/ **1.** *adj.* causing abrasion. **2.** *n.* a material used to grind or wear away.

abrasiveness /ə brā′sĭv nĭs/ **1.** a feature of a substance that abrades by friction. **2.** the ability of a material to abrade or scrape another material.

abreaction /ăb′rē ăk′shən/ the release of emotions following the recollection of a repressed unpleasant experience. [ab- + reaction]

ABR test *abbreviation.* auditory brainstem response test.

abruptio placentae /ə brŭp′shē ō′ plə sĕn′tē/ premature separation of the placenta from the uterine wall, frequently with massive maternal hemorrhage.

abscess /ăb′sĕs/ **1.** pus collected in an infected site, usually accompanied by inflammation and pain. **2.** a collection of liquefied dead tissue within solid tissue.

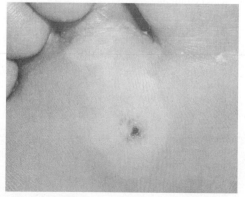

Abscess (on a Foot)

abscission /ăb sĭsh′ən, -sĭzh′-/ removal by cutting away.

abscopal /ăb skō′pəl/ having an effect on another part (said of radiated tissue on non-radiated tissue).

absence /ăb′səns/ state of clouded consciousness (usually referring to the time during a seizure).

absence seizure /sē′zhər/ a brief seizure causing unconsciousness or slowed thinking.

absorb /ăb sôrb′, -zôrb′/ to take up a liquid by absorption.

absorbance /ăb sôr′bəns, -zôr′-/ or **absorbancy** /ăb sôr′bən sē, -zôr′-/ capacity for absorbing liquids.

absorbed dose /ăb sôrbd′, -zôrbd′/ the amount of energy that has been absorbed per unit mass of irradiated substance at a specific location of the body.

absorbent /ăb sôr′bənt, -zôr′-/ **1.** *adj.* capable of absorbing a gas, liquid, light rays, or heat; absorptive. **2.** *n.* a substance capable of absorbing.

absorption /ăb sôrp′shən, -zôrp′-/ **1.** incorporating, receiving, or taking in gases, liquids, light, or heat. **2.** the taking in of radiation energy by a tissue it passes through. **3.** the ability of cells in the GI tract to absorb nutrients and other substances.

absorptive /ăb sôrp′tĭv, -zôrp′-/ capable of absorbing; absorbent.

abstemious /ăb stē′mē əs/ resistant to consuming too much food or alcohol.

abstinence /ăb′stə nəns/ voluntary restraint of a desire or appetite, especially with respect to something pleasurable, such as alcohol or sexual intercourse.

abstinence syndrome symptoms of withdrawal from a drug habit, such as a narcotic addiction.

AB type blood a member of the ABO blood group characterized by antigens denoted by the letters A and B and lacking antibodies against these antigens.

abulia /ə byōō′lē ə, ə bōō′-/ loss or weakening of the ability to make independent decisions.

abuse *n.* /ə byōōs′/ **1.** excessive use of something such as a drug. **2.** violent treatment of a child or other person. **3.** in billing, the misuse of funds meant for patient care. *v.* /ə byōōz′/ **4.** to use something, as a drug or alcohol, in excess. **5.** to treat someone, especially a child, violenty or in a sexually inappropriate way.

abutment /ə bŭt′mənt/ something, such as a tooth or implant, used to attach a fixed or removable prosthesis.

a.c. *abbreviation.* Latin *ante cibum*, before meals.

AC *abbreviation*. air conduction.

acanth- *combining form*. thorny or having spines: *for example*, acanthosis.

acanthocyte /ə kăn′thə sīt′/ an abnormal red blood cell with thorny projections. [acantho- + -cyte]

acanthoid /ə kăn′thoid/ shaped like a spine or thorn. [acanth- + -oid]

acantholysis /ăk′ăn thŏl′ə sĭs/ breakdown of the prickle-cell layer of cells in the epidermis. [acantho- + -lysis]

acanthoma /ăk′ăn thō′mə/ a tumor created by the rapid growth of flat, scaly cells on a surface of the body. [acanth- + -oma]

acanthorrhexis /ə kăn′thə rĕk′sĭs/ rupture of the connections of the prickle cell in the epidermis. [acantho- + -rrhexis]

acanthosis /ăk′ăn thō′sĭs/ a thickening of one of the five layers of the skin, the layer known as the prickle-cell layer. [acanth- + -osis]

acanthotic /ăk′ăn thŏt′ĭk/ of or having acanthosis. [acantho- + -tic]

acapnia /ə kăp′nē ə/ the absence of carbon dioxide in the blood during circulatory arrest. [a- + -capnia]

acariasis /ăk′ə rī′ə sĭs/ a disease caused by mites.

acaricide /ə kăr′ə sīd′/ a poison used to kill ticks.

acarid /ăk′ə rĭd/ a mite or tick.

accelerator globulin (AcG, ac-g) /glŏb′yə lĭn/ a protein in serum that promotes the conversion of prothrombin to thrombin.

access /ăk′sĕs/ a way of approaching or gaining admittance to or use of.

accessory /ăk sĕs′ə rē/ referring to a gland, muscle, nerve, or other part that is auxiliary to a more important structure.

accessory gland a small gland lying near, but unattached to, a larger gland.

accessory nerve cranial nerve XI; either of pair of motor nerves that transmit impulses to the pharynx, larynx, and soft palate and muscles of the upper thorax, back, and shoulders.

accessory organ an extra organ, in addition to the main organ; these organs, such as an accessory spleen, are abnormal, but do not usually cause disease.

accident /ăk′sĭ dənt/ an unexpected medical event (as a cardiovascular accident).

acclimatization /ə klī′mə tə zā′shən/ physiological adaptation to a variation in the environment.

accommodation /ə kŏm′ə dā′shən/ **1.** adjustment or adaptation to some change in the environment, in particular the change in the eye's lens for different focal distances. **2.** a change in expectations more in line with experience than hope.

accretion /ə krē′shən/ a build-up of foreign material, such as a calculus or plaque, in a body cavity or on a tooth.

accuracy /ăk′yər ə sē/ the quality of exactness in a measurement.

ACE *abbreviation*. angiotensin-converting enzyme.

ACE inhibitor /ās′ ĭn hĭb′ĭ tər/ one of a class of drugs that dilates the veins as a treatment for hypertension and heart failure.

ACE-inhibitor drug ACE inhibitor.

acentric /ā sĕn′trĭk/ having no center or located away from the center.

ACE2 *abbreviation*. angiotensin-converting enzyme 2.

acephalia /ā′sə făl′ē ə/ congenital lack of a head.

acephaly /ā sĕf′ə lē/ or **acephalism** /ā sĕf′ə lĭz′əm/ acephalia. [a- + -cephaly]

acet-, aceto- *combining form*. two-carbon fragment of acetic acid: *for example*, acetic acid.

acetabular /ăs′ĭ tăb′yə lər/ of or involving the acetabulum.

acetabulectomy /ăs′ĭ tăb′yə lĕk′tə mē/ surgical removal of the acetabulum.

acetabuloplasty /ăs′ĭ tăb′yə lō plăs′tē/ plastic surgery that tries to restore the acetabulum to its normal state.

acetabulum /ăs′ĭ tăb′yə ləm/ (*pl*. **acetabula** /ăs′ĭ tăb′yə lə/) a rounded space at the top of the hipbone, lined with cartilage, where the femur fits.

acetaminophen /ə sē′tə mĭn′ə fən, -fĕn′/ a crystalline anti-inflammatory compound that reduces fever and relieves pain.

acetate /ăs′ĭ tāt′/ an ester or salt of acetic acid.

acetic acid /ə sē′tĭk, ə sĕt′ĭk/ a clear, colorless organic acid with a distinctive pungent odor, found in vinegar. [acet- + -ic]

acetone /ăs′ĭ tōn′/ a colorless inflammable liquid normally found in urine, but occurring in excessive amounts in the urine and blood of people with diabetes.

acetonemia /ăs′ĭ tō nē′mē ə/ an abnormal increase of ketone bodies in the blood.

acetonuria /ăs′ĭ tō nŏŏr′ē ə/ an abnormal increase of ketone bodies in the urine.

acetylcholine (Ach) /ə sē′təl kō′lēn/ a chemical found in neurons that transmits information across the space between two nerve cells.

acetylsalicylic acid /ə sē′təl săl ə sĭl′ĭk/ aspirin.

AcG, ac-g *abbreviation*. accelerator globulin.

Ach *abbreviation*. acetylcholine.

achalasia /ăk′ə lā′zhə/ failure to relax, used especially to refer to organ openings. [a- + chalasia]

ache /āk/ a pain.

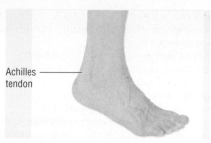

Achilles tendon

Achilles Tendon

Achilles tendon /ə kĭl′ēz tĕn′dən/   the tendon that connects the heel bone to the foot. *Also called* tendo calcaneus.

Achilles tendonitis /tĕn′də nī′tĭs/   inflammation of the Achilles tendon. [tendon + -itis]

achlorhydria /ā′klôr hī′drē ə/   a lack of hydrochloric acid in the stomach juices, associated with pernicious anemia (B_{12} deficiency). [a- + chlor- + -hydr- + -ia]

acholia /ā kō′lē ə/   an absence or severe decrease of secreted bile. [a- + chol- + -ia]

acholic /ā kŏl′ĭk/   lacking bile.

acholuria /ā′kə lŏŏr′ē ə/   absence of bile pigments in the urine.

acholuric /ā′kə lŏŏr′ĭk/   lacking bile pigments in the urine.

achondroplasia /ā kŏn′drə plā′zhə/   a type of congenital dwarfism caused by abnormal growth of cartilage at the ends of the long bones. [a- + chondro- + -plasia]

achondroplastic /ā kŏn′drə plăs′tĭk/   of or involving achondroplasia.

achromatopsia   /ā krō′mə tŏp′sēə/   severe lack of color perception; color-blindness. [a- + chromat- + -opsia]

Person with Achondroplasia

achromaturia /ā krō′mə tŏŏr′ē ə/   the production of clear or almost colorless urine. [a- + chromat- + -uria]

achromic /ā krō′mĭk/   having no color. [a- + chrom- + -ic]

acid /ăs′ĭd/   *n.* **1.** any of a class of substances having a sour taste when dissolved in water, able to turn blue litmus red, and capable of reacting with bases and some metals to form salts. **2.** a substance yielding hydrogen ions when dissolved in water. *adj.* **3.** of or involving acid.

acid-base balance   the normal balance between acid and the nonacid (basic) elements of salts expressed as the blood pH and bicarbonate; it is a function of the relative quantities of acidic and basic substances taken in and produced by metabolism compared to the quantities of acidic and basic substances excreted and taken up by metabolism.

acidemia /ăs′ĭ dē′mē ə/   an increase in the concentration of H-ions in the blood measured as an abnormal decrease in pH; abnormal acidity. [acid + -emia]

acid-fast bacilli smear /bə sĭl′ī/   a test in which spit or sputum (coughed or aspirated) from the chest (or stomach in children) is stained and examined under a microscope for the presence of tuberculosis or another bacterial infection.

acid-fast bacillus (AFB) /bə sĭl′əs/ (*pl.* **bacilli** /bə sĭl′ī/)   a bacterium that does not lose its color when treated with acid-alcohol following the application of a dye, such as tubercle bacillus (*Mycobacterium tuberculosis*).

acid indigestion /ĭn′dĭ jĕs′chən/   indigestion caused by too much hydrochloric acid in the stomach, often treated with calcium carbonate or other antacid.

acidity /ə sĭd′ĭ tē/   **1.** the quality of being acid. **2.** the acid in (or pH of) a liquid.

acidophilus /ăs′ĭ dŏf′ə ləs/   a bacterium normally found in the intestinal tract and vagina and in dairy products. When the intestinal tract or vagina has been stripped of acidophilus by disease or antibiotics, ingesting acidophilus (found in some yogurts) can return the intestinal tract to its normal condition or prevent vaginal yeast infections.

acidosis /ăs′ĭ dō′sĭs/   an abnormal condition caused by an increase of acid or a decrease in the alkaline reserve in the blood and body tissues. [acid + -osis]

acid phosphatase /fŏs′fə tās′/   an enzyme found in prostate tissue that is elevated in prostate inflammatory conditions.

acid reflux /rē′flŭks/   the return of stomach contents back up into the esophagus, which causes a burning sensation when stomach acid irritates the esophagus. *Also called* gastroesophageal reflux disease, GERD.

aciduria /ăs´ĭ dŏŏr´ē ə/ **1.** excretion of acidic urine. **2.** excretion of an excessive amount of a specific type of acid in the urine, as in ketoaciduria. [acid + -uria]

acinous gland /ăs´ə nəs/ a gland with a grape-shaped secreting part and a narrow passageway.

ACL *abbreviation.* anterior cruciate ligament.

acne /ăk´nē/ an inflammatory disease of unknown origin, characterized by pimples on the face, chest, and back, frequently found in adolescents.

acne rosacea /rō zā´shē ə/ chronic facial dermatitis characterized by a rosy coloring of the nose and cheeks. *Also called* rosacea.

acne vulgaris /vŭl gâr´ĭs/ a disease typical of adolescence characterized by a proliferation of inflamed cysts and pimples on the face, chest, and upper back and caused by androgenic stimulation of oils secreted by the sebaceous glands.

-acousis *See* -acusis.

acoustic /ə kōō´stĭk/ relating to hearing and the sense of sound.

acoustic aphasia /ə fā´zhə/ a hearing impairment that affects the ability to understand aural components of language use and communication, including an inability to write from dictation even though the hearing is normal. Frequently included in "receptive aphasia," which includes visual input as well. *Also called* auditory aphasia.

acoustic meatus /mē ā´təs/ **1.** the outer opening of the auditory canal, leading from the ear to the ear drum. **2.** the internal opening of the auditory canal, a channel that passes through the hard portion of the temporal bone through which the facial nerves and veins run.

acoustic nerve cranial nerve VIII; either of a pair of sensory nerves involved in equilibruim and hearing. *Also called* vestibulocochlear nerve, vestibular nerve.

acoustic neurofibromatosis /nŏŏr´ō fī brō´mə tō´sĭs/ a genetic disease characterized by the growth of usually noncancerous tumors in the acoustic nerve, composed chiefly of Schwann cells, and sometimes accompanied by physical deformity and a predisposition to brain tumors and various forms of cancer.

acoustic neuroma /nŏŏ rō´mə/ acoustic schwannoma.

acoustic schwannoma /shwä nō´mə/ a noncancerous encapsulated tumor composed chiefly of Schwann cells in the acoustic nerve, and often causing edema of the optic disc, dizzyness, and unsteady gait; acoustic neuroma.

acquired /ə kwīrd´/ referring to a disease, condition, or other abnormality that has not been inherited.

acquired active immunity /ĭ myōō´nĭ tē/ resistance to disease acquired from an earlier infection or a vaccination.

acquired immunity /ĭ myōō´nĭ tē/ resistance to a disease, either active or passive.

acquired immunodeficiency syndrome or **disease (AIDS)** a disease in which the immune system is compromised by a retrovirus (HIV), characterized by a lessening in helper T cells and exposure to opportunistic and potentially life-threatening diseases.

acquired passive immunity /păs´ĭv ĭ myōō´nĭ tē/ resistance to a disease acquired as a result of antibodies transferred from another individual or animal, as from a mother to infant.

ACR *abbreviation.* American College of Radiology.

acranial /ā krā´nē əl/ lacking a skull. [a- + cranial]

acro- *prefix.* **1.** end, tip, or peak: *for example,* acrocephaly. **2.** extremity: *for example,* acrocyanosis.

acrocentric /ăk´rō sĕn´trĭk/ having the centromere (the part of a chromosome that divides it into two arms) located near one end, so that there is a long and a short arm. [acro- + centric]

acrocephaly /ăk´rō sĕf´ə lē/ a congenital skull abnormality where the skull is unusually pointed. *Also called* oxycephaly. [acro- + cephaly]

acrocyanosis /ăk´rō sī´ə nō´sĭs/ a diagnostic finding involving the circulation in the hands, and sometimes the feet, in which the hands are always cold and blue. *Also called* Raynaud's disease, Raynaud's phenomenon. [acro- + cyanosis]

acrodermatitis /ăk´rō dûr mə tī´tĭs/ inflammation of the skin on the hands and feet. [acro- + dermatitis]

acrodynia /ăk´rō dĭn´ē ə/ **1.** pain in the hands and feet. **2.** a syndrome almost always caused by mercury poisoning. [acro- + -dynia]

acrohyperhidrosis /ăk´rō hī´pər hī drō´sĭs/ an abnormal amount of sweating from the hands and feet. [acro- + hyper- + hidrosis]

acrokeratosis /ăk´rō kĕr´ə tō´sĭs/ abnormal growths on the horny layer of skin, especially on the backs of the fingers. [acro- + -keratosis]

acromegaly /ăk´rō mĕg´ə lē/ a disorder characterized by a gradual increase in the size of the head, hands, jaw, and feet caused by excessive amounts of secretion of somatotropin by the pituitary gland. [acro- + -megaly]

acromi-, acromio- *combining form.* the acromion: *for example,* acromial, acromiohumeral.

acromial /ə krō′mē əl/ of or involving the acromion. [acromi- + -al]

acromioclavicular dislocation /ə krō′mē ŏ klə vĭk′yə lər dĭs′lō kā′shən/ displacement of the acromion and clavicle at the joint.

acromioclavicular joint the point where the acromion and clavicle bones meet.

acromiohumeral /ə krō′mē ō hyōō′mər əl/ of or involving the acromion and the humerus. [acromio- + humeral]

acromion /ə krō′mē ən/ the flat end of the spine of the scapula that articulates with the clavicle and provides a point of attachment for the deltoid and trapezius muscles.

acromioscapular /ə krō′mē ō skăp′yə lər/ of or involving the acromion and the body of the scapula. [acromio- + scapular]

acrophobia /ăk′rə fō′bē ə/ a disabling fear of heights. [acro- + -phobia]

acrosclerosis /ăk′rō sklĭ rō′sĭs/ a localized type of gradual hardening throughout the body and associated with Raynaud's phenomenon, involving increasing stiffness and immobility of the skin of the fingers, with loss of the soft tissue and bone mass of the long bones in the hands and feet. [acro- + sclerosis]

acrosome /ăk′rə som′/ the caplike compartment at the head of a sperm that enables the sperm to penetrate the outer wall of the egg. [acro- + -some]

acrotism /ăk′rə tĭz′əm/ a nonexistent or hard-to-detect pulse.

ACTH *abbreviation.* adrenocorticotropic hormone.

actin-, actino- *combining form.* ray, beam; having raylike structures: *for example,* actinotherapy.

— Acrosome

Acrosome

actinic /ăk tĭn′ĭk/ of or involving the chemically active rays emitted by the electromagnetic band, especially those of sunlight. [actin- + -ic]

actinic granuloma /grăn′yə lō′mə/ a ring-shaped skin lesion on skin that has been exposed to the sun in which very large cells can be seen consuming the skin's elastic fibers when looked at with a microscope.

actinic keratosis (AK) /kĕr′ə tō′sĭs/ a premalignant growth on the sun-exposed skin of middle-aged and elderly light-skinned people that may develop into a carcinoma if untreated.

actinotherapy /ăk′tə nō thĕr′ə pē/ a treatment using ultraviolet light. [actino- + therapy]

action /ăk′shən/ the performance of a function, the way the performance is carried out, or its result.

activated charcoal an agent given by mouth to neutralize an ingested poison or an overdose of a drug.

activated partial thromboplastin time (APTT) /thrŏm′bō plăs′tĭn/ a blood test that measures how long it takes a patient's blood to clot.

active acquired immunity /ĭ myōō′nĭ tē/ the immune system's ability to produce antibodies to repel a specific agent, acquired by contracting an infectious disease such as mumps or by vaccination. *Also called* active immunity.

active exercises exercises that stimulate the cardiovascular system, strengthen muscles, and improve lung capacity.

active immunity /ĭ myōō′nĭ tē/ active acquired immunity.

active range of motion (AROM) the full range of voluntary motion a given joint can perform.

active stage of labor the second phase of the early stage when contractions are still four or five minutes apart and can last up to 60 seconds. Women who have decided to be medicated during labor usually go to the hospital during this stage.

active tuberculosis /tōō bûr′kyə lō′sĭs/ the presence of *Mycobacterium tuberculosis* infection confirmed by a positive chest x-ray and a sputum culture. U.S. law requires treatment for active turberculosis.

activities of daily living (ADLs) the daily routines of life, such as bathing, getting dressed, and preparing meals, that require mobility and the ability to perform them independently.

acuity /ə kyōō′ĭ tē/ sharpness; clarity; severity (as of pain).

acupressure /ăk′yōō prĕsh′ər/ a therapeutic method for treating pain or tension in which pressure is applied along meridians to change or open energy flow.

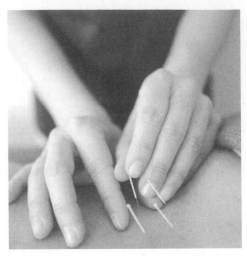

Acupuncturist

acupuncture /ăk′yo͞o pŭngk′chər/ a Chinese therapeutic treatment in which fine needles are inserted into specific sites along meridians on the body to bring about change in the energy flow to stimulate, disperse, or regulate the life force energy to restore a healthy energy balance.

acupuncturist /ăk′yo͞o pŭngk′chər ĭst/ a person trained to perform acupuncture.

-acusis, -acousis *suffix.* hearing: *for example,* anacusis, presbyacousis.

acustimulation /ăk′yo͞o stĭm′yə lā′shən/ therapeutic stimulation at acupuncture points using mild electric current, used to control symptoms such as nausea and vomiting.

acute /ə kyo͞ot′/ **1.** used to denote a serious disease or infection that appears suddenly. **2.** used to denote brief, but intense, treatment.

acute abdomen /ăb′də mən, ăb dō′mən/ a serious abdominal condition, such as appendicitis, characterized by pain, tenderness, and rigid muscles, that indicates a possible need for surgery.

acute angle-closure glaucoma /glô kō′mə/ abnormal pressure in the front chamber of the eye occurring when normal circulation of fluid within the eye is suddenly blocked at the angle formed by the junction in the anterior chamber of the cornea and the iris.

acute arterial occlusion /är têr′ē əl ə klo͞o′zhən/ the sudden blockage of an artery by a blood clot; if a coronary artery is blocked, a heart attack occurs.

acute ascending paralysis /pə răl′ə sĭs/ an acute disorder that usually follows a viral infection or immunization and is marked by a symmetric paralysis of the legs that progresses rapidly upward, ascending to the arms, and

sometimes the breathing muscles and neck. Some consider it a form of Guillain-Barre syndrome. *Also called* Landry's paralysis.

acute bacterial endocarditis /băk têr′ē əl ĕn′dō kär dī′tĭs/ a serious infection of one of the four heart valves, characterized by fever, fatigue, malaise, shortness of breath, and sometimes scattered small skin lesions.

acute care short-term intensive care provided for a serious disease or trauma.

acute illness a serious illness that appears suddenly but usually does not last long.

acute lymphoblastic leukemia (ALL) /lĭm′fō blăs′tĭk lo͞o kē′mē ə/ a sudden-onset type of leukemia—the most common cancer among children—characterized by the rapid growth of many immature white blood cells in the blood and bone marrow that would normally develop into lymphocytes; acute lymphocytic leukemia.

acute lymphocytic leukemia (ALL) /lĭm′fō sĭt′ĭk lo͞o kē′mē ə/ acute lymphoblastic leukemia.

acute myeloblastic leukemia (AML) /mī′ə lō blăs′tĭk lo͞o kē′mē ə/ acute myelogenous leukemia.

acute myelocytic leukemia (AML) /mī′ə lō sĭt′ĭk lo͞o kē′mē ə/ cancer of the white blood cells that occurs suddenly and, if not treated, progresses rapidly. There are two major types of acute leukemia: acute lymphoblastic leukemia and acute myelogenous leukemia.

acute myelogenous leukemia (AML) /mī′ə lŏj′ə nəs lo͞o kē′mē ə/ a malignant disease that progresses rapidly in which white blood cells, which fight infection, are overproduced but fail to mature, causing too many immature blood-forming cells in the blood and bone marrow. *Also called* acute myeloblastic leukemia, acute myeloid leukemia, acute non-lymphocytic leukemia.

acute myeloid leukemia (AML) /mī′ə loid′ lo͞o kē′mē ə/ a malignant disease that progresses rapidly in which white blood cells, which fight infection, are overproduced but fail to mature, causing too many immature blood-forming cells in the blood and bone marrow. *Also called* acute myelogenous leukemia, acute myeloblastic leukemia, acute nonlymphocytic leukemia.

acute necrotizing gingivitis (AGN) /nĕk′rə tī′zĭng jĭn′jə vī′tĭs/ acute infection of the respiratory tract and mouth, marked by lesions of the mucous membranes. *Also called* trench mouth, Vincent's angina.

acute necrotizing ulcerative gingivitis (ANUG) /nĕk′rə tī′zĭng ŭl′sə rā′tĭv jĭn′jə vī′tĭs, ŭl′sər ə tĭv/ acute infection of the respiratory tract and mouth, marked by lesions of the mucous membranes. *Also called* trench mouth, Vincent's angina.

acute nonlymphocytic leukemia / nŏn′ lĭm fō sĭt′ĭk lōō kē′mē ə/ a malignant disease that progresses rapidly in which white blood cells, which fight infection, are overproduced but fail to mature, causing too many immature blood-forming cells in the blood and bone marrow. *Also called* acute myelogenous leukemia, acute myeloid leukemia, acute myeloblastic leukemia.

acute promyelocytic leukemia /prō′mī ə lō sĭt′ĭk lōō kē′mē ə/ a bone marrow cancer in which there are too many immature blood cells and too few mature blood cells.

acute respiratory distress syndrome (ARDS) /rĕs′pər ə tôr′ē/ a rapid-onset disorder in which the lungs fail to function as they should. *Also called* adult respiratory distress syndrome, wet lung.

acute respiratory failure (ARF) /rĕs′pər ə tôr′ē/ loss of lung function that causes an imbalance in the amounts of oxygen and carbon dioxide in arterial blood.

acute undifferentiated leukemia (AUL) /ŭn′dĭf ə rĕn′shē ā′tĭd lōō kē′mē ə/ acute undifferentiated leukemia is usually diagnosed after acute myelogenous leukemia and acute lymphoblastic leukemia have been ruled out.

ad- *prefix.* to, toward, near the midline: *for example*, adduction.

AD *abbreviation.* Alzheimer's disease.

A.D. *abbreviation.* Latin *auris dextra*, right ear.

-ad *suffix.* toward, in the direction of: *for example*, cephalad.

ADA *abbreviation* **1.** American Dental Association (www.ada.org). **2.** Americans with Disabilities Act.

ADAA *abbreviation.* American Dental Assistants Association (www.dentalassistant.org).

adactyly /ā dăk′tə lē/ congenital lack of fingers. [a- + -dactyly]

adamantine /ăd′ə măn′tēn/ extremely hard, used to describe tooth enamel.

Adam's apple /ăd′əmz/ an informal term used to refer to the thyroid cartilage visible in men's throats.

Adams-Stokes /ăd′əmz stōks′/ **disease** or **syndrome** a syndrome in which the pulse rate falls below 40, and fainting occurs due to inadequate blood and oxygen reaching the brain.

adaptation /ăd′əp tā′shən/ **1.** a change in the function of an organ or tissue to respond to new conditions. **2.** the ability of sensory organs to change in the presence of repeated stimuli.

adaptive equipment /ə dăp′tĭv/ special

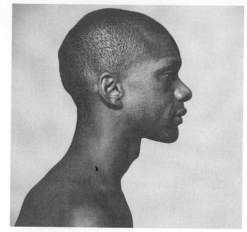

Adam's Apple

devices that improve the ability of disabled people to function.

ADD *abbreviation.* attention deficit disorder.

addict /ăd′ĭkt/ a person addicted to a specific substance or practice.

addiction /ə dĭk′shən/ physical and psychological dependence on a specific substance or practice.

Addisonian anemia /ăd′ə sō′nē ən ə nē′mē ə/ a disorder of the blood caused by lack of vitamin B$_{12}$.

Addison('s) disease /ăd′ə sən(z)/ a disease with failure of adrenocortical function characterized by anemia, low blood pressure, and weakness, usually resulting from destruction or loss of both adrenal glands. *Also called* chronic adrenocortical insufficiency.

adduct /ə dŭkt/ to draw toward the middle (midline).

adduction /ə dŭk′shən/ **1.** movement of a part toward the midline of the body. **2.** rotation of an eye toward the nose.

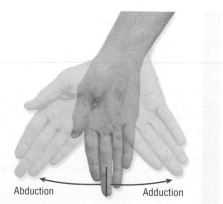

Abduction   Adduction

Adduction and Abduction

adductor (muscle) /ə dŭk′tər/ a muscle that pulls a body part toward the body's midline.

adductor spasmodic dysphonia /spăz mŏd′ĭk dĭs fō′nē ə/ a disorder in which sudden muscle spasms cause the vocal cords to draw together violently.

aden-, adeno- *combining form*. gland or glandular: *for example*, adenitis, adeniform.

adenalgia /ăd′ə năl′jə, -jē ə/ pain in a gland. [aden- + -algia]

adenectomy /ăd′ə něk′tə me/ surgical removal of a gland. [aden- + -ectomy]

adeniform /ə děn′ə fôrm′/ adenoid.

adenine (A) /ăd′ə nēn′/ one of the four bases in DNA (where it pairs with thymine) and in RNA (where it pairs with uracil).

adenitis /ăd′ə nī′tĭs/ inflammation of a lymph node or gland. [aden- + -itis]

adenocarcinoma /ăd′ə nō kär′sə nō′mə/ (*pl.* **adenocarcinomas** or **adenocarcinomata** /ăd′ə nō kär′sə nō′mə tə/) a cancer derived from glandular tissue or in which the tumor cells form familiar glandular structures. [adeno- + carcinoma]

adenohypophysis /ăd′ə nō hī pŏf′ə sĭs/ the frontal lobe of the pituitary gland, which secretes important hormones; anterior (lobe of) pituitary. [adeno- + hypophysis]

adenoid cystic carcinoma /ăd′ə noid′ sĭs′tĭk kär′sə nō′mə/ a cancer made up of large epithelial masses with round, glandlike spaces or cysts frequently filled with mucus or collagen.

adenoidectomy /ăd′ə noi děk′tə mē/ surgical removal of the adenoids. [adenoid + -ectomy]

adenoiditis /ăd′ə noi dī′tĭs/ inflammation of the adenoids. [adenoid + -itis]

adenoids /ăd′ə noidz′/ unencapsulated lymphoid tissue found in the nasopharynx.

adenoma /ăd′ə nō′mə/ (*pl.* **adenomas** or **adenomata** /ăd′ə nō′mə tə/) a usually benign growth of epithelial tissue. [aden- + -oma]

adenomatous goiter /ăd′ə nŏm′ə təs goi′tər, -nō′mə təs/ an enlarged thyroid gland.

adenomyoma /ăd′ə nō mī ō′mə/ (*pl.* **adenomyomas** or **adenomyomata** /ăd′ə nō mī ō′mə tə/) a benign growth of muscle tissue. [adeno- + myoma]

adenomyosis /ăd′ə nō mī ō′sĭs/ a benign condition in which the mucous (inner) membrane of the uterus (endometrium) grows into the uterine musculature adjacent to the endometrium. [adeno- + myosis]

adenopathy /ăd′ə nŏp′ə thē/ swelling of the lymph nodes. [adeno- + -pathy]

adenosarcoma /ăd′ə nō sär kō′mə/ a malignant tumor arising in glandular tissue; adenocarcinoma. [adeno- + sarcoma]

adenosine /ə děn′ə sēn′/ a compound of adenine and a sugar.

adenosine triphosphate (ATP) /trī fŏs′fāt/ an enzyme found in muscle tissue and a potent store of energy.

adenosis /ăd′ə nō′sĭs/ an abnormal occurrence of glandular tissue. [aden- + -osis]

adenotomy /ăd′ə nŏt′ə mē/ surgical procedure on a gland. [adeno- + -tomy]

adenovirus /ăd′ə nō vī′rəs/ any of a group of viruses that cause upper respiratory infections. [adeno- + virus]

adermogenesis /ə dûr′mō jěn′ə sĭs/ failure of damaged skin to regenerate.

ADH *abbreviation*. antidiuretic hormone.

ADHD *abbreviation*. attention deficit hyperactivity disorder.

adhesiolysis /ăd hē′zē ŏl′ə sĭs/ surgical cutting of adhesions performed by laparoscopy or laparotomy.

adhesion /ăd hē′zhən/ **1.** the uniting of two surfaces or parts following surgery. **2.** inflammatory bands in the pleural or peritoneal cavity.

adhesiotomy /ăd hē′zē ŏt′ə mē/ surgical separation of adhesions.

adhesive capsulitis /ăd hē′sĭv kăp′sə lī′tĭs/ a painful condition characterized by inflammation of the cartilage and the development of fibrous bands in the shoulder joint. *Also called* frozen shoulder.

adipo- *combining form*. fat, fatty: *for example*, adipocyte.

adipocyte /ăd′ə pō sīt′/ a connective tissue cell that specializes in making and storing fat for the body. *Also called* fat cell. [adipo- + -cyte]

adipokines /ăd′ə pō kīnz′/ substances released from fatty tissue.

adiponectin /ăd′ə pō něk′tĭn/ a substance that reduces the accumulation of fatty tissue.

adipose /ăd′ə pōs′/ fatty.

adipose tissue fatty connective tissue.

adjacent /ə jā′sənt/ having a shared border; next to; nearby.

adjustment disorder **1.** a class of mental and behavioral disorders caused by an event or stress factors in the immediate environment and expected to disappear when the stressors are gone. **2.** a maladaptive reaction to an environmental stress factor occurring within weeks of the appearance of the stressor and expected to last for up to six months.

adjuvant /ăj′ə vənt/ **1.** a substance added to a (prescription) drug that improves its therapeutic effects. **2.** adjuvant chemotherapy.

adjuvant chemotherapy /kē′mō thěr′ə pē/ chemotherapy following surgical removal of a cancerous growth.

ADLs *abbreviation*. activities of daily living.

ad lib. *abbreviation*. Latin *ad libitum*, freely.

Adm *abbreviation*. admission.

admission (Adm) /ăd mĭsh′ən/ the process of admitting a patient to a hospital.

admitting diagnosis the reason a patient has been admitted to a hospital.

admitting physician the doctor responsible for admitting a patient to the hospital.

adneural /ăd nŏŏr′əl/ toward or in the direction of a nerve. [ad- + neural]

adnexa /ăd nĕk′sə/ (*pl. of* **adnexum** /ăd nĕk′səm/) those parts near to an organ or structure, especially the uterus; for example, uterine adnexa are fallopian tubes and ovaries.

ADR *abbreviation.* adverse drug reaction.

adren-, adreno-, adrenal-, adrenalo- *combining form.* adrenal gland: *for example,* adrenalectomy, adrenocortical.

adrenal /ə drē′nəl/ of or relating to the adrenal gland. [adren- + -al]

adrenal angiography /ăn′jē ŏg′rə fē/ x-ray examination of the blood vessels of an adrenal gland following IV injection of a radiopaque contrast substance; adrenal arteriography.

adrenal arteriography /är têr′ē ŏg′rə fē/ adrenal angiography.

adrenal cortex /kôr′tĕks/ the outer portion of the adrenal glands that produces several steroid hormones.

adrenalectomy /ə drē′nə lĕk′tə mē/ surgical removal of one or both adrenal glands. [adrenal- + -ectomy]

adrenal failure failure of one or both adrenal glands to function.

adrenal gland one of two endocrine glands located above each kidney that secrete important substances such as epinephrine. *Also called* suprarenal gland.

adrenaline /ə drĕn′ə lĭn/ a hormone secreted by the adrenal medulla in response to physical or mental stress that causes increased heart rate and increased blood pressure. *Also called* epinephrine.

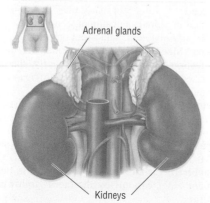

Adrenal glands

Kidneys

Adrenal Glands

adrenalitis /ə drĕn′ə lī′tĭs/ inflammation of an adrenal gland. [adren- + -itis]

adrenal medulla /mĭ dŭl′ə/ the central part of the adrenal gland that releases adrenaline (epinephrine) and noradrenaline (norepinephrine).

adrenals /ə drē′nəlz/ adrenal glands.

adrenal vein catheterization /văn′ kăth ĭ tər ə zā′shən/ a method of identifying the cause of overproduction of aldosterone using radiography and a venous blood sampling catheter.

adrenergic /ăd′rə nûr′jĭk/ activated by or having similar effects to epinephrine.

adrenocortical /ə drē′nō kôr′tĭ kəl/ of or involving the cortex of an adrenal gland. [adreno- + cortical]

adrenocortical steroids /stĕr′oidz/ steroids, such as cortisone, produced by the adrenal cortex.

adrenocorticohyperplasia /ə drē′nō kôr′tĭ kō hī′pər plā′zhə/ increased growth of one of the adrenal glands. [adreno- + cortico- + hyperplasia]

adrenocorticoid /ə drē′nō kôr′tĭ koid′/ any steroid produced by the adrenal glands.

adrenocorticotropic hormone (ACTH) /ə drē′nō kôr′tĭ kō trō′pĭk, -trŏp′ik/ a hormone produced by the pituitary gland that stimulates the adrenal cortex to produce steroids; adrenocotricotropin; corticotrophin. [adreno- + cortico- + -tropic]

adrenocorticotropin /ə drē′nō kôr′tĭ kō trō′pĭn/ adrenocorticotropic hormone.

adrenomegaly /ə drē′nō mĕg′ə lē/ an increase in the size of one or both adrenal glands. [adreno- + -megaly]

adrenopathy /ə drē nŏp′ə thē/ a disease of one or both adrenal glands. [adreno- + -pathy]

adult-onset diabetes /dī′ə bē′tĭs, -tēz/ a mild form of diabetes mellitus, with diminished sensitivity to insulin, often treatable by diet and exercise. *Also called* non-insulin-dependent diabetes mellitus, Type 2 diabetes.

adult respiratory distress syndrome (ARDS) /rĕs′pər ə tôr′ē/ a rapid-onset disorder in which the lungs fail to function as they should. *Also called* acute respiratory distress syndrome, wet lung.

adult T-cell leukemia (ATL) /lōō kē′mē ə/ a disease of mature T-cells that occurs in adulthood, characterized by swollen lymph nodes, spleen, and liver, skin and bone lesions, and a susceptibility to infection. Also called adult T-cell lymphoma, adult T-cell leukemia/lymphoma.

adult T-cell leukemia/lymphoma (ATL) /lĭm fō′mə/ or **adult T-cell lymphoma (ATL)** adult T-cell leukemia.

advance directive or advance medical directive a legal document signed by the patient or patient's agent, specifying the acceptable kinds of medical measures that may be used to prolong life in a life-threatening situation. *Also called* durable power of attorney, living will.

adventitia /ăd′věn tǐsh′ə/ the external connective tissue of an organ.

adventitious /ăd′věn tǐsh′əs/ **1.** caused by an external agent or arising in an unusual place. **2.** happening accidentally.

adverse drug event /ăd′vûrs/ adverse drug reaction.

adverse drug reaction (ADR) any unwanted, harmful side effect of a drug.

adverse effect adverse drug reaction.

adverse event or reaction adverse drug reaction.

aero- *combining form.* air: *for example,* aerophobia.

aerobe /âr′ōb/ microorganism that can only live in the presence of air or free oxygen.

aerobic /â rō′bǐk/ **1.** living in the air and using oxygen. **2.** of or involving an aerobe.

aerobic exercise aerobics.

aerobics /â rō′bǐks/ a type of exercise that improves cardiovascular and respiratory functioning; aerobic exercises.

aerocele /âr′ə sēl′/ expansion of a small body cavity by gas, especially in the larynx or trachea. [aero- + -cele]

aerophagia /âr′o fā′jə, -je ə/ or aerophagy /â rŏf′ə jē/ the swallowing of an abnormal amount of air. [aero- + -phagia]

aerophobia /âr′ō fō′bē ə/ an abnormal fear of drafts. [aero- + -phobia]

aerosinusitis /âr′ō sī′nə sī′tǐs/ inflammation of the sinuses caused by a quick change in air pressure, as when flying. [aero- + sinusitis]

aerosol /âr′ə sôl′/ liquid or solid matter medicinal applications packaged under pressure in order to be delivered as a gas or spray.

aerosolization /âr′ə sô lǐ zā′shən/ packaging a medicine under pressure.

aerospace medicine /âr′ō spās′/ the branch of medicine concerned with the ability of the body to function in outer space. [aero- + space]

aerotherapy /âr′ō thěr′ə pē/ a naturopathic method of improving the functioning of the cardiovascular system using oxygen therapy. [aero- + therapy]

aerotitis /âr′ō tī′tǐs/ problems of the middle ear caused by rapid changes in air pressure, as when flying; aerotitis media.

aerotitis media /mē′dē ə/ aerotitis.

aetiology /ē′tē ŏl′ə jē/ the origins and causes of disease; etiology.

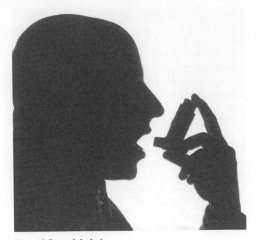

Aerosol (in an Inhaler)

AF *abbreviation.* atrial fibrillation

AFB *abbreviation.* acid-fast bacillus.

afebrile /ā fěb′rǐl/ without fever. [a- + febrile]

affect /ăf′ěkt/ the feeling or mood connected with an idea.

afferent /ăf′ər ənt/ flowing or carrying toward a center, used of some arteries, veins, nerves, and lymphatics.

afferent arteriole /är têr′ē ōl′/ a small artery that carries blood to the capillary bed.

afferent nerve a nerve that carries information from the periphery to the central nervous system. *Also called* sensory nerve.

afferent neuron /nŏŏr′ŏn/ a neuron that carries information from sensory receptors at its peripheral endings to the central nervous system. *Also called* sensory neuron.

afferent vessel /věs′əl/ an artery that carries blood to a part.

affinity /ə fǐn′ǐ tē/ **1.** the attraction that makes some atoms unite with others. **2.** highly specific staining of a tissue by a dye.

aflatoxin /ăf′lə tŏk′sǐn/ a cancerous toxin produced by fungi, in particular *Aspergillus*, found in peanuts and animal feed.

AFO *abbreviation.* ankle-foot orthotic.

African sleeping sickness a potentially fatal infection transmitted by the tsetse fly, characterized by fever and deep coma; African trypanosomiasis.

African tickbite fever /tǐk′bīt′/ a disease caused by a bacterium, *Rickettsia africae*, in southern Africa.

African trypanosomiasis /trǐ păn′ō sə mī′ə sǐs/ African sleeping sickness.

afterbirth /ăf′tər bûrth′/ the placenta and membranes cast off by the uterus following birth.

Ag *abbreviation.* silver.

A/G *abbreviation*. albumin : globulin ratio.

agammaglobulinemia /ā′găm ə glŏb′yə lə nē′mē ə/ the lack of, or low levels of, serum gamma globulin.

agar-agar /ä′gär ä′gär, ā′gär ā′gär/ an extract of seaweed, used as the main ingredient in dental impressions.

age-related deafness age-related hearing loss, usually in both ears, with gradually progressive inability to hear. *Also called* presbycusis.

age-related macular degeneration /măk′yə lər dĭ jĕn′ə rā′shən/ an eye disease, usually appearing after age 60, that progressively destroys the central portion of the retina, impairing the ability to see straight ahead.

agenesis /ā jĕn′ə sĭs/ the failure to develop, or absence of, some part. [a- + -genesis]

agent /ā′jənt/ **1.** a force or substance that can produce an effect. **2.** something, such as a microorganism or chemical substance, whose presence or absence causes a disease or more advanced disease.

ageusia /ə gyōō′zē ə/ loss of the ability to taste.

agglutin-, agglutino- *combining form.* adhere or combine: *for example,* agglutinogen.

agglutinate *v.* /ə glōō′tə nāt′/ **1.** to cause to adhere. **2.** to combine or unite in a group or mass. *n.* /ə glōō′tə nĭt/ **3.** a clump of combined material.

agglutination /ə glōō′tə nā′shən/ **1.** the action or process of agglutinating. **2.** a mass or group formed of separate elements. **3.** a reaction in which particles suspended in a liquid clump together.

agglutinin /ə glōō′tə nĭn/ a substance capable of causing agglutination.

agglutinogen /ăg′lōō tĭn′ə jən, -jĕn′, ə glōō′tə nə-/ an antigen that causes an agglutinin to form. [agglutino- + -gen]

aggression /ə grĕsh′ən/ extremely hostile or destructive behavior.

aggressive /ə grĕs′ĭv/ **1.** developing or spreading rapidly. **2.** more intense or thoroughgoing, as a treatment.

aggressive angiomyxoma /ăn′jē ō mĭk sō′mə/ an invasive tumor found in the genitals of young women that does not spread to other parts of the body.

aggressive lymphoma /lĭm fō′mə/ a rapidly spreading tumor of lymph tissue, usually malignant.

aggressiveness /ə grĕs′ĭv nĭs/ **1.** the ability to develop or spread rapidly. **2.** the intense or more comprehensive approach to treatment of a disease.

aging /ā′jĭng/ the process of growing older.

agita /ăj′ĭ tə/ an informal term used to refer to heartburn or acid indigestion.

agitated depression depression characterized by agitation and restlessness.

agitation /ăj′ĭ tā′shən/ restless emotional disturbance.

aglossia /ā glŏs′ē ə/ lacking a tongue.

aglycosuria / ā glī′kō sōōr′ē ə/ lack of sugar in the urine.

AGN *abbreviation*. **1.** acute glomerulonephritis. **2.** acute necrotizing gingivitis.

agnathia /ăg nā′thē ə/ lack of the lower jaw at birth.

agnathous /ăg′nə thəs/ lacking a lower jaw from birth.

agnosia /ăg nō′zhə/ an inability to recognize or understand sensory information.

agonist /ăg′ə nĭst/ **1.** a drug or compound that acts on a receptor the way a natural hormone might. **2.** a drug that increases the potency of other drugs.

agoraphobia /ăg′ər ə fō′bē ə/ an abnormal fear of leaving safe surroundings; excessive fear of public places.

agranulocyte /ə grăn′yə lə sīt′/ a type of white blood cell that has no granules.

agranulocytosis /ə grăn′yə lō sī tō′sĭs/ a serious condition characterized by a low white cell count.

agraphia /ə grăf′ē ə/ the inability to write.

ague /ā′gyōō/ an old-fashioned term for a fever that comes and goes.

AHD *abbreviation*. atherosclerotic heart disease.

AHIMA *abbreviation*. American Health Information Management Association (www. ahima.org)

AI *abbreviation*. aortic insufficiency.

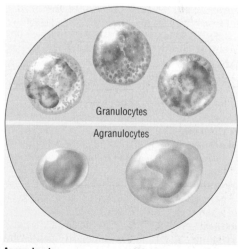

Agranulocyte

AID *abbreviation.* artificial insemination by donor.

aided exercise physical exercising performed with the aid of mechanical devices.

AIDS /ādz/ *abbreviation.* acquired immunodeficiency syndrome or acquired immunodeficiency disease.

AIDS dementia complex /dĭ měn′shə kŏm′ plĕks/ a progressive syndrome associated with AIDS, characterized by memory loss, an inability to concentrate, and the loss of other intellectual functions.

AIDS-related complex (ARC) an early stage in AIDS characterized by mild symptoms.

AIDS wasting syndrome a syndrome associated with AIDS, characterized by abnormal involuntary weight loss plus either chronic diarrhea or chronic weakness and persistent fever that cannot be explained except by HIV infection.

AIH *abbreviation.* artificial insemination, homologous (using the husband's semen).

ailurophobia /ī lōōr′ə fō′bē ə, ā lōōr′-/ an intense irrational fear of cats.

air-conditioner lung /lŭng/ an inflammation of the lung alveoli caused by breathing contaminated forced air.

air conduction (AC) /kən dŭk′shən/ the carrying of sound to the inner ear via the auditory canal and middle ear.

air contrast enema /ĕn′ə mə/ air contrast barium enema.

air contrast barium enema /bâr′ē əm ĕn′ə mə, băr′-/ an x-ray diagnostic examination in which air is injected into the colon after it has been coated with a thick liquid containing barium. *Also called* double-contrast barium enema.

airway /âr′wā′/ any part of the respiratory system that allows the passage of air.

airway obstruction /əb strŭk′shən/ a respiratory dysfunction in which airflow is obstructed, usually when breathing out.

AK *abbreviation.* actinic keratosis.

A-K *abbreviation.* above-the-knee.

AKA *abbreviation.* above-the-knee amputation.

akaryocyte /ā kăr′ē ə sīt′/ a cell without a nucleus. [a- + karyo- + -cyte]

akathisia /ăk′ə thĭzh′ə, -thĭz′ē ə/ inability to sit for long periods due to quivering and restlessness in the muscles.

akeratosis /ə kĕr′ə tō′sĭs/ a deficiency or complete lack of the horny layer of skin. [a- + keratosis]

akinesia /ā′kĭ nē′zhə/ or **akinesis** /ā′kĭ nē′sĭs/ the inability to move voluntarily caused by brain dysfunction. [a- + -kinesia]

akinesthesia /ā kin′əs thē′zhə/ loss of the ability to perceive motion.

akinetic /ā′kĭ nĕt′ĭk/ or **akinesic** /ā′kĭ nē′zĭk, -sĭk/ of or involving akinesia.

akinetic mutism /myōō′tĭz əm/ a mild or chronic state of consciousness in which the person seems alert but is incapable of responding to stimuli.

-al of or involving; process: *for example,* adrenal.

Ala *abbreviation.* alanine.

alalia /ə lā′lē ə/ the inability to speak.

alanine (A, Ala) /ăl′ə nēn′/ an amino acid building block in producing protein.

alanine aminotransferase (ALT) /ə mē′nō trăns′fə rās′/ an enzyme normally found in liver and heart cells that is released into the bloodstream when liver or heart damage occurs. *Also called* alanine transaminase, glutamic-pyruvic transaminase; serum glutamic pyruvic transaminase.

alanine-glyoxylate aminotransferase /ăl′ ə nēn′ glī ŏk′sə lāt′ ə mē′nō trăns′fə rās′/ a liver enzyme.

alanine transaminase (ALT) /trănz ăm′ə nās′/ alanine aminotransferase. *Also called* glutamic-pyruvic transaminase, serum glutamic pyruvic transaminase.

alb *abbreviation.* serum albumin.

albinism /ăl′bə nĭz′əm/ any of several inherited disorders characterized by little or no skin color.

albino /ăl bī′nō/ a person who has albinism.

albuginea /ăl′byōō jĭn′ē ə/ a layer of white fibrous tissue, especially the tissue covering the testicle.

albumen /ăl byōō′mən/ 1. albumin. 2. the white of an egg.

albumin /ăl byōō′mən/ a water-soluble protein, especially one in the blood which carries or binds many drugs and other compounds.

albumin : globulin ratio (A/G) /ăl byōō′mən glŏb′yə lĭn rā′shē ō/ the ratio of albumin to globulin in the serum or urine, information used to diagnose kidney disease.

albuminuria /ăl byōō′mə nōōr′ē ə/ the presence of protein in the urine, often indicative of disease. *Also called* proteinuria. [albumin + -uria]

alcohol /ăl′kə hôl′/ 1. ethanol, often used to sterilize septic wounds. 2. a drink containing ethanol, such as wine or beer.

alcohol abuse alcoholism.

alcohol dependence alcoholism.

alcoholic cirrhosis /ăl′kə hô′lĭk sĭ rō′sĭs/ a liver disease caused by alcoholism.

alcoholism /ăl′kə hô lĭz′əm/ a chronic disorder characterized by excessive and uncontrolled consumption of alcohol; alcohol abuse; alcohol dependence.

alcohol poisoning a toxic condition caused by drinking a large amount of alcohol, usually in a short period of time, occasionally causing death.

aldosterone /ăl dŏs′tə rōn′/ a hormone produced by the adrenal cortex which causes the kidney to conserve sodium (salt) and water.

aldosteronism /ăl dŏs′tər ə nĭz′əm/ a disorder characterized by the secretion of too much aldosterone.

Alexander technique /ăl′ĭg zăn′dər/ physical exercises that improve various bodily functions, such as breathing.

alexia /ə lĕk′sē ə/ the inability to understand spoken or written language, caused by a brain lesion.

alexic /ə lĕk′sĭk/ of or involving alexia.

algae /ăl′jē/ a group of one-celled organisms capable of photosynthesis that includes seaweeds.

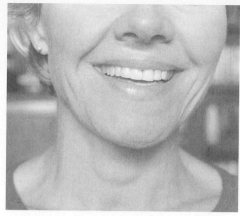

Alignment (of upper and lower Teeth)

algesio- *combining form.* pain: *for example,* algesiometer.

-algesia *suffix.* pain: *for example,* analgisia.

algesia /ăl jē′zē ə/ pain.

algesic /ăl jē′zĭk/ painful.

algesiometer /ăl jē′zē ŏm′ĭ tər/ or **algesimeter** /ăl′jə sĭm′ĭ tər/ a device that measures sensitivity to painful stimuli; algometer. [algesio- + -meter]

algesthesia /ăl′jəs thē′zhə/ or **algesthesis** /ăl′jəs thē′sĭs/ sensitivity to pain; algesia.

-algia *suffix.* pain or a specific painful condition: *for example,* neuralgia.

algo- *combining form.* pain: *for example,* algophobia.

algometer /ăl gŏm′ĭ tər/ algesiometer.

algophilia /ăl′gə fĭl′ē ə/ pleasure derived from the thought of pain experienced by oneself or others. [algo- + -philia]

algophobia /ăl′gə fō′bē ə/ an abnormal fear of pain. [algo- + -phobia]

alienation /āl′yə nā′shən/ a psychological condition characterized by an inability to experience meaningful relationships with others.

alignment /ə līn′mənt/ **1.** the proper longitudinal positioning of a bone or limb. **2.** the proper positioning of the teeth with respect to the jaws and other teeth.

alimentary /ăl′ə mĕn′tə rē/ of or relating to food.

alimentary canal digestive tract.

alkalemia /ăl′kə lē′mē ə/ a rise in the pH of the blood caused by a decrease in hydrogen ions.

alkali /ăl′kə lī′/ any substance having strong base or non-acid properties.

alkaline /ăl′kə līn′/ of or containing an alkali.

alkaline phosphatase /ăl′kə līn′ fŏs′fə tās′/ a phosphatase normally found in liver, heart, and lung tissue, measured as a blood level.

alkaloid /ăl′kə loid′/ one of hundreds of plant products characterized by alkaline reactions.

alkalosis /ăl′kə lō′sĭs/ a state characterized by a fall in the hydrogen ion concentration in arterial blood, indicating either a metabolic or respiratory abnormality.

alkaptonuria /ăl kăp′tō nŏŏr′ē ə/ an inherited metabolic disorder caused by lack of a particular enzyme (homogentisic acid [HGA] dioxygenase), characterized by a certain acid (homogentisic acid) in the urine, bluish-black color in connective tissue, and arthritis.

ALL *abbreviation.* acute lymphoblastic leukemia; acute lymphocytic leukemia.

allele /ə lēl′/ one of a series of different genes capable of occurring at the same site on a chromosome.

allelic /ə lē′lĭk, ə lĕl′ĭk/ of or involving an allele.

allergen /ăl′ər jən, -jĕn′/ a substance that causes an allergic reaction.

allergic /ə lûr′jĭk/ of, pertaining to, or having an allergy.

allergic reaction a reaction to an allergen following contact with it.

allergic rhinitis /rī nī′tĭs/ inflammation of the mucous membrane of the nose (a runny nose) caused by exposure to an allergen, such as pollen.

allergist /ăl′ər jĭst/ a physician who specializes in treating allergies.

allergy /ăl′ər jē/ a potentially dangerous (when extreme) sensitivity to a specific allergen caused by exposure to it that typically causes an increased sensitivity to the allergen when exposed to it again. The allergy is manifested by symptoms such as rash, itching, runny nose, swelling of the face, mouth or tongue, or sometimes as an asthma attack or difficulty breathing.

allergy desensitization /dē sĕn′sĭ tə zā′shən/ or **allergy immunotherapy** /ĭm′yə nō thĕr′ə pē/ stimulation of the immune system by gradually introducing larger amounts of the allergens to which a person is sensitive; allergy shots.

allergy scratch test a skin test that identifies the allergen that causes an allergic reaction. A small amount of the suspected allergen is placed on the skin, which is then gently scratched with a sterile needle.

allergy shots allergy immunotherapy.

allergy skin test administration of diluted amounts of an allergen under the skin to test for a reaction.

allergy testing administering allergy skin tests.

allied health /ăl′līd hĕlth/ the careers in health care that support or complement health care practitioners: for example, medical assistant, physical therapist, laboratory technician, dental assistant, medical billing specialist, medical coder, nurse's aide, and medical receptionist.

allo- *prefix.* of the same species: *for example,* allograft.

allodynia /ăl′ō dĭn′ē ə/ a condition in which nonpainful stimuli cause pain.

allogeneic /ăl′ō jə nē′ĭk/ or **allogenic** /ăl′ō jĕn′ĭk/ from different individuals belonging to the same species.

allogeneic graft allograft.

allogenic transplant /trăns′plănt′/ allograft.

allograft /ăl′ə grăft′/ the transplantation of an organ or tissue from one person to another of the same species with different genetic makeup; allogeneic graft, allogenic transplant. [allo- + graft]

allopath /ăl′ə păth′/ allopathist.

allopathic /ăl′ə păth′ĭk/ of or involving the principles of allopathy.

allopathic medicine /mĕd′ə sĭn/ a system of medical treatment in which diseases are treated by the introduction of another disease antagonistic to them; allopathy.

allopathist /ə lŏp′ə thĭst/ a person trained to treat diseases using the principles of allopathy; allopath.

allopathy /ə lŏp′ə thē/ allopathic medicine. [allo- + -pathy]

aloe /ăl′ō/ aloe vera.

aloe vera /vĕr′ə, vêr′ə/ a succulent plant whose leaves produce a soothing, slimy liquid used in cosmetics and skin preparations; it is particularly effective in treating burns.

alogia /ə lō′jə, -jē ə/ **1.** a speech disorder characterized by an impairment of verbal expression and comprehension; aphasia. **2.** an inability to speak caused by mental deficit or dementia.

Alopecia (as normal part of Aging)

alopecia /ăl′ō pē′shē ə/ partial or total loss of hair; baldness; may be normal (as in aging) or may be part of a disease process.

alopecia areata /ăr′ē ā′tə/ a condition of hair loss characterized by limited irregular bald patches in the scalp, eyebrows, and beard.

alopecia (capitis) totalis /(kăp′ĭ tĭs) tō tăl′ĭs/ total hair loss on the scalp.

alopecia universalis /yōō′nə vər sā′lĭs/ total hair loss all over the body.

alpha-adrenergic blocker /ăl′fə ăd′rə nûr′jĭk/ a drug used to treat high blood pressure that blocks alpha receptors in arteries and smooth muscle, resulting in lowered blood pressure and a decrease in the symptoms of fright, such as sweating, shaking, and tachycardia; alpha blocker.

alpha blocker alpha-adrenergic blocker.

alpha cells endocrine cells in the pancreas that make and secrete glucagon, which causes the liver to release glucose, raising glucose levels in the blood.

alpha-fetoprotein /ăl′fə fē′tō prō′tēn, -tē ĭn/ a protein normally produced during fetal development.

alpha-fetoprotein analysis /ə năl′ə sĭs/ a blood test that screens pregnant women to identify those at an increased risk of having babies with certain problems.

alpha-galactosidase A deficiency /ăl′fə gə lăk′tō sī′dās ā′/ an enzyme essential to the metabolism of molecules known as glycosphingolipids; lack of this enzyme is associated with Fabry's disease.

alpha globulin /glŏb′yə lĭn/ a type of globulin found in blood plasma.

alpha-glucosidase inhibitor /ăl′fə glōō′kō sī′dās/ oral medications prescribed for type 2 diabetes that decrease the absorption of carbohydrates from the intestine.

alpha-hydroxy acid /ăl′fə hī drŏk′sē/ any of the so-called "fruit acids," including glycolic and lactic acid, sometimes used to treat skin conditions.

alpha interferon /ĭn′tər fêr′ŏn/   a protein produced by the body in response to an infection.

alpha linolenic acid /lĭn′ō lē′nĭk, -lĕn′ĭk/   an essential fatty acid found in flaxseed oil, canola oil, and walnuts.

alpha receptor   a site on cells in the heart that interacts with epinephrine or norepinephrine to increase heart rate, and on cells in the skin and GI tract that interacts with these hormones to cause vasoconstriction.

Alport syndrome /ôl′pôrt/   a hereditary disease characterized by progressive kidney disease, deafness, and eye defects.

ALS   *abbreviation.*   amyotrophic   lateral sclerosis.

Alström syndrome /äl′strəm/   a progressive genetic disorder characterized by obesity, deafness, and visual problems in childhood, followed by type 2 diabetes and kidney failure in adulthood.

ALT   *abbreviation.* alanine aminotransferase; alanine transaminase.

alternate hemiplegia /hĕm′ĭ plē′jə, -jē ə/   a rare neurological disorder of infants, characterized by temporary episodes of paralysis of one side of the body (hemiplegia).

alternative medical system   a system of alternative medicine with a system of theory and practice.

alternative medicine   any practice thought to have therapeutic benefits, such as doses of megavitamins or massage therapy, used instead of standard medical treatments.

altitude sickness   a disorder brought on by high altitudes in which the body is not able to get enough oxygen.

alveol-, alveolo-   *combining form.* alveolus: *for example,* alveolitis, alveoloplasty.

alveolar /ăl vē′ə lər/   of or involving an alveolus.

alveolar bone   spongy bone located in the mandible.

alveolar proteinosis /prō′tē nō′sĭs, -tē ə nō′-/   a lung disease characterized by progressive breathing difficulty and coughing due to blockage by lipoprotein material in the alveoli.

alveolectomy /ăl′vē ə lĕk′tə mē/   partial or complete removal of alveolar bone. [alveol- + -ectomy]

alveolitis /ăl′vē ə lī′tĭs/   **1.** inflammation of the alveoli. **2.** inflammation of a tooth socket. [alveol- + -itis]

alveoloplasty   /ăl vē′ə lə plăs′tē/   surgical shaping and smoothing of sockets prior to the use of dentures. [alveolo- + -plasty]

alveolotomy /ăl′vē ə lŏt′ə mē/   surgical opening of a tooth socket to drain pus. [alveolo- + -tomy]

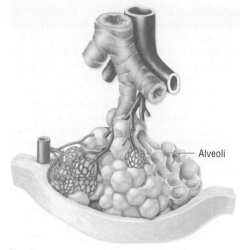

Alveoli

alveolus /ăl vē′ə ləs/   (*pl.* **alveoli** /ăl vē′ə lī′/) **1.** a tiny air sac in the lungs. **2.** a small cell or cavity such as a tooth socket.

Alzheimer('s) disease /ôlts′hī mər(z)/   progressive neurologic disease of the brain that causes irreversible loss of neurons and eventual dementia characterized by loss of memory, impairment of judgment, decision-making, language use, and awareness of surroundings.

a.m., AM   *abbreviation.* Latin *ante meridiem,* before noon.

AMA   *abbreviation.* American Medical Association (www.ama-assn.org).

amalgam /ə măl′gəm/   a combination of mercury with another metal used in fillings of teeth.

amastia /ə măs′tē ə/   congenital lack of one or both breasts.

amaurosis /ăm′ô rō′sĭs/   blindness, especially when the cause is not found in the eye.

amaurosis fugax /fyōō′găks/   brief episode of visual loss, usually due to small clots breaking off atherosclerotic plaques in the carotid artery.

ambi-   *combining form.* **1.** around, on all sides: *for example,* ambient. **2.** both, double: *for example,* ambidextrous, ambivalent.

ambidextrous /ăm′bĭ dĕks′trəs/   capable of using both hands equally well. [ambi- + dextrous]

ambient /am′bē ənt/   of or relating to the environment in which an organism lives.

ambivalence /ăm bĭv′ə ləns/   a lack of certainty caused by coexisting contradictory feelings or attitudes.

ambivalent /ăm bĭv′ə lənt/   of or involving ambivalence.

amblyopia /ăm′blē ō′pē ə/   visual impairment in which there is no apparent damage to the eye.

ambulance /ăm′byə ləns/ a vehicle that transports sick or injured people to a treatment center.

ambulant /ăm′byə lənt/ ambulatory.

ambulate /ăm′byə lāt′/ to walk.

ambulation /ăm′byə lā′shən/ the act of walking.

ambulatory /ăm′byə lə tôr′ē/ capable of walking; ambulant.

ambulatory care medical or surgical treatment when hospitalization is not necessary; outpatient care.

ambulatory phlebectomy /flə běk′tə mē/ a minimally invasive type of surgery that removes swollen veins through small punctures.

ambulatory surgery an operation that is performed in an outpatient clinic, doctor's office, or ambulatory surgery center without overnight hospitalization.

AMC *abbreviation.* arthrogryposis multiplex congenita.

ameba /ə mē′bə/ (*pl.* **amebae** /ə mē′bē/ or **amebas**) the common name for a one-celled organism and similar protozoans; amoeba.

amebiasis /ăm′ē bī′ə sĭs/ disease or illness caused by amebas; amoebiasis.

amebic /ə mē′bĭk/ related to or caused by amebas; amoebic.

amebic colitis /kə lī′tĭs/ inflammation of the colon caused by amebas.

amebic dysentery /dĭs′ən tĕr′ē/ diarrhea caused by amebas.

amelanotic /ā mĕl′ə nŏt′ĭk/ lacking melanin; colorless. [a- + melanotic]

amelanotic melanoma /mĕl′ə nō′mə/ a form of skin cancer in which melanin is not produced by the malignant cells.

amelia /ā mē′lē ə/ congenital lack of limbs.

amelioration /ə mēl′yə rā′shən/ improvement.

amelogenesis /ăm′ə lō jĕn′ə sĭs/ the development of tooth enamel.

amenorrhea /ā mĕn′ə rē′ə/ the abnormal end of or lack of menstruation. *Also called* menostasis. [a- + menorrhea]

American Sign Language (ASL) the language used by deaf people in the United States, in which communication relies on signs and gestures made using the hands.

Americans with Disabilities Act (ADA) a Congressional law that protects the rights of people with disabilities and sets forth basic requirements for accessibilities and services (www. ada.gov).

Ames test /āmz/ a test that identifies possible chemical carcinogens by examining their mutagenic effect on Salmonella bacteria.

ametria /ə mē′trē ə/ congenital lack of a uterus.

AMI *abbreviation.* acute myocardial infarction.

amine /ə mēn′, ăm′ĭn/ any of a class of basic organic compounds produced from ammonia.

amino acid (AA, aa) /ə mē′nō, ăm′ĭ nō′/ one of 20 compounds required to create protein.

aminotransferase /ə mē′nō trăns′fə rās′, ăm′ə nō-/ an enzyme that catalyzes the transfer of an amino group from a donor molecule to a recipient molecule; transaminase.

amitriptyline /ăm′ĭ trĭp′tə lēn′/ an antidepressant medication that can raise mood by increasing the neurotransmitters in brain tissue, and sometimes used for pain relief in neuropathic pain.

AML *abbreviation.* acute myelogenous lymphocytic leukemia; acute myeloblastic leukemia; acute myelocytic leukemia; acute myeloid leukemia.

ammoniuria /ə mō′nē yŏŏr′ē ə/ producing urine that contains too much ammonia.

amnesia /ăm nē′zhə/ the inability to recall information stored in long-term memory.

amnio- *combining form.* amnion: *for example,* amniography.

amniocentesis /ăm′nē ō sĕn tē′sĭs/ removal of fluid from the amniotic sac for diagnostic purposes. [amnio- + -centesis]

amniochorial /ăm′nē ō kôr′ē əl/ of or involving both amnion and chorion.

amniogenesis /ăm′nē ō jĕn′ə sĭs/ development of the amnion. [amnio- + -genesis]

amniography /ăm′nē ŏg′rə fē/ making an x-ray of the amniotic cavity and fetus, after a contrast medium has been injected into the amniotic fluid. [amnio- + -graphy]

amnion /ăm′nē ən/ the innermost membrane enclosing a fetus in utero; it contains the amniotic fluid.

amnionic sac /ăm′nē ŏn′ĭk săk′/ amnion.

amnionitis /ăm′nē ə nī′tĭs/ inflammation of the amnion. [amnion + -itis]

amnioreduction /ăm′nē ō rĭ dŭk′shən/ the removal of a large amount of amniotic fluid. [amnio- + reduction]

amniorrhea /ăm′nē ə rē′ə/ the leakage of amniotic fluid. [amnio- + -rrhea]

amniorrhexis /ăm′nē ə rĕk′sĭs/ a tear in the amnion. [amnio- + -rrhexis]

amnioscope /ăm′nē ə skōp′/ an endoscope used to examine amniotic fluid without removing it. [amnio- + -scope]

amnioscopy /ăm′nē ŏs′kə pē/ using an endoscope to examine amniotic fluid. [amnio- + -scopy]

amniotic cavity /ăm′nē ŏt′ĭk/ the fluid-filled sac inside the amnion.

amniotic fluid /flŏŏ′ĭd/ the protective fluid surrounding the fetus inside the amniotic sac.

amniotic sac /săk/   the sac that provides a fluid environment to protect the fetus

amniotomy /ăm′nē ŏt′ə mē/   a deliberate tearing of the fetal membranes in order to cause labor to start or to make it less difficult. [amnio- + -tomy]

amoeba /ə mē′bə/   the common name for a one-celled organism and similar protozoans; ameba.

amoebiasis /ăm′ē bī′ə sĭs/   disease or illness caused by amebas; amebiasis.

amoebic /ə mē′bĭk/   related to or caused by amebas; amebic.

amorphous /ə môr′fəs/   **1.** having no definite form. **2.** uncrystallized.

amoxicillin   /ə mŏk′sə sĭl′ĭn/   a broad-spectrum antibiotic.

amphetamine /ăm fĕt′ə mēn′, -mĭn/   a highly addictive drug that acts by increasing dopamine in the uppermost part of the brainstem.

amphiarthrosis /ăm′fē är thrō′sĭs/   (*pl.* **amphiarthroses** /ăm′fē är thrō′sēz/)   a kind of connection between bony surfaces, ligaments, or elastic cartilage, that allows only limited motion; found in adult humans in the intervertebral joints with discs and the pubic symphysis.

amplification /ăm′plə fĭ kā′shən/   enlarging or increasing a visual or auditory stimulus to make it easier to perceive.

amplification device   something that makes a visual stimulus larger or an auditory stimulus louder.

ampule /am′ pyōōl/   a small medicine vial for liquids.

ampulla /ăm pŭl′ə/ (*pl.* **ampullae** /ăm pŭl′ē/)   a widening of a canal or duct.

ampulla of Vater /fä′tər/   portion of the bile duct where it joins the duodenum

amputation /ăm′pyōō tā′shən/   removal of a limb or part of a limb.

amputee /ăm′pyōō tē′/   a person who has lost one or more limbs.

Amsler /ämz′lər/ **grid** or **chart**   a pattern of small squares used to identify defects in the central visual field.

amyelia /ā′mī ē′lē ə/   congenital lack of a spinal cord.

amyelination /ā mī′ə lə nā′shən/   congenital lack of myelin sheath covering a nerve or nerves.

amygdala   /ə mĭg′də lə/   (*pl.*   **amygdalae** /ə mĭg′də lē′/)   small rounded structure of the primitive temporal lobe concerned with feeding, fighting, flight, and mating behavior.

amygdaloid /ə mĭg′də loid′/   having a shape similar to an almond or a tonsil.

amygdaloid body or **amygdaloid nucleus**   amygdala.

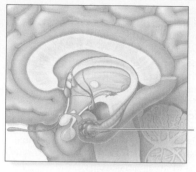

— Amygdala

Amygdala

amylase /ăm′ə lās′/   an enzyme that splits starch.

amyloidosis   /ăm′ə loi dō′sĭs/   a disorder caused by the abnormal deposition of the protein amyloid in various tissues.

amyotonia /ā′mī ə tō′nē ə/   a generalized loss of muscle tone.

amyotrophic   lateral   sclerosis   (ALS) /ā′mī ə trŏf′ĭk lăt′ər əl sklĭ rō′sĭs/   a progressive degenerative disease of the lateral columns of the spinal cord leading to weakness, paralysis, and death. *Also called* Lou Gehrig's disease.

amyotrophy /ā′mī ŏt′rə fē/   atrophy of muscular tissue. [a- + myo- + -trophy]

an-[1]   *prefix.* not: *for example,* anemia.

an-[2], **ana-**   *prefix.* up; upward: back; backward: *for example,* anabiosis.

ANA   *abbreviation.* antinuclear antibody titer, elevated in connective tissue disease.

anabiosis /ăn′ə bī ō′sĭs/   a bringing back to life from a deathlike condition; resuscitation. [ana- + -biosis]

anabolic steroids /ăn′ə bŏl′ĭk stĕr′oidz/   a prescription drug used by some athletes, often illegally, to increase their muscle mass.

anabolism /ə năb′ə lĭz′əm/   **1.** the buildup of substances in the body, a metabolic process. **2.** all synthetic metabolic reactions.

anacusis or **anakusis** /ăn′ə kyōō′sĭs/   the inability to hear.

anaerobe /ăn′ə rōb′, ăn âr′ōb/   microorganism capable of living without oxygen.

anaerobic /ăn′ə rō′bĭk/   **1.** capable of living without oxygen. **2.** of or involving an anaerobe.

anaesthesia /ăn′əs thē′zhə/   total or partial loss of sensation or awareness caused by disease, injury, or an anesthetic drug; anesthesia.

anaesthetic /ăn′əs thĕt′ĭk/   **1.** *n.* a drug or chemical agent that causes partial or total loss of sensation, with or without loss of consciousness; anesthetic. **2.** *adj.* of or involving loss of bodily sensation; anesthetic.

anal /ā′nəl/ of or involving the anus.

anal atresia /ə trē′zhə/ congenital lack of an anus or of the anal canal. *Also called* atresia ani.

analbuminemia /ăn′ăl byoō′mə nē′mē ə/ a lack of albumin from blood serum.

anal canal the last part of the digestive tract, up to the anus.

analeptic /ăn′ə lĕp′tĭk/ a medication that stimulates the central nervous system.

anal fissure /fĭsh′ər/ a tear in the anal canal.

anal fissurectomy /fĭsh′ə rĕk′tə mē/ surgical removal of an anal fissure.

anal fistula /fĭs′chə lə/ an abnormal opening near the anus.

anal fistulectomy /fĭs′chə lĕk′tə mē/ surgical removal or closure of a fistula.

analgesia /ăn′əl jē′zē ə/ the inability to feel pain even though it is present. [an- + -algesia]

analgesic /ăn′əl jē′zĭk/ 1. *adj.* characterized by a limited ability to respond to pain. 2. *n.* an analgesic drug.

analgesic drug a pain reliever.

anal incontinence /ĭn kŏn′tə nəns/ inability to control the anal sphincters, making it difficult to retain feces in the rectum. *Also called* fecal incontinence, rectal incontinence.

analog or **analogue** /ăn′ə lôg′/ one of two compounds that have the same elements but a different structure or properties.

analogous /ə năl′ə gəs/ sharing a functional similarity but differing in origin or structure.

analysis /ə năl′ə sĭs/ 1. the breaking down of a compound into its basic elements. 2. the study of a whole by examination of its distinct parts. 3. treatment of mental disorders through in-depth talk therapy; psychoanalysis. 4. the organizing of data in order to proceed with research or make a judgment regarding patient care.

analyst /ăn′ə lĭst/ a medical practitioner trained in analysis.

analytic sensitivity /ăn′ə lĭt′ĭk/ the ability of a test to identify a substance or some small change in it.

analytic specificity /spĕs′ə fĭs′ĭ tē/ the ability of a test to react only to a specific element.

anaphia /ăn ā′fē ə/ the lack of sense of touch.

anaphylactic reaction /ăn′ə fə lăk′tĭk/ a severe allergic reaction to foreign material.

anaphylactic shock an extreme allergic reaction with circulatory failure.

anaphylaxis /ăn′ə fə lăk′sĭs/ an immediate allergic reaction.

anaplasia /ăn′ə plā′zhə/ loss of differentiation in a cell, usually in association with cancer. [ana- + -plasia]

anaplastic /ăn′ə plăs′tĭk/ 1. of or involving anaplasty. 2. relating to or characterized by anaplasia. 3. developing without form, as in the loss of cell differentiation associated with cancers.

anaplastology /ăn′ə plă stŏl′ə jē/ the use of prostheses to replace or reconstruct missing body parts or the medical specialty concerned with the making or fitting of prosthetic devices.

anaplasty /ăn′ə plăs′tē/ the restoration of a part to its normal shape with the use of healthy tissue. [ana- + -plasty]

anapophysis /ăn ə pŏf′ə sĭs/ an auxiliary process of thoracic or lumbar vertebrae.

anastomosis /ə năs′tə mō′sĭs/ 1. a natural connection between two blood vessels or other tubular structures. 2. a functioning link between tubular structures. 3. an opening between two or more spaces or organs that are usually distinct.

anat. *abbreviation.* anatomy.

ANA test a test that identifies unusual antibodies directed against structures of the cell nucleus.

anatomical crown /ăn′ə tŏm′ĭ kəl/ portion of the tooth covered with enamel.

anatomical position upright position of the body with arms at the side, feet together, and the head, palms, and toes facing forward, used as a reference when describing parts of the body in relation to each other.

anatomy /ə năt′ə mē/ 1. the science that studies the physical structure of organisms. 2. dissection. See anatomy plates starting after page 264.

Anderson-Fabry(′s) disease /ăn′dər sən fă′brē(z) dĭ zēz′/ a sex-linked genetic disorder due to deficiency of an enzyme that leads to a number of progressive symptoms, including renal disfunction, a rash on the thighs, buttocks and genitals, fevers, and hypertension; death results from renal, cardiac, or cerebrovascular complications. *Also called* Fabry disease. *See also* alpha-galactosidase A deficiency.

andr-, andro- *combining form.* masculine: *for example,* android, androphobia.

androblastoma /ăn′drō blă stō′mə/ 1. a testicular tumor. 2. an ovarian tumor containing some properties that may cause masculinization. [andro- + blastoma]

androgen /ăn′drə jən/ a male sex hormone that controls the development and maintenance of masculine characteristics. [andro- + -gen]

androgenic /ăn′drə jĕn′ĭk/ of or relating to the male sex hormone androgen. [andro- + -genic]

androgen suppression the reduction or blocking of androgen production by taking antiandrogen drugs, female sex hormones, or by surgical removal of the testicles, used in treatment of prostate cancer.

androgen suppression therapy treatment to reduce or block androgen production by taking antiandrogen drugs, female sex hormones, or by surgical removal of the testicles.

androgynous /ăn drŏj′ə nəs/ of or involving androgeny.

androgyny /ăn drŏj′ə nē/ showing characteristics of both sexes, such as hermaphroditism and bisexuality.

android /ăn′droid/ having human features and form. [andr- + -oid]

android pelvis /pĕl′vĭs/ a masculine-shaped pelvis.

androphobia /ăn′drə fō′bē ə/ an abnormal fear of men. [andro- + -phobia]

androstenedione /ăn′drō stēn′dī ōn′/ a pivotal androgenic steroid secreted by the testes, adrenal cortex, and ovary.

androsterone /ăn drŏs′tə rōn′/ a steroid hormone formed in the testes and excreted in urine that reinforces masculine characteristics.

anemia /ə nē′mē ə/ any of various conditions marked by deficiency in red blood cells or hemoglobin. [an- + -emia]

anemic /ə nē′mĭk/ relating to or suffering from anemia.

anencephaly /ăn′ĕn sĕf′ə lē/ a birth defect of the central nervous system, in which most of the brain and spinal cord are missing.

anergy /ăn′ər jē/ **1.** a state of reduced (below normal) immune response to an allergen or antigen. **2.** lack or absence of energy.

anesthesia /ăn′əs thē′zhə/ total or partial loss of sensation or awareness caused by disease, injury, or an anesthetic drug; anaesthesia. [an- + -esthesia]

anesthesia awareness a situation occurring rarely during surgery in which the patient becomes conscious but is unable to move, and can later recall sounds and sensations.

anesthesiologist /ăn′əs thē′zē ŏl′ə jĭst/ a physician who specializes in the practice of anesthesiology; anaesthesiologist.

anesthesiology /ăn′əs thē′zē ŏl′ə jē/ the branch of medicine concerned with the study and application of anesthesia.

anesthetic /ăn′əs thĕt′ĭk/ **1.** *n.* a drug or chemical agent that causes partial or total loss of sensation, with or without loss of consciousness; anesthetic agent. **2.** *adj.* of or involving loss of bodily sensation.

anesthetic agent a drug or chemical that causes partial or total loss of bodily sensation; an anesthetic.

anesthetist /ə nĕs′thĭ tĭst/ a person who is trained in the practice of anesthesiology.

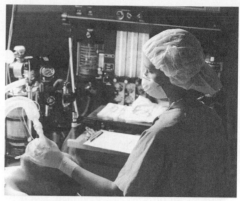
Anesthesiologist

anesthetize /ə nĕs′thĭ tīz′/ to treat with an anesthetic or to cause anesthesia.

anesthetized /ə nĕs′thĭ tīzd′/ rendered insensible by the application of anesthetics.

anetoderma /ăn′ĭ tō dûr′mə/ a condition in which the areas of the skin become bag-like, due to the deterioration or loss of elastic fibers in the skin.

aneuploid /ăn′yoo ploid′/ a cell or organism that has a chromosome number that is not an exact multiple of the usually haploid number.

aneurysm /ăn′yoo rĭz′əm/ a blood-filled bulge in a blood vessel caused by disease or a weakening in the vessel wall.

aneurysmal bruit /ăn′yoo rĭz′məl broot′/ a blowing sound heard with a stethoscope when blood passes through an aneurysm

angi-, angio- *combining form.* blood or lymph vessel: *for example*, angioma, angioedema.

angiectasia /ăn′jē ĕk sta′zhə/ dilation of a lymphatic or blood vessel. [angi- + -ecstasia]

angiitis /ăn′jē ĭ′tĭs/ inflammation of a blood or lymph vessel. [angi- + -itis]

angina /ăn′jə nə, ăn jī′nə/ severe acute chest pain caused by inadequate supply of oxygen to part of the heart; angina pectoris.

angina pectoris (AP) /pĕk′tər ĭs/ angina.

angioblast /ăn′jē ə blăst′/ a cell that participates in the making of blood vessels. [angio- + -blast]

angiocardiography /ăn′je o kăr′dē ŏg′rə fē/ x-ray examination of blood vessels using a contrast medium; angiography. [angio- + cardio- + -graphy]

angioedema /ăn′jē ō ĭ dē′mə/ an allergic reaction of the skin characterized by hive-like patches in the subcutaneous layer; angioneurotic edema. [angio- + edema]

angiofibroma /ăn′jē ō fī brō′mə/ a benign tumor-like growth having numerous, frequently dilated, vascular channels. *Also called* telangiectatic fibroma. [angio- + fibroma]

angiogenesis /ăn′jē ō jĕn′ə sĭs/ development or birth of new blood vessels. [angio- + -genesis]

angioglioma /ăn′jē ō glī ō′mə/ a tumor with both angioma and glioma characteristics. [angio- + glioma]

angiogram /ăn′jē ə grăm′/ an angiographic x-ray of blood vessels used to examine and diagnose cardiovascular conditions. [angio- + -gram]

angiography /ăn′jē ŏg′rə fē/ x-ray examination of blood vessels using a contrast medium; angiocardiography. [angio- + -graphy]

angiohemophilia /ăn′jē ō hē′mə fĭl′ē ə/ a genetic blood disorder in which there is a deficiency in the blood proteins that control clotting. *Also called* Von Willebrand('s) disease. [angio- + hemophilia]

angioid /ăn′jē oid′/ resembling a blood or lymph vessel. [angi- + -oid]

angiology /ăn′jē ŏl′ə jē/ the scientific study of blood and lymph vessels. [angio- + -logy]

angiolysis /ăn′jē ŏl′ə sĭs/ the destruction of a blood vessel, as in the cutting of the umbilical chord. [angio- + -lysis]

angioma /an′jē ō′mə/ (*pl.* **angiomas** or **angiomata** /ăn′jē ō′mə tə/) a benign tumor composed of blood or lymph vessels. [angi- + -oma]

angiomatosis /ăn′jē ō mə tō′sĭs/ condition with multiple angiomas.

angioneurotic edema /ăn′jē ō nŏŏ rŏt′ĭk ĭ dē′mə/ an allergic reaction of the skin characterized by hive-like patches in the subcutaneous layer; angioedema.

angiopathy /ăn′jē ŏp′ə thē/ any disease of blood or lymph vessels. [angio- + -pathy]

angioplasty /ăn′jē ə plăs′tē/ surgical repair of a blood vessel by replacing a section of it, or by using a balloon-tipped catheter to expand or unclog it. [angio- + -plasty]

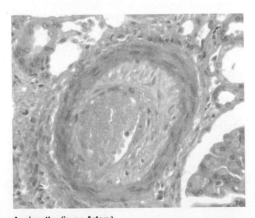

Angiopathy (in an Artery)

angiopoiesis /ăn′jē ō poi ē′sĭs/ formation of blood or lymph vessels. [angio- + -poiesis]

angiopoietic /ăn′jē ō poi ĕt′ĭk/ of or relating to angiopoiesis.

angiorrhaphy /ăn′jē ôr′ə fē/ surgical repair of a blood vessel using sutures. [angio- + -rrhaphy]

angiosarcoma /ăn′jē ō sär kō′mə/ a rare malignant tumor forming in vascular tissue. [angio- + sarcoma]

angioscopy /ăn′jē ŏs′kə pē/ radiographic imaging of injected substances passing through the capillaries. [angio- + -scopy]

angiospasm /ăn′jē ə spăz′əm/ sudden contraction of a blood vessel causing an increase in blood pressure. [angio- + spasm]

angiostatin /ăn′jē ō stăt′ən/ a fragment of plasminogen protein secreted by tumors that stops the formation of new blood vessels.

angiostenosis /ăn′jē ō stĭ nō′sĭs/ narrowing of one or more blood vessels. [angio- + stenosis]

angiotensin /ăn′jē ō tĕn′sĭn/ a hormone that functions in the body in controlling arterial pressure.

angiotensin-converting enzyme /ăn′jē ō tĕn′sĭn kən vûr′tĭng en′zim/ an enzyme that converts angiotensin I into angiotensin II.

angiotensin receptor blocker (ARB) a medication that blocks the action of angiotensin II, helping the blood vessels to relax and widen, lowering blood pressure.

angiotomy /ăn′jē ŏt′ə mē/ incision into a blood vessel. [angio- + -tomy]

angle-closure glaucoma /glô kō′mə/ primary glaucoma in which circulation and drainage of fluids in the eye is blocked by the iris.

angulation /ăng′gyə lā′shən/ the bending of an organ or part into an abnormal angle.

anhedonia /ăn′hē dō′nē ə/ uncharacteristic loss of pleasure doing activities which are normally pleasurable.

anhidrosis /ăn′hī drō′sĭs/ absence of sweat glands, making heat intolerable.

anhidrotic /ăn′hī drŏt′ĭk/ of or relating to anhidrosis.

anhydrous /ăn hī′drəs/ absence of water. [an- + -hydrous]

aniline /ăn′ə lĭn, -lēn′/ an oily, colorless, and highly toxic substance used in the making of dyes, resins, explosives, and pharmaceuticals.

anilingus /ā′nə lĭng′gəs/ oral sexual stimulation of the anus.

aniso- *combining form.* not equal, disimilar: *for example,* anisocytosis.

anisocoria /ăn′ə sō kôr′ē ə/ a condition in which the two pupils are different sizes.

anisocytosis /ăn′ə sō sī tō′sĭs/ significant difference in size between cells that are normally the same size, especially in reference to blood cells. [aniso- + -cytosis]

anisomastia /ăn′ə sō măs′tē ə/ breasts of unequal size.

anisomelia /ăn′ə sō mē′lē ə/ condition with unequal sizes of two paired limbs.

anisometropia /ăn′ə sō mĭ trō′pē ə/ a condition in which the refractive power of the two eyes is different.

anisotonic /ăn′ī sō tŏn′ĭk/ having unequal osmotic pressure.

ankle /ăng′kəl/ the joint connecting the lower leg to the foot.

ankle bone or **anklebone** /ăng′kəl bōn′/ the bone in the ankle that articulates with (connects to) the tibia and fibula to form the ankle joint. *Also called* talus.

ankle joint the joint connecting the lower leg to the foot.

ankyl-, anklyo- *combining form.* fused; stiffened: *for example,* ankylosis, ankylostoma.

ankyloglossia /ăng′kə lō glŏs′ē ə/ partial or complete fusion of the tongue to the floor of the mouth.

ankylose /ăng′kə lōz′, -lōs′/ to stiffen or fuse together, as in an injured joint. [ankyl- + -ose]

ankylosing spondylitis /ăng′kə lō′zĭng spŏn′də lī′tĭs, -sĭng/ arthritis of the spine that causes the vertebrae to fuse and become inflexible.

ankylosis /ăng′kə lō′sĭs/ the fusion of a joint caused by disease, injury, or surgical procedure. [ankyl- + -osis]

ankylostoma /ăng′kə lŏs′tə mə/ a bloodsucking parasitic hookworm that migrates to the intestines when ingested and can cause anemia. [ankylo- + -stoma]

anlage /än′lä′gə/ (*pl.* **anlagen** /än′lä′gən/) an organ or structure in its earliest stage of development.

annexa /ə něk′sə/ (*pl. of* **annexum** /ə něk′səm/) accessory or adjoining parts to a main structure; adnexa.

annuloplasty /ăn′yə lō plăs′tē/ reconstructive surgery of a leaking cardiac valve to narrow the opening and diminish the leak.

annulus /ăn′yə ləs/ (*pl.* **annuli** /ăn′yə lī′/ or **annuluses**) a ring-shaped structure.

anomaly /ə nŏm′ə lē/ something that deviates from the norm, or is contrary to a rule.

anomia /ə nō′mē ə/ a mental condition characterized by an inability to name objects or to recognize written or spoken names of objects.

anomic aphasia /ə nŏm′ĭk ə fā′zhə/ a mental condition caused by lesions in the language area of the brain, characterized by difficulty in naming people or objects.

anonymous reporting acquisition and reporting of certain data excluding patients identities.

anonymous testing a method of testing in which the identity of patient is not disclosed.

anophthalmia /ăn′ŏf thăl′mē ə/ a birth defect in which all the tissues of the eyes are absent. [an- + ophthalmia]

anoplasty /ā′nə plăs′tē/ plastic surgery of the anus.

anorchia /ăn ôr′kē ə/ congenital lack of one or two testicles.

anorchism /ăn ôr′kĭz əm/ absence of one or both testes. [an- + orch- + -ism]

anorectic /ăn′ə rěk′tĭk/ of or relating to anorexia.

anorexia /ăn′ə rěk′sē ə/ aversion to food with persistent loss of appetite.

anorexia nervosa /nûr vō′sə/ a mental disorder marked by an extreme fear of becoming obese, leading to extreme dieting and other eating disorders, which can result in life-threatening weight loss.

anorexic /ăn′ə rěk′sĭk/ of or relating to anorexia nervosa.

anorexigenic /ăn′ə rěk′sĭ jěn′ĭk/ causing or promoting anorexia. [anorexi(a) + -genic]

anorgasmia /ăn′ôr găz′mē ə/ inability to experience orgasm due to physical or psychological disorder. [an- + orgasm + -ia]

anosmatic /ăn′ŏz măt′ĭk/ partially or totally lacking the sense of smell.

anosmia /ăn ŏz′me ə/ partial or complete loss of smell caused by either a lesion on the olfactory nerve, obstruction of the nasal fossae, or disease.

anovulation /ăn ŏv′yōō lā′shən/ suspension or cessation of ovulation due to a medical condition, medication, or menopause. [an- + ovulation]

anovulatory /ăn ŏv′yōō lə tôr′ē/ absence of discharge of an ovum from the ovary during an ovarian cycle.

anovulatory menstruation /měn′strōō ā′shən/ menstrual bleeding without recent ovulation.

anoxemia /ăn′ŏk sē′mē ə/ absence of oxygen in the blood flowing through the arteries.

anoxia /ăn ŏk′sē ə/ partial or complete absence of oxygen from inspired gases, arterial blood, or tissues.

anoxic /ăn ŏk′sĭk/ of or relating to anoxia.

ant- *See* anti-.

antacid /ănt ăs′ĭd/ an agent that prevents, reduces, or neutralizes acidity. [ant- + acid]

antagonism /ăn tăg′ə nĭz′əm/ mutual opposition in action between two or more substances, diseases, or processes.

antagonist /ăn tăg′ə nĭst/ something opposing the action of another, causing antagonism.

ante- *prefix.* 1. before: *for example,* antepartum. 2. in front of: *for example,* anteflexion.

ante cibum (a.c.) /ăn′tē sī′bəm/ before a meal

anteflexion /ăn′tē flĕk′shən/ a sharp forward curve or bend. [ante- + flexion]

antegrade /ăn′tĭ grād′/ movement in a normal direction. [ante- + grade]

antegrade amnesia /ăm nē′zhə/ loss of memory of events following the trauma or disease that caused the condition.

ante meridiem (a.m., AM) /ăn′te mə rĭd′ē əm, -ĕm/ before noon.

ante mortem /ăn′tē môr′tĕm/ before death; generally used for dying declarations.

antenatal /ăn′tē nā′təl/ during pregnancy; preceding birth. *Also called* prenatal. [ante- + natal]

antenatal surgery surgical operation performed on an unborn fetus in the womb, or partially removed from the womb.

antepartum /ăn′tē pär′təm/ preceding labor or childbirth. [ante- + partum]

anteposition /ăn′tē pə zĭsh′ən/ forward or anterior position. [ante- + position]

anterior /ăn tēr′ē ər/ frontal; in front of, or before.

anterior chamber the space in the eye between the cornea and the iris.

anterior cruciate ligament (ACL) /krōō′shē ĭt lĭg′ə mənt, -shē āt′/ the ligament that extends from the top of the tibia to the underside of the femur.

anterior fontanelle /fŏn′tə nĕl′/ the soft spot in the front of a newborn baby's head where the cranial bones have not yet fused.

anterior pituitary (AP) /pĭ tōō′ĭ tĕr′ē/ the frontal lobe of the pituitary gland that secretes hormones. *Also called* adenohypophysis.

anterior plane of body a term of anatomic orientation referring to the front plane of the body.

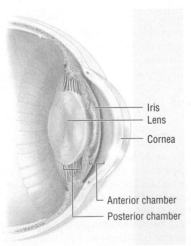

Iris
Lens
Cornea

Anterior chamber
Posterior chamber

Anterior Chamber

anterior tibial artery /tĭb′ē əl är′tə rē/ a small artery that passes between the tibia and the fibula, before becoming the dorsalis pedis artery at the ankle joint.

antero- *prefix.* anterior: *for example,* anteroposterior.

anterograde /ăn′tə rō grād′/ moving or extending forward from a point in time. [antero- + grade]

anterograde amnesia /ăm nē′zhə/ amnesia of events following the trauma or disease that caused the condition.

anterograde memory memory of events following an event, such as brain surgery.

anterolateral /ăn′tə rō lăt′ər əl/ in front of and away from the center. [antero- + lateral]

anteromedial /ăn′tə rō mē′dē əl/ in front of and toward the center. [antero- + medial]

anteroposterior (AP) /ăn′tə rō pŏ stēr′ē ər/ of or relating to both the front and the rear. [antero- + posterior]

anteroposterior and lateral (AP & LAT) /lăt′ər əl/ an anatomical orientation term meaning front to back and side to side.

anteroposterior (AP) view view from front to back.

anterosuperior /ăn′tə rō sōō pêr′ē ər/ in front and above. [antero- + superior]

anteversion /ăn′tē vûr′zhən/ leaning forward as a whole, without bending. [ante- + -version]

anthrac-, anthraco- *combining form.* coal; carbon; carbuncle: *for example,* anthracosis, anthracosilicosis.

anthracosilicosis /ăn′thrə kō sĭl′ĭ kō′sĭs/ a disease of miners, in which deposits of carbon and silica accumulate in the lungs. [anthraco- + silicosis]

anthracosis /ăn′thrə kō′sĭs/ inflammation of the lungs, caused by inhalation and accumulation of carbon from inhaled smoke or coal dust. [anthrac- + -osis]

anthrax /ăn′thrăks/ a highly infectious fatal disease caused by the bacterium *Bacillus anthracis*, characterized by skin ulcers, serous effusions in various organs and body cavities and by symptoms of extreme prostration and death. *Also called* splenic fever.

anti- *prefix.* against, opposite: *for example,* antibiotic.

antiandrogen drug /ăn′tē ăn′drə jən/ an agent given to reduce or block the production of androgens.

antianemic /ăn′tē ə nē′mĭk/ any substance that prevents or corrects anemic conditions. [anti- + anemic]

antianginal /ăn′tē ăn′jə nəl, -ăn jī′nəl/ an agent counteracting or preventing angina. [anti- + anginal]

antiangiogenic /ăn'tē ăn'jē ō jĕn'ĭk/ an agent that can destroy or interfere with the fine network of blood vessels needed by tumors to grow and metastasize. [anti- + angiogenic]

antianxiety /ăn'tē ăng zī'ĭ tē/ tending to prevent or relieve anxiety. [anti- + anxiety]

antiarrhythmic /ăn'tē ə rĭth'mĭk/ a drug or procedure that prevents or corrects irregularities in heart activity. [anti- + arrythmi(a) + -ic]

antiarthritic /ăn'tē är thrĭt'ĭk/ a substance or therapy that is used to remedy arthritis. [anti- + arthritic]

antiasthmatic /ăn'tē ăz măt'ĭk/ an agent that prevents or relieves an asthmatic attack. [anti- + asthmatic]

antibacterial /ăn'tē băk têr'ē əl/ an agent that prevents or slows the growth of bacteria or kills them directly. [anti- + bacterial]

antibiotic /ăn'tē bī ŏt'ĭk/ a substance capable of killing bacteria, widely used in the treatment of infections. [anti- + biotic]

antibiotic resistance the ability of microorganisms to withstand an antibiotic that once killed them.

antibiotic-resistant tuberculosis /ăn'tē bī ŏt'ĭk rĭ zĭs'tənt tōō bûr'kyə lō'sĭs/ a form of tuberculosis that withstands one or more of the antibiotics normally used to treat it.

antibody /ăn'tĭ bŏd'ē/ a specialized immune protein that is produced in response to an antigen, which it then neutralizes. [anti- + body]

antibody-dependent cell-mediated cytotoxicity /sī'tō tŏk sĭs'ĭ tē/ a response of the immune system in which an antibody coats an antigen, making it more vulnerable to attack by immune cells.

anticholinergic /ăn'te kŏl'ə nûr'jĭk/ an agent that blocks the action of parasympathetic or other cholinergic nerve fibers. [anti- + cholinergic]

anticipation /ăn tĭs'ə pā'shən/ **1.** the appearance of a symptom before the normal expected time. **2.** in hereditary diseases, the earlier occurrence of a disease in each successive generation.

anticlotting /ăn'tē klŏt'ĭng/ inhibiting the bloods ability to clot. [anti- + clotting]

anticoagulant /ăn'tē kō ăg'yə lənt/ any agent that prevents the formation of blood clots. [anti- + coagulant]

anticonvulsant /ăn'tē kən vŭl'sənt/ a drug that treats or prevents seizures. [anti- + convulsant]

anticonvulsive /ăn'tē kən vŭl'sĭv/ tending to lessen or prevent seizures. [anti- + convulsive]

antidepressant /ăn'tē dĭ prĕs'ənt/ a drug used to treat or prevent clinical depression. [anti- + depressant]

antidiabetic /ăn'tē dī'ə bĕt'ĭk/ a drug used to treat diabetes. [anti- + diabetic]

antidiarrheal /ăn'tē dī'ə rē'əl/ a drug used to treat or prevent diarrhea. [anti- + diarrheal]

antidiuretic /ăn'tē dī'ə rĕt'ĭk/ a drug used to reduce the production of urine. [anti- + diuretic]

antidiuretic hormone (ADH) /hôr'mōn/ a hormone secreted by the pituitary gland that affects blood pressure by stimulating capillary muscles and reduces urine flow by affecting reabsorption of water by kidneys. *Also called* vasodepressin.

antidote /ăn'tĭ dōt'/ an agent that neutralizes a poison.

antiemetic /ăn'tē ə mĕt'ĭk/ **1.** *n.* a drug that prevents nausea and vomiting **2.** *adj.* providing relief from nausea and vomiting. [anti- + emetic]

antiestrogen /ăn'tē ĕs'trə jən/ any substance capable of preventing the full biological effects of estrogenic hormones. [anti- + estrogen]

antifibrinolysin /ăn'tē fī'brĭ nō lī'sĭn/ any substance capable of preventing the full effects of plasmin; antiplasmin.

antifibrinolytic /ăn'tē fī'brĭ nō lĭt'ĭk/ any substance that slows the breakdown of fibrin. [anti- + fibrinolytic]

antifungal /ăn'tē fŭng'gəl/ an agent that kills, prevents, or treats fungal infections. [anti- + fungal]

antigen /ăn'tĭ jən/ any substance that stimulates the production of antibodies. [anti- + -gen]

antigen-antibody complex /ăn'tĭ jən ăn'tĭ bŏd'ē/ the large network of molecules formed by the binding of antibodies and antigens, that acts as mediators in immune response. *Also called* immune complex.

antigenic drift /ăn'tĭ jĕn'ĭk/ the molecular changes that take place in microorganisms when they pass from one host to another, making them more resistant to antibodies.

antigenic shift a sudden molecular mutation of a virus that produces new strains of itself, making it more resistant to immune response.

antigen-presenting cell (APC) a cell that processes antigens into a form recognizable to T cells.

antiglobulin /ăn'tē glŏb'yə lĭn/ an antibody that combines with and precipitates globulin. [anti- + globulin]

anti-HB /ăn'te āch'bē'/ the antibody to the hepatitis B antigen.

antihemorrhagic /ăn'tē hĕm'ə răj'ĭk/ preventing or reducing hemorrhage. *Also called* hemostatic. [anti- + hemorrhagic]

antihistamine /ăn'tē hĭs'tə mēn', -mĭn/ a drug used to prevent or counteract the effects of histamine, especially in treating allergies. [anti- + histamine]

antihormone /ăn'tē hôr'mōn/ a drug that prevents or inhibits the affects of a hormone. [anti- + hormone]

antihyperlipidemic /ăn'tē hī'pər lĭp'ĭ dē'mĭk/ **1.** *adj.* preventing or reducing the buildup of lipids in the blood. **2.** *n.* a drug that reduces the buildup of lipids in the blood.

antihypertensive /ăn'tē hī'pər tĕn'sĭv/ a drug or treatment that lowers blood pressure. [anti- + hypertensive]

anti-infective /ăn'tē ĭn fĕk'tĭv/ an agent that kills or slows the spread of infection.

anti-inflammatory /ăn'tē ĭn flăm'ə tôr'ē/ **1.** *n.* a drug that prevents or reduces inflammation. **2.** *adj.* preventing or reducing inflammation.

antimalarial /ăn'tē mə lâr'ē əl/ a drug or treatment that prevents or kills malaria. [anti- + malarial]

antimetabolite /ăn'tē mə tăb'ə līt'/ a substance that inhibits the normal metabolic process. [anti- + metabolite]

antimicrobial /ăn'tē mī krō'bē əl/ **1.** *adj.* preventing or inhibiting microbial infection. **2.** *n.* a drug that prevents or inhibits microbial infection. [anti- + microbial]

antimicrobial resistance the result of microbial mutation, making the microbes more resistant to antimicrobial agents.

antineoplastic /ăn'tē nē'ō plăs'tĭk/ preventing or inhibiting the growth and spread of a tumor. [anti- + neoplastic]

antinuclear antibody (ANA) /ăn'tē noo'klē ər ăn'tĭ bŏd'ē/ an unusual antibody that attacks the nucleus of a cell; their numbers are elevated in connective tissue diseases.

antinuclear antibody (ANA) test a test for the presence of antinuclear antibodies.

antioxidant /ăn'tē ŏk'sĭ dənt/ an agent that prevents or reduces the oxidative damage of free radicals. [anti- + oxidant]

antiparasitic /ăn'tē păr'ə sĭt'ĭk/ preventing or destroying parasites or parasitic infection. [anti- + parasitic]

antiphospholipid antibody syndrome /ăn'tē fŏs'fō lĭp'ĭd ăn'tĭ bŏd'ē/ a disorder of the immune system characterized by abnormal blood clotting, migraine headaches, spontaneous abortion, and low blood platelet counts, caused by abnormal antibodies in the blood.

antiplatelet agent /ăn'tē plăt'lĭt/ a drug that prevents or reduces platelet buildup in blood vessels. [anti- + platelet]

antipruritic /ăn'tē proo rĭt'ĭk/ preventing or relieving itching. [anti- + pruritic]

antipsoriatic /ăn'tē sôr'ē ăt'ĭk/ preventing or treating psoriasis. [anti- + psoriatic]

antipsychotic /ăn'tē sī kŏt'ĭk/ **1.** *adj.* preventing or treating psychosis. **2.** *n.* an agent that

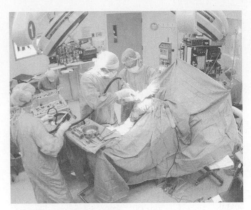

Antisepsis (during Surgery)

prevents or treats the symptoms of psychosis. [anti- + psychotic]

antipyretic /ăn'tē pī rĕt'ĭk/ **1.** *adj.* preventing or reducing fever. **2.** *n.* an agent that reduces fever, such as aspirin. [anti- + pyretic]

antireflux surgery /ăn'tē rē'flŭks/ surgical procedure in which the fundus of the stomach is sutured to the esophagus to narrow the esophagus and prevent or reduce acid reflux. *Also called* fundoplication, reflux surgery.

antiretroviral /ăn'tē rĕt'rō vī'rəl/ medication used in the treatment of a retrovirus usually HIV. [anti- + retroviral]

antiretroviral therapy (ART) treatment that inhibits or arrests a retrovirus.

antisepsis /ăn'tə sĕp'sĭs/ preventing infection by arresting the growth and spread of germs. [anti- + sepsis]

antiseptic /ăn'tə sĕp'tĭk/ **1.** *adj.* of or relating to sepsis. **2.** *n.* an agent capable of arresting the growth and spread of germs. [anti- + septic]

antisocial personality disorder /ăn'tē sō'shəl/ a personality disorder characterized by complete and aggressive disregard for the rights of others, and an inability to exhibit normal behavior.

antispasmodic /ăn'tē spăz mŏd'ĭk/ an agent or substance that reduces the occurrence and severity of muscle spasms and seizures. [anti- + spasmodic]

antitoxin /ăn'tē tŏk'sĭn/ an antibody capable of neutralizing toxin produced by bacteria and viruses. [anti- + toxin]

antitubercular /ăn'tē too bûr'kyə lər/ a vaccine or drug used to prevent or treat tuberculosis. [anti- + tubercular]

antitussive /ăn'tē tŭs'ĭv/ a drug that relieves or suppresses coughing.

antivenin /ăn'tē vĕn'ĭn/ an antitoxin used to neutralize animal or insect venom.

antiviral /ăn′tē vī′rəl/ capable of destroying or inhibiting the growth of a virus. [anti- + viral]

antrectomy /ăn trĕk′tə mē/ surgical removal of all or a portion of an antrum, such as the stomach.

antrum /ăn′trəm/ a cavity or chamber.

ANUG *abbreviation.* acute necrotizing ulcerative gingivitis.

anuria /ə nyōōr′ē ə/ absence of urine production. [an- + -uria]

anuric /ə nyōōr′ĭk/ of or relating to anuria.

anus /ā′nəs/ the end of the digestive tract, through which feces matter exits the body.

anvil /ăn′vĭl/ an anvil-shaped bone in the middle ear, located between the malleus and the stapes. *Also called* incus.

anxiety /ăng zī′ĭ tē/ apprehension and fear manifested as palpitations, sweating, tension, and stress.

anxiety disorder a group of several chronic mental illnesses with biological and environmental causes, characterized by excessive and persistent apprehension and fear, manifested as sweating, palpitations, tension, and stress.

anxiolytic /ăng′zē ə lĭt′ĭk/ **1.** *adj.* reducing tension and anxiety. **2.** *n.* an agent or substance that reduces tension and anxiety.

aort-, aorto- *combining form.* aorta: *for example,* aortitis.

aorta /ā ôr′tə/ the largest artery in the body; it carries blood from the heart to the arteries of all limbs and organs except the lungs.

aortal /ā ôr′təl/ of or relating to the aorta.

aortalgia /ā′ôr tăl′jə, -jē ə/ pain attributed to the aorta.

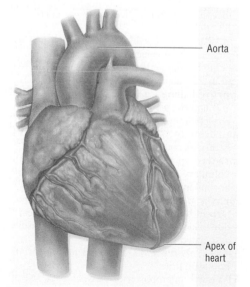

Aorta

Apex of heart

Aorta

aortic /ā ôr′tĭk/ of or relating to the aorta.

aortic aneurysm /ăn′yə rĭz′əm/ a blood-filled bulge in the aorta caused by disease or a weakening in the vessel wall.

aortic arch **1.** the curved portion of the aorta between the ascending and descending aorta. **2.** any of several pairs of arteries encircling the embryonic pharynx in the mesenchyme of the branchial arches.

aortic atresia /ə trē′zhə/ a birth defect of the heart in which the normal valve between the left ventricle and the aorta is absent.

aortic dissection /dĭ sĕk′shən, dī-/ a tear in the middle wall of the aorta, leading to an aortic aneurysm.

aortic insufficiency (AI) /ĭn′sə fĭsh′ən sē/ incomplete closure of the aortic valve, causing blood from the aorta to leak into the left ventricle of the heart.

aortic regurgitation /rĭ gûr′jĭ tā′shən/ leakage of blood from the aorta into the left ventricle caused by aortic insufficiency.

aortic stenosis /stĭ nō′sĭs/ narrowing of the heart valve between the left ventricle and the aorta, slowing blood flow and increasing stress on the heart.

aortic valve the valve connecting the left ventricle of the heart to the aorta.

aortitis /ā′ôr tī′tĭs/ inflammation of the aorta. [aort- + -itic]

aortogram /ā ôr′tə grăm′/ an image produced by aortography. [aorto- + -gram]

aortography /ā′ôr tŏg′rə fē/ x-ray examination of the aorta injected with a contrast medium. [aorto- + -graphy]

AP *abbreviation.* **1.** angina pectoris. **2.** arterial pressure. **3.** anterior pituitary. **4.** anteroposterior.

AP & LAT anteposterior and lateral.

apathy /ăp′ə thē/ lack of interest or emotion, often an early sign of cerebral disease. [a- + -pathy]

APC *abbreviation.* **1.** acetylsalicylic acid, phenacetin, and caffeine, combined to make an analgesic. **2.** antigen-presenting cells.

Apert syndrome /ä pâr′/ a malformation syndrome characterized by deformity of the skull and midface, fused fingers and toes, fusion of the neck vertebrae, and mental retardation.

apertura /ăp′ər tōōr′ə/ in anatomy, any opening.

apex /ā′pĕks/ the tip of a pyramidal or rounded structure, like the lung or the heart.

Apgar /ăp′gär/ or **Apgar score** an evaluation of the physical condition of a newborn infant immediately following delivery, by scoring the heart rate, respiratory effort, muscle tone, skin color, and response to noxious stimulation.

aphagia /ə fā′jē ə/   inability to swallow or eat. [a- + -phagia]

aphakia /ə fā′kē ə/   absence or loss of the lens of the eye.

aphasia /ə fā′zhə/   a speech disorder characterized by an impairment of verbal expression and comprehension. [a- + -phasia]

-apheresis   *combining form.* removal, separation: *for example,* leukapheresis.

apheresis /ăf′ə rē′sĭs/   reinfusion of a patient's own blood from which certain cellular or fluid elements have been removed.

aphonia /ə fō′nē ə/   inability to speak.

aphrasia /ə frā′zhə/   inability to speak or understand spoken words.

aphrodisiac /ăf′rə dĭz′ē ăk′, -dē′zē-/   something that increases sexual desire.

aphthous stomatitis /ăf′thəs stō′mə tī′tĭs/   a sore throat characterized by small painful ulcers in the mouth and throat.

aphthous ulcer /ŭl′sər/   a painful oral ulcer commonly called a canker sore.

apic-, apico-   *combining form.* apex: *for example,* apical, apicolysis.

apical /ā′pĭ kəl/   of or relating to an apex. [apic- + -al]

apical pulse   a pulse heard through a stethoscope placed directly over the apex of the heart.

apicoectomy /ā′pĭ kō ĕk′tə mē/   surgical removal of the apical portion of the tooth by way of an incision made through the gums.

apicolysis /ā′pĭ kŏl′ə sĭs/   surgical collapse of the upper portion of the lung. [apico- + -lysis]

aplasia /ə plā′zhə/   failure to develop. [a- + -plasia]

aplastic /ā plăs′tĭk, ə plăs′-/   of or relating to aplasia. [a- + -plastic]

aplastic anemia /ə nē′mē ə/   anemia caused by failure of the bone marrow to produce blood cells and platelets.

apnea /ăp′nē ə/   a period of reduced or absent breathing.

apo-   *prefix.* separated from; derived from: *for example,* apocrine.

apocrine /ăp′ə krĭn/   of or relating to an apocrine gland and its secretions. [apo- + -crine]

apocrine gland   a large sweat gland located in hairy regions of the body that produces both a fluid and an apical secretion.

apolipoprotein /ăp′ō lĭp′ō prō′tēn, -tē ĭn/   a major protein component of HDL abundant in plasma, and instrumental in promoting the transfer of cholesterol into the liver.

aponeur-, aponeuro-   *combining form.* tendon-like: *for example,* aponeurosis.

aponeurorrhaphy /ăp′ō nōō rôr′ə fē/   suture of a fascia or of an aponeurosis. [aponeuro- + -rrhaphy]

aponeurosis /ăp′ō nōō rō′sĭs/   a membrane resembling a flattened tendon that attaches muscle to bone. [aponeur- + -osis]

apophysis /ə pŏf′ə sĭs/   an outgrowth or projection, especially of bone.

apoplexy /ăp′ə plĕk′sē/   a rarely used term for a cerebral stroke most often due to intracerebral hemorrhage.

apoptosis /ăp′ŏp tō′sĭs, ăp′ə tō′-/   type of cell death in which the cell uses specialized cellular processes to kill itself.

apothecary /ə pŏth′ĭ kĕr′ē/   1. person who prepares and sells medicines; pharmacist. 2. store that prepares and sells medicines; pharmacy.

append-   *combining form.* appendage, appendix: *for example,* appendectomy.

appendage /ə pĕn′dĭj/   any subordinate part attached to a main body or structure.

appendectomy /ăp′ĕn dĕk′tə mē/   surgical removal of the appendix. [append- + -ectomy]

appendic-, appendico-   *combining form.* appendix: *for example,* appendicitis, appendicolith.

appendiceal /ăp′ĕn dĭsh′əl, ə pĕn′də sē′əl/   of or relating to the appendix.

appendicitis /ə pĕn′də sī′tĭs/   inflammation of the appendix. [appendic- + -itis]

appendicolith /ə pĕn′dĭ kə lĭth/   a calcification in the appendix. [appendico- + -lith]

appendicular skeleton /ăp′ĕn dĭk′yə lər/   the bones of the limbs, shoulders, and pelvis.

appendix /ə pĕn′dĭks/   a small wormlike appendage of the colon, formally called the vermiform appendix.

appetite suppressant /sə prĕs′ənt/   a drug that reduces appetite.

appliance /ə plī′əns/   a dental or surgical device used as for a therapeutic or corrective function.

apposition /ăp′ə zĭsh′ən/   1. the fitting together of two substances. 2. the condition of being fitted together. 3. the relationship of two or more fracture fragments.

approved drug   a drug that has been tested and approved for sale by the U.S. Food and Drug Administration.

approximate /ə prŏk′sə māt′/   to join together, as cut tissue.

apraxia /ə prăk′sē ə/   an inability to perform voluntary motor functions, while retaining normal muscle function.

apraxia of speech   a speech disorder characterized by inability to speak or speak clearly due to lack of voluntary control of the muscles associated with speech.

APTT   *abbreviation.* activated partial thromboplastin time.

AP view   anteroposterior view.

apyrexia /ā′pī rĕk′sē ə/   lack of fever.

aq. *abbreviation.* water.

aqueous humor /ā′kwē əs hyōō′mər, ăk′wē-/ the fluid that fills the front and rear chambers of the eye.

arachnodactyly /ə răk′nō dăk′tə lē/ abnormally slender and long fingers, often associated with Marfan's syndrome.

arachnoid /ə răk′noid/ or **arachnoid membrane** /mĕm′brān/ the middle layer of the three membranes surrounding the central nervous system.

arachnoiditis /ə răk′noi dī′tĭs/ inflammation of the arachnoid.

arachnophobia /ə răk′nə fō′bē ə/ intense fear of spiders.

ARB *abbreviation.* angiotensin II receptor blocker.

arbovirus /är′bō vī′rəs/ any of a group of RNA viruses usually transmitted by insects that feed on the blood, such as mosquitoes or ticks.

ARC *abbreviation.* AIDS-related complex.

arch /ärch/ **1.** any structure shaped like a bow. **2.** the archlike part of the foot structure.

arcuate /är′kyōō ĭt/ having an arched or bow-like shape.

arcuate nucleus /nōō′klē əs/ any of several specialized groups of neurons in either the thalamus, hypothalamus, or medulla oblongata.

ARDS *abbreviation.* adult respiratory distress syndrome or acute respiratory distress syndrome.

areflexia /ā rĭ flĕk′sē ə/ absence of reflexes.

arenavirus /är′ə nə vī′rəs/ any of a family of RNA viruses usually transmitted from rodents to humans.

areola /ə rē′ə lə/ (*pl.* **areolas** or **areoli** /ə rē′ə lē/) the pigmented area surrounding the nipple.

ARF *abbreviation.* **1.** acute renal failure. **2.** acute respiratory failure.

Arg *abbreviation.* arginine.

arginine /är′jə nēn′/ one of the 20 amino acids found within proteins.

argon laser /är′gŏn lā′zər/ a laser that uses argon as its active medium, used in eye surgery.

Argyll-Robertson pupil /är′gĭl rŏb′ərt sən/ a condition where the pupil loses its response to light.

argyria /är jĭr′ē ə/ skin discoloration caused by the ingestion of silver.

arhinia, arrhinia /ā rĭn′ē ə/ congenital lack of a nose.

arm /ärm/ the part of the upper limb between the shoulder and the elbow.

AROM *abbreviation.* active range of motion.

aromatherapy /ə rō′mə thĕr′ə pē/ inhalation or application of essential oils, thought to promote health.

arrector pili /ə rĕk′tôr pī′lī (*pl.* **arrectores pilorum** /ə rĕk tôr′ēz pĭ lôr′əm/) muscle that connects the hair to the skin, contraction of which causes "goose bumps".

arrest /ə rĕst′/ to stop or interfere with.

arrhythmia /ə rĭth′mē ə/ irregular rhythm of the heart. [a- + -rrhythmia]

ART *abbreviation.* **1.** antiretroviral therapy. **2.** assisted reproductive technology.

arteri-, arterio- *combining form.* artery: *for example,* arterioplasty.

arteria /är tēr′ē ə/ in anatomy, an artery.

arterial /är tēr′ē əl/ relating to one or more arteries. [arteri- + -al]

arterial aneurysm /ăn′yə rĭz′əm/ a bulge in an artery causing the arterial walls to weaken.

arterial blood gas (ABG) the measure of oxygen and carbon dioxide levels and pH in a sample of blood taken from an artery.

arterial tension blood pressure in an artery.

arteriogram /är tēr′ē ə grăm′/ an x-ray of an artery after the injection of a contrast medium. [arterio- + -gram]

arteriography /är tēr′ē ŏg′rə fē/ radiographic imaging of a substance flowing through an artery. [arterio- + -graphy]

arteriol-, arteriolo- *combining form.* arteriole: *for example,* arteriolitis, arteriololith.

arteriolar /är tēr′ē ō′lər/ relating to one or more arterioles.

arteriole /är tēr′ē ōl′/ a small extension of an artery that leads to a capillary.

arteriololith /är tēr′ē ə lĭth/ a chalky deposit in an arterial wall. [arteriolo- + -lith]

arteriolitis /är tēr′ē ə lī′tĭs/ inflammation of an arteriole. [arteriol- + -itis]

arterioplasty /är tēr′ē ə plăs′tē/ surgery to reconstruct the wall of an artery. [arterio- + -plasty]

arteriorrhaphy /är tēr′ē ôr′ə fē/ suture of an artery. [arterio- + -rrhaphy]

arteriorrhexis /är tēr′ē ō rĕk′sĭs/ rupture of an artery. [arterio- + -rrhexis]

arteriosclerosis /är tēr′ē ō sklĭ rō′sĭs/ hardening of the arteries. [arterio- + -sclerosis]

arteriosclerotic /är tēr′ē ō sklĭ rŏt′ĭk/ relating to or affected by arteriosclerosis.

arteriospasm /är tēr′ē ə spăz′əm/ a sudden contraction of an artery. [arterio- + spasm]

arteriotomy /är tēr′ē ŏt′ə mē/ a surgical incision into an artery. [arterio- + -tomy]

arteriovenous /är tēr′ē ō vē′nəs/ pertaining to arteries and veins. [arterio- + venous]

arteriovenous malformation (AVM) /măl′fôr mā′shən/ a tangled cluster of blood vessels, usually found in the brain, where arteries and veins connect directly with no connecting capillaries.

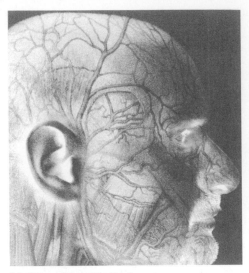

Arteries and Veins of the Head

arteritis /är'tə rī'tĭs/   inflammation of an artery. [arter(io)- + -itis]

artery /är'tə rē/   any blood vessel that carries oxygenated blood from the heart to any part of the body.

arthr-, arthro-   *combining form.* joint: *for example,* arthritis, arthrocentesis.

arthralgia /är thrăl'jə, -jē ə/   joint pain. [arthr- + -algia]

arthrectomy /är thrĕk'tə mē/   surgical removal of a joint. [arthr- + -ectomy]

arthritic /är thrĭt'ĭk/   relating to arthritis.

arthritis /är thrī'tĭs/   inflammation of one or more joints. [arthr- + -itis]

arthrocentesis /är'thrō sĕn tē'sĭs/   surgical puncture of a joint with a needle to remove fluid. [arthro- + -centesis]

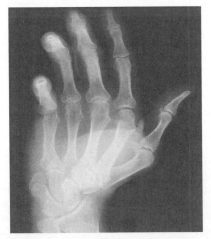

Arthritis (in X-Ray of the Hand)

arthrochondritis /är'thrō kŏn drī'tĭs/   inflammation of an articular cartilage. [arthro- + chondritis]

arthrodesis /är thrŏd'ə sĭs, är'thrō dē'sĭs/   surgical immobilization of a joint. *See also* spondylodesis. [arthro- + -desis]

arthrography /är thrŏg'rə fē/   x-ray of a joint after the injection of a contrast medium. [arthro- + -graphy]

arthrogryposis /är'thrō grĭ pō'sĭs/   a congenital disease with progressive loss of joint motion.

arthrogryposis multiplex congenita (AMC) /mŭl'tə plĕks' kən jĕn'ĭ tə/   congenital disorder where multiple joints have limited range of motion.

arthropathy /är thrŏp'ə thē/   any disease relating to the joints. [arthro- + -pathy]

arthoplasty /är'thrə plăs'tē/   surgical replacement or reconstruction of a joint. [arthro- + -plasty]

arthrosclerosis /är'thrō sklĭ rō'sĭs/   joint stiffness. [arthro- + -sclerosis]

arthroscope /är'thrə skōp'/   an instrument that is used to visually examine the inside of a joint. [arthro- + -scope]

arthroscopy /är thrŏs'kə pē/   surgical examination of a joint in which an arthroscope is inserted into a joint. [arthro- + -scopy]

arthrosis /är thrō'sĭs/   condition where a joint deteriorates. [arthro- + -osis]

arthrostomy /är thrŏs'tə mē/   temporary surgical opening into a joint. [arthro- + -stomy]

arthrotomy /är thrŏt'ə mē/   incision into a joint. [arthro- + -tomy]

articular /är tĭk'yə lər/   relating to a joint.

articular cartilage /kär'tə lĭj/   cartilage lining a joint.

articulate 1. *v.* /är tĭk'yə lāt'/   to join together as in a joint. **2.** *adj.* /är tĭk'yə lĭt/   capable of producing proper speech.

articulation /är tĭk'yə lā'shən/   **1.** a joint. **2.** the production of the sounds used for speech.

artifact /är'tə făkt'/   a self-inflicted marking or perpetuation of a skin lesion.

artificial abortion /ə bôr'shən/   a forced or induced abortion.

artificial acquired immunity /ĭ myōō'nĭ tē/   medically induced immunity, such as by a dose of gamma globulin or vaccination.

artificial heart   a device capable of performing the functions of a heart.

artificial insemination (AIH) /ĭn sĕm'ə nā'shən/   a fertilization procedure during which semen is placed in the vagina with a catheter for the purposes of fertilization.

artificial knee a manufactured replacement for the knee joint.

artificial nose a manufactured replacement for part or all of the nose.

artificial pacemaker /pās′mā′kər/ a manufactured device that controls the rhythm of the heart through electrical impulses. *Also called* pacemaker.

artificial pancreas /păn′krē əs, păng′-/ a manufactured device that continuously monitors blood sugar levels and releases insulin when necessary.

artificial ventilation forced breathing, such as mouth to mouth resuscitation.

aryepiglottic fold /ăr′ē ĕp′ĭ glŏt′ĭk′/ mucous membrane that stretches between the epiglottis and the arytenoid cartilage.

A.S. *abbreviation*. Latin *auris sinister*, left ear.

ASA (drug caution code) abbreviation of acetylsalycylic acid (aspirin), placed on the label of a medication as a warning that it contains acytylsalysylic acid, which can cause complications for someone with specific medical conditions.

asbestos /ăs bĕs′təs, ăz-/ a fibrous mineral that can be harmful when inhaled.

asbestosis /ăs′bĕs tō′sĭs, ăz′-/ scarring of the lungs as a result of asbestos inhalation.

ascariasis /ăs′kə rī′ə sĭs/ a disease caused by infection with intestinal roundworms.

ascending aorta /ə sĕn′dĭng ā ôr′tə/ the first section of the aorta originating from the heart and to the coronary arteries.

ascending colon /kō′lən/ the part of the colon on the right side of the abdomen, between the cecum and the transverse colon.

ascites /ə sī′tēz/ buildup of fluid in the abdomen.

ascitic fluid /ə sĭt′ĭk/ the fluid that accumulates during ascites.

ascorbic acid /ə skôr′bĭk/ vitamin C.

ASD *abbreviation*. atrial septal defect.

asepsis /ə sĕp′sĭs, ā sĕp′-/ the absence of pathogenic microorganisms. [a- + sepsis]

aseptic /ə sĕp′tĭk, ā sĕp′-/ relating to asepsis.

aseptic necrosis /nə krō′sĭs/ death of tissue caused by an inadequate supply of blood when no infection is present.

aseptic technique sterile procedures used to reduce the patient's risk of infection during surgery.

asexual /ā sĕk′shōō əl/ **1.** having no sex or sexual organs. **2.** lacking sexual attraction or desire.

Asian influenza /ĭn′flōō ĕn′zə/ or **Asian flu** /flōō/ influenza virus that usually appears first in an Asian country.

ASL *abbreviation*. American Sign Language.

asocial /ā sō′shəl/ unwilling or unable to adhere to normal standards of social behavior. [a- + social]

ASP *abbreviation*. aspartic acid.

aspartate aminotransferase (AST) /ăs pär′tāt ə mē′nō trăns′fə rās′/ an enzyme usually present in cells of the liver and the heart. *Also called* glutamic oxaloacetic transaminase, serum glutamic oxaloacetic transaminase.

aspartic acid (ASP) /ăs pär′tĭk/ one of the 20 amino acids found in proteins.

Asperger('s) syndrome /ăs′pər gər(z)/ an autistic disorder that affects social interaction.

aspergillosis /ăs′pər jĭ lō′sĭs/ serious fungal infection, usually in the lungs.

aspermia /ā spûr′mē ə, ə spûr′-/ inability to produce or ejaculate semen.

asphyxia /ăs fĭk′sē ə/ lack of oxygen due to impaired breathing.

asphyxiate /ăs fĭk′sē āt′/ to smother, choke, or otherwise obstruct breathing.

aspirate /ăs′pə rāt′/ to suck in, especially to suck a food particle into the airway.

aspiration /ăs′pə rā′shən/ **1.** removal of gas or fluid through suction, such as fluid buildup in a joint. **2.** accidental sucking in of fluids or food particles into the airway.

aspiration biopsy /bī′ŏp sē/ the use of a needle to collect samples for examination.

aspiration pneumonia /nōō mōn′yə/ pneumonia resulting from the inhalation of foreign particles into the lungs.

aspirator /ăs′pə rā′tər/ a device that removes fluid through aspiration.

asplenia /ā splē′nē ə/ absence of the spleen.

asplenic /ā splĕn′ĭk/ having no spleen.

assay /ăs′ā/ an analysis.

assignment of benefits directive giving permission for insurance benefits to be paid directly to a health care provider.

assistant /ə sĭs′tənt/ a person trained or certified to work in a particular position, as a medical assistant.

assisted living accommodations that provide room and board and care for the elderly or the disabled.

assisted reproductive technology (ART) /rē′prə dŭk′tĭv/ medical procedures designed to help infertile couples conceive.

assisted suicide help in committing suicide given to a terminally ill person by a doctor or another person, usually by providing medication.

assistive device any device used to help someone perform a task, such as a cane or a wheelchair.

assistive technology equipment designed to help a disabled person function more easily.

AST *abbreviation.* aspartate aminotransferase.

astasia /ə stā′zhə/ inability to stand due to a motor difficulty.

asthenia /ăs thē′nē ə/ weakness.

asthenic /ăs thĕn′ĭk/ relating to asthenia.

asthenopia /ăs′thə nō′pē ə/ eye weakness; eyestrain.

asthma /ăz′mə/ chronic inflammation of the bronchial tubes, causing difficulty in breathing.

asthmatic /ăz măt′ĭk/ **1.** *adj.* of or relating to asthma. **2.** *n.* a person suffering from asthma.

astigmatic /ăs′tĭg măt′ĭk/ **1.** *adj.* of or relating to astigmatism. **2.** *n.* a person suffering from astigmatism.

astigmatism /ə stĭg′mə tĭz′əm/ abnormal curvature of the cornea resulting in blurred vision.

astringent /ə strĭn′jənt/ causing constricting of tissues, which can control bleeding or fluid secretion.

astro- *combining form.* star: *for example,* astrocyte.

astroblast /ăs′trə blăst′/ a primitive cell that develops into an astrocyte. [astro- + -blast]

astrocyte /ăs′trə sīt′/ a star-shaped cell of the nervous system; astroglia. *Also called* macroglia. [astro- + -cyte]

astrocytoma /ăs′trō sī tō′mə/ a brain tumor, composed of astrocytes. [astrocyte + -oma]

astroglia /ăs trŏg′lē ə, ăs trō glī′ə/ astrocyte.

asymptomatic /ā′sĭmp tə măt′ĭk/ without symptoms. [a- + symptomatic]

asystole /ā sĭs′tə lē/ cardiac arrest where there is no electrical activity in the heart.

ataractic /ăt′ə răk′tĭk/ any drug that is used to reduce stress, a tranquilizer.

ataxia /ə tăk′sē ə/ poor coordination.

-ate replaces "-ic" in acids after the acid has been neutralized, such as nitrate from nitric acid.

atelectasis /ăt′ə lĕk′tə sĭs/ collapse of part or all of a lung.

atelectatic /ăt′ə lĕk tăt′ĭk/ relating to atelectasis.

atelia /ā tē′lē ə/ incomplete development of the body or any of its parts.

athelia /ə thē′lē ə/ congenital absence of the nipples.

ather-, athero- *combining form.* soft fatty deposit: *for example,* atheroma, atherosclerosis.

atherectomy /ăth′ə rĕk′tə mē/ removal of an atheroma. [ather- + -ectomy]

atherogenesis /ăth′ə rō jĕn′ə sĭs/ formation of an atheroma. [athero- + -genesis]

atheroma /ăth′ə rō′mə/ (*pl.* **atheromas** or **atheromata** /ăth′ə rō′mə tə/) fatty deposit in an artery. [ather- + -oma]

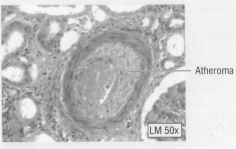

Atheroma

LM 50x

Atheroma

atheromatous /ăth′ə rō′mə təs, -rŏm′ə-/ affected by an atheroma.

atherosclerosis /ăth′ə rō sklĭ rō′sĭs/ thickening and hardening of the artery walls due to fatty deposits, or atheromas.

atherosclerotic /ăth′ə rō sklĭ rŏt′ĭk/ relating to or affected by atherosclerosis.

atherosclerotic heart disease (AHD) the gradual thickening and hardening of the walls of arteries from fat deposits.

athetoid /ăth′ī toid′/ affected by athetosis.

athetosis /ăth′ī tō′sĭs/ involuntary slow writhing movements of the limbs, especially the arms and hands, usually the result of a brain lesion or secondary effect of a drug.

athlete's foot fungal infection of the feet that causes itching and burning. *Also called* tinea pedis.

athymia /ə thī′mē ə/ **1.** absence of the thymus. **2.** absence of emotion.

athymic /ə thī′mĭk/ lacking a thymus.

ATL *abbreviation.* adult T-cell leukemia, adult T-cell leukemia/lymphoma, or adult T-cell lymphoma.

atlantoaxial /ăt lăn′tō ăk′sē əl/ relating to both the first and second cervical vertebrae or the joint between them.

atlas /ăt′ləs/ the first cervical vertebrae.

atom /ăt′əm/ the basic unit of matter.

atomizer /ăt′ə mī′zər/ a device that delivers medication in a fine spray or mist.

atonic /ə tŏn′ĭk, ā tŏn′-/ without muscle tone or strength, relaxed.

atonic seizure a sudden loss of muscle strength resulting in collapse. *Also called* drop attack, drop seizure.

atopic /ə tŏp′ĭk, ā tŏp′-/ prone to allergies.

atopic dermatitis /dûr′mə tī′tĭs/ a chronic skin disease with itching, redness, loss of the skin's surface, and scaling.

atopy /ăt′ə pē/ hypersensitivity to environmental allergens.

ATP *abbreviation.* adenosine triphosphate.

atresia /ə trē′zhə/ absence of development of a tube or a normal opening such as the anus or duodenum.

atresia ani /ā′nī/ congenital lack of an anus or of the anal canal. *Also called* anal atresia.

atri-, atrio- *combining form.* atrium: *for example,* atrioventricular.

atria /ā′trē ə/ plural of atrium.

atrial /ā′trē əl/ of or pertaining to the atrium.

atrial fibrillation (AF) /fĭb′rə lā′shən/ rapid, irregular contractions of the atria of the heart causing cardiac arrhythmia and, often, the formation of clots.

atrial flutter rapid contractions of the atria of the heart.

atrial septal defect (ASD) /sĕp′təl dē′fĕkt, dĭ fĕkt′/ a hole between the two atria of the heart present as a congenital defect at birth.

atrial septum /sĕp′təm/ the wall or septum between the two atria of the heart.

atrioventricular (AV) /ā′trē ō vĕn trĭk′yə lər/ of or pertaining to the atria and ventricles of the heart.

atrioventricular block partial or complete block of electrical impulses from the atria to the ventricles of the heart.

atrioventricular bundle the bundle of muscle fibers starting in the atrioventricular node.

atrioventricular (AV) node a small bundle of muscle fiber that sends electrical impulses from the atria to the ventricles of the heart.

atrioventricular valve either of the two valves (tricuspid valve, mitral valve) between the atria and the ventricles of the heart.

atrium /ā′trē əm/ (*pl.* **atria** /ā′trē ə/) **1.** either of the two upper chambers of the heart through which blood is circulated. **2.** any chamberlike entrance to an organ.

atrophic /ə trŏf′ĭk/ of or pertaining to atrophy.

atrophy /ăt′rə fē/ a wasting of something, as an organ, tissue, or the body.

attack /ə tăk′/ an episode or sudden onset of a disease or condition.

attending physician the hospital physician responsible for primary care of patients during their hospital stay.

attention deficit disorder (ADD) a psychological disorder characterized by an inability to pay attention and by lack of impulse control.

attention deficit hyperactivity disorder (ADHD) /hī′pər ăk tĭv′ĭ tē/ a psychological disorder characterized by an inability to pay attention, lack of impulse control, and hyperactivity.

A type blood one of the common blood groups.

atypical /ā tĭp′ĭ kəl/ unusual, as symptoms of a disease.

A.U. *abbreviation.* Latin *auris unitas,* both ears.

audio- *combining form.* sound, hearing: *for example,* audiometer.

audiogram /ô′dē ə grăm′/ the graphic result of a hearing test. [audio- + -gram]

audiologist /ô′dē ŏl′ə jĭst/ a specialist who evaluates and provides mechanical treatment to patients with hearing loss.

audiology /ô′dē ŏl′ə jē/ the study of hearing disorders. [audio- + -logy]

audiometer /ô′dē ŏm′ĭ tər/ a device for measuring hearing ability. [audio- + -meter]

audiometry /ô′dē ŏm′ĭ trē/ the measurement of hearing ability.

auditory /ô′dĭ tôr′ē/ having to do with hearing.

auditory aphasia /ə fā′zhə/ a hearing impairment that affects the ability to understand aural components of language use and communication, including an inability to write from dictation even though the hearing is normal; acoustic aphasia.

auditory brainstem response (ABR) test /brān′stĕm′/ a test for hearing and brain function integrity in which electrodes attached to the head can record electrical activity from the auditory nerve and other parts of the brain. *Also called* brainstem auditory evoked potentials.

auditory feedback unwanted feedback sound picked up by a microphone, annoying in hearing aids.

auditory integration training therapeutic training designed for people who have difficulty processing acoustic signals.

auditory nerve a nerve in the ear that attaches to the cochlea; cochlear nerve.

auditory ossicles /ŏs′ĭ kəlz/ a group of three small bones in the middle ear that transmit sound to the oval window in the ear.

AUL *abbreviation.* acute undifferentiated leukemia.

aura /ôr′ə/ symptoms such as flashing lights, numbness, or weakness that signal the onset of a migraine headache or a seizure.

aural /ôr′əl/ **1.** of or pertaining to the ear. **2.** of or pertaining to an aura.

auricle /ôr′ĭ kəl/ the shell-like outer structure of the ear visible on the side of the head. *Also called* pinna.

auricular /ô rĭk′yə lər/ of or pertaining to the auricle.

auris dexter (A.D.) /ôr′ĭs dĕk′stər/ right ear.

auris sinister (A.S.) /sĭn′ĭ stər/ left ear.

auris unitas (A.U.) /yōō′nĭ tăs′/ both ears.

auscultate /ôs kŭl′tāt/ to make a diagnosis by listening to the sounds produced by various bodily functions, usually with a stethoscope.

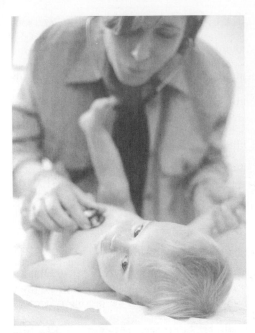

Auscultation

auscultation /ôs'kŭl tā'shən/ listening to the sounds produced by various body functions, usually through a stethoscope, in order to make a diagnosis.

Austin Flint murmur /ô stən flĭnt' mûr'mər/ a murmur caused by aortic regurgitation, a sound originating at the aortic valve.

aut-, auto- *combining form.* self, same: *for example,* autoimmune.

autism /ô'tĭz əm/ a developmental disorder characterized by abnormal absorption with the self, impaired communication ability, and a preoccupation with fantasy rather than reality. [aut- + -ism]

autistic /ô tĭs'tĭk/ pertaining to or characterized by autism.

autoantibody /ô'tō ăn'tĭ bŏd'ē/ an antibody that attacks the tissue of the organism that produced it. [auto- + antibody]

autoclave /ô'tə klāv'/ **1.** *n.* a device that sterilizes by using compressed steam. **2.** *v.* to sterilize with such a device.

autogenous /ô tŏj'ə nəs/ referring to something that originates within the individual to which it is applied, as with a graft or a vaccine. [auto- + -genous]

autograft /ô'tō grăft'/ an organ or tissue grafted into a new position in the body of the individual from which it came; autotransplant. [auto- + graft]

autografting /ô'tō grăf'tĭng/ the act of performing an autograft.

autohemotherapy /ô'tō hē'mō thĕr'ə pē/ a treatment involving the removal and reinsertion of an individual's own blood. [auto- + hemo- + therapy]

autoimmune /ô'tō ĭ myōōn'/ denoting an immune system response by the body against one or more of its own tissues. [auto- + immune]

autoimmune disease or **disorder** any of a number of disorders caused by the patient's immune system attacking his or her own body; autoimmune disorder.

autoimmune hemolytic anemia /hē'mə lĭt'ĭk ə nē'mē ə/ a condition in which the red blood cells are attacked by one's own immune system.

autoimmunity /ô'tō ĭ myōō'nĭ tē/ a condition in which the tissues of the body are attacked by one's own immune system.

autoinoculation /ô'tō ĭ nŏk'yə lā'shən/ **1.** inoculation using substances taken from the patient's own body. **2.** a new infection caused by the spread of an already present infection to other parts of the patient's body.

autologous /ô tŏl'ə gəs/ derived or transferred from one's own body.

autologous blood donation a blood transfusion in which an individual both provides and receives the transfused blood; autologous transfusion.

autologous transfusion /trăns fyōō'zhən/ autologous blood donation.

autologous transplant /trăns'plănt'/ a transplant in which an individual serves as both donor and recipient.

autolysis /ô tŏl'ə sĭs/ the breakdown of cells or tissues caused by substances found within them. [auto- + -lysis]

automated external defibrillator /dē fĭb'rə lā'tər/ a device that applies a brief electric shock to the heart muscle in order to stop fibrillation and restore a normal heart rhythm.

automated white cell differential /dĭf'ə rĕn'shəl/ a machine-generated listing of the percentages of the various white blood cell types.

automatism /ô tŏm'ə tĭz'əm/ any movement or functioning of an organ or body part that is outside of the conscious control of the individual in which it occurs.

autonomic /ô'tə nŏm'ĭk/ of or relating to the autonomic nervous system.

autonomic failure failure of the autonomic nervous system to function properly.

autonomic nervous system the part of the nervous system that regulates involuntary body functions, such as heart function.

autonomic neuropathy /nōō rŏp'ə thē/ disease of the nerves that are not under the

Tissue Preparation during an Autopsy

conscious control of the patient, such as those that control digestion and the cardiovascular system.

autophagia /ô′tō fā′jə, -jē ə/ **1.** the biting of one's own skin. **2.** the consumption, by the body, of some of its own tissues to maintain nutrition. [auto- + -phagia]

autopsy /ô′tŏp sē/ an examination of a corpse in order to determine the cause of death. *Also called* necropsy, postmortem examination.

autoradiography /ô′tō rā′dē ŏg′rə fē/ a photographic record of the radiation emitted from a specimen after it has been injected or exposed to a radioactive substance.

autosomal /ô′tō sō′məl/ of or relating to an autosome.

autosome /ô′tə sōm′/ any chromosome other than the sex chromosomes.

autosuggestion /ô′tō səg jĕs′chən/ the process of focusing on an idea or concept in order to cause a mental or physical change in oneself.

autotransplant /ô′tō trăns′plănt/ an organ or tissue grafted into a new position in the body of the individual from which it came; autograft.

autotransplantation /ô′tō trăns′plăn tā′shən/ the process of performing an autotransplant.

AV *abbreviation.* atrioventricular.

avascular /ə văs′kyə lər, ā văs′-/ lacking blood vessels. [a- + vascular]

avian flu /ā′vē ən floo′/ avian influenza.

avian influenza /ĭn′floo ĕn′zə/ a highly contagious disease caused by the influenza virus, found initially almost exclusively in birds; avian flu. *Also called* bird flu.

AVM *abbreviation.* arteriovenous malformation.

avulse /ə vŭls′/ to separate by avulsion.

avulsion /ə vŭl′shən/ the removal of a body part by a forcible tearing, as in trauma or surgery.

ax *abbreviation.* axis.

axial /ăk′sē əl/ **1.** relating to an axis. **2.** located in or relating to the central part of the body.

axial skeleton /skĕl′ĭ tən/ the bones of the head and trunk of the body.

axilla /ăk sĭl′ə/ (*pl.* **axillae** /ăk sĭl′ē/ the armpit.

axillary /ăk′sə lĕr′ē/ of or relating to the axilla.

axillary artery /är′tə rē/ the section of the major artery in the arm that is found in the armpit.

axillary lymph nodes /lĭmf′ nōdz′/ lymph nodes located in the axilla.

axis /ăk′sĭs/ **1.** an imaginary line through the center of the body or any of its parts. **2.** the spinal column. **3.** the central nervous system. **4.** the second of the cervical vertebrae. **5.** an artery that splits into a number of branch arteries immediately after its point of origin.

axon /ăk′sŏn/ a long nerve fiber that conducts impulses away from a neuron.

Ayurveda /ä′yər vā′də, -vē′də/ an ancient Hindu medicinal science.

Ayurvedic medicine /ä′yər vā′dĭk, -vē′dĭk/ a system of medicine that aims to treat body, mind, and spirit, involving music, herbal treatments, massage, and so on.

azoospermia /ā′zō ō spûr′mē ə/ the absence of live spermatozoa in the semen.

azotemia /ăz′ō tē′mē ə/ presence of high levels of urea in the blood. *Also called* uremia.

azoturia /ăz′ō tŏŏr′e ə/ an excess of urea in the urine.

AZT *abbreviation.* azidothymadine, also known as zidovudine, a drug used in the treatment of HIV.

azygous /ăz′ĭ gəs, ā zī′gəs/ occurring singly, not paired.

Ba *abbreviation.* barium.

babesiosis /bə bē'zē ō'sĭs/ a disease caused by a tick-borne parasite, usually occurring in the Northeast or Midwest and marked by fevers and sweating, chills, fatigue, anemia, and enlargement of the liver and spleen.

Babinski('s) /bə bĭn'skē(z)/ **reflex** or **sign** a response to the stroking of the sole of the foot from the heel toward the toes, in which the big toe flexes upward; normal in infants but abnormal in older children and adults, where it indicates a neurological problem; a common diagnostic technique.

baby blues a common temporary mental state occurring in the mother of a newborn shortly after delivery, with mood swings varying from depression to elation and back, accompanied by anxiety and irritability.

baby teeth the first set of teeth that start to grow in infancy. *Also called* primary teeth, primary dentition.

bacillary angiomatosis /băs'ə lĕr'ē ăn'jē ō mə tō'sĭs/ a usually mild bacterial infection caused by a cat scratch, with swollen lymph glands, fevers and sweats, chills, and vomiting. *Also called* cat-scratch fever, cat-scratch disease.

bacilliform /bə sĭl'ə fôrm'/ rod-shaped.

bacillus /bə sĭl'əs/ (*pl.* **bacilli** /bə sĭl'ī/) any rod-shaped bacterium.

back /băk/ the rear side of the body from the neck to the bottom of the spine.

backache /băk'āk'/ pain, generally in the lower back, usually caused by sore muscles or strained ligaments.

backbone /băk'bōn'/ the long series of connected vertebrae running down the middle of the back. *Also called* spine.

background radiation ionizing radiation occurring naturally (cosmic rays, radioactive material in the earth, etc.) and which is measured before a test in which a radioactive drug is administered so that it can be subtracted from the resulting clinical counts.

back pain pain in the upper or lower back, having many possible causes.

bacteremia /băk'tə rē'mē ə/ the presence of bacteria in the blood. [bacter(i)- + -emia]

bacteri-, bacterio- *combining form.* bacteria: *for example,* bactericide, bacteriology.

bacteria /băk têr'ē ə/ (*sing.* **bacterium** /băk têr'ē əm/) any of a large class of single-celled microorganisms, most of which multiply by cell division; some cause disease.

bacterial /băk têr'ē əl/ of or involving bacteria. [bacteri- + -al]

bacterial endocarditis /ĕn'dō kär dī'tĭs/ infection of the inner lining of the heart, usually of the valves, with fever, enlarged spleen, and heart murmur, caused by a bacterium. *See also* acute bacterial endocarditis, subacute bacterial endocarditis.

bacterial meningitis /mĕn'ĭn jī'tĭs/ a potentially lethal inflammation of the membranes that cover the brain and spinal cord, caused by a bacterium such as *Streptococcus pneumoniae* or *Neisseria meningitides,* and marked by high fever, headache, and stiff neck.

bacterial pneumonia /nōō mōn'yə/ infection of one or both lungs, caused by a bacterium, such as *Streptococcus pneumoniae,* also known as pneumococcus.

bactericidal /băk têr'ə sī'dəl/ of or involving a substance that can kill bacteria. An antibiotic can be either bactericidal or bacteriostatic.

bactericide /băk têr'ə sīd'/ a substance that can kill bacteria. [bacteri- + -cide]

bacteriogenic /băk têr'ē ō jĕn'ĭk/ caused by bacteria. [bacterio- + -genic]

bacteriology /băk têr'ē ŏl'ə jē/ the branch of science that studies bacteria. [bacterio- + -logy]

bacteriolysis /băk têr'ē ŏl'ə sĭs/ destruction of bacteria. [bacterio- + -lysis]

bacteriophage /băk têr'ē ə fāj'/ a virus-like particle that can infect a bacterium. [bacterio- + -phage]

bacteriosis /băk têr'ē ō'sĭs/ condition, such as an infection, caused by bacteria. [bacteri- + -osis]

bacteriostatic /băk têr'ē ō stăt'ĭk/ **1.** *adj.* slowing down or preventing the growth of bacteria. **2.** *n.* an agent that slows down or prevents the growth of bacteria.

bacterium /băk têr'ē əm/ the singular of bacteria.

bacteriuria /băk têr'ē yōōr'ē ə/ the presence of bacteria in the urine. [bacteri- + -uria]

BaE, Ba enema *abbreviation.* barium enema.

BAEP *abbreviation.* brainstem auditory evoked potentials.

BAER *abbreviation.* brainstem auditory evoked response.

bag of waters the amniotic fluid-filled sac that cushions the fetus and usually breaks shortly before labor begins.

Baker cyst /bā′kər sĭst′/ a sac filled with synovial fluid that forms behind the knee.

balan-, balano- *combining form.* glans penis: *for example,* balanitis, balanoplasty.

balance /băl′əns/ **1.** the act of retaining an upright posture. **2.** the system of equilibrium maintained by complex structures in the inner ear and input from proprioceptors (position sensors) in the joints of the feet, ankles, and knees.

balanitis /băl′ə nī′tĭs/ inflammation of the glans penis. [balan- + -itis]

balanoplasty /băl′ə nō plăs′tē/ surgical repair of the glans penis. [balano- + -plasty]

baldness /bôld′nĭs/ partial or total loss of hair. *Also called* alopecia.

ball-and-socket joint a joint, such as at the shoulder or hip, in which the rounded end of one bone sits in a cuplike indentation in another.

balloon angioplasty /ăn′jē ə plăs′tē/ a procedure to open a blocked or narrowed artery, in which a balloon-tipped catheter is snaked into the artery up to the affected area, and then inflated to force open the blocked portion.

balloon catheter dilation /kăth′ĭ tər dī lā′shən/ or **dilitation** /dĭl′ĭ tā′shən/ a procedure to enlarge a vessel, tube, or duct in the body, in which a balloon is attached to a catheter, snaked to the affected area, and then inflated to force open the vessel, tube, or duct.

balloon tamponade /tăm′pə nād′/ a procedure to stop bleeding in the esophagus or stomach, in which a balloon-tipped catheter is snaked to the appropriate position and inflated to put pressure on the bleeding artery or vein in order to compress it and to stop the bleeding.

balloon valvuloplasty /văl′vyə lō plăs′tē/ a procedure to open a narrowed heart valve, in which a balloon-tipped catheter is snaked to the appropriate valve, and then inflated to open the valve.

ballottement /bə lŏt′mənt/ **1.** a palpation technique used to examine a floating organ that is not near the surface. **2.** a diagnostic technique in pregnancy, in which a light tap of the uterus is made through the vagina wall.

balm /bäm/ an oily or resinous medicinal liquid made from a plant or tree, used especially to soothe itching or inflamed skin.

band /bănd/ in anatomy, a cordlike strip that holds tissue or structures together.

Bandage

bandage /băn′dĭj/ **1.** *n.* a piece of cloth applied to a body part to provide compression, absorb drainage, and protect from contamination of a wound, or to prevent the movement of a body part (for example to immobilize an arm or fingers) or of another dressing that has been applied directly on a wound. **2.** *v.* to apply a bandage to a wound or body part.

band cells any of three kinds of white blood cells with granular cytoplasm and a lobed nucleus, found in bone marrow and peripheral blood. Their numbers are elevated during certain infections.

banding of chromosomes /krō′mə sōmz′/ the use of chemicals to stain chromosomes so that the individual chromosomes can be identified.

bar-, baro- *combining form.* weight, pressure: *for example,* bariatric, barostat.

barber's itch a fungal infection of bearded areas on the face or neck. *Also called* tinea barbae.

barbiturate /bär bĭch′ər ĭt/ any of a group of chemically related medicines used to prevent convulsions, relieve anxiety, and produce sleep.

bariatric /băr′ē ăt′rĭk/ of or involving the branch of medicine specializing in issues of obesity and weight control. [bar- + iatr- + -ic]

bariatrician /băr′ē ə trĭsh′ən/ bariatric physician.

bariatric physician /fĭ zĭsh′ən/ a doctor specializing in issues of obesity and weight control; bariatrician.

bariatric surgery a weight-loss operation, such as a gastric bypass or gastric banding, to reduce the size of the stomach and sometimes bypassing a portion of the intestines as well.

bariatrics /băr′ē ăt′rĭks/ the branch of medicine specializing in obesity and weight control.

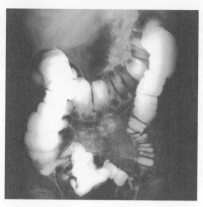

Barium Enema X-Ray

barium (Ba) /bâr′ē əm/ a chemical element in a liquid of the same name which shows up white on x-rays, and is used in imaging the body, especially the alimentary tract, from mouth to anus.

barium enema (BaE, BE) /cn′ə mə/ an enema of the lower intestine and rectum with a chalky solution that contains barium, enabling the intestine to be seen clearly on x-rays. *See also* air contrast barium enema.

barium enema x-ray a series of x-rays of the three parts of the colon and the rectum after the patient has had a barium enema. *Also called* lower gastrointestinal series.

barium solution a liquid that contains barium sulfate, swallowed or given as an enema, which makes various organs of the body visible on x-rays.

barium sulfate /sŭl′fāt/ a tasteless, odorless, non-gritty white powder, BaSO₄, mixed with water and swallowed or given as an enema, allowing the digestive tract to be x-rayed.

barium swallow a series of x-rays of the esophagus, stomach, and small intestines after the patient has swallowed barium sulfate. *Also called* upper gastrointestinal series.

Barlow('s) syndrome /bär′lō(z)/ the most common heart defect, with abnormal movement of one or both valve's lips during ventricular systole, usually with no symptoms or treatment but sometimes with fatigue and palpitations. *Also called* mitral valve prolapse.

baro- *See* bar-.

barosinusitis /băr′ō sī′nə sī′tĭs/ sinus problems, especially pain, due to changes in atmospheric pressures, such as when going up or down in a plane. [baro- + sinusitis]

barostat /băr′ə stăt′/ a structure composed of pressure-sensitive receptors, located in the area of the carotid artery where it splits into inner and outer carotids, that helps people adjust to changing pressure.

barotitis /băr′ə tī′tĭs/ inflammation of the barostat.

barotrauma /băr′ō trou′mə/ injury of an organ, especially in the ear, due to changes in atmospheric pressure or injury to the lungs during mechanical ventilation with high pressures.

Barr body /bär/ the shriveled, inactive remnant of the X-chromosome found in the nucleus of the cells (except sex cells) of most female mammals.

Barrett('s) esophagus /băr′ĭt(s) ĭ sŏf′ə gəs/ chronic peptic ulcers in the esophagus, often a result of long-term GERD.

barrier method the use of a physical barrier, such as a diaphragm or condom, to prevent sperm from entering the cervix where there is a chance to come into contact with a mature egg.

Bartholin('s) adenitis /bär′tə lĭn(z) ăd′ə nī′tĭs/ inflammation of a Bartholin gland.

Bartholin('s) glands a pair of glands located on the labia minora at the side of and below the vaginal opening that secrete a lubricating fluid when stimulated.

bas-, baso- *combining form.* base; foundation: *for example,* basal, basophil.

basal /bā′səl, -zəl/ of or involving a base. [bas- + -al]

basal cell a cell at the bottom of the top layer of the skin.

basal cell carcinoma /kär′sə nō′mə/ a slow-growing cancer of the basal cells of the skin, usually caused by overexposure to sunlight.

basal cell nevus syndrome /nē′vəs/ a genetic disorder marked by a broad face, skeletal abnormalities, and the occurrence of basal cell carcinomas.

basal ganglia /găng′glē ə/ large groups of nerve cell bodies located deep within the brain, involved in musculoskeletal movement; basal nuclei.

basal metabolic rate (BMR) /mĕt′ə bŏl′ĭk/ the rate at which energy is used when the body is completely at rest, usually measured in calories per kilogram per hour.

basal nuclei /nōō′klē ī′/ basal ganglia.

basal temperature body temperature on waking up, used to determine when ovulation is occurring.

base /bās/ **1.** the bottom of a structure. **2.** in pharmacy, the main ingredient in a medication. **3.** any of the four bases in DNA: adenine, cytosine, guanine, thymine. **4.** any of the four bases in RNA: adenine, cytosine, guanine, uracil. **5.** a liquid with a pH over 7, contrasted with an acid.

BASE breast cancer gene /bās/ a gene that encodes a protein produced only by the salivary glands and by breast cells in breast cancer; the level of this protein can be used to screen for and track the progression of treatment for breast cancer. [*b*reast *a*nd *s*alivary gland *e*xpression]

baseline /bās′līn′/ a value representing the initial or normal level of a measurable aspect of something, used especially in medical studies.

basement membrane a thin membrane made of protein held together by collagen, on which lies a single layer of epithelial or endothelial cells, for example at the bottom of the epidermis or beneath the endothelium of blood vessels.

base pair either of two pairs of DNA bases—adenine and thymine or cytosine and guanine—that bond, keeping the double-helix structure of a chromosome aligned.

baseplate wax preformed shape representing the base of the denture, used for taking bite registration during the fitting of a complete denture.

basic /bā′sĭk/ **1.** of or involving a starting point or base. **2.** not acidic; having a pH greater than 7.

basilar /băs′ə lər/ of or involving a base.

basilar membrane a membrane in the inner ear that transmits sound vibrations to hair cells in the organ of Corti and, ultimately, to the auditory nerve and brain.

baso- *See* bas-.

basophil /bā′sə fĭl/ a type of white blood cell that releases heparin (an anticlotting factor) and histamines (involved in allergic reactions) and whose cytoplasm stains with basic dyes. *See also* eosinophil, neutrophil. [baso- + -phil]

basophilia /bā′sə fĭl′ē ə/ an increase in basophils in peripheral blood found in some types of leukemia.

basophilic /bā′sə fĭl′ĭk/ pertaining to the ability to stain with basic dyes.

battered child syndrome a form of child abuse in which physical damage, including pinching, punching, striking, kicking, beating, shaking, etc., is inflicted on the child.

battle fatigue an emotional disorder caused by the stresses of combat, occurring among soldiers.

BBB *abbreviation.* blood-brain barrier.

BC *abbreviation.* bone conduction.

B cell a type of white blood cell that matures either into a plasma cell, which produces antibodies, or into a memory B cell, which creates an enhanced immunological reaction on reexposure to a antigen. *Also called* B lymphocyte, beta cell.

BCG *abbreviation.* bacillus of Calmette and Guerin (vaccination for tuberculosis).

BE *abbreviation.* barium enema.

beat /bēt/ a pulsation or throbbing, as in a heartbeat.

Beau('s) lines /bō(z)/ horizontal grooves that sometimes cross the fingernails due to nail disease, malnutrition, trauma, or severe illness.

Beckwith-Wiedemann syndrome /bĕk′wĭth wē′də mən/ a genetic disease disorder with giantism, a large tongue, and the protrusion of a part of the intestine and sometimes the liver and spleen at the navel.

bedbug /bed′bŭg′/ a bloodsucking wingless bug, *Cimex lectularius,* that inhabits houses and especially beds with a bite that causes itching.

bed rest staying in bed for medical reasons, such as to minimize the occurrence of certain complications of pregnancy or to aid in recuperation from a disease such as tuberculosis.

bedside manner the attitude and behavior of a doctor toward a patient.

bedsore /bĕd′sôr′/ a skin lesion resulting from pressure on the skin, especially over a bony prominence, as from long bed rest. *Also called* decubitus ulcer, pressure sore.

bedwetting /bĕd′wet′ĭng/ an informal term for enuresis, involuntary urination in bed, especially at night.

bee sting the painful sting of the bee, to which some people are highly allergic.

behavior modification the conscious changing of undesired behavior through various feedback mechanisms, including rewards, biofeedback, conditioning, etc.

behavior therapy a form of psychotherapy that focuses on substituting desirable responses for unwanted or destructive behaviors through a variety of learning techniques, including rewards, negative consequences, relaxation, and biofeedback.

behavioral medicine a field of medicine that specializes in the interaction of behavior and health.

behaviorism /bē hāv′yə rĭz′əm/ a school of psychology that focuses on observable behaviors rather than on emotions or underlying motivations.

Behcet('s) /bā′sət(s), bə shĕt(s)′/ **disease** or **syndrome** a group of symptoms that include painful recurring ulcers of the mouth and genitalia, inflammation of the eye, and frequently arthritis.

behind-the-ear hearing aid a clear plastic hearing aid that sits behind the external ear.

belch /bĕlch/ **1.** *v.* to expel wind from the stomach; eructate. **2.** *n.* eructation.

Bell('s) palsy /bĕl(z) pôl′zē/ a paralysis of the facial nerve on one side of the face, believed caused by a virus, that usually improves greatly with passage of time and physical therapy.

belly /bel′ē/   the abdomen.

belly button   the navel. *Also called* umbilicus.

belly pain   acute or chronic abdominal pain.

below-knee amputation (BKA)   surgical removal of the leg below the knee, not uncommon in diabetes.

Bence-Jones protein /bens′ jōnz′ prō′tēn, -tē ĭn/   low-weight protein fragments found in the urine of patients with multiple myeloma.

Bender-Gestalt Test /běn′dər gə shtält′/   a test in which a person is asked to copy geometric designs; the results can indicate visual-motor neurological difficulties.

bends /běndz/   informal term for decompression sickness.

benign /bĭ nīn′/   not malignant; used especially with cancers to indicate that they are not invasive and spreading.

benign melanoma /měl′ə nō′mə/   a nonmalignant tumor of cells in the epidermis that produce melanin.

benign paroxysmal positional vertigo /păr′ək sĭz′məl pə zĭsh′ə nəl vûr′tĭ gō′/   a balance disorder that causes the sensation of dizziness or spinning on moving the head.

benign prostatic hyperplasia /prŏ stăt′ĭk hī′pər plā′zhə/ or **benign prostatic hypertrophy (BPH)** /hī pûr′trə fē/   a noncancerous growth of normal cells in the prostate, which can cause compression of the urethra and incomplete, frequent urination.

benign tumor   a nonmalignant tumor.

benzodiazepines (BZD) /běn′zō dī ăz′ə pēnz′/   a family of chemically related medications that reduce anxiety and act as sedatives and muscle relaxants and that can be used to treat convulsions.

benzothiazides /běn′zō thī′ə zīdz′/   a family of chemically related diuretics that increase the excretion of sodium and chloride and, therefore, water, and also act to reduce blood pressure.

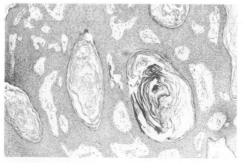

Benign Skin Tumor

bereavement /bĭ rēv′mənt/   a state of acute grieving that often accompanies the death of a loved one.

beriberi /běr′ē běr′ē/   a syndrome with inflammation of many nerves, heart disease, and swelling, caused by a lack of vitamin B_1 (thiamine).

Bernard('s) syndrome /bär när(z)′/   a disorder marked by a sunken eye accompanied by a drooping eyelid and contracted pupil on one side of the face, along with flushing and a lack of sweating on that side of the face, caused by paralysis of certain facial nerves.

berry aneurysm /ăn′yə rĭz′əm/   a pouch-shaped widening and weakness in an artery in the brain, usually found where a cerebral artery departs from the circular artery at the base of the brain.

berylliosis /bə rĭl′ē ō′sĭs/   **1.** poisoning by acute exposure to toxic fumes of the metal beryllium, which can cause severe and even fatal inflammation of the lungs. **2.** the more common poisoning by chronic overexposure to beryllium, which causes a general inflammatory reaction in the lungs and results in tumors, scarring, and increasing shortness of breath.

beta adrenergic blocking agent /bā′tə ăd′rə nûr′jĭk/   beta blocker.

beta blocker   one of a number of drugs that interfere with the stimulation of beta receptors, resulting in slowing the heart rate and reducing blood vessel muscle tone and used to treat abnormal heart rhythms, abnormally fast heart rates, high blood pressure, and angina; beta adrenergic blocking agent.

beta carotene /kăr′ə tēn′/   a vitamin, abundant in carrots, sweet potatoes, spinach, cantaloupe, and more, that protects cells against oxidation and is turned into vitamin A within the body.

beta cell   **1.** a type of white blood cell that matures either into a plasma cell, which produces antibodies, or into a memory B cell, which creates an enhanced immunological reaction on reexposure to an antigen. *Also called* B lymphocyte, B cell. **2.** a cell in the islet of Langerhans in the pancreas that produces insulin.

beta globulin /glŏb′yə lĭn/   a kind of globulin that transports fats and fat-soluble vitamins, such as A, D, and E, through the blood.

beta-human chorionic gonadotropin (HCG) /kôr′ē ŏn′ĭk gō năd′ə trō′pĭn/   **1.** a hormone produced by the placenta and used in pregnancy testing of either urine or blood. **2.** a hormone produced by some tumors, whose presence can indicate cancer of uterus, ovary, liver, pancreas, lung, or testis.

beta particle an electron or positron emitted from an atomic nucleus in a certain type of radioactive decay.

beta ray a stream of beta particles.

beta receptor a site on a cell that interacts with epinephrine or norepinephrine to increase heart rate and strength of heart contractions, increase blood flow to skeletal muscles, and decrease peripheral vascular resistance by dilating capillaries.

bi- *prefix.* twice, double: *for example,* bifocal.

BIA *abbreviation.* bioelectric impedance analysis.

bicameral /bī kăm′ər əl/ having two chambers, as an abscess divided into two sections by a septum.

bicellular /bī sĕl′yə lər/ having two cells or two cellular divisions. [bi- + cellular]

biceps /bī′sĕps/ informal term for the biceps brachii muscle.

biceps brachii muscle /brā′kē ī′/ the muscle that flexes and brings up the forearm.

biceps femoris muscle /fē′mər ĭs, fĕm′ər-/ the muscle that flexes the knee and rotates the leg to the side.

biconcave /bī′ kŏn kāv′/ bowing in on two sides [bi- + concave].

biconvex /bī′kŏn vĕks′/ bowing out on two sides. [bi- + convex]

bicornuate /bī kôrn′yōō āt′/ having two horns or two projections.

bicuspid /bī kŭs′pĭd/ **1.** *adj.* having two points or cusps. **2.** *n.* any of eight teeth located on each side of the upper and lower jaws between the cuspids and the molars.

bicuspid valve a valve between the upper and lower chambers on the left side of the heart, made of two triangular flaps. *Also called* mitral valve.

b.i.d., bid, BID *abbreviation.* Latin *bis in die,* two times a day (on prescriptions).

bifid /bī′fĭd/ separated into two equal lobes.

bifocals /bī fō′kəlz/ eyeglasses that have two focus points, one for seeing things close up, such as when reading or sewing, the other for viewing things at a distance, such as when driving or watching a movie. [bi- + focal]

bifurcate /bī′fər kāt′/ **1.** *v.* to divide into two branches. **2.** *adj.,* also, **bifurcated** (/bī′fər kā′tĭd/) divided into two branches.

bifurcation /bī′fər kā′shən/ **1.** the point at which something divides into two branches. **2.** division into two branches.

bigeminal /bī jĕm′ə nəl/ paired.

bigeminy /bī jĕm′ə nē/ repeated pairs of atrial and ventricular beats.

big toe the innermost digit of the foot. *Also called* great toe, hallux.

Bifocals

bilateral /bī lăt′ər əl/ involving two sides. [bi- + lateral]

bile /bīl/ a bitter, yellowish-brown to green fluid secreted in the liver, stored in the gallbladder, and released into the beginning of the small intestine to aid in digestive function, especially the absorption of fats.

bile acid any of certain complex acids secreted in the liver that are active in the breakdown of fats and are reabsorbed from the intestine to be used again by the liver.

bile ducts small passages between the cells of the liver that transport bile to the hepatic duct, where it joins the cystic duct coming from the gallbladder and becomes the common bile duct, discharging into the upper small intestine.

biliary /bĭl′ē ĕr′ē/ of or involving bile, bile ducts, or the gallbladder.

biliary atresia /ə trē′zhə/ a birth defect in which there is an absence of the major bile ducts draining bile from the liver, usually discovered two or three weeks after birth with yellowing of the eyes and skin.

biliary colic /kŏl′ĭk/ pain caused by obstruction of the bile ducts, usually by gallstones.

biliary duct any of the bile ducts.

bilious /bĭl′yəs/ of or involving bile or excess secretion of bile.

bilirubin /bĭl′ə rōō′bĭn/ the yellow-orange pigment in bile, an end product of red cell metabolism that is normally excreted in feces.

bilirubinemia /bĭl′ə rōō bə nē′mē ə/ excess amounts of bilirubin in the blood.

bilirubinuria /bĭl′ə rōō bə nōōr′ē ə/ presence of bilirubin in the urine.

biliverdin /bĭl′ə vûr′dĭn/ a greenish pigment in bile.

Billroth('s) I /bĭl′rôth(s)/   surgical widening of the narrowed bottom of the stomach (pylorus) and direct reconnection of the stomach to the initial portion of the duodenum (first part of small intestine).

Billroth('s) II /bĭl′rôth(s)/   surgical removal of the narrowed bottom of the stomach (pylorus) and direct connection of the stomach to the middle part of the small intestine.

binaural /bī nôr′əl/   of or involving both ears.

binder / bīnd′ər/   **1.** a bandage or wrap that encircles something. **2.** a substance that adheres to another substance.

binge drinking   drinking more than 4 (women) or 5 (men) drinks at one time.

binge eating disorder   an eating disorder characterized by episodes of eating very large quantities of food, often accompanied by self-induced vomiting. *See also* bulimia.

binocular   /bĭ nŏk′yə lər/   adapted for or involving both eyes.

binocularity /bĭ nŏk′yə lăr′ĭ tə/   the ability to see a single, three-dimensional image when using both eyes.

binocular vision   seeing a single, three-dimensional image when using both eyes.

bio-   *combining form.* life, living: *for example,* biochemistry.

bioactive /bī′ō ăk′tĭv/   affecting or interacting with living tissue. [bio- + active]

bioavailability /bī′ō ə vā′lə bĭl′ĭ tē/   the percentage of an administered drug that is absorbed and available to the body, important in pharmacy for calculating effective dosages. [bio- + availability]

biochemical /bī′ō kĕm′ĭ kəl/   of or involving biochemistry. [bio- + chemical]

biochemistry /bī′ō kĕm′ĭ strē/   the study of the chemistry of living organisms. [bio- + chemistry]

biochemistry panel   a group of automated tests for various common diseases or disorders.

bioelectric impedance analysis (BIA) /bī′ō ĭ lĕk′trĭk   ĭm pē′dəns   ə năl′ ə sĭs/   a measure of body fat by determining how quickly an impulse travels through the body— the slower the travel the more body fat, the higher the less body fat. *Also called* fat scales.

bioelectromagnetic-based therapy /bī ō ĭ lĕk′trō măg nĕt′ĭk/   any of several techniques in complementary and alternate medicine using electromagnetic fields to improve health. [bio- + electromagnetic]

bioethics /bī′ō ĕth′ĭks/   a field of study specializing in the potential ethical and philosophical consequences of the application of certain medical technology and treatment, such as euthanasia, genetic engineering, and stem cell research. [bio- + ethics]

Biohazard Container

biofeedback /bī′ō fēd′băk/   a technique of learning to control one's own body by monitoring one's brain waves, blood pressure, or other physiological measurement. [bio- + feedback]

biofield therapy /bī′o fēld′/   any of a variety of therapies used in complementary and alternate medicine that try to affect the energy fields that are believed to surround and flow through the body.

biohazard /bī′ō hăz′ərd/   **1.** potential danger from exposure to an infectious organism, as in blood or waste, especially in a laboratory or research setting. **2.** the infectious organism itself. [bio- + hazard]

bioinformatics /bī′ō ĭn fər măt′ĭks/   the use of computer science and mathematical and statistical techniques in the collection, processing, and analysis of biological data. [bio- + informat(ion) + -ics]

biological response modifiers   medications or activities such as exercise, which has been shown to reduce recurrence of breast cancers, that help the body fight cancer by boosting the immune system.

biological rhythm   natural body cycles, such as the sleep-wake cycle or the menstrual cycle; biorhythm.

biological therapy   treatments that use the body's immune system to fight cancer or to moderate the effects of cancer treatment. *Also called* biotherapy.

biologically based therapy   the complementary and alternative medical use of substances found in nature, such as herbs, dietary supplements, and megadoses of vitamins, to prevent illness and restore health.

biomagnetic therapy /bī′ō măg nĕt′ĭk/   a complementary and alternative form of treatment that uses magnets to relieve pain and improve health. [bio- + magnetic]

biomarker /bī′ō mär′kər/ a substance, such as human chorionic gonadotropin or alpha-fetoprotein, that when present in abnormal amounts in serum may indicate the presence of disease, as that caused by a malignancy. [bio(logical) + marker]

biomedical /bī′ō mĕd′ĭ kəl/ the study of how natural sciences and particularly the environment affects clinical medical. [bio- + medical]

biopsy (bx, BX, Bx, Bx.) /bī′ŏp sē/ **1.** *n.* the removal of a small piece of living tissue for analysis, or the specimen itself. **2.** *v.* to remove living tissue for analysis.

biorhythm /bī′ō rĭth′əm/ natural body cycles, such as the sleep-wake cycle or the menstrual cycle; biological rhythm.

bioterrorism /bī′o tĕr′ə rĭz′əm/ terrorism using biological agents or toxins, especially those that can be easily introduced and transmitted and that have a high death rate.

biotherapy /bī′ō thĕr′ə pē/ biological therapy.

biotransformation /bī′ō trăns fər mā′shən/ chemical alteration of a substance within the body. [bio- + transformation]

biparous /bĭp′ər əs/ bearing twins. [bi- + -parous]

bipolar /bī pō′lər/ **1.** having two poles or ends, as a nerve or cell. **2.** of or involving a psychological disorder with recurrent bouts of depression and elation (mania). [bi- + polar]

bipolar disease or **disorder** a kind of psychological disorder with recurring bouts of depression and elation. *Also called* manic depressive disorder/disease/illness.

bird flu avian influenza, occasionally transmissible to humans, as in the recent appearance of the H5N1 strain.

birth /bûrth/ the act or process of being born or bringing forth offspring.

birth control any of a variety of physical barriers to the meeting of sperm and egg or pharmacological pills or implants that control hormone flow to prevent ovulation or implantation.

birth control implant medication that prevents the flow of certain hormones in order to block ovulation.

birth control pill any of various pills that prevent the flow of certain hormones in order to block ovulation.

birth defect any physical or mental abnormality that is present at birth. *Also called* congenital defect.

birthmark or **birth mark** /bûrth′märk′/ a localized skin discoloration or overgrowth present at birth, such as a mole or port-wine stain.

birth rate the number of live births over the course of a year, divided by the average population for that year, usually expressed in number of births per thousand people.

birth weight the weight of an infant at birth.

bisected-angle /bī sĕk′tĭd/ the technique for taking radiographs based on the principle of directing the central rays perpendicular to an imaginary line which bisects the angle formed by the long axis of the teeth and the plane of the film.

bisexual /bī sĕk′shoo əl/ *n.* **1.** a person with the gonads of both male and female. **2.** a person who has sexual attraction to both men and women. *adj.* **3.** of or involving a person with both male and female gonads. **4.** of or involving a person who has sex with men and women.

bis in die (b.i.d., bid, BID) /bĭs′ ĭn dē′ā/ twice a day (on prescriptions).

bite /bīt/ **1.** *n.* the fit of the teeth of the upper jaw with those of the lower jaw when the jaws are closed. **2.** *n.* a breaking of the skin caused by teeth. **3.** *v.* to break the skin using teeth.

biteplate or **bite plate** /bīt′plāt′/ a removable dental appliance worn to gradually correct the positioning of the teeth when they come together

bite-wing film x-ray film that has been prepared in such a way that the patient can hold it between the teeth in a particular position during the x-ray.

biventricular assist device /bī′vĕn trĭk′yə lər/ a mechanical pump that helps damaged ventricles of the heart by helping the right ventricle pump blood to the lungs and the left ventricle pump blood to the body. [bi- + ventricular]

B-K *abbreviation.* below the knee.

BKA *abbreviation.* below-knee amputation.

Black Death one of three varieties of severe bacterial infection caused by *Yersinia pestis,* transmitted by the bite of fleas living on infected rats, with painfully swollen glands especially in the groin, fever, headache, and gangrene of the nose, fingers, and toes. *Also called* Great Plague, bubonic plague. *See also* pneumonic plague.

black eye darkening of the skin around the eye, resulting from a blow, bruise, or other trauma, such as facial surgery.

blackhead /blăk′hĕd′/ a small plug of sebum blocking the duct of a sebaceous gland especially on the face. *Also called* comedo.

black lung (disease) an occupational disease of the lungs, which can be disabling and even fatal, caused by prolonged breathing of coal dust. *Also called* miner's lung. *See also* pneumoconiosis.

blackout /blăk′ out / a condition of sudden unconsciousness, as in a fainting spell.

black tongue a black or brownish discoloration of the upper surface of the tongue, sometimes with elongation of the small bumps

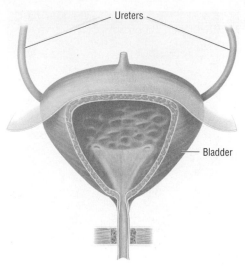

Ureters

Bladder

Bladder

(papillae) of the tongue, caused by tobacco or as a reaction to antibiotics.

bladder /blăd′ər/ **1.** urinary bladder; the organ where urine collects before being excreted from the body. **2.** gallbladder; the pear-shaped organ that stores bile from the liver and excretes it into the duodenum as needed to assist in the absorption of fat. **3.** any membranous organ or sac that contains water or air.

bladder cancer a malignant tumor that begins in the lining of the bladder.

blast-, blasto- *combining form.* immature cell: *for example,* blastoma, blastocyte.

-blast *suffix.* immature, forming: *for example,* erythroblast.

blastema /blă stē′mə/ (*pl.* **blastemas** or **blastemata** /blă stē′mə tə/) group of imma ture cells in the embryo, before differentiation.

blastocele /blăs′tə sēl′/ the cavity in the embryo of the developing ovum. [blasto- + -cele]

blastocyst /blăs′tə sĭst′/ a modified stage of the blastula, in which there is an inner cell mass and a thin layer of cells enclosing the blastocele. [blasto- + -cyst]

blastocyte /blăs′tə sīt′/ an undifferentiated cell in the embryo. [blasto- + -cyte]

blastocytoma /blăs′tō sī tō′mə/ a tumor made of undifferentiated immature cells. [blasto-cyt(e) + -oma]

blastoderm /blăs′tə dûrm′/ a disk of cells lying between the yolk sac and the amniotic cavity from which the embryo develops; it gives rise to the ectoderm, mesoderm, and endoderm.

blastogenesis /blăs′tō jĕn′ə sĭs/ the change from small lymphocytes into larger cells capable of undergoing mitosis. [blasto + -genesis]

-blastoma *combining form.* a tumor made of undifferentiated immature cells: *for example,* neuroblastoma, retinoblastoma. [blast- + -oma]

blastomycosis /blăs′tō mī kō′sĭs/ a fungal infection with inflammatory lesions of the skin or lungs and sometimes becoming a chronic infection of lungs, skin and mucous membranes, central nervous system, bones, and liver, kidneys, or other organs. [blasto- + mycosis]

blastula /blăs′chə lə/ the embryo in an early stage in development, in which the ovum consists of a hollow sphere of cells enclosing a cavity, the blastocele.

bleb /blĕb/ a usually fluid-filled blister on the skin or on the lining of the lungs.

bleed /blēd/ **1.** *v.* to lose blood because of a break in a blood vessel. **2.** *n.* a blood vessel that is bleeding.

bleeding time a test measuring platelet function: the speed at which small blood vessels close off to stop bleeding, having been blocked by platelet aggregation.

blemish /blĕm′ĭsh/ a small change in or discoloration of the skin that may detract from appearance but is otherwise medically insignificant.

blephar-, blepharo- *combining form.* eyelid: *for example,* blepharedema, blapharoplasty.

blepharectomy /blĕf′ə rĕk′tə mē/ surgical removal of all or part of an eyelid. [blephar- + -ectomy]

blepharedema /blĕf′ər ĭ dē′mə/ swelling of the eyelid. [blephar- + edema]

blepharitis /blĕf′ə rī′tĭs/ inflamation of the eyelid. [blephar- + -itis]

blepharochalasis /blĕf′ə rō kăl′ə sĭs/ excess skin of the upper eyelid that can block vision. [blepharo- + chalasis]

blepharophimosis /blĕf′ə rō fĭ mō′sĭs/ narrowed eye slits. [blepharo- + phimosis]

blepharoplasty /blĕf′ə rō plăs′tē/ surgical repair of the eyelid. [blepharo- + -plasty]

blepharoptosis /blĕf′ə rŏp tō′sĭs/ drooping of the upper eyelid. [blephar- + -ptosis]

blepharorrhaphy /blĕf′ə rôr′ə fē/ a suturing of the eyelid. [blepharo- + -rrhaphy]

blepharospasm /blĕf′ə rō spăz′əm/ an involutary twitch of the eyelid. [blepharo- + spasm]

blepharotomy /blef′ə rŏt′ə mē/ a surgical incision into the eyelid. [blepharo- + -tomy]

blind /blīnd/ being completely or partially unable to see.

blind gut informal term for the pouchy, slightly distended beginning of the large intestine, which connects with the ileum and from which the vermiform appendix extends. *Also called* cecum.

B

blindness /blīnd′nĭs/ total or partial absence of vision.

blind spot the region on the back of the eyeball where the optic nerve connects to the retina; there are no visual receptor cells at that junction. *Also called* optic disc/disk.

blink /blĭngk/ a usually involuntary rapid closing and reopening of the eye, generally for removing dirt or moisturizing the eyes.

blister /blĭs′tər/ a thin bubble-like sac on the surface of the skin, usually filled with watery liquid or serum.

blister agent or **blistering agent** a synthetic or organic substance that causes blistering of the skin, lungs, or eyes on contact.

bloat /blōt/ or **bloating** /blō′tĭng/ abdominal swelling caused by the retention of gas.

block /blŏk/ or **blockage** /blŏk′ĭj/ any obstruction, as one in a blood vessel caused by plaque.

block anesthesia /ăn′əs thē′zhə/ regional anesthesia, such as a spinal or epidural, using local anesthetic to block nerve transmission to and from the brain.

blood /blŭd/ fluid containing plasma, red and white blood cells, and platelets, pumped throughout the body, delivering oxygen and nutrients to and removing wastes from the cells.

blood and heart scan a scan tracing a radioactive drug to show blood flow through the heart and indicate disease or impaired function.

blood bank a location, often part of a hospital, where whole blood and certain components are processed, typed, and stored for later use.

blood blister a small blister on the surface or just underneath the skin filled with blood from a broken blood vessel, often due to friction.

blood-brain barrier (BBB) the tightly packed cells in the walls of the capillaries in the brain that prevent substances, such as most drugs and other matter, from migrating from the bloodstream (diffusing) into the cells of the brain itself.

blood cells any of the solids suspended in the blood. *See also* red blood cell, white blood cell, platelet.

blood chemistry or **blood chemistry profile** a standard test of plasma for the presence of most substances normally found in plasma, such as glucose, cholesterol, uric acids, and electrolytes, which can indicate a variety of common disorders, such as diabetes, kidney or liver problems, circulatory problems, etc.

blood clot a coagulation of blood in a vessel. *See also* embolism, thrombus.

blood clotting coagulation.

blood count the numerical count of the number of red blood cells, white blood cells, and platelets in a specific volume of blood.

blood culture a test to look for microorganisms such as bacteria or fungi in the blood.

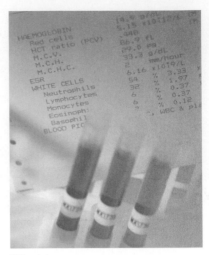
Blood Chemistry

blood dyscrasia /dĭs krā′zhə/ any blood disease.

blood flow the movement of blood through blood vessels and organs in the body.

blood gas analysis analysis of the acidity (pH), carbon dioxide and oxygen concentrations, and oxygen saturation of the blood to diagnose certain metabolic and respiratory disorders.

blood gases a determination of the respective amounts of oxygen and carbon dioxide in the blood during metabolic processes.

blood glucose /glōō′kōs/ **1.** the sugar that is carried in the blood to provide energy to cells; blood sugar. **2.** a test that measures the level of blood glucose present in the blood at a given point in time. *See also* fasting blood glucose, glucose tolerance test.

blood group any of several systems of classifying blood, based on presence or absence of antigens located on the surface of red blood cells; blood type. *See also* ABO blood group.

blood grouping the process of classifying blood samples into blood groups; blood typing.

bloodless surgery surgery performed with almost no loss of blood, usually using a laser.

blood poisoning a systemic disease caused by infection of the blood by pathogenic organisms. *Also called* sepsis, septicemia.

blood pressure (BP, bp) the maximum arterial pressure (systolic) during the contraction of the left ventricle in relation to the arterial pressure in between heartbeats (diastolic pressure). *See also* diastolic pressure, systolic pressure.

bloodshot /blŭd′shŏt′/ reddened or inflamed, as the blood vessels of the eye.

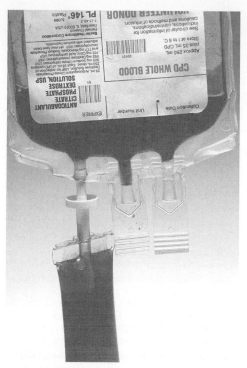

Blood Transfusion

blood slide or **blood smear** a specimen of blood spread thinly on a glass slide and examined in the lab for number and shape of blood cells.

bloodstream /blŭd′strēm′/ the blood flowing through the circulatory system of the body.

blood sugar blood glucose.

blood system the body system that includes the blood and all of its component parts.

blood thinner any agent that prevents the formation of blood clots, such as heparin or coumadin. *Also called* anticoagulant.

blood transfusion the replacement of blood or of one of its components after having matched the blood groups of the recipient and the blood or blood product being transfused.

blood type any of several systems of classifying blood, based on presence or absence of antigens located on the surface of red blood cells; blood group.

blood typing the process of classifying blood samples into blood groups; blood grouping.

blood urea nitrogen (BUN) /yoo rē′ə nī′trə jən/ a determination of the amount of nitrogen (in the form of urea) present in the blood, providing a quick rough estimate of kidney function.

blood vessel any of the passageways—arteries, veins, and capillaries—through which blood circulates in the body.

bloody nose bleeding from the nose. *Also called* epistaxis.

blue baby a baby born with poorly oxygenated blood as a result of a heart or lung defect.

blunted affect /ăf′ĕkt/ a mood disorder marked by reduced expression of emotion.

blurred vision loss of sharpness of vision and the ability to see details.

blush /blŭsh/ a sudden, usually brief, redness of the face and neck and sometimes the chest.

B lymphocyte /lĭm′fə sīt′/ a type of white blood cell that matures either into a plasma cell, which produces antibodies, or into a memory B cell, which creates an enhanced immunological reaction on reexposure to a antigen. *Also called* B cell, beta cell.

BM *abbreviation*. bowel movement.

BMD *abbreviation*. bone mass density or bone mineral density.

BMI *abbreviation*. body mass index.

BMI calculation a person's weight in kilograms (kg) divided by their height in meters squared (m^2).

BMR *abbreviation*. basal metabolic rate.

board certified having passed a medical exam in a specialty, administered and assessed by a board of specialists in that field, necessary for permission to practice in a hospital.

body /bŏd′ē/ **1.** the physical structure of a being. **2.** the main part of any structure.

body-based therapies complementary and alternative medicine approaches to resolving illness and promoting health that involve manipulation of the soft tissue (massage) or bones (chiropractic) of the body.

body cavity 1. one of two major spaces in the body: the dorsal cavity (at the back of the body) or the ventral cavity (at the front of the body). **2.** one of three spaces within the cavity

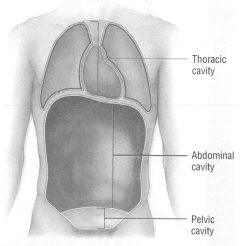

Thoracic cavity

Abdominal cavity

Pelvic cavity

Body Cavities

at the front of the body: the thoracic cavity, the abdominal cavity, or the pelvic cavity.

body dysmorphic disorder /dĭs môr′fĭk/ a psychological disorder in which the patient is obsessed with one or several real or fancied body imperfections.

body fat monitor a device that measures changes in voltage when a harmless amount of electrical current passes between two parts of the body, used to calculate the percentage of that person's body fat.

body fat scale a special scale with footpads on which a person stands that measures the changes in voltage when a harmless amount of electrical current is sent through the body, used to calculate the percentage of that person's body fat.

body habitus /hăb′ĭ təs/ the general physique of a person.

body integrity identity disorder a condition in which the patient wants to undergo medically unnecessary amputations.

body language nonverbal communication through the usually unconscious use of gestures, facial expressions, postures, etc.

body mass index (BMI) a general measure of nutritional status, giving a general measurement of the amount of fat in a person's body, calculated by dividing the person's weight in kilograms (kg) by the square of their height in meters (m^2).

body mechanics the application of the principles of physics and anatomy to body movement in order to prevent and correct problems caused by posture and lifting and to increase coordination and endurance.

Boerhaave('s) syndrome /bŏŏr′hä və(z)/ tearing open of the esophagus for no apparent reason.

Bogorad('s) syndrome /bō′gə räd(z)′/ a disorder in which tears are produced when a person salivates during eating.

boil /boil/ dome-shaped lesion; furuncle.

bolus /bō′ləs/ **1.** a single large dose of a diagnostic or therapeutic substance administered orally or intravenously. **2.** a mouthful of chewed food, ready to be swallowed.

bone /bōn/ the hard connective tissue that forms the skeleton; there are 206 bones in the human body. *See also* osseous tissue, osteocyte. *See* plate 7 following page 264.

bone cancer one of several types of rare tumors that arise in bone tissue: osteosarcoma, chondrosarcoma, Ewing('s) sarcoma, myeloma, fibrosarcoma.

bone conduction (BC) /kən dŭk′shən/ transmission of sound to the inner ear through vibration of the bones of the skull.

bone densitometry /dĕn′sĭ tŏm′ĭ trē/ measurement of the amount of bone tissue in a

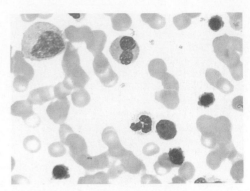

Bone Marrow

certain volume of bone, used especially to assess risk for osteoporosis.

bone density amount of mineral content in a certain volume of bone, determined by a special x-ray called a quantitative computed tomogram.

bone depression any of five types of hole or indentation in bone: fossa, foramen, fissure, sulcus, and sinus.

bone grafting transplantation of bone from one site on the body to another (autograft) or from donated bone (allograft), in order to repair the bone or to fuse it, as in the spine, to prevent movement.

bone head the often rounded end of a bone where it attaches to other bones or connective material.

bone marrow either of two types of soft connective tissue found in the inner cavity of a bone: red bone marrow, yellow bone marrow.

bone marrow transplant /trăns′plănt′/ grafting of bone marrow tissue.

bone mineral density or **bone mass density (BMD)** a measure of the amount of calcium in bone.

bone phagocyte /făg′ə sīt′/ bone cell that ingests dead bone and bone debris.

bone process any of seven extensions on most bones: bone head, crest, process, tubercle, trochanter, tuberosity, condyle.

bone projection an extension of or protuberance on a bone.

bone scan x-ray examination of the skeleton after radioactive material has been injected, frequently to locate a site of infection, which shows up as an area of increased metabolic (and radioactive marker) activity.

bone spur an abnormal projection that grows on a bone.

bone tumor a malignant or benign abnormal growth of cells within a bone.

bone type any of many categories of bone; the five most common types are: long bones, short bones, flat bones, irregular bones, and sesamoid bones.

bony necrosis /nə krō′sĭs/ death of bone cells.

booster or **booster shot** or **booster dose** an injection of an antigen administered after a primary inoculation, in order to enhance or renew the effect of the primary inoculation.

borborygmus /bôr′bə rĭg′məs/ (*pl.* **borborygmi** /bôr′bə rĭg′mī/) rumbling or gurgling noises in the stomach or intestines, made by the peristaltic movement of gases and/or fluid through the digestive tract. *Also called* bowel sounds.

borderline personality disorder a psychological disorder with unstable moods, self-image, behavior, and identity and often inappropriate anger, impulsive behavior, and depression.

Bornholm('s) disease /bôrn′hōlm(z)/ a temporary illness with fever, severe chest pain, and headache, usually caused by a coxsackievirus. *Also called* pleurodynia.

bottlefeeding /bŏt′əl fē′dĭng/ feeding an infant milk or other liquid nutritional preparation with a bottle rather than by breastfeeding.

botulinum toxin /bŏch′ə lī′nəm tŏk′sĭn/ the toxin produced by a bacterium, *Clostridium botulinum,* lethal when accidentally ingested in certain spoiled foods; used medically in tiny quantities to relieve muscle spasms and to minimize wrinkling by injection into specific muscle sites.

botulism /bŏch′ə lĭz′əm/ a potentially fatal diseased caused by the ingestion of botulinum toxin in improperly canned or preserved foods.

bougie /bōō′zhē/ a flexible rod that is used to dilate, examine, or medicate any narrow tubular passageway of the body, such as the urethra or esophagus.

bougienage or **bouginage** /bōō′zhē näzh′/ the use of a bougie to dilate, examine, or medicate a narrow tubular passageway of the body.

boutonneuse /bōō′tə nû(r)z′/ a tick-borne disease caused by a bacterium of the *Rickettsia* genus, with fever, black spots at the bite, and swollen glands in the area surrounding the bite.

bowel /bou′əl/ or **bowels** /bou′əlz/ the intestine or a part of it.

bowel movement (BM) **1.** the evacuation of feces from the intestines. **2.** feces.

bowel sounds rumbling or gurgling noises in the stomach or intestines, made by the peristaltic movement of gases and/or fluid through the digestive tract. *Also called* borborygmus.

Bowen('s) disease /bō′ən(z)/ an early stage of skin or mucous membrane malignancy, in which slightly raised, red, scaly or crusted patches are found.

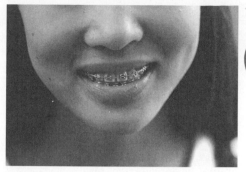

Braces

bow-legs /bō′ lĕgz′/ an outward curving of the legs, causing a separation of the knees when the ankles are close together.

Bowman('s) capsule /bō′mən(z)/ a membranous structure that surrounds each glomerulus of the kidney, in which water, urea, and certain solids collect before passing into a renal tubule and, ultimately, being excreted as urine.

BP, bp *abbreviation.* blood pressure.

BPD *abbreviation.* bronchopulmonary dysplasia.

BPH *abbreviation.* benign prostatic hyperplasia or benign prostatic hypertrophy.

braces /brā′sĭz/ **1.** appliances put on the teeth by an orthodontist in order to shift the teeth or underlying bone for better bite or for cosmetic purposes. **2.** *sing.* **brace** /brās/ any orthotic appliance used to shape or hold a body part in place.

brachi-, brachio- *combining form.* arm: *for example,* brachiocephalic.

brachial /brā′kē əl/ of or involving the arm.

brachial artery the artery that runs from the shoulder to the elbow.

brachial neuritis /nōō rī′tĭs/ inflammation of the nerves of the arm, with pain and muscle weakness.

brachial palsy /pôl′zē/ or **brachial paralysis** /pə răl′ə sĭs/ brachial plexus palsy.

brachial plexus /plĕk′səs/ the group of nerves, arising in the upper spine, that power the arms.

brachial plexus palsy or **brachial plexus paralysis** paralysis of the arm due to damage to the brachial plexus.

brachial vein the vein that runs from the elbow to the shoulder.

brachiocephalic /brā′kē ō sə făl′ĭk/ of or involving both the arm and the head. [brachio- + cephalic]

brachium /brā′kē əm/ (*pl.* **brachia** /brā′kē ə/) in anatomy, the arm or an armlike structure.

brachy- *prefix.* short: *for example,* brachytherapy.

brachycephaly /brăk′ē sĕf′ə lē/ a head that is shorter than normal in its measurement from back to front. [brachy- + -cephaly]

brachydactyly /brăk′ē dăk′tə lē/ fingers that are shorter than normal. [brachy- + -dactyly]

brachymelia /brăk′ē mē′lē ə/ abnormal shortness of limbs.

brachytherapy /brăk′ē thĕr′ə pē/ radiation therapy performed close to the site being irradiated, for example by implantation of radioactive seeds into a prostate tumor. [brachy- + therapy]

brady- *prefix.* slow: *for example,* bradypnea.

bradycardia /brăd′ē kär′dē ə/ a slow heart rate, less than 60 beats a minute. [brady- + -cardia]

bradyesthesia /brăd′ē ĕs thē′zhə/ slow in perceiving sensations. [brady- + -esthesia]

bradykinesia /brăd′ē kĭ nē′zhə/ slowness of movement. [brady- + -kinesia]

bradykinetic /brăd′ē kĭ nĕt′ĭk/ marked by slow movement. [brady- + -kinetic]

bradypnea /brăd′ĭp nē′ə/ slow breathing. [brady- + -pnea]

Braille system /brāl/ a system of reading and writing for the blind in which combinations of raised dots represent letters and are read by touch.

brain /brān/ the part of the central nervous system enclosed in the skull and consisting of soft gray and white tissue that serves to control the body's functions and interactions with the outside world. *See also* brainstem, cerebellum, cerebrum, diencephalon.

brain abscess /ăb′sĕs/ a localized collection of pus surrounded by inflamed tissue, found in the brain.

brain aneurysm /ăn′yŏŏ rĭz′əm/ the thinning and ballooning out of a wall in an artery or vein in the brain.

brain biopsy /bī′ŏp sē/ removal of a small piece of brain tissue for analysis and diagnosis.

brain cancer a malignant tumor in the brain.

brain death absence of brain function as indicated by a flat electroencephalogram for 24 hours.

brain edema /ĭ dē′mə/ swelling in the brain; cerebral edema.

brain scan any of several technologies for producing images of the brain: CAT scan, MRI, fMRI, PET scan, SPECT scan.

brainstem or **brain stem** /brān′stĕm′/ the stalk-like portion at the bottom of the brain that connects to the spinal cord, made up of the midbrain, the pons, and the medulla oblongata.

brainstem auditory evoked potentials (BAEP) or **responses (BAER)** a test measuring responses triggered by click (auditory) stimuli measured across the skull and used to test hearing and neurologic soundness in infants and in comatose adults. *Also called* ABR test.

brain swelling *swelling in the brain;* cerebral edema.

brain tumor /tōō′mər/ a benign or malignant growth in the brain.

brain ventricle /vĕn′trĭ kəl/ any of four connected cavities in the brain, filled with cerebrospinal fluid and forming part of the central canal of the spinal cord as it leaves the brain: lateral ventricles, third ventricle, fourth ventricle.

brainwashing /brān′wôsh′ĭng/ the use of undue pressure or torture to get someone to change their beliefs.

branch /brănch/ any offshoot, as of a blood vessel or nerve.

branchial cleft cyst /brăng′kē əl klĕft′ sĭst′/ or **branchial cyst** a cyst located on either side of the neck that becomes noticeable in adolescent although it is present from birth; it is an embryonic remnant of gills.

brand name the name given to a particular drug by a manufacturer and copyrighted for sole use by that manufacturer.

Braxton Hicks contractions /brăk′stən hĭks′/ irregular contractions of the uterus that can occur during the middle of a first pregnancy or at the end of the first trimester in later pregnancies, not indicative of the onset of labor. *Also called* false labor.

Brazelton Neonatal Behavior Assessment Scale /brā′zəl tən nē′ō nā′təl/ or the **Brazelton** a scale used in the sensorimotor, neurologic, emotional, and developmental assessment of infants at or shortly after birth.

BRCA breast cancer gene one of two genes—BRCA-1 and BRCA-2—whose mutations are linked to breast and ovarian cancers; breast cancer gene.

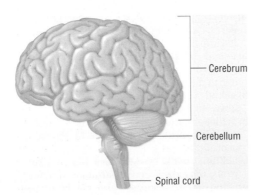

Cerebrum

Cerebellum

Spinal cord

Brain

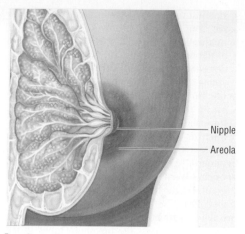

Nipple

Areola

Breast

breast /brĕst/ either of the two mammary glands that project outward from the chest in mature women.

breast augmentation plastic surgery to insert a silicone cup (usually filled with saline solution), performed to enlarge the breasts.

breast biopsy /bī'ŏp sē/ the removal of a small piece of living tissue or the extraction of cells by needle and aspiration for laboratory analysis.

breastbone /brĕst'bōn'/ a long, flat bone located in the center of the thorax to which the ribs attach. *Also called* sternum.

breast cancer any of many types of cancer that originate in the breast.

breast cancer gene BRCA breast cancer gene.

breastfeeding or **breast-feeding** /brĕst' fē'dĭng/ to suckle (nurse at the breast) an infant.

breast lump a swelling or knot in the breast that can occur at any time in either sex; usually benign, occasionally indicates a malignant tumor.

breast milk milk from the human breast, which contains excellent nutrition for an infant and provides immunological benefits.

breast pump a device used by lactating mothers to withdraw milk from their breasts.

breast reconstruction /rē'kən strŭk'shən/ surgical repair of a female breast, usually after a cancerous breast has been removed. *Also called* mammoplasty.

breast reduction surgical reduction in the size of the breasts.

breast self-examination the monthly examining of her breasts by a woman who has been taught the techniques of breast palpation for the purpose of detecting abnormalities.

breast surgeon a surgeon who specializes in operating on the breast.

breast trauma /trou'mə/ physical damage, such as that caused by a blow or an impact, which may cause blood vessels to rupture and blood to collect in one place or fat cells to die; either result can cause a perceptible, noncancerous lump.

breath /brĕth/ **1.** a single act of inhaling air and then exhaling it. **2.** the air inhaled or exhaled.

breathing /brē'thĭng/ the process of inhaling air; respiration.

breath sounds noises that can be heard when listening through a stethoscope to a patient's lungs, such as crackles or rales, wheezes or rhonchi, and stridor

breech /brēch/ of a birth position in which the buttocks are the presenting part in second stage of labor.

breech birth birth in which the feet or buttocks emerge before the head.

breech presentation a position in which the fetus is in the birth canal with the feet or buttocks closest to the cervix; labor often ends with a cesarean section.

Breslow('s) thickness /brĕs'lō(z)/ a measure of the 5-year survival rate in melanoma; the thicker the tumor, the lower the survival rate.

brevicollis /brĕv'ĭ kŏl'ĭs/ abnormal shortness of the neck.

brevis /brĕv'ĭs/ short; used with muscles and tendons. *See also* longus.

bridge /brĭj/ a permanent dental appliance that replaces or restores one or more teeth and is attached to the patient's own teeth or roots.

bridgework /brĭj'wŭrk'/ in dentistry, a bridge.

Bright('s) disease /brīts/ chronic inflammation of the kidney, with albumin in the urine.

bristle brush an attachment to the dental handpiece to remove stain from occlusal surfaces (the upper and lower surfaces of teeth where they come together).

brittle diabetes /dī'ə bē'tĭs, -tēz/ a form of insulin-dependent diabetes with dangerous rapid shifts in blood glucose level. *Also called* unstable diabetes.

Broca('s) aphasia /brō'kə(z) ə fā'zhə/ difficulty in speaking (although comprehension is usually fine) caused by damage to Broca's area (the speech area) in the cerebral cortex.

Broca('s) area the part of the cerebral cortex that governs the production of speech, located on the left side of the brain.

broken hip a fractured bone in the hip, frequent among the elderly.

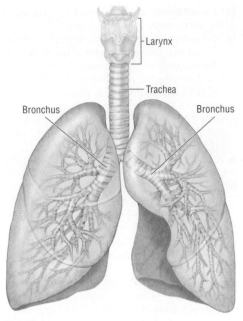

Larynx

Trachea

Bronchus   Bronchus

Bronchi

bronch-, bronchi-, broncho- *combining form.* bronchus, bronchi: *for example,* bronchitis, bronchogenic.

bronchi /brŏng′kī / plural of bronchus.

bronchial alveolar lavage /brŏng′kē əl ăl vē′ə lər lə vazh′/ the injection into and removal of fluid from the bronchi and alveoli to collect cells for analysis or remove protein debris; bronchial washing. [bronchi- + -al]

bronchial asthma /ăz′mə/ a lung condition, frequently an allergic reaction, with narrowing of the bronchi due to inflammation and spasm of the smooth muscle, swelling of the mucosal lining, and the presence of mucus in the bronchi and bronchioles.

bronchial brushing a type of biopsy using a brush on the end of a bronchoscope.

bronchial pneumonia /nōō mōn′yə/ acute inflammation of the walls of the smaller bronchial tubes that can spread into the air sacs; bronchopneumonia.

bronchial tree a bronchus and its branches.

bronchial tube a bronchus or any of its branches.

bronchial washing bronchial alveolar lavage.

bronchiectasis /brong′kē ek′tə sis / permanent widening of the bronchi, following chronic inflammation or obstruction. [bronchi- + -ectasis]

bronchiol-, bronchiolo- *combining form.* bronchiole: *for example,* bronchiolitis.

bronchiole /brong′kē ōl′/ one of the many smallest tubes of a bronchus, ending in an air sac.

bronchiolitis /brong′kə lī′tis/ inflammation of the bronchioles, usually due to viral infection and potentially very serious in very young children. [bronchiol- + -itis]

bronchioloalveolar /brŏng′kē ō′lō ăl vē′ə lər/ of or relating to bronchioles and alveoli. [bronchiolo- + alviolar]

bronchitis /brong kī′tis/ inflammation of the bronchi. [bronch- + -itis]

broncho- *See* bronch-.

bronchoalveolar /brong′kō ăl vē′ə lər/ of or involving the bronchi and alveoli. [broncho- + alveolar]

bronchoconstrictor /brong′kō kən strĭk′tər/ a drug that narrows the breathing tubes in the lungs. [broncho- + constrictor]

bronchodilation /brŏng′kō dī lā′shən/ a widening of the bronchi and bronchioles in response to a drug. [broncho- + dilation]

bronchodilator /brŏng′kō dī lā′tər/ a drug that opens the breathing tubes in the lungs. [broncho- + dilator]

bronchogenic /brŏng′kō jĕn′ĭk/ originating in the bronchi. [broncho- + -genic]

bronchogenic carcinoma /kär′sə nō′mə/ a cancer arising from the lining of the bronchi.

bronchogram /brŏng′kə grăm′/ an x-ray image of the trachea and bronchi made by instillation of a contrast medium. [broncho- + gram]

bronchography /brŏng kŏg′rə fē/ the process of recording an x-ray image of the trachea and bronchi after instilling a contrast medium. [broncho- + graphy]

broncholith /brŏng′kə lĭth/ a stone in a branch of a bronchus or in the bronchus itself. [broncho- + -lith].

broncholithiasis /brŏng′kō lĭ thī′ə sĭs/ inflammation or obstruction caused by the presence of stones within the bronchial tubes. [broncho- + -lithiasis]

bronchomalacia /brŏng′kō mə lā′shə/ a degeneration of the cartilage in the walls of the trachea and bronchi. [broncho- + -malacia]

bronchoplasty /brŏng′kə plăs′tē/ the surgical repair of a bonchus. [broncho- + -plasty]

bronchopneumonia /brŏng′kō nōō mōn′yə/ acute inflammation of the walls of the smaller bronchial tubes that can spread into the air sacs. [broncho- + pneumonia]

bronchopulmonary /brŏng′kō pŭl′mə něr′ē/ of or involving the lungs and their air passages. [broncho- + pulmonary]

bronchopulmonary dysplasia (BPD) /dĭs plā′zhə/ a disease of infants, especially in those at least four weeks premature with low birth weight, marked by shallow rapid breathing, sucked in ribs and chest, and wheezing, craning the neck, and periodically turning blue from lack of oxygen.

bronchoscope /brong′kə skōp′/ a rigid and flexible instrument used to examine the bronchi. [broncho- + -scope]

bronchoscopy /brŏng kŏs′kə pē/ a visual examination of the bronchi. [broncho- + -scopy]

bronchospasm /brŏng′kə spăz′əm/ involuntary contraction of the smooth muscles of the broncial tubes, as in asthma. [broncho- + spasm]

bronchospirometer /brŏng′kō spī rŏm′ĭ tər/ a device that measures the changes in size (volume) and rate of airflow of each lung separately, used to measure respiratory functioning. [broncho- + spirometer]

bronchostenosis /brŏng′kō stĭ nō′sĭs/ narrowing of a bronchus. [broncho- + -stenosis]

bronchostomy /brŏng kŏs′tə mē/ surgical creation of an opening into a bronchial tube. [broncho- + -stomy]

bronchotomy /brŏng kŏt′ə mē/ surgical incision into a bronchus. [broncho- + -tomy]

bronchus /brŏng′kəs/ (pl. **bronchi** /brŏng′kī/) either of two airways from the trachea to the lungs.

brow /brou/ **1.** eyebrow. **2.** forehead.

brucellosis /brōō′sə lō′sĭs/ a disease caused by infection with bacteria of the genus Brucella, with fevers that come and go, aches, sweating, fatigue, and weakness, caused by contact with infected animals and untreated contaminated milk and milk products. Also called undulant fever.

Bruce('s) protocol /brōōs′(ĭz) prō′tə kôl′/ a test used to evaluate cardiovascular health, using a treadmill that increases in steepness and speed through seven stages.

Brudzinski('s) sign /brōō jĭn′skē(z)/ either of two occurrences in meningitis, when the opposite leg imitates the passively flexed leg while lying down or when lying on one's back, the involuntary flexing of the hips and knees after flexing the neck.

bruise /brōōz/ an informal term for ecchymosis, a discoloration of the skin caused by blood escaping from ruptured blood vessels even though the skin itself is not broken.

bruit /brōōt/ an abnormal sound heard when listening to the flow of blood in an artery or vein.

brush biopsy /bī′ŏp sē/ the collecting of cells with a slightly abrasive brush for microscopic examination

Brushfield('s) spots /brŭsh′fēld(z)/ light spots in the iris, seen in people with Down syndrome.

bruxism /brŭk′sĭz əm/ grinding the teeth together, especially while sleeping

BSA abbreviation. body surface area.

BSE abbreviation. bovine spongiform encephalopathy.

B Type blood the red blood cells of a person with two B genes, whose plasma will have anti-A antibodies in it.

bubble boy disease a congenital deficiency in the ability to produce both antibodies and T-cells, making the infant incapable of fighting off infection and reqired to live in an enclosed sterile environment; severe combined immunological deficiency.

bubo /bōō′bō/ (pl. **buboes** /bōō′bōz/) a painful and tender swollen gland, most frequently in the groin or armpit.

bubonic plague /bōō bŏn′ĭk/ one of three varieties of severe bacterial infection caused by Yersinia pestis, transmitted by the bite of fleas living on infected rats, with painfully swollen glands especially in the groin, fever, headache, and gangrene of the nose, fingers, and toes. Also called Black Death. See also pneumonic plague.

bucc-, bucco- combining form. cheek: for example, buccogingival.

buccal /bŭk′əl/ of or involving the cheek.

bucally /bŭk′ə lē/ left to dissolve inside the check (as a way of administering a tablet).

buccinator muscle /bŭk′sə nā′tər/ the cheek muscle in the mouth.

buccogingival /bŭk′ō jĭn′jə vəl, -jĭn jī′vəl/ of or involving the inside of the cheek and the gums. [bucco- + gingival]

buck tooth an upper front tooth that sticks out beyond the lower lip.

bulbar /bŭl′bär/ **1.** bulb-shaped. **2.** of or involving the medulla oblongata.

bulbourethral /bŭl′bo yŏŏ re′thrəl/ of or involving the base of the penis and the urethra.

bulbourethral gland one of two glands below the prostate that secrete a fluid to lubricate the inside of the urethra. Also called Cowper's glands.

bulimia /bōō lē′mē ə/ or **bulimia nervosa** /nûr vō′sə/ a psychological disorder involving bouts of uncontrolled eating and then self-induced vomiting to prevent weight gain. See also binge eating disorder.

bulimic /bōō lē′mĭk/ **1.** adj. involving or having bulimia. **2.** n. a person with bulimia.

bulla /bŭl′ə/ (pl. **bullae** /bŭl′ē/) a large blister filled with fluid or air as in the lungs.

bullous /bŭl′əs/ of or involving large blisters filled with fluid.

bullous pemphigoid /pĕm′fĭ goid′/ a disease with fluid-filled blisters on the skin, usually affecting the elderly.

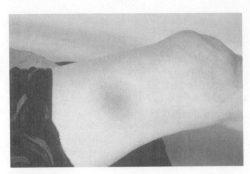

Bull's Eye Rash

bull's eye rash   a rash with two or more reddened rings around a common center.

BUN   *abbreviation.* blood urea nitrogen.

bundle branch block   a disorder of the electrical conduction of the heart, occurring when
either of the ventricular bundles have been
damaged by a heart attack or underlying heart
disease.

bundle of His /hĭs/   a bundle of fibers in the
muscle wall between the two ventricles that
transmit electrical charges through the heart
muscle.

bunion /bŭn′yən/   a painful swelling at the
base of the big toe, usually due to inflammation of a bursa or arthritis.

bunionectomy /bŭn′yə nĕk′tə mē/   the surgical removal of a bunion.

Burkitt('s) lymphoma /bûr′kĭt(s) lĭm fō′mə/
a type of non-Hodgkin cancer of the lymph
system, most often seen in young people between 12 and 30, usually as a fast-growing tumor in the abdomen of B-cell origin.

burn /bûrn/   damage of varying severity to the
skin and other body part caused by heat,
flame, chemicals, or electricity. *See also* first-
degree burn, second-degree burn, third-
degree burn.

burning mouth syndrome   a condition in
which the patient complains about a burning
sensation in the mouth, although no cause for
these sensations can be found.

burnishing /bûr′nĭng/   smoothing the surface
of dental amalgam with a smooth, flat
instrument.

burp /bûrp/   **1.** *n.* a belch. **2.** *v.* to emit a belch
or to cause to do so, such as by patting a baby
on the back.

burr hole   the round hole where a drill or saw
has been used to cut through a hard material,
such as a skull, to drain a hematoma or
biopsy a brain tumor.

burs-, burso-   *combining form.* bursa, bursae:
for example, bursitis, bursolith.

bursa /bûr′sə/ (*pl.* **bursae** /bûr′sē/)   a sac
lined with a synovial membrane and filled
with fluid found in the space adjacent to
joints.

bursal /bûr′səl/   of or involving a bursa.

bursectomy /bûr sĕk′tə mē/   the surgical
removal of a bursa. [burs- + -ectomy]

bursitis /bûr sī′tĭs/   inflammation of a bursa.
[burs- + -itis]

bursolith /bûr′sə lĭth/   a stone that forms in a
bursa. [burso- + -lith]

butterfly rash   a red rash on each cheek that
crosses the bridge of the nose; seen frequently
in systemic lupus erythematosis.

buttocks /bŭt′əks/   the two fleshy parts behind
the hips that form the lower back trunk of the
body.

bx, BX, Bx, Bx.   *abbreviation.* biopsy.

bypass /bī′păs′/   *n.* **1.** an operation in which an
alternate tubular passage is created for the
movement of body fluids or other material.
2. a coronary bypass. *v.* **3.** to create an alternate passage for the movement of fluids or
other material.

bypass surgery   an operation, such as a coronary bypass or liver shunt, to create an
alternate passage in the body for fluid or other
matter

byssinosis /bĭs′ə nō′sĭs/   an occupational disease that impairs breathing due to a reaction
to the dust of unprocessed cotton, flax, and
hemp.

BZD   *abbreviation.* benzodiazepine.

C

C *abbreviation.* **1.** calorie (kilocalorie). **2.** carbon. **3.** Celsius/centigrade. **4.** cervical vertebra/vertebrae. **5.** cytosine.

c *abbreviation.* **1.** small calorie (gram calorie). **2.** centi-.

Ca *abbreviation.* calcium.

CA *abbreviation.* **1.** (also **ca**) cancer/carcinoma. **2.** chronological age. **3.** coronary artery.

CA-125 *abbreviation.* cancer antigen 125.

CABG *abbreviation.* coronary artery bypass graft.

cachectic /kə kĕk′tĭk/ **1.** of or pertaining to cachexia. **2.** having or showing cachexia.

cachexia /kə kĕk′sē ə/ or **cachexy** /kə kĕk′sē/ the state of general poor health with significant weight loss, wasting, and weakness seen in persons who have a severe or terminal illness, such as cancer or kidney failure.

cacomelia /kăk′ō mē′lē ə/ congenital limb deformity. *Also called* dysmelia.

cacosmia /kə kŏz′mē ə/ unpleasant odor.

CAD *abbreviation.* coronary artery disease.

cadaver /kə dăv′ər/ a dead body, especially one that is to be dissected.

cadaverous /kə dăv′ər əs/ having the appearance of a dead body; extremely pale.

caduceus /kə doo′sē əs/ a symbol often used to represent the medical profession or a physician, consisting of two snakes entwined around a staff with two wings at its top.

caecum /sē′kəm/ (*pl.* **caeca** /sē′kə/) the pouchy, slightly distended beginning of the large intestine; cecum.

caesarean/cesarean /sĭ zâr′ē ən/ a cesarean section.

caesarean/cesarean section (C/S) extraction of a fetus through an abdominal incision.

caffeine /kă fēn′, kăf′ēn/ a compound found in coffee, tea, cola beverages, and some drugs that acts as a stimulant, bronchodilator, and a diuretic and can produce undesirable side effects ranging from sleeplessness or stomach upset, to extra heart beats (premature ventricular contractions).

calcanea /kăl kā′nē ə/ plural of calcaneum.

calcaneal /kăl kā′nē əl/ of or pertaining to the calcaneus.

calcaneal spur a small projection of bone from the calcaneus that can cause pain when walking.

calcaneo- *combining form.* heel: *for example,* calcaneodynia.

calcaneodynia /kăl kā′nē ō dĭn′ē ə/ heel pain. [calcaneo- + -dynia]

calcaneum /kăl kā′nē əm/ (*pl.* **calcanea** /kăl kā′nē ə/) calcaneus.

calcaneus /kăl kā′nē əs/ (*pl.* **calcanei** /kăl kā′nē ī/) the four-sided bone at the back of the foot, the largest of the tarsal bones; calcaneum. *Also called* heel.

calcar /kăl′kär/ (*pl.* **calcaria** /kăl kâr′ē ə/) any small projection or spur, especially from a bone.

calcification /kăl′sə fĭ kā′shən/ a hardening, usually due to deposits of calcium salts.

calcify /kăl′sə fī′/ to harden or become inflexible due to deposits of calcium salts.

calcinosis /kăl′sə nō′sĭs/ abnormal deposit of calcium salts in tissue, often causing inflexibility.

calcitonin /kăl′sĭ tō′nĭn/ a hormone secreted in the thyroid gland whose function is related to the increasing or lowering of serum calcium levels to maintain homeostasis.

calcium (Ca) /kăl′sē əm/ a mineral important for the development of bone.

calcium channel blocker any of a group of cardiovascular drugs used to treat hypertension.

calcium deficiency lack of sufficient calcium in the body.

calciuria /kăl′sē yoor′ē ə/ excretion of calcium in the urine.

calculus /kăl′kyə ləs/ (*pl.* **calculi** /kăl′kyə lī/ or **calculuses**) **1.** a small stone-like mass of material in a body cavity or organ, usually formed of mineral salts and typically found in the urinary bladder or gallbladder. *Also called* gallstone. **2.** hard, yellowish deposit on the teeth. *Also called* tartar.

calefacient /kăl′ə fā′shənt/ **1.** *adj.* producing warmth or heat. **2.** *n.* an agent that produces warmth or heat.

calf /kăf/ the muscular part of the leg between the knee and the ankle.

calf bone informal term for fibula, the outside bone of the two long bones in the lower leg.

calibrate /kăl′ə brāt′/ to set a measuring instrument to a standard.

calic-, calico-, calio- *combining form.* calyx: *for example,* calioplasty.

calicecstasis /kăl'ə sĕk'stə sĭs/ dilation of the calices. [calic- + -ecstasis]

calicectomy /kăl'ə sĕk'tə mē/ calicotomy. [cali- + -ectomy]

calicotomy /kăl'ə kŏt'ə mē/ surgical incision into a calyx. [calico- + -tomy]

calioplasty /kā'lē ə plas'tē/ surgical repair of a calyx. [calio- + -plasty]

caliorrhaphy /kā'lē ôr'ə fē/ suturing of a ca-lyx. [calio + -rrhaphy]

calipers /kăl'ə pərz/ an instrument with two curved opposing legs, used to measure size or width.

calix /kā'lĭks/ (pl. **calices** /kăl'ə sēz'/) a flower-shaped structure, especially one in the pelvis of the kidney; calyx

callosity /kə lŏs'ĭ tē/ a callus.

callus /kăl'əs/ a generally small, hardened area of the skin caused by friction or pressure; callosity.

calor /kăl'ôr, kā'lôr/ heat in the body, as one of the four classic symptoms indicating the presence of inflammation. *See also* dolor, ru-bor, tumor.

calorie (C) /kăl'ə rē/ a unit of food energy. *Also called* kilocalorie.

calx /kălks/ posterior of the foot; heel.

calyx /kā'lĭks/ (pl. **calyces** /kăl'ə sēz'/) a flower-shaped structure, especially one in the pelvis of the kidney; calix.

CAM *abbreviation*. complementary and alternative medicine.

camera /kăm'ər ə/ (pl. **camerae** /kăm'ə rē'/) any anatomical chamber, such as of the eye or heart.

campylobacteriosis /kăm'pə lō băk têr'ē ō'sĭs/ any infection caused by a bacteria of the genus *Campylobacter*, such as an acute type of enteritis.

canal /kə năl'/ any narrow, tubular structure, such as the ear canal.

canaliculus /kăn'ə lĭk'yə ləs/ (pl. **canaliculi** / kăn'ə lĭk'yə lī'/) a small canal or duct, as in some bones.

canalis /kə năl'ĭs, -nä'lĭs/ (pl. **canales** /kə năl' ēz, -nä'lās/) a canal (used especially in anatomical descriptions, such as *canalis analis*, anal canal).

cancellated bone /kăn'sə lā'tĭd/ or **cancellous bone** /kăn'sə ləs/ bone formed in a lattice-like shape with bone marrow or tissue in the interstices. *Also called* spongy bone.

cancer /kăn'sər/(**CA**) any of a number of dis-eases that include malignant tumors with the capability of growing and invading surround-ing tissue. *See also* carcinoma.

cancer antigen 125 (CA-125) /ăn'tĭ jən/ an antigen found on the surface of certain cells associated with certain cancers and other dis-eases.

Type of Cancer (for asymptomatic people)	Early Detection Guidelines from the American Cancer Society (www.cancer.org)
breast cancer	yearly mammograms after age 40; monthly self-exam; clinical exam every 3 years.
colorectal cancer	▪ yearly fecal occult blood test ▪ flexible sigmoidoscopy every 5 years ▪ double-contrast barium enema every 5 years ▪ colonoscopy every 10 years
cervical cancer	Pap test every year after first sexual intercourse or by age 21 (liquid Pap test every 2 years)
uterine cancer	For high-risk women, screening should start at age 35.
prostrate	starting between age 40 and 50, depending on risk, annual PSA tests.

Recommended Cancer Prevention Tests

cancer cluster a unusual cluster of occurrences of cancers in a certain location or among a cer-tain group.

cancer in situ /ĭn sī'tōō, sĭt'ōō/ a cancer that is still confined to the place where it first de-veloped, without having spread to another site in the body. *See also* carcinoma in situ.

cancerous /kăn'sər əs/ having cancer cells; invaded by cancer.

cancer survivor a person who has been treated successfully for cancer and lives a relatively normal life, especially one who has lived for five years after the original diagnosis.

cancrum /kăng'krəm/ (pl. **cancra** /kăng'krə/) an inflammatory lesion, usually gangrenous.

candidiasis /kăn'dĭ dī'ə sĭs/ infection of the skin, mucous membranes, or gastrointestinal tract by a fungus of the genus *Candida*, espe-cially the species *Candida albicans*, found in people with immunosuppressive disease, oth-erwise healthy women, and infants. *Also called* moniliasis, monilial vaginitis, vulvo-vaginal candidiasis. *See also* thrush.

cane /kān/ a stick or rod used as an aid in walking.

canine tooth /kā'nīn/ either of two long, oval, slightly pointed teeth in both the upper and lower jaws, between the second incisor and the first premolars. *See also* eyetooth.

canker or **canker sore** /kăng'kər/ a small ul-cer on a mucous membrane, especially in the mouth. *Also called* aphthous ulcer.

cannabis /kăn'ə bĭs/ the dried flowers of the *Cannabis sativa* plant used in some medica-tions (often legally restricted) and smoked as an illegal drug informally known as marijuana. It is thought to help relieve nausea associated with some cancer treatments.

cannonball pulse   a jerky pulse marked by a strong beat followed by collapse, a sign of a malfunctioning aortic valve. *Also called* Corrigan's pulse, water-hammer pulse.

cannula /kăn′yə lə/   a small tube that can be inserted into a vein or cavity, often used for the transport of fluid.

cannulation /kăn′yə lā′shən/   insertion of a cannula.

canthus /kăn′thəs/   the inner angle of the eye.

cantilever bridge /kăn′tə lē′vər/   a dental bridge that is attached to a natural tooth at one end only.

cap   *abbreviation.* capsule.

cap /kăp/   informal term for a restorative covering of a tooth or crown.

CAPD   *abbreviation.* continuous ambulatory peritoneal dialysis.

capillary /kăp′ə lĕr′ē/   a very small vessel, especially a blood capillary.

capillary bed   capillaries collectively.

capitate /kăp′ĭ tāt′/   **1.** *adj.* having a rounded, knoblike head. **2.** *n.* the largest bone of the wrist.

capitation /kăp′ĭ tā′shən/   a system of insurance payment for managed care in which providers are paid for each subscriber no matter what services are performed.

capitulum /kə pĭch′ə ləm/   (*pl.* **capitula** /kə pĭch′ə lə/)   a small round end at the head of a bone.

capno-   *combining form.* carbon dioxide: *for example,* capnometer.

capnogram /kăp′nə grăm′/   a graph of carbon dioxide content in exhaled air. [capno- + -gram]

capnometer /kăp nŏm′ĭ tər/   an instrument for measuring carbon dioxide in exhaled air. [capno- + -meter]

capnometry /kăp nŏm′ĭ trē/   the process of measuring with a capnometer.

capsula /kăp′sə lə/   (*pl.* **capsulae** /kăp′sə lē′/)   membranous structure, usually made of dense collagenous connective tissue, that envelops an organ.

capsular /kăp′sə lər/   of or pertaining to capsules.

capsule /kăp′səl, -sool/ (**cap**)   **1.** a tissue layer that encloses an organ, joint, or neoplasm. **2.** medicine dose contained in a hard or soft shell of soluble material.

capsulitis /kăp′sə lī′tĭs/   inflammation of the capsule of an organ or part.

capsulotomy /kăp′sə lŏt′ə mē/   incision into a capsule (as during a cataract operation).

caput /kăp′ət, kä′poot/   (*pl.* **capita** /kăp′ĭ tə, kä′pĭ tä′/)   the upper extremity or head of an anatomical part.

carb /kärb/   informal term for carbohydrate.

carbamide /kär′bə mīd′/   a nitrogen compound resulting from the breakdown of protein that is excreted in the urine. *Also called* urea.

carbohydrate /kär′bō hī′drāt/   any of various sugars and starches, mostly found in or produced from green plants, and a primary source of food.

carbohydrate-loading   the eating of large amounts of foods that are high in carbohydrates, such as pasta, for one or more days before taking part in a long-distance race or other strenuous physical activity.

carbon dioxide (CO₂) /kär′bən dī ŏk′sīd/   a compound of carbon and oxygen found in exhaled air.

carbon monoxide (CO) /mə nŏk′sīd/   colorless, odorless gas that can be poisonous.

carbuncle /kär′bŭng kəl/   **1.** an infection of the skin and underlying tissues usually caused by a staphylococcus and consisting of a grouping of painful, pus-filled boils sometimes accompanied by fever. **2.** an infectious, fatal animal disease that can be transmitted to humans. *Also called* anthrax.

carcin-, carcino-   *combining form.* cancer: *for example,* carcinoma, carcinogen.

carcinoembryonic antigen (CEA) /kär′sə nō ĕm′brē ŏn′ĭk ăn′tĭ jən/   an antigen found in some carcinomas.

carcinogen /kär sĭn′ə jən/   any substance or factor that is known or believed to cause cancer, such as cigarette smoking, chemical

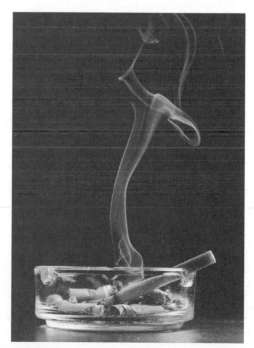

Carcinogen

pollution, or overexposure to the sun. [carcino- + -gen]

carcinogenesis /kär′sə nə jĕn′ə sĭs/ the development of cancer. [carcino- + -genesis]

carcinogenic /kär′sə nə jĕn′ĭk/ causing cancer. [carcino- + -genic]

carcinoid tumor /kär′sə noid′/ a kind of tumor of the gastroenteric tract, lungs, or especially the appendix, that often spreads to the liver and releases much serotonin.

carcinoma /kär′sə nō′mə/ (*pl.* **carcinomas** or **carcinomata** /kär′sə nō′mə tə/) any of various malignant cancer tumors that begin in the skin or certain other tissues. [carcin- + -oma]

carcinoma in situ /ĭn sī′tōō, sĭt′ōō/ (**CIS**) carcinoma that is still confined to the place where it first developed, without having spread to another site in the body. *See also* cancer in situ.

card-, cardi-, cardio- *combining form.* heart: *for example,* carditis, cardiology.

-cardia *suffix.* the condition of having a specific kind of heart or heartbeat: *for example,* bradycardia.

cardiac /kär′dē ăk′/ of or pertaining to the heart.

cardiac arrest cessation of cardiac activity.

cardiac arrhythmia /ə rĭth′mē ə/ abnormality in the heart's rate or rhythm.

cardiac catheterization /kăth′ĭ tər ə zā′shən/ insertion of a catheter into a vein, usually of the leg or arm, to investigate the condition of the heart, the coronary arteries, and surrounding blood vessels, to take blood samples, and to plan for surgery.

cardiac conduction system the system that conducts electrical impulses throughout the heart, causing the muscle to pump blood.

cardiac cycle the complete cycle of a heartbeat including systole (contraction) and diastole (relaxation).

cardiac insufficiency **1.** the inability of the heart to function normally. **2.** heart failure.

cardiac muscle the heart muscle or the myocardium that contracts and pumps blood

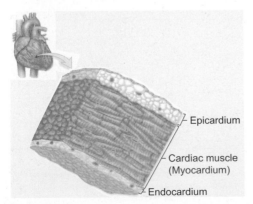

Cardiac Muscle

out of the heart, into the aorta and to the body, and to the heart itself through the coronary arteries which branch off the aorta.

cardiac output the amount of blood pumped by the left side of the heart in liters per minute.

cardiac region the area of the stomach closest to the heart.

cardiac rehabilitation /rē′hə bĭl′ĭ tā′shən/ a program of rehabilitation—including exercise and behavioral and nutritional changes—prescribed to patients with cardiovascular disease.

cardiac scan electronic imaging of the heart to determine how it is functioning.

cardiac sphincter /sfĭngk′tər/ the muscular ring between the esophagus and the cardiac region of the stomach.

cardiac stress test a test for heart function, usually performed on a treadmill; stress test.

cardiac tamponade /tăm′pə nād′/ limited functioning of the heart caused by compression of the heart by a large build-up of fluid in the pericardium, the sac surrounding the heart muscle. *Also called* pericardial tamponade.

cardiac valve any of the four valves of the heart: aortic, mitral, pulmonary, and tricuspid.

cardio- *See* cardi-.

cardiogenic /kär′dē ō jĕn′ĭk/ arising from or caused by the heart. [cardio- + -genic]

cardiologist /kär′dē ŏl′ə jĭst/ a physician who specializes in cardiology. [cardio- + -logist]

cardiology /kär′dē ŏl′ə jē/ the branch of medicine that specializes in the diagnosis and treatment of diseases of the heart. [cardio- + -logy]

cardiomalacia /kär′dē ō mə lā′shə/ softening of the heart muscle. [cardio- + -malacia]

cardiomegaly /kär′dē ō mĕg′ə lē/ abnormal enlargement of the heart. *Also called* megalocardia. [cardio- + -megaly]

cardiomyopathy /kär′dē ō mī ŏp′ə thē/ chronic disease of the heart muscle. *Also called* myocardiopathy. [cardio- + myo- + -pathy]

cardiopathy /kär′dē ŏp′ə thē/ any disease of the heart. [cardio- + -pathy]

cardioplegia /kär′dē ō plē′jē ə, -jə/ temporarily induced cardiac arrest, as during a surgical procedure. [cardio- + -plegia]

cardiopulmonary /kär′dē ō pŭl′mə nĕr′ē/ of or pertaining to both the heart and the lungs. [cardio- + pulmonary]

cardiopulmonary bypass /bī′păs′/ a surgical procedure to divert blood that is blocked from returning to the heart.

cardiopulmonary resuscitation (**CPR**) /rĭ sŭs′ĭ tā′shən/ a mechanical restoration of cardiac function after a cardiac arrest.

cardiorrhaphy /kär′dē ôr′ə fē/ suturing of the heart wall. [cardio- + -rrhaphy]

cardiorrhexis /kär′dē ō rĕk′sĭs/ rupture of the heart wall. [cardio- + -rrhexis]

cardiotonic /kär′dē ō tŏn′ĭk/ having a positive effect on the function of heart muscle. [cardio- + tonic]

cardiovascular /kär′dē ō văs′kyə lər/ of or pertaining to the heart and the blood vessels. [cardio- + vascular]

cardiovascular disease (CVD) disease of the heart and blood vessels.

cardiovascular system the circulatory system including the heart and blood vessels.

cardioversion /kär′dē ō vûr′zhən/ restoration of a normal heartbeat through the use of a machine or device that delivers an electrical shock to the heart. [cardio- + -version]

cardioverter /kär′dē ō vûr′tər/ a machine or device used in performing cardioversion.

carditis /kär dī′tĭs/ inflammation of the heart. [card- + -itis]

caries /kâr′ēz/ decay of a bone, especially a tooth, as in dental caries.

cariogenesis /kăr′ē ō jĕn′ə sĭs/ the production of caries.

cariogenic /kăr′ē ō jĕn′ĭk/ causing caries, often said of specific foods.

carminative /kär mĭn′ə tĭv/ **1.** *n.* an agent that expels gas from the digestive system. **2.** *adj.* causing the expulsion of gas from the digestive system.

carnitine /kär′nĭ tēn′/ a compound present in muscle and involved in the transfer of fatty acids.

carotene /kăr′ə tēn′/ any of three pigments found in plants and animals that convert to vitamin A in the body.

carotenemia /kăr′ə tə ne′mē ə/ excessive carotene in the blood, a harmless condition seen as a yellow tint to the skin, usually in infants, caused by eating carrots and pumpkin or other yellow-orange vegetables. *Also called* xanthemia.

carotenoid /kə rŏt′ə noid′/ any of the carotenes.

carotid /kə rŏt′ĭd/ **1.** *adj.* of or pertaining to a carotid artery. **2.** *n.* the carotid artery.

carotid artery either of two main arteries that supply blood to the head. *Also called* common carotid artery. *See also* external carotid artery, internal carotid artery.

carotid body a small sensory structure at the point where the carotid artery branches in the neck into the internal and external carotid arteries. The carotid body is rich in blood vessels and contains certain cells that sense changes in blood pressure and other cells that sense levels of oxygen, carbon dioxide, pH,

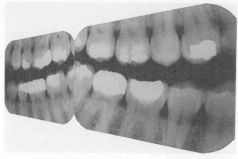

Caries (on Dental X-Ray)

and temperature; both groups of cells send regulatory messages to the brainstem.

carotid sinus an area in the neck where the carotid artery divides into the internal and external carotid arteries. It contains nerves important to the regulation of heart rate and blood pressure.

carp-, carpo- *combining form.* wrist: *for example,* carpal, carpopedal.

carpal /kär′pəl/ of, pertaining to, or associated with the wrist or any of its bones. [carp- + -al]

carpal bone any of the eight bones in the wrist.

carpal tunnel a space in the wrist through which the median nerve and the flexor tendons pass.

carpal tunnel syndrome (CTS) continual pain along with burning, tingling, or other sensations in the wrist, hand, and fingers, caused by compression of the median nerve in the carpal tunnel.

carpectomy /kär pĕk′tə mē/ removal of some or all of the carpus. [carp- + -ectomy]

carpometacarpal /kär′pō mĕt′ə kär′pəl/ of or pertaining to the carpus and the metacarpus. [carpo- + metacarpal]

carpopedal /kär′pō pĕd′əl/ **1.** of or pertaining to the hands and feet. **2.** of or pertaining to the wrist and foot. [carpo- + -pedal]

carpus /kär′pəs/ (*pl.* **carpi** /kär′pī/) the wrist.

carrier /kăr′ē ər/ **1.** a person or animal that is infected with a certain disease-causing organism but has no symptoms of the illness and can pass the infection to another. **2.** a person or animal that has the gene for a particular trait but does not show that trait, and whose offspring can receive the gene and will show that trait if the other parent also has the gene and passes it on.

cartilage /kär′tə lĭj/ elastic tissue that makes up most of the fetal skeleton and later changes to bone. In the body, it is the slippery, shiny substance that comprises the surface of joints; also found in most tubular structures, and other semisolid structures (nose and ears).

cartilaginous /kär'tə lăj'ə nəs/   containing or composed of cartilage.

cartilaginous joint   a joint in which the opposing bones are connected by a layer of cartilage, as the vertebrae of the spinal column.

cartilago /kär'tə lā'gō/ (*pl.* **cartilagines** /kär'tə lăj'ə nēz'/)   cartilage (used especially in anatomical descriptions, such as *cartilage thyroidea*, thyroid cartilage).

caruncle /kăr'ŭng kəl/   or **caruncula** /kə rŭng'kyə lə/   any small fleshy protuberance.

cascade /kăs kād'/   a sequence of events in a process in which each step or stage starts the next one until the process is complete.

casein /kā'sēn, -sē ĭn/   the main protein in milk and the basis of cheese and curd.

case management   1. the supervision or coordination of a patient's care by a doctor or other health care provider. 2. in a managed care organization, the supervision of a patient's treatment by a gatekeeper.

cast   1. a dressing of gauze and wet plaster (or fiberglass) that hardens into a firm shape when it dries, applied to a part of the body to protect it while it heals, as from a broken bone or surgery. 2. an article made from a mold or impression, as a reproduction of the upper or lower teeth in dentistry. 3. a slight squint. *Also called* strabismus.

castrate /kăs'trāt/   to perform castration on (a person or animal).

castration /kă strā'shən/   surgical removal of the testes or ovaries.

CAT   *abbreviation.* computerized axial tomography.

cata-   *prefix.* down: *for example,* catalepsy.

catabolism /kə tăb'ə lĭz'əm/   the breakdown of compounds in the body for use as energy as part of the metabolic process.

catalepsy /kăt'ə lĕp'sē/   loss of the ability to perform voluntary movement, usually associated with a mental illness. [cata- + -lepsy]

catalyst /kăt'ə lĭst/   material that initiates or accelerates chemical reactions without being consumed itself, as enzymes in intracellular metabolic reactions or the activating chemical compound in the preparation of dental materials.

cataplexy /kăt'ə plĕk'sē/   sudden muscle weakness, usually due to shock or trauma.

cataract /kăt'ə răkt'/   a clouding of the lens or lens capsule of the eye, which prevents incoming light from reaching the retina and can lead to impaired vision or blindness.

cataract surgery   an operation to correct a cataract, usually by removing the natural lens and replacing it with an artificial one.

catarrh /kə tär'/   inflammation or infection of the membranes of the nose or throat, usually involving overproduction of mucus.

catatonia /kăt'ə tō'nē ə/   a state of rigidity or bizarre movements usually associated with a mental disorder such as schizophrenia.

catatonic /kăt'ə tŏn'ĭk/   1. of, pertaining to, or characteristic of catatonia. 2. affected by or displaying catatonia.

catecholamine /kăt'ə kŏl'ə mēn'/   any of various compounds that act as both hormones and neurotransmitters and play a role in reactions to stress.

catgut /kăt'gŭt'/   absorbable suture material made from the collagen of animals, such as sheep and cows.

Cath, cath   *abbreviation.* catheter.

catharsis /kə thär'sĭs/   the purging of something, especially of emotional tension.

cathartic /kə thär'tĭk/   1. *adj.* having the effect of catharsis. 2. *n.* an agent that purges something.

catheter /kăth'ĭ tər/   a slender tube inserted into a bodily space or blood vessel for various purposes, such as to administer medications, withdraw fluids, or explore functioning.

catheterization /kăth'ĭ tər ə zā'shən/   the process or procedure of inserting a catheter.

catheterized specimen /kăth'ĭ tə rīzd'/   a sample of urine taken from the urinary bladder using a catheter.

cathexis /kə thĕk'sĭs/   an investment or attachment of emotional energy, as to a person or idea.

cathode /kăth'ōd/   negative electrode, used in dental x-ray tubes.

cathode ray   the ray of electrons leaving a cathode tube aimed at a target.

CAT scan   an image of the body done by computerized axial tomography.

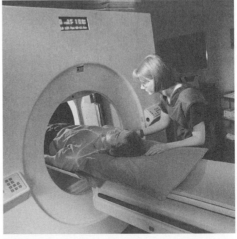

CAT Scan

cat-scratch disease or **cat-scratch fever** a usually mild, self-limited infection resulting from the bite or scratch of a cat, marked by fever, inflammation of the lymph nodes, chills and vomiting, and a pustule at the site of the wound. *Also called* bacillary angiomatosis.

cauda equina /kô′də ĭ kwī′nə/ tail portion, especially the ending of the spinal cord.

caudal /kô′dəl/ **1.** of, pertaining to, or at the tail. **2.** like a tail.

caudal anesthesia /ăn′əs thē′zhə/ or **caudal block** an anesthetic injected at the end of the spinal column to numb the lower part of the body, as during childbirth or in pediatric surgery involving the feet, legs, or genitourinary tract.

caudate nucleus /kô′dāt noo′klē əs/ a part of each basal ganglia in the cerebral hemisphere, associated with body movement.

caul /kôl/ **1.** (or **cowl** /koul/) a piece of the amniotic sac covering the head or face of an infant at birth. *Also called* veil. **2.** a fold of the peritoneum that hangs in front of the intestines. *Also called* greater omentum.

cauliflower ear a deformed outer ear resulting from repeated injuries, especially the punches received in the boxing ring.

causalgia /kô zăl′jē ə, -jə/ a painful burning sensation resulting from injury to a nerve, which persists after the injury appears to have healed.

cauterization /kô′tər ə zā′shən/ the destruction of tissue with a chemical, electricity, or hot or cold instrumentation, usually to stop excessive bleeding or seal off a wound. *Also called* cautery.

cauterize /kô′tə rīz′/ to do cauterization on (a person, a tissue, etc.).

cautery /kô′tə rē/ **1.** any substance or instrument used in cauterizing. **2.** cauterization.

cavernous /kăv′ər nəs/ having hollow spaces.

cavernous hemangioma /hĭ măn′jē ō′mə/ or **cavernous angioma** /ăn′jē ō′mə/ a tumor made up of large blood vessels with much blood in them, found in or on the skin, in the internal organs, and sometimes in the brain and ranging in color from bright red to blue.

cavernous sinus /sī′nəs/ one of a pair of sinuses found on either side of the sphenoid bone in the skull.

cavernous sinus thrombosis /thrŏm bō′sĭs/ a blood clot formed or found in a cavernous sinus.

cavity **1.** a space within the body or a hollow organ. **2.** a hole or pit in a tooth caused by dental caries.

CBC *abbreviation.* complete blood count.

CBT *abbreviation.* cognitive behavioral therapy.

cc *abbreviation.* cubic centimeter.

CCPD *abbreviation.* continuous cycling peritoneal dialysis.

CCS *abbreviation* certified coding specialist (hospital).

CCS-P *abbreviation* certified coding specialist—physician.

CCU *abbreviation.* coronary care unit.

CDA *abbreviation.* certified dental assistant.

CDC *abbreviation.* Centers for Disease Control and Prevention.

CEA *abbreviation.* carcinoembryonic antigen.

cec-, ceco- *combining form.* cecum: *for example,* cecectomy, cecopexy.

cecal /sē′kəl/ of, pertaining to, or of the nature of the cecum. [cec- + -al]

cecectomy /sē sĕk′tə mē/ surgical removal or all or part of the cecum. [cec- + -ectomy]

cecopexy /sē′kə pĕk′sē/ surgical attachment of the cecum to the abdominal wall to keep it in place. [ceco- + -pexy]

cecostomy /sē kŏs′tə mē/ **1.** a surgically created opening in the cecum. **2.** the surgery itself. [ceco- + -stomy]

cecotomy /sē kŏt′ə mē/ incision into the cecum. [ceco- + -tomy]

cecum or **caecum** /sē′kəm/ (*pl.* **ceca** or **caeca** /sē′kə /) **1.** the pouchy, slightly distended beginning of the large intestine, which connects with the ileum and from which the vermiform appendix extends. *Also called* blind gut. **2.** any pouch or sac with only one opening or entry.

-cele *suffix.* **1.** tumor or swelling: *for example,* varicocele. **2.** cavity: *for example,* hydrocele.

celiac /se′lē ăk′/ of or pertaining to the abdomen; abdominal.

celiac artery celiac trunk.

celiac disease a digestive disorder caused by eating gluten (a wheat protein), seen in both children and adults and marked generally by diarrhea, distention of the abdomen, gas, and weakness, treated by dietary manipulation. *Also called* gluten enteropathy.

celiac trunk the artery that arises from the abdominal aorta below the diaphragm and branches into or serves arteries to the stomach, liver, spleen, esophagus, pancreas, gallbladder, and other internal organs. *Also called* celiac artery.

celio- *combining form.* abdomen: *for example,* celiotomy.

celiorrhaphy /sē′lē ôr′ə fē/ suture of an abdominal wound. [celio- + -rrhaphy]

celiotomy /sē′lē ŏt′ə mē/ surgical incision into the abdomen. *Also called* laparotomy. [celio- + -tomy]

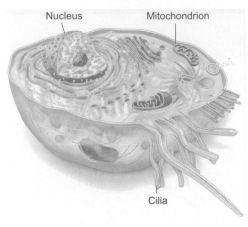

Cell

cell /sĕl/   the basic structure of living tissue, visible only with a microscope, that consists of a nucleus, cytoplasm with various structures in it, and a membrane that encloses the cytoplasm.

cell body   only the portion of a cell containing the nucleus and the cytoplasm, without any structures that may extend from it, such as the axons and dendrites of a nerve cell.

cell count   a measure of the number of cells in a given volume or area, especially of the red and white cells in the blood.

cell cycle   the sequence of physical and chemical changes that occur as a cell with a nucleus grows and reproduces.

cell lineage /lĭn′ē ĭj/   the tracing of the development of cells to or from the original cell that produced them.

cell-mediated immunity (CMI) /sĕl′ mē′ dē ā tĭd ĭ myoō′nĭ tē/   immune response involving T lymphocytes. *Also called* cellular immunity.

cell membrane   the thin tissue that encloses the contents of a cell, through which some molecules can pass passively while others require active transport.

cell therapy   the injection of stem cells into a diseased or malfunctioning organ or tissue to restore it to a healthy state.

cellular /sĕl′yə lər/   of, pertaining to, or of the nature of a cell.

cellular immunity /ĭ myoō′nĭ tē/   cell-mediated immunity.

cellulite /sĕl′yə līt′, -lĕt′/   lumpy deposits of fat in the skin that make the flesh look dimpled, occurring most often in the thighs and buttocks, especially of women.

cell wall   a rigid structure that supports the cells of plants and certain other organisms but is not found in animal cells.

Celsius /sĕl′sē əs/   of or indicating a scale of temperatures at which 0 degrees is the freezing

point of water and 100 degrees is its boiling point at normal atmospheric pressure. *Also called* centigrade

cement /sĭ mĕnt′/   **1.** any substance that causes two pieces or parts to adhere to each other; glue. **2.** in dentistry, any of various compounds used in filling a tooth or attaching a crown or restoration.

cementum /sĭ mĕn′təm/   a layer of bonelike tissue covering the root of a tooth.

centenarian /sĕn′tə nâr′ē ən/   **1.** a person who has reached the age of 100 years or more.

Centers for Medicaid and Medicare Service (CMS)   the part of the U.S. Department of Health and Human Services responsible for administering Medicare and Medicaid (www.cms.hhs.gov). *Formerly,* Health Care Financing Administration.

-centesis   *suffix.* puncture: *for example,* amniocentesis, colocentesis.

centesis /sĕn tē′sĭs/   the insertion of a needle or similar instrument into a bodily space or organ to add or withdraw fluids; tap.

centi-   *prefix.* one hundred: *for example,* centigram.

centigrade /sĕn′tĭ grād′/   of or indicating a scale of temperatures at which 0 degrees is the freezing point of water and 100 degrees is its boiling point at normal atmospheric pressure. *Also called* Celsius.

centigram /sĕn′tĭ grăm′/   one one-hundredth of a gram. [centi- + gram]

centimeter (cm) /sĕn′tə mē′tər/   one one-hundredth of a meter. [centi- + meter]

central /sĕn′trəl/   **1.** of, pertaining to, in, or at the center. **2.** pertaining to the brain.

central auditory disease /ô′dĭ tôr′ē/   any disorder of hearing or perception stemming from a disorder or malfunction in the brain or the neural pathways to the brain.

central auditory processing disorder   a condition marked by below-average language skills, usually associated with another condition, such as deafness or brain disease.

central core disease   an inherited disease of infants and children, marked by abnormalities in the muscle fibers, muscle weakness, and delays in motor development.

central incisor /ĭn sī′zər/   either of the two teeth directly at the front of each jaw, on the midline of the body.

central nervous system (CNS)   that part of the nervous system composed of the brain and the spinal cord. *See also* peripheral nervous system.

central retinal artery /rĕt′ə nəl är′tə rē/   a branch of the ophthalmic artery of the eye that penetrates the optic nerve.

central venous catheter (CVC) /vē′nəs kăth′ĭ tər/   a catheter inserted into the heart or the venous trunk through a large vein, as of the arm, leg, neck, or shoulder, for long-term IV use. *Also called* vascular access device.

central venous pressure (CVP) the blood pressure in the superior and inferior vena cava.

central vision vision formed by an image on the fovea centralis; direct vision.

centric /sĕn′trĭk/ in dentisty, having all teeth of both jaws meet in a normal manner and having the forces exerted by the lower on the upper jaw perfectly distributed in the dental arch.

centrifugal /sĕn trĭf′yə gəl, -trĭf′ə-/ **1.** moving away from a center. **2.** of or involving a centrifuge.

centrifuge /sĕn′trə fyo͞oj′/ an apparatus used to spin fluids to separate out parts, such as blood parts: red cells, white cells (buffy coat), platelets, and plasma.

centromere /sĕn′trə mêr′/ the cinched-together part of a chromosome that divides it into two parts.

cephal-, cephalo- *combining form.* head: *for example,* cephalgia, cephalomegaly.

cephalad /sĕf′ə lăd′/ toward the head. [cephal- + -ad]

cephalalgia /sĕf′ə lăl′jē ə, -jə/ head pain. *Also called* headache. [cephal- + -algia]

cephalic /sə făl′ĭk/ of or relating to the head. [cephal- + -ic]

cephalic index a ratio of maximum length to maximum width of the head, multiplied by 100.

cephalic presentation a complication during childbirth in which any part of the head, such as the face, presents first instead of the normal back of the head (occiput).

cephalomegaly /sĕf′ə lō mĕg′ə lē/ abnormal enlargement of the head. *Also called* macrocephaly, megacephaly, megalocephaly. [cephal- + -megaly]

cephalometer /sĕf′ə lŏm′ĭ tər/ an instrument used to position the head before imaging. [cephalo- + -meter]

cephalometrics /sĕf′ə lō mĕt′rĭks/ the interpretation of lateral skull radiographs taken under standardized conditions.

cephalopelvic /sĕf′ə lō pĕl′vĭk/ of the relationship between the size of the head of the fetus and the pelvis of the mother. [cephalo- + pelvic]

cephalopelvic disproportion (CPD) a condition in which the fetal head is too large to pass through the maternal pelvis, necessitating a cesarean birth.

-cephaly *suffix.* head; *for example,* megalocephaly.

cerclage /sâr klăzh′/ binding together with a loop or a ring, usually used for encircling the cervix or binding together fractured bone. Cerclage is used by obstetricians to prevent an incompetent cervix from dilating early in pregnancy and causing miscarriage or premature birth.

cerebellar /sĕr′ə bĕl′ər/ of or relating to the cerebellum.

cerebellitis /sĕr′ə bĕ lī′tĭs/ inflammation of the cerebellum.

cerebellum /sĕr′ə bĕl′əm/ the large posterior portion of the brain, consisting of two hemispheres, which controls coordination and maintains balance.

cerebr-, cerebri-, cerebro- *combining form.* cerebrum: *for example,* cerebral, cerebrospinal.

cerebral /sə rē′brəl, sĕr′ə brəl/ of or relating to the cerebrum. [cerebr- + -al]

cerebral cortex /kôr′tĕks/ the gray covering of the cerebrum containing nerve cells where thought processes occur.

cerebral edema /ĭ dē′mə/ swelling in the brain.

cerebral hemispheres the two halves of the cerebrum.

cerebral hemorrhage /hĕm′ər ĭj, hĕm′rĭj/ hemorrhage in the cerebrum.

cerebral palsy (CP) /pôl′zē/ a condition usually caused by critical lack of oxygen during childbirth, affecting coordination and motor skills, usually diagnosed in the first three years of life.

cerebral vascular accident (CVA) /văs′kyə lər/ sudden loss of circulation to the brain, usually affecting brain functions either temporarily or permanently. *Also called* cerebrovascular accident, stroke.

cerebration /sĕr′ə brā′shən/ the process of thought; cognition.

cerebriform /sə rē′brə fôrm′/ resembling the brain, particularly in its contour with fissures and convolutions. [cerebri- + -form]

cerebritis /sĕr′ə brī′tĭs/ inflammation of the cerebrum or brain. [cerebr- + -itis]

cerebrosclerosis /sə rē′brō sklĭ rō′sĭs/ hardening of the two halves of the cerebrum. [cerebro- + -sclerosis]

cerebrospinal /sə rē′brō spī′nəl/ of or relating to the brain and spinal cord. [cerebro- + spinal]

cerebrospinal fluid (CSF) fluid that fills the brain ventricles and the cavities of the spinal cord.

cerebrotomy /sĕr′ə brŏt′ə mē/ incision into the brain. [cerebro- + -tomy]

cerebrovascular /sə rē′brō văs′kyə lər/ of or relating to the blood circulation to the brain. [cerebro- + vascular]

cerebrovascular accident (CVA) sudden loss of circulation to the brain, usually affecting

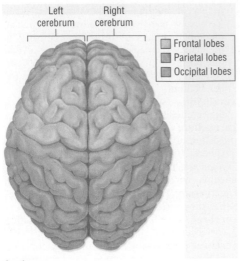

Left cerebrum   Right cerebrum

☐ Frontal lobes
☐ Parietal lobes
☐ Occipital lobes

Cerebrum

brain functions either temporarily or permanently. *Also called* cerebral vascular accident, stroke.

cerebrovascular disease any condition caused by a disruption in blood circulation to the brain.

cerebrum /sə rē′brəm/ (*pl.* **cerebrums** or **cerebra** /sə rē′brə/) the largest part of the brain consisting of two hemispheres.

certification /sûr′tə fĭ kā′shən/ **1.** The process of taking an examination and receiving a license or official standing in a specialty; *for example,* board certification in surgery. **2.** a legal procedure in which a person is deemed to need involuntary hospitalization for a mental condition.

ceruloplasmin /sə rōō′lō plăz′mĭn/ a protein in blood plasma that carries copper.

cerumen /sə rōō′mən/ a waxy secretion produced by glands in the outer ear canal that protects the ear by repelling water and trapping dust and other particles. *Also called* earwax, wax.

ceruminolytic /sə rōō′mə nō lĭt′ĭk/ a substance that softens cerumen in the ear.

ceruminosis /sə rōō′mə nō′sĭs/ excessive formation of cerumen in the ears.

ceruminous gland /sə rōō′mə nəs/ any of several glands in the external auditory meatus of the ear that secrete cerumen.

cervic-, cervico- *combining form.* neck; cervix: *for example,* cervicitis, cervicothoracic.

cervical /sûr′vĭ kəl/ of or relating to the neck or cervix. [cervic- + -al]

cervical cancer cancer of the cervix, usually detectable by a Pap smear.

cervical vertebrae /vûr′tə brē′/ the vertebrae of the neck.

cervicectomy /sûr′və sĕk′tə mē/ removal of the cervix of the uterus. *Also called* trachelectomy. [cervic- + -ectomy]

cervicitis /sûr′və sī′tĭs/ inflammation of the cervix of the uterus. [cervic- + -itis]

cervicobrachial /sûr′vĭ kō brā′kē əl/ of or relating to the neck and arm. [cervico- + brachial]

cervicodynia /sûr′vĭ kō dĭn′ē ə/ neck pain. [cervico- + -dynia]

cervicothoracic /sûr′vĭ kō thô răs′ĭk/ of or relating to the cervix and the thorax. [cervico- + thoracic]

cervix /sûr′vĭks/ (*pl.* **cervices** /sûr′vĭ sēz′/) any necklike structure, especially the lower part of the uterus extending into the vagina.

cesarean/caesarean /sĭ zâr′ē ən/ a cesarean section.

cesarean/caeserean section extraction of a fetus through an abdominal incision.

Chadwick('s) sign /chăd′wĭk(s)/ bluish tinting of the cervix and vagina, usually indicating pregnancy.

chakra /chŭk′rə/ according to an ancient Indian system of therapy, any of seven vital energy centers of the body starting from the base of the spine to the crown of the head, which respond to sounds, emotions, colors, etc.

chalasia /kə lā′zhə/ or **chalasis** /kə lā′sĭs/ relaxation of a contracted muscle.

chalazion /kə lā′zē ən/ (*pl.* **chalazia** /kə lā′zē ə/) a cyst of the little glands of the eyelid. *Also called* meibomian cyst.

chamber /chām′bər/ an enclosed space such as one of the areas of the heart.

chancre /shăng′kər/ a painless ulcer, usually in the genital area, that is the first sign of a syphilis infection.

chancroid /shăng′kroid/ an infectious ulcer seen in venereal diseases. *Also called* soft chancre.

chancrous /shăng′krəs/ having a chancre.

change of life an informal term for menopause.

chapped /chăpt/ having rough, dry, scaly skin, usually as a result of exposure to cold.

CHARGE syndrome /chärj/ a complex of disorders in infants with four of the seven symptoms of CHARGE: **c**oloboma or cleft of the eye, **h**eart defects, **a**tresia of the nasal passageways, **r**etarded growth and development, **g**enital hypoplasia, **e**ar anomalies, deafness.

charlatan /shär′lə tən/ a fraudulent practitioner who claims to have medical training and usually claims to have miracle cures.

charley horse pain or muscle stiffness after exertion.

chart /chärt/ a patient's record, usually including symptoms, diagnoses, treatments, observations, and written records of interactions with medical personnel.

checkup /chĕk′ŭp′/ a general physical examination performed by a doctor, often on a yearly basis.

cheeks /chēks/ the walls of the mouth that form both sides of the face. *Also called* mala.

cheil-, cheilo- *combining form*. lips: *for example,* cheiloplasty.

cheilitis /kī li′tĭs/ inflammation of the lips. [cheil- + -itis]

cheiloplasty /kī′lə plăs′tē/ plastic surgery of the lips. [cheilo- + -plasty]

cheilorrhaphy /kī lôr′ə fē/ suturing of the lips. [cheilo- + -rrhaphy]

cheilosis /kī lō′sĭs/ extreme dryness of the lips, with cracking. [cheil- + -osis]

cheilotomy /kī lŏt′ə mē/ incision into the lips. [cheilo- + -tomy]

chelation therapy /kē lā′shən/ a therapy that uses a substance to bind with toxic and other metals to make them less harmful to or remove them from the body.

chemical dependence condition of extreme reliance on chemicals or drugs. *Also called* addiction.

chemical peel the application of chemicals to the face to eliminate blemishes or wrinkled skin.

chemo- *combining form*. chemical: *for example,* chemokinesis.

chemo /kē′mō/ informal term for chemotherapy.

chemokine /kē′mə kīn′/ chemicals that stimulate leukocyte movement.

chemokinesis /kē′mō kī nē′sĭs/ stimulation of movement by a chemical. [chemo- + -kinesis]

chemoprophylaxis /kē′mō prō′fə lăk′sĭs/ the use of drugs to prevent disease. [chemo- + prophylaxis]

chemosurgery /kē′mō sûr′jə rē/ Removal of tissue using chemicals. [chemo- + surgery]

chemotherapy /ke′mo thĕr′ə pe/ treatment of disease using chemicals or drugs, especially treatment of cancer using antineoplastic drugs. [chemo- + therapy]

cherry angioma /ăn′jē ō′mə/ a red skin lesion, usually formed from weakening of capillaries as aging occurs.

chest /chĕst/ the area of the body between the neck and the abdomen enclosed by the ribs and breastbone. *Also called* thorax.

chest film most common x-ray which shows the chest area including the heart, lungs, ribs and thoracic spine. *Also called* chest x-ray.

chest pain pain in the chest area that is sometimes the signal of something more serious such as a heart attack. *Also called* angina.

chest tube a tube introduced into the chest cavity next to the lung, usually to remove fluid or air and allow the lungs to expand normally.

chest x-ray (CXR) chest film.

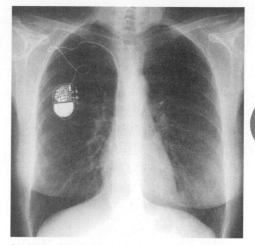
Chest Film (Showing Pacemaker)

Cheyne-Stokes respiration /chān′ stōks′/ a breathing pattern with deep breaths alternating with apnea, often found in patients in coma.

CHF *abbreviation*. congestive heart failure.

chickenpox or **chicken pox** /chĭk′ən pŏks′/ a highly contagious childhood disease with pustules caused by the varicella-zoster virus. *Also called* varicella.

chilblain /chĭl′blān/ a skin injury caused by exposure to cold, usually marked by redness, itching, and burning.

child abuse physical, psychological, or sexual abuse of a child.

childbearing /chīld′bâr′ĭng/ pregnancy and birth.

childbed fever a potentially lethal bacterial infection occurring in the mother immediately after childbirth, most often caused by unsterile conditions. *Also called* puerperal fever.

childbirth /chīld′bûrth′/ the process of giving birth to a child.

childhood /chīld′hŏŏd/ the period of life between infancy and puberty.

chill /chĭl/ a sudden sensation of cold.

chimera /kī mêr′ə/ a person who carries two genetically distinct types of cells, for example a dizygotic (fraternal) twin who carries two genetically different red cell populations.

chin /chĭn/ the prominence of the lower jaw just below the lower lip. *Also called* mentum.

Chinese medicine system of medicine founded in China based on qi or chi, the energy in the body, that uses herbs, meditiation, acupuncture, and other methods to achieve balance in the body. *Also called* traditional Chinese medicine.

Chinese restaurant syndrome facial pain, headache, chest pain, and burning in the esophagus, usually caused by a sensitivity to MSG, a taste-enhancing additive often used in Chinese cooking.

chiropodist /kĭ rŏp′ə dĭst/ a person trained and licensed to treat the feet. *Also called* podiatrist.

chiropody /kĭ rŏp′ə dē/ the diagnosis and treatment of diseases of the foot. *Also called* podiatry.

chiropractic /kī′rə prăk′tĭk/ alternative health practice based on manipulation of the spine and the relationship between the body's structure and its own recuperative powers and health.

chiropractor /kī′rə prăk′tər/ a health practitioner trained in chiropractic.

chlamydia /klə mĭd′ē ə/ a common sexually transmitted disease, which, if left untreated in the female, may result in sterility.

chloasma /klō ăz′mə/ brownish patches on the face and elsewhere, usually a sign of pregnancy. *Also called* melasma, mask of pregnancy.

chlor-, chloro- *combining form.* **1.** green. **2.** chlorine. *For example,* chloruresis.

chlorine /klôr′ēn/ (**CL**) a greenish, gaseous, toxic element, used in disinfectants and bleaches.

chloruresis /klôr′yŏŏ rē′sĭs/ the presence of chlorine in the urine. [chlor- + -uresis]

choana /kō′ə nə/ (*pl.* **choanae** /kō′ə nē′/) the passageway on either side of the back of the nose leading to the throat.

choanal /kō′ə nəl/ of or pertaining to the choanae.

choke /chōk/ to obstruct respiration by blocking of the larynx or trachea.

chol-, chole-, cholo- *combining form.* bile: *for example,* cholemia.

cholang-, cholangi-, cholangio- *combining form.* bile duct: *for example,* cholangioma, cholangiography.

cholangiogram /kō lăn′jē ə grăm′/ a radiographic image of the bile ducts. [cholangio- + -gram]

cholangiography /kō lăn′jē ŏg′rə fē/ radiographic imaging of the bile ducts. [cholangio- + -graphy]

cholangioma /kō lăn′jē ō′mə/ tumor of the bile ducts. [cholangi- + -oma]

cholangiopancreatography /kə lăn′jē ō păng′ krē ə tŏg′rə fē/ radiographic imaging of the bile ducts and pancreas. [cholangio- + pancreato- + -graphy]

cholangiostomy /kə lăn′jē ŏs′tə mē/ surgical formation of a fistula into a bile duct. [cholangio- + -stomy]

cholangiotomy /kə lăn′jē ŏt′ə mē/ incision into a bile duct. [cholangio- + -tomy]

cholangitis /kō′lăn jī′tĭs/ inflammation of a bile duct. [cholang- + -itis]

cholecyst /kō′lə sĭst/ gallbladder.

cholecyst-, cholecysto- gallbladder: *for example,* cholecystitis, cholecystogram.

cholecystectomy /kō′lə sĭ stĕk′tə mē/ removal of the gallbladder. [cholecyst- + -ectomy]

cholecystitis /kō′lə sĭ stī′tĭs/ inflammation of the gallbladder. [cholecyst- + -itis]

cholecystoduodenostomy /kō′lə sĭs′tō dōō′ō dē nŏs′tə mē/ establishment of an opening between the gallbladder and the duodenum, performed when the bile duct is obstructed, perhaps by tumor, to permit the bile to flow into the intestine. [cholecysto- + duoden(um) + -ostomy]

cholecystogram /kō′lə sĭs′tə grăm′/ radiographic image of the gallbladder. [cholecysto- + -gram]

cholecystography /kō′lə sĭ stŏg′rə fē/ radiographic imaging of the gallbladder. [cholecysto- + -graphy]

cholecystopexy /kō′lə sĭs′tə pĕk′sē/ surgical fixing of the gallbladder against the abdominal wall. [cholecysto- + -pexy]

cholecystorrhaphy /kō lə sĭ stôr′ə fē/ suturing of the gallbladder. [cholecysto- + -rrhaphy]

cholecystostomy /kō′lə sĭ stŏs′tə mē/ surgical formation of a fistula into the gallbladder. [cholecysto- + -stomy]

cholecystotomy /kō′lə sĭ stŏt′ə mē/ incision into the gallbladder. [cholecysto- + -tomy]

choledoch-, choledocho- *combining form.* the common bile duct: *for example,* choledochotomy.

choledochitis /kō lĕd′ə kī′tĭs/ inflammation of the common bile duct. [choledoch- + -itis]

choledocholithiasis /kō lĕd′ə kō lĭ thī′ə sĭs/ presence of a gallstone in the common bile duct. [choledocho- + lith- + -iasis]

choledocholithotomy /kō lĕd′ə kō lĭ thŏt′ə mē/ removal of a gallstone via an incision into the common bile duct. [choledocho- + litho- + -tomy]

choledochorrhaphy /kō lĕd′ə kôr′ə fē/ suturing of the ends of the common bile duct. [choledocho- + -rrhaphy]

choledochotomy /kō lĕd′ə kŏt′ə mē/ incision into the common bile duct. [choledocho- + -tomy]

cholelith /kō′lə lĭth/ a calcification of substances in bile, such as cholesterol and mineral salts, formed in the gallbladder or a bile duct. *Also called* gallstone.

cholelithiasis /kō′lə lĭ thī′ə sĭs/ presence of gallstone in the gallbladder or the bile ducts. [cholelith- + -iasis]

cholelithotomy /kō lə lĭ thŏt′ə mē/ surgical removal of a gallbladder stone. [chole- + lithotomy]

cholelithotripsy /kō′lə lĭth′ə trĭp′sē/ crushing of a gallstone.

cholemia /kō lē′mē ə/ presence of bile in the blood, usually indicating liver disease. [chol- + -emia]

cholepoiesis /kō'lĭ poi ē'sĭs/   formation of bile. [chole- + -poiesis]

cholera /kŏl'ər ə/   an infectious epidemic disease caused by a bacteria and mostly found in India and Asia.

cholestasis /kō'lə stā'sĭs/   a stopping of the flow of bile, usually resulting in jaundice.

cholesteatoma /kō lĕs'tē ə tō'mə/ (*pl.* **cholesteatomas** or **cholesteatomata** /kō lĕs'tē ə tō'mə tə/)   a fatty cyst (tumor) in the mastoid bone adjacent to the middle ear.

cholesterol /kə lĕs'tə rōl', -rôl'/   the most common type of steroid found in the body. There are two types of cholesterol, one of which is beneficial, the other harmful. *See* high-density lipoproteins (HDLs) and low-density lipoproteins (LDLs).

cholesterol-lowering drugs   drugs that lower harmful cholesterol in the bloodstream, usually "statins."

cholic /kō'lĭk/   of or pertaining to the bile.

choline /kō'lēn/   a B-complex vitamin important to metabolizing fat.

cholinergic /kŏl'ə nûr'; ĭk/   having stimulating effect similar to that of a release of acetylcholine.

chondr-, chondro- *combining form.* cartilage: *for example,* chondrectomy, chondrocyte.

chondralgia /kŏn drăl'jə, -jē ə/   cartilage pain. *Also called* chondrodynia. [chondr- + -algia]

chondrectomy /kŏn drĕk'tə mē/   removal of cartilage. [chondr- + -ectomy]

chondritis /kŏn drī' tĭs/   inflammation of cartilage. [chondr- + -itis]

chondrocyte /kŏn'drə sīt'/   specialized cells that form cartilage. [chondro- + -cyte]

chondrodynia /kŏn'drō dĭn'ē ə/   cartilage pain. *Also called* chondralgia. [chondro-_-dynia]

chondrodysplasia /kŏn'drō dĭs plā'zhə/   a form of dwarfism with skeletal deformities thought to result from the underdevelopment of cartilage. *Also called* chondrodystrophy. [chondro- + dysplasia]

chondrodystrophy /kŏn'drō dĭs'trə fē/   chondrodysplasia. [chondro- + dystrophy]

chondrogenesis /kŏn'drō jĕn'ə sĭs/   formation of cartilage. [chondro- + -genesis]

chondroid /kŏn'droid/   resembling cartilage. [chondr- + -oid]

chondroma /kŏn drō'mə / (*pl.* **chondromas** or **chondromata** /kŏn drō'mə tə/)   tumor formed from cartilage. [chondr- + -oma]

chondromalacia /kŏn'drō mə lā'shə/   softening of cartilage. [chondro- + -malacia]

chondromalacia patellae /pə tĕl'ē/   degenerative conditions with loss of cartilage at the contact between the kneecap (patella) and the knee joint.

chondroplasia /kŏn'drə plā'zhə/   formation of cartilage. [chondro- + -plasia]

chondroplasty /kŏn'drə plăs'tē/   surgical repair of cartilage. [chondro- + -plasty]

chondrosarcoma /kŏn'drō sär kō'mə/ (*pl.* **chondrosarcomas** or **chondrosarcomata** /kŏn'drō sär kō'mə tə /)   a malignant tumor formed from cells in cartilage. [chondro- + sarcoma]

chorda /kôr də/   in anatomy, a chordlike or tendinous structure.

chordee /kôr dē'/   painful erection of the penis, usually with curvature due to a fibrous band, often seen with gonorrhea or Peyronie's disease.

chorditis /kôr dī'tĭs/   inflammation of the vocal cords. *Also called* laryngitis.

chordoma /kôr dō'mə/   a type of cancer that usually starts in the spinal cord.

chordotomy /kôr dŏt'ə mē/   surgical transaction of a portion of the spinal cord for relief of severe pain; cordotomy.

chorea /kô rē'ə/   condition with spastic movements of the face and limbs thought to be caused by a brain lesion.

chorio- *combining form.* membrane, especially the chorion: *for example,* choriocarcinoma.

chorioamnionitis /kôr'ē ō ăm'nē ə nī'tĭs/   inflammation of the chorion and amnion. [chorio- + amnion + itis]

choriocarcinoma /kôr'ē ō kär'sə nō'mə/ (*pl.* **choriocarcinomas** or **choriocarcinomata** /kôr'ē ō kär'sə nō'mə tə /)   highly malignant tumor developing from cells in the uterus following a pregnancy. [chorio- + carcinoma]

chorion /kôr'ē ŏn'/   the outermost fetal membrane that forms part of the placenta.

chorionic villi /kôr'e ŏn'ĭk vĭl'ī/   the vascular fingers of the chorion.

chorionic villus sampling /vĭl'əs/   a biopsy taken from the chorionic villi during the first trimester of pregnancy to test for genetic abnormalities.

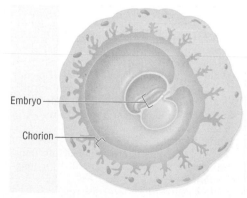

Chorion (in Week 3 Embryo)

Embryo

Chorion

choroid /kôr′oid/ the vascular layer between the retina and sclera of the eye. *Also called* choroid layer.

choroidal /kə roi′dəl/ of or pertaining to the choroid.

choroiditis /kôr′oi dī′tĭs/ inflammation of the choroid.

choroid layer choroid.

chrom-, chromat-, chromato-, chromo- *combining form.* color: *for example,* chromocyte.

chromatid /krō′mə tĭd/ one of the two strands of chromosomes that later each become a separate chromosome.

chromatin /krō′mə tĭn/ material in the nucleus of a cell that contains genetic information.

chromatism /krō′mə tĭz′əm/ abnormal color or pigmentation. [chromat- + -ism]

chromatogram /krō măt′ə grăm′/ the pattern formed by the separation of substances in chromatography. [chromato- + -gram]

chromatography /krō′mə tŏg′rə fē/ a process for separating out chemical substances in a solution by passing the solution over various mediums to which the parts are attracted. [chromato- + -graphy]

chromatolysis /krō′mə tŏl′ə sĭs/ the disintegration of chromatin within a cell, especially a nerve cell. [chromato- + -lysis]

chromatopsia /krō′mə tŏp′sē ə/ a vision disturbance in which objects appear incorrectly colored. [chromat- + -opsia]

chromaturia /krō′mə toor′ē ə/ abnormal urine color. [chromat- + -uria]

chromesthesia /krō′mĕs thē′zhə/ a condition in which color sense is stimulated by another sense, such as sound. [chrom- + -esthesia]

chromium (Cr) /krō′mē əm/ a metallic element important in the metabolism of glucose.

chromocyte /krō′mə sīt′/ a pigmented cell, such as a red blood cell. [chromo- + -cyte]

chromosomal /krō′mə sō′məl/ of or pertaining to chromosomes.

chromosomes /krō′mə sōmz′/ the strands of DNA in the nucleus of a cell that contain all the genetic information.

chron-, chrono- *combining form.* time: *for example,* chronobiology.

chronic /krŏn′ĭk/ long-term, persistent or recurring, said of disease.

chronic adrenocortical insufficiency /ə drē′nō kôr′tĭ kəl/ adrenocortical insufficiency usually resulting from destruction or loss of both adrenal glands from disease. *Also called* Addison's disease.

chronic bronchitis /brŏng kī′tĭs/ persistent bronchitis with recurring bronchial infections.

chronic care health care provided for long-term illnesses.

chronic disease long-term disease.

chronic fatigue syndrome /fə tēg′/ a complex of symptoms including debilitating fatigue lasting for a long time, thought to be caused by the Epstein-Barr virus.

chronic granulocytic leukemia /grăn′yə lō sĭt′ĭk loo kē′mē ə/ chronic myelogenous leukemia.

chronic illness any long-term or recurring disease.

chronic lymphocytic leukemia (CLL) /lĭm′fō sĭt′ĭk loo kē′mē ə/ a form of leukemia most commonly found in people over 60, usually a slowly progressing form of the disease.

chronic myelocytic leukemia (CML) /mī′ə lō sĭt′ĭk loo kē′mē ə/ or **chronic myelogenous leukemia (CML)** /mī′ə lŏj′ə nəs/ a chronic form of leukemia whose early symptoms include night sweats and fatigue.

chronic obstructive pulmonary disease (COPD) or **chronic obstructive lung disease (COLD)** any chronic lung disorder with persistent airflow obstruction.

chronobiology /krŏn′ō bī ŏl′ə jē/ the study of time and biological rhythms and how they affect individuals. [chrono- + biology]

chronooncology /krŏn′ō ŏng kŏl′ə jē/ the study of time and biological rhythms and how they affect the growth of tumors and how they can be used to time treatment more effectively.

chronotropic /krŏn′ə trō′pĭk/ affecting the tuning or rate of something, such as a heartbeat.

chrysotherapy /krĭs′ō thĕr′ə pē/ of gold salts in the treatment of disease, especially rheumatoid arthritis.

chyl-, chylo- *combining form.* chyle: *for example,* chylemia, chylopoiesis.

chyle /kīl/ a milky fluid transported from the intestines during digestion to the lymph system.

chylemia /kī lē′mē ə/ chyle in the blood. [chyl- + -emia]

chylopoiesis /kī′lō poi ē′sĭs/ formation of chyle in the intestines. [chylo- + -poesis]

chyluria /kī loor′ē ə/ excretion of chyle in the urine. [chyl- + -uria]

chyme /kīm/ the semifluid mass of partly digested food passing out of the stomach into the duodenum.

CIC *abbreviation.* completely in the canal (said of hearing aids).

cicatrix /sĭk′ə trĭks, sĭ kā′trĭks/ (*pl.* **cicatrices** /sĭk′ə trī′sēz, sĭ kā′trĭ sēz′/) a scar.

-cidal *suffix.* killing; *for example,* suicidal, bactericidal.

-cide *suffix.* one that kills; *for example,* suicide, fungicide.

cilia /sĭl′ē ə/ (*sing.* **cilium** /sĭl′ē əm/) hairlike projections from a cell.

ciliary body /sĭl′ē ĕr′ē/ vascular layer of the eye between the sclera and the cyrstalline lens.

ciliary muscle the smooth muscle part of the ciliary body that aids in focusing the lens.

cine- *combining form.* movement: *for example,* cineangiogram.

cineangiogram /sĭn′ē ăn′jē ə grăm′/ video taken in cineradiography. [cine- + angiogram]

cineradiography /sĭn′ə rā′dē ŏg′rə fē/ radiographic imaging taken while a body part is in motion. [cine- + radiography]

cingulum /sĭng′gyə ləm/ any beltlike structure, such as the bony ridge around the base of a tooth.

circadian rhythm /sûr kā′dē ən/ a biological rhythm that takes place in a 24-hour cycle.

circinate /sûr′sə nāt′/ having a circular shape.

circle /sûr′ kəl/ any ring-shaped part.

circulation /sûr′kyə lā′shən/ movement through a circular course, such as the movement of blood throughout the body (blood circulation).

circulatory /sûr′kyə lə tôr′ē/ of or pertaining to circulation.

circulatory system the body system that circulates blood throughout the body, including the heart and all the blood vessels; cardiovascular system.

circum- *prefix*. around: *for example*, circumarticular.

circumarticular /sûr′kəm är tĭk′yə lər/ surrounding a joint. [circum- + articular]

circumcise /sûr′kəm sīz′/ to perform circumcision.

circumcision /sûr′kəm sĭzh′ən/ surgical removal of all or part of the prepuce (foreskin) of the penis.

circumduction /sûr′kəm dŭk′shən/ movement in a circular direction, as the movement of some joints.

circumflex /sûr′kəm flĕks′/ bending or winding around as the branch of an artery.

cirrhosis /sĭ rō′sĭs/ degenerative liver disease, often resulting from alcoholism or hepatitis.

cirrhotic /sĭ rŏt′ĭk/ having cirrhosis.

CIS *abbreviation*. carcinoma in situ.

cistern /sĭs′tərn/ or **cisterna** /sĭs tûr′nə/ a sac or cavity containing fluid.

CJD *abbreviation*. Creutzfeldt-Jakob's disease.

CK *abbreviation*. creatinine kinase.

Cl *abbreviation*. chlorine.

clamps /klămps/ instrument for grasping; forceps.

clap /klăp/ informal name for gonorrhea.

Clarke('s) sign /klärk(s)/ a diagnostic maneuver that determines the condition of knee cartilage.

-clasis *suffix*. breaking; *for example*, osteoclasis.

clasp /klăsp/ in dentistry, a fastener that holds a denture in place.

classification of diseases the systemic grouping of diseases by similarities in cause or symptoms.

-clast *suffix*. breaking; *for example*, osteoclast.

claudication /klô′dĭ kā′shən/ limping, frequently due to insufficient blood flow (oxygen delivery) to the leg muscles.

Clamps

claustral /klô′strəl/ of or pertaining to a claustrum.

claustrophobia /klô′strə fō′bē ə/ abnormal fear of enclosed spaces.

claustrophobic /klô′strə fō′bĭk/ of or having claustrophobia.

claustrum /klô′strəm/ any barrierlike structure, especially a thin layer of gray matter in each cerebral hemisphere of the brain.

clavicle /klăv′ĭ kəl/ the curved long bone that forms the anterior part of the shoulder. *Also called* collarbone.

clavicular /klə vĭk′yə lər/ of or pertaining to the clavicle.

clavus /kla′vəs/ (*pl*. **clavi** /klā′vī/) small callous formed from localized pressure. *Also called* corn.

claw foot or **claw hand** a symptom of disease with fixed contracture of the foot or hand.

clean-catch specimen /spĕs′ə mən / a urine specimen taken after cleaning of the external urinary opening (urethral orifice).

clearance /klêr′əns/ the removal of a substance from the blood, especially by the kidneys.

cleft /klĕft/ a fissure or split, as in the chin.

cleft lip a birth defect of the upper lip sometimes associated with a fissue in the alveolar ridge (which later holds the teeth) and a cleft palate.

cleft palate /păl′ĭt/ birth defect with a fissure in the middle of the palate, often including a fissure in the lip. *Also called* palatoschisis, uranoschisis.

cleido- *combining form*. clavicle: *for example*, cleidocostal.

cleidocostal /klī′dō kŏs′təl/ of or relating to the clavicle and the ribs. [cleido- + costal]

cleidocranial /klī′dō krā′nē əl/ of or relating to the clavicle and the cranium. [cleido- + cranial]

climacteric /klī măk′tər ĭk, klī′măk tĕr′ĭk/   the period of cessation of menstruation. *Also called* menopause.

climax /klī′măks/   **1.** the most severe stage of a disease. **2.** orgasm.

clinic /klĭn′ĭk/   a health care facility for the treatment of patients.

clinical /klĭn′ĭ kəl/   having to do with or applicable to patients.

clinical depression /dĭ prĕsh′ən/   depression with symptoms that meet the criteria set forth in the *Diagnostic and Statistical Manual (DSM)*.

clinical psychologist /sī kŏl′ə jĭst/   a professional specialist in clinical psychology.

clinical psychology /sī kŏl′ə jē/   a professional specialty that uses talk therapy to treat patients with emotional and behavioral disorders.

clinical social worker   a social worker trained in and usually licensed to practice psychotherapy.

clinical trial   a trial of a medication, medical device, or treatment method performed on a large group of people to determine effectiveness.

clinician /klĭ nĭsh′ən/   a health care professional who treats patients as opposed to one in other areas, such as research.

clino- *combining form.* sloping; curving: *for example*, clinodactyly.

clinocephaly /klī′nō sĕf′ə lē/   a congenital defect in which the head is concave. [clino- + -cephaly]

clinodactyly /klī′nō dăk′tə lē/   permanent curving (usually from birth) of one or more fingers. [clino- + -dactyly]

clip /klĭp/   a medical device use to hold a part together or to close off something such as a small blood vessel.

clitoral /klĭt′ər əl, klĭ tôr′əl/   of or pertaining to the clitoris.

clitoral amputation   removal of the clitoris; clitoridectomy, clotorectomy.

clitoridectomy /klĭt′ər ĭ dĕk′tə mē/ or **clitorectomy** /klĭt′ə rĕk′tə mē/   removal of the clitoris.

clitoriditis /klĭt′ər ĭ dī′tĭs/   inflammation of the clitoris.

clitoris /klĭt′ər ĭs/   a small erectile mass of tissue located at the top anterior part of the vulva, the primary site of female arousal.

clivus /klī′vəs/   a downward sloping part, as the upper part of a sphenoid bone.

CLL *abbreviation.* chronic lymphocytic leukemia.

cloaca /klō ā′kə/   a common passageway for feces and urine in early embryos.

clone /klōn/   *n.* **1.** a fragment of DNA or something developed from that fragment. **2.** a

Clinic (Reception Area)

colony of organisms or cells derived from a single organism or cell by asexual reproduction. *v.* **3.** to produce a living cell or organism using such a fragment.

clonic /klŏn′ĭk/   of or pertaining to clonus.

clonic seizure   a type of seizure that includes involuntary muscle movements or clonus.

cloning   the production of a living part or organisim using a clone.

clonism /klō′nĭz əm/   a condition with repetitious clonus.

clonus /klō′nəs/   spastic, involuntary muscle movement.

closed fracture   a fracture with no skin break. *Also called* simple fracture.

closed head trauma   a head trauma or injury with the skull remaining intact.

closed reduction   manipulation of a fracture without opening the skin.

closed surgery   surgery without skin penetration, such as a closed reduction.

clostridium /klŏ strĭd′ē əm/ (*pl.* **clostridia** /klŏ strĭd′ē ə/)   any of a group of bacteria that cause infections, particularly of the large bowel.

closure /klō′zhər/   the closing up of, as sutures.

clot /klŏt/   **1.** *v.* to form a mass, especially to coagulate (blood). *n.* **2.** a mass formed by coagulation, especially of blood.

clotbuster /klŏt′bŭs′tər/   informal term for a medicine that dissolves clots. *Also called* thrombolytic agent.

clotting factor any of the various components of plasma involved in clotting.

clotting time the time it takes for a blood clot to form; prothrombin time (PTT) is one measure of clotting factors.

clubfoot or **club foot** /klŭb'foot'/ birth defect with the foot turned inward, often correctable by surgery. *Also called* talipes equinovarus.

clubhand or **club hand** /klŭb'hănd'/ a congenital defect with a shortened, misshapen hand.

clumping /klŭm'pĭng/ a thick massing, as of bacteria in a fluid.

clunes /kloo'nēz/ the buttocks.

cluster /klŭs'tər/ any unusual occurrence of something, such as an abnormally high rate of occurrence of a particular disease in a small area.

cluster headache frequent, reccurring headaches.

cluttering /klŭt'ər ĭng/ a speech disorder with rapid, erratic and unclear speech.

clysis /klī'sĭs/ an infusion of fluid, as for hydration.

cm *abbreviation.* centimeter.

CMA *abbreviation.* certified medical assistant.

CMI *abbreviation.* cell-mediated immunity.

CML *abbreviation.* chronic myelogenous leukemia.

CMS *abbreviation.* Centers for Medicare and Medicaid Services (www.cms.hhs.gov).

CMT *abbreviation.* certified medical transcriptionist.

CMV *abbreviation.* cytomegalovirus.

CNS *abbreviation.* central nervous system.

CO *abbreviation.* carbon monoxide.

CO$_2$ *abbreviation.* carbon dioxide.

co-, com-, con- *prefix.* with, together: *for example*, coenzyme.

CoA *abbreviation.* coarctation of the aorta.

coagulant /kō ăg'yə lənt/ an agent that causes or aids in coagulation.

coagulate /kō ăg'yə lāt'/ to change from a liquid into a thickened mass; clot.

coagulation /kō ăg'yə lā'shən/ the change from a liquid into a thickening mass, as in blood clotting.

coagulation time the time required for blood to clot.

coarctation /kō'ärk tā'shən/ constriction or severe narrowing of an artery.

coarctation of the aorta (CoA) /ā ôr'tə/ narrowing of the aorta at its connection to the ductus arteriosus, a structure which is functional in the fetus, but closes soon after birth.

coat /kōt/ an outer covering, as the outer layer of an organ.

coated stent a tiny medicated tube used to prop open an artery following angioplasty.

COBRA /kō'brə/ *abbreviation.* U.S. federal Consolidated Omnibus Budget Reconciliation Act.

cocaine /kō kān'/ a substance extracted from coca leaves, used as a topical anesthestic, and widely used as an illegal stimulant.

coccal /kŏk'əl/ of or relating to cocci.

cocci /kŏk'sī/ plural of coccus.

coccidioidomycosis /kŏk sĭd'ē oi'dō mī kō'sĭs/ fungal disease contracted through the inhalation of a fungus.

coccoid /kŏk'oid/ of or similar to a coccus.

-coccus *suffix.* belonging to a group of bacteria having a spherical shape: *for example*, streptococcus.

coccus /kŏk'əs/ (*pl.* **cocci** /kŏk'sī/) a bacteria of spherical shape.

coccydynia /kŏk'sī dĭn'ē ə/ pain in the region of the coccyx.

coccygeal /kŏk sĭj'ē əl/ of or relating to the coccyx.

coccygeal plexus /plĕk'səs/ a small nerve network formed by the fifth sacral and coccygeal nerves.

coccygeal vertebrae /vûr'tə brē'/ the four small vertebrae at the bottom of the spine that form the tail bone, called the coccyx.

coccygectomy /kŏk'sī jĕk'tə mē/ surgical removal of the coccyx.

coccyx /kŏk'sĭks/ the small bone at the base of the vertebral column formed by the fusion of the coccygeal vertebrae.

cochle-, cochleo- *combining form.* of or relating to the inner ear: *for example*, cochleovestibular.

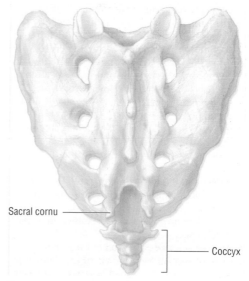

Sacral cornu

Coccyx

Coccyx

cochlea /kŏ′klē ə/ (*pl.* **cochleae** /kŏ′klē ē′/) a small conical structure of the inner ear that mediates the sense of hearing by converting vibrations into nerve impulses sent to the brain.

cochlear /kŏ′klē ər/ of or relating to the cochlea.

cochlear implant /ĭm′plănt′/ a small electronic device functioning as an advanced hearing aid, surgically implanted into a nonfunctioning cochlea.

cochlear nerve a part of the acoustic nerve involved in transmission of auditory stimuli to the brain.

cochleovestibular /kŏ′klē ō vĕ stĭb′yə lər/ of or relating to the cochlea and the vestibule of the ear. [cochleo- + vestibular]

code /kōd/ 1. a set of rules, principles, or ethics. 2. a system designed to transmit information or aid in communication. 3. a term used by hospital staff to describe an emergency situation requiring resuscitation. 4. a numeric system used in medical documentation to indicate a visit, diagnosis, or procedure.

codeine /kō′dēn/ a narcotic pain reliever derived from morphine.

coding /kō′dĭng/ the assignment of numbers to visits, diagnoses, or procedures in medical documentation for the purpose of receiving reimbursement.

codon /kō′dŏn/ a sequence of three items on a strand of DNA that provides genetic information.

coefficient /kō′ĭ fĭsh′ənt/ a constant number that serves as a measure of something, such as absorption.

coelom /sē′ləm/ (*pl.* **coeloms** or **coelomata** /sē lō′mə tə/) body cavity in an embryo that becomes several important cavities in the fetus.

coenzyme /kō ĕn′zīm/ small molecule that enhances the action of an enzyme. [co- + enzyme]

coenzyme Q10 an antioxidant that protects cells from free radicals and helps in the production of the energy necessary for cell growth and maintenance. *Also called* CoQ10, ubiquinone.

cognition /kŏg nĭsh′ən/ the mental process of being aware, learning, thinking, and memory.

cognitive /kŏg′nĭ tĭv/ of or relating to cognition.

cognitive behavioral therapy (CBT) a form of psychotherapy that deals with the connection between thoughts and emotions, with a focus on present behavior rather than past experience.

cognitive science the study of the mind,

cognitive therapy any form of psychotherapy that focuses on self-discovery and self-instruction as the main treatment technique.

cohort /kō′hôrt/ a well-defined group of a population that shares a common exposure or period of birth, by which they are identified, such as any designated group followed for a long period of time.

coil /koil/ a spiral-shaped item, especially an informal name for an intrauterine device.

coinsurance that part of an insurance plan for which the patient is responsible or two insurance plans that share the cost of insuring one patient.

coital /kō′ĭ təl/ of or relating to coitus.

coitus /kō′ĭ təs/ sexual intercourse.

coitus interruptus /ĭn′tə rŭp′təs/ an undependable form of contraception in which sexual intercourse is interrupted before the male ejaculates.

col-, colo- *combining form.* colon: *for example,* colitis, colostomy.

colchicine /kŏl′chə sēn′/ a substance extracted from a plant that is used in the treatment of gout and to stop cell division in laboratory studies.

cold /kōld/ 1. a low temperature. 2. a common term for a viral infection in the upper respiratory tract.

COLD *abbreviation.* chronic obstructive lung disease.

cold sore a small, painful sore on the face or mouth caused by herpes simplex.

colectomy /kə lĕk′tə mē/ surgical removal of part or all of the colon. [col- + -ectomy]

colic /kŏl′ĭk/ 1. *adj.* of or relating to the colon. 2. *n.* an attack of apparent abdominal pain in infants characterized by prolonged episodes of loud crying.

colicky /kŏl′ĭ kē/ exhibiting symptoms of colic.

colitis /kə lī′tĭs/ inflammation of the colon. [col- + -itis]

collagen /kŏl′ə jən/ the major protein of the skin, tendons, cartilage, bone, and connective tissue.

collagen disease any one of a group of diseases that attack the connective tissues, such as lupus erythematosus and rheumatoid arthritis.

collagen injection a form of cosmetic surgery in which collagen is injected under the skin to repair scars, wrinkles, or to enlarge tissues, such as the lips.

collapsed lung a lung that is unable to fully expand due to an air leak or fluid in the chest cavity next to the lung.

collarbone /kŏl′ər bōn′/ the bone that extends from the breastbone to the shoulder. *Also called* clavicle.

collateral /kə lăt′ər əl/ 1. *adj.* subordinate, side by side. 2. *n.* a side branch of a nerve or blood vessel.

Colles' fracture /kŏl′ēz/ a fracture of the wrist caused by using an outstretched arm to brace a fall.

collimator /kŏl′ə mā′tər/ in the dental x-ray machine, the usually lead diaphragm placed at the base of the cone to restrict the size of the beam.

colloid /kŏl′oid/ gelatinous material, as produced by the thyroid gland or as present as tissue degenerates.

colo- *See* col-.

coloboma /kŏl′ə bō′mə/ a defect of the eye due to incomplete closure of the optic fissure.

colocentesis /kō′lə sĕn tē′sĭs/ surgical procedure in which the colon is pierced to relieve pressure and swelling. [colo- + -centesis]

colon-, colono- *combining form.* colon: *for example,* colonic, colonoscopy.

colon /kō′lən/ part of the large intestines from the cecum to the rectum, that removes (reabsorbs) water from digested food before it exits the body.

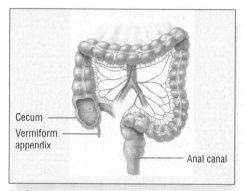

Cecum

Vermiform appendix

Anal canal

(a) Colon

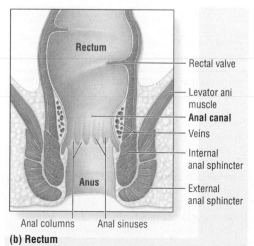

Rectum

Rectal valve

Levator ani muscle

Anal canal

Veins

Internal anal sphincter

Anus

External anal sphincter

Anal columns   Anal sinuses

(b) Rectum

colon cancer a malignant tumor of the colon.

colonic /kō lŏn′ĭk, kə-/ **1.** *adj.* of or pertaining to the colon. **2.** *n.* a procedure to cleanse the colon by flushing it with water. [colon + -ic]

colonic polyposis /pŏl′ĭ pō′sĭs/ a disease in which multiple polyps erupt in the lining or the colon.

colonoscope /kō lŏn′ə skōp′/ a flexible fiber optic instrument used to inspect the inside of the colon. [colono- + scope]

colonoscopy /kō′lə nŏs′kə pē/ inspection of the inside of the colon using a colonoscope. [colono- + -scopy]

colon polyp /pŏl′ĭp/ small growth on the inside of the colon that can lead to cancer if not removed.

colon therapy the administering of an enema to cleanse the colon.

colony count the exact number of colonies in a bacterial culture.

colony-stimulating factors (CSF) a group of molecules made of sugar and protein (glycoproteins) that stimulate blood cell production.

colopexy /kŏl′ə pĕk′sē/ surgical procedure to attach the colon to the abdominal wall. [colo- + -pexy]

coloptosis /kō′lŏp tō′sĭs/ downward displacement of the colon. [colo- + -ptosis]

color blindness or **colorblindness** /kŭl′ər blīnd′nĭs/ a sight disorder caused by an insufficient number of cone photoreceptors in the retinas, causing a partial or total inability to distinguish certain colors. *See also* deuteranopia, deuteranomaly.

colorectal /kō′lə rĕk′təl/ of or relating to the large bowel. [colo- + rectal]

colorectal cancer cancer of the colon and rectum. [colo- + -rectal]

colorectal polyp /pŏl′ĭp/ a small growth on the inside of the colon and rectum that can lead to cancer if not removed.

colorrhagia /kō′lə rā′jə, -jē ə/ unusual discharge from the colon. [colo- + -rrhagia]

colorrhaphy /kō lôr′ə fē/ suturing of the colon. [colo- + -rrhaphy]

coloscopy /kə lŏs′kə pē/ inspection of the inside of the colon using a colonoscope. [colo- + -scopy]

colostomy /kə lŏs′tə mē/ a surgical procedure creating an opening in the colon through the abdominal wall to redirect waste out of the body into an external receptacle. [colo- + -stomy]

colostomy bag a removable bag attached to the end of a colostomy to collect feces.

colostrum /kə lŏs′trəm/ a thin white fluid secreted from the breasts immediately following childbirth, before the production of breast milk.

colp-, colpo- *combining form.* vagina: *for example,* colpitis, colpodynia.

colpecstasis /kŏl pĕk′tə sĭs/ dilation of the vagina. [colp- + -ecstasis]

colpectomy /kŏl pĕk′tə mē/ surgical removal of part or all of the vagina. *Also called* vaginectomy. [colp- + -ectomy]

colpitis /kŏl pī′tĭs/ inflammation of the vagina. *Also called* vaginitis. [colp- + -itis]

colpocele /kŏl′pə sēl′/ hernia protruding into the vaginal wall. [colpo- + -cele]

colpocleisis /kŏl′pə klī′sĭs/ surgical opening of the lumen of the vagina. [colpo- + -cleisis]

colpodynia /kŏl′pə dĭn′ē ə/ vaginal pain. *Also called* vaginodynia. [colpo- + -dynia]

colpoperineorrhaphy /kŏl′pō pĕr′ə nē ôr′ə fē/ surgical repair of a lacerated vagina. [colpo- + perineorrhaphy]

colpopexy /kŏl′pə pĕk′sē/ surgical procedure to attach a prolapsed vagina to the abdominal wall. [colpo- + -pexy]

colpoplasty /kŏl′pə plăs′tē/ plastic surgery of the vagina. *Also called* vaginoplasty. [colpo- + -plasty]

colpopoiesis /kŏl′poi ē′sĭs/ formation of a vagina. [colpo- + -poiesis]

colpoptosis /kŏl′pŏp tō′sĭs/ a condition in which the vagina has prolapsed against the abdominal wall. [colpo- + -ptosis]

colporrhagia /kŏl′pə rā′jə, -jē ə/ unusual discharge from the vagina. [colpo- + -rrhagia]

colporrhaphy /kŏl pôr′ə fē/ surgical repair and suture of a tear in the vagina. [colpo- + -rrhaphy]

colporrhexis /kŏl′pə rĕk′sĭs/ tearing of the vaginal wall. [colpo- + -rrhexis]

colposcope /kŏl′pə skōp′/ an instrument used to magnify and examine cells in the vagina. [colpo- + -scope]

colposcopy /kŏl pŏs′kə pē/ examination of the vagina using a colposcope. [colpo- + -scopy]

colpospasm /kŏl′pə spăz′əm/ spasm that causes contraction of the vagina. [colpo- + -spasm]

colpostenosis /kŏl′pō stĭ nō′sĭs/ narrowing of the vaginal opening. [colpo- + -stenosis]

colpotomy /kŏl pŏt′ə mē/ surgical procedure to correct abnormal narrowing of the lumen of the vagina. [colpo- + -tomy]

column /kŏl′əm/ or **columna** /kə lŭm′nə/ an anatomical structure shaped like a tube.

com- *prefix.* with, together: *for example,* compress.

coma /kō′mə/ prolonged state of total unconsciousness resulting from trauma, disease, or poisoning.

comatose /kō′mə tōs′/ in a coma.

combined oral contraceptive /kŏn′trə sĕp′tĭv/ a common birth control pill that includes an estrogen and a progestin and suppresses ovulation.

comedo /kŏm′ĭ dō′/ (*pl.* **comedones** /kŏm′ĭ dō′nēz/) a small plug of sebum blocking the duct of a sebaceous gland especially on the face. *Also called* blackhead.

comminuted fracture /kŏm′ə nōō′tĭd/ a fracture in which the bone is broken into several fragments.

commissure /kŏm′ə shōōr′/ a line of junction between two anatomical parts, such as eye lids, lips, or cardiac valves.

commissurotomy /kŏm′ə shōō rŏt′ə mē/ surgical division of a commisure.

common bile duct the duct formed by the joining of the cystic duct of the gall bladder and the hepatic duct of the liver.

common carotid artery /kə rŏt′ĭd/ either of two main arteries, right and left carotid, that supply blood to the brain and head.

common cold any viral infection in the upper respiratory tract.

common hepatic duct /hĭ păt′ĭk/ the duct formed by the junction or the left and right hepatic ducts of the liver.

communicable disease any disease or infection that can be transmitted directly from one person to another.

communication /kə myōō′nĭ kā′shən/ **1.** an opening or passage between two anatomical structures. **2.** the exchange of thoughts and information through speech or behavior.

comorbidity /kō′môr bĭd′ĭ tē/ coexistence of two unrelated disease processes. [co- + morbidity]

compact bone hard dense bone tissue that forms the outer shell of bones.

compartment syndrome a condition in which there is swelling and inflammation isolated to one section of the body, such as an arm or leg, causing compression of blood supply and nerves, usually requiring immediate surgery.

compensation an increase or change in activity in one part of the body to adjust for a dysfunction or injury in another part.

competence /kŏm′pĭ təns/ Ability to perform a function, especially the ability to respond immunologically.

complaint a disorder, disease, or symptom.

complementary medicine a term for alternative therapies used alongside conventional medicine.

complete blood count (CBC) one of the most common diagnostic laboratory tests that measures red blood cells, white blood cells, hematocrit, hemoglobin, platelets, and other elements in a certain volume of blood. *See* form on page 75.

Elyse Armadian, M.D.	Laboratory Report	
3 South Windsor Street	Sunview Diagnostics	
Fairfield, MN 00219	6712 Adams Drive	
300-546-7890	Fairfield, MN 00220	
	300-546-7000	

Patient: Janine Josephs	Patient ID: 099-00-1200	Date of Birth: 08/07/43
Date Collected: 09/30/XXXX	Time Collected: 16:05	Total Volume: 2000
Date Received: 09/30/XXXX	Date Reported: 10/06/XXXX	

Test	Result	Flag	Reference
Complete Blood Count			
WBC	4.0		3.9-11.1
RBC	4.11		3.80-5.20
HCT	39.7		34.0-47.0
MCV	96.5		80.0-98.0
MCH	32.9		27.1-34.0
MCHC	34.0		32.0-36.0
MPV	8.6		7.5-11.5
NEUTROPHILS %	45.6		38.0-80.0
NEUTROPHILS ABS.	1.82		1.70-8.50
LYMPHOCYTES %	36.1		15.0-49.0
LYMPHOCYTES ABS.	1.44		1.00 3.50
EOSINOPHILS %	4.5		0.0-8.0
EOSINOPHILS ABS.	0.18		0.03-0.55
BASOPHILS %	0.7		0.0-2.0
BASOPHILS ABS.	0.03		0.000-0.185
PLATELET COUNT	229		150-400
Automated Chemistries			
GLUCOSE	80		65-109
UREA NITROGEN	17		6-30
CREATININE (SERUM)	0.6		0.5-1.3
UREA NITROGEN/CREATININE	28		10-29
SODIUM	140		135-145
POTASSIUM	4.4		3.5-5.3
CHLORIDE	106		96-109
CO$_2$	28		20-31
ANION GAP	6		3-19
CALCIUM	9.8		8.6-10.4
PHOSPHORUS	3.6		2.2-4.6
AST (SGOT)	28		0-30
ALT (SGPT)	19		0-34
BILIRUBIN, TOTAL	0.5		0.2-1.2
PROTEIN, TOTAL	7.8		6.2-8.2
ALBUMIN	4.3		3.5-5.0
GLOBULIN	3.5		2.1-3.8
URIC ACID	2.4		2.0-7.5
CHOLESTEROL	232	*	120-199
TRIGLYCERIDES	68		40-199
IRON	85		30-150
HDL CHOLESTEROL	73	*	35-59
CHOLESTEROL/HDL RATIO	3.2		3.2-5.7
LDL, CALCULATED	148	*	70-129
T3, UPTAKE	32		24-37
T4, TOTAL	6.9		4.5-12.8

Complete Blood Count (Patient with High Cholesterol)

complete fracture   a break of the entire width of the bone.

complete hysterectomy /hĭs'tə rĕk'tə mē/ complete surgical removal of the uterus and cervix.

complex /kŏm'plĕks/ **1.** a group of ideas that form a dominant part of one's personality, often in a negative way. **2.** a group of symptoms that form a syndrome.

complex fracture   a fracture with extensive damage to soft tissue.

complexion /kəm plĕk'shən/ the natural appearance of the skin of the face.

complex partial seizure   a form of seizure in which the person loses awareness, but not consciousness, and can carry out normal activities such as walking and talking, but without any memory of it following the seizure.

compliance /kəm plī'əns/   the act of adhering to official requirements.

complicated fracture   a bone fracture causing damage to an artery, nerve, or joint.

complication /kŏm'plĭ kā'shən/   any medical event influenced by or resulting from a disease, but not directly caused by it.

compos mentis /kŏm'pəs mĕn'tĭs/ of sound mind.

compound /kŏm'pound/   any substance formed from two or more very different components brought together by a covalent or electrostatic bond.

compound fracture   a fracture in which part of the broken bone pierces the skin.

comprehension /kŏm'prĭ hĕn'shən/ the ability to understand.

compress /kŏm'prĕs/   a pad applied for local pressure. [com- + press]

compression /kəm prĕsh'ən/   **1.** the application of pressure so as to hold in place or to stop bleeding. **2.** a deep tissue massage technique in which controlled pressure is used to compress a muscle.

compression fracture   a bone fracture, usually of the spine, causing loss of height.

compressor /kəm prĕs'ər/ something that compresses by squeezing together, as a device (such as clamps) or muscle.

compulsion /kəm pŭl'shən/   extreme anxiety manifested in an obsessive impulse to repeatedly perform an act.

compulsive /kəm pŭl'sĭv/   of or relating to compulsion.

computed tomography (CT) /tə mŏg'rə fē/ an x-ray technique using several x-ray beams in different positions and computer processing to produce cross-sectional images of the body. *Also called* computerized (axial) tomography.

computed tomography (CT) scan   an x-ray of the body using computed tomography.

computerized axial tomography (CAT) /ăk'sē əl/ computed tomography.

computerized tomography computed tomography.

con- *prefix.* with, together: *for example,* concentric.

concave /kŏn kāv'/ curved inward.

concentration /kŏn'sən trā'shən/ The increasing in strength of something, such as a pharmaceutical preparation; the preparation itself.

concentric /kən sĕn'trĭk/ sharing a common center. [con- + centric]

conception /kən sĕp'shən/ **1.** act of forming an abstract idea or notion. **2.** act of becoming pregnant.

conceptus /kən sĕp'təs/ the product of conception.

concordance /kən kôr'dəns/ agreement (as in data) occurring between two different things.

concordant /kən kôr'dənt/ showing concordance.

concrescence /kən krĕs'əns/ a growing together, as of tissue or parts.

concretion /kən krē'shən/ a mass formed by concrescence.

concussion /kən kŭsh'ən/ a traumatic injury to tissues, such as the brain, caused by violent shaking or a severe blow.

condensation /kŏn'dĕn sā'shən, -dən-/ **1.** the act of condensing, as from a gas to a liquid.

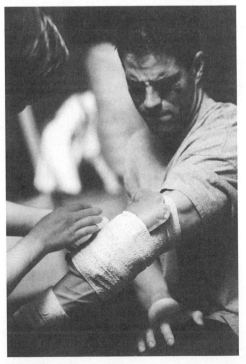

Compress

2. a psychological process of association of emotions with one word or thought. **3.** abnormal hardening of an organ or part.

condenser /kən dĕn′sər/ in dentistry, an instrument for packing material into a cavity.

condition /kən dĭsh′ən/ *n.* **1.** a state of being. **2.** a stimulus necessary for a certain response to occur. **3.** any of several methods of learning in behavioral psychology. *v.* **4.** to undergo gradual training.

conditioning /kən dĭsh′ə nĭng/ the process of controlling or influencing new responses in a person through gradual training.

condom /kŏn′dəm/ a sheath or cover for the penis or vagina used to prevent conception or transmission of infection during sexual intercourse.

conduction /kən dŭk′shən/ the transmission of energy from one object or part to another without significant movement of the objects.

conductive /kən dŭk′tĭv/ of or relating to conduction.

conductive hearing loss hearing loss caused by an obstruction or lesion in the ear.

conductivity /kŏn′dŭk tĭv′ĭ tē/ the measure of an object's ability to transmit energy through conduction.

conductor /kən dŭk′tər/ something that transmits something, such as a nerve fiber.

condyl- *combining form.* rounded, knob-like, condyle: *for example,* condyloid.

condyle /kŏn′dīl/ the rounded surface at the end of a bone.

condylectomy /kŏn′də lĕk′tə mē/ surgical removal of the condyle. [condyl + ectomy]

condyloid /kŏn′də loid′/ of or resembling a condyle. [condyl- + -oid]

condyloma /kŏn′də lō′mə/ (*pl.* **condylomas** or **condylomata** /kŏn′də lō′mə tə/) sexually transmitted viral wart-like growths in genital area. [condyl- + -oma]

cone /kōn/ **1.** a shape with a circular base that tapers to a point at the top. **2.** a type of photoreceptor cell in the eye for color and daytime vision. **3.** metallic device used to focus a beam of x-rays.

cones /konz/ one of the receptors in the retina of the eye responsible for light and color.

confabulation /kən făb′yə lā′shən/ making completely foolish and irrelevant responses to any question, often associated with chronic alcoholism.

confidentiality /kŏn′fĭ dĕn′shē ăl′ĭ tē/ privileged right of a individual that no information shared with health professionals will be disclosed without out permission.

confinement /kən fīn′mənt/ **1.** the act of confining. **2.** the period of labor and childbirth.

confluent /kŏn′floo ənt/ flowing together, as the lesions in a skin inflammation.

confusion /kən fyoo′zhən/ impairment in orientation or mental state.

congenital /kən jĕn′ĭ təl/ present at birth, such as a birth defect.

congenital anemia /ə nē′mē ə/ anemia present at birth.

congenital anomaly /ə nŏm′ə lē/ an abnormality present at birth.

congenital defect /dē′fĕkt, dĭ fĕkt′/ a birth defect.

congenital heart condition a malformation of the heart present at birth.

congenital hemolytic jaundice /hē′mə lĭt′ĭk jôn′dĭs/ a genetic birth defect causing accelerated destruction of red blood cells, characterized by anemia, yellowing of the skin, and enlargement of the spleen.

congenital malformation /măl′fôr mā′shən/ a physical defect present at birth.

congenital septal defect /sĕp′təl/ a birth defect of the atrial or ventricular septum, between the left and right sides of the heart.

congested /kən jĕs′tĭd/ full of congestion.

congestion /kən jĕs′chən/ the excessive accumulation of fluid in an organ or body part.

congestive heart failure (CHF) /kən jĕs′tĭv/ the inability of the heart to pump sufficient blood flow to the organs resulting in weakness, shortness of breath, and poor circulation.

coniosis /kō′nē ō′sĭs/ any condition caused by dust.

conization /kō′nə zā′shən/ surgical removal of a cone of tissue from the cervix, usually for dysplasia, a premalignant lesion found on a PAP smear.

conjoined twins /kən joind′/ identical twins who did not fully separate during fetal development, with a varying extent and location of attachment.

conjugate /kŏn′jə gĭt, -gāt′/ joined together in pairs.

conjunctiva /kŏn′jŭngk tī′və/ (*pl.* **conjunctivae** /kŏn′jŭngk tī′vē/) mucous membrane on surface of the eyeball and lining the eyelid.

conjunctival /kŏn′jŭngk tī′vəl/ of or relating to the conjunctiva.

conjunctivitis /kən jŭngk′tə vī′tĭs/ inflammation of the conjunctiva, commonly called pinkeye.

conjunctivoplasty /kən jŭngk′tə vō plăs′tē/ plastic surgery of the conjuctiva.

connective tissue a material derived from mesoderm that forms the support structure for tissues and organs.

connective tissue disease any of several diseases that attack connective tissue.

Conn('s) /kŏn(z)/ **syndrome** or **disease** excessive secretion of aldosterone, characterized by headaches, fatigue, frequent urination, and more, caused by a tumor on the adrenal gland.

consanguinity /kŏn′săng gwĭn′ĭ tē/ relationship by blood.

conscious /kŏn′shəs/ aware of one's existence, thoughts, sensations, and environment.

consciousness /kŏn′shəs nĭs/ the state of being aware of one's surroundings.

consensual /kən sĕn′shōō əl/ **1.** agreed to by both parties, as sexual relations. **2.** working together, as the movement of voluntary and involuntary actions of body parts.

constipation /kŏn′stə pā′shən/ infrequent and incomplete bowel movements.

constitution /kŏn′stĭ tōō′shən/ the physical makeup of the body, including its functions, metabolic processes, reactions to stimuli, and resistance to pathogens.

constriction /kən strĭk′shən/ **1.** a point of narrowing that reduces the flow through a channel. **2.** the act or process of compression or tightening.

constrictor /kən strĭk′tər/ something that constricts, such as a muscle that compresses a body part.

consultant /kən sŭl′tənt/ a doctor or consultant to whom one turns for expert advice.

consultation /kŏn′səl tā′shən/ a discussion between two or more health professionals regarding diagnosis, treatment, etc.

consumption /kən sŭmp′shən/ **1.** the act or process of using something up. **2.** an old term for tuberculosis.

contact /kŏn′tăkt/ **1.** a touching or coming near something likely to cause an allergy or disease. **2.** a person recently exposed to something.

contact allergy /ăl′ər jē/ an allergic reaction caused by direct contact with an allergen.

contact area point at which teeth on the same arch touch each other (mesial and distal), protecting the gums and stabilizing the dental arch.

contact dermatitis /dûr′mə tī′tĭs/ an inflamed itching rash caused by the contact of an allergen or persistent irritation to the skin.

contact eczema /ĕk′sə mə, ĭg zē′-/ a skin rash caused by exposure to an allergen or chemical, characterized by redness, itching, and burning.

contact healing an ancient form of healing by touching the head, shoulders, or waist with the hands or palms.

contact lens a small lens that fits over the cornea of the eye to correct vision.

contagion /kən tā′jən/ disease transmission by direct or indirect contact.

contagious /kən tā′jəs/ transmissible by direct or indirect contact.

contaminant /kən tăm′ə nənt/ an impurity or infectious agent.

contaminate /kən tăm′ə nāt′/ to introduce an impurity or infectious agent into a clean environment.

contamination /kən tăm′ə nā′shən/ **1.** the presence of an impurity or infectious agent, rendering an object or environment harmful or impure. **2.** the situation that arises when a group under observation or study for one condition is altered in a way that modifies the study.

continence /kŏn′tə nəns/ control over the discharge of urine and feces.

continuous ambulatory peritoneal dialysis (CAPD) /ăm′byə lə tôr′ē pĕr′ĭ tə nē′əl dī ăl′ə sĭs/ a form of continuous dialysis in which fluid is exchanged at regular intervals throughout the day.

continuous cycling peritoneal dialysis (CCPD) /sī′klĭng pĕr′ĭ tə nē′əl dī ăl′ə sĭs/ a form of dialysis using a machine to deliver a special solution through an abdominal catheter to remove waste materials by diffusion from capillaries lining the abdominal cavity, usually performed at night during sleep.

continuous passive motion machine a machine used to rehabilitate a limb after surgery, especially after total knee replacement or knee injury, by providing constant movement within a preset range.

continuous positive airway pressure (CPAP) a technique of respiratory therapy in which a machine delivers constant air pressure into the nasal passages or the lungs, improving impaired respiratory function, frequently used to relieve symptoms of sleep apnea.

contra- *prefix.* opposed, against.

contraception /kŏn′trə sĕp′shən/ **1.** prevention of impregnation. **2.** any device or medication used to prevent conception.

contraceptive /kŏn′trə sĕp′tĭv/ of or relating to an agent that prevents conception.

contract *v.* /kən trăkt′/ **1.** to shorten or reduce. **2.** to acquire by contagion or infection. *n.* /kŏn′trăkt/ **3.** explicit agreement of patient and psychotherapist to follow a defined plan to achieve a specific goal through therapy.

Contraceptive (Condoms)

contraction /kən trăk′shən/ **1.** the tightening or shortening of a muscle. **2.** a shrinkage or reduction in size. **3.** during birth, wavelike tightening of the muscles of the uterus as part of the process of expelling the fetus.

contracture /kən trăk′chər/ a permanent shortening of a muscle, causing distortion or deformity.

contraindicate /kŏn′trə ĭn′dĭ kāt′/ to advise against a treatment or procedure because of the presence of a condition or circumstance. [contra- + indicate]

contraindication /kŏn′trə ĭn dĭ kā′shən/ any condition or circumstance that makes a treatment or procedure inadvisable. [contra- + indication]

contralateral /kŏn′trə lăt′ər əl/ of or relating to the opposite side. [contra- + lateral]

contrast 1. *v.* /kən trăst′/ to show differences through comparison. **2.** *n.* /kŏn′trăst/ the difference between the image densities of two areas.

contrast medium /kŏn′trăst/ an opaque substance internally administered to increase the contrast between tissues to enhance x-ray examination.

control /kən trōl′/ *v.* **1.** to limit, regulate, correct, or restore. **2.** ongoing operations or procedures aimed at reducing disease. *n.* **3.** member of a group under study or experimentation who does not partake in the procedures affecting the active treatment group, to serve as a reference for comparison.

controlled substance a drug whose manufacture, sale, prescription, and storage are subject to the U.S. Federal Controlled Substance Act.

contusion /kən tōō′zhən/ any injury causing damage to blood vessels beneath unbroken skin; a bruise.

convalescence /kŏn′və lĕs′əns/ the period of or the process of returning to health after an illness.

convalescent /kŏn′və lĕs′ənt/ returning to health after an illness.

conventional medicine medicine as practiced by holder of M.D. and D.O. degrees.

conversion /kən vûr′zhən/ **1.** a change in nature, form, or function. **2.** a psychological defense mechanism in which mental anxiety manifests itself as a physical symptom. **3.** the change in bacteria that takes place when it is infected by a virus (phage).

conversion disorder a mental disorder in which psychological conflict manifests itself as physical symptoms.

convolution /kŏn′və lōō′shən/ a twisting or coiling of an organ.

convulsion /kən vŭl′shən/ a violent spasm or seizure.

convulsive /kən vŭl′sĭv/ having convulsions.

Cooley('s) anemia /kōō′lē(z) ə nē′mē ə/ a disorder in which there is insufficient production of normal hemoglobin, resulting in profound anemia. *Also called* thalassemia major.

Coomb('s) test /kōōm(z)/ a procedure that measures the presence of antibodies on the surface of red blood cells, "positive" in a variety of diseases.

coordination /kō ôr′də nā′shən/ the act of coordinating, as the movements of muscles or, in insurance, the coordinating of benefits.

copay /kō′pā′, -pā′/ short for copayment.

copayment /kō′pā′mənt, -pā′-/ a fixed fee paid by the subscriber of a health insurance plan at the time of an office visit or when filling of a prescription. [co- + payment]

COPD *abbreviation.* chronic obstructive pulmonary disease.

copper (Cu) a metallic element naturally occurring in many proteins.

coprolalia /kŏp′rə lā′lē ə/ a symptom of Tourette's syndrome including uncontrollable outbursts of obscene language.

coprolith /kŏp′rə lĭth/ a hard mass of feces obstructing the appendix or in a diverticulum. *Also called* stercolith.

coprophobia /kŏp′rə fō′bē ə/ an abnormal fear of defecation and feces.

copula /kŏp′yə lə/ a narrow part between two structures.

copulation /kŏp′yə lā′shən/ **1.** sexual intercourse. **2.** the temporary union of two cells for mutual fertilization.

CoQ10 /sē′ō′kyōō′tĕn′/ an antioxidant that protects cells from free radicals and helps in the production of the energy necessary for cell growth and maintenance; coenzyme Q10. *Also called* ubiquinone.

cor /kôr/ in anatomy, the heart.

cor-, core-, coreo- *combining form.* pupil: *for example,* corelysis, coreoplasty.

cord /kôrd/ a slender, flexible structure, such as the spinal cord.

cordectomy /kôr dĕk′tə mē/ surgical removal of all or a portion of a cord. [cord + -ectomy]

cordotomy /kôr dŏt′ə mē/ **1.** any operation of the spinal chord. **2.** a surgical procedure on the larynx to treat vocal paralysis.

corectopia /kôr′ĕk tō′pē ə/ abnormal location of the pupil not in the center of the iris. [cor- + ectopia]

corelysis /kôr′ə lī′sĭs, kô rĕl′ə sĭs/ a surgical procedure to detach adhesions between the lens capsule and the iris. [core- + -lysis]

coreoplasty /kôr′ē ə plăs′tē/ plastic surgery to correct abnormalities in the pupil. [coreo- + -plasty]

corium /kôr′ē əm/ (*pl.* **coria** /kôr′ē ə/)   the inner layer of skin containing blood vessels, lymph vessels, hair follicles, and sweat glands, and sebum. Also called dermis.

corn /kôrn/   a calloused area of skin on the foot, caused by friction and pressure. *Also called* clavus.

corne-, corneo- *combining form.* cornea: *for example,* corneal, corneoscleral.

cornea /kôr′nē ə/   the transparent tissue covering the eyeball; it transmits and focuses light into the eye.

corneal /kôr′nē əl/   of or relating to the cornea. [corne- + -al]

corneal abrasion /ə brā′zhən/   a scratch on the cornea.

corneal transplant /trăns′plănt′/   surgical replacement of a damaged cornea with a healthy one.

corneoscleral /kôr′nē ō sklêr′əl/   of or relating to the cornea and sclera. [corneo- + -scleral]

cornu /kôr′nōō, kôrn′yōō/   any hornlike structure, such as a bone protuberance.

corona /kə rō′nə/   in anatomy, a crownlike upper part, such as the top of the head.

coronal /kôr′ə nəl/   of or relating to the coronal plane.

coronal plane   a vertical plane parallel to the shoulders, running from head to foot, dividing the body into front and rear halves

coronal structure   the point at which the frontal and parietal bones of the skull meet.

coronary /kôr′ə nĕr′ē/   *adj.* **1.** resembling a crown. **2.** of or relating to blood vessels surrounding the heart. *n.* **3.** myocardial infarction; coronary occlusion.

coronary angiography /ăn′jē ŏg′rə fē/   the best test for evaluating and defining coronary artery disease, in which a contrast medium is injected through a catheter into each coronary artery, and clear x-ray images are produced.

coronary angioplasty /ăn′jē ə plăs′tē/   a procedure using a balloon-tipped catheter to expand a narrowing in a coronary artery.

coronary artery   one of several arteries branching from the aorta that supply blood to the heart muscle.

coronary artery bypass (surgery)   a surgical procedure in which a new blood vessel (vein or artery) is grafted onto the heart to bridge a blockage of an artery. *Also called* coronary bypass (surgery), coronary artery bypass graft, CABG.

coronary artery bypass graft (CABG)   a surgical procedure in which a new blood vessel (vein or artery) is grafted onto the heart to bridge a blockage of an artery.

coronary artery disease (CAD)   a disease in which plaque builds up in a coronary artery, impeding blood flow and often leading to myocardial infarction.

coronary artery occlusion /ə klōō′zhən/   partial or complete blockage in a coronary artery, caused by a blood clot, plaque buildup, or spasm, often resulting in a myocardial infarction. *Also called* coronary occlusion.

coronary bypass (surgery)   a surgical procedure in which a blood vessel is grafted onto the heart to replace a blocked artery. *Also called* coronary artery bypass (surgery), coronary artery bypass graft, CABG.

coronary care unit (CCU)   a section of the hospital used exclusively to care for patients with cardiovascular disease.

coronary insufficiency /ĭn′sə fĭsh′ən sē/   inadequate blood flow through one or more coronary arteries.

coronary occlusion /ə klōō′zhən/   partial or complete blockage in a coronary artery, caused by a blood clot, plaque buildup, or spasm. *Also called* coronary artery occlusion.

coronary stent /stĕnt/   a stent inserted into a coronary artery to keep it open after angioplasty.

coronary thrombosis /thrŏm bō′sĭs/   blocking of a coronary artery by a blood clot, causing insufficient blood flow to the heart, resulting in a myocardial infarction.

coronavirus /kə rō′nə vī′rəs/   any one of a group of RNA viruses responsible for many illnesses including the common cold.

corporeal /kôr pôr′ē əl/   pertaining to the body of an organ, or to the entire body.

corpse /kôrps/   a dead body.

corpus /kôr′pəs/ (*pl.* **corpora** /kôr pôr′ə)/   **1.** the body. **2.** the main part of an organ.

corpus callosum /kə lō′səm/   the band of nerve tissue that connects the two halves of the brain.

corpuscle /kôr′pŭs əl/   a cell in the body, such as a blood cell.

corpus luteum /lōō′tē əm/   a mass of cells that secrete progesterone, formed from an ovarian follicle after the release of a mature egg.

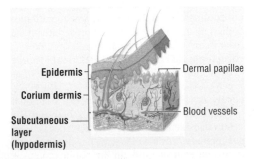

Epidermis — Dermal papillae

Corium dermis —

Subcutaneous layer (hypodermis) — Blood vessels

Corium

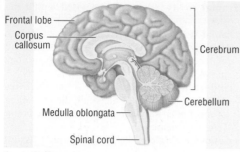

Frontal lobe
Corpus callosum
Cerebrum
Cerebellum
Medulla oblongata
Spinal cord

Corpus Callosum

corpus striatum /strī ā′təm/　either of two groups of nerve fibers in the lower portion of each cerebral hemisphere.

corpus uteri /yoo′tə rī′/　the womb.

corrective /kə rĕk′tĭv/　serving to correct, as lenses.

correspondence /(kôr′ĭ spŏn′dəns/　communication between two things, especially two points on the retina to produce a single image.

Corrigan('s) pulse /kôr′ĭ gən(z)/　a jerky carotid pulse marked by a strong beat followed by collapse, a sign of a malfunctioning aortic valve. *Also called* cannonball pulse, water-hammer pulse.

Corrigan('s) sign　a purple line appearing where the teeth meet the gums indicating copper poisoning.

corrosive /kə rō′sĭv/　causing destruction, especially through a chemical reaction.

corrugator /kôr′ĭ gā′tər/　a muscle that pulls the skin together causing wrinkles.

cortex /kôr′tĕks/　the outer portion of an organ, as the outer layer of the cerebral hemisphere of the brain.

cortic-, cortico-　*combining form.* cortex: *for example,* cortical, corticosteroid.

cortical /kôr′tĭ kəl/　of or relating to a cortex. [cortic- + -al]

cortical blindness　loss of vision resulting from injury to the visual cortex, caused by a traumatic brain damage.

cortical bone　the thin outer layer of bones, also called cortical substance.

corticoid /kôr′tĭ koid/　corticosteroid.

corticopontine /kôr′tĭ kō pŏn′tēn, -tĭn/　bridge connecting the cerebral cortex with the pons.

corticosteroid /kôr′tĭ kō stĕr′oid, -stêr′-/　any of the steroid hormones made by the outer layer of the adrenal gland. [cortico- + -steroid]

corticotropin /kôr′tĭ kō trō′pĭn/　a hormone made in the hypothalamus.

corticotropin-releasing hormone (CRH)　a hormone made by the hypothalamus that stimulates the release of corticotropin by the pituitary gland.

cortisol /kôr′tĭ sôl′/　the primary stress hormone, produced in the cortex of the adrenal gland.

cortisone /kôr′tĭ sōn′, -zōn′/　a naturally occurring hormone produced and secreted by the adrenal gland.

corynebacterium /kôr′ə nē băk têr′ē əm/　any of various bacteria, one of which causes diphtheria.

coryza /kə rī′zə/　a head cold.

cosmeceutical /kŏz′mə soo′tĭ kəl/　a cosmetic product that claims to have medicinal effects, such as an antiwrinkle cream.

cosmesis /kŏz mē′sĭs/　a concern in surgical operations for the appearance of the patient.

cosmetic /kŏz mĕt′ĭk/　**1.** *adj.* of or relating to physical appearance. **2.** *n.* an agent that improves the appearance of a feature, defect, or abnormality.

cosmetic surgery　surgery that improves appearance of a feature or corrects a defect or abnormality.

cost-, costo-　*combining form.* rib: *for example,* costalgia, costochondritis.

costa /kös′tə/ (*pl.* **costae** /kös′te/)　rib or rib-like part.

costal /kŏs′təl/　of, relating to, or near a rib. [cost- + -al]

costal cartilage /kär′tə lĭj/　the cartilage that connects the ribs to the sternum.

costalgia /kŏ stăl′jē ə, -jə/　pain in the ribs. [cost- + -algia]

costal margin　the bottom edge of the rib cage.

costectomy /kŏ stĕk′tə mē/　surgical removal of a rib. [cost- + -ectomy]

costochondral /kŏs′tō kŏn′drəl/　of or relating to the ribs and their cartilage.

costochondritis /kŏs′tō kŏn drī′tĭs/　inflammation of the ribs and their cartilage. *Also called* Tietze syndrome. [costo- + chrondritis]

costosternal /kŏs′tō stûr′nəl/　of or pertaining to the ribs and the sternum. [costo- + -sternal]

costotomy /kŏs tŏt′ə mē/　surgical division of a rib. [costo- + -tomy]

costovertebral /kŏs′tō vûr′tə brəl/　of or relating to the ribs and vertebra. [costo- + vertebral]

cough /kôf/　a rapid expulsion of air from the lungs to free the respiratory passages of irritating material.

cough suppressant /sə prĕs′ənt/　a medicine used to reduce coughing, especially an unproductive (dry) cough.

counter-　*prefix.* against: *for example,* countertraction.

counterpulsation /koun′tər pŭl sā′shən/　a technique used to reduce stress on the heart by setting an external machine to pump blood between heartbeats, providing constant, steady circulation.

countertraction /koun'tər trăk'shən/ traction used to oppose other traction to reduce a fracture.

coupling /kŭp'lĭng/ the joint between the last lumbar vertebra and the sacrum.

coverage /kŭv'ər ĭj/ inclusion as payable in an insurance plan.

Cowper('s) glands /kou'pər(z)/ tiny glands that secrete a component of seminal fluid into the urethra. *Also called* bulbourethral glands.

cowpox /kou'pŏks'/ a mild skin disease of cattle, characterized by a pustular rash, capable of immunizing humans against smallpox.

coxa /kŏk'sə/ (*pl.* **coxae** /kŏk'sē/) in anatomy, the hip.

coxsackievirus or **Coxsackie virus** /kŏk săk'ē vī'rəs/ any of various enteroviruses associated with several diseases, including meningitis, myocarditis, and pericarditis.

CP *abbreviation.* cerebral palsy.

CPAP *abbreviation.* continuous positive airway pressure.

CPC *abbreviation.* certified professional coder.

CPC-H *abbreviation.* certified profession coder, hospital.

CPD *abbreviation.* cephalopelvic disproportion.

CPK *abbreviation.* creatine phosphokinase.

CPR *abbreviation.* cardiopulmonary resuscitation.

CPT *abbreviation.* Current

Cr *abbreviation.* chromium.

crabs /krăbz/ slang for pubic lice, a parasitic insect that lives in the genital area of humans, typically spread through sexual contact.

crack /krăk/ cocaine that has been processed into a form that can be smoked.

cracked tooth syndrome severe toothache caused by a tooth fracture.

crackles /krăk'əlz/ short, rough inspiratory sounds produced by inflamed or fluid overloaded lungs, as heard through a stethoscope.

cradle cap an inflammation of the scalp in infants, characterized by redness and flaking skin, caused by overactive sebaceous glands.

cramp /krămp/ the sudden, often painful, contraction of a muscle caused by strain or chill.

crani-, cranio- *combining form.* skull: *for example,* craniectomy, craniofacial.

cranial /krā'nē əl/ of or relating to the skull. [crani- + -al]

cranial arteritis /är'tə rī'tĭs/ a serious disease characterized by inflammation of the temporal arteries of the brain. *Also called* temporal arteritis.

cranial bones the bones surrounding the brain, forming the cranium.

cranial cavity the space enclosed within the skull.

cranial nerve one of twelve pairs of nerves that travels directly from the brain through the skull, including the optic nerve and auditory nerve. See chart below.

craniectomy /krā'nē ĕk'tə mē/ surgical removal of a portion of the skull, the first stage of most neurosurgical operations on the brain. [crani- + -ectomy]

craniocele /krā'nē ə sēl'/ a congenital fissure in the skull through which the brain protrudes. [cranio- + -cele]

craniocerebral /krā'nē ō sə rē'brəl, -sĕr'ə brəl/ of or relating to the skull and the brain. [cranio- + cerebral]

craniocleidodysostosis /krā'nē ō klī'dō dĭs'ŏs tō'sĭs/ a birth defect of bone development characterized by underdeveloped collar bones, misshaped skull, and poor tooth formation.

Cranial Nerve	Major Functions
I Olfactory	smell
II Optic	vision
III Oculomotor	eyelid and eyeball movement
IV Trochlear	innervates superior oblique turns eye downward and laterally
V Trigeminal	chewing face and mouth touch and sensation of pain
VI Abducens	turns eye laterally
VII Facial	controls most facial expressions secretion of tears and saliva taste
VIII Vestibulo-cochlear (auditory)	hearing equilibrium
IX Glosso-pharyngeal	taste senses carotid blood pressure
X Vagus	senses aortic blood pressure slows heart rate stimulates digestive organs taste
XI Spinal Accessory	controls trapezius muscles to raise head and shoulders controls neck muscles that rotate and flex the head controls swallowing movements
XII Hypoglossal	controls tongue movements

Cranial Nerves

craniofacial /krā′nē ō fā′shəl/ of or relating to both the skull and the face. [cranio- + facial]

craniology /krā′nē ŏl′ə jē/ the scientific study of the skull. [cranio- + -logy]

craniomalacia /krā′nē ō mə lā′shə/ softening of the bones of the skull. [cranio- + -malacia]

craniometer /krā′nē ŏm′ĭ tər/ an instrument used to measure the skull. [cranio- + -meter]

craniometry /krā′nē ŏm′ĭ trē/ measurement of the bones of the skull. [cranio- + -metry]

craniopagus /krā′nē ŏp′ə gəs/ conjoined twins whose skulls are fused together.

craniopathy /krā′nē ŏp′ə thē/ any disease affecting the bones of the skull. [cranio- + -pathy]

cranioplasty /krā′nē ə plăs′tē/ surgical correction of skull defects. [cranio- + -plasty]

craniopuncture /krā′nē ə pŭngk′chər/ puncture of the skull for exploratory surgery. [cranio- + puncture]

craniosacral /krā′nē ō sā′krəl/ of or relating to both the cranium and sacrum. [cranio- + sacral].

cranioschisis /krā′nē ŏs′kə sĭs/ a birth defect in which the skull bones do not fuse together, often accompanied by defective brain development. [cranio- + -schisis]

craniosclerosis /krā′nē ō sklĭ rō′sĭs/ thickening of the skull. [cranio- + -sclerosis]

craniospinal /krā′nē ō spī′nəl/ of or relating to the skull and spinal column. [cranio- + spinal]

craniotomy /krā′nē ŏt′ə mē/ surgical incision of the skull. [cranio- + -tomy]

cranium /krā′nē əm/ (*pl.* **craniums** or **crania** /krā′nē ə/) the skull.

crash cart /krăsh′ kärt′/ informal term for a movable cart containing resuscitation equipment.

C-reactive protein (CRP) a plasma protein that increases in concentration in the presence of inflammation.

cream /krēm/ a semisolid pharmaceutical preparation meant for topical use.

crease /krēs/ a line or mark made by folding as of the skin.

creatine /krē′ə tēn′, -tĭn/ an organic acid found in muscle tissue that supplies energy for muscle contraction.

creatine kinase (CK) /kī′nās/ an enzyme found in skeletal tissue and heart muscle; its presence indicates that a myocardial infarction has recently taken place. *Also called* creatine phospohokinase.

creatine phosphokinase (CPK) /fŏs′fō kī′nās/ creatine kinase.

creatinine /krē ăt′ə nēn′, -nĭn/ a waste molecule byproduct of the metabolism of creatine.

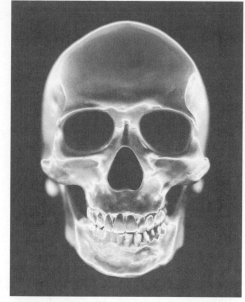

Cranium (in X-Ray)

creatinine clearance test a test used to determine the quality of kidney function by measuring how rapidly creatine is filtered out of the blood by the kidneys and excreted in urine.

creatinuria /krē ăt′ə nŏŏr′ē ə/ an increase in the amount of creatine in the urine.

crena /krē′nə/ (*pl.* **crenae** /krē′nē/) any of the opposing notches in cranial sutures.

crenated /krē′nā tĭd/ having a margin with small rounded projections.

crepitation /krĕp′ĭ tā′shən/ a crackling sound as produced by rubbing two irregular surfaces together, such as cartilage, fractured bone, or hair. *Also called* crepitus.

crepitus /krĕp′ĭ təs/ **1.** crepitation. **2.** a noisy discharge of gas from the intestines.

crest /krĕst/ a ridge of bone.

CREST syndrome /krĕst/ an acronym for calcinosis, Raynaud's phenomenon, esophagus, sclerodactyly, telangiectasias; a disease of the connective tissue characterized by the formation of scar tissue under the skin and sometimes in organs.

cretin /krē′tən/ a person afflicted with cretinism.

cretinism /krē′tə nĭz′əm/ congenital deficiency of the thyroid hormone resulting in dwarfed stature, mental retardation, dystrophy of the bones, and low basal metabolism.

Creutzfeldt-Jakob('s) disease /kroits′fĕlt yä′ kəb(z)/ (**CJD**) a rare and fatal brain disorder marked by mental degeneration, blindness, muscle spasms, dementia, and eventually paralysis and coma, for which there is no treatment; caused by a viral-like particle called a prion, and perhaps the same as or similar to the agent causing mad cow disease.

CRF *abbreviation.* corticotropin-releasing factor.

CRH *abbreviation.* corticotropin-releasing horomone.

crib death the sudden unexplained death of an infant with no known illness while sleeping. *Also called* sudden infant death syndrome (SIDS).

cricoid /krī′koid/ **1.** ring-shaped. **2.** denoting the small ring of cartilage of the lower larynx.

cricothyroid /krī′kō thī′roid/ of or relating to the cricoid and thyroid cartilages, two segments of the trachea in the neck.

cricothyrotomy /krī′kō thī rŏt′ə mē/ incision through the skin and the cricothyroid membrane to provide emergency relief of an upper respiratory obstruction.

-crine *suffix.* secreting: *for example,* endocrine, apocrine.

cripple /krĭp′əl/ an informal and often offensive term for person who is partially disabled.

crippled /krĭp′əld/ disabled or impaired.

crisis /krī′sĭs/ a sudden downturn in the course of an illness or condition.

critical care intensive care of patients in life-threatening conditions and in need constant monitoring.

critical incident stress management crisis counseling for people who have been exposed to a traumatic event.

CRNA *abbreviation.* Certified Registered Nurse Anesthetist.

Crohn('s) disease /krōn(z)/ an inflammatory disease of the digestive system characterized by intestinal ulcers, abdominal pain, diarrhea, vomiting, fever, and weight loss. *Also called* granulomatous colitis, regional enteritis.

crossbite /krôs′bīt′/ reverse position of one or more teeth.

cross-dressing /krôs′ drĕs′ĭng/ to dress in clothing customarily worn by the opposite sex.

crossed eyes a form of strabismus in which the eyes deviate inwards.

cross-eye an eye that deviates inward.

cross-matching a test of compatibility between a donor's and recipient's blood, by mixing a sample of each.

crossover study a type of clinical study in which the subjects serve as their own control by receiving each treatment in a random order.

cross section a two-dimensional surface formed by cutting a slice (actually or by imaging) through a structure.

Cross-Eyes

cross-species transplantation /trăns′plăn tā′ shən/ transplant of an organ or tissue from one species to a different species.

crotch /krŏch/ slang term for the perineal area.

croup /kro͞op/ a viral or bacterial infection of the upper respiratory tract, occurring most often in young children.

crown /kroun/ **1.** the portion of the tooth that is covered with enamel. **2.** an artificial substitute for the natural crown of the tooth. **3.** any structure with a crownlike shape.

crowning /krou′nĭng/ **1.** dental procedure in which the natural crown of the tooth is replaced with an artificial substance, such as gold, porcelain, or stainless steel. **2.** a stage in childbirth in which the largest part of the fetal head has emerged from the vaginal orifice.

CRP *abbreviation.* cAMP receptor protein; C-reactive protein.

cruciate /kro͞o′shē ĭt/ having a crosslike shape.

cruciate ligaments /lĭg′ə mənts/ the two large ligaments known as anterior and posterior crisscrossing in the knee joint providing stability.

crus /kro͞os/ (*pl.* **crura** /kro͞or′ə/) in anatomy, any structure similar to a leg.

crust /krŭst/ a hard outer layer or covering, such as a scab.

crutch /krŭch/ a device used to assist in walking.

crux /krŭks/ (*pl.* **cruxes** or **cruces** /kro͞o′sēz/) a junction or crossing.

cryo- *combining form.* cold: *for example,* cryogenic.

cryocardioplegia /krī′ō kär′dē ō plē′jē ə, -jə/ paralysis of the heart due to exposure to extreme cold. [cryo- + -cardio- + -plegia]

cryocautery /krī′ō kô′tə rē/ any extremely cold substance or instrument capable of destroying tissue on contact by freezing. [cryo- + cautery]

cryogenic /krī′ō jĕn′ĭk/ having or relating to extremely low temperatures. [cryo- + -genic]

cryoglobulin /krī′ō glŏb′yə lĭn/ any of various abnormal globulins that precipitate or crystallize from plasma when cooled. [cryo- + globulin]

cryoglobulinemia /krī′ō glŏb′yə lĭ nē′mē ə/ the presence of high quantities of cryoglobulin in blood plasma. [cryo- + globulin + -emia]

cryolysis /krī ŏl′ə sĭs/ destruction by cold. [cryo- + -lysis]

cryopexy /krī′ə pĕk′sē/ surgical reattachment of the sensory retina to the pigment epithelium and choroid by applying a freezing probe to the sclera. [cryo- + -pexy]

cryopreservation /krī′ō prĕz′ər vā′shən/ the process of storing tissues at very low temperatures to preserve their viability. [cryo- + preservation]

cryoprobe /krī′ə prōb′/ an instrument used in cryosurgery capable of applying extremely low temperature to a selected area. [cryo- + probe]

cryoprotectant /krī′ō prə tĕk′tənt/ a chemical used in cryopreservation that protects the tissue from freeze damage. [cryo- + protectant]

cryostat /krī′ə stăt′/ a chamber used in cryopreservation that holds frozen tissue samples and maintains the temperature. [cryo- + -stat]

cryosurgery /krī′ō sûr′jə rē/ an operation using freezing temperature in the form of carbon dioxide or liquid nitrogen to destroy tissue. [cryo- + surgery]

cryotherapy /krī′ō thĕr′ə pē/ the use of cold temperatures to treat injury or disease. [cryo- + therapy]

crypt /kript/ a small recess or depression or cavity.

crypt-, crypto- *combining form.* hidden or obscure: *for example,* cryptitis, crytococcus.

cryptic /krĭp′tĭk/ hidden or concealed.

cryptitis /krĭp tī′tĭs/ inflammation of a follicle or of a tubular structure such as the rectum. [crypt- + -itis]

cryptococcus /krĭp′tə kŏk′əs/ any of several yeast-like fungi. [crypto- + -coccus]

cryptography /krĭp tŏg′rə fē/ encoding or decoding of a secret message, such as genetic decoding of DNA. [crypto- + -graphy]

cryptolith /krĭp′tə lĭth/ a hidden concretion as in a follicle. [crypto- + -lith]

cryptorchidism /krĭp tôr′kĭ dĭz′əm/ or **cryptorchism** /krĭp tôr′kĭz əm/ failure of one or both of the testes to descend into the scrotum. *Also called* undescended testicle.

cryptosporidiosis /krĭp tō spôr′ĭ dī ō′sĭs/ a parasitic infection of the intestines causing diarrhea.

cryptosporidium /krĭp′tō spô rĭd′ē əm/ the microscopic parasite that causes cryptosporidiosis.

C/S *abbreviation.* C-section.

C-section /sē′ sĕk′shən/ short for cesarean section (C/S), a surgical extraction of the fetus from the uterus.

CSF *abbreviation.* cerebrospinal fluid.

CSF *abbreviation.* colony-stimulating factor.

CT *abbreviation.* computed tomography.

CT cell short for cytotoxic T-lymphocyte, a type of T-cell capable of seeking out and destroying virus infected cells.

CTS *abbreviation.* carpal tunnel syndrome.

CT scan or **CAT scan** short for computerized (axial) tomography scan, an x-ray technique using several x-ray beams in different positions and computer processing, to produce cross-sectional images of the body.

Cu *abbreviation.* cooper.

cubic centimeter (cc) /sĕn′tə mē′tər/ one thousandth of a liter; one milliliter.

cubital /kyoo′bĭ təl/ of or relating to the elbow or the ulna.

cubital tunnel the opening formed by the meeting of the two heads of the forearm muscles, through which the ulnar nerve passes at the elbow and enters the forearm.

cubital tunnel syndrome compression of the ulner nerve in the cubital tunnel, causing pain and numbness in the forearm and hand.

cubitus /kyoo′bĭ təs/ elbow; ulna.

cubitus valgus /văl′gəs/ a deformity of the elbow causing deviation of the extended forearm away from the center of the body.

cubitus varus /văr′əs/ a deformity of the elbow causing deviation of the extended forearm inwards toward the center of the body.

cuboid bone /kyoo′boid/ the cube-shaped bone on the outer side of the instep.

cuff /kŭf/ the inflatable band used with a sphygmanometer to measure blood pressure.

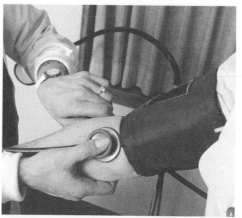

Cuff (in Sphymanometer)

culdo- *combining form.* pouch: *for example,* culdoscope.

culdocentesis /kŭl'dō sĕn tē'sĭs/ withdrawal of fluid through a puncture of the vaginal wall. [culdo- + -centesis]

culdoplasty /kŭl'də plăs'tē/ plastic surgery on the vagina. [culdo- + -plasty]

culdoscope /kŭl'də skōp'/ endoscopic instrument used in culdoscopy. [culdo- + -scope]

culdoscopy /kŭl dŏs'kə pē/ visual examination of a woman's pelvic organs by the insertion of a culdoscope through the vaginal wall. [culdo- + -scopy]

culture /kŭl'chər/ **1.** reproduction of cells or microorganisms in a growth media. **2.** a mass of microorganisms in a growth media. **3.** the beliefs, customs, and social behavior of a particular group of people.

cuneiform /kyoō nē'ə fôrm'/ having a triangular or wedge shape; used to describe the three wedge-shaped bones of the ankle.

cunnilingus /kŭn'ə lĭng'gəs/ oral stimulation of the clitoris or vulva.

cup /kŭp/ to treat by cupping.

cupping /kŭp'ĭng/ formation of a cup-shaped hollow or depression.

curable /kyoōr'ə bəl/ capable of being healed and made well.

curative /kyoōr'ə tĭv/ healing or restoring to health.

cure /kyoōr/ *v.* **1.** to heal and make well. *n.* **2.** a method of treatment that restores and heals. **3.** hardening of a substance over time, or by applying heat, light or chemical agents.

curettage /kyoōr'ĭ täzh'/ the excavation of growths in a body cavity such as the uterus, by scraping. *Also called* curettement.

curette /kyoō rĕt'/ an instrument used for curettage, shaped like a loop or ring attached to a rod-shaped handle.

curettement /kyoō rĕt'mənt/ curettage.

curing /kyoōr'ĭng/ the process of hardening of materials.

Current Procedural Terminology (CPT) the list of billing codes maintained by the American Medical Association.

curvature /kûr'və chər/ a bending or flexure, often abnormal, as of the spine.

Cushing('s) disease /koōsh'ĭng(z)/ a form of Cushing's syndrome caused by excessive secretion of cortisol hormone by the pituitary gland.

Cushing('s) syndrome a disorder caused by an increased production of corticosteroids from a tumor of the adrenal cortex or of the pituitary gland, characterized by obesity, fatigue, and weakening of the muscles.

-cusis *suffix.* hearing; *for example,* paracusis.

cusp /kŭsp/ **1.** a conic ridge on a tooth. **2.** a leaflet of a cardiac valve.

cuspid /kŭs'pĭd/ a pointed tooth between the incisors and the bicuspids, in both the upper and lower jaw. Also *called* canine tooth.

custodial care /kŭ stō'dē əl/ nonskilled long-term personal care to assist with the activities of daily living.

cut /kŭt/ **1.** *n.* an area of severed skin. **2.** *v.* to make an incision or to sever.

cutaneous /kyoō tā'nē əs/ of or relating to the skin.

cutdown /kŭt'doun'/ dissection of a vein for insertion of a catheter to administer intravenous fluids or medication.

cuticle /kyoō'tĭ kəl/ **1.** a thin outer layer. **2.** a hardened noncellular layer covering the epidermis. **3.** a thin layer of tissue covering part of a nail. *Also called* eponychium, perionychium.

cutis /kyoō'tĭs/ skin.

CVA *abbreviation.* cerebrovascular attack; cerebrovascular accident.

CVC *abbreviation.* central venous catheter.

CVD *abbreviation.* cardiovascular disease.

CVP *abbreviation.* central venous pressure.

CXR *abbreviation.* chest x-ray.

cyan- *combining form.* blue: *for example,* cyanosis.

cyanopsia /sī'ə nŏp'sē ə/ condition in which all objects appear blue; may temporarily occur after cataract surgery. [cyan- + -opsia]

cyanosis /sī'ə nō'sĭs/ a condition in which the skin and mucous membranes take on a blue or purple color due to deficient oxygen in the blood. [cyan- + -osis]

cyanotic /sī'ə not' ĭk/ of or relating to cyanosis; having a bluish discoloration. [cyan- + -otic]

cycl-, cyclo- *combining form.* circle; cycle; ciliary body: *for example,* cyclectomy, cycloplegia.

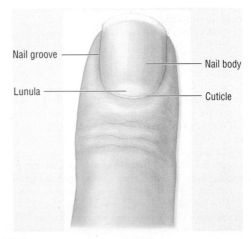

Nail groove

Nail body

Lunula

Cuticle

Cuticle

cycle /sī′kəl/ a series of events or stages that recur, such as the menstrual cycle.

cyclectomy /sī klĕk′tə mē/ surgical removal of a portion of the muscle surrounding the lens of the eye. [cycl- + -ectomy]

cyclodialysis /sī′klō dī ăl′ə sĭs/ surgical opening of a passage between the anterior chamber and the suprachoroidal space in order to reduce pressure within the eye in glaucoma. [cyclo- + dialysis]

cyclopia /sī klō′pē ə/ a rare birth defect in which both eye sockets are fused together. [cycl- + -opia]

cycloplegia /sī′klə plē′jē ə, -jə/ paralysis of the ciliary muscle of the eye, usually from drops used to facilitate examination of the eye. [cyclo- + -plegia]

cycloplegic /sī′klə plē′jĭk/ **1.** adj. of or relating to cycloplegia. **2.** n. a drug that paralyzes the ciliary muscle. [cyclo- + -plegic]

cyclothymia /sī′klə thī′mē ə/ a form of bipolar disorder in which mood swings are less drastic. [cyclo- + -thymia]

cyclothymic disorder /sī′klə thī′mĭk/ a mental disorder characterized by mood swings from depression to elation. [cyclo- + -thymic]

cyclotropia /sī′klə trō′pē ə/ a disorder of the eye in which one eye rolls outward or inward on its visual axis. [cyclo- + -tropia]

cylindroma /sĭl′ĭn drō′mə/ a benign tumor of skin glands, arising as a nodule on the scalp, face, or limbs.

cylindruria /sĭl′ĭn drōōr′ē ə/ the presence of renal cylinders or casts in the urine.

cyst-, cysti-, cysto- combining form. **1.** the bladder: for example, cystitis. **2.** cyst: for example, cystadenoma.

cyst /sĭst/ an abnormal sac-like structure containing fluid, gas, or a semisolid material.

cystadenocarcinoma /sī stăd′ə nō kär′sə nō′mə/ a malignant tumor derived from glandular tissue, in which secretions are retained and accumulate in cysts. [cyst- + adenocarcinoma]

cystadenoma /sī stăd′ə nō′mə/ (pl. **cystadenomas** or **cystadenomata** /sī stăd′ə nō′mə tə/) a low-grade tumor derived from glandular tissue, in which secretions are retained and accumulate in cysts. [cyst- + adenoma]

cystectomy /sī stĕk′tə mē/ **1.** surgical removal of the bladder. **2.** surgical removal of the gallbladder. **3.** surgical removal of a cyst. [cyst- + -ectomy]

cysteine /sĭs′tē ēn′, -ĭn/ an amino acid found in most proteins.

cystic /sĭs′tĭk/ of or relating to the bladder, gallbladder, or a cyst. [cyst- + -ic]

cystic duct the gallbladder duct that joins the hepatic duct, to form the common bile duct.

cysticercosis /sĭs′tĭ sər kō′sĭs/ infection caused by ingestion of pig tapeworm larvae, which can cause the formation of cysts in the brain, muscles, eyes.

cystic fibrosis /fī brō′sĭs/ one of the most common genetic diseases with no cure, in which the lungs, intestines, and pancreas become clogged with thick mucus, caused by abnormal secretions from the exocrine glands.

cystiform /sĭs′tə fôrm′/ cystoid. [cysti- + -form]

cystine /sĭs′tēn, -tĭn/ a white crystalline amino acid found in many proteins, especially keratin, and often found in kidney stones.

cystine kidney stones crystallized cystine in the kidneys due to cystinuria.

cystinuria /sĭs′tĭ nōōr′ē ə/ a genetic disorder characterized by excessive urinary excretion of the amino acids cystine, lysine, arginine, and ornithine.

cystitis /sī stī′tĭs/ inflammation of the bladder. [cyst- + -itis]

cysto- See cyst-.

cystocele /sĭs′tə sēl′/ hernia of the bladder through the vaginal wall. Also called vesicocele. [cysto- + -cele]

cystogram /sĭs′tə grăm′/ an x-ray image of the bladder using cystography. [cysto- + -gram]

cystography /sī stŏg′rə fē/ x-ray of the bladder injected with a contrast medium. [cysto- + -graphy]

cystolith /sĭs′tə lĭth/ a hard mass of mineral salts in the urinary tract. Also called urinary calculus. [cysto- + -lith]

cystometer /sī stŏm′ĭ tər/ a device used to measure bladder capacity, sensation, pressure, and residual urine. [cysto- + -meter]

cystometrography /sĭs′tō mə trŏg′rə fē/ the measuring of bladder function using a cystometer. [cysto- + metro- + -graphy]

cystopexy /sĭs′tə pĕk′sē/ surgical attachment of the bladder or gallbladder to the abdominal wall. [cysto- + -pexy]

cystoplasty /sĭs′tə plăs′tē/ reconstructive surgery of the bladder. [cysto- + -plasty]

cystoplegia /sĭs′tə plē′jɔ, -jē ə/ paralysis of the bladder. [cysto- + -plegia]

cystopyelography /sĭs′tō pī′ə lŏg′rə fē/ x-ray images of the bladder, ureter, and renal pelvis after injection with a contrast medium. [cysto- + pyelo- + -graphy]

cystorrhaphy /sī stôr′ə fē/ suture of a wound or defect in the bladder. [cysto- + -rrhaphy]

cystorrhea /sĭs′tə rē′ə/ unusual discharge from the bladder. [cysto- + -rrhea]

cystoscope /sĭs′tə skōp′/ a thin tubular instrument with a light used to examine the interior of the bladder. [cysto- + -scope]

cystoscopic /sĭs'tə skŏp'ĭk/ of or relating to a cystoscope.

cystoscopy /sĭ stŏs'kə pē/ examination of the bladder using a cystoscope. [cysto- + -scopy]

cystostomy /sĭ stŏs'tə mē/ surgical creation of a hole in the bladder, to drain urine while allowing surgery on the urethra to heal. [cysto- + -stomy]

cystotomy /sĭ stŏt'tə mē/ surgical incision into the bladder. *Also called* vesicotomy.

cystoureteritis /sĭs'tō yŏŏ rē'tə rī'tĭs/ inflammation of the bladder and ureters. [cysto- + ureteritis]

cystoureterogram /sĭs'tō yŏŏ rē'tər ə grăm'/ radiographic image produced by cystoureterography. [cysto- + uretero- + -gram]

cystoureterography /sis'tō yŏŏ rē'tə rŏg'rə fē/ radiographic imaging of the bladder and ureters. [cysto- + uretero- + -graphy]

cystourethrogram /sĭs'tō yŏŏ rē'thrə grăm'/ x-ray image of the bladder and urethra made after a contrast medium has been injected. [cysto- + urethro- + -gram]

cystourethroscopy /sĭs'tō yŏŏr'ə thrŏs'kə pē/ examination of the bladder and urethra using both a cystoscope and a urethroscope. [cysto- + urethro- + -scopy]

cyt-, cyto- *combining form.* a cell: *for example,* cytosis, cytology.

-cyte *suffix.* a cell: *for example,* blastocyte.

cytodiagnosis /sī'tō dī'əg nō'sĭs/ diagnosis by microscopic viewing of cells. [cyto- + diagnosis]

cytogenesis /sī'tō jĕn'ə sĭs/ the origin and development of cells. [cyto- + genesis]

cytogenetics /sī'tō jə nĕt'ĭks/ the branch of genetics focusing on the study of the structure and function of the cell, particularly the chromosome. [cyto- + genetics]

cytogenic /sī'tə jĕn'ĭk/ of or relating to cytogenetics. [cyto- + -genic]

cytoid /sī'toid/ resembling a cell. [cyt- + -oid]

cytokine /sī'tə kīn'/ any of several proteins that regulate immune response, secreted by cells particularly of the immune system.

cytokinesis /sī'tō kĭ nē'sĭs/ the division of the cytoplasm of a cell following the division of its nucleus. [cyto- + -kinesis]

cytologic /sī'tə lŏj'ĭk/ of or relating to cytology. [cyto- + -logic]

cytology /sī tŏl'ə jē/ the science and study of the cell. [cyto- + -logy]

cytolysis /sī tŏl'ə sĭs/ the disintegration of a cell. [cyto- + -lysis]

cytolytic /sī'tə lĭt'ĭk/ destructive of cells. [cyto- + -lytic]

cytomegalovirus (CMV) /sī'tō mĕg'ə lō vī'rəs/ any of several herpes viruses that attack and

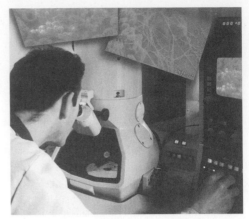
Cytopathologist

enlarge epithelial cells and can cause birth defects. [cyto- + megalo- + virus]

cytometer /sī tŏm'ĭ tər/ a device used to count and measure cells, especially blood cells. [cyto- + -meter]

cytometry /sī tŏm'ĭ trē/ the counting of cells, especially blood cells, using a cytometer. [cyto- + -metry]

cytopathologist /sī'tō pə thŏl'ə jĭst/ specialist trained in cytopathology. [cyto- + pathologist]

cytopathology /sī'tō pə thŏl'ə jē/ the study of how disease changes individual cells. [cyto- + pathology]

cytopathy /sī tŏp'ə thē/ cell disease. [cyto- + -pathy]

cytophagy /sī tŏf'ə jē/ the ingestion of cells by phagocytes in the blood. [cyto- + -phagy]

cytoplasm /sī'tə plăz'əm/ the protoplasm outside the nucleus of a cell. [cyto- + -plasm]

cytosine (C) /sī'tə sēn'/ one of the four bases in DNA and RNA, where it pairs with guanine.

cytosis /sī tō'sĭs/ a condition in which there is more than the usual number of cells. [cyt- + -osis]

cytoskeleton /sī'tō skĕl'ĭ tən/ the internal framework of a cell. [cyto- + skeleton]

cytostasis /sī stŏs'tə sĭs, sī'tō stā'sĭs/ the arrest of cellular movement, growth, and reproduction. [cyto- + -stasis]

cytotechnologist /sī'tō tĕk nŏl'ə jĭst/ a person specializing in medical examination and identification of cellular abnormalities. [cyto- + technologist]

cytotoxic /sī'tō tŏk'sĭk/ of or relating to any agent or process that is destructive or toxic to cells. [cyto- + toxic]

cytotoxin /sī'tō tŏk'sĭn/ any substance that is toxic to cells. [cyto- + toxin]

D

D (drug caution code) found on the label of some medication, indicating that it may cause drowsiness.

dacryo- *combining form.* tear or tears; lacrymal sac or duct: *for example*, dacryocyst.

dacryoadenitis /dăk′rē ō ăd′ə nī′tĭs/ inflammation of the tear gland. [dacryo- + adenitis]

dacryocyst /dăk′rē ə sĭst/ the upper portion of the nasolacrimal duct, into which tears pass before reaching the nasal cavity. *Also called* lacrimal sac. [dacryo- + -cyst]

dacryocyst-, dacryocysto- *combining form.* of or involving the lacrimal sac: *for example*, dacryocystitis.

dacryocystectomy /dăk′rē ō sĭ stĕk′tə mē/ surgical removal of the lacrimal sac. [dacryocyst- + -ectomy]

dacryocystitis /dăk′rē ō sĭ stī′tĭs/ inflammation of the lacrimal sac. [dacryocyst- + -itis]

dacryocystocele /dăk′rē ō sĭs′tə sēl′/ a weakness in the wall of the lacrimal sac. [dacryocysto- + -cele]

dacryocystorhinostomy /dăk′rē ō sĭs′tō rī nŏs′tə mē/ the surgical creation of an opening between the lacrimal sac and the nasal lining to relieve chronic tearing. [dacryocysto- + rhino- + -stomy]

dacryocystotome /dăk′rē ō sĭs′tə tōm′/ an instrument for cutting into the lacrimal sac. [dacryocysto- + -tome]

dacryocystotomy /dăk′rē ō sĭ stŏt′ə mē/ a surgical incision into the lacrimal sac. [dacryocysto- + -tomy]

dacryohemorrhea /dăk′rē ō hĕm′ə rē′ə/ discharge of tears with blood. [dacryo- + hemo- + -rrhea]

dacryolith /dăk′rə lĭth/ a calculus (stone) in the lacrimal sac or duct. [dacryo- + -lith]

dacryopyorrhea /dăk′rē ō pī′ə rē′ə/ a discharge of tears that contain white blood cells. [dacryo- + pyorrhea]

dacryorrhea /dăk′rē ə rē′ə/ excessive tears. [dacryo- + -rrhea]

dacryostenosis /dăk′rē ō stĭ nō′sĭs/ narrowing of the tear duct [dacryo- + -stenosis]

dactyl-, dactylo- *combining form.* fingers; toes: *for example*, dactyledema, dactylospasm.

dactyledema /dăk′tĭl ĭ dē′mə/ swelling of the fingers or toes. [dactyl- + edema]

dactylitis /dăk′tə lī′tĭs/ inflammation of a finger or toe. [dactyl- + -itis]

dactylomegaly /dăk′tə lō mĕg′ə lē/ an abnormal enlargement of the fingers or toes. *Also called* macrodactylia. [dactylo- + -megaly]

dactylospasm /dăk′tə lə spăz′əm/ the cramping of a finger or toe. [dactylo- + spasm]

-dactyly *suffix.* the condition of have a specified kind or number of fingers or toes: *for example*, syndactyly.

D & C, D and C *abbreviation.* dilation and curettage.

D & E *abbreviation.* dilation and evacuation.

dander /dăn′dər/ thin plates of surface skin shed by certain animals, to which some people are allergic.

dandruff /dăn′drəf/ a mild skin condition of the scalp, in which white flakes of skin are shed.

date of service the date that a patient receives medical care.

date rape forcible oral, anal, or vaginal intercourse, by an acquaintance with whom one is on a date.

dB *abbreviation.* decibel.

DC *abbreviation.* **1.** also **d.c.** direct current. **2.** Doctor of Chiropractic.

DDS *abbreviation.* **1.** Doctor of Dental Surgery. **2.** Denver Developmental Screening Test.

de- *prefix.* away from: *for example*, decompression.

dead /dĕd/ having no pulse or respirations; no longer alive.

dead-man switch a switch on the dental x-ray machine so constructed that a circuit-closing contact can only be maintained by continuous pressure by the operator.

dead on arrival (DOA) having no signs of life upon arrival at the hospital.

deaf /dĕf/ having diminished hearing or being unable to hear.

deafness /dĕf′nĭs/ diminished or absent sense of hearing.

death /dĕth/ the point at which heart activity and respirations cease, or the point when the EEG (electroencephalogram) has shown no activity for a period of 24 or more hours. *Also called* brain death.

Deciduous Teeth

death rate the rate of death for a particular age group, population, location, or condition, usually measured per 1000 people.

debilitated /dĭ bĭl′ĭ tā′tĭd/ weakened, as from an illness or condition.

debride /dĭ brēd′/ to remove dead and dying tissue from a wound or burn, to help the healing process.

debridement /dĭ brēd′mənt/ removal of dead and dying tissue from a wound or burn to help the healing process.

debulk /dē bŭlk′/ to remove a section of a large tumor that cannot be completely removed by surgery to make the remaining tumor more vulnerable to or accessible to later radioactive or chemical treatments.

decalcification /dē kăl′sə fĭ kā′shən/ removal or loss of calcium, as from bones, in conditions such as osteoporosis.

decapitation /dĭ kăp′ĭ tā′shən/ the removal of the head.

decay /dĭ kā′/ **1.** *v.* to break down, disintegrate, or decompose, usually caused by bacteria. **2.** *n.* the product of such decomposition, as tooth decay.

deceased /dĭ sēst′/ no longer alive; dead.

decibel (Db) /dĕs′ə bĕl′/ a measure of the intensity of sound.

deciduous teeth /dĭ sĭj′o͞o əs/ the first set of teeth that begins to erupt through the gums in infants at around 6 months old. *Also called* primary teeth, baby teeth.

deciliter (dL) /dĕs′ə lē′tər/ a tenth of a liter.

decompensate /dē kŏm′pən sāt′/ to fail to maintain adequate blood circulation resulting in labored breathing and other severe symptoms.

decompression /dē′kəm prĕsh′ən/ removal of pressure. [de- + compression]

decompression sickness sometimes fatal bubbling of dissolved nitrogen in the blood when the atmospheric pressure decreases too rapidly, as when coming to the surface rapidly after deep-sea diving while breathing compressed air.

decongestant /dē′kən jĕs′tənt/ agent that reduces congestion.

decortication /dē kôr′tĭ kā′shən/ removal of all or part of the outer surface of an organ.

decubitus /dĭ kyo͞o′bĭ təs/ or **decubitus ulcer** /ŭl′sər/ a skin lesion that results from the pressure of lying in the same position for a long time, especially on a bony prominence. *Also called* bedsore, pressure sore.

decussation /dē′kŭ sā′shən/ in anatomy, any x-shaped crossing, especially of bands of nerve fibers across the spinal cord.

deductible /dĭ dŭk′tə bəl/ the amount of payment for health care that is a patient's responsibility before the insurance pays.

deep tissue massage /tĭsh′o͞o mə säzh′/ a massage therapy technique that focuses on releasing muscle tension in deep muscle tissue by deep pressure or friction applied across the grain of muscles.

deep vein thrombosis (DVT) /thrŏm bō′sĭs/ the forming of thrombi (blood clots) in the deep veins, especially of the legs, usually related to a period of inactivity but on very rare occasion a signal of an undiagnosed cancer.

def, DEF *abbreviation.* decayed, extracted, and filled, said of teeth.

defecation /dĕf′ĭ kā′shən/ the discharge of feces from the rectum.

defect /dē′fĕkt/ any abnormality or malformation, especially one present at birth.

defense mechanism an unconscious psychological process, such as denial, used means of coping with situations, while not necessarily dealing with an underlying problem.

defensive /dĭ fĕn′sĭv/ in psychology, overly protective of oneself from the criticism of others.

defensiveness /dĭ fĕn′sĭv nĭs/ in psychology, the condition of being constantly defensive.

defibrillation /dē fĭb′rə lā′shən/ attempted restoration of normal heart rhythm with an electrical shock.

defibrillator /dē fĭb′rə lā′tər/ an electronic device that may restore the heart to its normal rhythm by shocking it.

Defibrillator Paddles

deficiency /dĭ fĭsh′ən sē/ a lack or shortage of a substance (such as a vitamin or mineral).

deficit /dĕf′ə sĭt/ impairment, as in function or intellectual capacity.

deformation /dē′fôr mā′shən/ any anatomical structure that is deviated from normal; any body distortion.

deformity /dĭ fôr′mĭ tē/ any anatomical structure that is not of normal size or shape; anything that deviates from normal size or shape.

degenerative /dĭ gĕn′ər ə tĭv/ worsening in mental or physical qualities, said of disease or condition.

degenerative disk the gradual weakening and compression of a vertebral disk.

degenerative disorder or **disease** any disease or disorder that is getting worse.

degenerative joint disease (DJD) arthritis that involves degeneration of the joints. *Also called* osteoarthritis.

deglutition /dē′glōō tĭsh′ən/ the process of passing food or drink from the mouth into the digestive tract; swallowing.

degradation /dĕg′rĭ dā′shən/ progression to a worse condition or a lesser state.

degree /dĭ grē′/ a measure of damage, as in first-degree burn.

dehisce /dĭ hĭs′/ to tear open, as a recently sutured surgical incision.

dehydrated /dē hī′drā tĭd/ suffering from dehydration.

dehydration /dē′hī drā′shən/ lack or loss of water, as from lack of intake of sufficient water or from a disorder that causes vomiting and/or diarrhea and a subsequent loss of body fluids.

dehydroepiandrosterone (DHEA) /dē hī′drō ĕp′ē ăn drŏs′tə rōn′/ a steroid released by the adrenal glands that acts on the body in a way similar to testosterone. Reputed to have antiaging benefits.

deinstitutionalization /dē ĭn′stĭ tōō′shə nə lə zā′shən/ discharge of patients from a mental institution into other facilities or programs.

dejection /dĭ jĕk′shən/ **1.** lowness of spirits; extreme sadness. **2.** feces; excrement.

deleterious /dĕl′ĭ têr′ē əs/ causing injury; harmful.

deliriousness /dĭ lêr′ē əs nĭs/ delirium.

delirium /dĭ lêr′ē əm/ an altered mental state that includes confusion, disorientation, and hallucinations and may have either a physical or emotional cause.

delirium tremens (DTs) /trē′mənz/ a severe form of delirium resulting from withdrawal of alcohol after a long period of intoxication, often with classical hallucinations, such as seeing pink elephants.

deliver /dĭ lĭv′ər/ to give birth to or to assist in giving birth to (an infant).

delivery /dĭ lĭv′ə rē/ the act of giving birth.

delts informally term for the deltoids.

deltoid /dĕl′toid/ or **deltoid muscle** the large, triangular shoulder muscle that stretches from the collarbone to the humerus.

delusion /dĭ lōō′zhən/ a false belief usually held as part of a mental disorder.

delusional /dĭ lōō′zhə nəl/ having delusions.

dementia /dĭ mĕn′shə/ the progressive loss of cognitive functions, usually associated with old age or a brain disease.

demulcent /dĭ mŭl′sənt/ a soothing agent, especially one used on mucous surfaces, such as glycerine or lanolin.

demyelination /dē mī′ə lə nā′shən/ loss of myelin from the nerve sheath, causing a slowing of conduction and associated with certain diseases, such as multiple sclerosis.

dendrite /dĕn′drīt/ small protuberance extending from a nerve cell that conducts impulses inward toward the cell body. *Also called* dendron.

dendritic /dĕn drĭt′ĭk/ of or pertaining to dendrites.

dendron /dĕn′drŏn/ dendrite.

denervate /dē nûr′vāt/ to lose nerve supply, as by cutting of a nerve during surgery or from a drug that blocks nerve supply.

denervation /dē′nûr vā′shən/ loss of nerve supply.

dengue /dĕng′gā/ or **dengue fever** or **dengue hemorrhagic fever (DHF)** /hĕm′ə răj′ĭk/ an infectious tropical disease caused by an arbovirus, with high fever and severe joint pain and muscle aches.

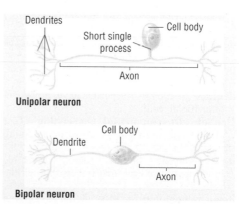

Unipolar neuron

Bipolar neuron

dens /dĕnz/ (pl. **dentes** /dĕn′tēz/) **1.** tooth. **2.** a toothlike projection from the C2 vertebra that allows it to articulate with the C1.

densitometer /dĕn′sĭ tŏm′ĭ tər/ a device that measures bone density using light and x-rays.

densitometry /dĕn′sĭ tŏm′ĭ trē/ measurement of bone density (the amount of bone tissue in a certain volume of bone), used especially to assess risk for osteoporosis.

dent-, denti- combining form. teeth: for example, dentalgia, dentilabial.

dental /dĕn′təl/ of or relating to teeth. [dent- + -al]

dental calculus /kăl′kyə ləs/ deposits of hardened material that forms around the teeth, often causing gum disease and/or decay. Also called tartar.

dental caries /kâr′ēz/ holes in the enamel and dentin of a tooth, caused by decay. Also called cavities.

dentalgia /dĕn tăl′jə/ tooth pain; toothache. [dent- + -algia]

dental hygienist a technician trained to educate patients in oral health, clean teeth, take dental x-rays, and perform certain other related services.

dental operatory /ŏp′ər ə tôr′ē/ dental treatment area where treatment is performed on patients.

dental radiography /rā′dē ŏg′rə fē/ the method of recording images of dental structures by the use of roentgen rays or x-rays.

dentifrice /dĕn′tə frĭs/ any substance used in the cleaning of teeth.

dentilabial /dĕn′tĭ lā′bē əl/ of or relating to the teeth and lips. [denti- + labial]

dentilingual /dĕn′tə lĭng′gwəl/ of or pertaining to the teeth and tongue. [denti- + lingual]

dentin /dĕn′tĭn/ the hard, calcified tissue forming the mass of the tooth.

dentist /dĕn′tĭst/ a licensed practitioner of dentistry.

dentistry /dĕn′tə strē/ the branch of medicine concerned with the prevention, diagnosis, and treatment of diseases of the teeth, gums, and related structures of the mouth. Also called odontology.

dentition /dĕn tĭsh′ən/ the natural arrangement of teeth in the dental arch.

dentoid /dĕn′toid/ having the form of a tooth. [dent- + -oid]

denture /dĕn′chər/ a partial or complete set of artificial teeth.

Denver Developmental Screening Test (DDS) an examination used for assessing the developmental progress of children.

deoxygenated blood /dē ŏk′sĭ jə nā′tĭd/ blood low in oxygen that travels through the veins.

deoxyhemoglobin /dē ŏk′sē hē′mə glō′bĭn/ a form of hemoglobin without oxygen.

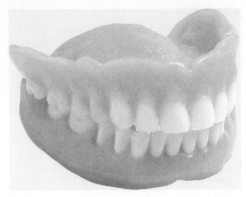

Dentures

deoxyribonucleic acid (DNA) /dē ŏk′sē rī′bō noo klē′ĭk/ a long linear polymer shaped like a double helix found in the nucleus of a cell, which transmits genetic information.

dependence /dĭ pĕn′dəns/ the state of being reliant upon another person or object for a particular need.

dependent /dĭ pĕn′dənt/ **1.** n. a person other than the insured, such as a spouse or child, who is covered under a health plan. **2.** adj. needing something such as insulin or being addicted to something such as heroine, for maintenance.

dependent edema /ĭ dē′mə/ a detectable increase in fluid volume in a lower area such as a foot and ankle, characterized by swelling or pitting because fluid has migrated by gravity and diffusion to this area.

depigmentation /dē pĭg′mən tā′shən/ the partial or total loss of coloring. [de- + pigmentation]

depilation /dĕp′ə lā′shən/ the removal of hair from the body.

depilatory /dĭ pĭl′ə tôr′ē/ an agent containing alkaline used in the removal of hair.

depression /dĭ prĕsh′ən/ **1.** any sunken area. **2.** a mental state with feelings of despair, loneliness, and hopelessness.

depressive disorder /dĭ prĕs′ĭv/ a chronic state of depression that can be clinically diagnosed according to certain established symptoms.

depressor /dĭ prĕs′ər/ **1.** any muscle that flattens or draws a part down. **2.** an instrument used to push a part down or aside during an examination or operation, such as a tongue depressor. **3.** anything that depresses or slows functional activity.

deprivation /dĕp′rə vā′shən/ the state of lacking essential things for physical and emotional well-being.

Using a Tongue Depressor

derm-, derma-, dermo- *combining form.* skin: *for example,* dermatome, dermoplasty.

-derma *suffix.* skin: *for example,* scleroderma, keratoderma.

dermabrasion /dûr′mə brā′zhən/ a surgical procedure using controlled abrasion of the skin, performed to remove small scars and other skin defects. [derm- + abrasion]

dermal /dûr′məl/ of or relating to the skin.

dermat-, dermato- *combining form.* skin: *for example,* dermatosis, dermatomycosis.

dermatitis /dûr′mə tī′tĭs/ inflammation of the skin. [dermat- + -itis]

dermatoautoplasty /dər măt′ō ô′tō plăs′tē, dûr′mə tō-/ the grafting of skin from one part of the body to another. [dermato- + auto- + -plasty]

dermatofibroma /dər măt′ō fī brō′mə, dûr′mə tō-/ a small benign skin tumor that is most often found on the legs. [dermato- + fibroma]

dermatoglyphics /dər măt′ə glĭf′ĭks, dûr′mə tə-/ the study of dermal ridges on the fingers, palms, toes, and soles.

dermatographism /dər măt′ə grăf′ĭz əm, dûr′mə tə-/ the development of skin welts along the lines where one has been stroked or scratched.

dermatoid /dûr′mə toid′/ resembling skin. [dermat- + -oid]

dermatologic /dûr′mə tə lŏj′ĭk/ having to do with the skin.

dermatologist /dûr′mə tŏl′ə jĭst/ a doctor who specializes in the diagnosis and treatment of the skin. [dermato- + -logist]

dermatology /dûr′mə tŏl′ə jē/ the branch of medicine that deals with the study and treatment of the skin. [dermato- + -logy]

dermatolysis /dûr′mə tŏl′ə sĭs/ loosening or hardening of skin, usually caused by disease. [dermato- + -lysis]

dermatome /dûr′mə tōm′/ **1.** a cutting instrument used for removing thin slices of skin. **2.** an area of skin that gets its sensation from a single spinal nerve. [derma- + -tome]

dermatomegaly /dər măt′ō měg′ə lē, dûr′mə tō-/ congenital defect with excess skin hanging in folds. [dermato- + -megaly]

dermatomycosis /dər măt′ō mī kō′sĭs, dûr′mə tō-/ an infection of the skin caused by fungus. [dermato- + -mycosis]

dermatomyositis /dər măt′ō mī′ə sī′tĭs, dûr′mə tō-/ a progressive inflammatory condition of the skin and muscle characterized by muscular weakness, skin rash, and swelling of the eyelids.

dermatopathy /dûr′mə tŏp′ə thē/ any disease of the skin. [dermato- + -pathy]

dermatophylaxis /dər măt′ō fĭ lăk′sĭs, dûr′mə tō-/ protection of the skin from harm, as with the use of sunscreen. [dermato- + -phylaxis]

dermatophyte /dər măt′ə fīt′, dûr′mə tə-/ any fungus capable of causing an infection of the skin, hair, or nails. [dermato- + -phyte]

dermatophytosis /dər măt′ə fī tō′sĭs, dûr′mə tə-/ an infection caused by a dermatophyte.

dermatoplasty /dər măt′ə plăs′tē, dûr′mə tə-/ the use of skin grafts in plastic surgery. [dermato- + -plasty]

dermatosclerosis /dər măt′ō sklĭ rō′sĭs, dûr′mə tō-/ hardening of the skin. [dermato- + -sclerosis]

dermatoscopy /dûr′mə tŏs′kə pē/ noninvasive inspection of the skin for early diagnosis of melanoma and other skin abnormalities. [dermato- + -scopy]

dermatosis /dûr′mə tō′sĭs/ any noninflammatory skin disease involving lesions or eruptions of the skin. [dermat- + -osis]

dermatotherapy /dər măt′ō thěr′ə pē, dûr′mə tō-/ treatment of skin ailments. [dermato- + therapy]

dermis /dûr′mĭs/ the inner layer skin containing blood vessels, lymph vessels, hair follicles, sweat glands, and sebum.

dermoblast /dûr′mə blăst′/ mesoderm cells that develop in the dermis. [dermo- + -blast]

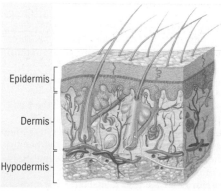

Epidermis —

Dermis —

Hypodermis —

Dermis

dermoid /dûr′moid/   **1.** *adj.* resembling skin. **2.** *n.* a dermoid cyst. [derm- + -oid]

dermoid cyst /sĭst/   a benign tumor found in the skin or ovary that may contain hair, teeth, bone, and sebum. *Also called* dermoid.

dermopathy /dûr mŏp′ə thē/   any disease of the skin. [dermo- + -pathy]

dermoplasty /dûr′mə plăs′tē/   the use of skin grafts in plastic surgery. [dermo- + -plasty]

dermovascular /dûr′mō văs′kyə lər/   of or pertaining to the blood vessels of the skin. [dermo- + vascular]

DES *abbreviation.* diethylstilbestrol.

descending aorta /ā ôr′tə/   the part of the aorta that runs down through the chest and the abdomen.

descending colon /kō′lən/   the section of the colon extending from the left colic flexure to the pelvic brim.

descending pathway   the nerves running down the spinal cord that allow the brain to control the body below the head.

desensitize /dē sĕn′sĭ tīz′/   to reduce or remove sensitivity, especially to an antigen in the treatment of allergies.

desiccant /dĕs′ĭ kənt/   a substance used as a drying agent, such as a small bag of silica gel put in bottles of medicine to keep the pills dry.

desiccate /dĕs′ĭ kāt′/   to dry thoroughly; to remove all moisture.

-desis *suffix.* binding: *for example,* arthrodesis, pleurodesis.

desm-, desmo- *combining form.* fibrous connection; ligament: *for example,* desmoplasia.

desmoid /dĕz′moid/   **1.** *adj.* made of fiber or ligament. **2.** *n.* also **desmoid tumor** a benign tumor of dense connective tissue, most often found in the abdominal muscles of women. [desm- + -oid]

desmopathy /dĕz mŏp′ə thē/   disease of the ligaments. [desmo- + -pathy]

desmoplasia /dĕz′mə plā′zhə/   the dense growth of fibrous or connective tissue, especially in tumors. [desmo- + -plasia]

desmoplastic /dĕz′mə plăs′tĭk/   causing or producing adhesions or formation of fibrous tissue. [desmo- + -plastic]

desmopressin /dĕz′mō prĕs′ĭn/   a synthetic hormone used as a medication for its antidiuretic effects.

desquamate /dĕs′kwə māt′/   to shed the outer layer of skin in scales.

desquamation /dĕs′kwə mā′shən/   the shedding or scaling of the outer layer of skin.

detached retina /rĕt′ə nə/   a retina that has separated from its connection to the back of the eye (including its own blood supply), resulting in visual impairment.

deterioration /dĭ têr′ē ə rā′shən/   the process or condition of getting worse.

detox /dē′tŏks′/   removal of the toxic properties and effects of a poison.

detoxication /dē tŏk′sĭ kā′shən/   recovery from the toxic effects of something, such as a drug.

detoxification /dē tŏk′sə fĭ kā′shən/   the process of detoxifying.

detoxify /dē tŏk′sə fī′/   to counteract, diminish, or eliminate a toxic substance, as in treatment for drug addiction.

detrition /dĭ trĭsh′ən/   a wearing away, as by friction.

detritus /dĭ trī′təs/   matter, such as tissue, that is the result of detrition.

detrusor /dĭ trōō′zər, -sər/   any muscle that pushes down, such as muscles in the walls of the bladder.

detumescence /dē′tōō mĕs′əns/   lessening of swelling, as of an organ.

deuteranomaly /dōō′tər ə nŏm′ə lē/   colorblindness of the red-green type.

deuteranopia /dōō′tər ə nō′pē ə/   a form of colorblindness characterized by a low sensitivity to red and green.

deuteropathy /dōō′tə rŏp′ə thē/   a secondary disease that occurs after another.

development /dĭ vĕl′əp mənt/   the natural process of growth from a simpler early stage to a more complex stage.

developmental delay /dĭ vĕl′əp mĕn′təl/   a slowing in the normal progression of childhood development.

developmental disorder   any disorder that disrupts the normal progression of childhood development.

developmentally disabled   having a physical or mental handicap affecting cognitive, language, motor, or social skills, that becomes apparent at a young age.

deviance /dē′vē əns/   behavior that varies from accepted social norms.

deviant /dē′vē ənt/   **1.** *n.* person whose behavior varies from accepted social norms. **2.** *adj.* varying from accepted social norms.

deviated septum /dē′vē ā′tĭd sĕp′təm/   abnormal displacement of the midline wall in the nose to one side or the other.

deviation /dē′vē ā′shən/   deviant behavior.

device /dĭ vīs′/   equipment meant for a specific purpose.

DEXA scan /dĕk′sə/   the image or data produced by a special x-ray machine, used to measure bone density. [*d*ual-*e*nergy *x*-ray *ab*sorptiometry]

dexter /dĕk′stər/   located on or in relation to the right side of the body.

dextr-, dextro-   right.

dextro- *combining form.* right; on the right side: *for example,* dextroamphetamine.

dextroamphetamine /dĕk'strō ăm fĕt'ə mēn', -mĭn/ the white crystalline isomer of amphetamine that is used as a central nervous system stimulant. [dextro- + amphetamine]

dextrocardia /dĕk'strō kär'dē ə/ abnormal orientation of the heart to the right side, resulting in a mirror image of a normal heart. [dextro- + -cardia]

dextroposition of the heart /dĕk'strō pə zĭsh'ən/ abnormal position of the heart to the right side of the chest. [dextro- + position]

dextrose /dĕk'strōs/ a sugar that is the chief source of energy in the body. *Also called* glucose.

dextroversion /dĕk'strə vûr'zhən/ **1.** a turning to the right. **2.** rotation of both eyes to the right. [dextro- + -version]

DHEA *abbreviation.* dehydroepiandrosterone.

DHF *abbreviation.* dengue hemorrhagic fever.

di- *prefix.* two, twice: *for example,* diplegia.

DI *abbreviation.* diabetes insipidus.

dia- *prefix.* through, throughout, completely: *for example,* diaphoresis.

diabetes /dī'ə bē'tĭs, -tēz/ any of several metabolic disorders marked by polyuria (excessive urination) and polydipsia (persistent thirst).

diabetes insipidus (DI) /ĭn sĭp'ĭ dəs/ a chronic metabolic disorder caused by a deficiency of the pituitary hormone vasopressin, characterized by intense thirst and excessive urination.

diabetes intermittens /ĭn'tər mĭt'ənz/ a form of diabetes mellitus in which there are periods of normal carbohydrate metabolism followed by relapses back to a diabetic state.

diabetes mellitus (DM) /mĕl'ĭ təs, mə lī'təs/ a chronic form of diabetes characterized by high levels of sugar in the blood and inability to transport it into cells ("starvation in the midst of plenty"), caused by low insulin production (referred to as type 1), or low sensitivity of the cells to normal levels of insulin (referred to as type 2). *See also* type 1 diabetes mellitus, type 2 diabetes mellitus, non-insulin-dependent diabetes mellitus, insulin-dependent diabetes mellitus.

diabetic /dī'ə bĕt'ĭk/ **1.** *adj.* relating to or suffering from diabetes. **2.** *n.* a person who suffers from some form of diabetes.

diabetic coma a coma that develops in inadequately treated cases of severe diabetes mellitus, caused by the buildup of glucose and ketones in the bloodstream.

diabetic dermopathy /dûr mŏp'ə thē/ a skin disorder often appearing on the shins of people with diabetes mellitus, in which small discolored patches of skin become pigmented and ulcerated, often resulting in scarring.

Diabetic Testing Blood Sugar

diabetic eye disease a disease of the eye in which capillaries leak into the retina causing impaired vision or blindness.

diabetic ketoacidosis /kē'tō ăs'ĭ dō'sĭs/ a complication of diabetes mellitus characterized by the buildup of glucose, ketones, and lactic acid in the blood, sometimes resulting in diabetic coma.

diabetic macular edema /măk'yə lər ĭ dē'mə/ swelling of the retina due to the leakage of fluid from capillaries into the macula, a consequence of microcirculatory damage that can occur in people with diabetes.

diabetic musculoskeletal disorder /mŭs'kyə lō skĕl'ĭ təl/ a disorder associated with diabetes mellitus resulting in limited joint mobility.

diabetic nephropathy /nə frŏp'ə the/ kidney disease associated with long-standing diabetes.

diabetic neuropathy /nŏŏ rŏp'ə thē/ a generic term for any disorder of the nervous system related to diabetes mellitus.

diabetic retinopathy /rĕt'ə nŏp'ə thē/ a common complication of diabetes affecting the blood vessels of the retina, in which capillaries leak into the retina, causing impaired vision or blindness.

diabetic shock extreme hypoglycemia associated with diabetes, characterized by tremulousness, faintness, and sometimes loss of consciousness.

diabetic skin disease any of many skin disorders caused by, or affected by, diabetes.

diagnose /dī'əg nōs'/ to come to a medical conclusion by diagnosis.

diagnosis /dī'əg nō'sĭs/ (**dx, DX**) the determination of the nature of a medical problem through observation and/or testing.

diagnosis-related group (DRG) payment categories of patient diagnoses used by hospitals in charging fees to insurers.

Diagnostician Viewing X-Rays

diagnostic /dī'əg nŏs'tĭk/   *adj.* **1.** relating to or used in diagnosis. **2.** establishing or confirming a diagnosis. *n.* **3.** something used in the analysis or determination of medical condition.

***Diagnostic and Statistical Manual of Mental Disorders* (*DSM*)**   official manual of psychiatric disorders used by mental health professionals to ensure uniformity of diagnosic criteria.

diagnostician /dī'əg nŏ stĭsh'ən/   a person who specializes in diagnosing medical conditions.

diagnostic imaging   the use of imaging techniques in the diagnostic process.

diakinesis /dī'ə kĭ nē'sĭs/   a stage in cell division (meiosis) in which the paired chromosomes shorten and thicken.

dialysate /dī ăl'ə sāt'/   the fluid and electrolyte mixture that passes on one side of a dialyzing membrane while blood passes on the other side.

dialysis /dī ăl'ə sĭs/   the process of cleansing the blood, by passing it through a special machine (hemodialysis) or by filling the peritoneum with a cleansing solution (peritoneal dialysis).

dialysis machine   a machine that treats blood to remove excess water and waste products in patients with kidney failure.

dialyzer /dī'ə lī'zər/   a machine used to perform dialysis.

diapedesis /dī'ə pĭ dē'sĭs/   the passage of blood through the walls of blood vessels and into surrounding body tissue.

diaper rash   dermatitis on the buttocks and thighs caused by prolonged exposure to urine and feces in a child's diaper.

diaphoresis /dī'ə fə rē'sĭs/   the excretion of fluid by the sweat glands through pores in the skin; perspiration. [dia- + -phoresis]

diaphoretic /dī'ə fə rĕt'ĭk/   relating to or causing perspiration; sweating.

diaphragm /dī'ə frăm'/   **1.** the main muscle of respiration, separating the chest cavity from

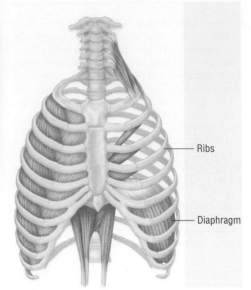

Diaphragm

the abdomen; when it contracts, the abdominal contents move downwards and the lungs fill with air. As it relaxes, the lungs empty by elastic recoil. **2.** a thin disc with a small hole designed to restrict the amount of light passing through the lens of an optic instrument. **3.** a thin flexible rubber disk used in the vagina, capping the cervix, to prevent pregnancy.

diaphragmatic /dī'ə frăg măt'ĭk/   of or relating to the diaphragm.

diaphragmatic hernia /hûr'nē ə/   a type of hernia in which the contents of the abdomen protrude into the chest through a weak spot in the diaphragm.

diaphysis /dī ăf'ə sĭs/   shaft, as in a long bone.

diarrhea /dī'ə rē'ə/   unusually frequent or abnormally liquid bowel movements. [dia- + -rrhea]

diarthrosis /dī'är thrō'sĭs/ (*pl.* **diarthroses** /dī'är thrō'sēz/)   freely movable joint; a subclassification of synovial joints characterized by presence of a synovial membrane, synovial fluid, and a joint capsule.

diaschisis /dī ăs'kə sĭs/   a sudden loss of partial brain function, due to an injury. [dia- + -schisis]

diascope /dī'ə skōp'/   a flat glass plate used to examine skin lesions by pressing against the skin. [dia- + -scope].

diastalsis /dī'ə stôl'sĭs/   a type of digestive peristalsis in which a wave of restraint is followed by a contraction.

diastasis /dī ăs'tə sĭs/   **1.** any separation of normally joined parts. **2.** the last stage of diastole in the heart, during which little additional blood enters the ventricle.

diastatic /dī′ə stăt′ĭk/ of or pertaining to diastasis.

diastema /dī′ə stē′mə/ an abnormal space between two teeth, usually the maxillary central incisors.

diastole /dī ăs′tə lē/ the normally occurring state of relaxation and dilation of the heart ventricles, during which they fill with blood.

diastolic /dī′ə stŏl′ĭk/ of or relating to diastole.

diastolic pressure the lowest arterial blood pressure, after the contraction of the heart, as the chambers of the heart refill with blood.

diastrophic dysplasia /dī′ə strŏf′ĭk dĭs plā′zhə/ an inherited form of dwarfism characterized by clubfoot, curved spine, incomplete bone growth, cleft palate, and shortening of the Achilles tendon.

diathermy /dī′ə thûr′mē/ a therapy in which heat is applied to muscle tissue through electromagnetic currents.

diathesis /dī ăth′ə sĭs/ a predisposition to a disease or disorder.

dicentric chromosome /dī sĕn′trĭk krō′mə sōm′/ an abnormal chromosome with two centromeres rather than one.

dichromatic /dī′krə măt′ĭk/ of or pertaining to dichromatism.

dichromatism /dī krō′mə tĭz′əm/ a form of color blindness in which only two of the three primary colors can be perceived.

Dick(′s) test /dĭk(s)/ a skin test used to determine susceptibility to scarlet fever (testing for antibodies to the streptococci that cause it).

dicrotism /dī′krə tĭz′əm/ a condition in which each heartbeat is felt in the pulse as two beats.

diencephalon /dī′ĕn sĕf′ə lŏn′/ the deep section of the brain composed of the epithalamus, dorsal thalamus, subthalamus, and hypothalamus.

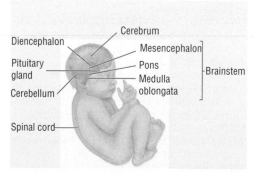

Diencephalon
Cerebrum
Mesencephalon
Pituitary gland
Pons
Brainstem
Medulla oblongata
Cerebellum
Spinal cord

Diencephalon

diet /dī′ĭt/ n. **1.** a specific program of foods that may or may not be eaten, often including times at which they must be eaten or avoided, for therapeutic reasons. **2.** a specific program of foods to eat, often in specific quantities, or to avoid, usually in order to lose weight. v. **3.** to follow a diet.

dietary /dī′ĭ tĕr′ē/ of or relating to diet.

dietary fiber indigestible plant matter, which stimulates digestion when eaten.

Dietary Reference Intake (DRI) a set of dietary values serving as a reference for healthy nutrient intake for individuals in the United States and Canada.

dietetic /dī′ĭ tĕt′ĭk/ **1.** relating to diet. **2.** relating to food having low caloric content.

diethylstilbestrol (DES) /dī ĕth′əl stĭl bĕs′trôl/ the first synthetic form of the hormone estrogen, once erroneously thought to prevent premature birth and miscarriage but which was the cause of vaginal and cervical cancers in some of the female offspring of women so treated.

dietician /dī′ĭ tĭsh′ən/ an expert in dietetics.

diff *abbreviation.* differential

diff dx differential diagnosis.

differential /dĭf′ə rĕn′shəl/ of, relating to, or showing a difference.

differential diagnosis /dī′əg nō′sĭs/ the determination of a patient's illness by weighing the probability of one disease versus other diseases with similar symptoms; a list of possible diseases with the patient's symptoms in order of likelihood.

differential white cell count the proportions of the different kinds of white cells in the blood.

differentiated cancer /dĭf′ə rĕn′shē ā′tĭd/ a cancer whose cells are mature and more or less look like the cells of the organ in which it originated.

digastric /dī găs′trĭk/ **1.** n. a muscle with two fleshy ends separated by a thinner tendinous section. **2.** adj. of or relating to the digastric muscle. [di- + gastric]

DiGeorge(′s) syndrome /dī jôrj′(ĭz)/ congenital absence of the thymus gland.

digest /dī jĕst, dī-/ **1.** to soften by moisture and heat. **2.** to break down into smaller parts by means of hydrolysis or chemical action.

digestant /dī jĕs′tənt/ a substance that aids digestion.

digestion /dī jĕs′chən, dī-/ the mechanical, chemical, and enzymatic process in which food is broken down, absorbed, and converted into energy in the body.

digestive system /dī jĕs′tĭv, dī-/ the digestive tract and all related glands and organs.

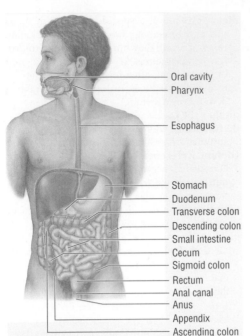

Digestive Tract

digestive tract the passage leading from the mouth to the anus, through which food passes and is digested.

digit /dĭj′ĭt/ a finger or toe.

digitalis /dĭj′ĭ tăl′ĭs/ **1.** a perennial flowering plant from which a cardiac medicine is prepared. **2.** the medicine itself.

digital radiography /rā′dē ŏg′rə fē/ computer processing of a digital x-ray image.

digital rectal examination (DRE) an examination using a finger to detect abnormalities in the rectum.

digital subtraction angiography (DSA) /ăn′jē ŏg′rə fē/ an x-ray that uses a computer to subtract images of bone and soft tissue to provide a clearer picture of the cardiovascular system.

digital thermometer a thermometer with a digital readout.

diglossia /dī glŏs′ē ə/ congenital condition with a cleft or divided tongue.

dilate /dī lāt′/ or **dilatate** /dĭl′ĭ tāt′, dī′lĭ-/ to perform or undergo dilation

dilating /dī lā′tĭng/ or **dilatating** /dĭl′ĭ tā′tĭng, dī′lĭ-/ the widening and opening of the cervix caused by uterine contractions.

dilation /dī lā′shən/ or **dilatation** /dĭl′ĭ tā′shən, dī′lə-/ the process of stretching, enlarging, or expanding an opening, as the cervix.

dilation and curettage (D&C) /kyŏŏr′ĭ täzh′/ or **dilitation and curettage (D and C)** a procedure in which the cervix is dilated and the uterine lining scraped with a curette, performed to diagnose and treat uterine conditions.

dilation and evacuation (D & E) surgical dilation of the cervix and removal of the fetus and other products of conception; used to terminate a pregnancy usually during the second trimester.

dilator /dī lā′tər/ or **dilatator** /dĭl′ĭ tā′tər, dī′lĭ-/ **1.** an instrument designed to enlarge or stretch open a hollow structure. **2.** a muscle that pulls open an orifice. **3.** a substance that aids in dilating.

diluent /dĭl′yŏŏ ənt/ substance that dilutes the strength of a solution.

dilute /dī lŏŏt′/ to reduce the concentration, quality, or purity of a solution.

dilution /dī lŏŏ′shən/ **1.** the act of diluting. **2.** a solution that has been diluted.

dimorphic /dī môr′fĭk/ occurring in two distinct forms.

dimorphism /dī môr′fĭz əm/ existing in two different forms.

dimple /dĭm′pəl/ **1.** *n.* a small round indentation on the body, occurring naturally or as a result of trauma or scaring. **2.** *v.* to cause dimples.

dimpling /dĭm′plĭng/ **1.** *adj.* causing dimples. **2.** *n.* a natural or artificial condition marked by dimples.

diopter /dī ŏp′tər/ a unit of measure of the refracting power of lenses.

diphtheria /dĭf thêr′ē ə/ an acute infectious bacterial disease of the upper respiratory system, against which children are usually immunized.

diphtheria, pertussis /pər tŭs′ĭs/, **and tetanus** /tĕt′ə nəs/ **(DPT)** a vaccine used for immunization of diphtheria, pertussis, and tetanus.

dipl-, diplo- *combining form.* double, twofold: *for example,* diploid, diplococcus.

diplegia /dī plē′jē ə, -jə/ paralysis of corresponding parts on both sides of the body. [di- + -plegia]

diplobacillus /dĭp′lō bə sĭl′əs/ a pair of rodshaped bacterial cells joined end to end. [diplo- + -bacillus]

diplococcus /dĭp′lə kŏk′əs/ (*pl.* **diplococci** /dĭp′lə kŏk′sī/) spherical bacterial cells joined in pairs. [diplo- + -coccus]

diploid /dĭp′loid/ denoting a cell whose nucleus contains a paired set of chromosomes, twice the number of sperm or egg cells; all cells except sex cells are diploid (in humans, contain 46 chromosomes). *See also* haploid. [dipl- + -oid]

diplopia /dī plō′pē ə/ double vision, seeing one object as two. [dipl- + -opia]

dips-, dipso- *combining form.* thirst: *for example,* dipsomania.

Image labels: Oral cavity, Pharynx, Esophagus, Stomach, Duodenum, Transverse colon, Descending colon, Small intestine, Cecum, Sigmoid colon, Rectum, Anal canal, Anus, Appendix, Ascending colon

dipsomania /dĭp′sə mā′nē ə/ an insatiable craving for alcoholic beverages. [dipso- + -mania]

dipsosis /dĭp sō′sĭs/ an insatiable thirst, or a craving for unusual forms of drink. [dips- + -osis]

direct vision vision formed by an image on the fovea centralis. *Also called* central vision.

dis- *prefix.* in two, apart: *for example,* dislocation.

disability /dĭs′ə bĭl′ĭ tē/ inability to perform within a prescribed range of normal due to a deficiency or impairment. [dis- + ability]

disabled /dĭs ā′bəld/ to be incapacitated by injury or illness.

disarticulation /dĭs′är tĭk′yə lā′shən/ the amputation of a limb at the joint, without cutting the bone. [dis- + articulation]

disc/disk /dĭsk/ a thick, round piece of cartilage (fibrous tissue) separating the vertebrae (bones of the spinal column).

discharge /dĭs′chärj/ **1.** the excretion or secretion of fluid from the body. **2.** the release of a patient from treatment or care.

discharge planning the collaborative process of evaluating a patient's needs and developing a plan for follow-up and future care after discharge from treatment or care.

disciform /dĭs′ə fôrm′, dĭs′kə-/ shaped like a disc.

disclosing solution a solution that stains plaque red, used in dentistry to show patients the location of plaque.

discoid /dĭs′koid/ shaped like a disc/disk.

discoid lupus erythematosus (DLE) /dĭs′koid lōō′pəs ĕr′ə thē′mə tō′səs/ a chronic inflammatory condition that causes skin lesions to appear on the face and elsewhere. *See also* lupus erythematosus, systemic lupus erythematosus.

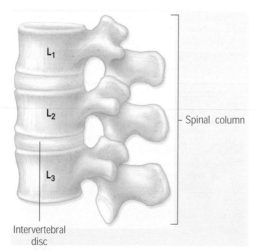

L₁

L₂ — Spinal column

L₃

Intervertebral disc

Disc/Disk

discordance /dĭs kôr′dəns/ the presence of any condition in only one member of a pair of twins, as used in genetic studies.

discordant /dĭs kôr′dənt/ of or showing discordance.

disease /dĭ zēz′/ an impairment in the normal state of health or a condition of abnormal functioning; a state of ill health with specific symptoms.

disinfect /dĭs′ĭn fĕkt′/ to destroy or inhibit the growth of pathogenic microorganisms. [dis- + infect]

disinfectant /dĭs′ĭn fĕk′tənt/ an agent capable of disinfecting.

disinfected /dĭs′ĭn fĕk′tĭd/ condition of being rid of pathogenic microorganisms through disinfection.

disinfection /dĭs′ĭn fĕk′shən/ the destruction of pathogenic microorganisms by direct exposure to a disinfectant.

disintegrate /dĭs ĭn′tĭ grāt′/ to reduce a substance into smaller parts or fragments.

disk/disc /dĭsk/ a thick, round piece of cartilage (fibrous tissue) separating the vertebrae (bones of the spinal column).

diskectomy /dĭs kĕk′tə mē/ the surgical removal of a disc from between the vertebrae. [disk + -ectomy]

diskitis /dĭs kī′tĭs/ inflammation of a disc or disc space. [disk + -itis]

dislocation /dĭs′lō kā′shən/ the displacement of a bone from its normal position in a joint. [dis- + location]

dislocation fracture /frăk′chər/ a bone fracture plus the dislocation of a joint. *Also called* fracture dislocation.

dismember /dĭs mĕm′bər/ to amputate a limb from.

disorder /dĭs ôr′dər/ a condition in which there is a disturbance of function or structure due to a genetic failure, trauma, or disease.

disorganized schizophrenia /skĭt′sə frē′nē ə/ a severe form of schizophrenia characterized by erratic speech, childish mannerisms and bizarre behavior.

disorganized thinking a lack of logical continuity of thought, with the inability to focus or concentrate.

disorientation /dĭs ôr′ē ən tā′shən/ a state of confusion in regards to one's surroundings, resulting from a medical or psychological condition or, sometimes, from a reaction to medication.

dispensary /dĭ spĕn′sə rē/ the office of a physician or part of a hospital where medicines are dispensed.

displaced fracture /frăk′chər/ a fracture resulting in fragments of bone that are out of alignment.

displacement /dĭs plās'mənt/ **1.** the act of moving something out of its normal location or position. **2.** the redirection of an emotional impulse from one target to another.

disposition /dĭs'pə zĭsh'ən/ a person's usual mood or temperament.

dissect /dĭ sĕkt', dī-/ to cut open or separate tissue for surgical study or treatment.

dissected /dĭ sĕk'tĭd, dī-/ divided into parts by one or more incisions.

dissecting aneurysm /ăn'yə rĭz'əm/ a tear in an arterial wall through which blood escapes.

dissecting aortic aneurysm /ā ôr'tĭk/ a tear in the aortic wall through which blood escapes.

dissection /dĭ sĕk'shən, dī-/ act of dissecting.

disseminate /dĭ sĕm'ə nāt'/ to spread throughout an organ or tissue of the body.

dissociate /dĭ sō'shē āt'/ to separate or remove from association.

dissociation /dĭ sō'shē ā'shən/ **1.** separation into parts. **2.** a mental condition in which there is an unconscious separation of the personality into two or more parts.

dissociative identity disorder a psychological disorder in which the personality becomes split into two or more parts, each with its own distinct behavior. *Also called* multiple personality disorder.

dissonance /dĭs'ə nəns/ in psychology, inconsistency or conflict between a person's beliefs and actions.

distal /dĭs'təl/ **1.** more or most distant from a point of attachment or origin. **2.** situated away from the front center section of the jaw.

distended /dĭ stĕn'dĭd/ abnormally swollen or extended due to internal pressure from fluid or gas.

distention /dĭ stĕn'shən/ the act or state of being swollen or extended.

distortion /dĭ stôr'shən/ on an x-ray film, an increase or decrease in the size and shape of the object.

distracted /dĭ străk'tĭd/ **1.** having difficulty staying focused or unable to concentrate. **2.** stretched to the point of separation, said of a joint or broken bone.

distribution /dĭs'trĭ byōō'shən/ **1.** the extension of arteries or nerves into tissue and organs. **2.** the area in which the branches of arteries and nerves end. **3.** arrival of a medicine into the blood (from the stomach or from an intravenous tube) and its spread throughout the body. **4.** the relative number of people spread throughout several categories or groups.

diuresis /dī'ə rē'sĭs/ large production and excretion of urine.

diuretic /dī'ə rĕt'ĭk/ an agent that increases the production and excretion of urine.

diurnal /dī ûr'nəl/ **1.** of or concerning the daylight hours. *See also* nocturnal. **2.** recurring every 24 hours; daily.

divergence /dĭ vûr'jəns, dī-/ **1.** a spreading apart from a common point. **2.** the branching out of a neuron to make connections with other neurons.

divergent strabismus /strə bĭz'məs/ a condition with one or both eyes are directed outward.

diverticula /dī'vər tĭk'yə lə/ plural of diverticulum

diverticular /dī'vər tĭk'yə lər/ lə of or relating to the diverticulum.

diverticulectomy /dī'vər tĭk'yə lĕk'tə mē/ a surgical procedure used to remove a diverticulum.

diverticulitis /dī'vər tĭk'yə lī'tĭs/ infection and inflammation of a diverticulum.

diverticulosis /dī'vər tĭk'yə lō'sĭs/ the presence of several diverticula.

diverticulum /dī'vər tĭk'yə ləm/ (*pl.* **diverticula** /dī'vər tĭk'yə lə/) a small bulging sac protruding from the bladder or intestines, in which fecal matter may collect and cause inflammation.

divulsion /dĭ vŭl'shən/ **1.** forcible dilation, as of the walls of a canal. **2.** removal by tearing.

divulsor /dĭ vŭl'sər/ instrument used in divulsion (forcible dilation).

dizygotic twins /dī'zī gŏt'ĭk/ twins formed from two separate eggs and two separate sperm. *Also called* fraternal twins. *See also* identical twins.

dizziness /dĭz'ē nĭs/ a general term used to describe unsteadiness and loss of equilibrium.

DJD *abbreviation.* degenerative joint disease.

dL *abbreviation.* deciliter.

DLE *abbreviation.* discoid lupus erythematosus.

DM *abbreviation.* diabetes mellitus.

DNA *abbreviation.* deoxyribonucleic acid.

DNA cloning a procedure used to copy a gene or segment of DNA.

Dizygotic Twins

DNR *abbreviation* do not resuscitate.

D.O. *abbreviation*. Doctor of Osteopathy.

DOA *abbreviation*. dead on arrival.

doctor /dŏk′tər/ **1.** a person who is trained in the art and science of healing, and licensed to practice.

doctor-assisted suicide a situation in which a physician provides a seriously ill patient with the means needed to end their own life.

dolor /dō′lər/ pain, as one of the four classic signs of inflammation. *See also* calor, rubor, tumor.

do not resuscitate (DNR) /rĭ sŭs′ĭ tāt′/ a written order indicating a patient's wish to not receive any lifesaving procedures.

domestic violence physical abuse of one's partner or spouse.

dominant /dŏm′ə nənt/ ruling or controlling, as a characteristic or a gene.

donor /dō′nər/ a person who gives their blood, tissue, or organs for transplant.

donor insemination /ĭn sĕm′ə nā′shən/ a procedure in which a donor's sperm is inserted into the uterus through a thin catheter to achieve pregnancy.

dopa /dō′pə/ a precursor of dopamine, used in the treatment of Parkinson's disease.

dopamine /dō′pə mēn′/ an important neurotransmitter in the brain, essential to central nervous system functioning. A reduction in dopamine is associated with Parkinson's disease.

doping /dō′pĭng/ the illegal use of drugs, especially to increase athletic performance.

Doppler effect /dŏp′lər/ an apparent change in the frequency of a sound wave due to the relative motion of the source and the observer.

Doppler ultrasonography /ŭl′trə sō nŏg′rə fē/ the use of the doppler effect in ultrasound technology to track the movement of targets in the bloodstream.

Doppler ultrasound /ŭl′trə sound′/ a form of ultrasound that utilizes the Doppler effect to track the movement of blood, especially in the heart.

dormant /dôr′mənt/ in a state of biological rest; having suspended growth and development.

dors-, dorsi-, dorso- *combining form.* back: *for example,* dorsalgia, dorsiflexion.

dorsal /dôr′səl/ pertaining to the back. [dors- + -al]

dorsalgia /dôr săl′jē ə, -jə/ back pain. [dors- + -algia]

dorsalis pedis artery /dôr sā′lĭs pē′dĭs/ the lowest section of the tibial artery, lying across the front of the ankle joint.

dorsal vertebrae /vûr′tə brē′/ the 12 bones in the spine between the cervical vertebrae of the neck and the lumbar vertebrae of the back, labeled T1 to T12. *Also called* thoracic vertebrae.

dorsiflexion /dôr′sə flĕk′shən/ bending back the hands or fingers, or the foot or toes. [dorsi- + flexion]

dorsocephalad /dôr′sō sĕf′ə lăd′/ toward the back of the skull. [dorso- + cephalad]

dorsolumbar /dôr′sō lŭm′bər, -bär/ of or pertaining to the dorsal and lumbar vertebrae. [dorso- + lumbar]

dorsum /dôr′səm/ the back side or rear of a structure.

dosage /dō′sĭj/ **1.** the administering of medication in prescribed doses. **2.** the amount of medicine administered at one time.

dose /dōs/ the exact measure of a medicine to be administered, often including the timing of administration.

dosimeter /dō sĭm′ĭ tər/ an instrument that measures the absorption of x-rays.

dosimetry /dō sĭm′ĭ trē/ the accurate measurement of radiation exposure.

double-blind a term used to describe a study in which both the observer and the subjects are unaware of the treatment—test drug or placebo—being administered.

double-blinded study a form of study in which both the observer and the subject are unaware of the nature of the treatment being tested.

double-contrast barium enema /bâr′ē əm/ a procedure in which a barium enema and injection of air are administered to enhance x-rays of the colon and rectum. *Also called* air contrast barium enema.

double helix /hē′lĭks/ two parallel strands of DNA connected, forming a structure resembling a coiled ladder.

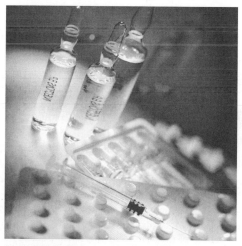

Doses of Medicine in Capsules and Ampules

double-jointed a nonmedical term used to describe a condition with joints that are hyperflexible.

double-masked a double-blind study in which both the observer and the subject are unaware of the identity of the control or the variable.

double pneumonia /noo mōn'yə/ pneumonia occurring in both lungs at the same time.

douche /doosh/ **1.** a stream of water, gas or vapor projected onto the body or into a body cavity for cleansing purposes. **2.** an instrument used to deliver a douche.

douching /doo'shǐng/ using a douche to clean or medicate.

dowager('s) hump /dou'ə jər(z)/ an outward curvature of the upper spine caused by osteoporosis and compression fractures.

Down('s) syndrome /doun(z)/ a chromosomal disorder caused by the existence of an extra, third, chromosome number 21, affecting both intellectual and physical development.

DPT *abbreviation.* **1.** diphtheria-pertussis-tetanus, a vaccine used for immunization of diphtheria, pertussis, and tetanus. **2.** Doctor of Physical Therapy.

DPT immunization or **injections** a series of five injections (four between 2 and 8 months of age, and one between 4 and 6 years of age) to protect against diphtheria, pertussis, and tetanus. *Also called* DTaP immunization.

Dr/ Dr. *abbreviation.* doctor.

dracunculiasis /drə kŭngk'yə lī'ə sǐs/ an infection caused by a parasitic roundworm that lives in the abdomen or under the skin.

draft /drăft/ a single dose of medication.

drain /drān/ **1.** *v.* to discharge fluid from a wound or cavity. **2.** *n.* an instrument used to draw off a fluid.

drainage /drā'nǐj/ the removal of fluid (especially pus) from a body cavity.

dram (dr) /drăm/ a unit of weight equal to 1/16 ounce in the U.S. Customary System, and having an apothecary weight of 1/8 ounce.

drape /drāp/ **1.** *v.* to cover or conceal parts of the body not under examination, **2.** *n.* the material used to drape a patient for examination.

DRE *abbreviation.* digital rectal exam.

dream /drēm/ **1.** *n.* thoughts, emotions, and images created by the involuntary activity of the brain during sleep. **2.** *v.* to have such thoughts, emotions, and images during sleep.

dressing /drĕs'ĭng/ material, such as gauze, used to cover injured parts.

Dressler('s) syndrome /drĕs'lər(z)/ inflammation of the heart following a heart attack or other injury to the heart.

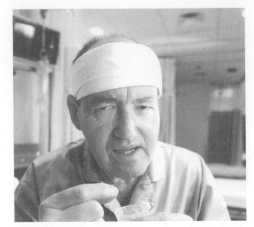
Dressing on a Head Wound

DRG *abbreviation.* diagnosis-related group, payment categories used by hospitals to charge fees to insurers.

DRI *abbreviation.* dietary reference intake.

drill /drĭl/ **1.** *n.* an instrument used in dentistry to scrape away a portion of a tooth for filling. **2.** *v.* to scrape away a portion of a tooth to fill it.

drip /drĭp/ **1.** *v.* to flow one drop at a time. **2.** *n.* a device used to deliver a fluid one drop at a time.

drive /drīv/ in psychology, a strong motivation towards a particular goal.

drop /drŏp/ **1.** the smallest amount of liquid heavy enough to form a globule. **2.** a small liquid dosage of medicine.

drop attack a sudden loss of muscle strength resulting in collapse. *Also called* atonic seizure, drop seizure.

drop foot partial or total lack of flexion in the foot, usually due to nerve injury, resulting in a dragging of the foot. *Also called* foot-drop.

drop hand partial or total lack of flexion in the hand, usually due to nerve injury, resulting in a hanging down of the hand. *Also called* hand-drop.

droplet /drŏp'lĭt/ a small particle, or drop, of moisture.

dropper /drŏp'ər/ a tubular device used to deliver liquid medicine in drops.

drop seizure drop attack. *Also called* atonic seizure.

drowning /drou'nĭng/ suffocation caused by fluid filling the lungs.

drowsiness /drou'zē nĭs/ a state of impaired awareness; sleepiness.

drug /drŭg/ *n.* **1.** an agent administered to prevent, diagnose, treat, or cure disease. **2.** general term for narcotics. *v.* **3.** to administer a drug.

drug abuse   habitual use of a drug, especially an illegal one, for nontherapeutic purposes.

drug-eluting stent /ē loō'tǐng/   a stent (a device surgically implanted to hold open a blocked blood vessel) that delivers medication over a period of time.

druggist /drŭg'ĭst/   a person trained and licensed to prepare and dispense drugs. *Also called* pharmacist.

drug interaction   the desirable or undesirable side effect of drugs reacting to each other, or with other chemical agents, in the body.

drug resistance   the ability of a disease or bacteria to tolerate or withstand a drug that was once capable of destroying it.

drug-resistant tuberculosis /toō bûr'kyə lō'sĭs/   tuberculosis that is immune to routine drug treatment.

drug therapy   the administration of drugs or chemicals for the treatment of disease.

drusen /droō'zən/   small yellow or white structures found in the retina or optic disc.

dry cough   a nonproductive cough in which nothing is expelled.

dry eye   itching and burning of the eye caused by a tear deficiency.

dry gangrene /găng'grēn, găng grēn'/   a form of gangrene caused by a lack of blood supply, characterized by dry shriveled dead tissue.

dry ice   carbon dioxide in its solid form, used as a coolant.

dry mouth   an abnormally dry feeling in the mouth, a symptom of inadequate salivary gland function.

dry skin   abnormal moisture loss in the skin caused by climate, vitamin deficiency, illness, or medication.

DSA   *abbreviation.* digital subtraction angiography.

DSM   *abbreviation. Diagnostic and Statistical Manual.*

DT   *abbreviation.* **1.** duration tetany, the spasm of degenerated muscle upon application of electrical current. **2.** diphtheria tetanus, a vaccine used for immunization of diphtheria and tetanus.

DTaP immunization   a series of five injections (four between 2 and 8 months of age, and one between 4 and 6 years of age) to protect against diphtheria, pertussis, and tetanus. *Also called* DPT immunization or injections.

DT immunization   a vaccine used for immunization of diphtheria and tetanus.

DTs   *abbreviation.* delirium tremens.

dual-energy X-ray absorptiometry (DEXA) /ăb sôrp'shē ŏm'ǐ trē, -zôrp'-/   a technique for measuring bone mineral density using two x-ray beams of different strengths.

Dubowitz for newborns /doō'bə wĭts/   an examination used to estimate the gestational age

of a newborn by evaluating the baby's appearance, skin texture, motor function, and reflexes.

Duchenne('s) dystrophy /doō shĕn(z)'/   the most common form of muscular dystrophy, usually appearing between the age of two and six, caused by a mutation in the X chromosome that prevents normal muscle protein production and development of muscle strength; it affects males but is transmitted by females.

duct /dŭkt/   a tubular structure in the body capable of conveying a gas or liquid.

ductal /dŭk'təl/   of or relating to a duct.

ductile /dŭk'təl, -tīl/   able to be easily bent or otherwise misshapen.

ductless gland   a gland that delivers a hormonal secretion directly into the bloodstream, such as the islands of Langerhans, which secrete insulin directly into the bloodstream in response to glucose concentration.

ductus /dŭk'təs/   duct.

ductus arteriosus /är têr'ē ō'sĭs/   a small arterial duct that redirects blood from the pulmonary artery to the aorta in fetal life.

ductus deferens /dĕf'ə rĕnz'/   a duct that carries sperm from the epididymis to the ejaculatory duct.

ductus venosus /və nō'səs/   a fetal vein that travels through the liver to the inferior vena cava.

due date   the estimated day a baby will be born. *Also called* estimated date of confinement.

dull /dŭl/   not sharp or acute, as vision, hearing, or mental acuity.

duoden-, duodeno-   *combining form.* duodenum: *for example,* duodenostomy.

duodenal /doō'ə dē'nəl, doō ŏd'ə nəl/   of or relating to the duodenum. [duoden- + -al]

duodenal ulcer   a hole in the lining of the duodenum.

duodenectomy /doō ŏd'ə nĕk'tə mē/   surgical procedure to remove the duodenum. [duoden- + -ectomy]

duodenitis /doō ŏd'ə nī'tĭs/   inflammation of the duodenum. [duoden- + -itis]

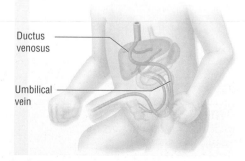

Ductus venosus

Umbilical vein

Ductus Venosus

Medical Power of Attorney
Effective Upon Date of Execution

I, [NAME], a resident of [ADDRESS. COUNTY, STATE]; Social Security Number [NUMBER] designate [NAME], presently residing at [ADDRESS], telephone number [PHONE NUMBER] as my agent to make any and all health care decisions for me, except to the extent I state otherwise in this document. For the purposes of this document, "health care decision" means consent, refusal of consent, or withdrawal of consent to any care, treatment, service, or procedure to maintain, diagnose, or treat an individual's physical or mental condition. This medical power of attorney takes effect if I become unable to make my own health care decisions.

Limitations: [Describe any desired limitations, for example, concerning life support, life-prolonging care, treatment, services, and procedures.]

Disclosure of Information Relating to My Physical or Mental Health: Subject to any limitations in this document, my agent has the power and authority to do all of the following:

1. Request, review, and receive any information, verbal or written, regarding my physical or mental health, including, but not limited to, medical and hospital records;
2. Execute on my behalf any releases or other documents that may be required in order to obtain this information;
3. Consent to the disclosure of this information.

Additional Powers: Where necessary to implement the health care decisions that my agent is authorized by this document to make, my agent has the power and authority to execute on my behalf all of the following:

1. Documents titled or purporting to be a "Refusal to Permit Treatment" and "Leaving Hospital Against Medical Advice";
2. Any necessary waiver or release from liability required by a hospital or physician.

Duration: This power of attorney exists indefinitely from its date of execution, unless I establish herein a shorter time or revoke the power of attorney.

[**If applicable:** This power of attorney expires on [DATE]. If I am unable to make health care decisions for myself when this power of attorney expires, the authority I have granted my agent shall continue to exist until such time as I become able to make health care decisions for myself.]

Alternative Agent: In the event that my designated agent becomes unable, unwilling, or ineligible to serve, I hereby designate [NAME], presently residing at [ADDRESS], telephone number [PHONE NUMBER] as my as my first alternate agent, and [NAME], presently residing at [ADDRESS], telephone number [PHONE NUMBER] as my as my second alternate agent.

Prior Designations Revoked: I revoke any prior Medical Power of Attorney.

Location of Documents:

The original copy of this Medical Power of Attorney is located at [Location].

Signed copies of this Medical Power of Attorney have been filed with the following individuals and institutions: [Names and Addresses].

I sign my name to this Medical Power of attorney on the date of [DATE], at [ADDRESS, COUNTY, STATE].

_____
NAME

Statement of Witnesses

I hereby declare under penalty of perjury that the person who signed or acknowledged this document is personally known to me (or proved to me on the basis of convincing evidence) to be the principal, that the principal signed or acknowledged this durable medical power of attorney in my presence, that the principal appears to be of sound mind and under no duress, fraud, or undue influence. I am not the person appointed an agent by this document. I am not related to the principal by blood, marriage, or adoption. I would not be entitled to any portion of the principal's estate on the principal's death. I am not the attending physician of the principal or an employee of the attending physician. I have no claim against any portion of the principal's estate on the principal's death. Furthermore, if I am an employee of a health care facility in which the principal is a patient, I am not involved in providing direct patient care to the principal and am not an officer, director, partner, or business office employee of the health care facility or of any parent organization of the health care facility.

_____
Witness
_____
Witness

Subscribed and sworn to before me on [DATE].

_____
Notary Public, [COUNTY, STATE]
My commission expires _____.

Durable Power of Attorney

duodenojejunostomy /doo ŏd′ə nō jĭ joo nŏs′tə mē/ surgical creation of a passage between the duodenum and the jejunum. [duodeno- + jejuno- + -stomy]

duodenolysis /doo ŏd′ə nŏl′ə sĭs/ surgical breaking or removal of adhesions from the duodenum. [duodeno- + -lysis]

duodenorrhaphy /doo ŏd′ə nôr′ə fē/ suturing of the duodenum. [dudeno- + -rrhaphy]

duodenoscopy /doo ŏd′ə nŏs′kə pē/ the use of an endoscope to visually examine the duodenum. [duodeno- + -scopy]

duodenostomy /doo ŏd′ə nŏs′tə mē/ a surgical procedure to create an opening in the duodenum. [duodeno- + -stomy]

duodenotomy /doo ŏd′ə nŏt′ə mē/ incision into the duodenum. [duodeno- + -tomy]

duodenum /doo′ə dē′nəm, doo ŏd′ə nəm/ the first part of the small intestines, running from the stomach to the jejunum.

Dupuytren('s) contracture /doo pwē trĕn(z)′ kən trăk′chər/ a disease of the hand causing the formation of scar tissue around the tendons, resulting in a flexion deformity of the fingers.

dura /door′ə/ dura mater.

durable medical equipment reusable medical equipment bought or rented for use in the home.

durable power of attorney a legal document giving an individual the legal authority to handle all legal decisions on behalf of a person incapacitated by a medical condition. *See* form on page 104.

dural /door′əl/ of or relating to the dura mater.

dural sac /săk/ the membrane that encases the spinal cord within the vertebral column.

dura mater /mā′tər/ a strong membrane covering the central nervous system; the outer layer of meninges that protect the brain and spinal cord.

DV *abbreviation.* daily value, as the recommended intake of a nutrient.

DVT *abbreviation.* deep vein thrombosis.

dwarf /dwôrf/ a person with dwarfism.

dwarfism /dwôr′fĭz əm/ any of several genetic conditions characterized by abnormally short stature.

dx, DX *abbreviation.* diagnosis.

DXA *abbreviation.* dual x-ray absorptiometry.

DXA bone scan a technique for measuring bone mineral density using two x-ray beams of different strengths.

dyad /dī′ăd/ **1.** a pair. **2.** a double chromosome resulting from the splitting of a quadruple chromosome.

dye /dī′nə mō′/ an agent or compound used to stain or color.

dynamo- *combining form.* strength or force; energy: *for example,* dynamometer.

dynamograph /dī năm′ə grăf′/ an instrument that measures muscle strength. [dynamo- + -graph]

dynamometer /dī′nə mŏm′ĭ tər/ an instrument that measures muscle strength. [dynamo- + -meter]

-dynia *suffix.* pain: *for example,* coccydynia.

dys- *prefix.* abnormal, difficult: *for example,* dysethesia.

dysarthria /dĭs är′thrē ə/ a disorder caused by the paralysis or inadequate function of mouth muscles, causing disturbances in speech.

dysarthrosis /dĭs′är thrō′sĭs/ **1.** dysarthria. **2.** a false or malformed joint.

dysautonomia /dĭs ô′tə nō′mē ə/ abnormal functioning of the autonomic nervous system, usually resulting from a disease.

dyscephalia /dĭs′sə fā′lē ə/ congenital malformation of the head.

dyscrasia /dĭs krā′zhə/ an abnormal or unbalanced state of the body, especially of the blood.

dysdiadokokinesia /dĭs′dī ăd′ə kō kĭ nē′zhə/ impairment in performing normal voluntary movements as a result of cerebellar impairment.

dysentery /dĭs′ən tĕr′ē/ inflammation of the intestines marked by pain, fever, watery stool, and dehydration.

dysesthesia /dĭs′əs thē′zhə/ **1.** impairment of sensation, especially touch. **2.** abnormal, unpleasant sensations produced by ordinary stimuli. **3.** abnormal, unpleasant sensations felt in the absence of stimuli. [dys- + -esthesia]

dysfunction /dĭs fŭngk′shən/ difficult or abnormal function. [dys- + function]

dysgenesis /dĭs jĕn′ə sĭs/ congenital abnormal development of an organ. [dys- + -genesis]

dysgraphia /dĭs grăf′ē ə/ a developmental disorder affecting the ability to write.

dyskeratosis /dĭs′kĕr ə tō′sĭs/ faulty development of the skin, in which cells keratinize prematurely.

dyskinesia /dĭs′kĭ nē′zhə/ impairment in performing normal voluntary movements.

Therapist with Patient with Dyskinesia

dyslexia /dĭs lĕk′sē ə/   a reading impairment caused by the brain's inability to process graphic symbols.

dyslipidemia /dĭs′lĭp ĭ dē′mē ə/   any condition marked by abnormal levels of blood lipids. [dys- + lipid + -emia]

dysmelia /dĭs mē′lē ə/   a birth defect characterized by missing or abnormally short limbs, sometimes associated with spinal abnormalities.

dysmenorrhea /dĭs′mĕn ə rē′ə/   difficult and painful menstruation. [dys- + menorrhea]

dysmenorrheal /dĭs′mĕn ə rē′əl/   of or relating to dysmenorrhea.

dysmorphism /dĭs môr′fĭz əm/   of abnormal size or shape.

dysmorphology /dĭs′môr fŏl′ə jē/   a branch of clinical genetics concerned with the study of birth defects. [dys- + -morpho- + -logy]

dysmyotonia /dĭs′mī ə tō′nē ə/   abnormal muscle tone.

dyspareunia /dĭs′pə rōō′nē ə/   pain during sexual intercourse.

dyspepsia /dĭs pĕp′shə, -sē ə/   stomach condition marked by abdominal pain and bloating. [dys- + -pepsia]

dyspeptic /dĭs pĕp′tĭk/   of or relating to dyspepsia.

dysphagia /dĭs fā′jē ə, -jə/   difficulty swallowing. [dys- + -phagia]

dysphasia /dĭs fā′zhə/   a speech disorder in which there is an impairment of verbal expression and comprehension. [dys- + -phasia]

dysphonia /dĭs fō′nē ə/   any disorder affecting voice production. [dys- + -phonia]

dysplasia /dĭs plā′zhə/   abnormal tissue or cell development, often found in various cancers. [dys- + -plasia]

dysplastic /dĭs plăs′tĭk/   of or relating to dysplasia. [dys- + -plastic]

dyspnea /dĭsp nē′ə/   shortness of breath associated with heart or lung disease, but naturally occurring during intense physical activity or at high altitudes. [dys- + -pnea]

dyspraxia /dĭs prăk′sē ə/   **1.** impaired or painful organ function. **2.** impairment of coordinated movements, often resulting from stroke, tumor, or brain injury.

dysrhythmia /dĭs rĭ*th*′mē ə/   defective or abnormal rhythm, said of the heart. [dys- + -rhythmia]

dysthymia /dĭs thī′mē ə/   a chronic mood disorder marked by depression, fatigue, and abnormal eating and sleeping habits.

dysthymic disorder /dĭs thī′mĭk/   a chronic disturbance or mood characterized by recurring periods of mild depression.

dystocia /dĭs tō′shə/   difficult childbirth.

dystonia /dĭs tō′nē ə/   abnormal muscle contractions and tremors. [dys- + -tonia]

dystrophic /dĭs trŏf′ĭk, -trō′fĭk/   of or relating to faulty nutrition. [dys- + -trophic]

dystrophy /dĭs′trə fē/   abnormal tissue or organ growth caused by nutritional deficiency. [dys- + -trophy]

dysuria /dĭs yōōr′ē ə/   difficulty or pain in urination. [dys- + -uria]

E

ear /êr/   the organ of hearing that is used to sense sound and maintain equilibrium, divided into the external, middle, and inner ear. *see illustration* on page 108.

earache /êr'āk'/   pain in the ear. *Also called* otalgia, otodynia.

ear bones   a group of small bones in the middle ear; auditory ossicles.

eardrum/ear drum /êr'drŭm'/   the membrane that separates the external ear from the middle ear. *Also called* tympanic membrane, tympanum.

earmold/ear mold /êr'mōld'/   a plastic mold designed to fit inside the auricle of the ear and conduct amplified sound from a hearing aid into the ear canal.

earplug /êr'plŭg'/   a soft object, usually made of cotton or rubber, designed to fit inside the ear in order to block out water or excess sound.

ear thermometer   a thermometer that measures body temperature through the ear canal.

ear tubes   very small plastic tubes that are placed through an incision in the eardrum, creating an airway into the middle ear in order to allow pressure to equalize and built-up fluids to escape.

earwax /êr'wăks'/   a wax-like secretion produced by the outer part of the ear canal that protects the ear by repelling water and trapping dust and other particles. *Also called* cerumen, wax.

eastern equine encephalitis (EEE) /ē'kwīn ĕn sĕf'ə lī'tĭs/   a potentially fatal viral disease transmitted by mosquitoes that can cause permanent brain damage.

eating disorder   a psychological disorder, such as anorexia nervosa or bulimia nervosa, that affects eating habits.

EBCT   *abbreviation.* electron beam computerized tomography.

Ebola virus /ĭ bō'lə/   a deadly virus found mainly in African countries that can cause hemorrhagic fever and kills more than 90% of those infected.

eburnitis /ē'bər nī'tĭs, ĕb'ər-/   condition with unusual hardness of dentin in the teeth.

EBV   *abbreviation.* Epstein-Barr virus.

ECC   *abbreviation.* extracorporeal circulation.

ecchymoma /ĕk'ə mō'mə/   a small hematoma resulting from a bruise.

ecchymosed /ĕk'ə mōzd', -mōst'/   of or having ecchymosis.

ecchymosis /ĕk'ə mō'sĭs/ (*pl.* **ecchymoses** /ĕk'ə mō'sēz/)   a discoloration of the skin or mucous membranes caused by blood escaping from ruptured blood vessels; informally called a black and blue mark. *Also called* bruise.

ecchymotic /ĕk'ə mŏt'ĭk/   relating to an ecchymosis.

eccrine glands /ĕk'rĭn/   sweat glands occurring in the skin throughout the body that are shaped like a coiled tube, excrete water and salt, and cool the body by evaporation of sweat.

ECG, EKG   *abbreviation.* electrocardiogram.

echinacca /ĕk'ə nā'shə/   an herb that supposedly boosts immune system function and is commonly used as an alternative treatment for infections such as the common cold.

echinococcosis /ĭ kī'nō kŏ kō'sĭs/   a disease caused by a parasitic tapeworm.

ECHO /ĕk'ō/   *abbreviation.* echocardiogram.

echo-   *prefix.* sound: *for example,* echoencaphalogram.

echo   *abbreviaton.* echocardiogram.

echoacousia /ĕk'ō ə kōō'zhə/   a hearing disturbance with sounds appearing to be echoed constantly.

echocardiogram   **(ECHO)**   /ĕk'ō kär'dē ə grăm'/   the record obtained by echocardiography. [echo- + cardio- + -gram]

echocardiograph /ĕk'ō kär'dē ə grăf'/   the device used to perform echocardiography. [echo- + cardio- + -graph]

echocardiography   /ĕk'ō kär'dē ŏg'rə fē/   a technique of monitoring the heart that uses ultrasound to take two-dimensional images of the heart both at rest and during exercise. It can demonstrate blood flow direction, such as with a leaky valve. [echo- + cardio- + -graphy]

echoencephalogram   /ĕk'ō ĕn sĕf'ə lə grăm'/   the record obtained by echoencephalography. [echo- + encephalogram]

echoencephalography /ĕk'ō ĕn sĕf'ə lŏg'rə fē/   the use of reflected ultrasound in examining the brain for measuring size of ventricles, shift of midline due to tumor, etc. [echo- + encephalography]

echogram /ĕk'ō grăm'/   the record obtained by echography. [echo- + -gram]

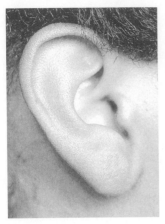

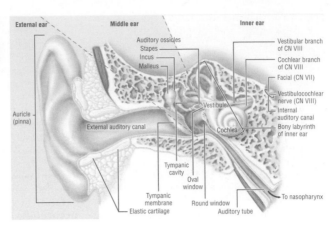

Ear

echography /ĕ kŏg′rə fē/ imaging using ultrasound. *Also called* ultrasonography. [echo- + -graphy]

echolalia /ĕk′ō lā′lē ə/ involuntary repetition of words or phrases spoken by another person, often observed in patients with schizophrenia or Tourette's syndrome.

echopraxia /ĕk′ō prăk′sē ə/ involuntary imitation of the physical movements of others, often observed in patients with schizophrenia or Tourette's syndrome.

echovirus /ĕk′ō vī′rəs/ any of a number of viruses found in the gastrointestinal tract and associated with a number of diseases. [echo- + virus]

eclampsia /ĭ klămp′sē ə/ hypertension, proteinuria, and convulsions or seizures, associated with third-trimester pregnancy, not caused by epilepsy or other cerebral conditions, and potentially life-threatening to both mother and fetus.

ECMO /ĕk′mō/ *abbreviation.* extracorporeal-membrane oxygenation, a complex therapeutic tool used in extreme ICU conditions where lung function has failed but is expected to recover within a few days.

E. coli /ē kō′lī/ a bacillus with numerous strains found normally in the intestinal tract but, in some strains, responsible for gastrointestinal ailments, usually including diarrhea. *Also called* Escherichia coli.

E. coli diarrhea /dī′ə rē′ə/ hemorrhagic diarrhea caused by the bacteria *Escherichia coli*.

ECT *abbreviation.* electroconvulsive therapy; electroshock therapy.

-ectasia, -ectasis *suffix.* dilation, expansion: *for example,* gastrectasia, atelectasis.

ecthyma /ĕk thī′mə/ a staphylococcus infection that causes pyogenic crusts on the skin.

ecto- *prefix.* outer, on the outside: *for example,* ectoderm.

ectocardia /ĕk′tō kär′dē ə/ congenitally abnormal placement of the heart. *Also called* exocardia.

ectoderm /ĕk′tə dûrm′/ the outermost layer of germ cells in an embryo, from which develop skin, nervous system, and sense organs. *See also* endoderm, mesoderm. [ecto- + -derm]

ectodermal /ĕk′tə dûr′məl/ relating to the ectoderm.

ectomorph /ĕk′tə môrf′/ an individual who is lean and non-muscular, in which the tissues from the ectoderm predominate. [ecto- + -morph]

-ectomy *suffix.* excision, removal: *for example,* prostatectomy.

ectoparasite /ĕk′tō păr′ə sīt′/ a parasite that lives on the exterior or outer surfaces of another organism, as fleas or lice. [ecto- + parasite]

ectopia /ĕk tō′pē ə/ an abnormal positioning or location of an organ or body part, which can be a congenital defect or the result of an injury.

ectopic /ĕk tŏp′ĭk/ **1.** out of place, referring to an organ or body part. **2.** of or relating to a heartbeat that does not originate in the sinoatrial node, as in ectopic heartbeats.

ectopic pregnancy a pregnancy that occurs outside of the cavity of the uterus, either in the fallopian tube or rarely, in the abdomen.

ectoplasm /ĕk′tə plăz′əm/ the granule-free outer layer of cytoplasm in a cell. *See also* endoplasm. [ecto- + -plasm]

ectro- *combining form.* missing (usually from birth).

ectrodactyly /ĕk′trō dăk′tə lē/ a birth defect in which one or more of the fingers or toes are partially or completely missing. [ectro- + -dactyly]

ectromelia /ĕk′trō mē′lē ə/ a birth defect in which an infant is missing one or more limbs. [ectro- + -melia]

ectropion /ĕk trō′pē ŏn′/ the abnormal turning outward of the edge of the lower eyelid, especially after plastic surgery on lower lid pouches. *See also* entropion.

eczema /ĕk′sə mə, ĭg zē′-/ any non-contagious inflammation of the skin, often involving redness, itchiness, and the appearance of scaly lesions.

ED *abbreviation.* **1.** effective dose. **2.** emergency department. **3.** erectile dysfunction.

EDC *abbreviation.* estimated date of confinement.

-edema *suffix.* swelling: *for example,* myxedema.

edema /ĭ dē′mə/ an accumulation of excess fluids in cells, tissues, or cavities.

edematous /ĭ dĕm′ə təs/ marked by edema.

edentulous /ĭ dĕn′chə ləs/ a condition in which the natural teeth are absent.

Edward('s) syndrome /ĕd′wərd(z)/ a severely detrimental syndrome present at birth in which a child is born with an extra chromosome 18, characterized by widespread birth defects and extreme mental retardation.

EEE *abbreviation.* eastern equine encephalitis.

EEG *abbreviation.* electroencephalogram.

EENT *abbreviation.* eye, ear, nose, and throat. *See also* ENT.

EF *abbreviation.* ejection fraction.

effacement /ĭ fās′mənt/ the thinning of the cervix just before or during labor.

effective dose (ED) the quantity of a medication or other treatment needed to produce the desired effect, frequently designated as ED50, meaning that a given dose is effective in 50% of patients, or ED95 (effective in 95%), etc.

effeminate /ĭ fĕm′ə nĭt/ having qualities associated more with females than with males.

efferent /ĕf′ər ənt/ conducting away from a central organ or body part.

efferent nerve a nerve that relays impulses away from the central nervous system.

effleurage /ĕf′lōō räzh′/ in massage therapy, a long unbroken massage stroke that follows the muscle fibers and can be superficial or deep but always aimed toward the heart and is used to relax or warm up the muscles to allow for a deeper technique.

effluvium /ĭ flōō′vē əm/ an outflow of waste, especially of noxious vapors or gas.

effusion /ĭ fyōō′zhən/ **1.** the seeping of fluid into a body cavity or tissue. **2.** the effused fluid itself.

EGD *abbreviation.* esophagogastroduodenoscopy.

egg /ĕg/ a female gamete or sex cell.

ego /ē′gō/ in psychoanalysis, the most conscious component of the psyche and the most immediately responsible for thoughts, behaviors, and interaction with the outside world.

egocentric /ē′gō sĕn′trĭk/ extremely self-centered.

egomania /ē′gō mā′nē ə/ in psychology, an obsessive interest in oneself.

Ehlers-Danlos syndrome /ā′lərz dăn′lŏs/ a genetic disorder of fibroelastic tissue characterized by loose joints and skin, aortic valve incompetency, and aortic aneurysm.

ehrlichiosis /ĕr lĭk′ē ō′sĭs/ an acute bacterial infection caused by various species of the genus Erlichia and commonly transmitted to humans by the brown dog tick.

EIA *abbreviation.* enzyme immunoassay.

eicosanoid /ī kō′sə noid′/ any of a number of compounds derived from fatty acids and involved in cellular activity.

ejaculate /ĭ jăk′yə lāt′/ to expel suddenly, as semen from the penis.

ejaculation /ĭ jăk′yə lā′shən/ the expulsion of semen during orgasm.

ejaculatory duct /ĭ jăk′yə lə tôr′ē/ the duct in males that passes through the prostate and through which the semen passes during ejaculation.

ejection fraction (EF) during a heartbeat, the blood pumped out of a filled ventricle when the heart contracts, expressed as a percentage of ventricular volume.

EKG, ECG *abbreviation.* electrocardiogram.

elastic /ĭ lăs′tĭk/ having the property of returning to an original shape after being expanded, compressed, or distorted in some way.

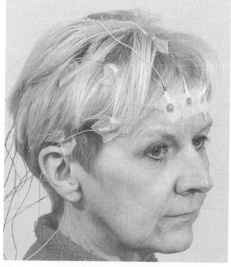

EEG

elasticity /ē′lă stĭs′ĭ tē/   the degree to which an object possesses the property of being elastic.

elastin /ĭ lăs′tĭn/   a yellow, elastic protein that is the major component in the connective tissue of elastic structures in the body, found in skin and damaged by UV (sun light), leading to wrinkles.

elastoma /ĭ lă stō′mə/   tumorlike deposits of connective tissue, especially around the neck, armpits, and thighs.

elbow /ĕl′bō/   the bend in the arm between the upper arm with the forearm.

elbow joint   the compound hinge joint in the elbow that connects the upper arm, humerus, and the two bones of the forearm, radius, and ulna.

elder abuse   physical or emotional abuse, or financial exploitation, of an elderly person by the person's family, medical caregivers, or others.

elective /ĭ lĕk′tĭv/   indicating a procedure or treatment that is voluntarily undergone by a patient and may be advantageous without being urgently needed.

elective surgery   any surgery performed on a patient at his or her request that is not vital or urgent.

electro-   *combining form.* electrical: *for example,* electrocardiogram.

electrocardiogram (ECG, EKG) /ĭ lĕk′trō kär′dē ə grăm′/   the graphic record, created by electrocardiography, of the electrical activity in the heart. [electro- + cardio- + -gram]

electrocardiograph   /ĭ lĕk′trō kär′dē ə grăf′/   a device that records the electrical activity in the heart. [electro- + cardio- + -graph]

electrocardiography /ĭ lĕk′trō kär′dē ŏg′rə fē/   the method of examining the heart by recording and studying electrical currents that pass through it. [electro- + cardio- + -graphy]

electrocauterization /ĭ lĕk′trō kô′tər ə zā′shən/   the method of cauterization by passing a high-frequency current through tissue or a piece of metal in contact with the tissue. [electro- + cauterization]

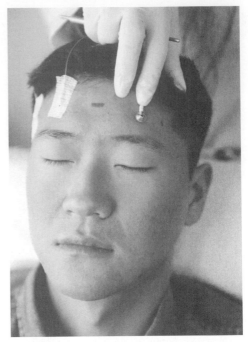
Electrode

electrocautery /ĭ lĕk′trō kô′tə rē/   an instrument for passing a high-frequency current through a local area of tissue. [electro- + cautery]

electrocoagulation /ĭ lĕk′trō kō ăg′yə lā′shən/   coagulation achieved by use of an electrocautery.

electrocochleography   /ĭ lĕk′trō kō′klē ŏg′rə fē/   the process of measuring the electrical activity in the inner ear caused by sound stimuli. [electro- + cochleo- + -graphy]

electroconvulsive therapy (ECT) /ĭ lĕk′trō kən vŭl′sĭv/   electroshock therapy, sometimes used for severe depression unresponsive to drug therapy.

electrode /ĭ lĕk′trōd/   a device that makes contact with or measures one of the two ends of an electrical circuit.

electrodesiccation   /ĭ lĕk′trō dĕs′ĭ kā′shən/   the use of a high-frequency electrical current in order to dry tissue, destroy lesions, or seal off blood vessels.

electrodiagnosis   /ĭ lĕk′trō dī′əg nō′sĭs/   the use of electronic imaging in the diagnosis of disease. [electro- + diagnosis]

electroencephalogram (EEG) /ĭ lĕk′trō ĕn sĕf′ə lə grăm′/   the record obtained by an electroencephalograph. [electro- + encephalogram]

electroencephalograph   /ĭ lĕk′trō ĕn sĕf′ə lə grăf′/   an instrument that measures the electrical activity in the brain through electrodes

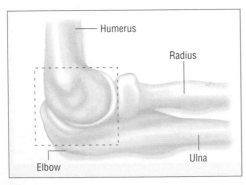

Humerus

Radius

Elbow

Ulna

Elbow

attached to the scalp. [electro- + encephalo- + -graph]

electroencephalography (EEG) /ĭ lĕk′trō ĕn sĕf′ə lŏg rə fē/ the registration of electrical potentials measured by an electroencephalograph. [electro- + encephalography]

electrogram /ĭ lĕk′trə grăm′/ graphic image made by tracing of electrical events in the body. [electro- + -gram]

electrolysis /ĭ lĕk trŏl′ə sĭs/ **1.** the breaking down of a chemical compound by the passing through of an electrical current. **2.** the removal of hair by the application of an electrical current to the hair follicle, destroying it. [electro- + -lysis]

electrolyte /ĭ lĕk′trə līt′/ any substance in a solution that is broken down by an electrical current, such as dissolved atoms or molecules in blood (for example, sodium, potassium, calcium, bicarbonate, chloride, and others), allowing the current to pass through the solution.

electromagnetic field therapy /ĭ lĕk′trō măg nĕt′ĭk/ an alternative therapy, in which magnetic fields are applied to various parts of the body, used to treat a wide range of afflictions.

electromyogram (EMG) /ĭ lĕk′trō mī′ə grăm′/ the record of the electrical currents associated with muscular activity, produced during electromyography. [electro- + myo- + -gram]

electromyograph /ĭ lĕk′trō mī ŏ grăf′/ device for imaging of the electrical activity of muscles, used in diagnosing neuromuscular disorders. [electro- + myo- + -graph]

electromyography /ĭ lĕk′trō mī ŏg′rə fē/ the process of recording electrical activity produced by the muscles for diagnostic purposes. [electro- + myo- + -graphy]

electron beam computerized tomography (EBCT) /tə mŏg′rə fē/ a non-invasive test that detects coronary artery disease by scanning for calcium deposits in the coronary arteries.

electronic medical record (EMR) a patient's record stored in electronic form in a computer database.

electrophoresis /ĭ lĕk′trō fə rē′sĭs/ a process by which an electric current is passed through a solution in order to separate particles related to their molecular size and electrical charge. [electro- + -phoresis]

electrophoretic /ĭ lĕk′trō fə rĕt′ĭk/ of or relating to electrophoresis.

electrophrenic respiration /ĭ lĕk′trō frĕn′ĭk/ respiration induced by electrical stimulation of the phrenic nerve, the motor nerve of the diaphragm, used in patients where the respiratory center has been paralyzed. [electro- + phrenic]

electrophysiologic /ĭ lĕk′trō fĭz′ē ə lŏj′ĭk/ of or relating to electrophysiology.

electrophysiology /ĭ lĕk′trō fĭz′ē ŏl′ə jē/ the field of medicine that studies electrical activity in the body and its direct effects. [electro- + physiology]

electroshock /ĭ lĕk′trō shŏk′/ electroshock therapy. [electro- + shock]

electroshock therapy (ECT) a treatment for various mental disorders, but especially severe depression, in which an electric current is passed through the brain while under brief anesthesia. *Also called* electroconvulsive therapy, shock therapy.

electrosurgery /ĭ lĕk′trō sûr′jə rē/ surgery in which a high-frequency electrical current is used to separate tissue instead of a scalpel. [electro- + surgery]

electrotherapy /ĭ lĕk′trō thĕr′ə pē/ the use of electricity in the treatment of disease. [electro- + therapy]

elephantiasis /ĕl′ə fən tī′ə sĭs/ a disease caused by parasitic worms that invade the lymphatic system, resulting in fluid buildup in parts of the body, and often swelling the limbs or genitals to an enormous size.

elevated /ĕl′ə vā′tĭd/ higher than normal, as fever.

elevator /ĕl′ə vā′tər/ in a dental extraction, an instrument used to apply leverage against the tooth to loosen it from the periodontal ligament.

elimination /ĭ lĭm′ə nā′shən/ the expulsion of waste material from the body.

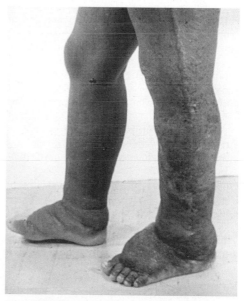

Elephantiasis

ELISA /ĭ lī′zə, ĭ lĭs′ə/ *abbreviation.* enzyme-linked immunosorbent assay.

elix. *abbreviation.* elixir.

elixir /ĭ lĭk′sər/ a sweet, fragrant liquid solution containing alcohol and water that serves as a vehicle for medicine.

elliptocytosis /ĭ lĭp′tō sī tō′sĭs/ a rare congenital disorder in which most of the patient's red blood cells are elliptically shaped, resulting in anemia. *Also called* ovalocytosis.

emaciation /ĭ mā′shē ā′shən/ the process of becoming abnormally thin.

emasculate /ĭ măs′kyə lāt′/ **1.** to castrate. **2.** to weaken or cause to lose vigor.

emasculation /ĭ măs′kyə lā′shən/ the act of emasculating.

embalm /ĕm bäm′/ to prevent a dead body from decaying by treating it with chemicals.

embolectomy /ĕm′bə lĕk′tə mē/ the surgical removal of an embolus.

embolic stroke /ĕm bŏl′ĭk/ a stroke caused by an embolus disrupting the flow of blood to the brain.

embolism /ĕm′bə lĭz′əm/ the obstruction of a blood vessel by an embolus (clot).

embolization /ĕm′bə lə zā′shən/ the process by which blood flow to a tumor is disrupted by injection of embolic material into the artery that flows into the tumor.

embolus /ĕm′bə ləs/ (*pl.* **emboli** /ĕm′bə lī′/) a blood clot or small particle of bone marrow fat that travels in the bloodstream and lodges in a smaller vessel, obstructing the flow of blood.

embrasure /ĕm brā′zhər/ a v-shaped opening to adjacent or opposing teeth.

embryo- *combining form.* of or relating to an embryo: *for example,* embryogenesis.

embryo /ĕm′brē ō′/ an organism in the early stages of its development, especially a developing ovum in the eight weeks before it becomes a fetus.

embryogenic /ĕm′brē ō jĕn′ĭk/ **1.** of or relating to the creation of an embryo. **2.** capable of producing an embryo. [embryo- + -genic.]

embryogenesis /ĕm′brē ō jĕn′ə sĭs/ the creation and development of an embryo. [embryo- + -genesis]

embryologist /ĕm′brē ŏl′ə jĭst/ specialist in embryology. [embryo + -logist]

embryology /ĕm′brē ŏl′ə jē/ science that deals with the development and functioning of the embryo. [embryo + -logy]

embryonal /ĕm′brē ə nəl, ĕm′brē ō′nəl/ relating to or being an embryo.

embryonic /ĕm′brē ŏn′ĭk/ embryonal.

embryopathy /ĕm′brē ŏp′ə thē/ any disease of the embryo. [embryo- + -pathy]

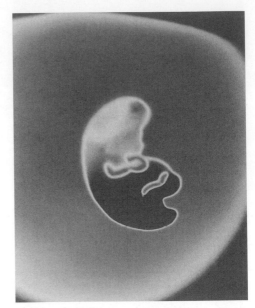

Embryo (eight-weeks)

emergency /ĭ mûr′jən sē/ a situation in which a delay in the treatment of the patient would lead to a significant increase in the threat to life or body part.

emergency birth control emergency contraception.

emergency contraception /kŏn′trə sĕp′shən/ the prevention of pregnancy, whether by drugs or a device, after unprotected intercourse, usually within the first 24 hours.

emergency department the department of a hospital designated for the immediate treatment of injuries and sudden illnesses. *Also called* emergency room.

emergency medical technician (EMT) a medical technician who is trained and certified to provide emergency medical care at the scene of an accident or sudden illness or medical event before a patient reaches a hospital. *Also called* paramedic.

emergency medicine the branch of medicine concerned with the treatment of sudden illnesses or injuries.

emergency physician a physician who directs the care of patients both in the emergency department of a hospital and those under the care of emergency medical technicians.

emergency room (ER) the department of a hospital designated for the immediate treatment of injuries and sudden illnesses. *Also called* emergency department.

emergency surgery surgery that is unexpectedly and urgently required.

-emesis *suffix.* vomit: *for example,* hematemesis.

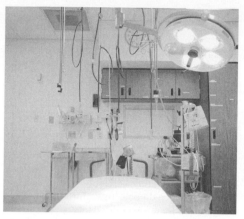

Emergency Room

emesis /ĕm′ə sĭs/ the sudden expelling of the stomach contents; vomiting.

emetic /ə mĕt′ĭk/ **1.** a medication that induces vomiting. **2.** causing or relating to vomiting.

EMG *abbreviation.* electromyogram.

-emia *suffix.* blood: *for example,* hyperglycemia.

emission /ĭ mĭsh′ən/ something that is emitted or discharged from the body, especially semen during ejaculation.

emmetropia /ĕm′ĭ trō′pē ə/ the condition of normal eyes in which parallel rays of light are focused on the retina, resulting in perfect vision.

emollient /ĭ mŏl′yənt/ **1.** *n.* an agent that softens or soothes the skin. **2.** *adj.* softening and soothing to the skin.

emotion /ĭ mō′shən/ a spontaneous, intense mental state that is often accompanied by physiological changes.

emotional /ĭ mō′shə nəl/ of or relating to emotion.

empathic /ĕm păth′ĭk/ of or pertaining to empathy.

empathize /ĕm′pə thīz′/ to show empathy for.

empathy /ĕm′pə thē/ identification with and understanding of another person's emotional state.

emphysema /ĕm′fə sē′mə/ a condition in which there is an increased accumulation of air in the organs and tissues, especially in the lungs, resulting in loss of lung elasticity and decreased gas exchange.

empyema /ĕm′pī ē′mə, ĕm′pē-/ the accumulation of pus in a body cavity, usually the thorax.

empyesis /ĕm′pī ē′sĭs/ skin eruption with pustules.

EMR *abbreviation.* electronic medical record.

EMT *abbreviation.* emergency medical technician.

emulsify /ĭ mŭl′sĭ fī′/ to make into an emulsion; to make a greasy or fatty material water-soluble by dispersing one liquid into another.

emulsion /ĭ mŭl′shən/ a forced suspension of molecules of one liquid into another, usually water-based liquid, by vigorous shaking, as is done for oil into vinegar and water in a salad dressing.

enamel /ĭ năm′əl/ the hard substance covering the exposed portion of the teeth.

enanthem /ĭ năn′thəm/ a mucous membrane eruption, especially one occurring in an exanthematous viral rash.

encapsulated /ĕn kăp′sə lā′tĭd/ covered by a membrane or protective coating.

encephal-, encephalo- *combining form.* the brain: *for example,* encephalitis, encephalogram.

encephalatrophy /ĕn sĕf′ə lăt′rə fē/ atrophy of the brain. [encephal- + atrophy]

encephalitis /ĕn sĕf′ə lī′tĭs/ inflammation of the brain. [encephal- + -itis]

encephalocele /ĕn sĕf′ə lə sēl′/ a congenital gap in the skull, usually resulting in a protrusion of the brain. [encephalo- + -cele]

encephalogram /ĕn sĕf′ə lə grăm′/ the record obtained during encephalography. [encephalo- + -gram]

encephalography /ĕn sĕf′ə lŏg′rə fē/ radiographic imaging of the brain. [encephalo- + -graphy]

encephalomalacia /ĕn sĕf′ə lō mə lā′shə/ softening of the brain tissue. [encephalo- + -malacia]

encephalomeningitis /ĕn sĕf′ə lō mĕn′ĭn jī′tĭs/ inflammation of the brain and meninges. *Also called* meningoencephalitis. [encephalo- + meningitis]

encephalomyelitis /ĕn sĕf′ə lō mī′ə lī′tĭs/ inflammation of the brain and spinal cord. [encephalo- + myelitis]

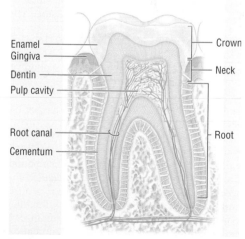

Enamel — — Crown
Gingiva
 — — Neck
Dentin —
Pulp cavity —
Root canal — — Root
Cementum —

Enamel

encephalomyelopathy /ĕn sĕf′ə lō mī′ə lŏp′ə thē/ any disease that affects both the brain and spinal cord. [encephalo- + myelo- + -pathy]

encephalomyeloradiculitis /ĕn sĕf′ə lō mī′ə lō rə dĭk′yə lī′tĭs/ inflammation of the brain, spinal cord, and spinal roots. [encephalo- + myelo- + radiculitis]

encephalopathy /ĕn sĕf′ə lŏp′ə thē/ any disease of the brain. [encephalo- + -pathy]

encephalosclerosis /ĕn sĕf′ə lō sklĭ rō′sĭs/ a hardening of the brain. [encephalo- + -sclerosis]

encephalotomy /ĕn sĕf′ə lŏt′ə mē/ incision into the brain. [encephalo- + -tomy]

enchondroma /ĕn′kŏn drō′mə/ (pl. **enchondromas** or **enchondromata** /ĕn′kŏn drō′mə tə/) a benign growth of cartilage originating in the interior of a bone.

enchondromatosis /ĕn′kŏn drō′mə tō′sĭs/ a congenital disorder in which benign growths of cartilage cause distortions or fractures in the bones.

encopresis /ĕn′kə prē′sĭs/ repeated defecation caused by psychological reasons or fecal retention and soiling.

encounter /ĕn koun′tər/ 1. in psychology, a group therapy meeting usually involving emotional confrontation. 2. in health care, a face-to-face contact between a client and a provider.

end-, endo- prefix. within, inner, absorbing, or containing: for example, endarterectomy, endocervical.

endangitis /ĕn′dăn jī′tĭs/ inflammation of the inner lining of a blood vessel. [end- + angitis]

endarterectomy /ĕn där′tə rĕk′tə mē/ the surgical removal of the inner lining of an artery; carotid endarterectomy.

endarteritis /ĕn där′tə rī′tĭs/ inflammation of the inner lining of an artery. Also called endoarteritis. [end- + arteritis]

endaural /ĕn dôr′əl/ within the ear. [end- + aural]

endbrain /ĕnd′brān′/ the anterior section of the forebrain including the cerebrum. [end- + brain]

endemic /ĕn dĕm′ĭk/ confined to a specific community or region.

ending /en′dĭng/ the terminal part of something, as a nerve ending.

endoarteritis /ĕn′dō är′tə rī′tĭs/ inflammation of the inner lining of an artery. Also called endarteritis. [endo- + arteritis]

endocardial /ĕn′dō kär′dē əl/ 1. within the heart 2. of or relating to the endocardium.

endocarditis /ĕn′dō kär dī′tĭs/ inflammation of the endocardium, including heart valves.

endocardium /ĕn′dō kär′dē əm/ (pl. **endocardia** /ĕn′dō kär′dē ə/) the lining of the cavities of the heart, which also forms part of the heart valves.

endocervical /ĕn′dō sûr′vĭ kəl/ 1. within the cervix. 2. of or relating to the endocervix. [endo- + cervical]

endocervicitis /ĕn′dō sûr′və sī′tĭs/ inflammation of the endocervix.

endocervix /ĕn′dō sûr′vĭks/ the mucous membrane lining the uterine cervical canal. [endo- + cervix]

endochondral /ĕn′dō kŏn′drəl/ growing or developing within cartilage.

endocolitis /ĕn′dō kə lī′tĭs/ inflammation of the colon. [endo- + colitis]

endocranial /ĕn′do krā′nē əl/ of or pertaining to the area within the cranium. [endo- + cranial]

endocranium /ĕn′dō krā′nē əl/ the inner part of the cranium. [endo- + cranium]

endocrine /ĕn′də krĭn/ 1. secreting internally, as certain glands. 2. of or relating to the endocrine system.

endocrine gland glands that have no ducts and secrete directly into the blood.

endocrine system all of the tissues in the body that secrete hormones internally and control much of the metabolic activity of the body, including, among others, the adrenal, pituitary, thyroid, and reproductive glands, and the islets of Langerhans.

endocrinologist /ĕn′dō krĭ nŏl′ə jĭst/ a medical professional who specializes in the endocrine system.

endocrinology /ĕn′dō krĭ nŏl′ə jē/ the study of the glands and hormones of the body and diseases and disorders that affect them.

endocrinopathy /ĕn′dō krĭ nŏp′ə thē/ any disorder affecting an endocrine gland.

endocystitis /ĕn′dō sĭ stī′tĭs/ inflammation of the mucous membrane within the bladder. [endo- + cystitis]

endocytosis /ĕn′dō sī tō′sĭs/ the process of ingesting substances into a cell by a folding inward of the pasma membrane. [endo- + cyt- + -osis]

endoderm /ĕn′də dûrm′/ the innermost layer of germ cells of an embryo, developing into the digestive tract, lungs and associated structures. See also ectoderm, mesoderm. [endo- + -derm]

endodermal /ĕn′dō dûr′məl/ of or relating to the endoderm.

endodontics /ĕn′dō dŏn′tĭks/ a specialty within dentistry concerned with the dental pulp, especially with root canal work.

endodontist /ĕn′dō dŏn′tĭst/ a dentist who specializes in the pulp of the teeth, including performing root canals.

end-of-life care physical and emotional care of a patient who is terminally ill, particularly in a hospice setting.

endogenous /ĕn dŏj'ə nəs/ originating from within an organism.

endolith /ĕn'də lĭth/ calcification found within the dental pulp.

endolymph /ĕn'də lĭmf'/ the fluid contained within the inner ear. [endo- + lymph]

endometrial biopsy /ĕn'dō mē'trē əl bī'ŏp sē/ a procedure for sampling and testing the endometrium.

endometrial cancer cancer of the lining of the uterus. *Also called* endometrial carcinoma.

endometrial carcinoma /kär'sə nō'mə/ endometrial cancer.

endometrial hyperplasia /hī'pər plā'zhə/ overgrowth of the lining of the uterus.

endometrioma /ĕn'dō mē'trē ō'mə/ a tumor composed of endometrial tissue. [endo- + metri- + -oma]

endometriosis /ĕn'dō mē'trē ō'sĭs/ a condition in which tissue of the endometrium is present outside the uterus, in the fallopian tubes or abdominal cavity.

endometritis /ĕn'dō mĭ trī'tĭs/ inflammation of the endometrium.

endometrium /ĕn'dō mē'trē əm/ the mucous membrane lining the uterus.

endomorph /ĕn'də môrf'/ an individual who has a heavy body build, in which the tissues from the ectoderm are relatively predominant. *See also* ectomorph, mesomorph. [ecto- + -morph]

endomyocarditis /ĕn'dō mī'ō kär dī'tĭs/ inflammation of the heart muscle and heart lining. [endo- + myocarditis]

endomyometritis /ĕn'dō mī'ō mĭ trī'tĭs/ infection in the lining of the uterus after a cesarean. [endo + myo- + metritis]

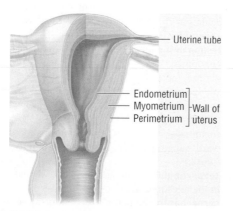

— Uterine tube

Endometrium
Myometrium } Wall of
Perimetrium } uterus

Endometrium

endomysium /ĕn'dō mĭz'ē əl/ fine connective tissue around muscle fibers.

endopericarditis /ĕn'dō pĕr'ĭ kär dī'tĭs/ inflammation of both the endocardium and the pericardium. [endo- + pericarditis]

endoperimyocarditis /ĕn'dō pĕr'ē mī'ō kär dī'tĭs/ inflammation of the heart muscle as well as the endocardium and pericardium. [endo- + peri- + myocarditis]

endoplasm /ĕn'də plăz'əm/ the inner, less viscous portion of the cytoplasm. *See also* ectoplasm. [endo- + -plasm]

endorphin /ĕn dôr'fĭn/ a naturally occurring neurochemical found in the brain that causes euphoria and analgesia; levels rise during exercise and when "in love."

endoscope /ĕn'də skōp'/ an instrument used to examine the interior of a hollow organ, such as the stomach or bladder. [endo- + -scope]

endoscopic /ĕn'də skŏp'ĭk/ of, relating to, or performed by use of an endoscope.

endoscopic retrograde cholangiopancreatography (ERCP) /kə lăn'jē ō păn'krē ə tŏg'rə fē/ a procedure that uses a combination of x-rays and an endoscope to diagnose disorders of the liver, gallbladder, bile ducts, and pancreas; also used to remove stones blocking the common bile duct and occasionally to insert a stent into the common bile duct when blocked by a pancreatic tumor.

endoscopic surgery surgery involving the use of an endoscope.

endoscopic ultrasound a procedure involving the use of an endoscope and ultrasound in order to examine the digestive tract and the surrounding tissue.

endoscopy /ĕn dŏs'kə pē/ the visual inspection of a body cavity or canal with an endoscope.

endoskeleton /ĕn'dō skĕl'ĭ tən/ the internal framework of the body. [endo- + skeleton]

endosteoma /ĕn dŏs'tē ō'mə/ a benign tumor within the medullary cavity of a bone. [end- + osteoma]

endosteum /ĕn dŏs'tē əm/ the thin layer of cells lining the interior of long bones.

endothelial /ĕn'dō thē'lē əl/ of, relating to, or produced by the endothelium.

endothelioma /ĕn'dō thē'lē ō'mə/ a tumor originating in the endothelium.

endothelium /ĕn'dō thē'lē əm/ (*pl.* **endothelia** /ĕn'dō thē'lē ə/) a thin layer of cells that lines some of the cavities in the body and all blood vessels.

endotoxin /ĕn'dō tŏk'sən/ a bacterial toxin produced after the destruction of the bacterial cells. [endo- + toxin]

endotracheal /en′dō trā′kē əl/ within the trachea.

endotracheal intubation /ĭn′tōō bā′shən/ the passage of a tube from the nose or mouth through the trachea in order to maintain the airway, as during anesthesia.

endotracheal (ET) tube a tube passed into the trachea during endotracheal intubation.

endovascular surgery /ĕn′dō văs′kyə lər/ a surgical procedure in which a catheter containing medication or miniature instruments is inserted into a blood vessel in order to treat a vascular disease.

end stage the final phase in the course of an illness, particularly one that results in death.

end-stage renal disease (ESRD) /rē′nəl/ chronic, irreversible kidney failure.

endurance /ĕn dōōr′əns/ the ability to last through physical exertion; stamina.

enema /ĕn′ə mə/ the injection of liquid into the rectum for cleansing or other therapeutic purposes.

energy medicine a type of alternative medicine that focuses on the energy for healing either through another's touch or by utilizing the client's own energy.

energy therapy any of various types of therapy used in energy medicine.

enervate /ĕn′ər vāt′/ to weaken.

enervation /ĕn′ər vā′shən/ the loss of energy; weakening.

engagement /ĕn gāj′mənt/ the point at which the fetus drops and engages into the mother's pelvis usually several weeks before onset of labor.

engorged /ĕn gôrjd′/ filled with excessive blood or other fluid.

enophthalmos /ĕn′ŏf thăl′məs/ sunken eyeball.

ENT *abbreviation.* ear, nose, throat. *See also* EENT.

enter-, entero- *combining form.* intestines: *for example,* enteritis, enterocele.

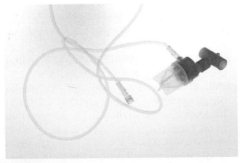

Endotracheal Tube

enteral /ĕn′tər əl/ of or pertaining to the intestines.

enterectomy /ĕn′tə rĕk′tə mē/ surgical removal of part of the intestines. [enter- + -ectomy]

enteric /ĕn tĕr′ĭk/ of or pertaining to the intestines.

enteric-coated coated with a substance that delays a medication's release until it passes into the intestines, thereby avoiding stomach irritation, as with enteric-coated aspirin.

enteritis /ĕn′tə rī′tĭs/ inflammation of the intestines. [enter- + -itis]

enterobiasis /ĕn′tə rō bī′ə sĭs/ intestinal pinworm infection.

enterocele /ĕn′tər ə sēl′/ a hernia sac containing a portion of the small intestine. [entero- + -cele]

enterocentesis /ĕn′tə rō sĕn tē′sĭs/ puncture of the intestines to withdraw fluids or gas. [entero- + -centesis]

enteroclysis /ĕn′tə rŏk′lə sĭs/ an enema that reaches high into the colon.

enterococcus /ĕn′tə rō kŏk′əs/ (*pl.* **enterococci** /ĕn′tə rō kŏk′sī/) bacteria normally found in intestines. [entero- + -coccus]

enterocolitis /ĕn′tə rō kə lī′tĭs/ inflammation of both the colon and small intestines. [entero- + colitis]

enterocolostomy /ĕn′tə rō kə lŏs′tə mē/ surgical connection of the small intestines and colon. [entero- + colostomy]

enterocyst /ĕn′tər ə sĭst/ a cyst within the intestines. *Also called* enterocystoma. [entero- + cyst]

enterocystocele /ĕn′tə rō sĭs′tə sēl′/ hernia of both the intestines and bladder. [entero- + cysto- + -cele]

enterocystoma /ĕn′tə rō sĭ stō′mə/ a cyst within the intestines. *Also called* enterocyst. [entero- + cyst- + -oma]

enterology /ĕn′tə rŏl′ə jē/ medical specialty dealing with the intestines. [entero- + -logy]

enteromycosis /ĕn′tə rō mī kō′sĭs/ fungal infection of the intestines. [entero- + mycosis]

enteropathy /ĕn′tə rŏp′ə thē/ any intestinal disease. [entero- + -pathy]

enteropexy /ĕn′tər ə pĕk′sē/ surgical fixing of part of the intestines to the abdominal wall. [entero- + -pexy]

enteroptosis /ĕn′tər ŏp tō′sĭs/ abnormal downward sagging of the intestines. [entero- + -ptosis]

enterorrhagia /ĕn′tər ə rā′jə, -jē ə/ bleeding in the intestines. [entero- + -rrhagia]

enterorrhaphy /ĕn′tə rôr′ə fē/ suturing of the intestines. [etnero- + -rrhaphy]

enteroscope /ĕn'tər ə skōp'/ a flexible device used to examine the small intestine. [entero- + -scope]

enteroscopy /ĕn'tə rŏs'kə pē/ the examination of the small intestine with a flexible device. [entero- + -scopy]

enterosepsis /ĕn'tər ə sĕp'sĭs/ sepsis of the intestines. [entero- + sepsis]

enterospasm /ĕn'tər ə spăz'əm/ a painful intestinal contraction. [entero- + -spasm]

enterostasis /ĕn'tə rŏs'tə sĭs/ an intestinal obstruction. [entero- + -stasis]

enterostenosis /ĕn'tə rō stĭ nō'sĭs/ narrowing of the intestines. [entero- + -stenosis]

enterostomy /ĕn'tə rŏs'tə mē/ surgical creation of a new opening into the small intestine that bypasses the oral-gastric route, to permit draining, or the opposite, to nourish the patient by infusing liquid meals. [entero- + -stomy]

enterotomy /ĕn'tə rŏt'ə mē/ incision into the intestines. [entero- + -tomy]

enterovirus /ĕn'tə rō vī'rəs/ an intestinal virus.

entropion /ĕn trō'pē ŏn'/ a turning inward, as the eyelid turning inward toward the eye. *See also* ectropion.

enucleation /ĭ nōō'klē ā'shən/ the surgical removal of an eye.

enuresis /ĕn'yōō rē'sĭs/ urinary incontinence, especially bedwetting at night.

environmental medicine the practice of medicine that focuses on the relationship between health and environmental factors including lifestyle.

enzyme /ĕn'zīm/ a protein that acts as a catalyst for chemical reactions in living things.

enzyme defect any disorder caused by a deficient genetic abnormality of a necessary enzyme.

enzyme immunoassay (EIA) a text that uses an enzyme bonded to an antigen as a marker.

enzyme-linked immunosorbent assay (ELISA) /ĭm'yə nō sôr'bənt ăs'ā/ a test using enzymes to detect antibodies or antigens.

enzyme therapy the use of oral enzymes to replace those missing due to disease, such as enzymes taken with each meal in cystic fibrosis, in which pancreatic enzymes are lacking.

eosinophil /ē'ō sĭn'ə fĭl/ a type of white blood cell that stains red with dye.

eosinophilia /ē'ō sĭn'ə fĭl'ē ə/ an abnormal increase in eosinophils in the blood, often present in allergic conditions.

eosinophilic /ē'ō sĭn'ə fĭl'ĭk/ of or pertaining to an eosinophil.

ependyma /ə pĕn'də mə/ membrane that lines the ventricles of the brain and the central canal of the spinal cord.

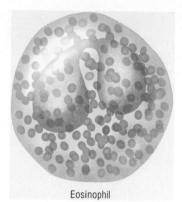

Eosinophil

Eosinophil

ependymoma /ə pĕn'də mō'mə/ a tumor that originates in cells from the ependyma.

epi- *prefix.* over: *for example,* epicondyle.

epicanthal fold /ĕp'ĭ kăn'thəl/ a vertical fold of skin that comes across the inner angle of the eye and is normally found in Mongolian peoples, and also found in people with birth defects such as Down syndrome.

epicanthus /ĕp'ĭ kăn'thəs/ (*pl.* **epicanthi** /ĕp'ĭ kăn'thī/) a vertical fold of skin over the nasal canthus (portion of eye near to the nose).

epicardium /ĕp'ĭ kär'dē əm/ (*pl.* **epicardia** /ĕp'ĭ kär'dē ə/) the outer layer of tissue that forms the heart wall.

epicondyle /ĕp'ĭ kŏn'dīl/ a bony projection above the condyle. [epi- + condyle]

epicranial /ĕp'ĭ krā'nē əl/ above or covering the cranium. [epi- + cranial]

epicranium /ĕp'ĭ krā'nē əm/ (*pl.* **epicrania** /ĕp'ĭ krā'nē ə/) the scalp or cover of the cranium. [epi- + cranium]

epidemic /ĕp'ĭ dĕm'ĭk/ 1. *n.* a disease that spreads rapidly and over a wide area. 2. *adj.* spreading rapidly and widely.

epidemic hemorrhagic fever /hĕm'ə răj'ĭk/ any of various epidemic fevers accompanied by high fever, pain, vomiting, and bleeding; usually spread by rodents.

epidemiologist /ĕp'ĭ dē'mē ŏl'ə jĭst/ a specialist who studies the spread and control of epidemics.

epidemiology /ĕp'ĭ dē'mē ŏl'ə jē/ the study of the spread and control of epidemics.

epidermal /ĕp'ĭ dûr'məl/ of or pertaining to the epidermis or skin.

epidermis /ĕp'ĭ dûr'mĭs/ the outer layer of skin cells, mostly made up of squamous cells.

epididym-, epididymo- *combining form.* epididymis: *for example,* epididymitis, epididymoplasty.

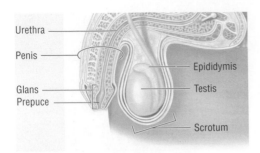

Epididymis

epididymis /ĕp′ĭ dĭd′ə mĭs/ (*pl.* **epididymides** /ĕp′ĭ dĭ dĭm′ĭ dēz′/) a coiled structure in the testis for the storage and transport of sperm to the vas deferens.

epididymitis /ĕp′ĭ dĭd′ə mī′tĭs/ inflammation of the epididymis. [epdidym- + -itis]

epididymoplasty /ĕp′ĭ dĭd′ə mə plăs′tē/ surgical repair of the epididymis. [epididymo- + -plasty]

epidural /ĕp′ĭ dōōr′əl/ **1.** *adj.* above or outside of the dura mater. **2.** *n.* an epidural anesthetic.

epidural anesthesia /ăn′əs thē′zhə/ a type of local anesthesia injected into the epidural space, often used in labor and birth and postoperative pain management.

epidural anesthetic /ăn′əs thĕt′ĭk/ a type of local anesthesia injected into the epidural space, blocking sensation from the point of insertion downward.

epidural block epidural anesthesia.

epidural space the space surrounding the dura mater.

epigastric /ĕp′ĭ găs′trĭk/ of or pertaining to the epigastrium.

epigastric region the part of the abdomen immediately above the stomach.

epigastrium /ĕp′ĭ găs′trē əm/ the part of the abdomen between the bottom of the rib cage and the belly button.

epiglottis /ĕp′ĭ glŏt′ĭs/ the cartilaginous flap that covers the trachea during swallowing to prevent food from entering the trachea.

epiglottitis /ĕp′ĭ glŏ tī′tĭs/ inflammation of the epiglottis.

epilation /ĕp′ə lā′shən/ removal of body hair including the hair root.

epilepsy /ĕp′ə lĕp′sē/ a seizure disorder in which the brain's nerve cells fire electrical impulses at a very high rate, causing disturbances in brain function and often convulsions.

epileptic /ĕp′ə lĕp′tĭk/ a person with epilepsy.

epinephrine /ĕp′ə nĕf′rĭn/ a substance that is produced in the medulla of the adrenal gland in response to danger, excitement, etc. and has various effects, such as a quickening of the heartbeat and increasing blood pressure. *Also called* adrenaline.

epineurium /ĕp′ĭ nōōr′ē əm/ the connective tissue surrounding the trunk of a nerve.

epipharynx /ĕp′ə făr′ĭngks/ the part of the pharynx lying above the soft palate. *Also called* nasopharynx. [epi- + pharynx]

epiphora /ĭ pĭf′ər ə/ overflow of tears, usually due to an obstruction of the lacrimal ducts.

epiphyseal /ĕp′ə fĭz′əl/ of or pertaining to the epiphysis.

epiphyseal plate a layer of cartilage between the epiphysis and the bone shaft which is the growth center for the bone.

epiphysis /ĭ pĭf′ə sĭs/ the distal and proximal ends of a long bone.

epiphysitis /ĭ pĭf′ĭ sī′tĭs/ inflammation of an epiphysis.

episclera /ĕp′ə sklêr′ə/ a thin membrane covering the sclera.

episcleritis /ĕp′ə sklĭ rī′tĭs/ inflammation of the episclera.

episio- *combining form.* vulva: *for example,* episiotomy.

episioplasty /ĭ pē′zē ə plăs′tē/ surgical repair of the vulva. [episio- + -plasty]

episiorrhaphy /ĭ pē′zē ôr′ə fē/ suturing of an injured vulva. [episio- + -rrhaphy]

episiotomy /ĭ pē′zē ŏt′ə mē/ a surgical widening of the end of the birth canal during delivery to avoid tearing of the perineum. [episio- + -tomy]

episode /ĕp′ə sōd′/ one incident in a recurring pathological condition, as a psychotic episode or a cardiac episode.

episodic /ĕp′ə sŏd′ĭk/ not constant, as care provided only as needed.

epispadias /ĕp′ə spā′dē əs/ a congenital defect with the urethra opening on the top side of the penis.

epistaxis /ĕp′ə stăk′sĭs/ bleeding from the nose. *Also called* nosebleed, rhinorrhagia.

epithalamus /ĕp′ə thăl′ə məs/ the uppermost part of the diencephalons of the brain.

epithelial /(ĕp′ə thē′lē əl/ of or pertaining to the epithelium.

epithelioma /ĕp′ə thē′lē ō′mə/ a tumor composed of epithelial cells.

epithelium /(ĕp′ə thē′lē əm/ the outermost layer of skin cells.

EPO *abbreviation.* erythropoietin.

eponychium /ĕp′ə nĭk′ē əm/ (*pl.* **eponychia** /ĕp′ə nĭk′ē ə/) the cuticle of a nail. *Also called* perionychium.

eponym /ĕp′ə nĭm/ a name given to something, such as a disease, that includes the name

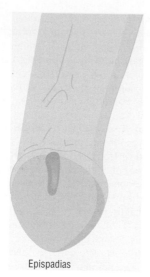

Epispadias

Epispadias

of a person, often the person who discovered the disease, such as Parkinson's disease.

Epstein-Barr virus (EBV) /ĕp′stīn bär′/ a type of herpes virus that causes mononucleosis and is associated with other conditions, as Burkitt's lymphoma and nasopharyngeal cancer.

equilibrium /ē′kwə lĭb′rē əm/ a state of balance, either physical or emotional.

ER *abbreviation.* **1.** emergency room. **2.** estrogen receptor.

Erb('s) /ârb(z)/ **palsy** /pôl′zē/ or **paralysis** /pə răl′ə sĭs/ damage by stretching to part of the brachial plexus (nerves between the neck and the armpit) that occurs during birth, producing weakness of the shoulder and arm of the newborn but frequently resolving spontaneously.

ERCP *abbreviation.* endoscopic retrograde cholangiopancreatography.

erectile dysfunction /ĭ rĕk′tīl, -tĭl/ difficulty in achieving or sustaining an erection for sexual intercourse or the inability to achieve ejaculation.

erection /ĭ rĕk′shən/ the condition of sexual arousal in the penis or clitoris with swelling and/or hardness.

erector /ĭ rĕk′tər/ a muscle that erects a part of the body.

ergograph /ûr′gə grăf′/ a device for measuring the work capacity of muscles.

ergonomics /ûr′gə nŏm′ĭks/ the design of devices and working conditions to minimize physical and psychological damage to the worker.

ergot /ûr′gət, -gŏt/ a grain fungus, some of whose alkaloids can be used to treat migraines, induce contractions, and control bleeding. Other alkaloids can induce hallucinations and physical discomfort.

ergotism /ûr′gə tĭz′əm/ a severe condition with intestinal distress and possible hallucinations caused by the ingestion of excessive amounts of ergot.

erogenous /ĭ rŏj′ə nəs/ causing sexual stimulation, referring especially to areas of the body that are sensitive to sexual stimulation.

erosion /ĭ rō′zhən/ any wearing away of a surface, especially of an area of skin.

erotomania /ĭ rō′tə mā′nē ə, ĭ rŏt′ə-/ obsessive interest in a love object (often someone famous) who is not responsive.

ERT *abbreviation.* estrogen replacement therapy.

eructation /ĭ rŭk tā′shən/ the expulsion of air from the stomach. *Also called* belching.

eruption /ĭ rŭp′shən/ a breaking out of a rash.

erysipelas /ĕr′ə sĭp′ə ləs/ streptococcus infection characterized by red, blotchy skin.

erythema /ĕr′ə thē′mə/ a redness of the skin, as caused by inflammation or sunburn.

erythematous /ĕr′ə thĕm′ə təs, -thē′mə-/ red or ruddy, as skin.

erythralgia /ĕr′ə thrăl′jə, -jē ə/ a reddening of the skin. [erythr- + -algia]

erythro- *combining form.* red, redness: *for example,* erythrocyte.

erythroblast /ĭ rĭth′rə blăst′/ immature red blood cell. [erythro- + -blast]

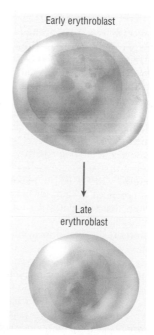

Early erythroblast

Late
erythroblast

Erythroblast

erythroblastosis fetalis /ĭ rĭth′rō blă stō′sĭs fĭ tăl′ĭs/ an incompatibility disorder between a mother and fetus with differing Rh positive (baby) and Rh negative (mother) factors.

erythrocyanosis /ĭ rĭth′rō sī′ə nō′sĭs/ reddishblue discoloration of the skin in response to cold. [erythro- + cyanosis]

erythrocyte /ĭ rĭth′rə sīt′/ mature red blood cell. [erythro- + -cyte]

erythrocyte sedimentation rate (ESR) a test for inflammation that measures the rate at which red blood cells separate from blood serum when allowed to stand vertically in a pipette for an hour.

erythrocytopenia /ĭ rĭth′rō sī′tə pē′nē ə/ deficiency in the number of erythrocytes. [erythro- + cyto- + -penia]

erythrocytosis /ĭ rĭth′rō sī tō′sĭs/ abnormal increase in erythrocytes. [erythro- + -cyt- + -osis]

erythroderma /ĭ rĭth′rō dûr′mə/ abnormal skin redness. [erythro- + -derma]

erythrodesis /ĕr′ə thrŏd′ə sĭs, ĭ rĭth′rō dē′sĭs/ the breaking down of red blood cells. [erythro- + -desis]

erythroleukemia /ĭ rĭth′rō loō kē′mē ə/ a rare type of acute myeloid leukemia in which there is an overproduction of abnormal immature red blood cells. [erythro- + leukemia]

erythromycin /ĭ rĭth′rə mī′sĭn/ a commonly used antibiotic, often given to people allergic to penicillin, and famous for causing stomach upset.

erythropenia /ĭ rĭth′rō pē′nē ə/ deficiency in red blood cells. [erythro- + -penia]

erythrophagia /ĭ rĭth′rō fā′jə, -jē ə/ destruction of red blood cells by cells such as macrophages. [erythro- + -phagia]

erythroplakia /ĭ rĭth′rə plā′kē ə/ reddish patch found in the mouth. [erythro- + -plakia]

erythroplasia /ĭ rĭth′rō plā′zhə/ reddish patch on the skin, often a precursor to skin cancer.

erythropoiesis /ĭ rĭth′rō poi ē′sĭs/ production of erythrocytes in the bone marrow. [erythro- + -poesis]

erythropoietin (EPO) /ĭ rĭth′rə poi′ĭ tĭn/ a hormone produced in the kidney or given as an injection that stimulates the formation of red blood cells.

erythropoietin test a test for erythropoietin in the blood.

erythropsia /ĕr′ə thrŏp′sē ə/ a visual impairment with all objects appearing reddish. [erythro- + -opsia]

eschar /ĕs′kär/ scab formed from cautery (burning).

escharotomy /ĕs′kə rŏt′ə mē/ incision into an eschar.

Escherichia coli /ĕsh′ə rĭk′ē ə kō′lī/ a bacillus with numerous strains found normally in the intestinal tract but, in some strains, responsible for gastrointestinal ailments, usually including diarrhea. *Also called* E. coli.

esophag-, esophago- *combining form.* esophagus: *for example,* esophagitis, esophagoscope.

esophageal /ĭ sŏf′ə jē′əl, ē′sə făj′ē əl/ of or pertaining to the esophagus.

esophageal reflux a condition with reflux (regurgitation) of acid stomach contents back up into the esophagus.

esophagectomy /ĭ sŏf′ə jĕk′tə mē/ removal of the esophagus. [esophag- + -ectomy]

esophagitis /ĭ sŏf′ə jī′tĭs/ inflammation of the esophagus. [esophag- + -itis]

esophagocele /ĭ sŏf′ə gə sēl′/ hernia of the mucous membrane of the esophagus. [esophago- + -cele]

esophagoenterostomy /ĭ sŏf′ə gō ĕn′tə rŏs′tə mē/ surgical formation of a connection between the esophagus and the intestines.

esophagogastrectomy /ĭ sŏf′ə gō gă strĕk′tə mē/ surgical removal of part of the stomach and the esophagus. [esophago- + gastrectomy]

esophagogastroduodenoscopy (EGD) /ĭ sŏf′ə gō găs′trō doō′ō dĭ nŏs′kə pē/ a viewing of the esophagus, stomach, and duodenum with the use of a thin, flexible scope.

esophagastrostomy /ĭ sŏf′ə gō gă strŏs′tə mē/ surgical formation of a connection between the mouth and stomach. [esophago- + gasto- + -stomy]

esophagomalacia /ĭ sŏf′ə gō mə lā′shə, -shē ə/ softening of the esophagus. [esophago- + -malacia]

esophagoplasty /ĭ sŏf′ə gə plăs′tē/ surgical repair of the esophagus. [esophago- + -plasty]

esophagoscope /ĭ sŏf′ə gə skōp′/ thin, flexible scope used to examine the esophagus. [esophago- + -scope]

esophagoscopy /ĭ sŏf′ə gŏs′kə pē/ examination of the esophagus using an esophagoscope. [esophago- + -scopy]

esophagospasm /ĭ sŏf′ə gō spăz′əm/ spasming of the esophageal walls. [esophago- + -spasm]

esophagostenosis /ĭ sŏf′ə gō stĭ nō′sĭs/ narrowing of the esophagus. [esophago- + -stenosis]

esophagostomy /ĭ sŏf′ə gŏs′tə mē/ creation of a surgical opening directly into the esophagus. [esophago- + -stomy]

esophagotomy /ĭ sŏf′ə gŏt′ə mē/ incision into the esophagus. [esophago- + -tomy]

esophagus /ĭ sŏf'ə gəs/ the tubular passageway from the pharynx (back of the mouth) to the stomach through which food passes. *Also called* gullet.

esophoria /ĕs'ə fôr'ē ə/ abnormal turning inward of the eyes.

esotropia /ĕs'ə trō'pē ə/ condition with one eye crossing inward or outward. *Also called* strabismus, cross-eye.

ESP *abbreviation.* extrasensory perception.

ESR *abbreviation.* erythrocyte sedimentation rate.

ESRD *abbreviation.* end-stage renal disease.

essential amino acid compound not made in the body but essential for growth in infants and children and for protein synthesis in adults; must be supplied in the natural diet or by dietary supplement.

essential fatty acid an acid that is essential in the diet for proper body functioning.

essential hypertension /hī'pər tĕn'shən/ hypertension (high blood pressure) for which no cause can be found.

essential tremor /trĕm'ər, trē'mər/ an inherited movement disorder with shaking of the hands and head.

-esthesia *suffix.* sensation, perception: *for example,* paresthesia.

estimated date of confinement (EDC) the projected date of birth. *Also called* due date.

estradiol /ĕs'trə dī'ôl/ a hormone produced by the ovaries, synthesized and used to treat hormone deficiencies.

estriol /ĕs'trē ôl'/ a hormone produced during pregnancy, synthesized and used to treat hormone deficiencies.

estrogen /ĕs'trə jən/ the female hormone produced by the ovaries, important for the development and maintenance of secondary sex characteristics.

estrogen/progestin therapy /prō jĕs'tĭn/ or **estrogen-progestin therapy** the use of the hormones estrogen and progestin to alleviate symptoms of menopause and to prevent osteoporosis.

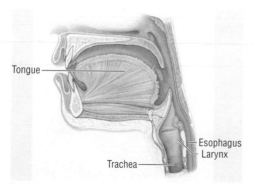

Tongue

Esophagus
Larynx

Trachea

Esophagus

estrogen receptor any cell to which estrogen molecules can become easily bound.

estrogen replacement therapy (ERT) the treatment of the symptoms of lowered estrogen (either from removal of ovaries or from menopause) with estrogen and, often, progestin.

ESWL *abbreviation.* extracorporeal shock wave lithotripsy.

ether /ē'thər/ a colorless substance formerly widely used as an anesthestic.

ethics /ĕth'ĭks/ rules or standards governing a profession.

ethmoid /ĕth'moid/ **1.** spongy, latticelike. **2.** of or pertaining to the ethmoid bone.

ethmoid bone spongy bone at the roof of the nasal cavity and the floor of the skull.

ethmoid sinuses air-filled cavities located at the top of the nasal cavities between the eyes.

etiology /ē'tē ŏl'ə jē/ the origins and causes for the development of a disease.

ETT *abbreviation.* exercise tolerance test.

ET tube endotracheal intubation tube.

eu- *prefix.* well, good, normal: *for example,* eupnea.

eucholia /yōō kō'lē ə/ a normal quantity and quality of bile.

eugenics /yōō jĕn'ĭks/ the study of methods for controlling population through selective breeding.

eunuch /yōō'nək/ a male whose testicles never developed or have been removed or destroyed.

eupepsia /yōō pĕp'shə, -sē ə/ normal digestion. [eu- + -pepsia]

euphoria /yōō fôr'ē ə/ a state of happiness and well-being; when excessive, euphoria is linked to several mental disorders.

eupnea /yōōp nē'ə/ normal breathing. [eu- + -pnea]

eupraxia /yōō prăk'sē ə/ normal ability to move in a coordinated way.

eustachian tube /yōō stā'shən, -shē ən/ tube that connects the middle ear to the pharynx. *Also called* otopharyngeal tube.

euthanasia /yōō'thə nā'zhə/ assisting in the death of a person with an incurable or painful disease.

euthyroid /yōō thī'roid/ normal function of the thyroid gland. [eu- + thyroid]

evacuation /ĭ văk'yōō ā'shən/ the act of discharging, especially from the bowels.

event /ĭ vĕnt'/ a moment when something of medical importance has occurred.

eversion /ĭ vûr'zhən/ a turning outward, as of the foot.

evidence-based medicine the combining of clinical expertise, patient values, and the best available research to determine patient care.

Examination

eviscerate /ĭ vĭs'ə rāt'/ to remove the bowels or contents of a body organ from.

evisceration /ĭ vĭs'ə rā'shən/ the act of eviscerating.

evoked potential electrical wave pattern observed in an EEG in response to a controlled stimulus, used in testing for neurological disorders.

evoked potential study study of a person with sensory deficits by using electrical stimulation.

Ewing('s) sarcoma /yōō'ĭng(z) sär kō'mə/ a type of bone tumor that occurs in children and adolescents.

exacerbate /ĭg zăs'ər bāt'/ to make worse; increase the seriousness of.

exacerbation /ĭg zăs'ər bā'shən/ a sudden increase in the seriousness of or worsening, as of a symptom or disease.

exam /ĭg zăm'/ short for examination.

examination /ĭg zăm'ə nā'shən/ an in-person screening usually using a prescribed system or method and often including both observations and tests.

exanthematous viral disease /ĕg'zăn thĕm'ə təs/ a viral disease, such as measles, that causes a skin rash.

excavation /ĕks'kə vā'shən/ a cavity formed by a pathological or purposeful process.

exchange list a list of groups of foods that can be exchanged for similar amounts of carbohydrates, proteins, or fats in a dietary program, used especially in the management of diabetes.

excimer laser treatment /ĕk'sə mər/ treatment with a laser that uses very concentrated light to vaporize or destroy tissue.

excipient /ĭk sĭp'ē ənt/ in pharmacology, an inert substance used to bind a pill or tablet.

excise /ĭk sīz', ĕk'sīz/ to remove completely.

excision /ĭk sĭzh'ən/ the complete removal of something, as by surgery.

excisional biopsy /ĭk sĭzh'ə nəl bī'ŏp sē/ a biopsy which includes an entire lesion with a little surrounding tissue.

excitability /ĭk sī'tə bĭl'ĭ tē/ the property of something or someone that enables it to react to stimulation.

excitation /ĕk'sī tā'shən/ The complete stimulation of a nerve or muscle or the state of such stimulation.

excoriation /ĭk skôr'ē ā'shən/ a surface injury, such as an abrasion or a scratch.

excrement /ĕk'skrə mənt/ waste matter; feces.

excrescence /ĭk skrĕs'əns/ an outgrowth from a surface that may be normal, such as a fingernail, or abnormal, such as a wart.

excrete /ĭk skrēt'/ to expel, as waste matter from the body.

excretion /ĭk skrē'shən/ anything that is expelled, as waste matter from the body.

excretory system /ĕk'skrĭ tôr'ē/ the organs involved with the excretion of waste matter from the body.

exemia /ĭk sē'mē ə, ĭg zē'-/ a condition with loss of blood in general circulation, as in shock. [ex- + -emia]

exencephaly /ĕk'sĕn sĕf'ə lē/ a condition with a defective skull allowing exposure of the brain.

exenteritis /ĭk sĕn'tə rī'tĭs, ĭg zĕn'-/ inflammation of the outer covering of the intestines. [ex- + enteritis]

exercise-induced asthma an attack of asthma that results from the exertion of exercise.

exercise stress test a test for heart function taken while a person is exercising on a treadmill.

exercise tolerance test (ETT) exercise stress test.

exfoliate /ĕks fō'lē āt'/ **1.** to peel or slough off skin cells. **2.** to lose primary teeth as part of normal development.

exfoliation /ĕks fō'lē ā'shən/ **1.** the peeling or sloughing off of skin cells. **2.** the loss of primary teeth as part of normal development.

exfoliative biopsy /ĕks fō'lē ā'tĭv bī'ŏp sē/ the scraping of skin cells from the surface for examination.

Exercise Stress Test

exhalation /ĕks'hə lā'shən/ the process of breathing out.

exhale /ĕks hāl'/ to breathe out.

exhaustion /ĭg zôs'chən/ **1.** extreme fatigue. **2.** the removal of the active parts of a drug by treating it with a solvent.

exhibitionism /ĕk'sə bĭsh'ə nĭz'əm/ an intense need to expose the sexual organs in public.

exo- *prefix.* external, on the outside: *for example*, exotropia.

exocardia /ĕk'sō kär'dē ə/ congenitally abnormal placement of the heart. *Also called* ectocardia.

exocrine /ĕk'sə krĭn/ exocrine gland.

exocrine gland any gland that secretes substances through ducts to a specific location or to the outside of the body, as the sweat gland or the pancreas.

exodontia /ĕk'sō dŏn'shə/ or **exodontics** /ĕk'sō dŏn'tĭks/ the branch of dentristry concerned with tooth extraction.

exogenous /ĕk sŏj'ə nəs/ originating from outside the body.

exophoria /ĕk'sō fôr'ē ə/ strabismus in which the eyes deviate outward.

exophthalmos or **exophthalmus** /ĕk'sŏf thăl'məs/ protruding eyeball, usually resulting from hyperthyroidism.

exostosis /ĕk'sŏ stō'sĭs/ a benign growth on a bone, especially the one on the calcaneus (heel), informally called a heel spur.

exotropia /ĕk'sə trō'pē ə/ an eye condition in which one eye looks outward. [exo- + -tropia]

expected date of delivery estimated date of birth; due date.

expectorant /ĭk spĕk'tər ənt/ agent that promotes the expelling of mucus from the lungs, bronchi, or trachea.

expectoration /ĭk spĕk'tə rā'shən/ the act of expelling or coughing up mucus from the lungs, bronchi, or trachea.

expendable /ĭk spĕn'də bəl/ able to be used and disposed, as medical or dental supplies.

experimental psychology the study of mental processes using experimental data to form conclusions.

expiration /ĕks'pə rā'shən/ **1.** the process of breathing out. **2.** death.

expiration date the last date something (as a medication) should be used before it spoils or loses its effectiveness.

expire /ĭk spīr'/ **1.** to breath out. **2.** to die.

exploratory surgery surgery to examine the interior or to find the cause of a disease or condition.

exstrophy /ĕk'strə fē/ the turning inside out of an organ at birth, for example, exstrophy of the bladder, a congenital malformation

extend /ĭk stĕnd'/ to stretch out, as a limb.

extended care care over a long period of time, particularly care given in a long-term care facility.

extension /ĭk stĕn'shən/ the process of straightening, as an arm at the elbow or the leg at the knee; opposite of flexion.

extensor /ĭk stĕn'sər, -sôr/ any part, such as a muscle, that extends.

external /ĭk stûr'nəl/ on the outside of; acting from the outside.

external auditory meatus /mē ā'təs/ the external part of the ear, which opens into the ear canal.

external carotid artery /kə rŏt'ĭd är'tə rē/ one of the two branches of each of the two common carotid arteries; it is located near the surface of the neck and branches into smaller arteries.

external ear the spiral, shell-like structure of the outside part of the ear on each side of the head. *Also called* auricle, pinna.

external fixation device a device used externally to hold a fractured limb in place.

extirpation /ĕk'stər pā'shən/ the removal of a diseased part or organ.

extra- *prefix.* without, outside of: *for example*, extracellular.

extracellular /ĕk'strə sĕl'yə lər/ taking place outside of a cell. [extra- + cellular]

extracorporeal /ĕk'strə kôr pôr'ē əl/ outside of the body.

extracorporeal circulation (ECC) circulation of a patient's blood outside of the body as to a heart-lung machine.

extracorporeal shock wave lithotripsy (ESWL) /lĭth'ə trĭp'sē/ the breaking up of calculi in the urinary tract or gallbladder using sound waves.

extract 1. *n.* /ĕk'străkt/ a plant or animal ingredient used as part of a medication. **2.** *v.* /ĭk străkt'/ to remove a tooth by extraction.

extraction /ĭk străk'shən/ the removal of a tooth using a forceps or other device.

extractor /ĭk străk'tər/ a device used to pull out something, especially a dental instrument used to extract teeth.

extradural /ĕk'strə dŏŏr'əl/ outside of the dura mater.

extraocular /ĕk'strə ŏk'yə lər/ outside of the eye.

extraoral /ĕk'strə ôr'əl/ outside of the mouth. [extra- + oral]

extrasensory perception /ĕk'strə sĕn'sə rē pər sĕp'shən/ **(ESP)** perceptions received by senses outside of the normal five senses, for example, by telepathy.

extrasystole /ĕk'strə sĭs'tə lē/ a premature heartbeat. [extra- + systole]

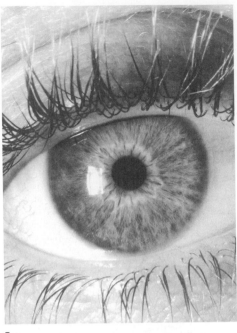

Eye

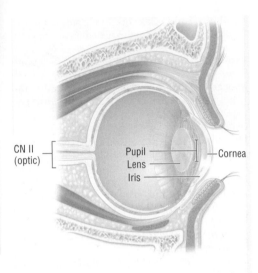

extrauterine pregnancy /ĕk′strə yōō′tər ĭn/ any pregnancy that does not implant in the uterus. *Also called* ectopic pregnancy, tubal pregnancy.

extravasate /ĭk străv′ə sāt′/ to pass through vessel walls to surrounding tissue.

extravasation /ĭk străv′ə sā′shən/ the passage through vessel walls into tissue or blood cells or plasma.

extremity /ĭk strĕm′ĭ tē/ hand or foot.

extrinsic /ĭk strĭn′sĭk/ originating outside of; not an essential part of.

extroversion /ĕk′strə vûr′zhən/ concern with things outside of the self.

extrovert /ĕk′strə vûrt′/ a person concerned with things outside of the self, generally, an outgoing person.

extrusion /ĭk strōō′zhən/ the eruption of a tooth into an abnormal position.

extubate /ĕk′stōō bāt′/ to remove a tube from the body.

extubation /ĕk′stōō bā′shən/ the removal of a tube from the body, usually from the trachea.

exudate /ĕks′yōō dāt′/ fluid and white cells slowly oozing from blood vessels in response to injury or inflammation.

exude /ĭk sōōd′, ĭg zōōd′/ to emit, as sweat through pores.

eye /ī/ one of the two organs of sight, located in the front of the skull.

eyeball /ī′bôl′/ the globe of the eye or the eye itself.

eye bank a facility for storing eyes or corneas for transplantation.

eyebrow /ī′brou′/ the arch of hair that grows along the ridge formed by the upper part of the orbital bone that encases the eye.

eye color the color of the iris of the eye.

eyecup /ī′kŭp′/ a small cup that is shaped to fit over the eye, filled with liquid and used to bathe the exposed surface of the eye.

eyeglasses /ī′glăs′ĭz/ a set of corrective lenses in a frame worn in front of the eye to correct vision or protect the eyes.

eyelash /ī′lăsh′/ one of a group of stiff hairs that grow along the edge of the eyelid.

eyelid /ī′lĭd′/ the movable fold of skin that opens and closes to protect, humidify, and nourish the cornea of the eye and to keep light from entering the eyes. *Also called* palpebra.

eye socket the bony cavity in the skull in which the eyeball sits and the associated muscles, nerves, and blood vessels. *Also called* orbit, orbital cavity.

eyestrain /ī′strān′/ a tired feeling in the eyes, usually after long use.

eyetooth /ī′tōōth′/ either of two long, oval, slightly pointed teeth (one on the right and one on the left) in the upper jaw between the second incisor and the first premolar. *Also called* canine tooth.

F

F *abbreviation.* Fahrenheit.

Fabry('s) disease /fä'brē(z)/ a sex-linked genetic disorder of lipid metabolism caused by an enzyme deficiency that leads to a number of progressive symptoms, including renal disfunction, fevers, and hypertension; death results from renal, cardiac, or cerebrovascular complications.

face /fās/ the front of the head, from the forehead down to the chin.

facelift /fās'lĭft'/ plastic surgery performed for cosmetic purposes to remove signs of aging in the face, such as wrinkles and sagging skin. *Also called* rhytidectomy, rhytidioplasty.

facial bone any of the 14 bones that make up the face of the skull.

facial muscle any of the many muscles that are attached to the skin of the face and are responsible for creating facial expression.

facial nerve cranial nerve VII; one of a pair of mixed sensory and motor nerves that give feeling to much of the face and are also responsible for the taste buds at the anterior two-thirds of the tongue.

facial nerve paralysis /pə răl'ə sĭs/ loss of voluntary control of the facial muscles, which are supplied by cranial nerve VII, usually on one side of the face. *Also called* Bell's palsy.

facies /fā'shē ēz'/ facial characteristics or expression usually indicative of a particular disease.

facing /fā'sĭng/ the front part of the head, from the forehead to the chin.

factor /făk'tər/ **1.** something that contributes to a result. **2.** a substance or element that takes part in a specific physiological process or bodily system, for example, blood coagulation.

FAE *abbreviation.* fetal alcohol effects.

Fahrenheit (F) /făr'ən hīt'/ a temperature scale in which the boiling point of water is 212° and the freezing point is 32° at sea level. Normal human temperature has long been regarded as 98.6° F; however, now a range around that number is considered normal.

failure to thrive (FTT) a condition in which an infant's growth, development, and weight gain are far below average. This condition may result from neglect, abuse, or a medical condition.

faint /fānt/ **1.** *adj.* weak, light-headed. **2.** *v.* to lose consciousness because of a transient lack of blood to the brain, as in a syncopal attack. **3.** *n.* a syncopal episode.

fainting /fān'tĭng/ a temporary lapse in consciousness because of a decrease in the blood supply to the brain. *Also called* syncope.

fallopian tube /fə lō'pē ən/ one of a pair of slender tubes that extend from each ovary to the side of the uterus and through which an ovum is carried to the uterus. *Also called* oviduct, uterine tube.

false labor occasional contractions that occur during pregnancy without dilation of the cervix. *Also called* Braxton-Hicks contractions.

false negative test result that wrongly indicates a negative result, or normal condition, even though an abnormal condition is present in the subject.

false positive test result that wrongly indicates a positive result, or abnormal condition, in the subject even though there is no abnormal condition present.

false rib any of the five pairs of lower ribs that are not directly connected to the sternum with bone. *See also* true rib, floating rib.

falx /fălks, fôlks/ (*pl.* **falces** /făl'sēz, fôl'-/) in anatomy, any sickle-shaped structure, such as the folds in the dura mater of the brain.

familial /fə mĭl'yəl/ of a disease or characteristic that tends to occur in many members of a family, more than would be expected by chance; often hereditary.

familial adenomatous polyposis (FAP) /ăd'ə nŏm'ə təs pŏl'ə pō'sĭs/ an inherited disorder caused by a gene mutation that results in thousands of polyps forming in the colon and rectum, usually beginning at puberty and almost inevitably developing into cancer of the colon by the time the person is 30.

familial amyotrophic lateral sclerosis (ALS) /ā'mī ə trŏf'ĭk lăt'ər əl sklĭ rō'sĭs/ ALS in a person with a family history of the disease; between 5 and 10 percent of ALS cases are of the familial type.

family history part of a patient's medical history that includes information on the incidence of specific diseases in the family, used to predict whether the patient may have a tendency toward a certain disease or disorder.

family practice a medical practice or specialty that coordinates the total health care for the individual and/or family.

family therapy a type of psychological therapy in which a therapist works with several or all family members as a group to help them resolve the conflicts they face with each other.

Fanconi('s) anemia /făn kō′nē(z)/ a rare genetic disease, usually congenital, that is characterized by aplastic anemia in childhood or early adult life. *Also called* Fanconi's pancytopenia.

Fanconi('s) pancytopenia /păn′sī tə pē′ne ə/ Fanconi anemia.

FAP *abbreviation.* **1.** familial adenomatous polyposis. **2.** functional ambulation profile (analysis of a patient's ability to walk).

farsightedness /fär′sī′tĭd nĭs/ a vision disorder in which distant objects can be seen more clearly than closer objects. *Also called* hyperopia, hypermetropia.

FAS *abbreviation.* fetal alcohol syndrome.

FAS diagnosis fetal alcohol syndrome diagnosis.

fasci-, fascio- *combining form.* a band of fibrous tissue: *for example,* fasciitis, fasciotomy.

fascia /făsh′ē ə/ (*pl.* **fasciae** /făsh′ē ē′/) a sheet of connective tissue that envelops parts of the body underneath the skin; it covers or binds muscles together and supports soft structures in the body, such as organs.

fascicle /făs′ĭ kəl/ a small bundle of nerve or muscle fibers.

fasciculation /fə sĭk′yə lā′shən/ involuntary muscle contraction, or twitching, of a single, localized muscle group.

fasciculus /fə sĭk′yə ləs/ (*pl.* **fasciculi** /fə sĭk′yə lī′/) a slender bundle of fibers, usually muscle, tendon, or nerve fibers.

fasciectomy /făsh′ē ĕk′tə mē/ surgical removal of strips of fascia. [fasci- + -ectomy]

fasciitis /făsh′ē ī′tĭs/ inflammation of the fascia. [fasci- + -itis]

fasciodesis /făs′ē ŏd′ə sĭs/ the surgical attachment of a fascia to another or to a tendon. [fascio- + -desis]

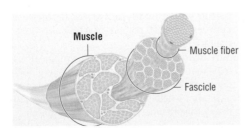

Fascicle

fasciola /fə sē′ə lə/ a small band of fibers.

fascioplasty /făsh′ē ə plăs′tē/ plastic surgery on a fascia. [fascio- + -plasty]

fasciorrhaphy /făsh′ē ôr′ə fē/ suture of a fascia. [fascio- + -rrhaphy]

fasciotomy /făsh′ē ŏt′ə mē/ surgical incision into or through a fascia. [fascio- + -tomy]

fastigium /fă stĭj′ē əm/ the point of greatest intensity of a disease, as when the highest fever occurs.

fasting /făs′tĭng/ abstaining from food, or from certain foods, for a period of time; usually done for therapeutic or religious reasons or in preparation for a diagnostic test.

fasting blood glucose (FBG) /glōō′kōs/ a measurement of the amount of glucose (sugar) found in a sample of blood taken after the patient has fasted overnight (at least 8 hours), commonly used to detect diabetes mellitus.

fasting blood sugar (FBS) fasting blood glucose.

fat /făt/ **1.** a type of body tissue (adipose tissue) in which fat is stored, insulating the body and acting as a cushion for the vital organs **2.** compounds formed from fatty acids that are found in animal tissues and in some plants and which act as a source of energy. *Also called* lipid.

fatal /fā′təl/ causing death; deadly.

fat cell a connective tissue cell that specializes in making and storing fat for the body. *Also called* adipocyte.

fatigue /fə tēg′/ a state of exhaustion and loss of strength following prolonged physical and/or mental activity; may also be confined to a single organ.

fat pad an accumulation of closely packed fat cells surrounded by fibrous tissue, such as the plantar surface of the heel.

fat scales bioelectric impedance analysis (BIA). This measures body fat by measuring how quickly an impulse travels through the body—the slower the travel the more body fat, the higher the less body fat.

fatty acid any of a large group of organic acids derived from fats through hydrolysis; some are manufactured by the body while others, known as essential fatty acids, are synthesized by plants and must be included in the diet.

fatty liver yellow discoloration of the liver because of an accumulation of certain fats in the liver.

fauces /fô′sēz/ (*pl.* **fauces**) the narrow passage at the back of the mouth that opens into the pharynx.

favus /fā′vəs, fä′-/ a scalp disease with yellow, odorous crusts.

FBG *abbreviation.* fasting blood glucose.

FBS *abbreviation.* fasting blood sugar.

FDA *abbreviation.* Food and Drug Administration (www.fda.gov).

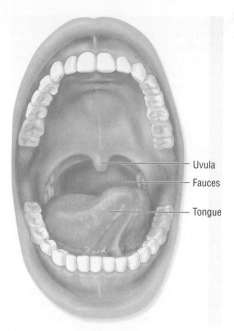

Uvula

Fauces

Tongue

Fauces

FDA recall a product, such as a new drug, food substance, cosmetic, or medical device, that the FDA has withdrawn from the marketplace for health and safety reasons, having found it unfit for consumers.

febrile /fē′brəl, -brīl, fĕb′rəl/ of or relating to fever.

febrile seizure a short convulsion associated with fever, usually less than 15 minutes long, occurring commonly in infants or young children because of a rapid increase in body temperature.

fecal /fē′kəl/ related to feces or excrement.

fecal incontinence /ĭn kŏn′tə nəns/ inability to control the emptying of the bowels due to lack of voluntary control of the anal sphincters (muscles of the anus). *Also called* anal incontinence, rectal incontinence.

fecalith /fē′kə lĭth/ a hard stonelike mass of feces. [feca(l) + -lith]

fecal matter feces.

fecal occult blood /ə kŭlt′/ hidden (occult) blood detected in a stool sample.

fecal occult blood test a test that examines a small sample of stool for hidden (occult) blood, which would indicate bleeding somewhere in the gastrointestinal tract.

fecaluria /fē′kə loōr′ē ə/ presence of feces in the urine.

feces /fē′sēz/ the waste or excrement from the digestive tract that is expelled from the bowels during defecation (emptying the bowels). *Also called* stool.

fecund /fĕk′ənd, fē′kənd/ fertile.

fecundity /fĭ kŭn′dĭ tē/ the ability to produce offspring.

feedback /fēd′băk′/ the return of information from a system in which input has been given.

feeding tube a flexible tube passed through the nose and into the esophagus and stomach for introducing liquid food into the stomach.

fee for service a system of payment in health care in which a provider is paid for each individual service delivered to the patient; often the payment is expected at the time the service is delivered.

feet /fēt/ plural of foot.

FEF *abbreviation.* forced expiratory flow.

fellatio /fə lā′shē ō′/ oral stimulation of the penis.

Felty('s) syndrome /fĕl′tē(z)/ a condition that occurs with adult rheumatoid arthritis, characterized in addition by an enlarged spleen and an abnormally low white blood cell count.

female /fē′māl/ **1.** *n.* a member of the sex that produces eggs and therefore can bear young; a woman or girl. **2.** *adj.* of or relating to the feminine sex.

female condom /kŏn′dəm/ a condom, shaped like a male condom, the closed end of which is inserted into the vagina, with the open end remaining outside; a non-prescription form of birth control designed for one-time use.

female genitalia /jĕn′ĭ tāl′yə/ the female organs of reproduction, both internal and external: the external organs are the vulva and clitoris, and the internal organs are the ovaries, fallopian tubes, uterus, and vagina.

female gonads /gō′nădz/ the reproductive glands in females, i.e., the ovaries, which are responsible for producing sex cells (gametes) and female hormones.

female orgasmic dysfunction /ôr găz′mĭk dĭs fŭngk′shən/ disorder in which the female cannot achieve orgasm after normal arousal.

female reproductive system the organs responsible for sexual reproduction in females, which include the ovaries, fallopian tubes, uterus, vagina, clitoris, and vulva.

female urethral meatus /yoō rē′thrəl mē ā′təs/ the opening (meatus) of the female urethra, just above the vaginal opening, where urine passes out of the body.

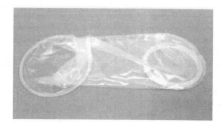

Female Condom

female urethral opening female urethral meatus.

feminization /fĕm′ə nə zā′shən/ development of female secondary sex characteristics, for example breast enlargement, in a male because of a hormonal disorder or in response to certain drugs.

femor-, femoro- *combining form.* relating to the femur or thigh: *for example,* femoral, femorpopliteal.

femoral /fĕm′ər əl/ of or relating to the femur or thigh. [femor- + -al]

femoral angiography /ăn′jē ŏg′rə fē/ x-rays of the femoral artery taken after the injection of a contrast medium.

femoral artery /är′tə rē/ the large artery in the thigh that supplies blood to the groin and lower extremities.

femoral hernia /hûr′nē ə/ a hernia in which a portion of the intestine pushes through the fascia enclosing the femoral vessels and into the groin.

femoral nerve the main nerve of the front of the thigh, supplying the muscles and nerves to the area.

femoral vein the large vein in the thigh that transports blood from the leg back to the inferior vena cava and heart.

femoropopliteal bypass /fĕm′ə rō pŏp lĭt′ē əl/ a passage created surgically from the popliteal artery to the popliteal artery to circumvent blocked or damaged vascular segments. [femoro- + popliteal]

femur /fē′mər/ (*pl.* **femurs** or **femora** /fĕm′ər ə/) **1.** thigh. **2.** the bone of the thigh, the longest and strongest bone in the body.

fenestra /fə nĕs′trə/ (*pl.* **fenestrae** /fə nĕs′trē/) in anatomy, a small windowlike opening, especially one in the bones of the middle ear.

fenestration /fĕn′ə strā′shən/ **1.** a surgical procedure in which an opening or window is made into an organ or bone, such as the bony part of the inner ear, to gain access to a cavity inside. **2.** the making of openings in a dressing or cast to allow access to a wound or part.

ferning /fûr′nĭng/ a fernlike secretion of cervical mucus during midcycle.

-ferous *suffix.* carrying, yielding: *for example,* lactiferous.

ferritin /fĕr′ĭ tĭn/ an iron-protein complex formed in the intestine and stored mainly in the liver, spleen, and bone marrow; the primary means of storing iron in the body.

ferrugination /fə rōō′jə nā′shən/ the deposit of iron salts in the walls of small blood vessels.

fertile /fûr′təl/ **1.** capable of conceiving and bearing offspring. **2.** impregnated or fertilized.

fertility /fər tĭl′ĭ tē/ the ability to conceive and bear young or to induce conception.

fertilization /fûr′tə lə zā′shən/ the union of the male and female sex cells (the spermatozoon and ovum) to form a zygote (fertilized ovum), which eventually develops into the fetus.

fester /fĕs′tər/ to produce pus, as from an ulcer.

FET *abbreviation.* forced expiratory time.

fet-, feti-, feto- *combining form.* fetus: *for example,* fetal, fetoscope.

fetal /fē′təl/ **1.** of or relating to a fetus. **2.** in humans, pertaining to the period of development in the uterus following the embryonic period—from the end of the eighth week to the time of birth. [fet- + -al]

fetal alcohol effects (FAE) malformations similar to those associated with a diagnosis of fetal alcohol syndrome (FAS) but not serious enough to be classified as FAS.

fetal alcohol syndrome (FAS) a set of birth defects, including impaired mental ability, short limbs, a somewhat malformed face and head, and sometimes specific heart defects, that may appear in infants whose mothers consumed alchohol during pregnancy.

fetal circulation the pathway (blood vessels and structures) for the circulation of blood in

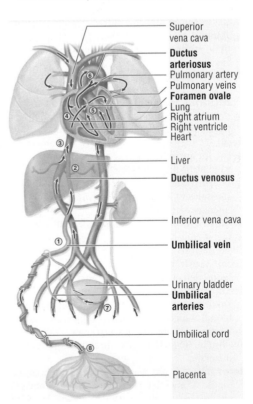

Superior vena cava
Ductus arteriosus
Pulmonary artery
Pulmonary veins
Foramen ovale
Lung
Right atrium
Right ventricle
Heart
Liver
Ductus venosus
Inferior vena cava
Umbilical vein
Urinary bladder
Umbilical arteries
Umbilical cord
Placenta

Fetal Circulation

the fetus. The system is set up to direct the blood with the highest oxygen concentration to the most vital organs.

fetal distress an abnormal condition of the fetus, often discovered during labor, in which the heart rate or rhythm is markedly altered because of low oxygen levels in the fetus.

fetal dystocia /dĭ stō′shə/ a delivery that is difficult because of the large size, shape, or position of the fetus.

fetal heart rate (FHR) the number of heart beats that occur in the fetus during a given time, normally between 100 beats/minute and 160 beats/minute.

fetal heart tone (FHT) the tone or sound produced by the heart of the fetus, which begins beating after about two weeks of intrauterine life.

fetal monitor an electronic device used most often during labor to observe the fetal heart rate and the maternal uterine contractions.

fetal monitoring observation with a fetal monitor of fetal heart rate response to movement, external stimuli, or uterine contractions.

fetal surgery surgery performed on a fetus before birth.

fetal ultrasound /ŭl′trə sound′/ an ultrasound scan performed to determine the status of the fetus. *See also* fetal monitor, fetal monitoring.

feticide /fē′tə sīd′/ the killing of a fetus. [feti- + -cide]

fetishism /fĕt′ĭ shĭz′əm/ the act of fixating on or receiving erotic gratification from a fetish (an inanimate object or body part that is not ordinarily considered to be of a sexual nature but whose presence is required for sexual gratification).

fetometry /fē tŏm′ĭ trē/ measurement of a fetus, especially the diameter of the head, prior to delivery. [feto- + -metry]

fetopathy /fē tŏp′ə thē/ fetal disease. [feto- + -pathy]

fetoprotein /fē′tō prō′tēn, -tē ĭn/ an antigen normally present in the fetus but abnormal when found in adults. [feto- + protein]

fetor /fē′tər, -tôr/ an offensive odor.

fetoscope /fē′tə skōp′/ **1.** a special endoscope (fiberoptic device) inserted through a small incision in the pregnant woman's abdomen to observe the fetus in the uterus and to withdraw fetal blood for analysis. **2.** a stethoscope placed on the mother's abdomen that monitors the fetal heartbeat. [feto- + -scope]

fetoscopy /fē tŏs′kə pē/ use of a fetoscope to observe a fetus and to withdraw fetal blood for analysis. [feto- + -scopy]

fetus /fē′təs/ the live offspring that develops inside the mother after the embryonic period, that is, from the end of the eighth week of pregnancy until the moment of birth.

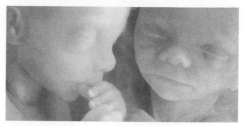
Fetus (Twins)

FEV₁ abbreviation for forced expiratory volume measured during first second of expiration, useful in quantifying pulmonary disability.

fever /fē′vər/ a body temperature above the normal 98.6° F.

fever blister cold sore caused by the herpes virus.

feverfew /fē′vər fyōo′/ a perennial herb most often used to treat migraines, fevers, headaches, psoriasis, and inflammation.

feverish /fē′vər ĭsh/ having fever or feeling as though one has a fever.

fever of undetermined origin (FUO) having an elevated body temperature, lasting two weeks or longer, for which no cause or origin can be found even with extensive testing.

FHR *abbreviation.* fetal heart rate.

FHT *abbreviation.* fetal heart tone.

fiber /fī′bər/ **1.** a long, threadlike structure found in tissue, especially the elastic strands of connective tissue, a strand of nerve tissue, or the elongated cells of muscle tissue. **2.** foods such as whole-grain cereals, fruits, and vegetables that add roughage (indigestible plant matter that stimulates the bowels) to one's diet.

Fiber (in Plant Foods)

fiberoptics /fī′bər ŏp′tĭks/ the transmission of light signals through glass fibers, used in imaging.

fiberscope /fī′bər skōp′/ an optic instrument that transmits light and carries images back to the viewer using a flexible bundle of small glass or plastic fibers; the light is able to go around curves and reach into corners in the internal body part being viewed.

fibr-, fibro- *combining form.* fiber: *for example*, fibroid, fibrosarcoma.

fibremia /fī brē′mē ə/ the presence of fibrin in blood. [fibr- + -emia]

fibril /fī′brəl/ a minute fiber or small thread of a fiber.

fibrillation /fĭb′rə lā′shən/ an abnormal muscle contraction or muscular twitching usually occurring in the atria of the heart and requiring treatment. If the ventricles fibrillate, this rhythm must be terminated by countershock (cardioversion) immediately, or death ensues.

fibrillin 1 /fĭb′rə lĭn/ a protein in the body that is used to build the elastic fibers found in flexible structures such as the blood vessels, lungs, and skin.

fibrin-, fibrino- *combining form.* fibrin: *for example*, fibrinogen.

fibrin /fī′brĭn/ the whitish, insoluble, elastic protein in blood that forms an interlacing fibrous network during normal blood clotting and accounts for the semisolid nature of a blood clot.

fibrinogen /fī brĭn′ə jən/ a protein present in blood plasma that is converted into fibrin in the presence of other substances, such as thrombin, during normal blood clotting. [fibrino- + -gen]

fibrinogenesis /fī′brə nō jĕn′ə sĭs/ the production of fibrin. [fibrino- + -genesis]

fibrinoid /fī′brə noid′/ of or like fibrin. [fibrin- + -oid]

fibrinuria /fī′brə nŏŏr′ē ə/ presence of fibrin in urine. [fibrin- + -uria]

fibroadenoma /fī′brō ăd′ə nō′mə/ (*pl.* **fibroadenomas** or **fibroadenomata** /fī′brō ăd′ə nō′mə tə/) a benign tumor made up of dense fibrous tissue. [fibro- + adenoma]

fibroblast /fī′brə blăst′/ an undifferentiated cell in connective tissue that produces substances which are the precursors of bone, collagen, and other connective tissue cells. [fibro- + -blast]

fibrocartilage /fī′brō kär′tə lĭj/ cartilage that is very fibrous. [fibro- + cartilage]

fibrocyst /fī′brō sĭst/ a cyst containing a large amount of fibrous tissue. [fibro- + cyst]

fibrocystic disease of the breast /fī′brō sĭs′tĭk/ a common benign condition among women in which the breast contains one or more cysts. [fibro- + cyst(ic)]

fibrocystoma /fī′brō sĭ stō′mə/ (*pl.* **fibrocystomas, fibrocystomata** /fī′brō sĭ stō′mə tə/) a benign cyst containing fibrous tissue. [fibro- + cyst + -oma]

fibroid /fī′broid/ 1. *adj.* resembling or made up of fibers or fibrous tissue. 2. *n.* a fibroid tumor. [fibr- + -oid]

fibroidectomy /fī′broi dĕk′tə mē/ surgical removal of a fibroid. [fibroid + -ectomy]

fibroid tumor a fibroma or fibromyoma, especially in the wall of the uterus; fibroid. *Also called* leiomyoma uteri.

fibroma /fī brō′mə/ (*pl.* **fibromas** or **fibromata** /fī brō′mə tə/) a benign tumor made up primarily of fibrous tissue. [fibr- + -oma]

fibromatoid /fī brō′mə toid′/ of or pertaining to a fibroma.

fibromatosis /fī′brō mə tō′sĭs/ condition with multiple fibromas.

fibromyalgia /fī′brō mī ăl′jē ə, -jə/ a syndrome characterized by chronic musculoskeletal pain and stiffness with no detectable inflammation, tenderness at specific sites of the body (trigger points), fatigue, and severe sleep disturbance; the exact cause is unknown. *Also called* fibrositis. [fibro- + -my(o) + -algia]

fibromyectomy /fī′brō mī ĕk′tə mē/ surgical removal of a fibromyoma. [fibro- + my- = -ectomy]

fibromyoma /fī′brō mī ō′mə/ a tumor containing both fibrous and muscle tissue. [fibro- + myoma]

fibromyositis /fī′brō mī′ə sī′tĭs/ chronic muscle inflammation with overgrowth of connective tissue.

fibromyxoma /fī′brō mĭk sō′mə/ (*pl.* **fibromyxomas, fibromyxomata** /fī′brō mĭk sō′mə tə/) a benign tumor containing a lot of fibrous tissue. [fibro- + myxoma]

fibronectin /fī′brə nĕk′tən/ a fibrous protein that binds collagen and other substances to cell membranes.

fibroplasia /fī′brō plā′zhə/ the formation of fibrous tissue. [fibro- + -plasia]

fibroplastic /fī′brō plăs′tĭk/ forming or producing fibrous tissue. [fibro- + -plastic]

fibrosarcoma /fī′brō sär kō′mə/ a malignant tumor formed from deep fibrous tissue. [fibro- + sarcoma]

fibrosis /fī brō′sĭs/ formation of extra fibrous tissue as a reactive process or in repair of something, rather than as part of normal tissue building. [fibr- + -osis]

fibrositis /fī′brə sī′tĭs/ 1. inflammation of fibrous tissue. 2. fibromyalgia.

fibrous joint /fī′brəs/ a fusion of two bones by fibrous tissue resulting in an almost immovable joint, such as those of the skull segments.

fibula /fĭb′yə lə/   the lateral (outside) bone of the two long bones in the lower leg that extend from the knee to the lateral malleolus of the ankle. The fibula supports about 10% of the body's weight. *Also called* calf bone.

fifth disease   a viral disease, usually affecting children and characterized by a red rash starting on the cheeks, so named because, in the time before routine vaccinations were given, it was often the fifth disease a child would contract.

filariasis /fĭl′ə rī′ə sĭs/   infection by worms of the genus *Filariae*; if left untreated may lead to blindness.

filial /fĭl′ē əl/   pertaining to the relationship of sons and daughters to their parents.

filler /fĭl′ər/   a substance used to fill space when packing something, such as an inactive ingredient that is added to a pill to make it bigger and easier to handle when the active ingredient is too small.

filling /fĭl′ĭng/   material, such as a silver or porcelain amalgam, that is used to fill a cavity in a tooth.

film /fĭlm/   an abbreviated form of "x-ray film," referring to an x-ray or radiograph.

film badge   a small pack of x-ray film, sensitive to ionizing radiation, worn by personnel working with x-rays and other sources of radiation to measure their exposure on a regular basis.

filovirus /fē′lō vī′rəs/   a genus of RNA virus that includes the Ebola and Marburg viruses.

filtration   /fĭl trā′shən/   in radiology, the process of adding a filter, such as a sheet of aluminum or copper, between the radiation source and the object being irradiated to increase the penetrating ability of the radiation.

filum /fī′ləm/ (*pl.* **fila** /fī′lə/)   in anatomy, a threadlike structure.

fimbria /fĭm′brē ə/ (*pl.* **fimbriae** /fĭm′brē ē′/)   any structure resembling a bordering fringe, especially the one found at the entrance of the fallopian tubes.

fine-needle aspiration /ăs′pə rā′shən/ (**FNA**)   the technique of removing tissue with a very thin needle and gentle suction to obtain tissue samples.

finger /fĭng′gər/   any of the terminal structures at the end of the hand, except the thumb.

fingernail /fĭng′gər nāl′/   the flattened plate made out of keratin, a hardened protein, at the end of each finger; usually clear with a pinkish coloration from the blood vessels underneath. Discolorations can indicate a condition or disease.

finger prick or **finger stick**   a procedure in which the tip of the finger is pricked with a needle to obtain a droplet blood sample, as for checking glucose in a diabetic.

fingerprint /fĭng′gər prĭnt′/   an impression made of the surface of a fingertip or thumb.

fingerspelling /fĭng′gər spĕl′ĭng/   a method of communicating with a severely hearing-impaired person, in which words are spelled using the positions of the fingers to represent letters of the alphabet.

first aid   emergency care given in the case of injury or sudden illness before regular medical care by trained medical personnel can be administered.

first-degree burn   a mild or superficial burn that is marked by pain, a sensation of heat, and redness of the skin, but no blisters. *See also* second-degree burn, third-degree burn.

fissure /fĭsh′ər/   a normal or abnormal groove or crack.

fissure fracture or **fissured fracture**   a fracture that runs parallel to the long axis of the bone. *Also called* linear fracture.

fistula /fĭs′chə lə/ (*pl.* **fistulas** or **fistulae** /fĭs′chə lē′/)   an abnormal duct or passageway leading from an organ to the body surface, or to another organ, usually resulting from an injury or disease.

fistulectomy /fĭs′chə lĕk′tə mē/   surgical removal of a fistula.

fistulize /fĭs′chə līz′/   to create or form a fistula.

fistulotomy /fĭs′chə lŏt′ə mē/   a surgical incision into a fistula.

fitness /fĭt′nĭs/   **1.** health. **2.** ability of the body to distribute oxygen to muscle tissue during physical exertion.

fixation /fĭk′sā shən/   putting of something in a fixed position, especially a surgical technique where a body part or organ is attached permanently in place.

fixative /fik′sə tĭv/   any solution that preserves tissue and cell samples, especially when used for microscopic examination.

flaccid /flăk′sĭd, flăs′ĭd/   limp, lacking firmness or muscle tone.

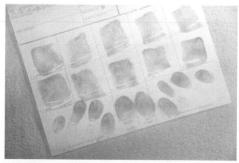

Fingerprints

flagellate /flăj′ə lĭt, -lāt′/ *adj.* **1.** also, **flagellated** /flăj′ə lā′tĭd/ having flagella. **2.** involving or caused by flagella. *n.* **3.** an organism having a flagellum. *v.* /flăj′ə lāt′/ **4.** to whip.

flagellation /flăj′ə lā′shən/ **1.** the way an organism's flagella are organized. **2.** the act or process of whipping.

flagellum /flə jĕl′əm/ (*pl.* **flagella** /flə jĕl′ə/) a threadlike projection from a cell that functions in movement.

flail /flāl/ **chest** loss of chest structure due to multiple rib fractures.

flange /flănj/ the portion of the base of the denture extending from the cervical ends of the teeth to the edge of the denture.

flap /flăp/ a piece of tissue, as skin or muscle, that is partially detached.

flare-up /flâr′ ŭp′/ a recurrence of a disease or condition or an intensification of its process.

flat affect /ăf′ĕkt/ the facial appearance of depression or schizophrenia characterized by a drastic reduction in emotional expression.

flat bone any thin broad bone such as a rib, breastbone, or scapula.

flatfoot /flăt′fŏŏt′/ or flat feet /flăt′ fēt′/ a condition in which the arch of the foot is absent and the entire bottom surface of the foot touches the ground. *Also called* pes planus.

flatulence /flăch′ə ləns/ excess gas in the digestive tract.

flatulent /flăch′ə lənt/ of or relating to flatulence.

flatus /flā′təs/ gas in or expelled from the digestive tract.

flavin /flā′vən/ or **flavine** /flā′vēn/ a ketone that forms part of certain yellow nitrogenous enzymes, such as riboflavin.

flax seed a seed of the flax plant, rich in alpha-linolenic acid and used as a dietary supplement.

flesh /flĕsh/ muscle and fat in humans or other animals.

flesh-eating bacteria an invasive group A streptococcus that quickly destroys tissue and causes death if an infection with this bacterium goes untreated.

flex /flĕks/ **1.** to bend a part of the body. **2.** to tighten a muscle.

flexion /flĕk′shən/ the act of bending a joint or limb.

flexor /flĕk′sər, -sôr/ a muscle that flexes.

flexure /flĕk′shər/ **1.** the act of flexing or condition of being flexed. **2.** the part that is flexed; the bend.

floater /flō′tər/ a small dark spot that seems to float in front of the eye, not impairing vision, caused by a small piece of debris in the gel-like substance in the eye (vitreous humor), casting a shadow on the retina.

floating kidney a kidney that is displaced and movable.

floating rib either of the two bottom pair of ribs, which are not attached to the sternum at all. *See also* true rib, false rib.

flood /flŭd/ **1.** to hemorrhage from the uterus in childbirth. **2.** to have a very heavy menstrual flow.

flooding /flŭd′ĭng/ **1.** an abnormally heavy discharge of blood from the uterus. **2.** in behavioral psychotherapy, a sudden and intense exposure to an anxiety-producing situation.

floppy baby syndrome an abnormal condition of newborns, characterized by insufficient muscle tone due to neurological or muscular problems.

floppy valve syndrome a disorder of the heart in which one or both of the mitral valve leaflets do not close completely.

flora /flôr′ə/ the microorganisms that inhabit the body.

floss /flôs/ thread pulled through the teeth in order to remove particles of food.

flossing /flô′sĭng/ the act of cleaning between the teeth with dental floss.

flow /flō/ *n.* **1.** the menstrual discharge of blood and mucosal tissue. **2.** the volume of a gas or liquid moving past a point over a given unit of time. *v.* **3.** to circulate, as blood. **4.** to menstruate.

flow meter an instrument that measures the volume of a gas or liquid moving past a point over a given unit of time.

flu /flŏŏ/ short for influenza, an illness caused by a group of viruses that infect the respiratory tract.

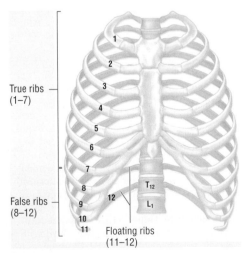

True ribs (1–7)

False ribs (8–12)

Floating ribs (11–12)

Floating Ribs

flu shot   a dose of the influenza vaccine.

flu vaccine   the medicine used to vaccinate against influenza.

fluor-, fluoro-   *combining form.* **1.** fluorine: *for example,* fluoride. **2.** fluorescence: *for example,* fluoroscopy.

fluorescein angiography   /floo rĕs'ē ĭn ăn'jē ŏg'rə fē/   a procedure to examine the blood vessels of the retina, by injecting a dye into a vein in the arm and taking pictures of the back of the eye as the dye passes through the retinal vessels.

fluorescent   /floo rĕs'ənt/   having the property of emitting visible light when exposed to external radiation such as x-rays or light.

fluorescent treponemal antibody absorbed test   /trĕp'ə nē'məl ăn'tē bŏd'ē/   a blood test for syphilis.

fluoridation   /floor'ĭ dā'shən/   the addition of fluorine to drinking water for dental health.

fluoride   /floor'īd/   a compound containing fluorine, added to toothpaste, drinking water, and some foods for dental health. [fluor- + -ide]

fluorine   /floor'ēn/   a toxic gas used in certain diagnostic tests and, as a compound with other substances, to treat disease. Its most important medical use is in the form of fluoride, where it fights caries (plaque) and hence tooth decay.

fluoroscope   /floor'ə skōp'/   a device containing a screen covered with a fluorescent substance that allows the observer to see the pattern revealed by x-rays, used for viewing structures within the body

fluoroscopy   /floo rŏs'kə pē/   examination of the body using a fluoroscope. [fluoro- + -scopy]

fluorosis   /floo rō'sĭs/   an irreversible condition characterized by mottling of the teeth, caused by excessive fluorine intake. [fluor- + -osis]

fluorouracil   /floor'ō yoor'ə sĭl/   a fluorine-containing agent used to treat cancers of the skin, breast, and digestive system.

flush   /flŭsh/   **1.** *n.* temporary redness of the skin over the cheeks or neck, triggered by excitement, fever, or physical exertion. **2.** *v.* to wash or rinse.

flutamide   /floo'tə mīd'/   an antiandrogen drug used to treat prostate cancer.

flutter   /flŭt'ər/   an abnormal, constant, rapid vibration.

flux   /flŭks/   **1.** the discharge of fluid material from the body, especially the discharge of watery feces from the bowel. **2.** the material so discharged. **3.** the rate of flow of a fluid, gas, or energy.

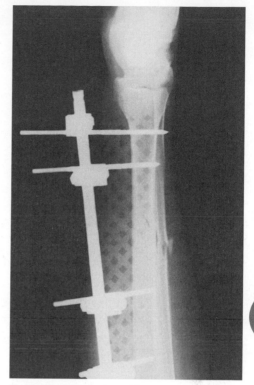

Fluoroscope (of Reconstructed Bone)

fMRI   *abbreviation.* functional magnetic resonance imaging, a type of magnetic resonance imaging that demonstrates the correlation between physical changes and mental functioning.

FNA   *abbreviation.* fine needle aspiration biopsy.

focal   /fō'kəl/   of or relating to a focus.

focal seizure   a seizure in only one part of the brain, affecting one side of the body.

focus   /fō'kəs/   (*pl.* **foci** /fō'sī/)   **1.** in optometry, the point where an image is clear and sharply defined. **2.** the primary center where a disease process starts, or where it concentrates.

folate   /fō'lāt/   folic acid, a B vitamin essential in the production of DNA and RNA.

fold   /fōld/   a ridge formed by the doubling back on itself of a thin plate or layer of skin or other flat body part.

Foley catheter   /fō'lē kăth'ĭ tər/   a catheter with a balloon tip used to secure it in the bladder.

folia   /fō'lē ə/   plural of folium.

folic acid   /fō'lĭk, fŏl'ĭk/   a B vitamin essential in the production of DNA and RNA. *Also called* folate.

folinic acid /fō lĭn′ĭk/ the form of folic acid that is metabolically active in the body.

folium /fō′lē əm/ (*pl.* **folia** /fō′lē ə/) a thin, broad structure, as in the cerebellum.

follicle /fŏl′ĭ kəl/ a small cavity or sac.

follicle-stimulating hormone (FSH) a hormone produced by the pituitary gland that stimulates the production of graafian follicles, and activates sperm-forming cells.

follicular /fə lĭk′yə lər/ of or relating to a follicle.

follicular cyst a cyst caused by an accumulation of follicular secretions due to a duct blockage.

folliculitis /fə lĭk′yə lī′tĭs/ an inflammation of the hair follicles.

folliculosis /fə lĭk′yə lō′sĭs/ the presence of abnormally large numbers of lymph follicles.

folliculus /fə lĭk′yə ləs/ (*pl.* **folliculi** /fə lĭk′ yə lī′/) a small cavity or sac; a follicle.

fomentation /fō′měn tā′shən/ **1.** a warm liquid or ointment therapeutically applied to the body; poultice. **2.** the therapeutic application of such a substance.

fontanel/fontanelle /fŏn′tə něl′/ any of the soft spaces between the undeveloped cranial bones of an fetus or infant, commonly called "soft spots."

Fontan('s) /fŏn tän(z)′/ **operation** or **procedure** surgical formation of a channel from the right atrium to the main pulmonary artery, bypassing an undeveloped right ventricle.

Food and Drug Administration (FDA) the government agency responsible for ensuring the safety and effectiveness of all drugs and medical devices (www.fda.gov).

foodborne disease /fōod′bôrn′/ any of a group of over 250 known diseases caused by consuming contaminated food or drink.

food poisoning infection transmitted through food or drink, typically characterized by nausea, vomiting, and diarrhea.

foot /fŏot/ (*pl.* **feet** /fēt/) the lower extremity of the leg that is in contact with the ground when standing or walking.

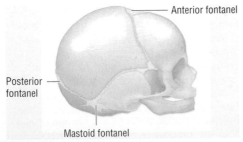

Anterior fontanel

Posterior fontanel

Mastoid fontanel

Fontanels

foot-and-mouth disease a disease caused by a highly infectious virus, infecting livestock more often than humans, characterized by skin lesions, fever, mouth blisters, appetite loss, weight loss, and foot sores.

foot-drop/footdrop/foot drop /fŏot′drŏp′/ sinking of the front of the foot due to weak or paralyzed muscles in the lower leg because of peroneal nerve injury. *Also called* drop foot.

foot-drop brace a brace worn on the lower leg to hold the foot in place to correct foot-drop.

foot fungus /fŭng′gəs/ an infectious fungus causing burning, itching, and scaling, commonly referred to as athlete's foot.

footling presentation /fŏot′lĭng/ a feet-first position of a fetus during birth.

foramen /fô rā′mən/ (*pl.* **foramina** /fô răm′ə nə/) a natural opening in tissue or bone.

foramen magnum /măg′nəm/ the large opening at the base of the skull through which the spinal cord passes.

foramen of Magendie /mə zhän dē′/ an opening in the roof of the fourth ventricle of the brain, through which the cerebrospinal fluid passes.

foramen ovale /ō vā′lē/ an opening in the septum between the left and right atria in a fetus that closes soon after birth.

foramina /fô răm′ə nə/ plural of foramen.

foramina of Luschka /lōōsh′kə/ the two openings in the fourth ventricle of the brain.

forced expiratory flow (FEF) /ĭk spī′rə tôr′ē/ the flow of air from the lungs during a test to measure forced vital capacity, as an indicator of how well the lungs are working

forced expiratory volume (FEV) the amount of air that can be expelled from the lungs following maximum inspiration. Also expressed as a percentage of total volume exhaled, i.e. $FEV_1\%$. *See also* FEV_1.

forced vital capacity (FVC) the maximum volume of air that can be forcibly expelled after a full inspiration or forcibly inhaled following a full expiration.

forceps /fôr′sěps/ a tong-like instrument used to grasp, manipulate, or extract, especially during surgery.

forearm /fôr′ärm′/ the part of the arm between the wrist and the elbow, including the ulna and radius.

forebrain /fôr′brān′/ **1.** one of the three primary regions of the embryonic brain, from which the diencephalon and telencephalon develop. **2.** the segment of the adult brain that develops from the embryonic forebrain; it includes the thalamus, hypothalamus, and cerebrum.

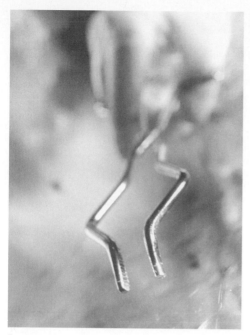

Forceps

forehead /fôr′hĕd′, -ĭd/ the region of the face between the eyebrows and the hairline.

foreign body an object that has been introduced into the body that doesn't belong in it, as a catheter in the bladder, a prosthetic heart valve, etc.

foreign body airway obstruction partial or complete blockage of the breathing passages by a foreign object, often a peanut in young children.

forensic /fə rĕn′sĭk/ used in legal proceedings or courts of law, as expert scientific or medical testimony.

forensic anthropology scientific identification and study of skeletal or decomposed human remains for use in a court of law.

forensic dentist application of dentistry, such as to identify the dead, to aid police investigation and for use in a court of law.

forensic genetics application of genetic science to legal proceedings and in courts of law.

forensic medicine application of medical science to legal proceedings and in courts of law.

forensic psychiatrist application of psychiatry to legal proceedings and in courts of law.

foreplay /fôr′plā′/ sexual stimulation, often leading to sexual intercourse.

foreshortening /fôr shôr′tə nĭng/ in radiology, a distortion on an x-ray in which an object appears shorter than it actually is.

foreskin /fôr′skĭn′/ the fold of skin that covers the glans of the penis. *Also called* prepuce.

Forestier('s) disease /fôr′ĕs tyā(z)′/ a form of arthritis characterized by calcification of the spine and tendons.

-form *suffix.* having the form of: *for example*, fungiform.

formaldehyde /fôr măl′də hīd′/ a gaseous poisonous compound combined with water, used to preserve biological specimens.

formalin /fôr′mə lĭn/ a clear liquid solution of formaldehyde containing a small amount of methanol, used to preserve biological specimens.

formed element a blood cell or platelet, differentiated from the fluid portion of the blood.

formication /fôr′mĭ kā′shən/ a sensation described as insects running around on or in the skin, felt by individuals with spinal cord or nerve disorders or during intoxication.

formula feeding the feeding to an infant of prepared formula in addition to, or as an alternative to breast feeding.

formulary /fôrm′yə lĕr′ē/ a compilation of pharmaceutical substances with their formulas, uses, and recipes.

fornication /fôr′nĭ kā′shən/ sexual intercourse between two people who are not married to each other.

fornix /fôr′nĭks/ (*pl.* **fornices** /fôr′nə sēz′/) an arch-shaped structure, such as the band of white matter located below the corpus callosum in the brain.

fornix cerebri /sə rē′brī/ a compact arching band of white nerve fiber beneath the corpus callosum connecting the two cerebral lobes of the brain. *Also called* fornix of the brain.

fornix conjunctivae /kŏn′jŭngk tī′vē/ the arching folds connecting the membrane of the inner eyelid to the membrane covering the eyeball.

fornix of the brain fornix cerebri.

fornix uteri /yōō′tə rī′/ the front and back recesses of the upper vagina.

fornix vaginae /və jī′nē/ the front and back recesses of the upper vagina.

fossa /fŏs′ə/ (*pl.* **fossae** /fŏs′ē/) a cavity or depression.

foulage /fōō läzh′/ a form of massage, in which the muscles are kneaded and pressed.

foundation /foun dā′shən/ a base or supporting structure.

four-finger crease or **line** a single crease in the palm as opposed to two, associated with several disorders, most commonly with Down syndrome.

Fournier('s) gangrene /fōōrn yā(z)′ găng grēn′/ a severe bacterial infection of the perineum and genitalia, lethal if untreated, characterized by extreme pain and redness.

fourth disease a mild childhood disorder caused by bacterial infection of *Staphylococcus aureus*, characterized by a rash.

fourth stage of labor the period following delivery during which the uterus contracts, expelling any remaining contents including the placenta.

fourth ventricle /věn′trĭ kəl/ the lowest of the four communicating cavities in the brain.

fovea /fō′vē ə/ (*pl.* **foveae** /fō′vē ē′/) fovea centralis.

fovea centralis /sěn trā′lĭs/ the tiny depression in retina of the eye through which light falls directly onto the cones that provide the clearest image; fovea.

foveation /fō′vē ā′shən/ the formation of pitted scars, as in chickenpox or acne.

fowl plague a highly contagious, extremely deadly viral disease in birds. Also called avian influenza, bird flu.

FP *abbreviation*. **1.** freezing point. **2.** family physician. **3.** family practice.

fractionation /frăk′shə nā′shən/ **1.** in radiology, the use of therapeutic radiation in a series of small doses, which are calculated fractions of a total dose, in order to minimize tissue damage. **2.** separation of a mixture into its components.

fracture /frăk′chər/ **1.** *n.* a break or crack, especially in bone. **2.** *v.* the act of breaking.

fracture dislocation a bone fracture plus the dislocation of a joint. *Also called* dislocation fracture.

fragile site the point on a chromosome where gaps and breaks usually occur.

fragile X-chromosome /ěks′ krō′mə sōm/ an X-chromosome with a fragile site at the end of the long arm, giving the illusion of a detached fragment.

fragile X syndrome a mutation of a fragile X-chromosome that is the most common genetic cause of mental retardation.

fragment /frăg′mənt/ a small part broken off something larger, as a bone fragment.

frailty syndrome /frāl′tē, frā′əl-/ a condition particularly affecting the elderly characterized by lethargy, mood disturbances, accelerated osteoporosis, weakness, and high susceptibility to disease.

frame /frām/ **1.** the human body, referring especially to size. **2.** a structure made of parts fitted together, usually meant for support.

Framingham Study /frā′mĭng hăm′/ a long-term study beginning in 1948, involving over 12,000 residents of Framingham, MA, from which a wealth of health information has been

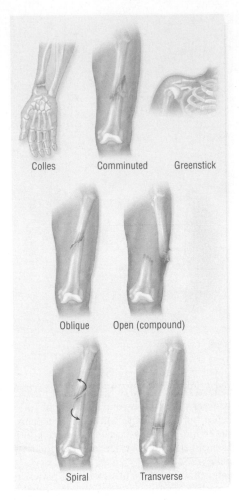

Colles   Comminuted   Greenstick

Oblique   Open (compound)

Spiral   Transverse

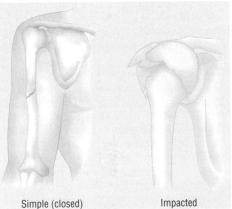

Simple (closed)   Impacted

Fractures

extracted, such as causes of heart disease and cancer.

fraternal twins twins due to fertilization of two different ova by two different sperm. *Also* *called* dizygotic twins. *See also* identical twins.

freckle /frĕk′əl/ a flat circular spot of dark pigment on the skin due to excessive exposure to sunlight, or of hereditary origin.

free association a technique used in psychoanalysis in which the patient continuously speaks or writes down the ideas in his or her head without reservation.

fremitus /frĕm′ĭ təs/ (*pl.* **fremitus**) a vibration generated in the body that can be felt by a hand resting or pressing on the body.

frenal /frē′nəl/ of or involving a frenum.

French /frĕnch/ a unit of measure equal to one-third millimeter, for measuring the diameter of tubular instruments.

French paradox referring to the low rate of heart disease and long life expectancy of the French population, despite having a diet high in saturated fats.

frenectomy /frĭ nĕk′tə mē/ surgical removal of a frenum.

frenotomy /frĭ nŏt′ə mē/ surgical division of a frenum.

frenulum /frĕn′yə ləm/ (*pl.* **frenula** /frĕn′yə lə/) a small frenum.

frenum /frē′nəm/ (*pl.* **frena** /frē′nə/) a structure that serves to restrain or support another structure, especially the fibrous connection between the underside of the tongue and the floor of the mouth.

frequency /frē′kwən sē/ the number of regular recurrences during a period of time.

Freudian /froi′dē ən/ of or relating to the theories of Sigmund Freud and to a type of psychoanalysis based on those theories.

Frey syndrome /frī/ a syndrome characterized by sweating on only one side of the head or neck after eating, caused by a damaged nerve in the cheek.

friable /frī′ə bəl/ **1.** crumbling easily; easy to reduce to powder; brittle. **2.** used of tissue that tears or fragments easily. **3.** in bacteriology, used of brittle cultures that crumble easily.

friction /frĭk′shən/ in massage therapy, the application of finger pressure directly to a lesion and transverse to muscle fibers.

friction rub **1.** a skin disorder characterized by redness, burning, and itching, caused by friction between two areas of skin, such as the folds of the neck, groin, armpit, breasts, and toes. **2.** cardiac murmur caused by pericarditis.

frigid /frĭj′ĭd/ **1.** extremely cold. **2.** used of a woman who is unable to experience sexual excitement or who does not respond to sexual advances.

frigidity /frĭ jĭd′ĭ tē/ failure of a female to respond to sexual stimulus for reasons of psychological or emotional origin.

frons /frŏnz/ (*pl.* **frontes** /frŏn′tēz/) the forehead; the region of the face between the *eyebrows* and the hairline.

frontal /frŭn′təl/ pertaining to the forehead.

frontal bone the large bone of the forehead.

frontal lobe the front part of each of the two cerebral hemispheres, located directly behind the forehead, that controls voluntary movement, emotional expression, and moral behavior.

frontal plane the plane that divides the body into front and back portions.

frontal sinus either of the two mucous membrane-lined cavities within the frontal bone.

frontes /frŏn′tēz/ plural of frons.

frostbite /frôst′bīt′/ destruction of skin and muscle tissue caused by prolonged exposure to freezing temperatures.

frozen section a thin cross section of a frozen specimen used for microscopic diagnosis.

frozen shoulder a painful condition characterized by inflammation of the cartilage and the development of fibrous bands in the shoulder joint. *Also called* adhesive capsulitis.

fructose /frŭk′tōs, frook′-/ a kind of sugar found in honey and many fruits.

fructosuria /frŭk′tō soor′ē ə, frook′-/ the presence of the sugar fructose in the urine.

FSH *abbreviation.* follicle-stimulating hormone.

ft. *abbreviation.* foot; feet.

FTT *abbreviation.* failure to thrive.

fugue /fyoog/ a condition in which a person suddenly changes lifestyle for a short period of time, later having no memory of what happened during that period.

fugue state a state of altered consciousness in which an individual is not fully aware of reality, yet can walk around or even talk.

fulguration /fŭl′gyə rā′shən/ destruction of tissue, such as a tumor, by applying electrical current.

functional genomics /fŭngk′shə nəl jē nō′mĭks/ the study of genes and the role their resulting proteins play in the body.

fundoplication /fŭn′dō plĭ kā′shən/ a surgical technique that fortifies the barrier between the stomach and the lower esophagus to prevent acid reflux. *Also called* antireflux surgery, reflux surgery.

fundoscopy /fŭn dŏs′kə pē/ examination of the optic disc, retina, and blood vessels.

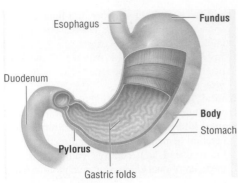

Esophagus — — Fundus

Duodenum

— Body

— Stomach

Pylorus

Gastric folds

Fundus (of Stomach)

fundus /fŭn′dəs/ the portion of an organ farthest from its opening.

fung-, fungi-, fungo- *combining form.* fungus: *for example,* fungiform.

fungal /fŭng′gəl/ of or relating to fungus. [fung- + al]

fungal nail infection common fungal infection of the nails characterized by thickened, brittle, and opaque nails. *Also called* onychomycosis.

fungemia /fŭn jē′mē ə/ a fungal infection in the bloodstream.

fungi /fŭn′jī/ plural of fungus.

fungicidal /fŭn′jə sī′dəl/ capable of destroying or inhibiting the growth of fungi.

fungicide /fŭn′jə sīd′/ a substance capable of destroying or inhibiting the growth of fungi. [fungi- + -cide]

fungiform /fŭn′jə fôrm′/ shaped like a mushroom, as the fungiform papilla. [fungi + form]

fungiform papilla /pə pĭl′ə/ the tiny mushroom-shaped protrusions on the back of the tongue.

fungistat /fŭn′jə stăt′/ a substance that inhibits the growth of fungi. [fungi + -stat]

fungistatic /fŭn′jə stăt′ĭk/ capable of inhibiting the growth of fungi without killing them. [fungi + static]

fungus /fŭng′gəs/ (*pl.* **fungi** /fŭn′jī/) any of a large group organisms, such as yeasts, molds, and mildews that can cause infections such as athlete's foot, ringworm, and candidiasis.

funiculus /fyōō nĭk′yə ləs/ (*pl.* **funiculi** /fyōō nĭk′yə lī′/) any long ropelike structure within the body; cord.

funnel chest a depressed or caved-in chest. *Also called* pectus excavatum.

funny bone the part of the elbow where the ulnar nerve travels, referring to the sensation felt when is bumped.

FUO *abbreviation.* fever of unknown origin.

furuncle /fyōōr′ŭng kəl/ medical term for a boil.

fusiform /fyōō′zə fôrm′/ having a form like a spindle.

fusion inhibitor an antiretroviral drug that prevents any virus (especially HIV) from fusing with a cell and infecting it.

fusospirillary gingivitis /fyōō′zō spī′rə lĕr′ē jĭn′jə vī′tĭs/ a painful mouth infection with swelling and shedding of dead mouth tissues. *Also called* trench mouth, Vincent's angina.

fusospirillosis /fyōō′zō spī′rə lō′sĭs/ a painful mouth infection with swelling and shedding of dead mouth tissues. *Also called* trench mouth, Vincent's angina.

fusospirochetal gingivitis /fyōō′zō spī′rə kē′təl jĭn′jə vī′tĭs/ a painful mouth infection with swelling and shedding of dead mouth tissues. *Also called* trench mouth, Vincent's angina.

FVC *abbreviation.* forced vital capacity.

G

G 1. (drug caution code) abbreviation of glaucoma, placed on the label of a medication as a warning that it can cause complications for someone with the disease. 2. *abbreviation.* gravida.

g *abbreviation.* gram; grams.

gag reflex involuntary contraction of the muscles of the throat caused by the contact of a foreign object with the mucous membrane of the back of the mouth and pharynx.

gait /gāt/ a particular manner of walking.

galact-, galacto- *combining form.* milk: *for example,* galactorrhea.

galactocele /gə lăk'tə sēl'/ a cyst caused by an obstruction to a lactiferous duct. *Also called* lactocele. [galacto- + -cele]

galactopoiesis /gə lăk'tō poi ē'sĭs/ milk production. [galacto- + -poiesis]

galactorrhea /gə lăk'tə rē'ə/ spontaneous or excessive flow of milk at any time other than during nursing, sometimes a sign of a pituitary adenoma. *Also called* lactorrhea. [galacto- + -rrhea]

galactose /gə lăk'tōs/ a simple sugar contained in milk, a component of lactose. [galact- + -ose]

galactosemia /gə lăk'tə sē'mē ə/ a metabolic disease in which there is a defect in the body's ability to use galactose due to a deficiency of an enzyme.

galactosis /găl'ək tō'sĭs/ secretion of milk by the mammary glands. [galact- + -osis]

galactosuria /gə lăk'tə soor'ē ə/ the presence of milk in the urine.

gall /gôl/ older term for bile, which is a bitter, yellowish-brown to green fluid secreted in the liver, stored in the gallbladder, and released into the beginning of the small intestine to aid in digestive function, especially the absorption of fats; not in use today.

gallbladder (GB) /gôl'blăd'ər/ a pear-shaped organ just below the liver that stores bile until it is needed in the small intestine to aid in the digestion of fats. [gall + bladder]

gallop /găl'əp/ a triple beat of the heart, usually indicative of serious heart disease.

gallop rhythm a triple beat of the heart, usually indicative of serious heart disease.

gallstone /gôl'stōn'/ a hard calcification of substances in bile formed in the gallbladder or a bile duct. *Also called* cholelith, calculus.

galvanic skin response /găl văn'ĭk/ (**GSR**) a change in the electrical conductivity of the skin in response to emotional stimuli.

gamete /găm'ēt, gə mēt'/ a reproductive cell; the sperm or the egg.

gamete intrafallopian transfer (GIFT) /ĭn'trə fə lō'pē ən/ a technique used to assist conception in which sperm and eggs are inserted into a woman's fallopian tubes where fertilization can occur.

gameto- *combining form.* gamete: *for example,* gametocyte.

gametocide /gə mē'tə sīd'/ substance capable of destroying gametes or gametocytes. [gameto- + -cide]

gametocyte /gə mē'tə sīt'/ a cell that develops into a gamete by meiosis. [gameto- + -cyte]

gametogenesis /gə mē'tə jĕn'ə sĭs/ the development and production of gametes. [gameto- + -genesis]

gamma-aminobutyric acid /găm'ə ə mē'nō byoo tîr'ĭk, -ăm'ə nō-/ an amino acid found in the central nervous system and associated with the transmission of nerve impulses; used in epilepsy as an inhibitory neurotransmitter.

gamma globulin /glŏb'yə lĭn/ a class of antibody or immunoglobulin found in the blood.

gamma hydroxybutyrate (GHB) /hī drŏk'sē byoo'tə rāt'/ a central nervous system depressant drug commonly called a "date rape drug"; so called because it is slipped into drinks to make it easier to rape a potential victim.

gamma knife a radiation therapy machine that works by focusing low-dose gamma rays from several locations at one small target.

gamma linoleic acid /lĭn'ə lē'ĭk/ a fatty acid found in some plant seed oils, used as an adjunct to treat several disorders, such as heart disease and diabetes.

gamma rays high-energy electromagnetic radiation.

gangli-, ganglio- *combining form.* ganglion: *for example,* gangliitis.

ganglia /găng'glē ə/ plural of ganglion.

gangliectomy /găng'glē ĕk'tə mē/ surgical removal of a ganglion. [gangli- + -ectomy]

gangliform /găng'glə fôrm'/ having the form or appearance of a ganglion. [gangli- + form]

gangliitis /găng′glē ī′tĭs/ inflammation of a ganglion. [gangli- + -itis]

ganglioblast /găng′glē ə blăst′/ an embryonic cell that develops into ganglion cells. [ganglio- + -blast]

gangliolysis /găng′glē ŏl′ə sĭs/ the destruction or dissolution of a ganglion. [ganglio- + -lysis]

ganglion /găng′glē ən/ (*pl.* **ganglia** /găng′glē ə/) **1.** a mass of nerve cells forming a nerve center. **2.** a knot-like cyst (usually benign) formed from tendon sheath or synovial tissue.

ganglion cyst a knot-like cyst formed from tendon sheath or synovial tissue.

ganglionectomy /găng′lē ə něk′tə mē/ surgical removal of a ganglion. [ganglion + -ectomy]

ganglioneuroma /găng′glē ō nŏŏ rō′mə/ a benign neuroma containing ganglionic cells. [ganglio- + neur- + -oma]

ganglionitis /găng′glē ə nī′tĭs/ inflammation of a ganglion. [ganglion- + -itis]

gangrene /găng′grēn, găng grēn′/ death and decay of tissue due to insufficient blood supply, frequently infected by bacteria of the genus *Clostridium*.

gap junction the area of contact between adjacent cell membranes that facilitates the intercellular passage of ions, hormones, and neurotransmitters.

gargle /gär′gəl/ **1.** *v.* to rinse the throat with a liquid (often an antiseptic) by exhaling air with the head back to produce a bubbling effect. **2.** *n.* the liquid agent used for gargling.

garlic /gär′lĭk/ an edible herb of the lily family commonly used as a food and regarded by some as having medicinal properties.

gas /găs/ a fluid in vapor form, without shape or fixed volume.

gas chromatography (GC) /krō′mə tŏg′rə fē/ a technique used to separate complex mixtures by vaporizing the mixture and sending it through a detection device.

gas-liquid chromatography (GLC) a technique in which a gas moves over a liquid, and chemical substances are separated by their different adsorption rates.

gaseous /găs′ē əs, găsh′əs/ of or relating to gas.

gastr-, gastro- *combining form.* stomach: *for example,* gastritis.

gastralgia /gă străl′jē ə, -jə/ pain in the stomach, commonly called a stomachache. [gastr- + -algia]

gastrectasia /găs′trĕk tā′zhə/ dilation of the stomach. [gastr- + -ectasia]

gastrectomy /gă strĕk′tə mē/ surgical removal of all or a portion of the stomach. [gastr- + -ectomy]

gastric /găs′trĭk/ of or relating to the stomach. [gastr- + -ic]

gastric adenocarcinoma /ăd′ə nō kär′sə nō′mə/ cancer developing in the inner lining of the stomach; previously common and thought to be related to carcinogens in smoked meat; now rare.

gastric analysis measurement of the pH and acid output of the contents of the stomach.

gastric atrophy shrinkage and weakening of the stomach muscles resulting in insufficient production of digestive juices.

gastric banding a surgical procedure in which an adjustable band is placed around the stomach to limit the amount of food that can be ingested at one time, used to aid weight loss.

gastric bypass surgical division of the stomach to limit food consumption, used for treatment of extreme obesity. *Also called* gastroplasty.

gastric cancer or **gastric carcinoma** /kär′sə nō′mə/ cancer of the stomach.

gastric emptying study a test in which the patient eats a meal to which a small amount of radioactive material has been added so that the passage of the food to the intestines can be timed.

gastric gland one of many glands in the stomach wall that secrete gastric juice.

gastric hemorrhage hemorrhage from the stomach. *Also called* gastrorrhagia.

gastric juice acidic fluid secreted by the gastric gland that aid in digestion.

gastric lavage /lə väzh′/ washing out of the stomach with sterile water to remove blood or toxins (as in overdose).

gastric outlet the passage out of the stomach into the duodenum, the first part of the small intestine.

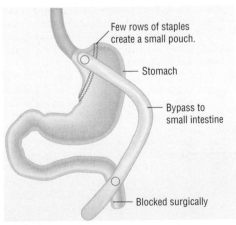

Few rows of staples create a small pouch.

Stomach

Bypass to small intestine

Blocked surgically

Gastric Bypass

gastric outlet obstruction   any blockage that impedes the emptying of food from the stomach to the duodenum.

gastric resection /rĭ sĕk'shən/   surgical removal of a portion of the stomach, used as a treatment for obesity.

gastric stapling   a surgical procedure similar to gastric banding, in which the sections of the stomach are stapled together to limit the amount of food that can be ingested at one time, used to aid weight loss.

gastric ulcer   a hole in the lining of the stomach caused by gastric juices.

gastric volvulus /vŏl'vyə ləs/   abnormal twisting of the stomach impairing its blood flow, causing pain, and leading to a surgical emergency.

gastrin /găs'trĭn/   a hormone secreted by certain stomach glands that stimulates production of gastric juices.

gastritis /gă strī'tĭs/   inflammation of the stomach. [gastr- + -itis]

gastro-   *See* gastr-.

gastrocnemius muscle /găs'trŏk nē'mē əs, găs'trə nē'-/   the fleshy muscle that forms the large portion of the calf.

gastrocolitis /găs'trō kə lī'tĭs/   inflammation of the stomach and colon. [gastro- + col- + -itis]

gastrocolostomy /găs'trō kə lŏs'tə mē/   surgical creation of a passageway between the stomach and the colon. [gastro- + colo- + -stomy]

gastroduodenitis /găs'trō dŏŏ ŏd'ə nī'tĭs/   inflammation of the stomach and duodenum. [gastro- + duoden- + itis]

gastroduodenoscopy /găs'trō dŏŏ ŏd'ə nŏs'kə pē/   examination of the stomach and duodenum [gastro- + duodeno- + -scopy]

gastroduodenostomy /găs'trō dŏŏ'ō də nŏs'tə mē/   surgical formation of a passage from the stomach to the duodenum.

gastrodynia /găs'trō dĭn'ē ə/   pain in the stomach. *Also called* gastralgia. [gastro- + -dynia]

gastroenteric /găs'trō ĕn tĕr'ĭk/   of or relating to the gastrointestinal tract. [gastro- + enteric]

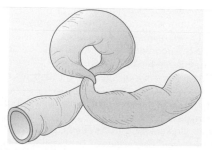

Gastric Volvulus

gastroenteritis /găs'trō ĕn'tə rī'tĭs/   inflammation of the stomach and intestines. [gastro- + enteritis]

gastroenterocolitis /găs'trō ĕn'tə rō kə lī'tĭs/   inflammatory disease involving the stomach and intestines. [gastro- + entero- + colitis]

gastroenterologic disease /găs'trō ĕn'tər ə lŏj'ĭk/   any disease of the digestive system.

gastroenterologist /găs'trō ĕn'tə rŏl'ə jĭst/   a physician who specializes in diseases of the gastrointestinal tract.

gastroenterology /găs'trō ĕn'tə rŏl'ə jē/   the branch of medicine concerned with the study, diagnosis, and treatment of the gastrointestinal tract. [gastro- + -entero- + -logy]

gastroenteroplasty /găs'trō ĕn'tər ə plăs'tē/   surgical repair of the stomach and instestine. [gastro- + entero- + -plasty]

gastroenteroptosis /găs'trō ĕn'tər ŏp tō'sĭs, -tər ə tō'-/   prolapse of the stomach and intestine. [gastro- + entero- + -ptosis]

gastroenterostomy /găs'trō ĕn'tə rŏs'tə mē/   surgical formation of a passage from the stomach to the intestines. [gastro- + entero- + colostomy]

gastroenterotomy /găs'trō ĕn'tə rŏt'ə mē/   surgical incision into the stomach and intestine. [gastro- + entero- + -tomy]

gastroesophageal /găs'trō ĭ sŏf'ə jē'əl, -ē'sə făj'ē əl/   of or relating to both the stomach and esophagus. [gastro- + esophageal]

gastroesophageal junction   the location where the esophagus connects to the stomach.

gastroesophageal reflux /rē'flŭks/   backwards flow of stomach acids into the esophagus, causing burning pain and discomfort, and sometimes ulcers, neoplastic changes, and stricture. *See also* Barrett's esophagus.

gastroesophageal reflux disease (GERD)   a disease in which there is recurrent backwards flow of stomach acids into the esophagus, causing burning pain and discomfort.

gastroesophageal sphincter /sfĭngk'tər/   a ring of muscle fibers at the junction of the esophagus and stomach. *Also called* lower esophageal sphincter.

gastroesophagitis /găs'trō ĭ sŏf'ə jī'tĭs/   inflammation of the stomach and esophagus. [gastro- + esophag- + -itis]

gastroileitis /găs'trō ĭl'ē ī'tĭs/   inflammation of the stomach and ilium. [gastro- + ile- + -itis]

gastroileostomy /găs'trō ĭl'ē ŏs'tə mē/   surgical creation of a passage between the stomach and the ileum. [gastro- + ileo- + -stomy]

gastrointestinal (GI) /găs'trō ĭn tĕs'tə nəl/   of or relating to the stomach and intestines.

gastrointestinal (GI) endoscopy /ĕn dŏs'kə pē/   examination of the esophagus, stomach, and intestines using an endoscope.

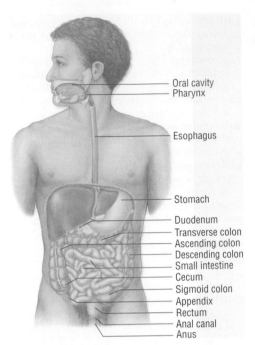

Oral cavity
Pharynx
Esophagus
Stomach
Duodenum
Transverse colon
Ascending colon
Descending colon
Small intestine
Cecum
Sigmoid colon
Appendix
Rectum
Anal canal
Anus

Gastrointestinal Tract

gastrointestinal (GI) series   x-ray examination of the esophagus, stomach, and intestines following the ingestion of a barium mixture.

gastrointestinal (GI) tract or **system**   the entire passage leading from the mouth to the esophagus, stomach, intestines, rectum, and anus, through which food is ingested, digested, absorbed, and expelled from the body.

gastrojejunostomy   /găs′trō jĭ jōō nŏs′tə mē/   surgical formation of a passageway from the stomach to the jejunum, the second portion of the small intestine. [gastro- + jejunostomy]

gastrolith /găs′trə lĭth/   a calculus in the stomach. [gastro- + -lith]

gastromalacia /găs′trō mə lā′shə/   softening of the stomach walls. [gastro- + -malacia]

gastromegaly /găs′trō mĕg′ə lē/   enlargement of the stomach. *Also called* megalogastria. [gastro- + -megaly]

gastroparalysis /găs′trō pə răl′ə sĭs/   paralysis of the stomach walls.

gastroparesis /găs′trō pə rē′sĭs/   partial paralysis of the stomach muscles; occurs in long-standing diabetes. [gastro- + -paresis]

gastropathy /gă strŏp′ə thē/   a disease of the stomach. [gastro- + -pathy]

gastroplasty /găs′trə plăs′tē/   **1.** surgical repair of the stomach. 2. surgical division of the stomach to limit food consumption, used for treatment of extreme obesity. *Also called* gastric bypass. [gastro- + -plasty]

gastroptosis /găs′trŏp tō′sĭs, -trə tō′-/   prolapse of the stomach. [gastro- + -ptosis]

gastrorrhagia   /găs′trə rā′jē ə/   hemorrhage from the stomach. *Also called* gastric hemorrhage. [gastro- + -rrhagia]

gastrorrhaphy /gă strôr′ə fē/   suture of a ruptured stomach. [gastro- + -rrhaphy]

gastrorrhea   /gă strôr′ē ə/   oversecretion of gastric juices in the stomach. [gastro- + -rrhea]

gastroschisis /gă strŏs′kə sĭs/   a birth defect in which there is a defect in the abdominal wall through which a portion of the intestines protrudes. [gastro- + -schisis]

gastroscope /găs′trə skōp′/   a type of endoscope used to examine the inside of the stomach. [gastro- + -scope]

gastroscopy /gă strŏs′kə pē/   examination of the inside of the stomach using a gastroscope. [gastro- + -scopy]

gastrospasm   /găs′trə spăz′əm/   spasmodic contraction of the stomach walls. [gastro- + -spasm]

gastrostomy /gă strŏs′tə mē/   surgical formation of a hole through the abdominal wall and into the stomach, usually for nutrition in a patient who cannot swallow. [gastro- + -stomy]

gastrotomy /gă strŏt′ə mē/   surgical incision into the stomach. [gastro- + -tomy]

gatekeeper /gāt′kē′pər/   a health care professional who establishes the first encounter with a patient and regulates the patient's activities within the health care system.

gating /gā′tĭng/   the process by which a channel in a cell membrane opens and closes.

Gaucher('s) disease /gō shā(z)′/   a group of five rare hereditary diseases caused by a defect in lipid metabolism characterized by enlargement of the liver, spleen, and lymph nodes, and bone deterioration.

gauze /gôz/   a soft, open-weave, bleached cotton cloth used for surgical dressing, bandages, and sponges.

gavage feeding /gə väzh′/   introduction of nutritive material through a nasogastric (stomach) tube, used with infants. *See also* tube feeding.

gay /gā/   a homosexual individual, especially a male.

GB   *abbreviation.* gallbladder

GC   *abbreviation.* gas chromatography.

g-cal   *abbreviation.* gram calorie.

G-CSF   *abbreviation.* granulocyte colony-stimulating factor.

GDM   *abbreviation.* gestational diabetes mellitus.

gel /jĕl/   **1.** the semisolid state of a colloidal suspension. **2.** a substance in this state.

-gen   precursor of: *for example,* glycogen.

gender /jĕn′ dər/   the sex or sexual identity of a person.

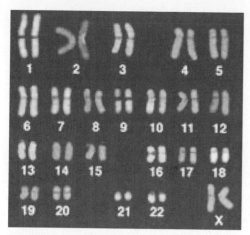

Gene Mapping (done on Karyotype of Human Chromosomes)

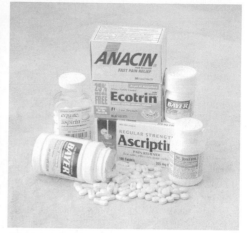

Generic Drugs (Aspirin)

gender identity disorder a mental disorder characterized by an overwhelming desire to change anatomical sex.

gene /jēn/ a segment of DNA in a specific place on a chromosome that determines (often in combination with other genes) a particular characteristic in an organism by controlling the formation of an enzyme or protein, and is capable of replicating itself exactly at each cell division.

gene deletion a total absence or loss of a gene, which may result in severe health problems or deformities.

gene duplication an extra copy of a gene, which may lead to severe health problems or deformities.

gene expression the translation of information encoded in a gene into protein or RNA.

gene mapping a representation of the relative positions of genes on a chromosome and of the distances between the genes.

gene markers detectable segments of DNA that serve as landmarks for a target gene.

gene product the RNA or protein produced by the expression of a gene.

genera /jĕn′ər ə/ the plural of genus.

general anesthetic a drug that puts the person to sleep (for certain kinds of surgery) as opposed to a local anesthetic, which only numbs a particular area.

general paresis /pə rē′sĭs/ a condition caused by inflammation of the brain in the last (tertiary) stage of syphilis, characterized by progressive dementia, tremors, and paralysis.

generalized anxiety disorder a condition characterized by chronic worrying and tension lasting several months or years.

generalized tonic-clonic seizure /klŏn′ĭk, klō′nĭk/ a two-phase seizure in which the body becomes rigid followed by uncontrolled jerking.

generation /jĕn′ə rā′shən/ 1. the process of producing offspring; procreation. 2. the offspring of a couple, considered as the first of their descendants.

generic /jə nĕr′ĭk/ 1. of or relating to a genus. 2. general. 3. characteristic or distinctive.

generic drug a drug that is labeled by its chemical name and is not sold under the ownership restrictions of a trade name drug.

generic name the chemical name or makeup of a drug.

gene silencing a mechanism by which cells suppress large sections of chromosomal DNA.

-genesis origin; production: *for example*, embryogenesis.

gene testing testing a sample of blood or tissue for the presence of a gene.

gene therapy insertion of normal, healthy DNA into cells to correct a genetic defect or treat a disease, sometimes accomplished by inserting a piece of corrected DNA into a virus, and infecting the target cells, leaving behind new information after the infection has cleared.

genetic /jə nĕt′ĭk/ of or relating to genes or to the information carried by the genes.

genetic code the sequence of nucleotides (building blocks of DNA) that determines the sequence of amino acids in protein synthesis.

genetic counseling education and guidance provided by health care professionals to those who have a genetic disease, are at risk of developing a genetic disease, or are concerned about the possibility of passing a genetic disease to their children.

genetic counselor a health care professional specializing in medical genetics and trained to provide genetic counseling.

genetic disease a disease caused by an abnormal or missing gene, such as Huntington's chorea and cystic fibrosis.

geneticist /jə nĕt'ə sĭst/ an expert or specialist in genetics.

genetic predisposition /prē'dĭs pə zĭsh'ən/ an inherited genetic pattern that makes one susceptible to a certain disease.

genetics /jə nĕt'ĭks/ the scientific study of heredity.

genetic screening testing to determine susceptibility to a genetic disease.

genetic testing a group of tests to diagnose a genetic disease, identify future risk of getting or passing on a genetic disease, and to predict drug responses to a genetic disease.

genetic transformation the transformation or altering of genetic material in a cell due to the incorporation of foreign DNA.

-genic producing; generating: *for example,* embryogenic.

geniculum /jə nĭk'yə ləm/ (*pl.* **genicula** /jə nĭk'yə lə/) **1.** any small anatomical structure bent like a knee. **2.** a kneelike bend in an organ.

genital /jĕn'ĭ təl/ of or relating to the genitalia.

genital herpes /hûr'pēz/ a viral infection (*herpes simplex virus*) transmitted during sexual contact with the genitals and characterized by painful skin eruptions. *Also called* herpes genitalis.

genitalia /jĕn'ĭ tāl'yə/ the male and female external sex organs.

genitals /jĕn'ĭ təlz/ the male and female external sex organs.

genital wart a wart in the area of the genitals or anus caused by a viral infection (*human papilloma virus*) transmitted during sexual contact.

genitourinary (GU) /jĕn'ĭ tō yŏŏr'ə nĕr'ē/ of or relating to the genital and urinary organs and their functions.

genitourinary system all the organs involved in reproduction and the formation and evacuation of urine.

geno- *combining form.* gene, genetic: *for example,* genoblast.

genoblast /jē'nə blăst'/ the nucleus of the fertilized ovum. [geno- + -blast]

genome /jē'nōm/ a complete set of chromosomes of an organism, with the associated genes.

Genome Database the official worldwide repository for genomic mapping data located at Johns Hopkins University in Baltimore, Maryland.

genomic /jē nō'mĭk, -nŏm'ĭk/ of or relating to a genome or the study of genomes.

genomics /jē nō'mĭks, -nŏm'ĭks/ the science and study of genes and their function.

genomic segment any specific region of the genome.

genoplasty /jē'nə plăs'tē/ an alternative to traditional gene therapy, a repair technology that uses short DNA fragments to induce a cell to repair its genome. [geno- + -plasty]

genotoxin /jē'nō tŏk'sĭn/ a substance that damages or causes mutations in DNA. [geno- + toxin]

genotype /jē'nə tīp'/ the genetic makeup of a cell, organism, or individual.

genus /jē'nəs/ (*pl.* **genera** /jĕn'ər ə/) in biology, a group of related organisms containing one or more species. The species within the genus share various characteristics.

genu valgum /jē'nōō văl'gəm/ a condition where the knees are abnormally close together and the ankles are far apart. *Also called* knock-kneed.

geode /jē'ōd/ a bony cyst sometimes found in patients with arthritis.

GERD /gûrd/ *abbreviation.* gastroesophageal reflux disease.

GERD surgery a surgical technique that fortifies the barrier between the stomach and the lower esophagus to prevent acid reflux. *Also called* fundoplication.

geriatric /jĕr'ē ăt'rĭk/ of or relating to old age or the aging process.

geriatric medicine the branch of medicine concerned with the diagnosis, treatment, and prevention of diseases specific to aging, or occurring in the elderly.

geriatrician /jĕr'ē ə trĭsh'ən/ a physician who specializes in geriatrics.

geriatrics /jĕr'ē ăt'rĭks/ the branch of medicine concerned with the diagnosis, treatment, and prevention of diseases specific to aging, or occurring in the elderly.

germ /jûrm/ **1.** a microorganism, especially a pathogen that can cause disease or infection. **2.** a small mass of cells which are capable of developing into a new organism or one of its parts.

Germ (cells in a culture)

germ cell   the female and male reproductive cells; the eggs and sperm.

germ cell tumor   a tumor arising from a germ cell.

German measles /mē′zəlz/   a virus capable of causing birth defects in a fetus if occurring in the first trimester of pregnancy. The disease itself is mild with a rash and some lymph node swelling. *Also called* rubella.

German measles immunization /ĭm′yə nə zā′ shən/   a part of the MMR vaccine, a standard vaccine given to prevent measles, mumps, and rubella, administered in two doses.

German measles vaccine /văk sēn′/   a vaccine administered to prevent rubella.

germanium /jûr mā′nē əm/   a nonessential chemical element some claim to be beneficial as an alternative treatment for some diseases; it can cause kidney damage and death if used chronically.

germicide /jûr′mə sīd′/   agent that kills germs; disinfectant.

germinoma /jûr′mə nō′mə/   a type of germ cell tumor.

germline mutation /jûrm′līn′/   a change in the DNA of a germ cell at the single-cell stage of its development, that will exist in every cell in the body it is transmitted to.

geronto-   *combining form.* old age: *for example,* gerontology.

gerontologist /jĕr′ən tŏl′ə jĭst/   a specialist in gerontology.

gerontology /jĕr′ən tŏl′ə jē/   the scientific study of the process and problems of aging. [geronto- + -logy]

gerontophobia /jə rŏn′tō fō′bē ə/   abnormal fear of old people. [geronto- + phobia]

gestalt therapy /gə shtält′/   a type of psychotherapy that emphasizes treatment by focusing on the structure and organization of living in terms of present awareness and one's relationship with the outside world.

gestation /jĕ stā′shən/   the period between conception and birth.

gestational diabetes /jĕ stā′shə nəl dī′ə bē′tĭs, -tēz/   a form of diabetes mellitus that appears during pregnancy and usually disappears after delivery; it can predispose the mother to later Type 2 diabetes.

gestational diabetes mellitus (GDM) /mĕl′ĭ təs, mə lī′təs/   a form of diabetes mellitus that appears during pregnancy and usually disappears after delivery.

gestational hypertension /hī′pər tĕn′shən/   high blood pressure that develops during pregnancy and usually subsides after delivery; it can indicate the onset of toxemia, consisting

of edema, hypertension, and proteinuria and can also predispose the mother to later hypertension.

gestational period   the period of human development between conception and birth.

gestosis /jĕ stō′sĭs/   any disorder of pregnancy.

GH   *abbreviation.* growth hormone.

GHB   *abbreviation.* gamma hydroxybutyrate.

GHz   *abbreviation.* gigahertz.

GI   *abbreviation.* gastrointestinal.

GI series   *abbreviation.* gastrointestinal series; gingival index.

GI tract   *abbreviation.* gastrointestinal tract.

giardia /jē är′dē ə/   a single-celled organism that infects the GI tract, causing diarrhea.

giardiasis /jē′är dī′ə sĭs/   infection with giardia; a common diarrheal disease caused by a single-celled organism (*Giardia lamblia*) and often spread by a contaminated water supply.

GIFT /gĭft/   *abbreviation.* gamete intrafallopian transfer.

gigahertz (Ghz) /gĭg′ə hûrts′, jĭg′-/   a unit of frequency equal to one billion hertz, i.e., one billion cycles per second.

gigantism /jī găn′tĭz əm/   excessive growth of the body or any of its parts.

gingiv-, gingivo-   *combining form.* gum: *for example,* gingivitis.

gingiva /jĭn′jə və/   (*pl.* **gingivae** /jĭn′jə vē′/) the firm tissue surrounding the base of the teeth. *Also called* gums.

gingival /jĭn′jə vəl/   of or relating to the gums. [gingiv- + -al]

gingivectomy /jĭn′jə vĕk′tə mē/   surgical removal of gum tissue. [gingiv- + -ectomy]

gingivitis /jĭn′jə vī′tĭs/   inflammation of the gums. [gingiv- + -itis]

gingivoglossitis /jĭn′jə vō glŏ sī′tĭs/   inflammation of the tongue and gums.

gingivoplasty /jĭn′jə və plăs′tē/   surgical repair of the gums. [gingivo- + -plasty]

gingko biloba /gĭng′kō bə lō′bə/   an herb purported to serve as a treatment for dementia, to

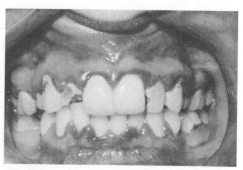

Gingivitis

improve memory, and to improve mental focus.

ginseng /jĭn′sĕng/ a Chinese herb believed to have medicinal powers, used to increase energy by stimulating the adrenal gland.

girdle /gûr′dəl/ the bony framework that unites the arms and legs to the trunk.

gland /glănd/ an organ that produces a secretion.

glandula /glăn′jə lə/ (pl. **glandulae** /glăn′jə lē′/) a small gland.

glandular fever /glăn′jə lər/ a self-limited illness commonly called mono (or mononucleosis), caused by the Epstein-Barr virus, characterized by fever, fatigue, sore throat, swollen lymph glands, liver inflammation, and spleen enlargement. *Also called* infectious mononucleosis, mononucleosis.

glans /glănz/ (pl. **glandes** /glăn′dēz/) **1.** the rounded head of the penis. **2.** the rounded head of the clitoris.

glans penis the rounded head of the penis.

glaucoma /glô kō′mə/ a common eye condition in which insufficient drainage of the fluid in the eye causes increased pressure and damage to the optic nerve, leading to impaired vision and eventual blindness.

glaucoma detection an eye test in which intraocular pressure is measured with a tonometer to aid in early detection of glaucoma.

GLC *abbreviation.* gas-liquid chromatography

Gleason('s) score /glē′sən(z)/ a grading system for prostate cancer used to predict its degree of malignancy and degree of spread.

glenohumeral /glē′nō hyōō′mər əl/ of or relating to the shoulder joint, where the glenoid fossa and humerus meet.

glenoid fossa /glē′noid fŏs′ə/ the socket part of the shoulder joint that is attached to the scapula.

glenoid labrum /lā′brəm/ the ring of cartilage lining the glenoid fossa that provides stability for the shoulder joint.

gli-, glia- glio- *combining form.* neuroglia: *for example,* glioma.

gliacyte /glī′ə sīt′/ a neuroglial cell.

glial cell /glī′əl/ a cell of the central nervous system that supports and insulates the neurons of the brain and spinal chord. [gli- + -al]

glioblast /glī′ə blăst′/ an early neural cell that gives rise to neuroglial cells and to the cells that line the central canal of the spine and ventricles of the brain. [glio- + -blast]

glioblastoma /glī′ō blă stō′mə/ a malignant tumor of the central nervous system usually occurring in the brain, and almost always fatal. [glio- + blastoma]

glioblastoma multiforme /mŭl′tə fôr′mē/ a fast-moving malignant tumor of the glial tissues in the brain.

glioma /glī ō′mə/ (pl. **gliomas** or **gliomata** /glī ō′mə tə/) a brain tumor developing in the glial tissues. [gli- + -oma]

gliomatosis /glī ō′mə tō′sĭs/ abnormal growth of glial tissues.

glioneuroma /glī′ō nōō rō′mə/ a ganglioneuroma with fibers and glial cells in the matrix. [glio- + neur- + -oma]

gliosarcoma /glī′ō sär kō′mə/ a tumor derived from neuroglia. [glio- + sarc- + -oma]

gliosis /glī ō′sĭs/ excessive growth of neuroglia. [gli- + -osis]

Glisson('s) capsule /glĭs′ən(z)/ the connective tissue encapsulating the liver.

globin /glō′bĭn/ the protein component of hemoglobin and myoglobin.

-globin *suffix.* protein: *for example,* hemoglobin.

globulin /glŏb′yə lĭn/ any of several proteins found in blood, milk, muscle, and plant seeds.

-globulin *suffix.* protein: *for example,* immunoglobulin.

globus pallidus /glō′bəs păl′ĭ dəs/ the inner pale yellow part of the lenticular nucleus, at the base of the cerebral hemisphere. *Also called* pallidum.

glomerular /glō měr′yə lər/ of or relating to glomeruli.

glomerular filtration the filtering of water and waste products out of plasma through glomerular capillary walls into a blind sac called Bowman's capsule, which is the first part of the kidney's urine collecting system.

glomerulonephritis /glō měr′yə lō nə frī′tĭs/ a kidney disease characterized by inflammation of the renal glomeruli.

glomerulus /glō měr′yə ləs/ (pl. **glomeruli** /glō měr′yə lī′/) **1.** a network of capillaries.

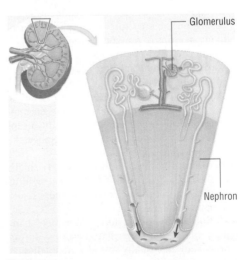

Glomerulus

Nephron

Glomerulus

2. the spherical structure of capillaries found in the kidneys that filter urine out of blood.

glomus /glō'məs/ (*pl.* **glomera** /glŏm'ər ə/) a small round swelling, especially one surrounded by nerve fibers.

gloss-, glosso- *combining form.* tongue: *for example*, glossitis, glossopathy.

glossal /glŏs'əl/ of or relating to the tongue. [gloss- + -al]

glossalgia /glŏ săl'gē ə, -jə/ pain or burning sensation of the tongue. [gloss- + -algia]

glossectomy /glŏ sĕk'tə mē/ surgical removal of all or a portion of the tongue. [gloss- + -ectomy]

glossitis /glŏ sī'tĭs/ inflammation of the tongue. [gloss- + -itis]

glossolalia /glŏs'ə lā'lē ə/ meaningless speech or muttering during sleep, trance-like states, or certain schizophrenic syndromes.

glossopathy /glŏ sŏp'ə thē/ any disease of the tongue. [glosso- + -pathy]

glossopharyngeal /glŏs'ō fə rĭn'jəl, -jē əl/ involving the tongue and the pharynx. [glosso- + pharyng- + -al]

glossopharyngeal nerve /glŏs'ō fə rĭn'jē əl, -jəl/ the cranial nerve IX (CN IX) supplying the tongue, throat, and salivary glands.

glossoplegia /glŏs'ō plē'jē ə, -jə/ paralysis of the tongue. [glosso- + -plegia]

glossoptosis /glŏs'ŏp tō'sĭs/ abnormal drooping forward of the tongue out of the mouth. [glosso- + -ptosis]

glossorrhaphy /glŏ sôr'ə fē/ suture to repair a wound of the tongue. [glosso- + -rrhaphy]

glossotomy /glŏ sŏt'ə mē/ a surgical incision into the tongue. [glosso- + -tomy]

glottal /glŏt'əl/ denoting or involving the glottis.

glottis /glŏt'ĭs/ the central portion of the larynx where the vocal cords are located.

glottitis /glŏ tī'tĭs/ inflammation of the glottis. [glott- + -itis]

gluc-, gluco- glucose.

glucagon /glōō'kə gŏn'/ a hormone produced by the pancreas that triggers a rise in blood sugar levels by stimulating the liver to release glucose stored there as glycogen, thus opposing the action of insulin.

glucocorticoid /glōō'kō kôr'tĭ koid'/ any of a group of steroid hormones produced by the cortex of the adrenal gland and predominantly affecting carbohydrate metabolism. [gluco- + corticoids]

glucogenesis /glōō'kō jĕn'ə sĭs/ the formation of glucose. [gluco- + -genesis]

gluconeogenesis /glōō'kō nē'ō jĕn'ə sĭs/ the formation of glucose from protein or fat. [gluco- + neo- + -genesis]

glucoprotein /glōō'kō prō'tēn, -tē ĭn/ a glycoprotein in which the sugar is glucose. [gluco- + protein]

glucosamine /glōō kō'sə mēn', -mĭn/ an amino derivative of glucose that is a component of several structures including cartilage.

glucose /glōō'kōs/ the sugar that is the main source of energy in the body; a simple sugar found in certain foods (mainly fruits) and found in normal blood of all animals. Its utilization is controlled by insulin.

glucose monitor device for measuring levels of glucose in the blood; most commonly used in controlling diabetes.

glucose tolerance test (GTT) a standard blood test to make a diagnosis of diabetes mellitus or reactive hypoglycemia.

glucosuria /glōō'kōs yōō rē'ə/ excretion of glucose in the urine; normally it is not present.

glue-sniffing /glōō' snĭf'ĭng/ the deliberate inhaling of volatile fumes from plastic cements to induce central nervous system stimulation, producing symptoms from euphoria to coma.

glutamate /glōō'tə māt'/ or **glutamic acid** /glōō tăm'ĭk/ a nonessential amino acid.

glutamic oxaloacetic transaminase (GOT) /ok'sə lō ə sē'tĭk trăn săm'ə nās'/ an enzyme released into the blood after injury to the liver or heart. *Also called* aspertate aminotransferase, serum glutamic oxaloacetic transaminase (SGOT).

glutamic-pyruvic transaminase /glōō tăm'ĭk pī rōō'vĭk/ a serum enzyme that is elevated in certain liver and cardiac conditions. *Also called* alanine aminotransferase, serum glutamic pyruvic transaminase.

glutamine /glōō'tə mēn', -mĭn/ a nonessential amino acid.

glutathione S-transferase /glōō'tə thī'ōn ĕs' trăns'fə rās'/ a group of amino acids that play a key role in detoxification, especially of carcinogens and certain drugs.

gluteal /glōō'tē əl/ of or relating to the buttocks.

Glucose Monitor

gluten /gloo'tən/   a protein found in wheat, grains, and many other foods.

gluten enteropathy /ĕn'tə rŏp'ə thē/   a condition in which an allergic reaction to gluten impairs the absorption of nutrients in the small intestine; manifested by diarrhea, steatorrhea (fat in the stool), and nutritional and vitamin deficiencies. *Also called* celiac disease.

gluteus maximus /gloo'tē əs măk'sə məs/   the largest muscle in the body forming the bulk of the buttocks, controlling movement of the upper leg, as in extending the thigh when rising from a sitting position.

gluteus medius /mē'dē əs/   the middle of the three gluteal muscles (muscles of the buttocks) controlling rotation of the thigh.

gluteus minimus /mĭn'ə məs/   the innermost of the three gluteal muscles (muscles of the buttocks).

glyc-, glyco- *combining form.* sugar, glycogen: *for example,* glycemia.

glycated hemoglobin /glī'kā tĭd hē'mə glō'bĭn/   the binding of hemoglobin with glucose; an elevated level is a sign of poorly treated long-term diabetes, measured as "hemoglobin A1c"; glycohemoglobin.

glycemia /glī sē'mē ə/   the presence of glucose in the blood. [glyc- + -emia]

glycemic index /glī sē'mĭk/   a measure of the ability of different foods to raise blood sugar levels within a two-hour period.

glycerin /glĭs'ər ĭn/   a thick syruplike liquid derived from fats and oils, used, among other things, as a solvent, to soften skin, to alleviate constipation, and to reduce ocular pressure. *Also called* glycerol.

glycerol /glĭs'ə rôl'/   glycerin.

glycine /glī'sēn/   the simplest nonessential amino acid found in protein.

glycobiology /glī'kō bī ŏl'ə jē/   the scientific study of sugars and their role in biology. [glyco- + biology]

glycogen /glī'kə jən/   the main form in which carbohydrate is stored, primarily in the liver, and which is then broken down into glucose for energy as needed. [glyco + -gen]

glycogenesis /glī'kə jĕn'ə sĭs/   the formation of glycogen. [glyco- + -genesis]

glycogen storage disease   one of fourteen known diseases that interfere with the storage of glycogen in the body.

glycogenolysis /glī'kō jə nŏl'ə sĭs/   the hydrolysis of glycogen to glucose.

glycogenosis /glī'kō jə nō'sĭs/   a disorder in which normal and abnormal forms of glycogen are stored in body tissue. [glycogen- + -osis]

glycohemoglobin /glī'kō hē'mə glō'bĭn/   the binding of hemoglobin with glucose; an elevated level is a sign of poorly treated long-term diabetes, measured as "hemoglobin A1c"; glycated hemoglobin.

glycolipid /glī'kō lĭp'ĭd/   a lipid that contains carbohydrate groups. [glyco- + lipid]

glycolysis /glī kŏl'ə sĭs/   the metabolic process in which carbohydrates are converted into pyruvic acid and lactate. [glyco- + -lysis]

glycopenia /glī'kə pē'nē ə/   a deficiency of sugar in an organ or tissue. [glyco- + -penia]

glycoprotein /glī'kō prō'tēn, -tē ĭn/   a molecule consisting of a sugar molecule attached to an amino acid. [glyco- + protein]

glycorrhea /glī'kə rē'ə/   discharge of abnormal amounts of sugar from the body, as in glycosuria. [glyco- + -rrhea]

glycosuria /glī'kōs yoo rē'ə/   excess sugar in the urine.

glycosylated hemoglobin test /glī kō'sə lā'tĭd hē'mə glō'bĭn/   a blood test to measure the percentage of hemoglobin bound with glucose to monitor treatment of diabetes mellitus. *Also called* hemoglobin A1c.

gm.   *abbreviation.* gram; grams.

GM-CSF   *abbreviation.*   granulocyte macrophage colony-stimulating factor.

gnatho-   *combining form.* jaw: *for example,* gnathoplasty.

gnathoplasty /năth'ə plăs'tē/   surgical repair of the jaw. [gnatho- + -plasty]

gnathostomiasis /năth'ō stō mī'ə sĭs/   a disease caused by an infestation of roundworms underneath the skin and sometimes within internal organs, characterized by pain, itching, swelling, and, in serious cases, meningitis and encephalitis.

goiter /goi'tər/   enlargement of the thyroid gland associated with iodine deficiency. *Also called* struma.

gold (Au) /gōld/   a metallic element used in imaging and in the treatment of certain tumors.

Goldenhar('s) syndrome /gōl'dən här(z)'/   a birth defect of the jaw, cheek, and ear on one side, associated with vertebral defects in the neck.

gonad /gō'năd/   the ovary and testes.

gonadotropic hormone /gō năd'ə trŏp'ĭk/   a hormone secreted by the pituitary gland and the placenta that stimulates the gonads.

gonadotropin /gō năd'ə trō'pĭn/   a hormone that stimulates the growth and activity of the gonads.

gonarthritis /gŏn'är thrī'tĭs/   inflammation of the knee.

Goiter

Goniometer

gonio- *combining form.* angle: *for example,* goniometer.

goniometer /gō′nē ŏm′ĭ tər/ an instrument used to measure the range of motion of a joint. [gonio- + -meter]

gonioscope /gō′nē ə skōp′/ a type of ophthalmoscope for examining the anterior chamber of the eye. [gonio- + -scope]

gonioscopy /gō′nē ŏs′kə pē/ examination of the anterior chamber of the eye, measuring the angle where the cornea meets the iris, using a gonioscope. [gonio- + -scopy]

goniotomy /gŏn′ē ŏt′ə mē/ surgical incision into the trabecular tissue of the eye.

gonocele /gŏn′ə sēl′/ a cystic lesion of the epididymis or testis.

gonococcus /gŏn′ə kŏk′əs/ (*pl.* **gonococci** /gŏn′ ə kŏk′sī/) the pus-producing bacterium that causes gonorrhea, identified by culture of vaginal or penile secretions, or a Gram stain showing Gram-negative diplococci.

gonorrhea /gŏn′ə rē′ə/ a sexually transmitted disease caused by the bacterium *Neisseria gonorhoeae,* characterized by painful urination and inflammation of the genital mucous membrane.

Goodell′(s) sign /gŏŏ dĕl(z′)/ softening of the cervix and vagina, indicating pregnancy.

Goodpasture(′s) syndrome /gŏŏd′păs′chər(z)/ an autoimmune disease characterized by inflammation and bleeding in the lungs and kidneys.

goose bumps/goosebumps /gŏŏs′ or **gooseflesh** /gŏŏs′flĕsh′/ an erection of tiny muscles in the skin due to temperature or excitement.

GOT *abbreviation.* glutamic-oxaloacetic transaminase.

gouge /gouj/ a curved chisel used on bone.

gout /gout/ a metabolic disease characterized by high levels of uric acid in the blood, inflammation of joints, kidney stones, and kidney failure; most often occurs in men.

gouty arthritis painful condition characterized by needle-like uric acid crystals in the fluid and lining of the joints, causing severe pain and inflammation; most often affects the big toe.

Gower(′s) syndrome /gou′ər(z)/ a condition characterized by random fainting during relatively normal activities, caused by a reflex of the autonomic (involuntary) nervous system.

graafian follicle /grä′fē ən fŏl′ĭ kəl/ a fluid-filled cavity on the ovary enclosing a developing egg that bursts open at ovulation to release the egg.

grade /grād/ a measure of severity of a disease or abnormal condition, used especially in the evaluation of the severity of a tumor.

grading of tumors a measure of abnormality or differentiation of cancer cells to aid in treatment and prognosis.

graft /grăft/ healthy tissue taken from one part of the body to replace diseased or damaged tissue in another location.

-gram a written record; *for example,* echocardiogram.

gram (g, gm.) /grăm/ a unit of measurement of weight and mass in the metric system, equal to a thousandth of a kilogram, or a thousandth of a liter.

gram calorie (g-cal) a measure of energy equal to that necessary to raise the temperature of one gram of water by one degree centigrade. *Also called* small calorie. *See also* kilocalorie.

Gram-negative of or relating to a bacterium that does not retain a violet stain when being tested for with a dye.

Gram-positive of or relating to a bacterium that retains a violet stain when being tested for with a dye.

Gram stain a technique used to classify bacteria by applying a violet stain.

grand mal /grăn′ măl′, grănd/ a form of epilepsy characterized by tonic-clonic seizures, two-phase seizures in which the body becomes rigid and then starts to jerk uncontrollably.

grand mal epilepsy /ĕp′ə lĕp′sē/ a form of epilepsy characterized by tonic-clonic seizures, two-phase seizures in which the body becomes rigid and then starts to jerk uncontrollably.

grand mal seizure a type of epilepsy seizure characterized by two phases, in which first the body becomes rigid and then starts to jerk uncontrollably.

grand multipara /grănd′ mŭl tĭp′ər ə/ a woman who has given birth five or more times.

grand rounds an official meeting at which two or more doctors discuss the clinical case of one or more patients.

granul-, granulo- *combining form.* granule or granular: *for example,* granuloma.

granular leukocyte /grăn′yə lər loō′kə sīt′/ granulocyte.

granulation /grăn′yə lā′shən/ a normal stage in the healing process in which new tissue and blood vessels form around a wound.

granule /grăn′yoōl/ **1.** a small, grainlike mass. **2.** a small mass having no internal structure. **3.** in pharmacology, a very small pill containing a tiny dose of a medication.

granulocyte /grăn′yə lə sīt′/ one of three kinds of white blood cells that contain granular enzymes which digest microorganisms: neutrophils, basophils, eosinophils; granular leukocyte. [granulo- + -cyte]

granulocyte colony-stimulating factor (G-CSF) a naturally occurring (and genetically manufactured) protein that stimulates the production of white blood cells to boost immune function.

granulocyte-macrophage colony-stimulating factor (GM-CSF) /măk′rə fāj′/ a naturally occurring protein that stimulates the production of white blood cells to boost immune system function.

granulocytopenia /grăn′yə lō sī′tə pē′nē ə/ insufficient numbers of granulocytes, usually due to bacterial infection or chemotherapy. [granulo- + cyto- + -penia]

granulocytosis /grăn′yə lō sī tō′sĭs/ abnormally high levels of granulocytes. [granulo- + -cytosis]

granuloma /grăn′yə lō′mə/ (*pl.* **granulomas** or **granulomata** /grăn′yə lō′mə tə/) a tumor or granular tissue, usually due to an ulcerated infection. [granul- + -oma]

granuloma annulare /ăn′yoō lâr′ē/ a ring-shaped rash of unknown cause, usually on the extremities.

granulomatous /grăn′yə lŏm′ə təs/ having small grainy nodules.

granulomatous colitis /grăn′yə lŏm′ə təs kə lī′tĭs/ an inflammatory disease of the large intestines. *Also called* Crohn's disease, regional enteritis.

-graph *suffix.* instrument: *for example,* echocardiograph.

-graphy *suffix.* printout or representation: *for example,* echocardiography.

Graves(') disease /grāv(z)/ hyperactivity of the thyroid gland, the leading cause of goiter, characterized by protruding eyeballs and a nervous excitability.

gravid /grăv′ĭd/ pregnant.

gravida (G) /grăv′ĭ də/ a pregnant woman.

gray (Gy) /grā/ a measure of radiation absorption equal to one joule per kilogram.

gray matter nerve tissue of the brain and spinal cord made of nerve cell bodies, their dendrites, and supportive tissues.

gray syndrome or **gray baby syndrome** a syndrome in the newborn caused by toxic levels of an antibiotic drug (chloramphenicol) ingested by the mother before delivery, and due to insufficient liver enzymes to metabolize it, causing low blood pressure, blue-colored skin and lips, and usually death.

great toe the largest, innermost toe. *Also called* big toe, hallux.

greater omentum /ō mĕn′təm/ a fold of the peritoneum that hangs in front of the intestines. *Also called* caul.

greenstick fracture a fracture in which one side of the bone is broken but the other is not.

grief therapy psychological treatment for individuals who have experienced the death of a close relative or friend.

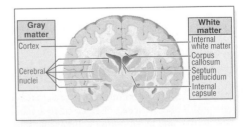

Gray Matter

grinding /grīn′dĭng/ the wearing away by friction and force of superficial layers of a surface, as the teeth.

grippe /grĭp/ an old-fashioned word for influenza.

groin /groin/ the area of the body where the interior upper legs meet the torso.

groove /grōōv/ a long and narrow channel or furrow.

gross anatomy study of structures that can be seen without the aid of a magnifying instrument.

group practice the practice of medicine by a group of doctors in the same field each with their own subspecialty.

group therapy a form of psychotherapy in which several patients discuss their problems together, with the guidance of a therapist.

growing pains pains in the limbs and joints of children usually occurring at night, once thought to be caused by rapid growth, but actually due to unrelated causes.

growth /grōth/ **1.** the process of mental and physical development and maturity. **2.** an increase. **3.** an abnormal mass of tissue forming on or in an organism.

growth hormone (GH) a hormone produced in the pituitary gland that stimulates the excretion of a hormone by the liver, which in turn stimulates growth of long bones.

GSR *abbreviation.* galvanic skin response.

gtt *abbreviation.* Latin *guttae*, drops.

GTT *abbreviation.* glucose tolerance test.

GU *abbreviation.* genitourinary.

guanine /gwä′nēn/ one of the four bases in DNA and in RNA, where it pairs with cytosine.

guarding /gär′dĭng/ tension of muscles to minimize movement in injured or painful areas of the body.

guided imagery an alternative medicine therapy in which patients use their minds to heal themselves and attack disease.

guidewire /gīd′wīr′/ a usually metal or plastic wire used to assist in inserting, positioning, and moving a catheter, especially an angiographic catheter.

Guillain-Barre (Barré) syndrome /gē an′ bä rā′/ a disorder characterized by progressive paralysis, usually beginning in the legs and sometimes ascending to involve arms and respiratory muscles, caused by misdirected immune response that impairs nerve function.

Gulf War syndrome a syndrome experienced by veterans of the Gulf War with many varying symptoms and no known cause.

gullet /gŭl′it/ an informal term for the esophagus, the tubular passageway from the pharynx (back of the mouth) to the stomach through which food passes.

gum disease inflammation of the gums and loss of the bone surrounding the teeth.

gums /gŭmz/ the firm tissue surrounding the base of the teeth.

gurney /gûr′nē/ a flat stretcher or table with wheels for moving hospital patients.

gustation /gŭ stā′shən/ the act of tasting or the ability to taste.

gustatory /gŭs′tə tôr′ē/ of or related to taste.

gut /gŭt/ an informal term for the digestive tract, especially from the stomach to the anus.

Guthrie test /gŭth′rē/ a screening blood test for phenylketonuria.

guts /gŭts/ an informal term for the intestine.

guttate /gŭt′āt/ having the shape of, or resembling, drops.

Gy *abbreviation.* gray.

GYN *abbreviation.* gynecology; gynecologist.

gyne-, gynec-, gyneco- *combining form.* woman: *for example,* gynecology.

gynecoid /gī′nĭ koid′/ characteristic of a woman. [gynec- + - oid]

gynecologic /gī′nĭ kə lŏj′ĭk/ of or relating to the study and practice of gynecology.

gynecologist /gī′nĭ kŏl′ə jĭst/ (**GYN**) a physician specializing in gynecology. [gyneco- + logist]

gynecology /gī′nĭ kŏl′ə jē/ (**GYN**) the branch of medicine dealing with the diagnosis and treatment of disorders affecting the female reproductive organs. [gyneco- + -logy]

gynecomastia /gī′nĭ kō măs′tē ə/ enlargement of breast tissue in males.

gynephobia /gī′nə fō′bē ə/ abnormal fear of women. [gyne- + -phobia]

gyrus /jī′rəs/ (*pl.* **gyri** /jī′rī/) a convoluted ridge in the surface of the brain.

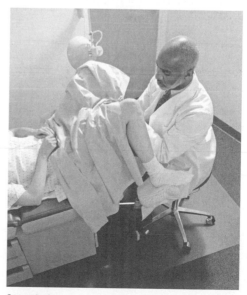

Gynecologist

H

H *abbreviation.* **1.** hyperopia; hyperopic. **2.** hydrogen. **3.** (drug caution code) found on the label of medication indicating that it can be habit forming.

h *abbreviation.* **1.** height. **2.** hour.

H₂O the chemical formula for water.

habit /hăb′ĭt/ **1.** a behavior pattern so regularly used that it is almost involuntary. **2.** an informal term for addiction to a drug.

habitual abortion three consecutive miscarriages.

Haemophilus influenzae **type B (HIB)** /hē mŏf′ə ləs ĭn′floo ĕn′zē/ a bacterium responsible for a range of serious diseases, including meningitis, epiglottitis, pneumonia, and joint or skin infection, mostly affecting children under the age of 5.

hair /hâr/ the cylindrical pigmented filaments that grow from the hair follicles of the epidermis. Hair can be external as on the scalp or internal as the cilia of the nose. *See illustration on page 154.*

hair follicle /fŏl′ĭ kəl/ the saclike cavity containing a hair root from which the hair grows.

hairline fracture a break so fine that the bone does not separate; similar to a crack in a bone and often resulting from overuse.

hair root the portion of a hair that is embedded in a hair follicle.

hair shaft the portion of a hair extending beyond the skin.

hairy cell/hairy-cell leukemia /loo kē′mē ə/ a form of chronic leukemia in which the malignant blood cells appear to be covered in tiny hairs.

halitosis /hăl′ĭ tō′sĭs/ condition of having abnormally bad breath, resulting either from poor dental hygiene or a medical condition.

hallucination /hə loo′sə nā′shən/ false or distorted perception of reality caused by a mental disorder or a drug.

hallucinogen /hə loo′sə nə jən/ a substance, especially a drug, that induces hallucination.

hallucinogenic /hə loo′sə nə jĕn′ĭk/ capable of causing hallucinations.

hallux /hăl′əks/ (*pl.* **halluces** /hăl′yə sēz′/) the innermost digit of the foot. *Also called* big toe, great toe.

hallux valgus /văl′gəs/ deviation of the big toe in the direction of the little toe.

hallux varus /văr′əs/ deviation of the big toe away from the other toes.

hamartoma /hăm′ăr tō′mə/ (*pl.* **hamartomas** or **hamartomata** /hăm′ăr tō′mə tə/) a self-limiting tumor made of new cell growth but with no division at cell maturity.

hammer /hăm′ər/ the tiny hammer-shaped bone in the middle ear, responsible for transmitting sound vibrations from the eardrum to the incus and stapes. *Also called* malleus.

hammertoe / hammer toe /hăm′ər tō′/ a deformed toe that is permanently flexed at the proximal interphalangeal joint; the deformed joint is pushed up against the top of one's shoe and is often painful.

hamstring /hăm′strĭng′/ the tendons or muscles at the back of the knee, the site of many sports-related injuries.

hand /hănd/ the lower extremity of the upper limb, consisting of the wrist, palm, fingers, and thumb.

hand drop partial or total lack of flexion in the hand, usually due to nerve injury, resulting in a hanging down of the hand. *Also called* drop hand.

handedness /hăn′dĭd nĭs/ the preference of using one hand over the other.

hand, foot, and mouth / hand-foot-and-mouth disease or **syndrome** a common illness occurring in infants, characterized by fever and rash in the mouth and on the hands and feet, caused by infection with coxsackievirus.

handicap /hăn′dē kăp′/ the inability to carry out certain tasks or access certain aspects of the environment due to one or more impairments; disability.

hangman('s) injury or fracture a dislocation or fracture of the upper cervical vertebrae.

hangnail /hăng′nāl′/ a partially detached piece of skin at the root or side of a fingernail or toenail.

hangover /hăng′ō′vər/ the unpleasant physical side effects that follow heavy alcohol consumption.

Hansen('s) disease /hăn′sən(z)/ a chronic, mildly contagious bacterial disease that especially affects the nerves and skin; found mostly in tropical and subtropical regions of the world. *Also called* leprosy.

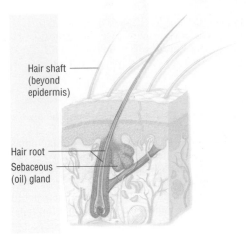

Hair shaft
(beyond
epidermis)

Hair root
Sebaceous
(oil) gland

Hair

hantavirus /hăn′tə vī′rəs/   a family of viruses that cause hemorrhagic fever and pneumonia, transmitted by rodent feces.

hantavirus pulmonary syndrome /pōͦl′mə nĕr′ē/   a respiratory disease caused by a hantavirus, characterized by fever, muscle pain, headache, cough, vomiting, and chills, which can quickly lead to fluid buildup in the lungs and, if untreated, death.

haploid /hăp′loid/   denoting a cell having a single, unpaired set of chromosomes as does a germ cell (a sperm or ovum), (which in humans contains 23 chromosomes). *See also* diploid.

hard of hearing   informal term for partial hearing loss.

hard palate   the bony portion of the roof of the mouth, consisting of the bony palate covered above by the mucous membrane of the nose and below by the roof of the mouth.

harelip /hâr′lĭp′/   a nonmedical term for cleft lip.

Hashimoto(′s) disease /hä′shē mō′tō(z)/ or **Hashimoto(′s) thyroiditis** /thī′roi dī′tĭs/   an autoimmune disease of the thyroid gland in which lymphocytes infiltrate the thyroid, characterized by goiter, inflammation of the thyroid, and hypothyroidism. *Also called* struma lymphomatosa.

HAV   *abbreviation.* hepatitis A virus, the RNA virus that causes hepatitis A.

Haversian canals /hə vûr′zhən/   the small canals through which blood vessels branch out in bone.

hay fever   an allergy to airborne pollen, characterized by itchy eyes, runny nose, nasal congestion, sneezing, itchy throat, and excess mucus.

HB   *abbreviation.* hepatitis B vaccine.

Hb   *abbreviation.* hemoglobin.

HBIG   *abbreviation.* hepatitis B immune globulin.

HBV   *abbreviation.* hepatitis B virus, the DNA virus that causes hepatitis B.

HCFA   *abbreviation.* Health Care Finance Administration, now the Centers for Medicare and Medicaid Services.

HCG, hCG   *abbreviation.* human chorionic gonadotropin.

hct, HCT   *abbreviation.* hematocrit.

HCV   *abbreviation.* hepatitis C virus, the RNA virus that causes hepatitus C.

HD   *abbreviation.* Hodgkin's disease.

HDL   *abbreviation.* high-density lipoprotein.

HDN   *abbreviation.* hemolytic disease of the newborn.

HDV   *abbreviation.* hepatitis D virus, the RNA virus that causes hepatitis D.

head /hĕd/   **1.** the uppermost part of the body containing the skull, brain, eyes, ears, nose, mouth, and jaws. **2.** the tip or end of a structure, such as the head of a bone.

headache /hĕd′āk′/   a pain in the upper and/or rear portion of the head above the eyes and ears.

head lice   any parasitic insect found on the scalp of humans.

heal /hēl/   **1.** to cure, as a wound or illness, or to restore to health. **2.** to become healthy.

healing touch   a type of alternative medicine therapy involving touch or work in a client's energy field to bring about relaxation and pain relief.

health /hĕlth/   the overall condition of a person or organ.

Health and Human Services (HHS)   the U.S. Department of Health and Human Services whose agencies have authority for creating and enforcing HIPAA regulations (www.hhs.gov).

Health Care Financing Administration (HCFA)   formerly, the part of the U.S. Department of Health and Human Services that was responsible for administering Medicare and Medicaid. Now called the Centers for Medicare and Medicaid Services (CMS).

health care provider   any hospital, institution, or health professional that provides health care.

health care proxy   a legal document giving an individual legal permission to make health care decisions on behalf of patients if the patients are incapable of making decisions for themselves.

health insurance   an insurance providing compensation for medical expenses and against loss due to illness or injury.

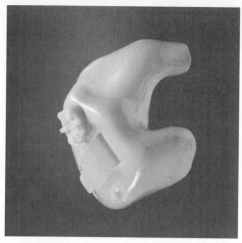

Hearing Aid

**Health Insurance Portability and Account-
ability Act (HIPAA) of 1966** U.S. law providing uniform privacy, security, and electronic transaction standards regarding patients'
medical records and other health related information, and allowing continuation of health
insurance after termination of employment for
a prescribed period.

health maintenance organization (HMO) a
corporation that provides comprehensive
health care to voluntarily enrolled, paying
members through a specific network of physicians and specialists.

healthy /hĕl'thē/ conducive to or possessing
good health.

hearing /hêr'ĭng/ the sense by which sound is
perceived.

hearing aid a small electronic device worn in
or behind the ear, used to amplify sound to
compensate for poor hearing.

hearing impaired having partial to complete
hearing loss.

hearing instrument a hearing aid.

hearing loss partial or complete hearing impairment; may result from a birth defect, illness, or aging.

heart /härt/ the chambered muscular organ
that pumps blood received from veins into the
lungs for oxygenation and then into arteries,
thereby circulating blood throughout the circulatory system. The heart is essential to life.

heart attack a sudden interruption of blood
supply to part of the heart muscle due to an
obstructed or constricted coronary artery,
characterized by severe chest pain that can radiate to the left shoulder and arm or upper
back and by shortness of breath. *Also called*
myocardial infarction.

heartbeat /härt'bēt'/ a single complete contraction and relaxation of the heart muscle; the
number of heartbeats is reflected in the pulse.

heart block a condition characterized by un-
coordinated contractions of the atria and ventricles of the heart.

heartburn /härt'bûrn'/ a burning sensation
felt in the chest, caused by acid reflux. *Also
called* pyrosis.

heart conduction system the system of electrical impulses that control heart contractions.

heart disease any structural or functional impairment of the heart or coronary blood vessels.

heart failure inability of the heart to provide
adequate blood circulation, causing weakness,
edema, and shortness of breath.

heart-lung machine a device that oxygenates
and circulates blood throughout the body during heart surgery.

heart monitor a device for observing functioning of the heart.

heart murmur an abnormal sound of the
heart which may be a sign of disease.

heart muscle the muscle tissue of the heart.
Also called myocardium.

heart rate the number of heartbeats per
minute.

heart sounds any of the sounds heard when
listening to the heart through a stethoscope,
generally used for diagnostic purposes.

heart transplant or **heart transplantation** a
surgical procedure in which a diseased or
damaged heart is removed and replaced with a
healthy heart from a recently deceased person.

heart valve any of the four valves that control
blood flow through the heart: tricuspid, bicuspid, pulmonary, aortic.

heat /hēt/ a form of energy perceived as
warmth or hotness.

heat cramps painful muscle spasms caused by
dehydration, especially following hard work
in intense heat.

Heart Monitor

heat exhaustion a condition caused by prolonged exposure to intense heat or by dehydration, characterized by dehydration, weakness, exhaustion, and collapse. *Also called* heat prostration.

heating pad a soft, flexible pad containing electrical heating elements, used to provide localized heat.

heat prostration heat exhaustion.

heat rash an inflammatory skin condition caused by obstructed sweat ducts during prolonged exposure to intense heat and humidity.

heat-related illness any illness or condition caused by prolonged exposure to intense heat.

heat stroke a condition caused by prolonged exposure to intense heat in which the core body temperature rises above 104 degrees Fahrenheit, characterized by severe headache, delirium, convulsions, coma, and sometimes, death. Heat stroke damages the body's ability to regulate its internal temperature.

hebephrenia /hē′bə frē′nē ə, -frĕn′ē ə/ a severe schizophrenia, often beginning in adolescence, characterized by inappropriate, silly, and erratic speech, behavior, affect, and mannerisms; now called disorganized schizophrenia.

heel /hēl/ the rounded portion of the foot beneath and behind the ankle. *Also called* calcaneus.

heel spur a bone spur or overgrowth of bone on the back or underside of the heel generally from overuse and usually very painful. *Also called* exostosis.

heel stick the most common technique for drawing blood from newborns in which a small needle pricks the bottom of the heel and the blood is collected in a tiny glass tube.

Hegar's sign /hā′gärz/ softening of the lower portion of the uterus in early pregnancy.

height /hīt/ the distance from the bottom of the foot to the top of the head.

Heimlich maneuver /hīm′lĭk/ an emergency technique used to discharge an object from the trachea, using firm upwards thrusts below the rib cage of a choking person, which forces air from the lungs to travel upward. *Also called* abdominal thrust maneuver.

HeLa cell /hē′lə/ any of the cells of the first continuously cultured carcinoma strain used in cancer studies.

helical /hĕl′ĭ kəl, hē′lĭ-/ of, relating to, of having the form of a helix.

Helicobacter pylori /hĕl′ĭ kō băk′tər pī lôr′/ a gram-negative bacteria associated with several gastrointestinal disorders, especially ulcers.

helix /hē′lĭks/ **1.** a spiral form or structure. **2.** the rim of skin and cartilage around the outer car.

helper T cell a type of lymphocyte (immune system cell) that secretes substances called cytokines, which contribute to the immune response by regulating other immune system cells, such as T cells and B cells. The HIV virus attacks helper T cells, weakening the body's immune response. *Also called* T helper cell.

hem- hemo- *combining form.* blood: *for example,* hemarthrosis.

hemangi-, hemangio- *combining form.* blood vessel: *for example,* hemangioma.

hemangioblast /hĭ măn′jē ə blăst′/ a mesodermal cell in the embroyo that can give rise to either vascular endothelial cells or hemocytoblasts.

hemangioblastoma /hĭ măn′jē ō blă stō′mə/ (*pl.* **hemangioblastomas** or **hemangioblastomata** / hĭ măn′jē ō blă stō′mə tə/) a benign, slow-growing tumor in the cerebellum, usually occurring among middle-aged people. [hemangio- + blast- + -oma]

hemangioma /hĭ măn′jē ō′mə/ (*pl.* **hemangiomas** or **hemangiomata** /hĭ măn′jē ō′mə tə/) a benign skin lesion composed of dense dilated blood vessels. [hemangi- + -oma]

hemangiosarcoma /hĭ măn′jē ō sär kō′mə/ (*pl.* **hemangiosarcomas** or **hemangiosarcomata** /hĭ măn′jē ō sär kō′mə tə/) a rare, malignant fast-growing tumor composed of invasive structureless cells derived from blood vessels. [hemangio- + sarc- + -oma]

hemarthrosis /hē′mär thrō′sĭs/ blood accumulation or hemorrhage in a joint. [hem- + -arthrosis]

hemat-, hemato- *combining form.* blood: *for example,* hematemesis.

hematemesis /hē′mə tĕm′ə sĭs/ the vomiting of blood. [hemat- + -emesis]

hematic /hĭ măt′ĭk/ **1.** *adj.* of or involving blood. **2.** *n.* an agent that promotes the growth of red blood cells

Heimlich Maneuver

hematoblast /hĭ măt′ə blăst′/ an undifferentiated cell from which all blood cells are derived; a stem cell. *Also called* hemocytoblast, hemoblast, hematocytoblast. [hemato- + -blast]

hematocele /hĭ măt′ə sēl′/ hemorrhage into a body cavity, as into the testis.

hematochezia /hē′mə tə kē′zhə/ passage of blood in the feces.

hematocrit (Hct, HCT) /hĭ măt′ə krĭt/ the percentage of red blood cells in a blood sample after centrifugation.

hematocytoblast /hĭ măt′ō sī′tə blăst′/ hematoblast. *Also called* hemoblast, hemocytoblast. [hemato- + cyto- + blast]

hematologist /hē′mə tŏl′ə jĭst/ a physician specializing in hematology.

hematology /hē′mə tŏl′ə jē/ the branch of medicine concerned with the study of blood and blood-producing organs. [hemato- + -logy]

hematology-oncology /ŏng kŏl′ə jē/ the diagnosis, treatment, and prevention of diseases of the blood and cancer.

hematolysis /hē′mə tŏl′ə sĭs/ hemolysis. [hemato- + -lysis]

hematoma /hē′mə tō′mə/ a blood clot caused by a broken blood vessel. [hemat- + -oma]

hematometry /hē′mə tŏm′ĭ tre/ blood test to find the number and proportions of different types of blood cells and the amount of hemoglobin. [hemato- + -metry]

hematopathology /hĭ măt′ō pə thŏl′ə jē/ blood disease. [hemato- + pathology]

hematopoiesis /hĭ măt′ō poi ē′sĭs/ the formation of blood or blood cells. [hemato- + -poiesis]

hematopoietic /hĭ măt′ō poi ĕt′Ĭk/ of or relating to the formation of blood or blood cells. [hemato- + -poietic]

hematostaxis /hĭ măt′ə stăk′sĭs/ spontaneous bleeding as a result of a blood disease.

hematuria /hē′mə tōōr′ē ə/ the presence of blood in the urine. [hemat- + -uria]

hemi- *combining form.* half: *for example,* hemiplegia.

hemianesthesia /hĕm′ē ăn′əs thē′zhə/ loss of feeling on one side of the body. [hemi- + anesthesia]

hemianopia /hĕm′ē ə nō′pē ə/ loss of vision in half of the visual field, occurring in one or in both eyes. [hemi- + an- + -opia]

hemianopsia /hĕm′ē ə nŏp′sē ə/ loss of vision in half of the visual field, occurring in one or in both eyes. [hemi- + an- + -opsia]

hemiapraxia /hē′mē ə prăk′sē ə/ inability to perform purposeful movement on one side of the body. [hemi- + apraxia]

hemiarthroplasty /hĕm′ē är′thrə plăs′tē/ replacement of one-half of a component of a joint. [hemi- + arthro- + -plasty]

hemicolectomy /hĕm′ē kə lĕk′tə mē/ surgical removal of half of the colon. [hemi- + colectomy]

hemifacial /hĕm′ē fā′shəl/ of or relating to one side of the face. [hemi- + facial]

hemigastrectomy /hĕm′ē gă strĕk′tə mē/ surgical removal of half of the stomach. [hemi- + gastr- + -ectomy]

hemihypertrophy /hĕm′ē hī pûr′trə fē/ hypertrophy of half of a body part, or half of the entire body. [hemi- + hypertrophy]

hemiparesis /hĕm′ē pə rē′sĭs/ weakness or mild paralysis of one side of the body. [hemi- + paresis]

hemiplegia /hĕm′ĭ plē′jē ə, -jə/ paralysis of one side of the body. [hemi- + -plegia]

hemiplegic /hĕm′ĭ plē′jĭk/ of or relating to hemiplegia.

hemisphere /hĕm′ə sfêr′/ half of a symmetrical ball-shaped structure, especially one-half of the cerebrum of the brain. [hemi- + sphere]

hemithorax /hĕm′ē thôr′ăks/ one side of the chest. [hemi- + thorax]

hemizygous /hĕm′ē zī′gəs/ having only one copy of a gene instead of two.

hemo- *combining form.* blood: *for example,* hemodialysis.

hemoblast /hē′mə blăst′/ an undifferentiated cell from which all blood cells are derived; a stem cell. *Also called* hematoblast, hemocytoblast, hematocytoblast.

Hemoccult test /hē′mō ə kŭlt′/ trade name of the test for detecting hidden blood in feces.

hemochromatosis /hē′mō krō′mə tō′sĭs/ a condition caused by abnormal iron metabolism, characterized by high levels of iron in tissues, diabetes, liver dysfunction, and bronze coloration of the skin. [hemo- + chromat- + -osis]

hemoclasis /hē mŏk′lə sĭs/ the destruction of blood cells. [hemo- + -clasis]

hemocyte /hē′mə sīt′/ **1.** a blood cell, especially of an arthropod. **2.** a blood cell of a vertebrate, especially a red blood cell. [hemo- + -cyte]

hemocytoblast /hē′mō sī′tə blăst′/ an undifferentiated cell from which all blood cells are derived; a stem cell. *Also called* hematoblast, hematocytoblast.

hemocytolysis /hē′mō sī tŏl′ə sĭs/ the breaking down or dissolving of blood cells. [hemo- + cyto- + -lysis]

hemodiagnosis /hē′mō dī′əg nō′sĭs/ diagnosis by blood tests. [hemo- + diagnosis]

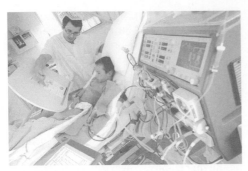

Hemodialysis

hemodialysis /hē'mō dī ăl'ə sĭs/ a type of dialysis in which waste material and toxic substances are filtered out of the blood using a dialysis machine. [hemo- + dialysis]

hemodialysis catheter /kăth'ĭ tər/ a catheter in a vein used for dialysis.

hemoglobin (Hb, Hgb, HGB) /hē'mə glō'bĭn/ the oxygen-carrying protein pigment in red blood cells measured in grams/100 ml. [hemo- + -globin]

hemoglobin A1c a blood test to measure the percentage of hemoglobin bound with glucose, to monitor treatment of diabetes mellitus. *Also called* glycosylated hemoglobin test.

hemoglobinemia /hē'mō glō'bə nē'mē ə/ the presence of hemoglobin in plasma. [hemo- + globin- + -emia]

hemoglobinopathy /hē'mə glō'bə nŏp'ə thē/ any disease characterized by the presence of abnormal hemoglobin in the blood.

hemoglobinuria /hē'mə glō'bə nōōr'ē ə/ the presence of hemoglobin in the urine. [hemoglobin + -uria]

hemogram /hē'mə grăm'/ a record of the results of a blood test. [hemo- + -gram]

hemolith /hē'mə lĭth/ a calculus in a blood vessel wall. [hemo- + -lith]

hemolysis /hĭ mŏl'ə sĭs/ the destruction of red blood cells, releasing hemoglobin into the bloodstream. [hemo- + -lysis]

hemolytic /hē'mə lĭt'ĭk/ of, relating to, or causing hemolysis.

hemolytic anemia anemia caused by abnormal hemolysis.

hemolytic disease of the newborn (HDN) abnormal destruction of red blood cells in a fetus due to antibodies transmitted from the mother through the placenta.

hemolytic uremic syndrome /yōō rē'mĭk/ a condition with many causes including bacterial infection and, in adults, complications of pregnancy; it is characterized by hemolysis and kidney failure.

hemopathy /hē mŏp'ə thē/ disease of the blood. [hemo- + -pathy]

hemophilia /hē'mə fĭl'ē ə, -fēl'yə/ any of a group of diseases characterized by delayed blood clotting. [hemo- + -philia]

hemophilic /hē'mə fĭl'ĭk/ **1.** of or involving hemophilia. **2.** of microorganisms, thriving in blood or a blood medium. [hemo- + -philic]

hemopneumothorax /hē'mō nōō'mə thôr'ăks/ the presence of blood and air in the pleural cavity. [hemo- + pneumo- + -thorax]

hemopoiesis /hē'mō poi ē'sĭs/ the formation of blood or blood cells. [hemo- + -poiesis]

hemopoietic /hē'mō poi ĕt'ĭk/ of or relating to hemopoiesis.

hemoptysis /hĭ mŏp'tə sĭs/ coughing up blood from the respiratory tract. [hemo- + -ptysis]

hemorrhage /hĕm'ə rĭj, hĕm'rĭj/ severe excessive bleeding. [hemo- + -rrhage]

hemorrhagic /hĕm'ə răj'ĭk/ of or relating to hemorrhage.

hemorrhagic fever a syndrome caused by a viral infection, characterized by excessive bleeding from the mouth or through the skin, high fever, muscle pain, weakness, dizziness, and if untreated, shock, coma, seizure, and death.

hemorrhagic stroke a stroke caused by a ruptured blood vessel in the brain. *Also called* cerebrovascular accident, ischemic stroke, stroke.

hemorrhoids /hĕm'ə roidz', hĕm'roidz/ a mass of dilated veins in anal tissue, causing inflammation, pain, and itching. *Also called* piles.

hemorrhoidectomy /hĕm'ə roi dĕk'tə mē, hĕm'roi-/ surgical removal of hemorrhoids. [hemorrhoid + -ectomy]

hemostasis /hĭ mŏs'tə sĭs, hē'mō stā'sĭs/ the stoppage of bleeding or blood flow. [hemo- + stasis]

hemostat /hē'mə stăt'/ **1.** a surgical instrument, such as forceps, that compresses a blood vessel to stop bleeding. **2.** a hemostatic.

hemostatic /hē'mō stăt'ĭk/ **1.** *adj.* of or relating to hemostasis. **2.** *n.* an agent that stops or slows blood flow.

hemothorax /hē'mō thôr'ăks/ blood accumulation in the pleural cavity. [hemo- + thorax]

hepar /hē'pär/ a former word for the liver.

heparin /hĕp'ə rĭn/ an anticoagulant (blood-thinner).

hepat-, hepatico-, hepato- *combining form.* liver: *for example,* hepatectomy.

hepatectomy /hĕp'ə tĕk'tə mē/ surgical removal of all or a portion of the liver. [hepat- + -ectomy]

hepatic /hĭ păt'ĭk/ of or relating to the liver. [hepat- + -ic]

hepatic artery the artery that supplies blood to the liver, pancreas, gallbladder, stomach, and small intestine.

hepatic biopsy /bǐ'ŏp sē/   a liver biopsy performed by removing a small piece of the liver for diagnosis.

hepatic duct   the ducts that transport bile from the liver to the common bile duct.

hepatic flexure /flěk'shər/   the bend in the colon at the point in which the ascending colon and transverse colon meet. *Also called* right colic flexure.

hepaticostomy /hǐ păt'ǐ kǒs'tə mē/   the surgical creation of an opening into the hepatic duct. . [hepatico- + -stomy]

hepaticotomy /hǐ păt'ǐ kǒt'ə mē/   a surgical incision into the hepatic duct. . [hepatico- + -tomy]

hepatic portal system   the veins that transport blood from the stomach, intestine, spleen, and pancreas to the liver back to the inferior vena cava and then to the heart.

hepatic transplant   a liver transplant.

hepatic vein   any of the veins that drain the liver.

hepatitis /hěp'ə tī'tǐs/   inflammation of the liver caused by toxin or infection, causing fever, jaundice, liver enlargement, and pain. [hepat- + -itis]

hepatitis A (HAV)   inflammation of the liver caused by an RNA virus, transmitted through contaminated food, drink, and rarely blood; usually resolves itself quickly.

hepatitis B (HBV)   inflammation of the liver caused by a DNA virus, transmitted through

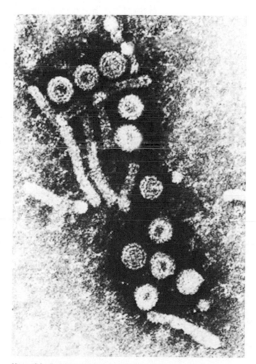

Hepatitis B (cells under a microscope)

infected blood, sexual contact, and from mother to child during childbirth; has long-term effects but a vaccine is available.

hepatitis C (HCV)   inflammation of the liver caused by an RNA virus, transmitted through infected blood and, less commonly, through sexual contact. No vaccine is available at this time.

hepatitis D (HDV)   inflammation of the liver caused by an RNA virus, occurring only as an additional infection in individual with hepatitis B.

hepatitis E (HEV)   inflammation of the liver caused by a virus, transmitted through sewage-contaminated water.

hepatitis F (HFV)   untreatable inflammation of the liver caused by a rare mutated virus.

hepatitis G (HGV)   a virus related to the hepatitis C virus that does not cause liver inflammation or any other disease.

hepato-   *See* hepat-.

hepatobiliary /hǐ păt'ō bǐl'ē ěr'ē, hěp'ə tō-/   of or relating to the liver, gallbladder, bile ducts, and bile. [hepato- + biliary]

hepatoblastoma /hǐ păt'ō blă stō'mə, hěp'ə tō-/   a malignant liver tumor occurring in young children. [hepato- + blastoma]

hepatocarcinoma /hǐ păt'ō kär'sə nō'mə, hěp'ə tō-/   carcinoma of the liver. [hepato- + carcinoma]

hepatocele /hǐ păt'ə sel', hěp'ə tə-/   hernia of the liver. [hepato- + -cele]

hepatocyte /hǐ păt'ə sīt', hěp'ə tə-/   a functional cell of the liver. [hepato- + -cyte]

hepatogastric /hǐ păt'ə găs'trǐk/   of or involving the liver and the stomach. [hepato- + -gastric]

hepatology /hěp'ə tŏl'ə jē/   the branch of medicine concerned with the study of the liver and the diagnosis, treatment, and prevention of its diseases. [hepato- + -logy]

hepatoma /hěp'ə tō'mə/ (*pl.* **hepatomas** or **hepatomata** /hěp'ə tō'mə tə/)   a malignant liver tumor. [hepat- + -oma]

hepatography /hěp'ə tŏg'rə fē/   x-ray examination of the liver. [hepato- + -graphy]

hepatomegaly /hǐ păt'ō měg'ə lē, hěp'ə tō-/   abnormal liver enlargement. [hepato- + -megaly]

hepatopexy /hǐ păt'ə pěk'sē/   the fixing of the liver into position. [hepato- + -pexy]

hepatorrhagia /hǐ păt'ō rā'jē ə, -jə, hěp'ə tō-/   hemorrhage in the liver. [hepato- + -rrhagia]

hepatorrhaphy /hěp'ə tôr'ə fē/   surgical suture of a wound of the liver. [hepato- + -rrhaphy]

hepatorrhexis /hǐ păt'ō rěk'sǐs, hěp'ə tō-/   rupture of the liver. [hepato- + -rrhexis]

hepatoscopy /hěp'ə tŏs'kə pē/   visual examination of the liver. [hepato- + -scopy]

hepatosplenomegaly /hĭ păt′ō splē′nō mĕg′ə lē, hĕp′ə tō-/ simultaneous enlargement of the liver and spleen. [hepato- + spleno- + -megaly]

hepatotomy /hĕp′ə tŏt′ə mē/ surgical incision into the liver. [hepato- + -tomy]

hepatotoxic /hĭ păt′ō tŏk′sĭk, hĕp′ə tō-/ destructive or toxic to the liver. [hepato- + toxic]

herbal /ûr′bəl, hûr′-/ of or relating to herbs.

herbalism /ûr′bə lĭz′əm, hûr′-/ herbal medicine.

herbalist /ûr′bə lĭst, hûr′-/ one who specializes in herbal medicine.

herbal medicine the study and use of herbs to prevent and treat disease, and to enhance overall health; a form of complementary and alternative medicine.

herbal remedy an herbal preparation used to prevent or treat an ailment or a disease; not generally approved by the FDA.

hereditary /hə rĕd′ĭ tĕr′ē/ transmitted genetically from parent to child, as a disease such as cystic fibrosis or a characteristic such as eye color.

heredity /hə rĕd′ĭ tē/ the genetic transmission of characteristics, qualities, diseases, and predispositions from parent to child.

heritability /hĕr′ĭ tə bĭl′ĭ tē/ the degree to which a quality or state is heritable.

heritable /hĕr′ĭ tə bəl/ capable of being transmitted from parent to child.

hermaphrodite /hûr măf′rə dīt′/ an individual with both male and female reproductive organs.

hermaphroditism /hûr măf′rə dī tĭz′əm/ the presence in one individual of both male and female reproductive tissue.

hernia /hûr′nē ə/ the protrusion of a bodily structure through a perforation or tear in the wall that normally contains it, as a hiatal hernia.

hernial /hûr′nē əl/ of or involving a hernia.

hernia repair surgical suture of a hernia. *Also called* herniorrhaphy.

herniate /hûr′nē āt′/ to protrude abnormally from an organ or body structure within which something is normally located.

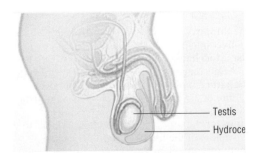

Testis

Hydroce

Hernia

herniated disc/disk /hûr′nē ā′tĭd/ a rupture of the connective tissue between two or more vertebral bones or a bulging of the tissue from the interior of a disk.

herniation /hûr′nē ā′shən/ the act or process of herniating.

hernio- *combining form.* hernia: *for example,* herniorrhaphy.

hernioplasty /hûr′nē ə plăs′tē/ surgical repair of a hernia. *Also called* herniorrhaphy. [hernio- + -plasty]

herniorrhaphy /hûr′nē ôr′ə fē/ hernia repair.

herniotomy /hûr′nē ŏt′ə mē/ operation to correct an irreducible hernia, especially a strangulated hernia. [hernio- + -tomy]

heroic /hĕ rō′ĭk/ denoting an aggressive and dangerous procedure with a very ill patient.

heroin /hĕr′ō ĭn/ a highly addictive narcotic derived from morphine.

heroin addiction a physical and psychological dependence on heroin.

herpes /hûr′pēz/ any of a group of viral diseases that cause blister-like eruptions on the skin and mucous membranes; after primary infection, herpes viruses can remain dormant in nerve cells, and eruptions may recur at times of stress.

herpes genitalis /jĕn′ĭ tā′lĭs/ a viral infection caused by the herpes simplex virus, which is transmitted through sexual contact and causes painful, blister-like eruptions in the genital area. *Also called* genital herpes.

herpes simplex type 1 or **herpes simplex virus Type 1** /sĭm′plĕks/ a virus that causes cold sores and fever blisters in and around the mouth.

herpes simplex type 2 or **herpes simplex virus Type 2** a virus that causes genital herpes, or herpes genitalis.

herpes simplex virus (HSV) either of the two viruses that cause herpes.

herpes zoster /zŏs′tər/ painful nerve infection in adults caused by the varicella-zoster virus that causes chickenpox in children. *Also called* shingles.

herpetic /hûr pĕt′ĭk/ of or relating to herpes.

hertz (Hz) /hûrts/ a unit of frequency equal to one cycle per second.

hetero- *combining form.* other; different: *for example,* heterograft.

heteroblastic /hĕt′ər ə blăs′tĭk/ developing from two different kinds of tissue. [hetero- + -blastic]

heterochromia /hĕt′ə rō krō′mē ə/ an abnormal color difference between two structures.

heterogeneous /hĕt′ər ə jē′nē əs/ composed of dissimilar parts; not uniform.

heterogenesis /hĕt′ə rō jĕn′ə sĭs/ the production of offspring unlike the parents. [hetero- + genesis]

heterograft /hĕt′ər ə grăft′/ a graft of tissue from one species onto a different species. *Also called* xenograft. [hetero- + graft]

heterometropia /hĕt′ə rō mĭ trō′pē ə/ vision in which one eye refracts differently from the other eye. [hetero- + metr- + -opia]

heteropia /hĕt′ə rō′pē ə/ abnormal alignment of one or both eyes. *Also called* strabismus.

heteroplasia /hĕt′ə rō plā′zhə/ the growth of abnormal tissue, or the growth of normal tissue in the wrong place. [hetero- + -plasia]

heterosexual /hĕt′ə rō sĕk′shōō əl/ a person sexually attracted to members of the opposite sex, as opposed to a homosexual, who is attracted to members of the same sex. [hetero- + sexual]

heterosexuality /hĕt′ə rō sĕk′shōō ăl′ĭ tē/ sexuality towards the opposite sex. [hetero- + sexuality]

heterotaxy /hĕt′ər ə tăk′sē/ abnormal positioning of body parts, particularly organs, due to birth defects. [hetero- + -taxy]

heterotopic /hĕt′ə rō tŏp′ĭk/ occurring in an abnormal location.

heterozygote /hĕt′ə rō zī′gōt/ an individual having two different forms of a gene, one inherited from the mother and one from the father. [hetero- + zygote]

heterozygous /hĕt′ə rō zī′gəs/ of or relating to a heterozygote. [hetero- + -zygous]

HEV *abbreviation.* hepatitis E virus, the RNA virus that causes hepatitis E.

hexadactyly /hĕk′sə dăk′tə lē/ a common birth defect of having an extra toe or finger. *Also called* polydactyly.

Hg *abbreviation.* mercury.

HGB, Hgb, HB *abbreviation.* hemoglobin.

HGH *abbreviation.* human growth hormone.

HHS *abbreviation.* U.S. Department of Health and Human Services (www.hhs.gov).

hiatal /hī ā′təl/ of or relating to a hiatus.

hiatal hernia /hûr′nē ə/ a hernia in which a portion of the stomach protrudes through the diaphragm into the chest.

hiatus /hī ā′təs/ a gap, perforation, or opening.

HIB bacteria *Haemophilus influenzae* type B bacteria.

HIB immunization an immunization to prevent diseases caused by the HIB bacteria, such as meningitis in children.

hiccup/hiccough /hĭk′ŭp/ involuntary contraction of the diaphragm and simultaneous closure of the glottis resulting in a sudden inspiration of air that is almost immediately halted. *Also called* singultus.

hidr-, hidro- *combining for.* sweat; sweat glands: *for example,* hidrosis.

hidradenitis /hī drăd′ə nī′tĭs/ infection or inflammation of the sweat glands. [hidr- + adenitis]

hidradenoma /hī drăd′ə nō′mə/ a benign tumor arising from sweat glands. [hidr- + adenoma]

hidrocystoma /hī′drō sĭ stō′mə/ a cystic form of hidradenoma. *Also called* syringocystoma. [hidro- + cyst + -oma]

hidropoiesis /hī′drō poi ē′sĭs/ the formation of sweat. [hidro- + -poiesis]

hidrosis /hī drō′sĭs/ the formation and excretion of sweat, especially in abnormal amounts. [hidr- + -osis]

hidrotic /hī drŏt′ĭk/ of, relating to, or causing hidrosis.

high blood pressure blood pressure consistently over 140/90 mm Hg. *Also called* hypertension.

high blood sugar excessive glucose in the blood. Also called hyperglycemia.

high-density lipoproteins (HDLs) /lĭp′ō prō′tēnz, -tē ĭnz/ a type of lipoprotein responsible for transporting cholesterol from body tissues to the liver; regarded as the healthy part of cholesterol readings.

high-fiber diet a diet high in fibrous foods that aid in removal of solid waste from the body.

high risk register (HRR) a checklist of conditions that can lead to hearing loss, used in audiology to determine relative future risk.

hilum /hī′ləm/ (*pl.* **hila** /hī′lə/) or **hilus** /hī′ləs/ (*pl.* **hili** /hī′lī/) the thin opening in an organ or gland through which nerves, ducts, and blood vessels pass, especially the hilum of the right or left lung. *Also called* porta.

hindbrain /hīnd′brān′/ the lower rear portion of the brain including the cerebellum and the brainstem.

hinge joint a uniaxial joint such as an elbow and knee that allows motion on only one plane.

hip /hĭp/ **1.** the joint where the acetabulum and femur meet. **2.** an informal term for the

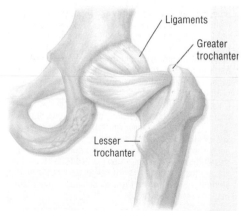

Ligaments

Greater trochanter

Lesser trochanter

Hip

area of the body between the waist and the thigh.

HIPAA *abbreviation.* Health Insurance Portability and Accountability Act.

hip bone the portion of the pelvis between the waist and the thigh that composes the cup-like cavity where the acetabulum meets the femur.

hip fracture a broken bone in the hip, generally the acetabulum or at the top of the femur.

hip joint the ball-and-socket joint formed by the round head of the femur and the cup-like cavity of the acetabulum (hip bone).

hippocampus /hĭp′ō kăm′pəs/ the complex nerve structure at the base of each lateral ventricle of the brain that helps regulate emotion and memory.

Hippocratic Oath /hĭp′ə krăt′ĭk/ a sacred oath sworn by all physicians to observe medical ethics, including *Primum non nocere — first, do no harm!*

hirsute /hûr′so͞ot/ having excessive facial and body hair.

hirsutism /hûr′so͞o tĭz′əm, hûr so͞o′-/ abnor-

I swear by Apollo the physician and Asklepios, and health, and All-Heal, and all the gods and goddesses, that, according to my ability and judgment.

I will keep this Oath and this stipulation—to reckon him who taught me this Art equally dear to me as my parents, to share my substance with him, and relieve his necessities if required, to look upon his offspring in the same footing as my own brothers, and to teach them this Art, if they shall wish to learn it, without fee or stipulation; and that by precept, lecture, and every other mode of instruction, I will impart a knowledge of the Art to my own sons, and those of my teachers, and to disciples bound by a stipulation and oath according to the law of medicine, but to none others.

I will follow that system of regimen which, according to my ability and judgment, I consider for the benefit of my patients, and abstain from whatever is deleterious and mischievous, I will give no deadly medicine to any one if asked, nor suggest any such counsel; and in like manner I will not give to a woman a pessary to produce abortion. With purity and holiness I will pass my life and practice my Art.

I will not cut persons laboring under the stone, but will leave this to be done by men who are practitioners of this work. Into whatever houses I enter, I will go into them for the benefit of the sick, and will abstain from every voluntary act of mischief and corruption; and, further, from the seduction of females or males, of freemen and slaves. whatever, in connection with my professional practice, or not in connection with it, I see or hear, in the life of men, which ought not to be spoken of abroad, I will not divulge, as reckoning that all such should be kept secret. While I continue to keep this Oath unviolated, may it be granted to me to enjoy life and the practice of the Art, respected by all men, in all times! But should I trespass and violate this Oath, may the reverse be my lot!

Hippocratic Oath

---

mal excessive hair growth, especially in women.

hirudin /hĭ ro͞o′dĭn, hĭr′yo͞o-/ an anticoagulant extracted from leech saliva.

His *abbreviation.* histidine.

hist-, histo- *combining form.* body tissue: *for example,* histamine, histoblast.

histamine /hĭs′tə mēn′, -mĭn/ a substance released from the immune system which mediates an allergic reaction, that dilates blood vessels and increases their permeability. [hist- + amine]

histi-, histio- *combining form.* body tissue, especially connective tissue: *for example,* histiocyte.

histidine (His) /hĭs′tĭ dēn′, -dĭn/ an amino acid essential for the growth and repair of tissues.

histioblast /hĭs′tē ə blăst′/ a tissue-forming cell. *Also called* histoblast. [histo- + -blast]

histiocyte /hĭs′tē ə sīt′/ an inactive macrophage found in connective tissue. *Also called* histocyte. [histio- + -cyte]

histiocytic lymphoma /hĭs′tē ə sĭt′ĭk lĭm fō′mə/ a malignant tumor of connective tissue made of neoplastic histiocytes.

histiocytoma /hĭs′tē ō sĭ tō′mə/ a tumor containing histiocytes. [histio- + cyt- + -oma]

histiocytosis /hĭs′tē ōsĭ tō′sĭs/ any disorder characterized by the presence of histiocytes in tissues or blood. [histio- + cytosis]

histo- *see* hist-.

histoblast /hĭs′tə blăst′/ a tissue-forming cell. *Also called* histioblast. [histo- + -blast]

histocompatibility /hĭs′tō kəm păt′ə bĭl′ĭ tē/ ability to tolerate tissue grafts and blood transfusions without rejections.

histocompatible /hĭs′tō kəm păt′ə bəl/ tissue and blood compatible.

histocyte /hĭs′tə sīt′/ an inactive macrophage found in connective tissue. *Also called* histiocyte. [histo- + -cyte]

histogenesis /hĭs′tō jĕn′ə sĭs/ the formation and development of tissue.

histogenous /hĭ stŏj′ə nəs/ formed by tissues.

histoid /hĭs′toid/ resembling normal tissue. [hist- + -oid]

histologist /hĭ stŏl′ə jĭst/ a specialist in histology. [histo- + -logist]

histology /hĭ stŏl′ə jē/ the study of the microscopic structure and function of bodily tissues, work often done by pathologists. [histo- + -logy]

histone /hĭs′tōn/ any of a group of five simple proteins rich in basic amino acids that are found in the nucleus associated with the DNA.

histonuria /hĭs′tō no͞or′ē ə/ excretion of histones in the urine.

Hives

histopathology /hĭs'tō pə thŏl'ə jē/ the microscopic study of diseased tissue. [histo- + -patho- + -logy]

histoplasmosis /hĭs'tō plăz mō'sĭs/ an infectious disease of the respiratory system contracted by inhaling spores, causing an influenza-like sickness.

histrionic /hĭs'trē ŏn'ĭk/ excessively emotional, usually with loud outbursts.

HIV *abbreviation.* human immunodeficiency virus.

hives /hīvz/ an allergic reaction of the skin characterized by the formation of small, red, itching bumps. *Also called* urticaria.

HIV-positive having a positive blood test result for the human immunodeficiency virus.

HIV test a test to detect antibodies to the HIV virus or the HIV virus itself.

HMD *abbreviation.* hyaline membrane disease.

HMO *abbreviation.* health maintenance organization.

hoarse /hôrs/ a rough or husky voice, often due to a sore throat, overuse of the vocal cords, or smoking.

Hodgkin('s) disease (HD) /hŏj'kĭn(z)/ or **Hodgkin('s) lymphoma** /lĭm fō'mə/ a malignant disease characterized by enlargement of the lymph nodes, spleen, and liver, with anemia and fever.

holistic medicine /hō lĭs'tĭk/ a type of alternative medicine that considers the entire person including his or her physical, social, and emotional well-being.

Holter monitor /hōl'tər/ a portable device (ECG) that continuously records heart activity for a 24-hour period, used to detect rhythm abnormalities.

Homan('s) sign /hō'mən(z)/ pain in the calf or knee when bent while the foot is dorsiflexed, usually indicating thrombosis in the leg veins.

homeo-, homo- *combining form.* like; similar: *for example,* homeostasis.

homeopathic medicine /hō'mē ō păth'ĭk/ the practice of using minute doses of medication thought capable of producing symptoms similar to the disease symptoms in healthy individuals, in order to cure the person suffering from those symptoms.

homeoplasia /hō'mē ō plā'zhə/ the formation of new tissue similar to existing tissue in the same area. [homeo- + -plasia]

homeostasis /hō'mē ō stā'sĭs/ the ability of the body to maintain constant equilibrium by constantly adjusting physiological processes. [homeo- + -stasis]

homeotherapy /hō'mē ō thĕr'ə pē/ the use of homeopathic principles in the treatment and prevention of disease.

homogeneous /hō'mə jē'nē əs, -jēn'yəs/ of a similar nature or structure.

homogenesis /hō'mə jĕn'ə sĭs/ reproduction in which the offspring are similar to the parents. [homo- + -genesis]

homograft /hō'mə grăft'/ a tissue graft from a donor of the same species as the recipient. *Also called* allograft. [homo- + graft]

homolateral /hō'mə lăt'ər əl/ located on, or affecting the same side of the body, also called ipsilateral. [homo- + lateral]

homosexual /hō'mə sĕk'shoo əl/ of, relating to, or having a sexual attraction to the same sex, as opposed to heterosexual, attraction to someone of the opposite sex. [homo- + sexual]

homosexuality /hō'mə sĕk'shoo ăl'ĭ tē/ sexuality toward the same sex.

hordeolum /hôr dē'ə ləm/ (*pl.* **hordeola** /hôr dē'ə lə/) a small grain-like tumor on the eyelid; inflammation of one of the sebaceous glands of the eyelid. *Also called* sty.

hormonal /hôr mō'nəl/ of or relating to hormones.

hormone /hôr'mōn/ a substance secreted into the blood stream by one tissue to effect a physiological activity.

hormone replacement therapy (HRT) the administration of estrogen and progestin to women to relieve the symptoms of menopause, prevent osteoporosis, and thought to reduce the risk of heart disease (however some studies dispute this).

hormone therapy the therapeutic use of hormones.

horn /hôrn/ **1.** a hard, tapering projection composed chiefly of keratin. **2.** something in the shape of a horn.

horn cell a nerve cell found in the gray columns of the spinal cord.

horny layer the outermost layer of the skin consisting of dead cells that slough off.

hose /hōz/ tight, fitted leggings used to promote blood flow back to the heart.

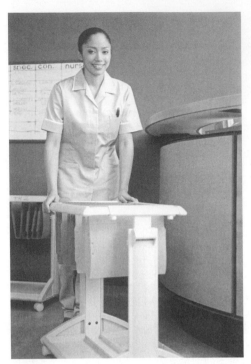

Hospital

hospice /hŏs′pĭs/ a facility that provides hospice care or the care itself.

hospice care physical, psychological, social, and spiritual care administered to dying patients and their families.

hospital /hŏs′pĭ təl/ a facility that provides medical, surgical, psychological, and often emergency care to the sick or injured, usually on an in-patient basis.

Hospital Formulary /fôrm′yə lĕr′ē/ a list of medications and treatments that are available on site to the hospital's medical staff.

hospitalist /hŏs′pĭ tə lĭst/ **1.** a physician who works exclusively in a hospital. **2.** a physician who assumes the role of primary care doctor while a patient is in a hospital, returning care of the patient to his or her normal primary care doctor upon discharge.

hospitalization /hŏs′pĭ tə lə zā′shən/ the placing of a patient within a hospital for observation or treatment.

hospitalize /hŏs′pĭ tə līz′/ the act of placing a patient in hospitalization.

hot flash a sudden sensation of heat, often throughout the entire body, experienced by some women during menopause.

house officer a hospital employee who treats patients while receiving specialized medical training.

house staff physicians or surgeons undergoing specialized training at a hospital, while caring for patients.

house surgeon a surgeon who works entirely at a hospital.

H&P *abbreviation.* history and physical.

HPV *abbreviation.* human papilloma virus.

H. pylori /pī lôr′ī/ a bacteria, *Helicobacter pylori*, associated with several gastrointestinal disorders, especially ulcers.

HRR *abbreviation.* high-risk register.

HRT *abbreviation.* hormone replacement therapy.

HSG *abbreviation.* hysterosalpingography.

HSV *abbreviation.* herpes simplex virus.

HTLV *abbreviation.* human T-cell leukemia virus.

HTN *abbreviation.* hypertension.

human chorionic gonadotropin (HCG, hCG) /kôr′ē ŏn′ĭk gō năd′ə trō′pĭn/ a hormone produced early in pregnancy by the placenta, detected by certain pregnancy tests.

human gene map the locations of the human genes.

human gene therapy the treatment of a genetic defect by the introduction of normal DNA into the cells of the patient.

human genome /jē′nōm/ all of the DNA found within a human.

Human Genome Project an international project whose goal is to identify and order all of the base pairs in the human genome.

human growth hormone (HGH) a hormone produced in the pituitary gland that stimulates growth; sometimes given to stimulate growth in underdeveloped children.

human immunodeficiency virus (HIV) /ĭm′yə nō dĭ fĭsh′ən sē/ a retrovirus that causes AIDS in humans.

human papilloma virus (HPV) /păp′ə lō′mə/ a group of over 100 viruses that cause a range of afflictions, such as warts and cervical cancer.

human T-cell leukemia virus (HTLV) /lōō kē′ mē ə/ a retrovirus that causes adult T-cell leukemia.

humectant /hyōō mĕk′tənt/ a substance that promotes the retention of moisture; used in certain lotions and creams.

humeral /hyōō′mər əl/ of, relating to, or found within the area of the body around the humerus and shoulder.

humerus /hyōō′mər əs/ (*pl.* **humeri** /hyōō′ mə rī′/) the long bone in the arm that extends from the shoulder to the elbow.

humidifier /hyōō mĭd′ə fī′ər/ a device used to increase the amount of moisture in the air of an enclosed space, such as a bedroom or a greenhouse.

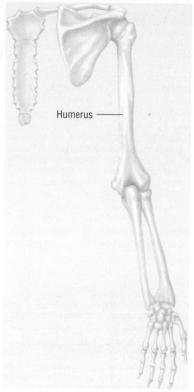

Humerus

Humerus

humor /hyo͞o′mər/   any body fluid.

humoral /hyo͞o′mər əl/   of or relating to the fluids of the body.

humoral immunity   the component of the immune system comprised by antibodies that are secreted and circulate in the blood.

hump /hŭmp/   nonmedical term for the bulge found on the upper back of a person suffering from kyphosis.

humpback /hŭmp′băk′/   nonmedical term for kyphosis, the abnormal curvature of the spine resulting in a bulging hump on the upper back.

hunchback /hŭnch′băk′/   nonmedical term for kyphosis, the abnormal curvature of the spine resulting in a a bulging hump on the upper back.

hunger pain   a cramp in the upper abdomen caused by hunger.

Huntington('s) chorea /hŭn′tĭng tən(z) kə rē′ə/ or **Huntington('s) disease**   a rare genetic disorder that appears at age 30-40, characterized by neurological degeneration and usually resulting in death.

hyal-, hyals-   *combining form.* glassy: *for example,* hyalinuria.

hyaline /hī′ə lēn′, -lĭn/ or **hyalin** /hī′ə lĭn/   a translucent substance that forms in certain cartilage and some skin conditions.

hyaline membrane disease (HMD)   a respiratory disease of infants where alveoli (tiny air sacs in the lung) collapse because of lack of surfactant. *Also called* respiratory distress syndrome.

hyalinuria /hī′ə lĭ no͞or′ē ə/   presence of hyaline casts in urine.

hyaloid /hī′ə loid′/   glassy, translucent. [hyal- + oid]

hyalosis /hī′ə lō′sĭs/   pathological changes in the vitreous body of the eye. [hyal- + -osis]

hybrid /hī′brĭd/   an offspring resulting from the mating of two different species or anything composed of heterogeneous parts.

hybridoma /hī′brĭ dō′mə/   a hybrid cell line formed from an antibody-producing lymphocyte and a non-antibody-producing myeloma cell.

hydatid cyst /hī′də tĭd sĭst′/   a cyst formed around the larva of a parasitic tapeworm, usually in the liver.

hydr-, hydro-   *combining form.* water, liquid: *for example,* hydrocele.

hydradenitis /hī′drăd ə nī′tĭs/   inflammation of the sweat glands. [hydr- + adenitis]

hydranencephaly /hī′drăn ĕn sĕf′ə lē/   a birth defect in which the cerebral hemispheres of the brain are lacking. [hydr- + anencephaly]

hydrarthrosis /hī′drär thro′sĭs/   a collection of fluid in a joint cavity. [hydr- + arthrosis]

hydrate /hī′drāt/   **1.** *n.* any of a large class of compounds containing chemically combined water. **2.** *v.* to combine chemically with water.

hydration /hī drā′shən/   **1.** the chemical addition of water. **2.** the drinking of water, especially to reduce dehydration.

hydremia /hī drē′mē ə/   an increase in the water content of plasma. [hydr- + -emia]

hydrocarbon /hī′drə kär′bən/   an organic compound containing only hydrogen and carbon. [hydro- + carbon]

hydrocele /hī′drə sēl′/   a fluid-filled cavity or duct, especially in the scrotum. [hydro- + -cele]

hydrocelectomy /hī′drō sē lĕk′tə mē/   surgical removal of a hydrocele.

hydrocephalic /hī′drō sə făl′ĭk/   having hydrocephalus. [hydro- + cephalic]

hydrocephalus /hī′drə sĕf′ə lĭs/   condition with an abnormal accumulation of cerebrospinal fluid in the brain under increased pressure, causing enlargement of the skull and destruction of neural tissue; hydrocephaly.

hydrocephaly /hī′drə sĕf′ə lē/   hydrocephalus. [hydro- + -cephaly]

hydrocortisone /hī′drō kôr′tə zōn′/   a topical corticosteroid used in treatment of skin ailments. [hydro- + cortisone]

A. Handwashing

1. Wash hands after touching blood, body fluids, secretions, excretions, and contaminated items, whether or not gloves are worn. Wash hands immediately after gloves are removed, between patient contacts, and when otherwise indicated to avoid transfer of microorganisms to other patients or environments. It may be necessary to wash hands between tasks and procedures on the same patient to prevent cross-contamination of different body sites.
2. Use a plain (nonantimicrobial) soap for routine handwashing.
3. Use an antimicrobial agent or a waterless antiseptic agent for specific circumstances (e.g., control of outbreaks or hyperendemic infections), as defined by the infection control program. (See Contact Precautions for additional recommendations on using antimicrobial and antiseptic agents.)

B. Gloves

Wear gloves (clean, nonsterile gloves are adequate) when touching blood, body fluids, secretions, excretions, and contaminated items. Put on clean gloves just before touching mucous membranes and nonintact skin. Change gloves between tasks and procedures on the same patient after contact with material that may contain a high concentration of microorganisms. Remove gloves promptly after use, before touching noncontaminated items and environmental surfaces, and before going to another patient, and wash hands immediately to avoid transfer of microorganisms to other patients or environments.

C. Mask, Eye Protection, Face Shield

Wear a mask and eye protection or a face shield to protect mucous membranes of the eyes, nose, and mouth during procedures and patient-care activities that are likely to generate splashes or sprays of blood, body fluids, secretions, and excretions.

D. Gown

Wear a gown (a clean, nonsterile gown is adequate) to protect skin and to prevent soiling of clothing during procedures and patient-care activities that are likely to generate splashes or sprays of blood, body fluids, secretions, or excretions. Select a gown that is appropriate for the activity and amount of fluid likely to be encountered. Remove a soiled gown as promptly as possible, and wash hands to avoid transfer of microorganisms to other patients or environments.

E. Patient-Care Equipment

Handle used patient-care equipment soiled with blood, body fluids, secretions, and excretions in a manner that prevents skin and mucous membrane exposures, contamination of clothing, and transfer of microorganisms to other patients and environments. Ensure that reusable equipment is not used for the care of another patient until it has been cleaned and reprocessed appropriately. Ensure that single-use items are discarded properly.

F. Environmental Control

Ensure that the hospital has adequate procedures for the routine care, cleaning, and disinfection of environmental surfaces, beds, bedrails, bedside equipment, and other frequently touched surfaces, and ensure that these procedures are being followed.

G. Linen

Handle, transport, and process used linen soiled with blood, body fluids, secretions, and excretions in a manner that prevents skin and mucous membrane exposures and contamination of clothing, and that avoids transfer of microorganisms to other patients and environments.

H. Occupational Health and Bloodborne Pathogens

1. Take care to prevent injuries when using needles, scalpels, and other sharp instruments or devices; when handling sharp instruments after procedures; when cleaning used instruments; and when disposing of used needles. Never recap used needles, or otherwise manipulate them using both hands, or use any other technique that involves directing the point of a needle toward any part of the body; rather, use either a one-handed "scoop" technique or a mechanical device designed for holding the needle sheath. Do not remove used needles from disposable syringes by hand, and do not bend, break, or otherwise manipulate used needles by hand. Place used disposable syringes and needles, scalpel blades, and other sharp items in appropriate puncture-resistant containers, which are located as close as practical to the area in which the items were used, and place reusable syringes and needles in a puncture-resistant container for transport to the reprocessing area.
2. Use mouthpieces, resuscitation bags, or other ventilation devices as an alternative to mouth-to-mouth resuscitation methods in areas where the need for resuscitation is predictable.

I. Patient Placement

Place a patient who contaminates the environment or who does not (or cannot be expected to) assist in maintaining appropriate hygiene or environmental control in a private room. If a private room is not available, consult with infection control professionals regarding patient placement or other alternatives.

Hygiene (federal standards—www.cdc.gov)

hydrogen (H) /hī′drə jən/ the lightest element and a component of water.

hydrogen peroxide a topical anti-infective.

hydrolysis /hī′drōl′ə sĭs/ chemical decomposition in which a compound is split into other compounds by reacting with water.

hydronephrosis /hī′drō nə frō′sĭs/ condition with accumulation of excess urine in the kidneys due to obstruction in urine outflow. [hydro- + nephrosis]

hydrophilia /hī′drə fĭl′ē ə/ **1.** tendency of tissue to absorb water. **2.** attraction to water. [hydro- + -philia]

hydrophobia /hī′drə fō′bē ə/ **1.** extreme fear of water. **2.** viral disease transmitted by a bite from an infected animal; this highly infectious disease leads to fatal paralysis if not treated. *Also called* rabies. [hydro- + -phobia]

hydrops /hī′drŏps/ abnormal accumulation of fluid in a body cavity.

hydrorrhea /hī′drə rē′ə/ copious discharge of watery fluid from the body. [hydro- + -rrhea]

hydrosalpinx /hī′drō săl′pĭngks/ condition of fluid accumulation in a fallopian tube. [hydro- + salpinx]

hydrotherapy /hī′drō thĕr′ə pē/ therapy using water externally, as in a whirlpool bath. [hydro- + therapy]

hydrothionemia /hī′drō thī′ə nē′mē ə/ the presence of hydrogen sulfur in the blood.

hydrothionuria /hī′drō thī′ə nŏŏr′ē ə/ the presence of hydrogen sulfur in the urine.

hydrothorax /hī′drō thôr′ăks/ condition of fluid accumulation in the pleural cavity. [hydro- + thorax]

hygiene /hī′jēn/ **1.** the science of the preservation of health. **2.** practices or conditions that preserve health, particularly cleanliness. *See guidelines* for hygiene on page 166.

hygienic /hī′jē ĕn′ĭk, hī jĕn′-/ **1.** conducive to good health. **2.** of or relating to hygiene.

hygienist /hī′jē ĕn′ĭst, hī jĕn′-/ **1.** an expert in hygiene. **2.** a dental hygienist.

hymen-, hymeno- *combining form.* hymen: *for example,* hymenitis.

hymen /hī′mən/ membranous tissue that covers the introitus of the vagina.

hymenectomy /hī′mə nĕk′tə mē/ surgical removal of the hymen. [hymen- + -ectomy]

hymenitis /hī′mə nī′tĭs/ inflammation of the hymen. [hymen- + -itis]

hymenotomy /hī′mə nŏt′ə mē/ surgical incision into the hymen. [hymeno- + -tomy]

hyoglossus /hī′ō glŏs′əs/ a muscle of the tongue arising from the hyoid bone.

hyoid bone /hī′oid/ a U-shaped bone at the base of the tongue that supports the muscles of the tongue.

hyper- *prefix.* excessive or above normal: *for example,* hyperacusis.

hyperactive /hī′pər ăk′tĭv/ overly active, especially said of a child regarded as having attention deficit disorder.

hyperactivity /hī′pər ăk tĭv′ĭ tē/ an excessive amount of activity, especially in a child regarded as having attention deficit disorder.

hyperacusis /hī′pər ə kyŏŏ′sĭs/ an abnormally heightened sense of hearing. [hyper- + -acusis]

hyperadrenalism /hī′pər ə drĕn′ə līz′əm/ a glandular disorder where the adrenal gland overproduces one of its hormones. [hyper- + adrenal + -ism]

hyperadrenocorticism /hī′pər ə drē′nō kôr′tə sĭz′əm/ an excess of adrenocortical substances in the body.

hyperalbuminemia /hī′pər ăl byŏŏ′mə nē′mē ə/ an abnormally high level of albumin in the blood.

hyperaldosteronism /hī′pər ăl dŏs′tər ə nĭz′əm/ a disorder characterized by excessive production of aldosterone.

hyperalimentation /hī′pər ăl′ə mĕn tā′shən/ complete nutrition given solely by intravenous means. *Also called* total parenteral nutrition. [hyper- + alimentation]

hyperbaric /hī′pər băr′ĭk/ of, relating to, or occurring at higher than normal atmospheric pressures.

hyperbaric chamber a large chamber in which oxygen levels are higher than normal; used to treat carbon monoxide poisoning and certain other conditions.

hyperbaric oxygen therapy treatment during which a patient is exposed to oxygen in a sealed chamber at a pressure greater than 1 atmosphere, used to treat infections caused by anaerobic organisms.

hyperbilirubinemia /hī′pər bĭl′ə rŏŏ′bə nē′mē ə/ excessive bilirubin in the blood. [hyper- + bilirubinemia]

hypercalcemia /hī′pər kăl sē′mē ə/ excessive calcium in the blood.

hypercalciuria /hī′pər kăl sē yŏŏr′ē ə/ excessive calcium in the urine.

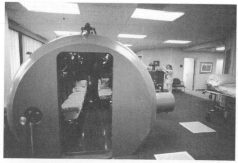

Hyperbaric Chamber

hypercapnia /hīʹpər kăpʹnē ə/ excessive carbon dioxide in the blood.

hypercementosis /hīʹpər sēʹmĕn tōʹsĭs/ excessive deposition of cementum on a tooth.

hyperchloremia /hīʹpər klô rēʹmē ə/ excessive chloride ions in the blood.

hypercholesterolemia /hīʹpər kə lĕsʹtər ə lēʹ mē ə/ excessive cholesterol in the blood.

hypercholia /hīʹpər kōʹlē ə/ secretion of an excessive amount of bile in the liver. [hyper- + chol- + -ia]

hyperemesis /hīʹpər ĕmʹə sĭs/ excessive vomiting. [hyper- + emesis]

hyperemesis gravidarum /grăvʹĭ dârʹəm/ excessive nausea and vomiting during pregnancy, resulting in dehydration and acidosis.

hyperemia /hīʹpə rēʹmē ə/ an excessive accumulation of blood in a body part. [hyper- + -emia]

hyperesthesia /hīʹpər ĕs thēʹzhə/ an abnormally heightened sensitivity to sensory stimuli, such as touch to the skin or sound. [hyper- + -esthesia]

hyperextension /hīʹpər ĭk stĕnʹshən/ the abnormal extension of a limb beyond its normal range of motion.

hyperglycemia /hīʹpər glī sēʹmē ə/ excessive glucose in the blood. *Also called* high blood sugar.

hyperglycemic response /hīʹpər glī sēʹmĭk/ a response to a carbohydrate meal resulting in abnormally elevated levels of blood glucose.

hypergonadism /hīʹpər gōʹnă dĭzʹəm/ excessive secretion of gonadal hormones.

hyperhidrosis /hīʹpər hī drōʹsĭs/ excessive sweating. [hyper- + hidrosis]

hyperhidrotic /hīʹpər hī drŏtʹĭk/ of or pertaining to hyperhidrosis.

hyperinsulinism /hīʹpər ĭnʹsə lə nĭzʹəm/ excessive insulin in the blood, resulting in hypoglycemia.

hyperkalemia /hīʹpər kə lēʹmē ə/ an excessive amount of potassium ions in the blood. [hyper- + kalemia]

hyperkeratosis /hīʹpər kĕrʹə tōʹsĭs/ thickening of the horny layer of the epidermis. [hyper- + keratosis]

hyperkinesia /hīʹpər kĭ nēʹzhə/ or **hyperkinesis** /hīʹpər kĭ nēʹsĭs/ excessive muscular activity, usually resulting from a pathological condition. [hyper- + -kinesia *or* -kinesis]

hyperlipemia /hīʹpər lĭ pēʹmē ə/ hyperlipidemia. [hyper- + lip- + -emia]

hyperlipidemia /hīʹpər lĭpʹĭ dēʹmē ə/ an excessive amount of lipids in the blood; hyperlipemia.

hyperlipoproteinemia /hīʹpər lĭpʹō prōʹtē nēʹ mē ə, -līʹpō-/ the presence of increased amounts of lipids in the blood, due either to decreased breakdown of lipoproteins or increased production of lipids. [hyper- + lipo- + protein + -emia]

hyperlordosis /hīʹpər lôr dōʹsĭs/ extreme lumbar curvature of the spine. [hyper- + lordosis]

hypermania /hīʹpər māʹnē ə/ an extreme mental state characterized by disorentation and violent behavior. [hyper- + mania]

hypermetropia /hīʹpər mĭ trōʹpē ə/ hyperopia. *Also called* farsightedness.

hypermobility syndrome /hīʹpər mō bĭlʹĭ tē/ a benign childhood condition where the joints are flexible beyond the normal range of motion.

hypernatremia /hīʹpər nā trēʹmē ə/ excessive sodium in the blood.

hypernephroma /hīʹpər nĭ frōʹmə/ a tumor of the kidney. [hyper- + nephroma]

hyperopia (H) /hīʹpə rōʹpē ə/ a vision disorder in which distant objects can be seen more clearly than closer objects. *Also called* hypermetropia, farsightedness. [hyper- + -opia]

hyperopic /hīʹpə rŏpʹĭk/ of or pertaining to hyperopia.

hyperostosis /hīʹpər ŏ stōʹsĭs/ abnormal growth of bone tissue.

hyperoxaluria /hīʹpər ŏkʹsə lo͝orʹē ə/ excessive oxalic acid in urine.

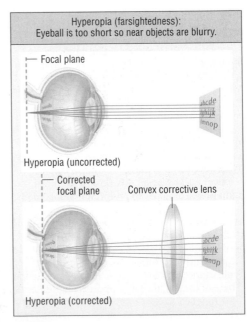

Hyperopia (farsightedness):
Eyeball is too short so near objects are blurry.

Focal plane

Hyperopia (uncorrected)

Corrected focal plane   Convex corrective lens

Hyperopia (corrected)

Hyperopia

hyperparathyroidism /hī′pər păr′ə thī′roi dĭz′ əm/ an abnormal increase in hormone secretions from the parathyroid glands, causing high levels of calcium in the blood. [hyper- + parathyroid + -ism]

hyperpigmentation /hī′pər pĭg′mĕn tā′shən/ abnormal darkening of the skin as a result of heredity, sun exposure, drug reaction, or disease. [hyper- + pigmentation]

hyperpituitarism /hī′pər pĭ tōō′ĭ tə rĭz′əm/ overactivity of the pituitary gland leading to several conditions, such as gigantism and acromegaly.

hyperplasia /hī′pər plā′zhə/ an abnormal increase in cell division. [hyper- + -plasia]

hyperplastic /hī′pər plăs′tĭk/ of or relating to hyperplasia.

hyperpnea /hī′pər nē′ə, -pərp-/ abnormally deep, labored breathing. [hyper- + -pnea]

hyperpyrexia /hī′pər pī rĕk′sē ə/ extremely high fever.

hypersecretion /hī′pər sĭ krē′shən/ abnormally high levels of secretion. [hyper- + secretion]

hypersensitivity /hī′pər sĕn′sĭ tĭv′ĭ tē/ an exaggerated immune response to an antigen. [hyper- + sensitivity]

hypersplenism /hī′pər splē′nĭz əm/ a condition in which the spleen is enlarged due to overactive sequestration (removal and destruction) of blood elements, such as red cells and platelets.

hypertension (HTN) /hī′pər tĕn′shən/ blood pressure consistently over 140/90 mm Hg. *Also called* high blood pressure.

hypertensive /hī′pər tĕn′sĭv/ having blood pressure readings consistently over 140/90 mm Hg.

hypertensive retinopathy /rĕt′ə nŏp′ə thē/ changes in the retina of the eye resulting from hypertension.

hyperthermia /hī′pər thûr′mē ə/ elevated body temperature.

hyperthyroid /hī′pər thī′roid/ having an overactive thyroid gland. [hyper- + thyroid]

hyperthyroidism /hī′pər thī′roi dĭz′əm/ overactivity of the thyroid gland, characterized by increased metabolism and weight loss and protruding eyeballs.

hypertonia /hī′pər tō′nē ə/ abnormally increased muscle tone.

hypertrophic /hī′pər trŏf′ĭk/ having an abnormal increase in size or function. [hyper- + -trophic]

hypertrophy /hī pûr′trə fē/ an abnormal increase in the size of an organ's cells. [hyper- + -trophy]

hypertropia /hī′pər trō′pē ə/ upward deviation in the line of sight of one eye in relation to the other.

hyperuricemia /hī′pər yōōr′ə sē′mē ə/ excessive amount of uric acid in the blood, characteristic of gout.

hyperuricosuria /hī′pər yōōr′ĭ kōs yōōr′ē ə/ abnormally high levels of uric acid in the urine, often an indicator of gout. *Also called* uricaciduria.

hyperventilation /hī′pər vĕn′tə lā′shən/ abnormally fast and/or deep breathing, sometimes resulting in fainting.

hypervitaminosis /hī′pər vī′tə mĭ nō′sĭs/ a condition caused by the excessive intake of vitamins, usually through excessive intake of fat-soluble vitamins as a dietary supplement; symptoms depend on which vitamin has been ingested.

hypervolemia /hī′pər vō lē′mē ə/ an abnormal increase in fluid volume, especially circulating blood.

hypervolemic /hī′pər vō lē′mĭk/ having hypervolemia.

hyphema /hī fē′mə/ bleeding in the anterior chamber of the eye.

hypn-, hypno- *combining form.* sleep: *for example,* hypnotherapy.

hypnagogic /hĭp′nə gŏj′ĭk/ of or relating to the drowsy state of intermediate consciousness before sleep.

hypnogenesis /hĭp′nō jĕn′ə sĭs/ the process of inducing sleep or a hypnotic state. [hypno- + -genesis]

hypnosis /hĭp nō′sĭs/ an altered state of consciousness resembling sleep, often used as a therapeutic measure. [hypn- + -osis]

hypnotherapy /hĭp′nō thĕr′ə pē/ the use of hypnosis as a therapeutic measure. [hypno- + therapy]

hypnotic /hĭp nŏt′ĭk/ *adj.* **1.** inducing sleep or hypnosis. **2.** of or involving hypnosis. *n.* **3.** an agent that relieves pain and induces sleep.

hypnotism /hĭp′nə tĭz′əm/ the act, practice, or study of inducing hypnosis.

hypnotist /hĭp′nə tĭst/ someone who practices hypnotism.

Hypnotherapy

hypnotize /hĭp′nə tīz′/ to cause to fall into a hypnotic state.

hypo- *prefix.* low, below normal: *for example,* hypohidrosis.

hypoadrenalism /hī′pō ə drē′nə lĭz′əm/ below normal activity of the adrenal glands.

hypoalbuminemia /hī′pō ăl byōō′mə nē′mē ə/ abnormally low level of albumin in the blood.

hypocalcemia /hī′pō kăl sē′mē ə/ low level of calcium in the blood.

hypocapnia /hī′pō kăp′nē ə/ low level of carbon dioxide in the blood.

hypochloremia /hī′pō klô rē′mē ə/ low level of chloride in the blood.

hypochondria /hī′pō kŏn′drē ə/ psychological disorder where the patient either fears or believes he or she is suffering from a serious illness. *Also called* hypochondriasis.

hypochondriac /hī′pō kŏn′drē ăk′/ a person suffering from hypochondria.

hypochondriac region area beneath the ribs.

hypochondriasis /hī′pō kən drī′ə sĭs/ hypochondria.

hypochondroplasia /hī′pō kŏn′drə plā′zhə/ dwarfism with shortening of the ends of the limbs. [hypo- + chondro- + -plasia]

hypochromia /hī′pō krō′mē ə/ abnormally low levels of hemoglobin in the red blood cells.

hypodermic /hī′pə dûr′mĭk/ **1.** *adj.* beneath the skin. *Also called* subcutaneous. **2.** *n.* a hypodermic syringe.

hypodermic injection a subcutaneous injection using a small syringe and short needle.

hypodermic syringe /sə rĭnj′/ or **needle** an instument with a hollow tube and a short needle, used to give injections or withdraw blood.

hypodontia /hī′pō dŏn′chə/ a condition where a person has less than the normal number of teeth.

hypoesthesia /hī′pō ĕs thē′zhə/ partial loss of sensation. [hypo- + -esthesia]

hypogastric /hī′pō găs′trĭk/ of or relating to the hypogastric region. [hypo- + gastric]

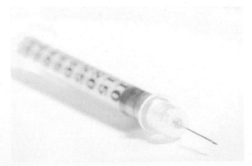

Hypodermic Syringe

hypogastric region the lower part of the abdomen; the lowest of the three regions of the abdomen.

hypogeusia /hī′pō gyōō′sē ə/ the condition of having a diminished sense of taste.

hypoglossal /hī′pō glŏs′əl/ of or relating to structures under the tongue.

hypoglossal nerve cranial nerve XII; one of two cranial nerves essential for swallowing and tongue movement.

hypoglycemia /hī′pō glī sē′mē ə/ abnormally low blood glucose level (below 70), which can produce shakiness, sweating, tiredness, hunger, and, at very low levels, confusion and loss of consciousness.

hypoglycemic /hī′pō glī sē′mĭk/ having hypoglycemia.

hypogonadism /hī′pō gō′nă dĭz′əm/ condition with abnormally low levels of secretions, as estrogen or testosterone, from the gonads.

hypohidrosis /hī′pō hī drō′sĭs/ abnormally low level of perspiration. [hype- + hidrosis]

hypohidrotic /hī′pō hī drŏt′ĭk/ having hypohidrosis.

hypokalemia /hī′pō kə lē′mē ə/ condition with abnormally low levels of potassium in the bloodstream. [hypo- + kalemia]

hypomania /hī′pō mā′nē ə/ a mild degree of mania. [hypo- + mania]

hypomanic /hī′pō măn′ĭk/ having hypomania.

hyponatremia /hī′pō nā trē′mē ə/ a potentially lethal condition of having excessive fluid in the bloodstream, often caused by overconsumption of liquids during extreme exercise.

hypoparathyroidism /hī′pō păr′ə thī′roi dĭz′əm/ abnormally low secretions of parathyroid hormone, which regulates calcium and phosphorus metabolism, from the parathyroid glands. [hypo- + parathyroid + -ism]

hypopharynx /hī′pō făr′ĭngks/ the lower part of the pharynx between the epiglottis and larynx. [hypo- + pharynx]

hypophoria /hī′pə fôr′ē ə/ the tendency of the visual axis of one eye to fall below the visual axis of the other eye. [hypo- + -phoria]

hypophysectomy /hī pŏf′ə sĕk′tə mē/ surgical removal of the hypophysis.

hypophysis /hī pŏf′ə sĭs/ a gland made up of a posterior and an anterior lobe that secretes many different hormones. *Also called* pituitary gland. *See also* adenohypophysis, neurohypophysis.

hypopigmentation /hī′pō pĭg′mĕn tā′shən/ abnormally low level of skin pigmentation. [hypo- + pigmentation]

hypopituitarism /hī′pō pĭ tōō′ĭ tə rĭz′əm/ condition of abnormally low level of pituitary activity.

Hypospadias

Hypospadias

hypoplasia /hī′pō plā′zhə/ underdevelopment due to an abnormally low number of cells in tissue or an organ. [hypo- + -plasia]

hypoplastic /hī′pō plăs′tĭk/ of or relating to hypoplasia. [hypo- + -plastic]

hypoplastic anemia progressive anemia due to hypoplastic (underactive) bone marrow.

hypopnea /hī′pō nē′ə, -pŏp-/ abnormally slow or shallow breathing. [hypo- + -pnea]

hyposecretion /hī′pō sĭ krē′shən/ abnormally low level of secretion. [hypo- + secretion]

hyposmia /hī pŏz′mē ə/ diminished sense of smell.

hypospadias /hī′pō spā′dē əs/ a birth defect in which the urethra opens on the underside of the penis. *See also* epispadias.

hyposplenism /hī′po sple′nĭz əm/ reduced or absent functioning of the spleen. [hypo- + splen- + -ism]

hypotension /hī′pō těn′shən/ blood pressure with readings that indicate there is not enough pressure in the blood to provide oxygen to the tissues. *Also called* low blood pressure.

hypotensive /hī′pō těn′sĭv/ having hypotension.

hypothalamus /hī′pō thăl′ə məs/ the bottom part of the diencephalons of the brain, involved in controlling body temperature and the autonomic nervous system. [hypo- + thalamus]

hypothermia /hī′pō thûr′mē ə/ abnormally low body temperature.

hypothyroidism /hī′pō thī′roi dĭz′əm/ condition of having abnormally low thyroid activity, often accompanied by weight gain and lethargy.

hypotonia /hī′pō tō′nē ə/ diminished muscle tone.

hypotropia /hī′pō trō′pē ə/ downward deviation in the line of sight of one eye in relation to the other.

hypoventilation /hī′pō věn′tə lā′shən/ abnormally slow or shallow respiration causing an increase of carbon dioxide in the blood. [hypo- + ventilation]

hypovitaminosis /hī′pō vī′tə mĭ nō′sĭs/ condition caused by lack of adequate intake or processing of vitamins in the diet. [hypo- + vitamin + -osis]

hypovolemia /hī′pō vō lē′mē ə/ abnormally low volume of circulating blood.

hypovolemic /hī′pō vō lē′mĭk/ having a low volume of circulating blood.

hypovolemic shock shock caused by a massive loss of blood.

hypoxemia /hī′pŏk sē′mē ə/ abnormally low concentration of oxygen in the blood.

hypoxia /hī pŏk′sē ə/ diminished levels of oxygen in blood or tissue.

hypoxic /hī pŏk′sĭk/ of or relating to hypoxia.

hyster-, hystero- *combining form.* uterus: *for example,* hysterocele.

hysteratresia /hĭs′tər ə trē′zhə/ congenital absence of the endocervical canal (opening of the uterus). [hyster- + atresia]

hysterectomy /hĭs′tə rěk′tə mē/ surgical removal of the uterus. [hyster- + -ectomy]

hysteria /hĭ stěr′ē ə/ **1.** formerly, a name for conversion disorder. **2.** a nonmedical term for an uncontrollable outburst of emotion.

hysterocele /hĭs′tər ə sēl′/ an abdominal hernia involving all or part of the uterus. [hystero- + -cele]

hysterogram /hĭs′tər ə grăm′/ radiologic examination of the uterus. [hystero- + -gram]

hysteropathy /hĭs′tə rŏp′ə thē/ any uterine disease. [hystero- + -pathy]

hysteropexy /hĭs′tər ə pěk′sē/ surgical fixing of an abnormally movable uterus. [hystero- + -pexy]

hysteroplasty /hĭs′tər ə plăs′tē/ surgical repair of the uterus. [hystero- + -plasty]

hysterorrhaphy /hĭs′tə rôr′ə fē/ suture of the uterus. [hystero- + -rrhaphy]

hysterorrhexis /hĭs′tə rō rěk′sĭs/ rupture of the uterus. [hystero- + -rrhexis]

hysterosalpingectomy /hĭs′tə rō săl′pĭn jěk′tə mē/ surgical removal of the uterus and one or both of the fallopian tubes. [hystero- + salping- + -ectomy]

hysterosalpingogram /hĭs′tə rō săl pĭng′gə grăm′/ the radiographic image obtained in hysterosalpingography.

hysterosalpingography (HSG) /hĭs′tə rō săl′pĭng gŏg′rə fē/ radiographic imaging of the uterus and fallopian tubes.

hysterosalpingo-oophorectomy /hĭs′tə rō săl pĭng′gō ō′ə fə rĕk′tə mē/   surgical removal of the uterus, oviducts, and ovaries.

hysteroscope /hĭs′tər ə skōp′/   visual examination of the uterine cavity using an endoscope. [hystero- + -scope]

hysteroscopy /hĭs′tə rŏs′kə pē/   visual inspection of the uterine cavity. [hystero- + -scopy]

hysterospasm /hĭs′tər ə spăz′əm/   a spasm of the uterus. [hystero- + spasm]

hysterotomy /hĭs′tə rŏt′ə mē/   incision into the uterus. [hystero- + -tomy]

Hz *abbreviation.* hertz.

I (drug caution code) a symbol placed on the label of a medication, indicating possible adverse interaction if taken with other drugs.

-ia *suffix.* condition; disease: *for example,* atresia, iridomalacia.

-iasis *suffix.* pathological condition characterized or produced by: *for example,* lithiasis.

iatrogenic /ī ăt′trə jĕn′ĭk, ē ăt′-/ induced by a doctor's actions, words, or therapy, especially said of a complication caused by treatment.

IBD *abbreviation.* inflammatory bowel disease.

IBS *abbreviation.* irritable bowel syndrome.

-ic of, pertaining to, relating to, or characterized by: *for example,* lactic.

ICD-9-CM *abbreviation.* title of *International Classification of Diseases, 9th Revision, Clinical Modification;* system for diagnosis classification now in use for medical coding. ICD-10 is under review and expected to be adopted by 2010.

ICF *abbreviation.* **1.** intermediate care facility. **2.** intracellular fluid.

ichthy-, ichthyo- *combining form.* fish or fish-like: *for example,* ichthyosis.

icthyoid /ĭk′thē oid′/ characteristic of a fish. [itchy- + -oid]

ichthyosis /ĭk′thē ō′sĭs/ a skin disorder characterized by dry flaking or scaling of the skin. [itchy- + -osis]

ichthyotoxism /ĭk′thē ō tŏk′sĭz əm/ poisoning by a substance derived from fish.

ICP *abbreviation.* intracranial pressure.

ictal /ĭk′təl/ of or relating to a seizure or stroke.

icterus /ĭk′tər əs/ yellowish discoloration of the skin or whites of the eyes due to high levels of bilirubin in the blood. *Also called* jaundice.

ICU *abbreviation.* intensive care unit.

id /ĭd/ the unconscious division of the psyche that serves as the source of primitive instinctual impulses needing immediate satisfaction, according to Freudian theory.

IDDM *abbreviation.* insulin-dependant diabetes mellitus.

identical twins twins that originate from a single fertilized egg. *Also called* monozygotic twins, monozygous twins. *See also* fraternal twins.

idio- *combining form.* unknown: *for example,* idiopathy.

idiopathic /ĭd′ē ə păth′ĭk/ of or relating to a disease with no known cause.

idiopathy /ĭd′ē ŏp′ə thē/ a disease of unknown cause. [idio- + -pathy]

idiosyncrasy /ĭd′ē ə sĭng′krə sē/ **1.** a peculiar trait. **2.** a peculiar reaction to a food or drug.

idiot savant /să vänt′/ older term for savant, an autistic individual who is exceptionally gifted in a particular field.

Ig *abbreviation.* immunoglobulin.

IgA *abbreviation.* immunoglobulin A.

IgD *abbreviation.* immunoglobulin D.

IgE *abbreviation.* immunoglobulin E.

IGF *abbreviation.* insulin-like growth factor(s).

IgG *abbreviation.* immunoglobulin G.

IgM *abbreviation.* immunoglobulin M.

IL *abbreviation.* interleukin.

ile-, ileo- *combining form.* ileum: *for example,* ileitis.

ileac /ĭl′ē ăk′/ **1.** of or relating to ileus. **2.** of or relating to the ileum; ileal. [ilie- + -ac]

ileal /ĭl′ē əl/ of or relating to the ileum. [ile- + -al]

ileal loop a loop of ileum removed and used to surgically create a urinary conduit to the skin, bypassing a diseased (or removed) bladder. *Also called* neobladder.

ileectomy /ĭl′ē ĕk′tə mē/ surgical removal of the ileum. [ile- + -ectomy]

ileitis /ĭl′ē ī′tĭs/ inflammation of the ileum. [ile- + -itis]

ileocecal /ĭl′ē ō sē′kəl/ of or relating to the ileum and the cecum. [ileo- + cecal]

ileocecal valve valve between the ileum and the cecum.

ileopexy /ĭl′ē ə pĕk′sē/ surgical fixing in position of the ileum. [ileo- + -pexy]

ileorrhaphy /ĭl′ē ôr′ə fē/ suturing of the ileum. [ileo- + -rrhaphy]

ileostomy /ĭl′ē ŏs′tə mē/ surgical creation of an opening through the abdomen into the ileum. [ileo- + -stomy]

ileotomy /ĭl′ē ŏt′ə mē/ surgical incision into the ileum. [ileo- + -tomy]

ileum /ĭl′ē əm/ the lowest (third) part of the small intestine.

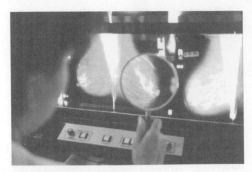
Imaging (Breast Diagnosis)

ileus /ĭl′ē əs/   obstruction or blockage of the ileum.

iliac /ĭl′ē ăk′/   of, relating to, or near the ilium.

iliofemoral /ĭl′ē ō fĕm′ər əl/   of or relating to the ilium of the pelvis and the femur.

ilium /ĭl′ē əm/   the uppermost and widest of the three bones of the pelvis.

illness /ĭl′nĭs/   sickness; lack of health; disease.

illusion /ĭ lōō′zhən/   a false concept, belief, or perception of reality.

IM   *abbreviation.* intramuscular.

image /ĭm′ĭj/   *n.* **1.** a mental picture of an object or concept. **2.** a picture of an object as reflected in a mirror or refracted by a lens. **3.** the representation of internal structures by radiographic or other physical means, such as x-rays, CAT scan, or ultrasound. *v.* **4.** to make such an image.

imagery /ĭm′ĭj re/   any thought or mental imagery, or the use of such imagery in behavioral therapy.

imaging /ĭm′ĭ jĭng/   **1.** internal examination of the body using specialized instruments. **2.** the use of mental imagery to affect bodily processes or pain.

imbalance /ĭm băl′əns/   lack of balance.

immersion /ĭ mûr′zhən/   **1.** positioning a body or body part completely under water or other fluid. **2.** in microscopy, the placing of the object of study in water or oil, to reduce refraction around the edges.

immobilize /ĭ mō′bə līz′/   to make something incapable of moving.

immovable joint   a union of two bones by fibrous tissue. *Also called* synarthrosis.

immune /ĭ myōōn′/   protected against infection.

immune complex   the large network of molecules formed by the binding of an antibodies and antigens, that act as mediators in immune response. *Also called* antigen-antibody complex.

immune reaction   binding of an antigen by its antibody as an immune system response to an invading substance.

immune response   immune system recognition and attack of an antigen by specific antibodies.

immune system   the complex system of organs, tissues, and cells that protects the body from pathogenic substances and infection.

immunity /ĭ myōō′nĭ tē/   **1.** the condition of being immune. **2.** natural or induced resistance to infection.

immunization /ĭm′yə nə zā′shən/   treatment to create immunity.

immuno-   *combining form.* immune; immunity: *for example,* immunodeficient.

immunocompetent   /ĭm′yə nō kŏm′pĭ tənt/   having the capacity to develop an immune response. [immuno- + competent]

immunocompromised   /ĭm′yə nō kŏm′prə mīzd′/   impairment or insufficient development of immune response. [immuno- + compromised]

immunocyte /ĭm′yə nə sīt′/   a white blood cell that can produce antibodies. [immuno- + -cyte]

immunodeficiency /ĭm′yə nō dĭ fĭsh′ən sē/   a weakened or deficient immune response. [immuno- + deficiency]

immunodeficient /ĭm′yə nō dĭ fĭsh′ənt/   having a suppressed or reduced immune system. [immuno- + deficient]

immunodepressant /ĭm′yə nō dĭ prĕs′ənt/   a substance capable of suppressing immune function. [immuno- + depressant]

immunodepression   /ĭm′yə nō dĭ prĕsh′ən/   intentional suppression of the immune response to prevent the body's natural rejection of grafts or transplants. [immuno- + depression]

immunogenetics   /ĭm′yə nō jə nĕt′ĭks/   the branch of immunology concerned with the relation between immune response and heredity. [immuno- + genetics]

immunoglobulin (Ig) /ĭm′yə nō glŏb′yə lĭn/   any in the family of glycoproteins (molecules consisting of a simple sugar attached to an amino acid) that function as antibodies in immune response. [immuno- + -globulin]

immunoglobulin A (IgA)   one of the five classes of immunoglobulins; found in the gastrointestinal tract and the respiratory tract.

immunoglobulin D (IgD)   one of the five classes of immunoglobulins; found on the surface of B cells.

immunoglobulin E (IgE)   one of the five classes of immunoglobulins; found in the skin and mucous membranes, responsible for allergic reactions.

immunoglobulin G (IgG)   one of the five classes of immunoglobulins; found in blood serum and lymph, used against bacteria, viruses, fungi, and foreign substances.

immunoglobulin M (IgM) one of the five classes of immunoglobulins; found in circulating bodily fluids, and the first sent to attack an antigen.

immunologist /ĭm′yə nŏl′ə jĭst/ a physician specializing in immunology.

immunology /ĭm′yə nŏl′ə jē/ the branch of medicine concerned with the structure, function, and disorders of the immune system. [immuno- + -logy]

immunosuppressant /ĭm′yə nō sə prĕs′ənt/ an agent that suppresses the immune system. [immuno- + suppressant]

immunosuppression /ĭm′yə nō sə prĕsh′ən/ intentional suppression of the immune response to prevent the body's natural rejection of grafts or transplants. [immuno- + suppression]

immunosuppressive /ĭm′yə nō sə prĕs′ĭv/ causing or characterized by immunosuppression. [immuno- + suppressive]

immunosuppressive agent an agent that slows immune response to prevent the body's natural rejection of grafts or transplants.

immunotherapy /ĭm′yə nō thĕr′ə pē/ treatment of a disease by triggering, enhancing, or suppressing the immune system. [immuno- + therapy]

immunotoxin /ĭm′yə nō tŏk′sĭn/ a toxin bonded to a monoclonal antibody, used to attack tumor cells. [immuno- + toxin]

impacted /ĭm păk′tĭd/ wedged together as to fuse, fill, or block, as an impacted tooth.

impacted fracture a fracture in which the bone fragments are wedged together.

impacted tooth a tooth wedged against another, preventing normal eruption.

impairment /ĭm pâr′mənt/ a weakness or deterioration due to injury or disease.

impetigo /ĭm′pĭ tī′gō/ a very contagious skin infection characterized by patches of red itchy skin, pustules, and sores usually on the face, caused by the *Staphylococcus aureus* bacteria or by a group A streptococcus bacteria.

implant *v.* /ĭm plănt′/ **1.** to insert or graft by surgery. **2.** to become attached to the uterine lining, as of a fertilized egg. *n.* /ĭm′plănt′/ **3.** a device or material used to repair or replace part of the body. **4.** medication inserted into tissue for long-term treatment.

implantation /ĭm′plăn tā′shən/ the act of implanting, especially of a fertilized egg implanting in the uterus.

impotence /ĭm′pə təns/ a condition occurring in men, characterized by an inability to achieve or sustain an erection long enough for sexual intercourse.

impotent /ĭm′pə tənt/ unable to achieve or sustain an erection long enough for sexual intercourse.

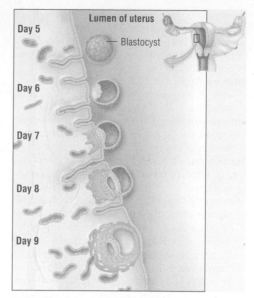

Implantation

impregnation /ĭm′prĕg nā′shən/ the process or act of making pregnant.

imprinting /ĭm prĭn′tĭng/ the process, shortly after birth, in which offspring model specific behavioral patterns after a parent or role model.

impulse /ĭm′pŭls/ a sudden impelling force, urge, or desire that triggers an abrupt, unpremeditated action.

impulsive /ĭm pŭl′sĭv/ involving or based on impulse rather than reason.

impulsivity /ĭm′pŭl sĭv′ĭ tē/ actions based on sudden impulse rather than rational or premeditated thought.

in- *prefix. into or not: for example,* inbreeding.

inborn /ĭn′bôrn′/ present at birth; innate; congenital. [in- + born]

inbred /ĭn′brĕd′/ **1.** resulting from inbreeding. **2.** naturally inherent; innate. [in- + bred]

inbreeding /ĭn′brē′dĭng/ **1.** breeding between closely related individual animals in a stock, to preserve desirable characteristics and remove undesirable ones, but occasionally accentuating undesirable traits or illnesses. **2.** mating between close cousins, increasing the appearance of usually undesirable recessive traits. [in- + breeding]

incarcerated (hernia) /ĭn kär′sə rā tĭd (hûr′nē ə)/ constricted or trapped, as a hernia.

incest /ĭn′sĕst/ sexual intercourse between individuals too closely related to legally marry.

incestuous /ĭn sĕs′chōō əs/ denoting or involving incest.

incidence /ĭn′sĭ dəns/ **1.** the rate at which something occurs in a group over a period of time. **2.** the arrival of radiation at a surface.

incision /ĭn sĭzh′ən/ a cut in body tissue, or the scar resulting from such a cut.

incisional biopsy /ĭn sĭzh′ə nəl bī′ŏp sē/ a biopsy in which a sample of the tissue in question is cut away and tested.

incisive /ĭn sī′sĭv/ 1. of or involving the incisors. 2. able to cut or pierce, as a surgical instrument.

incisor /ĭn sī′zər/ any the four front teeth shaped for cutting, located in both the upper and lower jaws.

incoherent /ĭn′kō hêr′ənt/ lacking clarity or any logical connection, usually due to emotional stress.

incompatible /ĭn′kəm păt′ə bəl/ 1. unsuitable to use with or together, as in blood transfusion or organ transplantation. 2. not able to be together, emotionally or physically, in a friendly, productive way. [in- + compatible]

incompetence /ĭn kŏm′pĭ təns/ the condition or quality of being unable or incapable of performing a physical or mental function. [in- + competence]

incompetent /ĭn kŏm′pĭ tənt/ not capable of performing a function or serving a particular purpose. [in- + competent]

incomplete fracture a break that does not extend though the entire width of the bone. [in- + complete]

incontinence /ĭn kŏn′tə nəns/ lack of the ability to control urination or defecation.

incontinent /ĭn kŏn′tə nənt/ uncontrollable or involuntary, especially in the ability to control urination or defecation.

incubation period /ĭn′kyə bā′shən/ the period between infection and manifestation of a disease.

incubator /ĭng′kyə bā′tər/ a climate-controlled chamber used for growing cultures, hatching eggs, creating chemical or biological reactions, and for maintaining temperature and protecting an ill or premature infant.

incurable /ĭn kyoor′ə bəl/ impossible to cure; not curable.

Incubator

incus /ĭng′kəs/ (pl. **incudes** /ĭn kyoo′dēz/) the anvil-shaped middle bone between the malleus and the stapes in the middle ear. *Also called* anvil.

index /ĭn′dĕks/ (pl. **indices** /ĭn′də sēz′/ or **indexes**) 1. the index finger. 2. the ratio of the size, frequency, capacity, etc., of an object or substance in relation to a fixed standard. 3. a rating scale. 4. a mold used to maintain the relative position of one tooth to another. 5. a plaster guide used to reposition teeth, casts, etc.

index finger the finger next to the thumb.

indication /ĭn′dĭ kā′shən/ 1. something that suggests the cause or the correct treatment of a disease. 2. the measurement taken by an instrument.

indigestion /ĭn′dĭ jĕs′chən/ pain or discomfort resulting from a difficulty in digesting something. [in- + digestion]

indolent /ĭn′də lənt/ slow-growing; relatively inactive; sluggish.

induce /ĭn doos′/ to cause something to happen, especially to cause labor to begin.

induced abortion intentional abortion by medicinal or mechanical means.

induction /ĭn dŭk′shən/ the act or process of inducing or causing to occur, such as in enzyme production and anesthesia administration.

induration /ĭn′doo rā′shən/ an area of soft tissue or organ hardening.

indwelling /ĭn′dwĕl′ĭng/ existing or placed in the body to serve as a vessel for drainage, as a catheter, or for the administration of food and medications. [in- + dwelling]

indwelling catheter /kăth′ĭ tər/ a soft plastic tube inserted into the bladder to provide drainage for an extended period of time.

inebriated /ĭ nē′brē ā′tĭd/ cognitively impaired due to the consumption of too much alcohol.

in extremis /ĭn ĭk strē′mĭs/ about to die.

infancy /ĭn′fən sē/ the earliest stage of childhood.

infant /ĭn′fənt/ a child up to two years of age.

infant formula a cow or goat milk or soy-based substitute for breast milk.

infanticide /ĭn făn′tə sīd′/ 1. the act or practice of killing infants. 2. a person who kills an infant.

infantile /ĭn′fən tīl′, -tĭl/ of or relating to infants or infancy.

infantile autism /ô′tĭz əm/ one of a family of neuropsychiatric disorders characterized by a lack of social interaction and communication, withdrawal, speech impairments, and repetitive abnormal behavior.

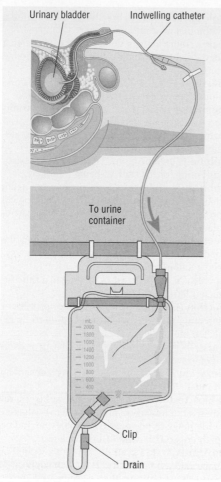

Indwelling Catheter

infantile paralysis /pə răl′ə sĭs/ a viral disease found only in humans, characterized by inflammation of the central nervous system, fever, vomiting, headache, sore throat, and paralysis. *Also called* polio, poliomyelitis.

infantilism /ĭn′fən tə lĭz′əm, ĭn făn′-/ extreme immaturity in an adult characterized by infantile mentality, stunted growth or dwarfism, and sexual immaturity.

infant mortality rate the ratio of deaths to live births during the first year of life; the number of deaths before their first birthday per 1000 live births.

infarct /ĭn′färkt/ an area of dead tissue, usually in an organ, caused by insufficient blood flow, often as a result of an embolus or thrombus.

infarction /ĭn färk′shən/ the formation of an infarct.

infect /ĭn fĕkt′/ to invade the body with pathogenic microorganisms.

infection /ĭn fĕk′shən/ invasion of pathogenic microorganisms in the body.

infectious disease /ĭn fĕk′shəs/ any disease caused by the invasion, growth, and reproduction of a pathogenic microorganism and usually transmissible from one person to another.

infectious mononucleosis /mŏn′ō nōō′klē ō′ sĭs/ an infection with the Epstein-Barr virus, a herpes virus, commonly called mono, characterized by fever, sore throat, fatigue, and swollen lymph nodes. *Also called* glandular fever, mononucleosis.

inferior /ĭn fêr′ē ər/ below, lower.

inferior vena cava /vē′nə kā′və/ the large vein that carries deoxygenated blood from below the waist to the right atrium of the heart. The superior vena cava carries deoxygenated blood from the upper part of the body.

infertile /ĭn fûr′təl/ unable to conceive. [in- + fertile]

infertility /ĭn′fər tĭl′ĭ tē/ the inability to conceive.

infestation /ĭn′fĕ stā′shən/ the state of being invaded and overrun.

infiltrate /ĭn fĭl′trāt, ĭn′fĭl trāt′/ to penetrate or permeate with a liquid or gas.

infiltration /ĭn′fĭl trā′shən/ the act or process of infiltrating.

infirm /ĭn fûrm′/ feeble because of ill health or old age.

inflamed /ĭn flāmd′/ resulting from or affected by inflammation.

inflammation /ĭn′flə mā′shən/ a tissue reaction to injury or infection, characterized by pain, swelling, and redness.

inflammatory /ĭn flăm′ə tôr′ē/ characterized by or caused by inflammation.

inflammatory bowel disease (IBD) any of a group of intestinal diseases characterized by inflammation of the intestines, abdominal pain, and diarrhea.

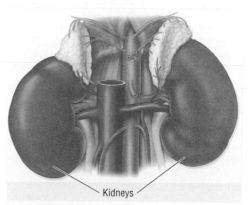

Inferior Vena Cava

influenza /ĭn'floo ĕn'zə/   a viral infection of the respiratory tract. *Also called* flu.

informed consent   agreement to undergo a treatment, study, or surgery by a patient who has fully understood all the details, risks, and relevant facts.

infra-   *prefix.* inferior, below, or beneath: *for example,* infracostal.

infrabulge /ĭn'frə bŭlj'/   the area of the tooth where the retaining clasp for a removable denture is placed.

infraclusion /ĭn'frə kloo'zhən/   position of a tooth that does not reach the line of occlusion.

infracostal /ĭn'frə kŏs'təl/   beneath the ribs. [infra- + costal]

infraction /ĭn frăk'shən/   a fracture, especially an incomplete fracture with no displacement of bone.

infraorbital /ĭn'frə ôr'bĭ təl/   below the orbital cavity. [infra- + orbital]

infrapatellar /ĭn'frə pə tĕl'ər/   below the kneecap. [infra- + patellar]

infraspinatus muscle /ĭn'frə spī nā'təs/   a muscle in the rotator cuff group of the shoulder that moves the humerus, as during external rotation.

infrasternal /ĭn'frə stûr'nəl/   below the sternum. [infra- + sternal]

infundibulum /ĭn'fŭn dĭb'yə ləm/   (*pl.* **infundibula** /ĭn'fŭn dĭb'yə lə/)   any of various funnel-shaped passages or structures of the body.

infuse /ĭn fyooz'/   **1.** to extract by soaking. **2.** to introduce a fluid into the body through a vein.

infusion /ĭn fyoo'zhən/   **1.** the act or process of infusing. **2.** a medicinal preparation to be infused.

ingestion /ĭn jĕs'chən/   **1.** the act of introducing food and drink into the body through the mouth. **2.** the taking in of particles by a phagocytic cell.

ingrown toenail   a condition that occurs when the edge of the toenail becomes embedded in the surrounding flesh.

inguinal /ĭng'gwə nəl/   of or relating to the groin.

inguinal canal   a passage in the lower abdominal wall that allows the passage of the spermatic cord in the male and contains the round ligament in the female.

inguinal hernia /hûr'nē ə/   a hernia in the inguinal canal.

inguinal region   the lower region of the abdomen on either side of the pubic region.

inhalant /ĭn hā'lənt/   something that is used in or for inhaling, especially a drug.

inhalation /ĭn'hə lā'shən/   **1.** the act or process of inhaling. **2.** a medicinal preparation administered by inhaling.

inhale /ĭn hāl'/   **1.** to breathe in. **2.** to inspire a medicinal mist into the lungs.

inhaler /ĭn hā'lər/   a device used to disperse a medicinal mist which is then breathed into the lungs.

inheritance /ĭn hĕr'ĭ təns/   genetic transmission, as of a disease, from parents to child.

inherited /ĭn hĕr'ĭ tĭd/   having been transmitted from parents to child.

inhibit /ĭn hĭb'ĭt/   to suppress, restrain, decrease, or prevent.

inhibition /ĭn'hĭ bĭsh'ən/   the act or process of inhibiting, or the state of being inhibited.

inhibitor /ĭn hĭb'ĭ tər/   **1.** a drug or other agent that stops or slows a chemical or physiological process. **2.** a nerve that stops or slows a particular action when stimulated.

inject /ĭn jĕkt'/   to introduce a fluid into the body by means of injection, usually with a syringe and needle.

injected /ĭn jĕk'tĭd/   of or relating to a fluid injected into the body.

injection /ĭn jĕk'shən/   **1.** the act or process of injecting. **2.** a medicinal preparation to be injected into the body.

injure /ĭn'jər/   to inflict physical harm or damage; to wound.

injury /ĭn'jə rē/   damage or loss caused by trauma.

inkblot test   a test in which a subject's responses to inkblot prints are used to evaluate a wide range of personality variables, including pathology. *Also called* Rorschach test.

inlay /ĭn'lā'/   **1.** a graft of skin into a wound or bone into a bone cavity. **2.** an arch support. **3.** a preshaped filling that is cemented into a tooth cavity.

innate immunity   naturally occurring immunity not due to vaccination or infection.

inner ear   the most complex portion of the ear, involved in hearing and balance, located within the temporal bone, composed of the semicircular canals, vestibule, and cochlea.

innervate /ĭ nûr'vāt, ĭn'ər vāt'/   **1.** to supply with nerves. **2.** to stimulate action.

Injection

innervation /ĭn'ûr vā'shən/ **1.** the distribution of nerves. **2.** the degree of stimulation.

innominate bone /ĭ nŏm'ə nĭt/ either of the two bones making up the pelvis. *Also called* hip bone.

inoculate /ĭ nŏk'yə lāt'/ to implant (a disease agent or antigen) in someone to stimulate disease resistance. *Also called* vaccinate.

inoculation /ĭ nŏk'yə lā'shən/ the implanting of a disease agent or antigen in someone to stimulate disease resistance. *Also called* vaccination.

inotropic /ĭn'ō trŏp'ĭk/ affecting muscle contraction, especially of the heart muscle.

inpatient /ĭn'pā'shənt/ a patient admitted to a hospital for treatment while staying for a period of time, usually at least 48 hours. [in- + patient]

inquest /ĭn'kwĕst'/ a legal inquiry into a death.

insane /ĭn sān'/ afflicted with or showing signs of insanity.

insanity /ĭn săn'ĭ tē/ **1.** persistent mental derangement involving the inability to distinguish the real from the imagined. **2.** a degree of mental malfunctioning sufficient to excuse an individual of legal responsibility for a crime.

inseminate /ĭn sĕm'ə nāt'/ to introduce semen into the female reproductive tract.

insemination /ĭn sĕm'ə nə'shən/ the introduction of semen into the female reproductive tract.

insertion /ĭn sûr'shən/ **1.** the point at which a muscle attaches to the bone or other part that it moves. **2.** the application of a dental prosthesis into the mouth.

insidious /ĭn sĭd'ē əsn/ said of a disease that progresses without showing symptoms, so that a patient often presents with an already advanced illness.

insight /ĭn'sīt'/ understanding of the factors that motivate one's behavior.

in situ /ĭn sī'tōō, sĭt'ōō/ in the original place or position, as a tumor (carcinoma in situ).

insomnia /ĭn sŏm'nē ə/ chronic condition characterized by an inability to fall asleep for any significant length of time.

inspiration /ĭn'spə rā'shən/ inhalation of air into the lungs.

inspire /ĭn spīr'/ to draw air into the lungs.

instability /ĭn'stə bĭl'ĭ tē/ **1.** lacking stability. **2.** of a joint, dislocating easily during normal activity. [in- + stability]

instep /ĭn'stĕp'/ the arched upper surface of the foot between the ankle and the toes.

instillation /ĭn'stə lā'shən/ pouring or injecting a liquid one drop at a time.

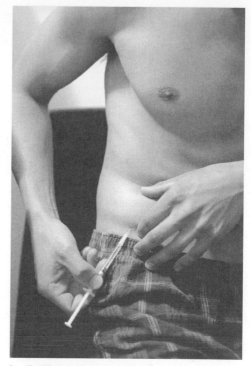

Insulin (Diabetic Self-Injecting)

instinct /ĭn'stĭngkt/ a pattern of behavior with which all members of a given species are born.

instrument /ĭn'strə mənt/ a tool, especially a surgical tool.

insufficiency /ĭn'sə fĭsh'ən sē/ **1.** inadequate supply or amount of. **2.** lack of complete function or power. [in- + sufficiency]

insulin /ĭn'sə lĭn/ a hormone secreted by the pancreas that regulates glycogen storage in the liver, facilitates the entry of glucose into cells, and helps regulate carbohydrate and fat metabolism, especially in converting glucose to glycogen; also produced as a medication for people with diabetes.

insulin-dependent diabetes /dī'ə bē'tĭs, -tēz/ or **insulin-dependent diabetes mellitus (IDDM)** /mĕl'ĭ təs, mə lī'tĭs/ a chronic autoimmune disease caused by insufficient insulin production, characterized by high sugar (glucose) levels in the blood, excessive thirst, frequent urination, and weight loss. *Also called* diabetes mellitus, juvenile diabetes, Type 1 diabetes.

insulin-like growth factor (IGF) either of two polypeptides similar to insulin in structure, secreted during early childhood, that regulate growth hormones.

insulinoma /ĭn'sə lə nō'mə/ a benign islet tumor that secretes insulin. [insulin + -oma]

insulin pump a portable device that infuses insulin continuously, with additional doses to cover meals, used by people with diabetes to control blood sugar levels.

insulin reaction low blood sugar due to excessive insulin, causing coma.

insulin resistance a state of reduced effectiveness of insulin in lowering blood sugar levels.

insulin shock extremely low blood sugar level caused by an insulin overdose, characterized by fatigue, dizziness, fainting, convulsions, and coma.

intake /ĭn′tāk′/ **1.** the process of taking in or consuming. **2.** the amount taken in.

integument /ĭn tĕg′yə mənt/ the outer protective membrane of the body including the skin, hair, and nails.

integumentary system /ĭn tĕg′yə mĕn′tə rē/ the skin and all of its structures.

intelligence /ĭn tĕl′ə jəns/ the capacity to learn and apply that knowledge toward a goal.

intelligence quotient (IQ) a measurement of the capacity to learn using a standardized test.

intensive care unit (ICU) a section of the hospital containing the equipment and professionals needed to provide critical care.

inter- *prefix.* between; within: *for example,* intercostal.

interaction /ĭn′tər ăk′shən/ the effects of actions that take place between two entities. [inter- + action]

interatrial septum /ĭn′tər ā′trē əl sĕp′təm/ the wall between the left and right atria of the heart.

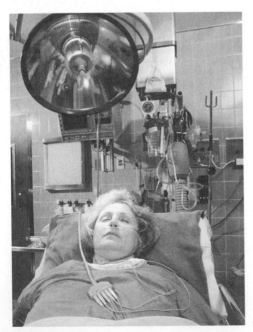

Intensive Care Unit

intercellular /ĭn′tər sĕl′yə lər/ located among or between cells. [inter- + cellular]

intercostal /ĭn′tər kŏs′təl/ located between the ribs. [inter- + costal]

intercostal muscle the skeletal muscle located between the ribs.

intercourse /ĭn′tər kôrs′/ **1.** sexual intercourse. *Also called* coitus. **2.** communications or interactions occurring between people.

intercurrent disease /ĭn′tər kûr′ənt/ a disease that occurs during the course of another disease.

interdental /ĭn′tər dĕn′təl/ **1.** of, relating to, or located between the teeth. **2.** designed to be used between the teeth. [inter- + dental]

interdigit /ĭn′tər dĭj′ĭt/ the area between two contiguous fingers or toes. [inter- + digit]

interdisciplinary /ĭn′tər dĭs′ə plə nĕr′ē/ involving two or more specialties in medicine and science.

interferon /ĭn′tər fêr′ŏn/ a protein capable of inhibiting viral penetration of cells, produced by cells that have been infected by a virus.

interictal /ĭn′tər ĭk′təl/ of, relating to, or occurring during, the interval between seizures. [inter- + ictal]

interleukin /ĭn′tər lōō′kĭn/ **(IL)** any of a class of proteins called lymphokines that function in regulating the immune system.

intermediate care facility (ICF) a care setting for patients who do not require the skilled nursing provided in a hospital or skilled nursing facility.

intermittent claudication /ĭn′tər mĭt′ənt klô′dĭ kā′shən/ a condition caused by inadequate blood supply to the legs, characterized by pain, cramping, and weakness in the legs while walking.

intermittent positive-pressure breathing (IPPB) or **ventilation (IPPV)** mechanical inflation of the lungs using a bag and mask or an endotracheal tube and a ventilator to supply the lungs with air.

intern /ĭn′tûrn/ an advanced student or graduate of medical school who assists in medical care in a hospital.

internal /ĭn tûr′nəl/ located or effective within the body.

internal cardiac defibrillator /kär′dē ăk′ dē fĭb′rə lā′tər/ a device implanted within the body to recognize and correct abnormal heart rhythms.

internal carotid artery /kə rŏt′ĭd är′tə rē/ one of the two branches of each of the two common carotid arteries; it is located deep within the neck and branches into smaller arteries.

International Class of Disease (ICD) *See* IDC-9-CM.

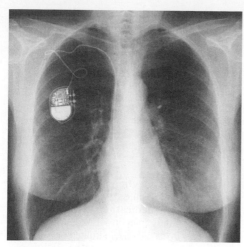

Internal Pacemaker

internal ear the most complex portion of the ear, involved in hearing and balance; it is located within the temporal bone and composed of the semicircular canals, vestibule, and cochlea.

internal fixation the stabilization of fractured bones using wires, screws, pins, and plates to attach them to each other and maintain this position for healing.

internal genitalia /jĕn′ĭ tāl′yə/ **1.** the ovaries, fallopian tubes, uterus, cervix, and vagina of the female. **2.** the testes, epididymis, vas deferens, seminal vesicle, ejaculatory duct, bulbourethral gland, and the prostate of the male.

internal medicine the branch of medicine concerned with the diagnosis and treatment of the internal organs, primarily in adults.

internal organ a main organ located inside the body.

internal pacemaker a small, oval electrical device that is implanted within the body to regulate heart rhythm or maintain a minimum heart rate.

internal respiration the exchange of gases that takes place between blood and tissues.

international unit (IU) an internationally standardized measure or amount of a substance.

internist /ĭn′tûr nĭst, ĭn tûr′-/ a physician who specializes in the diagnoses and treatment of adults.

interphalangeal joint /ĭn′tər fə lăn′jē əl, -făl′ ən jē′əl/ the joint of the finger or where each of the fingers meets the hand, made more prominent when the fist is closed. *Also called* knuckle, metacarpophalangeal joint.

interstice /ĭn tûr′stĭs/ the small spaces, cracks, crevices, and gaps between things.

interstitial /ĭn′tər stĭsh′əl/ being between things that are close together.

interstitial cystitis /sĭ stī′tĭs/ a chronic condition characterized by inflammation of the bladder, causing reduced bladder capacity.

interstitial fluid the fluid filling the spaces between tissue cells.

intertrigo /ĭn′tər trī′gō/ inflammation of adjacent areas of skin caused by friction and chafing, occurring in folds of skin, beneath the breast, in axillae (armpits), etc.

interval /ĭn′tər vəl/ the time or space between two events or objects.

intervention /ĭn′tər vĕn′shən/ the process of interfering with the intent to modify a process or situation, especially referring to a confrontation with a person addicted to illegal drugs.

interventional /ĭn′tər vĕn′shə nəl/ of or relating to intervention.

interventricular foramen /ĭn′tər vĕn trĭk′yə lər fə rā′mən/ the small openings from the left and right ventricle of the brain that connects the third ventricle in the diencephalon with the lateral ventricle in the cerebral hemisphere.

interventricular septal defect /sĕp′təl dē′fĕkt/ common heart malformation consisting of a small or sometimes large opening between the two ventricles. *Also called* ventricular septal defect.

interventricular septum /sĕp′təm/ the curved wall between the ventricles of the heart. *Also called* ventricular septum.

intervertebral /ĭn′tər vûr′tə brəl/ located between vertebrae. [inter + vertebral]

intervertebral disk any of the fibrocartilage disks located between vertebrae.

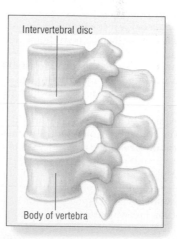

Intervertebral disc

Body of vertebra

Intervertebral Disk

intestinal /ĭn tĕs′tə nəl/   of, relating to, or constituting the intestine.

intestinal gas   vapors located in the intestines and expelled through the rectum.

intestinal obstruction   any form of intestinal blockage including infolding, malformation, tumor, a foreign body, or inflammation.

intestine /ĭn tĕs′tĭn/   the tubular organ in the abdomen that completes digestion, consisting of the large and small intestines.

in-the-canal hearing aid   an instrument used to aid mild to moderate hearing loss, custom-made to fit in the canal of the ear.

in-the-ear aid   in-the-ear hearing aid.

in-the-ear hearing aid   an instrument used to aid mild to moderate hearing loss, custom-made to fit in the outer ear.

intoxication /ĭn tŏk′sĭ kā′shən/   **1.** a state produced by any toxic substance or poison, especially by drugs or alcohol. **2.** a state of emotional excitement.

intra-   *prefix. within: for example,* intracardiac.

intra-aortic /ĭn′trə ā ôr′tĭk/   situated or occurring within the aorta.

intra-arterial /ĭn′trə är têr′ē əl/   within an artery or arteries.

intracapsular /ĭn′trə kăp′sə lər/   situated or occurring within a capsule. [intra- + capsular]

intracardiac /ĭn′trə kär′dē ăk′/   situated or occurring within the heart. [intra- + cardiac]

intracavitary /ĭn′trə kăv′ĭ tĕr′ē/   situated or occurring within an organ or body cavity.

intracellular /ĭn′trə sĕl′yə lər/   situated or occurring within a cell or cells. [intra- + cellular]

intracerebral /ĭn trə sə rē′brəl, -sĕr′ə-/   situated or occurring within the brain. [intra- + cerebral]

intracoronary /ĭn′trə kôr′ə nĕr′ē/   situated or occurring within the arteries of the heart. [intra- + coronary]

intracorporeal /ĭn′trə kôr pôr′ē əl/   situated or occurring within the body. [intra- + corporeal]

intracorporeal electrohydraulic lithotripsy /ĭ lĕk′trō hī drô′lĭk lĭth′ə trĭp′sē/   use of an endoscope to break up stones within the urinary system.

intracranial /ĭn′trə krā′nē əl/   situated or occurring within the skull. [intra- + cranial]

intracranial pressure (ICP)   pressure within the cavity of the skull.

intractable /ĭn trăk′tə bəl/   stubborn; difficult to alleviate, cure, or control.

intracutaneous /ĭn′trə kyōō tā′nē əs/   situated or occurring within the skin. [intra- + cutaneous]

intracytoplasmic sperm injection (ICSI) /ĭn′ trə sī′tō plăz′mĭk/   fertilization outside the body by injecting a single sperm into an egg, and then implanting the egg into the uterus.

intradermal /ĭn′trə dûr′məl/   situated or occurring within the layers of the skin; location for TB skin test. [intra- + dermal]

intradermal injection   an injection into the skin.

intradermal test   a test for allergy in which a small amount of the possible allergen is injected into the skin.

intramuscular (IM) /ĭn′trə mŭs′kyə lər/   situated or occurring within a muscle. [intra- + muscular]

intramuscular injection   an injection of a medication into a muscle.

intramuscular medication   any medication administered by injecting it into a muscle.

intranasal /ĭn′trə nā′zəl/   situated or occurring within the nose. [intra- + nasal]

intraocular /ĭn′trə ŏk′yə lər/   situated or occurring within the eyeball. [intra- + ocular]

intraocular lens (IOL)   an artificial lens implanted into the eye to replace a damaged natural lens, or during cataract surgery.

intraocular pressure (IOP) or **intraocular tension**   the pressure of the intraocular fluid within the eyeball that sustains its firm round shape; measured in testing for glaucoma.

intraoral /ĭn′trə ôr′əl/   situated or occurring within the mouth. [intra- + oral]

intraosseous /ĭn′trə ŏs′ē əs/   situated or occurring within a bone. [intra- + osseous]

intrapartum /ĭn′trə pär′təm/   occurring during labor and delivery.

intraperitoneal /ĭn′trə pĕr′ĭ tə nē′əl/   situated or occurring within the peritoneum. [intra- + peritoneal]

intraspinal /ĭn′trə spī′nəl/   situated or occurring within the spine.

intrathecal /ĭn′trə thē′kəl/   situated or occurring under the arachnoid membrane of the brain or spinal cord; location of spinal fluid.

intrathecal injection   an injection through the lumbar and beneath the arachnoid membrane, as for spinal anesthesia.

intrathoracic /ĭn′trə thô răs′ĭk/   situated or occurring within the thorax. [intra- + thoracic]

intrauterine /ĭn′trə yōō′tər ĭn/   situated or occurring within the uterus. [intra- + uterine]

intrauterine contraceptive device (IUD) /kŏn′trə sĕp′tĭv/   intrauterine device.

intrauterine device (IUD)   a birth control device inserted and left in the uterus to prevent conception.

intrauterine insemination (IUI) /ĭn sĕm′ə nā′shən/   a procedure in which sperm is inserted directly into the womb through a thin catheter.

intravenous (IV) /ĭn′trə vē′nəs/   situated, occurring, or administered into a vein. [intra- + venous]

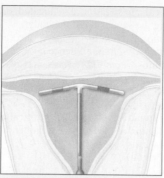

Intrauterine device (IUD)

Intrauterine Device

intravenous drip   continuous administration of medication, nutrients, saline solution, etc., at a measured rate through a vein

intravenous feeding   delivery of a nutrient-rich solution through a vein.

intravenous injection (IV)   an injection into a vein.

intravenous medication   any medication administered by intravenous injection.

intravenous pyelogram (IVP) /pī′ə lə grăm′/ x-ray image of the kidneys and ureters taken after intravenous injection of a contrast medium as it is excreted by the kidneys.

intravenous pyelography /pī′ə lŏg′rə fē/ x-ray photography of the kidneys and ureters after intravenous injection of a contrast medium.

intraventricular /ĭn′trə vĕn trĭk′yə lər/ situated or occurring within or between the ventricles in the brain. [intra- + ventricular]

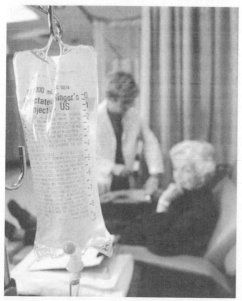

Intravenous Medication

intraventricular septal defect /sĕp′təl dē′fĕkt/ an abnormal opening in the ventricular septum, usually congenital and generally requiring surgical repair. *Also called* ventricular septal defect.

intraventricular septum /sĕp′təm/ the membranous, muscular partition that separates the right and left ventricles of the heart. *Also called* ventricular septum.

intrinsic /ĭn trĭn′sĭk, -zĭk/ **1.** of or relating to the essential nature or constitution of a thing. **2.** situated within or belonging only to the body part on which it acts.

introitus /ĭn trō′ĭ təs/ the orifice or opening into a canal or hollow organ.

introjection /ĭn′trō jĕk′shən/ the unconscious process of internalizing the characteristics of a person into one's psyche.

introversion /ĭn′trə vûr′zhən/ **1.** in psychology, the quality of being concerned only with one's own needs, thoughts, desires, etc. **2.** the turning inside out of a part or organ.

introvert 1. *n.* /ĭn′trə vûrt′/ in psychology, someone who is only involved with his or her own needs, thoughts, desires, etc. **2.** *v.* /ĭn′trə vûrt′/ to turn a part or organ inside out.

intubate /ĭn′tōō bāt′/ to insert a tube into a hollow organ or passageway.

intubation /ĭn′tōō bā′shən/ the insertion of a tube into a hollow organ or passageway to hold it open or prevent obstruction, especially into the trachea.

intussusception /ĭn′təs sə sĕp′shən/ **1.** the folding in of an outer layer to form a pocket, especially the telescoping of the intestine into itself. **2.** incorporation of new substances among existing components of living tissue. **3.** disease of toddlers: passage of a portion of intestine into the next portion by means of peristalsis, and causing compression of the

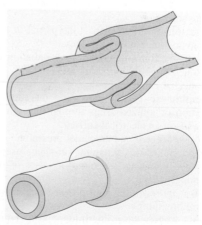

Intussusception

blood supply, obstruction, sometimes sepsis and death if not reduced (pushed back out) surgically or by barium enema.

in utero /ĭn yōō′tə rō′/   in the uterus.

invalid /ĭn′və lĭd/   **1.** *n.* a person who is too weak or sick to take care of him- or herself. **2.** *adj.* of, for, or involving a person who is very weak or sick.

invasive /ĭn vā′sĭv/   **1.** having the tendency to spread and infect healthy tissue. **2.** entering the body by incision or puncture, said of surgery.

inversion /ĭn vûr′zhən/   the state of being, or act of inverting, reversing, or changing direction.

in vitro /ĭn vē′trō/   outside the body, in an artificial environment, in a test tube.

in vitro fertilization (IVF)   fertilization of an egg by a sperm, occurring outside the body, in a laboratory dish or test tube.

in vivo /ĭn vē′vō/   within the body.

involuntary /ĭn vŏl′ən tĕr′ē/   without control, or against one's will. [in- + voluntary]

involuntary muscle   any muscle that functions without conscious control.

involute /ĭn′və lōōt′/   **1.** to curve or roll inward. **2.** to decrease and return to normal size after being enlarged.

involution /ĭn′və lōō′shən/   **1.** inward rolling or curving. **2.** shrinking; returning to normal size.

iodine /ī′ə dīn′/   **1.** a nonmetallic element, component of certain intravenous dyes used for x-rays (IVP dye). **2.** a solution of iodine and ethyl alcohol used as an antiseptic for wounds.

IOL   *abbreviation.* intraocular lens.

ion /ī′ŏn, ī′ən/   an atom or group of atoms that has acquired an electrical charge by gaining or losing one or more electrons.

ion channel   a protein that serves as a channel in and out of cell membranes through which ions may pass.

ionization /ī′ə nə zā′shən/   the partial or total conversion of atoms into ions.

ionizing radiation   high-energy radiation capable of producing ionization in the substances it passes through.

iontophoresis /ī ŏn′tō fə rē′sĭs/   the administration of ionized drugs through the skin by means of an electrical current.

IOP   *abbreviation.* intraocular pressure.

ipecac /ĭp′ĭ kăk′/   a natural substance used to induce vomiting, especially in cases of poisoning.

IPPB   *abbreviation.* intermittent positive-pressure breathing.

IPPV   *abbreviation.* intermittent positive-pressure ventilation.

ipsilateral /ĭp′sə lăt′ər əl/   located on or affecting the same side of the body.

IPV   *abbreviation.* inactivated polio vaccine.

IQ   *abbreviation.* intelligence quotient.

irid-, irido-   *combining form.* iris of the eye: *for example,* iridalgia.

iridalgia /ĭr′ĭ dăl′jē ə, -jə/   pain in the iris or irises. [irid- + -algia]

iridectomy /ĭr′ĭ dĕk′tə mē/   surgical removal of a portion of the iris, one treatment for glaucoma. [irid- + -ectomy]

irides /ĭr′ĭ dēz′/   a plural of iris.

iriditis /ĭr′ĭ dī′tĭs/   inflammation of the iris. [irid- + -itis]

iridocele /ĭr′ĭ də sēl′/   protrusion of a portion of the iris through a corneal defect. [irido- + -cele]

iridocyclitis /ĭr′ĭ dō sī klī′tĭs/   inflammation of the iris and the ciliary body.

iridodilator /ĭr′ĭ dō dī lā′tər/   a substance that causes the pupil of the eye to dilate. [irido- + dilator]

iridology /ĭr′ĭ dŏl′ə jē/   the study of the iris of the eye; in some types of alternative medicine, this is a diagnostic tool. [irido- + -logy]

iridomalacia /ĭr′ĭ dō mə lā′shə/   degenerative softening of the iris. [irido- + malacia]

iridopathy /ĭr′ĭ dŏp′ə thē/   disease of the iris. [irido- + -pathy]

iridoplegia /ĭr′ĭ dō plē′jē ə, -jə/ or **iridoparalysis** /ĭr′ĭ dō pə răl′ə sĭs/   paralysis of the sphincter of the iris. [irido- + -plegia *or* paralysis]

iridoptosis /ĭr′ĭ dŏp tō′sĭs/   prolapse or drooping of the iris. [irido- + -ptosis]

iridorrhexis /ĭr′ĭ dō rĕk′sĭs/   surgical detachment of the iris from its peripheral attachment. [irido- + -rrhexis]

iridoschisis /ĭr′ĭ dŏs′kə sĭs/   separation of the front layer of the iris from the back layer. [irido- + -schisis]

iridotomy /ĭr′ĭ dŏt′ə mē/   artificial formation or enlargement of the pupil by cutting the iris. [irido- + -tomy]

iris /ī′rĭs/ (*pl.* **irises** or **irides** /ĭr′ĭ dēz′/)   the round muscular pigmented curtain of the eye, the center of which is perforated by the pupil.

iritis /ī rī′tĭs/   inflammation of the iris of the eye.

iron /ī′ərn/   an essential mineral necessary for synthesis of hemoglobin, the protein which carries oxygen in the blood.

iron deficiency anemia /ə nē′mē ə/   low levels of red blood cells and hemoglobin due to insufficient iron in the diet.

irradiated /ĭ rā′dē ā′tĭd/   exposed to or treated with radiation.

irradiation /ĭ rā′dē ā′shən/   the act or process of exposing or treating with radiation.

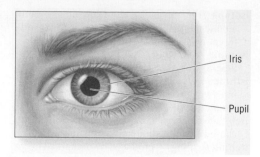

Iris

Pupil

Iris

irrational /ĭ răsh′ə nəl/ not governed by reason; not rational. [ir- + rational]

irreducible hernia /ĭr′ĭ dōō′sə bəl hûr′nē ə/ a hernia that cannot be fixed by manually returning it to its proper position.

irregular bones those bones with complex form, such as the vertebrae.

irrigate /ĭr′ĭ gāt′/ to wash out a cavity or wound with saline or some other sterile solution.

irrigation /ĭr′ĭ gā′shən/ the act or process of washing out.

irritable bowel syndrome (IBS) a gastrointestinal disorder characterized by abdominal contractions, pain, bloating, irregular bowel movements, diarrhea, and constipation.

irritant /ĭr′ĭ tənt/ something that causes irritation.

irritant contact dermatitis /dûr′mə tī′tĭs/ an inflamed itchy rash caused by the contact of an allergen or persistent irritation to the skin.

irritation /ĭr′ĭ tā′shən/ **1.** the normal response of a nerve to a stimulus. **2.** the inflammatory reaction of tissue to toxin or injury.

irruption /ĭ rŭp′shən/ the breaking through to the surface, as of the skin or gums.

ischemia /ĭ skē′mē ə/ insufficient circulation due to blockage of a blood vessel.

ischemic stroke /ĭ skē′mik/ sudden damage to nerve cells in the brain resulting from hemorrage into a part of the brain, or a clot in a blood vessel causing damage to brain tissue deprived of blood flow. *Also called* cerebrovascular accident, hemorrhagic stroke.

ischi-, ischio- *combining form.* ischium: *for example,* ischiodynia.

ischial /ĭs′kē əl/ of or relating to the ischium. [ischi- + -al]

ischial bursitis /bər sī′tĭs/ inflammation of the bursa of the buttocks due to prolonged sitting on a hard surface.

ischialgia /ĭs′kē ăl′jē ə, -jə/ pain in the ischium. *Also called* ischiodynia. [ischi- + -algia]

ischiodynia /ĭs′kē ō dĭn′ē ə/ pain in the ischium. *Also called* ischialgia. [ischio- + -dynia]

ischiofemoral /ĭs′kē ō fĕm′ər əl/ of or relating to the ischium and the femur. [ischio- + femoral]

ischioneuralgia /ĭs′kē ō nōō răl′jē ə, -jə/ sharp pain in the ischium. [ischio- + neuralgia]

ischium /ĭs′kē əm/ the bone that constitutes the inferior and posterior portion of the pelvis and constitutes a small part of the acetabulum, articulating with the femur.

islet cell /ī′lĭt/ **cancer** or **carcinoma** /kär′sə nō′mə/ a malignant but often treatable form of islet cell tumor.

islet cell tumor an endocrine tumor composed of cells similar to those in the normal islet of Langerhans; may be benign or malignant and usually hormonally active, producing insulin, glucagon, or other active molecules.

islets of Langerhans /läng′ər häns′, -hänz′/ the endocrine cell clusters of the pancreas that secrete insulin and glucagon.

-ism *suffix.* state or condition of: *for example,* icthyotoxism.

iso- *prefix.* equal; uniform: *for example,* isocellular.

isocellular /ī′sō sĕl′yə lər/ composed of cells of uniform size and character. [iso- + cellular]

isoflavones /ī′sō flā′vōnz/ a group of phytoestrogens found in soybeans; currently being studied for health benefits.

isokinetic /ī′sō kĭ nĕt′ĭk/ **1.** being equal in force. **2.** contracting against a constant resistance, said of a muscle.

isokinetic exercise a muscle-building exercise performed by contracting muscle against a constant resistance.

isolate /ī′sə lāt′/ to remove and set apart; to quarantine.

isolation /ī′sə lā′shən/ **1.** the act of isolating or the state of being isolated. **2.** a room in which an infectious patient is isolated.

isoleucine /ī′sō lōō′sēn/ an essential amino acid that is isomeric with leucine.

isomer /ī′sə mər/ one of two or more organic compounds having the same molecular composition, but which differ in placement of one or more individual molecules within the compound.

isomeric /ī′sə měr′ĭk/ being an isomer.

isometric /ī′sə mět′rĭk/ **1.** being equal in dimension and measure. **2.** sustained muscle length during contraction against resistance.

isometric exercise a muscle-building exercise performed by sustaining muscle contraction against resistance, without changing the length of the muscle.

Isotonic Exercise

isometropia /ĭ′sō mĭ trō′pē ə/　uniform refraction in both eyes.

isopathy /ĭ sŏp′ə thē/　**1.** treatment of viral or bacterial disease with small, dilute doses of the infecting microorganism. **2.** treatment of a diseased organ by having the patient consume the same organ from a healthy animal. [iso- + -pathy]

isothermal /ĭ′sō thûr′məl/　equal or constant temperature. [iso- + thermal]

isotonic /ĭ′sə tŏn′ĭk/　**1.** of equal tension. **2.** having an equal concentration of solutes as the blood. **3.** maintaining constant muscle contraction while the muscle length changes. [iso- + tonic]

isotonic exercise a muscle-building and mobility-increasing exercise involving isotonic contraction.

isotope /ī′sə tōp′/　an atom having the same atomic number (thus the same name) but a different mass number from similar atoms.

isotopic /ī′sə tŏp′ĭk/　of or relating to an isotope.

isthmus /ĭs′məs/　a narrow passage connecting two larger structures or cavities, as the isthmus of the thyroid.

itch /ĭch/　an irritating sensation of the skin, caused by mild stimulation of pain receptors.

itching /ĭch′ĭng/　produced by or marked by an itch.

-itis　*suffix.* inflammation or disease of: *for example,* iritis.

IU　*abbreviation.* international unit.

IUD　*abbreviation.* intrauterine contraceptive device.

IUI　*abbreviation.* intrauterine insemination.

IV　*abbreviation. adj.* **1.** intravenous. *n.* **2.** intravenous injection. **3.** intravenous drip.

IVF　*abbreviation.* in vitro fertilization.

IVP　*abbreviation.* intravenous pyelogram.

J

jacket /jăk'ĭt/ **1.** a bandage applied to the trunk of the body to immobilize it. **2.** a dental crown made of porcelain or acrylic resin.

Jacksonian seizure /jăk sō'nē ən/ a seizure in which abnormal movements or sensations spread from a focused area to adjacent points on the body.

Jakob-Creutzfeldt disease /yä'kəp kroits'fĕlt/ a severely degenerative disease that affects the brain, transmitted by a particle known as a prion; related to mad cow disease.

janiceps /jăn'ə sĕps'/ conjoined twins who have their heads fused together, but their faces looking in opposite directions.

Japanese encephalitis /ĕn sĕf'ə lī'tĭs/ a viral form of encephalitis that occurs in Japan and other Asian countries, transmitted by mosquitoes.

jaundice /jôn'dĭs/ a yellowish discoloration of the skin or whites of the eyes, due to high levels of bilirubin in the blood. *Also called* icterus.

jaw /jô/ or **jawbone** /jô'bōn'/ either of the two structures (upper and lower) in the mouth of vertebrates that form the framework of the mouth and which hold the teeth. *Also called* mandible, maxilla.

JCAHO *abbreviation.* Joint Commission on Accreditation of Healthcare Organizations, an organization that inspects hospitals and reviews and gives accreditation to healthcare organizations (www.jcaho.org).

jejun-, jejuno- *combining form.* jejunum: *for example,* jejunostomy.

jejunal /jĭ jōō'nəl/ of or relating to the jejunum. [jejun- + -al]

jejunectomy /jĭ jōō nĕk'tə mē/ surgical removal of all or part of the jejunum. [jejun- + -ectomy]

jejunoileitis /jĭ jōō'nō ĭl'ē ī'tĭs/ inflammation of the jejunum and the ileum. [jejuno- + ileitis]

jejunoileostomy /jĭ jōō'nō ĭl'ē ŏs'tə mē/ a surgical procedure to create a passageway between the jejunum and the ileum. [jejuno- + ileo- + -ostomy]

jejunoplasty /jĭ jōō'nə plăs'tē/ surgical repair of the jejunum. [jejuno- + -plasty]

jejunostomy /jĭ jōō nŏs'tə mē/ a surgical procedure during which an opening is formed between the abdominal wall and the jejunum, allowing artificial feeding. [jejuno- + -stomy]

jejunotomy /jĭ jōō nŏt'ə mē/ surgical incision into the jejunum. [jejuno- + -tomy]

jejunum /jĭ jōō'nəm/ the section of the small intestine that lies between the duodenum and the ileum, usually measuring about eight feet in length. *See illustration* on page 188.

Jenner's method /jĕn'ərz/ the process of immunizing a patient to a serious disease by inoculating them with a less serious form of the disease. Jenner vaccinated people against smallpox by using the much less severe cowpox.

Jewett staging system /jōō'ĭt/ a system, using the letters A, B, C, and D, for identifying the stage of prostate cancer, A being the least advanced, D being the most advanced.

Jin shin do /jĭn' shĭn' dō'/ a type of alternative medicine therapy that combines acupressure, breathing, and an understanding of how emotional tension affects the body with the goal of releasing the physical and emotional tension to relieve the physical problems.

jock itch a fungal infection of the groin area, usually occurring in men. *Also called* tinea cruris.

johnny /jŏn'ē/ a hospital gown, usually with an opening in the back.

joint /joint/ the point where two or more bones are connected, usually at least somewhat flexible. *See illustration* on page 188.

J-tube /jā'tōōb'/ a tube used for artificial feeding directly into the jejunum.

jugular /jŭg'yə lər/ **1.** *adj.* of, relating to, or found within the throat or neck. **2.** *n.* a jugular vein.

jugular vein a vein found in the neck that carries blood back from the head.

junction /jŭngk'shən/ the point or surface at which two parts, usually bones or layers of tissue, join together.

juncture /jŭngk'chər/ the point at which any two or more anatomical structures meet.

juvenile /jōō'və nəl, -nīl'/ occurring between infancy and adulthood.

juvenile diabetes /dī'ə bē'tĭs, -tēz/ a chronic autoimmune disease caused by insufficient insulin production, characterized by high sugar (glucose) levels in the blood, excessive

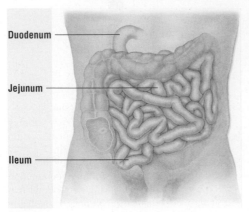

Jejunum

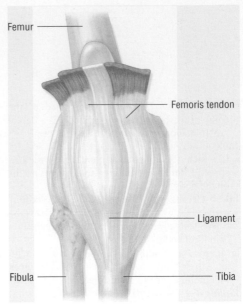

Joint

thirst, frequent urination, and weight loss, with a very early onset. *Also called* insulin-dependent diabetes, insulin-dependent diabetes mellitus, Type 1 diabetes.

juvenile rheumatoid arthritis /rōō′mə toid′ är thrī′tĭs/ a chronic autoimmune disease characterized by pain, inflammation, and stiffness in the joints, muscles, or connective tissue, with onset prior to adulthood. *See also* rheumatoid arthritis.

juxtaglomerular apparatus /jŭk′stə glŏ mer′ yə lər/ the collection of cells found near the glomerulus in the kidney that stimulate the secretion of aldonsterone, which plays a role in the self-regulation of kidney function.

K *abbreviation.* potassium.

kalemia /kə lē′mē ə/ the presence of potassium in the blood: excess is hyperkalemia; low potassium is hypokalemia.

Kaposi('s) sarcoma /kăp′ə zē(z) sär kō′mə, kə pō′sē(z)/ a malignant, vascular tumor of the skin, rare until recently appearing in patients with AIDS, because of their immunocompromised status.

Kartagener('s) syndrome /kär tä′gə nər(z)/ an inherited syndrome characterized by chronic sinusitis (inflammation of the sinuses) and bronchiectasis (permanent widening of the bronchi).

karyo- *combining form.* nucleus: *for example,* karyotype.

karyocyte /kăr′ē ə sīt′/ any cell containing a nucleus. [karyo- + -cyte]

karyogenesis /kăr′ē ō jĕn′ə sĭs/ the formation and development of a cell nucleus. [karyo- + -genesis]

karyokinesis /kăr′ē ō kĭ nē′sĭs/ the division of a cell nucleus into daughter cells. [karyo- + -kinesis]

karyoplasm /kăr′ē ə plăz′əm/ the protoplasm that comprises the nucleus of a cell. [karyo- + -plasm]

karyotype /kăr′ē ə tīp′/ the complete set of chromosomes of a cell or organism. [karyo- + type]

karyotyping /kăr′ē ə tī′pĭng/ the process of studying or making a representation of karyotypes.

Kawasaki('s) disease /kä′wə sä′kē(z)/ a childhood disease, mostly found in people of Asian descent, characterized by a rash, conjunctivitis, swollen lymph nodes, and fever.

Kearns-Sayre('s) syndrome /kûrnz′ sâr′(z)/ a disease caused by defects in mitochondrial DNA, resulting in a wide range of effects, including paralysis of the eye muscles, heart disease, and hearing loss.

Kegel exercises /kā′gəl/ exercises of the perineal muscles, performed either for prevention of or as a treatment for urinary incontinence.

keloid /kē′loid/ a scar formation of raised, reddish skin tissue, usually resulting from burns or excessive tissue repair.

keloplasty /kē′lə plăs′tē/ surgical removal of scar tissue.

kerat-, kerato- *combining form.* **1.** the cornea. **2.** horny tissue or cells: *for example,* keratitis, keratoderma.

keratectasia /kĕr′ə tĕk tā′zhə/ an abnormal bulging of the cornea. [kerat- + -ectasia]

keratectomy /kĕr′ə tĕk′tə mē/ the removal of tissue from the cornea. [kerat- + -ectomy]

keratin /kĕr′ə tĭn/ a tough, water-resistant protein found in the nails, hair, and outer layers of the skin.

keratitis /kĕr′ə tī′tĭs/ inflammation of the cornea. [kerat- + -itis]

keratoconjunctivitis /kĕr′ə tō kən jŭngk′tə vī′tĭs/ inflammation of the cornea and conjunctiva. [kerato- + conjunctivitis]

keratoconus /kĕr′ə tō kō′nəs/ abnormal conical protrusion of the cornea, usually affecting both eyes, treated with "hard" contact lenses or corneal transplant.

keratocyst /kĕr′ə tə sĭst′/ cyst in the jaw derived from dental lamina. [kerato- + cyst]

keratocyte /kĕr′ə tə sīt′/ **1.** a connective tissue cell of the cornea. **2.** a spiky or spindle-shaped red blood cell sometimes found in the blood of certain anemia patients. [kerato- + -cyte]

keratoderma /kĕr′ə tō dûr′mə/ **1.** any horny growth, especially on the skin. **2.** a thickening of the horny layer of the skin. [kerato- + -derma]

keratogenic /kĕr′ə tə jĕn′ĭk/ causing the growth of horny tissue, skin, and hair. [kerato- + -genic]

keratolysis /kĕr′ə tŏl′ə sĭs/ **1.** the destruction or dissolution of keratin. **2.** a loosening or periodic shedding of the horny layer of the skin. [kerato- + -lysis]

keratolytic /kĕr′ə tə lĭt′ĭk/ of, relating to, or causing keratolysis. [kerato- + -lytic]

keratoma /kĕr′ə tō′mə/ (*pl.* **keratomas** or **keratomata** /kĕr′ə tō′mə tə/) a horny tumor. kerat- + -oma]

keratomalacia /kĕr′ə tō mə lā′shə/ softening of the cornea specifically due to lack of vitamin A, sometimes found in young children suffering from severe malnutrition. [kerato- + -malacia]

keratometer /kĕr′ə tŏm′ĭ tər/ an instrument used to measure the curvature of the cornea. [kerato- + -meter]

keratometry /kĕr′ə tŏm′ĭ trē/ the measurement of the curvature of the cornea.

keratomycosis /kĕr′ə tō mī kō′sĭs/ a fungal infection of the cornea. [kerato- + mycosis]

keratopathy /kĕr′ə tŏp′ə thē/ disease of the cornea. [kerato- + pathy]

keratoplasty /kĕr′ə tə plăs′tē/ the surgical removal and replacement of any portion of the cornea. [kerato- + -plasty]

keratorrhexis /kĕr′ə tə rĕk′sĭs/ a rupture of the cornea. [kerato- + -rrhexis]

keratoscleritits /kĕr′ə tō sklĭ rī′tĭs/ inflammation of the cornea and the sclera. [kerato- + scleritis]

keratoscope /kĕr′ə tə skōp′/ an instrument for examining the cornea. [kerato- + -scope]

keratoscopy /kĕr′ə tŏs′kə pē/ visual examination of the cornea, especially to determine astigmatism. [kerato- + -scopy]

keratosis /kĕr′ə tō′sĭs/ excessive growth of the horny layers of the skin. [kerat- + -osis]

keratotomy /kĕr′ə tŏt′ə mē/ an incision through the cornea. [kerato- + -tomy]

kernicterus /kər nĭk′tər əs/ a type of brain damage caused by severe jaundice in the newborn period.

Kernig('s) sign /kĕr′nĭg(z)/ the inability to extend the leg at the knee due to pain, which may indicate meningitis.

ket-, keto- *combining form.* ketone or ketone group: *for example,* ketosis.

ketoacidosis /kē′tō ăs′ĭ dō′sĭs/ acidosis caused by the excessive production of ketones or ketone bodies, as in uncontrolled diabetes or starvation. [keto- + acidosis]

ketogenesis /kē′tə jĕn′ə sĭs/ metabolic production of ketones or ketone bodies. [keto- + -genesis]

ketogenic diet /kē′tə jĕn′ĭk/ a diet that is very low in carbohydrates, which promotes ketosis. The Atkin's diet is an example of this.

ketone /kē′tōn/ a by-product of fat metabolism.

ketone body one of three organic substances that contain ketones, found in blood and urine in abnormal quantities in certain conditions, such as diabetes mellitus.

ketonuria /kē′tə nōōr′ē ə/ presence of ketone bodies in the urine.

ketosis /kē tō′sĭs/ an increase of ketone bodies in the blood. [ket- + -osis]

kg *abbreviation.* kilogram; kilograms.

kidney /kĭd′nē/ one of the two bean-shaped organs that filters blood and excretes urine.

kidney failure inability of the kidneys to excrete waste from the body. *Also called* renal failure.

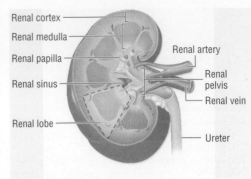

Kidney

kidney stone a stone-like mass formed in the excretory passages of the kidney. *Also called* nephrolith, renal calculus.

kidney transplant the surgical transplant of a kidney from a donor.

killer cell or **killer T cell** a T cell that attaches itself to a target cell and destroys it.

kilocalorie (C) /kĭl′ə kăl′ə rē/ a calorie, the unit used to measure the energy potential in food, equal to the amount of energy required to raise one liter of water one degree centigrade at sea level.

kilogram (kg) /kĭl′ə grăm′/ the base unit of mass in the international system, equal to 1000 grams or approximately 2.2 pounds.

Kimmelstiel-Wilson('s) /kĭm′əl stēl′ wĭl′ sən(z)/ **disease** or **syndrome** kidney disease caused by long-term, poorly controlled diabetes.

-kinesia *suffix.* motion: *for example,* hyperkinesia.

kinesin /kĭ nē′sĭn/ cellular proteins that convert chemical energy into mechanical force.

kinesiology /kĭ nē′sē ŏl′ə jē, -nē′zē-/ the study of the movement of the body and particularly of the muscles.

-kinesis *suffix.* movement or activation: *for example,* hyperkinesis.

kinesthesia /kĭn′əs thē′zhə/ the perception of the position and movement of the body, body parts, and muscles.

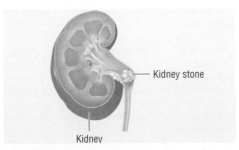

Kidney Stones

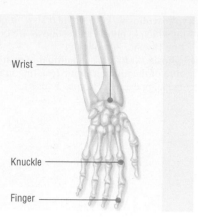

Knuckle

-kinetic *suffix.* of or relating to motion or movement: *for example,* bradykinetic.

kinetic /kĭ nĕt′ĭk/ of or relating to motion or movement.

kinetics /kĭ nĕt′ĭks/ the study of motion, or the effects that forces have on the motion of a body or system of bodies.

kinky hair syndrome or **disease** a congenital disorder that first manifests itself with sparse, short, abnormally pigmented hair, and leads to physical and mental degeneration and death. *Also called* Menkes disease.

kleptomania /klĕp′tə mā′nē ə/ an obsessive need to steal without any economic motivations, considered a symptom of obsessive-compulsive disorder.

kleptomaniac /klĕp′tə mā′nē ăk′/ a person with kleptomania.

Klinefelter('s) syndrome /klīn′fĕl tər(z)/ a genetic abnormality found in males, characterized by infertility, abnormally small testes, lack of facial and body hair, and enlarged breasts, caused by an additional X chromosome in a male, XXY, as opposed to the normal XY.

Klippel-Feil /klĭp′əl fīl′, klĭ pĕl′/ **anomaly** or **sequence** a defect in the development of the spinal column in the neck where the cervical vertebrae fuse, resulting in a short neck, low hairline at the base of the neck, and restricted movement of the head.

Klumpke('s) palsy /klo͞omp′kē(z) pôl′zē/ or **Klumpke(s) paralysis** /pə răl′ə sĭs/ paralysis of the muscles in the forearm and the hand, due to an injury of certain spinal nerves.

knee /nē/ the region between the thigh and lower leg consisting of the knee joint and patella.

kneecap /nē′kăp′/ a flat, triangular bone at the front of the knee joint. *Also called* patella.

knee jerk the reflexive extension of the leg as a result of a tap on the patellar tendon, a test for neurological function.

knee joint the joint found at the meeting of the femur and tibia.

knock-kneed /nŏk′ nēd′/ a condition where the knees are abnormally close together and the ankles are far apart. *Also called* genu valgum.

knot /nŏt/ a node, nodule, swelling, or other formation similar to a knot.

knuckle /nŭk′əl/ the joint of the finger or where each of the fingers meets the hand (at the head of the metacarpals), made more prominent when the fist is closed. *Also called* interphalangeal or metacarpophalangeal joint.

Koplik('s) spots /kŏp′lĭk(s)/ spots found in the mouth, indicative especially of the measles.

Korsakoff('s) /kôr′sə kôf(s)′/ **syndrome** or **psychosis** /sī kō′sĭs/ a disorder that occurs after prolonged periods of heavy alcohol consumption, characterized by a loss of short-term memory and confabulation; a symptom of acute thiamine deficiency.

Krebs /krĕbz/ **cycle** a series of organism reactions that are the main source of cellular energy.

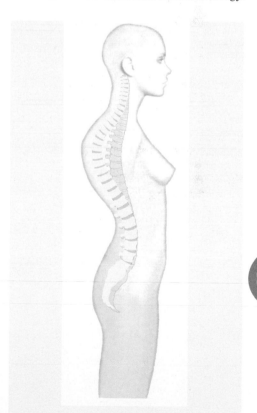

Kyphosis

KUB *abbreviation*. kidneys, ureter, and bladder.

kuru /ko͞or′o͞o/   a fatal brain disease found in New Guinea, transmitted by a prion and resulting from ritual cannibalism.

Kussmaul('s) respiration /ko͞os′moul(z)/ rapid, deep breathing, resulting from diabetic acidosis or some other form of acidosis.

Kveim('s) test /kvām(z)/   a test of the skin used to diagnose sarcoidosis.

kwashiorkor /kwäsh′ē ôr′kôr/   a childhood disease caused by protein deprivation, a prominent sign of which is a greatly distended abdomen that is fluid filled.

kyph-, kypho- *combining form*. abnormal curvature of the spine; hunchback: *for example*, kyphosis.

kyphoscoliosis /kī′fō skō′lē ō′sĭs/   a condition in which kyphosis and scoliosis are both present. [kypho- + scoliosis]

kyphosis /kī fō′sĭs/   abnormal outward curvature of the thoracic spine resulting in a hunchback appearance. [kyph- + -osis]

l, L *abbreviation.* **1.** liter; liters. **2.** left.

lab /lăb/ short for laboratory

labeled compound a chemical compound with a special substance (such as radioactive material) incorporated into it that is easily detected so that the distribution of the compound or its fragments can be traced in the body during a physiologic process.

labi-, labio- *combining form.* lips: *for example,* labiodental.

labia /lā′bē ə/ plural of labium.

labial /lā′bē əl/ related to the lips.

labia majora /mə jôr′ə/ (*sing.* **labium majus** /lā′bē əm mā′jəs/) two liplike folds of skin, one on either side of the opening to the vagina, located outside the labia minora; they are longer and thicker than the labia minora.

labia minora /mə nôr′ə/ (*sing.* **labium minus** /mī′nəs/) two thin liplike folds of skin, one on either side of the opening to the vagina, which are located inside the labia majora, closest to the vaginal opening.

labile /lā′bīl, -bəl/ **1.** readily changing, unstable **2.** in psychology, emotionally unstable.

lability /lā bĭl′ĭ tē/ the state of being labile; instability or a tendency to change frequently.

labiodental /lā′bē ō dĕn′təl/ **1.** pertaining to the lips and teeth, especially the front teeth whose surfaces face the lips. **2.** referring to certain letters, for example *f* and *v*, the sounds of which are formed with a combination of the lower lip and upper teeth. [labio- + dental]

labiogingival /lā′bē ō jĭn′jə vəl/ of or involving the lips and the gums. [labio- + gingiv- + -al]

labioplasty /lā′bē ə plăs′tē/ plastic surgery of the lip(s), especially of the vagina. [labio- + -plasty]

labium /lā′bē əm/ (*pl.* **labia** /lā′bē ə/) **1.** a lip; the liplike edge of an organ or tissue; a lipshaped structure. **2.** one fold of either of two sets of liplike folds of skin at the opening of the vagina. *See also* labia majora and labia minora.

labor /lā′bər/ **1.** the physical processes involved in giving birth by dilating the cervix, and expelling the fetus and placenta from the uterus through the vagina. **2.** the length of time required for this process to complete.

laboratory /lăb′rə tôr′ē/ a facility designed to perform tests, experiments, and scientific research. Medical laboratories follow set criteria. Normal laboratory values are available in Appendix C starting on page 431.

labra /lā′brə/ plural of labrum.

lab result the outcome of a clinical test. *See also* lab test.

labrum /lā′brəm/ (*pl.* **labra** /lā′brə/) a lipshaped edge or structure, especially the fibrous cartilage around the lip or rim of some joints.

lab test a clinical procedure, usually performed in a laboratory, that is designed to examine blood, tissue, bodily secretions, or the like to help in establishing or confirming a diagnosis or as a tool for managing a known condition or illness.

labyrinth /lăb′ə rĭnth/ the intricate intercommunicating canals of the inner ear, which are responsible for sensing balance.

labyrinthectomy /lăb′ə rĭn thĕk′tə mē/ surgical removal of the labyrinth of the inner ear. [labyrinth + -ectomy]

labyrinthitis /lăb′ə rĭn thī′tĭs/ inflammation of the canals of the inner ear, often resulting in lack of balance, nausea and vomiting, and vertigo. [labyrinth + -itis]

laceration /lăs′ə rā′shən/ **1.** a wound or cut, often having a jagged edge. **2.** the act of tearing tissue.

lacrimal /lăk′rə məl/ relating to tears.

lacrimal bone small, thin, fragile bone in the face located near the inner part of the eye socket (orbital cavity); it joins with another bone, the maxilla, to form the groove for the lacrimal sac.

lacrimal ducts the two pairs of channels, one pair in the corner of each eye, through which tears pass as they are carried away from the eye into the lacrimal sac.

lacrimal gland one of a pair of almondshaped glands that secrete tears; the glands are located below each eyebrow, on the upper outer side of each eye.

lacrimal sac /săk/ the upper portion of the nasolacrimal duct into which tears from the two lacrimal ducts in the corner of each eye empty; they pass from here into the nasal cavity.

lacrimation /lăk′rə mā′shən/ the secretion of tears, especially in abundance as in weeping or due to a disease.

lact-, lacti-, lacto- *combining form.* milk: *for example,* lactiferous.

lactase /lăk′tās/ an enzyme concentrated in the intestinal juices that converts lactose (milk sugar) into other simpler sugars as part of the digestive process.

lactate /lăk′tāt/ **1.** *n.* a salt of lactic acid. **2.** *v.* to secrete milk.

lactate dehydrogenase (LDH) /dē hī′drə jə nās′/ a group of enzymes found in the cells of almost all body tissues where they are a catalyst in converting lactate to pyruvate (a salt of pyruvic acid, an intermediate in protein and carbohydrate metabolism); a rise of LDH in blood may indicate a disease or injury in an organ, such as the kidneys or heart.

lactation /lăk tā′shən/ the production and secretion of milk from the mammary glands of the breast after giving birth.

lactic /lăk′tik/ relating to milk. [lact- + -ic]

lactic acid a water-soluble liquid found in muscles and blood, sour milk and wines, and used in various beverages and pharmaceuticals.

lactic acidosis /ăs′ĭ dō′sĭs/ a condition marked by the buildup of lactic acid, because of the absence of adequate oxygen to further metabolize the lactate to carbon dioxide and water.

lactiferous /lăk tĭf′ər əs/ milk-producing or milk-conveying. [lacti- + -ferous]

lactiferous ducts the numerous ducts, or channels, that carry milk from the lobes of each breast to the nipple.

lactobacillus /lăk′tō bə sĭl′əs/ any one of a group of bacteria known for producing lactic acid from carbohydrates; many species are

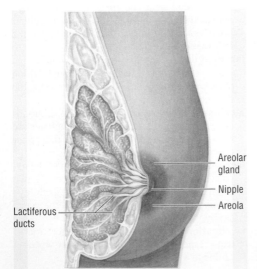

Lactiferous ducts
Areolar gland
Nipple
Areola

Lactiferous Ducts

part of the normal flora of the mouth, intestine, and vagina; also found in fermented food products such as yogurt and sourdough. [lacto- + bacillus]

lactocele /lăk′tə sēl′/ a cyst caused by an obstruction to a lactiferous duct. *Also called* galactocele. [lacto- + -cele]

lactogen /lăk′tə jən/ a substance, such as a drug or hormone, that stimulates the production or secretion of milk. [lacto- + -gen]

lactogenesis /lăk′tō jĕn′ə sĭs/ the production of milk. [lacto- + -genesis]

lactogenic /lăk′tə jĕn′ik/ of or relating to the production of milk. [lacto- + -genic]

lactogenic hormone a pituitary hormone that stimulates the secretion of breast milk in women after childbirth. *Also called* prolactin.

lactorrhea /lăk′tə rē′ə/ a flow of milk from the breasts that is not connected with nursing or giving birth, or a continued discharge between periods of nursing or after weaning. *Also called* galactorrhea. [lacto- + -rrhea]

lactose /lăk′tōs/ a sugar that is found only in cow's milk.

lactose intolerance an inability to digest lactose (milk sugar, as found in dairy products) because of a lack of the enzyme lactase.

lactosuria /lăk′tə sŏŏr′ē ə/ the presence of lactose in the urine. [lactos- + -uria]

lacuna /lə kyōō′nə/ (*pl.* **lacunae** /lə kyōō′nē/) **1.** a small depression, pit or cavity, especially in bone. **2.** a defect, discontinuity, or gap.

lame /lām/ physically disabled in a foot or leg, so that walking is difficult and jerky.

lamella (*pl.* **lamellas** or **lamellae** /lə mĕl′ē/) **1.** thin, platelike layer of bone or tissue. **2.** a medicated disk containing gelatin and glycerin that is placed under the eyelid for local absorption.

lamina /lăm′ə nə/ (*pl.* **laminae** /lăm′ə nē′/) a thin, flat layer, especially the part of the vertebral arch from the pedicle to the midline.

laminectomy /lăm′ə nĕk′tə mē/ surgical procedure during which the laminae (bony arches) of one or more vertebrae are removed in order to alleviate compression of the spinal cord. *Also called* rachiotomy. [lamin(a) + -ectomy]

laminitis /lăm′ə nī′tĭs/ inflammation of a lamina. [lamin- + -itis]

laminotomy /lăm′ə nŏt′ə mē/ the surgical division of a vertebral lamina. [lamino- + -tomy]

lance /lăns/ to cut into or open, or to pierce, as a boil, vein, or abscess, usually for drainage.

lancet /lăn′sĭt/ a surgical knife that has a sharp tip, is short, wide, and usually two-edged; used to make small incisions and punctures.

Landau-Kleffner syndrome /lăn′dou klĕf′nər/ a childhood disorder of unknown cause characterized by seizures, psychomotor abnormalities, and impaired language ability (aphasia), especially an inability to comprehend spoken language that may result in mutism. It begins in early childhood and lasts to about age 15, with some language problems usually carrying over into adulthood.

Landry('s) paralysis /lăn′drē(z) pə răl′ə sĭs/ an acute disorder that usually follows a viral infection or immunization and is marked by a symmetric paralysis of the legs that progresses rapidly upward, ascending to the arms, and sometimes the breathing muscles and neck. Considered by some to be a form of Guillain-Barre syndrome. *Also called* acute ascending paralysis.

Langerhans cells /läng′ər hänz′, -häns′/ dendritic cells found in the interstitial spaces of the epidermis, believed to have an immune function.

lanugo /lə nōō′gō/ fine, soft, downy hair that appears on the body of the fetus at about the fourth or fifth month of gestation; it is usually entirely shed before birth, but is occasionally found on some newborns.

laparo- *combining form.* abdomen, abdominal wall: *for example,* laparoscope.

laparoscope /lăp′ər ə skōp′/ an endoscope (fiberoptic instrument with an illuminated tube) designed for examining the abdominal cavity. [laparo- + -scope]

laparoscopic /lăp′ər ə skŏp′ĭk/ of or relating to a laparoscope.

laparoscopic hysterectomy /hĭs′tə rĕk′tə mē/ surgical removal of the uterus (hysterectomy) with the use of a laparoscope as a visual guide within the abdomen.

laparoscopic surgery an operation that uses a laparoscope as a guide while carrying out surgical procedures inside the abdominal cavity.

laparoscopy /lăp′ə rŏs′kə pē/ visual examination of the abdominal cavity using a laparoscope passed through a small incision in the wall of the abdomen. [laparo- + -scopy]

laparotomy /lăp′ə rŏt′ə mē/ a surgical incision into the abdominal wall, often for exploratory purposes. [laparo- + -tomy]

large bowel large intestine.

large cell/large-cell carcinoma /kär′sə nō′mə/ a group of cancers originating in the bronchi of the lungs and made up of large undifferentiated cells.

large cell/large-cell lymphoma /lĭm fō′mə/ cancer of the lymphatic tissue composed of large cells of an undetermined type.

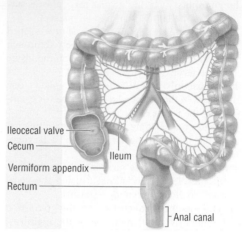

Ileocecal valve
Cecum
Ileum
Vermiform appendix
Rectum
Anal canal

Large Intestine

large intestine (LI) the part of the digestive tract that extends from the ileocecal valve to the rectum; it includes the cecum, colon, and rectum, and is wider and shorter than the small intestine that precedes it.

laryng-, laryngo- *combining form.* the larynx: *for example,* laryngectomy.

laryngeal /lə rĭn′jē əl, -jəl/ pertaining to the larynx.

laryngectomy /lăr′ĭn jĕk′tə mē/ surgical procedure to remove all or part of the larynx, usually for cancer. [laryng- + -ectomy]

laryngitis /lăr′ĭn jī′tĭs/ inflammation of the mucous membrane that lines the larynx, accompanied by swollen vocal cords, resulting in hoarseness. *Also called* chorditis. [laryng- + -itis]

laryngocele /lə rĭng′gə sēl′/ an abnormal air sac connected to the larynx through the laryngeal ventricle and sometimes visible as a bulge on the outside of the neck. [laryngo- + -cele]

laryngocentesis /lə rĭng′gō sĕn tē′sĭs/ a surgical procedure in which the larynx is punctured. [laryngo- + -centesis]

laryngomalacia /lə rĭng′gō mə lā′shē ə, -shə/ having soft laryngeal cartilage, most often seen in young children, characterized by occasional stridorous breathing. [laryngo- + -malacia]

laryngopharynx /lə rĭng′gō făr′ĭngks/ (*pl.* **laringopharynges** /lə rĭng′gō fə rĭn′jēz/ or **laryngopharynxes**) the portion of the pharynx that is situated behind and below the larynx, extending from the hyoid bone at the top of the larynx down to the esophagus. [laryngo- + pharynx]

laryngoplasty /lə rĭng′gə plăs′tē/   plastic surgery of the larynx. [laryngo- + -plasty]

laryngoscope /lə rĭng′gə skōp′/   a tube-shaped instrument with a light that is inserted through the mouth to examine or operate on the inside of the larynx. [laryngo- + -scope]

laryngoscopist   /lăr′ĭng gŏs′kə pĭst/   one trained in the use of a laryngoscope for examining the inside of the larynx.

laryngoscopy /lăr′ĭng gŏs′kə pē/   examination of the inside of the larynx using a laryngoscope. [laryngo- + -scopy]

laryngospasm /lə rĭng′gə spăz′əm/   a spasm in the muscles of the larynx, causing the vocal cords to close. [laryngo- + spasm]

laryngotracheobronchitis   /lə rĭng′gō trā′kē ō brŏng kī′tĭs/   inflammation of the main respiratory passages—the larynx, trachea, and bronchi—due to a viral or bacterial infection, particularly symptomatic in young children; it is a form of croup. [laryngo- + tracheo- + bronchitis]

laryngotracheotomy /lə rĭng′gō trā′kē ŏt′ə mē/   a surgical incision in the larynx and trachea. [laryngo- + tracheo- + -tomy]

larynx /lăr′ĭngks/ (*pl.* **larynges** /lə rĭn′jēz/)   the upper part of the respiratory tract that houses the vocal cords and is responsible for producing sounds (often called the voice box); it is also part of the air passageway that connects the pharynx and the trachea.

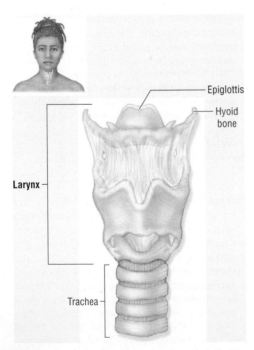

Epiglottis

Hyoid bone

Larynx

Trachea

Larynx

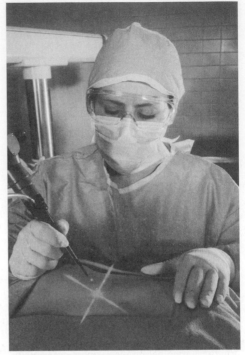

Laser Surgery

laser /lā′zər/   an instrument that produces a powerful beam of light with a very thin ray (of one wavelength), which when focused at close range produces intense heat; it is used in surgery to cut or separate parts of tissue or to destroy tissue. [*l*ight *a*mplification by *s*timulated *e*mission of *r*adiation]

laser-assisted in situ keratomileusis (LASIK) /ĭn sī′tōō kĕr′ə tō mī lōō′sĭs, ĭn sĭt′ōō/   eye surgery to correct severe myopia (nearsightedness) and more recently hyperopia (farsightedness), in which a laser is used to reshape the cornea; a flap of corneal epithelium is made, the exposed cornea is reshaped, and the flap is laid back in place to heal without sutures.

laser surgery   surgery that uses the power of a laser beam to cut, separate, cauterize, or dissolve tissue or to remove lesions on the skin.

laser therapy   a pain management method that uses a laser on specific acupuncture points to relieve pain.

LASIK /lā′sĭk/   *abbreviation.* laser-assisted in situ keratomileusis.

Lassa fever /lä′sə, lăs′ə/   a highly contagious and often fatal disease found in West Africa that is caused by a viral infection acquired through contact with rodents as well as through person-to-person transmission;

marked by fever, sore throat, small hemorrhages under the skin (bruises), and often with kidney and heart failure that end in death.

Lassa virus an arenavirus (an RNA virus transmitted from rodents to humans) that causes the highly fatal Lassa fever.

lassitude /lăs'ĭ tōōd'/ condition of listlessness or weariness.

latent /lā'tənt/ dormant, capable of developing or manifesting, as of a disease.

later-, latero- *combining form.* side: *for example,* lateral.

lateral /lăt'ər əl/ at or toward the side of. [later- + -al]

lateral plane in anatomy, for denoting orientation, the plane parallel to the medial plane that divides the body into left and right sides. *Also called* sagittal plane.

lateral view in medical drawings, images, and x-rays, the side view of a body part or system; for example, a lateral view of the human skeleton.

lateroversion /lăt'ə rō vûr'zhən/ inclining or tilting to one side or the other, said especially of a malposition of the uterus. [latero- + -version]

latex /lā'tĕks/ **1.** an emulsion produced in the vessels of certain plants that contains resins, proteins, and other substances and is used to make adhesives and rubber products. **2.** similar synthetic materials used to make synthetic rubbers, which are potent allergens.

latissimus dorsi muscle /lə tĭs'ə məs dôr'sī/ a large, wide, triangular-shaped muscle that attaches to the thoracic and lumbar areas of the back and that is used to pull the arm toward the body or extend or rotate it medially.

laughing gas informal term for nitrous oxide, a mild anesthetic used in dentistry.

lavage /lə văzh'/ the washing out of an organ or empty cavity in the body, such as the stomach, bladder, or paranasal sinuses.

laxative /lăk'sə tĭv/ any substance that is taken to loosen and move the bowels slightly.

laxity /lăk'sĭ stē/ degree of freedom of movement in a joint.

lazy eye abnormal alignment of one or both eyes. An informal term for strabismus.

lb. *abbreviation.* pound; pounds.

LD *abbreviation.* lethal dose, often LD50 or LD95 to describe the dose at which 50% or 95% of the subjects (usually lab animals) die.

LDH *abbreviation.* lactate dehydrogenase.

LDL *abbreviation.* low-density lipoprotein.

LDL (low-density lipoprotein) cholesterol cholesterol composed mainly of low-density lipoprotein; known as the "bad cholesterol" because elevated levels, which usually develop from a diet high in saturated fats, are associated with an increased risk in coronary heart disease. It contains relatively more fats and less protein than high-density lipoprotein (HDL) cholesterol, the "good cholesterol."

LE *abbreviation.* **1.** left eye (usually abbreviated OS or o.s.). **2.** lupus erythematosus (usually abbreviated SLE)

lead (Pb) /lĕd/ a metallic element that is toxic; one isotope, however, has been used to treat certain eye conditions.

lead poisoning a toxic condition capable of causing brain damage that can be chronic or acute and is caused from absorbing excessive amounts of lead or lead compounds from the environment, for example, from lead-based paint or lead fumes in an industrial setting.

lean body mass an estimated measurement of the mass of the body (bones, muscles, organs, and so on) minus the storage fat of the body.

learning disability an abnormal condition of children that can carry on into adult life in which there is difficulty learning one or more specific scholastic skills such as reading, writing, or math despite average or above-average learning abilities in other areas. *Also called* learning problem.

learning disabled having a learning disability.

learning problem learning disability.

lecithin /lĕs'ə thĭn/ any of a group of compounds, common in plants and animals, that are an essential part of all cell membranes and necessary for the metabolism of fats; foods rich in lecithin include egg yolk, corn, and soybeans.

leech /lēch/ a bloodsucking parasitic worm usually found in fresh water; in the past, commonly used in medicine to let out blood as a therapeutic treatment; now used sometimes in plastic and reconstructive surgery to promote blood flow to damaged tissue, because the leech injects an anticoagulant as it removes edema and blood from its point of attachment.

LEEP /lēp/ *abbreviation.* loop electrosurgical excision procedure.

left atrium /ā'trē əm/ the upper chamber on the left side of the heart into which the oxygenated blood flows from the lungs via the pulmonary veins; the blood is pumped into the left ventricle below, which sends it to the body.

left colic flexure /kŏl'ĭk flĕk'shər/ the curve at the junction of the transverse colon and descending colon. *Also called* splenic flexure.

left-handed having the natural tendency to use the left hand rather than the right for writing and other manual tasks.

left heart the left atrium and the left ventricle.

left hepatic duct /hĭ păt'ĭk/ the duct that transmits bile to the common hepatic duct from the left side of the liver and the left part of the caudate lobe.

left lower quadrant (LLQ)   designation used in anatomy to signify the lower left quarter of an organ or body part. For example, the abdomen is divided into four quarters described as left lower quadrant (LLQ), left upper quadrant (LUQ), right lower quadrant (RLQ), and right upper quadrant (RUQ).

left umbilical vein /ŭm bĭl′ĭ kəl vān′/   vein through which blood is returned from the placenta to the fetus. *Also called* umbilical vein.

left upper quadrant (LUQ)   designation used in anatomy to signify the left upper quarter of an organ or body part, especially the abdomen.

left ventricle (LV) /vĕn′trĭ kəl/   the thick-walled lower chamber on the left side of the heart that receives blood from the left atrium and pumps it out to the body through the aorta.

left ventricular assist device (LVAD) /vĕn trĭk′yə lər/   a mechanical pump designed to temporarily assist the left ventricle in pumping blood out into the body.

leg /lĕg/   **1.** in anatomy, the portion of the lower limb between the knee and the ankle. **2.** in ordinary usage, the entire lower limb, from the top of the thigh to the foot.

legal blindness   blindness as defined by the law (for use in determining eligibility for government disability benefits, for example); in the United States, most states define this as visual acuity in the better eye, using the best possible corrective lenses, of no better than 20/200, or a visual field restriction to 20 degrees or less in the better eye.

Legionnaire('s) disease /lē′jə nâr(z)′/   an acute and sometimes fatal pneumonia caused by a bacterium (*Legionella*) that is transmitted through contaminated water and then is airborne, for example, in water vaporizers or the moist air that comes from air-conditioning ducts.

leiodermia /lī′ō dûr′mē ə/   smooth, shiny skin.

leiomy-, leiomyo-   *combining form.* smooth muscle: *for example,* leiomyosarcoma.

leiomyofibroma /lī′ō mī′ō fī brō′mə/   (*pl.* **leiomyofibromas** or **leiomyofibromata** /lī′ō mī′ō fī brō′mə tə/)   benign tumor made of smooth muscle cells and fibrous tissue, most often found in the uterus. *See also* fibroid tumor. [leiomyo- + fibroma]

leiomyoma /lī′ō mī ō′mə/   (*pl.* **leiomyomas** or **leiomyomata** /lī′ō mī ō′mə tə/)   benign tumor originating in smooth muscle, most often found in the uterus, stomach, esophagus, or small intestine. [leiomy- + -oma]

leiomyoma uteri /yōō′tə rī′/   a benign tumor found in the smooth muscle of the uterus, occurring in women between 30 and 50 years of age. *Also called* fibroid, fibroid tumor.

leiomyosarcoma /lī′ō mī′ō sär kō′mə/   a malignant (cancerous) tumor originating in smooth muscle cells, most often found in the uterus or digestive tract. [leiomyo- + -sarcoma]

leishmaniasis /lēsh′mə nī′ə sĭs/   a group of diseases caused by infection with a species of parasite, transmitted through the bite of sand flies. The disease may affect the skin (cutaneous leishmaniasis) with one or more sores, or the organs (visceral leishmaniasis) resulting in an enlarged spleen and liver, or a combination of skin and mucous membranes (mucocutaneous leishmaniasis).

lemniscus /lĕm nĭs′kəs/   (*pl.* **lemnisci** /lĕm nĭs′ī/)   a band of nerve fibers, especially one of two bundles of sensory nerve fibers that ascend to the thalamus.

lens /lĕnz/   **1.** the transparent, crystalline portion of the eye, lying directly behind the pupil, that focuses light rays entering the eye through the pupil onto the retina. **2.** transparent glass, plastic, or other material that is shaped and ground to refract light in a specific way, as found in eyeglasses, microscopes, or cameras.

lenticular /lĕn tĭk′yə lər/   **1.** of or related to a lens. **2.** resembling a lens.

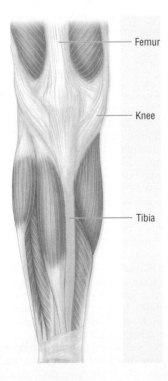

Femur

Knee

Tibia

Leg

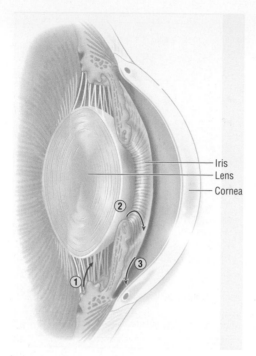

Iris
Lens
Cornea

Lens

lenticular nucleus the cone-shaped central core of the cerebral cortex, containing both the putamen and the two segments of the globus pallidus.

lentigo /lĕn tī′gō/ (*pl.* **lentigines** /lĕn tĭj′ə nēz′/) a flat brown spot on the skin found in elderly or middle age people, usually on parts of the body exposed to the sun.

leper /lĕp′ər/ an outdated term for a person suffering from leprosy, or Hansen('s) disease caused by the bacteria *Mycobacterium laprae*.

leprosy /lĕp′rə sē/ a chronic, mildly contagious bacterial disease that especially affects the nerves and skin; found mostly in tropical and subtropical regions of the world. *Also called* Hansen('s) disease.

-lepsy *suffix.* seizure: *for example,* narcolepsy.

lept-, lepto- *combining form.* thin, narrow, weak, delicate: *for example,* leptomeninges.

-leptic *suffix.* a type of seizure: *for example,* epileptic, neuroleptic.

leptin /lĕp′tĭn/ a hormone associated with obesity that plays a role in the metabolism of fat; if a person's metabolism is functioning properly, leptin should act to curb the appetite.

leptomeningeal /lĕp′tō mə nĭn′jē əl, -mĕn′ən jē′əl/ of or relating to the leptomeninges.

leptomeninges /lĕp′tō mə nĭn′jēz/ (*sing.* **leptomeninx** /lĕp′tō mā′nĭnks, -mĕn′ingks/) two of the three membranous layers (meninges) that cover the brain and spinal cord; the two innermost layers, called the arachnoid membrane and the pia mater, are jointly known as leptomeninges. [lepto- + meninges]

leptomeningitis /lĕp′tō mĕn′ĭn jī′tĭs/ inflammation of the leptomeninges. [leptomening(es) + -itis]

leptospirosis /lĕp′tō spī rō′sĭs/ an acute disease caused by infection with a type of bacteria called a spirochete; acquired most often in the tropics, but found worldwide, it is transmitted through the urine of infected cattle, dogs, vermin, or wild animals.

LES *abbreviation.* lower esophageal sphincter.

lesbian /lĕz′bē ən/ a female whose sexual orientation is towards other women; a female homosexual.

lesbianism /lĕz′bē ə nĭz′əm/ sexual preference or orientation of women for other women; female homosexuality.

Lesch-Nyhan disease /lĕsh′ nī′ən/ a rare, inherited metabolic disease of males caused by overproduction of uric acid due to a deficiency of an enzyme essential for the metabolism of purine; it leads to mental retardation, renal failure, and self-mutilation.

lesion /lē′zhən/ **1.** an injury or wound; may be internal, as a vascular lesion, or external, as a skin lesion. **2.** a visible abnormality of skin tissue, such as a sore, rash, or boil. *See illustration on page 200.*

lesser omentum /ō mĕn′təm/ a fold of the peritoneum that joins part of the stomach and duodenum to the liver.

let-down reflex a normal reflex in a nursing woman that releases milk from the glands of the breast in response to the infant's crying or sucking.

lethal /lē′thəl/ relating to or causing death.

lethal dose (LD) the amount of a chemical or biological toxin that is likely to produce death.

lethargy /lĕth′ər jē/ state of dullness, extreme drowsiness, sluggishness, apathy.

leucine /loo′sēn/ an essential amino acid important for growth in children and nitrogen balance in adults.

leuk-, leuko- *combining form.* white; white blood cell: *for example,* leukoblast.

leukapheresis /loo′kə fə rē′sĭs/ a procedure in which blood is drawn, leukocytes are selectively removed, and then the blood is retransfused into the donor; may be done to treat the donor, for other patients, or for research purposes. [leuk- + -apheresis]

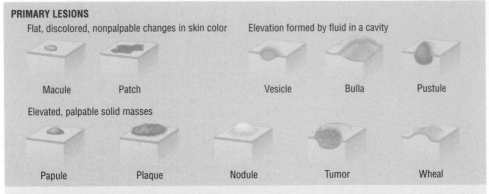

PRIMARY LESIONS

Flat, discolored, nonpalpable changes in skin color

Macule   Patch

Elevation formed by fluid in a cavity

Vesicle   Bulla   Pustule

Elevated, palpable solid masses

Papule   Plaque   Nodule   Tumor   Wheal

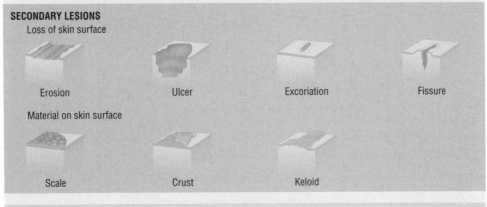

SECONDARY LESIONS

Loss of skin surface

Erosion   Ulcer   Excoriation   Fissure

Material on skin surface

Scale   Crust   Keloid

VASCULAR LESIONS

Cherry angioma   Telangiectasia   Petechiae   Purpura   Ecchymosis

Lesions

leukemia /loo kē′mē ə/ a group of cancerous diseases involving the blood-forming tissues (also referred to as "cancer of the blood") that may be acute or chronic, and that is marked by uncontrolled proliferation of white blood cells with unusual forms; infiltration occurs in the bone marrow, lymph nodes, spleen, and liver. [leuk- + -emia]

leukoblast /loo′kə blăst′/ an immature white blood cell. [leuko- + -blast]

leukocoria /loo′kō kôr′ē ə/ a condition in which a whitish mass reflected within the eye makes the pupil look white; associated with several eye diseases.

leukocyte /loo′kə sīt′/ any of various blood cells that separate into a thin white layer when whole blood is centrifuged, and help protect the body from infection and disease. Leukocytes include neutrophils, eosinophils, basophils, lymphocytes, and monocytes. *Also called* white blood cell. [leuko- + -cyte]

leukocytopenia /loo′kō sī′tə pē′nē ə/ having a lower than normal number of white blood cells in the circulating blood. *Also called* leukopenia. [leuko- + -cyto- + -penia]

leukocytopoiesis /loo′kō sī′tō poi ē′sĭs/ formation of white blood cells. [leuko- + cyto- + -poesis]

leukocytosis /loo′kō sī tō′sĭs/ an increase in the number of white blood cells in the circulating blood. [leuko- + cyt- + -osis]

leukoderma /loo′kə dûr′mə/ a loss of skin pigment that produces patches of white skin. [leuko- + -derma]

leukodystrophy /loo′kō dĭs′trə fē/ any of a group of diseases caused by degeneration of the brain's white matter, which is involved in the conduction of nerve impulses. [leuko- + dystrophy]

leukoencephalopathy /loo′kō ĕn sĕf′ə lŏp′ə thē/ damage to white matter of the brain. [leuko- + encephalo- + -pathy]

leukopenia /lōō′kə pē′nē ə/ having a lower than normal number of white blood cells in the circulating blood. *Also called* leukocytopenia. [leuko- + -penia]

leukoplakia /lōō′kə plā′kē ə/ a change in a mucous membrane in the mouth, for example on the cheeks or gums, that is often associated with pipe smoking and is characterized by a raised white patch that is hardened and irregular in shape and which may be cancerous or precancerous. [leuko- + -plakia]

leukoreduction /lōō′kō rĭ dŭk′shən/ the process of filtering and taking out the white blood cells from whole blood before transfusion so that the receiver can avoid bacteria and viruses that may be passed on through the donated blood. [leuko- + reduction]

leukorrhagia /lōō′kə rā′jə, -jē ə/ leukorrhea. [leuko- + -rrhagia]

leukorrhea /lōō′kə rē′ə/ a white or yellowish vaginal discharge normally present in smaller amounts during different points in the menstrual cycle and during pregnancy; a large increase may indicate infection. [leuko- + -rrhea]

leukotriene /lōō′kə trī′ēn/ any of a group of biologically active substances that play an inhibitory role in the physiology of inflammation and allergic reactions.

levo- *combining form.* left: *for example,* levorotation.

levorotation /lē′vō rō tā′shən/ a turning or twisting counterclockwise, or to the left.

levoversion /lē′vō vûr′zhən/ **1.** a turning to the left. **2.** rotation of both eyes to the left. [levo- + -version]

LFT *abbreviation.* liver function test.

LI *abbreviation.* large intestine.

libido /lĭ bē′dō/ **1.** sexual drive. **2.** in psychoanalysis, the psychic energy behind all instinctual drives.

licensed clinical social worker a person who has obtained a master's degree in social work and is trained in psychotherapy and the behavioral sciences to help individuals deal with problems in everyday living.

licensed practical nurse (LPN) a person who has graduated from an accredited program in practical nursing and is licensed by a public authority to practice basic nursing techniques and patient care under the supervision of a registered nurse.

lifespan /līf′spăn′/ the length of life for an individual.

lifestyle disease a disorder associated with certain risk factors that are part of an individual's habits or customs, such as drinking, smoking, or lack of exercise; an example is lung cancer, which is associated with the use of tobacco.

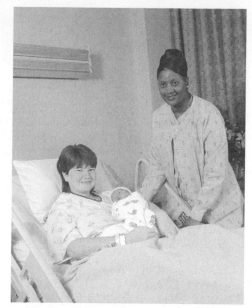

Licensed Practical Nurse

life support **1.** *n.* the use of medical equipment or other techniques that sustain life by taking over basic life functions when a major body system fails, without which the person would not survive; for example, the use of a ventilator for breathing. **2.** (*also* **life-support**) *adj.* of or relating to life support, as in a life-support system.

ligament /lĭg′ə mənt/ **1.** one of many bands of tough white connective tissue that binds joints together and connects bones and cartilage, facilitating movement. **2.** a layer of membrane that extends between visceral organs, such as a band of peritoneum, to give support.

ligate /lī′gāt/ to bind or tie off with a ligature.

ligation /lī gā′shən/ the act of applying a ligature.

ligature /lĭg′ə chər, -chŏŏr′/ **1.** a wire, cord, or bandage used to tie or bind. **2.** a surgical thread, wire, or filament used to tie off a vessel, such as an artery, or to tie off a tube or duct.

lightheadedness /līt′hĕd′ĭd nĭs/ the state of feeling giddy, as though about to faint.

light therapy the use of infrared, ultraviolet, or colored light to treat pain and, especially in the winter months, certain depressive disorders, such as seasonal affective disorder.

Likert scale /lĭ′kərt/ a rating scale that uses numbers representing responses from strongly negative to strongly positive, such as 1 = strongly disagree to 10 = strongly agree, for gauging a respondent's attitudes or reactions to a set of statements; used mainly in psychiatry and the behavioral sciences.

limb /lĭm/ **1.** an extremity of the body; an arm or leg. **2.** a branch of an internal organ or other structure in the body.

liminal /lĭm′ə nəl/ relating to a threshold, as of a response to either physical or psychological stimuli.

limp /lĭmp/ **1.** *v.* to walk with a jerky motion. **2.** *n.* a jerky gait.

line /līn/ **1.** a narrow mark that differs from its surroundings in color, texture, elevation, etc. **2.** a strain of cells or organisms descended from a single ancestor. **3.** an imaginary line connecting two anatomical points, used to establish a plane or axis. **4.** a catheter or intravenous line. **5.** tubing.

linea /lĭn′ē ə/ (*pl.* **lineae** /lĭn′ē ē′/) in anatomy, a line.

linea nigra /lĭn′ē ə nī′grə/ the linea alba (the ridge of white connective tissue that runs midway down the entire front of the abdominal wall), which during pregnancy becomes pigmented, appearing as a long, thin, dark line.

linear fracture a fracture that runs parallel to the long axis of the bone. *Also called* fissure fracture.

lingua /lĭng′gwə/ (*pl.* **linguae** /lĭng′gwē/) in anatomy, a tongue.

lingual /lĭng′gwəl/ pertaining or next to the tongue.

lingual tonsils two masses of lymphoid tissue located near the root of the tongue on either side of the throat, each made up of a group of small nodules.

lip /lĭp/ **1.** one of two muscular structures around the outside of the mouth, forming an upper and lower fleshy border; labium. **2.** a liplike structure around a cavity or groove.

lip-, lipo- *combining form.* fat: *for example,* lipectomy, lipodystrophy.

lipase /lĭp′ās, lī′pās/ any of several enzymes produced by the digestive system that act as a catalyst in the breakdown of lipids (fats).

lipectomy /lĭ pĕk′tə mē, lī-/ a surgical procedure to remove subcutaneous fat, for example, from the abdominal wall. [lip- + ectomy]

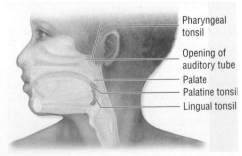

Pharyngeal tonsil
Opening of auditory tube
Palate
Palatine tonsil
Lingual tonsil

Lingual Tonsils

lipid /lĭp′ĭd, lī′pĭd/ any of a number of fatty organic compounds, including cholesterol, phospholipids, triglycerides, and fatty acids, that are insoluble in water. Some lipids are stored in the body as energy reserves; all play an important role in the structure of a cell. *Also called* fat.

lipid-lowering agent a medication taken to lower the level of lipids such as cholesterol and triglycerides in the blood, because high levels are associated with a higher risk for coronary artery disease.

lipid profile a group of blood tests performed together to analyze the breakdown of lipids in the blood; the lipid profile is performed after fasting and measures total cholesterol, HDL cholesterol, LDL cholesterol, and triglycerides; usually done to assess the risk of heart disease.

lipid storage diseases a group of disorders, including diseases such as metachromatic leukodystrophy and Fabry's disease, that are caused by congenital problems in lipid metabolism resulting in an abnormal accumulation of lipids in misplaced areas of the body.

lipid tests blood tests performed after fasting to check the amount of lipids in the blood; basic lipid tests measure cholesterol and triglycerides.

lipo- *See* lip-.

lipoatrophy /lĭp′ō ăt′rə fē, lī′pō-/ loss of subcutaneous fat in some diabetic patients at the site of insulin injections. [lipo- + atrophy]

lipoblast /lĭp′ə blăst′, lī′pə-/ an embryonic, or developing, fat cell. [lipo- + -blast]

lipocyte /lĭp′ə sīt′, lī′pə-/ **1.** a cell specialized to make and store fat. **2.** a fat-storing cell found in the liver. [lipo- + -cyte]

lipodystrophy /lĭp′ō dĭs′trə fē, lī′pō-/ an inherited or acquired disorder of fat metabolism; in most forms, marked by a loss of fatty tissue in the body. [lipo- + -dystrophy]

lipoid /lĭp′oid, lī′poid/ lipid-like; resembling fat. [lip- + -oid]

lipolysis /lĭ pŏl′ə sĭs, lī-/ the breakdown of fats. [lipo- + -lysis]

lipoma /lĭ pō′mə, lī-/ (*pl.* **lipomas** or **lipomata** /lĭ pō′mə tə, lī-/) a benign tumor made of mature fat cells. [lip- + -oma]

lipoprotein /lĭp′ō prō′tēn, -tē ĭn, lī′pō-/ a compound composed of lipid and protein that provides the principal means by which lipids are transported in the blood; lipoproteins are classified according to their density—high, low, and very low density (HDL, LDL, and VLDL). LDLs contain relatively more fats and less protein than HDLs. [lipo- + protein]

liposarcoma /lĭp′ō sär kō′mə, lī′pō-/ a malignant tumor occurring in adults that is primarily made of primitive fat cells. [lipo- + sarcoma]

liposuction /lĭp'ō sŭk'shən, lī'pō-/ a surgical procedure that suctions out fatty deposits in specific parts of the body, commonly the abdomen, buttocks, and hips and thighs, using a high-pressure vacuum. [lipo- + suction]

lipuria /lĭ poŏr'ē ə/ the presence of lipids in the urine. [lip- + -uria]

listeriosis /lĭ stêr'ē ō'sĭs/ an infectious and serious worldwide disease caused by bacteria, occuring in animals and sometimes transmitted to humans, often through contaminated food and usually to newborns or those with weak immune systems. In severe cases in humans it can result in miscarriage as well as in symptoms such as a dark red rash, fever, and enlargement of the spleen and liver, and often progresses to meningitis and encephalitis. It is treated with antibiotics.

liter (l, L) /lē'tər/ a measure of capacity in the metric system that is equivalent to slightly more than one quart (1.057 U.S. liquid quarts); also equal to 1000 cubic centimeters.

lith-, litho- *combining form.* stone, calculus, calcification: *for example,* lithogenesis.

-lith *suffix.* stone, calculus: *for example,* prostatolith.

lithiasis /lĭ thī'ə sĭs/ the formation of stones in an internal organ, occurring most often in the gallbladder, kidney, and urinary tract. [lith- + -iasis]

-lithiasis *suffix.* stone formation or condition: *for example,* ureterolithiasis.

lithium /lĭth'ē əm/ a silver-white metal that is the lightest known metal; lithium carbonate, a salt of lithium, is used as a mood stabilizer in the treatment of bipolar disorder, in which it lessens the intensity of the manic episodes.

lithogenesis /lĭth'o jĕn'ə sĭs/ the formation of stones. [litho- + -genesis]

lithogenic /lĭth'ō jĕn'ĭk/ causing or promoting the formation of stones. [litho- + -genic]

litholysis /lĭ thŏl'ə sĭs/ destruction or dissolving of stones. [litho- + -lysis]

lithotomy /lĭ thŏt'ə mē/ surgical procedure to remove a stone by making an incision, especially into the urinary bladder. [litho- + tomy]

lithotomy position a surgical position in which the patient is lying on his or her back, with knees bent, thighs turned out, and heels elevated and resting in straps at the end of the table, as is used for a vaginal or rectal exam.

lithotripsy /lĭth'ə trĭp'sē/ the breaking up of a stone within the body, usually in the urinary tract, through the use of mechanical force during surgery or with less invasive means such as focused sound waves, shock waves, lasers, or ultrasound; the broken particles can then be passed in the urine.

lithuresis /lĭth'yoo rē'sĭs/ presence of calculi in the urine.

litmus /lĭt'məs/ a blue dye obtained from lichens that is used as an acid/alkaline indicator; it turns red in acid solutions and blue in alkaline solutions.

litmus test a test for determining the pH of a solution. An absorbent strip of paper treated with litmus (litmus paper) is submerged in the solution; the resulting shade of red or blue determines the pH on a scale of 4.5 (red) to 8.5 (blue).

liver /lĭv'ər/ a dark reddish-brown organ weighing from 40 to 60 ounces that is located in the upper right portion of the abdominal cavity, beneath the diaphragm, and is the largest gland in the body; among the hundreds of functions it performs, the liver regulates blood sugar levels and secretes bile for the gallbladder to aid digestion; it metabolizes proteins, carbohydrates, and fats; it manufactures certain blood proteins; and it cleans the blood of toxins.

liver function test (LFT) any of various tests to determine how the liver is functioning, sometimes also including the functioning of the pancreas.

liver scan 1. examination of the liver by a sensing device such as magnetic resonance imaging (MRI) or computerized axial tomography (CAT). **2.** the information obtained by this means.

liver spot a small, benign, brownish discoloration of the skin, usually on the backs of the hands or on the forehead, caused by overexposure to the sun and commonly appearing in persons as they age. *Also called* senile lentigo.

liver transplant 1. the surgical replacement of a diseased or failing liver with a healthy liver. **2.** the new liver itself.

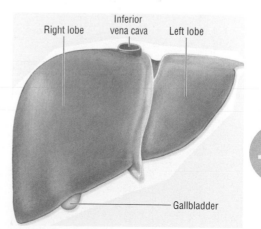

Liver

livid /lĭv′ĭd/ **1.** black-and-blue, as from an injury or congestion. **2.** pale; ashy.

living donor a healthy person who donates an organ, such as a kidney or part of a liver, to another person whose organ is diseased or has failed to function.

living will a document, legally valid in most states, in which a person describes in advance the type of medical treatment that should be given if he or she is unable to communicate during a severe health crisis or at the end of life.

LLQ *abbreviation.* left lower quadrant.

lob-, lobo- *combining form.* lobe: *for example,* lobectomy.

lobar /lō′bər, -bär/ of, relating to, or involving a lobe.

lobar pneumonia /nŏŏ mōn′yə/ a bacterial pneumonia occurring in one lobe of a lung, especially pneumococcal pneumonia.

lobe /lōb/ **1.** a distinct, usually rounded part of an organ, such as a lung or the liver, set off by fissures, connective tissue, or other structures. **2.** the fleshy lower portion of the external ear; earlobe. **3.** a division of the crown of a tooth.

lobectomy /lō bĕk′tə mē/ the surgical removal of a lobe of an organ, especially of a lung. [lob- + -ectomy]

lobi /lō′bī/ plural of lobus.

lobotomy /lə bŏt′ə mē/ **1.** an incision into a lobe of an organ. **2.** the surgical severing of nerve fibers in the frontal lobe of the brain, once commonly performed as a treatment for some types of mental illness. Now regarded as unnecessary since the development of psychiatric drugs. [lobo- + -tomy]

lobule /lŏb′yōōl/ a small lobe or a subdivision of a lobe.

lobulus /lŏb′yə ləs/ (*pl.* **lobuli** /lŏb′yə lī′/) lobule.

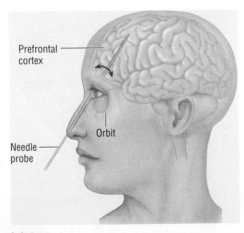

Lobotomy

lobus /lō′bəs/ (*pl.* **lobi** /lō′bī/) in anatomy, a lobe.

local anesthetic any of various anesthetics that block sensation in one part of the body while allowing the patient to remain conscious, typically applied on the skin or given by injection.

localized /lō′kə līzd′/ limited to a particular area, part, or organ.

local reaction a response or reaction to some stimulus, such as a drug or an allergen, that is confined to one area or part of the body.

lochia /lō′kē ə/ (*pl.* **lochia**) the normal discharge of blood, tissue, and other fluid from the uterus following childbirth, ranging in color from dark to light and lasting for several weeks.

locked-in syndrome a condition caused by a lesion in a blood vessel of the brain, marked by paralysis of all four limbs, inability to speak, eye movements limited to vertical direction, and preservation of consciousness. *Also called* pseudocoma.

lockjaw /lŏk′jô′/ informal term for **1.** tetanus, an acute disease with spasmodic contraction of the muscles of the neck and jaw. **2.** trismus, a spasmodic locking of the jaw muscles, an early sign of tetanus.

locus /lō′kəs/ (*pl.* **loci** /lō′sī/) **1.** the specific place where something is situated; site. **2.** in genetics, the place on a chromosome where a specific gene is situated.

-logy *suffix.* the science or study of (the subject specified): *for example,* dermatology.

loiasis /lō ī′ə sĭs/ infection by an African worm, which invades the connective tissue, causes itching and swelling, and often migrates to the eye.

loin /loin/ the part of the back and side between the bottom of the ribs and the pelvis. *Also called* lumbus.

loins /loinz/ an informal term for the genital and pubic region.

long bone any of the longer bones of the extremities, such as a thigh bone or an arm bone, with a lengthy shaft and an enlarged portion at either end that articulates with other bones.

longevity /lŏn jĕv′ĭ tē/ the state or condition of living or lasting for a very long time.

long-term care (LTC) the provision of full-time health care and support services to persons who are too ill or disabled to care for themselves, usually in a facility where such persons live permanently.

long-term care facility an establishment for the care and support of persons who are unable to live independently because of illness or disability.

Long-Term Care Facility

long-term memory (LTM) the ability to recall to the conscious mind information and experience that have been stored in the brain for a long period of time.

longus /lông'gəs/ long; used with muscles and tendons. *See also* brevis.

loop electrosurgical excision procedure (LEEP) /ĭ lĕk'trō sûr'jĭ kəl ĭk sĭzh'ən/ surgical removal of external genital warts using a thin loop of low-voltage electrified wire.

lordosis /lôr dō'sĭs/ **1.** the normal forward curve of the cervical and lumbar vertebrae of the spine. **2.** an abnormally deep forward curve of the lumbar vertebrae.

lotion /lō'shən/ in pharmacology, a liquid containing insoluble particles in suspension or emulsion, for external application without rubbing.

Lou Gehrig('s) disease /loo' gĕr'ĭg(z)/ a progressive disease with gradual loss of voluntary muscle function and paralysis, leading to death. *Also called* amyotrophic lateral sclerosis.

low back pain pain or discomfort in the lumbar or sacral areas of the spine, usually resulting from muscle strain or weakness, arthritis, injury, or degeneration of the vertebral disks.

low birth weight the weight of a full-term infant at birth below 5.5 lb.

low blood pressure consistent blood pressure readings that are below normal. *Also called* hypotension.

low blood sugar a blood glucose level below 70, which can produce shakiness, sweating, tiredness, hunger, and, at very low levels, confusion and loss of consciousness. *Also called* hypoglycemia.

low-density lipoprotein (LDL) /lĭp'ō prō'tēn, -tē ĭn, lī'pō-/ a fatty blood protein that transports cholesterol throughout the body and is associated with the depositing of cholesterol in the arteries and with heart disease.

lower esophageal sphincter (LES) /ĭ sŏf'ə jē' əl sfĭngk'tər/ a ring of muscle fibers at the junction of the esophagus and stomach. *Also called* gastroesophageal sphincter.

lower extremities the two limbs of the body between the buttocks and the feet; the legs.

lower gastrointestinal (GI) series /găs'trō ĭn tĕs'tə nəl/ examination of the lower part of the digestive tract in which an enema of contrast medium barium is given and images of the colon and the rectum are obtained by x-ray or fluoroscope.

lower leg the part of the leg between the knee and the ankle.

lower motor neuron a motor neuron within the spinal cord that connects directly to a muscle and stimulates it.

low-grade at the lower end of a range of numbers that indicate the nature of a condition, such as a fever; not serious or advanced.

low-tension glaucoma /glô kō'mə/ open-angle glaucoma without increased pressure within the eye, but with the retinal changes typical of glaucoma.

low vision eyesight that is impaired in some way, as by inability to focus clearly, but can still see enough to be useful.

low vision device any of a variety of mechanical or electronic products that help persons with low vision or lack of sight to perform tasks, such as magnifiers, voice-activated appliances, talking clocks and watches, and large-print or Braille labels and books.

lozenge /lŏz'ĭnj/ a small, hard, pleasantly flavored tablet or disk containing medication that is sucked on slowly to soothe a sore throat or deliver the medication to the mouth itself. *Also called* troche.

LP *abbreviation.* **1.** latency period. **2.** lipoprotein/low protein. **3.** lumbar puncture.

LPN *abbreviation.* licensed practical nurse.

LR *abbreviation.* **1.** labor room. **2.** light reaction or light reflex.

LRM *abbreviation.* left radical mastectomy.

LRT *abbreviation.* lower respiratory tract.

LS *abbreviation.* **1.** left side. **2.** liver and spleen. **3.** lumbosacral. **4.** lymphosarcoma.

LSH *abbreviation.* lutein-stimulating hormone.

LTC *abbreviation.* long-term care.

LTM *abbreviation.* long-term memory.

lubricant /loo'brĭ kənt/ a substance applied to a surface or between two surfaces to reduce irritation, prevent dryness, and allow smooth movement.

lucidity /loo sĭd'ĭ tē/ state or condition characterized by mental clarity.

LUL *abbreviation.* **1.** left upper limb. **2.** left upper lobe (of lung).

lumb-, lumbo- *combining form.* loins: *for example,* lumbocostal.

lumbago /lŭm bā′gō/ pain in the lumbar region.

lumbar /lŭm′bər, -bär/ of, pertaining to, or occurring in the back and sides between the bottom of the ribs and the pelvis.

lumbar nerves the five pairs of nerves arising from the spinal cord in the lumbar region of the body.

lumbar plexus /plĕk′səs/ **1.** a network formed by the lumbar nerves in the psoas major muscle of the lower back. **2.** a network of lymphatic nodes and vessels in the lumbar region.

lumbar puncture (LP) the insertion of a needle into the space between two lumbar vertebrae, usually the third and fourth, to withdraw spinal fluid for examination and sometimes to inject medication. *Also called* spinal puncture, spinal tap.

lumbar region the area of the back along the sides of the lumbar vertebrae.

lumbar vertebrae /vûr′tə brē′, -brā′/ the five vertebrae (typically designated L1-L5) of the spinal column lying between the thoracic vertebrae and the sacrum.

lumboabdominal /lŭm′bō ăb dŏm′ə nəl/ of or pertaining to both the lumbar region of the back and the abdomen. [lumbo- + abdominal]

lumbocostal /lŭm′bō kŏs′təl/ of or pertaining to both the lumbar region and the ribs. [lumbo- + costal]

lumbodynia /lŭm′bō dĭn′ē ə/ pain in the lumbar region. *Also called* lumbago. [lumbo- + -dynia]

lumbosacral /lŭm′bō săk′rəl, -sā′krəl/ of or pertaining to both the lumbar region and the sacrum. [lumbo- + sacral]

lumbus /lŭm′bəs/ the part of the back and side between the bottom of the ribs and the pelvis. *Also called* loin.

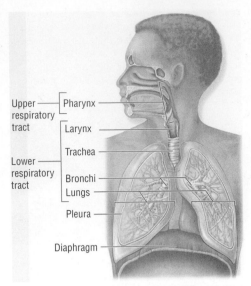

Lungs

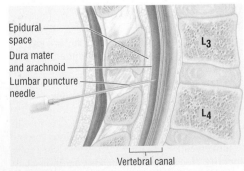

Lumbar Puncture

lumen /lōō′mən/ (*pl.* **lumina** /lōō′mə nə/ or **lumens**) the space or cavity inside a tubular organ or instrument.

lumenal or **luminal** /lōō′mə nəl/ of, relating to, or of the nature of a lumen.

lumpectomy /lŭm pĕk′tə mē/ surgical removal of a malignant tumor with little or no destruction of surrounding tissue, especially excision of a breast cancer without removing the breast itself. [lump + -ectomy]

lung /lŭng/ either of the pair of lobed, balloon-like organs of respiration in the chest that inhale air containing oxygen and exhale carbon dioxide and water.

lung cancer malignancy in one or both lungs, often caused by smoking or exposure to certain chemicals (as asbestos) or pollution.

lung transplant **1.** surgical replacement of diseased or failing lungs with healthy lungs. **2.** the new lungs themselves.

lung volume reduction surgery (LVRS) an operation to remove part of one or both lungs, used to improve breathing in certain patients with severe emphysema.

lunula /lōōn′yə lə/ (*pl.* **lunulae** /lōōn′yə lē′/) a small area shaped like a crescent, such as the curved white portion of the base of the nails.

lunule /lōōn′yōōl/ lunula.

lupus /lōō′pəs/ any of various diseases involving the skin and joints and sometimes other systems and organs of the body.

lupus erythematosus /ĕr′ə thē′mə tō′səs/ any of several connective tissue disorders. *See also* systemic lupus erythematosus, discoid lupus erythmatosus.

lupus vulgaris /vŭl gâr′əs/ tuberculosis of the skin, characterized by reddish brown patches and nodules in the nose, cheeks, and sometimes the membranes of the eyes.

LUQ *abbreviation.* left upper quadrant.

luteal /loō′tē əl/ of, pertaining to, or associated with the corpus luteum (a mass of cells that secrete progesterone, formed from an ovarian follicle after the release of a mature egg).

luteinizing hormone /loō′tē ə nī′zĭng/ a hormone produced by the pituitary gland that stimulates ovulation and the formation of the corpus luteum in females and the production of testosterone in males.

luxation /lŭk sā′shən/ dislocation, as of a joint.

LV *abbreviation.* **1.** left ventricle. **2.** leukemia virus. **3.** live virus.

LVAD *abbreviation.* left ventricular assist device.

LVN *abbreviation.* licensed vocational/visiting nurse.

LVRS *abbreviation.* lung volume reduction surgery.

lycopene /lī′kə pēn′/ a red carotenoid pigment found in tomatoes and some berries and fruits.

Lyme arthritis /līm/ arthritis resulting from Lyme disease.

Lyme disease a bacterial disease transmitted by the bite of a tick *(Borrelia burgdorferi)* and marked by a distinctive rash, headache, fever, muscle aches, inflammation and pain in the joints, and sometimes chronic arthritis and nerve and cardiac damage.

lymph-, lympho- *combining form.* lymph: *for example,* lymphocyte.

lymph /lĭmf/ a clear to yellowish fluid containing white blood cells that circulates through the body in the vessels of the lymphatic system, clearing bacteria and other products from the tissues and providing lymphocytes to the blood.

lymphaden-, lymphadeno- *combining form.* lymph node: *for example,* lymphadenectomy.

lymphadenectomy /lĭm făd′ə něk′tə mē/ surgical removal of a lymph node. *Also called* lymph node dissection. [lymphaden- + -ectomy]

lymphadenitis /lĭm făd′ə nī′tĭs/ inflammation of one or more lymph nodes resulting from infection. [lymphaden- + -itis]

lymphadenography /lĭm făd′ə nŏg′rə fē/ radiography of lymph nodes that have been injected with a contrast medium. [lymphadeno- + -graphy]

lymphadenopathy /lĭm făd′ə nŏp′ə thē/ any abnormal or diseased condition of the lymph nodes. [lymphadeno- + -pathy]

lymphangi-, lymphangio- *combining form.* lymphatic vessel: *for example,* lyphangioma.

lymphangiogram /lĭm făn′jē ə grăm′/ the radiographic film produced by lymphangiography. [lymphangio- + -gram]

lymphangiography /lĭm făn′jē ŏg′rə fē/ radiographic imaging of lymph vessels through the injection of a contrast substance into the vessels. *Also called* lymphography. [lymphangio- + -graphy]

lymphangioleiomyomatosis /lĭm făn′jē ō lī′ō mī′ō mə tō′sĭs/ or **lymphangiomyomatosis** /lĭm făn′jē ō mī′ō mə tō′sĭs/ a rare and progressive disease of women of childbearing age, marked by tumors of the smooth muscle in the lungs and chest cavity.

lymphangioma /lĭm făn′jē ō′mə/ a malformation of lymphatic channels and spaces that resembles a tumor and is benign, but may cause serious symptoms by compression, of the airway, for example, in the newborn. [lymphangi- + -oma]

lymphangitis /lĭm′făn jī′tĭs/ inflammation of one or more lymphatic vessels. [lymphang(i)- + -itis]

lymphatic /lĭm făt′ĭk/ of or pertaining to lymph or to the tissues or vessels that contain or carry it.

lymphatic drainage massage in massage therapy, a technique that uses very light rhythmic strokes to move lymph towards the nodes to encourage healing.

lymphatic duct either of two vessels that carry lymph to the bloodstream.

lymphatic system taken together, the vessels, glands, and tissues that contain or carry lymph throughout the body.

lymphatic tissue or **lymphoid tissue** /lĭm′foid/ the netlike cells and fibers of the lymphatic system containing the lymphocytes in the interstices.

lymphatic vessels taken together, the network of channels that carry lymph throughout the body.

lymphedema /lĭm′fĭ dē′mə/ swelling resulting from the accumulation of lymph in the tissues, often occurring in the legs. [lymph- + -edema]

lymph node or **lymph gland** one of the small, roundish bodies of lymphatic tissue that lie along the lymphatic vessels and are the primary producers of lymphocytes.

lymph node dissection /dĭ sěk′shən/ surgical removal of a lymph node. *Also called* lymphadenectomy.

lymphoblast /lĭm′fə blăst′/ an immature lymphocyte. [lympho- + -blast]

lymphoblastic leukemia /lĭm′fə blăs′tĭk loō kē′mē ə/ leukemia characterized by increased growth and activity of the lymphatic

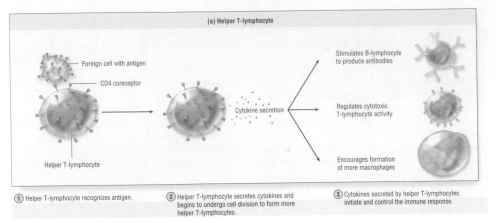

Lymphocyte

tissue and high numbers of malignant lympho-cytes and lymphoblasts. *Also called* lympho-cytic leukemia. *See also* acute lymphoblastic leukemia.

lymphocyte /lĭm′fə sīt′/   the primary cell pro-duced by the lymphatic tissue, a type of white blood cell that is part of the body's immune system and functions to clear infection.

lymphocytic /lĭm′fə sĭt′ik/   of, pertaining to, typical of, or involving lymphocytes.

lymphocytic leukemia /loō kē′mē ə/   lym-phoblastic leukemia.

lymphocytosis /lĭm′fō sī tō′sĭs/   an abnor-mally high number of lymphocytes in the blood or other bodily fluids, usually associ-ated with an infection or inflammation. [lym-pho- + -cytosis]

lymphography /lĭm fŏg′rə fē/   radiographic imaging of lymph vessels through the injec-tion of a substance not penetrable by x-rays into the vessels. *Also called* lyphangiography. [lympho- + -graphy]

lymphoid /lĭm′foid/   of, pertaining to, or like lymph or lymphatic tissue. [lymph- + -oid]

lymphoid tissue   lymphatic tissue.

lymphokine /lĭm′fə kīn′/   a type of protein re-leased by certain lymphocytes as part of the body's immune response.

lymphokinesis /lĭm′fō kĭ nē′sĭs/   **1.** circulation of lymph throughout the lymphatic system. **2.** movement of lymph within the semicircular canals of the inner ear. [lympho- + -kinesis]

lymphoma /lĭm fō′mə/ (*pl.* **lymphomas** or **lym-phomata** /lĭm fō′mə tə/)   a usually malig-nant tumor of the lymphatic tissue.

lymphomatosis /lĭm fō′mə tō′sĭs/   condition in which there are multiple sites of lymphoma distributed throughout the body. [lymph- + -omat- + -osis]

lymphopathy /lĭm fŏp′ə thē/   disease of the lymph nodes or vessels. [lympho- + -pathy]

lymphosarcoma /lĭm′fō sär kō′mə/ (*pl.* **lym-phosarcomas** or **lymphosarcomata** /lĭm′fō sär kō′mə tə/)   a malignant lymphoma that has spread widely. [lympho- + sarcoma]

lymphostasis /lĭm fŏs′tə sĭs/   blockage of the flow of lymph. [lympho- + stasis]

lymph vessel   any of the channels through which lymph is carried.

Lys   *abbreviation.* lysine.

lysine /lī′sēn/   one of the essential amino acids, necessary for growth in infants and for nitrogen balance in adults.

-lysis   *suffix.* lysis: *for example,* electrolysis.

lysis /lī′sĭs/   **1.** destruction or dissolution, as of a chemical compound or a cell, by a specific agent; disintegration; decomposition. **2.** the gradual diminishing or easing of the symp-toms of an illness..

lysosome /lī′sə sōm′/   a small structure in the cytoplasm of many cells that contains en-zymes involved in the digestive process inside the cell.

-lytic   *suffix.* involving or pertaining to lysis (of the matter or type specified): *for example,* hemolytic.

M

macerate /măs′ə rāt′/   to soften something, as tissue or an organ, by steeping or soaking.

Macewen('s) sign /mə kyōō′ən(z)/   a dull sound heard on percussion (tapping) of the skull, indicating hydrocephalus.

Machado-Joseph disease /mə chä′dō jō′zəf, -səf/   a degenerative disease of the central nervous system that tends to occur in families of Portuguese ancestry.

macro- *prefix.* large; long: *for example,* macrocephaly.

macroadenoma /măk′rō ăd′ə nō′mə/   a pituitary tumor larger than ten millimeters in diameter. [macro- + adenoma]

macrobiotic /măk′rō bī ŏt′ĭk/   **diet** a highly restricted diet consisting mostly of whole grains and beans thought to promote well-being and longevity.

macrocephalic /măk′rō sə făl′ĭk/   of or related to macrocephaly.

macrocephalus /măk′rō sĕf′ə ləs/ or **macrocephaly** /măk′rō sĕf′ə lē/   having an abnormally large skull, acquired either after or prior to birth. *See also* megacephaly. [macro- + -cephaly]

macrocheilia /măk′rō kī′lē ə/   having abnormally enlarged lips.

macrocranium /măk′rō krā′nē əm/   an overly large skull, especially the bones of the skull that contain the brain, often seen in hydrocephaly. [macro- + -cranium]

macrocyte /măk′rə sīt′/   an unusually large red blood cell, indicative of certain diseases, such as pernicious anemia (a disease with vitamin B12 deficiency). [macro- + -cyte]

macrocytic /măk′rə sĭt′ĭk/   of or pertaining to macrocytes.

macrocytosis /măk′rō sī tō′sĭs/   a condition marked by unusually large numbers of macrocytes in the blood. [macro- + -cytosis]

macrodactylia /măk′rō dăk tĭl′ē ə/   a condition with unusual enlargement of one or more digits (fingers or toes).

macrodontia /măk′rō dŏn′shē ə/   condition in which one or several teeth are enlarged.

macroglia /mă krŏg′lē ə/   a large star-shaped neuroglia (nerve cell) with many branches. *Also called* astrocyte.

macroglobulin /măk′rō glŏb′yə lĭn/   a globulin (a type of protein found in the body) of high molecular weight. [macro- + globulin]

macroglobulinemia /măk′rō glŏb′yə lĭ nē′mē ə/   increased levels of macroglobulins in the blood serum. [macro- + globulin + -emia]

macroglossia /măk′rō glŏs′ē ə/   having an abnormally large tongue, either by birth or as a result of a pathology.

macrognathia /măk′rō nā′thē ə/   having an unusually large or elongated jaw.

macrolides /măk′rō līdz/   any of several common antibiotics that are produced by a certain species of *Streptomyces,* such as erythromycin.

macromastia /măk′rō măs′tē ə/   having abnormally large breasts.

macrophage /măk′rə fāj′/   any of the large phagocytes (scavenger cells) that rid the body of unwanted microorganisms and cell debris by engulfing and devouring them (phagocytosis). [macro- + -phage]

macrorhinia /măk′rō rĭn′ē ə/   having an unusually large nose, either by birth or resulting from a pathology.

macroscopic /măk′rə skŏp′ĭk/   large enough to be examined with the naked eye, i.e., without the use of a microscope. [macro- + -scopic]

macrosomia /măk′rə sō′mē ə/   having an abnormally large-sized body, as in gigantism.

macrovascular /măk′rō văs′kyə lər/   of or related to the large blood vessels. [macro- + vascular]

macula /măk′yə lə/   (*pl.* **maculae** /măk′yə lē′/)   **1.** a small spot **2.** a discolored flat spot or patch on the skin; macule **3.** the macula lutea of the eye.

macula lutea /lōō′tē ə/   (*pl.* **maculae luteae** /lōō′tē ē/)   a small yellowish spot on the retina of the eye where vision is most acute.

macular /măk′yə lər/   of or related to the macula.

macular cyst /sĭst/   a hole in the macula lutea of the eye, usually caused by the shrinking of the vitreous humor (jellylike substance) in the eye.

macular degeneration /dĭ jĕn′ə rā′shən/   a disease in which the macula lutea of the eye degenerates, resulting in a progressive loss of sharp, central vision. *Also known as* age-related macular degeneration.

macular retinopathy /rĕt'ə nŏp'ə thē/   any of various diseases of the macula lutea.

macular vision   central vision, as is used for reading, driving, and carrying out activities that require keen straight-ahead seeing.

macule /măk'yōōl/   a small discolored spot or patch on the skin; usually flat.

maculopathy /măk'yə lŏp'ə thē/   any of various diseases of the macula lutea.

mad cow disease   a severely degenerative disease that affects the brain, transmitted by a particle known as a prion, thought to be transmitted by eating meat from an infected cow; related to Jakob-Creutzfeldt disease.

Madelung('s) disease /mä'də lōōng(z)'/   disorder with a symmetrical accumulation of fatty deposits on the upper back, shoulders, and neck.

magistral /măj'ə strəl/   in pharmacology, said of a prescription that has been specially formulated for a particular patient.

magnesium (Mg) /măg nē'zē əm/   a mineral essential to normal bodily metabolism and functioning, including the development of healthy bones and normal muscle contraction.

magnesium deficiency   a shortage of the mineral magnesium in the body, which leads to irritability of the nervous system and muscle spasm; often seen in malnutrition, persistant diarrhea, and kidney disease.

magnet therapy   an alternative therapy used to treat a wide variety of disorders, such as arthritis, immune dysfunction, and cancer; magnets are applied to different parts of the body to generate magnetic fields thought to be helpful in reducing inflammation and curing disease. *Also called* magnetic field therapy.

magnetic field therapy   magnet therapy.

magnetic resonance angiography (MRA) /ăn'jē ŏg'rə fē/   a diagnostic technique that generates computer images of blood vessels using a magnetic resonance imaging (MRI) machine; a contrast medium is injected into the bloodstream before the scan is done, making the blood vessels easier to see.

magnetic resonance cholangiopancreatography /kə lăn'jē ō păn'krē ə tŏg'rə fē/   a diagnostic technique that generates computer images of the bile and pancreatic ducts using a magnetic resonance imaging (MRI) machine [chol- + angio- + pancreato- + -graphy].

magnetic resonance elastography /ĭ lăs tŏg' rə fē/   a diagnostic technique that gently shakes tissue in a magnetic resonance imaging (MRI) machine to measure the elasticity of the tissue; for example, harder, less elastic tissue in the breast could indicate a tumor.

magnetic resonance imaging (MRI)   a non-invasive diagnostic technique used to generate

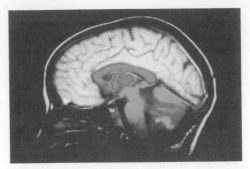
Magnetic Resonance Imaging

computerized images of internal body tissues and organs while the patient lies inside a large magnetic tube; the images are obtained through the use of a scanner that relies on magnetism and the application of radio waves to create an image.

magnetic resonance perfusion imaging /pər fyōō'zhən/   a magnetic resonance imaging technique that uses a dye in order to see blood flow in tissues.

magnetic resonance spectroscopic imaging /spĕk'trə skŏp'ĭk/   a noninvasive diagnostic technique that generates computer images of cellular activity in tissue using a magnetic resonance imaging (MRI) machine.

maintenance dose   the lowest effective amount of a medicine that will maintain a gradual healing process but will also protect against a flaring up of the condition being treated.

major depressive disorder   a psychiatric disorder characterized by chronic, severe depression.

major surgery   surgery involving risk to the life of the patient, especially surgery on a major organ such as the heart or brain.

mal-   *prefix.* bad, ill; abnormal: *for example,* malabsorption.

mala /mā'lə, -lä/   cheek.

malabsorption /măl'ăb sôrp'shən, -zôrp'-/   inadequate or ineffective absorption of nutrients from the intestinal tract; often occurring in disorders such as celiac disease and cystic fibrosis. [mal- + absorption]

-malacia   *suffix.* softening: *for example,* osteomalacia.

malacia /mə lā'shə/   abnormal softening in a tissue or organ.

maladaptive behavior /măl'ə dăp'tĭv/   an inability to adjust to the stresses of everyday living, resulting in abnormal behavior.

maladjusted /măl'ə jŭs'tĭd/   unable to deal well with the difficulties and challenges of daily life. [mal- + adjusted]

malady /măl′ə dē/   disease, illness, disorder.

malaise /mə lāz′, -lĕz′/   feeling of fatigue and ill health, often at the onset of an illness.

malalignment /măl′ə līn′mənt/   poor alignment of a structure, as the pieces of a bone, or of teeth within the jaw. [mal- + alignment]

malar /mā′lər, -lär/   of or relating to the cheek or cheek bone (mala).

malaria /mə lâr′ē ə/   an infectious disease, mostly confined to tropical regions, that is caused by a parasite (*Plasmodium* protozoa) and is carried through the bite of an infected female mosquito; characterized by recurrent bouts of severe chills and high fever, may be fatal if untreated.

malarial /mə lâr′ē əl/   pertaining to or affected with malaria.

male /māl/   **1.** *n.* a member of the sex that produces sperm to fertilize the female's eggs; a man or boy. **2.** *adj.* of or relating to the masculine sex.

male birth control pills   hormone-based pills, still in the developmental stage, that will temporarily decrease or prevent sperm production in the body, thereby limiting the male's ability to fertilize an egg.

male condom   a type of birth control in the form of a thin rubber sheath that is placed over the penis to prevent sperm from making contact with the female's egg and also as a protection against sexually transmitted diseases.

male external genitalia /jĕn′ĭ tāl′yə/   the external reproductive organs of the male—the penis and scrotum.

male genitalia   male reproductive organs, external and internal. *See* male external genitalia and male internal genitalia.

male internal genitalia   the internal reproductive organs of the male—the testes, epididymides, deferent ducts, seminal vesicles, bulbourethral (Cowper's) glands, and prostate.

male pattern baldness   hereditary baldness on the crown and temples in the male. *See also* alopecia.

male reproductive system   the male reproductive organs (including the male internal and external genitalia) involved in producing, storing, and delivering sperm to the female egg for fertilization.

maleruption /măl′ĭ rŭp′shən/   incorrect eruption of teeth through the gum. [mal- + eruption]

malformation /măl′fôr mā′shən/   an irregular or abnormal structural development; physical deformity. [mal- + formation]

malfunction /măl fŭngk′shən/   **1.** *n.* failure to function in the normal way. **2.** *v.* to function imperfectly or improperly. [mal- + function]

malignancy /mə lĭg′nən sē/   **1.** the state of being malignant or cancerous. **2.** a malignant tumor.

malignant /mə lĭg′nənt/   tending to cause destruction and death, especially used to describe a cancer that is invasive and spreading.

malignant hypertension /hī′pər tĕn′shən/   severe hypertension that occurs rapidly and leads to rapid deterioration in the blood vessels.

malignant melanoma /mĕl′ə nō′mə/   a rapidly spreading skin tumor that arises from a pigment-producing cell (melanocyte) in the skin. *Also called* melanocarcinoma, melanoma. [melan- + -oma]

malignant tumor /tōō′mər/   a locally invasive and destructive growth (usually a form of cancer) that tends to spread to other body parts and is likely to cause death if not adequately treated.

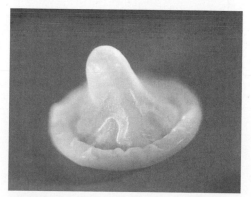

Male Condom

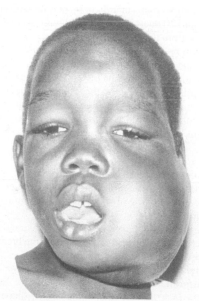

Malignant Tumor

M

malingering /mə lĭng′gər ĭng/   pretending to be ill or otherwise disabled in order to avoid work or draw sympathy.

malleolus /mə lē′ə ləs/ (*pl.* **malleoli** /mə lē′ə lī′/)   a rounded bony projection, as on either side of the ankle; the medial malleolus is the distal end of the tibia, the lateral malleolus is the distal end of the fibula.

malleus /măl′ē əs/ (*pl.* **mallei** /măl′ē ī′/)   the outermost of the three small bones of the middle ear; it resembles a mallet or hammer and transmits sound vibrations from the eardrum to the incus and then the stapes—the other two small bones of the middle ear. *Also called* hammer.

malnutrition /măl′nōō trĭsh′ən/   state of poor nutrition as a result of a poor diet or an inability to absorb foods. [mal- + nutrition]

malocclusion /măl′ə klōō′zhən/   improper alignment between the upper and lower teeth so that the teeth do not contact normally when the jaw is closed. [mal- + occlusion]

malodorous /măl ō′dər əs/   having a bad odor.

malrotation /măl′rō tā′shən/   failure of an organ or body part, especially the intestinal tract, to rotate normally during embryonic development. [mal- + rotation]

malunion /măl yōō′n yən/   incomplete coming together or healing, as of a fracture or wound.

mamm-,   **mamma-**,   **mammo-** *combining form.* breast: *for example,* mammogram.

mammaplasty /măm′ə plăs′tē/   surgical alteration or repair of a breast. *Also called* mammoplasty. [mamma- + -plasty]

mammary duct /măm′ə rē/   one of between 15 and 20 ducts in the female breast that carry milk from the mammary gland to the nipple.

mammary gland   milk-secreting gland in the female breast. *Also called* milk gland.

mammary papilla /pə pĭl′ə/ (*pl.* **mammary papillae** /pə pĭl′ē/)   the small projection from the center of the breast that contains the openings for the mammary ducts; it is surrounded by a round pigmented area called the areola. *Also called* nipple.

mammectomy /mə mĕk′tə mē/   surgical removal of a breast. [mamm- + -ectomy]

mammogram /măm′ə grăm′/   x-ray image of the soft tissues of the breasts. [mammo- + -gram]

mammography /mə mŏg′rə fē/   diagnostic technique that uses x-rays to screen the breasts for abnormalities, particularly for those that might be cancerous. [mammo- + -graphy]

mammoplasty /măm′ə plăs′tē/   plastic surgery to rebuild or change the size or shape of

Mammography

the breast. *Also called* mammaplasty, mastoplasty. [mammo- + -plasty]

Mammotome /măm′ə tōm′/   a minimally invasive technique for breast biopsy, known as the Mammotome® Breast Biopsy System, that uses a small probe guided by ultrasound images to locate abnormalities in the breast and obtain tissue samples.

mammotomy /mə mŏt′ə mē/   surgical incision into a breast. *Also called* mastotomy.

managed care   a system of providing health care that attempts to lower costs by using an outside party—such as an insurance company or a doctor-hospital network—to mediate between the patient and the doctor in managing the patient's care; a variety of cost-containment methods are followed. *Also called* managed health care.

managed health care   managed care.

mandible /măn′də bəl/   large, U-shaped bone of the lower jaw. *Also called* mandibular bone.

mandibular /măn dĭb′yə lər/   of or involving the mandible.

mandibular bone   mandible.

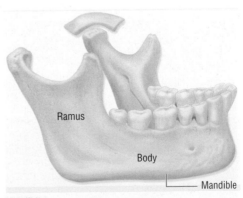

Ramus

Body

Mandible

Mandible

mandibular nerve   one of three branches of the trigeminal nerve (cranial nerve V) that supplies nerve fibers to most of the face; the mandibular nerve is the lowermost branch and brings sensory fibers to the teeth, the mandible, the floor of the mouth, part of the tongue, and the skin of the cheek, lower lip, and chin, as well as motor fibers to the muscles for chewing.

mandrin /măn′drĭn/   guide that supplies shape and firmness to a flexible catheter, especially for use in the urinary meatus.

manganese (Mn) /măng′gə nēz′, -nēs′/   a metallic element necessary for normal bone metabolism and many enzyme reactions; certain salts of manganese are used in medicine.

mange /mānj/   a communicable skin disease of domestic animals, including dogs and cats, caused by various mites, such as *Chorioptes, Psoroptes,* and *Sarcoptes*; in humans, known as scabies.

mania /mā′nē ə/   mood disorder in which the person's behavior is mentally and physically hyperactive and disorganized due to an abnormally elevated mood; the euphoric (manic) phase in manic-depressive disease.

-mania   *suffix.* having an extreme compulsion for something: *for example,* dipsomania.

manic /măn′ĭk/   of or affected with mania.

manic-depressive disease or **disorder** or **illness**   mental disorder characterized by periodic mood swings from mania to depression. *Also called* bipolar disease, bipolar disorder.

manic episode   in manic-depressive disease, a period marked by an abnormally elevated mood, increased speed of thought and speech, excitability, agitation, and other indications of mania.

manifestation /măn′ə fĕ stā′shən/   a symptom or sign of a disease.

manipulation /mə nĭp′yə lā′shən/   skillful use of the hands in examining or for therapeutic reasons, as in repositioning a fractured bone.

manipulation therapy   manipulative therapy.

manipulative /mə nĭp′yə lə tĭv/   of or relating to manipulation.

manipulative therapy   in complementary and alternative medicine, the physical manipulation of the body for healing; there are many forms, such as massage therapy, chiropractic medicine, osteopathy, and acupressure. *Also called* manipulation therapy.

Mantoux test /măn tōō′/   a clinical test in which an intradermal (under the skin) injection of a small amount of tuberculin is given to test for past or present infection with tuberculosis.

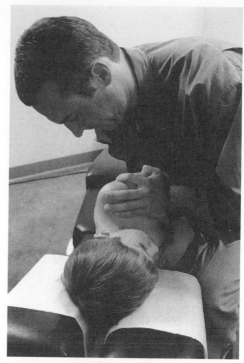

Manipulative Therapy (chiropractor)

Test is given annually to all medical personnel who come in contact with potentially infected patients. *Also called* PPD skin test, PPD test.

manual /măn′yōō əl/   of, relating to, or done with the hands.

manubrium /mə nōō′brē əm/   (*pl.* **manubria** /mə nōō′brē ə/)   the upper part of the sternum (the breastbone); it connects to the clavicle and the first two pairs of ribs.

marasmus /mə răz′məs/   severe malnutrition, especially in children, usually because of insufficient protein and calorie intake; characterized by the wasting away of body tissues.

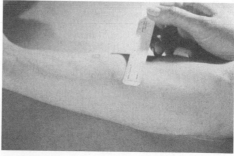

Positive Mantoux Test

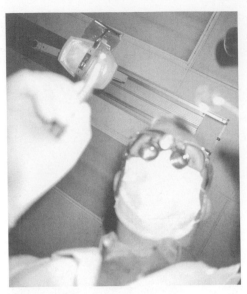

Mask (on dentist)

Marburg('s) disease /mär′bərg(z)/   often fatal viral disease in humans that produces, among other symptoms, a fever, prominent rash, and gastrointestinal hemorrhaging; first seen in Marburg, Germany, in 1967 among laboratory workers who were working with green monkeys that carried the virus from Africa.

Marburg('s) virus   a virus, indigenous to Africa, known to cause Marburg('s) disease, or green monkey disease.

Marfan('s) syndrome /mär′făn(z)/   an inherited disorder of the body's connective tissue resulting in abnormally long bones, especially in the limbs; excessive joint mobility; and defects in the eyes and cardiovascular system.

margin /mär′jĭn/   an edge or border, as of an organ or tumor.

marginal /mär′jə nəl/   of or involving a margin.

margination /mär′jə nā′shən/   the adhering of leukocytes to the walls of blood vessels during the early stages of inflammation.

marijuana or **marihuana** /măr′ə wä′nə/   the dried leaves and flowers of the female hemp plant *Cannabis sativa*, smoked or occasionally ingested for its intoxicating effect. It is classified as an illegal drug but is allowed for very limited medical use in some places.

marker /mär′kər/   something that serves to identify or distinguish; for example, a genetic marker.

marrow /măr′ō/   the soft, pulpy connective tissue found within bone. *See also* bone marrow.

masculine /măs′kyə lĭn/   characteristic of the male sex or gender.

mask /măsk/   **1.** *n.* a covering for the mouth and nose used to protect against inhaling toxic substances, to administer oxygen or anesthesia, or to prevent the spread of infection. **2.** *v.* to cover something, as with a mask.

masklike face   an expressionless facial appearance such as Parkinson's facies, resulting from a disease such as Parkinson's disease.

mask of pregnancy   brown blotches that develop on the cheeks and forehead of many women during pregnancy, likely due to hormonal changes; the same kind of hyperpigmentation may appear in women taking oral contraceptives or using hormone therapy. *Also called* chloasma, melasma.

masochism /măs′ə kĭz′əm/   a disorder in which a person derives sexual gratification from being physically or emotionally maltreated.

masochist /măs′ə kĭst/   a person who practices masochism.

massage /mə säzh′/   the practice of kneading the muscles and connective tissue of the body for therapeutic purposes, as to relieve muscle spasms, increase circulation, or for general well-being.

massage therapist   one who practices massage therapy.

Massage Therapist

massage therapy   the practice of using massage to treat various illnesses and conditions. *Also called* myotherapy.

masseter /mə sĕt′ər/   the large muscle that raises the lower jaw and assists in chewing.

masseteric nerve /măs′ĭ tĕr′ĭk/   the major nerve in the masseter.

mass spect /spĕkt/   short for mass spectrometry.

mass spectrometer /spĕk trŏm′ĭ tər/   a device that detects ions by measuring electrical current.

mass spectrometry /spĕk trŏm′ĭ trē/   the procedure of using a mass spectrometer to observe and measure the weight (mass) and charge of molecules in a substance in order to identify its chemical makeup.

MASS syndrome /măs/   an inherited disorder of the body's connective tissue that results in the following group of symptoms: *m*itral valve prolapse, *a*ortic anomalies, *s*keletal changes, and *s*kin changes (MASS); it closely resembles Marfan('s) syndrome.

mast-, masto-   *combining form.* breast: *for example,* mastitis.

mastalgia /mă stăl′jə/   pain in the breast. *Also called* mastodynia.

mast cell   a cell found in connective tissue that contains substances, including histamine and heparin, that are released as part of an allergic reaction or in response to inflammation or injury to bodily tissues. *Also called* mastocyte.

mast cell tumor   a collection of mast cells resembling a tumor. *Also called* mastocytoma.

mastectomy /mă stĕk′tə mē/   surgical removal of all or part of a breast, and in some cases the nearby associated tissue in the pectoral muscles and lymph nodes, as a treatment for cancer. *See also* modified radical mastectomy, radical mastectomy, simple mastectomy. [mast- + -ectomy]

masticate /măs′tĭ kāt′/   to chew food to prepare it for swallowing.

mastication /măs′tĭ kā′shən/   the process of chewing food to prepare it for swallowing.

mastitis /mă stī′tĭs/   inflammation of the breast, usually caused by infection. [mast- + -itis]

mastocyte /măs′tə sīt′/   a cell found in connective tissue that contains substances, including histamine and heparin, that are released as part of an allergic reaction or in response to inflammation or injury to bodily tissues. *Also called* mast cell. [masto- + -cyte]

mastocytoma /măs′tō sī tō′mə/   a collection of mast cells resembling a tumor. *Also called* mast cell tumor. [masto- + cyt- + -oma]

mastocytosis /măs′tō sī tō′sĭs/   excessive proliferation of mast cells in various tissues of the body. [masto- + -cytosis]

mastodynia /măs′tə dĭn′ē ə/   pain in the breast. *Also called* mastalgia. [masto- + -dynia]

mastoid-, mastoido-   *combining form.* breast: *for example,* mastoidotomy.

mastoid /măs′toid/   **1.** resembling a breast. **2.** of or relating to the mastoid process or bone.

mastoid antrotomy /ăn trŏt′ə mē/   a surgical procedure in which an opening is made into the mastoid antrum (a large cavity in the temporal bone) to create drainage.

mastoid bone   a rounded projection of the temporal bone just behind the ear that also serves as the attachment for various muscles. *Also called* mastoid process.

mastoid cell   one of numerous small cavities in the mastoid process that communicate with each other; because they are filled with air, they are also called mastoid air cells.

mastoidectomy /măs′toi dĕk′tə mē/   a group of operations aimed at hollowing out the mastoid process of the temporal bone and middle ear for purposes of drainage, exposure, or removal of a growth such as a cholesteatoma.

mastoiditis /măs′toi dī′tĭs/   inflammation of any part of the mastoid process, usually resulting from an ear infection. [mastoid- + -itis]

mastoidotomy /măs′toi dŏt′ə mē/   a surgical procedure that involves cutting into the mastoid process. [mastoido- + -tomy]

mastoid process   a rounded projection of the temporal bone just behind the ear that also serves as the attachment for various muscles; so-named because of its somewhat conical or nipplelike shape.

mastopexy /măs′tə pĕk′sē/   plastic surgery to lift sagging breasts; usually with some improvement to the shape as well. [masto- + -pexy]

mastoplasty /măs′tə plăs′tē/   surgical alteration or repair of a breast. *Also called* mammaplasty, mammoplasty. [masto- + -plasty]

mastoptosis /măs′tŏp tō′sĭs/   sagging of the breast. [masto- + -ptosis]

mastorrhagia /măs′tə rā′jə, -jē ə/   hemorrhage from a breast. [masto- + -rrhagia]

mastotomy /mə stŏt′ə mē/   surgical incision into a breast. *Also called* mammotomy. [masto- + -tomy]

mast syndrome   a birth defect, inherited through a recessive gene, that results in presenile dementia and spastic paraplegia (motor

M

disturbances); onset is usually during early adulthood, with the disease progressing slowly; first noted among the Old Order Amish population.

masturbate /măs′tər bāt′/ to practice masturbation.

masturbation /măs′tər bā′shən/ stimulation of one's own genitals for sexual pleasure.

maternal /mə tûr′nəl/ inherited from, related to, or derived from a mother.

maternity /mə tûr′nĭ tē/ **1.** the state or fact of being a mother; motherhood. **2.** the section of a hospital dedicated to childbirth and the care of mothers and their newborns.

matrix /mā′trĭks/ (*pl.* **matrices** /mā′trə sēz′/, **matrixes**) **1.** intercellular material. **2.** the basic structure of a tooth or nail.

maturation /măch′ə rā′shən/ the process of reaching full development.

mature /mə choͤor′/ **1.** *adj.* fully developed; ripe. **2.** *v.* to reach full development, to ripen.

maturity /mə choͤor′ĭ tē/ having reached full development or total growth.

maturity onset/maturity-onset diabetes /dī′ə bē′tĭs, -tēz/ a form of diabetes mellitus, with diminished sensitivity to insulin, precipitated or exacerbated by increasing obesity and often treatable by diet and exercise. *Also called* non-insulin-dependent diabetes, Type II diabetes.

maxill-, maxillo- *combining form.* maxilla: *for example,* maxillofacial.

maxilla /măk sĭl′ə/ (*pl.* **maxillae** /măk sĭl′ē/) one of a pair of bones that make up the upper jaw; the bones hold the upper teeth and also form part of the eye sockets, hard palate, and nasal cavity. *Also called* maxillary bone.

maxillary /măk′sə lĕr′ē, măk sĭl′ə rē/ related to maxilla.

maxillary bone maxilla.

maxillary nerve the middle branch of the three divisions of the trigeminal nerve (cranial nerve V) that supplies nerve fibers to most of the face; the maxillary nerve supplies nerve fibers to the skin of the middle part of the face, the upper jaw and teeth, and the mucous membrane of the maxillary sinus and nasal cavity.

maxillary sinus one of a pair of air cavities in the maxilla (upper jaw) that connect with the nose.

maxillectomy /măk′sə lĕk′tə mē/ surgical removal of the maxilla. [maxill- + -ectomy]

maxillitis /măk′sə lī′tĭs/ inflammation of the maxilla. [maxill- + -itis]

maxillofacial /măk sĭl′ō fā′shəl/ of or relating to the jaws and the face. [maxillo- + facial]

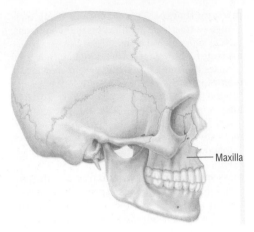

Maxilla — Maxilla

Maxilla

maxillotomy /măk′sə lŏt′ə mē/ surgical sectioning of the maxilla in order to reposition it. [maxillo- + -tomy]

Mb *abbreviation.* myoglobin.

MBC *abbreviation.* maximum breathing capacity.

McBurney('s) point /mək bûr′nē(z)/ a site on the abdomen of a patient with acute appendicitis that is notably sensitive when the pressure of a finger is applied; located several inches below and to the right of the umbilicus, in the right lower quadrant.

McBurney('s) incision /mək bûr′nē(z) ĭn sĭzh′ən/ surgical incision used for appendectomy.

mcg *abbreviation.* microgram; micrograms, one-millionth of a gram.

MCH *abbreviation.* **1.** mean corpuscular hemoglobin. **2.** maternal and child health (services).

MCHC *abbreviation.* mean corpuscular hemoglobin concentration.

MCP *abbreviation.* Metacarpophalangeal.

MCS *abbreviation.* multiple chemical sensitivity.

MCV *abbreviation.* mean corpuscular volume.

MD *abbreviation.* **1.** (*also* M.D.) Doctor of Medicine. **2.** muscular dystrophy.

MDI *abbreviation.* metered-dose inhaler.

ME *abbreviation.* medical examiner.

Meadow('s) syndrome /mĕd′ō(z)/ a condition in which a parent or caregiver falsely claims that a child or incompetent adult is sick in order to receive medical attention and treatment. *Also called* Munchausen syndrome by proxy.

mean corpuscular hemoglobin (MCH) /kôr
pŭs′kyə lər   hē′mə glō′bĭn/   a   calculated
value that measures the amount of hemoglobin in the average red blood cell (RBC); part
of a CBC (complete blood count).

**mean corpuscular hemoglobin concentration
(MCHC)**   a calculated value that measures
the average concentration of hemoglobin in a
given volume of blood; part of a CBC (complete blood count).

mean corpuscular volume (MCV)   a calculated value that measures the average volume
of a red blood cell; part of a CBC (complete
blood count).

measles   an acute and contagious disease,
caused by the varicella virus, that usually occurs during childhood; it is marked by a
cough, fever, and rash of red spots on the skin;
vaccination can often prevent it. *Also called*
rubeola.

meat-, meato-   *combining form.* meatus: *for
example,* meatoplasty.

meatal /mē ā′təl/   pertaining to a meatus.

meatoplasty /mē ăt′ə plăs′tē/   surgical repair
or alteration of a meatus. [meato- + -plasty]

meatorrhaphy /mē′ə tôr′ə fē/   surgical suturing of a meatus. [meato- + -rrhaphy]

meatoscope /mē ăt′ə skōp′/   a viewing instrument used to examine a meatus. [meato- +
-scope]

meatotomy /mē′ə tŏt′ə mē/   an incision to enlarge a meatus, esp. the urethral meatus.
[meato- + -tomy]

meatus /mē ā′təs/   a naturally occurring external opening of a canal or duct in the body.

mechanical ventilation   a machine or other device that forces air into and out of the lungs of
a person who cannot breathe on their own.

Meckel('s) diverticulum /měk′əl(z) dī′vər tĭk′
yə ləm/   a small sac or pouch occurring inside the end of the small intestine or the beginning of the large intestine.

meconium /mĭ kō′nē əm/   a greenish sterile
substance that accumulates in the intestines of
a fetus and is expelled around the time of
birth.

meconium ileus /ĭl′ē əs/   an intestinal obstruction in a newborn baby due to thickening
of the meconium.

medi-, medio-   *combining form.* middle; central: *for example,* mediolateral.

media /mē′dē ə/   plural of medium.

medial /mē′dē əl/   of, in, or toward the middle
or middle layer of something. [medi- + -al]

median /mē′dē ən/   *adj.* **1.** medial. *n.* **2.** the
middle or center. **3.** a number or value in a

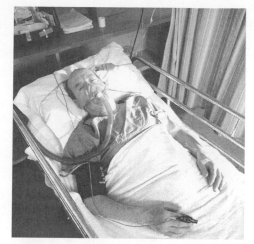
Mechanical Ventilation

range of numbers at which there are as many
values above that number as below it.

median plane   a vertical plane through the
midline of the body, dividing the right half
from the left. *Also called* midsagittal plane.

mediastin-, mediastino-   *combining form.*
mediastinum: *for example,* mediastinoscope.

mediastinal /mē′dē ə stī′nəl/   of or relating to
a mediastinum. [mediastin- + -al]

mediastinal lymph nodes /lĭmf/   lymph
nodes that receive lymph from the lungs and
vessels throughout the mediastinum.

mediastinitis /mē′dē ăs′tə nī′tĭs/   inflammation of the tissues of the mediastinum. [medi-
astin- + -itis]

mediastinoscope   /mē′dē ăs tĭn′ə skōp′/   an
endoscope used to explore the mediastinum,
inserted through an incision above the sternum. [mediastino- + -scope]

mediastinoscopy /mē′dē ăs′tĭ nŏs′kə pē/   examination of the mediastinum with a mediastinoscope. [mediastino- + -scopy]

mediastinotomy /mē′dē ăs′tĭ nŏt′ə mē/   an incision into the mediastinum. [mediastino- +
-tomy]

mediastinum /mē′dē ə stī′nəm/   (*pl.* **medi-
astina** /mē′dē ə stī′nə/)   **1.** a thin membrane
or cartilage evenly dividing a space or soft tissue in the body. **2.** the medial area of the thorax, from about the top of the rib cage to the
diaphragm, with all its organs, vessels, and tissues (thymus, esophagus, aorta, and bronchi)
except the lungs.

medic /měd′ĭk/   **1.** military doctor. **2.** paramedic. **3.** medical doctor. **4.** medical student
or intern.

M

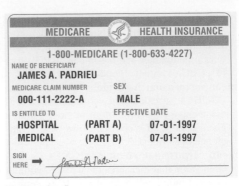

Medicare (card)

Medical Assistant

Medicaid /mĕd′ĭ kād′/ a program of the federal and state governments that pays for medical care and health-related services of persons who qualify because of their low income or lack of financial assets.

medical /mĕd′ĭ kəl/ **1.** of or pertaining to medicine or to treatment for disease. **2.** of or pertaining to the profession or practice of medicine.

medical assistant a person trained in certain office and clinical tasks to assist medical professionals.

medical errors mistakes made by physicians, nurses, or other providers in caring for patients, preparing or administering medications, or by failing to follow correct procedures or apply the right treatment, often resulting in harm to the patient, and/or legal actions against the practitioner.

medical examiner (ME) a physician employed by a city, state, or the like to officially determine the cause of death of certain persons, often by performing an autopsy and doing laboratory tests.

medical records all the notes, charts, test results, and other documents relating to a patient's state of health, family history of disease, treatments for specific conditions, hospitalizations, surgeries, and so on. Medical

records must be signed by the physician before becoming part of the patient's permanent record.

medical transcriptionist a person trained to transcribe medical information dictated by physicians.

Medicare /mĕd′ĭ kâr′/ a program of the U.S. government that provides health insurance to all persons aged 65 and older, to some younger persons with disabilities, and to all persons with end-stage renal disease.

Medicare Part A that portion of Medicare insurance that applies to the costs of hospital stays, care in a skilled nursing facility, hospice care, and some home health care.

Medicare Part B that portion of Medicare insurance that applies to the costs of care by physicians, outpatient hospital care, durable medical equipment, and certain other medical services.

Medicare Part D that portion of Medicare which pays for some or all of prescription drugs.

medication /mĕd′ĭ kā′shən/ **1.** a medicine; medicament. **2.** treatment with medicine.

medicinal /mə dĭs′ə nəl/ of or like a medicine; curative.

medicine /mĕd′ə sĭn/ **1.** a drug or other substance used in treating illness or injury; medication. **2.** the branch of science concerned with preserving health and diagnosing and treating illness or injury. **3.** the profession or practice of this science. **4.** the treatment of illness or injury without surgery.

Medigap policy /mĕd′ĭ găp′/ health insurance sold by a private company to pay certain medical costs not covered by the original Medicare plan, such as copayments and deductibles.

medio- *See* medi-.

mediolateral /mē′dē ō lăt′ər əl/ of or indicating the middle point and one side. [medio- + lateral]

meditation /mĕd′ĭ tā′shən/ **1.** the act or exercise of focusing the mind on one idea, image, theme, or the like, done silently and usually in private as a religious or spiritual practice or as a way to calm or heal oneself. **2.** the specific thought or prayer used during this act.

Mediterranean diet /mĕd′ĭ tə rā′nē ən/ the foods regularly eaten in the countries around the Mediterranean Sea, consisting of fruits, vegetables, grains, olive oil, fish, dairy, poultry, and wine but very little red meat, butter, and eggs and considered by some experts to protect against heart disease.

medium /mē′dē əm/ (pl. **media** /mē′dē ə/) **1.** sa substance in which microorganisms are cultured. **2.** the solution in which a substance is held in suspension.

MEDLINE /mĕd′līn′/ a system that links many medical libraries in the United States and makes massive amounts of medical information available online; part of the National Library of Medicine (www.nlm.nih.gov).

meds /mĕdz/ short for medication.

medulla /mə dŭl′ə/ (pl. **medullae** /mə dŭl′ē/) the soft, innermost part of an organ or structure.

medulla oblongata /ŏb′lông gä′tə/ (pl. **medullae oblongatae** /ŏb lông gä′tē/) the bottom portion of the brain stem, continuous with the upper end of the spinal cord in the skull, containing nerves that control respiration, circulation, and certain other functions.

medullary /mĕd′ə lĕr′ē, mə dŭl′ə rē/ **1.** of or pertaining to a medulla. **2.** of or pertaining to bone marrow. **3.** of or pertaining to the spinal cord.

medullary cavity the space inside the shaft of a long bone that contains the marrow.

medulloblastoma /mə dŭl′ō blä stō′mə/ a malignant brain tumor usually situated in the

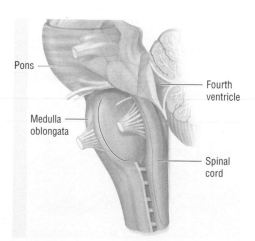

Pons

Fourth ventricle

Medulla oblongata

Spinal cord

Medulla Oblongata

cerebellum and occurring most often in children.

mega- prefix. **1.** very large; great; huge. **2.** abnormally large; enlarged; oversize. **3.** in the metric system, one million. For example, megacephaly.

megacephaly /mĕg′ə sĕf′ə lē/ or **megacephalia** /mĕg′ə sə făl′yə/ abnormal enlargement of the head. Also called megalocephaly, cephalomegaly. [mega- + -cephaly]

megacolon /mĕg′ə kō′lən/ a greatly distended and enlarged condition of the colon. [mega- + colon]

megacystis /mĕg′ə sĭs′tĭs/ an abnormally enlarged bladder, especially in children.

megadactyly /mĕg′ə dăk′tə lē/ abnormal enlargement of the fingers or toes. Also called dactylomegaly, macrodactylia. [mega- + -dactyly]

megahertz (mh, MHz) /mĕg′ə hûrts′/ a unit of frequency equal to one million hertz, i.e., one million cycles per second. [mega- + hertz]

megakaryoblast /mĕg′ə kăr′ē ə blăst′/ a cell that develops into a megakaryocyte. [mega- + karyo- + -blast]

megakaryocyte /mĕg′ə kăr′ē ə sīt′/ a giant cell of the bone marrow that has a many-lobed nucleus and produces blood platelets. [mega- + karyocyte]

megalo- prefix. **1.** very large; huge. **2.** abnormally large; enlarged. For example, megalocephaly.

megaloblast /mĕg′ə lə blăst′/ a large cell with a nucleus that occurs in the formation of the abnormal red blood cells seen in some types of anemia and vitamin deficiencies. [megalo- + -blast]

megalocardia /mĕg′ə lō kär′dē ə/ abnormal enlargement of the heart. Also called cardiomegaly.

megalocephaly /mĕg′ə lō sĕf′ə lē/ abnormally large size of the head. Also called macrocephaly, megacephaly, cephalomegaly. [megalo- + -cephaly]

megalogastria /mĕg′ə lō găs′trē ə/ abnormal enlargement of the stomach. Also called gastromegaly.

megalomania /mĕg′ə lō mā′nē ə/ an abnormal mental state in which a person unrealistically believes he or she is extremely powerful, gifted, or good or has special knowledge and abilities that others do not. [megalo- + mania]

-megaly suffix. abnormal enlargement or growth: for example, cephalomegaly.

megavitamin therapy /mĕg′ə vī′tə mĭn/ treatment of diseases and physical conditions with doses of vitamins much greater than the recommended daily allowances. In some cases, such therapy has contributed to severe

M

medical problems, while some people claim great benefit.

meibomian cyst /mī bō'mē ən/ a cyst formed on the meibomian glands. *Also called* chalazion.

meibomian gland any of the sebaceous glands in the rims of the eyelids. *Also called* tarsal gland.

meibomianitis /mī bō'mē ə nī'tĭs/ or **meibomitis** /mī'bō mī'tĭs/ inflammation of the meibomian glands. [meibomian + -itis]

meiosis /mī ō'sĭs/ (*pl.* **meioses** /mī ō'sēz/) the process of cell division by which the reproductive cells of the body are formed, with each sex cell containing only half the number of chromosomes as the body's regular cells. *See also* mitosis.

meiotic /mī ŏt'ĭk/ of, by, pertaining to, or typical of meiosis.

melan-, melano- *combining form.* melanin: *for example,* melanocyte.

melancholia /mĕl'ən kō'lē ə/ a severe form of major depressive disorder.

melanin /mĕl'ə nĭn/ any of various naturally occurring pigments responsible for skin, hair, and eye colors.

melanism /mĕl'ə nĭz'əm/ darkening of the skin or tissues. *Also called* melanosis. [melan- + -ism]

melanoblast /mə lăn'ə blăst', mĕl'ə nə-/ a cell that develops into a melanocyte. [melano- + -cyte]

melanocarcinoma /mĕl'ə nō kär'sə nō'mə/ a rapidly spreading skin tumor that arises from a pigment-producing cell (melanocyte) in the skin. *Also called* malignant melanoma, melanoma. [melano- + carcinoma]

melanocyte /mə lăn'ə sīt', mĕl'ə nə-/ an epidermal cell that produces melanin. [melano- + -cyte]

melanocytoma /mĕl'ə nō sī tō'mə/ a neoplasm or other growth that consists of melanocytes and is usually benign. [melano- + cyt- + -oma]

melanoderma /mĕl'ə nō dûr'mə/ darkening of the skin caused by an abnormal increase in the number of melanocytes present or in the melanin they contain. [melano- + -derma]

melanoid /mĕl'ə noid'/ *adj.* **1.** resembling or suggesting melanin; dark or black. **2.** having or occurring in melanosis. *n.* **3.** a dark pigment resembling melanin. [melan- + -oid]

melanoma /mĕl'ə nō'mə/ a rapidly spreading skin tumor that arises from a melanocyte (pigment-producing cell) in the skin. *Also called* malignant melanoma, melanocarcinoma. [melan- + -oma]

melanosis /mĕl'ə nō'sĭs/ darkening of the skin or tissues caused by the production of too much melanin or other pigment. *Also called* melanism. [melan- + -osis]

melanotic /mĕl'ə nŏt'ĭk/ **1.** relating to or indicating the presence of melanin or other dark pigment. **2.** having or marked by melanosis.

melanuria /mĕl'ə no͞or'ē ə/ the presence of dark pigment in the urine. [melan- + -uria]

melasma /mə lăz'mə/ patchy brownish pigmentation on the forehead, cheeks, and sometimes the neck, seen most often in women who are pregnant or taking oral contraceptives. *Also called* chloasma, mask of pregnancy.

melatonin /mĕl'ə tō'nĭn/ a hormone formed in the pineal gland, thought to be involved in regulating sleep, mood, puberty, and ovarian cycles.

melena /mə lē'nə/ feces that are black and tarry due to the presence of blood, often from internal bleeding.

-melia *suffix.* limb: *for example,* phocomelia.

membrana /mĕm brā'nə/ (*pl.* **membranae** /mĕm brā'nē/) in anatomy, a membrane.

membrane /mĕm'brān/ a thin layer of tissue that covers, lines, or separates a part of the body, such as a cell, an organ, or a space.

membranous /mĕm'brə nəs/ **1.** of or pertaining to a membrane. **2.** like a membrane.

membranous labyrinth /lăb'ə rĭnth/ a cluster of fluid-filled ducts and sacs in the part of the inner ear that helps maintain balance and equilibrium.

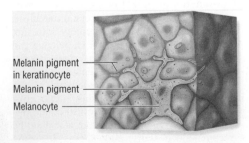

Melanin pigment in keratinocyte
Melanin pigment
Melanocyte

Melanocyte

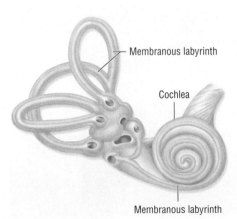

Membranous labyrinth
Cochlea
Membranous labyrinth

Membranous Labyrinth

memory /měm′ə rē/ **1.** the mental capacity to recall what one has previously experienced, known, or learned. **2.** a particular thing remembered; recollection.

memory B cell a white blood cell that creates an enhanced immunological reaction on reexposure to an antigen.

menarche /mə när′kē/ the first menstrual period occurring in puberty, usually between the ages of 9 and 16 years.

Mendelsohn('s) maneuver /měn′dəl sən(z)/ a technique for swallowing taught to patients whose normal ability to eat or drink has been impaired by illness, injury, surgery, etc. In some cases, a thickened solution is used to retrain the muscles.

Ménière('s) /mān yâr(z)′, mən-/ **disease** or **syndrome** a disease of the inner ear marked by ringing of the ears, dizziness, and progressive loss of hearing.

mening-, meningi-, meningo- *combining form.* meninges; membrane: *for example,* meningioma.

meningeal /měn′ĭn jē′əl, mə nĭn′jē-/ of, pertaining to, or affecting the meninges.

meninges /mə nĭn′jēz/ (*sing.* **meninx** /mē′nĭngks, měn′ĭngks)* the three layers of membrane that surround and protect the brain and spinal cord; the arachnoid, dura mater, pia mater.

meningioma /mə nĭn′jē ō′mə/ a tumor of the meninges that grows slowly and is usually benign but can compress and damage the tissues. [meningi- + -oma]

meningitis /měn′ĭn jī′tĭs/ inflammation of the meninges of the brain or spinal cord caused by bacterial or viral infection; can be fatal. *See also* bacterial meningitis, viral meningitis. [mening- + -itis]

meningitis vaccine either of two vaccines that protect against meningococcal meningitis, given to children, adolescents, and certain others who are at risk of infection.

meningocele /mə nĭng′gə sēl′/ a birth defect in which the meninges protrude through an abnormal opening in the skull or spinal column, forming a fluid-filled sac. [meningo- + -cele]

meningococcal meningitis /mə nĭng′gə kŏk′əl/ bacterial meningitis caused by meningococci (*Neisseria meningitidis*), typically accompanied by a petechial rash (composed of small red spots).

meningococcus /mə nĭng′gə kŏk′əs/ (*pl.* **meningococci** /mə nĭng′gə kŏk′sī/) a bacterium of the species *Neisseria meningitidis,* which causes meningococcal meningitis. [meningo- + -coccus]

meningoencephalitis /mə nĭng′gō ěn sěf′ə lī′tĭs/ inflammation of the brain and its meninges. *Also called* encephalomeningitis. [meningo- + encephalitis]

meningomalacia /mə nĭng′gō mə lā′shə/ abnormal softening of a membrane. [meningo- + -malacia]

meningomyelitis /mə nĭng′gō mī′ə lī′tĭs/ inflammation of the spinal cord and its meninges. [meningo- + myelitis]

meningomyelocele /mə nĭng′gō mī′ə lə sēl′/ protrusion of the spinal cord and its meninges through a defective opening in the spinal column. [meningo- + myelocele]

meningorrhagia /mə nĭng′gō rā′jē ə, -jə/ hemorrhaging in or from the meninges. [meningo- + -rrhagia]

meninx /mē′nĭngks, měn′ĭngks/ singular of meninges.

meniscectomy /měn′ə sěk′tə mē/ surgery to remove or trim the meniscus of the knee (patella). [menisc(us) + -ectomy]

meniscitis /měn′ə sī′tĭs/ inflammation of the meniscus of the knee. [menisc(us) + -itis]

meniscus /mə nĭs′kəs/ (*pl.* **menisci** /mə nĭs′ī, -nĭs′kī/ or **meniscuses**) a crescent-shaped disk of cartilage in a joint, especially in the knee joint.

Menke('s) /měng′kəz/ **disease** or **syndrome** a congenital disorder that first manifests itself with sparse, short, abnormally pigmented hair, and leads to physical and mental degeneration and death. *Also called* kinky hair syndrome.

meno- *combining form.* menses; menstruation: *for example,* menometrorrhagia.

menometrorrhagia /měn′ō mē′trə rā′jē ə, -jə/ excessive bleeding during the menstrual period and between menstrual periods; usually accompanied by pain. [meno- + metrorrhagia]

menopause /měn′ə pôz′/ **1.** the point at which a woman stops menstruating permanently, occurring sometime before or around the age of 50 years. **2.** the span of time before menstruation stops completely, often marked by hot flashes, irregular periods, mood changes, decreased sexual drive, and other symptoms. *Also called* climacteric.

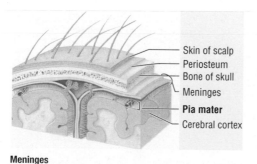

Skin of scalp
Periosteum
Bone of skull
Meninges
Pia mater
Cerebral cortex

Meninges

M

menorrhagia /měn′ə rā′jē ə, -jə/ abnormally heavy or prolonged menstrual flow. [meno- + -rrhagia]

menorrhea /měn′ə rē′ə/ **1.** normal menstrual discharge. **2.** excessive menstrual discharge. [meno- + -rrhea]

menostasis /mə nŏs′tə sĭs/ the abnormal end of or lack of menstruation. *Also called* amenorrhea. [meno- + stasis]

menses /měn′sēz/ the flow of blood and other matter from the uterus during menstruation. *Also called* menstrual period.

menstrual /měn′strōō əl/ of or relating to the menses or to menstruation.

menstrual cramps spasms of the muscles in the uterus as the menstrual flow is being discharged, often very painful; can usually be treated with NSAIDS, heating pad, and rest.

menstrual cycle the regular sequence of hormonal changes in the female body that takes place about every 28 days from puberty to menopause, counted from the first day of a menstrual period, ending just before the next period starts, and including ovulation at its midpoint.

menstrual irregularity any event or symptom that is not normal for the menstrual cycle, such as bleeding between periods or infrequent periods.

menstrual period the flow of blood and other matter from the uterus during menstruation. *Also called* menses.

menstrual phase the point in the menstrual cycle when the menstrual period takes place.

menstruate /měn′strōō āt′/ to get menstrual periods or be having a menstrual period; undergo menstruation.

menstruation /měn′strōō ā′shən/ the process of discharging a flow of blood during the menstrual cycle, approximately every 28 days.

mental /měn′təl/ **1.** of, pertaining to, or characteristic of the mind or psyche. **2.** taking place in the mind or psyche. **3.** of or relating to disorders of the mind or treatment for them. **3.** of or pertaining to the chin.

mental disease or **disorder** mental illness.

mental health **1.** the state of being able to think and behave in an organized, realistic, rational, and generally positive way without being distracted by one's own unwanted ideas or impulses. **2.** the branch of health care concerned with maintaining psychological wellness and treating disorders of the mind.

mental illness any of various diseases or disorders of the mind generally marked by disorganized, unrealistic thinking and uncontrolled behavior or by abnormal changes in mood or emotion. *Also called* mental disease, mental disorder.

mental retardation /rē′tär dā′shən/ below-average intellectual functioning resulting from fetal development, generally regarded as an IQ below 70.

mento- *combining form.* chin: *for example,* mentoposterior.

mentoanterior /měn′tō ăn têr′ē ər/ of or referring to a position of a fetus during labor in which the head or face presents first in the birth canal with the chin pointing toward the front right or left of the mother's pelvis. [mento- + anterior]

mentoplasty /měn′tə plăs′tē/ surgery to correct deformities of or improve the appearance of the chin. [mento- + -plasty]

mentoposterior /měn′tō pŏ stêr′ē ər/ of or referring to a position of a fetus during labor in which the head or face presents first in the birth canal with the chin pointing toward the back right or left of the mother's pelvis. [mento- + posterior]

mentum /měn′təm/ (*pl.* **menta** /měn′tə/) the the prominence of the lower jaw just below the lower lip. *Also called* chin.

MEP *abbreviation.* maximum expiratory pressure.

meralgia /mə răl′jē ə, -jə/ pain in the thigh.

mercury (Hg) /mûr′kyə rē/ a toxic, silvery metallic element that turns liquid at room temperatures and is used in thermometers.

mercury poisoning poisoning caused by ingesting or inhaling mercury or substances containing mercury.

meridian /mə rĭd′ē ən/ in acupuncture, one of the specific pathways in the body along which

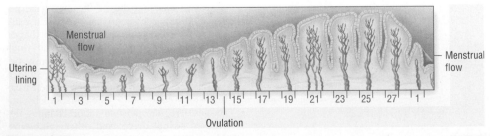

Menstrual Cycle

the qi energy must flow freely to maintain health.

merocrine gland /mĕr′ə krĭn, -krīn′/ a type of gland in which the secretion produced does not destroy any of the cells of the gland itself.

mes-, meso- *combining form.* **1.** middle; central: *for example*, mesaortitis. **2.** intermediate; in between. **3.** mesentery: *for example*, mesenteritis.

mesangium /mĕ zăn′jē əm/ (*pl.* **mesangia** /mĕ zăn′jē ə/) a supporting membrane of the capillaries of a glomerulus of the kidney.

mesaortitis /mĕz′ā ôr tī′tĭs/ inflammation of the middle layer of the aorta. [mes- + aortitis]

mesencephalon /mĕz′ĕn sĕf′ə lŏn′/ the middle division of the brain. *Also called* midbrain. [mes- + encephalon]

mesenchyme /mĕz′ĕn kīm′/ the part of the embryo from which the connective tissues, blood and lymphatic vessels, and bones and cartilage develop.

mesenteric /mĕz′ĕn tĕr′ĭk/ of or relating to the mesentery.

mesenteritis /mĕz′ĕn tə rī′tĭs/ inflammation of the mesentery. [mes- + enteritis]

mesenterium /mĕz′ən tĕr′ē əm/ mesentery (def. 1).

mesentery /mĕz′ən tĕr′ē/ **1.** the fold of membrane that attaches the small intestine to the back of the abdominal wall and carries its blood supply. *Also called* mesenterium. **2.** any membranous fold that attaches a part of the body to the body wall.

mesial /mē′zē əl/ **1.** of, relating to, in, or toward the middle. **2.** of or toward the midline of the dental arch.

mesio- *combining form.* mesial: *for example*, mesiobuccal.

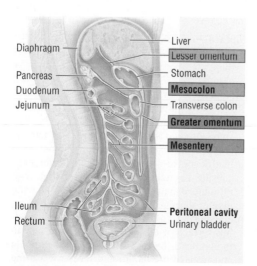

Diaphragm — Liver
Lesser omentum
Pancreas — Stomach
Duodenum — **Mesocolon**
Jejunum — Transverse colon
Greater omentum
Mesentery
Ileum — **Peritoneal cavity**
Rectum — Urinary bladder

Mesentery

mesiobuccal /mē′zē ō bŭk′əl/ of, pertaining to, or formed by the mesial and buccal surfaces or walls of a tooth. [mesio- + buccal]

mesiocervical /mē′zē ō sûr′vĭ kəl/ **1.** of or relating to the mesial surface of the neck of a tooth. **2.** mesiogingival. [mesio- + cervical]

mesiocclusal /mē′zē ə klōō′səl, -zəl/ denoting the angle formed at the junction of the mesial, lingual, and occlusal surfaces of a molar or premolar. [mesio- + occlusal]

mesiocclusion /mē′zē ə klōō′zhən/ malocclusion of the lower teeth, in which they are located in a position anterior to the upper or maxillary teeth. [mesio- + occlusion]

mesiodistal /mē′zē ō dĭs′təl/ of or relating to the mesial and distal surfaces of a tooth. [mesio- + distal]

mesiogingival /mē′zē ō jĭn′jə vəl/ of or relating to the place where the mesial surface of a tooth and the gum line meet. *Also called* mesiocervical. [mesio- + gingival]

mesiolabial /mē′zē ō lā′bē əl/ of or relating to the mesial and labial surfaces of a tooth or the point where they meet. [mesio- + labial]

mesiolingual /mē′zē ō lĭng′gwəl/ of or relating to the mesial and lingual surfaces of a tooth or the point where they meet. [mesio- + lingual]

mesmerism /mĕz′mə rĭz′əm/ **1.** hypnotism. **2.** any form or practice of hypnotism based on the concept of animal magnetism, an influential power supposed to exist in certain practitioners.

meso- *See* mes-.

mesocardium /mĕz′ō kär′dē əm/ (*pl.* **mesocardia meso-** /mĕz′ō kär′dē ə/) the double-layered membrane that supports the heart in an embryo.

mesocecum /mĕz′ō sē′kəm/ the portion of the mesentery that supports the cecum. [meso- + cecum]

mesocephalic /mĕz′ō sə făl′ĭk/ having or indicating a skull in the medium or average range of the cephalic index. [meso- + cephalic]

mesocolon /mĕz′ō kō′lən/ the portion of the peritoneum that attaches the colon to the back of the abdominal wall. [meso- + colon]

mesoderm /mĕz′ə dûrm′/ the middle layer of germ cells in an embryo, developing into the muscles, bones and cartilage, blood and blood vessels, connective tissue, lymphatic system, kidneys, sex glands, and associated structures of the internal organs. *See also* ectoderm, endoderm. [meso- + -derm]

mesodermal /mĕz′ō dûr′məl/ or **mesodermic** /mĕz′ō dûr′mĭk/ of, relating to, characteristic of, or arising from the mesoderm.

M

mesodontic /měz′ō dŏn′tĭk/ having teeth of a medium size.

mesoduodenum /měz′ō dōō′ə dē′nəm, -dōō ŏd′ə nəm/ (*pl.* **mesoduodena** /měz′ō dōō′ə dē′nə, -dōō ŏd′ə nə/) the fold of the mesentery of the embryo that attaches the duodenum to the abdominal wall. [meso- + duodenum]

mesogastrium /měz′ō găs′trē əm/ (*pl.* **mesogastria** /měz′ō găs′trē ə/) the part of the mesentery of the embryo enfolding the organ that will develop into the stomach.

mesometrium /měz′ō mē′trē əm/ the portion of the broad ligament that supports the body of the uterus.

mesomorph /měz′ə môrf′/ a person whose body is naturally muscular, lean, sturdy, and well proportioned, indicating the dominance of the mesoderm in embryonic development. *See also* ectomorph, endomorph. [meso- + -morph]

mesothelioma /měz′ō thē′lē ō′mə/ a rare, benign or malignant tumor that arises from the tissues of the mesothelium and grows in a sheetlike cover on the internal organs; this tumor occurs in the lung as a result of asbestos exposure.

mesothelium /měz′ō thē′lē əm/ (*pl.* **mesothelia** /měz′ō thē′lē ə/) the surface layer of flat cells in the membrane that lines the internal spaces of the body, such as the cavities containing the lungs and the heart.

MET *abbreviation.* **1.** metabolic equivalent. **2.** muscle energy technique.

meta- *prefix.* after, behind, altered: *for example,* metaplasia.

metabolic /mět′ə bŏl′ĭk/ relating to metabolism

metabolic equivalent (MET) the amount of oxygen used while lying down.

metabolic syndrome a group of health risks that make one susceptible to diabetes, heart disease, or stroke.

metabolism /mə tăb′ə lĭz′əm/ **1.** the sum of all of the chemical changes in living cells that provide energy for important processes, activities, and the incorporation of new material. **2.** the sum of all of the ways a substance can be changed in a living body. *See also* anabolism, catabolism. **3.** all physical and chemical changes that take place within an organism.

metabolite /mə tăb′ə līt′/ **1.** something produced by metabolic change. **2.** something required for an organism's metabolic processes or necessary for a metabolic change to occur.

metabolize /mə tăb′ə līz′/ to alter foods by chemical processes so that they can be used to fuel activities.

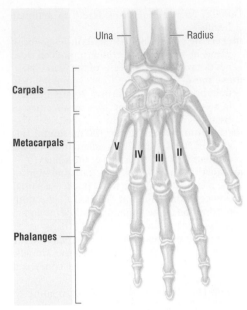

Metacarpals

metacarpal /mět′ə kär′pəl/ **1.** *adj.* relating to the metacarpus. **2.** *n.* any of the five long bones in the palm of the hand.

metacarpectomy /mět′ə kär pěk′tə mē/ the removal of any or all of the metacarpals.

metacarpophalangeal (**MCP**) /mět′ə kär′pō fə lăn′jē əl/ **1.** involving the bones of the metacarpus and fingers of the human hand. **2.** relating to the connections that enable metacarpophalangeal bones to move.

metacarpophalangeal joint the joint of the finger or where each of the fingers meets the hand, made more prominent when the fist is closed. *Also called* knuckle, interphalangeal joint.

metacarpus /mět′ə kär′pəs/ the part of the human hand between the wrist and the fingers that has five lengthened bones. [meta- + carpus]

metacentric chromosome /mět′ə sěn′trĭk krō′mə sōm′/ a chromosome that has a narrow section in the middle that divides the chromosome into two arms of about the same length.

metachromatic leukodystrophy /mět′ə krə măt′ĭk lōō′kō dĭs′trə fē/ a genetic disorder causing a certain enzyme to be missing, with ultimate damage to various organs and the myelin sheaths of nerves.

metacone /mět′ə kōn′/ the point on the grinding surface of an upper molar in the human mouth that is located farthest from the middle and front of the mouth and faces toward the back of the mouth.

metamorphic /mĕt′ə môr′fĭk/ of or relating to metamorphosis.

metamorphosis /mĕt′ə môr′fə sĭs/ a marked change in structure, function, or appearance.

metamyelocyte /mĕt′ə mī′ə lə sīt′/ a type of bone marrow cell intermediate between the mature bone marrow cell and the immature cell. [meta- + myelo- + -cyte]

metaphase /mĕt′ə fāz′/ an intermediate phase in the process of cell division in which the chromosomes align themselves in the cell. [meta- + phase]

metaphysis /mə tăf′ə sĭs/ (*pl.* **metaphyses** /mə tăf′ə sēz′/) a cone-shaped section between the part of a bone where growth occurs (epiphysis) and the main shaft (diaphysis).

metaplasia /mĕt′ə plā′zhə/ an acquired condition in which a fully developed tissue abnormally changes into a different kind of adult tissue. [meta- + -plasia]

metastasis /mə tăs′tə sĭs/ (*pl.* **metastases** /mə tăs′tə sēz′/) **1.** the movement or spread of a disease from one part of the body to another (especially said of cancer). **2.** the spread of bacteria from one part of the body to another, either through the bloodstream or the lymph channels. [meta- + stasis]

metastasize /mə tăs′tə sīz′/ to move or spread from one part of the body to another.

metastatic /mĕt′ə stăt′ĭk/ relating to or involving dispersal from one part of the body to another.

metatarsal /mĕt′ə tär′səl/ **1.** *adj.* concerning or involving the metatarsus. **2.** any of the bones in the metatarsus.

metatarsal bone one of the long bones in the foot.

metatarsalgia /mĕt′ə tär săl′jē ə, -jə/ pain in the metatarsus.

metatarsophalangeal /mĕt′ə tär′sō fə lăn′jē əl/ one of the joints between the metatarsals and the toes.

metatarsus /mĕt′ə tär′səs/ the part of the foot between the tarsus and toes. [meta- + tarsus]

metencephalon /mĕt′ĕn sĕf′ə lŏn′/ the part of the adult brain where the cerebellum and pons are located.

-meter *suffix.* instrument for or method of measuring: *for example,* thermometer.

metered dose/metered-dose inhaler (MDI) an inhaler that delivers medicine in measured doses.

methadone /mĕth′ə dōn′/ a drug used as a substitute for heroin and morphine.

methadone treatment program a program that provides methadone to people addicted to heroin and morphine.

methamphetamine /mĕth′ăm fĕt′ə mēn′/ a highly addictive stimulant drug originally prescribed for losing weight.

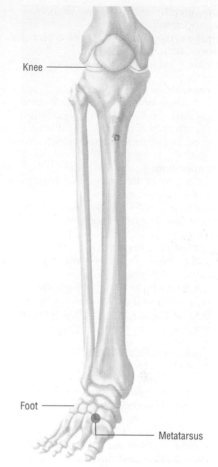

Knee

Foot

Metatarsus

Metatarsus

methemoglobin /mĕt hē′mə glō′bĭn/ a form of hemoglobin found in red blood cells that cannot combine with oxygen. It is sometimes found in the bloodstream when someone has been poisoned with a chemical such as cyanide.

methemoglobinemia /mĕt hē′mə glō bə nē′ mē ə/ methemoglobin found in the bloodstream, indicated by shortness of breath, a blue tinge to the lips, dizziness, etc. If present in large amounts, death may follow.

methemoglobinuria /mĕt hē′mə glō bə noŏr′ ē ə/ methemoglobin found in the urine because cyanide or another chemical poison was ingested.

methionine /mĕth thī′ə nēn′/ an essential amino acid found in most proteins and essential to nutrition.

method /mĕth′əd/ the technique, order, system, or manner of doing something, as performing a procedure.

M

metr-, metri-, metro- *prefix.* uterus: *for example,* metroplasty.

metralgia /mĭ trăl′jē ə, -jə/ pain or tenderness in the uterus. [metr- + -algia]

metritis /mĭ trī′tĭs/ inflammation of the uterus. [metr- + -itis]

metroparalysis /mē′trō pə răl′ə sĭs/ paralysis or weakness of the uterine muscle during or right after childbirth. [metro- + paralysis]

metropathy /mĭ trŏp′ə thē/ any disease of the uterus, especially the uterine muscle. [metro- + -pathy]

metroperitonitis /mē′trō pĕr′ĭ tə nī′tĭs/ inflammation of the uterus and peritoneum. [metro- + peritonitis]

metroplasty /mē′trə plăs′tē/ surgical repair of the uterus. *Also called* uteroplasty. [metro- + -plasty]

metrorrhagia /mē′trə rā′jē ə, -jə/ abnormal bleeding from the uterus between periods. [metro- + -rrhagia]

metrorrhea /mē′trə rē′ə/ a discharge of mucus or pus from the uterus. [metro- + -rrhea]

-metry *suffix.* process or method of measuring something: *for example,* optometry.

mets short for metastasis.

mg *abbreviation.* milligram.

MG *abbreviation.* myasthenia gravis.

Mg *abbreviation.* magnesium

mGy *abbreviation.* milligray.

mh *abbreviation.* megahertz.

MHz *abbreviation.* megahertz.

MI *abbreviation.* **1.** myocardial infarction. **2.** mitral incompetence or inadequacy.

micro- *prefix.* meaning small: *for example,* microblast.

microabscess /mī′krō ăb′sĕs/ a very small abscess. [micro- + abscess]

microalbuminuria /mī′krō ăl byoō′mə noōr′ ē ə/ a very small amount of protein in the urine. [micro- + albuminuria]

microaneurysm /mī′krō ăn′yə rĭz′əm/ **1.** enlargement of the venous end of a retinal capillary, found in diabetes mellitus, retinal vein obstruction, and absolute glaucoma. **2.** any microscopic aneurysm. [micro- + aneurysm]

microangiopathy /mī′krō ăn′jē ŏp′ə thē/ a disease of the capillaries, present in long-standing diabetes. [micro- + angiopathy]

microbe /mī′krōb/ bacterium; germ.

microblast /mī′krə blăst′/ a small red blood cell. [micro- + -blast]

microcardia /mī′krō kär′dē ə/ abnormal smallness of the heart. [micro- + -cardia]

microcephalic /mī′krō sə făl′ĭk/ having an abnormally small head. [micro- + -cephalic]

microcephaly /mī′krō sĕf′ə lē/ or **microcephalus** /mī′krō sĕf′ə ləs/ the condition of having an abnormally small head, usually related to mental defects. [micro- + -cephaly]

microchimerism /mī′krō kī′mə rĭz′əm, -kī mêr′ĭz əm/ **1.** the presence of donor cells in someone who has received a graft. **2.** the presence of fetal cells in the mother's bloodstream.

microcirculation /mī′krō sûr′kyə lā′shən/ blood flow in the capillaries. [micro- + circulation]

micrococcus /mī′krə kŏk′əs/ (*pl.* **micrococci** /mī′krə kŏk′sī/) a small, round, gram-positive bacterium. [micro- + -coccus]

microcyst /mī′krə sĭst/ a very small cyst. [micro- + cyst]

microcyte /mī′krə sīt′/ an abnormally small red blood cell, found in some types of anemia, such as iron deficiency. [micro- + -cyte]

microcytic /mī′krə sĭt′ĭk/ relating to, being, or typical of microcytes.

microcytosis /mī′krō sī tō′sĭs/ a decrease in the size of red blood cells. [micro- + cytosis]

microdactyly /mī′krō dăk′tə lē/ abnormally small fingers or toes. [micro- + -dactyly]

microdontia /mī′krə dŏn′shē ə, -shə/ or **microdontism** /mī′krə dŏn′tĭz əm/ an abnormally small tooth or set of teeth.

microglia /mī krŏg′lē ə/ small cells of the nervous system that are not nerves, found where there is neural damage or inflammation, capable of consuming foreign material. *Also called* microglial cells. [micro- + -glia]

microglial cells /mī krŏg′lē əl/ microglia.

micrometer /mī′krō mē′tər/ one millionth of a meter. *Also called* micron. [micro- + -meter]

micromyelia /mī′krō mī ē′lē ə/ abnormal smallness or shortness of the spine. [micro- + myel- + -ia]

micromyeloblast /mī′krō mī′ə lə blăst′/ a very small immature bone marrow cell, often the predominant cell found in myeloblastic leukemia. [micro- + myeloblast]

micron /mī′krŏn/ one millionth of a meter. *Also called* micrometer.

microorganism /mī′krō ôr′gə nĭz′əm/ a very small plant or animal. [micro- + organism]

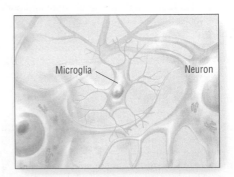

Microglia

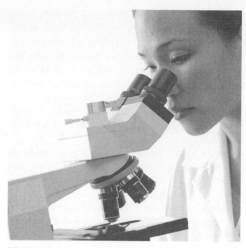

Microscope

micropenis /mī′krō pē′nĭs/ an abnormally small penis. *Also called* microphallus. [micro- + penis]

microphage /mī′krə fāj′/ a type of small leukocyte capable of consuming bacteria, foreign material, or other cells. [micro- + -phage]

microphallus /mī′krō făl′əs/ micropenis. [micro- + phallus]

microphthalmia /mī′krŏf thăl′mē ə/ or **microphthalmos** /mī′krŏf thăl′məs/ abnormal smallness of one or both eyes.

micropodia /mī′krə pō′dē ə/ abnormal smallness of the feet.

microscope /mī′krə skōp′/ an instrument used to examine extremely small things. [micro- + -scope]

microscopic /mī′krə skŏp′ĭk/ so small that a microscope is needed to see it.

microscopic laser surgery laser surgery performed using the magnification provided by a surgical microscope.

microscopy /mī krŏs′kə pē/ use of a microscope to examine very small objects. [micro- + -scopy]

microsomia /mī′krə sō′mē ə/ abnormal smallness of the body.

microsurgery /mī′krō sûr′jə rē/ an operation performed using the magnification provided by a surgical microscope. [micro- + surgery]

microtia /mī krō′shē ə, -shə/ abnormal smallness of the pinna (external ear).

microvascular /mī′krō văs′kyə lər/ of, relating to, or being a part of the circulatory system made up of very small blood vessels, the capillaries. [micro- + vascular]

micturate /mĭk′chə rāt′/ urinate.

micturition /mĭk′chə rĭsh′ən/ the act or process of discharging urine from the urinary bladder to the outside of the body. *Also called* urination.

mid- *prefix.* middle: *for example,* midbrain.

midbrain /mĭd′brān′/ the middle division of the brain. *Also called* mesencephalon. [mid- + brain]

middle ear the small membrane-lined cavity that carries sound waves from the eardrum to the inner ear via three small bones: malleus, incus, stapes. *Also called* tympanic cavity.

midget /mĭj′ĭt/ a very small person with a well-proportioned physique; this term is considered offensive.

midgut /mĭd′gŭt/ the middle part of the digestive tube containing the end of the duodenum, the small intestine, and the central part of the colon. [mid- + gut]

mid-life crisis a period during middle age when some people experience anxiety when thinking about events and trends in their life that failed to happen or did not turn out as they had hoped.

midsagittal /mĭd săj′ĭ təl/ midsagittal plane.

midsagittal plane plane that divides the body into equal right and left halves. *Also called* median plane.

midstream urine specimen a urine specimen taken from the middle of the urine stream rather than the beginning or end, used to culture bacteria and test sensitivity to antibiotics.

midwife /mĭd′wīf′/ (*pl.* **midwives** /mĭd′wīvz′/) someone who is qualified to practice midwifery.

midwifery /mĭd wĭf′ə rē/ independent care of mothers and infants, often in the home or a birth center, that generally treats childbirth as a normal event requiring little or no intervention.

migraine /mī′grān/ a type of recurring intense headache characterized by dizziness, nausea and vomiting, spots or bright flashes before the eyes, and sensitivity to light. *Also called* migraine headache.

migraine aura /ôr′ə/ an abnormal sensory sensation preceding a migraine.

migraine headache migraine.

miliary aneurysm /mĭl′ē ĕr′ē ăn′yŏŏ rĭz′əm/ an abnormal stretching of a blood vessel's wall, especially an artery, characterized by numerous small injuries.

miliary tuberculosis /tōō bûr′kyə lō′sĭs/ an acute form of tuberculosis in which small lumps are formed in one or more of the body's organs by tubercle cells, usually spread by the blood.

milk /mĭlk/ the nourishing fluid produced by mammary glands

milk fever a mild infection following childbirth and the beginning of lactation, characterized by fever.

M

Milk Teeth

milk gland   gland in the breast that secretes milk. *Also called* mammary gland.

milk of magnesia /măg nē′zhə/   a thick chalky liquid containing magnesium hydroxide, used to absorb excess stomach acid or relieve constipation.

milk teeth   a baby's temporary teeth that will be gradually replaced by permanent teeth during childhood.

milli-   *prefix.* one thousand, especially in the metric system.

milligram (mg) /mĭl′ĭ grăm′/   one thousandth of a gram. [milli- + -gram]

milligray (mGy) /mĭl′ĭ grā′/   a unit of absorbed radiation.

milliliter (ml, mL) /mĭl′ə lē′tər/   one thousandth of a liter. [milli- + liter]

millimeter (mm) /mĭl′ə mē′tər/   one thousandth of a meter. [milli- + -meter]

mimesis /mĭ mē′sĭs/   the condition of having symptoms imitative of a disease while not actually having the disease, usually caused by psychological disturbances.

mimetic /mĭ mĕt′ĭk/   of or about a disease that imitates the symptoms of another disease.

Minamata disease /mĭn′ə mä′tə/   a degenerative condition of the nervous system caused by eating food (often seafood) made toxic by methylmercury and characterized by loss of neural functions, narrowing of vision, and gradual loss of muscle tone; referred to as SMON (subacute-myelo-optico-neuropathy).

mind /mīnd/   the complex of neural pathways in the brain that feels, perceives, thinks, wills, and reasons, interpreting and making sense of information received on the basis of past experience.

mind-altering substance   any substance, usually a drug such as LSD or marijuana, that affects the mind and behavior. *See also* hallucinogen.

mind-body intervention   a variety of techniques, previously characterized as alternative medicine, designed to enhance the mind's capacity to affect bodily function and symptoms. Some methods, for example, patient support groups and cognitive-behavioral therapy, are now mainstream, while others, such as meditation, prayer, and creative therapies such as art, music, or dance, remain peripheral.

mineral /mĭn′ər əl/   any homogeneous chemical compound that is neither animal nor vegetable.

miner's lung   a fibrous condition of the lungs caused by prolonged inhalation of quartz and coal dust. *Also called* black lung (disease). *See also* pneumoconiosis.

minimally invasive   any medical procedure or treatment that requires minimal disruption or alteration of the body.

minimally invasive surgery   any operation that requires a tiny incision, often less than an inch, using a miniaturized device such as an endoscope.

ministroke /mĭn′ē strōk′/   informal term for a transient ischemic attack, a temporary blockage of a cerebral blood vessel resulting in dizziness and numbness on one side of the body or temporary loss of vision.

Minnesota Multiphasic Personality Inventory (MMPI) /mŭl′tĭ fā′zĭk/   a psychological test used with people aged 16 and older, consisting of 550 true-false questions.

minor /mī′nər/   not serious or life-threatening.

miosis /mī ō′sĭs/   abnormal smallness of the pupil of the eye.

miotic /mī ŏt′ĭk/   something that causes miosis, especially certain drugs to treat glaucoma.

mirror-image cell   a cell with two identical nuclei situated similarly in the cytoplasm.

MIS   *abbreviation.* medical information system.

miscarriage /mĭs kăr′ĭj, mĭs′kăr′ĭj/   spontaneous loss of the womb's contents before the middle of the second trimester. *Also called* spontaneous abortion.

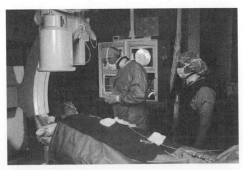

Minimally Invasive Surgery

misdiagnose /mĭs′dī əg nōs′/ to diagnose incorrectly. [mis- + diagnose]

misdiagnosis /mĭs′dī əg nō′sĭs/ an incorrect diagnosis. [mis- + diagnosis]

missed abortion an abortive condition in which a dead fetus remains in the womb for two or more months.

miticide /mĭt′ə sīd′/ a substance that kills mites.

mitochondria /mī′tə kŏn′drē ə/ plural of mitochondrion.

mitochondrial /mī′tə kŏn′drē əl/ of or relating to mitochondria.

mitochondrial disorder any of several hereditary disorders caused by genetic mutation of mitochondrial DNA.

mitochondrial DNA a strand of genetic code inside a cytoplasmic organelle, which programs the organelle's functions, most of which involve managing cellular energy.

mitochondrion /mī′tə kŏn′drē ən/ (pl. **mitochondria** /mī′tə kŏn′drē ə/) a specialized organelle found in cytoplasm that supplies most of a cell's energy; it is the location in which pyruvate (or lactate) is metabolized by the Kreb's cycle into CO_2 and water, producing a large amount of ATP (adenosine triphosphate), the key source of energy for many cellular processes; this is the site in the cell where oxygen is consumed.

mitosis /mī tō′sĭs/ the process of cell division consisting of a series of changes to the cell nucleus that produces two identical cells with the same chromosome and DNA content as the original cell.

mitotic /mī tŏt′ĭk/ of or relating to mitosis.

mitral /mī′trəl/ of or relating to the mitral valve of the heart.

mitral atresia /ə trē′zhə/ absence or failure of development of the heart's mitral valve.

mitral insufficiency (MI) /ĭn′sə fĭsh′ən sē/ inability of the heart's mitral valve to close properly, allowing blood to flow back into the auricle, sometimes leading to heart failure. *Also called* mitral regurgitation, mitral reflux.

mitral prolapse /prō′lăps, prō lăps′/ abnormal bulging of the mitral valve's leaflets during contractions.

mitral reflux /rē′flŭks/ mitral regurgitation.

mitral regurgitation (MR) /rĭ gûr′jĭ tā′shən/ a condition caused by damage to mitral valve leaflets, in which the mitral valve does not close properly, allowing blood to flow back into the auricle. *Also called* mitral insufficiency.

mitral stenosis (MS) /stĭ nō′sĭs/ mitral valve stenosis.

mitral valve the valve located on the left side of the heart, between the auricle and the ventricle, having two triangular flaps. *Also called* bicuspid valve.

mitral valve prolapse (MVP) /prō′lăps, prō lăps′/ abnormal movement of one or both of the mitral valve's leaflets during ventricular systole, sometimes with no symptoms or treatment but sometimes with fatigue and palpitations and often causing mitral regurgitation. *Also called* Barlow's syndrome.

mitral valve stenosis /stĭ nō′sĭs/ narrowing of the mitral valve's opening, usually caused by rheumatic fever. *Also called* mitral stenosis.

mittelschmerz /mĭt′əl shmârts/ abdominal pain during ovulation, caused by irritation of the peritoneum by bleeding from the site of ovulation.

mixed-tissue tumor /mĭkst′ tĭsh′oo toomər/ a tumor made up of two or more kinds of tissue.

ml, mL *abbreviation.* milliliter; milliliters.

mm *abbreviation.* millimeter; millimeters.

MMPI *abbreviation.* Minnesota Multiphasic Personality Inventory, a psychological personality test.

MMR vaccine a vaccine against measles, mumps, and rubella, administered in two doses; the first between 12 and 15 months, the second between 4 and 6 years.

Mn *abbreviation.* manganese.

mobility /mō bĭl′ĭ tē/ ability of a joint to move.

Möbius sign /mû(r)′bē əs, mō′-/ in Graves disease, loss of coordinated motion of the two eyes causing the images of a single point to fall on different areas of the retinas; ocular convergence is impaired.

modality /mō dăl′ĭ tē/ **1.** a form of use or application of a treatment or program of treatment. **2.** any of the modes of sensing such as sight or touch.

modified radical mastectomy /mă stĕk′tə mē/ surgical removal of an entire breast without removing the pectoral muscles lying underneath.

Mohs surgery /mōz/ a method for removing skin tumors by first killing the abnormal tissue with zinc chloride paste, then gradually cutting out thin layers of tissue and examining them under a microscope until only healthy tissue remains, that is, until the borders of the incision are clear of tumor.

moist gangrene /găng′grēn, găng grēn′/ a type of gangrene that is accompanied by a moist, foul-smelling discharge.

moisturize /mois′chə rīz′/ to add moisture, for example, to dry skin, by applying a cream or salve to the area.

M

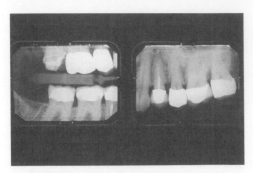

Molars (on left)

molar /mō′lər/ or **molar tooth**   one of the twelve adult teeth used to grind food, 6 in the upper jaw and 6 in the lower jaw at the back of the mouth.

mole /mōl/   a benign overgrowth of pigmented cells on the skin present at birth or appearing early in life.

molecule /mŏl′ĭ kyōōl′/   the smallest amount of a substance that has all its chemical properties and is composed of one or more atoms.

molluscum contagiosum /mə lŭs′kəm kən tā′jē ō′səm/   an infectious viral skin disease characterized by small bumps; in adults it is usually sexually transmitted and appears on or near the genitals.

mon-, mono-   *combining form.* involving one element or part; single; alone: *for example,* monaural, monoblast.

monaural /mŏn ôr′əl/   relating to, affecting, or made for use with one ear. [mon- + aural]

mongolism   /mŏng′gə lĭz′əm/   an old-fashioned term for Down Syndrome; no longer in use

Monilia /mə nĭl′ē ə/   a class of fungus that includes the genus *Candida.*

moniliasis /mō′nə lī′ə sĭs, mŏn′ə-/ or **monilial vaginitis** /mə nĭl′ē əl văj′ə nī′tĭs/   overgrowth in the vagina of the naturally occurring yeast fungus *Candida albicans,* usually found in women who have been taking antibiotics for other illnesses or who are immunosuppressed. *Also called* candidiasis, vulvovaginal candidiasis.

monitor /mŏn′ĭ tər/   **1.** *n.* a device for observing, detecting, and recording the functioning or condition of something, to assure proper functioning. **2.** *v.* to use a device to observe, record, or detect the functioning or process or condition of something.

monkeypox /mŭng′kē pŏks′/   a rare infectious viral disease caused by exposure to infected prairie dogs or someone who has it; symptoms include a rash, chills, sweats, headaches, sore throat, cough, backache, and shortness of breath.

mono-   *See* mon-.

mono /mŏn′ō/   short for infectious mononucleosis.

monoblast /mŏn′ə blăst′/   an immature cell that becomes a large mononuclear leukocyte (white blood cell). [mono- + -blast]

monocellular /mŏn′ō sĕl′yə lər/   of, relating to, consisting of, or caused by a single-celled organism. [mono- + cellular]

monocular /mə nŏk′yə lər/   relating to, affecting, or visible to only one eye. [mon- + ocular]

monocular diplopia /dĭ plō′pē ə/   a double image or ghost image produced in one eye alone; (diplopia usually occurs because of a failure of convergence of the two eyes).

monocyte /mŏn′ə sīt′/   a large leukocyte (white blood cell) having only one nucleus. [mono- + -cyte]

monocytopenia /mŏn′ə sī′tə pē′nē ə/   an abnormal decrease in the number of monocytes in the bloodstream. [mono- + cyto- + -penia]

monocytosis /mŏn′ō sī tō′sĭs/   an abnormal increase in the number of monocytes in the bloodstream. [mono- + cytosis]

monogamous /mə nŏg′ə məs/   the practice of having only one sexual partner for a period of time.

monogenic /mŏn′ə jĕn′ĭk/   relating to a hereditary disease, syndrome, or inherited characteristic controlled by a single gene. [mono- + -genic]

monomania /mŏn′ə mā′nē ə/   an obsession with one idea or subject. [mono- + mania]

monomyoplegia   /mŏn′ō mī′ə ple′je ə,   -jə/   paralysis of only one muscle. [mono- + myo- + -plegia]

mononeural /mŏn′ō nŏŏr′əl/   **1.** having one neuron. **2.** supplied by one nerve. [mono- + neural]

mononeuritis /mŏn′ō nŏŏ rī′tĭs/   inflammation that affects only one nerve. [mono- + neuritis]

mononeuropathy   /mŏn′ō nŏŏ rŏp′ə thē/   a disorder in which only one nerve is involved. [mono- + neuropathy]

mononuclear /mŏn′ō nōō′klē ər/   having one nucleus, said especially of blood cells.

mononuclear phagocytic system /făg′ə sīt′ĭk/   a widely distributed group of free and fixed bone marrow cells that protect the body from infections and toxic substances.

mononucleosis /mŏn′ō nōō′klē ō′sĭs/   an infectious viral disease characterized by abnormally high numbers of leukocytes in the bloodstream. *Also called* infectious mononucleosis, glandular fever.

monoparesis /mŏn′ō pə rē′sĭs/   slight or partial paralysis of one or part of one hand or foot. [mono- + -paresis]

Monozygotic Twins

monopathy /mə nŏp′ə thē/   a single disease or a disease that affects a single part or organ. [mono- + -pathy]

monoplegia /mŏn′ə plē′jē ə, -jə/   paralysis of one arm or leg. [mono- + -plegia]

monozygotic /mŏn′ō zī gŏt′ĭk/ or **monozygous** /mŏn′ō zī′gəs/ **twins**   twins that develop from the splitting of one egg shortly after it has been fertilized. *Also called* identical twins. *See also* dizygotic twins.

mons pubis /mŏnz′ pyoo′bĭs/ (*pl.* **montes pubis** /mŏn′tēz/)   the pad of fatty tissue women have over the joint where the two pubic bones meet.

Montgomery('s) tubercles /mŏnt gŭm′ə rē(z) too̅bər kəlz/   excessive redness of the ring around the nipple, associated with pregnancy.

mood /moo̅d/   a predominant state of mind that, when impaired, can cause distorted perceptions of situations and events and radical changes in behavior.

mood-altering drug   a drug capable of changing a person's emotional state.

mood disorder   a psychological condition with lack of control over one's emotions.

mood stabilizer   a class of drugs capable of reducing abrupt mood changes.

mood swing   alternation between elation and depression, or between depression and elation.

morbid /môr′bĭd/   1. diseased. 2. prone to gloomy feelings.

morbidity /môr bĭd′ĭ tē/   1. a diseased condition. 2. the frequency with which complications occur after an operation or other medical treatment.

morbid obesity /ō bē′sĭ tē/   overweight as to impair normal activities or to cause diseased conditions.

morgue /môrg/   a place where the dead are kept before being turned over to a funeral home for burial or cremation and where autopsies are performed.

moribund /môr′ə bŭnd′/   near death.

morning-after pill   a pill that prevents implantation of an ovum, taken the morning after unprotected intercourse.

morning sickness   nausea and vomiting associated with early pregnancy.

-morph   *suffix.* having a specified form or shape: *for example,* ectomorph.

morphea /môr fē′ə/   localized form of scleroderma with hardened patches of thick skin.

morphine /môr′fēn/   a potentially addictive drug, derived from opium, used to relieve pain and induce sleep.

morpho-   *combining form.* form, shape, or structure: *for example,* morphogenesis.

morphogenesis /môr′fō jěn′ə sĭs/   differentiation of cells and tissues in the embryo that determine the form of the organs and parts of the body. [morpho- + -genesis]

morphology /môr fŏl′ə jē/   the study of the structure of plants and animals. [morpho- + -logy]

mortal /môr′təl/   1. relating to or causing death. 2. subject to death.

mortality /môr tăl′ĭ tē/   1. the quality of being mortal. 2. death rate.

Morton('s) neuroma /môr′tən(z) noo̅ rō′mə/ or **Morton('s) disease**   a swollen inflamed nerve in the ball of the foot, usually between the second and third toes, especially common in women who wear high-heeled and/or narrow shoes.

Morton('s) syndrome   a congenital condition with a shortened first metatarsal, which causes pain in the foot.

Morton('s) toe   a second toe that is longer than the big toe.

mortuary /môr′choo ěr′ē/   a place where bodies are prepared for burial or cremation and where sometimes funeral services are held.

mother /mŭ*th*′ər/   1. female parent. 2. any cell or part that produces similar cells or parts.

motile /mō′tĭl/   capable of spontaneous movement.

motility /mō tĭl′ĭ tē/   the ability to move spontaneously.

motion sickness   nausea and vomiting caused by travel or excessive motion.

motive /mō′tĭv/   the emotion or desire or reason that moves a person to perform an action.

motor /mō′tər/   of or referring to neural structures that generate and transmit signals that cause muscles to contract or glands to secrete.

motor aphasia /ə fā′zhə/   inability to pronounce words or to speak.

motor dysfunction /dĭs fŭngk′shən/   interruption or malfunction of muscular movement.

motor nerve   a nerve that causes muscles to move or glands to secrete.

M

Mouth-to-Mouth Resuscitation

motor neuron /nŏŏr'ŏn/ a neuron that sends signals to muscle or glandular tissue thereby causing activity.

motor neuron disease any progressive dysfunction of the nerves controlling movement, often inherited, such as amyotrophic lateral sclerosis.

mottling /mŏt'lĭng/ an area of skin having spots of various colors.

mouth /mouth/ **1.** the oral cavity. **2.** any opening of a cavity or canal.

mouth-to-mouth resuscitation /rĭ sŭs'ĭ tā' shən/ emergency help with breathing provided by breathing into another's mouth, often accompanying cardiopulmonary resuscitation (CPR).

mouthwash /mouth'wôsh'/ a solution, usually containing astringent, antiseptic, antibacterial agents as well as breath-sweeteners, used to clean the mouth and as a gargle.

movement disorders any change in movement, sensation, or nerve function caused by abnormal electrical activity in a specific area of the brain.

moxibustion /mŏk'sə bŭs'chən/ in traditional Chinese medicine, the burning of a soft preparation of young wormwood leaves on the skin in order to burn or destroy tissue.

moyamoya disease /moi'ə moi'ə/ a rare, progressive cerebrovascular disorder in which the major blood vessels leading into the brain become narrow or blocked, accompanied by the formation of abnormal blood vessels called moyamoya vessels. The cause of the disease is unknown, although researchers suspect a genetic link. *Moyamoya* means "cloud of smoke" in Japanese, derived from the way the abnormal vessels look in diagnostic tests.

MP *abbreviation*. mentoposterior position.

MPD *abbreviation*. **1.** multiple personality disorder. **2.** medical program director. **3.** maximum permissible dose.

MR *abbreviation*. mitral regurgitation.

MRA *abbreviation*. magnetic resonance angiography.

MRI *abbreviation*. magnetic resonance imaging.

MS *abbreviation*. **1.** multiple sclerosis. **2.** mitral stenosis.

muc-, muci-, muco- *combining form*. mucus; mucous: *for example,* mucocele.

muciform /myŏŏ'sə fôrm'/ resembling mucus. [muci- + -form]

mucilage /myŏŏ'sə lĭj/ a thick, liquid plant substance used in pharmacy as a vehicle for delivering drugs and in medicine as a soothing or softening ointment.

mucin /myŏŏ'sĭn/ any of a group of mucoproteins found in human secretions, such as saliva, and in the stomach lining.

mucinoid /myŏŏ'sə noid'/ **1.** mucoid **2.** resembling mucin.

mucinous /myŏŏ'sə nəs/ of, relating to, similar to, or containing mucin.

muco- *See* muc-.

mucocele /myŏŏ'kə sēl'/ an abnormal swelling caused by excessive mucus in a hollow organ or body cavity. [muco- + -cele]

mucocutaneous /myŏŏ'kō kyŏŏ tā'nē əs/ **1.** relating to or made up of skin and mucous membrane. **2.** referring to the point at which the two meet at the nasal, oral, vaginal, and anal orifices. [muco- + cutaneous]

mucoid /myŏŏ'koid/ **1.** referring to a mucin, mucoprotein, or glycoprotein. **2.** muciform. **3.** mucinous. [muc- + -oid]

mucopolysaccharidosis /myŏŏ'kō pŏl'ē săk'ər ĭ dō'sĭs/ any of a group of hereditary disorders of carbohydrate metabolic processes characterized by accumulation of polysaccharides (complex carbohydrates, such as starches) in tissues and their excretion in urine.

mucoprotein /myŏŏ'kō prō'tēn, -tē ĭn/ any of a group of proteins that break down in water into carbohydrates as well as amino acids.

mucopurulent /pyŏŏr'ə lənt, -yə lənt/ relating to infected matter that oozes from blood vessels into an inflamed area, primarily made up of pus but also containing mucus. [muco- + purulent]

mucosa /myŏŏ kō'sə/ mucous membrane.

mucosal /myŏŏ kō'səl/ relating to the mucous membrane.

mucositis /myŏŏ'kə sī'tĭs/ inflammation of a mucous membrane.

mucous /myŏŏ'kəs/ relating to mucus or a mucous membrane.

mucous membrane /mĕm'brān/ a membrane containing mucous glands that lines body cavities and serves a protective function. *Also called* mucosa.

mucus /myŏŏ'kəs/ a thick, slippery liquid secreted by mucous membranes that moistens and protects them.

MUGA /mōō'gə/ *abbreviation.* multiple-gated acquisition scan.

multi- *prefix.* many: *for example,* multipara.

multicellular /mŭl'tē sĕl'yə lər/ made up of many cells. [multi- + cellular]

multicentric /mŭl'tī sĕn'trĭk/ having many centers of origin.

multifocal /mŭl'tē fō'kəl/ relating to or occurring in many places. [multi- + focal]

multigravida /mŭl'tē grăv'ĭ də/ a pregnant woman who has already had one or more pregnancies. [multi- + gravida]

multinuclear /mŭl'tē nōō'klē ər/ having more than one nuclei.

multipara /mŭl tĭp'ər ə/ a woman who has had at least two children.

multiparous /mŭl tĭp'ər əs/ relating to a multipara.

multiple chemical sensitivity (MCS) idiopathic environmental intolerance or allergy.

multiple-gated acquisition (MUGA) scan a noninvasive test that uses technetium, a radioactive isotope, to evaluate how well the heart's ventricles are functioning.

multiple myeloma /mī'ə lō'mə/ a bone marrow cancer characterized by weakness, hemorrhage, frequent infections, and anemia, and presence of Bence-Jones protein in the urine; it affects men more often than women.

multiple organ failure simultaneous failure of more than one vital organ, often fatal.

multiple personality disorder (MPD) a psychological disorder in which the personality has developed two or more complex socially integrated parts.

multiple pregnancy an instance of carrying two or more fetuses at the same time.

multiple sclerosis (MS) /sklĭ rō'sĭs/ a chronic demyelinating disease of the nervous system that may cause partial paralysis, changes in speaking ability, inability to walk, etc.

multiple system atrophy /ăt'rə fē/ a group of nonhereditary degenerative diseases of the autonomic nervous system of unknown origin, characterized by uncontrolled trembling and lack of muscle coordination. *Also called* Shy-Drager syndrome.

multiple system failure simultaneous failure of two or more vital systems.

mumps /mŭmps/ an extremely contagious, acute viral disease that causes swelling of the parotid glands at the angles of the jaws; when occurring after childhood in males, may cause sterility.

Munchausen('s) syndrome /mōōn'chou zən(z)/ a condition characterized by faking the symptoms of a disease or injury in order to receive medical attention and treatment.

Munchausen('s) syndrome by proxy a condition in which a parent or caregiver falsely

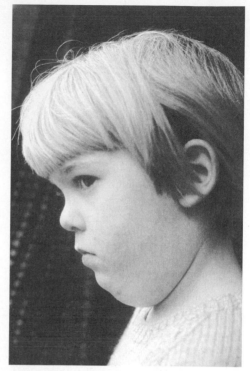

Mumps

claims that a child or incompetent adult is sick or induces symptoms of disease or injury in them in order to receive medical attention and treatment.

Munro('s) point /mŭn rō(z)'/ a point where tenderness in response to pressure is indicative of appendicitis.

mural thrombus /myōōr'əl thrŏm'bəs/ a blood clot formed on and attached to the lining of the heart; dangerous because parts of clot that break off can migrate through the aorta to brain and cause embolic stroke.

murine typhus /myōōr'ĭn tī'fəs, myōō rēn'/ a form of epidemic typhus transmitted by fleas living on rodents.

murmur /mûr'mər/ an abnormal sound heard when listening to the heart or blood vessels with a stethoscope.

Murray Valley encephalitis /mûr'ē văl'ē ĕn sĕf'ə lī'tĭs/ a severe, usually fatal, encephalitis that especially affects children living in Australia's Murray Valley.

muscle /mŭs'əl/ any of several types of primary tissue comprised of specialized cells that contract, causing various organs and other parts of the body to move.

muscle cramp an extremely painful muscle contraction usually occurring in the uterus (during menstruation) or in the calf muscles;

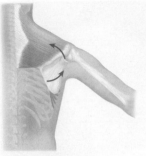
Superior Rotators

Inferior rotators

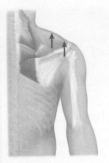
Elevators

Depressors

Muscles (in shoulder)

may result from dehydration or electrolyte imbalance.

muscle fiber one of two types of muscle cells: slow-twitch (type I), which contract slowly with little accompanying tension, and fast-twitch (type II), which contract quickly and develop high tension.

muscle relaxant /rǐ lăk′sənt/ any of a class of drugs prescribed to ease muscle spasms and relieve the pain of strains and sprains. *Also called* relaxant.

muscle tissue /tǐsh′ōō/ any of the three types of contractile tissue that cause body movements: striated, smooth, or cardiac.

muscular /mŭs′kyə lər/ **1.** involving one or more muscles. **2.** having well-developed muscles.

muscular dystrophy (MD) /dǐs′trə fē/ any one of several degenerative hereditary disorders affecting the skeletal muscles or organs.

musculoskeletal system /mŭs′kyə lō skĕl′ĭ təl/ the system of muscles, tendons, ligaments, bones, joints, and associated tissues that move the body and maintain its shape.

music therapy the use of music to assist in therapeutic treatment of psychological problems.

Musset('s) sign /myōō′sā(z), myōō sā(z)′/ the rhythmic nodding of the head when the ventricle contracts, indicating aortic insufficiency and regurgitation caused by a leaky aortic valve.

mutagen /myōō′tə jən/ anything that causes a mutation or an increase in mutations.

mutagenesis /myōō′tə jĕn′ə sĭs/ production of a mutation, usually by radiation or chemicals.

mutagenic /myōō′tə jĕn′ĭk/ likely to cause mutations or an increase in mutations.

mutant /myōō′tənt/ **1.** *n.* an abnormal animal produced by chromosomal change. **2.** *adj.* tending to undergo or resulting from mutation.

mutate /myōō′tāt/ to produce a change in the sequence of base pairs in the chromosomal molecule that is retained in future divisions.

mutation /myōō tā′shən/ a change in the sequence of base pairs in the chromosomal molecule.

mute /myōōt/ incapable of speech; silent.

mutilating keratoderma /myōō′tə lā′tĭng kĕr′ə tō dûr′mə/ a skin disorder characterized by the growth of constricting fibers around the middle bone of the fingers or toes that can cause spontaneous amputation.

mutilation /myōō′tə lā′shən/ a deliberate injury or distortion of an obvious or necessary part of the body.

mutism /myōō′tĭz əm/ inability to speak.

MVP *abbreviation.* mitral valve prolapse.

my-, myo- *prefix.* muscle: *for example,* myalgia.

myalgia /mī ăl′jē ə, -jə/ pain in one or more muscles. *Also called* myodynia. [my- + -algia]

myasthenia /mī′əs thē′nē ə/ weakness in one or more muscles.

myasthenia gravis (MG) /grăv′ĭs/ an immune system disorder affecting signals between the nerves and the muscles and characterized by varying weakness, especially of the eye muscles and those in the arms and legs. The weakness typically becomes worse as a result of activity.

myatonia /mī′ə tō′nē ə/ or **myatony** /mī ăt′ə nē/ abnormal capacity of a muscle to stretch.

myc-, myco- *combining form.* fungus: *for example,* mycodermatitis.

mycelium /mī sē′lē əm/ the mass of thread-like filaments forming a colony of fungi.

mycetoma /mī′sē tō′mə/ a chronic foot infection caused by a bacterium or fungus and characterized by a yellow, white, red, brown, or black substance oozing from lesions.

mycobacteria /mī′kō băk tēr′ēə/ (*sing.* **mycobacterium** /mī′kō băk tēr′ē əm/) any of a number of species of rod-shaped, aerobic bacteria belonging to the genus Mycobacterium, some of which are pathogenic to humans.

mycobacteriosis /mī′kō băk têr′ē ō′sĭs/ infection caused by parasitic mycobacteria.

mycodermatitis /mī′kō dûr′mə tī′tĭs/ any rash caused by a fungus, yeast, or mold. [myco- + dermatitis]

mycoid /mī′koid/ resembling a fungus. [myc- + -oid]

mycology /mī kŏl′ə jē/ the study of fungi, especially their capacity to cause disease. [myco- + -logy]

mycophage /mī′kə fāj′/ a virus that infects fungi. *See also* mycovirus. [myco- + -phage]

mycosis /mī kō′sĭs/ a disease caused by a fungus. [myc- + -osis]

mycotoxin /mī′kō tŏk′sĭn/ a poisonous substance produced by some fungi. Some have therapeutic uses. [myco- + toxin]

mycovirus /mī′kō vī′rəs/ a virus that infects fungi. [myco- + virus]

mydriasis /mĭ drī′ə sĭs/ dilation of the pupil, as for an eye examination.

mydriatic /mĭd′rē ăt′ĭk/ **1.** *adj.* causing the pupil to dilate. **2.** *n.* something (such as a solution) that causes the pupil to dilate.

myel-, myelo- **1.** bone marrow: *for example,* myelitis. **2.** the spinal cord and medulla oblongata: *for example,* myelocele. **3.** the myelin sheath enclosing nerve fibers: *for example,* myelination.

myelin /mī′ə lĭn/ the lipid material that forms the sheath enclosing nerve fibers, composed of alternating membranes of fat and protein; its presence greatly accelerates the speed of nerve conduction.

myelin sheath the protective envelope that encloses nerve fibers and protects the fibers while messages travel in proper progression.

myelinated /mī′ə lĭ nā′tĭd/ enclosed by a myelin sheath.

myelination /mī′ə lĭ nā′shən/ or **myelinization** /mī′ə lə nə zā′shən/ the process of acquiring or developing a myelin sheath around a nerve fiber.

myelitis /mī′ə lī′tĭs/ **1.** inflammation of the spinal cord. **2.** inflammation of the bone marrow. [myel- + -itis]

myelo- *See* myel-.

myeloblast /mī′ə lə blăst′/ an immature cell normally occurring in bone marrow but not in the blood. [myelo- + -blast]

myeloblastic leukemia /mī′ə lə blăs′tĭk lōō kē′mē ə/ a form of leukemia characterized by uncontrolled growth of myeloblasts in the bone marrow and in various tissues, organs, and circulating blood.

myelocele /mī′ə lə sēl′/ **1.** protrusion of the spinal cord in spinal bifida. **2.** the spinal cord's central canal. [myelo- + -cele]

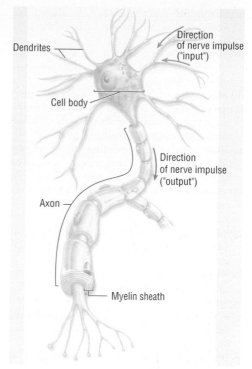

Myelin Sheath

myelocyst /mī′ə lə sĭst′/ any cyst that develops from a vestigial duct in the central nervous system. [myelo- + cyst]

myelocyte /mī′ə lə sīt′/ an immature cell that becomes a white blood cell. [myelo- + -cyte]

myelocytic /mī′ə lə sĭt′ĭk/ relating to or characterized by myelocytes.

myelocytosis /mī′ə lō sī tō′sĭs/ the presence of excessive numbers of myelocytes in the bloodstream or tissues or both. [myelo- + cytosis]

myelodysplasia /mī′ə lō dĭs plā′zhə/ **1.** abnormal development of the lower spinal cord. **2.** a bone marrow disorder characterized by the rapid growth of stem cells, which can develop into a type of leukemia. [myelo- + dysplasia]

myeloencephalitis /mī′ə lō ĕn sĕf′ə lī′tĭs/ inflammation of the spinal cord and brain, often caused by a viral infection. [myelo- + encephalitis]

myelofibrosis /mī′ə lō fī brō′sĭs/ proliferation of fibroblastic cells in bone marrow, causing anemia and sometimes enlargement of the spleen and liver. [myelo- + fibrosis]

myelogenesis /mī′ə lō jĕn′ə sĭs/ **1.** bone marrow development. **2.** central nervous system development. **3.** formation of a myelin sheath around an axon. [myelo- + -genesis]

myelogenous /mī'ə lŏj'ə nəs/ produced by, relating to, or originating in bone marrow. [myelo- + -genous]

myelogram /mī'ə lə grăm'/ an x-ray examination of the spinal canal and its contents using a dye. [myelo- + -gram]

myelography /mī'ə lŏg'rə fē/ x-ray examination of the spinal cord and nerve roots following injection (usually lumbar) of a dye into the subarachnoid space. [myelo- + -graphy]

myeloid /mī'ə loid'/ relating to, developed from, or exhibiting characteristics associated with bone marrow. [myel- + -oid]

myeloma /mī'ə lō'mə/ a cancer of the bone marrow involving white blood cells. [myel- + -oma]

myelomalacia /mī'ə lō mə lā'shə/ gradual softening of the spinal cord. [myelo- + -malacia]

myelopathy /mī'ə lŏp'ə thē/ disease of the spinal cord. [hyelo- + -pathy]

myelopoiesis /mī'ə lō poi ē'sĭs/ **1.** formation of bone marrow or bone marrow cells. **2.** production of blood cells in bone marrow. [myelo- + -poiesis]

myelorrhaphy /mī'ə lôr'ə fē/ suture of a spinal cord wound. [myelo- + -rrhaphy]

myelosis /mī'ə lō'sĭs/ condition with abnormal growth of bone marrow cells or tissue. [myel- + -osis]

myelotomy /mī'ə lŏt'ə mē/ a surgical incision of the spinal cord. [myelo- + -tomy]

myenteric /mī'ĕn tĕr'ĭk/ relating to the myenteron.

myenteron /mī ĕn'tə rŏn'/ the muscular coat of the intestine.

myesthesia /mī'əs thē'zhə/ awareness of motion or action in joints or muscles.

myo- *combining form.* muscle: *for example,* myocele.

myoblastoma /mī'ō blă stō'mə/ a tumor in immature muscle cells. [myo- + blastoma]

myocardi, mycardio- *combining form.* myocardium: *for example,* myocarditis.

myocardia /mī'ō kär'dē ə/ plural of myocardium.

myocardial /mī'ō kär'dē əl/ relating to the myocardium.

myocardial bridge muscle fibers of the heart that extend over the coronary artery.

myocardial infarction (MI) /ĭn färk'shən/ a sudden interruption of blood supply to part of the heart muscle due to an obstructed or constricted coronary artery, characterized by severe chest pain that can radiate to the left shoulder and arm or upper back and by shortness of breath. Informally called heart attack.

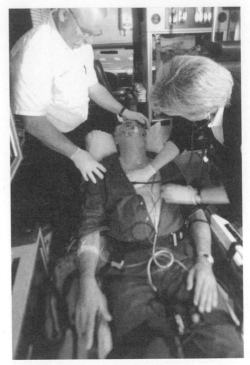

Myocardial Infarction (patient in ambulance)

myocardial perfusion /pər fyōō'zhən/ passage of a fluid (usually blood) through the myocardium.

myocardiopathy /mī'ō kär'dē ŏp'ə thē/ chronic disease of the heart muscle. *Also called* cardiomyopathy.

myocarditis /mī'ō kär dī'tĭs/ inflammation of the myocardium. [myocard- + -itis]

myocardium /mī'ō kär'dē əm/ (*pl.* **myocardia** /mī'ō kär'dē ə/) the middle muscular layer of the heart wall. *Also called* heart muscle.

myocele /mī'ə sēl'/ muscle that sticks out of a tear in the sheath. [myo- + -cele]

myoclonic /mī'ə klŏn'ĭk/ exhibiting myoclonus.

myoclonus /mī'ə klō'nəs/ one or several sharp contractions of a group of muscles, usually caused by a central nervous system lesion.

myocyte /mī'ə sīt'/ a muscle cell. [myo- + -cyte]

myocytoma /mī'ō sī tō'mə/ a benign growth of tissue derived from muscle. [myo- + cyt- + -oma]

myodynia /mī'ə dĭn'ē ə/ muscle pain. *Also called* myalgia. [myo- + -dynia]

myofascial /mī'ō făsh'ē əl/ of or relating to the connective tissue found around and between muscle tissues.

myofascial release   in massage therapy, the application of sustained pressure to an immobilized muscle to release tissue that may be trapped within.

myofibroma   /mī′ō fī brō′mə/   a benign growth of fibrous muscle tissue. [myo- + fibroma]

myofibrosis /mī′ō fī brō′sĭs/   a condition in which fibrous tissue has replaced muscle tissue, often indicating prolonged inflammation of the muscle. [myo- + fibrosis]

myogenesis /mī′ō jĕn′ə sĭs/   a developmental sequence in the embryo that leads to the formation of muscle cells or fibers. [myo- + -genesis]

myoglobin   /mī′ə glō′bĭn/(**Mb**)   the protein found in muscle that carries and stores oxygen. [myo- + -globin]

myogram /mī′ə grăm′/   the record produced by a myograph. [myo- + -gram]

myograph /mī′ə grăf′/   an instrument that records muscle contractions. [myo- + -graph]

myography /mī ŏg′rə fē/   the recording of muscle contractions made by a myograph. [myo- + -graphy]

myoid /mī′oid/   similar to muscle. [my- + -oid]

myokymia /mī′ə kĭm′ē ə/   ongoing involuntary motions of muscles at rest.

myolipoma /mī′ō lĭ pō′mə/   a benign growth made primarily of fat cells and including some muscle cells. [myo- + lipoma]

myolysis /mī ŏl′ə sĭs/   the deterioration of muscle tissue. [myo- + -lysis]

myoma /mī ō′mə/   (*pl.* **myomas, myomata** /mī ō′mə tə/)   a benign growth composed of muscle tissue. [my- + -oma]

myomalacia /mī′ō mə lā′shə/   softening of muscle tissue. [myo- + -malacia]

myomectomy /mī′ə mĕk′tə mē/   removal of a myoma from the uterus.

myometritis /mī′ō mī trī′tĭs/   inflammation of the myometrium.

myometrium /mī′ə mē′trē əm/   the muscular wall of the uterus.

myopathy /mī ŏp′ə thē/   any abnormal condition or disease of the muscles. [myo + -pathy]

myopia /mī ō′pē ə/   a refractive disorder in which distant objects appear blurry because focusing takes place in the front of the retina. *Also called* nearsightedness, shortsightedness.

myopic /mī ŏp′ĭk/   relating to or having myopia.

myoplasty /mī′ə plăs′tē/   reconstructive surgery performed on muscle tissue. [myo- + -plasty]

myorrhaphy /mī ôr′ə fē/   suture of muscle tissue. [myo- + -rrhaphy]

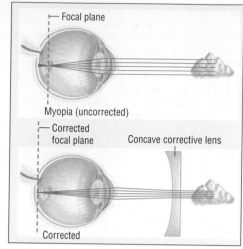

Myopia

myosarcoma /mī′ō sär kō′mə/   a malignant growth derived from muscle tissue. [myo- + sarcoma]

myosclerosis /mī′ō sklī rō′sĭs/   chronic muscular inflammation with abnormal proliferation of connective tissue cells in the affected muscle. [myo- + -sclerosis]

myositis /mī′ə sī′tĭs/   inflammation of a muscle.

myospasm /mī′ə spăz′əm/   involuntary, irregular muscle contractions. [myo- + -spasm]

myotasis /mī ŏt′ə sĭs/   extension or stretching of a muscle.

myotatic /mī′ə tăt′ĭk/   of or relating to myotasis.

myotherapy /mī′ō thĕr′ə pē/   the practice of using massage to treat various illnesses and conditions. *Also called* massage therapy. [myo- + therapy]

myotonia /mī′ə tō′nē ə/   prolonged contraction or delayed relaxation of a muscle caused by an abnormality of the muscle membrane.

myring-, myringo-   *combining form.* eardrum: *for example*, myringitis.

myringectomy /mĭr′ĭn jĕk′tə mē/   surgical removal of the eardrum. *Also called* tympanostomy, tympanotomy. [myring- + -ectomy.

myringitis /mĭr′ĭn jī′tĭs/   inflammation of the eardrum. [myring- + -itis]

myringoplasty /mī rĭng′gə plăs′tē/   repair or reconstructive surgery of a damaged eardrum. [myringo- + -plasty]

myringotomy   /mĭr′ĭng gŏt′ə mē/   surgical puncturing of the eardrum to release fluid. *Also called* tympanostomy, tympanotomy. [myringo- + -tomy]

myx-, myxo-   *combining form.* mucus: *for example*, myxosarcoma.

myxedema /mĭk′sə dē′mə/ an abnormal accumulation of watery liquid in the skin, often most noticeable in the face and shins, characteristic of hypothyroidism. [myx- + edema]

myxofibroma /mĭk′sō fī brō′mə/ a benign growth composed of fibrous connective tissue. [myxo- + fibroma]

myxoid /mĭk′soid/ resembling mucus. [mix- + -oid]

myxoma /mĭk sō′mə/ (*pl.* **myxomata** /mĭk sō′mə tə/) a benign growth composed of connective tissue. [myx- + -oma]

myxosarcoma /mĭk′sō sär kō′mə/ a malignant tumor found in connective tissue. [myxo- + sarcoma]

N *abbreviation.* nitrogen.

Na *abbreviation.* sodium.

Naegele('s) rule /nā′gə lə(z)/ a formula for determining an estimated delivery date for a pregnancy.

nail /nāl/ a thin plate of hard epithelial cells containing keratin that grows on the upper side of the tip of each finger and toe.

nail bed the part of the finger or toe on which the nail sits.

narc-, narco- *combining form.* numbness or drowsiness: *for example,* narcosis.

narcissism /när′sə sĭz′əm/ a personality disorder in which one is too involved with oneself; having too much self-love.

narcoleptic /när′kə lĕp′tĭk/ a person who has narcolepsy. [narco- + -leptic]

narcolepsy /när′kə lĕp′sē/ a disorder with sudden great sleepiness and sometimes temporary paralysis in the middle of daily activity. [narco- + -lepsy]

narcosis /när kō′sĭs/ unconsciousness as a result of a drug. [narc- + -osis]

narcotic /när kŏt′ik/ **1.** *adj.* producing decreased sensitivity to pain or inducing sleep. **2.** *n.* a drug that produces numbness or sleep by depressing the central nervous system; in current usage, a "hypnotic" drug causes sleep, and a "narcotic" drug relieves pain.

nares /nâr′ēz/ (*sing.* **naris** /nâr′ĭs/) the two external openings at the base of the nose; the nostrils.

NARP *abbreviation.* neuropathy, ataxia, and retinitis pigmentosa, a genetic disease inherited from the mother, featuring weakness of the muscles near the trunk, ataxia (wobbliness), seizure, disease of the retina, and sometimes retardation or developmental delay.

nas-, naso- *combining form.* nose: *for example,* nasogastric.

nasal /nā′zəl/ of or relating to the nose.

nasal bone either of two small bones that form the bridge of the nose.

nasal cavity either of two cavities in the nose, through which air enters and exits the body.

nasal decongestant /dē′kən jĕs′tənt/ a drug that reduces swollen tissue in the nose.

nasal flu vaccine /văk sēn′/ a weakened strain of a flu virus serving as a vaccine and administered by spraying it into the nose.

nasal mucus /myōō′kəs/ the thick wet secretions of the membranes lining the inside of the nose.

nasal septum /sĕp′təm/ the ridge of bone and cartilage that divides the nasal cavity in two parts.

nasoantritis /nā′zō ăn trī′tĭs/ inflammation of the nose and the maxillary sinuses (the large sinuses below the eyes on either side of the nose).

nasoenteral tube /nā′zō ĕn′tər əl/ a thin flexible tube that goes from the nose to the stomach or small intestine, usually for feeding. *Also called* nasogastric tube. [naso- + enteral]

nasofrontal /nā′zō frŭn′təl/ involving the frontal bone of the skull; of the bones of the nose and the forehead. [naso- + frontal]

nasogastric (NG) /nā′zō găs′trĭk/ from the nose to the stomach. [naso- + gastric]

nasogastric (NG) intubation /ĭn′tōō bā′shən/ insertion of a thin flexible tube into the stomach through the nose, generally for feeding.

nasogastric (NG) tube a thin flexible tube that goes from the nose to the stomach, either for keeping the stomach empty of gastric secretions, or for feeding. *Also called* nasoenteral tube.

nasolacrimal /nā′zō lăk′rə məl/ involving the nose and the tear glands or tear ducts. [naso- + lacrimal]

nasolacrimal duct the narrow tube that channels tears from the lacrimal sac to the nasal cavity.

nasopharyngeal /nā′zō fə rĭn′jē əl/ involving the nasopharynx. [naso- + pharyngeal]

nasopharyngitis /nā′zō făr′ĭn jī′tĭs/ inflammation of the nasopharynx. [naso- + pharyng- + -itis]

nasopharyngoscopy /nā′zō făr′ĭng gŏs′kə pē/ examination of the nasopharynx using an optical instrument. [naso- + pharyngo- + -scopy]

nasopharynx /nā′zō făr′ingks/ the part of the pharynx lying above the soft palate. *Also called* epipharynx. [naso- + pharynx]

natal /nā′təl/ relating to birth.

natremia /nā trē′mē ə/ the presence of sodium in the blood. [natr- + -emia]

natriuresis /nā′trē yōō rē′sĭs/ the rate of excretion of sodium in the urine. [*natri(um)*, sodium + ur- + -esis]

natriuretic /nā′trē yōō rĕt′ĭk/ a drug that increases the excretion of sodium in the urine. [*natri(um)*, sodium + ur- + -etic]

natural acquired immunity natural immunity.

natural family planning a system of determining when sexual intercourse may result in pregnancy and abstaining from intercourse at those times. *Also called* rhythm method.

natural immunity /ĭ myōō′nĭ tē/ immunity (resistance to infection) that is present in the body without immunization.

natural killer (NK) cell a lymphocyte that attaches to cells and destroys them.

naturopath /nā′chə rō păth′/ a practitioner of naturopathic medicine.

naturopathic /nā′chə rō păth′ĭk/ of or relating to naturopathic medicine; involving practices that augment the body's ability to heal itself.

naturopathic medicine a system of medical practice that uses the body's own powers to maintain and restore health through nutrition, exercise, and various other alternative medical practices. *Also called* naturopathy.

naturopathy /nā′chə rŏp′ə thē/ naturopathic medicine.

nausea /nô′zē ə, -zhə/ an unpleasant feeling in the stomach that can often precede vomiting.

nauseate /nô′zē āt′, -zhē āt′/ to cause the feeling of being about to vomit.

nauseous /nô′shəs, -zē əs/ **1.** feeling about to vomit. **2.** causing the feeling of being about to vomit.

navel /nā′vəl/ the scar in the center of the abdomen showing where the umbilical cord was attached during fetal development. *Also called* belly button, umbilicus.

ND *abbreviation.* Doctor of Naturopathic Medicine.

nearsightedness /nêr′sī′tĭd nĭs/ a refractive disorder in which distant objects appear blurry because focusing takes place in the front of the retina. *Also called* myopia, shortsightedness.

nebulizer /nĕb′yə lī′zər/ a device that delivers a liquid medication as a very fine spray.

NEC *abbreviation.* not elsewhere classified (used in medical coding).

neck /nĕk/ **1.** the part of the body that connects the head to the shoulders. **2.** any elongated part, such as the neck of the cervix.

necr-, necro- *combining form.* death or corpse: *for example,* necrophilia.

necrobiosis /nĕk′rō bī ō′sĭs/ cell or tissue death due to natural processes such as development and aging. [necro- + -biosis]

necrocytosis /nĕk′rō sī tō′sĭs/ the abnormal death or decay of cells. [necro- + -cytosis]

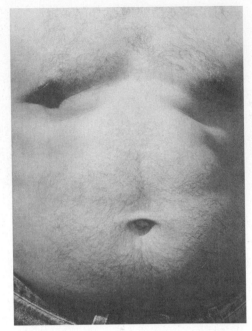
Navel

necrology /nĕ krŏl′ə jē/ the study of or a record of deaths and statistics about death. [necro- + -logy]

necrophilia /nĕk′rō fĭl′ē ə/ **1.** sexual attraction to corpses. **2.** sexual contact with a corpse. [necro- + -philia]

necrophobia /nĕk′rō fō′bē ə/ abnormal fear of death. [necro- + -phobia]

necropsy /nĕk′rŏp sē/ the examination of a dead body to determine the cause of death. *Also called* autopsy, postmortem examination. [necr- + -opsy]

necrosis /nĕ krō′sĭs/ the death of tissue or organs caused by ischemia (loss or decrease of blood flow). [necr- + -osis]

necrotic /nĕ krŏt′ĭk/ involving dead tissue or organs.

necrotizing fasciitis /nĕk′rə tī′zĭng făsh′ē ī′tĭs, făs′-/ an infection of soft tissue, usually of the limbs or abdominal wall, that is potentially life-threatening.

necrotizing gingivitis /jĭn jĭ vī′tĭs/ a painful infection by two bacteria of the gums that causes ulceration and swelling in the mouth. *Also called* trench mouth, Vincent's angina, acute necrotizing (ulcerative) gingivitis.

needle /nē′dəl/ a sharp, pointed tool for puncturing or suturing.

needle biopsy /bī′ŏp sē/ the removal of material for analysis by withdrawing it out through a large bore needle or trocar attached to a syringe.

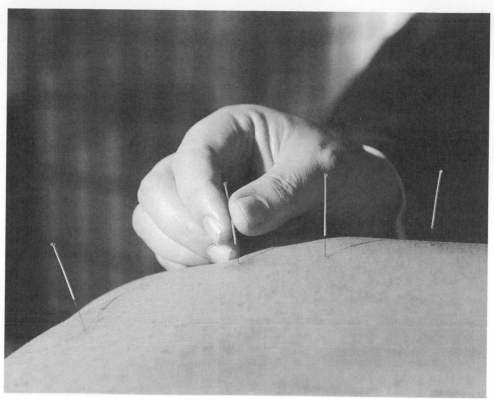

Needles (used in acupuncture)

needle holder an instrument used to hold the needle when suturing.

needle stick accidental puncture of the skin with an unsterilized needle.

needle thoracotomy /thôr′ə kŏt′ə mē/ placing a needle in the chest to decompress trapped air.

neg, neg. *abbreviation.* negative.

negative /nĕg′ə tĭv/ **1.** lacking a positive result in a test for a specific disease. **2.** not possessing the quality in question.

neglect /nĭ glĕkt′/ **1.** *v.* to pay too little or no attention to. **2.** *n.* negligence.

negligence /nĕg′lĭ jəns/ failure to perform duties properly according to the national or state required standard of care.

nematode /nĕm′ə tōd′/ a roundworm of the phylum Nemetoda, which can infest humans.

neo- *prefix.* new, recent: *for example,* neonatal.

neobladder /nē′ō blăd′ər/ a surgically constructed sac (usually with ileum) for storing urine when the bladder has been removed or destroyed. *Also called* ileal loop.

neocyte /nē′ə sīt′/ a young cell. [neo- + -cyte]

neologism /nē ŏl′ə jĭz′əm/ a new word or phrase created by a patient, often seen as a sign of schizophrenia.

neonatal /nē′ō nā′təl/ of, for, or involving a newborn. [neo- + natal]

neonatal hyperbilirubinemia /hī′pər bĭl′ə rōō′ bə nē′mē ə/ a condition of newborns in which the bilirubin level is too high, causing yellowish skin and sclerae (whites of the eyes).

neonatal intensive care unit (NICU) a hospital unit designed specifically for the treatment of ill newborns and babies born prematurely.

neonatal jaundice /jôn′dĭs/ a condition in which the skin and sclerae (whites of the eyes) of a newborn are yellowish, caused by lysis of red cells, and release of hemoglobin, which is metabolized to bilirubin in the liver.

neonate /nē′ə nāt′/ a newborn infant in the first four weeks of life.

neonatologist /nē′ō nā tŏl′ə jĭst/ doctor who specializes in diagnosis and treatment of diseases in newborns.

neonatology /nē′ō nā tŏl′ə jē/ the branch of medicine that specializes in the diagnosis and treatment of deseases in newborns.

neoplasia /nē′ō plā′zhə/ **1.** abnormal tissue growth. **2.** new tissue growth. [neo- + -plasia]

neoplasm /nē′ə plăz′əm/ a new growth or tumor. [neo- + -plasm]

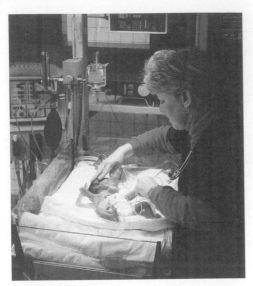

Neonatal Intensive Care Unit

neoplastic /nē′ō plăs′tĭk/ of or involving a neoplasm. [neo- + -plastic]

nephr-, nephro- *combining form.* kidney: *for example,* nephralgia.

nephralgia /nĕ frăl′jē ə, -jə/ pain in a kidney. [nephr- + -algia]

nephrectomy /nĕ frĕk′tə mē/ surgical removal of a kidney. [nephr- + -ectomy]

nephritis /nĕ frī′tĭs/ inflammation of the kidney. [nephr- + -itis]

nephroblastoma /nĕf′rō blă stō′mə/ malignant tumor of the kidney found primarily in children. [nephro- + blastoma]

nephroblastomatosis /nĕf′rō blă stō′mə tō′sĭs/ condition of having fragments of embryonic tissue in the kidneys, one or more of which may develop into malignant tumors. [nephro- + blastomat(a) + -osis]

nephrocalcinosis /nĕf′rō kăl′sə nō′sĭs/ the depositing of calcium in the kidneys, which can impair kidney function or become the beginnings of kidney stones. [nephro- + calcinosis]

nephrocele /nĕf′rə sēl′/ a hernia of the kidney. [nephro- + -cele]

nephrogenous /nĕ frŏj′ə nəs/ developing from kidney tissue. [nephro- + -genous]

nephrogram /nĕf′rə grăm′/ an x-ray image of a kidney. [nephro- + -gram]

nephrography /nĕ frŏg′rə fē/ radiographic imaging of the kidney. [nephro- + -graphy]

nephroid /nĕf′roid/ relating to or having or resembling the shape of a kidney. [nephr- + -oid]

nephrolith /nĕf′rə lĭth/ a stone of hard mineral and crystal that forms in the kidney. *Also called* kidney stone, renal calculus. [nephro- + -lith]

nephrolithiasis /nĕf′rō lĭ thī′ə sĭs/ condition of having calculi (stones) in the kidney. [nephro- + -lith + -iasis]

nephrolithotomy /nĕf′rō lĭ thŏt′ə mē/ surgical incision into the kidney to remove a stone. [nephro- + litho- + -tomy]

nephrologist /nĕ frŏl′ə jĭst/ doctor who specializes in diagnosis and treatment of diseases of the kidney. [nephro- + -logist]

nephrology /nĕ frŏl′ə jē/ branch of medicine that specializes in diagnosis and treatment of diseases of the kidney. [nephro- + -logy]

nephrolysis /nĕ frŏl′ə sĭs/ **1.** destruction of cells in the kidney. **2.** surgical detachment of a kidney from inflamed adhesions. [nephro- + -lysis]

nephrolytic /nĕf′rō lĭt′ĭk/ involving destruction of cells in the kidney. [nephro- + -lytic]

nephroma /nĕ frō′mə/ a kidney tumor. [nephr- + -oma]

nephromegaly /nĕf′rō mĕg′ə lē/ extreme enlargement of a kidney or kidneys. [nephr- + -megaly]

nephron /nĕf′rŏn/ one of about a million convoluted tubular structures in each kidney in which the filtering process takes place.

nephronic loop /nĕ frŏn′ĭk/ the U-shaped structure of a nephron that helps in maintaining the concentration of urine.

nephropathy /nĕ frŏp′ə thē/ any disease or disorder of the kidneys. *Also called* renopathy. [nephro- + -pathy]

nephropexy /nĕf′rō pĕk′sē/ surgical fixation of a kidney in a particular location. [nephr- + -pexy]

nephrophthisis /nĕ frŏf′thĭ sĭs/ an inherited disease of the kidneys leading to loss of kidney function. [nephr- + -phthisis]

nephroptosis /nĕf′rŏp tō′sĭs/ the falling of a kidney down from its proper position in the body. [nephro- + -ptosis]

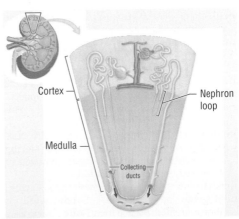

Nephron

nephrorrhaphy /nĕf rôr′ə fē/ suturing a kidney laceration. [nephro- + -rraphy]

nephrosclerosis /nĕf′rō sklĭ rō′sĭs/ hardening of the kidneys often resulting from long-term hypertension. [nephro- + -sclerosis]

nephroscope /nĕf′rə skōp′/ an optical instrument passed into the kidney, either through the ureter or through a surgical incision. [nephro- + -scope]

nephroscopy /nĕ frŏs′kə pē/ examination of a kidney using an optical instrument passed through a surgical incision or through the ureter. [nephro- + -scopy]

nephrosis /nĕ frō′sĭs/ **1.** nephropathy. **2.** nephrotic syndrome.

nephrosonography /nĕf′rō sə nŏg′rə fē/ an image of the kidney using ultrasound.

nephrostomy /nĕ frŏs′tə mē/ creation of an opening between a kidney and the outside of the body. [nephro- + -stomy]

nephrotic syndrome /nĕ frŏt′ĭk sĭn′drōm/ a group of symptoms of kidney disease including excess protein in the urine, low blood protein, and high cholesterol.

nephrotomy /nĕ frŏt′ə mē/ a surgical incision into a kidney. [nephro- + -tomy]

nephrotoxic /nĕf′rō tŏk′sĭk/ poisonous to kidney cells. [nephro- + toxic]

nerve /nûrv/ a bundle of nerve fibers that transmit electrical impulses to the organs and muscles of the body.

nerve block the stopping of electrical transmission along a nerve by local anesthesia or pressure.

nerve cell the basic element of the nervous system, consisting of a cell body, dendrites, and an axon. *Also called* neuron, neurocyte.

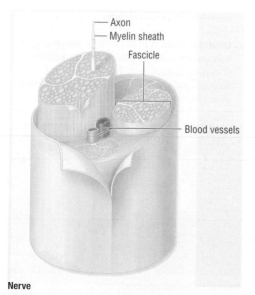

— Axon
— Myelin sheath
— Fascicle
— Blood vessels

Nerve

nerve conduction /kən dŭk′shən/ the transmission of electrical impulses through a bundle of nerve cells.

nerve fiber one of the long, thin extensions of a nerve cell that transmit electrical impulses.

nerve strokes a massage therapy technique used to encourage healing after a stroke, performed by dragging the full palm of the hand with fingers trailing, slowly and lightly from head to feet or down the arms to the hands.

nerve tissue cells working together that carry messages to and from the brain and spinal cord to all parts of the body.

nervi /nûr′vī/ plural of nervus.

nervous /nûr′vəs/ **1.** involving nerves or a nervous system. **2.** feeling anxious or uncomfortable.

nervous breakdown a nonscientific term for a sudden, disabling mental disorder, usually including extreme depression.

nervous system either of two body systems that direct the voluntary or involuntary activities of the body by electrical messages sent to and from the brain and spinal cord to all parts of the body. *See also* central nervous system, peripheral nervous system, autonomic nervous system.

nervus /nûr′vəs/ (*pl.* **nervi** /nûr′vī/) in anatomy, a nerve.

network /nĕt′wûrk′/ net-like arrangement of fiber within a structure.

neur-, neuri-, neuro- *combining form.* nerve, nervous system: *for example,* neurology.

neural /nŏŏr′əl/ of, for, or involving a nerve or nerves.

neural canal the space between the front and back of the vertebrae of the spinal column, through which the spinal cord passes.

neuralgia /nŏŏ răl′jē ə, -jə/ sharp stabbing or throbbing pain along the path of a nerve. [neur- + -algia]

neural tube defect (NTD) one of a number of very serious birth defects, such as spina bifida and anencephaly, caused by the abnormal development of the embryonic neural tissue from which the spinal cord and brain develop.

neurasthenia /nŏŏr′əs thē′nē ə/ a psychological disorder with general weakness, depression, and apathy. [neur- + -asthenia]

neurectomy /nŏŏ rĕk′tə mē/ surgical removal of a nerve or part of a nerve. [neur- + -ectomy]

neurilemma /nŏŏr′ə lĕm′ə/ the membranous covering that protects the myelin sheath of a nerve's axon.

neuritis /nŏŏ rī′tĭs/ inflammation of a nerve or nerves. [neur- + -itis]

neuro- *See* neur-.

neuroarthropathy /nŏŏr′ō är thrŏp′ə thē/ joint disease caused by loss of sensation in a joint. [neuro- + athro- + -pathy]

neuroblast /nŏŏr′ə blăst′/ an immature nerve cell. [neuro- + -blast]

neuroblastoma /nŏŏr′ō blă stō′mə/ a malignant tumor of immature nerve cells. [neuro- + blastoma]

neurochemical /nŏŏr′ō kĕm′ĭ kəl/ **1.** *n.* a drug that affects the nervous system. **2.** *adj.* of or relating to neurochemistry or neurochemicals.

neurochemistry /nŏŏr′ō kĕm′ə strē/ the study of the chemistry of the brain and nervous system.

neurocyte /nŏŏr′ə sīt′/ the basic element of the nervous system, consisting of a cell body, dendrites, and an axon. *Also called* neuron, nerve cell. [neuro- + -cyte]

neurocytoma /nŏŏr′ō sī tō′mə/ (*pl.* **neurocytomas** or **neurocytomata** /nŏŏr′ō sī tō′mə tə/) tumor made up of cells derived from nerve cells, usually ganglia. [neruo- + cyt- + -oma]

neurodermatitis /nŏŏr′ō dûr′mə tī′tĭs/ scaly patches of skin, located especially on the ankles, wrists, forearms, and head, that become very itchy when scratched. [neuro- + dermat- + -itis]

neuroendocrine /nŏŏr′ō ĕn′də krĭn/ **1.** of or involving the interaction of the nervous system and the endocrine system. **2.** involving cells that release hormones into the bloodstream in response to a neural signal. [neuro- + endocrine]

neuroendocrinology /nŏŏr′ō ĕn′dō krĭ nŏl′ə jē/ the medical specialty involved in the interactions between the nervous system and the endocrine system. [neuro- + endocrinology]

neuroepithelial /nŏŏr′ō ĕp′ĭ thē′lē əl/ involving the neuroepithelium. [neuro- + epithelial]

neuroepithelium /nŏŏr′ō ĕp′ĭ thē′lē əm/ **1.** tissue made of specialized epithelial cells that receive sensory stimuli, such as rods and cones in the eye. **2.** the portion of the embryonic ectoderm that develops into the nervous system. [neuro- + epithelium]

neurofibroma /nŏŏr′ō fĭ brō′mə/ a benign tumor of a nerve sheath. [neuro- + fibroma]

neurofibromatosis /nŏŏr′ō fĭ brō′mə tō′sĭs/ **1.** a genetic disorder with dark patches on the skin and benign but potentially disfiguring tumors of nerve sheaths. **2.** a genetic disorder with tumors in the nerves of the ear that can cause deafness, often accompanied by cranial and spinal tumors.

neurogastroenterology /nŏŏr′ō găs′trō ĕn′tə rŏl′ə jē/ study of the interaction between the brain and the enteric nervous system (the nervous system that controls the stomach and the intestines). [neuro- + gastroenterology]

neurogenesis /nŏŏr′ō jĕn′ə sĭs/ the development of nerve tissue or the nervous system. [neuro- + -genesis]

neurogenic /nŏŏr′ō jĕn′ĭk/ or **neurogenetic** /nŏŏr′ō jə nĕt′ĭk/ or **neurogenous** /nŏŏ rŏj′ə nəs/ originating in nerve tissue or in a nerve.

neuroglia /nŏŏ rŏg′lē ə/ a class of cells in the nervous system that do not transmit electrical impulses but that support, connect, protect, and remove debris from the nervous system. *See also* astroglia (astrocytes), oligodendroglia, microglia.

neuroglial /nŏŏ rŏg′lē əl/ of or involving neuroglia.

neurohypophysis /nŏŏr′ō hī pŏf′ə sĭs/ the hind lobe of the pituitary gland, which produces hormones governing water balance in the cells, uterine contractions and lactation, and melanin production. *Also called* posterior lobe. [neuro- + hypophysis]

neuroleptic /nŏŏr′ō lĕp′tĭk/ any of a class of drugs used to treat schizophrenia and other psychoses. [neuro- + -leptic]

neurologic /nŏŏr′ə lŏj′ĭk/ or **neurological** /nŏŏr′ə lŏj′ĭ kəl/ of or involving the nervous system.

neurologic assessment examination and evaluation of the nervous system, usually involving testing of reflexes, balance, and other neurological indicators.

neurologist /nŏŏ rŏl′ə jĭst/ a doctor specializing in disorders of the nervous system and their treatment. [neuro- + -logist]

neurology /nŏŏ rŏl′ə jē/ the study of the nervous system and its disorders. [neuro- + -logy]

neurolysis /nŏŏ rŏl′ə sĭs/ **1.** destruction of nerve cells. **2.** surgical removal of a nerve from inflammatory adhesions. [neuro- + -lysis]

neurolytic /nŏŏr′ō lĭt′ĭk/ of or involving neurolysis, as a neurolytic block to relieve unremitting cancer pain. [neuro- + -lytic]

neuroma /nŏŏ rō′mə/ any tumor originating in nerve tissue. [neur- + -oma]

Neurologist (reviewing scans)

neuromatosis /nŏŏ rō′mə tō′ sĭs/ the condition of having multiple neuromas.

neuromuscular /nŏŏ′rō mŭs′kyə lər/ of or involving the connection between nerves and the muscles, that is, the neuromuscular conduction of signals. [neuro- + muscular]

neuromuscular electrical stimulation stimulation of skeletal muscles using electrical current.

neuromyelitis /nŏŏ′rō mī′ə lī′tĭs/ inflammation of nerves and the spinal cord. [neuro- + myelitis]

neuromyopathy /nŏŏr′ō mī ŏp′ə thē/ disease or disorder involving muscles and their nerves. [neuro- + myo- + -pathy]

neuron /nŏŏr′ŏn/ the basic element of the nervous system, consisting of a cell body, dendrites, and an axon. *Also called* nerve cell.

neuronal /nŏŏr′ə nəl, nŏŏ rō′nəl/ of or involving neurons.

neuronitis /nŏŏr′ō nī′tĭs/ inflammation of a neuron. [neuron + -itis]

neuro-oncology /nŏŏr′ō ŏng kŏl′ə jē/ branch of medicine that specializes in cancers of the nervous system and their treatment. [neuro- + oncology]

neuro-otology /nŏŏr′ō ō tŏl′ə jē/ branch of medicine that specializes in diseases of the nerves of the ear and their treatment. [neuro- + otology]

neuropathic /nŏŏr′ō păth′ĭk/ of or involving neuropathy.

neuropathologist /nŏŏr′ō pă thŏl′ə jĭst/ doctor who specializes in diseases of the nerves and their treatment. [neuro- + pathologist]

neuropathology /nŏŏr′ō pə thŏl′ə jē/ the branch of pathology that studies diseases of the nervous system. [neuro- + pathology]

neuropathy /nŏŏ rŏp′ə thē/ **1.** any disease or disorder of a nerve or nerves. **2.** a painful condition usually of feet, in which a disorder of sensory nerves causes hypersensitivity to tactile stimuli; often present in diabetes. [neuro- + -pathy]

neuropharmacology /nŏŏr′ō fär′mə kŏl′ə jē/ the study of drugs that affect nerve tissue or the nervous system. [neuro- + pharmacology]

neurophysiology /nŏŏr′ō fĭz′ē ŏl′ə jē/ the branch of physiology that studies the nervous system. [neuro- + physiology]

neuroplasty /nŏŏr′ō plăs′tē/ surgical repair of a nerve. [neuro- + -plasty]

neuropsychiatrist /nŏŏr′ō sī kī′ə trĭst/ doctor specializing in diagnosis and treatment of mental disorders of both neurological and psychological origin. [neuro- + psychiatrist]

neuropsychologist /nŏŏr′ō sī kŏl′ə jĭst/ psychologist specializing in the relationship between the body and the brain. [neuro- + psychologist]

neuroradiologist /nŏŏr′ō rā′dē ŏl′ə jĭst/ doctor specializing in diagnostic imaging of the head, neck, and spine. [neuro- + radiologist]

neuroradiology /nŏŏr′ō rā′dē ŏl′ə jē/ subbranch of medicine that specializes in diagnostic imaging of the head, neck and spine. [neuro- + radiology]

neuroretinitis /nŏŏr′ō rĕt′ə nī′tĭs/ inflammation of the optic nerve and retina. [neuro- + retinitis]

neurorrhaphy /nŏŏ rôr′ə fē/ sewing together two parts of a cut nerve. [neuro- + -rraphy]

neuroscience /nŏŏr′ō sī′əns/ a branch of science that studies the chemistry, physiology, function, growth and development, pathology, structure and molecular structure, etc., of the nervous system. [neuro- + biology]

neurosis /nŏŏ rō′sĭs/ (*pl.* **neuroses** /nŏŏ rō′ sēz/) any of various emotional or mental disorders, usually involving anxiety, insecurity, irrational fears, and hypochondra, that do not include grossly distorted reality or disordered thinking. *Also called* psychoneurosis. [neur- + -osis]

neurosurgeon /nŏŏr′ō sûr′jən/ surgeon specializing in operations on the brain and spinal cord. [neuro- + surgeon]

neurosurgery /nŏŏr′ō sûr′jə rē/ branch of surgery that specializes in the brain and spinal cord. [neuro- + surgery]

neurotic /nŏŏ rŏt′ĭk/ **1.** *adj.* of or relating to a neurosis. **2.** *n.* a person who has neuroses.

neurotomy /nŏŏ rŏt′ə mē/ a surgical incision into a nerve. [neuro- + -tomy]

neurotoxic /nŏŏr′ō tŏk′sĭk/ poisonous to nerve tissue or the nervous system. [neuro- + toxic]

neurotoxin /nŏŏr′ō tŏk′sĭn/ a substance that is poisonous to nerve tissue or the nervous system. [neuro- + toxin]

neurotransmitter /nŏŏr′ō trănz mĭt′ər/ any of a number of chemical substances, such as acetylcholine or dopamine, that transmit nerve impulses across the gap between one nerve and its neighboring nerve. [neuro- + transmitter]

neurotropic /nŏŏr′ō trŏp′ĭk/ seeking out or preferentially affecting nerve tissue. [neuro- + -tropic]

neurovascular /nŏŏr′ō văs′kyə lər/ of or pertaining to structures that have both a neurological and a vascular function. [neuro- + vascular]

neutropenia /nŏŏ′trō pē′nē ə/ disorder with abnormally low number of neutrophils in the bloodstream.

neutropenic /nŏŏ′trə pē′nĭk/ of or having neutropenia.

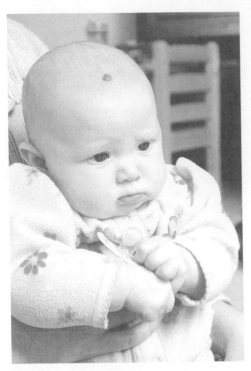

Nevus

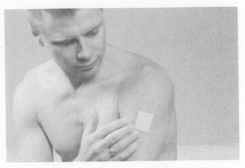

Nicotine Patch

neutrophil /nŏŏ′trə fĭl/ a kind of white blood cell making up over 50% of the white blood cells in the bloodstream.

neutrophilia /nŏŏ′trə fĭl′ē ə/ a disorder with an abnormal increase in neutrophils in the bloodstream.

nevoid /nē′void/ having the appearance of a mole or birthmark or malformation.

nevus /nē′vəs/ (*pl.* **nevi** /nē′vī/) any localized abnormal area of pigmented skin present at birth, such as a mole or a birthmark.

newborn /nŏŏ′bôrn′/ an infant from birth to 4 weeks of age.

newborn screening state-mandated tests of newborns to pick up certain treatable, frequently genetic diseases, such as hypothyroidism, PKU, and sickle cell disease; varies from state to state.

NG *abbreviation.* nasogastric.

NG intubation /ĭn′tŏŏ bā′shən/ inserting a thin flexible tube into the stomach through the nose; nasogastric intubation.

NG tube a thin flexible tube that is inserted into the stomach through the nose; nasogastric tube.

NHL *abbreviation.* non-Hodgkin's lymphoma.

niacin /nī′ə sĭn/ one of the vitamins in the vitamin-B complex; nicotinic acid.

niacin deficiency /dĭ fĭsh′ən sē/ a lack of adequate amounts of nicotinic acid in the body, causing pellagra.

niche /nĭch, nēsh/ an erosion in the wall of an organ, detectable by x-ray.

nicotine /nĭk′ə tēn′, nĭk′ə tēn′/ substance found in the tobacco plant to which smokers become addicted.

nicotine patch a patch containing medication that curbs the addiction to nicotine and thereby helps smokers quit the habit.

nicotinic acid /nĭk′ə tĭn′ĭk/ the part of the vitamin B-complex that prevents pellagra.

nictitate /nĭk′tĭ tāt′/ to wink the eye.

NICU *abbreviation.* neonatal intensive care unit.

nidation /nī dā′shən/ the implantation of an embryo in the uterine lining.

NIDDM *abbreviation.* non-insulin-dependant diabetes mellitus.

nidus /nī′dəs/ **1.** point of origin of a nerve. **2.** focal point of an infection. **3.** focal point around which a crystalline or mineralogical deposit, such as a kidney stone, develops.

Niemann-Pick('s) disease (NPC) /nē′män pĭk(s)′/ genetic disorder affecting the storage of lipids.

night blindness reduced ability to see in dim light or at night, due to impaired function of the rods in the retina, caused by lack of adequate vitamin A in the diet or by heredity. *Also called* nyctalopia, nyctanopia.

nightmare /nīt′mâr′/ a terrifying dream, in which the dreamer experiences severe anxiety and a sense of helplessness.

night sweats bouts of sweating during sleep that accompany many inflammatory disorders and, in women, sometimes occur in the months and years before and during menopause in response to fluctuating hormones.

night terrors a sleep disorder in children, where a severe nightmare causes the child to appear to be awake screaming, with persisting deep distress, while in fact still asleep.

nihilism /nī′ə lĭz′əm/ **1.** a mental delusion that nothing, including the self, exists. **2.** a lack of belief in the usefulness of medical treatments.

nil per os (NPO, n.p.o.) /nĭl′ pər ŏs′/ nothing by mouth.

nipple /nĭp′əl/ tissue at the tip of the breast through which milk flows during lactation.

nipple shield a protective cap through which milk can flow, placed over the nipple to protect it during nursing.

nitrituria /nī′trĭ tŏŏr′ē ə/ the presence of nitrites in the urine.

nitrogen (N) /nī′ trə jən/ a nonmetallic element present in all living cells.

nitrogenous /nī trəj′ēn əs/ containing nitrogen.

nitrous oxide /nī′trəs ŏk′sīd/ an odorless gas sometimes inhaled as an anesthetic, especially in dentistry. Informally called laughing gas.

NK cell *abbreviation.* natural killer cell.

NMR *abbreviation.* nuclear magnetic resonance.

noc. *abbreviation.* Latin *nocte,* at night.

noc, n.o.c. not otherwise classified.

nocardia infection /nō kär′dē ə/ an infection by any of various filamentous or rod-shaped bacteria of the genus *Nocardia.*

nocardiosis /nō kär′dē ō′sĭs/ a serious disease, usually beginning in the lungs but frequently spreading to other body organs including the brain, caused by one of several bacteria of the genus *Nocardia.*

nocebo /nō sē′bō/ an unexpected and unpleasant outcome or side effect of a placebo.

noct-, nocti-, nocto- *combining form.* night: *for example,* noctiphobia.

noctambulism /nŏk tăm′byə lĭz′əm/ a brief episode of motor behavior while asleep, usually in children, usually walking and sometimes talking. *Also called* sleepwalking, somnambulism.

nocte (noc.) /nŏk′tā/ at night (in prescriptions).

noctiphobia /nŏk′tĭ fō′bē ə/ abnormal fear of darkness and/or night. *Also called* nyctophobia. [nocti- + -phobia]

nocturia /nŏk tŏŏr′ē ə/ excessive urination at night. *Also called* nycturia. [noct- + -uria]

nocturnal /nŏk tûr′nəl/ taking place at night. *See also* diurnal (def. 1).

nocturnal amblyopia /ăm′blē ō′pē ə/ poor vision in dim light, not attributable to any physical cause.

nocturnal enuresis /ĕn′yŏŏ rē′sĭs/ nightime urinary incontinence. *Also called* bedwetting.

node /nōd/ **1.** a limited tissue mass or swelling that may be normal or pathological. **2.** a limited mass of differentiated tissue, especially a lymph node.

nodular /nŏj′ə lər/ **1.** made of or involving a node or nodes. **2.** shaped like a node.

nodule /nŏj′ōōl/ a small, solid node.

nodulus /nŏj′ə ləs/ a nodule or small knot.

non- *prefix.* the reverse or opposite of something; not: *for example,* nondegenerative.

nonagenarian /nŏn′ə jə nâr′ē ən/ a person between 90 and 100 years old.

noncompliance /nŏn′kəm plī′əns/ failure to comply with the rules and regulations governing a hospital, clinic, or the like.

non compos mentis /nŏn′ cŏm′pəs mĕn′tĭs/ not of sound mind.

nondegenerative disorder /nŏn′dĭ jĕn′ər ə tĭv/ a disease or disorder in which the organ or system affected does not get worse over time. [non- + degenerative]

nondisjunction /nŏn′dĭs jŭngk′shən/ the failure of one or more pairs of chromosomes to separate during cell division (either meiosis or mitosis), such that one of the two daughter cells receives both copies of that chromosome and the other receives none.

non-Hodgkin('s) lymphoma (NHL) /nŏn′hŏj′ kĭn(z) lĭm fō′mə/ any of several cancers of the lymphatic system that have some of the same symptoms as Hodgkin's disease.

non-insulin-dependent diabetes mellitus (NIDDM) /nŏn ĭn′sə lĭn di pĕn′dənt dī′ə bē′ tĭs mĕl′ĭ təs, mə lī′tĭs, dī′ə bē′tēz/ a form of diabetes mellitus, with diminished sensitivity to insulin, precipitated or exacerbated by increasing obesity and often treatable by diet and exercise. *Also called* Type II diabetes, maturity onset diabetes.

noninvasive /nŏn′ĭn vā′sĭv/ referring to a medical test or procedure or treatment that does not involve entering a body opening or breaking the skin.

nonpathogenic /nŏn′păth ə jĕn′ĭk/ not disease-causing. [non- + pathogenic]

nonprescription drugs /nŏn′prĭ skrĭp′shən/ drugs that can be purchased without a prescription.

nonproductive cough /nŏn′prə dŭk′tĭv/ a cough that does not bring mucus up into the throat.

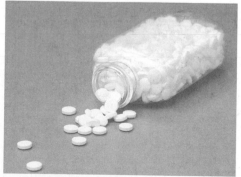

Nonprescription Drug (aspirin)

nonproprietary name /nŏn′prə prī′ĭ tĕr′ē/ the generic name of a drug, which cannot be trademarked and is used by government agencies and national organizations.

non-rapid eye movement (NREM or non-REM) sleep /nŏn′răp′ĭd/ a period of deep sleep during which a person does not dream.

nonsteroidal anti-inflammatory drug (NSAID) /nŏn′stĭ roi′dəl ăn′tē ĭn flăm′ə tôr′ē/ any of a group of drugs, such as aspirin and ibuprofen, that do not contain steroids, used to treat inflammation, pain, and fever.

nonunion /nŏn yōōn′yən/ the failure of a fracture to heal together normally.

nonviable /nŏn vī′ə bəl/ not capable of living and growing.

Noonan('s) syndrome (NS) /nōō′nən(z) sĭn′ drōm/ a group of symptoms that includes congenital heart abnormalities, low-set ears, webbed neck, a deformity of elbows, and often mental retardation, similar to Turner's syndrome but without the chromosomal abnormality.

noradrenaline /nôr′ə drĕn′ə lĭn/ norepinephrine.

norepinephrine /nôr′ĕp ə nĕf′rĭn/ a hormone produced in the adrenal medulla (the inner, central part of the adrenal gland) in response to stress; it constricts blood vessels, thereby raising blood pressure, and dilates the bronchi. *Also called* noradrenaline.

norm-, normo- *combining form.* normal: *for example,* normocyte.

normal /nôr′məl/ **1.** in psychology, average in intelligence and other psychological traits and not suffering from mental illness or emotional disorder. **2.** in medicine, free from infection, disease, or malformation and not subject to experimental therapy.

normal growth rate the rate of normal growth of bone in both the fetus, measured in length, and after birth, measured in height.

normal range the limits between which normal test values for a healthy population are found.

normal sinus rhythm the regular rhythm of the heart.

normal tension glaucoma /glô kō′mə/ a form of glaucoma in which the pressure within the eye is normal but the optic nerve is progressively damaged as it is in classic glaucoma, with increasing loss of field of vision.

normoblast /nôr′mə blăst′/ a cell in the third of four sequential stages in the development of a mature red blood cell. [normo- + -blast]

normocyte /nôr′mə sĭt′/ a red blood cell that is normal in color, shape, and size. [normo- + -cyte]

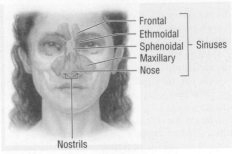

Nose

normotensive /nôr′mō tĕn′sĭv/ **1.** *adj.* marked by normal tension or pressure. **2.** *n.* a person with normal blood pressure.

Northern blot a procedure used to separate and identify fragments of DNA.

Norwalk virus /nôr′wôk vī′rəs/ a member of a family of small round viruses that cause gastroenteritis.

NOS *abbreviation.* not otherwise specified (used in medical coding).

nose /nōz/ a structure on the face through which air is humidified as it enters the respiratory system; the external organ of the sense of smell.

nosebleed /nōz′blēd′/ bleeding from the nose. *Also called* epistaxis, rhinorrhagia.

nose job informal term for rhinoplasty (surgical repair or cosmetic alteration of the nose).

nosocomial /nŏs′ō kō′mē əl/ hospital-acquired.

nosocomial infection /ĭn fĕk′shən/ infection that was not present on admission but appears 72 hours or more after hospitalization for an unrelated reason.

nosology /nō sŏl′ə jē/ **1.** scientific classification of disease. **2.** classification of sick people into groups, based on some stated criterion or criteria.

nostrils /nŏs′trəlz/ two external openings at the base of the external nose. *Also called* nares.

nostrum /nŏs′trəm/ **1.** a general remedy, either patented or secret, offered as a cure: not used of prescription or general over-the-counter drugs. **2.** a worthless remedy sold with exaggerated claims.

notifiable disease /nō′tə fī′ə bəl/ a disease, such as AIDS, gonorrhea, hepatitis, or tuberculosis, whose presence in a patient must be reported to Centers for Disease Control and often state and local authorities. *Also called* reportable disease.

nourish /nûr′ĭsh/ to provide with food or other life-sustaining substances; feed.

nourishment /nûr′ĭsh mənt/ food and/or other substances necessary to maintain life.

novocaine /nō′və kān′/ an anesthetic commonly used in dentistry.

noxious /nŏk′shəs/ injurious to health, such as chemical fumes.

NPC *abbreviation.* Niemann-Pick's disease.

NPO, n.p.o. *abbreviation.* Latin *nil per os,* nothing by mouth.

NREM sleep /ĕn′rĕm′/ or **nonREM sleep** /nŏn′rĕm′/ *abbreviation.* non-rapid eye movement sleep.

NS *abbreviation.* Noonan's syndrome.

NSAID *abbreviation.* nonsteroidal anti-inflammatory drug.

NTD *abbreviation.* neural tube defect.

nucha /nōō′kə/ the back of the neck.

nuchal /nōō′kəl/ of or involving the back of the neck.

nuchal rigidity stiffness in the neck; stiff neck.

nuclear medicine /nōō′klē ər/ the branch of medicine that uses radioactivity to diagnose and treat disease.

nucleic acid /nōō klē′ĭk/ any of a group of very large molecules, DNA or RNA, that contain genetic information, coded as a sequence of proteins and directing cellular functioning.

nucleolus /nōō klē′ə ləs/ a clearly visible rounded mass within the cell nucleus that contains the DNA templates for RNA production.

nucleotide /nōō′klē ə tīd′/ any of a group of molecules that form the building blocks of DNA.

nucleus /nōō′klē əs/ the central portion of a cell, directing the cell's activities and containing genetic information in the form of DNA chromosomes.

nulligravida /nŭl′ĭ grăv′ĭ də/ a woman who has never been pregnant.

nullipara /nŭ lĭp′ər ə/ a woman who has never given birth.

nulliparous /nŭ lĭp′ər əs/ having never conceived a child.

nummular eczema /nŭm′yōō lər ĕk′sə mə, ĕg zē′mə/ a chronic skin condition consisting of itchy coin-shaped patches.

nurse /nûrs/ *n.* **1.** a person formally educated in the scientific methods of nursing the sick and the infirm. *v.* **2.** to provide nursing care to the sick and the infirm. **3.** to suckle an infant.

nurse practitioner /prăk tĭsh′ə nər/ a registered nurse with advanced education in the primary care of people with certain conditions.

nurse-midwife /nûrs′mĭd′wīf′/ a nurse with advanced training in prenatal care and skilled in assisting a woman in childbirth.

nursing /nûr′sĭng/ **1.** breastfeeding. **2.** the profession and duties of a nurse.

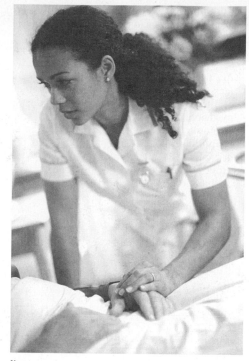

Nurse

nursing assistant a person trained to assist patients both in facilities and at home who need help due to disability, illness, or physical or cognitive limitations.

nursing home or **nursing facility** an institution in which sick and elderly people who cannot live independently or who require skilled nursing care live.

nutraceutical /nōō′trə sōō′tĭ kəl/ a food or a dietary supplement derived from a food that is believed to provide medical benefits, including preventing and treating disease.

nutrients /nōō′trē ənts/ components of food that are necessary for normal body health and function, such as vitamins and minerals, protein, fats, fiber, and carbohydrates.

nutrition /nōō trĭsh′ən/ the science of dietary requirements for healthy body functioning and for activity, growth and development, and reproduction and lactation.

nutritional neuroscience /nōō trĭsh′ə nəl nōōr′ ō sī′əns/ the study of nutrition, including dietary supplements and food additives, as it relates to neurochemistry, neurobiology, behavior, emotions, etc.

nutritionist /nōō trĭsh′ə nĭst/ someone trained in the science of dietary requirements for health.

nyct-, nycto- *combining form.* night: *for example,* nyctophobia.

nyctalbuminuria /nĭk′tăl byo͞o′mĭ no͞or′ē ə/ excessive albumin in the urine at night. [nyct- + albuminuria]

nyctalopia /nĭk′tə lō′pē ə/ reduced ability to see in dim light or at night, due to impaired function of the rods in the retina, caused by lack of adequate vitamin A in the diet or by heredity. *Also called* night blindness, nyctanopia.

nyctanopia /nĭk′tə nō′pē ə/ nyctalopia.

nyctophilia /nĭk′tō fĭl′ē ə/ a preference for darkness or the night. [nycto- + -philia]

nyctophobia /nĭk′tō fō′bē ə/ abnormal fear of darkness or the night. *Also called* noctophobia. [nycto- + -phobia]

nycturia /nĭk to͞or′ē ə/ excessive urination at night. *Also called* nocturia. [nyct- + -uria]

nymphomania /nĭm′fō mā′nē ə/ obsessive sexual desire in a woman.

nystagmus /nĭ stăg′məs/ excessive involuntary movement of the eyeball.

nyxis /nĭk′sĭs/ the surgical insertion of a needle or other instrument into a body cavity, especially the abdomen, to withdraw fluid from it; a puncture. *Also called* paracentesis.

O₂ *abbreviation.* oxygen.

oat cell carcinoma /kär′sə nō′mə/ a highly malignant cancer, usually of the lungs, made of small egg-shaped cells.

OB *abbreviation.* obstetrics; obstetrician.

obese /ō bēs′/ **1.** having a body mass index of ≥30. **2.** seriously overweight.

obesity /ō bē′sĭ tē/ **1.** the condition of having a body mass index of ≥30. **2.** the condition of being seriously overweight.

OB/GYN *abbreviation.* obstetrics and gynecology.

objective /əb jĕk′tĭv/ **1.** able to be perceived by people other than the patient, said of symptoms. **2.** factual, such as data; not open to interpretation.

oblique /ō blēk′/ at a slant or at an angle.

oblique fracture /frăk′chər/ a bone break in a direction that slants across a central line running the length of the bone.

oblique x-ray /ĕks′rā′/ an x-ray taken at a particular angle other than anterior-posterior or lateral.

OBS *abbreviation.* organic brain syndrome.

obsession /əb sĕsh′ən/ domination of thoughts and feelings by an image, object, or concept.

obsessive-compulsive disorder (OCD) /əb sĕs′ĭv kəm pŭl′sĭv/ a condition with persistent thoughts, ideas, and actions that lead to repetitive, ritualistic, and time-consuming behaviors.

obstetric /əb stĕt′rĭk/ or **obstetrical** /əb stĕt′ rĭ kəl/ for or involving obstetrics.

obstetrician /ŏb′stĭ trĭsh′ən/ a doctor who diagnoses and treats pregnancies and childbirths.

obstetrician/gynecologist /gī′nə kŏl′ə jĭst/ a doctor who is qualified to practice both obstetrics and gynecology.

obstetrics (OB) /əb stĕt′rĭks/ the diagnosis and treatment of fertility, pregnancy, and childbirth.

obstruction /əb strŭk′shən/ blockage, as by a narrowing or closing.

obstructive sleep apnea (OSA) /ăp′nē ə/ a recurrent brief suspension of breathing, due to temporary obstruction of the air passage by a lax soft palate, uvula, or tonsils.

obtund /ŏb tŭnd′/ to dull or deaden the senses.

obturation /ŏb′tōō rā′shən/ the blocking or obstruction of a passageway.

obturator /ŏb′tōō rā′tər/ anything that covers an opening or blocks a passageway, either something organic, such as the soft palate or something manufactured, such as a prosthetic.

occipital /ŏk sĭp′ĭ təl/ of or involving the occiput.

occipital bone the bone covering the posterior and base of the skull.

occipital lobe the posterior portion of the brain.

occiput /ŏk′sĭ pŭt′/ the posterior and base of the skull.

occlude /ə klōōd′/ to close off or block.

occlusal /ə klōō′zəl/ **1.** of or about occlusion. **2.** of or involving the surfaces of the upper and lower teeth where they contact one another.

occlusion /ə klōō′zhən/ **1.** the closing off of a blood vessel due to a blockage. **2.** the fit of the teeth of the upper jaw with those of the lower jaw when the jaws are closed.

occlusive /ə klōō′sĭv/ tending to occlude.

occult /ə kŭlt′/ hidden; not known or not visible.

occult blood blood that is present in amounts that are too small to be seen.

occult stool blood test a chemical test of a stool specimen for the presence of blood.

occupational disease /ŏk′yōō pā′shə nəl/ any disorder associated with or caused by a person's work.

occupational medicine the branch of medicine specializing in occupational disease.

Occupational Safety and Health Administration (OSHA) Federal agency that regulates workers' health and safety in the workplace (www.osha.gov).

occupational therapist (OT) /thĕr′ə pĭst/ a person trained in the assessment and treatment of people whose condition, disease, or injury has interfered with their performance of activities of daily living. *See illustration* on page 252.

occupational therapy (OT) activities designed to help people develop, maintain, or regain skills necessary for the performance of activities of daily living, usually performed in a social setting.

Occupational Therapist

OCD *abbreviation.* obsessive-compulsive disorder.

ochronosis /ŏk′rə nō′sĭs/ a disorder in which cartilage and sometimes the white of the eyes, lips, and skin of the ears and hands turn a dark brownish-yellow.

octogenarian /ŏk′tə jə nâr′ē ən/ a person between the ages of 80 and 90.

ocul-, oculo- *combining form. eye: for example,* oculodynia.

ocular /ŏk′yə lər/ of or involving the eye.

ocular albinism /ăl′bə nĭz′əm/ a genetic disorder with lack of pigment in the eyes and deafness.

oculocutaneous /ŏk′yə lō kyōō tā′nē əs/ involving the eyes and skin. [oculo- + cutaneous]

oculodynia /ŏk′yə lō dĭn′ē ə/ pain in an eye or eyes. [oculo- + -dynia]

oculomotor /ŏk′yə lō mō′tər/ of or pertaining to movement of the eye. [oculo- + motor]

oculomotor nerve cranial nerve III; one of two motor nerves that produces movement of the eyes as well as the eyelid muscles. It also supplies the iris (which is the sphincter muscle through which light enters the eye) and the ciliary muscles (which change the shape of the lens to accommodate for near and far vision). Damage to this nerve may result in double vision, dilated pupils, blurred vision, and droopy eyelids (ptosis).

oculus /ŏk′yə ləs/ *(pl.* **oculi** /ŏk′yə lī′/) the eye.

oculus dexter (o.d.) /dĕk′stər/ the right eye (in optometry)

oculus sinister (o.s.) /sĭn′ĭ stər/ the left eye (in optometry)

oculus uterque (o.u.) /yōō tûr′kwē, -kwā/ each eye (in optometry)

OD *abbreviation.* 1. *n.* an overdose. 2. *v.* to overdose.

o.d. *abbreviation.* Latin *oculus dexter,* the right eye (in optometry).

odont-, odonto- *combining form.* tooth, teeth: *for example,* odontoplasty.

odontalgia /ō′dŏn tăl′jē ə, -jə/ a toothache. [odont- + -algia]

odontoblast /ō dŏn′tə blăst′/ a cell that lines the pulp cavity of the tooth and forms dentin. [odonto- + -blast]

odontoblastoma /ō dŏn′tō blă stō′mə/ *(pl.* **odontoblastomas** or **odontoblastomata** /ō dŏn′tō blă stō′mə tə/) 1. an odontoma that is just beginning to grow. 2. a tumor largely made up of odontoblasts. [odonto- + blast- + -oma]

odontodysplasia /ō dŏn′tō dĭs plā′zhə/ a localized developmental abnormalilty of teeth, usually affecting some of the incisors on one side only, characterized by insufficient production of enamel and dentin. [odonto- + dysplasia

odontogenesis /ō dŏn′tō jĕn′ə sĭs/ the development of the teeth. [odonto- + genesis]

odontoma /ō′dŏn tō′mə/ *(pl.* **odontomas** or **odontomata** /ō′dŏn tō′mə tə/) a tumor originating in dental tissue. [odont- + -oma]

odontoneuralgia /ō dŏn′tō nōō răl′jē ə, -jə/ sharp stabbing or throbbing pain in the face caused by a decayed tooth. [odonto- + neuralgia]

odontopathy /ō′dŏn tŏp′ə thē/ tooth disease. [odonto- + -pathy]

odontoplasty /ō dŏn′tə plăs′tē/ surgical repair or reshaping of the tooth. [odonto- + -plasty]

odontology /ō′dŏn tŏl′ə jē/ the study of the structure and development of teeth and of the prevention and cure of their diseases. [odont- + -logy]

odor /ō′dər/ anything that stimulates the sense of smell; smell.

-odynia *suffix.* pain: *for example,* gastrodynia.

odynophagia /ō dĭn′ō fā′jē ə, -jə/ pain on swallowing.

off-label use the prescribing of a drug for a purpose other than those purposes approved by the FDA.

offspring /ôf′sprĭng′/ the children of a particular individual.

-oid *suffix.* like, resembling: *for example,* nephroid.

oil /oil/ any of many greasy liquids that mix with alcohol and ether but not with water, combustible at room temperature; oils are classified by their source as animal, vegetable, or mineral, and are further divided into volatile and fixed (or fatty) oils.

oint, oint. *abbreviation.* ointment.

ointment /oint′mənt/ a thick, semisolid preparation that is applied to the skin and contains medication.

olecranon /ō lĕk′rə nŏn′, ō′lĭ krā′nŏn/ the end of the ulna (the larger of the two long bones of

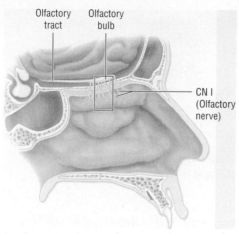

Olfactory tract   Olfactory bulb

CN I (Olfactory nerve)

Olfactory Bulb

the forearm) that projects out behind the elbow; it rotates in the trochlea (a groove) of the humerus (the other of the two long bones).

olecranon process   the bony protrusion of the olecranon that forms the outer bump in the elbow.

olfaction /ŏl făk′shən/   the sense of smell.

olfactory /ŏl făk′tə rē/   of or involving the sense of smell.

olfactory apparatus /ăp′ə răt′əs/   the entire apparatus needed to smell, from the nostrils to the olfactory lobes of the brain. *Also called* olfactory system.

olfactory bulb   the enlarged bulb-shaped ending of the nerve leading to the area of the brain under the frontal lobe, where the olfactory messages are processed.

olfactory disorder   any dysfunction or disease of the olfactory system.

olfactory lobe   a projection at the inferior front of each cerebral hemisphere where messages from the olfactory nerve are processed.

olfactory nerve   cranial nerve I; either of the two sensory nerves that conduct information from the olfactory receptors to an area under each of the frontal lobes of the brain.

olfactory receptors   neurons covered with cilia that send messages to the area in the brain where olfactory messages are processed.

olfactory system   the entire apparatus needed to smell, from the nostrils to the olfactory lobes of the brain. *Also called* olfactory apparatus.

olig-, oligo-   *combining form.* too few, too little; scanty: *for example,* oligomenorrhea.

oligoarthritis /ŏl′ĭ gō är thrī′tĭs/   inflammation of fewer than five joints. [oligo- + arthitis]

oligodactyly /ŏl′ĭ gō dăk′tə lē/   having fewer than five fingers or toes on a hand or foot. [oligo- + -dactyly]

oligodendrocyte /ŏl′ĭ gō děn′drō sīt′/   one of many projecting cells on the surface of oligendroglia. [oligo- + -dactyly]

oligodendroglia /ŏl′ĭ gō děn drog′lē ə/   cells in the brain that do not transmit electrical impulses but that produce myelin and help in supporting neurons. *Also called* oligodendroglial cells.

oligodendroglial cells /ŏl′ĭ gō děn drog′lē əl/   oligodendroglia.

oligodendroglioma /ŏl′ĭ gō děn drog′lē ō′mə/   a slow-growing tumor made up of oligodendrogial cells. [oligodendrogli(a) + -oma]

oligomenorrhea /ŏl′ĭ gō měn′ə rē′ə/   infrequent or scanty menstrual periods. [oligo- + menorrhea]

oligo-ovulation /ŏl′ĭ gō ŏv′yoo lā′shən/   irregular and infrequent ovulation. [oligo- + ovulation]

oligopeptide /ŏl′ĭ gō pěp′tīd/   a molecule made from a few amino acids.

oligospermia /ŏl′ĭ gō spûr′mē ə/   abnormally few spermatozoa in the semen.

oliguria /ŏl′ĭ goor′ē ə/   excretion of a very small amount of urine relative to fluid intake (less than 1 cc of urine output per hour per kg of body weight).

oliva /ō lī′və/ (*pl.* **olivae** /ō lī′vē/)   the olive. *Also called* olivary body.

olivary /ŏl′ə vâr′ē/   of or involving the olivary body.

olivary body   the olive. *Also called* oliva.

olive /ŏl′ĭv/   either of the two small protuberances located on either side of the medulla oblongata in the brain. *Also called* oliva.

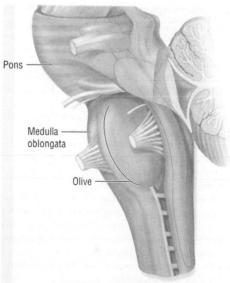

Pons

Medulla oblongata

Olive

Longitudinal section (cut-away)

Olive

-oma (*pl.* **-omas** or **-omata** /-ō′mə tə/) *suffix.* tumor, neoplasm: *for example,* myeloma.

omega-3 fatty acids /ō mā′gə thrē′/ a group of fatty acids in the oil of certain saltwater fish that have been shown to reduce the amount of very-low-density lipoprotein cholesterol.

oment-, omento- *combining form.* omentum: *for example,* omentectomy.

omentectomy /ō′měn těk′tə mē/ a surgical removal of all or part of the lining of the abdominal cavity. [oment- + -ectomy]

omentitis /ō′měn tī′tĭs/ inflammation of the lining of the abdominal cavity. [oment- + -itis]

omentopexy /ō měn′tə pěk′sē/ the surgical fixing in place of the omentum. [omento- + -pexy]

omentoplasty /ō měn′tə plăs′tē/ surgical repair of the omentum. [omento- + -plasty]

omentum /ō měn′təm/ (*pl.* **omenta** /ō měn′tə)/ a fat-laden fold of the membrane that lies in the abdominal cavity from the stomach to below the transverse colon. *See also* lesser omentum, greater omentum.

omnifocal lens /ŏm′nĭ fō′kəl/ an eyeglass or lens for both near and distant vision.

omphal-, omphalo- *combining form.* navel; umbilicus: *for example,* omphalocele.

omphalectomy /ŏm′fə lěk′tə mē/ surgical removal of the navel. [omphalo- + -ectomy]

omphalic /ŏm făl′ĭk/ of or relating to the navel. [omphal- + -ic]

omphalitis /ŏm′fə lī′tĭs/ inflammation of the navel. [omphal- + -itis]

omphalocele /ŏm′fə lə sēl′/ a birth defect in which a piece of the intestine protrudes from the abdominal cavity at the navel.

omphalorrhagia /ŏm′fə lō rā′jē ə, -jə/ bleeding from the navel. [omphalo- + -rrhagia]

omphalorrhea /ŏm′fə lō rē′ə/ the discharge of lymph at the navel. [omphalo- + -rrhea]

omphalorrhexis /ŏm′fə lō rěk′sĭs/ rupture of the umbilical cord. [omphalo- + -rrhexis]

omphalos /ŏm′fə lŏs′/ the navel. *Also called* umbilicus.

omphalotomy /ŏm′fə lŏt′ə mē/ a surgical incision into the navel. [omphalo- + -tomy]

onanism /ō′nə nĭz′əm/ **1.** withdrawal of the penis from the vagina prior to ejaculation, a method used to control impregnation. **2.** masturbation, especially male masturbation.

onchocerciasis /ŏng′kō sər kī′ə sĭs/ an infestation of threadlike roundworms of the species *Onchocerca volvulus* that live in nodules under the skin and ultimately cause blindness. *Also called* river blindness.

onco- *combining form.* tumor, mass, swelling: *for example,* oncogene.

oncogene /ŏng′kə jēn′/ a gene that causes a host cell to become cancerous. [onco- + gene]

Oncologist

oncogenic /ŏng′kə jěn′ĭk/ of or involving an oncogene. [onco- + gen(e) + -ic]

oncogenic agent anything that causes a gene to mutate into an oncogene.

oncogenic viruses viruses that are capable of causing tumors.

oncologist /ŏng kŏl′ə jĭst/ a doctor specializing in the diagnosis and treatment of cancers. [onco- + -logist]

oncology /ŏng kŏl′ə jē/ the branch of medicine that studies, diagnoses, and treats people with cancer. [onco- + -logy]

oncosis /ŏng kō′sĭs/ the formation of a tumor or tumors. [onc- + -osis]

Ondine('s) curse /ŏn dēn(z)′/ hypoventilation during sleep, thought to be due to a brainstem defect in sensitivity to CO_2.

oneirism /ō nīr′ĭz əm/ a dreamlike state of consciousness.

oneirophrenia /ō nīr′ō frē′nē ə/ a type of schizophrenia marked by being in a dreamlike state.

onset /ŏn′sět′/ a beginning.

onych-, onycho- *combinng form.* nail: *for example,* onychalgia.

onychalgia /ŏn′ĭ kăl′jē ə, -jə/ pain in a nail or nails. [onych- + -algia]

onychectomy /ŏn′ĭ kěk′tə mē/ surgical removal of a nail or nail bed. [onych- + -ectomy]

onychia /ō nĭk′ē ə/ inflammation of the nail bed. *Also called* onychitis. [onych- + -ia]

onychitis /ŏn′ĭ kī′tĭs/ onychia. [onych- + -itis]

onychocryptosis /ŏn′ĭ kō krĭp tō′sĭs/ an ingrown nail. [onycho- + crypt- + -osis]

onychodystrophy /ŏn′ĭ kō dĭs′trə fē/ malformation of a nail, sometimes caused by trauma to the nail bed. [onycho- + dystrophy]

onychogryphosis /ŏn′ĭ kō grĭ fō′sĭs/ or **onychogryposis** /ŏn′ĭ kō grĭ pō′sĭs/ abnormal thickening and curving of a nail.

onychoid /ŏn′ĭ koid′/ resembling a nail. [onych- + -oid]

onycholysis /ŏn′ĭ kŏl′ə sĭs/ separation of the nail plate from the nail bed. [onycho- + -lysis]

onychoma /ŏn´ĭ kō´mə/   a tumor of the nail bed. [onych- + -oma]

onychomalacia /ŏn´ĭ kō mə lā´shē ə, -shə/   softening of the nails. [onycho- + -malacia]

onychomycosis /ŏn´ĭ kō mī kō´sĭs/   one of many fungal infections of the nails. [onycho- + micosis]

onychopathy /ŏn´ĭ kŏp´ə thē/   disease or deformity of the nails. *Also called* onychosis. [onycho- + -pathy]

onychophagia /ŏn´ĭ kō fā´jē ə, -jə/ or **onychophagy** /ŏn´ĭ kŏf´ə jē/   the habit of nail biting. [onycho- + -phagia *or* -phagy]

onychoplasty /ŏn´ĭ kō plăs´tē/   surgical repair of the nail bed. [onycho- + -plasty]

onychosis /ŏn´ĭ kō´sĭs/   disease or deformity of the nails. *Also called* onychopathy. [onych- + -osis]

oo-   *combining form.* egg: *for example,* oocyte.

ooblast /ō´ə blăst´/   the immature cell from which an ovum develops. [oo- + -blast]

oocyte /ō´ə sīt´/   a not-completely-developed egg cell. [oo- + -cyte]

oogenesis /ō´ə jĕn´ə sĭs/   the development of egg cells. [oo- + -genesis]

oogonium /ō´ə gō´nē əm/ (*pl.* **oogonia** /ō´ə gō´nē ə/)   an undeveloped egg cell before it has become an oocyte.

oophor-, oophoro-   *combining form.* ovary: *for example,* oophorectomy.

oophorectomy /ō´ə fə rĕk´tə mē/   surgical removal of one or both ovaries. [oophor- + -ectomy]

oophoritis /ō´ə fə rī´tĭs/   inflammation of an ovary. [oophor- + -itis]

oophoropexy /ō ŏf´ər ō pĕk´sē/   surgical fixation of a displaced ovary. [oophoro- + -pexy]

oophoroplasty /ō ŏf´ər ə plăs´tē/   surgical repair of an ovary. [oophoro- + -plasty]

opacity /ō păs´ĭ tē/   a dark spot in normally clear or transparent tissue.

opaque /ō pāk´/   not letting light through; not transparent; cloudy.

open-angle glaucoma /glô kō´mə/   the most common type of glaucoma, characterized by increased intraocular pressure, an enlarged depression in the center of the optic disk, and consequent damage to the optic nerve.

open biopsy /bī´ŏp sē/   a biopsy that requires a surgical incision.

open fracture /frăk´chər/   a fracture in which a bone protrudes through the skin.

open heart surgery   surgery performed on an exposed heart while a heart-lung machine circulates and oxygenates the blood.

opening /ō´pə nĭng/   a hole, gap, or open space in a body structure.

open reduction /rĭ dŭk´shən/ or **open reduction and fixation**   setting a fractured bone after cutting into the skin and manipulating muscle to free the site of the fracture and put the fragments in anatomical position.

open wound /wo͞ond/   a wound where tissue is exposed.

operable /ŏp´ər ə bəl/   able to be removed, repaired, cured, or improved by surgical procedure.

operate /ŏp´ə rāt´/   to perform surgery.

operating room (OR) /ŏp´ə rā´tĭng/   a specially equipped and sterilized room in a hospital or other medical facility where surgical procedures are performed.

operation /ŏp´ə rā´shən/   the surgical removal, transplant, or manipulation of tissue.

operculum /ō pûr´kyo͞o ləm/ (*pl.* **opercula** /ō pûr´kyo͞o lə/)   **1.** a covering. **2.** the opening at the top of the thoracic cavity. **3.** a plug of mucus that lodges in the opening of the cervix upon fertilization and seals it off. **4.** the attached flap of tissue in a retinal tear.

ophthalm-, ophthalmo-   *combining form.* eye: *for example,* ophthalmology.

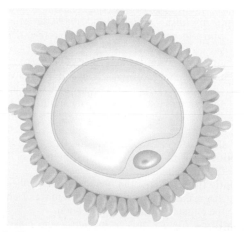

Oocyte

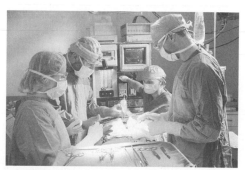

Operating Room

ophthalmalgia /ŏf′thăl măl′jē ə, -jə/ pain in the eye. *Also called* ophthalmodynia. [ophthalm- + -algia]

ophthalmia /ŏf thăl′mē ə/ inflammation of the eye, especially the conjunctiva.

ophthalmic /ŏf thăl′mĭk/ of or involving the eye. [ophthalm- + -ic]

ophthalmic artery /är′tə rē/ the blood vessel that brings oxygenated blood to the eye.

ophthalmic nerve the upper branch of the three divisions of the fifth cranial nerve (trigeminal nerve) that supplies nerve fibers to most of the face; the ophthalmic nerve is a sensory nerve and supplies nerve fibers to the cornia and iris, the lacrimal gland, the mucous membrane of the nasal cavity, and the skin of the eyelids, eyebrows, forehead and nose.

ophthalmic solution a sterile solution, sometimes containing medication, dispensed as eyedrops.

ophthalmitis /ŏf′thăl mī′tĭs/ inflammation of the eye. [ophthalm- + -itis]

ophthalmo- *See* ophthalm-.

ophthalmodynia /ŏf thăl′mō dĭn′ē ə/ pain in the eye. *Also called* ophthalmalgia. [ophthalmo- + -dynia]

ophthalmologist /ŏf′thăl mŏl′ə jĭst/ doctor who specializes in the diagnosis and treatment of diseases of the eye. [ophthalmo- + -logist]

ophthalmology /ŏf′thăl mŏl′ə jē/ the branch of medicine that studies the functions and structures of the eye, and its disorders and their treatment. [ophthalmo- + -logy]

ophthalmometer /ŏf′thăl mŏm′ĭ tər/ any of several instruments that measure different aspects of the eye, such as errors of refraction, volume of various parts, angles of curvature, and so on. [ophthalmo- + -meter]

ophthalmoplasty /ŏf thăl′mə plăs′tē/ surgical repair or reshaping of the eye or eyelid. [ophthalmo- + -plasty]

ophthalmoplegia /ŏf thăl′mō plē′jē ə, -jə/ paralysis of one or more of the muscles of the eye. [ophthalmo- + -plegia]

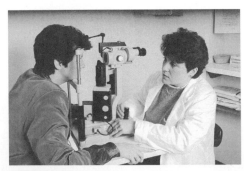

Ophthalmologist

ophthalmoptosis /ŏf thăl′mŏp tō′sĭs/ drooping of the upper eyelid. [ophthalmo- + -ptosis]

ophthalmoscope /ŏf thăl′mə skōp′/ an instrument for examining the interior of the eye. [ophthalmo- + -scope]

ophthalmoscopy /ŏf′thăl mŏs′kə pē/ visual examination of the interior of the eye. [ophthalmo- + -scopy]

-opia *suffix.* vision: *for example,* myopia.

opiate /ō′pē ĭt, -āt′/ a narcotic drug containing opium or any of its derivatives, used for pain relief.

opioid /ō′pē oid′/ **1.** any of a group of synthetic chemicals, such as methadone, that produces effects like those of an opiate. **2.** any of a group of substances produced in the body in response to stress, such as endorphin.

opioid antagonist /ăn tăg′ə nĭst/ a chemical compound specifically manufactured to block the effects of synthetic or organic opioids.

opisthotonos /ō′pĭs thŏt′ə nəs/ a spasm in which the head and the heels extend backward and the chest and abdomen are bowed forward.

opportunistic condition /ŏp′ər tōō nĭs′tĭk/ a condition, such as Kaposi′s sarcoma or cytomegalovirus (CMV), that occurs in someone as a result of a weakened immune system.

opportunistic infection /ĭn fĕk′shən/ an infection that can only take hold in the body of a person with a weakened immune system.

opportunistic microorganism /mī′krō ôr′gə nĭz′əm/ a microorganism that is only able to cause infection when a person′s immune system is weakened.

-opsia *suffix.* defect in vision or eyesight: *for example,* cyanopsia.

-opsy *suffix.* examination; viewing; process of viewing: *for example,* autopsy.

opt-, opto- *combining form.* vision: *for example,* optometry.

optic /ŏp′tĭk/ of or involving vision.

optic disc/disk a small round area of the retina where the optic nerve leaves the retina, that has no rods or cones and therefore can "see" nothing. *Also called* blind spot.

optic glioma /glī ō′mə/ a benign tumor of glial cells on an optic nerve or where the optic nerves cross to the opposite side of the brain.

optic nerve cranial nerve II; either of a pair of sensory nerves that travel from the retina to the visual cortex, where vision is "perceived."

optic neuroma /nōō rō′mə/ a benign tumor of the optic nerve.

optic tract /trăkt/ the bundle of nerve fibers that make up the optic nerve as it moves from the retina to the cortex of the brain.

optician /ŏp tĭsh′ən/ a specialist who makes and fits corrective lenses.

Optometrist

optics /ŏp′tĭks/ the branch of physics that deals with the properties of visible and invisible light and with vision.

optometrist /ŏp tŏm′ĭ trĭst/ a trained medical specialist who can examine people for vision problems and can prescribe corrective lenses.

optometry /ŏp tŏm′ĭ trē/ the specialty of examining and diagnosing certain vision disorders and providing preventive care and corrective lenses. [opto- + -metry]

or-, oro- *combining form.* mouth: *for example,* orofacial.

OR *abbreviation.* operating room.

oral /ôr′əl/ of or involving the mouth.

oral administration to give medication, as pills and some liquids, by mouth.

oral cavity the inside of the mouth.

oral contraceptive /kŏn′trə sĕp′tĭv/ any of several kinds of birth-control pill for women; most kinds suppress ovulation, but some prevent fertilization or implantation of the egg.

oral surgeon /sûr′jən/ a dentist who is additionally trained to perform surgery of the mouth, gums, and jaw.

oral temperature the temperature of the body as measured by placing the appropriate thermometer under the tongue.

orbit /ôr′bĭt/ the bony cavity in the skull in which the eyeball sits and the associated muscles, nerves, and blood vessels. *Also called* orbital cavity, eye socket.

orbital /ôr′bĭ təl/ of or involving the orbit.

orbital cavity /kăv′ĭ te/ the orbit. *Also called* eye socket.

orch-, orchi-, orchid-, orchido-, orchio- *combining form.* testicle: *for example,* orchialgia, orchidalgia.

orchectomy /ôr kĕk′tə mē/ surgical removal of a testical. *Also called* orchidectomy. [orch- + -ectomy]

orchialgia /ôr′kē ăl′jē ə, -jə/ orchidalgia. [orchi- + -algia]

orchidalgia /ôr′kĭ dăl′jē ə, -jə/ pain in a testicle. *Also called* orchialgia, orchidodynia, orchiodynia. [orchid- + -algia]

orchidectomy /ôr′kĭ dĕk′tə mē/ surgical removal of a testicle. [orchid- + -ectomy]

orchiditis /ôr′kĭ dī′tĭs/ inflammation of a testicle. *Also called* orchitis. [orchid- + -itis]

orchidocele /ôr′kĭ də sēl′, ôr kĭd′ə-/ a herniated testicle. [orchido- + -cele]

orchidodynia /ôr′kĭ dō dĭn′ē ə, ôr kĭd′ə-/ pain in a testical. *Also called* orchidalgia, orchialgia, orchiodynia. [orchido- + -dynia]

orchidopexy /ôr kĭd′ə pĕk′sē, ôr kĭd′ə/ fixing a testicle in position by surgery. *Also called* orchiopexy. [orchido- + -pexy]

orchidoplasty /ôr′kĭ də plăs′tē, ôr kĭd′ə-/ surgical repair or reshaping of a testicle. [orchido- + -plasty]

orchidotomy /ôr′kĭ dŏt′ə mē/ a surgical incision into a testicle. [orchido- + -tomy]

orchiectomy /ôr′kē ĕk′tə mē/ the surgical removal of a testicle. *Also called* orchectomy. [orchi- + -ectomy]

orchiodynia /ôr′kē ō dĭn′ē ə/ pain in a testicle. *Also called* orchidalgia, orchidodynia, orchialgia. [orchio- + -dynia]

orchiopexy /ôr′kē ō pĕk′sē/ fixing a testicle in position by surgery. *Also called* orchidopexy. [orchio- + -pexy]

orchitis /ôr kī′tĭs/ inflammation of a testicle. *Also called* orchiditis. [orch- + -itis]

orderly /ôr′dər lē/ a hospital worker who assists nurses in nonmedical patient care: transporting, lifting, shaving, etc.

organ /ôr′gən/ a group of cells working together to perform a specific function, as kidneys or the lungs.

organelle /ôr′gə nĕl′/ a specialized part of a cell that performs a particular function within the cell.

organ failure the inability of an organ to perform its function within the body.

organic /ôr găn′ĭk/ **1.** of or involving any chemical compound that contains carbon. **2.** of or involving living organisms. **3.** of or involving an organ. **4.** of or involving living tissue.

organic brain syndrome (OBS) any of various cognitive disorders caused by temporary or permanent brain dysfunction and usually characterized by dementia.

organo- *combining form.* organ: *for example,* organotherapy.

organ of Corti /kôr′tē/ a structure in the cochlea in the inner ear made up of fine hairlike receptor cells that translate sound vibrations into electrical impulses that are sent to the brain.

organ of hearing the ear.

organogenesis /ôr′gə nō jĕn′ə sĭs/ the embryologic development of an organ. [organo- + -genesis]

organ replacement organ transplantation.

organotherapy /ôr′gə nō thĕr′ə pē/ treatment of certain diseases by the administration of extracts from healthy organs or glands of certain animals. [organo- + therapy]

organ transplantation /trăns′plăn tā′shən/ or **organ transplant** /trăns′plănt′/ removal of a diseased organ and its replacement with a healthy organ from a donor. *Also called* organ replacement.

orgasm /ôr′găz əm/ the physical and emotional release that occurs as the climax of sexual stimulation, usually accompanied by ejaculation of semen in the male. *Also called* climax.

orgasmic /ôr găz′mĭk/ of or involving an orgasm.

orifice /ôr′ə fĭs/ any opening or entrance to any body cavity or organ.

origin /ôr′ĭ jĭn/ the beginning or source of something, especially the beginning of a cranial or spinal nerve or the more fixed attachment of a muscle.

oro-. *See* or-.

orofacial /ôr′ō fā′shəl/ of or involving the mouth and the face. [oro- + facial]

oromandibular /ôr′ō măn dĭb′yo͞o lər/ of or involving the mouth and the jaw. [oro- + mandibular]

oropharynx /ôr′ō făr′ĭngks/ the division of the pharynx lying between the soft palate and the upper edge of the epiglottis. [oro- + pharynx]

orphan disease a disease for which no treatment has been developed on account of its rarity (afflicts fewer than 200,000).

orphan drug a drug that is untested or undeveloped because its use is not known or it would be only used in rare circumstances.

orth-, ortho- *combining form.* straight, correct: *for example,* orthomolecular.

orth *abbreviation.* orthopedic surgeon.

orthodontic treatment /ôr′thə dŏn′tĭk/ corrective or preventive use of braces to straighten teeth or modify their seating in the jaw.

orthodontics /ôr′thə dŏn′tĭks/ the branch of dentistry dealing with the correction and prevention of crooked teeth and bad bites.

orthodontist /ôr′thə dŏn′tĭst/ a dentist who specializes in the correction and prevention of crooked teeth and bad bites.

orthomolecular medicine /ôr′thō mə lĕk′yə lər/ a form of alternative medicine that uses vitamins, amino acids, trace minerals, and other naturally occurring substances to preserve health and treat disease. [ortho- + molecular]

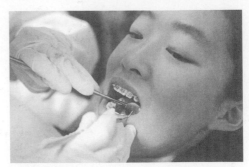

Orthodontist

orthopedic /ôr′thə pē′dĭk/ of or involving orthopedics.

orthopedics /ôr′thə pē′dĭks/ the branch of surgery that specializes in the correction of deformities and disorders in the function and structure of bones and associated muscles and ligaments.

orthopedic surgeon a surgeon who specializes in correcting deformities and disorders in the function and structure of bones and associated muscles and ligaments. *Also called* orthopedist.

orthopedist /ôr′thə pē′dĭst/ orthopedic surgeon.

orthopnea /ôr thŏp′nē ə/ difficulty breathing when not in an upright position. [ortho- + -pnea]

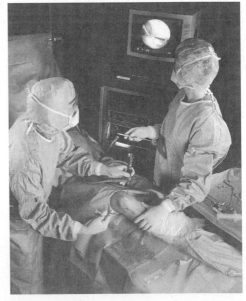

Orthopedic Surgeon

orthoscopic /ôr′thə skŏp′ĭk/ **1.** having correct vision; needing no corrective lenses. **2.** designed to correct vision.

orthosis /ôr thō′sĭs/ **1.** a device designed to correct or improve an orthopedic problem, especially used for the feet. *Also called* orthotic. **2.** the correcting or improving of an orthopedic problem. [orth- + -osis].

orthostatic hypotension /ôr′thō stăt′ĭk hī′pō těn′shən/ a drop in blood pressure on rapid change of position, such as standing up. [ortho- + static]

orthotic /ôr thŏt′ĭk/ **1.** *n.* a device designed to correct or improve an orthopedic problem, especially used for the feet. *Also called* orthosis. **2.** *adj.* serving to correct or improve an orthopedic problem.

orthotist /ôr thŏt′ĭst, ôr′thə tĭst/ a person trained in making and fitting orthotics.

OS, o.s. *abbreviation.* Latin *oculus smister,* the left eye (in optometry).

OSA *abbreviation.* obstructive sleep apnea.

os[1] /ŏs/ (*pl.* **ora** /ôr′ə/) the mouth.

os[2] (*pl.* **ossa** /ŏs′ə/) bone.

oscillometer /ŏs′ə lŏm′ĭ tər/ an instrument used to measure fluctuations, especially in the arterial blood.

oscilloscope /ə sĭl′ə skōp′/ an instrument that produces an image of oscillating current.

osculum /ŏs′kyə ləm/ (*pl.* **oscula** /ŏs′kyə lə/) a small pore or opening.

-ose *suffix.* **1.** full of. **2.** carbohydrate: *for example,* glucose.

OSHA /ō′shə/ *abbreviation.* Occupation Safety and Health Administration (www.osha.gov).

-osis *suffix.* condition; disorder: *for example,* orthosis.

Osler('s) nodes /ōs′lər(z)/ tender and swollen, raised, pea-sized lumps, usually bluish and usually found in the pads of the fingers and toes.

osmosis /ŏz mō′sĭs/ the diffusion of a liquid from areas of lower concentration to areas of higher concentration, through a semipermeable membrane.

osseous /ŏs′ē əs/ made of or resembling bone; bony.

osseous labyrinth /lăb′ə rĭnth/ the bony canal in the temporal bone within the inner ear.

osseous tissue specialized tissue that forms into bones. *Also called* bony tissue.

ossicle /ŏs′ĭ kəl/ a small bone, especially one in the middle ear.

ossiculectomy /ŏs′ĭk yə lěk′tə mē/ the surgical removal of one of the ossicles of the ear.

ossiculotomy /ŏs′ĭk yə lŏt′ə mē/ surgical incision into one of the ossicles of the ear.

ossiculum /ŏ sĭk′yə ləm/ (*pl.* **ossicula** /ŏ sĭk′yə lə/) an ossicle.

ossiferous /ŏ sĭf′ər əs/ forming or containing bone.

ossification /ŏs′ə fĭ kā′shən/ the process of changing from bony tissue into bone.

ossify /ŏs′ə fī′/ to turn into bone.

ost-, oste-, osteo- *combining form.* bone: *for example,* ostealgia.

ostealgia /ŏs′tē ăl′jē ə, -jə/ pain in a bone. *Also called* osteodynia. [oste- + -algia]

ostectomy /ŏ stĕk′tə mē/ surgical removal of a bone. [ost- + -ectomy]

osteitis /ŏs′tē ī′tĭs/ inflammation or infection of a bone. [oste- + -itis]

osteitis deformans /dĭ fôr′mănz/ a disease of the bones that affects older people and is marked by accelerated bone growth with thickening of the long bones and deformity of the flat bones.

osteitis fibrosa cystica /fī brō′sə sĭs′tĭ kə/ a bone disease caused by overactivity of the parathyroid glands, with softening of bone and the development of kidney stones and cysts and sometimes tumors.

osteoarthritis /ŏs′tē ō är thrī′tĭs/ a type of arthritis marked by deterioration of the cartilage in movable joints and vertebrae; usually as a result of gradual wear and tear. [osteo- + arthritis]

osteoarthropathy /ŏs′tē ō är thrŏp′ə thē/ any disease of the bones and joints. [osteo- + arthro- + -pathy]

osteoblast /ŏs′tē ə blăst′/ a cell that deposits calcium into bone. [osteo- + -blast]

osteoblastoma /ŏs′tē ō blă stō′mə/ a benign tumor made of osteoblasts, usually located in the spine. [osteo- + blast- + -oma]

osteocarcinoma /ŏs′tē ō kär′sə nō′mə/ bone cancer. [osteo- + carcinoma]

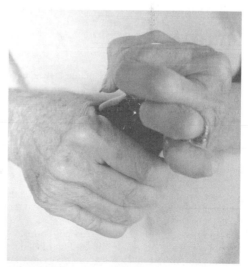

Osteoarthritis

osteochondritis /ŏs′tē ō kŏn drī′tĭs/   inflammation of bone and cartilage. [osteo- + chondr- + -itis]

osteochondroma /ŏs′tē ō kŏn drō′mə/   tumor made of bony and cartilaginous tissue. [osteo- + chondr- + -oma]

osteochondromatosis /ŏs′tē ō kŏn drō′mə tō′sĭs/   a condition marked by the presence of many osteochondromas. [osteochondromat(a) + -osis]

osteochondrosis /ŏs′tē ō kŏn drō′sĭs/   any of a group of disorders in children that cause degenerative changes in the growth centers at the ends of the bones normally surrounded by cartilage or cartilaginous coverings. [osteo- + chondr- + -osis]

osteoclasia /ŏs′tē ō klā′zē ə, -zhə/   the destruction and resorption of bone tissue, as when a bone fracture heals.

osteoclasis /ŏs′tē ŏk′lə sĭs/   the surgical breaking of a bone. [osteo- + -clasis]

osteoclast /ŏs′tē ə klăst′/   **1.** a giant cell with several nuclei that forms in the marrow of growing bones and absorbs dead osseous tissue; osteoclasts reabsorb calcium and bony structure, allowing osteoblasts to reconstruct bone at a fracture, for example. **2.** a surgical tool for breaking bones. [osteo- + -clast]

osteoclastoma /ŏs′tē ō klă stō′mə/   a sometimes malignant tumor containing osteoclasts and occurring at the ends of long bones. [osteoclast + -oma]

osteocyte /ŏs′tē ə sīt′/   a bone cell.

osteodynia /ŏs′tē ō dĭn′ē ə/   pain in a bone. *Also called* ostealgia. [osteo- + -dynia]

osteodystrophy /ŏs′tē ō dĭs′trə fē/   defective bone formation. [osteo- + dystrophy]

osteofibroma /ŏs′tē ō fĭ brō′mə/   a tumor made of bony and fibrous tissue. [osteo- + fibroma]

osteogenesis /ŏs′tē ō jĕn′ə sĭs/   the development of bone tissue. *Also called* ostosis. [osteo- + -genesis]

osteogenesis imperfecta /ĭm′pər fĕk′tə/   a connective tissue disorder causing brittle, easily fractured bones.

osteogenic sarcoma /ŏs′tē ō jĕn′ĭk sär kō′mə/   a malignant bone cancer, usually affecting the ends of the long bones, especially in people between the ages of 10 and 25. [osteo- + -genic]

osteoid /ŏs′tē oid′/   similar to or like a bone or bony tissue. [oste- + -oid]

osteoid osteoma /ŏs′tē ō′mə/   a benign but painful tumor usually occurring in a leg bone in teenagers and young adults.

osteology /ŏs′tē ŏl′ə jē/   the study of bones.

osteolysis /ŏs′tē ŏl′ə sĭs/   dissolution of bone.

osteolytic /ŏs′tē ō lĭt′ĭk/   of or involving the dissolution of bone.

osteoma /ŏs′tē ō′mə/ (*pl.* **osteomas** or **osteomata** / ŏs′tē ō′mə tə/)   a benign, slow-growing mass usually on the skull or jaw.

osteomalacia /ŏs′tē ō mə lā′shē ə, -shə/   a disease marked by softening and bending of bones. [osteo- + -malacia]

osteomyelitis /ŏs′tē ō mī′ə lī′tĭs/   an inflammation or infection of bone marrow and bone. [osteo- + myelitis]

osteonecrosis /ŏs′tē ō nĕ krō′sĭs/   extensive death of bone tissue.

osteopath (D.O.) /ŏs′tē ə păth′/   a medical doctor specializing in the musculoskeletal system who uses manipulation along with conventional diagnostic tools and treatments. *Also called* osteopathic physician.

osteopathic /ŏs′tē ō păth′ĭk/   of or involving osteopathy. [osteo- + -path(y) + -ic]

osteopathic physician /fĭ zĭsh′ən/   osteopath.

osteopathy /ŏs′tē ŏp′ə thē/   **1.** any disease of bone. **2.** a therapeutic system that believes that structural manipulation of muscles and bone can promote healing and health. [osteo- + -pathy]

osteopenia /ŏs′tē ō pē′nē ə/   a loss of bone density. [osteo- + -penia]

osteopetrosis /ŏs′tē ō pĕ trō′sĭs/   any of several hereditary disorders with thickening and abnormal density of bones due to an inability to remove old bone tissue as new bone tissue develops.

osteophyte /ŏs′tē ə fīt′/   a small outgrowth of bony tissue on a bone.

osteoplasty /ŏs′tē ə plăs′tē/   surgical repair of a bone. [osteo- + -plasty]

osteoporosis /ŏs′tē ō pə rō′sĭs/   a condition in which bones become increasingly porous and

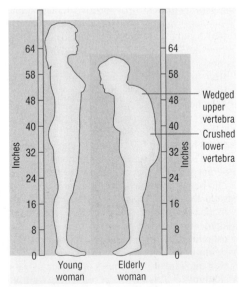

Osteoporosis

brittle, increasing the risk of fracture; occurs especially in post-menopausal women.

osteosarcoma /ŏs′tē ō sär kō′mə/ (*pl.* **osteosarcomas** or **osteosarcomata** /ŏs′tē ō sär kō′mă tə/) a malignant bone tumor, usually affecting the ends of the long bones, especially in people between the ages of 10 and 25. [osteo- + sarcoma]

osteosclerosis /ŏs′tē ō sklĭ rō′sĭs/ abnormal hardening and thickening of bone. [osteo- + sclerosis]

osteosis /ŏs′tē ō′sĭs/ the formation of bony tissue, often infiltrating connective tissue. [oste- + -osis]

osteosynthesis /ŏs′tē ō sĭn′thə sĭs/ internal repair of a bone fracture using a pin, plate, or other mechanical device. [osteo- + synthesis]

osteotome /ŏs′tē ə tōm′/ chisel-like surgical instrument for cutting into bone. [osteo- + -tome]

osteotomy /ŏs′tē ŏt′ə mē/ surgical incision into a bone. [osteo- + -tomy]

ostium /ŏs′tē əm/ (*pl.* **ostia** /ŏs′tē ə/) a small opening into a tubular organ.

ostomy /ŏs′tə mē/ any of several surgical procedures in which an opening into an organ is made to allow for drainage.

ostosis /ŏ stō′sĭs/ the development of bone; bone formation. *Also called* osteogenesis. [ost- + -osis]

OT occupational therapy; occupational therapist.

ot-, oto- *combining form.* ear: *for example,* otalgia.

otalgia /ō tăl′jē ə, -jə/ pain in an ear. *Also called* otodynia. [ot- + -algia]

OTC *abbreviation.* over-the-counter (for sale without a prescription).

otic solution /ō′tĭk, ŏt′ĭk/ ear drops.

otitis /ō tī′tĭs/ one of several inflammations of the ear. *See also* otitis externa, otitis interna, otitis media. [ot- + -itis]

otitis externa /ĕk stûr′nə/ inflammations of the outer ear or external auditory canal.

otitis interna /ĭn tûr′nə/ inflammation of the inner ear.

otitis media /mē′dē ə/ inflammation of the middle ear; commonly occurring in children, sometimes leading to a more severe ear infection.

oto- *See* ot-.

otoacoustic emission test /ō′tō ə kōō′stĭk ĭ mĭsh′ən/ a test of a newborn's ability to hear. [oto- + acoustic]

otodynia /ō′tō dĭn′ē ə/ pain in an ear. *Also called* otalgia. [oto- + -dynia]

otolaryngologist /ō′tō lăr′ĭng gŏl′ə jĭst/ a doctor who specializes in diseases of the ear and larynx. [oto- + -laryngo- + -logist]

otolaryngology /ō′tō lăr′ĭng gŏl′ə jē/ the branch of medicine that specializes in diseases of the ear and larynx. [oto- + -laryngo- + -logy]

otologist /ō tŏl′ə jĭst/ a doctor who specializes in diagnosis and treatment of ear disorders. [oto- + -logist]

otology /ō tŏl′ə jē/ the branch of medicine that specializes in disorders of the ear and their treatment. [oto- + -logy]

otomastoiditis /ō′tō măs′toi dī′tĭs/ inflammation of the mastoid process and the ear. [oto- + mastoid + -itis]

otomycosis /ō′tō mī kō′sĭs/ a fungal infection of the opening into the auditory canal. [oto- + mycosis]

otopharyngeal tube /ō′tō fə rĭn′jē əl, -jəl/ the tube running from the middle ear to the pharynx. *Also called* eustachian tube. [oto- + -pharyngeal]

otoplasty /ō′tō plăs′tē/ surgical repair of the outer ear. [oto- + -plasty]

otopyorrhea /ō′tō pī′ə rē′ə/ chronic infection of the middle ear with pus. [oto- + pyo- + rrhea]

otorhinolaryngologist /ō′tō rī′nō lăr′ĭng gŏl′ə jĭst/ ears, nose, and throat specialist. [oto- + rhino- + laryngo- + -logist]

otorrhagia /o′to ra′je ə, -jə/ bleeding in the ear. [oto- + -rrhagia]

otorrhea /ō′tō rē′ə/ discharge from the ear. [oto- + -rrhea]

otosclerosis /ō′tō sklĭ rō′sĭs/ hardening of bone inside the ear. [oto- + sclerosis]

otoscope /ō′tə skōp′/ a lighted viewing device for looking into the ear. [oto- + -scope]

otoscopy /ō tŏs′kə pē/ visual inspection of the ear using an otoscope. [oto- + -scopy]

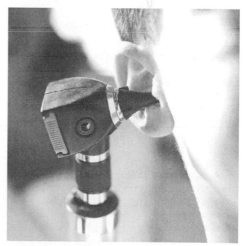

Otoscope

OU, o.u. *abbreviation.* Latin *oculus uterque,* each eye (in prescriptions)

ounce (oz.) /ouns/ a unit of weight equal to 28.3 grams.

-ous *suffix.* full of, possessing: *for example,* cartilagenous.

outer ear external ear or pinna and the external auditory canal.

out of network refers to a doctor or medical service that is not part of the network of providers covered by a person's medical insurance plan; under certain plans, the patient is reimbursed a certain percentage of the cost of the visit.

out-of-pocket costs /out′əv pŏk′ĭt/ costs paid by an insured patient as opposed to costs paid by the insurer.

outpatient /out′pā′shənt/ a patient who comes to a hospital or clinic for diagnosis and/or treatment but who is not hospitalized.

outpatient care medical treatment given to patients who are not admitted to a hospital. *Also called* ambulatory care.

outpatient procedure a medical procedure performed without admitting the patient to the hospital for an in-hospital stay.

ov-, ovi-, ovo- *combining form.* egg: *for example,* ovoid.

ova /ō′və/ (*sing.* **ovum** /ō′vəm/) female sex cells.

oval window /ō′vəl/ the membrane-covered opening between the middle ear and inner ear.

ovari-, ovario- *combining form.* ovary: *for example,* ovariocele.

ovarian /ō vâr′ē ən/ of or involving an ovary.

ovarian cancer cancer of an ovary.

ovarian cancer test CA 125 a test of blood or fluid from the abdominal or chest cavity, for an antibody, cancer antigen 125, that may indicate an ovarian cancer but that is also found in larger-than-normal quantities when other disease processes are present.

ovarian carcinoma /kär′sə nō′mə/ cancer of an ovary.

ovarian cyst /sĭst/ an enclosed growth, either solid or containing fluid, on or in an ovary.

ovarian cystectomy /sĭ stĕk′tə mē/ the surgical removal of a cyst on or in an ovary.

ovarian pregnancy /prĕg′nən sē/ a pregnancy that occurs within an ovary; a type of ectopic pregnancy.

ovarian teratoma /tĕr′ə tō′mə/ a usually benign tumor occurring in an ovary containing hair, bone, and other embryogenic tissue.

ovariectomy /ō vâr′ē ĕk′tə mē/ surgical removal of an ovary. [ovari- + -ectomy]

ovario- *See* ovari-.

ovariocele /ō vâr′ē ə sēl′/ a hernia (the intrusion of tissue through the wall) in an ovary. [ovario- + -cele]

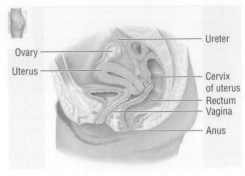

Ovary

ovariopexy /ō vâr′ē ə pĕk′sē/ surgical fixing an ovary in its proper position. [ovario- + -pexy]

ovary /ō′və rē/ either of two small oval structures in the pelvic cavity that produce eggs and female hormones.

over- *prefix.* excessive; above normal: *for example,* overdose.

overactive bladder /ō′vər ăk′tĭv/ a sudden contraction of the bladder, causing a need to urinate immediately.

overbreathing /ō′vər brē′thĭng/ hyperventilation; excessive breathing in and out, usually caused by anxiety or overexertion. [over- + breathing]

overdose (OD) /ō′vər dōs′/ *n.* **1.** a toxic dose of a drug. *v.* **2.** to ingest or inject a toxic dose of a drug. **3.** to die from having ingested or injected a toxic dose of a drug. [over- + dose]

over-the-counter (OTC) drug a drug that is available without a doctor's prescription.

overweight /ō′vər wāt′/ **1.** informally, weighing more than is considered normal for height and age. **2.** having a body mass index between 25 and 29.9, in an adult. [over- + weight]

oviduct /ō′vĭ dŭkt′/ one of a pair of slender tubes that extend from each ovary to the side of the uterus and through which an ovum is carried to the uterus. *Also called* fallopian tube, uterine tube.

oviferous /ō vĭf′ər əs/ egg-bearing; containing or producing eggs. [ovi- + -ferous]

ovoid /ō′void/ egg-shaped. [ov- + -oid]

ovulate /ŏv′yə lāt′/ to release a mature egg from an ovary.

ovulation /ŏv′yə lā′shən/ the monthly cycle of egg production and release from an ovary.

ovulatory /ŏv′yə lə tôr′ē/ of or involving ovulation.

ovum /ō′vəm/ (*pl.* **ova** /ō′və/) a female sex cell.

-oxia *suffix.* oxygen: *for example,* hypoxia.

oximeter /ŏk sĭm′ĭ tər/ an instrument used to measure the oxygen saturation of blood.

oxy- *combining form.* **1.** oxygen: *for example,* oxyhemoglobin. **2.** pointed: *for example,* oxycephaly.

oxycephaly /ŏk′sē sĕf′ə lē/ a congenital skull abnormality where the skull is unusually pointed. *Also called* acrocephaly. [oxy- + cephaly]

oxygen (O₂) /ŏk′sĭ jən/ a gas that makes up about 21% of the atmosphere and that is necessary for life.

oxygenate /ŏk′sĭ jə nāt′/ to enrich with oxygen.

oxygenated blood /ŏk′sĭ jə nā′tĭd/ bright red blood that comes from the lungs, flows through arteries, and is rich in oxygen.

oxygenating /ŏk′sĭ jə nā′tĭng/ **1.** adding oxygen. **2.** treating a patient by having him or her breath oxygen, or a medication combined with oxygen.

oxygenation /ŏk′sĭ jə nā′shən/ enrichment with oxygen.

oxygen mask a mask worn over the nose and mouth when inhaling supplementary oxygen.

oxygen tent a small tent placed over the head and upper body of a patient (or the entire crib of a young child), used to deliver high levels of oxygen to the patient.

oxygen therapy /thĕr′ə pē/ a treatment for diseases where patients are not getting adequate oxygen into their system when breathing on their own; the oxygen can be delivered through a nasal cannula, a mask, or catheter inserted directly into the trachea (windpipe).

oxyhemoglobin /ŏk′sē hē′mə glō′bĭn/ hemoglobin when carrying oxygen in the blood. [oxy- + hemo- + -globin]

oxytocin /ŏk′sē tō′sĭn/ a hormone produced in the posterior pituitary gland that stimulates contractions of the uterus and lactation; sometimes used to induce labor.

oz, oz. *abbreviation.* ounce; ounces.

THE HUMAN BODY

This 48-page insert illustrates the major parts of the human body and how they are treated in the health care professions. The first couple of pages cover general views of the body and body regions. The next sections are organized by body systems and, for each system, an overview table highlights the major structures, their functions, diagnostic tests and procedures, pathology, surgery, pharmacology, and specialists, practitioners, and careers. These are followed by dental, pharmacology, and complementary and alternative medicine.

Plate 1

Directional and Positioning Terms and Planes of the Body

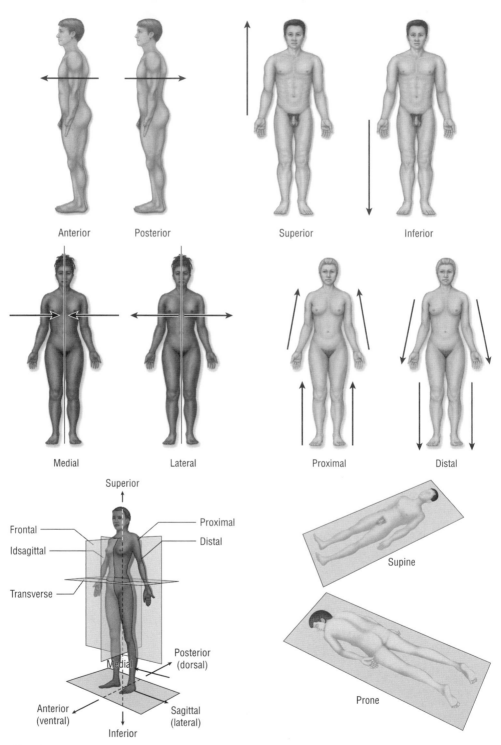

Anterior   Posterior   Superior   Inferior

Medial   Lateral   Proximal   Distal

Superior

Frontal

Idsagittal

Transverse

Proximal

Distal

Posterior (dorsal)

Medial

Anterior (ventral)

Sagittal (lateral)

Inferior

Supine

Prone

Directional terms are used in anatomy to describe the location and relative relationships of body parts. Positioning terms are used for patient examinations and procedures.

Plate 2

Body Regions and Cavities

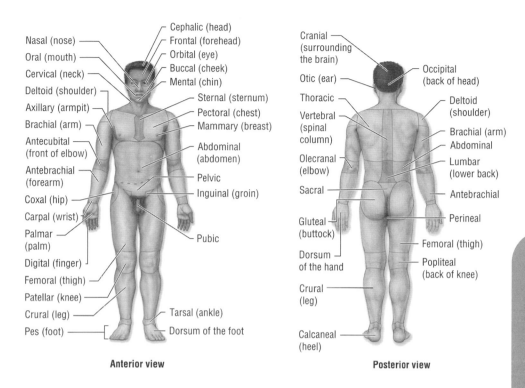

Nasal (nose)
Oral (mouth)
Cervical (neck)
Deltoid (shoulder)
Axillary (armpit)
Brachial (arm)
Antecubital (front of elbow)
Antebrachial (forearm)
Coxal (hip)
Carpal (wrist)
Palmar (palm)
Digital (finger)
Femoral (thigh)
Patellar (knee)
Crural (leg)
Pes (foot)

Cephalic (head)
Frontal (forehead)
Orbital (eye)
Buccal (cheek)
Mental (chin)
Sternal (sternum)
Pectoral (chest)
Mammary (breast)
Abdominal (abdomen)
Pelvic
Inguinal (groin)
Pubic
Tarsal (ankle)
Dorsum of the foot

Anterior view

Cranial (surrounding the brain)
Otic (ear)
Thoracic
Vertebral (spinal column)
Olecranal (elbow)
Sacral
Gluteal (buttock)
Dorsum of the hand
Crural (leg)
Calcaneal (heel)

Occipital (back of head)
Deltoid (shoulder)
Brachial (arm)
Abdominal
Lumbar (lower back)
Antebrachial
Perineal
Femoral (thigh)
Popliteal (back of knee)

Posterior view

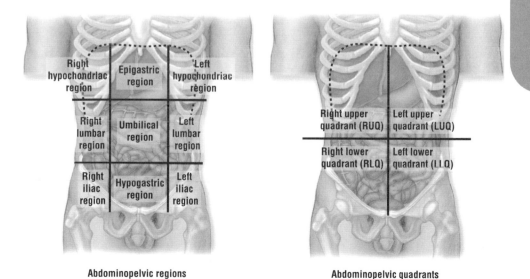

Right hypochondriac region
Epigastric region
Left hypochondriac region
Right lumbar region
Umbilical region
Left lumbar region
Right iliac region
Hypogastric region
Left iliac region

Abdominopelvic regions

Right upper quadrant (RUQ)
Left upper quadrant (LUQ)
Right lower quadrant (RLQ)
Left lower quadrant (LLQ)

Abdominopelvic quadrants

The anatomical names of the key regions of the body are shown in the anterior and posterior views. The abdominopelvic region can be subdivided into nine regions or four quadrants as shown here.

Plate 3

The Integumentary System

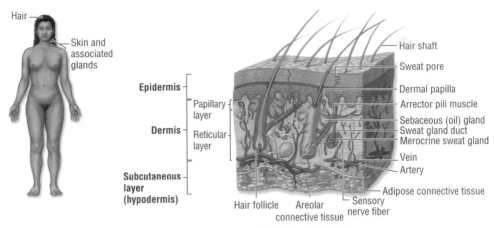

Hair

Skin and associated glands

Epidermis

Dermis
- Papillary layer
- Reticular layer

Subcutaneous layer (hypodermis)

Hair shaft

Sweat pore

Dermal papilla

Arrector pili muscle

Sebaceous (oil) gland

Sweat gland duct

Merocrine sweat gland

Vein

Artery

Adipose connective tissue

Hair follicle

Areolar connective tissue

Sensory nerve fiber

The Integument or Skin

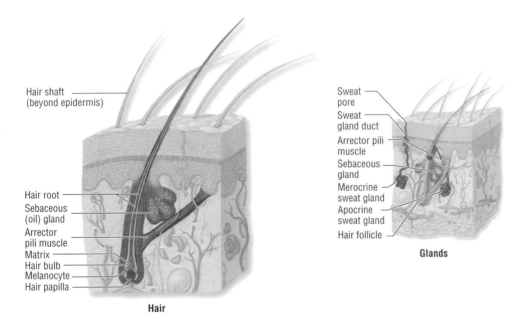

Hair shaft (beyond epidermis)

Hair root

Sebaceous (oil) gland

Arrector pili muscle

Matrix

Hair bulb

Melanocyte

Hair papilla

Hair

Sweat pore

Sweat gland duct

Arrector pili muscle

Sebaceous gland

Merocrine sweat gland

Apocrine sweat gland

Hair follicle

Glands

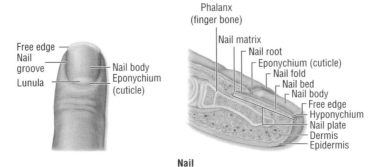

Free edge

Nail groove

Nail

Lunula

Nail body

Eponychium (cuticle)

Phalanx (finger bone)

Nail matrix

Nail root

Eponychium (cuticle)

Nail fold

Nail bed

Nail body

Free edge

Hyponychium

Nail plate

Dermis

Epidermis

Nail

Plate 4

Examples of pathology of the integumentary system. Most pathology is either a result of injury or caused by viruses, bacteria, or fungi.

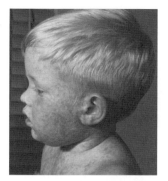

Measles

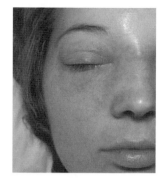

Cellulitis

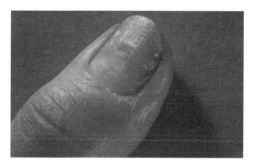

Nail Fungus

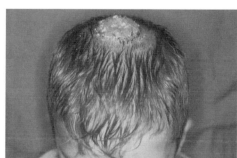

Ringworm (Tinea Capitis)

The Integumentary System—An Overview

System parts	Function	Major Tests	Major pathology	Major Procedures	Major Pharmaceutical agents	Specialists, Practitioners, and Allied Health Careers
skin	to serve as the protector of the body and its organs; to help regulate temperature and to serve as a sensory receptor.	visual examination allergy tests TB tine Schick test	lesions skin cancer acne burns psoriasis herpes shingles celluitis purpura	plastic surgery including grafts biopsy cauterization	anesthetic antifungal antihistamine antibacterial antipruritic anti-inflammatory	dermatologist medical assistant; medical receptionist; lab technician
hair	protective covering	visual examination	alopecia dandruff	hair replacement		
nails	protective covering	visual examination	onychitis fungal infections			
glands	excretion of wastes regulation of temperature					

Plate 5

The Musculoskeletal System

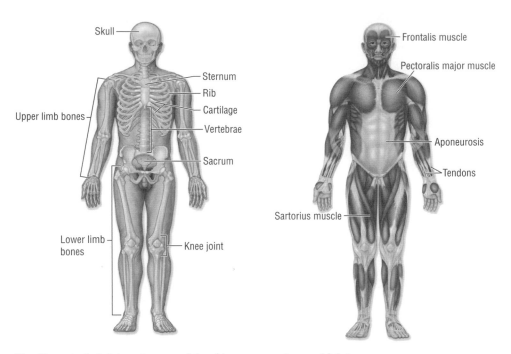

The Musculoskeletal system consists of bones, muscles, and joints.

The Musculoskeletal System—An Overview

System parts	Function	Major Tests	Major pathology	Major Procedures	Major Pharmaceutical agents	Specialists, Practitioners, and Allied Health Careers
bones	protect and support the organs of the body; allow movement	x-rays and scans as well as blood tests; biopsies	fractures; osteoporosis; cancer	casting; pins; replacement; removal of tumors; surgical repair	analgesics	orthopedist, orthopedic surgeon, osteopathic physician, osteopath, rheumatologists, sports medicine specialist, chiropractor, acupuncturist, radiologic technician; physical therapist; massage therapist, medical office assistant; medical receptionist
muscles	control the body's movements	imaging and blood tests	myalgia spasms	surgical repair	anti-inflammatory; muscle relaxant; NSAIDs	
joints	allow range of movement; connect bone to bone	imaging and blood tests	sprains; tendonitis; arthritis; bursitis	removal; repair; arthrocentesis	anti-inflammatory; NSAIDs	

Plate 6

Bones

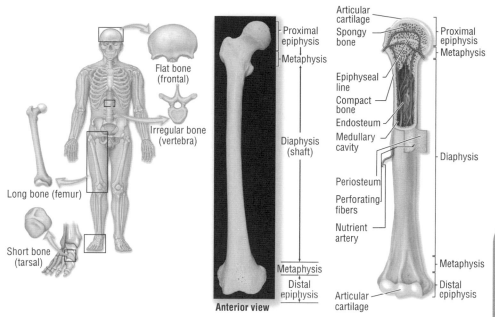

Classification of Bone by Shape

Anterior view

Anatomy of a Long Bone

Flat bone (frontal)

Irregular bone (vertebra)

Long bone (femur)

Short bone (tarsal)

Proximal epiphysis

Metaphysis

Diaphysis (shaft)

Metaphysis

Distal epiphysis

Articular cartilage

Spongy bone

Epiphyseal line

Compact bone

Endosteum

Medullary cavity

Periosteum

Perforating fibers

Nutrient artery

Articular cartilage

Proximal epiphysis

Metaphysis

Diaphysis

Metaphysis

Distal epiphysis

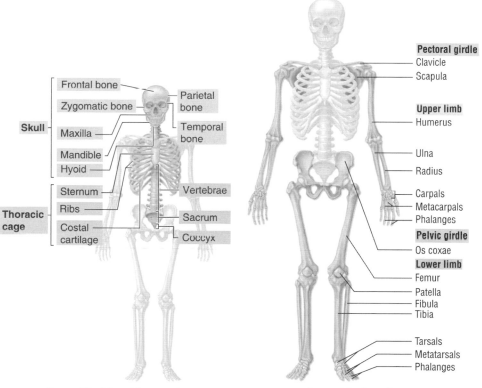

Bones of the Internal Framework

Bones of the Appendages

Frontal bone

Parietal bone

Zygomatic bone

Temporal bone

Maxilla

Mandible

Hyoid

Skull

Sternum

Ribs

Costal cartilage

Thoracic cage

Vertebrae

Sacrum

Coccyx

Pectoral girdle
Clavicle
Scapula

Upper limb
Humerus

Ulna
Radius

Carpals
Metacarpals
Phalanges

Pelvic girdle
Os coxae

Lower limb
Femur
Patella
Fibula
Tibia

Tarsals
Metatarsals
Phalanges

Plate 7

Joints and Cartilage

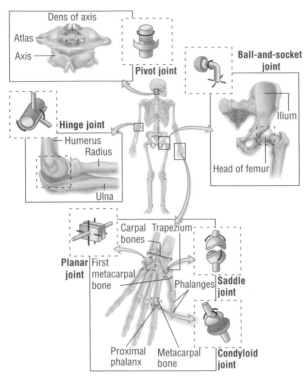

Types of Synovial Joints

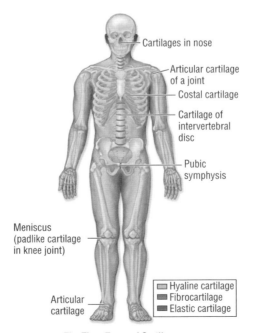

The Three Types of Cartilage

Plate 8

Muscles

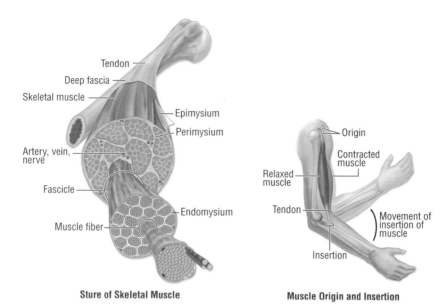

Sture of Skeletal Muscle

Muscle Origin and Insertion

There are three types of muscle: skeletal, cardiac, and smooth. Skeletal muscle is everywhere in the body except in the heart and in the lining of parts of the body, such as blood vessels, intestines, and the eyes.

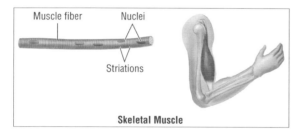

Skeletal Muscle

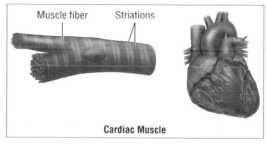

Cardiac Muscle

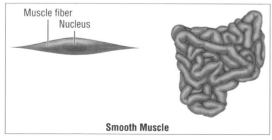

Smooth Muscle

Plate 9

The Cardiovascular System

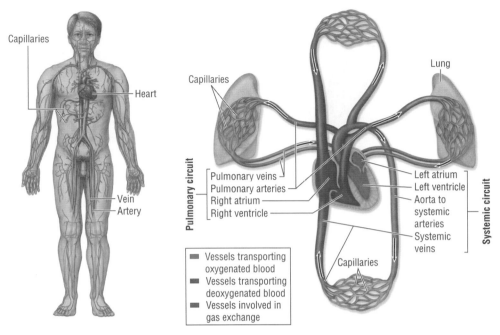

The cardiovascular system consists of the heart and all the blood vessels that are part of the circulation of blood throughout the body.

The Cardiovascular System—An Overview

System parts	Function	Major Tests	Major pathology	Major Procedures	Major Pharmaceutical agents	Specialists, Practitioners, and Allied Health Careers
heart	to serve as the pump that sends and receives blood to and from the entire body.	stress test electrocardiography cardiac MRI cardiac catheterization auscultation	myocardial infarction angina arrhythmia PVCs hypertension hypotension valve disorders	valve replacement heart transplant valvuloplasty cardiopulmonary bypass	ACE inhibitors beta blockers calcium channel blockers coronary vasodilators	cardiologist, cardiovascular surgeon, medical assistant; medical receptionist; radiologic technician; phlebotomist
blood vessels	the vehicle through which blood containing oxygen and nutrients circulates throughout the body and through which waste is removed from the cells.	angiography aortography arteriography venography lipid profile cardiac enzyme tests	aneurysm arteriosclerosis phlebitis thrombus embolus	bypass angioplasty endovascular surgery	coronary vasodilators thrombolytics lipid-lowering medications ACE inhibitors	

Plate 10

The Heart

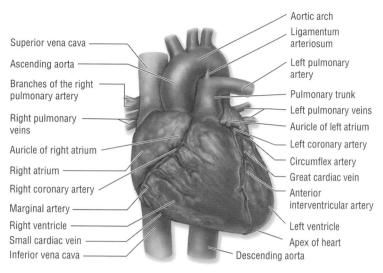

Aortic arch
Ligamentum arteriosum
Left pulmonary artery
Pulmonary trunk
Left pulmonary veins
Auricle of left atrium
Left coronary artery
Circumflex artery
Great cardiac vein
Anterior interventricular artery
Left ventricle
Apex of heart
Descending aorta

Superior vena cava
Ascending aorta
Branches of the right pulmonary artery
Right pulmonary veins
Auricle of right atrium
Right atrium
Right coronary artery
Marginal artery
Right ventricle
Small cardiac vein
Inferior vena cava

External Anatomy of the Heart

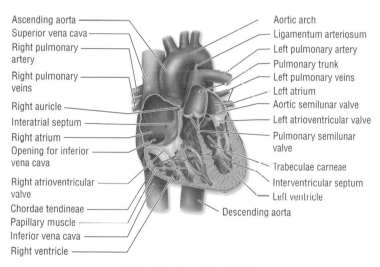

Ascending aorta
Superior vena cava
Right pulmonary artery
Right pulmonary veins
Right auricle
Interatrial septum
Right atrium
Opening for inferior vena cava
Right atrioventricular valve
Chordae tendineae
Papillary muscle
Inferior vena cava
Right ventricle

Aortic arch
Ligamentum arteriosum
Left pulmonary artery
Pulmonary trunk
Left pulmonary veins
Left atrium
Aortic semilunar valve
Left atrioventricular valve
Pulmonary semilunar valve
Trabeculae carneae
Interventricular septum
Left ventricle
Descending aorta

Internal Anatomy of the Heart

Posterior
Left AV valve (closed)
Left ventricle
Right AV valve (closed)
Right ventricle
Aortic semilunar valve (open)
Pulmonary semilunar valve (open)
Anterior
Ventricular Systole

Posterior
Left AV valve (open)
Left ventricle
Right AV valve (open)
Right ventricle
Aortic semilunar valve (closed)
Pulmonary semilunar valve (closed)
Anterior
Ventricular Diastole

Plate 11

Blood Vessels

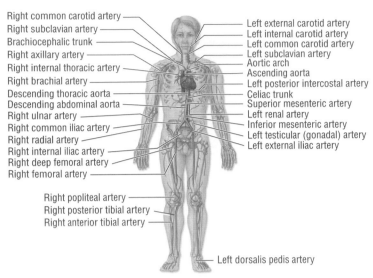

Right common carotid artery
Right subclavian artery
Brachiocephalic trunk
Right axillary artery
Right internal thoracic artery
Right brachial artery
Descending thoracic aorta
Descending abdominal aorta
Right ulnar artery
Right common iliac artery
Right radial artery
Right internal iliac artery
Right deep femoral artery
Right femoral artery

Left external carotid artery
Left internal carotid artery
Left common carotid artery
Left subclavian artery
Aortic arch
Ascending aorta
Left posterior intercostal artery
Celiac trunk
Superior mesenteric artery
Left renal artery
Inferior mesenteric artery
Left testicular (gonadal) artery
Left external iliac artery

Right popliteal artery
Right posterior tibial artery
Right anterior tibial artery

Left dorsalis pedis artery

Arteries

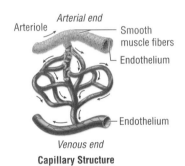

Arterial end
Arteriole
Smooth muscle fibers
Endothelium
Endothelium
Venous end

Capillary Structure

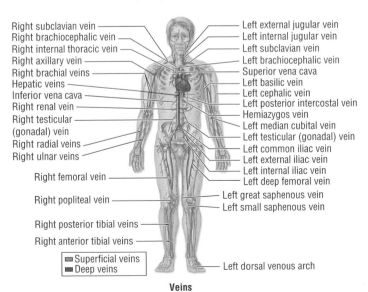

Right subclavian vein
Right brachiocephalic vein
Right internal thoracic vein
Right axillary vein
Right brachial veins
Hepatic veins
Inferior vena cava
Right renal vein
Right testicular (gonadal) vein
Right radial veins
Right ulnar veins

Left external jugular vein
Left internal jugular vein
Left subclavian vein
Left brachiocephalic vein
Superior vena cava
Left basilic vein
Left cephalic vein
Left posterior intercostal vein
Hemiazygos vein
Left median cubital vein
Left testicular (gonadal) vein
Left common iliac vein
Left external iliac vein
Left internal iliac vein
Left deep femoral vein

Right femoral vein
Right popliteal vein

Left great saphenous vein
Left small saphenous vein

Right posterior tibial veins
Right anterior tibial veins

■ Superficial veins
■ Deep veins

Left dorsal venous arch

Veins

Plate 12

Diagnosis and Pathology

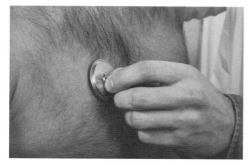
Auscultation

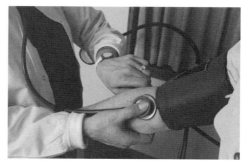
Blood Pressure

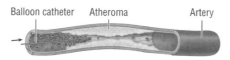

Balloon catheter   Atheroma   Artery

① Balloon catheter is used to carry an uninflated balloon
to the area in artery that is obstructed.

② Balloon inflates, compressing the atheroma.

③ Balloon is deflated following lumen widening, and
then catheter is withdrawn. A stent may be placed
in the artery as well.

Angioplasty

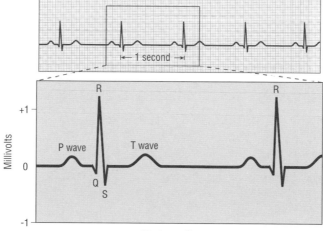

← 1 second →

Millivolts

+1

0

−1

P wave

R

Q
S

T wave

R

Electrocardiogram

Plate 13

The Respiratory System

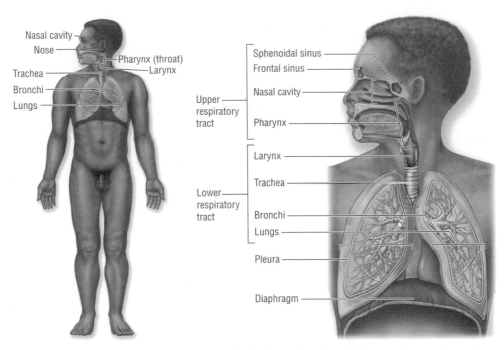

The respiratory system brings oxygen into the body and works with the cardiovascular system to supply oxygen to the body's cells. It then expels carbon dioxide into the atmosphere.

The Respiratory System—An Overview

System parts	Function	Major Tests	Major pathology	Major Procedures	Major Pharmaceutical agents	Specialists, Practitioners, and Allied Health Careers
nose and mouth	intake of air and exhalation of waste gases	visual examination; throat culture	strep throat; cancers	tonsillectomy		otorhinolaryngologist (ear, nose, and throat specialist), respiratory therapist; lab technician; radiologic technician; medical assistant; medical receptionist
larynx	inhalation and exhalation; vocal cords	endoscope	cancer	laryngectomy		
trachea and epiglottis	inhalation and exhalation and sending of food into the esophagus	endoscope	cancer; blockages	tracheostomy		
lungs	exchange of gases for getting oxygen into the body's cells and removing waste gases	endoscope; x-ray; peak flow meter; auscultation; pulmonary function tests	lung cancer; asthma; COPD; emphysema; pneumonia; tuberculosis; black lung	bronchotomy; lobectomy	bronchodilators; antitussives; decongestants; expectorants	

Plate 14

Upper Respiratory Tract

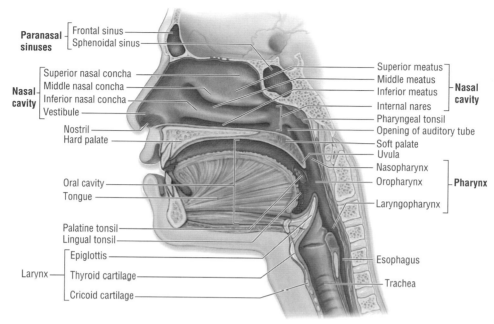

Paranasal sinuses
- Frontal sinus
- Sphenoidal sinus

Nasal cavity
- Superior nasal concha
- Middle nasal concha
- Inferior nasal concha
- Vestibule

- Nostril
- Hard palate

- Oral cavity
- Tongue

- Palatine tonsil
- Lingual tonsil

Larynx
- Epiglottis
- Thyroid cartilage
- Cricoid cartilage

Nasal cavity
- Superior meatus
- Middle meatus
- Inferior meatus
- Internal nares

- Pharyngeal tonsil
- Opening of auditory tube
- Soft palate
- Uvula

Pharynx
- Nasopharynx
- Oropharynx
- Laryngopharynx

- Esophagus
- Trachea

Upper Respiratory Tract

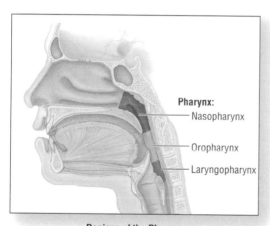

Pharynx:
- Nasopharynx
- Oropharynx
- Laryngopharynx

Regions of the Pharynx

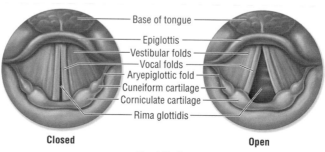

- Base of tongue
- Epiglottis
- Vestibular folds
- Vocal folds
- Aryepiglottic fold
- Cuneiform cartilage
- Corniculate cartilage
- Rima glottidis

Closed   **Open**

Vocal Cords

Plate 15

Lower Respiratory Tract

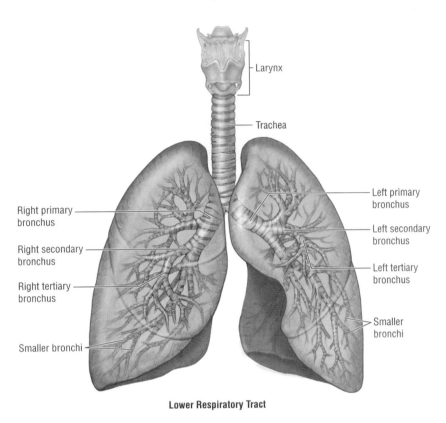

- Larynx
- Trachea
- Left primary bronchus
- Left secondary bronchus
- Left tertiary bronchus
- Smaller bronchi
- Right primary bronchus
- Right secondary bronchus
- Right tertiary bronchus
- Smaller bronchi

Lower Respiratory Tract

Primary bronchi
Secondary bronchi
Tertiary bronchi
Smaller bronchi

Bronchial Tree

- Bronchiole
- Branch of pulmonary artery
- Terminal bronchiole
- Respiratory bronchiole
- Branch of pulmonary vein
- Capillary beds
- Arteriole
- Alveolar duct
- Alveoli
- Connective tissue

Bronchioles and Alveoli

Plate 16

Inhalation and Exhalation and Pathology

Inhalation

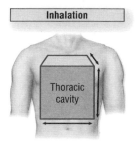

Exhalation

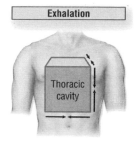

Thoracic cavity

Thoracic cavity

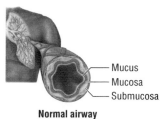

Mucus
Mucosa
Submucosa

Normal airway

Vertical changes

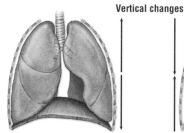

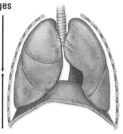

Diaphragm contracts; vertical dimensions of thoracic cavity increase.

Diaphragm relaxes; vertical dimensions of thoracic cavity narrow.

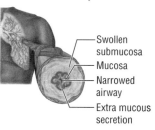

Swollen submucosa
Mucosa
Narrowed airway
Extra mucous secretion

Airway during an asthma attack

Asthma

Lateral changes

Ribs elevated and thoracic cavity widens.

Ribs depressed and thoracic cavity narrows.

Anterior-posterior changes

Inferior portion of sternum moves anteriorly.

Inferior portion of sternum moves posteriorly.

Mucus builds up and blocks the bronchial tree, leading to chronic respiratory infections.

Mucus buildup blocks the pancreatic ducts and prevents digestive enzymes from entering the small intestine.

Cystic Fibrosis

Plate 17

The Nervous System

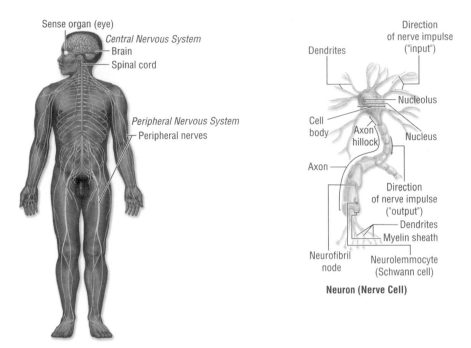

Sense organ (eye)

Central Nervous System
- Brain
- Spinal cord

Peripheral Nervous System
- Peripheral nerves

Direction of nerve impulse ("input")

Dendrites

Nucleolus

Cell body

Axon hillock

Nucleus

Axon

Direction of nerve impulse ("output")

Dendrites

Myelin sheath

Neurofibril node

Neurolemmocyte (Schwann cell)

Neuron (Nerve Cell)

The nervous system consists of the brain, spinal cord, and the body's network of nerves that send and receive messages to control the voluntary and involuntary activities of the body.

The Nervous System—An Overview

System parts	Function	Major Tests	Major pathology	Major Procedures	Major Pharmaceutical agents	Specialists, Practitioners, and Allied Health Careers
brain and meninges	master controller of all the body's activities; center of emotion and thought	electrodiagnosis and scans	trauma, congenital disorders; degenerative diseases; non-degenerative disorders; meningitis; cancer; vascular disorders; parkinson's disease; alzheimer's	surgery and electrostimulation	analgesic; anesthestics; anticonvulsants; sedatives	neurologist, neurosurgeon, psychiatrist, psychologist, therapist, counselor, acupuncturist, massage therapist, radiologic technician; occupational therapist; medical assistant; medical receptionist
spinal cord	link between brain and the rest of the body	imaging and blood tests	injuries; paralysis	surgical repair	analgesic	
nerves	send and receive messages to control voluntary and involuntary activities	imaging; reflex testing	shingles; neuritis; neuralgia; multiple sclerosis	surgery	analgesic; anesthetic; sedative	

Plate 18

The Brain

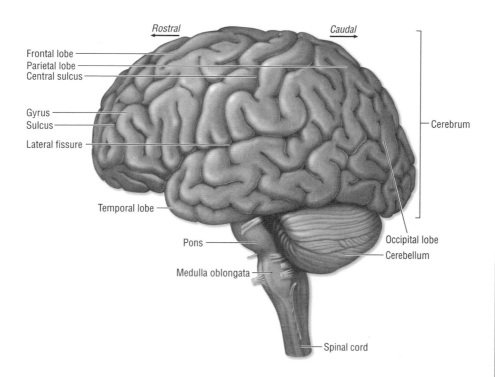

Rostral ← | → Caudal

Frontal lobe
Parietal lobe
Central sulcus

Gyrus
Sulcus
Lateral fissure

Temporal lobe

Pons
Medulla oblongata

Cerebrum

Occipital lobe
Cerebellum

Spinal cord

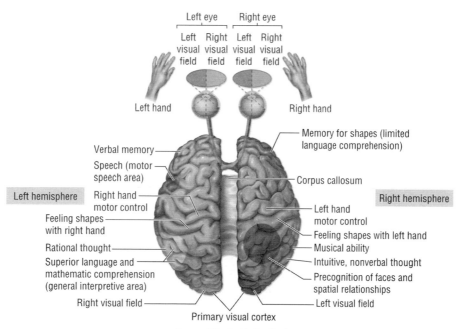

Left eye   Right eye

Left | Right | Left | Right
visual | visual | visual | visual
field | field | field | field

Left hand

Right hand

Verbal memory
Speech (motor speech area)

Left hemisphere   Right hand motor control

Feeling shapes with right hand

Rational thought

Superior language and mathematic comprehension (general interpretive area)

Right visual field

Memory for shapes (limited language comprehension)

Corpus callosum

Right hemisphere

Left hand motor control

Feeling shapes with left hand

Musical ability

Intuitive, nonverbal thought

Precognition of faces and spatial relationships

Left visual field

Primary visual cortex

Areas of Control in the Brain

Plate 19

The Spinal Cord

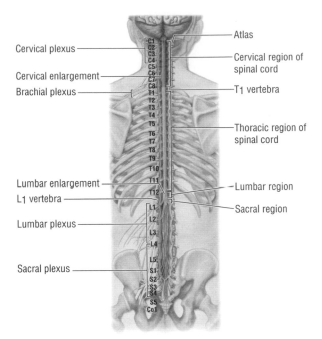

Cervical plexus

Cervical enlargement

Brachial plexus

Atlas

Cervical region of spinal cord

T1 vertebra

Thoracic region of spinal cord

Lumbar enlargement

L1 vertebra

Lumbar plexus

Lumbar region

Sacral region

Sacral plexus

Spinal Cord

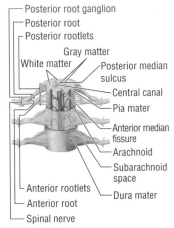

Epidural space

Spinous process of vertebra

Dura mater

Posterior

Spinal nerve

Arachnoid

Intervertebral foramen

Spinal cord

Body of vertebra

Subarachnoid space

Pia mater

Cross Section of Spinal Cord

Posterior root ganglion

Posterior root

Posterior rootlets

Gray matter

White matter

Posterior median sulcus

Central canal

Pia mater

Anterior median fissure

Arachnoid

Subarachnoid space

Anterior rootlets

Dura mater

Anterior root

Spinal nerve

Detail of Spinal Cord

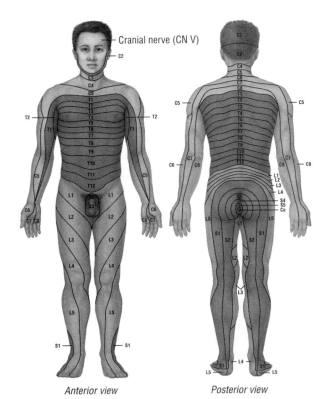

Cranial nerve (CN V)

Anterior view

Posterior view

Areas of Skin Controlled by Cranial and Spinal Nerves

Plate 20

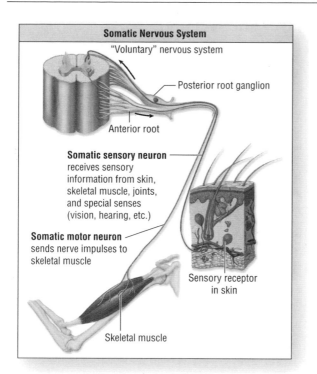

Somatic Nervous System

"Voluntary" nervous system

Posterior root ganglion

Anterior root

Somatic sensory neuron
receives sensory
information from skin,
skeletal muscle, joints,
and special senses
(vision, hearing, etc.)

Somatic motor neuron
sends nerve impulses to
skeletal muscle

Sensory receptor
in skin

Skeletal muscle

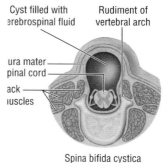

Cyst filled with
cerebrospinal fluid

Rudiment of
vertebral arch

Dura mater
Spinal cord

Back
muscles

Spina bifida cystica

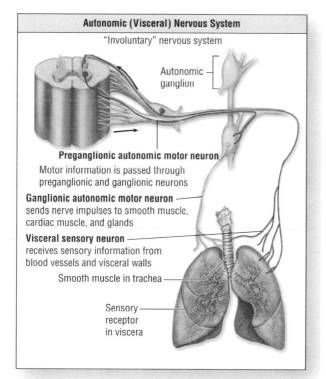

Autonomic (Visceral) Nervous System

"Involuntary" nervous system

Autonomic
ganglion

Preganglionic autonomic motor neuron
Motor information is passed through
preganglionic and ganglionic neurons

Ganglionic autonomic motor neuron
sends nerve impulses to smooth muscle,
cardiac muscle, and glands

Visceral sensory neuron
receives sensory information from
blood vessels and visceral walls

Smooth muscle in trachea

Sensory
receptor
in viscera

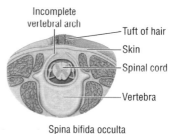

Incomplete
vertebral arch

Tuft of hair

Skin

Spinal cord

Vertebra

Spina bifida occulta

Plate 21

The Urinary System

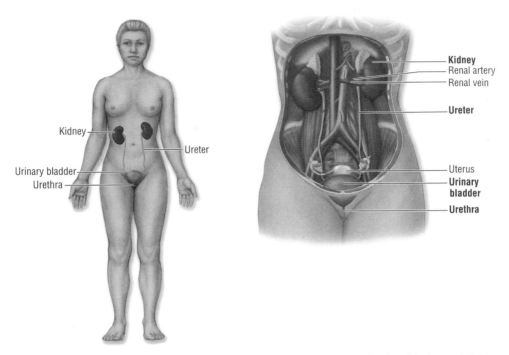

Kidney
Ureter
Urinary bladder
Urethra

Kidney
Renal artery
Renal vein
Ureter
Uterus
Urinary bladder
Urethra

The urinary system removes and excretes waste products from the blood and helps maintain homeostasis.

The Urinary System—An Overview

System parts	Function	Major Tests and Procedures	Major pathology	Major Procedures	Major Pharmaceutical agents	Specialists, Practitioners, and Allied Health Careers
kidney	distributor of and regulator of water and urinary waste throughout the body	imaging; blood tests; urinalysis; dialysis	infections; degenerative diseases; calculi; cancer	transplant; surgery to remove stones and repairs	analgesic; antibiotics; antidiuretics; diuretics	urologist, nephrologist, radiologic technician; lab technician; medical assistant; medical receptionist
bladder	storage of urine	imaging and blood tests	infections; calculi; malfunctioning; cancer	surgical repair	analgesic; antibiotic; antispasmodic	
ureters	passage of urine from the bladder to the urethra	imaging	infections; calculi; cancer	surgery	analgesic; antibiotic	
urethra	excretion of urine	imaging	infections; calculi; cancer	surgery	analgesic; antibiotic	

Plate 22

Kidneys

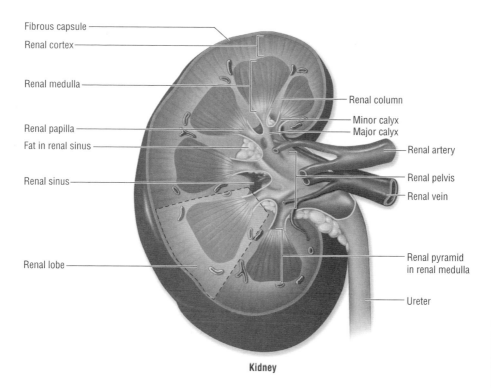

Fibrous capsule
Renal cortex
Renal medulla
Renal papilla
Fat in renal sinus
Renal sinus
Renal lobe

Renal column
Minor calyx
Major calyx
Renal artery
Renal pelvis
Renal vein
Renal pyramid
in renal medulla
Ureter

Kidney

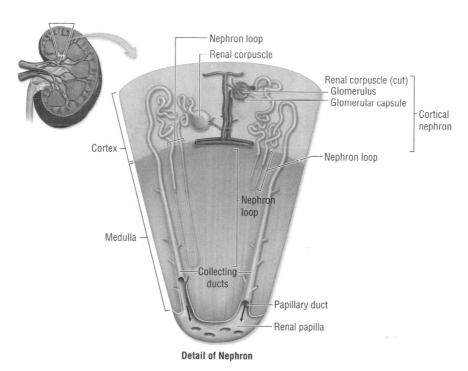

Nephron loop
Renal corpuscle

Renal corpuscle (cut)
Glomerulus
Glomerular capsule
Cortical nephron

Cortex

Nephron loop

Medulla

Nephron loop

Collecting ducts

Papillary duct

Renal papilla

Detail of Nephron

Plate 23

Bladder and Ureters

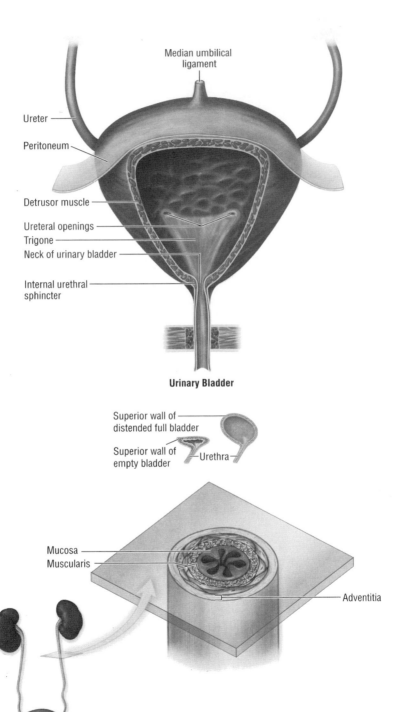

Median umbilical ligament

Ureter

Peritoneum

Detrusor muscle

Ureteral openings

Trigone

Neck of urinary bladder

Internal urethral sphincter

Urinary Bladder

Superior wall of distended full bladder

Superior wall of empty bladder

Urethra

Mucosa

Muscularis

Adventitia

Ureters

Plate 24

Urethra and Calculi

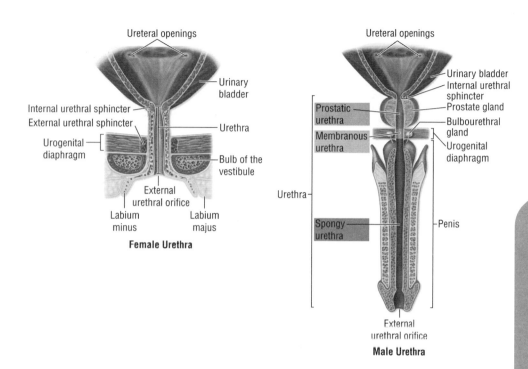

Ureteral openings

Urinary
bladder

Internal urethral sphincter

External urethral sphincter

Urogenital
diaphragm

Urethra

Bulb of the
vestibule

External
urethral orifice

Labium
minus

Labium
majus

Female Urethra

Ureteral openings

Urinary bladder

Internal urethral
sphincter

Prostatic
urethra

Prostate gland

Bulbourethral
gland

Membranous
urethra

Urogenital
diaphragm

Urethra

Spongy
urethra

Penis

External
urethral orifice

Male Urethra

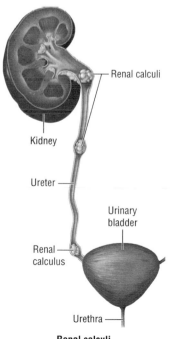

Renal calculi

Kidney

Ureter

Urinary
bladder

Renal
calculus

Urethra

Renal calculi

Plate 25

The Female Reproductive System

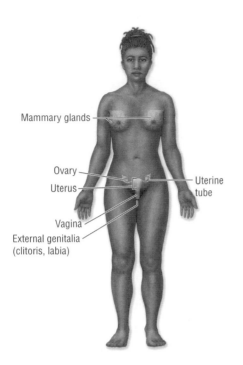

Mammary glands

Ovary

Uterus

Uterine tube

Vagina

External genitalia
(clitoris, labia)

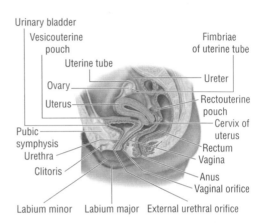

Urinary bladder

Vesicouterine pouch

Uterine tube

Ovary

Uterus

Pubic symphysis

Urethra

Clitoris

Labium minor

Labium major

External urethral orifice

Fimbriae of uterine tube

Ureter

Rectouterine pouch

Cervix of uterus

Rectum

Vagina

Anus

Vaginal orifice

The Female Reproductive System—An Overview

System parts	Function	Major Tests and Procedures	Major pathology	Major Procedures	Major Pharmaceutical agents	Specialist, Practitioners, and Allied Health Careers
ovaries or gonads	produce ova and release hormones	imaging; blood tests; urine tests	infections; malformations; cancer; infertility problems	corrective surgeries; removal of tumors and other abnormalities	hormones; birth control	obstetrician, gynecologist, midwife, radiologic technician; lab technician; medical assistant; medical receptionist
uterus	implantation and growth of embryo or release of its lining during menstruation	imaging; blood tests	infections; malformations; cancer	surgical repair; removal	birth control; oxytocin; tocolytic; abortifacient	
vagina	site of intercourse and of vaginal birth	imaging; blood tests	infections; cancer	surgery for birth control or repair	birth control	
breasts	lactation	imaging	infections; cancer	cosmetic surgery; removal of tumors		

Plate 26

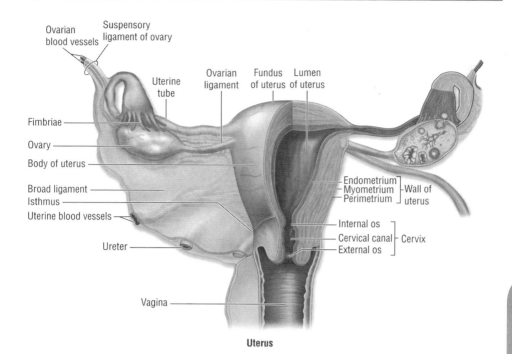

Uterus

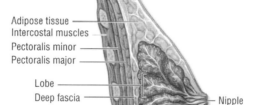

Mammary Gland

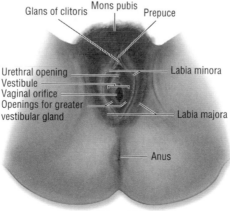

Female External Genitalia

Plate 27

The Male Reproductive System

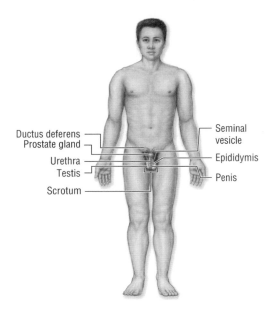

Ductus deferens
Prostate gland
Urethra
Testis
Scrotum

Seminal vesicle
Epididymis
Penis

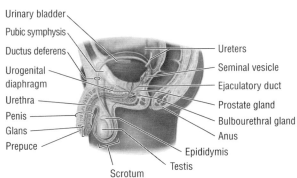

Urinary bladder
Pubic symphysis
Ductus deferens
Urogenital diaphragm
Urethra
Penis
Glans
Prepuce
Scrotum

Ureters
Seminal vesicle
Ejaculatory duct
Prostate gland
Bulbourethral gland
Anus
Epididymis
Testis

The Male Reproductive System—An Overview

System parts	Function	Major Tests and Procedures	Major pathology	Major Procedures	Major Pharmaceutical agents	Specialists, Practitioners, and Allied Health Careers
testes or testicles and scrotum	produce sperm and release hormones	imaging; blood tests; urine tests; palpation	infections; cancer; infertility problems	removal of tumors	hormones	urologist, radiologic technician, lab technician, medical assistant, medical receptionist
penis and urethra	ejaculation and excretion of urine	imaging; blood tests	infections; malformations; cancer	surgical repair; removal of tumors; birth control		
prostate	production of semen and muscular contractions	imaging; blood tests	infections; cancer	removal of tumors	treatments for hypertrophy	
vas deferens	movement of sperm	imaging	infections; cancer			

Plate 28

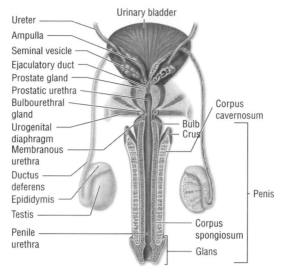

Ureter

Ampulla

Seminal vesicle

Ejaculatory duct

Prostate gland

Prostatic urethra

Bulbourethral gland

Urogenital diaphragm

Membranous urethra

Ductus deferens

Epididymis

Testis

Penile urethra

Urinary bladder

Corpus cavernosum

Bulb

Crus

Penis

Corpus spongiosum

Glans

Duct System

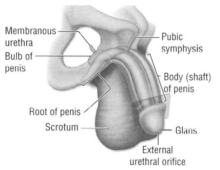

Membranous urethra

Bulb of penis

Root of penis

Scrotum

Pubic symphysis

Body (shaft) of penis

Glans

External urethral orifice

Male External Genitalia

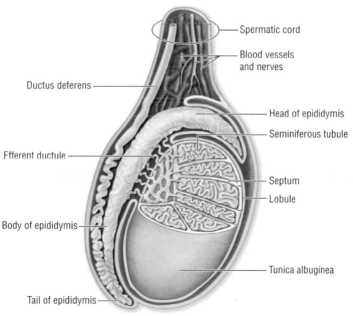

Spermatic cord

Blood vessels and nerves

Ductus deferens

Head of epididymis

Seminiferous tubule

Efferent ductule

Septum

Lobule

Body of epididymis

Tunica albuginea

Tail of epididymis

Testis

Plate 29

The Blood System

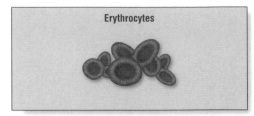

Erythrocytes

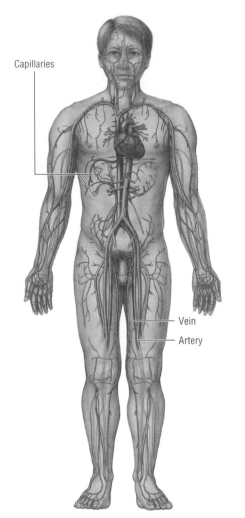

Capillaries

Vein

Artery

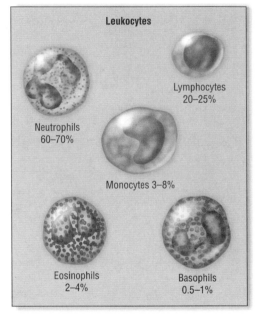

Leukocytes

Lymphocytes
20–25%

Neutrophils
60–70%

Monocytes 3–8%

Eosinophils
2–4%

Basophils
0.5–1%

The Blood System—An Overview

System parts	Function	Major Tests and Procedures	Major pathology	Major Procedures	Major Pharmaceutical agents	Specialists, Practitioners, and Allied Health Careers
blood	transports life-sustaining nutrients to cells and removes waste material	blood tests; other body system diseases	leukemia; hemophilia; infections; anemia	bone marrow transplant; bone marrow biopsy	anticoagulants; clotting agents; hemostatic thrombolytics	hematologist, phlebotomist, lab technician

Plate 30

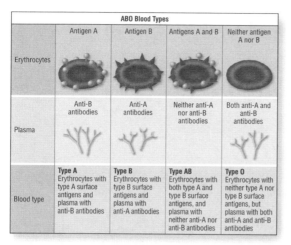

ABO Blood Types

	Antigen A	Antigen B	Antigens A and B	Neither antigen A nor B
Erythrocytes				
Plasma	Anti-B antibodies	Anti-A antibodies	Neither anti-A nor anti-B antibodies	Both anti-A and anti-B antibodies
Blood type	**Type A** Erythrocytes with type A surface antigens and plasma with anti-B antibodies	**Type B** Erythrocytes with type B surface antigens and plasma with anti-A antibodies	**Type AB** Erythrocytes with both type A and type B surface antigens, and plasma with neither anti-A nor anti-B antibodies	**Type O** Erythrocytes with neither type A nor type B surface antigens, but plasma with both anti-A and anti-B antibodies

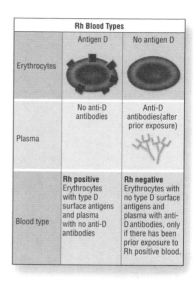

Rh Blood Types

	Antigen D	No antigen D
Erythrocytes		
Plasma	No anti-D antibodies	Anti-D antibodies(after prior exposure)
Blood type	**Rh positive** Erythrocytes with type D surface antigens and plasma with no anti-D antibodies	**Rh negative** Erythrocytes with no type D surface antigens and plasma with anti-D antibodies, only if there has been prior exposure to Rh positive blood.

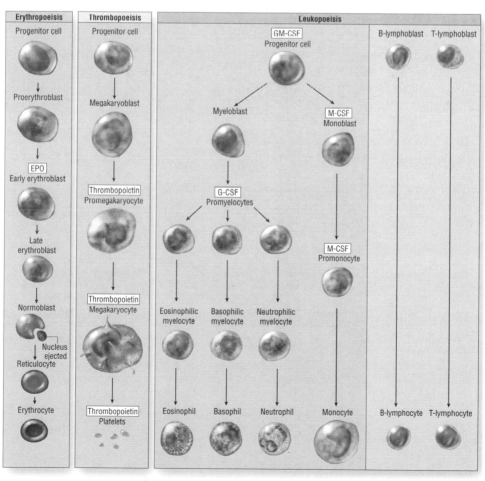

Blood Elements Formed from Hematocytoblasts

Plate 31

The Lymphatic and Immune Systems

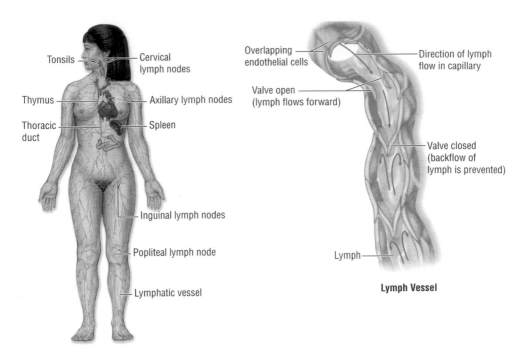

Tonsils

Cervical lymph nodes

Thymus

Thoracic duct

Axillary lymph nodes

Spleen

Inguinal lymph nodes

Popliteal lymph node

Lymphatic vessel

Overlapping endothelial cells

Valve open (lymph flows forward)

Direction of lymph flow in capillary

Valve closed (backflow of lymph is prevented)

Lymph

Lymph Vessel

The Lymphatic and Immune Systems—An Overview

System parts	Function	Major Tests and Procedures	Major pathology	Major Procedures	Specialists, Practitioners and Allied Health Careers
Lymphatic pathways and lymph nodes	deals with pathogens and other foreign substances that invade the body; maintains immunity	blood tests; scans	AIDS; cancer; autoimmune diseases; allergies	lymph node biopsy and removal	allergist, immunologist, radiologic technician, lab technician
thymus	important in childhood for immunity	scans		removal if cancerous	
spleen	filters waste from the blood	scans		removal if cancerous	
tonsils	play a role in immunity	visual examination	tonsillitis	removal	

Plate 32

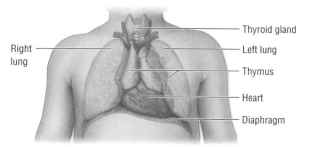

Right lung

Thyroid gland

Left lung

Thymus

Heart

Diaphragm

Thymus

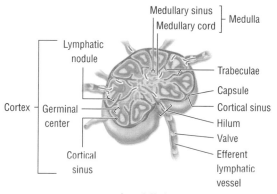

Medullary sinus
Medullary cord ⎱ Medulla

Lymphatic nodule

Trabeculae

Cortex

Germinal center

Capsule

Cortical sinus

Hilum

Valve

Efferent lymphatic vessel

Cortical sinus

Lymph Node

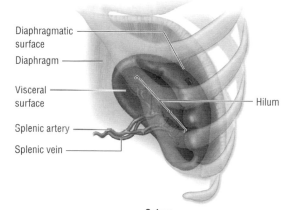

Diaphragmatic surface

Diaphragm

Visceral surface

Hilum

Splenic artery

Splenic vein

Spleen

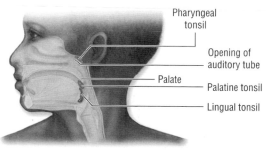

Pharyngeal tonsil

Opening of auditory tube

Palate

Palatine tonsil

Lingual tonsil

Tonsils

Plate 33

The Digestive System

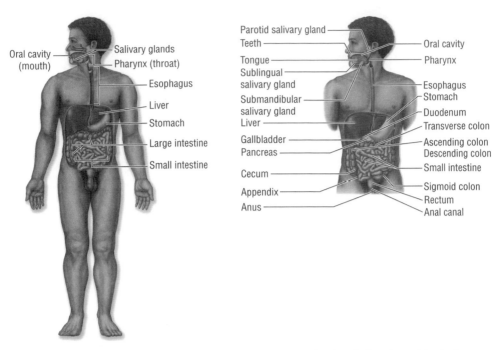

The digestive system mechanically and chemically digests food and absorbs nutrients for use in the body and expels waste products.

The Digestive System—An Overview

System parts	Function	Major Tests and Procedures	Major pathology	Major Procedures	Major Pharmaceutical agents	Specialists, Practitioners, and Allied Health Careers
upper digestive tract (mouth to stomach)	intake of food and conversion of it for use in the body	blood tests; imaging; endoscopes	sensitivities; infections; cancer; discomfort; hernias; ulcers	surgical repair or removal	agents to handle symptoms	gastroenterologist, bariatric surgeon, radiologic technician, lab technician, medical assistant, medical receptionist
lower digestive tract (intestines to anus)	completes digestive process and excretes waste	imaging; endoscopes; stool samples; blood tests	infections; cancer; colitis; structural disorders	surgical repair or removal	agents to handle symptoms	
liver	secretes bile	imaging; blood tests	cancer	partial removal		
gallbladder	stores bile	imaging	calculi; cancer	removal		
pancreas	secretes digestive fluids	imaging	cancer			

Plate 34

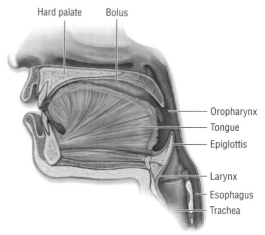

Hard palate   Bolus

Oropharynx
Tongue
Epiglottis
Larynx
Esophagus
Trachea

1. Food pushed by tongue

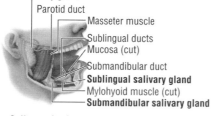

Parotid salivary gland
Parotid duct
Masseter muscle
Sublingual ducts
Mucosa (cut)
Submandibular duct
Sublingual salivary gland
Mylohyoid muscle (cut)
Submandibular salivary gland

Salivary glands

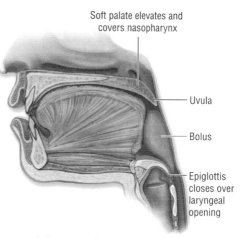

Soft palate elevates and
covers nasopharynx

Uvula

Bolus

Epiglottis
closes over
laryngeal
opening

2. Food moves to epiglottis

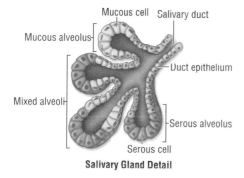

Mucous cell Salivary duct
Mucous alveolus
Duct epithelium
Mixed alveoli
Serous alveolus
Serous cell

Salivary Gland Detail

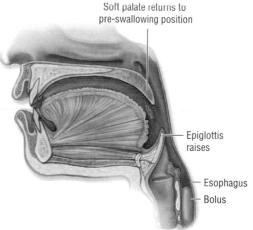

Soft palate returns to
pre-swallowing position

Epiglottis
raises

Esophagus
Bolus

3. Food enter esophagus

Swallowing

Plate 35

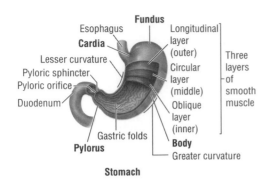

Stomach

Fundus
Esophagus
Cardia
Lesser curvature
Pyloric sphincter
Pyloric orifice
Duodenum
Gastric folds
Pylorus
Longitudinal layer (outer)
Circular layer (middle)
Oblique layer (inner)
Three layers of smooth muscle
Body
Greater curvature

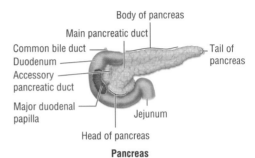

Pancreas

Body of pancreas
Main pancreatic duct
Common bile duct
Duodenum
Accessory pancreatic duct
Major duodenal papilla
Tail of pancreas
Jejunum
Head of pancreas

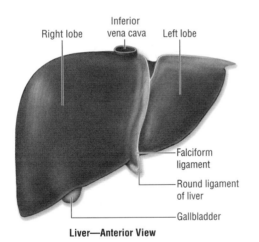

Liver—Anterior View

Right lobe
Inferior vena cava
Left lobe
Falciform ligament
Round ligament of liver
Gallbladder

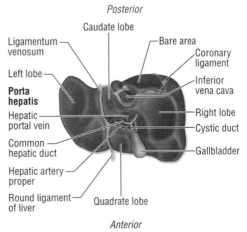

Liver—Posterior View

Posterior
Caudate lobe
Ligamentum venosum
Left lobe
Porta hepatis
Hepatic portal vein
Common hepatic duct
Hepatic artery proper
Round ligament of liver
Bare area
Coronary ligament
Inferior vena cava
Right lobe
Cystic duct
Gallbladder
Quadrate lobe
Anterior

Plate 36

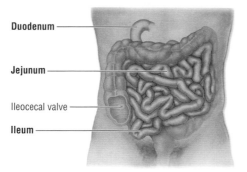

Small Intestine

Right colic flexure
Transverse mesocolon
Left colic flexure
Haustrum
Epiploic appendages
Superior mesenteric artery
Tenia coli
Ileocecal valve
Inferior mesenteric artery
Cecum
Ileum
Vermiform appendix
Sigmoid mesocolon
Anal canal
Rectum

Large Intestine

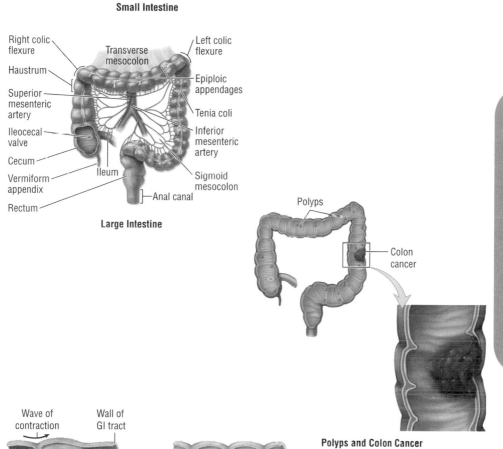

Polyps

Colon cancer

Polyps and Colon Cancer

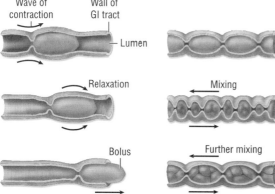

Wave of contraction
Wall of GI tract
Lumen
Relaxation
Mixing
Bolus
Further mixing

Peristalisis and Segmentation

Plate 37

The Endocrine System

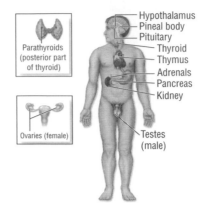

Hypothalamus
Pineal body
Pituitary
Thyroid
Thymus
Adrenals
Pancreas
Kidney

Parathyroids
(posterior part
of thyroid)

Ovaries (female)

Testes
(male)

The Endocrine System—An Overview

System parts	Function	Major Tests and Procedures	Major pathology	Major Procedures	Major Pharmaceutical agents	Specialists, Practitioners, and Allied Health Careers
pituitary gland	growth and metabolic functions as well as stimulation of other endocrine gland functions	blood tests; urine tests; serum tests	growth disorders; cancer; diabetes insipidus	surgical removal	agents to maintain homeostasis such as growth hormones	endocrinologists, lab technician, radiologic technician, medical assistant, medical receptionist
adrenal glands	regulates growth, metabolism and the nervous system	blood tests; urine tests; serum tests	overgrowth of hair, virilism, Addison's disease	surgical removal	agents to maintain homeostasis	
sex glands (testes and ovaries)	development of male and female sex characteristics; essential to human reproduction	blood tests; urine tests; serum tests	fertility problems; imbalanced sexual drives; cancer	surgical removal	hormone replacement therapy	
pancreas gland	regulates levels of blood glucose	blood tests; urine tests; serum tests	diabetes; pancreatitis; cancer	surgical removal	diabetes medications	
hypothalamus gland	stimulate pituitary functioning	blood tests; urine tests; serum tests	malfunctioning; cancer	surgical removal		
thyroid and parathyroid glands	metabolism, growth, and levels of blood calcium	blood tests; urine tests; serum tests	metabolic malfunctioning; cancer; impaired blood calcium affecting bone growth and other functions	surgical removal	hormone replacement therapy	
thymus gland	development of immunity in children	blood tests; urine tests; serum tests	malfunctioning; cancer	surgical removal		
pineal gland	secretes melatonin for wake and sleep cycles; sexual functioning; and skin pigmentation	blood tests; urine tests; serum tests	malfunctioning; cancer	surgical removal	melatonin	

Plate 38

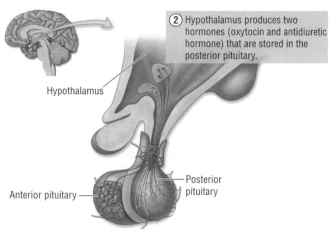

② Hypothalamus produces two hormones (oxytocin and antidiuretic hormone) that are stored in the posterior pituitary.

Hypothalamus

Posterior pituitary

Anterior pituitary

Hypothalamus

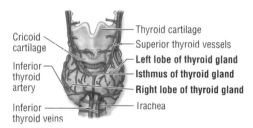

Cricoid cartilage

Inferior thyroid artery

Inferior thyroid veins

Thyroid cartilage

Superior thyroid vessels

Left lobe of thyroid gland

Isthmus of thyroid gland

Right lobe of thyroid gland

Trachea

Thyroid Gland

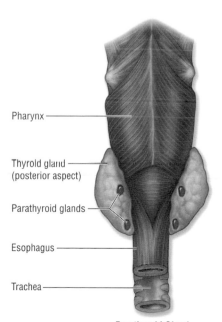

Pharynx

Thyroid gland (posterior aspect)

Parathyroid glands

Esophagus

Trachea

Parathyroid Gland

Plate 39

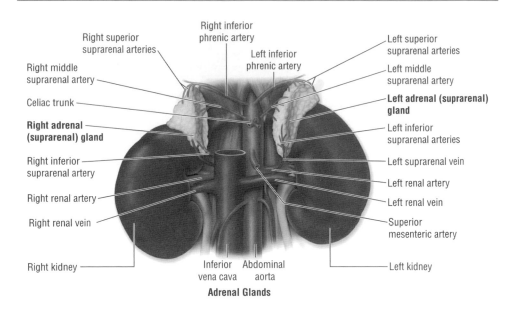

Right superior
suprarenal arteries

Right inferior
phrenic artery

Left inferior
phrenic artery

Left superior
suprarenal arteries

Right middle
suprarenal artery

Left middle
suprarenal artery

Celiac trunk

**Left adrenal (suprarenal)
gland**

**Right adrenal
(suprarenal) gland**

Left inferior
suprarenal arteries

Right inferior
suprarenal artery

Left suprarenal vein

Right renal artery

Left renal artery

Right renal vein

Left renal vein

Superior
mesenteric artery

Right kidney

Inferior
vena cava

Abdominal
aorta

Left kidney

Adrenal Glands

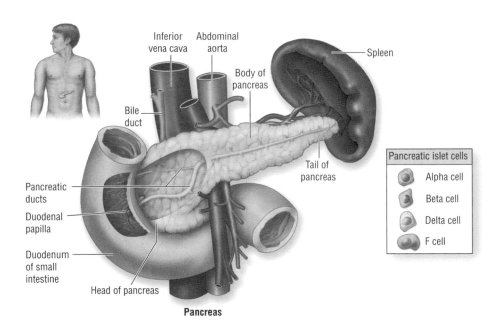

Inferior
vena cava

Abdominal
aorta

Spleen

Body of
pancreas

Bile
duct

Tail of
pancreas

Pancreatic
ducts

Duodenal
papilla

Duodenum
of small
intestine

Head of pancreas

Pancreatic islet cells
Alpha cell
Beta cell
Delta cell
F cell

Pancreas

Plate 40

Endocrine glands, their secretions, and their functions.

Endocrine Gland or Tissue	Hormone	Function
hypothalamus	pituitary-regulating hormones	either stimulate or inhibit pituitary secretions
neurohypophysis (pituitary gland—posterior)	antidiuretic hormone (ADH), vasopressin oxytocin melanocyte-stimulating hormone (MSH)	increase water reabsorption stimulates uterine contractions and lactation stimulates the production of melanin
adenohypophysis (pituitary gland—anterior)	growth hormone (GH), soma-totrophic hormone (STH), thyroid-stimulating hormone (TSH), adrenocorticotropic hormone (ACTH), follicle-stimulating hormone (FSH), luteinizing hormone (LH) prolactin	stimulate bone and muscle growth; regulate some metabolic functions such as the rate that cells utilize carbohydrates and fats stimulates thyroid gland to secrete hormones stimulates secretion of adrenal cortex hormones stimulate development of ova and production of female hormones stimulates breast development and milk production
thyroid	thyroxine (T4); triiodothyro-nine (T3) calcitonin	regulates metabolism; stimulates growth lowers blood calcium as necessary to maintain homeostasis
parathyroid	parathormone, parathyroid hormone (PTH)	increase blood calcium as neces-sary to maintain homeostasis
adrenal medulla	epinephrine (adrenaline), norepinephrine (*noradrenaline*)	work with the sympathetic nerv-ous system to react to stress
adrenal cortex	glucocorticoids (cortisol, corticosteroids, *corticosterone*), mineralocorticoids (aldosterone), gonadocorticoids (androgens)	affect metabolism, growth, and aid in electrolyte and fluid balances
pancreas (in islets of Langerhans)	insulin, glucagon	maintain homeostasis in blood glucose concentration
pineal gland	melatonin	affects sexual functions and wake-sleep cycles
ovaries	estrogen (estradiol, the most powerful estrogen), progesterone	promote development of female sex characteristics, menstrual cy-cle, reproductive functions
testes	androgen, testosterone	promote development of male sex characteristics, sperm production
thymus gland	thymosin, thymic humoral factor (THF), factor thymic serum (FTS)	aid in development of T cells and some B cells; function not well understood

Plate 41

The Sensory System

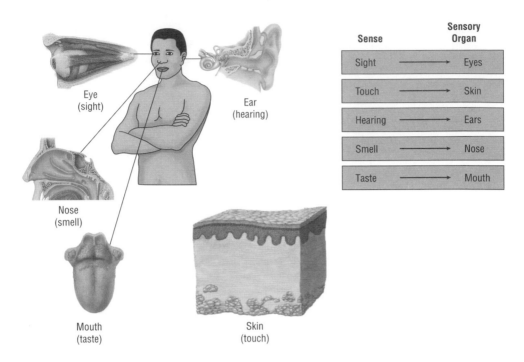

Sense		Sensory Organ
Sight	→	Eyes
Touch	→	Skin
Hearing	→	Ears
Smell	→	Nose
Taste	→	Mouth

Eye (sight)

Ear (hearing)

Nose (smell)

Mouth (taste)

Skin (touch)

The Sensory System—An Overview

System parts	Function	Major Tests and Procedures	Major pathology	Major Procedures	Major Pharmaceutical agents	Specialists, Practitioners, and Allied Health Careers
eyes	sight	eye exam; imaging	infections; vision defects or blindness	surgical sight correction; removal of lens; eye removal; replacement of parts	antibiotics; agents to relieve symptoms; miotic; mydriatic	ophthalmologist, optometrist, optician, optical assistant. medical assistant, medical receptionist
ears	hearing	hearing test; endoscope	infections; hearing defects or hearing loss	surgical defect correction; myringotomy	antibiotics; antiseptics	
nose	smell	endoscope	infections; loss of the sense of smell	surgical correction	decongestants	
taste buds	taste	visual examination	loss of taste sensation			
skin (touch)	touch	visual examination	loss of feeling			

Plate 42

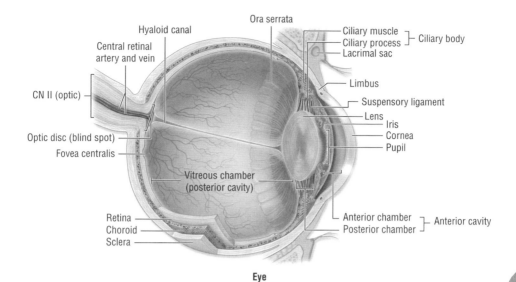

Eye

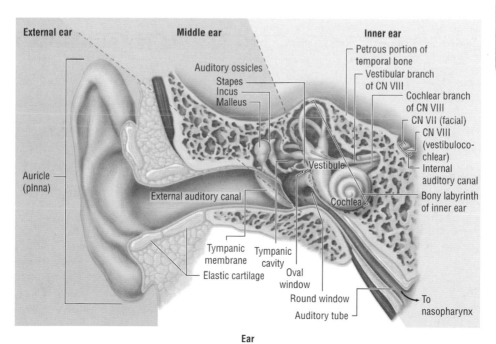

Ear

Plate 43

Dentistry

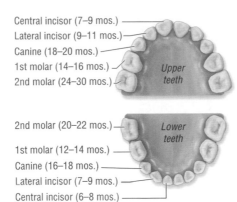

Central incisor (7–9 mos.)
Lateral incisor (9–11 mos.)
Canine (18–20 mos.)
1st molar (14–16 mos.)
2nd molar (24–30 mos.)

Upper teeth

2nd molar (20–22 mos.)

Lower teeth

1st molar (12–14 mos.)
Canine (16–18 mos.)
Lateral incisor (7–9 mos.)
Central incisor (6–8 mos.)

Deciduous Teeth

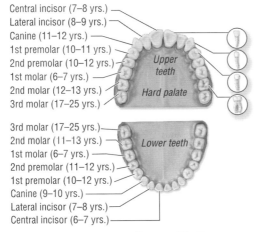

Central incisor (7–8 yrs.)
Lateral incisor (8–9 yrs.)
Canine (11–12 yrs.)
1st premolar (10–11 yrs.)
2nd premolar (10–12 yrs.)
1st molar (6–7 yrs.)
2nd molar (12–13 yrs.)
3rd molar (17–25 yrs.)

Upper teeth

Hard palate

3rd molar (17–25 yrs.)
2nd molar (11–13 yrs.)
1st molar (6–7 yrs.)
2nd premolar (11–12 yrs.)
1st premolar (10–12 yrs.)
Canine (9–10 yrs.)
Lateral incisor (7–8 yrs.)
Central incisor (6–7 yrs.)

Lower teeth

Permanent Teeth

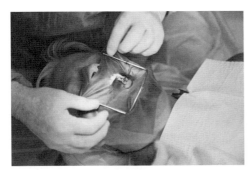

Dental Dam

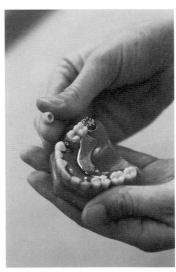

Dentures

Plate 44

Diagnostic Imaging

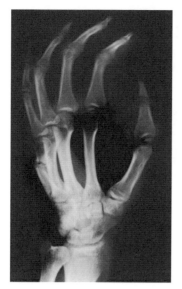

X-Ray

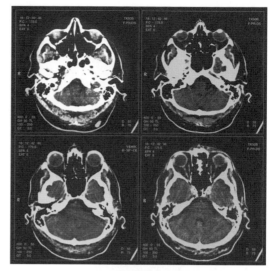

Cat Scan

MRI

Mammogram

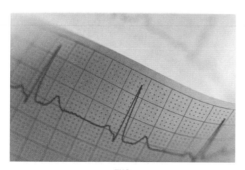

EKG

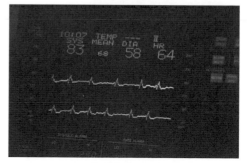

Cardiac Monitor

Plate 45

Surgery

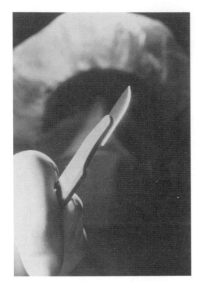

Scalpel

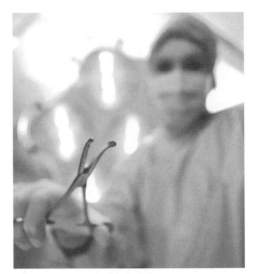

Surgical Tongs

Scrubs

Heart Surgery

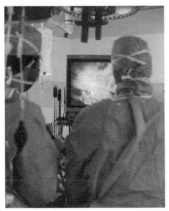

Surgical Monitor

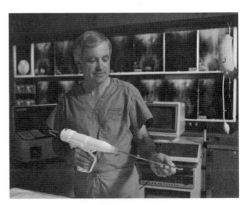

Medical Laser

Plate 46

Pharmacology

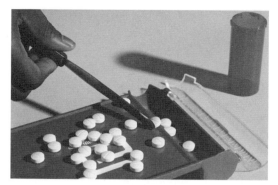

Counting Pills for a Prescription

Hospital Pharmacy

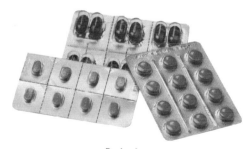

Packaging

Intramuscular

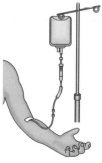

Intravenous

Intradermal

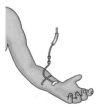

Intra-arterial

Plate 47

Complementary and Alternative Medicine (CAM)

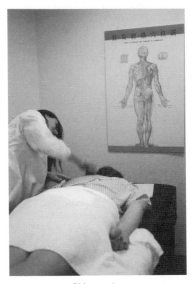

Chiropractor

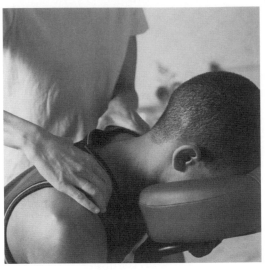

Massage Therapy

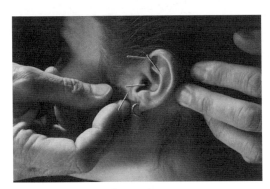

Acupuncture

Herbalist with Traditional Doctor

Yoga

Meditation

Plate 48

PA *abbreviation.* **1.** physician assistant. **2.** posteroanterior (as in a typical chest x-ray). **3.** pulmonary artery.

PAC *abbreviation.* premature atrial contraction.

pacemaker /pās'mā'kər/ **1.** any of various small, battery-driven devices surgically implanted in the chest to regulate the heart's rhythm or the rate at which it beats. *Also called* artificial pacemaker. **2.** the sinoatrial (SA) node of the heart muscle that naturally causes the heart to beat. *Also called* cardiac pacemaker. **3.** any biochemical substance that determines the rate at which a subsequent series of reactions will occur.

pachy- *combining form.* thick: *for example,* pachyonychia.

pachycephaly /păk'ē sĕf'ə lē/ excessive thickness of the skull. [pachy- + -cephaly]

pachydactyly /păk'ĭ dăk'tə lē/ abnormal thickness of the fingers or toes. [pachy- + -dactyly].

pachyderma /păk'ĭ dûr'mə/ abnormal thickness of the skin. [pachy- + -derma]

pachyglossia /păk'ē glos'ē ə/ excessive thickness of the tongue. [pachy- + -glossia]

pachymeningitis /păk'ē mĕn'ĭn jī'tĭs/ inflammation of the dura mater. [pachy- + -meningitis]

pachyonychia /păk'ē ō nĭk'ē ə/ abnormal thickening of the fingernails and toenails. [pachy- + onychia]

pack /păk/ **1.** *v.* to wrap a body in wet or dry, hot or cold sheet or blanket, for therapeutic purposes. **2.** *n.* the materials used for this purpose.

packed cell volume (PCV) the volume of blood cells remaining in a quantity of blood after centrifuging.

packed red blood cells (PRBC) the red blood cells that remain after the plasma has been removed from whole blood, used in blood transfusions; measured in a hematocrit.

PACU /păk'yōō'/ *abbreviation.* post-anesthesia care unit.

pad /păd/ **1.** a piece of absorbent material, such as gauze, folded and used to protect a wound. **2.** a thick mass of flesh that cushions a weight-bearing part of the body, as on the underside of a foot.

Paget('s) disease /păj'ĭt(s)/ **1.** either of two forms of cancer, one in the breast at the site of the nipples and areola and the other in the anal and genital region. **2.** a skeletal disease, chiefly of elderly people, marked by thickening and softening of the bones.

pain /pān/ **1.** a sensation ranging from mild discomfort to intense distress or agony, caused by disease, injury, pressure, constriction, or other damage and relayed to the brain through nerve pathways from the affected place in the body; usually rated on a scale of 1 to 10 with 10 being the most severe. **2.** any discomfort or distress caused by a particular condition or occurring at a particular place in the body, as a labor pain or a chest pain.

pain management the treatment and control of disabling or chronic pain, often using a combination of resources such as medication, physical therapy, biofeedback, meditation, acupuncture, and psychological support.

palate /păl'ĭt/ the partition between the oral and nasal cavities that forms the roof of the mouth, having a hard, bony front section and a soft, muscular back section.

palatine /păl'ĭ tēn'/ of or pertaining to the palate.

palatine bone either of two bones in the upper jaw forming the back of the hard palate and part of the eye socket and the nasal cavity.

palatine tonsil /tŏn'səl/ either of two small masses, one on each side of the opening to the throat, made up mostly of lymphoid tissue.

palato- *combining form.* palate: *for example,* palatoschisis.

palatoplasty /păl'ə tə plăs'tē/ surgery to repair defects or deformities of the hard palate. [palato- + -plasty]

palatoschisis /păl'ə tŏs'kə sĭs/ birth anomaly with a cleft in the middle of the palate, often including a fissure in the lip. *Also called* cleft palate, uranoschisis.

palliate /păl'ē āt'/ to lessen the severity of (a pain, disease, or condition) without curing; relieve or control somewhat; ease; provide comfort to someone with a terminal illness.

palliation /păl'ē ā'shən/ **1.** relief or moderation of the pain or progress of a disease or condition without attempting to cure the cause. **2.** the medication, therapy, or other means used for this purpose. **3.** comfort provided to patients with a terminal illness.

palliative /păl'ē ə tĭv/ **1.** *adj.* relieving or easing pain or distressing symptoms; bringing about palliation. **2.** *n.* something given to relieve or ease pain or distressing symptoms, especially a drug.

palliative care   1. care based on the principles of hospice care, to enable persons with terminal diseases or conditions to receive assistance, therapy, comfort, and guidance before their illness progresses to the hospice stage. **2.** any care given to ease pain or distressing symptoms without treating the cause.

pallidotomy /păl'ĭ dŏt'ə mē/   a surgical procedure on the pallidum, deep in the interior of the brain, done to relieve involuntary movements that occur in some disorders.

pallidum /păl'ĭ dəm/   the inner pale yellow part of the lenticular nucleus, at the base of the cerebral hemisphere of the brain. *Also called* globus pallidus.

pallor /păl'ər/   abnormal paleness of the skin.

palm /päm/   the fleshy, slightly concave inner surface of the hand, between the wrist and the bases of the fingers.

palmar /păl'mər, pä'mər/   of or relating to the palm of the hand. *Also called* volar.

palpate /păl'pāt/   to examine (a part of the body) by touching or gently pressing with one or both hands, normally used to take note of the integrity of tissue or structure.

palpation /păl pā'shən/   the action of palpating; examination with the hands.

palpebra /păl pē'brə/ (*pl.* **palpebrae** /păl pē'brē/)   the eyelid.

palpebral /păl pē'brəl/   of or relating to an eyelid.

palpitation /păl'pĭ tā'shən/   a sudden sensation that the heart is throbbing irregularly or harder or faster than normal, with the pulse going over 100 beats per minute.

palsy /pôl'zē/   paralysis of a muscle or muscles. *See also* Bell('s) palsy, cerebral palsy.

pan-   *prefix.* all; entire; the whole: *for example,* pancolitis.

panacea /păn'ə sē'ə/   a remedy claimed or believed to be a cure for all ailments; a cure-all.

pancolitis   /păn'kə lī'tĭs/   inflammation throughout the entire colon. [pan- + colitis]

pancreas /păng'krē əs/   a large, curved, elongated gland that lies behind the stomach between the spleen and the duodenum. Its islet cells secrete insulin and other hormones into the bloodstream, and the larger mass of the gland manufactures enzymes of digestion that pass through the pancreatic duct and the common bile duct, into the duodenum. It is thus both an exocrine and an endocrine gland.

pancreat-, pancreato-   *combining form.* pancreas: *for example,* pancreatitis.

pancreatectomy /păng'krē ə těk'tə mē/   surgical removal of the pancreas. [pancreat- + -ectomy]

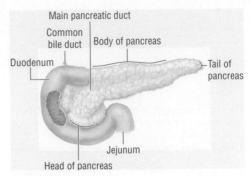

Pancreas

pancreatic /păng'krē ăt'ĭk/   of or relating to the pancreas.

pancreatic cancer   cancer of the pancreas.

pancreatic duct   the main duct of the pancreas, through which pancreatic enzymes flow, into the ampulla de Vater (part of the common bile duct) and from there into the duodenum.

pancreatic juice   a secretion of the pancreas containing enzymes that aid in digestion.

pancreatitis /păng'krē ə tī'tĭs/   inflammation of the pancreas. [pancreat- + -itis]

pancreatolysis /păng'krē ə tŏl'ə sĭs/   destruction of the tissues of the pancreas. [pancreato- + -lysis]

pancreatopathy /păng'krē ə tŏp'ə thē/   any disease of the pancreas. [pancreato- + -pathy]

pancreatotomy /păng'krē ə tŏt'ə mē/   surgical incision of the pancreas. [pancreato- + -tomy]

pancytopenia /păn'sī tō pē'nē ə/   a notable reduction in the number of all the cells normally found in circulating blood. [pan- + cytopenia]

pandemic /păn děm'ĭk/   **1.** *n.* an epidemic occurring worldwide or over a very large geographical area. **2.** *adj.* occurring throughout or affecting a very large geographical area or worldwide; widely distributed.

panencephalitis /păn'ěn sěf'ə lī'tĭs/   inflammation of both the white and gray matter of the brain. [pan- + encephal- + -itis]

pang /păng/   a sudden stab of pain.

panhypopituitarism /păn hĭ'pō pĭ tōō ĭ tə rĭz'əm/   hypopituitarism caused by destruction of the anterior pituitary gland, with the consequent failure to secrete important hormones: ACTH, TSH, LS and FSH, growth hormone, prolactin, vasopressin.

panic /păn'ĭk/   a sudden feeling of intense fear or anxiety, typically marked by the inability to think clearly or behave calmly.

panic attack   an episode of panic often accompanied by sweating, increased heart rate, rapid breathing, dizziness, feelings of unreality, fear of dying, etc., usually as a symptom of a mental illness or psychological disturbance.

panic disorder a psychological disorder marked by recurring panic attacks.

panniculitis /pə nĭk′yə lī′tĭs/ inflammation of subcutaneous fatty tissue.

panniculus /pə nĭk′yə ləs/ a layer of tissue, especially a layer of subcutaneous fat.

pannus /păn′əs/ **1.** superficial vascular inflammation of the cornea. **2.** inflamed synovial granulation tissue found in chronic rheumatoid arthritis.

pansinusitis /păn′sī nə sī′tĭs/ inflammation of all the sinuses around the nose. [pan- + sinusitis]

pantothenic acid /păn′tə thĕn′ĭk/ an acid, essential for cell growth, found in plant and animal tissues, rice, bran, etc., that is part of the B complex of vitamins.

Pap /păp/ short for **1.** Papanicolaou('s). **2.** (*also* **pap**) Pap test. **3.** (*also* **pap**) Pap smear.

PAP *abbreviation.* **1.** positive airway pressure. **2.** pulmonary artery pressure.

Papanicolaou('s) stain /păp′ə nĭk′ə lou(z)′/ a chemical preparation used to stain specimens for microscopic examination, as in the Pap test. *Also called* Pap/pap stain.

papilla /pə pĭl′ə/ (*pl.* **papillae** /pə pĭl′ē/) a small, nipple-shaped or conical formation of tissue, as on the skin, in the corner of the eye, or on the tongue.

papillary /păp′ə lĕr′ē/ of, pertaining to, or like a papilla.

papillary layer the outer layer of the dermis, which lies beneath the epidermis.

papillary muscle any of the conical muscular projections in the ventricles of the heart that attach to the valve leaflets and control their motion.

papillary tumor papilloma.

papilledema /pə pĭl′ə dē′mə/ edema of the optic disk.

papilloma /păp′ə lō′mə/ (*pl.* **papillomas** or **papillomata** /păp′ə lō′mə tə/) a benign tumor of epithelial tissue that grows in fingerlike projections. *Also called* papillary tumor.

papillomatosis /păp′ə lō′mə tō′sĭs/ the development of many papillomas.

Pap/pap /păp/ **test** or **smear** microscopic examination of cells scraped from the female cervix to determine whether cancer is present.

Pap/pap stain a chemical preparation used to stain specimens for microscopic examination, as in the Pap test. *Also called* Papanicolaou's stain.

papular /păp′yə lər/ of, pertaining to, or like a papule.

papule /păp′yōol/ a small, firm bump on the skin, often inflamed.

papulosis /păp′yə lō′sĭs/ the presences of a large number of widespread papules.

par-, para- *prefix.* **1.** near; beside. **2.** beyond; outside. **3.** assistant; associate. **4.** abnormal. *For example,* paramedical.

-para *suffix.* woman who has borne the indicated number of children: *for example,* primipara.

para /păr′ə/ a woman who has borne at least one child.

paracentesis /păr′ə sĕn tē′sĭs/ surgical insertion of a needle or other instrument into a body cavity, especially the abdomen, to withdraw fluid from it. *Also called* nyxis. [para- + -centesis]

paracusis /păr′ə kyōo′sĭs/ or **paracusia** /păr′ə kyōo′zhə/ **1.** defectiveness in the sense of hearing. **2.** an auditory hallucination.

paracystitis /păr′ə sĭ stī′tĭs/ inflammation in the various tissues around the urinary bladder. [para- + cystitis]

paraesthesia/paresthesia /păr′əs thē′zhə/ a sensation in the skin of burning, itching, tingling, insects crawling, or the like, without any apparent cause.

paraffin bath /păr′ə fĭn/ a type of therapy using immersion in warm wax to treat arthritis pain, inflammation, muscle spasms, dry skin, and other ailments.

paralalia /păr′ə lā′lē ə/ any speech defect characterized by distortion of the sound.

paralysis /pə răl′ə sĭs/ (*pl.* **paralyses** /pə răl′ə sēz′/) **1.** loss of the ability to voluntarily move the muscles in part or all of the body. **2.** loss of sensation in a part or area of the body.

paralytic /păr′ə lĭt′ĭk/ **1.** *adj.* of or related to paralysis. **2.** *n.* someone afflicted with paralysis; paraplegic or hemiplegic.

paralyze /păr′ə līz′/ to cause paralysis.

paramedic /păr′ə mĕd′ĭk/ a person who is trained to assist doctors and other health-care

Paramedic

providers by performing certain medical tasks or procedures, typically in an emergency situation where a doctor might not be present. [para- + medic]

paramedical /păr′ə mĕd′ĭ kəl/ of, pertaining to, or connected with the medical profession in a supporting or assisting role. [para- + medical]

parametritis /păr′ə mĭ trī′tĭs/ inflammation of the bands of broad ligament adjacent to the uterus. [para- + metr- + -itis]

parametrium /păr′ə mē′trē əm/ the connective tissue of the floor of the pelvis.

paranasal sinus /păr′ə nā′zəl sī′nəs/ any of the group of paired sinuses in the face that connect with the nasal cavity. *See also* ethmoid sinuses, frontal sinuses, maxillary sinuses, sphenoid sinuses. [para- + sinus]

paranoia /păr′ə noi′ə/ a mental illness marked by the irrational belief that one is being systematically persecuted or that one is extremely powerful or gifted, or both, usually without hallucinations.

paranoiac /păr′ə noi′ăk/ **1.** *n.* a person who has paranoia. **2.** *adj.* paranoid.

paranoid /păr′ə noid′/ **1.** *adj.* pertaining to, marked by, or resembling paranoia. **2.** *n.* paranoiac.

paranoid disorder delusional disorder including extreme paranoia.

paranoid schizophrenia /skĭt′sə frē′nē ə/ schizophrenia marked by one or more irrational and obsessive beliefs, as of being systematically persecuted, often with auditory hallucinations.

paraparesis /păr′ə pə rē′sĭs/ partial paralysis of the lower legs. [para- + paresis]

paraphasia /păr′ə fā′zhə/ an impairment of the ability to speak normally in which wrong words are used or words are combined illogically so that speech makes no sense. [para- + -phasia]

paraphilia /păr′ə fĭl′ē ə/ a disorder of sexual desire and behavior that takes many forms, such as exhibitionism, fetishism, pedophilia, and voyeurism. [para- + -philia]

paraphimosis /păr′ə fĭ mō′sĭs/ a condition in which the foreskin is retracted behind the glans penis and cannot be replaced over the glans, because the open end of the foreskin is narrowed (usually by scarring secondary to infection). [para- + phimosis]

paraplegia /păr′ə plē′jē ə, -jə/ paralysis of the legs and the lower part of the torso. [para- + -plegia]

paraplegic /păr′ə plē′jĭk/ **1.** *adj.* of, pertaining to, or having paraplegia. **2.** *n.* a person who has paraplegia.

parasite /păr′ə sīt′/ an organism that lives in or on another, obtaining all it needs to survive from this host.

Paraplegic

parasitemia /păr′ə sī tē′mē ə, -sĭ tē′-/ the presence of parasites in the blood. [parasit(e) + -emia]

parasitic /păr′ə sĭt′ĭk/ **1.** pertaining to or characteristic of a parasite or parasites. **2.** caused by a parasite or parasites.

parasitism /păr′ə sī tĭz′əm, -sĭ tĭz′-/ the condition of being completely dependent on another organism for survival with no benefit to the host and sometimes with injury.

parasitology /păr′ə sī tŏl′ə jē/ the study of parasites, their effect on their hosts, and treatments for the afflicted.

parasomnia /păr′ə sŏm′nē ə/ any of a group of sleep disorders, such as sleepwalking or persistent nightmares. [para- + -somnia]

parasympathetic /păr′ə sĭm′pə thĕt′ĭk/ of or pertaining to the parasympathetic nervous system. [para- + sympathetic]

parasympathetic nervous system one of the two divisions of the autonomic nervous system, with nerve fibers to the heart and various glands and internal organs that regulate, stimulate, or slow down vital physiologic functions. *See also* sympathetic nervous system.

parasympathomimetic /păr′ə sĭm′pə thō mĭ mĕt′ĭk/ having or producing effects similar to those resulting from stimulation of the parasympathetic nervous system.

parathormone /păr′ə thôr′mōn/ the hormone, secreted by the parathyroid glands, that regulates the metabolism of calcium and phosphorus. *Also called* parathyroid hormone.

parathyroid /păr′ə thī′roid/ *adj.* **1.** of, pertaining to, or coming from the parathyroid glands. **2.** next to the thyroid gland. *n.* **3.** parathyroid gland. [para- + thyroid]

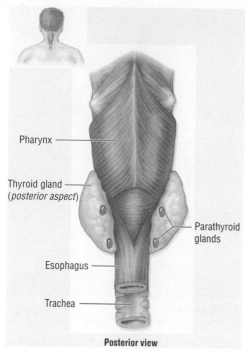

Parathyroid Gland

Posterior view

Pharynx

Thyroid gland
(*posterior aspect*)

Parathyroid
glands

Esophagus

Trachea

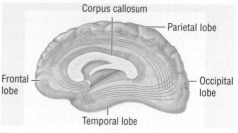

Parietal Lobe

Corpus callosum

Parietal lobe

Frontal
lobe

Occipital
lobe

Temporal lobe

parathyroidectomy /păr'ə thī'roi dĕk'tə mē/ surgical removal of one or more of the parathyroid glands. [parathyroid + -ectomy]

parathyroid gland any of four small, paired glands on or near the back of the thyroid gland that secrete parathyroid hormone.

parathyroid hormone the hormone, secreted by the parathyroid glands, that regulates the metabolism of calcium and phosphorus. *Also called* parathormone.

parenchyma /pə rĕng'kə mə/ the cells or tissues of an organ that perform its essential function, as opposed to the tissues that shape or support it. *See also* stroma.

parenchymal /pə rĕng'kə məl/ or **parenchymatous** /păr'əng kĭm'ĭ tŭs/ of, pertaining to, or characteristic of parenchyma.

parenteral /pə rĕn'tər əl/ delivered into the body by means other than the digestive tract, as intravenously or by injection.

parenteral administration the giving of a substance, as a drug, intravenously or by injection under the skin, into muscles, or other area of the body.

parenteral medication medication delivered to the body by parenteral route.

parenteral nutrition (PN) administration of nutritional fluids by parenteral route, usually intravenously.

paresis /pə rē'sĭs/ (*pl.* **pareses** /pə rē'sēz/) mild or partial paralysis.

paresthesia/paraesthesia /păr'əs thē'zhə/ a sensation in the skin of burning, itching, tingling, insects crawling, or the like, without any apparent cause. [par- + -esthesia]

pareunia /pə rōō'nē ə/ sexual intercourse.

parietal /pə rī'ĭ təl/ 1. pertaining to or forming the outer walls of a cavity. 2. of, relating to, or near the parietal bones.

parietal bone either of the two large, four-sided bones that form the sides and part of the top of the skull.

parietal lobe the central lobe of each cerebral hemisphere of the brain, between the frontal lobe and the occipital lobe.

parietal pleura /plŏŏr'ə/ the outermost of the two pleural membranes.

Parkinson('s) disease /pär'kĭn sən(z)/ a progressive neurologic disease occurring mostly in older adults, marked chiefly by tremors, muscle weakness and rigidity, and changes in posture and gait as a result of a deficiency of dopamine.

Parkinson('s) facies /fā'shē ēz', -shēz/ an expressionless facial appearance typically found in patients with Parkinson's disease.

parkinsonian /pär'kĭn sō'nē ən/ of or pertaining to parkinsonism.

parkinsonism/Parkinsonism /pär'kĭn sə nĭz'əm/ 1. Parkinson's disease. 2. any of a group of neurologic disorders having symptoms like those of Parkinson's disease.

paronychia /păr'ə nĭk'ē ə/ infection of the skin around a nail. [par- + -onychia]

parotid gland /pə rŏt'ĭd/ either of the largest of the paired salivary glands adjacent to the mouth, situated below and in front of the external ear.

parotitis /păr'ə tī'tĭs/ or **parotiditis** /pə rŏt'ĭ dī'tĭs/ inflammation of the parotid glands.

-parous *suffix.* giving birth to; bearing: *for example,* multiparous.

paroxysm /păr'ək sĭz'əm/ 1. a sudden spasm or seizure. 2. a sudden increase in or recurrence of the symptoms of a disease.

paroxysmal /păr'ək sĭz'məl/ occurring in paroxysms.

paroxysmal nocturnal dyspnea /nŏk tûr′nəl dĭsp nē′ə/ recurring attacks of breathing distress during sleep caused by fluid in the lungs or chronic lung disease.

paroxysmal tachycardia /tăk′ĭ kär′dē ə/ recurring attacks of rapid heartbeat that begin and end abruptly.

parrot fever a gastrointestinal infection in parrots and related birds that is caused by the *Chlamydia psittaci* bacterium; when transmitted to humans, it produces a fever and a respiratory disease. *Also called* psittacosis.

partial or **partial denture** /děn′chər/ an artificial denture that replaces one or more natural teeth but not all the teeth in the jaw and may be removable or fixed permanently.

partial hysterectomy /hĭs′tə rěk′tə mē/ surgical removal of all of the uterus except the cervix. *Also called* subtotal hysterectomy.

partial-thickness burn a burn that blisters the skin and is more severe than a first-degree burn. *Also called* second-degree burn.

partial thromboplastin time (PTT) /thrŏm′bō plăs′tĭn/ a measurement of certain coagulation factors in blood plasma.

participating provider a physician or other health-care provider who contracts with a health insurer to provide medical services to its subscribers.

-partum *suffix.* labor and childbirth: *for example,* postpartum.

parturition /pär′tŏŏ rĭsh′ən, -chŏŏ rĭsh′-/ the process of giving birth to a child, from labor through delivery; childbirth.

passive acquired immunity passive immunity acquired by injection of pooled gamma globulin, for example.

passive-aggressive of, pertaining to, or having passive-aggressive personality disorder.

passive-aggressive personality disorder a psychological disorder in which a person does not express negative feelings openly but rather shows them through uncooperative or obstructive behavior.

passive immunity immunity gained by receiving antibodies or lymphocytes from someone who already has them, for example, those maternal antibodies which pass through the placenta to the fetus.

passive range of motion (PROM) exercise done to a person by someone else or by a machine to put a part of the person's body through all the movements it is normally capable of.

passive stretching a type of stretching used in massage therapy in which a muscle is held in a position by the therapist or with the aid of an apparatus in order to stretch it.

Passive Stretching

patch /păch/ **1.** a small, usually flat area, as of skin, that is different in color or texture from the surface around it. **2.** a small piece of adhesive material containing a substance, as a hormone or a pain medication, that, when placed on the body, delivers this substance steadily through the skin. **3.** a dressing or covering to protect an injured or sensitive part.

patch test a test to detect allergies, using small strips of material placed on the skin.

patella /pə těl′ə/ (*pl.* **patellae** /pə těl′ē/ or **patellas**) a flat, triangular bone at the front of the knee joint. *Also called* kneecap.

patellar /pə těl′ər/ of or relating to the patella.

patellar ligament /lĭg′ə mənt/ that portion of the tendon of the quadriceps muscle of the thigh that extends from the patella to the tuberosity (rounded end) of the tibia. *Also called* patellar tendon.

patellar reflex an automatic forward kick of the lower leg produced by tapping the tendon just below the patella. Informally called *knee-jerk* reflex.

patellar tendon patellar ligament.

patellectomy /păt′ə lěk′tə mē/ surgical removal of the patella. [patell(a) + -ectomy]

patent 1. /pā′tənt/ open; not obstructed or closed. **2.** /păt′ənt/ of, pertaining to, or being a drug or medical preparation protected by a trademark or trade name.

patent ductus arteriosus /pā′tənt dŭk′təs är têr′ē ō′sĭs/ failure of the ductus arteriosus to close after birth.

paternal /pə tûr′nəl/ **1.** of, pertaining to, or of the nature of a father or fatherhood. **2.** related or connected through one's father. **3.** inherited from one's father.

-pathic *suffix.* of or pertaining to disease: *for example*, neuropathic.

patho- *combining form.* disease: *for example*, pathogenesis.

pathobiology /păth′ō bī ŏl′ə jē/ the branch of science concerned with the biological nature, causes, and effects of disease; pathology. [patho- + biology]

pathogen /păth′ə jən/ any agent that causes a disease, especially a microorganism such as a bacterium or virus. [patho- + -gen]

pathogenesis /păth′ə jĕn′ə sĭs/ the origin and development of a disease or morbid condition. [patho- + -genesis]

pathogenetic /păth′ō jə nĕt′ĭk/ **1.** of, pertaining to, or arising from pathogenesis. **2.** pathogenic.

pathogenic /păth′ə jĕn′ĭk/ causing disease or morbidity. *Also called* pathogenetic.

pathognomonic /păth′əg nə mŏn′ĭk, păth′ə nə-/ characteristic of a disease or morbid condition so distinctively as to confirm the diagnosis.

pathologic /păth′ə lŏj′ĭk/ or **pathological** /păth′ə lŏj′ĭ kəl/ **1.** causing disease or a diseased condition. **2.** of or relating to pathology.

pathologic fracture /frăk′chər/ fracture of a bone already weakened by existing disease.

pathologist /pə thŏl′ə jĭst/ a person who specializes in pathology, especially one who

Pathologist (preparing tissue samples)

works in a laboratory and examines specimens for the presence of disease.

pathology /pə thŏl′ə jē/ **1.** the signs and symptoms of a disease. **2.** the branch of medical science concerned with the nature, causes, and effects of disease. [patho- + -logy]

pathophysiology /păth′ō fĭz′ē ŏl′ə jē/ **1.** the changes in the body's functioning caused by a disease. **2.** the branch of medical science concerned with the nature, development, and progress of bodily changes caused by disease. [patho- + physiology]

pathway /păth′wā′/ the sequence of events by which one organic substance is converted to another.

-pathy *suffix.* disease or diseased condition: *for example,* myopathy.

patient /pā′shənt/ a person who is being examined or treated for illness or injury, as by a physician or at a hospital.

patient care technician (PCT) a person who is trained to perform medically related tasks such as blood collection, electrocardiograms, and catheterizations under the direct supervision of a registered nurse, usually in a hospital or rehabilitation facility.

patient-controlled/patient-controlled analgesia (PCA) /ăn′əl jē′zē ə/ a method for managing pain that allows a patient who is receiving intravenous pain medication to self-administer additional doses of this medication by pressing a button.

Pb *abbreviation.* lead.

p.c. *abbreviation.* Latin *post cibum,* after meals.

PCA *abbreviation.* **1.** patient-controlled analgesia. **2.** posterior cerebral artery.

PCL *abbreviation.* posterior cruciate ligament.

PCP *abbreviation.* **1.** *Pneumocystis carinii* pneumonia. **2.** primary care physician; primary care provider.

PCR *abbreviation.* polymerase chain reaction, commonly used in medical testing to amplify particular sequences of DNA.

PCT *abbreviation.* patient care technician.

PCV *abbreviation.* packed cell volume.

PD *abbreviation.* peritoneal dialysis.

PDR *abbreviation.* **1.** *Physicians' Desk Reference.* **2.** primary drug resistance.

PDT *abbreviation.* photodynamic therapy.

PE *abbreviation.* **1.** physical examination. **2.** pleural effusion. **3.** pulmonary edema. **4.** pulmonary embolism.

peak flow or **peak expiratory flow (PEFR)** /ĭk spī′rə tôr′ē/ the maximum rate of air flow at the start of expiration from fully expanded lungs.

peak flow meter an instrument that can detect decreases in air flow from the lungs, carried by people with asthma or other conditions that affect breathing capacity.

peau d'orange /pō′ dô ränj′/   a pitted or dimpled condition of the skin, like that of an orange, sometimes seen in inflammatory carcinoma of the breast.

pectoral muscles /pĕk′tər əl/   any of the greater or smaller muscles of the chest that control movements of the arm, shoulder, and some of the ribs.

pectus /pĕk′təs/ (*pl.* **pectora** /pĕk′tər ə/)   in anatomy, breast.

pectus carinatum /pĕk′təs kăr′ə nā′təm/   a deformity of the chest in which the breastbone juts out prominently.

pectus excavatum /ĕks′kə vā′təm/   a deformity of the front of the chest consisting of a deep hollow shaped like a funnel. *Also called* funnel chest.

PED   *abbreviation.* pediatric emergency department.

ped-, pedi-, pedo-   *combining form.* **1.** child: *for example,* pediatrician, pedodontics. **2.** foot or feet: *for example,* pedometer.

pederasty /pĕd′ə răs′tē/   sexual relations between a man and a boy.

pediatric /pē′dē ăt′rĭk/   of or pertaining to pediatrics.

pediatrician /pē′dē ə trĭsh′ən/   a physician whose specialty is pediatrics.

pediatric intensive care unit (PICU)   an intensive care unit for children.

Pediatrician

pediatrics /pē′dē ăt′rĭks/   the branch of medicine concerned with the development, care, and treatment of children.

pedicle /pĕd′ĭ kəl/   a stemlike part, as at the base of a tumor or on the bony structure of the vertebral arch.

pediculate /pə dĭk′yə lĭt, -lāt′/ or **pediculated** /pə dĭk′yə lā′tĭd/   having a pedicle or peduncle.

pediculicide /pə dĭk′yə lə sīd′/   a substance that kills lice.

pediculosis /pə dĭk′yə lō′sĭs/   infestation with lice.

pediculosis capitis /kăp′ĭ tĭs/   head lice.

pediculosis pubis /pyoo′bĭs/   pubic lice.

pedo-   *See* ped-.

pedodontics /pē′də dŏn′tĭks/   the branch of dentistry specializing in the diagnosis, care, and treatment of children's teeth.

pedodontist /pē′də dŏn′tĭst/   a dentist specializing in the diagnosis, care, and treatment of children's teeth.

pedometer /pĭ dŏm′ĭ tər/   a device that counts distance or the number of steps its wearer takes. [pedo- + -meter]

pedophilia /pē′də fĭl′ē ə, pĕd′ə-/   a sexual desire for children. [pedo- + -philia]

pedophobia /pē′də fō′bē ə, pĕd′ə-/   obsessive fear of children. [pedo- + -phobia]

peds   short for pediatrics.

peduncle /pĭ dŭng′kəl/   **1.** a stalk that attaches a growth to skin or body tissue. **2.** a stalklike bundle of neurons that connect different parts of the brain.

pedunculated /pĭ dŭng′kyə lā′tĭd/   having a stalk that attaches a growth to skin or body tissue.

peeling agent   a substance applied to the skin that produces a very mild surface burn and improves skin texture.

PEEP   *abbreviation.* positive end-expiratory pressure.

PEFR   *abbreviation.* peak expiratory flow rate.

PEG   *abbreviation.* percutaneous endoscopic gastrostomy.

PEG tube   a tube placed into the stomach through the abdominal wall, through which food, liquids, and medication can enter the digestive system; percutaneous endoscopic gastrostomy tube.

pellagra /pə lăg′rə, -lā′grə/   a condition resulting from severe deficiency of niacin (a B vitamin), marked by skin eruptions, inflammation of mucous membranes, diarrhea, and neurological symptoms including psychosis, confusion, and memory loss.

pelv-, pelvi-   *combining form.* pelvis: *for example,* pelvimeter.

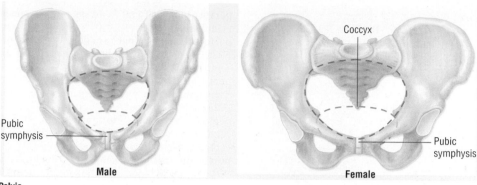

Pubic symphysis

Coccyx

Pubic symphysis

Male   **Female**

Pelvis

pelvic /pĕl'vĭk/ of or involving the pelvis.

pelvic bone hip bone.

pelvic cavity the space inside the pelvic girdle, where the female reproductive organs, the lower colon, the bladder, and the rectum are located.

pelvic exam or **pelvic examination** an examination of the female reproductive organs, partly visual and partly by palpation and usually including a removal of cervical cells (Pap smear) to be examined for cancer.

pelvic girdle the ring of bone that forms the skeleton of the pelvis, consisting of the fused hip bones (right and left ilium, ischium, and pubis) at the front and side and the lower spine and coccyx at the back. *Also called* pelvic bone.

pelvic inflammatory disease (PID) /ĭn flăm'ə tôr'ē/ sometimes painful and potentially scarring bacterial infection of the female reproductive system; can cause infertility.

pelvic ultrasonography /ŭl'trə sə nŏg'rə fē/ or **pelvic ultrasound** /ŭl'trə sound'/ imaging of the pelvic region using sound waves, used for fetal examination and to check for tumors.

pelvimeter /pĕl vĭm'ĭ tər/ an instrument used to measure the diameter and volume of the pelvis. [pelvi- + -meter]

pelvis /pĕl'vĭs/ **1.** the basinlike cavity in which the female reproductive organs, the bladder, the lower colon, and the rectum are located. **2.** the basinlike cavity in the kidney that holds urine before it passes into the ureter.

pelviscope /pĕl'və skōp'/ an optical device for viewing the contents of the pelvis. [pelvi- + -scope]

pemphigus /pĕm'fĭ gəs/ any of a group of skin diseases, some of them fatal, marked by successive recurring blisters on skin and mucous membranes.

pemphigus vulgaris /vŭl gâr'ĭs/ the most common and most severe form of pemphigus, with large nonhealing blisters.

-penia *suffix.* lack, deficiency: *for example,* leukopenia.

penicillin /pĕn'ə sĭl'ən/ an antibiotic produced naturally (by mold) and synthetically; it was the first antibiotic and is still widely used.

penicillin-resistant bacteria /băk têr'ē ə/ bacteria that are not affected by exposure to penicillin.

penile /pē'nīl/ of or involving the penis.

penile erectile dysfunction /ĭ rĕk'tīl dĭs fŭngk'shən/ the inability to achieve an erection or to maintain an erection until ejaculation.

penile implant or **penile prosthesis** /prŏs thē'sĭs/ a device surgically implanted within the shaft of the penis that enables the user to have an erection.

penis /pē'nĭs/ the male organ of copulation and urination.

Penrose drain /pĕn'rōz/ a soft rubber or silicone tube for preventing fluid from accumulating in a cavity.

-pepsia *suffix.* digestion: *for example,* dyspepsia.

pepsin /pĕp'sĭn/ a component of the gastric juice produced in the stomach that digests proteins.

peptic /pĕp'tĭk/ of or involving pepsin or digestion.

peptic ulcer /ŭl'sər/ an open sore or hole in the lining of the esophagus, stomach, or duodenum. *See illustration* on page 274.

peptic ulcer disease (PUD) the condition of having a peptic ulcer, frequently caused by a bacterium, *Helicobacter pylori.*

per- *prefix.* **1.** through. **2.** intensely. *For example,* percutaneous.

percentile /pər sĕn'tīl/ one of a hundred equal divisions of data.

perception /pər sĕp'shən/ the act of understanding through or sensing through the faculties of the mind.

perceptive /pər sĕp'tĭv/ able to sense through the faculties of the mind.

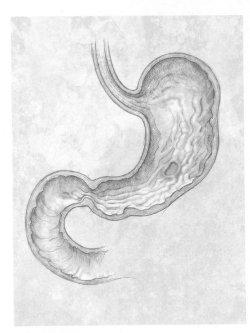

Peptic Ulcer

percussion /pər kŭsh'ən/ **1.** striking or tapping the surface of the body for diagnostic purposes. **2.** a technique for encouraging movement of secretions from the lung by striking the chest with cupped hands. **3.** a massage technique that involves light beating, hacking or cupping the hands or using tools that stimulate the muscles.

percutaneous /pûr'kyoo tā'nē əs/ administered through the skin by injection or a transdermal patch. [per- + cutaneous]

percutaneous balloon valvuloplasty /văl'vyə lə plăs'tē/ the opening of a blocked heart valve by inserting a balloon-tipped catheter into a vein, snaking it through to the heart, and inflating the balloon in the proper position to open the valve.

percutaneous endoscopic gastrostomy (PEG) /ĕn'də skŏp'ĭk gă strŏs'tə mē/ creating an opening in the abdominal wall to the stomach and inserting a tube through which a patient may be given food, liquids, and medication.

percutaneous transluminal angioplasty (PTA) /trănz loo'mə nəl ăn'jē ə plăs'tē/ the use of a balloon-tipped catheter to enlarge an artery.

percutaneous transluminal coronary angioplasty (PTCA) /kôr'ə nĕr'ə/ the use of a balloon-tipped catheter to enlarge a coronary artery.

perforate /pûr'fə rāt'/ to pierce or punch through.

perforated ulcer /pûr'fə rā'tĭd ŭl'sər/ an ulcer that has pierced through the wall of an organ.

perforation /pûr'fə rā'shən/ an abnormal opening in the wall of organ or vessel or through a body part.

perfuse /pər fyooz'/ to force a fluid, such as blood or saline solution, to flow through a blood vessel, organ, or tissue.

perfusion /pər fyoo'zhən/ the forcing of a fluid, such as blood or saline solution, through a blood vessel, organ, or tissue.

perfusion deficit /dĕf'ə sĭt/ inadequate supply of blood to a blood vessel, organ, or tissue.

peri- *prefix.* about, around, near: *for example,* perinatal.

periadenitis /pĕr'ē ăd'ə nī'tĭs/ inflammation of tissue surrounding a gland. [peri- + aden- + -itis]

perianal /pĕr'ē ā'nəl/ located beside the anus.

periaortic /pĕr'ē ā ôr'tĭk/ found behind the aorta.

pericardi-, pericardio- *combining form.* near the heart; pericardium: *for example,* pericardi-tis.

pericardiac /pĕr'ĭ kär'dē ăk'/ or **pericardial** /pĕr'ĭ kär'dē əl/ **1.** around the heart. **2.** of or involving the pericardium.

pericardial cavity the space between the visceral and parietal layers of the sac that covers the heart.

pericardial effusion /ĭ fyoo'zhən/ an excessive amount of fluid found in the pericardial sac.

pericardial fluid fluid located in the pericardial sac.

pericardial tamponade /tăm'pə nād'/ compression of the heart caused by an accumulation of blood or fluid in the space between the muscle of the heart and the pericardium; cardiac tamponade.

pericardiectomy /pĕr'ĭ kär'dē ĕk'tə mē/ surgical removal of part of the pericardium. [pericardi- + -ectomy]

pericardiostomy /pĕr'ĭ kär'dē ŏs'tə mē/ surgical creation of an opening in the pericardium. [pericardi- + -ostomy]

pericarditis /pĕr'ĭ kär dī'tĭs/ inflammation of the pericardium. [percard- + -itis]

pericardiotomy /pĕr'ē kär'dē ŏt'ə mē/ surgical incision into the periocardial sac. [pericardio- + -tomy]

pericardium /pĕr'ĭ kär'dē əm/ (*pl.* **pericardia** /pĕr'ĭ kär'dē ə/) the membrane that covers the heart and the beginnings of the large blood vessels. It consists of two layers: the visceral and parietal layers.

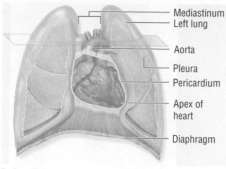

Labels: Mediastinum, Left lung, Aorta, Pleura, Pericardium, Apex of heart, Diaphragm

Pericardium

pericardotomy /pĕr′ĭ kär′dŏ′tə mē/ incision into the pericardial sac. [pericardo- + -tomy]

perichondral /pĕr′ĭ kŏn′drəl/ of or involving the perichondrium.

perichondritis /pĕr′ĭ kŏn drī′tĭs/ inflammation of the perichondrium.

perichondrium /pĕr′ĭ kŏn′drē əm/ the thin layer of tissue that surrounds cartilage and provides it with nutrients.

pericolitis /pĕr′ē kə lī′tĭs/ inflammation of tissue around the colon. [peri- + col- + -itis]

pericystitis /pĕr′ē sĭ stī′tĭs/ inflammation of tissue around the bladder. [peri- + cyst- + -itis]

perihepatitis /pĕr′ĭ hĕp′ə tī′tĭs/ inflammation of the peritoneal covering of the liver. [peri- + hepatitis]

perilymph /pĕr′ĭ lĭmf′/ the clear fluid found in the bony cavities of the inner ear. [peri- + lymph]

perimenopause /pĕr′ē mĕn′ə pôz′/ the period of time before menstruation ceases, during which menstrual periods may become irregular or scanty and hormonal changes begin. [peri- + menopause]

perimetrium /pĕr′ĭ mē′trē əm/ the thin covering of the outer layers of the uterine wall.

perinatal /pĕr′ĭ nā′təl/ occurring or involving the periods of time before, during, or following birth. [peri- + natal]

perinatal transmission transmittal of a disease or infection from mother to fetus prior to or during birth.

perinatologist /pĕr′ē nā tŏl′ə jĭst/ an obstetrician who specializes in perinatology.

perinatology /pĕr′ē nā tŏl′ə jē/ a subspecialty in obstetrics involving care of a mother and fetus from pregnancy to delivery.

perine-, perineo- *combining form.* perineum: *for example,* perineorrhaphy.

perineal /pĕr′ĭ nē′əl/ of or involving the perineum.

perineorrhaphy /pĕr′ē nē ôr′ə fē/ closing the perineum with sutures following surgery. [perineo- + -rrhaphy]

perineostomy /pĕr′ĭ nē ŏs′tə mē/ creation of an opening in the perineum. [perineo- + -stomy]

perineotomy /pĕr′ĭ nē ŏt′ə mē/ surgical incision into the perineum. [perineo- + -tomy]

perineum /pĕr′ĭ nē′əm/ (*pl.* **perinea** /pĕr′ĭ nē′ə/) **1.** the area between the thighs, below the pelvic diaphragm, between the coccyx and the pubis. **2.** the external surface of the perineum, between the anus and the vulva in women and the anus and scrotum in men.

period /pêr′ē əd/ **1.** the interval between two successive occurrences of any regularly recurring phenomenon or event; a cycle. **2.** time occupied by a stage of a disease, such as an incubation period or convalescent period. **3.** colloquial expression for the menstrual flow.

periodontal /pĕr′ē ə dŏn′təl/ near or around a tooth.

periodontal disease a disease or infection of the gums.

periodontal ligament /lĭg′ə mənt/ or **membrane** /mĕm′brān/ the connective tissue around the root of a tooth that secures it in its socket.

periodontics /pĕr′ē ə dŏn′tĭks/ the branch of dentistry concerned with treating gum diseases.

periodontist /pĕr′ē ə dŏn′tĭst/ a dentist who specializes in treating gum diseases.

periodontitis /pĕr′ē ə dŏn tī′tĭs/ inflammation of the gums.

perionychia /pĕr′ē ə nĭk′ē ə/ **1.** inflammation of the thin layer of skin at the base of a nail. **2.** plural of perionychium.

perionychium /pĕr′ē ə nĭk′ē əm/ (*pl.* **perionychia** /pĕr′ē ə nĭk′ē ə/) the thin layer of skin at the base of a nail; cuticle. *Also called* eponychium.

perioperative /pĕr′ē ŏp′ər ə tĭv/ at or near the time of an operation. [peri- + operative]

periosteal /pĕr′ē ŏs′tē əl/ of or involving the periosteum.

periosteum /pĕr′ē ŏs′tē əm/ (*pl.* **periostea** /pĕr′ē ŏs′tē ə/) a thick membrane covering all of a bone except the cartilage at the joint.

periostitis /pĕr′ē ŏ stī′tĭs/ inflammation of the periosteum.

peripheral /pə rĭf′ər əl/ of, involving, or located at an outer edge.

peripheral artery disease hardening of the arteries found outside the heart, for example, in the limbs or an organ; peripheral vascular disease.

peripheral nervous system (PNS) elements of the nervous system external to the brain and spinal cord, such as the ganglia.

peripheral vascular disease (PVD) /văs′kyə lər/ peripheral arterial or venous disease.

peripheral vision   vision produced by retinal stimulation around the macula.

periphery /pə rĭf'ə rē/   part of the body not at the center; an outer surface.

peristalsis /pĕr'ĭ stôl'sĭs/   waves of alternate contractions and relaxation of a tubular structure that move its contents, especially in the digestive tract.

peristaltic waves /pĕr'ĭ stôl'tĭk/   the alternating contraction and relaxation along the length of a tubular structure that moves the contents.

peristole /pə rĭs'tə lē/   the activity of the walls of the stomach in contracting around its contents.

peristolic /pĕr'ĭ stôl'ĭk/   denoting or involving the activity of the walls of the stomach in contracting around its contents

peritectomy /pĕr'ĭ tĕk'tə mē/   surgical removal of a ring of conjunctiva around the cornea of the eye.

peritone-, peritoneo-   *combining form.* peritoneum: *for example,* peritoneoscopy.

peritoneal /pĕr'ĭ tə nē'əl/   of or involving the peritoneum. [peritone- + -al]

peritoneal dialysis (PD) /dī ăl'ə sĭs/   removal of fluid from the body by alternately introducing and removing a dialysis solution from the peritoneum.

peritoneoscopy /pĕr'ĭ tō'nē ŏs'kə pē/   examination of the peritoneum using a laparoscope. [peritoneo- + -scopy]

peritoneotomy /pĕr'ĭ tō nē ŏt'ə mē/   surgical incision into the peritoneum. [peritoneo- + -tomy]

peritoneum /pĕr'ĭ tə nē'əm/ *(pl.* **peritonea** /pĕr'ĭ tə nē'ə/)   the membrane that lines the abdominal cavity and covers most of the organs within.

peritonitis /pĕr'ĭ tə nī'tĭs/   inflammation of the peritoneum.

peritonsillar abscess /pĕr'ĭ tŏn'sə lər ăb'sĕs/   occurrence of an infection in and around the tonsils.

peritonsillitis /pĕr'ĭ tŏn'sə lī'tĭs/   inflammation of tissue around the tonsils. [peri- + tonsill- + -itis]

permanent teeth   the 32 adult teeth in humans.

pernicious /pər nĭsh'əs/   very harmful; severe; destructive; potentially fatal if not treated.

pernicious anemia /ə nē'mē ə/   a chronic form of anemia caused by an inability to absorb B12.

peroneal muscular atrophy /pĕr'ə nē'əl mŭs'kyə lər ăt'rə fē/   a group of hereditary disorders that cause wasting of the muscles, especially those attached to the fibula, the long bone of the lower leg.

Permanent Teeth

peroral /pər ôr'əl/   through the mouth, referring to a treatment or method of giving medication. [per- + oral]

per os (PO, p.o.) /pər ŏs'/   through the mouth, in reference to a way of providing medication.

peroxide /pə rŏk'sīd'/   a compound containing a large amount of oxygen and often used as an antiseptic agent.

per rectum (PR) /pər rĕk'təm/   through the rectum, referring to a method of treatment or examination.

PERRL or **PERRLA**   *abbreviation.* pupils equally round and reactive to light or pupils equally round and reactive to light and accommodation.

Perry('s) syndrome /pĕr'ē(z)/   a hereditary type of Parkinson's disease characterized by depression, weight loss, and difficulty breathing due to failure of the central nervous system's control over breathing.

persistent vegetative state (PVS) /pər sĭs'tənt vĕj'ĭ tā'tĭv/   a prolonged state of unconsciousness, usually permanent.

persona /pər sō'nə/   a person's personality as it is presented to the world.

personality /pûr'sə năl'ĭ tē/   the unique combination of behaviors and attitudes that identifies an individual.

personality disorder   any one of several lifelong patterns of behavior characterized by an inability to function productively in social interactions and relationships.

perspiration /pûrs′pə rā′shən/ fluid produced by the sweat glands in the skin; sweat.

perspire /pər spīr′/ to produces perspiration; to sweat.

pertussis /pər tŭs′ĭs/ an acute infection of larynx, trachea, and bronchi caused by the bacteria *Bordetella pertussis,* characterized by spasms of repeated coughing. *Also called* whooping cough.

pes /pĕs/ (*pl.* **pedes** /pē′dēz/) in anatomy, a foot.

pes planus /pĕs′ plā′nəs/ feet that lack any arch, in which the entire bottom surface touches the ground. *Also called* flatfoot.

pessary /pĕs′ə rē/ **1.** a device placed in the vagina to support the uterus or hold it in position. **2.** a vaginal suppository.

pestilence /pĕs′tə ləns/ an epidemic of any disease; plague.

pestle /pĕs′əl/ a rod-shaped tool for grinding or crushing substances in a mortar, to prepare medications.

PET /pĕt/ *abbreviation.* positron emission tomography.

petechia /pə tē′kē ə/ (*pl.,* **petechiae** /pə tē′kē ē′/) a tiny red spot in the skin caused by capillary bleeding.

petechial hemorrhage /pə tē′kē əl hĕm′ər ĭj, hĕm′rĭj/ bleeding into the skin from the small blood vessels that cause petechiae. *Also called* punctate hemorrhage.

Peter Pan syndrome a popular psychology term for a dysfunctional male personality characterized by immaturity, dependence, narcissism, and irresponsibility.

petit mal /pĕt′ē măl, pə tē′/ a brief epileptic seizure.

Pestle

petit mal seizure petit mal.

petrissage /pā′trĭ säzh′/ somewhat deep massage technique that uses a rolling or kneading motion to relax tight muscles.

PET scan an image produced using radioactive isotopes and x-rays of soft tissue in a selected plane of the body.

PET scanner a diagnostic imaging device used to measure brain activity.

PE tube polyethylene tube.

-pexy *suffix.* fixation; attachment: *for example,* nephropexy.

Peyronie('s) disease /pā′rə nē′(z)/ a disease in which fibrous tissue grows in the shaft of the penis causing a curvature and pain during an erection.

PFT *abbreviation.* pulmonary function test.

pH a symbol for the logarithm that measures acidity and alkalinity.

phac-, phaco- *combining form.* shaped like a lens; birthmark: *for example,* phacoma.

phacoemulsification /făk′ō ĭ mŭl′sə fĭ kā′shən/ a surgical technique for removing a cataract from an eye using a low-frequency ultrasonic needle. [phaco- + emulsification]

phacoid /făk′oid/ having the shape of a lens. [phac- + -oid]

phacolysis /fă kŏl′ə sĭs/ dissection and removal of the lens of the eye in treatment of cataract. [phaco- + -lysis]

phacoma /fə kō′mə/ a benign growth involving an abnormal mixture of tissue elements. [phac- + -oma]

phacomalacia /fə kō′mə lā′shə/ softening of the lens of an eye. [phaco- + -malacia]

phag-, phago- *combining form.* consuming, eating: *for example,* phagocyte.

-phage, -phagia, -phagy *suffix.* consuming, eating: *for example,* macrophage.

phagocyte /făg′ə sīt′/ a cell capable of engulfing and digesting bacteria, foreign matter, and other cells. [phago- + -cyte]

phagocytic /făg′ə sīt′ĭk/ of or involving phagocytes.

phagocytosis /făg′ō sī tō′sĭs/ the cell process of engulfing and digesting other substances.

phalang-, phalango- *combining form.* finger, toe: *for example,* phalangectomy.

phalangeal /fə lăn′jē əl/ of or involving a finger or toe.

phalangectomy /făl′ən jĕk′tə mē, fā′lən-/ surgical removal of a finger or toe. [phalang- + -ectomy]

phalanges /fə lăn′jēz/ (*sing.* **phalanx** /fā′lăngks/) fingers or toes; digits.

phalanx /fā′lăngks/ (*pl.* **phalanges** /fə lăn′jēz/) singular of phalanges.

phallus /făl′əs/ penis.

phantom limb the sensation that an amputated limb is still attached to one's body.

Pharmacist

phantom pain the sensation of pain in a missing or paralyzed limb.

phantom sensation the sensation of feeling in a missing or paralyzed limb.

pharmaceutical /fär′mə sōō′tĭ kəl/ of or involving pharmacy or pharmaceutics.

pharmaceutics /fär′mə sōō′tĭks/ **1.** the science of preparing and dispensing drugs. **2.** the drugs themselves.

pharmacist /fär′mə sĭst/ someone who is licensed to prepare and dispense drugs. *Also called* druggist.

pharmaco- *combining form.* drugs: *for example,* pharmacogenetics.

pharmacodynamics /fär′mə kō dī năm′ĭks/ the study of the behavior and properties of drugs where they are active in the body.

pharmacogenetics /fär′mə kō jə nĕt′ĭks/ the study of varying responses to drugs that are genetically determined. [pharmaco- + genetics]

pharmacokinetics /fär′mə kō kĭ nĕt′ĭks/ the study of how drugs are distributed in the body after administration.

pharmacologic /fär′mə kə lŏj′ĭk/ or **pharmacological** /fär′mə kə lŏj′ĭ kəl/ or involving pharmacology or the characteristics and behaviors of drugs.

pharmacologist /fär′mə kŏl′ə jĭst/ someone who is trained in pharmacology.

pharmacology /fär′mə kŏl′ə jē/ the study of drugs and their chemistry, behaviors, and uses. [pharmaco- + -logy]

pharmacopeia/pharmacopoeia /fär′mə kə pē′ə/ a work that provides information about drugs.

pharmacotherapy /fär′mə kō thĕr′ə pē/ the use of drugs to treat illness. [pharmaco- + therapy]

pharmacy /fär′mə sē/ **1.** pharmaceutics. **2.** a business licensed to sell drugs.

pharyng-, pharyngo- *combining form.* pharynx: *for example,* pharyngoscope.

pharyngeal /fə rĭn′jē əl/ of or involving the pharynx.

pharyngeal tonsils /tŏn′səls/ the lymphoid nodules on the lateral wall of the pharynx.

pharyngectomy /făr′ĭn jĕk′tə mē/ surgical removal of the pharynx. [pharyng- + -ectomy]

pharyngitis /făr′ĭn jī′tĭs/ inflammation of the mucous membrane and parts of the pharynx. [pharyng- + -itis]

pharyngomycosis /fə rĭng′gō mī kō′sĭs/ a fungal infection of the mucous membrane of the pharynx. [pharyngo- + mycosis]

pharyngoplasty /fə rĭng′gə plăs′tē/ plastic surgery performed on the pharynx, sometimes to cure snoring. [pharyngo- + -plasty]

pharyngoscope /fə rĭng′gə skōp′/ an instrument used to examine the mucous membrane of the pharynx. [pharyngo- + -scope]

pharyngotomy /făr′ĭng gŏt′ə mē/ surgical incision into the pharynx. [pharyngo- + -tomy]

pharynx /făr′ĭngks/ the upper part of the digestive tube above the esophagus and below the mouth located in the throat.

-phasia *suffix.* speech disorder: *for example,* dysphasia.

phenocopy /fē′nə kŏp′ē/ something, such as a trait, caused by environmental factors, but resembling something of genetic origin.

phenotype /fē′nə tīp′/ everything observable about an organism including all the physical parts, metabolism, organs, reflexes, and behaviors.

phenylalanine /fĕn′əl ăl′ə nēn′/ an essential amino found in proteins and essential for nutrition.

phenylketonuria (PKU) /fĕn′əl kē′tə nŏŏr′ē ə/ a congenital inability to metabolize phenylalanine, a common amino acid of proteins, that can cause severe brain damage and mental retardation.

pheresis /fə rē′sĭs/ a procedure for removing blood from a donor, separating out and keeping a specific element, then returning the blood to the donor.

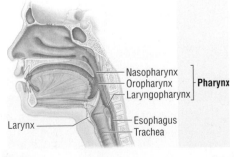

Pharynx

-phil, -phile, -philic, -philia *suffix.* love; desire for: *for example,* necrophilia.

phimosis /fĭ mō'sĭs/ (*pl.* **phimoses** /fĭ mō'sēz/) an abnormal constriction of the foreskin of the penis which results in the inability to uncover the glans penis.

phleb-, phlebo- *combining form.* vein: *for example,* phlebitis.

phlebectasia /flĕb'ĕk tā'zhə/ dilation of a vein. [phleb- + -ectasia]

phlebectomy /flə bĕk'tə mē/ surgical removal of a vein. [phleb- + -ectomy]

phlebitis /flə bī'tĭs/ inflammation of a vein. [phleb- + -itis]

phlebogram /flĕb'ə grăm'/ an x-ray image of a vein made after injection with a dye. *Also called* venogram. [phlebo- + -gram]

phlebography /flə bŏg'rə fē/ taking x-rays of a specific vein after a dye has been injected. *Also called* venography. [phlebo- + -graphy]

phlebosclerosis /flĕb'ō sklĭ rō'sĭs/ hardening of the walls of a vein. [phlebo- + -sclerosis]

phlebostasis /flə bŏs'tə sĭs/ **1.** sluggish movement of blood through the veins, frequently with dilation of the veins. **2.** compressing the veins in the hands and feet as a treatment for congestive heart failure. [phlebo- + -stasis]

phlebotomist /flə bŏt'ə mĭst/ a person trained to draw blood.

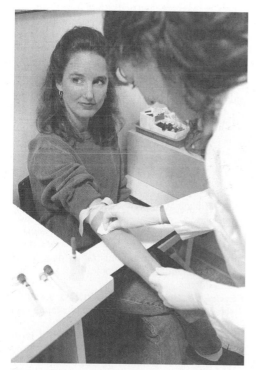

Phlebotomist

phlebotomy /flə bŏt'ə mē/ puncturing a vein to draw blood. *Also called* venotomy. [phlebo- + -tomy]

phlegm /flĕm/ mucus secreted in the lungs and throat and discharged through the mouth.

-phobia *suffix.* fear: *for example,* acrophobia.

phobia /fō'bē ə/ an excessive and irrational fear of an object, activity, or situation.

-phobic *suffix.* suffering from a phobia: *for example,* photophobic.

phobic /fō'bĭk/ **1.** *adj.* suffering from a phobia. **2.** *n.* a person who suffers from a phobia.

phocomelia /fō'kə mē'lē ə/ birth defect in which the arms and/or legs are foreshortened or are not separated from the body, and resemble the flippers of a seal. A side effect of an antinausea drug thalidomide, formerly used in pregnancy.

phon-, phono- *combining form.* sound, voice: *for example,* phonometer.

-phonia *suffix.* sound: *for example,* dysphonia.

phonic /fŏn'ĭk, fō'nĭk/ of or involving the production of sound.

phonology /fə nŏl'ə jē, fō-/ the scientific study of speech sounds. [phon- + -logy]

phonometer /fə nŏm'ĭ tər, fō-/ instrument for the measurement of the loudness of sounds. [phono- + -meter]

phonopathy /fə nŏp'ə thē, fō-/ a disease of the vocal apparatus. [phono- + -pathy]

phonopsia /fə nŏp'sē ə, fō-/ a condition where certain sounds cause the sensation of specific colors. [phon- + -opsia]

phonosurgery /fō'nō sûr'jə rē/ surgical procedures that restore or maintain the voice. [phono- + surgery]

-phoresis *suffix.* carrying, transmission: *for example,* electrophoresis.

-phoria *suffix.* feeling: *for example,* euphoria.

phorometer /fə rŏm'ĭ tər/ an instrument used to measure eye muscle balance, divergence, refraction, etc.

phot-, photo- *combining form.* light: *for example,* photophobia.

photocoagulation /fō'tō kō ăg'yə lā'shən/ a surgical technique used especially in eye surgery to seal tissue and blood vessels by the application of a beam of intense heat, as from a laser. [photo- + coagulation]

photodynamic therapy (PDT) /fō'tō dī năm'ĭk/ **1.** a laser-assisted procedure in eye surgery. **2.** a cancer treatment in which a photosensitizer is injected into the site of the cancer.

photokeratitis /fo'to kĕr'ə tĭ'tĭs/ inflammation of the cornea with burning, blurring, and sensitivity to light, caused by overexposure to ultraviolet light from the sun.

photophobia /fō'tə fō'bē ə/ abnormal sensitivity of the eye to light. [photo- + -phobia]

photophobic /fō′tō fō′bĭk/ of or pertaining to photophobia. [photo- + -phobic]

photopsia /fō tŏp′sē ə/ the condition of experiencing the sensation of flashing lights and colors, caused by electrical or mechanical stimulation of the optic nerve. [phot- + -opsia]

photorefractive keratectomy (PRK) /fō′tō rĭ frăk′tĭv kĕr′ə tĕk′tə mē/ surgical removal by laser of part of the cornea to correct for nearsightedness.

photosensitivity /fō′tō sĕn′sĭ tĭv′ĭ tē/ abnormal sensitivity of the skin to light. [photo- + sensitivity]

phototherapy /fō′tō thĕr′ə pē/ treatment with light, either ultraviolet or full-spectrum; used for newborns with high bilirubin, or adults with seasonal affective disorder. [photo- + therapy]

phren-, phreno- *combining form.* diaphragm. *for example,* phrenectomy.

phrenectomy /frə nĕk′tə mē/ surgical removal of part of the motor nerve controlling the diaphragm. [phren- + -ectomy]

-phrenia *suffix.* mental disorder: *for example,* schizophrenia.

phrenic /frĕn′ĭk/ **1.** of or involving the mind. **2.** of or involving the diaphragm. [phren- + -ic]

phrenic nerve the motor nerve of the diaphragm that arises from the fourth cervical nerve and sends sensory signals to the pericardium.

phrenitis /frə nī′tĭs/ inflammation of the diaphragm. [phren- + -itis]

phrenoplegia /frĕn′ə plē′jē ə/ paralysis of the diaphragm. [phreno- + -plegia]

-phthisis *suffix.* wasting away, shriveling: *for example,* nephrophthisis.

phthisis /thĭ′sĭs, thĭs′ĭs/ any disease marked by a wasting away of the body or a body part.

-phylaxis *suffix.* protection: *for example,* prophylaxis.

physiatrist /fĭ zī′ə trĭst/ a doctor who specializes in treatment of disease or injury by physical methods, such as heat and cold, light, water and electrical stimulation, exercise, manipulation, and mechanical devices.

physical /fĭz′ĭ kəl/ of or involving the body rather than the mind.

physical abuse bad treatment, such as hitting, slapping, pinching, or shaking.

physical examination (PE) examination of the body by auscultation and percussion, visual observation, touching and palpation, and smelling.

physical medicine the treatment of disease and injury mainly by mechanical or physical methods.

Physical Therapist

physical therapist (PT) a person trained in the evaluation and rehabilitation by use of exercise, massage, and active and passive movement to restore use of diseased, injured, or painful areas of the body.

physical therapy (PT) the evaluation and rehabilitation of people with disease, injury, and pain by exercise, massage, and active and passive movement.

physician /fĭ zĭsh′ən/ **1.** a graduate of a college of medicine or osteopathy who is licensed to practice medicine. **2.** a doctor who has a general medical practice as opposed to a surgeon.

physician('s) assistant (PA) a graduate of an accredited program who is licensed to perform certain duties of a physician, such as taking a medical history, making a physical examination, ordering diagnostic tests, etc., under the supervision of a licensed physician.

physician-assisted suicide killing oneself by ingestion or other administration of a lethal substance with the direct or indirect assistance of a doctor.

***Physician's Desk Reference* (PDR)** an annotated guide to prescription drugs available in the United States.

physiology /fĭz′ē ŏl′ə jē/ the branch of biology that studies the functions, activities, and physical and chemical processes within the body and its organs.

phyto- *combining form.* plant: *for example,* phytochemical.

phytochemical /fī′tō kĕm′ĭ kəl/ any of hundreds of health-promoting natural chemicals found in plants; phytonutrient. [phyto- + chemical]

phytodermatitis /fī′tō dûr′mə tī′tĭs/ inflammation of the skin caused by contact with or proximity to a plant. [phyto- + dermatitis]

phytonutrient /fī′tō noō′trē ənt/ phytochemical. [phyto- + nutrient]

phytotherapeutics /fī′tō thĕr′ə pyoō′tĭks/ the use of herbal remedies to prevent or cure diseases. [phyto- + therapeutics]

phytotoxin /fī′tō tŏk′sĭn/ any poisonous chemical compound produced by or derived from a plant. [phyto- + toxin]

pia mater /pī′ə mā′tər, pē′ə mä′tər/ the innermost of the three protective membranes that cover the brain and spinal cord, containing many blood vessels that nourish the tissue within.

pica /pī′kə/ a condition in which the sufferer, usually a young child, eats nonnutritive substances, as chalk or sand, over a long period of time; often associated with iron-deficient anemia.

Pick('s) disease /pĭk(s)/ a dementia caused by the progressive atrophy of parts of the frontal and temporal lobes.

Pickwickian syndrome /pĭk wĭk′ē ən/ a condition with extreme obesity, slow and shallow breathing with elevation of blood CO_2, right heart failure, and general weakness.

PICU *abbreviation.* pediatric intensive care unit.

PID *abbreviation.* pelvic inflammatory disease.

pigment /pĭg′mənt/ a substance that colors the cells it is present in, such as hair, skin, and the irises of the eyes.

pigmentation /pĭg′mən tā′shən/ the coloring of the hair, skin, and irises of the eyes.

pilar /pī′lər/ hairy.

piles /pīlz/ a mass of dilated veins in anal tissue causing inflammation, pain, and itching. *Also called* hemorrhoids.

pill /pĭl/ a medicinal substance in a small round compact mass for swallowing.

pill splitter a device for dividing a pill in half.

pilonidal /pī′lə nī′dəl/ of or involving the growth of hairs embedded under the skin.

pilonidal cyst a pocket within the flesh containing ingrown hairs, usually occurring in the crack of the buttocks just over the tailbone; often very painful.

pilonidal sinus /sī′nəs/ a channel from the surface to a cyst containing ingrown hairs.

pimple /pĭm′pəl/ a papule or pustule, usually found on the face and upper body, and often associated with acne.

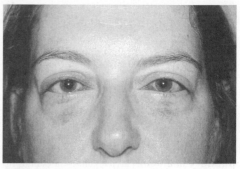

Pinkeye

pin /pĭn/ a plastic, wire, or metal object inserted into the body, used especially to hold pieces of fractured bone in position during healing.

pinch /pĭnch/ **1.** *v.* to squeeze between the tips of the fingers. **2.** *n.* a very small quantity, as of a powder.

pinched nerve pressure on the nerve, compressing it and causing pain.

pineal body /pĭn′ē əl/ pineal gland.

pineal gland an endocrine gland, located deep inside the brain, that releases melatonin, a hormone involved in sleep-wake cycles. *Also called* pineal body.

pinguicula /pĭn gwĭk′yə lə/ or **pinguecula** /pĭn gwĕk′yə lə/ (*pl.* **pinguiculae** /pĭn gwĭk′yə lē′/ or **pingueculae** /pĭn gwĕk′yə lē′/) a yellowish spot sometimes found in the white of the eye of the elderly, formed of thickened conjunctival tissue.

pinkeye /pĭngk′ī′/ an informal term for a very contagious form of acute viral conjunctivitis.

pinna /pĭn′ə/ the shell-like outer structure of the ear visible on the side of the head. *Also called* auricle.

pinocytosis /pĭn′ō sī tō′sĭs/ a process by which a cell membrane forms an indentation that fills with liquid, and then pinches off, leaving a little bubble of liquid inside the cell.

pinosome /pĭn′ə sōm′/ a little fluid-filled bubble within the cell, created by the process of pinocytosis.

pinworm infection an intestinal infection caused by *Enterobius vermicularis.*

PIP *abbreviation.* proximal interphalangeal joints.

piriformis muscle /pĭr′ə fôr′mĭs/ a muscle that begins in the front of the bone at the bottom of the spine just above the tailbone and ends near the top of the thighbone.

pit /pĭt/ **1.** any natural depression on the surface of the body, as a dimple or the armpit. **2.** a depression in the enamel of a tooth.

pitch /pĭch/ the apparent height or depth of the voice or tone, which depends on the relative rapidity of the vibration causing the tone.

pith /pĭth/ *n.* **1.** the center of a hair or feather. **2.** formerly, the medulla oblongata and spinal cord. *v.* **3.** to kill by piercing the medulla at the base of the skull.

pitting edema /ĭ dē'mə/ a kind of edema (swelling) where the flesh remains indented when it is pressed.

pituitary /pĭ tōō'ĭ tĕr'ē/ **1.** *n.* pituitary gland. **2.** *adj.* of or involving the pituitary gland.

pituitary adenoma /ăd'ə nō'mə/ a benign tumor of the pituitary gland, frequently removed so that it won't interfere with the functioning of the gland.

pituitary dwarfism /dwôr'fĭz əm/ lack of normal growth in childhood caused by a lack of growth hormone due to a malfunctioning pituitary gland.

pituitary gigantism /jī găn'tĭz əm/ excessive growth in childhood caused by the production of too much growth hormone by the pituitary gland.

pituitary gland a gland made up of a posterior and an anterior lobe that secretes many different hormones, some of which affect the body directly, such as growth hormone, and others that cause certain other glands to produce hormones, such as thyroid-stimulating hormone. *See also* neurohypophysis, adenohypophysis.

pityriasis alba /pĭt'ə rī'ə sĭs ăl'bə/ a chronic skin disorder of children, with itchy, flaky patches of lighter skin, usually on the face and sometimes the upper body.

pityriasis rosea /rō'zē ə/ a rash, usually on the torso, that begins with a large patch of reddish skin and is followed by 4 to 6 weeks of smaller, usually oval, patches.

PKD *abbreviation.* polycystic kidney disease.

PKU *abbreviation.* phenylketonuria.

placebo /plə sē'bō/ a substance that has no pharmacological effect on the body and is administered as a control in drug trials; patients (and doctors) in a double-blind experiment do not know who is receiving the experimental drug and who is receiving the placebo.

placebo effect a positive response to the taking of a placebo, such as improvement of symptoms, due to the psychological effect of a person believing that he or she has been given medication.

placenta /plə sĕn'tə/ a temporary organ that connects the fetus to the wall of the upper uterus in the mother and transfers oxygen-rich blood and nutrients from the mother to the fetus and waste products from the fetus to the mother, whose body excretes them.

placenta accreta /ə krē'tə/ the abnormal adherence of the fetal membrane that is part of the placenta to the wall of the uterus.

placental /plə sĕn'təl/ of or involving the placenta.

placental dystocia /dĭs tō'shə/ difficulty in ejecting or inability to eject the placenta after delivery.

placenta percreta /pər krē'tə/ the invasion of the uterine wall by the fetal membrane that is part of the placenta; this can lead to the rupture of the uterus.

placenta previa /prē'vē ə/ a condition in which the placenta is attached at the lower end of the uterus, which can lead to bleeding before or during labor and is one of the reasons for a cesarean section.

plague /plāg/ **1.** any epidemic disease having a high death rate. **2.** bubonic plague.

-plakia *suffix.* plaque (small patch on skin): *for example,* erythroplakia.

plan B emergency contraception meant to be taken after unprotected sexual intercourse.

plane /plān/ an imaginary surface that is used in anatomy to identify areas of the body, such as the midsagittal plane.

plantar /plăn'tər/ of or involving the sole of the foot. *Also called* volar.

plantar fasciitis /făsh'ē ĭ'tĭs/ inflammation of fascia on the sole of the foot, most often at the heel.

plantar flexion /flĕk'shən/ turning the toes down; extending the ankle so the foot and toes point downward.

plantar response the turning down of the toes in automatic response to a stroking of the lateral sole of the foot from heel to toes.

plantar wart /wôrt/ a usually painful wart on the sole of the foot.

plaque /plăk/ **1.** a patch of skin. **2.** a buildup of fatty material on the lining of an artery. **3.** microorganisms that grow on the teeth, causing tooth decay and breakdown of gums.

-plasia *suffix.* growth: *for example,* dysplasia.

-plasm *suffix.* tissue: *for example,* cytoplasm.

plasma /plăz'mə/ the fluid part of blood, consisting of water, proteins, salts, nutrients, clotting factors, and hormones.

plasma cell a blood cell that secretes antibodies called immunoglobulins.

plasmacytoma /plăz'mə sī tō'mə/ a malignant tumor of plasma cells that occurs in bone marrow.

plasma donation the sale, or occasionally donation, of blood that is separated immediately into plasma and blood cells by centrifuging; the blood cells are returned intravenously to the donor and the blood bank retains the plasma for transfusion into another patient.

plasmapheresis /plăz'mə fə rē'sĭs/ a process that uses centrifuging to separate the blood cells from plasma; the blood cells are then reintroduced to the patient. [plasma + -pheresis]

plasma protein   proteins, such as albumin, globulin, fibrinogen, and prothrombin, found in blood plasma.

plasmid /plăz′mĭd/   independent segments of DNA occurring in bacteria and yeasts, used in recombinant DNA technology to transfer genetic material from one species to another.

plaster /plăs′tər/   a material, usually plaster of Paris, that is applied to a body part and allowed to harden in order to immobilize that part or to make an impression or mold.

plaster of Paris /păr′ĭs/   calcined gypsum in a white powdery form, used to make casts and stiff bandages; sets rapidly when mixed with water.

-plastic   *suffix.* forming: *for example,* achondroplastic.

plastic surgeon   a surgeon who specializes in the construction, reconstruction, or other improvement in the shape and appearance of body structures that are missing, damaged, or misshapen.

plastic surgery   the surgical specialty involved in the construction, reconstruction, or other improvement in the shape and appearance of body structures that are missing, damaged, or misshapen. *Also called* rhytidoplasty.

-plasty   *suffix.* shaping, forming, repairing: *for example,* rhinoplasty.

plate /plāt/   *n.* **1.** a thin flattened part or portion, such as a flattened process of a bone. **2.** an incorrect reference to a full denture. **3.** a shallow covered dish for culturing microorganisms. *v.* **4.** to culture microorganisms in a culture plate.

platelet /plāt′lĭt/   an irregular-shaped fragment of certain very large cells (megakaryocytes) in bone marrow that functions in clotting in the bloodstream. *Also called* thrombocyte.

platelet aggregation   /ăg′rĭ gā′shən/   the clumping together of platelets in the bloodstream.

platelet count (PLT)   the number of platelets in a volume of whole blood, reported as platelets per cubic centimeter.

platinum (Pt) /plăt′ə nəm, plăt′nəm/   a metallic element, used to prevent or inhibit the growth of tumors.

play therapy   a kind of psychological therapy used mostly with young children, in which the child can express his or her feelings and problems through drawing, playing with dolls or clay figures, etc.

-plegia   *suffix.* paralysis: *for example,* paraplegia.

-plegic   *suffix.* a person who is paralyzed: *for example,* quadriplegic.

pleiotropic /plī′ə trŏp′ĭk/   (of a gene) affecting more than one genetic characteristic.

pleomorphic /plē′ə môr′fĭk/   (of a tumor) made up of many types of cells.

pleur-, pleuro-   *combining form.* **1.** pleura: *for example,* pleurocentesis. **2.** rib, side: *for example,* pleuralgia.

pleura /plŏŏr′ə/ (pl. **plurae** /plŏŏr′ē/)   a double layer of membrane on the outside of the lung and lining the chest wall. *See also* parietal pleura, visceral pleura.

pleural /plŏŏr′əl/   of or involving the pleura.

pleural cavity   the potential space between the lung and the chest wall; normally contains a little fluid. *Also called* pleural space.

Plastic Surgeon (holding breast implant)

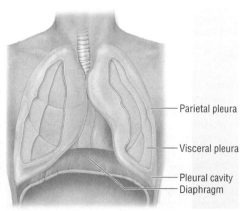

Parietal pleura

Visceral pleura

Pleural cavity
Diaphragm

Pleura

pleural effusion (PE) /ĭ fyōō'zhən/ accumulation of fluid in the pleural cavity.

pleuralgia /plōō răl'jē ə, -jə/ **1.** pain in the chest, often on one side only. **2.** pain in the side.

pleural rub a low-pitched grating or creaking sound that occurs when inflamed plurae rub together, especially when inhaling.

pleural space the potential space between the lung and the chest wall; normally contains a little fluid. *Also called* pleural cavity.

pleurectomy /plōō rĕk'tə mē/ the surgical removal of a part of the pleura. [pleur- + -ectomy]

pleurisy /plōōr'ə sē/ inflamation of the pleura. *Also called* pleuritis.

pleuritis /plōō rī'tĭs/ pleurisy. [pleur- + -itis]

pleurocentesis /plōōr'ō sĕn tē'sĭs/ a puncturing of the pleural cavity with a hollow instrument, such as a needle or trocar, to draw out excess fluid. *Also called* thoracentesis, thoracocentesis. [pleuro- + -centesis]

pleurodesis /plōō rŏd'ə sĭs/ a procedure to cause the two pleural membranes that line a lung to adhere to each other, eliminating the pleural cavity on purpose so that it can not fill up with fluid. [pleuro- + -desis]

pleurodynia /plōōr'ə dĭn'ē ə/ **1.** a virus infection causing fever, headache, and severe pain in the chest and abdomen. *Also called* Bornholm's disease. **2.** any pain in the chest or side. [pleuro- + -dynia]

pleurotomy /plōō rŏt'ə mē/ a surgical incision into the chest wall. *Also called* thoracotomy. [pleuro- + -tomy]

plexus /plĕk'səs/ a network of nerves or blood vessels.

PLT *abbreviation.* platelet count.

plug /plŭg/ any mass or clump of cells that closes an opening or fills a hole.

Plummer-Vinson('s) syndrome /plŭm'ər vĭn'sən(z)/ a disorder, with iron-deficiency anemia, cracks at the corners of the mouth, a painful tongue, and sometimes difficulties in eating, usually affecting middle-aged women.

PM, p.m. *abbreviation.* Latin *post meridian,* at night.

PMS *abbreviation.* premenstrual syndrome.

PN *abbreviation.* parenteral nutrition.

-pnea *suffix.* breath, breathing, respiration: *for example,* apnea.

pneum-, pneuma-, pneumat-, pneumato-, pneumo- *combining form.* **1.** breath. **2.** air. *For example,* pneumococcus.

pneumatic larynx /nōō măt'ĭk lăr'ĭngks/ a mechanical device that enables a person whose larynx has been removed to speak.

pneumatic otoscopy /ō tŏs'kə pē/ an examination of the ear with a device that emits air at various pressures to strike the eardrum.

pneumatocele /nōō măt'ə sēl'/ or **pneumocele** /nōō'mə sēl'/ **1.** intrusion of lung tissue through a hole in or a hernia in the chest wall. **2.** an abnormal gaseous or air-filled swelling. **3.** a thin-walled pocket within a lung. [pneumato- + -cele]

pneumobacillus /nōō'mō bə sĭl'əs/ a bacterium, *Klebsiella pneumoniae,* that causes pneumonia and some other diseases of the respiratory system. [pneumo- + bacillus]

pneumococcal meningitis /nōō'mə kŏk'əl mĕn'ĭn jī'tĭs/ meningitis caused by a pneumococcus bacteria.

pneumococcal pneumonia /nōō mōn'yə/ pneumonia caused by the bacterium *Diplococcus pneumoniae.*

pneumococcus /nōō'mə kŏk'əs/ (*pl.* **pneumococci** /nōō'mə kŏk'sī/) a bacteria of the species *Diplococcus pneumoniae,* causing pneumonia, inflammation of the middle ear, meningitis, and other diseases, especially of the respiratory tract. [pneumo- + -coccus]

pneumoconiosis /nōō'mō kō'nē ō'sĭs/ any chronic lung diseases, such as asbestosis and silicosis, caused by long-term inhalation of particulate matter, such as coal dust. *Also called* pneumoniosis.

pneumocystis /nōō'mə sĭs'tĭs/ a protozoan, *Pneumocystis jiroveci* (formerly *Pneumocystis carinii*), that causes pneumocystis pneumonia in immunosuppressed patients.

Pneumocystis carinii /kə rī'nē ī'/ the former classification of the species of protozoan that causes pneumocystis pneumonia in immunosuppressed patients.

pneumocystis carinii **pneumonia (PCP)** /nōō mōn'yə/ pneumocystis pneumonia.

pneumocystis pneumonia a lung infection caused by the protozoan *Pneumocystis jiroveci* in immunosuppressed patients.

pneumocyte /nōō'mə sīt'/ any of the specialized cells found in the alveoli. [pneumo- + -cyte]

pneumolith /nōō'mə lĭth/ a stone of hard mineral and crystal that forms in a lung. [pneumo- + -lith]

pneumomediastinum /nōō'mō mē'dē ə stī'nəm/ the presence of air or gas in the tissues between the lungs. [pneumo- + mediastinum]

pneumon-, pneumono- *combining form.* breath; lung: *for example,* pneumonectomy.

pneumonectomy /nōō'mə nĕk'tə mē/ surgical excision of all or part of a lung. [pneumon- + -ectomy]

pneumonia /nōō mōn'yə/ an inflammation of the lungs, with congestion, usually caused by a bacterial or viral infection. [pneumon- + -ia]

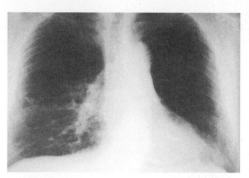

Pneumonia

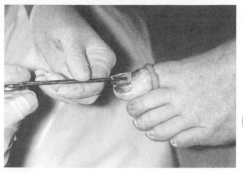

Podiatrist

pneumonic plague /nōō mŏn′ĭk plāg′/ a form of plague with hardening of the lungs, bloody mucus, and high fever.

pneumoniosis /nōō′mə nī′ə sĭs/ any chronic lung diseases, such as asbestosis and silicosis, caused by long-term inhalation of particulate matter, such as coal dust. *Also called* pneumoconiosis.

pneumonitis /nōō′mə nī′tĭs/ inflammation of the lungs. [pneumon- + -itis]

pneumonocentesis /nōō′mə nō sĕn tē′sĭs/ puncturing a lung with a hollow instrument, such as a needle or trocar, in order to withdraw fluid. [pneumono- + -centesis]

pneumonopathy /nōō′mə nŏp′ə the/ any disease or disorder of the lungs. [pneumono- + -pathy]

pneumonopexy /nōō′mə nə pĕk′sē/ the surgical fixing in place of a lung. [pneumono- + -pexy]

pneumonorrhagia /nōō′mə nə rā′jē ə/ a heavy discharge from the lungs. [pneumono- + -rrhagia]

pneumonotomy /nōō′mə nŏt′ə mē/ a surgical incision into a lung. [pneumono- + -tomy]

pneumopericardium /nōō′mō pĕr′ĭ kär′dē əm/ presence of gas or air in the pericardium (the protective membranous sac around the heart). [pneumo- + pericardium]

pneumothorax /nōō′mə thôr′ăks/ the presence of gas or air in a pleural cavity, i.e. between the lung and the chest wall; may cause the lung to collapse. [pneumo- + thorax]

PNF technique proprioceptive neuromuscular facilitation, a technique in massage therapy that relies on stimulating reflexes within muscles by alternating stretching and relaxing of muscles.

PNS *abbreviation.* peripheral nervous system.

p.o., PO *abbreviation.* Latin *per os,* by mouth.

pock /pŏk/ **1.** an eruptive skin pustule, such as the one in smallpox. **2.** the scar or pit left by such a pustule.

pocket /pŏk′ĭt/ a pouchlike cavity or hollow.

pockmarks /pŏk′märks′/ scars or pits left by the pocks in smallpox or chickenpox.

pod-, podo- *combining form.* foot, feet: *for example,* podocyte.

podagra /pō dăg′rə/ sharp pain in the foot, especially from gout.

podiatric /pō′dē ăt′rĭk/ of or involving podiatry.

podiatrist /pə dī′ə trĭst/ a person trained and licensed to diagnose and treat disorders of the foot. *Also called* chiropodist.

podiatry /pə dī′ə trē/ the diagnosis and treatment of diseases of the foot. *Also called* chiropody.

podocyte /pŏd′ə sīt′/ a cell with a club-shaped foot found in the tiny round structure at the end of the nephron in the kidney, through which blood is filtered. [podo- + -cyte]

-poiesis *suffix.* formation, production: *for example,* erythropoeisis.

-poietic *suffix.* forming, producing: *for example,* hemopoietic.

poikilo- *combining form.* varied, irregular: *for example,* poikilocyte.

poikilocyte /poi′kə lə sīt′/ an irregularly shaped red blood cell. [poikilo- + -cyte]

poikilocytosis /poi′kə lō sī tō′sĭs/ the presence of irregularly shaped red blood cells in the bloodstream.

poikiloderma /poi′kə lə dûr′mə/ a skin disorder with irregular patches of various coloration and dilation of blood vessels in those areas. [poikilo- + -derma]

point /point/ **1.** the sharp end of an object. **2.** a tiny spot different from surrounding tissue in color, texture, etc. **3.** the stage at which the surface of an abscess is about to rupture.

pointillage /pwăn′tē yäzh′/ massage with the fingertips.

point of service (POS) the location, such as a hospital, doctor's office, or clinic, where a patient sees a doctor or receives medical treatment.

poison /poi′zən/   a substance taken into the body that destroys or impairs normal functioning; may be fatal.

poisoning /poi′zə nĭng/   **1.** the illness caused by the introduction of a substance that destroys or impairs normal functioning. **2.** the administering of a substance that destroys or impairs normal functioning.

poison ivy   a leafy vine that produces an oily substance which causes severe itching and blistering on contact (contact dermatitis) and which may be spread from one part of the body to another by the patient's scratching.

polarity therapy /pō lăr′ĭ tē/   a type of energy-based therapy used in alternative medicine (particularly in massage therapy) in which it is thought that stress is released and health achieved when energy fields flow smoothly.

polio /pō′lē ō′/   poliomyelitis.

poliomyelitis /pō′lē ō mī′ə lī′tĭs/   an acute infectious viral gastrointestinal disease with fever, headache, sore throat, and vomiting and in some cases, paralysis, if the virus escapes the GI tract and infects the anterior horn cells of the spinal cord which direct muscle contraction. *Also called* polio.

pollen /pŏl′ən/   the microscopic spores of flowering plants, to which some people are allergic.

pollen count   a measure of air-borne pollen, averaged from the number of spores that are found on slides put outdoors for a certain amount of time.

pollenosis /pŏl′ə nō′sĭs/   pollinosis.

pollex /pŏl′ĕks/ (*pl.* **pollices** /pŏl′ə sēz′/)   the thumb.

pollinosis /pŏl′ə nō′sĭs/   hay fever caused by exposure to the pollen of certain plants, especially ragweed; pollenosis

poly-   *prefix.* many, much: *for example,* polyarthritis.

polyarteritis /pŏl′ē är′tə rī′tĭs/   inflammation of a number of arteries. [poly- + arteritis]

polyarthralgia /pŏl′ē är thrăl′jē ə, -jə/   pain in many joints. [poly- + arthralgia]

polyarthritis /pŏl′ē är thrī′tĭs/   arthritis occurring in more than one joint. [poly- + arthritis]

polyarticular /pŏl′ē är tĭk′yə lər/   involving or affecting many joints. [poly- + articular]

polyclonal /pŏl′ī klō′nəl/   coming from more than a single cell, as opposed to monoclonal.

polycystic /pŏl′ī sĭs′tĭk/   of or containing many cysts. [poly- + cystic]

polycystic kidney disease (PKD)   an inherited disease in which multiple pockets of fluid are found in the kidney, reducing kidney function.

polycystic ovary syndrome /ō′və rē/   a condition in woman marked by lack of ovulation, acne, obesity, and excess body hair.

polycythemia /pŏl′ī sī thē′mē ə/   the condition of having more than normal number of red blood cells.

polycythemia vera (PV) /vĭr′ə/   a disease in which the overproduction of red blood cells is caused by underlying bone marrow disorder.

polydactylism /pŏl′ĭ dăk′tə lĭz′əm/   having more than five fingers or toes. [poly- + dactyl- + -ism]

polydactyly /pŏl′ī dăk′tə lē/   the presence of more than five fingers or toes. *Also called* hexadactyly.

polydipsia /pŏl′ī dĭp′sē ə/   constant excessive thirst.

polyethylene (PE) tube /pŏl′ē ĕth′ə lēn′/   a tube made of plastic.

polygenic /pŏl′ī jĕn′ĭk/   of or involving a hereditary characteristic or disease that is controlled by many genes. [poly- + -genic]

polymorphic /pŏl′ī môr′fĭk/   occuring in more than one shape.

polymorphism /pŏl′ī môr′fĭz əm/   the existence of more than one form in a species.

polymyalgia /pŏl′ī mī ăl′jē ə, -jə/   pain in more than one muscle or muscle group. [poly- + myalgia]

polymyositis /pŏl′ī mī′ə sī′tĭs/   inflammation of a number of muscles at the same time. [poly- + myositis]

polyneuralgia /pŏl′ī nōō răl′jē ə, -jə/   sharp stabbing or throbbing pain along the paths of several nerves. [poly- + neuralgia]

polyneuritis /pŏl′ī nōō rī′tĭs/   inflammation of numerous nerves. [poly- + neuritis]

polyneuropathy /pŏl′ī nōō rŏp′ə thē/   any disease involving a number of nerves of the peripheral nervous system. [poly- + neuropathy]

polyp /pŏl′ĭp/   a growth on a mucosal lining, such as of the nose or colon.

polypectomy /pŏl′ī pĕk′tə mē/   the surgical removal of one or more polyps. [polyp + -ectomy]

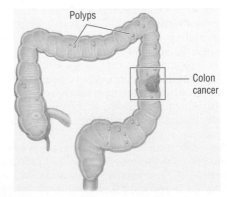

Polyp

polyphobia /pŏl′ĭ fō′bē ə/ excessive fear of many different things; having multiple phobias. [poly- + -phobia]

polyploid /pŏl′ĭ ploid′/ having more than twice the normal number of chromosomes.

polyposis /pŏl′ĭ pō′sĭs/ the growth of many polyps.

polysaccharide /pŏl′ē săk′ə rīd′/ a complex carbohydrate, such as starch, that can be broken down by acids or enzymes to simple sugars.

polysomnography (PSG) /pŏl′ĭ sŏm nŏg′rə fē/ the continuous recording of physiologic functions, such as electrical impulses in the brain and heart and eye movements, during sleep. [poly- + somno- + -graphy]

polyuria /pŏl′ē yoor′ē ə/ excessive urination, often a sign of diabetes. [poly- + -uria]

pons /pŏnz/ (pl. **pontes** /pŏn′tēz/) the round structure at the base of the brain, just above the medulla, involved in brainstem functions.

pool /pool/ n. **1.** the accumulation of blood in a body site. **2.** a source of similar cells or other substances. v. **3.** to mix blood from several donors. **4.** to contribute and share in financial and other resources.

popliteal /pŏp lĭt′ē əl, -lĭ tē′əl/ of or involving the back of the knee.

popliteal artery /är′tə rē/ the artery that passes through the back of the knee.

popliteal fossa /fŏs′ə/ the diamond-shaped channel behind the knee, through which the popliteal artery and vein and the tibial nerve run.

pore /pôr/ a tiny opening on the surface of the skin.

porencephaly /pôr′ĕn sĕf′ə lē/ the presence of cavities in the brain. [por(e) + encephal- + -y]

-porosis suffix. lessening in density; thinning out: for example, osteoporosis.

porphyria /pôr fêr′ē ə/ any of a group of usually inherited disorders in the production of heme (the part of hemoglobin that carries the oxygen).

porta /pôr′tə/ the thin opening into an organ or gland through which nerves, ducts, and blood vessels pass. Also called hilum, hilus.

portal /pôr′təl/ **1.** n. an opening into an organ. **2.** adj. of or involving an entrance, especially to the liver.

portal vein a large vein that carries blood to the liver from the stomach, intestine, pancreas, and spleen.

port wine stain a large purplish birthmark, usually on the face or neck.

POS abbreviation. point of service.

position /pə zĭsh′ən/ **1.** n. a particular way in which the body is placed for examination or therapeutic reasons, as in the Trendelenburg position. **2.** v. to place the body in a specific way for examination or therapy.

positive /pŏz′ĭ tĭv/ indicating a response to a test or other diagnostic procedure showing the presence of the tested substance or function

positive end-expiratory pressure (PEEP) /ĭk spī′rə tôr′ē/ a method of assisted breathing in which pressure in the airway remains higher than atmospheric pressure at the end of each exhalation.

positive pressure ventilation use of a mechanical respirator to provide oxygen to a patient whose own breathing is inadequate or paralyzed.

positron emission tomography (PET) /pŏz′ĭ trŏn ĭ mĭsh′ən tə mŏg′rə fē/ the process of making two-dimensional images of soft tissue, such as the brain, using radioactive isotopes and x-rays of a selected plane of the body.

positron emission tomography (PET) scan an image produced using radioactive isotopes and x-rays of soft tissue in a selected plane of the body.

posology /pə sŏl′ə jē/ the branch of pharmacology that specializes in determining the best doses of medications.

post- prefix. after, following: for example, postmortem.

post /pōst/ **1.** a slender rod inserted into a prepared root canal, cemented in place, on which a false tooth is mounted. **2.** a postmortem examination; an autopsy.

post-anesthesia care unit (PACU) a hospital unit where patients who have just had surgery are cared for, usually until they awaken from anesthesia. It was formerly called the recovery room.

postcibal /pōst sī′bəl/ after eating.

post cibum (p.c.) /pōst sī′bəm/ abbreviation. after a meal (in prescriptions).

postcoital /pōst kō′ĭ təl/ after intercourse. [post- + coital]

postcoital contraception /kŏn′trə sĕp′shən/ any of various techniques used to prevent implantation after intercourse has occurred, including various morning-after pills or the insertion of an IUD within 5 days after intercourse.

posterior /pŏ stêr′ē ər/ **1.** at the back of the body. **2.** nearest the back of the body.

posterior chamber a space in the eye behind the iris and the lens that is filled with vitreous humor (a transparent, jelly-like fluid).

posterior cruciate ligament (PCL) /kroo′shē ĭt lĭg′ə mənt/ a ligament of the knee joint that connects the bottom of the thigh bone to the top of the shin bone, crossing behind a similar ligament that crosses in front.

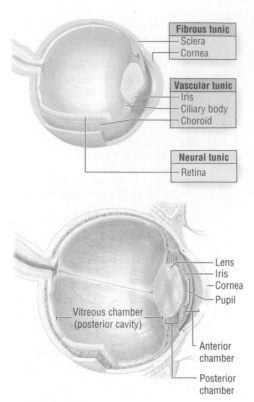

Posterior Chamber

posterior lobe the hind lobe of the pituitary gland that produces hormones governing water balance in the cells, uterine contractions and lactation, and melanin production. *Also called* neurohypophysis.

posteroanterior (PA) /pŏ stêr′ē ō ăn têr′ē ər/ in a direction from the back of a body part to the front.

posterolateral /pŏ stêr′ē ō lăt′ər əl/ behind and away from the midline.

postfebrile /pōst fē′brəl, -brīl, -fĕb′rəl/ taking place after a fever has returned to normal. [post- + febrile]

posthitis /pŏs thī′tĭs/ inflammation of the foreskin.

postictal /pōst ĭk′təl/ taking place after cessation of a seizure.

postmaturity /pōst mə chŏŏr′ĭ tē/ referring to a fetus that is more than one week late, that is, when a gestation has passed 42 weeks and the placenta may have become inadequate to provide all the nourishment the fetus needs. [post- + maturity]

postmenopausal /pōst′mĕn ə pô′zəl/ occurring after menses has stopped. [post- + menopausal]

postmenopause /pōst mĕn′ə pôz′/ the period after menses has stopped. [post- + menopause]

postmortem /pōst môr′təm/ **1.** *adv.* after death has occurred. **2.** *n.* a postmortem examination; autopsy.

postmortem examination a physical examination of a dead body to discover the cause of death. *Also called* autopsy, necropsy.

postnasal drip /pōst nā′zəl/ the secretion of mucus from the rear of the nasal cavity into the back of the throat.

postnatal /pōst nā′təl/ occurring after birth.

postop or **post-op** /pōst ŏp′/ postoperative.

postoperative /pōst ŏp′ər ə tĭv/ occurring after an operation.

postoperative care nursing and medical care given after surgery.

postpartum /pōst pär′təm/ occurring after giving birth. [post- + -partum]

postpartum depression (PPD) /dĭ prĕsh′ən/ a severe depression in the mother shortly after childbirth that can last for up to a year without treatment but is treatable with medication and talk therapy.

postpartum psychosis /sī kō′sĭs/ a severe mental illness in the mother within a few months of childbirth that may include hearing voices and visual hallucinations

postpolio muscular atrophy (PPMA) /pōst pō′ lē ō mŭs′kyə lər ăt′rə fē/ a wasting of muscle sometimes found as part of postpolio syndrome.

postpolio syndrome (PPS) progressive fatigue, pain, and sometimes muscle deterioration occurring 20 to 40 years after having polio, usually due to a new condition, such as diabetes or a spinal problem.

postprandial /pōst prăn′dē əl/ after a meal.

postprandial blood sugar a blood glucose test, taken a specified time after a meal, used in diabetes management.

posttraumatic stress /pōst′trə măt′ĭk/ severe anxiety occurring after a very disturbing or life-threatening situation, such as battle, a car accident, or a criminal assault.

posttraumatic stress disorder (PTSD) severe anxiety that may develop after a very disturbing or life-threatening experience, marked by flashbacks, horrifying memories, recurring fears, and feelings of helplessness.

postural /pŏs′chər əl/ of or involving posture.

postural drainage a treatment for congested lungs, in which the patient assumes a particular position (depending or which lobe is affected and where in the lobe), such that gravity will assist the drainage, while the patient coughs.

postural hypotension /hī′pō tĕn′shən/ a drop in blood pressure on standing up.

posture /pŏs′chər/ the position of the body and the relationship of its element.

Posture

potassium (K) /pə tăs′ē əm/ an element necessary for cells to function properly in the
body. *See also* hyperkalemia, hypokalemia.
potency /pō′tən sē/ the effectiveness or
strength of a drug.
potent /pō′tənt/ **1.** being strong and powerful.
2. of males, able to copulate. **3.** of medicine,
effective.
potentiation /pə tĕn′shē ā′shən/ the increase
in potency or strength; intensification.
potion /pō′shən/ **1.** a dose of liquid medicine.
2. a drink. **3.** a poison.
poultice /pōl′tĭs/ a moist paste of bread or
meat and herbs and other medications, ground
up and wet with oil or liquid, applied hot to the
afflicted area.
pound /pound/ a unit of weight equal to 16
ounces.
power of attorney a legal document written
by the patient assigning to someone else the
right to make decisions on his or her behalf.
pox /pŏks/ a disease, such as smallpox, having
many skin pustules.
poxvirus /pŏks′vī′rəs/ any of a group of large,
brick-shaped DNA-containing viruses that infect humans and other animals, including the
viruses of smallpox and various other poxes.
PPD *abbreviation.* **1.** postpartum depression.
2. purified protein derivative, used in a skin
test for tuberculosis.
PPD skin test or PPD test a skin test used to
determine if the tuberculosis-causing bacteria,

Mycobacterium tuberculosis, is present. *Also
called* Mantoux test.
PPMA *abbreviation.* postpolio muscular atrophy.
PPO *abbreviation.* preferred provider organization.
PPS *abbreviation.* postpolio syndrome.
PR *abbreviation.* per rectum.
practice /prăk′tĭs/ the use of knowledge and
skill by a trained and licensed health care professional to provide a service in the prevention, diagnosis, and treatment of illness and in
the maintenance of health.
practitioner /prăk tĭsh′ə nər/ a person who
has met the professional and legal requirements necessary to provide a health care
service, such as a physician or nurse or dental
hygienist.
Prader-Willi(′s) syndrome /prä′dər vĭl′ē(z)/
a group of congenital characteristics, including a lack of proper muscle tone, mental retardation, small hands, feet, and genitals, short
stature, and feeding difficulties that overcor-
rect later in infancy and can lead to obesity.
praxis /prăk′sĭs/ the process of planning and
carrying out a physical action in response to a
stimulus in the environment; a term used in
occupational therapy.
PRBC *abbreviation.* packed red blood cells.
pre- *prefix. before; for example,* preanesthetic.
preanesthetic /prē′ăn əs thĕt′ĭk/ occurring
before anesthesia is given. [pre- + anesthetic]
preauthorization /prē′ô thə rə zā′shən/ prior
authorization from a payer for services to be
provided; if not received, the procedure is
usually not covered by insurance. [pre- + au-
thorization]
precancerous /prē kăn′sər əs/ of a cell, in a
stage liable to become cancerous. *Also called*
premalignant. [pre- + cancerous]
preclinical /prē klĭn′ĭ kəl/ before a disease
can be observed. [pre- + clinical]
precocious /prĭ kō′shəs/ developing more
rapidly (earlier) than normal, especially
mentally.
precocious puberty /pyōō′bər tē/ reaching
puberty earlier than normal.
preconscious /prē kŏn′shəs/ in psychoanalysis, the part of the mind from which forgotten
thoughts, experiences, and memories can be
brought into awareness. [pre- + conscious]
precordial /prē kôr′dē əl/ of or involving the
precordium.
precordium /prē kôr′dē əm/ the surface of
the lower part of the thoracic cavity that lies
above the heart.
prediabetic /prē′dī ə bĕt′ĭk/ referring to a degree of impairment of carbohydrate metabolism that has not yet become full-fledged diabetes. [pre- + diabetic]

predispose /prē′dĭ spōz′/   to make or become susceptible to; have a tendency toward.

preeclampsia /prē′ĭ klămp′sē ə/   a condition of late pregnancy with high blood pressure, fluid retention, weight gain, albumin in the urine, sometimes progressing to eclampsia. [pre- + eclampsia]

preemie/premie /prē′mē/   an infant born prematurely.

preexcitation /prē′ĕk sī tā′shən/   early phase of activation of part of the heart muscle. [pre- + excitation]

preexisting condition /prē′ĭg sĭs′tĭng kən dĭsh′ən/   a patient's medical condition that existed prior to coverage by a new insurer.

preferred provider   a health care provider that is participating in a particular health insurance organization.

preferred provider organization (PPO)   a health care service that negotiates fixed rates for healthcare services to its insured clients.

pregnancy /prĕg′nən sē/   the period from conception to delivery, during which a woman carries the embryo/fetus in her uterus.

pregnancy test   any of a variety of tests of the blood or urine to determine if a woman is pregnant.

pregnant /prĕg′nənt/   having an embryo/fetus developing within the body.

prehypertension /prē′hī pər tĕn′shən/   blood pressure from 120–139 (systolic) over 80–89 (diastolic), commonly measured over a year. [pre- + hypertension]

preictal /prē ĭk′təl/   taking place before a stroke or seizure.

premalignant /prē′mə lĭg′nənt/   of a cell, in a stage liable to become cancerous. *Also called* precancerous. [pre- + malignant]

premature /prē′mə chŏŏr′/   **1.** referring to an infant born less than 37 weeks after conception. **2.** referring to anything that occurs before the expected time. [pre- + mature]

premature atrial contractions (PACs) /ā′trē əl kən trăc′shənz/   early contractions of upper chambers of the heart, caused by abnormal

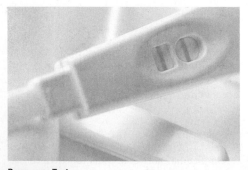

Pregnancy Test

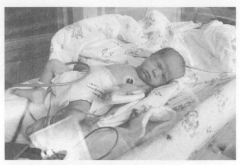

Premature Infant

electrical activity and disrupting normal heartbeat.

premature birth   delivering an infant after 20 weeks but less than 37 weeks after conception.

premature ejaculation   /ĭ jăk′yə lā′shən/   ejaculation that occurs before, at the moment of, or soon after penetration.

premature infant   an infant who was born after 20 but before 37 weeks of gestation.

premature menopause /mĕn′ə pôz′/   menopause that occurs before 40 years of age.

premature ventricular contractions (PVCs) /vĕn trĭk′yə lər kən trăk′shənz/   early contraction of the lower chambers of the heart, caused by abnormal electrical activity and sometimes experienced as palpitations.

prematurity /prē′mə chŏŏr′ĭ tē/   the condition of being born before 37 weeks of gestation.

premedication /prē′mĕd ĭ kā′shən/   **1.** medication given in advance of the administration of an anesthetic. **2.** administration of drugs before treatment to enhance their therapeutic effect and safety. [pre- + medication]

premenstrual /prē mĕn′strŏŏ əl/   taking place before a menstrual period. [pre- + menstrual]

premenstrual phase   the period of time preceding menstruation, when premenstrual syndrome occurs.

premenstrual syndrome (PMS)   a group of symptoms, one or more of which that may take place in the days leading up to a menstrual period, including depression, irritability, bloating, etc.

premie/preemie /prē′mē/   an infant born prematurely.

premolar /prē mō′lər/   any of eight teeth located between the molars in the back of the mouth and the cuspids.

prenatal /prē nā′təl/   before birth or before giving birth. [pre- + natal]

prenatal care   care given to mother and fetus during pregnancy.

preop / prē′ŏp′ / short for preoperative.

preoperative / prē ŏp′ər ə tĭv / before surgery.

prepatellar bursa / prē′pə tĕl′ər bûr′sə / a fluid-containing sac lying between the front of the kneecap and the skin. [pre- + patellar]

prepubertal / prē pyoo′bər təl / referring to the time before puberty has occurred.

prepubescent / prē′pyoo bĕs′ənt / involving or about the time prior to the onset of puberty.

prepuce / prē′pyoos / the fold of skin that covers the head of the penis. *Also called* foreskin.

presbycousis / prĕz′bĭ kyoo′sĭs / or **presbyacusia** / prĕz′bē ə kyoo′zhə / or **presbyacusis** / prĕz′bē ə kyoo′sĭs / age-related hearing loss.

presbyopia / prĕz′bē ō′pē ə / age-related loss of the ability to focus at close range, due to loss of elasticity of the lens.

prescribe / prĭ skrīb′ / to order the use of a particular medication, device, or other treatment.

prescription / prĭ skrĭp′shən / a doctor's order for the administration of a medication, device, or other treatment.

prescription drug a medication that requires a doctor's prescription before it can be dispensed.

present / prĭ zĕnt′ / **1.** (of the part of a fetus) to appear first at the cervix during labor. **2.** (of a patient) to appear for a medical or psychological examination showing a symptom or set of symptoms.

presentation / prē′zĕn tā′shən, prĕz′ən- / **1.** the position of the fetus in the uterus at the beginning of labor. **2.** the part of the fetus that first appears at the cervix during labor. **3.** the position of the fetus during a digital examination during pregnancy.

pressor / prĕs′ər / **1.** *adj.* increasing the activity of a part or function, as of a nerve. **2.** elevating blood pressure. **3.** *n.* any of several drugs, such as epinephrine, used to increase the blood pressure of a patient in shock.

pressure / prĕsh′ər / **1.** stress or force exerted on a body, as by tension, weight, or pulling. **2.** compression. **3.** the quotient obtained by dividing a force by the area of the surface on which it acts.

pressure point a point on the body where the application of pressure will slow or stop bleeding.

pressure sore or **pressure ulcer** / ŭl′sər / a chronic ulcer of the skin and flesh above a bony part, found in bedridden or immobile patients due to constant pressure from sitting or lying on the area. *Also called* bedsore, decubitus ulcer.

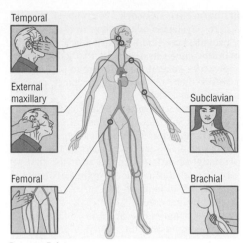

Pressure Points

presystole / prē sĭs′tə lē / the moments in the heart's cycle that just precede systole. [pre- + systole]

presystolic / prē′sĭ stŏl′ĭk / regarding or denoting the moments in the heart's cycle that just precede systole. [pre- + systolic]

preventative / prĭ vĕn′tə tĭv / **1.** *adj.* (*also* **preventive** / prĭ vĕn′tĭv /) intended to prevent disease. **2.** *n.* a drug or treatment intended to prevent a disease.

preventive medicine a branch of medicine specializing in the prevention of disease and the promotion of general health and well-being.

priapism / prī′ə pĭz′əm / a condition in which the penis remains abnormally and painfully erect, without sexual desire.

primary / prī′mĕr ē, -mə rē / first or most important in time or development.

primary amenorrhea / ā′mĕn ə rē′ə / absence of menstruation where there has never been a menstrual period.

primary amyloidosis / ăm′ə loi dō′sĭs / an accumulation of insoluble lipoprotein material in tissues and organs that is not a consequence of some other condition.

primary atelectasis / ăt′ə lĕk′tə sĭs / failure of the lungs to expand after birth.

primary biliary cirrhosis / bĭl′ē ĕr′ē sĭ rō′sĭs / a disease marked by inflammation and destruction of the small bile ducts in the liver, accompanied by itching and jaundice, and leading to cirrhosis of the liver.

primary care medical care provided by a general physician, pediatrician, or internist who provides diagnosis, treatment, and referrals to specialists as needed.

primary care network a group of primary care physicians who belong to a network of providers covered by a particular insurer.

primary care physician (PCP) a doctor who provides general medical care to patients and refers them to specialists or other medical services as needed.

primary care provider (PCP) a health care provider who provides medical care to patients and refers the patient to specialists or other medical services as needed.

primary dentition /děn tǐsh′ən/ the first set of 20 teeth that appear approximately between 6 and 28 months of life. *Also called* baby teeth, primary teeth.

primary progressive aphasia /ə fā′zhə/ an increasing loss of the ability to produce language, although the memory and intellect remain relatively intact in the early stages, that ultimately ends in an inability for the patient to care for him- or herself.

primary teeth any of the first set of 20 teeth in a human infant. *Also called* baby teeth, primary dentition.

primary tumor /tōō′mər/ a tumor that is located where it first developed.

primigravida /prī′mǐ grăv′ǐ də/ a woman who is in her first pregnancy.

primip /prī′mǐp, prī mǐp′/ short for primipara.

primipara /prī mǐp′ər ə/ a woman who has given birth one time.

primiparous /prī mǐp′ər əs/ relating to a woman who has given birth one time. *Also called* uniparous.

primordium /prī môr′dē əm/ a cluster of cells in an embryo that will give rise to an organ.

Prinzmetal('s) angina /prǐnz′mět əl(z) ăn′jə nə, ăn jī′nə/ chest pain due to a sudden spasm of one of the coronary arteries that supply oxygen-rich blood to the heart.

prion /prē′ŏn, prī′-/ a small, infectious, abnormally folded protein particle similar to a virus but lacking DNA, that causes degenerative diseases of the nervous system in animals and humans, such as mad cow disease, and Creutzfeldt Jakob disease.

prion disease any of several diseases caused by the accumulation of abnormally folded protein particles in the brain, such as Creutzfeldt-Jakob disease or kuru, acquired by eating an infected animal.

prior approval, prior authorization permission, in advance, from the medical insurer to a doctor to prescribe certain drugs or perform certain tests or procedures.

PRK *abbreviation.* photorefractive keratectomy.

PRN, p.r.n. *abbreviation.* Latin *pro re nata,* as needed (in prescriptions).

pro- *prefix.* before, forward: *for example,* procephalic.

probe /prōb/ a flexible rod with a blunt tip used to explore wounds, cavities, sinuses, etc.

probiotic /prō′bī ŏt′ĭk/ a bacteria, yeast, or other living agent, such as *Lactobacillus acidophilus* (a yeast found naturally in yoghurt), that promotes health or protects against disease.

procedural sedation /sə dā′shən/ management of a patient's pain during medical procedures.

procedure /prə sē′jər/ 1. an established method to achieve a particular result. 2. an operation.

procephalic /prō′sə făl′ĭk/ at the front of the head. [pro- + cephalic]

process /prŏs′ĕs, prō′sĕs/ 1. a protrusion or projection on a bone. 2. the natural development of a disease. 3. a disease or disorder. 4. a series of actions by a dental technician that convert a wax model into a final denture for installation in a patient's mouth.

proclivity /prō klǐv′ǐ tē/ an inclination, natural desire, or tendency.

proct-, procto- *combining form.* anus, rectum: *for example,* proctitis.

proctalgia /prŏk tăl′jə/ pain in the rectum. [proct- + -algia]

proctectomy /prŏk těk′tə mē/ surgical resection of the rectum. [proct- + -ectomy]

proctitis /prŏk tī′tǐs/ an inflammation of the anus and rectum. [proct- + -itis]

proctocele /prŏk′tə sēl′/ protrusion of the rectum into the vagina. *Also called* rectocele. [procto- + -cele]

proctologist /prŏk tŏl′ə jǐst/ a doctor specializing in diagnosis and treatment of diseases of the rectum and anus. [procto- + -logist]

proctology /prŏk tŏl′ə jē/ the branch of medicine that specializes in diseases of the rectum and anus. [procto- + -logy]

proctopexy /prŏk′tə pěk′sē/ the surgical fixing of the rectum to an adjacent structure. [procto- + -pexy]

proctoplasty /prŏk′tə plăs′tē/ surgical repair of the anus or rectum. *Also called* rectoplasty. [procto- + -plasty]

proctorrhea /prŏk′tô rē′ə/ a mucous discharge from the rectum. [procto- + -rrhea]

proctorrhaphy /prŏk tôr′ə fē/ suturing of a torn rectum or anus. [procto- + -rrhaphy]

proctoscope /prŏk′tə skōp′/ an instrument for visual examination of the rectum. *Also called* rectoscope. [procto- + -scope]

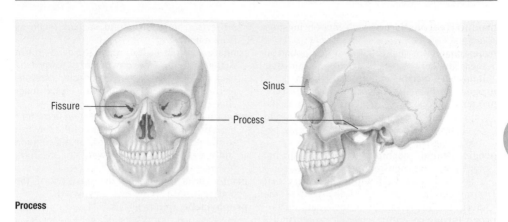

Process

General Structure	Anatomical Term	Description
Articulating surfaces	Condyle	Large, smooth, rounded articulating oval structure
	Facet	Small, flat, shallow articulating surface
	Head	Prominent, rounded epiphysis
	Trochlea	Smooth, grooved, pulley-like articular process
Depressions	Alveolus	Deep pit or socket in the maxillae or mandible
	Fossa	Flattened or shallow depression
	Sulcus	Narrow groove
Projections for tendon and ligament attachment	Crest	Narrow, prominent, ridgelike projection
	Epicondyle	Projection adjacent to a condyle
	Line	Low ridge
	Process	Any marked bony prominence
	Ramus	Angular extension of a bone relative to the rest of the structure
	Spine	Pointed, slender process
	Trochanter	Massive, rough projection found only on the femur
	Tubercle	Small, round projection
	Tuberosity	Large, rough projection
Openings and spaces	Canal (meatus)	Passageway through a bone
	Fissure	Narrow, slitlike opening through a bone
	Foramen	Rounded passageway through a bone
	Sinus	Cavity or hollow space in a bone

Various Processes, Projections, Depressions, and Openings in Bone.

proctoscopy /prŏk tŏs′kə pē/ a visual examination of the rectum. *Also called* rectoscopy. [procto- + -scopy]

proctosigmoidoscopy /prŏk′tō sĭg′moi dŏs′kə pē/ a visual examination of the rectum and lower colon. [procto- + -sigmoido- + -scopy]

prodromal /prō drō′məl/ relating to a symptom that signals the onset of a condition.

prodromal symptoms prodrome.

prodrome /prō′drōm/ a symptom or group of symptoms that signal the onset of a condition, such as that an aura may precede a migraine. *Also called* prodromal symptom(s).

prodrug /prō′drŭg′/ a chemically inactive substance that is converted within the body to a drug. [pro- + drug]

productive cough   a cough that brings up mucus.

proestrogen /prō ĕs'trə jən/   a compound in the body that behaves like a progesteron after it has been metabolized. [pro- + estrogen]

progeny /prŏj'ə nē/   offspring; descendants.

progeria /prō jêr'ē ə/   a disease in which the cells in the body age abnormally fast, and death from heart disease often occurring before the age of 10.

progestational hormone /prō'jě stā'shə nəl hôr'mōn/ or **progesterone** /prō jĕs'tə rōn'/ a hormone produced within the ovary that stimulates a thickening of the wall of the uterus and the formation of mammary ducts.

progesterone receptor   specific protein molecules to which progesterone can attach that are found on cancer cells in certain breast cancers.

progestin /prō jĕs'tĭn/   any natural or synthetic substance that acts like progesterone in the body.

prognathism /prŏg'nə thĭz'əm/   the condition of having forward-jutting jaws. [pro- + gnath- + -ism]

prognosis /prŏg nō'sĭs/   a forecast of the probable course and outcome of a disease.

prognostic /prŏg nŏs'tĭk/   of or involving a medical forecast.

program /prō'grăm, -grəm/   a set plan of actions or procedures meant to reach a goal, such as a dietary program.

progressive /prə grĕs'ĭv/   signifying a condition that will get worse.

projection /prə jĕk'shən/   **1.** something that protrudes or sticks out. **2.** in psychology, a defense mechanism whereby one unconsciously attributes to someone else a negative trait or feeling that one has about oneself but is in denial of.

prolactin /prō lăk'tĭn/   hormone produced by the anterior lobe of the pituitary gland; in females it stimulates and regulates the secretion of milk (lactation) after delivery. *Also called* lactogenic hormone.

prolactin hormone   *See* prolactin.

prolapse /prō lăps', prō'lăps/   the falling or slipping down of an organ, such as the uterus, from its normal position.

prolapsed umbilical cord /prō'lăpst ŭm bĭl'ĭ kəl kôrd'/   the appearance of a part of the umbilical cord ahead of the fetus during delivery; if the cord is compressed between the fetal head and the mother's pelvis, the condition can endanger the fetus.

prolapsed uterus /yōō'tər əs/   the slipping down of the uterus, because of weak underlying muscles, towards or into the vagina; often a result of advanced age or repeated full-term pregnancies.

PROM   *abbreviation.* passive range of motion.

prominence /prŏm'ə nəns/   something that projects from a structural surface, such as from a bone.

pronate /prō'nāt/   **1.** to rotate the hand or arm so that the palm faces downward or toward the back. **2.** to rotate the foot so the sole faces outward and the weight would fall on the inner edge of the foot when standing.

pronation /prō nā'shən/   **1.** being in or assuming a prone position. **2.** rotation of the forearm so the palm faces downward, or the rotation and eversion (turning outward) of the foot. *See also* supination.

prone /prōn/   denoting the position of the body when it is lying face downward.

prophylactic /prō'fə lăk'tĭk/   **1.** *adj.* preventing the spread of disease. **2.** *n.* an agent, such as a medicinal preparation, that prevents the spread of disease. **3.** common name for condom.

prophylaxis /prō'fə lăk'sĭs/   measures taken for the prevention of disease.

proprietary /prə prī'ĭ tĕr'ē/   (of a medicine) owned by an individual or a corporation under a patent or trademark.

proprietary name /prə prī'ĭ tĕr'ē/   the trademark or brand name under which a drug is manufactured and sold.

pro re nata (PRN, p.r.n.) /prō' rā' nā'tə/   as needed (in prescriptions).

prosencephalon /prŏs'ĕn sĕf'ə lŏn'/   the embryonic forebrain, which gives rise to the diencephalon and the telencephalon in the matured brain.

prostaglandin /prŏs'tə glăn'dĭn/   any of a group of fatty acids produced in various tissues in the body that act in very small amounts on certain organs and have a wide range of effects, such as the regulation of blood pressure and smooth muscle contraction.

prostate-, prostat-, prostato-   *combining form,* prostate gland: *for example,* prostatitis.

prostate /prŏs'tāt/   **1.** *adj.* of or relating to the prostate gland. **2.** *n.* the prostate gland.

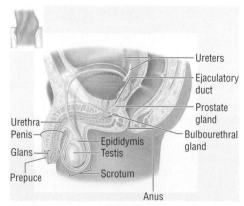

Ureters
Ejaculatory duct
Prostate gland
Bulbourethral gland
Urethra
Penis
Epididymis
Glans
Testis
Prepuce
Scrotum
Anus

Prostate

prostate cancer a slowly progressive malignancy (uncontrolled growth of cells) in the prostate gland, most common in males after age 50.

prostatectomy /prŏs'tə tĕk'tə mē/ the surgical removal of part of the prostate gland as, for example, in the case of benign prostatic hypertrophy (an enlarged prostate gland); or the surgical removal of the whole gland in the case of a malignancy. [prostat- + -ectomy]

prostate gland a chestnut-shaped gland located near the bladder and situated around the base of the male urethra that has two lobes; as part of the male reproductive system, it secretes a milky fluid into the urethra during the emission of semen.

prostate-specific antigen (PSA) test /ăn'tĭ jən/ a test used to detect prostate cancer and to monitor treatment of the disease by measuring the amount of prostate-specific antigen in the blood; elevated levels may indicate cancer or some other disease of the prostate gland.

prostatic /pɪŏ stăt'ĭk/ relating to the prostate gland.

prostatitis /prŏs'tə tī'tĭs/ inflammation of the prostate gland, often because of an infection. [prostat- + -itis]

prostatocystitis /prŏs'tə tō sĭ stī'tĭs/ inflammation of the prostate gland and the bladder. [prostato- + cystitis]

prostatomegaly /prŏs'tə tō mĕg'ə lē/ enlargement of the prostate gland. [prostato- + -megaly]

prostatorrhea /prŏs'tə tô rē'ə/ abnormal discharge from the prostate gland. [prostato- + -rrhea]

prostatotomy /prŏs'tə tŏt'ə mē/ surgical excision of part of all of the prostate gland. [prostato- + -tomy]

prostatovesiculectomy /prŏs'tə tō və sĭk'yə lĕk'tə mē/ surgical removal of the prostate gland and the seminal vesicles.

prostatovesiculitis /prŏs'tə tō və sĭk'yə lĭ'tĭs/ inflammation of the prostate gland and the seminal vesicles.

prosthesis /prŏs thē'sĭs/ (*pl.* **prostheses** /prŏs thē'sēz/) an artificial body part, such as a limb, hearing aid, or heart valve, that is designed to assume the function of a missing or diseased part.

prosthetic /prŏs thĕt'ĭk/ of or relating to a prosthesis.

prosthetics /prŏs thĕt'ĭks/ the designing, making, and fitting of prostheses.

prosthetist /prŏs'thĭ tĭst/ one who designs, makes, and fits artificial body parts as prescribed by a physician.

prosthodontics /prŏs'thə dŏn'tĭks/ the branch of dentistry that deals with the construction of

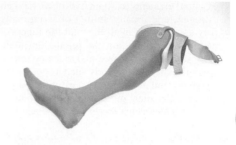

Prosthesis

artificial devices for replacing missing teeth or other structures in the mouth and jaw.

prosthodontist /prŏs'thə dŏn'tĭst/ a dentist who specializes in the practice of prosthodontics.

prostrate /prŏs'trāt/ weak from physical exhaustion.

prostration /prŏ strā'shən/ weakness from extreme physical exhaustion.

protease inhibitor /prō'tē ās'/ a class of drugs used to fight HIV infection by blocking the activity of the enzyme protease, needed in order for the virus to replicate.

protein /prō'tēn, -tē ĭn/ any of a group of large molecules made up of one or more chains of amino acids that contain all the

Protein (in foods)

essential elements (carbon, hydrogen, oxygen, nitrogen, and usually sulfur) of living cells; they are involved in all the vital life functions of the body, including the regulation of the cells, organs, and tissues, and make up important substances in the body such as hormones, enzymes, and antibodies. An essential part of an animal's diet, proteins can be obtained through protein-rich foods such as meat, fish, and milk.

proteinuria /prō′tē nŏor′ē ə, -tē ə nŏor′-/ having excessive amounts of protein, usually the protein albumin, in the urine. *Also called* albuminuria. [protein + -uria]

proteolytic /prō′tē ə lĭt′ĭk/ of or involving the process of breaking down proteins into simpler compounds, as happens in digestion.

prothrombin /prō thrŏm′bĭn/ a plasma protein, made and stored in the liver and present in blood plasma, that is required for the normal clotting (coagulation) of blood; during blood clotting, it is converted to thrombin. [pro- + thrombin]

prothrombin time (PT) a test that measures the time needed for clot formation in blood plasma; commonly used to monitor the effect of an anticoagulant (blood-thinning medication, such as Warfarin) on the clotting system.

protocol /prō′tə kôl′/ a written plan containing the precise procedures to be followed in a course of treatment or in a scientific experiment.

protoplasm /prō′tə plăz′əm/ the translucent, semi-fluid substance inside plant and animal cells and in which the life functions of cells take place; it includes the cytoplasm and nucleus of a cell.

protraction /prō trăk′shən/ the extension, especially of teeth, into an anterior position to normal.

protractor /prō trăk′tər/ a muscle that causes a part to protrude.

protrusion /prō trōo′zhən/ **1.** the state or condition of being thrust forward or projecting. **2.** in dentistry, projecting in relationship to the position of the mandible, as opposed to retrusion.

protuberance /prō tōo′bər əns/ a protruding outgrowth; a prominent bulge that extends beyond the surface.

provider /prə vī′dər/ a person or group of people providing services to patients; for example: a clinic, hospital, physician, or other health care professional.

proximal /prŏk′sə məl/ **1.** located nearest to the center or the place of origin or attachment; for example, the proximal end of a bone is the end nearest to the trunk of the body. **2.** in dental anatomy, used to indicate whether the

surface of a tooth is nearer or further from the median plane in the mouth.

prune belly syndrome partial or complete lack of abdominal muscles. *Also called* abdominal muscle deficiency syndrome.

prurigo /prŏo rī′gō/ a skin condition with itching papules.

pruritic /prŏo rĭt′ĭk/ relating to pruritus; extremely itchy.

pruritus /prŏo rī′tĭs/ any type of itch; may be caused by an infection, allergy, skin irritation, disease, or the like.

PSA prostate-specific antigen, a protein produced by the prostate gland that is used in the diagnosis of prostate cancer.

PSA blood test used to detect prostate cancer and to monitor treatment of the disease by measuring the amount of PSA in the blood; elevated levels may indicate cancer or some other disease of the prostate gland.

pseud-, pseudo- *combining form.* false: *for example,* pseudocoma.

pseudocoma /sŏo′dō kō′mə/ a condition caused by a lesion in a blood vessel of the brain, marked by paralysis of all four limbs, inability to speak, eye movements limited to vertical direction, and preservation of consciousness. *Also called* locked-in syndrome. [pseudo- + coma]

pseudocyesis /sŏo′dō sī ē′sĭs/ a condition in which a woman experiences symptoms of pregnancy, such as the cessation of menstruation and the enlargement of the belly and breasts, and believes herself to be pregnant although no conception has taken place; the condition is usually brought on by the hormonal changes of stress. Informally referred to as false pregnancy.

pseudocyst /sŏo′dō sĭst/ an accumulation of fluid or gas in an empty cavity or space in the body that resembles a cyst but has no lining. [pseudo- + cyst]

pseudodementia /sŏo′dō dĭ měn′shə/ a disorder that mimics dementia but is usually caused by a state of extreme apathy rather than by any dysfunction or deterioration of the brain. [pseudo- + dementia]

pseudoedema /sŏo′dō ĭ dē′mə/ a puffiness of skin due to something other than an accumulation of fluid. [pseudo- + edema]

pseudoesthesia /sŏo′dō ĕs thē′zhə/ the feeling that a limb which was amputated is still there; often accompanied by the sensation of pain or discomfort at the site. *Also called* phantom limb. [pseudo- + esthesia]

pseudoexfoliation syndrome /sŏo′dō ĕks fō′lē ā′shən/ a condition in which deposits on the surface of the lens of the eye look like exfoliation of the lens capsule; often leads to glaucoma. [pseudo- + exfoliation]

pseudogout /soo̅′do̅ gout′/ inflammation of the joints, such as in the knees, wrists, and hips, that results in attacks of acute swelling and pain resembling those associated with gout; however, the inflammation is caused by the deposit of crystalline salts rather than crystals of uric acid, as in actual gout. [pseudo- + gout]

pseudohypertrophic /soo̅′do̅ hī′pər trŏf′ĭk/ of or related to pseudohypertrophy.

pseudohypertrophy /soo̅′do̅ hī pûr′trə fē/ an enlargement at the site of an organ or of part of an organ due to an increase in fatty or fibrous tissue rather than to an increase in the size of the organ itself. [pseudo- + hypertrophy]

pseudomania /soo̅′do̅ mā′nē ə/ **1.** faked insanity. **2.** a disorder in which the person claims to have committed one or more crimes that he or she has not committed. [pseudo- + mania]

pseudomembranous colitis /soo̅′do̅ mĕm′brə nəs kə lī′tĭs/ inflammation of the lining of the colon that may follow treatment with antibiotics and is characterized by diarrhea containing a membranelike material of clotted blood and pus. [pseudo- + membranous]

pseudomonas infection /soo̅′do̅ mō′nəs/ any of several infections caused by bacteria of different species of the genus *Pseudomonas*, sometimes very resistant to antibiotics; usually found among patients with burns, a compromised immune system, or cystic fibrosis.

pseudoneuroma /soo̅′do̅ noo̅ rō′mə/ a tumor that is growing from a nerve but, unlike a true neuroma, does not contain nerve cells. [pseudo- + neuroma]

pseudoparalysis /soo̅′do̅ pə răl′ə sĭs/ a condition in which the patient cannot move the arms or legs, not because of actual paralysis, but rather because of pain, lack of coordination, or some other cause. [pseudo- + paralysis]

pseudotumor /soo̅′do̅ too̅′mər/ a swelling or enlargement that resembles a tumor.

PSG *abbreviation.* polysomnography.

psittacosis /sĭt′ə kō′sĭs/ a gastrointestinal infection in parrots and related birds that is caused by the *Chlamydia psittaci* bacterium; when transmitted to humans, it produces a fever and a respiratory disease. *Also called* parrot fever.

psoriasis /sə rī′ə sĭs/ a common, chronic skin disorder that flares up periodically and is marked by red, scale-covered patches of skin, especially on bony parts of the body such as the knees, elbows, scalp, and trunk; may be accompanied by a type of arthritis.

psoriatic arthritis /sôr′ē ăt′ĭk är thrī′tĭs/ inflammation of the joints that accompanies

Psoriasis

psoriasis; usually the small joints of the fingers and toes are affected.

psych-, psycho- *combining form.* mind: *for example,* psychology.

psyche /sī′kē/ the mind and its mental processes, conscious and unconscious, as distinct from the physical processes of the body.

psychedelic /sī′kə dĕl′ĭk/ **1.** *n.* a class of drugs (including, for example, mescaline) that produces a state of mind with altered sense perceptions and hallucinations that are thought to be mind-expanding. **2.** *adj.* a substance, visual display, or other sensory stimulant that produces this effect.

psychiatric /sī′kē ăt′rĭk/ of or pertaining to psychiatry.

psychiatric disorder any illness connected to one's mental state that results in abnormal behavior and/or impaired functioning; the origin may be biological, genetic, psychological, chemical, social, and so on.

psychiatric trauma a strong emotional shock that causes lasting mental and physical harm.

psychiatrist /sĭ kī′ə trĭst, sī-/ a medical doctor who specializes in psychiatry.

psychiatry /sĭ kī′ə trē, sī-/ the medical specialty concerned with the diagnosis and treatment of mental and emotional disorders.

psychoanalysis /sī′kō ə năl′ə sĭs/ a method, founded by Sigmund Freud, for studying the psychology of human behavior and for treating emotional disorders; it is based on the belief in a powerful and motivating unconscious; various techniques, such as dream interpretation, free association, and the analysis of defense mechanisms, are used to bring a person's unconscious matter to consciousness in an attempt to address emotional conflicts and ultimately change behavioral patterns. [psycho- + analysis]

psychoanalyst /sī′kō ăn′ə lĭst/ a psychiatrist or clinical psychologist who is trained in using psychoanalysis to treat emotional disorders.

psychodrama /sī′kō drä′mə, -drăm′ə/ a form of group therapy in which people act out their emotional problems through the use of improvisational acting techniques.

psychodynamics /sī'kō dī năm'ĭks/   the study of the motivational forces behind human behavior, especially the interaction between the unconscious and conscious aspects.

psychogenesis /sī'kō jĕn'ə sĭs/   **1.** the origin and development of mental processes, including personality and behavioral traits. **2.** development of a physical disease or symptom from a mental origin. [psycho- + -genesis]

psychogenic /sī'kō jĕn'ĭk/   **1.** originating in the mind. **2.** of or pertaining to psychogenesis.

psychological /sī'kə lŏj'ĭ kəl/   of or referring to psychology.

psychological test   any of a variety of standardized tests designed to obtain data about various aspects of a person's psychology, such as his or her vocational tendencies, possible learning disabilities, levels of anxiety, intelligence, or personality type.

psychologist /sī kŏl'ə jĭst/   a person licensed to practice clinical psychology or qualified to teach or conduct research in psychology.

psychology /sī kŏl'ə jē/   the science of the mind, especially as it affects behavior and emotion. [psycho- + -logy]

psychomotor /sī'kō mō'tər/   relating to the ability to produce voluntary muscle movements, requiring a combination of mental and motor activity. [psycho- + motor]

psychoneurosis /sī'kō nōō rō'sĭs/   (*pl.* **psychoneuroses** /sī'kō nōō rō'sēz/)   any of

Psychologist

various emotional or mental disorders, usually involving anxiety, insecurity, irrational fears, and hypochondra, that does not include grossly distorted reality or disordered thinking. *Also called* neurosis. [psycho- + neurosis]

psychoneurotic /sī'kō nōō rŏt'ĭk/   of or related to psychoneurosis.

psychopath /sī'kə păth'/   someone who is suffering from psychopathic personality disorder. *Also called* sociopath.

psychopathic personality /sī'kə păth'ĭk/   a person with a psychopathic personality disorder.

psychopathic personality disorder   a personality disorder characterized by complete and aggressive disregard for the rights of others, and an inability to exhibit normal behavior.

psychopathy /sī kŏp'ə thē/   a mental disorder, especially one resulting in antisocial behavior. [psycho- + -pathy]

psychopharmaceutical /sī'kō fär'mə sōō'tĭ kəl/   a drug used to treat a psychological disorder. [psycho- + pharmaceutical]

psychopharmacology /sī'kō fär'mə kŏl'ə jē/   **1.** the use of drugs, such as antidepressants, muscle relaxants, and antipsychotics, to treat mental disorders. **2.** the branch of pharmacology that studies the effect of drugs on the mind and behavior. [psycho- + pharmacology]

psychosexual /sī'kō sĕk'shōō əl/   pertaining to the emotional and mental aspects of sex. [psycho- + sexual]

psychosis /sī kō'sĭs/   (*pl.* **psychoses** /sī kō'sēz/)   a major mental disorder in which the person's perceptions, interpersonal relationships, and ideas of external reality are impaired; the person usually exhibits inappropriate mood and emotion and may suffer from hallucinations and delusions.

psychosocial /sī'kō sō'shəl/   pertaining to both psychological and social aspects of behavior. [psycho- + social]

psychosomatic /sī'kō sə măt'ĭk/   **1.** a physical manifestation of something psychological in origin. **2.** of or relating to the interaction of the mind and the body.

psychosomatic illness   a sickness that has physical symptoms and signs but which is psychological or emotional in origin.

psychotherapist /sī'kō thĕr'ə pĭst/   a person, such as a psychiatrist, clinical psychologist, nurse, social worker, or someone trained in a specific form of counseling, who practices a form of psychotherapy. Licensing for psychotherapy varies from state to state. [psycho- + therapist]

psychotherapy /sī'kō thĕr'ə pē/   any of a wide variety of therapies that attempt to treat emotional or behavioral disorders with psychological techniques rather than through traditional physical or chemical means. [psycho- + therapy]

psychotropic /sī'kō trō'pĭk/ capable of acting on the mind so as to alter mood and behavior; usually pertains to drugs used for treating mental disorders. [psycho- + -tropic]

psychotropic medication or **drug** a drug, legal or illegal, that is intended to alter the mind, mood, and behavior of the user.

pt *abbreviation.* patient.

PT *abbreviation.* **1.** physical therapy. **2.** physical therapist. **3.** prothrombin time.

Pt *abbreviation.* platinum.

PTA *abbreviation.* percutaneous transluminal angioplasty.

PTCA *abbreviation.* percutaneous transluminal coronary angioplasty.

pterygium /tə rĭj'ē əm/ a triangular-shaped flap of thick tissue that grows from the white of the eye, extending to the edge of the cornea or beyond, where it causes a problem in vision.

pterygoid muscle /tĕr'ĭ goid'/ a triangular-shaped muscle located near the sphenoid bone at the base of the skull.

-ptosis *suffix.* falling down or sagging of an organ: *for example,* blepharoptosis.

ptosis /tō'sĭs/ abnormal sinking or drooping of an organ or part; especially a drooping of the upper eyelid caused by a congenital or acquired weakness in the muscle or a paralysis of the oculomotor nerve.

PTSD *abbreviation.* posttraumatic stress disorder.

PTT *abbreviation.* partial thromboplastin time.

ptyalism /tī'ə lĭz əm/ having an excessive flow of saliva, as occurs sometimes in pregnancy. *Also called* sialism.

pub-, pubo- *combining form.* pubic, pubis: *for example,* puborectal.

pubarche /pyōō bär'kē/ the onset of puberty, marked by the growth of pubic hair.

puberty /pyōō'bər tē/ the developmental stage of adolescence when the physiological ability to reproduce is reached; it is marked by the maturity of the genital organs, development of the secondary sex characteristics, and in the female, the first occurrence of menstruation.

pubes /pyōō'bēz/ **1.** the region of the lower abdomen above the external genital organs where hair growth begins at puberty. **2.** the hair of this region (pubic hair).

pubescence /pyōō bĕs'əns/ puberty.

pubescent /pyōō bĕs'ənt/ having just reached puberty; in puberty.

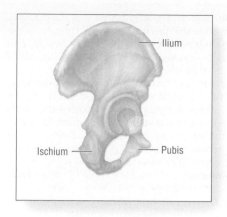

Pubis

pubic /pyōō'bĭk/ of or relating to the pubes or pubic bone.

pubic bone the forward part of the right and left hip bone; the two bones meet at the front of the pelvis. *Also called* pubis.

pubic lice any parasitic insect found on the pubic hair of humans.

pubic symphysis /sĭm'fə sĭs/ the strong fibrocartilaginous joint of the pelvis that lies between the two pubic bones in the front of the hips and connects them.

pubis /pyōō'bĭs/ (*pl.* **pubes** /pyōō'bēz/ the forward part of the right and left hip bone; the two bones meet at the front of the pelvis. *Also called* pubic bone.

public health the field of service, as well as the art and science, of protecting the health of a community; it includes areas such as preventive medicine, control of epidemic diseases, health education, sanitary measures, environmental hazards protection, and food and drug safety.

puborectal /pyōō'bō rĕk'təl/ pertaining to the pubic bone and the rectum. [pubo- + rectal]

PUBS percutaneous umbilical blood sampling, a technique used for diagnosing and treating a fetus in which a blood sample is taken from the umbilical vein by inserting a needle through the mother's abdominal and uterine walls.

PUD *abbreviation.* peptic ulcer disease.

pudendum /pyōō dĕn'dəm/ (*pl.* **pudenda** /pyōō dĕn'də/) the external genitals, especially those of the female.

puerpera /pyōō ûr'pər ə/ (*pl.* **puerperae** /pyōō ûr'pə rē'/) a woman who has just given birth.

puerperal fever /pyōō ûr'pər əl/ a bacterial infection that occurs in a woman after delivery, most often caused by unsterile conditions;

the infection usually begins near the placenta, within the uterus, and then spreads to the bloodstream (sepsis); it can be treated with large amounts of antibiotics. *Also called* childbed fever.

puerperium /pyo͞o′ər pêr′ē əm/ (*pl.* **puerperia** /pyo͞o′ər pêr′ē ə/) the period of time beginning immediately after childbirth and continuing up to the time the uterus returns to its normal size, usually defined as 42 days.

pulmon-, pulmono- *combining form.* the lungs: *for example,* pulmonology.

pulmonary /pŭl′mə nĕr′ē, po͞ol′-/ of or relating to the lungs or respiratory system.

pulmonary abscess /ăb′sĕs/ an infection in the lungs causing a pocket of pus.

pulmonary acinus /ăs′ə nəs/ the ending portion of a bronchiole (small airway) in the lung that contains the alveoli (air sacs).

pulmonary alveolar proteinosis /ăl vē′ə lər prō′tē nō′sĭs, -tē ĭ nō′sĭs/ a progressive lung disease marked by increased difficulty in breathing resulting from a build-up of protein and lipids in the alveoli (air sacs) for an unknown reason.

pulmonary arterial hypertension /är têr′ē əl hī′pər tĕn′shən/ high blood pressure in the pulmonary artery, which carries blood from the right ventricle of the heart to the lungs; may be primary or secondary to another disease. *Also called* pulmonary hypertension, pulmonary heart disease.

pulmonary artery (PA) /är′tə rē/ the blood vessel that carries deoxygenated blood from the right ventricle of the heart to the lungs, where it becomes oxygenated and returns to the heart. After it leaves the heart, the artery divides into two branches, called the right and left pulmonary arteries, which lead to the right and left lungs.

pulmonary artery catheter /kăth′ĭ tər/ a small balloon-tipped catheter inserted through the heart into the pulmonary artery for the purpose of measuring cardiac output and pulmonary artery pressure.

pulmonary artery stenosis /stĭ nō′sĭs/ an abnormal narrowing of the pulmonary artery; usually a congenital condition.

pulmonary circulation /sûr′kyə lā′shən/ the system of blood vessels that transports blood between the heart and the lungs. Deoxygenated blood goes out of the right ventricle of the heart through the pulmonary artery to the lungs, becomes oxygenated in the alveoli of the lungs, and then returns through the pulmonary veins to the left atrium of the heart, from where it will circulate throughout the body.

pulmonary edema (PE) /ĭ dē′mə/ abnormal accumulation of extravascular fluid—fluid

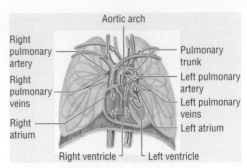

Pulmonary Circulation

outside of the blood vessels—in the tissues and alveoli (air sacs) of the lungs.

pulmonary embolism (PE) /ĕm′bə lĭz′əm/ a blockage in the pulmonary artery or one of its branches due to a blood clot, usually from the leg, or to foreign matter such as fat; it causes sudden closure of the vessel and results in difficult breathing and severe chest pain.

pulmonary embolus /ĕm′bə ləs/ blood clot or foreign matter, such as fat or tumor tissue, that travels through the blood and obstructs the pulmonary artery.

pulmonary fibrosis /fī brō′sĭs/ the formation of scar tissue in the lungs in response to lung inflammation or irritation; for example, as caused by tuberculosis.

pulmonary function test (PFT) a series of tests to assess the breathing function of the lungs. A spirometer is used to measure the ability of the lungs to move air in and out; other tests determine the efficiency of the lungs in exchanging oxygen and carbon dioxide.

pulmonary heart disease pulmonary hypertension.

pulmonary hypertension /hī′pər tĕn′shən/ high blood pressure in the pulmonary artery, which carries blood from the right ventricle of the heart to the lungs; may be primary or secondary to another disease. *Also called* pulmonary heart disease, pulmonary atrial hypertension.

pulmonary infarction /ĭn färk′shən/ death of lung tissue because of a lack of blood supply to the lung; the blood supply is cut off when a blockage occurs, usually a blood clot, in the pulmonary artery.

pulmonary insufficiency /ĭn′sə fĭsh′ən sē/ failure of the pulmonary valve to close properly, allowing some blood to flow backward from the pulmonary artery into the right ventricle.

pulmonary semilunar valve /sĕm′ē lo͞o′nər/ pulmonary valve.

pulmonary stenosis /stĭ nō′sĭs/ abnormal narrowing of the opening between the right ventricle and the pulmonary artery.

pulmonary trunk the short, wide portion of the pulmonary artery that carries deoxygenated blood out of the right ventricle of the heart and passes upward where it divides and becomes the right and left pulmonary arteries.

pulmonary valve or **pulmonic valve** a valve in the heart that separates the right ventricle from the pulmonary artery; made of three semilunar cusps that close during each heartbeat to prevent the blood headed through the artery to the lungs from flowing backward into the heart. *Also called* pulmonary semilunar valve.

pulmonary vein one of two sets of blood vessels that carry oxygenated blood from each lung back to the left atrium of the heart for circulation throughout the body.

pulmonic /pŭl mŏn′ĭk, pōol-/ of the lungs or respiratory system; pulmonary.

pulmono- *See* pulmon-.

pulmonology /pŭl′mə nŏl′ə jē, pōol′-/ the study of the anatomy, physiology, and pathology of the lungs. [pulmono- + -logy]

pulp /pŭlp/ **1.** any soft, spongy tissue in the body, such as is contained in the spleen or in the soft pads of the fingertips. **2.** the soft tissue found in the center of a tooth consisting of connective tissue containing nerves and blood vessels.

pulp canal a dental procedure to preserve a decayed tooth by replacing its root with a protective substance. *Also called* root canal.

pulp cavity the central hollow inside a tooth that contains the dental pulp; it is made up of the pulp chamber in the crown of the tooth and the root canal.

pulpotomy /pŭl pŏt′ə mē/ the removal of infected portions of dental pulp. [pulpo- + -tomy]

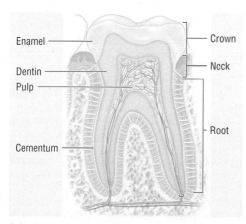

Enamel — Crown

Dentin — Neck

Pulp —

Cementum — Root

Pulp

pulse /pŭls/ the rhythmic beat produced in an artery from the regular pulsation (expansion and contraction) of the artery as the heart pumps blood through the system; each time the heart contracts, one pulsation can be detected on a superficial artery, as in the wrist or neck.

pulv. *abbreviation.* powder (used in prescriptions).

pump /pŭmp/ **1.** *n.* an apparatus, device, or organ, such as the heart, that transfers fluids or gases by pressure or suction. **2.** a system, as a sodium pump, that supplies energy for transport of ions across a chemical gradient, as across a cell membrane. **3.** *v.* to force fluid or gas along a certain pathway, as when the heart pumps blood.

pump oxygenator /ŏk′sĭ jə nā′tər/ a machine that substitutes for the heart and lungs during open heart surgery by pumping oxygenated blood through the body.

punch biopsy /bī′ŏp sē/ a method of removing live tissue in the shape of a small cylinder for examination; a circular punch is used to pierce the organ, skin, or a small incision in the skin.

punctate hemorrhage /pŭngk′tāt hĕm′ər ĭj, hĕm′rĭj/ bleeding into the skin from the small blood vessels that cause petechiae. *Also called* petechial hemorrhage

puncture /pŭngk′chər/ **1.** *v.* to make a hole with a sharp, pointed instrument. **2.** *n.* the hole made this way.

puncture wound /wōond/ a wound having much more depth than width; usually caused by a sharp pointed object.

pupil /pyōo′pəl/ an opening in the iris of the eye through which light passes before reaching the lens and retina; its diameter changes in response to changes in light and other stimuli.

pupill-, pupillo- *combining form.* pupil: *for example*, pupillometer.

pupillary /pyōo′pə lĕr′ē/ relating to the pupil of the eye.

pupillometer /pyōo′pə lŏm′ĭ tər/ an instrument that measures and records the diameter of the pupil. [pupillo- + -meter]

pupillometry /pyōo′pə lŏm′ĭ trē/ the measurement of the pupil of the eye. [pupillo- + -metry]

pupilloscope /pyōo′pə lə skōp′/ an instrument for observing the pupil, especially with regard to the refraction of light in the eye. [pupillo- + -scope]

purgative /pûr′gə tĭv/ a medicine, usually taken orally, to evacuate (purge) the bowels.

purge /pûrj/ **1.** *v.* to evacuate the bowels by using a purgative. **2.** *n.* something that purges, as in a medicinal purgative. **3.** the act of purging.

purified protein derivative (PPD) test /də rĭv′ə tĭv/ a clinical test in which a small amount of tuberculin is injected under the skin (intradermal injection) as a means of testing for past or present infection with tuberculosis. *Also called* Mantoux test. (Note: purified protein derivative refers to a dried purified form of tuberculin that is used for the test.)

purine /pyo͞or′ēn/ a base that is the parent compound of uric acid.

Purkinje fibers /pər kĭn′jē/ specialized cardiac muscle fibers that carry cardiac impulses from the atrioventricular node to the left and right ventricles of the heart, causing the ventricles to contract.

purpura /pûr′pyo͞o rə/ any of several types of bleeding disorders marked by hemorrhages under the skin and mucous membranes; the skin appears red at first and then changes to dark purple and brownish-yellow as it fades.

purulent /pyo͞or′ə lənt, -yə lənt/ containing or discharging pus.

pus /pŭs/ a viscous fluid that forms in infected tissue; it is usually yellowish and white in color and is made out of white blood cells and the debris of dead cells and tissue parts.

pustular /pŭs′chə lər/ consisting of or related to pustules.

pustule /pŭs′cho͞ol/ a round swollen area of skin (for example, a pimple or blister) that contains pus.

putamen /pyo͞o tā′mən/ (*pl.* **putamina** /pyo͞o tăm′ə nə/) part of a structure in the brain called the lentiform nucleus; of the three sections in the lentiform nucleus, it is the outer, larger, and darker gray section.

putrefaction /pyo͞o′trə făk′shən/ the act or process of rotting.

putrid /pyo͞o′trĭd/ in a state of rot and decay, accompanied by a foul smell.

PUVA *abbreviation.* psoralen and UVA, a treatment for psoriasis that combines the medication psoralen with carefully timed UVA (ultraviolet light of A wavelength) exposure.

PV *abbreviation.* **1.** polycythemia vera. **2.** peripheral vascular.

PVC *abbreviation.* premature ventricular contraction.

PVD *abbreviation.* peripheral vascular disease.

PVS *abbreviation.* persistent vegetative state.

py-, pyo- *combining form.* pus: *for example,* pyarthrosis.

pyarthrosis pus formation within a joint, usually caused by a bacterial infection. [py- + arthrosis]

pyel-, pyelo- *combining form.* pelvis (usually the renal pelvis): *for example,* pyelitis.

pyelitis /pī′ə lī′tĭs/ inflammation of the renal pelvis. [pyel- + -itis]

pyelogram /pī′ə lə grăm′/ an x-ray obtained through pyelography; [pyelo- + -gram]

pyelography /pī′ə lŏg′rə fē/ the technique of obtaining a series of x-rays of the renal pelvis and ureter after injecting a dye intravenously or into the ureter; used to detect abnormalities of the urinary tract such as tumors, cysts, or kidney stones. [pyelo- + -graphy]

pyelolithotomy /pī′ə lō lĭ thŏt′ə mē/ a surgical procedure in which an incision is made in the renal pelvis to remove a kidney stone (renal calculus). [pyelo- + litho- + -tomy]

pyelonephritis /pī′ə lō nə frī′tĭs/ inflammation of the renal pelvis due to an infection of the kidney; it can be acute (generally resulting from a bladder infection) or chronic (usually associated with a stone or other obstruction). [pyelo- + nephritis]

pyeloplasty /pī′ə lə plăs′tē/ surgical reconstruction of the renal pelvis and ureter. [pyelo- + -plasty]

pyelostomy /pī′ə los′tə mē/ the surgical creation of an opening into the pelvic kidney to create a channel for drainage. [pyelo- + -stomy]

pyelotomy /pī′ə lŏt′ə mē/ surgical incision into the renal pelvis. [pyelo- + -tomy]

pyeloureteritis /pī′ə lō yo͞o rē′tə rī′tĭs/ inflammation of a ureter and its associated renal pelvis (kidney). *Also called* ureteropyelitis, utereropyelonephritis. [pyelo- + ureteritis]

pyemia /pī ē′mē ə/ a form of septicemia with pyogenic bacteria circulating in the blood and often leading to internal abscesses. [py- + -emia]

pylor-, pyloro- *combining form.* the pylorus (outlet of the stomach): *for example,* pylorospasm.

pyloric region /pī lôr′ĭk/ the area at the bottom of the stomach that leads to the pylorus and pyloric sphincter.

pyloric sphincter /sfĭngk′tər/ a thick O-shaped muscular ring at the bottom of the stomach that separates the pylorus of the stomach from the duodenum.

pyloric stenosis /stĭ nō′sĭs/ a narrowing of the pyloric sphincter at the bottom of the stomach, preventing food from passing easily into the small intestine; it usually presents in the first 4–6 weeks of life and is treated surgically, and in an adult it may be the result of a stomach ulcer with associated edema and fibrosis at the outlet of the stomach.

pylorospasm /pī lôr′ə spăz′əm/ a spasm of the pyloric sphincter at the bottom of the stomach. [pyloro- + spasm]

pylorus /pī lôr′əs/ (*pl.* **pylori** /pī lôr′ī/) the lower, tubular portion of the stomach that is encircled by the rings of the pyloric sphincter

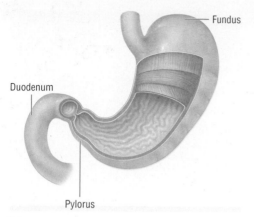

Fundus

Duodenum

Pylorus

Pylorus

and is the outlet to the duodenum (small intestine).

pyo- *See* py-.

pyoderma /pī'ə dûr'mə/ any pus-producing infection of the skin, such as impetigo. [pyo- + -derma]

pyogenic /pī'ə jĕn'ĭk/ producing pus. [pyo- + -genic]

pyonephritis /pī'ō nĕ frī'tĭs/ inflammation of the kidney with pus. [pyo- + nephr- + -itis]

pyonephrosis /pī'ō nĕ frō'sĭs/ collection of pus in the kidney, usually caused by obstruction. [pyo- + nephr- + -osis]

pyorrhea /pī'ə rē'ə/ **1.** a discharge of pus. **2.** pus-producing inflammation of the tissues that surround the teeth. [pyo- + -rrhea]

pyosalpinx /pī'ō săl'pĭngks/ an accumulation of pus in a fallopian tube. [pyo- + salpinx]

pyothorax /pī'ō thôr'ăks/ an accumulation of pus in the pleural cavity of the lung (the space between the outer surface of the lung and the chest wall). [pyo- + thorax]

pyoureter /pī'ō yōō rē'tər/ the build-up of pus in a ureter. *Also called* ureteropyosis. [pyo- + ureter]

pyrexia /pī rĕk'sē ə/ fever.

pyridoxine /pĭr'ĭ dŏk'sēn/ a water-soluble B vitamin (also known as B_6) that is an essential coenzyme in many metabolic processes, including the synthesis and breakdown of amino acids; found especially in whole-grain cereals, yeast, liver, meat, and fish.

pyro- *combining form.* fire, heat, or fever: *for example,* pyromania.

pyrolysis /pī rŏl'ə sĭs/ the decomposition of a chemical compound by applying heat. [pyro- + -lysis]

pyromania /pī'rō mā'nē ə/ having an uncontrollable urge to set fires. [pyro- + -mania]

pyromaniac /pī'rō mā'nē ăk'/ a person affected by pyromania. [pyro- + maniac]

pyrophilia /pī'rō fīl'ē ə/ an abnormal liking for fire. [pyro- + -philia]

pyrophobia /pī'rə fō'bē ə/ an abnormal fear of fire. [pyro- + -phobia]

pyrosis /pī rō'sĭs/ a burning sensation felt in the chest caused by acid reflux. *Also called* heartburn.

pyruvate /pī rōō'vāt/ a salt of pyruvic acid.

pyruvic acid /pī rōō'vĭk/ a water-soluble liquid important in many metabolic processes and used in biochemical research.

pyuria /pī yōōr'ē ə/ having pus in the urine; usually indicating a urinary tract infection. [py- + -uria]

Q

q, q. *abbreviation.* every.

qam, q.a.m. *abbreviation.* every morning.

Q angle angle measuring the quadriceps for abnormalities leading to knee pathology. Any angle greater than 15 degrees is considered suspicious in diagnosing knee problems.

q.d., qd *abbreviation.* Latin *quaque die,* every day.

Q fever an infectious disease that is transmitted to humans from animals—especially sheep, goats, and cattle—which are carrying a species of bacteria called *Coxiella burnetti;* the infection causes a high fever, muscle ache, malaise, and sometimes pneumonia.

q.h., qh *abbreviation.* Latin *quaque hora,* every hour.

q.2h. *abbreviation.* every 2 hours.

q.3h. *abbreviation.* every 3 hours.

q.i.d., qid *abbreviation.* Latin *quatuor in die,* four times a day.

Qi gong/Qigong/Qi Gong /chē′gŭng′/ an ancient Chinese healing practice that uses a combination of exercises—mental, physical, and breath-related—aimed at balancing the qi (subtle life force or energy system) in the body, for the purpose of promoting health and well-being.

q.n.s., QNS *abbreviation.* quantity not sufficient; used by a laboratory when an insufficient amount of specimen is received to perform a requested test.

qod, q.o.d. *abbreviation.* every other day.

qoh, q.o.h. *abbreviation.* every other hour.

qpm, q.p.m. *abbreviation.* every evening.

QRS complex on an electrocardiogram, the portion of the waveform representing a QRS wave.

QRS wave on an electrocardiogram, the QRS wave is comprised of waves Q, R, and S, depicting a series of deflections representing the electrical activity generated by the ventricles of the heart during contraction.

q.s., QS *abbreviation.* quantity sufficient; quantity required.

qt *abbreviation.* 1. (*also* **qt.**) quart; quarts. 2. interval in QRS complex.

quack /kwăk/ someone who pretends to have medical skills; a charlatan.

quadri- *prefix.* four: *for example,* quadriplegia.

quadrant /kwŏd′rənt/ 1. one quarter of a circle. 2. one of four equally divided regions that are mentally drawn in a (roughly circular) anatomical site of the body; for example: the four quadrants of the abdomen, referred to as the right upper, left upper, right lower, and left lower quadrants.

quadriceps /kwŏd′rə sĕps′/ the large four-part muscle at the front of the thigh whose function is to extend the leg; it covers the front and sides of the femur (thigh bone).

quadriparesis /kwŏd′rə pə rē′sĭs/ weakness of all four limbs (arms and legs), usually the result of a spinal cord injury or stroke. *Also called* tetraparesis.

quadriparetic /kwŏd′rə pə rĕt′ĭk/ of or affected with quadriparesis. *Also called* tetraparetic.

quadriplegia /kwŏd′rə plē′jē ə, -jə/ complete paralysis of all four limbs (arms and legs), usually the result of a spinal cord injury or stroke. [quadri- + -plegia] *See illustration* on page 306.

quadriplegic /kwŏd′rə plē′jĭk/ 1. *adj.* pertaining to quadriplegia. 2. *n.* a person affected with quadriplegia.

quadruplet /kwŏ drŭp′lĭt, -drōō′plĭt/ one of a set of four infants born in a multiple pregnancy.

qualititative /kwŏl′ĭ tā′tĭv/ of or relating to the quality of something, such as the kind of cells, kind of care, and so on.

quality of life the measure of a patient's overall mental and physical condition based on his or her ability to enjoy normal life activities.

quantitative /kwŏn′tĭ tā′tĭv/ of or relating to the quantity of something, such as the measurement of results of a study.

quantum touch /kwŏn′təm/ an alternative healing therapy that combines various breathing and body-awareness exercises to increase a patient's energy levels, encouraging the body to heal itself.

quaque die (q.d., qd) /kwä′kwä dē′ā/ every day.

quarantine /kwôr′ən tēn′/ isolation of a person, plant, or animal that has a known contagious disease, or exposure to such a disease, for a set period of time (until the incubation period passes) in an effort to halt the spread of the disease.

Quadriplegia

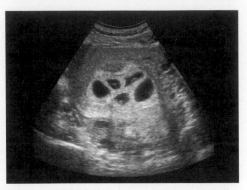

Quintuplets (fetuses)

quart (qt., qt) /kwôrt/ a unit of measure for liquid capacity equal to 32 ounces, ¼ gallon, or 0.946 liters.

quater in die (q.i.d, qid) /kwä′tĕr in dē′ā/ four times a day.

queasy /kwē′zē/ feeling sick to the stomach; nauseated.

Quellung reaction /kwĕl′əng, kvĕl′-/ swelling around a microorganism as a reaction to an antibody; used to test for the presence of certain microorganisms.

quickening /kwĭk′ə nĭng/ the first time during a pregnancy that a woman feels the baby moving inside the womb; it usually occurs 16–20 weeks into the pregnancy.

quiescent /kwī ĕs′ənt/ being at rest; inactive.

quinidine /kwĭn′ĭ dēn′/ a derivative of quinine, used to treat malaria and some heart disorders.

quinine /kwī′nīn/ a compound derived from certain tree barks, used to treat malaria.

quintuplet /kwĭn tŭp′lĭt, -tōō′plĭt/ any one of five offspring born together in the same pregnancy.

quotidian /kwō tĭd′ē ən/ occurring daily; for example, daily attacks of fever from malaria.

q wave a downward stroke in the QRS complex.

R

R, r *abbreviation.* roentgen.

Ra *abbreviation.* radium

RA *abbreviation.* rheumatoid arthritis.

rabies /rā'bēz/ viral disease transmitted by a bite from an infected animal; this highly infectious disease leads to fatal paralysis if not treated. *Also called* hydrophobia.

rach-, rachi-, rachio- *combining form.* spine: *for example,* rachiometer.

rachiometer /rā'kē ŏm'ĭ tər/ instrument used to measure spinal curvature. [rachio- + -meter]

rachiotomy /rā'kē ŏt'ə mē/ surgical removal of the lamina of a vertebral disc to relieve pain caused by compression of the nerve. *Also called* laminectomy. [rachio- + -tomy]

rachischisis /rə kĭs'kə sĭs/ congenital fissure of the spinal column, found in certain types of spina bifida. *Also called* spondyloschisis. [rachi- + -schisis]

rachitis /rə kī'tĭs/ 1. inflammation of the spinal column. 2. childhood bone disease caused by insufficient sunlight or vitamin D. *Also called* rickets. [rach- + -itis]

rad /răd/ *abbreviation.* radiation absorbed dose.

radi-, radio- *combining form.* radiation: *for example,* radioactive.

radial /rā'dē əl/ 1. parts spreading like rays from a common center. 2. the thumb side of the hand or forearm. 3. of or pertaining to the radius, the short thick bone in the forearm.

radial keratotomy /kĕr'ə tŏt'ə mē/ corneal surgery with symmetrical incisions into the cornea to correct myopia.

radiate /rā'dē āt'/ to spread like rays from a common center.

radiation /rā'dē ā'shən/ energy emission in the form of waves or particles as in the transmission of x-rays, ultraviolet light, or radio waves, used in diagnostic imaging.

radiation absorbed dose (rad) a unit of an absorbed dose of ionizing radiation, used in diagnostic imaging.

radiation oncology /ŏng kŏl'ə jē/ 1. the treatment of disease with radiation. *Also called* radiation therapy. 2. the medical specialty concerned with the use of radiation to treat disease.

radiation sickness fatigue, nausea, and vomiting from excessive radiation exposure; -

extreme exposure may lead to severe disease or death.

radiation therapy (XRT) treating disease with radiation, specifically x-rays. *Also called* radiation oncology.

radical /răd'ĭ kəl/ 1. extreme, said of the removal of all diseased tissue as well as some surrounding tissue, as in a radical mastectomy. 2. in biochemistry, a group of atoms having a certain structure in one molecule that moves as a group to another molecule maintaining that structure.

radical hysterectomy /hĭs'tə rĕk'tə mē/ surgical removal of the uterus, upper vagina, and parametrium.

radical mastectomy /mă stĕk'tə mē/ surgical removal of the entire breast, pectoral muscles, and often, neighboring lymph nodes and tissue; usually performed only when cancer has spread.

radical prostatectomy /prŏs'tə tĕk'tə mē/ surgical removal of the prostate gland and usually associated retroperitoneal lymph nodes.

radicul-, radiculo- *combining form.* relating to the root, as of a nerve or tooth: *for example,* radiculitis.

radiculectomy /rə dĭk'yə lĕk'tə mē/ surgical cutting of the spinal nerve roots to relieve pain. *Also called* rhizotomy. [radiculo- + -ectomy]

radiculitis /rə dĭk'yə lī'tĭs/ inflammation of the nerve root. [radicul- + -itis]

radiculopathy /rə dĭk'yə lŏp ə thē/ any disease of the nerve roots. [radiculo- + -pathy]

radioactive /rā'dē ō ăk'tĭv/ emitting alpha, beta, or gamma rays. [radio- + active]

radioallergosorbent test (RAST) /rā'dē ō ə lür'gō sŏr'bənt/ a test for allergies using radioimmunoassay procedures in which the patient's own serum reacts or does not react to an antigen.

radiocurable /rā'dē ō kyŏŏr'ə bəl/ curable with radiation therapy. [radio- + curable]

radiodiagnosis /rā'dē ō dī'əg nō'sĭs/ diagnostic imaging, such as x-ray, magnetic resonance, and sonar. [radio- + -diagnosis]

radiofrequency /rā'dē ō frē'kwən sē/ a range of electromagnetic wave frequencies. [radio- + frequency]

radiogram /rā′dē ə grăm′/ or **radiograph** /rā′dē ə grăf′/ an image produced by projecting x-rays (high-energy electromagnetic radiation) through the body onto film. *Also called* x-ray. [radio- + -gram *or* -graph]

radiographer /rā′dē ŏg′rə fər/ an x-ray technologist. [radio- + -grapher]

radiography /rā′dē ŏg′rə fē/ the process of examining part of the body via an x-ray or sonogram. [radio- + -graphy]

radioimmunoassay (RIA) /rā′dē ō ĭm′yə nō ə sā′, -ăs′ā/ identification of a substance that has been radioactively labeled based on its action as an antigen, used in diagnosis.

radiological /rā′dē ə lŏj′ĭ kəl/ or **radiologic** /rā′dē ə lŏj′ĭk/ of or relating to the use of radioactive substances to diagnose or treat disease. [radio- + -logic]

radiologic technologist or **radiologic technician (RT)**/tĕk nŏl′ə jĭst/ a technician trained in diagnostic imaging.

radiologist /rā′dē ŏl′ə jĭst/ a medical specialist trained to use radiological imaging in the diagnosis and treatment of disease. *Also called* roentgenologist.

radiology /rā′dē ŏl′ə jē/ the branch of medicine that uses radioactive imaging to diagnose and treat disease. *Also called* roentgenology. [radio- + -logy]

radiolucent /rā′dē ō lōō′sənt/ able to be penetrated by x-rays.

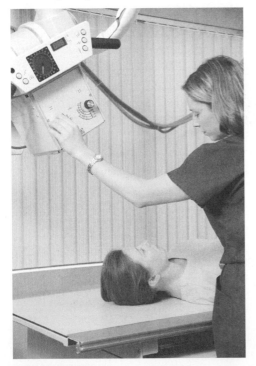

Radiologic Technician

radiopaque /rā′dē ō pāk′/ not able to be penetrated by x-rays and, therefore, visible on an x-ray exam. [radio- + opaque]

radiopharmaceutical /rā′dē ō fär′mə sōō′tĭ kəl/ a radioactive drug that is implanted, as in a joint. [radio- + pharmaceutical]

radioresistant /rā′dē ō rĭ zĭs′tənt/ resistant to radiation therapy. [radio- + resistant]

radiosensitive /rā′dē ō sĕn′sĭ tĭv/ treatable with radiation therapy. [radio- + sensitive]

radiotherapy /rā′dē ō thĕr′ə pē/ treatment of disease with radiation. [radio- + therapy]

radium (Ra) /rā′dē əm/ radioactive element used in cancer treatment.

radius /rā′dē əs/ the short, thick forearm bone located on the lateral side of the ulna.

radon (Rn) /rā′dŏn/ radioactive gaseous element formed when radium is broken down.

rales /rālz/ abnormal respiratory sound heard during auscultation.

raloxifene /rə lŏk′sə fēn′/ an estrogen modulating, oral preventive for osteoporosis also believed to counter the cancer-producing effects of estrogen on breast and uterine tissue.

ramus /rā′məs/ (*pl.* **rami** /rā′mī/) **1.** a branch of a nerve or blood vessel. **2.** the posterior part of the mandible. **3.** the primary divisions in the cerebral sulcus (grooves in the brain).

rancid /răn′sĭd/ having the unpleasant taste or odor of something, especially fats or oils, that is stale and decomposed.

random sample a group of subjects taken at random so as to understand the probability of certain outcomes in a particular population.

randomization /răn′də mə za′shən/ the arranging in a random manner of elements in an experiment.

random specimen a sample, such as a urine specimen to be tested for drugs, that is collected at any time, particularly when not expected.

range of motion (ROM) the area through which a joint is able to move freely.

rape /rāp/ the criminal act of forcing another person to submit to sexual intercourse.

rapid eye movement (REM) the rapid, jerky eye movements that occur while dreaming.

rash /răsh/ a red and patchy skin eruption.

RAST /răst/ *abbreviation.* radioallergosorbent test.

rate /rāt/ **1.** the speed or frequency of occurrence of an event, usually expressed with respect to time or some other known standard. **2.** a measure of the frequency of an event within a specified population, usually expressed with respect to the specified population.

rationalization /răsh′ə nə lə zā′shən/ a psychological defense mechanism in which the subject provides a plausible but untrue reason for his or her behavior.

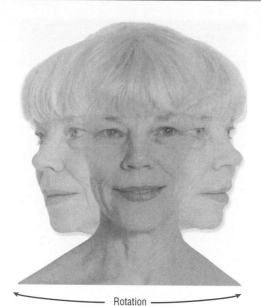

← Rotation →

Range of Motion (of head—sideways)

Raynaud('s) /rā nō(z)′/ **disease** or **phenome-non** a vascular disorder of the fingers and toes with blanching, bluish coloring, and numbness resulting from exposure to cold.

RBC *abbreviation.* **1.** red blood cells. **2.** red blood count.

RBC count red blood cell count.

RD *abbreviation.* registered dietitian.

RDA *abbreviation.* Recommended Daily Allowance; Recommended Dietary Allowance.

RDS *abbreviation.* respiratory distress syndrome.

re- *prefix.* **1.** again: *for example,* reabsorption. **2.** backward: *for example,* recessive.

reabsorption /rē′ăb sôrp′shən, -zôrp′-/ to absorb something previously secreted or emitted. [re- + absorption]

reaction /rē ăk′shən/ **1.** the response of an organism to a stimulus. **2.** a chemical process or change; transformation of one substance into another in response to a stimulus. **3.** an emotional and mental response to a stimulus. **4.** action of an antibody on a specific antigen, irrespective of the presence or absence of other components of the immunologic system.

reactive /rē ăk′tĭv/ capable of reacting to a stimulus. [re- + active]

reagent /rē ā′jənt/ a substance used in a chemical reaction to examine or produce another substance. [re- + agent]

reality testing the psychological process of understanding and appreciating one's relationship to the world through the experience of consequences.

rebound /rē′bound/ a return to a previous condition following the end of a course of treatment.

receptor /rĭ sĕp′tər/ **1.** a sensory organ, cell, or group of cells that responds to stimuli. **2.** a part of a cell that has an affinity for a specific chemical group, molecule, or virus.

recessive /rĭ sĕs′ĭv/ **1.** tending to recede (become more distant). **2.** an inherited trait that appears only when not masked by an inherited dominant characteristic.

recidivism /rĭ sĭd′ə vĭz′əm/ repeated lapsing into socially undesirable behaviors or situations.

recidivist /rĭ sĭd′ə vĭst/ **1.** someone who repeatedly relapses, as into criminal behavior. **2.** in psychiatry, someone who repeatedly relapses into antisocial behavior.

recipient /rĭ sĭp′ē ənt/ an individual who receives something, as an organ, blood, or tissue from a donor.

recombinant DNA /rē kŏm′bə nənt/ genetically engineered DNA made by combining DNA from organisms of different species.

Recommended Daily Allowance (RDA) the average daily nutrient and calorie intake recommended for good health by the federal government.

Recommended Dietary Allowance (RDA) the average daily nutrient and calorie intake recommended for good health by the federal government.

reconstruction /rē′kən strŭk′shən/ the rebuilding and correction of the appearance and function of damaged or defective body structures.

record /rĕk′ərd/ *n.* **1.** a written account of a patient's history with the supplier of medical care. **2.** in dentistry, the registration of jaw relations on a malleable material or on a device. *v.* /rĭ kôrd′/ *v.* **3.** to make a record.

recovery room a hospital unit for the care of patients who have just had surgery; usually used until the patient awakens from anesthesia, now called PACU (post-anesthesia care unit).

recrudescence /rē′kroo dĕs′əns/ the recurrence, or increased severity, of a disease after a remission. *Also called* relapse.

rect-, recto- *combining form.* rectum: *for example,* rectoabdominal.

rectal /rĕk′təl/ relating to the rectum.

rectal incontinence /ĭn kŏn′tə nəns/ the inability to control excretory functions. *Also called* anal incontinence, fecal incontinence.

rectoabdominal /rĕk′tō ăb dŏm′ə nəl/ relating to the *rectus abdominis* muscle, the vertical bands from the pubis to the lower sternal margin. [recto- + abdominal]

R

rectocele /rĕk′tə sēl′/   protrusion of the rectum into the vagina. *Also called* proctocele. [recto- + -cele]

rectoplasty /rĕk′tə plăs′tē/   reconstructive surgery of the rectum. *Also called* proctoplasty. [recto- + -plasty]

rectoscope /rĕk′tə skōp′/   an instrument, consisting of a tube and a light, used to examine the rectum. *Also called* proctoscope. [recto- + -scope]

rectoscopy /rĕk tŏs′kə pē/   the internal examination of the rectum. *Also called* proctoscopy. [recto- + -scopy]

rectourethral /rĕk′tō yoō rē′thrəl/   relating to or connecting the rectum and the urethra. [recto- + urethral]

rectouterine pouch /rĕk′to yoō′tər ĭn/   a sac between the rectum and the uterus formed by an abnormal fold in the peritoneum. [recto- + uterine]

rectum /rĕk′təm/   the end portion of the large intestine, from the sigmoid flexure to the anus.

rectus /rĕk′təs/   a straight muscle.

recumbent /rĭ kŭm′bənt/   reclining in a comfortable position.

recuperate /rĭ koō′pə rāt′/   to recover from an illness, injury, or surgery.

recurrence /rĭ kûr′əns/   a repeat occurrence, as the relapse of the symptoms of a disease.

recurrent /rĭ kûr′ənt/   **1.** occurring repeatedly. **2.** turning in a reverse direction, said of nerves and blood vessels.

red blood cell (RBC)   a cell that contains hemoglobin that carries oxygen to body tissues. *Also called* erythrocyte.

red blood cell (RBC) count   number of red blood cells per cubic millimeter of blood. *Also called* red blood count.

red blood count (RBC)   red blood cell count.

red cell   a red blood cell.

red corpuscle /kôr′pŭs əl/   a red blood cell.

reduction /rĭ dŭk′shən/   restoration of a body part or condition to normal by surgery or manipulation.

reduction mammaplasty /măm′ə plăs′tē/   plastic surgery to reduce the size of the breasts.

referral /rĭ fûr′əl/   **1.** the direction of a patient or case to a specialist for treatment. **2.** the patient who is referred.

referred pain /rĭ fûrd′/   pain related to an injury that is felt in area away from the site of the injury.

reflex /rē′flĕks/   an involuntary physiological response to a stimulus.

reflex sympathetic dystrophy (RSD) /sĭm′pə thĕt′ĭk dĭs′trə fē/   a sympathetic nervous system disorder following an injury, marked by motor and sensory disturbances of an extremity.

reflexology /rē′flĕk sŏl′ə jē/   **1.** the study of how reflex responses affect behavior. **2.** the application of pressure to specific points on the hands or feet believed to benefit specific, corresponding areas throughout the body.

reflux /rē′flŭks/   a flowing back or regurgitation, particularly of stomach acids into the esophagus.

reflux esophagitis /ĭ sŏf′ə jī′tĭs/   inflammation of the esophagus caused by the regurgitation of gastric acid.

reflux surgery /sûr′jə rē/   surgical procedure to fold the fundus of the stomach around the lower esophagus to block reflux. *Also called* antireflux surgery, fundoplication.

refract /rĭ frăkt′/   to change the direction of a ray of light.

refraction /rĭ frăk′shən/   the bending of a wave of light as it passes from one medium to another, said of the eye's ability to focus an image on the retina.

refractory /rĭ frăk′tə rē/   resistant to treatment, said of a disease.

refractory anemia /ə nē′mē ə/   a severe anemia that is not treatable with medication and that requires repeated blood transfusions to preserve life.

regeneration /rĭ jĕn′ə rā′shən/   **1.** the regrowth or restoration of a damaged or destroyed part or organic tissue. **2.** asexual reproduction, as when a worm is cut in two and both halves become new worms.

regimen /rĕj′ə mən/   a systematic plan for therapy, diet, and/or medication designed to promote the health of a patient.

regional anesthesia /rē′jə nəl ăn′əs thē′zhə/   use of a local anesthetic to produce loss of sensation in a limited area while the patient remains conscious.

regional enteritis /ĕn′tə rī′tĭs/   a chronic, progressive inflammation of the ileum. *Also called* Crohn's disease, granulomatous colitis.

registered dietitian (RD) /rĕj′ə stərd dī′ĭ tĭsh′ən/   a specialist in dietetics who has met the requirements for certification stipulated by the American Dietetic Association.

registered nurse (RN)   a trained nurse who is state-certified and licensed to practice nursing.

Red Blood Cell

registry /rĕj′ĭs trē/ **1.** a place where records, data, or lab samples are kept and made available for research or study. **2.** an organization that lists nurses seeking employment, and through which they can be hired.

regress /rĭ grĕs′/ to return to a previous, often worse, condition.

regression /rĭ grĕsh′ən/ **1.** a return to a less mature stage of psychosocial development **2.** a remission of the symptoms of a disease. **3.** an increase in the symptoms of a disease.

regulation /rĕg′yə lā′shən/ **1.** the act or condition of controlling or directing or of being controlled or directed. **2.** the ability of an embryo, to develop normally despite experimental modifications. **3.** a law or rule that legally regulates conduct of a person or institution.

regulatory gene /rĕg′yə lə tôr′ē jēn′/ a gene that produces a protein that inhibits an operator gene.

regulatory sequence /sē′kwəns/ a DNA sequence that regulates gene expression.

regurgitate /rĭ gûr′jĭ tāt′/ **1.** to flow backward, especially blood through a defective (leaking) heart valve. **2.** to bring up undigested, swallowed food into the mouth.

regurgitation /rĭ gûr′jĭ tā′shən/ **1.** backward flowing of blood through a defective (leaking) heart valve. **2.** bringing up undigested, swallowed food into the mouth.

rehab /rē′hăb/ short for rehabilitation.

rehabilitation /rē′hə bĭl′ĭ tā′shən/ **1.** restoration to physical health after an illness, through training and therapy, within the limitations of a person's disability. **2.** detoxification from alcohol or drug dependence through an intensive therapeutic (usually) inpatient program.

rehydrate /rē hī′drāt/ to restore fluids to the body lost through dehydration. [re- + hydrate]

rehydration /rē′hī drā′shən/ the restoration of fluids to the body that were lost through dehydration. [re- + hydration]

reiki /rā′kē/ Japanese technique for stress reduction, relaxation, and the promotion of healing; believed to benefit the body through the releasing of life force energy to move freely through the body.

reimbursement /rē′ĭm bûrs′mənt/ compensation paid for medical services, often refers to an overall plan such as how an institution provides care.

reimplantation /rē′ĭm plăn tā′shən/ replacement of a body part or tissue that has been removed back to its original site. *Also called* replantation. [re- + implantation]

reinfection /rē′ĭn fĕk′shən/ a second infection that follows recovery from a previous infection of the same type. [re- + infection]

reinnervate /rē′ĭ nûr′vāt, -ĭn′ər vāt′/ to restore function to a denervated body part by supplying it with nerves, through grafting or regrowth. [re- + innervate]

reinnervation /rē′ĭn ər vā′shən/ restoration of function to a denervated body part by supplying it with nerves, through grafting or regrowth.

rejection /rĭ jĕk′shən/ refusal to accept, said of an organ recipient's failure to accept a transplanted organ or tissue because of immunological incompatibility.

relapse 1. *v.* /rĭ lăps′/ return to a former state of illness after an apparent recovery. **2.** *n.* /rĭ lăps′, rē′lăps/ a recurrence of illness. *Also called* recrudescence. [re- + lapse]

relapsing fever /fē′vər/ an illness with periods of high fever transmitted by the bite of infected lice or ticks.

relaxant /rĭ lăk′sənt/ a drug that relaxes the body by relieving muscular tension. *Also called* muscle relaxant.

releasing factor a substance produced by the hypothalamus that stimulates the pituitary gland to accelerate the secretion of certain hormones.

relieve /rĭ lēv′/ to alleviate pain, discomfort, anxiety, distress, etc.

REM /rĕm/ *abbreviation.* rapid eye movements.

rem /rĕm/ the dosage of radiation needed to produce the same effect as one rad of x-rays. [roentgen equivalent in man]

REM sleep the sleep state during which dreaming occurs, characterized by rapid eye movements.

remedy /rĕm′ĭ dē/ agent that relieves a disease or disorder.

remission /rĭ mĭsh′ən/ the period during which symptoms of a disease subside.

remote telesurgery /tĕl′ə sûr′jə rē/ microsurgery using remote-controlled robotic instruments. *See illustration* on page 312.

ren-, reni-, reno- *combining form.* kidney: *for example,* renogram.

renal /rē′nəl/ relating to the kidneys.

Rehabilitation

Remote Telesurgery

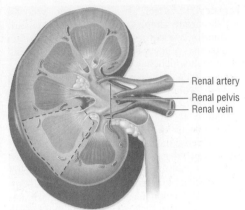

— Renal artery
— Renal pelvis
— Renal vein

Renal Pelvis

renal aneurysm /ăn′yə rĭz′əm/ an abnormal blood-filled dilation of a renal artery.

renal angiogram /ăn′jē ə grăm′/ an x-ray of the renal blood vessels, made after the injection of a radiopaque substance into the vessel, used in the diagnosis of pathological conditions.

renal angiography /ăn′jē ŏg′rə fē/ x-ray imaging of the renal blood vessels, made after the injection of a radiopaque substance into the vessel (usually via a femoral artery catheter), used in the diagnosis of pathological conditions.

renal artery /är′tə rē/ an artery originating from the aorta and distributing oxygenated blood to the kidneys, adrenal glands, and ureters.

renal calculus /kăl′kyə ləs/ a stone-like mass formed in the excretory passages of the kidney. *Also called* kidney stone, nephrolith.

renal capsule /kăp′səlz, -soolz/ the fibrous membrane surrounding each kidney.

renal colic /kŏl′ĭk/ the intense pain caused by the passage of a calculus through the ureter.

renal failure inability of the kidneys to excrete waste from the body. *Also called* kidney failure.

renal hypertension /hī′pər tĕn′shən/ hypertension resulting from kidney disease.

renal pelvis /pĕl′vĭs/ a funnel-shaped interior structure of the kidney into which urine is discharged before passing into the ureter.

renal tubule /toob′yool/ a convoluted tubular structure in the kidney for filtering blood and producing urine.

renal vein a vein that leaves the kidney from the renal hilum and drains into the vena cava.

renin /rē′nĭn/ an enzyme released by the kidneys that raises blood pressure by activating angiotensin.

rennin /rĕn′ĭn/ a digestive enzyme secreted in the gastric mucosa.

reno- *See* ren-.

renogram /rē′nō grăm′/ **1.** a graphic record of the passage of a radioactive tracer through the renal system, used in diagnosing kidney function. **2.** an x-ray of a kidney. [reno- + -gram]

renomegaly /rē′nō mĕg′ə lē/ the abnormal enlargement of a kidney. [reno- + -megaly]

repair /rĭ pâr′/ to heal, replace, improve, etc., damaged or diseased tissue or an organ or other body part.

repetitive stress injury /rĭ pĕt′ĭ tĭv/ a nerve or tendon disorder, such as carpal tunnel syndrome, caused by overexertion in repetitive motion activities.

replantation /rē′plăn tā′shən/ reattachment of a body part including the reestablishment of circulation. *Also called* reimplantation.

replication /rĕp′lĭ kā′shən/ **1.** the process of duplicating. **2.** repetition of an experiment to verify results.

repolarization /rē′pō lər ə zā′shən/ restoration of a polarized state across a membrane, with positive charges on the outer surface and negative charges on the inner surface. [re- + polarization]

reportable disease /rĭ pôr′tə bəl/ a disease, such as AIDS, gonorrhea, hepatitis, or tuberculosis, whose presence in a patient must be reported to Centers for Disease Control and often state and local authorities. *Also called* notifiable disease.

repress /rĭ prĕs′/ to expel or reject or otherwise inhibit, unconsciously, painful impulses, fears, memories, or desires from the conscious mind.

repression /rĭ prĕsh′ən/ **1.** the process of inhibiting **2.** the defense mechanism whereby the unconscious protects the conscious mind from painful impulses, fears, memories, or desires.

reproduce /rē′prə doos′/ to produce offspring, sexually or asexually. [re- + produce]

reproduction /rē′prə dŭk′shən/ **1.** the process of being reproduced. **2.** the sexual or asexual process by which organisms produce offspring. [re- + production]

reproductive system /rē′prə dŭk′tĭv/ the complex system of male or female organs and tissues involved in sexual reproduction. [re- + productive]

resect /rē sĕkt′/ to remove part or all of an organ or tissue through surgery.

resectable /rē sĕk′tə bəl/ capable of being surgically removed.

resection /rē sĕk′shən/ surgical removal of part or all of an organ or structure. [re- + section]

resectoscope /rē sĕk′tə skōp′/ tubular endoscopic instrument equipped with a sliding electrocautery loop, used for the surgical removal of lesions of the bladder, urethra, or prostate.

reservoir /rĕz′ər vwär′/ 1. fluid-containing sac. 2. an organism that transmits a pathogen while remaining unaffected by it. 3. an extra supply.

residency /rĕz′ĭ dən sē/ period during which a physician receives specialized clinical training in a hospital.

resident /rĕz′ĭ dənt/ a physician during residency.

residue /rĕz′ĭ dōō/ what remains after part of something has been removed.

residual urine /rĭ zĭj′ōō əl yŏŏr′ĭn/ urine that remains in the bladder after urination.

resistance /rĭ zĭs′təns/ the capacity of an organism to defend against disease, infection, or toxic agents.

resistant /rĭ zĭs′tənt/ incapable of being affected by a toxin or disease-causing agent.

resolution /rĕz′ə lōō′shən/ the subsidence of a pathological condition.

resorb /rē sôrb′, -zôrb′/ to break down and assimilate, as in damaged tissue.

resorption /rē sôrp′shən, -zôrp′-/ the process in which a body substance dissolves and undergoes assimilation.

respiration /rĕs′pə rā′shən/ the process of inhaling oxygen and exhaling carbon dioxide; breathing.

respirator /rĕs′pə rā′tər/ breathing device used in mechanical ventilation. *Also called* ventilator.

respiratory /rĕs′pər ə tôr′ē/ relating to respiration.

respiratory distress syndrome (RDS) acute respiratory disease of newborn babies, especially premature babies, in which the alveoli (tiny air sacs in the lungs) collapse because of lack of surfactant. *Also called* hyaline membrane disease.

respiratory rate the number of times per minute a person inhales and exhales.

respiratory system the system of organs involved in breathing, including the nose, pharynx, larynx, trachea, bronchial tubes, and lungs.

respiratory therapist (RT) /thĕr′ə pĭst/ a specialist in the therapeutic treatment of breathing disorders.

respiratory therapy /thĕr′ə pē/ the treatment of breathing disorders through the use of respirators or inhalant medication.

respiratory tract the organs involved in breathing, including the nose, nasal passages, nasopharynx, larynx, trachea, bronchi, and lungs.

respirometer /rĕs′pə rŏm′ĭ tər/ an instrument that measures the extent and characteristics of respiration.

response /rĭ spŏns′/ 1. any behavior that results from a stimulus. 2. the totality of a patient's reactions to a treatment, positive or negative.

rest /rĕst/ *n.* 1. repose of the body caused by sleep or by freedom from mental or physical labor. 2. a remnant of embryonic material that persists in the living organism after birth. 3. in dentistry, a support for a restoration. *v.* 4. to sit or lie down and relax.

restenosis /rē′stě nō′sĭs/ the recurrence of narrowing in a valve or duct after corrective surgery.

restitution /rĕs′tĭ tōō′shən/ a return to a previous state, said of the rotating movement of a newborn's head, during childbirth, to its position at the beginning of labor.

restless legs syndrome neurological disorder of unknown etiology characterized by dysaesthesias and restlessness in the legs, often occurring after going to bed, causing insomnia.

restoration /rĕs′tə rā′shən/ 1. a return to a healthy condition. 2. a dental replacement such as an implant, crown, partial denture, etc.

restraint /rĭ strānt′/ a device or means to restrict movement, especially a straitjacket or wrist straps used to restrain an agitated patient. *See illustration* on page 314.

resuscitate /rĭ sŭs′ĭ tāt′/ to revive a person from apparent death or unconsciousness.

resuscitation /rĭ sŭs′ĭ tā′shən/ the act of restoring a person to life or consciousness.

retain /rĭ tān′/ 1. to hold in position. 2. to hold in, as fluid.

retainer /rĭ tā′nər/ 1. the part of a dental bridge that is fastened to adjacent, natural teeth. 2. a device that holds teeth in position after orthodontic treatment.

retardation /rē′tär dā′shən/ 1. the condition of being slow in mental or physical development. 2. slowness in progress.

retch /rĕch/ 1. to involuntarily attempt to vomit. 2. to vomit.

R

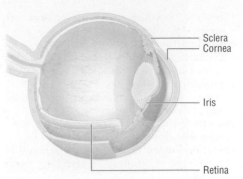

Retina

Restraint (straitjacket)

retention /rĭ tĕn′shən/ **1.** the act of retaining, as in the involuntary retaining of bodily wastes that are normally excreted. **2.** the ability to recall what has been experienced or learned.

retic-, reticulo- *combining form.* network: *for example,* reticulocyte.

reticular layer /rĭ tĭk′yə lər/ a deep fascial layer of the dermis.

reticulocyte /rĭ tĭk′yə lə sīt′/ an immature red blood cell consisting of a network of basophilic filaments (filaments that are easily stained with certain dyes). [reticulo- + -cyte]

reticulocytosis /rĭ tĭk′yə lō sī tō′sĭs/ an increase in the number of reticulocytes in the blood. [reticulo- + -cytosis]

retin-, retino- *combining form.* retina: *for example,* retinitis.

retina /rĕt′ə nə/ the light-sensitive membrane at the back of the eye that is the sensory end of the optic nerve; it receives the image formed by the lens and transmits the visual information to the brain via the optic nerve.

retinal /rĕt′ə nəl/ of or relating to the retina.

retinal detachment /dĭ tăch′mənt/ visual impairment in which the retina has separated from the choroid.

retinitis /rĕt′ə nī′tĭs/ inflammation of the retina. [retin- + -itis]

retinitis pigmentosa (RP) /pĭg′mĕn tō′sə/ a hereditary eye disease marked by night blindness, retinal atrophy, and pigment changes, constriction of the visual field, and eventual blindness.

retinoblastoma /rĕt′ə nō blăs tō′mə/ a hereditary malignant tumor of the retina that is present at birth or develops in childhood. [retino- + blastoma]

retinoid /rĕt′ə noid′/ any of various vitamin A derivatives used to treat acne and psoriasis. [retin- + -oid]

retinol /rĕt′ə nôl′/ an alcohol of vitamin A that plays an important role in the vision cycle.

retinopathy /rĕt′ə nŏp′ə thē/ any non-inflammatory degenerative condition of the retina. [retino- + -pathy]

retinopexy /rĕt′ə nō pĕk′sē/ surgical repair of a detached retina, by scleral band and/or cryopexy. [retino- + -pexy]

retinoschisis /rĕt′ə nŏs′kə sĭs/ degenerative splitting of the retina into layers. [retino- + -schisis]

retinoscope /rĕt′ə nə skōp′/ an instrument for examining light refraction in the eye. [retino- + -scope]

retraction /rĭ trăk′shən/ a drawing back or pulling inward, said of the movement of an organ or body part.

retractor /rĭ trăk′tər/ **1.** a surgical instrument used to hold back organs or tissues from the field of operation. **2.** a muscle that draws back an organ or body part.

retro- *prefix.* **1.** backward: *for example,* retroflexion. **2.** located behind: *for example,* retroperitoneal.

retroflexion /rĕt′rō flĕk′shən/ the backward bending of an organ or body part, said of the bending back of the uterus upon the cervix. [retro- + flexion]

retrograde /rĕt′rə grād′/ deteriorating from the normal order of development. [retro- + grade]

retrograde pyelogram /pī′ə lə grăm′/ a radiograph of the calyceal system of the kidney, made by injecting a radiopaque substance into the ureter. [retro- + grade]

retrogression /rĕt′rə grĕsh′ən/ **1.** degeneration; getting worse. **2.** a return to an earlier stage of development.

retroperitoneal /rĕt′rō pĕr′ĭ tə nē′əl/ located behind the peritoneum, as are the kidneys, ureters, bladder, uterus, etc. [retro- + peritoneal]

retroperitoneum /rĕt′rō pĕr′ĭ tə nē′əm/ the space behind the peritoneum. [retro- + peritoneum]

retroposition /rĕt′rō pə zĭsh′ən/ the backward displacement of an organ or structure, said especially of the uterus. [retro- + position]

retroversion /rĕt′rə vûr′zhən/ the tilting backward of an organ or body part, said of the uterus and cervix. [retro- + -version]

retrovirus /rĕt′rō vī′rəs/ any of a group of viruses, including HIV, that contain RNA and replicate in targeted host cells. [retro- + virus]

retrusion /rĭ trōō′zhən/ in dentistry, pushed backward or retracted in relationship to the position of the mandible, as opposed to protrusion.

reuptake/re-uptake /rē ŭp′tāk/ **1.** the process of using again. **2.** the reabsorption by a neuron of a neurotransmitter after a nerve impulse has been transmitted. [re- + uptake]

Reye('s) syndrome /rī(z), rā(z)/ an often fatal brain disorder in children with onset following an acute viral infection; may be precipitated by aspirin use in children.

RF *abbreviation.* rheumatoid factor.

rhabdoid /răb′doid/ rod-shaped.

rhabdomy-, rhabdomyo- *combining form.* striated muscle: *for example,* rhabdomyoma.

rhabdomyolysis /răb′dō mī ŏl′ə sĭs/ a disease that causes degeneration of skeletal muscle or an acute injury of skeletal muscle, like a crush injury, which liberates myoglobin and can cause renal failure. [rhabdomyo- + -lysis]

rhabdomyoma /răb′dō mī ō′mə/ a benign tumor composed of striated muscle fibers. [rhabdmyo- + -oma]

rhabdomyosarcoma /răb′dō mī′ō sär kō′mə/ a malignant tumor composed of striated muscle fibers. [rhabdomyo- + sarcoma]

Rh disease /är′āch′/ a fetal disease occurring when an Rh-negative mother produces antibodies to an antigen in the blood of her Rh-positive fetus which cross the placenta and destroy the red blood cells of the fetus.

rheumat-, rheumato- *combining form.* joint: *for example,* rheumatology.

rheumatic fever /rōō măt′ĭk/ an acute childhood disease characterized by fever, painful inflammation of the joints, and, damage to the heart valves that appears later in life; a sequela of untreated Group A streptococcal infection.

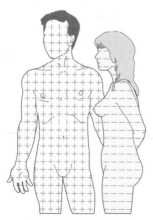

Rh-negative woman and Rh-positive man conceive a child.

Rh-negative woman with Rh-positive fetus

Cells from Rh-positive fetus enter mother's bloodstream.

Woman's antibodies form to fight Rh-positive blood cells.

In the next Rh-positive pregnancy, maternal antibodies attack fetal blood cells.

Rh Disease

rheumatic heart disease   damage to the heart valves caused by rheumatic fever, resulting in the reduced efficiency of the heart in pumping blood.

rheumatism /roo'mə tĭz'əm/   painful disorder of the joints, muscles, or connective tissue characterized by inflammation and disability.

rheumatoid arthritis (RA) /roo'mə toid' är thrĭ'tĭs/   a chronic autoimmune disease characterized by pain, inflammation, and stiffness in the joints, muscles, or connective tissue.

rheumatoid factor (RF)   autoantibody found in the blood serum of people with rheumatoid arthritis, used to diagnose the disease.

rheumatologist /roo'mə tŏl'ə jĭst/   a physician specializing in the diagnosis and treatment of rheumatic diseases.

rheumatology /roo'mə tŏl'ə jē/   the branch of medicine concerned with the study and treatment of rheumatic diseases. [rheumato- + -logy]

Rh factor   genetically determined red blood cell antigen capable of producing strong immunogenic reactions in individuals lacking the antigen.

Rh incompatibility   incompatibility of Rh blood types.

rhin-, rhino- *combining form.* the nose, nasal: *for example,* rhinitis.

rhinitis /rī nī'tĭs/   inflammation of the nasal mucous membranes. [rhin- + -itis]

rhinomycosis /rī'nō mī kō'sĭs/   fungal infection of the nasal mucous membranes. [rhino- + mycosis]

rhinophyma /rī'nō fī'mə/   enlargement of the nose resulting from an advanced stage of acne rosacea.

rhinoplasty /rī'nō plăs'tē/   plastic surgery of the nose. [rhino- + -plasty]

rhinorrhagia /rī'nō rā'jē ə/   a nosebleed. *Also called* epistaxis. [rhino- + -rrhagia]

rhinorrhea /rī'nō rē'ə/   excessive mucous discharge from the nose. *Also called* runny nose. [rhino- + -rrhea]

rhinotomy /rī nŏt'ə mē/   surgical incision into the nose. [rhino- + -tomy]

rhizotomy /rī zŏt'ə mē/   surgical procedure to cut the spinal nerve roots to relieve pain. *Also called* radiculectomy.

Rh negative/Rh-negative   the blood group whose red blood cells lack the Rh antigen.

rhonchus /rŏng'kəs/ (*pl.* **rhonchi** /rŏng'kī/)   a snoring sound in the chest, caused by secretions in a bronchial tube.

Rh positive/Rh-positive   the blood group whose red blood cells have the Rh antigen.

rhythm /rĭ_th_'əm/   **1.** measured time or movement; regular taking place of action or function. **2.** in electroencephalography, the regular

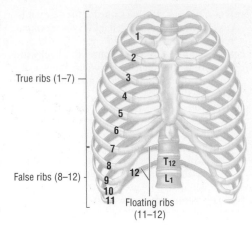

True ribs (1–7)
False ribs (8–12)
Floating ribs (11–12)

Rib Cage

occurrence of an impulse. **3.** the rhythm method.

rhythm method   birth control based on abstinence during ovulation.

rhytidectomy /rĭt'ĭ dĕk'tə mē/   plastic surgery to remove wrinkles from the face; a face lift.

rhytidoplasty /rĭt'ĭ dō plăs'tē/   plastic surgery to reduce sagging skin or wrinkles from the face. *Also called* plastic surgery.

RIA   *abbreviation.* radioimmunoassay.

rib /rĭb/   one of a series of long curved bones, extending from the spine to the sternum. *See also* false rib, floating rib, true rib.

rib cage   the enclosing structure of the chest, comprised of the ribs and the bones to which they attach. *Also called* thoracic cage.

ribonucleic acid (RNA) /rī'bō noo klē'ĭk/   any of various nucleic acids involved in the control of cellular chemical processes and in the transmission of genetic information.

ribonucleoprotein (RNP) /rī'bō noo'klē ō prō' tēn, -tē ĭn/   a compound of RNA and protein that is the primary component of the hereditary material in chromosomes.

ribosome /rī'bə sōm'/   RNA-containing organelles in a cell where protein synthesis occurs.

rickets /rĭk'ĭts/   a bone-softening disease of children caused by a Vitamin D deficiency. *Also called* rachitis.

rickettsia /rĭ kĕt'sē ə/   bacteria that live in lice and ticks and which transmit diseases including Rocky Mountain spotted fever and typhus to humans, when bitten by infected lice or ticks.

rickettsiosis /rĭ kĕt'sē ō'sĭs/   disease caused by rickettsia.

ridge /rĭj/   **1.** an elongated structure that projects above the surrounding surface; a crest.

2. a linear elevation on a tooth. **3.** the gums and bony process of the maxilla or mandible that contain the tooth sockets; the alveolar process without teeth present.

right atrium /ā′trē əm/ an upper chamber of the heart that receives blood from veins and passes it into the ventricles.

right colic flexure the bend in the colon at the point in which the ascending colon and transverse colon meet. *Also called* hepatic flexure.

right-handed /rīt′ hăn′dĭd/ having a more co-ordinated and skillful use of the right than the left hand, particularly for writing, and other manual tasks.

right heart the right atrium and ventricle.

right hepatic duct /hĭ păt′ĭk/ the duct that transmits bile to the common hepatic duct from the right side of the liver and the right part of the caudate lobe.

right lower quadrant (RLQ) /kwŏd′rənt/ the right lower quarter of any organ or part, especially the abdomen.

right upper quadrant (RUQ) the right upper quarter of any organ or part, especially the abdomen.

right ventricle /věn′trĭ kəl/ **(RV)** the lower right chamber of the heart which receives blood from the right atrium and pumps it through the pulmonary artery into the lungs.

rigidity /rĭ jĭd′ĭ tē/ the quality of being inflexible, as in muscle stiffness, or emotionally, as a resistance to change.

rigor /rĭg′ər/ a state of rigidity, as of muscles; inflexibility.

rigor mortis /môr′tĭs/ muscular rigidity of the body which develops 1–10 hours after death and lasts 3–6 days.

ring /rĭng/ a circular band, said of a circular anatomical opening.

ringworm /rĭng′wûrm′/ a fungal infection of the keratin of the skin, hair, or nails.

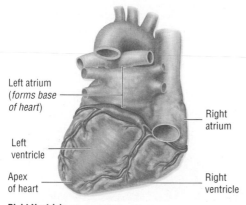

Left atrium (*forms base of heart*)

Right atrium

Left ventricle

Apex of heart

Right ventricle

Right Ventricle

Rinne test /rĭn′ə/ a hearing test using a tuning fork to determine conductive hearing loss.

risk factor a characteristic associated with the increased risk of susceptibility to disease or death; for example, smoking is a risk factor for cancer.

risk of recurrence the chance that an illness will come back again.

river blindness an infestation of threadlike roundworms of the species *Onchocerca volvulus* that live in nodules under the skin and ultimately cause blindness. *Also called* onchocerciasis.

RLL *abbreviation.* right lower lobe.

RLQ *abbreviation.* right lower quadrant.

RMSF *abbreviation.* Rocky Mountain spotted fever.

Rn *abbreviation.* radon.

RN *abbreviation.* registered nurse.

RNA *abbreviation.* ribonucleic acid.

RNA virus a group of viruses in which the core consists of RNA.

RNP *abbreviation.* ribonucleoprotein.

Rocky Mountain spotted fever (RMSF) an acute rickettsial disease caused by the bite of an infected tick.

rod /rŏd/ an elongated, cylindrical structure.

rods /rŏdz/ rod-shaped, photosensitive cells of the retina responsive in low light.

rods and cones the cells that form the photoreceptive layer of the retina.

roentgen (r, R) /rěnt′gən, -jən/ the international unit of exposure for x-rays or gamma-rays.

roentgenologist /rěnt′gə nŏl′ə jĭst, rěnt′jə-/ a specialist in the use of radiologic imaging techniques in the diagnosis and treatment of disease; radiologist.

roentgenology /rěnt′gə nŏl′ə jē, rěnt′jə-/ the branch of medicine that uses radiologic imaging techniques in the diagnosis and treatment of disease; radiology.

Rolfing /rŏl′fĭng/ a body restructuring technique that uses extremely deep and often painful manipulation of the fascia of the muscles and organs to reverse adhesions of muscle fascia to bones and to otherwise manipulate the myofascial system to reduce chronic stress and promote healing.

ROM *abbreviation.* range of motion.

Romberg('s) sign /rŏm′bərg(z)/ a diagnostic sign of certain neurologic diseases said to be positive when a subject sways when standing with feet close together and eyes closed.

roof /ro͞of/ the top part or covering structure, as of the mouth.

root /ro͞ot/ the origin of any part, as of a nerve where it begins from the spinal cord, or of a tooth.

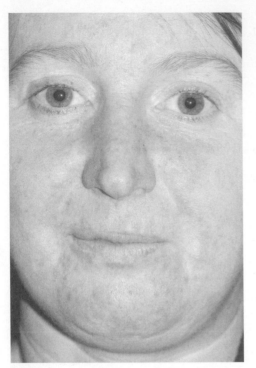

Rosacea

root canal a dental procedure to preserve a decayed tooth by replacing its root with a protective substance. *Also called* pulp canal.

rooting reflex a breast-feeding reflex in a newborn: when the cheek is stimulated, as by the nipple, the infant turns toward the nipple and takes it in the mouth and begins to suck.

Rorschach inkblot test /rôr′shäk/ Rorschach test.

Rorschach test a test in which a subject's responses to inkblot prints are used to evaluate a wide range of personality variables, including pathology. *Also called* inkblot test, Rorschach inkblot test.

rosacea /rō zā′shē ə/ a facial skin disorder resulting from chronic inflammation, and marked by red, acne-like eruptions.

roseola /rŏ zē′ə lə, rō′zē ō′lə/ a viral infection in children marked by a high fever and a red rash on the face and neck; usually mild and clears up in a few days.

rotation /rō tā′shən/ **1.** the motion of a body turning on its axis. **2.** recurrence, as in the symptoms of a periodic disease. **3.** during medical residency, a period of time spent in a particular specialty.

rotation diet a dietary regimen meant to control allergic reactions to food by rotating exposure to various substances.

rotator cuff /rō′tā tər/ the structure of tendons and muscles that secure the arm to the shoulder joint and allow the arm to rotate.

rotavirus /rō′tə vī′rəs/ a group of RNA viruses, including the human gastroenteritis viruses, which are the main cause of diarrhea and dehydration in children worldwide.

Roth's spots /rōts/ white spots surrounded by hemorrhage in the retina, symptomatic of bacterial endocarditis.

rounds /roundz/ a series of visits a doctor makes to his hospital patients.

round window an opening in the bone of the middle ear, covered by a membrane, and leading into the cochlea.

roundworm /round′wûrm′/ an infection of the skin or nails marked by round itchy patches.

route of administration the method of administering a remedy.

RP *abbreviation.* retinitis pigmentosa.

-rrhagia *suffix.* an excessive flow: *for example,* rhinorrhagia.

-rrhaphy *suffix.* suture: *for example,* proctorrhaphy.

-rrhea *suffix.* flow or discharge: *for example,* menorrhea.

-rrhexis *suffix.* rupture: *for example,* arteriorrhexis.

RSD *abbreviation.* reflex sympathetic dystrophy.

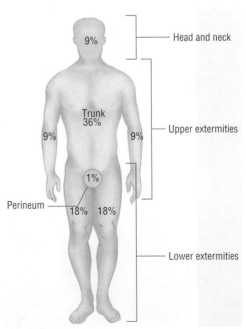

Rule of Nines

RT, rt *abbreviation.* **1.** radiologic technologist. **2.** reaction time. **3.** recreational therapy. **4.** respiratory therapist.

RU-486 a drug taken orally to induce abortion early in pregnancy.

rubella /ro͞o bĕl′ə/ a virus capable of causing birth defects in a fetus if occurring in the first trimester of pregnancy. The disease itself is mild with a rash and some lymph node swelling. *Also called* German measles.

rubeola /ro͞o bē′ə lə, ro͞o′bē ō′lə/ a highly contagious virus, occurring primarily in children, marked by distinct red spots that spread over the body. *Also called* measles.

rubor /ro͞o′bôr/ redness of body tissues, one of four classical symptoms of inflammation. *See also* calor, dolor, tumor.

rugae /ro͞o′gē, -jē/ anatomical folds, as in the lining of the stomach.

rule of nines method used to calculate the extent of burn injury by assigning values of 9 percent of surface areas to various parts of the body.

rule out to eliminate from consideration, as to rule out a particular disease.

runny nose a mucous discharge from the nose, as from the common cold. *Also called* rhinorrhea.

rupture /rŭp′chər/ **1.** *n.* a tear in an organ or tissue. **2.** *v.* to burst or tear open an organ or tissue.

ruptured disk or **ruptured vertebral disc** /vûr′tə brəl/ the abnormal protrusion of disk material from its capsule, sometimes causing painful compression of a nerve root.

RUQ *abbreviation.* right upper quadrant.

RV *abbreviation.* **1.** residual volume. **2.** right ventricle

Rx, RX *abbreviation.* medical prescription.

R

S

S *abbreviation.* sulfur.

SA *abbreviation.* sinoatrial.

Sabin vaccine /sā'bĭn văk sēn'/ an oral vaccine to immunize against poliomyelitis; no longer the preferred vaccine.

sac /săk/ **1.** a bursa or pouch-like structure, often filled with fluid. **2.** an abscess at the base of a tooth. **3.** the capsule of a tumor or cyst.

saccadic movement /sə kad'ik/ the short rapid movement of the eyes as they scan through several points in the visual field.

saccular /sak'yə lər/ having a sac-like form.

saccular aneurysm /an'yə riz'əm/ an aneurysm that has a sac-like bulge on an artery.

saccule /sak'yōōl/ **1.** a small sac. **2.** the smaller of the two membranous sacs in the vestibule of the inner ear.

sacculus /săk'yə ləs/ (*pl.* **sacculi** /săk'yə lī'/) in anatomy, saccule.

sacr-, sacro- *combining form.* sacrum: *for example,* sacrodynia.

sacral /sā'krəl, săk'rəl/ of or relating to the sacrum. [sacr- + -al]

sacral plexus /plek'səs/ a network of nerves supplying the pelvic region on lower limbs, formed by the 4th and 5th lumbar nerves and the 1st, 2nd, and 3rd sacral nerves.

sacrococcygeal /sā'krō kŏk sĭj'ē əl, -sĭj'ol, săk'rō-/ of or relating to the sacrum and the coccyx. [sacro- + coccygeal]

sacrodynia /sā'krə dĭn'ē ə, sā' krə-/ pain in the sacrum. [sacro- + -dynia]

sacroiliac /săk'rō ĭl'ē ăk', sā' krō-/ of or relating to the joint between the sacrum and the ilium. [sacro- + iliac]

sacrosciatic /săk'rō sī ăt'ĭk, sā' krō-/ of or relating to the sacrum and the ischium. [sacro- + sciatic]

sacrovertebral /săk'rō vûr'tə brəl, sā' krō-/ of or relating to the sacrum and all of the vertebrae above it. [sacro- + vertebral]

sacrum /săk'rəm, sāk'rəm/ the triangular bone at the base of the spinal column that forms the posterior portion of the pelvis.

SAD *abbreviation.* seasonal affective disorder.

saddle sore a sore on a horse or its rider caused by chafing of an improperly fitted saddle.

sadism /sā'dĭz əm, săd'ĭz-/ **1.** taking pleasure from being cruel. **2.** in psychiatry, achieving sexual gratification through inflicting pain and humiliation on another.

sadomasochism /sā'dō măs'ə kĭz'əm, săd'ō-/ the achieving of sexual gratification from inflicting pain on a person who achieves sexual stimulation or gratification from receiving it.

safe sex **1.** sexual activity using a contraceptive to reduce the risk of pregnancy. **2.** sexual activity using a condom to reduce the risk of sexually transmitted diseases.

sagittal /săj'ĭ təl/ **1.** of or relating to the suture holding together the two parietal bones of the skull. **2.** of or relating to the sagittal plane.

sagittal plane the plane that divides the body into right and left sections. *Also called* lateral plane.

salicylic acid /săl'ə sĭl'ĭk/ a white crystalline acid used in making aspirin, and in topical preparations used to treat eczema and other similar skin conditions.

saline /sā'lēn/ **1.** *adj.* of or relating to salt. **2.** *n.* a salt solution in the concentration similar to that found in plasma.

saliva /sə lī'və/ the secretions of the salivary glands and the oral mucous glands that keeps the mouth moist; begins the process of digestion.

salivary gland /săl'ə vĕr'ē/ any of three sets of exocrine glands that secrete saliva: the parotid, submaxillary, and sublingual glands.

Salk vaccine /sôk' văk sēn'/ an injectable killed vaccine used to immunize against poliomyelitis.

salmonella /săl'mə nĕl'ə/ (*pl.* **salmonellae** /săl'mə nĕl'ē/) any of several species of rod-shaped bacteria of the genus *Salmonella*, which are pathogenic to humans, usually causing vomiting and diarrhea.

salmonellosis /săl'mə nĕ lō'sĭs/ infection with salmonella bacteria, characterized by intestinal problems and fever.

salping-, salpingi-, salpingo- *combining form.* salpinx: *for example,* salpingectomy.

salpingectomy /săl'pĭn jĕk'tə mē/ surgical removal of one or both fallopian tubes. [salping- + -ectomy]

salpingitis /săl'pĭn jī'tĭs/ infection in one or both fallopian tubes. [salping- + -itis]

salpingocele /săl pĭng′gə sēl′/ hernia of a fallopian tube. [salpingo- + -cele]

salpingo-oophorectomy /săl pĭng′gō ō ŏf ə rĕk′tə mē/ surgical removal of an ovary and its fallopian tube.

salpingo-oophoritis /săl pĭng′gō ō ŏf′ə rī′tĭs/ inflammation of a fallopian tube and its ovary.

salpingo-oophorocele /săl pĭng′gō ō ŏf′ər ə sēl′/ hernia of an ovary and its fallopian tube.

salpingopexy /săl pĭng′gə pĕk′sē/ surgical fixing in place of an oviduct. [salpingo- + -pexy]

salpingoplasty /săl pĭng′gə plăs′tē/ surgical repair of a fallopian tube. [salpingo- + -plasty]

salpingostomy /săl′pĭng gŏs′tə mē/ a surgical formation of an opening in a fallopian tube to facilitate drainage of pus or to remove a tubal pregnancy [salpingo- + -stomy]

salpingotomy /săl′pĭng gŏt′ə mē/ incision into a fallopian tube. [salpingo- + -tomy]

salpinx /săl′pĭngks/ (pl. **salpinges** /săl pĭn′jēz/) **1.** fallopian tube. **2.** eustachian tube (connects the middle ear to the pharynx).

salt /sôlt/ a chemical compound, especially sodium chloride, used to season and preserve food.

salubrious /sə lōō′brē əs/ promoting good health.

salutary /săl′yə tĕr′ē/ wholesome; favorable to good health.

sample /săm′pəl/ **1.** *n.* a small part of a whole that contains the characteristics of the whole, such as a specimen of blood. **2.** in research, a portion of a population selected to represent the entire population. **3.** *v.* to take a sample or samples of, in order to determine something under research.

sanatorium /săn′ĭ tôr′ē əm/ an institution for the treatment of people with physical or mental problems. *Also called* sanitarium.

sand /sănd/ very small grains of disintegrated rock or a similar granular material.

sane /sān/ having a sound mental state; not mentally ill.

sanguineous /săn gwĭn′ē əs/ of or relating to blood.

sanitarium /săn′ĭ târ′ē əm/ an institution for the treatment of people with physical or mental problems. *Also called* sanatorium.

sanitary /săn′ĭ tĕr′ē/ free from dirt or infection.

SA node *abbreviation.* sinoatrial node, the natural pacemaker of the heart.

saphenous veins /sə fē′nəs/ the two main superficial veins of the leg originating at the foot and draining blood from the foot.

sarc-, sarco- *combining form.* flesh: *for example,* sarcocele.

sarcocele /sär′kə sēl′/ tumor of the testes. [sarco- + -cele]

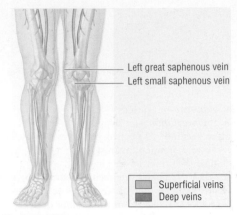

Left great saphenous vein
Left small saphenous vein

◻ Superficial veins
◼ Deep veins

Saphenous Veins

sarcoidosis /sär′koi dō′sĭs/ a disease with no known cause, characterized by firm, grainy or small, nodular lesions in the liver, lungs, shin, and lymph nodes.

sarcoma /sär kō′mə/ (pl. **sarcomas** or **sarcomata** /sär kō′mə tə/) a malignant tumor formed in connective tissue.

-sarcoma *suffix.* a malignant tumor formed in connective tissues: *for example,* angiosarcoma.

sarcoplasm /sär′kə plăz′əm/ the area outside the nucleus of a cell of a striated muscle fiber. [sarco- + -plasm]

sarcosis /sär kō′sĭs/ abnormal formation of flesh; fleshy tumor. [sarc- + -osis]

SARS /särz/ *abbreviation.* severe acute respiratory syndrome.

sartorius muscle /sär tôr′ē əs/ the longest muscle in the human body, found in the thigh and performing hip flexion, abduction, and external rotation. It helps rotate the leg and the thigh to assume the "tailor's position," sitting on the floor with the legs crossed.

saturated fat /săch′ə rā′tĭd/ a fat, such as butter, containing chains of saturated fatty acids. It increases cholesterol levels in the blood and is considered unhealthy. It is generally solid at room temperature.

SBC *abbreviation.* systolic blood pressure.

SBS *abbreviation.* shaken baby syndrome.

sc, SC *abbreviation.* subcutaneous.

scab /skăb/ a crust on the surface of a wound, caused by coagulation of discharge.

scabicide /skā′bə sīd′/ a medication that kills the mite that causes scabies.

scabies /skā′bēz/ a contagious skin disease caused by *Sarcoptes scabiei,* known as the itch mite, characterized by intense persistent itching.

scala /skā′lə/ (pl. **scalae** /skā′lē/) any of the spiral-shaped cavities of the cochlea of the ear.

scala tympani /tĭm'pə nē/   the division of the spiral canal of the cochlea below the spiral lamina.

scald /skôld/   to burn with hot liquid or steam.

scale /skāl/   **1.** *n.* a device for determining weight, particularly of a person. **2.** a standardized test used to measure ones mental state. **3.** a thin flake of skin. **4.** a thin plate of bone. **5.** *v.* to shed or peel in scaly layers; desquamate. **6.** to scrape tartar off teeth.

scaling /skā'lĭng/   the removal of tartar from tooth surfaces using a special instrument.

scalp /skălp/   the skin covering the top of the head.

scalpel /skăl'pəl/   an instrument with a thin sharp blade used in surgery and for dissection.

scan /skăn/   **1.** *v.* to examine or survey with a scanning instrument or apparatus. **2.** *n.* the image or data produced by such an instrument or apparatus.

scanner /skăn'ər/   an instrument or apparatus that scans.

scanning /skăn'ĭng/   the act of surveying with a scanner.

scapula /skăp'yə lə/ (*pl.* **scapulae** /skăp'yə lē'/)   one of the two large, flat, triangular bones forming the back portion of the shoulder. *Also called* shoulder blade.

scapulodynia /skăp'yə lō dĭn'ē ə/   pain in the shoulder blades.

scar /skär/   fibrous tissue that forms to heal and replace injured or destroyed tissues.

scarification /skăr'ĭ fĭ kā'shən/   the act of making small shallow cuts in the skin.

scarlatina /skär'lə tē'nə/   scarlet fever.

scarlet fever   an acute communicable disease (Group A streptococcus) usually occurring in children, characterized by high fever and a red (scarlet) rash. *Also called* scarlatina.

scatological /skăt'ə lŏj'ĭ kəl/   **1.** of or relating to scatology. **2.** using or involving obscenities, especially those referring to excrement.

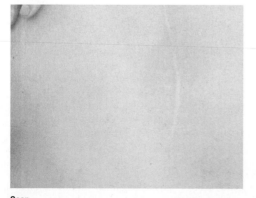

Scar

scatology /skă tŏl'ə jē/   **1.** the scientific study of feces. **2.** the obsession with excrement and pornography featuring it.

Schick test /shĭk/   a test to determine if an individual is immune to diphtheria, in which a small amount of diluted diphtheria toxin is injected into the skin and the skin is observed for a reaction.

Schilling test /shĭl'ĭng/   a test used to measure the level of vitamin B_{12} in the urine.

-schisis   *suffix.* splitting: *for example,* gastroschisis.

schisto-   *combining form.* split; cleft: *for example,* schistocyte.

schistocyte /shĭs'tə sīt', skĭs'-/   an abnormal, fragmented red blood cell. [shisto- + -cyte]

schistocytosis /shĭs'tō sī tō'sĭs, skĭs'-/   **1.** presence of schistocytes in the blood. **2.** fragmentation of a red blood cell. [shisto- + -cytosis]

schistoglossia /shĭs'tə glŏs'ē ə, skĭs'-/   a congenital splitting or cleft of the tongue.

schistosomiasis /shĭs'tō sō mī'ə sĭs/   any disease caused by infestation with schistosomes (tropical worms).

schiz-, schizo-   *combining form.* **1.** split; cleft: schizonychia. **2.** schizophrenia: *for example,* schizophasia.

schizoid /skĭt'soid/   **1.** schizophrenic. **2.** of, relating to, or having schizophrenia.

schizoid personality disorder   schizophrenia.

schizonychia /skĭt'sə nĭk'ē ə/   a condition characterized by irregular splitting of the nails. [schiz- + -onychia]

schizophasia /skĭt'sə fā'zhə/   the disordered speech characteristic of schizophrenia. [schizo- + -phasia]

schizophrenia /skĭt'sə frē'nē ə/   any of a group of psychotic disorders characterized by delusions, hallucinations, and withdrawal from reality, accompanied by emotional, behavioral, and intellectual abnormalities.

schizophrenic /skĭt'sə frĕn'ĭk/   **1.** *adj.* of or referring to schizophrenia. **2.** *n.* a person suffering from schizoprenia.

sciatica /sī ăt'ĭ kə/   pain along the sciatic nerve sometimes caused by a herniated disk.

sciatic nerve /sī ăt'ĭk/   a sensory and motor nerve that originates in the L2-S3 spinal segments and passes through the thigh where it splits into the common peroneal nerve and the tibial nerve; often the transmitter of lower back and posterior leg pain. *See illustration* on page 324.

scintigram /sĭn'tĭ grăm'/   the image obtained by scintography. *Also called* scintiscan.

scintigraphy /sĭn tĭg'rə fē/   an imaging technique in which a record of radioactive tracer counts in tissue or organ produces a scintigram image. *Also called* scintiphotography.

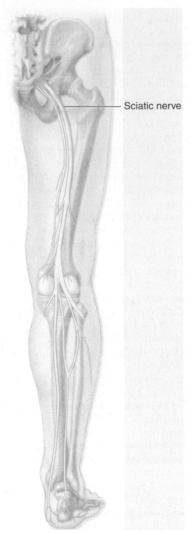

Sciatic nerve

Sciatic Nerve

scintillating scotoma /sĭn′tə lā′tĭng skə tō′mə/ an area of blindness accompanied by bright sparkling lights that sometimes precedes or accompanies a migraine.

scintimammography /sĭn′tə mă mŏg′rə fē/ an imaging technique used for detecting breast cancer by the use of scintigraphy.

scintiphotography /sĭn′tə fə tŏg′rə fē/ scintigraphy.

scintiscan /sĭn′tə skăn′/ a two-dimensional image of the distribution of a radioactive tracer in tissues. *Also called* scintigram.

scintiscanner /sĭn′tə skăn′ər/ the apparatus used to make a scintiscan.

scirrhous /skĭr′əs, sĭr′-/ hardened; dense.

scirrhous carcinoma /kär′sə nō′mə/ a dense cancerous growth formed in connective tissue.

scler-, sclero- *combining form.* **1.** hard: *for example,* scleroderma. **2.** sclera: *for example,* sclerectasia.

sclera /sklĕr′ə, sklêr′ə/ the white tough membranous tissue covering the entire eyeball except the cornea. *Also called* white of the eye.

scleral /sklĕr′əl, sklêr′əl/ of or relating to the sclera. [scler- + -al]

sclerectasia /sklĕr′ĕk tā′zhə, sklêr′-/ bulging of the sclera. [scler- + -ectasia]

scleredema /sklĕr′ə dē′mə, sklêr′-/ a disease characterized by hardened waxy pitting of the skin, often associated with diabetes mellitus. [scler- + edema]

sclerema /sklĭ rē′mə/ hardening of the skin.

scleritis /sklĭ rī′tĭs/ inflammation of the sclera. [scler- + -itis]

scleroconjunctival /sklĕr′ō kŏn′jŭngk tī′vəl, sklêr′-/ of or relating to the sclera and the conjunctiva. [sclero- + conjunctival]

sclerodactyly /sklĕr′ō dăk′tə lē′, sklêr′-/ scleroderma of the hands and feet. [sclero- + -dactyly]

scleroderma /sklĕr′ə dûr′mə, sklêr′-/ a pathological thickening and hardening of the skin. [sclero- + -derma]

scleromalacia /sklĕr′ō mə lā′shə, sklêr′-/ degenerative thinning of the sclera. [sclero- + -malacia]

sclerose /sklĕr′ōs, sklêr′-/ to cause or undergo sclerosis.

-sclerosis *suffix.* sclerosis: *for example,* encephalosclerosis.

sclerosis /sklĭ rō′sĭs/ any pathological hardening of a body part, such as an artery. [scler- + -osis]

sclerotherapy /sklĕr′ō thĕr′ə pē, sklêr′-/ a treatment for vericose veins in which a sclerosing solution is injected into the vessels. [sclero- + therapy]

scoli-, scolio- *combining form.* twisted; curved: *for example,* scoliometer.

scoliokyphosis /skō′lē ō kī fō′sĭs/ lateral and posterior curvature of the spine. [scolio- + kyphosis]

scoliometer /skō′lē ŏm′ĭ tər/ an instrument used to measure curves in the spine. [scolio- + -meter]

scoliosis /skō′lē ō′sĭs/ abnormal lateral curvature of the spine. [scoli- + -osis]

-scope *suffix.* an instrument used for viewing or examining: *for example,* endoscope.

-scopy *suffix.* viewing; seeing; observing: *for example,* endoscopy.

scorbutic /skôr byōō′tĭk/ of or relating to scurvy.

scot-, scoto- *combining form.* darkness: *for example,* scotoma.

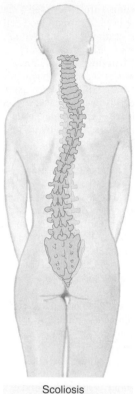

Scoliosis

Scoliosis

scotoma /skə tō′mə/ (*pl.* **scotomas** or **sco-tomata** /skə tō′mə tə/) an area of diminished vision; a dark or distorted area in the visual field, such as the scintillating scotoma that may accompany or precede a migraine. [scot- + -oma]

scotometer /skə tŏm′ĭ tər/ an instrument used to measure a scotoma. [scoto- + -meter]

scrape /skrāp/ *n.* **1.** a light scratch on the surface of the skin. **2.** a specimen obtained by being scraped off the surface of tissue. *v.* **3.** to remove by scratching from the surface, as to obtain a specimen for examination.

scratch test a skin test for allergy in which a small amount of an allergen is applied to a scrape on the skin.

screening /skrē′nĭng/ an examination or evaluation of a group or an individual to detect the probability of their developing a particular disease, or to determine their suitability for a particular treatment.

scrofula /skrŏf′yə lə/ a form of childhood tuberculosis primarily affecting the lymph nodes in the neck. *Also called* struma.

scrofulous /skrŏf′yə ləs/ of, relating to, or affected with scrofula.

scrotum /skrō′təm/ the sac of skin enclosing the testes.

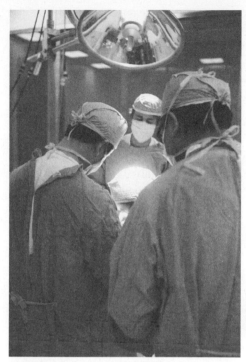

Scrubs

scrub /skrŭb/ to thoroughly wash and disinfect the hands and arms before performing surgery.

scrub in the procedure in which the hands and arms are scrubbed and sterile gloves, masks, and gowns are put on.

scrubs /skrŭbz/ protective garments worn by surgeons and other medical professionals and health care workers.

scrub typhus /tī′fəs/ an acute infectious disease transmitted by mites, characterized by fever, painfully swollen lymph glands, lesions, and rash.

scurvy /skûr′vē/ a disease caused by vitamin C deficiency, characterized by spongy bleeding gums, tooth loss, and fatigue.

Se *abbreviation.* selenium.

seasickness /sē′sĭk′nĭs/ nausea, dizzyness, and often vomiting; a form of motion sickness caused by the rocking or swaying motion of a boat.

seasonal affective disorder (SAD) a form of depression occurring during certain seasons of the year in which the person has less exposure to the sun, treated with light therapy.

sebaceous cyst /sə bā′shəs sĭst′/ a harmless cyst on the face or scalp containing fatty secretions from a sebaceous gland.

sebaceous gland any gland in the skin that produces and secretes sebum.

seborrhea /sĕb'ə rē'ə/ a disease of the sebaceous glands characterized by excessive secretion of sebum, and the formation of crusts or an oily film on the skin.

seborrheic dermatitis /sĕb'ə rē'ĭk dûr'mə tī'tĭs/ a chronic form of dermatitis characterized by the formation of itchy, discolored crusty patches, and greasy scaling of skin, usually on the scalp and face.

seborrheic eczema /ĕk'sə mə, ĭg zē'mə/ a chronic skin disease characterized by seborrhea of the scalp or eyelids.

seborrheic keratosis /kĕr'ə tō'sĭs/ a benign itchy wart-like lesion covered in a greasy crust, appearing on the face, torso, or extremities. *Also called* seborrheic wart.

seborrheic wart /wôrt/ seborrheic keratosis.

sebum /sē'bəm/ an oily secretion of the sebaceous glands consisting of fat, cellular material, and keratin.

secondary /sĕk'ən dĕr'ē/ **1.** not primary. **2.** inferior.

secondary amenorrhea /ā mĕn'ə rē'ə/ cessation of menstruation in a woman who has previously experienced normal menstruation.

secondary atelectasis /ăt'ə lĕk'tə sĭs/ collapse of a lung associated with a disease or procedure.

secondary cataract /kăt'ə răkt'/ a cataract that occurs in association with another disease or trauma, or that remains following cataract surgery.

secondary hypertension /hī'pər tĕn'shən/ high blood pressure that is secondary to another disease.

secondary sex characteristics any physical features or characteristics that distinguish between male and female without having direct reproductive function.

second-degree burn a burn that blisters the skin and is more severe than a first-degree burn. *Also called* partial-thickness burn. *See also* first-degree burn, third-degree burn.

secrete /sĭ krēt'/ to produce and release a substance.

secretion /sĭ krē'shən/ **1.** the process of secreting a substance. **2.** the substance that is secreted.

section /sĕk'shən/ **1.** *n.* the act of cutting or dividing. **2.** the segment or part that is cut away or separated. **3.** *v.* to divide surgically.

sedate /sĭ dāt'/ to reduce anxiety and stress by administering a sedative.

sedation /sĭ dā'shən/ reduction of anxiety and stress, especially by the administration of a sedative.

sedative /sĕd'ə tĭv/ a class of drugs that relieve anxiety and stress, having a tranquilizing effect.

sedimentation rate (SR) /sĕd'ə mən tā'shən/ the speed at which a red blood cell sinks in a specimen of drawn blood; used in diagnosing infections or inflammation.

segmental fracture /sĕg mĕn'təl/ a fracture in two parts of the same bone.

seizure /sē'zhər/ **(SZ)** a sudden spasm or convulsion, especially one associated with epilepsy.

seizure disorders a large group of medical conditions characterized by periods of uncontrolled electrical activity in the brain, causing sudden spasms or convulsions.

selective estrogen-receptor modulator (SERM) /sĭ lĕk'tĭv ĕs'trə jən rĭ sĕp'tər mŏj'ə lā'tər/ a drug that possesses some, but not all, of the actions of estrogen.

selective serotonin reuptake inhibitors (SSRIs) /sĕr ə tō'nin rē up'tāk ĭn hĭb'ə tərz/ a class of drugs that prevent the uptake of serotonin by the central nervous system, used to treat depression and obsessive compulsive disorder.

selenium (Se) /sə lē'nē əm/ a nonmetallic element chemically similar to sulfur and poisonous to animals.

sella turcica /sĕl'ə tûr'sĭ kə/ a saddle-like depression of the inner skull that houses the pituitary gland.

semen /sē'mən/ the white fluid excreted from the male reproductive organs during ejaculation that contains spermatozoa.

semi- *prefix.* **1.** half; partial; similar to: *for example,* semicomatose.

semicircular canals /sĕm'ē sûr'kyə lər, sĕm'ī-/ the three tubular parts of the inner ear associated with equilibrium.

semicomatose /sĕm'ē kōmə tōs', sĕm'ī-/ a partial or mild coma. [semi- + comatose]

semiconscious /sĕm'ē kon'shəs, sĕm'ī-/ not fully aware of sensations; partially conscious. [semi- + conscious]

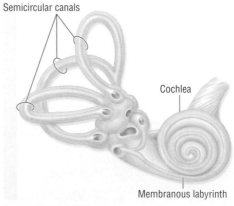

Semicircular canals

Cochlea

Membranous labyrinth

Semicircular Canals

semilunar valve /sĕm´ē loo´nər, sĕm´ī-/ one of two valves situated between the heart and the pulmonary artery, or between the heart and the aorta, that prevent blood from pouring back into the ventricles.

seminal /sĕm´ə nəl/ 1. of or relating to semen. 2. important and influencing the future.

seminal duct any of the ducts of the testes that carry semen.

seminal vesicle /vĕs´ĭ kəl/ one of two glandular pouches that secrete fluid into the ejaculatory duct.

seminiferous tubules /sĕm´ə nĭf´ər əs too´byoolz/ any of the curved tubules in the testes in which spermatozoa develops.

seminoma /sĕm´ə nō´mə/ (*pl.* **seminomas** or **seminomata** /sĕm´ə nō´mə tə/) a malignant tumor of the testis arising from sperm-forming tissue

seminormal /sĕm´ē nôr´məl, sĕm´ī-/ a solution that is half the strength of a normal solution. [semi- + normal]

semiprivate /sĕm´ē prī´vĭt, sĕm´ī-/ a hospital room shared by two or more patients. [semi- + private]

senescence /sĭ nĕs´əns/ the process of aging; growing old.

senile /sē´nīl/ 1. of, relating to, or resulting from old age, such as mental or physical deterioration. 2. showing mental and physical deterioration, especially short-term memory loss.

senile dementia /dĭ mĕn´shə/ a mental condition of old age characterized by progressive, abnormally accelerated mental and emotional deterioration.

senile lentigo /lĕn tī´gō/ a brown patch of skin, usually on the back of the hands and on the forehead, developed in old age, often due to sun damage. *Also called* liver spot.

senility /sə nĭlĭ tē/ 1. the state of being senile. 2. mental and physical deterioration associated with old age.

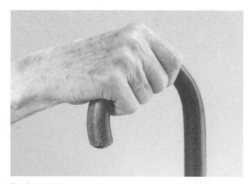

Senile Lentigo

sensation /sĕn sā´shən/ 1. a perception of a sense organ. 2. the faculty to feel or perceive.

sense /sĕns/ a perception produced by a stimulus.

sense of smell olfaction; the perception of an odor.

sense organ a receptor organ or structure having nerve endings that receive sensory stimulation (heat, pain, touch, and so on); the sense organ conveys it to the central nervous system.

sensitive /sĕn´sĭ tĭv/ 1. aware of and responsive to the feelings of others. 2. highly responsive to sensation. 3. abnormally susceptible to something, as a foreign protein or a drug.

sensitivity /sĕn´sĭ tĭv´ĭ tē/ 1. the condition of being sensitive. 2. the capacity of a sense organ to respond to stimulus.

sensitize /sĕn´sĭ tīz´/ 1. to make or become sensitive. 2. to make or become susceptible to an antigen.

sensitization /sĕn´sĭ tə zā´shən/ 1. to make or become sensitive. 2. the process of making a person susceptible to something by repeated injections of it.

sensorineural /sĕn´sə rē noor´əl/ of or relating to the sensory nerves.

sensorineural deafness total hearing loss due to damage to the sound receptors of the inner ear or to the acoustic nerve.

sensorineural hearing loss partial or total hearing loss due to damage to the sound receptors of the inner ear or to the auditory nerve.

sensorium /sĕn sôr´ē əm/ (*pl.* **sensoriums** or **sensoria** /sĕn sôr´ē ə/) the sensory system of the body, especially referring to the function of the brain of receiving and coordinating all stimuli.

sensory /sĕn´sə rē/ 1. of or relating to the senses, or to sensation. 2. transmitting impulses from sense organs to nerve centers.

sensory aphasia /ə fā´zhə/ inability to comprehend spoken or written words.

sensory integration /ĭn´tĭ grā´shən/ a form of occupational therapy in which special exercises are used to strengthen the patient's sense of touch, balance, physical awareness.

sensory nerve a nerve that conveys stimuli (such as pain, heat, temperature, and so on) from a sense organ to the central nervous system (brain or spinal cord). *Also called* afferent nerve.

sensory neuron /noor´ŏn/ a neuron that conducts nerve impulses along the nerve from a sense organ to the central nervous system (brain or spinal cord).

sensory receptor /rĭ sĕp´tər/ an organ that contains sensory nerve endings and responds to stimuli.

sensory system the body's network of sense organs.

sentinel lymph node /sen′tə nəl lĭmf′ nōd′/ or **sentinel node (SLN)** the first gland to filter lymphatic drainage from a tumor, identified by dye marker or radioactive marker.

sentinel lymph node (SLN) biopsy /bī′ŏp sē/ a procedure in which the sentinel lymph node is excised and tested for cancer cells. *Also called* sentinel node biopsy.

sentinel node biopsy a sentinel lymph node biopsy.

separation anxiety /sĕp′ə rā′shən ăng zī′ĭ tē/ a condition in which a child experiences anxiety or fear due to being separated from a parent or caretaker.

separation anxiety disorder excessive anxiety due to separation from a parent or care-taken.

separator /sĕp′ə rā′tər/ small elastic ring used in orthodontics to create space between the teeth for the fitting of orthodontic bands.

-sepsis *suffix.* sepsis.

sepsis /sĕp′sĭs/ **1.** the presence of pathogenic organisms or their toxins in the bloodstream. **2.** the poisoned condition resulting from path-ogenic organisms or their toxins in the bloodstream. *Also called* blood poisoning, septicemia.

septal defect /sĕp′təl dē′fĕkt, dĭ fĕkt′/ a birth defect or abnormality in the septum of the heart.

septate /sĕp′tāt/ divided by a septum or septa.

septic /sĕp′tĭk/ of, relating to, or causing sepsis.

septic arthritis /är thrī′tĭs/ inflammation in a joint caused by a bacterial infection.

septic bursitis /bər sī′tĭs/ bursitis caused by a bacterial infection in a bursa.

septicemia /sĕp′tə sē′mē ə/ a systemic dis-ease caused by infection of the blood by path-ogenic organisms. *Also called* blood poison-ing, sepsis.

septo- *combining form.* septum: *for example,* septostomy.

septoplasty /sĕp′tə plăs′tē/ plastic surgery on the nasal septum. [septo- + -plasty]

septorhinoplasty /sĕp′tō rī′nə plăs′tē/ plastic surgery on the septum and the internal nasal structure which may alter its outward appear-ance. [septo- + rhinoplasty]

septostomy /sĕp tŏs′tə mē/ the surgical for-mation of an opening in a septum. [septo- + -stomy]

septuagenarian /sĕp′twə jə när′ē ən/ a per-son in his or her seventies.

septum /sĕp′təm/ (*pl.* **septa** /sĕp′tə/) a carti-laginous or fibrous membrane that separates two cavities or tissues, especially the wall between the chambers of the heart or the di-viding wall between the nares.

sequela /sĭ kwĕl′ə/ (*pl.* **sequelae** /sĭ kwĕl′ē/) a pathological condition resulting from a pre-vious disease.

sequestrum /sĭ kwĕs′trəm/ a small piece of dead bone detached from healthy bone.

series /sêr′ēz/ in chemistry, a group of related elements arranged in order of increasing atomic number or a group of relative com-pounds differing in a constant ratio.

serine /sĕr′ēn/ an amino acid that is a com-mon constituent of many proteins.

SERM *abbreviation.* selective estrogen recep-tor modulator.

sero- *combining form.* serum: *for example,* serotype.

seroconversion /sêr′ō kən vur′zhən/ appear-ance of a specific antibody in blood serum against a newly acquired infective agent or vaccine. [sero- + conversion]

serology /sə rŏl′ə jē/ the science concerned with the study and use of serums. [sero- + -logy]

serosa /sə rō′sə/ a serous membrane.

serositis /sĕr′ə sī′tĭs, sêr′-/ inflammation of a serous membrane.

serotonin /sĕr′ə tō′nĭn, sêr′-/ a neurotransmit-ter found in the brain, blood serum, and gas-tric mucous membranes; inhibits gastric se-cretions, stimulates smooth muscle, and is involved in sleep, depression, and memory.

serotype /sĕr′ə tīp′, sêr′-/ a group of microor-ganisms distinguished by a common set of antigens. [sero- + type]

serous /sêr′əs/ containing, secreting, or re-sembling serum.

serous membrane /mĕm′brān/ a thin mem-brane lining a cavity that secretes a serous fluid and covers organs.

serous otitis /ō tī′tĭs/ inflammation of the middle ear with effusion.

serous otitis media /mē′dē ə/ inflammation of the middle ear with effusion.

serum /sêr′əm/ (*pl.* **serums** or **sera** (sêr′ə) **1.** the yellowish fluid component of blood which

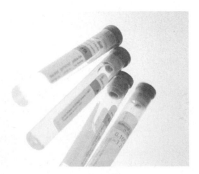

Serum

remains after it has clotted and cellular components have been removed. **2.** the fluid secreted to keep serous membranes moist. **3.** the antibody-rich fluid extracted from the tissues of animals to be used for immunization.

serum albumin /ăl byōō′mĭn/ the albumin occurring in blood serum that maintains the osmotic pressure of the blood. A low serum albumin is an indicator of liver disease or malnutrition.

serum glutamic oxaloacetic transaminase (SGOT) /glōō tăm′ĭk ŏk′sə lō ə sē′tĭk trăn zăm′ə nās′, ə sĕt′ĭk/ a serum enzyme that is elevated in certain conditions, such as acute hepatitis. *Also called* aspartate aminotransferase, glutamic oxaloacetic transaminase.

serum glutamic pyruvic transaminase (SGPT) /pī rōō′vĭk/ a liver enzyme that is elevated in many inflammatory liver conditions. *Also called* alanine aminotransferase, glutamic pyruvic transaminase.

sesamoid bone /sĕs′ə moid′/ a bone formed where a tendon passes over a joint. The largest sesamoid bone is the patella (knee).

sessile /sĕs′ĭl/ attached to the base directly rather than by a stalk.

sessile polyp /pŏl′ĭp/ a broad-based polyp.

severe acute respiratory syndrome (SARS) /rĕs′pər ə tôr′ē/ a highly contagious respiratory disease caused by the coronavirus. It first appeared in Asia and is sometimes fatal.

sex /sĕks/ **1.** either the female or male division of a species. **2.** the group of characteristics that distinguish males from females. *See also* gender. **3.** sexual intercourse.

sexagenarian /sĕk′sə jə nâr′ē ən/ a person in their sixties.

sex cell either of the basic organisms (a spermatozoon or an ovum) involved in reproduction.

sex chromosome /krō′mə sōm′/ chromosome that determines the sex of a person. In males, there are an X and Y chromosome, and in females, there are two X chromosomes.

sexual abuse /sĕk′shōō əl/ assault that includes sexual acts, especially when performed on a minor.

sexual intercourse /ĭn′tər kôrs′/ sexual connection between a male and a female with the penis inserted into the vagina. *Also called* coitus.

sexual preference /sĕk′shōō əl prĕf′ər əns/ the preferred sex of a potential or actual sexual partner.

sexual reproduction /rē′prə dŭk′shən/ the process of fertilization of an ovum by a sperm.

sexually transmitted disease (STD) or **sexually transmitted infection (STI)** any of

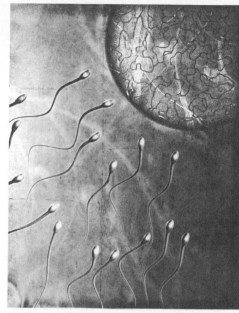

Sex Cell

various diseases that are transmitted through sexual contact, especially through sexual intercourse. *Also called* venereal disease.

SGOT *abbreviation.* serum glutamic oxaloacetic transaminase.

SGPT *abbreviation.* serum glutamic pyruvic transaminase.

shaft /shăft/ a long slender part, such as the shaft of a bone.

shaken baby syndrome (SBS) a set of injuries including damage to the brain, caused by severe shaking of an infant.

shank /shăngk/ the part of the leg from the knee to the foot. *Also called* shin.

sharps /shärps/ any sharp-pointed implements, especially needles that have been contaminated by use.

shave biopsy /bī′ŏp sē/ a biopsy that uses shavings taken by razor from an elevated growth, especially one on the skin.

sheath /shēth/ any protective covering.

shell shock psychological disorder resulting from the stress of a trauma, now usually called post-traumatic stress disorder.

shiatsu /shē ät′sōō/ a traditional Japanese healing art using pressure points to release chi (energy) and relaxation techniques to promote healing and wellness.

shigella /shĭ gĕl′ə/ (*pl.* **shigellae** /shĭ gĕl′ē/) a bacterium responsible for dysentery in humans.

shigellosis /shĭg'ə lō'sĭs/ dysentery caused by shigellae. It is rather common where hygiene is poor, there is a lack of sewers or no clean drinking water, etc.

shin /shĭn/ the bony part of the leg between the knee and foot. *Also called* shank.

shinbone/shin bone /shĭn'bōn'/ the large bone between the knee and the foot which is a major support of the body's weight. *Also called* tibia.

shingles /shĭng'gəlz/ painful nerve infection in adults caused by the herpes-varicella virus that causes chickenpox in children. *Also called* herpes zoster

shin splint an inflammation of the shinbone, usually caused by overuse.

shock /shŏk/ a sudden physical or mental disturbance.

shock lung the development of edema in the lungs as a result of shock.

shock therapy the passing of electrical currents through the brain as a treatment for mental disorders. *Also called* electroconvulsive therapy, electroschock therapy.

short bone any bone whose width and length are approximately the same.

short bowel syndrome a condition of malnutrition which exists because surgical resection of diseased small bowel has left too little absorptive surface to bring adequate nutrition into the body; treatment consists of additional intravenous nutrition.

shortness of breath (SOB) difficulty in breathing. *Also called* dyspnea.

shortsightedness /shôrt'sī'tĭd nĭs/ a refractive error in which light is focused in front of the retina; usually correctable by lenses. *Also called* myopia, nearsightedness.

short-term memory (STM) /shôrt'tûrm'/ memory of recent events; often lost or impaired in certain conditions, and very sensitive to diminished oxygen in the brain: for example, after a brief and rapidly resuscitated cardiac arrest, this facility is often damaged.

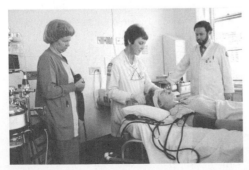

Shock Therapy

shoulder /shōl'dər/ the joint or the region of the joint where the head of the humerus connects to the body.

shoulder blade a large, triangular bone that forms the back portion of the shoulder. *Also called* scapula

shoulder joint shoulder.

show /shō/ **1.** *n.* a discharge of bloody mucus from the vagina shortly before labor begins. **2.** *v.* to be apparent, as a rounded belly of a pregnancy.

shunt /shŭnt/ **1.** a surgically created connection between an artery and a vein or the device used in such a surgery. **2.** the blood flowing through the lungs that does not get oxygenated because it does not flow through alveolar capillaries but through capillaries serving other pulmonary structures, expressed as *physiological shunt of 5%*.

Shy-Drager syndrome /shī drā'gər/ a degenerative neurological disease characterized by incontinence, tremors, and wasting. *Also called* multiple system atrophy.

SI units the international standard system of weights and measures.

SIADH *abbreviation.* syndrome of inappropriate ADH (antidiuretic hormone).

sial-, sialo- *combining form.* saliva, salivary gland: *for example*, sialogram.

sialidosis /sī ăl'ĭ dō'sis/ a rare childhood disorder resulting in periodic inflammation and discomfort in the salivary glands.

sialism /sī'ə lĭz'əm/ an excessive production of saliva. *Also called* ptyalism. [sial- + -ism]

sialoadenitis /sī ăl'ō ăd'ə nī'tĭs/ inflammation of a salivary gland. [sialo- + adenitis]

sialogram /sī ăl'ə grăm'/ x-ray image of the salivary glands. [sialo- + -gram]

sialolith /sī ăl'ə lĭth/ a calculus in the salivary glands. [sialo- + -lith]

sialosis /sī'ə lō'sĭs/ excessive secretion of saliva. [sial- + -osis]

sibling /sĭb'lĭng/ brother or sister.

sicca syndrome /sĭk'ə/ an immune disorder with progressive destruction of the secretory glands; symptoms include dry eyes, dry mouth, recurrent pneumonia, and dry mucous membranes throughout the body. *Also called* Sjogren's syndrome.

sick /sĭk/ **1.** being in ill health; suffering from a disease. **2.** experiencing nausea.

sick building syndrome a group of symptoms (such as respiratory ailments, headaches, and dry skin) that are prevalent among workers in a particular tightly enclosed energy-efficient building with recirculated air.

sickle cell /sĭk'əl sĕl'/ a crescent-shaped, elongated red blood cell.

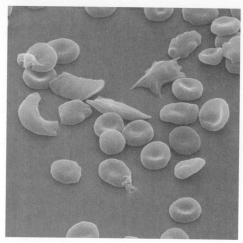

Sickle Cell Anemia

Sign Language (interpreter0

sickle cell anemia /ə nē′mē ə/ or **sickle cell disease**   a severe type of inherited anemia in which an abnormal hemoglobin molecule causes the red blood cell to take a crescent shape when in low oxygen conditions; usually only found in races indigenous to areas where malaria is prevalent. Called "SS disease," meaning that the gene comes from both parents; found most commonly in African Americans.

sickle cell trait   a genetic trait that does not cause any symptoms of sickle cell anemia. Called "SA disease," meaning that the gene comes from only one parent.

sickness /sĭk′nĭs/   ill health; disease.

side effects   unintended problems that occur when treatments (drugs, radiation, etc.) affect healthy cells.

sidero-   *combining form.* iron: *for example,* sideropenia.

sideroblast /sĭd′ər ə blăst′/   small red bloods cells containing iron. [sidero- + -blast]

sideropenia /sid′ər ə pē′nē ə/   an abnormally low level of iron in the blood. [sidero- + -penia]

SIDS /sĭdz/   *abbreviation.* sudden infant death syndrome.

sight /sīt/   the ability to perceive light and objects with the eye; vision.

sigmoid-, sigmoido-   *combining form.* sigmoid colon: *for example,* sigmoidoscopy.

sigmoid colon /sĭg′moid kō′lən/   the S-shaped portion of the colon that connects the descending colon to the rectum. *Also called* sigmoid flexure.

sigmoid flexure /flĕk′shər/   sigmoid colon.

sigmoidectomy /sĭg′moi dĕk′tə mē/   surgical removal of the sigmoid colon. [sigmoid- + -ectomy]

sigmoidoscope /sĭg moi′də skōp′/   endoscope used to examine the sigmoid colon. [sigmoid- + -scope]

sigmoidoscopy /sĭg′moi dŏs′kə pē/   examination with a sigmoidoscope. [sigmoido- + -scopy]

sign /sīn/   an objective finding found upon examination, especially something that points to a particular diagnosis.

signature /sĭg′nə chər/   an outward sign of a physical condition, such as a certain type of rash indicative of a particular illness.

sign language   a form of communication using fingers and hands to represent words and letters; used by the deaf.

silica /sĭl′ĭ kə/   fine, rock dust known to cause lung damage with long-term exposure.

silicosis /sĭl′ĭ kō′sĭs/   lung inflammation caused by inhalation of silica.

silver (Ag) /sĭl′vər/   a soft, white metallic element whose compounds, such as silver fluoride and silver nitrate, are used as antiseptics, astringents, or disinfectant.

silver nitrate /nī′trāt/   a powerful antiseptic used topically, as immediately after birth in the eyes (to prevent gonorrheal ophthalmitis), to prevent or cure certain infections.

simple fracture   a fracture in which the skin remains intact. *Also called* closed fracture.

simple mastectomy /mă stĕk′tə mē/   surgical removal of the whole breast, leaving the underlying muscles intact.

single-payer health care   health care reimbursement system with a single payer, such as the government.

single photon emission computed tomography (SPECT) brain scan /fō′tŏn ĭ mĭsh′ən kəm pyoo′tĭd tə mŏg′rə fē/   diagnostic imaging using emission from radionuclides to create images.

singultus /sĭng gŭl′təs/   spasmodic movement of the diaphragm that creates a noise. *Also called* hiccup.

sinsitr-, sinistro-   *combining form.* left: *for example,* sinistrocerebral.

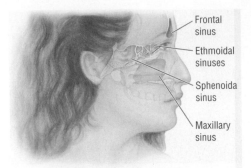

Frontal sinus
Ethmoidal sinuses
Sphenoidal sinus
Maxillary sinus

Sinus

sinistral /sĭn′ə strəl/ of or relating to thc left.

sinistrocerebral /sĭn′ə strō sə rē′brəl/ of or relating to the left cerebral hemisphere. [sinstro- + cerebral]

sinoatrial (SA) node /sī′nō ā′trē əl nōd′/ the cardiac muscle located in the posterior wall of the right atrium near the junction of the superior vena cava; it generates initial repeated electrical impulses in the heart's conduction system and is considered the heart's pacemaker. *Also called* sinus node.

sinus-, sinuso- *combining form.* sinus: *for example,* sinusitis.

sinus /sī′nəs/ a depression or cavity, as on the surface of an organ or, especially, any of the paranasal sinuses.

sinus bradycardia /brăd′ĭ kär′dē ə/ a slow heart rhythm (<60 beats/minute), which may be a feature of good health (athlete's heart) or a symptom of disease of the SA node.

sinus headache /hĕd′āk′/ a headache originating in the paranasal sinuses.

sinusitis /sī′nə sī′tĭs/ inflammation of a sinus, particularly one or more of the paranasal sinuses. [sinus- + -itis]

sinus node the cardiac muscle located in the posterior wall of the right atrium near the junction of the superior vena cava; it generates initial repeated electrical impulses in the heart's conduction system and is considered the heart's pacemaker. *Also called* sinoatrial node.

sinusotomy /sī′nə sŏt′ə mē/ incision into a sinus. [sinuso- + -tomy]

sinus rhythm (SR) the normal cardiac rhythm stimulated by the sinoatrial node.

sinus tachycardia /tăk′ĭ kär′dē ə/ a fast sinus rhythm (>100/minute), which may be due to stress, exercise, or some illness.

sixth disease a childhood viral disease caused by the herpes type 6 virus and characterized by a few days of high fever which subsides quickly.

Sjogren-Larsson's syndrome (SLS) /shû(r)′ grĕn lär′sənz/ a genetic disease characterized by icthyosis (thick and scaly skin), spasticity in the legs and sometimes arms, and mental retardation.

Sjogren('s) syndrome /shû(r)′grĕn(z)/ an immune disorder with progressive destruction of the secretory glands; symptoms include dry eyes, dry mouth, recurrent pneumonia, and dry mucous membranes throughout the body. *Also called* sicca syndrome.

skeletal /skĕl′ĭ təl/ of or relating to the skeleton.

skeletal muscle any voluntary muscle.

skeletal system the bones and muscle of the body; the musculoskeletal system.

skeleton /skĕl′ə tn/ the solid system of the body including the bones and muscles that allow for support and movement, protect vital organs, produce red blood cells, and store minerals.

skilled nursing facility a health-care institution for people who are unable to take care of their own daily needs that meets federal criteria for Medicaid and Medicare reimbursement for nursing care.

skin /skĭn/ the external membranous covering of the body; part of the integument.

skin graft skin that is transplanted from one part of the body to another.

skin tag a small benign growth on the skin.

skin test a method of testing for allergies by placing on or injecting an antigen into the skin and observing reactions.

skull /skŭl/ the bones and cartilage of the head.

skull fracture a fracture of any of the bones of the skull.

SL *abbreviation.* sublingual.

SLE *abbreviation.* systemic lupus erythematosus.

sleep /slēp/ a natural, temporary suspension or lowering of sensory reactions so as to allow rest.

sleep apnea /ăp′nē ə/ temporary stopping of breathing during sleep.

sleep disorder disturbance in a normal sleep pattern.

sleep studies testing during sleep to determine the cause of sleep disorders.

sleeping pill any medication that aids in getting a restful sleep.

sleeplessness /slēp′lĭs nĭs/ inability to get a restful night's sleep.

sleepwalking /slēp′wô′kĭng/ walking around while in an apparent state of sleep. *Also called* noctambulism, somnambulism.

sliding hiatal hernia /slī′dĭng hī ā′təl hûr′nē ə/ movement of the inital segment of the stomach up through the diaphragm into the lower

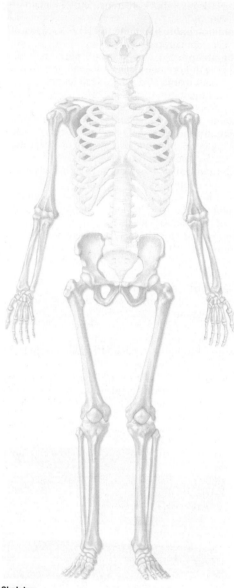

Skeleton

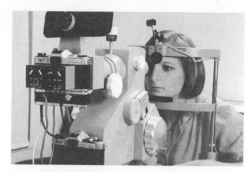

Slit Lamp Ocular Examination

SLN *abbreviation.* sentinel lymph node.

SLS *abbreviation.* Sjogren-Larsson's syndrome.

slurry /slûr′ē/ a mixture of water and pumice used in the practice of dental hygiene to remove plaque and stain.

small bowel /bou′əl/ small intestine.

small intestine /ĭn tĕs′tĭn/ the part of the digestive system between the stomach and the large intestine, made up of three sections—the duodenum, the jejunum, and the ileum.

smallpox /smôl′pŏks′/ a highly contagious, severe viral disease with fever and pimples that blister and form pocks; has been "globally eradicated" by vaccine. *Also called* variola.

smallpox vaccine a live virus vaccine (cow pox) that provides immunity against smallpox.

smear /smêr/ a small quantity of something, as blood or tissue, spread thinly on a plate for microscopic examination.

smell /smĕl/ the sense by which odors are detected in the olfactory organs.

smooth muscle generally involuntary muscle made of long tapering cells, found in the internal hollow organs and blood vessels and involved in constriction and dilation.

sneeze /snēz/ involuntary spasmodic contraction of the diaphragm and intercostal muscles.

Snellen('s) chart /snĕl′ən(z)/ a chart with letters, signs, and numbers used in testing vision. *Also called* Snellen's test type.

Snellen's test type Snellen's chart.

sniff test a test for diaphragm functioning involving rapid sniffing.

SNOMED /snō′mĕd′/ *abbreviation.* Systematized Nomenclature of Medical Terms, an international standardized system of medical terminology gradually being instituted worldwide.

snore /snôr/ to breathe during sleep making a hoarse nasal noise; a sign of partial upper airway obstruction.

snot /snŏt/ slang term for nasal mucus.

mediastinum, producing symptoms of "acid indigestion" and eructation. Previously thought to be an important feature of GERD, but has proved of little value in understanding or treating GERD.

sling /slĭng/ a triangular bandage for supporting an injured arm.

slipped disc/disk informal term for a herniated or ruptured disk in the vertebrae.

slit lamp ocular examination /ŏk′yə lər/ examination of the eye using a device with a high-intensity light beam focused on the eye structures.

SOAP method /sōp/ a method of keeping medical records that include *s*ubjective, *o*bjective, *a*ssessment, and *p*lan entries in the record.

SOB *abbreviation.* shortness of breath.

social anxiety disorder experiencing extreme discomfort in social situations. *Also called* social phobia.

social phobia social anxiety disorder.

social worker a person (usually with a degree in social work) who is trained to counsel individuals and families dealing with problems.

socio- *combining form.* social: *for example,* sociopathy.

sociopath /sō′sē ə păth′, sō′shē-/ a person with an antisocial personality disorder. *Also called* psychopath, sociopathic personality. [socio- + -path]

sociopathic personality a sociopath.

sociopathy /sō′sē ŏp′ə thē, sō′shē-/ antisocial behavioral pattern. [socio- + -pathy]

socket /sŏk′ĭt/ a hollow part, such as an eye socket or a tooth socket, into which another part fits.

sodium (Na) /sō′dē əm/ a highly reactive metallic element found naturally in the body as well as in foods.

sodomy /sŏd′ə mē/ **1.** having anal or oral sex. **2.** having sex with an animal.

soft chancre /shăng′kər/ a sexually transmitted disease with painful ulcers on the penis or vulva. *Also called* chancroid.

soft diet a normal diet limited to soft foods for people with swallowing difficulties.

soft palate /păl′ĭt/ the muscular part of the posterior portion of the roof of the mouth that has no bone.

sol, sol. *abbreviation.* solution.

solar plexus /sō′lər plĕk′səs/ the network of nerves in the back of the stomach.

sole /sōl/ the bottom surface of the foot.

soluble /sŏl′yə bəl/ able to be dissolved in a liquid.

solution /sə lo͞o′shən/ any liquid with dissolved material in it.

somat-, somato- *combining form.* body: *for example,* somatogenic.

somatic /sō măt′ĭk/ of or relating to the body.

somatic cell any cell of the body.

somatization /sō′mə tə zā′shən/ the expression of psychological needs through physical symptoms.

somatoform disorders /sō măt′ə fôrm′/ a group of disorders in which psychological problems express themselves through physical symptoms.

somatogenic /sō′mə tə jĕn′ĭk/ originating in the body. [somato- + -genic]

somatotherapy /sō′mə tə thĕr′ə pē/ treatment of mental illness using physical methods such as drugs, shock therapy, etc. [somato- + therapy]

somatotrophic hormone (STH) /sō′mə tə trŏf′ĭk/ somatropin.

somatropin /sō′mə tə trō′pĭn/ pituitary growth hormone (HGH—human growth hormone) that is also synthesized and given as a treatment for dwarfism. *Also called* somatotrophic hormone.

-some *suffix.* body: *for example,* chromosome.

somnambulism /sŏm năm′byə lĭz′əm/ walking around in an apparent state of sleep. *Also called* noctambulism, sleepwalking.

somnambulist /sŏm năm′byə lĭst/ a person who sleepwalks.

-somnia *suffix.* sleep: *for example,* insomnia.

somnolence /sŏm′nə ləns/ unnatural feeling of drowsiness; sleepiness.

somnolent /sŏm′nə lənt/ drowsy; sleepy.

Somogyi effect /sō′mō jē/ quick swings of blood sugar from high to low that occur in brittle or unstable diabetes.

son /sŭn/ male child.

sono- *combining form.* sound: *for example,* sonogram.

sonogram /sŏn′ə grăm′/ image obtained by sonography. [sono- + -gram]

sonographer /sə nŏg′rə fər/ technician trained in sonography.

sonography /sə nŏg′rə fē/ diagnostic imaging technique using sound waves to produce an

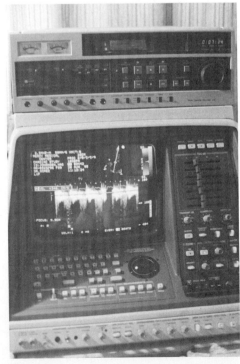

Sonography

image. *Also called* ultrasonography. [sono- + -graphy]

sopor /sō′pər/ an unnaturally deep sleep.

soporific /sŏp′ə rĭf′ĭk/ a drug that causes a state of deep sleep.

sore /sôr/ **1.** *adj.* inflamed; tender to the touch. **2.** *n.* a spot or area that is tender to the touch.

sore throat an inflammation of the throat that makes swallowing painful.

sound /sound/ **1.** *n.* a noise. **2.** an elongated instrument for probing body cavities. **3.** *adj.* well; healthy. **3.** *v.* to explore by observing with a sound or by listening as on auscultation.

Southern blot a diagnostic technique that searches for specific DNA fragments.

spasm /spăz′əm/ a sudden and strong, involuntary muscle contraction.

-spasm *suffix.* spasm: *for example,* bronchospasm.

spasmodic /spăz mŏd′ĭk/ of or having spasms.

spasmolytic /spăz′mə lĭt′ĭk/ an agent that controls spasms.

spastic /spăs′tĭk/ of or having spasms.

spastic colon /kō′lən/ a bowel disorder with abdominal pains and diarrhea, often caused by anxiety.

spastic dysphonia /dĭs fo′ne ə/ a disorder involving spastic contractions of the larynx.

spasticity /spă stĭs′ĭ tē/ an unusual involuntary increase in muscle tone, often resulting from illness, injury, or dehydration.

specialist /spĕsh′ə lĭst/ a medical practitioner who focuses his or her study and practice on a particular kind of disease, body part, type of patient, etc.

specialty /spĕsh′əl tē/ the particular medical field to which a medical professional devotes his or her studies and attention.

specific gravity the measure of a concentration of a substance in water.

specificity /spĕs′ə fĭs′ĭ tē/ the ability of an immune response to react to specific antigens.

specimen /spĕs′ə mən/ a sample, as of tissue, used for examination.

SPECT *abbreviation.* single photon emission computed tomography.

spectacles /spĕk′tə kəlz/ an old-fashioned term for a set of corrective lenses in a frame worn in front of the eye to correct vision or protect the eyes.

speculum /spĕk′yə ləm/ an instrument for dilating passages of the body either for examination or for surgical procedures.

speech /spēch/ the ability to articulate sounds or words.

speech disorder any disorder that affects speech.

speech pathologist /pə thŏl′ə jĭst/ professional trained to diagnose and treat people with speech disorders.

speech therapist professional trained in speech therapy.

speech therapy treatment to restore normal speech and communication.

sperm /spûrm/ the reproductive cell of the male produced in the testes.

sperm-, spermat-, spermato- spermo- *combining form.* sperm: *for example,* spermatogenesis.

spermatic cord /spər măt′ĭk/ the structures which go through the inguinal canal to the testis.

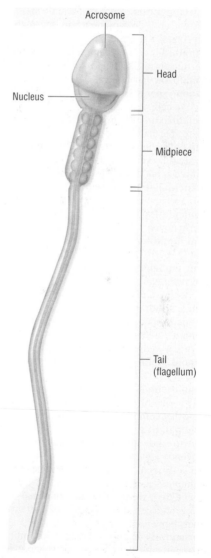

Sperm

spermatic duct the duct that carries sperm from the testis up to the seminal vesicle, where it becomes the ejaculatory duct and ends at the prostatic urethra. *Also called* vas deferens.

spermatid /spûr′mə tĭd/ one of a pair of haploid cells that become spermatozoa.

spermatocele /spər măt′ə sēl′/ a cyst on the epididymis. [spermato- + -cele]

spermatocide /spər măt′ə sīd′/ a birth control agent that kills sperm. [spermato- + -cide]

spermatocyst /spər măt′ə sĭst/ a cyst on the epididymis. [spermato- + -cyst]

spermatocyte /spər măt′ə sīt′/ a male germ cell that gives rise by meiosis to a pair of haploid cells, which in turn become spermatids. [spermato- + -cyte]

spermatogenesis /spər măt′ə jĕn′ə sĭs/ formation and development of spermatozoa. [spermato- + genesis]

spermatoid /spûr′mə toid′/ resembling sperm; sperm-like. [spermat- + -oid]

spermatozoa /spər măt′ə zō′ə/ (*sing.* **spermatozoon** /spər măt′ə zō′ŏn/) the male reproductive cell.

spermatozoan /spər măt′ə zō′ən/ of or relating to spermatozoa.

sperm cell the male reproductive cell.

spermicidal cream /spûr′mə sī′dəl/ a contraceptive agent that kills spermatozoa.

spermicidal jelly a contraceptive agent that kills spermatozoa.

spermicide /spûr′mə sīd′/ an agent that kills spermatozoa.

sperm motility /mō tĭl′ĭ tē/ the percentage of motile sperm in a semen sample.

sperm nucleus /nōō′klē əs/ the head of the spermatozoa.

SPF *abbreviation.* sun protection factor.

sphen- spheno- *combining form.* wedge; wedge-shaped: *for example,* sphenopalatine.

sphenoid /sfē′noid/ **1.** the sphenoid bone. **2.** having a wedge shape. [sphen- + -oid]

sphenoid bone a wing-shaped bone at the base of the skull.

sphenoid sinus or **sphenoidal sinus** /sfē noi′dəl/ one of two cavities in the sphenoid bone that communicate with the nasal cavities.

sphenopalatine /sfē′nō păl′ə tīn′/ of or relating to the sphenoid and palatine bones. [spheno- + palatine]

spher-, sphero- *combining form.* sphere: *for example,* spherocyte.

spherocyte /sfêr′ə sīt′/ an abnormal round red blood cell characteristic of certain anemias. [sphero- + -cyte]

spherocytosis /sfêr′ō sī tō′sĭs/ an inherited disorder with the presence of spherocytes in the blood. [sphero- + -cytosis]

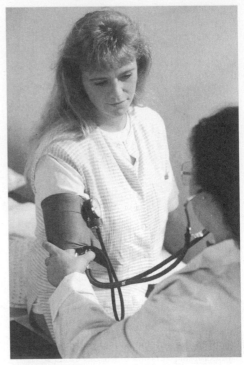

sphygmomanometer

spheroid /sfêr′oid/ having a spherical shape. [spher- + -oid]

sphincter /sfĭngk′tər/ a ring-shaped annular muscle that constricts and relaxes a body opening as part of normal functioning.

sphygm-, sphygmo- *combining form.* pulse: *for example,* sphygmoid.

sphygmoid /sfĭg′moid/ resembling a pulse. [sphygm- + -oid]

sphygmomanometer /sfĭg′mō mə nŏm′ĭ tər/ an instrument with a meter and cuff, used to measure arterial blood pressure.

spicule /spĭk′yōōl/ any needlelike structure or part.

spider angioma /ăn′jē ō′mə/ dilation of capillaries with a red dot in the center from which blood vessels branch out, usually visible just beneath the skin; may be present in advanced liver disease. *Also called* spider veins.

spider veins spider angioma.

spike /spīk/ **1.** the dominant peak in the record of an action potential or electroencephalogram. **2.** the narrow vertical tracing left on an electrocardiogram by a brief electrical event.

spin-, spino- *combining form.* spine, spinous: *for example,* spinocerebellar.

spinal /spī′nəl/ of, relating to, or near the spine or spinal cord.

spina bifida /spī′nə bĭf′ĭ də/　a birth defect in which the lower spinal column is not completely closed and the spinal cord or meninges may protrude; although the defect is corrected surgically, damage to nerve roots often leads to severe physical disabilities.

spina bifida cystica /sĭs′tĭ kə/　spina bifida with protrusion of the spinal cord or meninges.

spina bifida occulta /ə kŭl′tə/　spina bifida with no protrusion of the spinal cord or meninges.

spinal anesthesia /spī′nəl ăn′əs thē′zhə/　the injection of a local anesthetic drug directly into the cerebrospinal fluid in the spinal canal.

spinal canal　the canal through which the spinal cord, spinal meninges, and related structures pass. *Also called* vertebral canal.

spinal column　the series of articulated vertebrae and intervertebral disks that encase the spinal cord. *Also called* vertebral column.

spinal cord　the thick white cord of nerve tissue that passes through the spinal column, from which the spinal nerves branch off.

spinal cord compression　abnormal amount of pressure on the spinal cord due to injury or disease.

spinal curvature /kûr′və chər/　any abnormal curvature of the spine, such as scoliosis or kyphosis.

spinal fusion /fyōō′zhən/　a surgical procedure in which two or more vertebrae are joined.

spinal nerves　any of the 31 pairs of nerves that arise from the spinal cord.

spinal puncture or **spinal tap**　any diagnostic or therapeutic procedure involving the puncture of the subarachnoid space with a needle, sometimes to examine and culture the spinal fluid to identify the presence of infection, sometimes to inject a drug or dye for therapeutic or diagnostic purposes. *Also called* lumbar puncture.

spinal stenosis /stĭ nō′sĭs/　compression of the nerve roots or spinal cord due to spinal narrowing, due to arthritis, injury, Paget's disease, or fluorosis.

spindle cell　a spindle-shaped cell characteristic of certain tumors.

spindle neuron /nōōr′ŏn/　a large neuron found deep in the cortex of the brain.

spine /spīn/　the series of articulated vertebrae and intervertebral disks that encase the spinal cord. *Also called* backbone.

spinocerebellar /spī′nō sĕr′ə bĕl′ər/　of or relating to both the spinal cord and the cerebellum. [spino- + cerebellar]

spinoneural /spī′nō nōōr′əl/　of or relating to the spinal cord and its associated nerves. [spino- + neural]

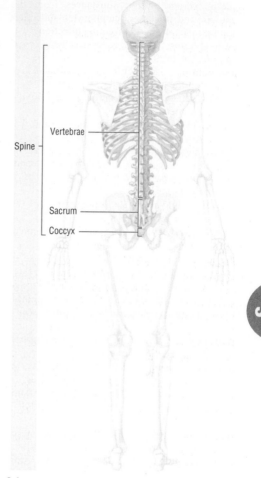

Spine

spinous /spī′nəs/　of or pertaining to the spine.

spinous process　the rear downward projections from each vertebral body, the nubby ends of which are seen and felt on external examination of the back.

spir-, spiro-　*combining form.* respiration: *for example,* spirometer.

spiral fracture　a fracture in which the bone has been twisted apart.

spirochete /spī′rə kēt′/　a microscopic spiral-shaped, worm-like bacterial organism, such as the bacterium that causes syphillis.

spirometer /spī rŏm′ĭ tər/　an instrument that measures the amount of air entering and exiting the lungs. [spiro- + -meter]

spirometry /spī rŏm′ĭ trē/　measuring the amount of air entering and exiting the lungs using a spirometer. [spiro- + -metry]

spit /spĭt/　to eject saliva from the mouth.

spleen /splēn/　the large lymphoid organ that sequesters and metabolizes old red blood cells, filters foreign substances from the blood, and produces lymphocytes and other compounds that aid in fighting infection.

splen- spleno- *combining form.* spleen: *for example,* splenectomy.

splenectomy /splĭ nĕk′tə mē/ surgical removal of the spleen. [splen- + -ectomy]

splenic /splĕn′ĭk/ of, relating to, or near the spleen. [splen- + -ic]

splenic fever a highly infectious animal disease. *Also called* anthrax.

splenic flexure /flĕk′shər/ the curve at the junction of the transverse colon and descending colon, adjacent to the spleen. *Also called* left colic flexure.

splenitis /splē nī′tĭs/ inflammation of the spleen. [splen- + -itis]

splenomegaly /splē′nə mĕg′ə lē/ enlargement of the spleen. [spleno- + -megaly]

splenopathy /splē nŏp′ə thē/ any disease of the spleen. [spleno- + -pathy]

splenorrhagia /splē′nə rā′jē ə/ hemorrhage from a ruptured spleen. [spleno- + -rrhagia]

splenorrhaphy /splē nôr′ə fē/ suture of a ruptured spleen. [spleno- + -rrhaphy]

splint /splĭnt/ a device used to prevent motion of a joint, a broken bone, or teeth.

spondyl-, spondylo- *combining form.* vertebra, vertebrae: *for example,* spondylolysis.

spondylarthritis /spŏn′dəl är thrī′tĭs/ inflammation of the joints of the spine. [spondyl- + arthritis]

spondylitis /spŏn′də lī′tĭs/ inflammation of the intervertebral joints. [spondyl- + -itis]

spondylolisthesis /spŏn′də lō lĭs′thə sĭs/ forward displacement of one of the lower lumbar vertebrae over the vertebra below it or on the sacrum, frequently causing nerve root compression and pain and/or weakness in the legs.

spondylolysis /spŏn′də lŏl′ə sĭs/ disintegration or dissolution of a vertebra. [spondylo- + -lysis]

spondyloschisis /spŏn′də lŏs′kə sĭs/ congenital fissure of the spinal column, found in certain types of spina bifida. *Also called* rachischisis.

spondylosis /spŏn′də lō′sĭs/ any of several degenerative diseases of the spinal column leading to immobilization of vertebral bones. [spondyl- + -osis]

spondylosyndesis /spŏn′də lō sĭn dē′sĭs/ a surgical procedure in which two or more vertebrae are joined; current terminology uses "arthrodesis" preceeded by the anatomical part, for example "L2-3 arthrodesis." [spondylo- + syndesis]

sponge /spŭnj/ **1.** a piece of absorbent porous material such as a gauze pad, used to wash or absorb. **2.** a form of birth control consisting

Sponge (contraceptive device)

of a small absorbent pad containing a spermicide.

spongiform /spŭn′jə fôrm′/ resembling a sponge.

spongiform encephalopathy /ĕn sĕf′ə lŏp′ə thē/ encephalopathy caused by a prion and characterized by progressive degeneration of the cerebral cortex into a spongelike substance: scrapie in sheep, kuru and Creutzfeldt-Jakob in humans, mad cow disease, and perhaps others. *Also called* TSEs (transmissible spongiform encephalopathies).

spongy bone a bone in which the spicules form a latticework, with interstices filled with embryonic connective tissue or bone marrow. *Also called* cancellated bone, cancellous bone.

spontaneous abortion /spŏn tā′nē əs ə bôr′shən/ an abortion occurring naturally. *Also called* miscarriage.

spontaneous amputation /ăm′pyōō tā′shən/ amputation of a limb either congenitally or as a result of a disease, not from an injury.

spoon nails a condition in which the fingernails are abnormally thin and concave, often related to anemia.

sporadic /spə răd′ĭk/ occurring at irregular intervals.

sporotrichosis /spôr′ō trĭ kō′sĭs/ a chronic parasitic fungal infection of the skin and lymph nodes.

sports massage massage therapy given before, during, and after athletic events to prepare the athlete, to lessen fatigue, to relieve swelling, to reduce muscle tension, to promote flexibility, and to prevent injuries.

spot /spŏt/ a small discolored round patch on the skin, or other surface, such as the eye.

spotted fever any of various diseases transmitted by ticks that are serious and can be fatal, such as Rocky Mountain spotted fever.

sprain /sprān/ an injury to a ligament.

sprained ankle an injury where the ligaments of the ankle are damaged, usually by stretching.

spur /spûr/ a bony projection. *Also called* calcar.

sputum /spyōō′təm/ mucus that comes up from the lungs.

sputum culture and sensitivity a test to determine whether the sputum is infected with bacteria and which antibiotic will be most effective.

sputum sample a sample of the mucus that is coughed up from the lungs.

sq *abbreviation.* subcutaneous.

squamous cell /skwā′məs/ flat, thin cell of epithelial tissue that resembles a fish scale.

squamous cell carcinoma /kär′sə nō′mə/ cancer that starts in squamous cells.

squamous epithelium /ĕp′ə thē′lē əm/ tissue layer that is composed of flat thin cells.

squint /skwĭnt/ **1.** *v.* to close the eyes partially while looking. **2.** *n.* an informal term for abnormal alignment of the eyes called strabismus or heteropia.

SR *abbreviation.* **1.** sedimentation rate. **2.** sinus rhythm.

SSPE *abbreviation.* subacute sclerosing panencephalitis.

SSRI *abbreviation.* selective serotonin reuptake inhibitor.

stabilize /stā′bə līz′/ to bring to a steady state.

staff /stăf/ **1.** all the people, medical and otherwise, who work at a hospital, clinic, etc. **2.** a tool that is inserted into the urethra and bladder as a guide to a surgical knife.

stage /stāj/ a point in the development of a disease, such as cancer.

staging /stā′jĭng/ determining what stage a disease has reached.

stain /stān/ **1.** *n.* a dye used to color tissue cells and other microscopic objects. **2.** any discoloration. **3.** *v.* to apply dye to tissue or other microscopic objects.

standard /stăn′dərd/ basis for comparison such as the quality or quantity of something, such as a treatment.

standard of care the level of care a physician is obligated to provide to a patient based on what other providers in the same situation would provide.

standard precautions set of procedures used to prevent the transmission of certain infection between patient and health care providers. *See standards* at hygiene on page 166.

Stanford-Binet intelligence scale /stăn′fərd bĭ nā′/ system used to measure a person's intelligence, mainly used for children.

stapedectomy /stā′pĭ dĕk′tə mē/ surgical removal of the stapes, one of three tiny bones in the middle ear.

stapes /stā′pēz/ (*pl.* **stapes** or **stapedes** /stə pē′dēz/) the innermost of the three small bones of the ear, shaped like a stirrup. *Also called* stirrup.

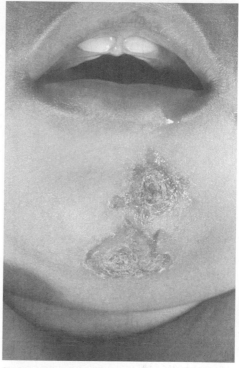

Staphylococcus (infection)

staph /stăf/ short for staphylococcus.

staph infection staphylococcal infection.

staphyl-, staphylo- *combining form.* **1.** relating to staphylococci. **2.** relating to the uvula (of the soft palate of the mouth): *for example,* staphyloplasty.

staphylitis /stăf′ə lī′tĭs/ inflammation of the uvula. [staphyl- + -itis]

staphylococcal /stăf′ə lə kŏk′əl/ of or relating to staphyllococcus.

staphylococcal infection infection caused by staphylococcus.

staphylococcus /stăf′ə lə kŏk′əs/ (*pl.* **staphylococci** /stăf′ə lə kŏk′sī/) round bacterium of the genus *Staphylloccus,* seen in bunches like grapes under the microscope, that is the cause of many infections, such as septicemia. [staphylo- + -coccus]

staphylococcus aureus /ôr′ē əs/ an antibiotic-resistant bacterium that is the cause of many infections.

staphyloplasty /stăf′ə lə plăs′tē/ surgical procedure to fix the uvula and soft palate. [staphylo- + -plasty]

staples /stā′pəlz/ surgical devices used to fasten tissue together.

startle reflex in infants, the reflex where the limbs contract suddenly in response to a loud noise or a startling motion.

stasis /stā′sĭs/ the slowing or stopping of the flow of blood or another body fluid.

stasis dermatitis /dûr′mə tī′tĭs/ skin irritation and breakdown as a result of decreased circulation.

STAT/stat /stăt/ term used in medicine meaning urgent or at once, short for the Latin word *statim,* which means immediately.

-stat *suffix.* implies something that prevents motion or change: *for example,* cryostat.

state /stāt/ condition of being, as of one's health or mental status.

statins /stăt′ĭnz/ class of drugs that lower cholesterol by inhibiting a certain enzyme; also improve tissue perfusion through increased levels of nitric oxide, which dilates capillaries.

stature /stăch′ər/ height when standing.

statutory rape /stăch′ə tôr′ē rāp′/ sexual intercourse between an adult and a minor, even if it is consensual.

STD *abbreviation.* sexually transmitted disease.

steat-, steato- *combining form.* fat: *for example,* steatorrhea.

steatohepatitis /stē ăt′ō hĕp′ə tī′tĭs/ fatty inflammation of the liver. [steato- + hepatitis]

steatoma /stī′ə tō′mə/ (*pl.* **steatomas** or **steatomata** /stī′ə tō′mə tə/) a tumor of the sebaceous glands. [steat- + -oma]

steatorrhea /stē ăt′ə rē′ə/ overactivity of any sebaceous gland, especially excessive discharge of undigested fat in the feces. [steato- + -rrhea]

steatosis /stē′ə tō′sĭs/ fatty deposits in the interstices of organ tissue. [steat- + -osis]

stem cell an undifferentiated (unspecialized) cell that can grow into any one of the body's cell types.

stem cell harvest the collection of stem cells for medical use, such as cancer treatment.

stem cell transplant replacement of stem cells in a patient.

stenosis /stĭ nō′sĭs/ (*pl.* **stenoses** /stĭ nō′sēz/ constriction; narrowing. *Also called* stricture.

-stenosis *suffix.* stenosis.

stenotic /stĭ nŏt′ĭk/ of or having stenosis.

stent /stĕnt/ a slender device used to hold open a structure, such as a blood vessel or a body orifice. Stents may be temporary or permanent and may contain medication *See also* drug-eluting stent.

step /stĕp/ one complete movement of the foot from one spot to another, as one movement in the series that comprises walking; one stage in any series.

stercolith /stûr′kə lĭth/ an intestinal mass of hard fecal matter. *Also called* coprolith.

stereo- *combining form.* solid; three-dimensional: *for example,* stereology.

stereology /stĕr′ē ŏl′ə jē/ the study of the three-dimensional properties of objects usually observed as two-dimensional. [stereo- + -logy]

stereotactic /stĕr′ē ə tăk′tĭk/ using of three planes in neurosurgery or neurology for locating points in the brain.

stereotactic frame a three-dimensional device used in neurosurgery or neurology for locating points in the brain for biopsy or radiation therapy.

stereotactic surgery surgery using a stereotactic frame.

stereotaxis /stĕr′ē ə tăk′sĭs/ stereotactic surgery. [stereo- + -taxis]

stereotaxy /stĕr′ē ə tăk′sē/ the use of a stereotactic frame to locate points in the brain.

sterile /stĕr′əl/ **1.** without germs; uncontaminated; antiseptic. **2.** unable to reproduce sexually.

sterility /stə rĭl′ĭ tē/ state of being sterile.

sterilization /stĕr′ə lə zā′shən/ to cause to become sterile, either by decontamination or by surgery.

stern-, sterno- *combining form.* sternum: *for example,* sternocostal.

sternal /stûr′nəl/ of or relating to the sternum.

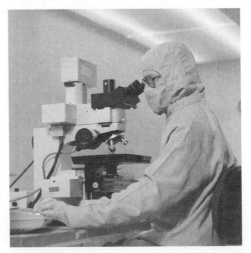

Sterile (laboratory)

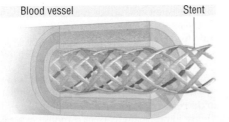

Blood vessel   Stent

Stent

sternalgia /stər năl′jē ə, -jə/   pain in the sternum. *Also called* sternodynia. [stern- + -algia]

sternoclavicular /stûr′nō klə vĭk′yə lər/   of or relating to the joint between the sternum and the clavicle.

sternocostal /stûr′nō kŏs′təl/   of or relating to the junction between the sternum and the ribs. [sterno- + costal]

sternodynia /stûr′nō dĭn′ē ə/   pain in the sternum. *Also called* sternalgia. [sterno- + -dynia]

sternoid /stûr′noid/   resembling the sternum. [stern- + -oid]

sternum /stûr′nəm/   a long, flat bone located in the center of the thorax to which the ribs attach. *Also called* breastbone.

sternutation /stûrn′yōō tā′shən/   sneezing.

steroid /stĕr′oid/   natural or synthetic fat-soluble organic compound, including various hormones, having important physiological effects and used in many drugs.

steroid abuse   the illegal use of androgenic steroids to build body mass, used by many athletes illegally to enhance performance.

stethoscope /stĕth′ə skōp′/   medical instrument for listening to sounds in the body.

STH   *abbreviation.* somatrophic hormone.

STI   *abbreviation.* sexually transmitted infection.

stiff neck   movement-constricting condition of the neck due to injury.

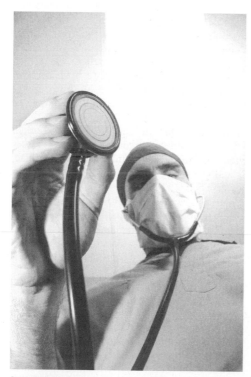

Stethoscope

stillbirth /stĭl′bûrth′/   birth of a infant who has died before delivery.

Still's disease /stĭlz/   rheumatoid arthritis found in children.

stimulant /stĭm′yə lənt/   any agent that stimulates or accelerates physiological activity.

stimulus /stĭm′yə ləs/ (*pl.* **stimuli** stĭm′yə lī′/) anything that arouses a response.

sting /stĭng/   **1.** *n.* acute pain from a sharp pointed object or structure such as the stinger of an insect. **2.** *v.* to burn or feel a sharp pain from a sting.

stirrup /stûr′əp, stĭr′-/   innermost small bone of the middle ear. *Also called* stapes.

St. John's Wort /sānt′ jŏnz′ wûrt′, wôrt′/ plant of the genus *Hypericum,* used in alternative medicine in the treatment of depression.

STM   *abbreviation.* short-term memory.

Stockholm syndrome /stŏk′hōlm/   psychological phenomenon in which a hostage bonds with his or her captor(s).

stoma /stō′mə/ (*pl.* **stomata** stō′mə tə/ or **stomas**)   an opening, as on the surface of a membrane, or one created surgically on the surface of the body.

stomach /stŭm′ək/   sac-like organ of the alimentary canal; the initial organ of digestion.

stomachache /stŭm′ək āk′/   vague nonmedical term for pain in the abdomen.

stomat-, stomato-   *combining form.* mouth; stoma: *for example,* stomatitis.

stomatitis /stō′mə tī′tĭs/   inflamation of the mucous membrane of the mouth. [stomat- + -itis]

stomatomycosis /stə măt′ō mī kō′sĭs/   fungal disease of the mouth. [stomato- + mycosis]

stomatoplasty /stə măt′ə plăs′tē/   reconstructive surgery of the mouth. [stomato- + -plasty]

-stomy   *suffix.* surgical opening in an organ or body part: *for example,* colostomy.

stone /stōn/   abnormal concretion in the body. *Also called* calculus.

stool /stōōl/   fecal matter.

stool culture   test of the stool to identify pathogenic organisms.

stool occult blood test /ə kŭlt′/   screen for colon cancer in which stool is examined for chemical evidence of blood.

strabismus /strə bĭz′məs/   abnormal alignment of one or both eyes. *Also called* heteropia.

strain /strān/   **1.** *v.* to injure through overuse. **2.** *n.* an injury to muscles and/or tendons resulting from overuse. **3.** group of organisms within a species that vary slightly from similar groups.

strait /strāt/   narrow passage, said of the upper or lower opening of the pelvic canal.

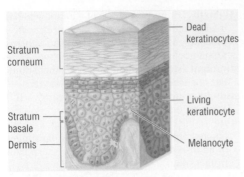

Stratum corneum

Dead keratinocytes

Stratum basale

Living keratinocyte

Dermis

Melanocyte

Stratum Basale

straitjacket /strāt′jăk′ĭt/ garment with closed sleeves which can be tied close to the body to restrain a violent or agitated person.

strangle /străng′gəl/ to prevent breathing by compressing the throat; suffocate.

strangulated hernia /străng′gyə lā′tĭd hûr′nē ə/ hernia to which the blood supply is compromised by swelling and congestion.

stratified /străt′ə fīd′/ arranged in layers, said of the layers of cells of the epithelium.

stratified squamous epithelium /skwā′məs ĕp′ə thē′lē əm/ layered cell structure of the epithelium.

stratum /strā′təm, străt′əm/ (*pl.* **strata** /strā′tə, străt′ə/) one of several horizontal layers, stacked on top of another.

stratum basale /bā sā′lē/ (*pl.* **strata basalia** /bā sā′lē ə/) innermost layer of the epidermis. *Also called* stratum germinativum.

stratum corneum /kôr′nē əm/ (*pl.* **strata cornea** /kôr′nē ə/) outermost layer of the epidermis, consisting of dead cells.

stratum germinativum /jûr′mə nə tī′vəm/ (*pl.* **strata germinativa** /jûr′mə nə tī′və/) innermost layer of the epidermis. *Also called* stratum basale.

strep /strĕp/ short for streptococcus.

strep throat infection of the throat and tonsils by streptococcus.

strepto- *combining form.* streptococcus: *for example,* streptobacillus.

streptobacillus /strĕp′tō bə sĭl′əs/ (*pl.* **streptobacilli** /strĕp′tō bə sĭl′ī/) any of the various rod-shaped, pathogenic bacteria that cause many infections. [strepto- + bacillus]

streptococcal /strĕp′tə kŏk′əl/ relating to or caused by streptococcus.

streptococcus /strĕp′tə kŏk′əs/ (*pl.* **streptococci** /strĕp′tə kŏk′sī/) any of various bacteria of the genus *Streptococcus*, which cause many common infections. [strepto- + -coccus]

streptokinase /strĕp′tō kī′nās/ proteolytic enzyme produced by hemolytic streptococci, used medicinally to dissolve blood clots.

streptolysin /strĕp′tō lī′sĭn/ any of several blood-destroying enzymes produced by streptococci.

stress /strĕs/ **1.** *v.* to exert pressure on. **2.** *n.* physiological and emotional responses to adverse stimuli, capable of disturbing normal functioning.

stress echocardiography /ĕk′ō kär′dē ŏg′rə fē/ echocardiographic monitoring of the body's circulation during exercise or chemically induced tachycardia.

stress fracture /frăk′chər/ hairline fracture of a bone due to excessive activity or injury; usually not visible on x-rays and mainly treated with rest.

stress incontinence /ĭn kŏn′tə nəns/ incontinence when involuntary pressure is exerted on the bladder by sneezing, coughing, laughing, or straining.

stressor /strĕs′ər/ an agent or situation that causes stress.

stress test test to measure heart function during physical activity, generally on a treadmill or stationery bicycle.

stretcher /strĕch′ər/ **1.** a kind of litter usually made of canvas stretched between two wooden poles with four handles for moving the sick and wounded, especially in war or over rough terrain. **2.** a metal table on wheels for the same purpose, used in hospitals and abulances. *Also called* gurney.

stretch marks striae on the skin from excessive expansion and rupture of elastin, especially from pregnancy or obesity.

stria /strī′ə/ (*pl.* **striae** /strī′ē/) **1.** narrow, parallel stripe of different color or texture, as of the skin. **2.** narrow structural band, especially of nerve fibers.

striae gravidarum /grăv′ĭ dâr′əm/ stretch marks resulting from pregnancy.

striated muscle /strī′ā tĭd/ skeletal, cardiac, and voluntary muscle, characterized by transverse bands of fibers.

striatum /strī ā′təm/ the caudate nucleus, putamen, and globus pallidus of the corpus striatum (of the cerebral hemispheres).

stricture /strĭk′chər/ narrowing of a bodily tube, duct or passage from scar tissue or a tumor. *Also called* stenosis.

stridor /strī′dər/ high-pitched sound heard during respiration indicating obstruction of the air passages.

strip /strĭp/ to remove a vein.

stripping /strĭp′ĭng/ a massage therapy technique using slow, deep, gliding pressure strokes along the length of the muscle fibers to release tightened muscles and relieve pain.

Stroke

stroke /strōk/   sudden damage to nerve cells in the brain resulting from hemorrage into a part of the brain, or from a clot in a blood vessel causing damage to brain tissue deprived of blood flow. *Also called* cerebrovascular accident. *See also* hemorrhagic stroke, ischemic stroke.

stroke volume   volume of blood pumped from the left ventricle in one heartbeat.

stroma /strō′mə/ (*pl.* **stromata** /strī′mə tə/)   **1.** supporting framework of connective tissue of a bodily structure. **2.** dense, spongy framework of a cell.

stromal /strō′məl/   relating to the stroma of a bodily structure or cell.

struma /strōō′mə/   an enlargement of the thyroid gland associated with iodine deficiency. *Also called* goiter.

struma lymphomatosa /lĭm fō′mə tō′sə/   an autoimmune disease of the thyroid gland in which lymphocytes infiltrate the thyroid, characterized by goiter, inflammation of the thyroid, and hypothyroidism. *Also called* Hashimoto's disease.

stump /stŭmp/   **1.** remaining part of a limb after a part has been removed. **2.** remaining stem after removing a tumor to which it was attached.

stupor /stōō′pər/   impaired consciousness marked by reduced responsiveness to stimuli.

stutter /stŭt′ər/   to speak with interruptions caused by repetitions of consonants or syllables, prolongations of sounds, hesitations before onset of following sounds, and sometimes accompanied by contortions.

St. Vitus dance /vī′təs/   chorea (spastic movement believed due to brain lesion) occurring in children, associated with rheumatic fever.

sty/stye /stī/   infection of the sebaceous gland of the eyelid. *Also called* hordeolum.

styl-, stylo- *combining form.* styloid process: *for example,* stylomastoid.

styloid /stī′loid/   slender and pointed. [styl- + -oid]

styloid process   any of the long, slender, pointed bone processes of the body. [styl- + -oid]

stylomastoid /stī′lō măs′toid/   of or relating to the styloid and mastoid processes of the temporal bone. [stylo- + mastoid]

sub- *prefix.* **1.** below. **2.** secondary. **3.** subdivision. **4.** not completely, almost. *For example,* submaxillary.

subacute /sŭb′ə kyōōt′/   somewhat acute; between acute and chronic. [sub- + acute]

subacute bacterial endocarditis /băk têr′ē əl ĕn′dō kär dī′tĭs /   condition usually involving abnormal cardiac valves and usually due to certain streptococci.

subacute sclerosing panencephalitis (SSPE) /sklĭ rō′sĭng păn′ ĕn sĕf′ə lī′tĭs/   chronic degenerative encephalitis occurring in children; rare complication of measles virus infection.

subacute spongiform encephalopathy /spŭn′ jĭ fôrm   ĕn sĕf′ə lŏp′ə thē/   transmissable progressive, fatal encephalopathy; a form of spongiform encepalopathy.

subarachnoid /sŭb′ə răk′noid/   space between the arachnoid and the pia mater in the tissue surrounding and protecting the brain and spinal cord. [sub- + arachnoid]

subarachnoid space   space between the arachnoid membrane and the pia mater through which the cerebrospinal fluid circulates.

subaural /sŭb ôr′əl/   below the ear. [sub- + aural]

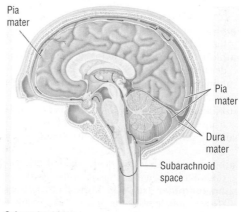

Subarachnoid Space

subclavian /sŭb klā′vē ən/ beneath the clavicle.

subclinical disease /sŭb klĭn′ĭ kəl/ an undetected illness due to a lack of clear clinical symptoms. [sub- + clinical]

subconscious /sŭb kŏn′shəs/ **1.** *adj.* below the level of conscious awareness. **2.** *n.* in psychology, mental processes that the individual is not knowingly aware of. [sub- + conscious]

subcostal /sŭb kŏs′təl/ located below the ribs. [sub- + costal]

subcutaneous /sŭb′kyoō tā′nē əs/ **(sc, SC, sq)** under the skin. [sub- + cutaneous]

subcutaneous injection an injection under the skin.

subcutaneous layer layer of soft tissue under the epidermis.

subcutaneous mastectomy /mă stĕk′tə mē/ surgical removal of breast tissue, leaving the overlying skin intact.

subcutaneous tissue soft tissue under the epidermis.

subdeltoid /sŭb dĕl′toid/ below the deltoid muscle. [sub- + deltoid]

subdural /sŭb doōr′əl/ located under the dura mater. [sub- + dural]

subdural hematoma /hē′mə tō′mə/ hematoma beneath the dura mater; may apply extreme pressure to the cerebral cortex after head trauma, especially in the elderly; often a surgical emergency.

subdural space the space between the dura mater and the arachnoid membrane.

subglottis /sŭb glŏt′ĭs/ the area beneath the vocal cords. [sub- + glottis]

subjacent /sŭb jā′sənt/ lying beneath another part.

subject /sŭb′jĕkt/ **1.** one whose responses are studied, as a patient in a clinical trial. **2.** a dead body used for anatomical study.

sublimation /sŭb′lə mā′shən/ **1.** expression of a primitive instinct in a socially acceptable way. **2.** process whereby a substance changes from a solid to a gas.

sublingual (SL) /sŭb lĭng′gwəl/ under the tongue. [sub- + lingual]

sublingual administration administered under the tongue.

sublingual gland either of two salivary glands located beneath the tongue.

sublingual medication /mĕd′ĭ kā′shən/ medication administered under the tongue.

sublingually /sŭb lĭng′gwə lē/ under the tongue.

subluxation /sŭb′lŭk sā′shən/ partial dislocation of a bone in a joint. [sub- + luxation]

submandibular /sŭb′măn dĭb′yə lər/ relating to the area below the lower jaw. [sub- + mandibular]

submandibular gland either of two major salivary glands inside the lower jaw, which discharge saliva into the mouth.

submaxillary /sŭb′măk sĭl′ə rē/ located beneath the maxilla. [sub- + maxillary]

submaxillary gland either of two major salivary glands inside the lower jaw, which discharge saliva into the mouth.

subpubic /sŭb pyoō′bĭk/ located under, or posterior to, the pubic bone. [sub- + pubic]

subscapular /sŭb skăp′yə lər/ **1.** located under the scapula. **2.** anterior surface of the scapula.

substance /sŭb′stəns/ material of a particular nature, especially said of a drug or agent.

substance abuse excessive and usually illegal use of a drug.

substance-related disorders disorders resulting from substance abuse, the side effects of medication, or from toxins.

subtotal hysterectomy /sŭb tō′təl hĭs′tə rĕk′tə mē/ surgical removal of all of the uterus except the cervix. *Also called* partial hysterectomy.

subungual /sŭb ŭng′gwəl/ beneath a fingernail or toenail. [sub- + ungual]

succumb /sə kŭm′/ **1.** to submit to an overwhelming force or desire. **2.** to die.

suction /sŭk′shən/ action of drawing out by aspiration, as fluid from a body cavity.

sudden infant death syndrome (SIDS) sudden death of a seemingly healthy infant during sleep, usually of unknown causes.

sudoriferous glands /soō′də rĭf′ər əs/ tiny glands of the subcutaneous tissue that secrete through the skin. *Also called* sweat glands.

suffocate /sŭf′ə kāt′/ to prevent from breathing; smother.

sugar /shoōg′ər/ any of a class of sweet, white, crystalline, carbohydrates.

suggestion /səg jĕs′chən/ **1.** the imparting of an idea to someone else indirectly or the idea thus imparted. **2.** the psychological process of having an individual adopt or accept an idea without argument or persuasion.

suicidal /soō′ə sī′dəl/ **1.** of or relating to suicide. **2.** wanting or likely to kill onself.

suicide /soō′ə sīd′/ act of intentionally killing oneself.

sulcus /sŭl′kəs/ (*pl.* **sulci** /sŭl′sī/) a narrow groove in an organ or tissue, especially of the surface of the brain.

sulfa drug /sŭl′fə/ any of various synthetic, antibacterial drugs.

sulfonamide /sŭl fŏn′ə mīd′/ any of a group of antibacterial sulfur compounds including sulfa drugs.

sulfonylurea /sŭl′fə nĭl yoōr′ē ə/ drug to treat diabetes that increases insulin secretion and reduces the level of glucose in the blood.

Sunscreens (with SPF)

sulfur (S) /sŭl′fər/ a nonmetallic element with a foul odor, used in medicine especially in the treatment of skin diseases.

sun protection factor (SPF) the degree to which a sunscreen protects the skin from ultraviolet rays; the higher the number, the greater the protection.

sunscreen /sŭn′skrēn′/ agent applied to protect the skin from the sun's ultraviolet rays.

super- *prefix.* **1.** above; upon. **2.** superior. **3.** exceeding. **4.** excessive. **5.** containing a large amount of a specific ingredient. *For example,* supernumery.

superbug /sōō′pər bŭg′/ disease-causing bacteria resistant to antibiotics. [super- + bug]

superego /sōō′pər ē′gō/ psychoanalytic term for the part of the unconscious that serves as a conscience. [super- + ego]

superficial /sōō′pər fĭsh′əl/ relating to or located near the surface.

superinfection /sōō′pər ĭn fĕk′shən/ an antibiotic-resistant infection that follows closely after another infection.

superior /sə pêr′ē ər/ located closer to the head and further from the feet.

superior lobe upper lobe of the right or left lung.

superior vena cava /vē′nə kā′və/ large vein that receives blood from the upper half of the body and empties into the right atrium of the heart.

supernumerary /sōō′pər nōō′mə rĕr′ē/ exceeding the normal number; extra.

superolateral /sōō′pə rō lăt′ər əl/ at the side and above.

supination /sōō′pə nā′shən/ **1.** being in or assuming the supine position. **2.** rotation of the forearm so that the palm faces upward, or the rotation and inversion (turning inward) of the foot. *See also* pronation.

supine /sōō pīn′/ lying on one's back.

supp. *abbreviation.* supplement.

supplement /sŭp′lə mənt/ something added to compensate for a deficiency, as a vitamin.

support system network of people who provide one with emotional or practical support.

suppository /sə pŏz′ĭ tôr′ē/ small, solid form of medication, meltable at body temperature, which is inserted into the vagina or rectum.

suppression /sə prĕsh′ən/ **1.** the curtailing of a bodily function. **2.** lack of development of a bodily structure. **3.** conscious omission of a thought or feeling from one's consciousness.

suppressor gene gene that suppresses expression of another, usually mutant, gene.

suppressor T cell T cell that inhibits the immune response of B cells or other T cells to an antigen. *Also called* T suppressor cell.

suppurate /sŭp′yə rāt′/ to form or discharge pus.

suppurative /sŭp′yə rā′tĭv/ tendency to form pus.

supra- *prefix.* above; over: supracostal.

supraclavicular /sōō′prə klə vĭk′yə lər/ located or occurring above the clavicle.

supracostal /sōō′prə kŏs′təl/ located or occurring above the ribs. [supra- + costal]

supraglottic /sōō′prə glŏt′ĭk/ located or occurring in the upper larynx or epiglottis.

suprainguinal /sōō′prə ĭng′gwə nəl/ located or occurring above the groin. [supra- + inguinal]

supramammary /sōō′prə măm′ə rē/ located or occurring above the mammary gland. [supra- + mammary]

suprapatellar /sōō′prə pə tĕl′ər/ located or occurring above the patella.

suprapubic /sōō′prə pyōō′bĭk/ located or occurring above the pubic bone. [supra- + pubic]

suprarenal /sōō′prə rē′nəl/ located or occurring above the kidney. [supra- + renal]

suprarenal gland one of two endocrine glands located just above the kidneys. *Also called* adrenal gland.

suprascapular /sōō′prə skăp′yə lər/ located or occurring above the scapula.

suprasternal /sōō′prə stûr′nəl/ located above or measured from the top of the sternum.

supraventricular /sōō′prə vĕn trĭk′yə lər/ located or occurring above the ventricles.

surfactant /sər făk′tənt/ **1.** a surface-active substance. **2.** a lipoprotein-based substance secreted in the lungs that reduces the surface tension of fluids that coat the lung; it is lacking in infants and premature babies with hyaline membrane disease.

surgeon /sûr′jən/   a physician specializing in surgery.

surgeon general (*pl.* **surgeons general**)   **1.** The chief general officer in the medical departments of the U.S. Army, Navy, or Air Force. **2.** The chief medical officer in the U.S. Public Health Service or in a state public health service.

surgery /sûr′jə rē/   **1.** the branch of medicine that uses surgical procedures to treat disease and repair injuries and deformities. **2.** a surgical procedure performed by a surgeon.

surgical menopause /sûr′jĭ kəl měn′ə pôz′/   surgically induced menopause, as in bilateral oophorectomy (removal of both ovaries).

surrogate /sûr′ə gĭt, -gāt′/   someone who substitutes for another, as someone who provides the nurturing care that is not supplied by an absent or incapable biological parent.

surrogate mother   **1.** a woman who acts as a surrogate. **2.** a woman who carries a child to term for another woman, either by implantation of a fertilized egg or by intercourse with the father and either carrying the child to term or donating the fertilized egg to the other woman.

susceptible /sə sěp′tə bəl/ especially sensitive to, or likely to be affected with, a disease, infection or condition.

susp.   *abbreviation.* suspension.

suspension /sə spěn′shən/   **1.** a dispersion of a solid in a liquid, as used in pharmaceutical preparations. **2.** the surgical attaching of an organ to surrounding tissue for support. **3.** the hanging of a part from a support, such as a limb in a cast.

suspensory ligament /sə spěn′sə rē lĭg′ə mənt/ a ligament that supports a body part.

suture /sōō′chər/   **1.** the process of joining two surfaces, as of a wound, by sewing them together. **2.** the fine thread or similar material used to close a wound or join two surfaces.

Sutures

suture needle   a needle designed to carry sutures.

swallow /swŏl′ō/   to pass something into the mouth, down the throat and into the stomach.

sweat /swět/   **1.** *v.* to excrete perspiration (water and salt) through the pores in the skin. **2.** *n.* the moisture excreted by the sweat glands.

sweat gland   any of the small, tubular glands found in the skin that secrete perspiration through the pores. *Also called* sudoriferous glands.

sweat test   a test for cystic fibrosis that involves measuring the subject's sweat for abnormally high sodium chloride content.

sweating /swět′ĭng/   the process by which the sweat glands excrete perspiration through the pores.

Swedish massage /swē′dĭsh mə säzh′/   gentle massage therapy techniques developed in Sweden.

swell /swěl/   to increase in size or volume due to internal pressure.

swimmer's ear   inflammation/infection of the external auditory canal due to water trapped in the ear.

symbiosis /sĭm′bē ō′sĭs, -bī ō′-/   a close relationship between two or more different organisms or species that may or may not benefit each member.

symbol /sĭm′bəl/   a printed or written sign used to represent something else.

symmetry /sĭm′ĭ trē/   exact correspondence of form and configuration on both sides of a center plane.

sympathectomy /sĭm′pə thěk′tə mē/   surgical removal of a part of the sympathetic nervous system.

sympathetic /sĭm′pə thět′ĭk/   of, relating to, or acting on the sympathetic nervous system.

sympathetic nerve   one of the nerves of the sympathetic nervous system.

sympathetic nervous system   the part of the autonomic nervous system, that inhibits the physiological effects of the parasympathetic nervous system. Examples: reducing digestive secretions and motility, speeding up the heart, and contracting blood vessels, allowing the bladder to fill and retain urine. *See also* parasympathetic nervous system.

sympathomimetic   /sĭm′pə thō mĭ mět′ĭk/ producing physiological effects resembling those caused by the action of the sympathetic nervous system.

sympathy /sĭm′pə thē/   **1.** relation between parts or organs by which a disease in one effects the other. **2.** mutual affection or compassion between two people arising from an affinity for one another.

symphysiotomy /sĭm fĭz′ē ŏt′ə mē/   surgical division of the pubic symphysis.

symphysis /sĭm'fə sĭs/ **1.** a union or meeting point of two structures, as of two bones that have grown together, and the junction thus formed. **2.** an abnormal adhesion or two or more structures.

symptom /sĭmp'təm/ an indication of a disease or disorder, especially when a deviation from a normal situation exists.

symptomatic /sĭmp'tə măt'ĭk/ **1.** of, relating to, or based on symptoms. **2.** constituting a symptom.

symptomatic treatment a therapy that eases the symptoms of a disease without treating the disease itself.

symptomatology /sĭmp'tə mə tŏl'ə jē/ **1.** the medical science of symptoms. **2.** the combined symptoms of a disease.

syn- **1.** together; united: *for example*, synarthrosis. **2.** same; similar: *for example*, synaesthesia.

synaesthesia/synesthesia /sĭn'əs thē'zhə/ a condition in which one type of stimulation evoke the sensation of another, as when a person sees various sounds as particular colors.

synapse /sĭn'ăps/ the junction across which a nerve impulse passes (using a transmitting molecule, such as acetyl choline) from an axon terminal to a neuron, muscle cell, or gland cell.

synapsis /sĭ năp'sĭs/ (*pl.* **synapses** /sĭ năp'sēz/) the side-by-side association of homologous paternal and maternal chromosomes during early meiotic prophase.

synarthrosis /sĭn'är thrō'sĭs/ (*pl.* **synarthoses** /sĭn'är thrō'sēz/) a union of two bones by fibrous tissue. *Also called* immovable joint.

syncephaly /sĭn sĕf'ə lē/ the condition of being conjoined at the head. [syn- + -cephaly]

synchronic study /sĭn krŏn'ĭk/ a study of the structure of a population at one point in time.

syncope /sĭng'kə pē/ a brief loss of consciousness caused by a sudden drop in blood pressure or failure of the cardiac systole, resulting in cerebral hypoxia. *Also called* fainting.

syndactylism /sĭn dăk'tə lĭz'əm/ or **syndactyly** /sĭn dăk'tə lē/ a condition in which two or more digits are fused.

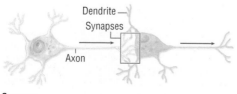

Synapse

syndrome /sĭn'drōm/ a group of symptoms that collectively indicate or characterize a disease, a psychological disorder, or another abnormal condition.

syndrome of inappropriate ADH (SIADH) a condition seen with certain diseases (particularly certain types of cancers) with the inappropriate secretion of antidiuretic hormone resulting in water retention, inhibition of urine excretion, and secondary symptoms like nausea or convulsions.

syndrome X angina pectoris of a usually benign form in which the coronary arteriogram is normal.

syndromic /sĭn drŏm'ĭk/ occurring as a syndrome or part of a syndrome.

synechia /sĭ nĕk'ē ə, -nē'kē-/ (*pl.* **synechiae** /sĭ nĕk'ē ē', -nē'kē-/) an adhesion of parts.

synergetic /sĭn'ər jĕt'ĭk/ synergistic.

synergism /sĭn'ər jĭz'əm/ synergy.

synergistic /sĭn'ər jĭs'tĭk/ **1.** of or relating to synergy or a synergist. **2.** producing or capable of producing synergy. *Also called* synergetic.

synergy /sĭn'ər jē/ the interactions of two things (such as treatments) such that the result is greater than the sum of the two parts.

synesthesia/synaesthesia /sĭn'əs thē'zhə/ a condition in which one type of stimulation evokes the sensation of another. [syn- + -esthesia]

synov-, synovo- *combining form.* synovial membrane: *for example*, synovectomy.

synovectomy /sĭn'ə vĕk'tə mē/ surgical removal of all or part of the synovial membrane of a joint. [synov- + -ectomy]

synovial /sĭ nō've əl/ of, relating to, or secreting synovial fluid.

synovial fluid clear, viscid lubricating fluid secreted by membranes in joint cavities, sheaths of tendons, and bursae.

synovial joint a joint in which the opposing bony surfaces are covered with a layer of hyaline cartilage or fibrocartilage and in which some degree of free movement is possible.

synovial membrane the connective-tissue membrane that lines the cavity of a synovial joint and produces the synovial fluid.

synovitis /sĭn'ə vī'tĭs/ inflammation of a synovial membrane. [synov- + -itis]

synthesis /sĭn'thə sĭs/ **1.** the combining of separate substances to form a coherent whole. **2.** formation of a chemical compound from simpler compounds. **3.** a period in the cell cycle.

syphilis /sĭf'ə lĭs/ a chronic infectious disease caused by a spirochete bacteria, *Treponema pallidum*, transmitted in sexual intercourse, or passed from mother to child in utero, with three stages characterized by local formation

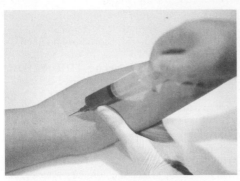

Syringe

of chancres (open sores, usually in the genital
region), ulcerous skin eruptions, and ultimately, if untreated, systemic infection that
leads to general paresis (paralysis).

syphilitic /sĭf'ə lĭt'ĭk/   of, relating to, or affected by syphilis.

syr.   *abbreviation*. syrup.

syringe /sə rĭnj'/   an instrument, such as a hypodermic needle, used to inject fluids into the
body, or draw fluids out of the body.

syringocystoma /sə rĭng'gō sĭ stō'mə/   a benign cystic tumor of the sweat glands. *Also
called* hidrocystoma.

syrup (syr.) /sĭr'əp/   in pharmacy, a concentrated sugar solution that contains medication
and usually a pleasant flavoring.

system /sĭs'təm/   **1.** a group of interacting, in-
terrelated, or interdependent elements forming

a whole. **2.** an organism or body considered as
a whole, especially with regard to its vital
processes or functions. **3.** a group of physio-
logically or anatomically complementary organs or parts.

systemic /sĭ stĕm'ĭk/   **1.** of or relating to a system. **2.** of, relating to, or affecting the entire
body. **3.** of, relating to, or affecting a specific
body system. **4.** of or relating to systemic
cirulation.

systemic circulation   the general circulation
of the blood through the body, as opposed to
the circulation of the blood from the heart to
the lungs and back to the heart.

systemic lupus erythematosus (SLE) /loo'pəs
ĕr'ə thē'mə tō'sĭs/   an inflammatory, multi-
systemic, autoimmune disease of the connective tissue, characterized by fever, skin lesions, joint pain or arthritis, and anemia, and
often affecting the kidneys, spleen, and other
organs. *See also* discoid lupus erythematosus,
lupus eythematosus.

systole /sĭs'tə lē'/   the period of contraction of
the heart, especially of the ventricles, during
which blood is driven out to the aorta and pulmonary artery after each dilation (refilling period) or diastole.

systolic /sĭ stŏl'ĭk/   of, relating to, or happening during a systole.

systolic blood pressure (SBC) or **systolic pressure**   the highest arterial blood pressure
reached during any given ventricular cycle.

sz   *abbreviation*. seizure.

T

T *abbreviation.* **1.** thymine. **2.** temperature. **3.** time. **4.** tablespoon; tablespoons.

t. *abbreviation.* teaspoon; teaspoons.

T3, T₃ *abbreviation.* triiodothyronine.

T4, T₄ *abbreviation.* thyroxine.

tab. *abbreviation.* tablet.

tabes /tā′bēz/ a wasting away; emaciation.

table /tā′bəl/ a presentation of numerical information in rows and columns, for easy comprehension.

tablespoon (T, tbsp, tbs.) /tā′bəl spōōn′/ a large spoon used to measure a dose of liquid medication equal to about 0.5 fluid ounces or 15 milliliters.

tablet /tăb′lĭt/ a pill containing a dose of solid medication.

tablet splitter a device for splitting tablets in half.

tache /tăsh/ a skin discoloration, as a freckle or macule.

tachometer /tă kŏm′ĭ tər/ a device that measures rate of speed, as of blood flow, heart rate, etc.

tachy- *prefix.* speedy; fast; rapid: *for example,* tachypnea.

tachycardia /tăk′ĭ kär′dē ə/ heart rate over 100 beats per minute. [tachy- + -cardia]

tachypnea /tăk′ĭp nē′ə/ abnormally fast breathing. [tachy- + -pnea]

tactile /tăk′tĭl, -tīl/ of or involving the sense of touch.

taeniasis /tē nī′ə sĭs/ an infection with a tapeworm of the genus *Taenia.*

tail /tāl/ the long tapering end of a structure, such as the end of the spine or certain organs.

tailbone /tāl′bōn′/ a small, final bone, consisting of four fused vertebrae, at the end of the spine. *Also called* coccyx.

tali /tā′lī/ plural of talus.

talipes /tăl′ə pēz / any of several deformities of the foot.

talipes calcaneus /kăl kā′nē əs/ deformity of the foot in which the toes are turned upward and only the heel touches the ground in walking.

talipes equinovarus /ĭ kwī′nō vâr′əs, ĕk′wĭ nō-/ deformity of the foot in which the foot is turned inward with the sole facing the other foot. *Also called* clubfoot.

talipes valgus /văl′gəs/ deformity of the foot in which the foot is turned outward.

talipes varus /vâr′əs/ deformity of the foot in which the foot is turned inward.

talk therapy psychological counseling for emotional problems using one-on-one sessions of talking as opposed to (or used in combination with) drug therapy.

talus /tā′ləs/ (*pl.* **tali** /tā′lī/) the bone in the ankle that attaches to the tibia and fibula above it and the calcaneus below it to form the ankle joint. *Also called* anklebone.

tamoxifen /tə mŏk′sə fən, -fĕn′/ the generic name of a drug that blocks estrogen receptors on cancer cells; used in the treatment of breast cancer.

tampon /tăm′pŏn/ **1.** a plug of absorbent material, such as cotton, inserted into a wound or opening to stop blood flow. **2.** a cylindrical plug inserted into the vagina to absorb menstrual blood.

tapeworm /tāp′wûrm′/ a parasitic worm that lives in the intestines.

tapotement /tə pŏt′mənt, tă′pôt mŏn′/ a massage technique that involves light beating, short chopping strokes, or cupping the hands or tools that stimulate the muscles.

tardive /tär′dĭv/ late, tardy; used to describe a condition or disease in which the characteristic symptom is observed late in the development of the condition, such as tardive dyskinesia.

tardive dyskinesia /dĭs′kə nē′zhə/ a movement disorder which sometimes occurs with the long-term use of antipsychotic medications.

target cell **1.** a cell with receptors that are compatible with a specific agent, such as a hormone or drug. **2.** a red blood cell with a dark center surrounded by a light band, occurring in certain diseases, such as anemia.

targeted radiation therapy radiation therapy using computers to pinpoint in three dimensions the location of a tumor for precise irradiation.

tars-, tarso- *combining form.* tarsus: *for example,* tarsectomy.

tarsal /tär′səl/ **1.** of or involving the ankle. **2.** of or involving the fibrous plates that form the edge of the eyelid.

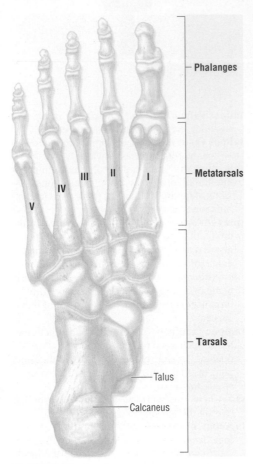

Phalanges

III II I
IV
V

Metatarsals

Tarsals

Talus

Calcaneus

Tarsal Bones

tarsal bones   the seven small bones that make up the ankle.

tarsal cyst /sĭst/   a cyst in the sebaceous glands of the eyelid.

tarsalgia /tär săl′jē ə, -jə/   pain in the tarsus. [tars- + -algia]

tarsal gland   a sebaceous gland in the eyelid. *Also called* meibomian gland.

tarsectomy /tär sĕk′tə mē/   **1.** surgical removal of the ankle. **2.** surgical removal of the tarsus of the eyelid. [tars- + -ectomy]

tarsomegaly /tär′sō mĕg′ə lē/   a congenital condition leading to excessively large ankles or wrists. [tarso- + -megaly]

tarsometatarsal /tär′sō mĕt′ə tär′səl/   of or pertaining to the tarsus and metatarsus. [tarso- + metatarsal]

tarsus /tär′səs/   **1.** the seven bones that make up the ankle. **2.** a plate of connective tissue that forms the edge of the eyelid.

tartar /tär′tər/   a hard, yellowy-brown deposit on the teeth consisting of mineralized plaque. *Also called* calculus.

taste /tāst/   the chemical sense, originating on the surface of the tongue and interpreted in the smell center of the brain, by which flavor is sensed.

taste bud   groups of receptor cells found in raised bumps, or papillae, on the surface of the tongue that can experience sweet, bitter, sour, and salty flavors.

taste cell   one of the receptor cells within a taste bud.

taxis /tăk′sĭs/   **1.** arrangment or order. **2.** non-surgical replacement of a part or organ that is out of position within the body or the reduction of a hernia, by manipulation. **3.** movement of an organism in response to a stimulus, as toward a light.

-taxy   *suffix.* order; arrangement: *for example,* heterotaxy.

Tay-Sachs disease /tā′ săks′/   a lethal inherited disease, found mostly in Jews of Eastern European ancestry, that affects neurological development in infants and usually causes death by age four.

TB   *abbreviation.* tuberculosis.

TBI   *abbreviation.* **1.** traumatic brain injury. **2.** total body irradiation.

Tbsp, tbsp.   *abbreviation.* tablespoon; tablespoons.

TB tine /tīn/   screening test for tuberculosis, in which a small dose of tuberculin is injected intradermally (four tines prick the skin) to check for a reaction indicating the presence of antibodies to tuberculosis. *Also called* tine test.

TBV   *abbreviation.* total blood volume.

TCA   *abbreviation.* tricyclic antidepressant.

T cell   one of three kinds of specialized white blood cells developed in the thymus that are responsible for cellular immunity and assist in humoral immunity. *Also called* T lymphocyte. *See also* helper T-cell, killer cell, suppressor T cell.

T-cell receptor   either of two kinds of receptors on the surface of T-cells that bind to foreign antigens.

TCM   *abbreviation.* traditional Chinese medicine.

TDD   *abbreviation.* telecommunications device for the deaf.

TDM   *abbreviation.* therapeutic drug monitoring.

tear duct /têr′ dŭkt′/   a canal that carries the tears from the lacrimal glands to the eye.

tears /têrz/   moisture secreted from the lacrimal glands located in the upper part of the eye socket to moisten the eye, wash out foreign particles, and distribute water and lubricate the eyelids.

teaspoon (t., tsp.) /tē′spo͞on′/   a small spoon used to measure a dose of liquid medication, equal to about one-sixth of a fluid ounce, or nearly 5 milliliters.

technique /tĕk nēk′/ the way an operation or experiment is performed.

teeth /tēth/ plural of tooth.

tel-, tele-, telo- *combining form.* **1.** distant: *for example,* telesurgery. **2.** end: *for example,* telomere.

telangiectasia /tĕl ăn′jē ĕk tā′zhə/ a permanent dilation of small blood vessels. [tel- + angi- + -ectasia]

telangiectatic fibroma /tĕl ăn′jē ĕk tăt′ĭk fī brō′ mə/ a benign tumor-like growth having numerous, frequently dilated, vascular channels. *Also called* angiofibroma

telangioma /tĕl ăn′jē ō′mə/ tumor of dilated blood vessels. [tel- + angioma]

telediagnosis /tĕl′ĭ dī′əg nō′sĭs/ diagnosis by evaluation of transmitted data from a remote site. [tele- + diagnosis]

telemedicine /tĕl′ə mĕd′ə sĭn/ the use of telecommunications technology to provide or improve medical care, as by teleconferencing or by the use of the computer to link to lab results or hospital records or to send images. [tele- + medicine]

telencephalon /tĕl′ĕn sĕf′ə lŏn′/ the frontal section of the embryonic forebrain, making up the cerebral hemispheres in the matured brain.

telepathy /tə lĕp′ə thē/ the ability to communicate by broadcasting or receiving thoughts rather than using written, spoken, or signed language. [tele- + -pathy]

telesurgery /tĕl′ə sûr′jə rē/ surgical procedures carried out at a distance by robots, usually operated under computer control of the distant surgeon. [tele- + surgery]

teletherapy /tĕl′ə thĕr′ə pē/ **1.** radiation therapy for cancer, with the source of radiation outside the body. **2.** psychotherapy conducted over the telephone. [tele- + therapy]

telo- *See* tel-.

telomere /tĕl′ə mêr′/ a segment of DNA at each end of the chromosome that repeats a sequence of letters that do not code for anything, but are shortened a little with each cell division—"the aging process at a chromosomal level."

telophase /tĕl′ə fāz′/ the final phase of mitosis, where the cytoplasm divides and two daughter cells are formed. [telo- + phase]

temp /tĕmp/ short for temperature.

temp. *abbreviation.* temperature.

temper /tĕm′pər/ **1.** state of mind given to outbursts of anger or irritation. **2.** a characteristic state of mind; disposition; temperament.

temperament /tĕm′pər ə mənt, -prə mənt/ an individual's characteristic way of thinking, reacting, feeling; predisposition.

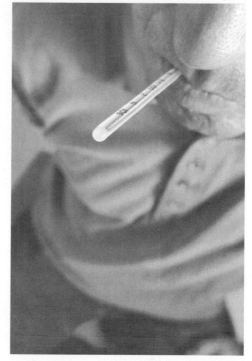

Temperature

temperature (T, temp.) /tĕm′pər ə chər, tĕm′ prə-/ a measure of the heat of the body, usually taken at certain points on the body, such as axilla (armpit), rectum, eardrum, or under the tongue; considered one of the vital signs. An elevated temperature is often an indicator of an infection.

temple /tĕm′pəl/ the flattish region on either side of the forehead.

temporal /tĕm′pər əl/ **1.** of or involving the temples. **2.** of or involving time.

temporal arteritis /är′tə rī′tĭs/ inflammation of the walls of the temporal arteries, marked by severe headaches and sometimes leading to stroke or blindness. *Also called* cranial arteritis.

temporal bone a large bone forming part of the base and the sides of the skull.

temporal lobe /lōb/ either of two lateral lobes, one in each of the cerebral hemispheres.

temporal muscle /mŭs′əl/ the muscle running from the temporal bone to the mandible that contracts to close the jaws.

temporomandibular joint (TMJ) /tĕm′pə rō măn dĭb′yə lər/ the joint of the lower jaw betweeen the temporal bone and the mandible; the condyloid process below is separated by an articular disk from the mandibular fossa above. A unique joint because the possible motions are opening, closing, protrusion, retraction, and lateral movement.

temporomandibular joint (TMJ) syndrome severe pain in the area of the temporomandibular joint.

ten-, teno- *combining form.* tendon: *for example,* tenodynia.

tenalgia /tə năl′jə, -jē ə/ pain in a tendon. *Also called* tenodynia. [ten- + -algia]

tender /tĕn′dər/ painful to the touch.

tendin-, tendino-, tendono- *combining form.* tendon: *for example,* tendonitis.

tendinitis /tĕn′də nī′tĭs/ inflammation of a tendon. [tendin- + -itis]

tendinoplasty /tĕn′də nō plăs′tē/ surgical repair of a tendon or tendons. *Also called* tendoplasty, tenontoplasty, tenoplasty. [tendino- + -plasty]

tendon /tĕn′dən/ the part of a muscle that connects its fleshy part with bone or another structure. The tendon itself is a fibrous band that does not have elasticity or contractile properties.

tendonitis /tĕn′də nī′tĭs/ inflammation of a tendon. [tendon + -itis]

tendoplasty /tĕn′dō plăs′tē/ surgical repair of a tendon or tendons. *Also called* tenindoplasty, tenontoplasty, tenoplasty.

tenesmus /tə nĕz′məs/ painful spasm of the anal sphincter with the urgency to defecate but the inability to do so.

tenia /tē′nē ə/ (*pl.* **teniae** /tē′nē ē′/) any ribbon-like band, as of muscle or tissue.

tennis elbow painful inflammation of the bursa at the elbow, usually caused by the strain of playing racket sports.

teno- *See* ten-.

tenodesis /tĕ nŏd′ə sĭs/ surgical fixation of a tendon. [teno- + -desis]

tenodynia /tĕn′ō dĭn′ē ə/ pain in the tendons. *Also called* tenalgia. [teno- + -dynia]

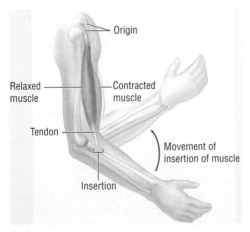

Origin

Relaxed muscle

Contracted muscle

Tendon

Movement of insertion of muscle

Insertion

Tendon

tenoplasty /tĕn′ō plăs′tē/ or **tenontoplasty** /tĕ nŏn′tō plăs′tē/ surgical repair of a tendon or tendons. *Also called* tendinoplasty, tendoplasty.

tenorrhaphy /tĕ nôr′ə fē/ suture of the ends of a tendon, as for repair of a ruptured Achille's tendon. [teno- + -rrhapy]

tenosynovitis /tĕn′ō sĭn′ō vī′tĭs/ inflammation of a tendon and its surrounding sheath. [teno- + synovitis]

tenotomy /tĕ nŏt′ə mē/ surgical cutting or division of a tendon, usually used to repair a congenitally shortened muscle. [teno- + -tomy]

TENS /tĕnz/ *abbreviation.* transcutaneous electrical nerve stimulation.

tension /tĕn′shən/ **1.** the stretching of something, as a muscle, until it is tight. **2.** emotional strain or strained relations between people or groups.

tension headache /hĕd′ăk′/ a headache associated with mental tension.

tension pneumothorax /nōō′mō thôr′ăks/ pneumothorax that results from a wound to the chest wall that allows air to enter the pleural cavity but prevents it from escaping, thus compressing the lung on that side, and even moving the heart away from that side, with compromise of blood flow.

tensor /tĕn′sôr/ a type of muscle that tightens a body part.

tent /tĕnt/ a tent-like covering used to control the amount of oxygen and humidity in the air being inspired during respiratory therapy.

terat-, terato- *combining form.* grossly deformed fetus or part: *for example,* teratoma.

teratocarcinoma /tĕr′ə tō kär′sə nō′mə/ a malignant teratoma. [terato- + carcinoma]

teratogen /tə răt′ə jən, -jĕn′/ a drug or other agent that causes a gross congenital abnormality. [terato- + -gen]

teratogenic /tĕr′ə tə jĕn′ĭk/ causing gross congenital abnormalities.

teratoma /tĕr′ə tō′mə/ (*pl.* **teratomas** or **teratomata** /tĕr′ə tō′mə tə/) a tumor with tissues not normally found in the organ or part in which it is located. [terat- + -oma]

terminal /tûr′mə nəl/ **1.** of or relating to the end of a part or structure. **2.** of or relating to something ultimately fatal.

terminal illness a fatal illness.

test /tĕst/ *n.* **1.** an examination. **2.** a particular process for assessing something. **3.** in psychology, a set of standardized questions or tasks used to measure emotional or intellectual traits and capacities of an individual. *v.* **4.** to conduct or undergo a test.

testes /tĕs′tēz/ plural of testis.

testicle /tĕs′tĭ kəl/ one of a pair of male reproductive glands located in the scrotal cavity. *Also called* testis.

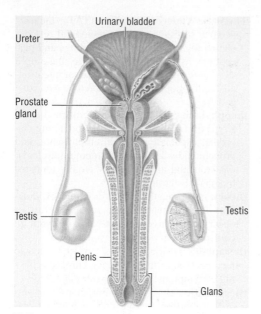

Testis

testicular /tĕs tĭk′yə lər/ of or relating to the testes.

testicular self-examination (TSE) /sĕlf′ ĭg zăm′ə nā′shən/ a procedure in which one palpates the testes to look for signs of abnormal growths.

testis /tĕs′tĭs/ (*pl.* testes /tĕs′tēz/) one of a pair of male reproductive glands located in the scrotal cavity. *Also called* testicle.

testosterone /tĕs tŏs′tə rōn′/ naturally occurring male sex hormone, produced mainly in the testes in response to stimulation by a pituitary hormone and responsible for the appearance and maintenance of male secondary sex characteristics.

tetanus /tĕt′ə nəs/ an acute and potentially fatal disease of the central nervous system that is caused by infection with the *Clostridium tetani* bacterium and results in painful muscle spasms. The bacterium is common in soil and infects wounds with dead tissue, such as puncture wounds, cuts, or burns. Informally called lockjaw.

tetanus shot a vaccine for immunization against tetanus.

tetany /tĕt′ə nē/ a disorder marked by periodic muscle twitching, tremors, and muscle spasms due to an abnormally low serum calcium levels.

tetr-, tetra- *combining form.* four: *for example,* tetraplegia.

tetracycline /tĕt′rə sī′klēn/ a broad-spectrum antibiotic used to treat a range of bacterial and rickettsial infections.

tetrahydrocannabinol (THC) /tĕt′rə hī′drō kə năb′ə nôl′/ the psychoactive component in the hemp plant *Cannabis sativa,* used in the preparation of substances such as marijuana, hashish, and bhang; a mild hallucinogen, it causes alterations in mood, including euphoria and paranoia, and in motor coordination, heart rate, and blood pressure. Nonintoxicating amounts have been used experimentally in the treatment of glaucoma because it lowers intraocular pressure and is thought to relieve the nausea and vomiting associated with chemotherapy.

tetraiodothyronine /tĕt′rə ī ō′dō thī′rə nēn′/ a hormone produced by the thyroid gland that controls oxidation in cells and regulates metabolism. *Also called* thyroxine (T_4).

tetralogy of Fallot /tĕ trăl′ə jē əv fä lō′/ congenital heart defect consisting of four abnormalities: right ventricular outflow obstruction, a defect in the ventricular septum, malposition of the aorta, and enlargement of the right ventricle.

tetraparesis /tĕt′rə pə rē′sĭs/ weakness of all four limbs (arms and legs), usually the result of a spinal cord injury or stroke. *Also called* quadriparesis.

tetraparetic /tĕt′rə pə rĕt′ĭk/ of or affected with tetraparesis. *Also called* quadriparetic.

tetraplegia /tĕt′rə plē′jə, -jē ə/ paralysis of all four limbs. *Also called* quadriplegia. [tetra- + plegia]

Texas catheter /tĕk′səs kăth′ĭ tər/ a catheter consisting of a condom worn on the penis connected to a tube leading to a container or leg bag. *Also called* condom catheter.

thalamo- *combining form.* the thalamus: *for example,* thalamotomy.

thalamocortical /thăl′ə mō kôr′tĭ kəl/ of or pertaining to the thalamus and the cerebral cortex.

thalamotomy /thăl′ə mŏt′ə mē/ a stereotactic surgical procedure to destroy a selected portion of the thalamus to provide relief from pain, involuntary movements, and epilepsy. [thalamo- + -tomy]

thalamus /thăl′ə məs/ (*pl.* **thalami** /thăl′ə mī′/) one of a pair of large oval masses composed of gray matter located deep within the brain that

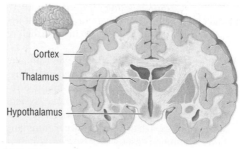

Thalamus

relay sensory impulses, for example, of pain and touch, to and from the cerebral cortex.

thalassemia /thăl'ə sē'mē ə/   hereditary form of anemia, with onset in infancy or childhood, caused by abnormal hemoglobin synthesis and found most often in people of Mediterranean origin. There are two forms: If inherited from both parents, the anemia is severe and the condition is referred to as thalassemia major, or Cooley('s) anemia. If inherited from one parent, symptoms may be few or none and the condition is called thalassemia minor.

thalidomide baby /thə lĭd'ə mīd'/   an infant born with severe birth defects, such as short flipper-like arms and/or legs, caused by prenatal exposure to the drug thalidomide. In Europe the drug was given to pregnant women to treat morning sickness until it was taken off the market in the early 1960s. Currently it is being used provisionally to treat leprosy and is being evaluated as a treatment for HIV and for aphthous mouth ulcers in advanced HIV disease.

thallium (TL) /thăl'ē əm/   a highly toxic, white, metallic element present in the environment mostly as a by-product of coal-burning; thallium sulfate is often used as rat poison.

thallium scan   an imaging method that uses a small amount of radioactive thallium as a tracer to determine if the blood supply to the myocardium (heart muscle) is diminished. *See also* thallium stress test.

thallium stress test   a procedure for assessing the effect of stress on the myocardium (heart muscle). The myocardium is stressed, either through exercise or by taking a medication, and a small amount of radioactive thallium is then injected into the subject intravenously as a tracer. The thallium adheres to the muscle cells of the heart allowing a series of scans to be taken that depict actual blood flow in the cardiac muscle.

thallium test   thallium stress test.

thanatology /thăn'ə tŏl'ə jē/   the study of death and dying.

thanatophobia /thə năt'ō fō'bē ə/   an abnormal fear of death.

THC   *abbreviation.* tetrahydrocannabinol.

thelarche /thē lär'kē/   beginning of breast development in the female, usually just before puberty.

T-helper cell   a type of lymphocyte (immune system cell) that secretes substances called cytokines, which contribute to the immune response by regulating other immune system cells, such as T cells and B cells. The HIV virus attacks T-helper cells, weakening the body's immune response. *Also called* helper T cell.

Thematic Apperception Test (TAT) /thē măt'ĭk ăp'ər sĕp'shən/   a psychological test designed to expose a person's feelings and perceptions by asking the subject to make up a story in response to viewing a set of intentionally ambiguous pictures depicting everyday situations.

theophylline /thē ŏf'ə lēn'/   a bronchodilator; a type of medicine used to treat breathing disorders, especially asthma, emphysema, and bronchitis, by relaxing the smooth muscles of the bronchial airways. Now largely replaced by inhaled steroid drugs.

theory /thē'ə rē, thêr'ē/   a possible explanation for a phenomenon, requiring further observation, investigation, and research to confirm.

therapeutic /thĕr'ə pyōō'tĭk/   of or related to therapeutics, or the treatment, cure, or relieving of symptoms of a disease or disorder.

therapeutic abortion /ə bôr'shən/   an induced abortion carried out for medical reasons to protect the mother's physical or mental health or, for example, in the case of rape.

therapeutic dose   the amount of a medicine required for it to be effective.

therapeutic drug monitoring (TDM)   careful measuring of a patient's response to a drug to determine the most effective dosages for treatment, rather than simply following the prescribed norm.

therapeutic massage /mə säzh'/   a natural healing method involving the manipulating of a person's muscles and other soft tissues with the intent of improving a person's health and well-being.

therapeutic touch   an alternative therapy that uses the laying on of hands to promote healing by the interaction between energy fields of health and patient. The goal is to balance and open the energy flow of the patient.

therapeutics /thĕr'ə pyōō'tĭks/   the branch of heath care and medical science concerned in particular with the treatment of a disease or disorder.

therapist /thĕr'ə pĭst/   a professional trained in the practice of a particular therapy.

therapy /thĕr'ə pē/   **1.** any method used to treat a disease or disorder, either curative or through the relief of symptoms. **2.** short for psychotherapy.

therm-, thermo-   *combining form.* heat: *for example,* thermogenesis.

thermal /thûr'məl/   of or pertaining to heat.

thermic /thûr'mĭk/   thermal.

thermogenesis /thûr'mō jĕn'ə sĭs/   the generation of heat, as by physiologic processes. [thermo- + -genesis]

thermography /thər mŏg′rə fē/ a technique of measuring heat in different areas of the body using an infrared camera to locate abnormalities. [thermo- + -graphy]

thermometer /thər mŏm′ĭ tər/ an instrument to measure temperature, especially one with a digital readout or a glass tube containing mercury and having graduated markings. [thermo- + -meter]

thermophobia /thûr′mō fō′bē ə/ fear of heat. [thermo- + -phobia]

thermoplastic /thûr′mō plăs′tĭk/ becoming softer with heating and harder with cooling. [thermo- + -plastic]

thermotherapy /thûr′mō thĕr′ə pē/ treatment using the application of heat. [thermo- + therapy]

thiamine /thī′ə mĭn/ a water-soluble vitamin (B_1) essential for carbohydrate metabolism and healthy neural activity.

thigh /thī/ the part of the leg between the hip and the knee; tissue surrounding the femur.

thigh bone large bone between the hip and knee; femur.

third-degree burn severe burn which destroys the skin and underlying tissues, and leaves the nerve endings exposed. *See also* first-degree burn, second-degree burn.

third molar /mō′lər/ the eighth tooth in both the upper and lower jaw, on either side of the mouth. *Also called* wisdom tooth.

third stage of labor the period from immediately following birth to the delivery of the placenta.

third ventricle /vĕn′trĭ kəl/ unpaired ventricle of the brain, bounded by parts of the telencephalon and diencephalons.

thirst /thûrst/ **1.** the sensation of dryness in the mouth and throat, causing a desire to drink. **2.** the condition of the body that creates this sensation.

thorac-, thoracico-, thoraco- *combining form.* chest or thorax: *for example,* thoracalgia.

thoracalgia /thôr′ə kăl′jə, -jē ə/ chest pain. *Also called* thoracodynia. [thorac- + -algia]

thoracentesis /thôr′ə sĕn tē′sĭs/ the removal of fluid from the chest for therapeutic or diagnostic purposes. *Also called* thoracocentesis, pleurocentesis. [thora(c)- + -centesis]

thoracic /thô răs′ĭk/ of or relating to the thorax or chest area. [thorac- + -ic]

thoracic aorta /ā ôr′tə/ a part of the aorta located within the thorax, beginning with the ascending aorta, then extending to the aortic arch, then to the descending aorta to the diaphragm. [thorac- + -ic]

thoracic cage the enclosing structure of the chest, comprised of the ribs and the bones to which they attach. *Also called* rib cage.

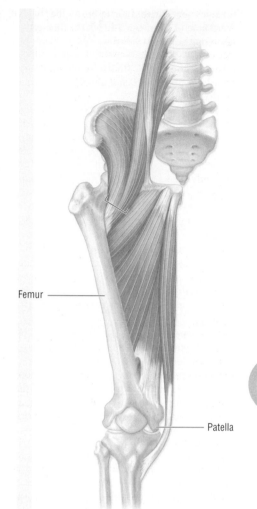

Femur

Patella

Thigh

thoracic cavity the cavity within the ribs, which encloses the lungs and heart.

thoracic duct the main duct of the lymphatic system; empties into the left subclavian vein.

thoracic medicine branch of medicine specializing in diseases of the organs contained within the thoracic cavity.

thoracic nerves the spinal nerves of the thoracic region.

thoracic outlet syndrome pain or numbness of the arm and hand, caused by compression of a nerve or blood vessel (by muscles attached to the first rib) as it passes from the neck to the arm.

thoracic surgeon /sûr′jən/ a physician specializing in thoracic surgery.

thoracic surgery /sûr′jə rē/ surgery involving the organs contained in the thoracic cavity.

thoracic vertebrae /vûr′tə brē/ the twelve vertebrae (T1 through T12) of the thoracic region that adjoin to the ribs.

thoraco- *See* thorac-

thoracoabdominal /thôr′ə kō ăb dŏm′ə nəl/ involving the thorax and abdomen. [thoraco- + abdominal]

thoracocentesis /thôr′ə kō sĕn tē′sĭs/ removal of fluid from the chest by puncturing for therapeutic or diagnostic purposes. *Also called* pleurocentesis, thoracentesis. [thoraco- + -centesis]

thoracodynia pain in the thorax. *Also called* thoracalgia. [thoraco- + -dynia]

thoracolumbar /thôr′ə kō lŭm′bär/ involving the thoracic and lumbar regions. [thoraco- + lumbar]

thoracometer /thôr′ə kŏm′ĭ tər/ instrument for measuring the circumference of the chest during respiration. [thoraco- + -meter]

thoracopathy /thôr′ə kŏp′ə thē/ any disease of the thoracic organs or tissues. [thoraco- + -pathy]

thoracoscope /thô răk′ə skōp′/ an endoscope used to examine the chest cavity. [thoraco- + -scope]

thoracoscopy /thôr′ə kŏs′kə pē/ endoscopic exam of the chest cavity and the lungs. [thoraco- + -scopy]

thoracostenosis narrowing of the thorax due to a loss of trunk muscles. [thoraco- + -stenosis]

thoracostomy /thôr′ə kŏs′tə mē/ surgical opening of the chest, as for drainage. [thoraco- + -stomy]

thoracostomy tube a tube inserted into the chest for drainage. [thoraco- + -stomy]

thoracotomy /thôr′ə kŏt′ə mē/ a surgical incision of the chest wall. *Also called* pleurotomy. [thoraco- + -tomy]

thorax /thôr′ăks/ the area between the neck and diaphragm containing the heart and lungs; the chest area.

Thr *abbreviation.* threonine.

THR *abbreviation.* **1.** target heart rate. **2.** threshold heart rate. **3.** total hip replacement. **4.** thyroid hormone receptor.

thready pulse /thrĕd′ē pŭls′/ a faint, rapid pulse that feels like a moving thread felt by the tip of the finger.

threonine (Thr) /thrē′ə nēn′/ an essential amino acid found in certain proteins.

threshold dose that dose of radiation below which there are no clinical effects of ionizing radiation.

thrill /thrĭl/ a tremor in the respiratory or circulatory system.

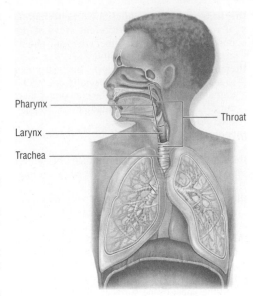

Pharynx

Larynx

Trachea

Throat

Throat

throat /thrōt/ passageway from the back of the mouth to the esophagus containing the pharynx, larynx, and trachea.

throat culture test to diagnose infections (especially streptococcal ones), consisting of the viewing of an incubated culture at 24–48 hours grown from material swabbed from the throat.

thromb-, thrombo- *combining form.* blood clot: *for example,* thrombocyte.

thrombectomy /thrŏm bĕk′tə mē/ surgical removal of a blood clot. [thromb- + -ectomy]

thrombi /thrŏm′bī/ plural of thrombus.

thrombin /thrŏm′bĭn/ proteolytic enzyme that converts fibrinogen to fibrin, thus causing blood to clot.

thrombin clotting time amount of time it takes for plasma to clot, used to determine the presence of inhibitory substances.

thrombinogen /thrŏm bĭn′ə jən, -jĕn′/ plasma protein needed for the normal clotting of blood.

thromboangiitis /thrŏm′bō ăn′jē ī′tĭs/ inflammation of the lining of a blood vessel (intima) with a concomittant blood clot. [thrombo- + angi- + -itis]

thrombocyte /throm′bə sīt′/ a small particle found in the blood plasma that helps in blood clotting. *Also called* platelet. [thrombo- + -cyte]

thrombocythemia /thrŏm′bō sī thē′mē ə/ thrombocytosis. [thrombo- + cyt- + -hemia]

thrombocytopenia /thrŏm′bō sī′tō pē′nē ə/ abnormal decrease in blood platelets, associated with hemorrhagic conditions. [thrombo- + cyto- + -penia]

thrombocytosis /thrŏm′bō sī tō′sĭs/ abnormal increase in blood platelets. *Also called* thrombocythemia. [thrombo- + -cytosis]

thromboembolism /thrŏm′bō ĕm′bə lĭz′əm/ blood clot that has broken away from a blood clot of another site and migrated, usually to the lungs. [thrombo- + embolism]

thrombogenic /thrŏm′bə jĕn′ĭk/ prone to forming a thrombus. [thrombo- + -genic]

thromboid /thrŏm′boid/ of or resembling a thrombus. [thromb- + -oid]

thrombokinase /thrŏm′bō kī′nās/ an enzyme present in platelets that converts prothrombin to thrombin in blood clotting.

thrombolysis /thrŏm bŏl′ə sĭs/ breaking up of a thrombus. [thrombo- + -lysis]

thrombolytic /thrŏm′bə lĭt′ĭk/ agent that dissolves a thrombus. [thrombo- + -lytic]

thrombolytic agent a drug administered to dissolve a thrombus. [thrombo- + -lytic]

thrombolytic therapy /thĕr′ə pē/ drug treatment to dissolve a thrombus. [thrombo- + -lytic]

thrombophilia /thrŏm′bō fĭl′ē ə/ increased tendency or predisposition to thrombosis. [thrombo- + -philia]

thrombophlebitis /thrŏm′bō flĭ bī′tĭs/ inflammation of a vein resulting in a thrombus; usual causes are venous stasis (blockage or cessation of circulation in a vein), injury to the vein, or a state where coagulation is likely to occur. [thrombo- + phlebitis]

thromboplastin /thrŏm′bō plăs′tĭn/ an enzyme in platelets that converts prothrombin to thrombin in blood clotting.

thrombosis /thrŏm bō′sĭs/ formation or presence of blood clot in a blood vessel. [thromb- + -osis]

thrombotic /thrŏm bŏt′ĭk/ forming a blood clot. [thromb- + -otic]

thrombotic thrombocytopenia /thrŏm′bō sī′tō pē′nē ə/ blood disease characterized by an abnormally low platelet count and diffuse thrombi. [thrombo- + cyto- + -penia]

thrombotic thrombocytopenic purpura (TTP) /thrŏm′bō sī′tō pē′nĭk pûr′pyər ə, -pər ə/ subcutaneous bleeding resulting from thrombocytopenia.

thrombus /thrŏm′bəs/ (*pl.* **thrombi** /thrŏm′bī/) blood clot in a blood vessel, remaining where it formed.

thrush /thrŭsh/ a superficial infection caused by the fungus *Candida albicans,* primarily in infants or in immunosuppressed adults, characterized by white patches of fungus in the mouth and throat. *Also called* candidiasis.

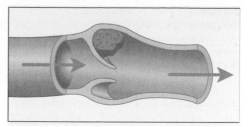

Thrombus

thumb /thŭm/ the short thick digit of the human hand, next to the index finger and opposable to each of the other four digits.

thym-, thymo- *combining form.* thymus: *for example,* thymocyte.

thymectomy /thī mĕk′tə mē/ surgical removal of the thymus, sometimes as a treatment for myasthenia gravis. [thym- + -ectomy]

thymine (T) /thī′mēn/ one of the four bases in DNA, where it pairs with adenine.

thymocyte /thī′mə sīt′/ a lymphocyte originating in the thymus. [thymo- + -cyte]

thymoma /thī mō′mə/ benign tumor of the thymus. [thym- + -oma]

thymosin /thī′mə sĭn/ a hormone produced from the thymus gland important for the maturation of the T lymphocytes.

thymus /thī′məs/ a lymphoid organ located below the base of the neck in the upper mediastinum, essential in the development of immunity before puberty, after which it becomes smaller and inactive. *Also called* thymus gland.

thymus gland thymus.

thyr-, thyro- *combining form.* thyroid: *for example,* thyroglobulin.

thyroglobulin /thī′rō glŏb′yə lĭn/ a protein of the thyroid gland. [thyro- + globulin]

thyroglossal /thī′rō glŏs′əl/ of or relating to the thyroid gland and the tongue. [thyro- + glossal]

thyroid-, *combining form.* the thyroid gland: *for example,* thyroidectomy.

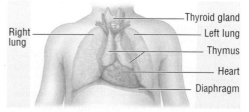

Thymus and Thyroid

thyroid /thī′roid/ thyroid gland.

thyroid cartilage /kär′tə lĭj/ main cartilage of the larynx with two processes that join to form the Adam's apple.

thyroidectomy /thī′roi dĕk′tə mē/ partial or total surgical removal of the thyroid gland. [thyroid- + -ectomy]

thyroid gland /glănd/ an endocrine gland with two lobes connected by an isthmus, located in front of and on either side of the trachea. The thyroid gland produces hormones important to metabolic functioning: thyroxine, triiodothyronine, calcitonin. *Also called* thyroid.

thyroiditis /thī′roi dī′tĭs/ inflammation of the thyroid gland. [thyroid- + -itis]

thyroid-stimulating hormone (TSH) a hormone secreted in the adenohypophysis (anterior pituitary gland) that stimulates the thyroid gland to secrete hormones.

thyromegaly /thī′rō mĕg′ə lē/ abnormal enlargement of the thyroid. [thyro- + -megaly]

thyroplasty /thī′rō plăs′tē/ surgical reshaping of the thyroid cartilage. [thyro- + -plasty]

thyrotoxic /thī′rō tŏk′sĭk/ overproducing thyroid hormone; suffering from thyrotoxicosis. [thyro- + toxic]

thyrotoxicosis /thī′rō tŏk′sĭ kō′sĭs/ condition resulting from an overproduction of thyroid hormone. *See also* hyperthyroidism. [thyro- + toxic + -osis]

thyrotropin /thī rŏt′rə pĭn, thī′rō trō′pĭn/ a hormone secreted by the pituitary gland that regulates the thyroid gland. [thyro- + -tropin]

thyroxin /thī rŏk′sĭn/ a hormone produced by the thyroid gland that controls oxidation in cells and regulates metabolism.

thyroxine (T₄, T4) /thī rŏk′sēn/ a hormone produced by the thyroid gland that controls oxidation in cells and regulates metabolism. *Also called* tetraiodothyronine.

Ti *abbreviation.* titanium.

TIA *abbreviation.* transient ischemic attack.

tibi-, tibio- *combining form.* of or relating to the tibia; *for example,* tibial.

tibia /tĭb′ē ə/ the larger of the two bones of the lower leg. *Also called* shinbone.

tibial /tĭb′ē əl/ of or relating to the tibia.

tibiofibular /tĭb′ē ō fĭb′yə lər/ relating to the tibia and the fibula.

tic /tĭk/ involuntary movement, especially in the face.

tic douloureux /tĭk′ dōō′lōō rōō′, -rōō′/ paroxysmal neuralgia of the trigeminal nerve.

tick /tĭk/ any of various bloodsucking arachnids, some of which transmit infectious diseases.

tick fever /fē′vər/ tick-borne febrile disease.

tid, t.i.d. *abbreviation.* three times a day, used in writing prescriptions.

Tietze('s) syndrome /tēt′sə(z)/ inflammation of the ribs and their cartilage. *Also called* costochondritis.

Tinct, tinct., tr. *abbreviation.* tincture.

tincture /tĭngk′chər/ medicinal substance in an alcohol solution.

tinea /tĭn′ē ə/ any of several fungal skin diseases, especially ringworm.

tinea barbae /bär′bē/ fungal infection of the neck and face.

tinea capitis /kăp′ĭ tĭs/ fungal infection of the scalp.

tinea corporis /kôr′pər ĭs/ fungal infection of parts of the body not covered with hair.

tinea cruris /krōōr′ĭs/ fungal infection of the groin and perineum. *Also called* jock itch.

tinea pedis /pe′dĭs/ fungal infection of the foot. *Also called* athlete's foot.

Tinel('s) sign /tĭ nĕl(z)′/ tingling sensation felt in an injured nerve, indicating regeneration of the nerve, or a partial lesion.

tine test /tīn/ intradermal skin test for tuberculosis using an implement with four tines (prongs) to puncture the skin and expose the patient to tuberculin antigen. *Also called* TB tine.

tinnitus /tĭ nī′təs/ ringing in the ears caused by a condition, such as Meniere's disease, aspirin overdose, infection, or injury.

tipped uterus /yōō′tər əs/ retroversion (a tilting backward) of the uterus.

tiredness /tīrd′nĭs, tī′ərd-/ loss of strength and energy.

tissue /tĭsh′ōō/ group of cells having similar structure and function. The four types of tissue are muscle, nerve, epithelial, and connective.

tissue plasminogen activator (tPA, TPA) /plăz mĭn′ə jən, -jĕn/ clot-dissolving enzyme found in blood vessels which can also be

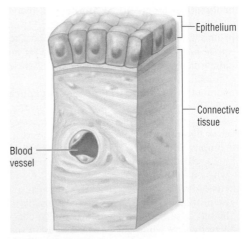

Tissue (connective)

genetically engineered and used as a drug to treat acute myocardial infarction.

titanium (Ti) /tī tā′nē əm/ a dark gray or silvery metallic element that is used in dental implants.

titer /tī′tər/ **1.** the concentration of a substance in solution as determined by titration. **2.** the strength of a solution as determined by titration.

titration /tī trā′shən/ the process of determining the amount of something in a solution by adding known amounts of a different solution and observing how much of the the second solution is needed to create a chemical reaction with the substance in question.

TL *abbreviation*. thallium.

TLC total lung capacity.

T lymphocyte /lĭm′fə sīt/ a cell produced in the thymus which functions in the immune response to infected cells. It is called a helper cell and works in conjunction with other cells in immune responses.

TMJ *abbreviation*. temporomandibular joint.

TNF *abbreviation*. tumor necrosis factor.

TNM *abbreviation*. tumor-node-metastasis.

TNM staging system for evaluating tumors, based on three variables: primary tumor (T), regional nodes (N), and metastasis (M).

toco- *combining form*. childbirth or labor: *for example*, tocolytic.

tocolysis /tō kŏl′ə sĭs/ drug-induced interruption of uterine contractions in (early) labor. [toco- + -lysis]

tocolytic /tō′kə lĭt′ĭk/ inhibiting uterine contractions in labor. [toco- + -lytic]

tocolytic agent or **tocolytic drug** medication that inhibits uterine contractions.

toddler /tŏd′lər/ a young child at the early stages of walking, especially a child between the ages of 1 and 3.

toe /tō/ any of the digits of the foot.

toenail /tō′nāl′/ the nail covering a toe.

tolerance /tŏl′ər əns/ the act of becoming less responsive to a substance through exposure to it.

-tome *suffix*. **1.** cutting instrument: *for example*, dermatome (def. 1). **2.** part, segment: *for example*, dermatome (def. 2).

tomo- *combining form*. cutting: *for example*, tomogram.

tomogram /tō′mə grăm′/ x-ray produced by tomography. [tomo- + -gram]

tomography /tə mŏg′rə fē/ technique for making x-rays of an isolated plane of the body. [tomo- + -graphy]

-tomy *suffix*. incision: *for example*, thoracotomy.

tone /tōn/ the normal state of tension in a relaxed muscle.

tone deafness /tōn′ dĕf′nĭs/ insensitivity to differences in tone.

tongue /tŭng/ the fleshy, sensory organ attached to the bottom of the mouth, which functions in tasting, eating, and speech.

-tonia *suffix*. pressure; tension: *for example*, dystonia.

tonic /tŏn′ĭk/ **1.** *n*. an agent that restores body tone or is refreshing. **2.** *adj*. characterized by continuous muscle tension, especially a convulsion or spasm.

tonicity /tō nĭs′ĭ tē/ body muscle or tone.

tono- *combining form*. tone; pressure; tension: *for example*, tonometer.

tonometer /tō nŏm′ĭ tər/ instrument that measures pressure within the eye. [tono- + -meter]

tonometry /tō nŏm′ĭ trē/ screening test for glaucoma that measures pressure within the eyes. [tono- + -metry]

tonotopic /tō′nō tŏp′ĭk/ arrangement of anatomical structures such that tonal frequencies are perceived at specific locations and are transmitted separately in the auditory pathway. [tono- + -topic]

tonsil /tŏn′səl/ one of two masses of lymphatic tissue on either side of the throat, thought to play an immunologic role in fighting upper respiratory infections.

tonsill-, tonsillo- *combining form*. tonsil: *for example*, tonsillitis.

tonsillectomy /tŏn′sə lĕk′tə mē/ surgical removal of the tonsils. [tonsill- + -ectomy]

tonsillitis /tŏn′sə lī′tĭs/ inflammation or infection of the tonsils. [tonsill- + -itis]

tonsillolith /tŏn sĭl′ə lĭth/ a calcium-containing formation in a tonsil. [tonsillo- + -lith]

tonsillotomy /tŏn′sə lŏt′ə mē/ surgical incision into a tonsil. [tonsillo- + -tomy]

tonus /tō′nəs/ body muscle or tone; tonicity.

tooth /tōōth/ (*pl*. **teeth** /tēth/) one of many bony structures in the sockets of the jaw, used for biting and chewing food. *See illustration on page 360.*

toothache /tōōth′āk′/ pain in or around a tooth.

tophaceous gout /tō fā′shəs gout′/ a form of gout in which deposits of urates form lumps in soft tissue, the ear, or around a joint.

tophus /tō′fəs/ (*pl*., **tophi** /tō′fī/) **1.** deposit of urates which forms in soft tissue, in the ear, or around a joint, that sometimes occur with gout. **2.** deposits on the surface of the teeth.

topical /tŏp′ĭ kəl/ pertaining to a specific area of the body or surface area of the skin.

topical anesthetic /ăn′əs thĕt′ĭk/ anesthetic applied to a sensitive surface, topical anesthetic drops to the cornea before measuring intraocular pressure with a tonometer.

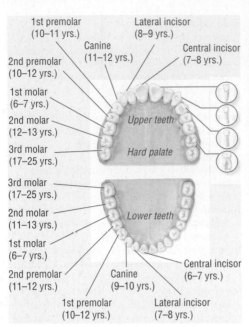

1st premolar (10–11 yrs.)
Lateral incisor (8–9 yrs.)
Canine (11–12 yrs.)
Central incisor (7–8 yrs.)
2nd premolar (10–12 yrs.)
1st molar (6–7 yrs.)
2nd molar (12–13 yrs.)
3rd molar (17–25 yrs.)
Upper teeth
Hard palate
3rd molar (17–25 yrs.)
2nd molar (11–13 yrs.)
Lower teeth
1st molar (6–7 yrs.)
2nd premolar (11–12 yrs.)
Canine (9–10 yrs.)
Central incisor (6–7 yrs.)
1st premolar (10–12 yrs.)
Lateral incisor (7–8 yrs.)

Teeth

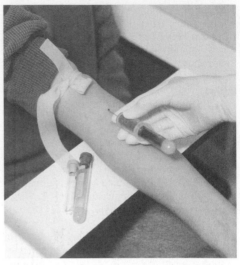

Tourniquet

topically /tŏp′ĭk lē/ pertaining to a specific part of the surface of the body.

TORCH syndrome /tôrch′/ a group of congenital infections with similar symptoms: toxoplasmosis (T), other infections (O), rubella (R), cytomegalovirus infection (C), and herpes simplex (H).

torpor /tôr′pər/ a state of mental or physical apathy; lethargy.

torsion /tôr′shən/ a twisting or turning of a part, as the torsion of the testis, requiring immediate surgical intervention.

torsion fracture bone fracture caused by the twisting of a limb.

torso /tôr′sō/ trunk of the body, excluding the head and limbs.

torticollis /tôr′tĭ kŏl′ĭs/ condition in which the head tilts to one side due to contraction of the neck muscles on that side.

torus fracture /tôr′əs/ a deformity caused by compression of the radial or ulnar soft bone tissue in children, with bulging in localized areas.

total lung capacity (TLC) /tō′təl lŭng′ kə păs′ĭ tē/ maximum amount of air the lungs can hold.

total parenteral nutrition (TPN) /pə rĕn′tər əl nōō trĭsh′ən/ complete nutrition given solely by intravenous means. *Also called* hyperalimentation.

totipotent /tō tĭp′ə tənt/ capable of generating a new organism or tissue, said of embryonic stem cells.

touch /tŭch/ to have contact with and feel, especially with the fingers.

Tourette('s) syndrome /tōō rĕt(s)′/ neuropsychiatric disorder characterized by facial tics and uncontrollable vocalizations, especially of offensive words.

tourniquet /tûr′nĭ kĭt/ device wrapped tightly around a limb to temporarily stop blood flow; bound tighter (higher) than arterial pressure to stop a wound from bleeding, or higher than venous pressure (quite low) to dilate veins for blood drawing or starting IVs.

tox-, toxi-, toxic-, toxico-, toxo- *combining form.* poison: *for example,* toxemia.

toxemia /tŏk sē′mē ə/ **1.** blood poisoning caused by toxins from a bacterial infection. **2.** a severe infection occurring during pregnancy. *See preclampsia* and *eclampsia.* [tox- + -emia]

toxic /tŏk′sĭk/ relating to or caused by a poison. [tox- + -ic]

toxicity /tŏk sĭs′ĭ tē/ the extent to which something is poisonous.

toxicogenic /tŏk′sĭ kō jĕn′ĭk/ producing toxic substances. [toxico- + -genic]

toxicology /tŏk′sĭ kŏl′ə jē/ study of the effects of poisons and treatments of poisoning. [toxico- + -logy]

toxicosis /tŏk′sĭ kō′sĭs/ pathological condition resulting from poisoning. [toxic- + -osis]

toxic shock toxic shock syndrome.

toxic shock syndrome (TSS) acute, severe, and often fatal bacterial infection marked by fever and shock; has occurred with the use of high-absorbency tampons. *Also called* toxic shock.

toxin /tŏk′sĭn/ poisonous protein capable of causing illness or stimulating production of neutralizing antibodies or antitoxins.

toxipathy /tŏk sĭp′ə thē/ any disease caused by poisoning, especially chronic poisoning. [toxi- + -pathy]

toxo- *See* tox-

toxoid /tŏk′soid/ toxin that has lost its toxicity but retained its antigenic properties and is therefore useful as a vaccine. [tox- + -oid]

toxoplasmosis /tŏk′sō plăz mō′sĭs/ neurologic disease caused by a parasite, especially harmful to a fetus in which it may cause blindness or neurological damage.

tPA, TPA *abbreviation.* tissue plasminogen activator.

TPN *abbreviation.* total parenteral nutrition.

TPR *abbreviation.* temperature, pulse, respiration.

trabecula /trə bĕk′yə lə/ (*pl.* **trabeculae** /trə bĕk′yə lē′/) **1.** rod-like bundle of connective fibers that provides support for an organ. **2.** any of the fine needlelike structures within cancellous bone.

trabecular /trə bĕk′yə lər/ involving or containing trabeculae.

trabeculectomy /trə bĕk′yə lĕk′tə mē/ surgical excision of trabecular tissue of the eye, to allow drainage of the aqueous humor, in the treatment of glaucoma.

trabeculoplasty /trə bĕk′yə lō plăs′tē/ laser surgery of the eye to create small holes in the trabecular network, to ease the intraocular pressure of glaucoma.

tracer study /trā′sər/ a diagnostic study using a traceable substance, such as a dye or a radioactive label, that can be followed through imaging.

trache-, tracheo- *combining form.* trachea: *for example,* tracheitis.

trachea /trā′kē ə/ membranous tube from the larynx to the bronchi through which inhaled air travels to and from the lungs. *Also called* windpipe.

tracheitis /trā′kē ī′tĭs/ inflammation of the trachea. [trache- + -itis]

trachel-, trachelo- *combining form.* neck, usually of the uterus; uterine cervix: *for example,* trachelorrhaphy.

trachelectomy /trăk′ə lĕk′tə mē/ surgical removal of the uterine cervix. *Also called* cervicectomy. [trachel- + -ectomy]

trachelorrhaphy /trăk′ə lôr′ə fē/ surgical suture of a laceration of the uterine cervix. [trachelo- + -rrhaphy]

tracheobronchial /trā′kē ō brŏng′kē əl/ of or pertaining to the trachea and bronchus. [tracheo- + bronchial]

tracheobronchoscopy /trā′kē ō brŏng kŏs′kə ē/ visual examination of the trachea and bronchi. [tracheo- + bronchoscopy]

tracheocele /trā′kē ə sēl′/ goiter; noncancerous enlargement of the thyroid gland. [tracheo- + -cele]

tracheoesophageal /trā′kē ō ĭ sŏf′ə jē′əl/ relating to or connecting the trachea and esophagus. [tracheo- + esophogeal]

tracheoplasty /trā′kē ə plăs′tē/ plastic surgery of the trachea. [tracheo- + -plasty]

tracheopyosis /trā′kē ō pī ō′sĭs/ tracheal inflammation with pus.

tracheorrhagia /trā′kē ō rā′jē ə, -jə/ hemorrhaging from the mucous membrane of the trachea. [tracheo- + -rrhagia]

tracheoscopy /trā′kē ŏs′kə pē/ internal exam of the trachea, as with a bronchoscope. [tracheo- + -scopy]

tracheostenosis /trā′kē ō stě nō′sĭs/ abnormal constriction of the tracheal lumen. [tracheo- + -stenosis]

tracheostomy /trā′kē ŏs′tə mē/ surgical opening of the trachea, through the tracheal cartilages in the neck, to facilitate breathing. [tracheo- + -stomy]

tracheotomy /trā′kē ŏt′ə mē/ surgical opening of the trachea, through the neck, to facilitate breathing. [tracheo- + -tomy]

trachoma /trə kō′mə/ contagious viral disease marked by inflammation of the conjuctiva and cornea of the eye; leading cause of blindness in African and Asian countries.

tract /trăkt/ **1.** a system made up of a series of related parts or organs, as the digestive tract or the upper repiratory tract. **2.** a bundle of nerve fibers having a common origin, function, and destination, as the optic tract or olfactory tract.

traction /trăk′shən/ a sustained pull exerted on a fractured, dislocated, or injured bone to aid in positioning, healing, or relieving pressure.

tractotomy /trə kŏt′ə mē/ surgical incision of a nerve tract in the spinal cord or brainstem to relieve pain.

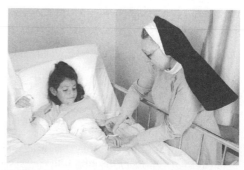

Traction

trade name proprietary name given to a product or service to identify it commercially, as opposed to a generic name, which is the official nonproprietary name of a drug.

traditional Chinese medicine (TCM) a system of medicine founded in China based on qi or chi, the energy in the body, that uses herbs, meditiation, acupuncture, and other methods to achieve balance in the body. *Also called* Chinese medicine.

tragus /trā′gəs/ (*pl.* **tragi** /trā′jī/) the cartilaginous projection in front of the external auditory meatus of the ear.

trait /trāt/ distinguishing characteristic.

trance /trăns/ semiconscious state, especially one induced by hypnosis.

tranquilizer /trăng′kwə lī′zər/ drug used to reduce tension and mental disturbance.

trans- *prefix.* across; through: *for example,* transdermal.

transaminase /trănz ăm′ə nās′/ enzyme that catalyzes the transfer of an amino group. *Also called* aminotransferase.

transcranial /trăns krā′nē əl/ through the skull. [trans- + cranial]

transcription /trăn skrĭp′shən/ synthesis of a type of RNA by copying the genetic information from a DNA sequence.

transcutaneous electrical nerve stimulation (TENS) /trăns′kyoo tā′nē əs/ electrical stimulation of the skin to relieve pain. [trans- + cutaneous]

transdermal /trănz dûr′məl/ through the skin. [trans- + dermal]

transesophageal /trănz′ĭ sŏf′ə jē′əl/ passing through the esophagus, especially said of a test performed through the esophagus.

trans fat/trans-fat /trăns′ făt′/ trans fatty acid.

trans fatty acid fatty acid produced by the hydrogenation of vegetable oil; common in processed foods and considered unhealthy.

transference /trăns fûr′əns, trăns′fər əns/ unconscious process whereby emotions associated with one person are felt toward another person.

transformer /trăns fôr′mər/ a device that steps up or steps down the voltage to levels needed to produce high kVp's (kilovolt peaks) or low mA's (milliamps) in the dental x-ray unit.

transfusion /trăns fyoo′zhən/ transfer of blood or plasma from one person to another.

transhepatic /trăns′hĭ păt′ĭk/ through the liver. [trans- + hepatic]

transient global amnesia /trăn′shənt glō′bəl ăm nē′zhə/ memory disorder with episodic amnesia and confusion.

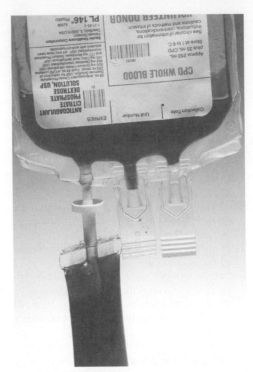

Transfusion

transient insomnia /ĭn sŏm′nē ə/ temporary insomnia.

transient ischemic attack (TIA) /ĭ skē′mĭk/ temporary blockage of a cerebral blood vessel resulting in dizziness and numbness on one side of the body or temporary loss of vision. Informally called a "ministroke."

transitional cell carcinoma /trăn zĭsh′ə nəl sĕl′ kär sə nō′mə/ malignancy derived from transitional epithelial tissue and usually occurring in the bladder, ureters or renal pelvis.

translation /trănz lā′shən/ the process in which the genetic information mRNA directs the production of a ribosomal protein.

translocation /trănz′lō kā′shən/ the transfer of a part of a chromosome to a different location within the same chromosome, or the exchange of parts between two chromosomes. [trans- + location]

transmissible /trănz mĭs′ə bəl/ capable of being transmitted, as a disease.

transmission /trănz mĭsh′ən/ act or process of conveying something, as a disease, from one being to another.

transplant /trăns′plănt′/ *v.* **1.** to transfer an organ or tissue from one person to another or from one body part to another. *n.* **2.** act or process of transferring an organ or tissue from one person to another or from one body part to another. *Also called* transplantation. **3.** the organ or tissue itself.

transplantation /trăns′plăn tā′shən/ act or process of transferring an organ or tissue from one person to another or from one body part to another.

transposition /trăns′pə zĭsh′ən/ the transfer of a DNA segment to a new site on the same or another chromosome or plasmid. [trans- + position]

transsexual /trăns sĕk′shoo əl/ person who has undergone a sex change. [trans- + sexual]

transthoracic /trăns′thô răs′ĭk/ through the thoracic cavity. [trans- + thoracic]

transudate /trăn′soo dāt′/ watery fluid passed through a membrane or extracted from tissue.

transurethral /trănz′yoo rē′thrəl/ through the urethra. [trans- + urethral]

transurethral resection (TUR) /rĭ sĕk′shən/ surgical removal of the prostate gland or bladder lesions using an endoscope inserted through the urethra.

transurethral resection of the prostate (TURP) /prŏs′tāt/ surgical removal of prostate tissue by transurethral resection.

transvaginal /trănz văj′ə nəl/ through the vagina. [trans- + vaginal]

transverse /trănz vûrs′/ being across from; crosswise.

transverse colon /kō′lən/ part of the large intestine that crosses the abdomen from the right side to the left and connects the ascending with the descending colon.

transverse fracture /frăk′chər/ fracture line of a bone that forms a right angle with the axis of the bone.

transverse plane horizontal plane dividing the body into an upper and lower section.

transverse process one of two processes projecting laterally from either side of a vertebra.

transvesical through the bladder. [trans- + vesical]

transvestism /trănz vĕs′tĭz əm/ adopting the dress and behavior of the opposite sex.

transvestite /trănz vĕs′tīt/ a person who adopts the dress and behavior of the opposite sex.

trapezius muscle /trə pē′zē əs mŭs′əl/ one of two flat triangular muscles of the upper back, involved in moving the shoulders and arms.

trauma /trou′mə, trô′mə/ **1.** serious physical injury. **2.** emotional wound with long-term effects.

trauma center specialized hospital unit for treatment of acute traumatic injuries.

traumatic /trə măt′ĭk/ relating to trauma.

traumatic brain injury (TBI) serious injury to the brain.

treadmill /trĕd′mĭl′/ exercise machine with a revolving belt for walking or running in place.

Trauma

treadmill test the monitoring of heart (ECG) and breathing rates of a patient exercising on a treadmill to determine heart function during physical activity. *Also called* stress test.

treat /trēt/ to deal with a patient or a disease in a manner designed to cure or alleviate the problem.

treatment /trēt′mənt/ process of providing medical, surgical, alternative, or psychological care for a disease or disorder or the care itself.

tremor /trĕm′ər/ an involuntary trembling or shaking.

tremulous /trĕm′yə ləs/ trembling; shaking.

trench fever acute infectious disease marked by fever and joint pain, transmitted by lice.

trench mouth acute infection by two bacteria of the mucous membranes of the mouth, characterized by ulcers, pain, bleeding, and foul breath. *Also called* (acute) necrotizing gingivitis, Vincent's angina.

Trendelenburg position /trĕn′də lən bûrg′/ position in which the head is lower than the body.

trephination /trĕf′ə nā′shən/ or **trepanation** /trĕp′ə nā′shən/ cranial opening made with a special surgical drill.

trephine /trə fīn′, -fēn′/ cylindrical surgical instrument used for making a round opening or cut, for example, precisely cutting the donor cornea from the donor eye or making a small round hole in the skull for a stereotactic brain biopsy.

tri- *prefix.* Three: *for example,* tricuspid.

triage /trē′äzh/ prioritizing treatment of patients based on urgency of care.

triceps /trī′sĕps/ three-headed skeletal muscle located along the back of the upper arm.

trich-, tricho- *combining form.* hair; thread: *for example,* trichogenous.

trichiasis /trĭ kī′ə sĭs/ condition in which hair near an orifice grows inward, especially a turning inward of the eyelashes often causing irritation of the eyeball. [trich- + -iasis]

trichinosis /trĭk′ə nō′sĭs/ intestinal and muscular infection transmitted by ingesting infected undercooked pork carrying trichina larvae.

trichoepithelioma /trĭk′ō ĕp′ə thē′lē ō′mə/ benign epithelial tumor, derived from the hair follicles. [tricho- + epithelioma]

trichogenous /trĭ kŏj′ə nəs/ promoting hair growth. [tricho- + -genous]

trichoglossia /trĭk′ō glŏs′ē ə/ benign condition of the tongue marked by an overgrowth of the papillae of the tongue.

trachomegaly /trăk′ō mĕg′ə lē/ abnormally long eyelashes. [tricho- + -megaly]

trichomoniasis /trĭk′ō mə nī′ə sĭs/ vaginal infection with itching and discharge caused by parasitical trichomonad protozoa.

trichomycosis /trĭk′ō mī kō′sĭs/ disease of the hair caused by a fungal infection. [tricho- + -mycosis]

trichophagy /trĭ kŏf′ə jē/ habit of biting the hair. [tricho- + -phagy]

trichophobia /trĭk′ō fō′bē ə/ phobia of loose hairs on the clothing or elsewhere. [tricho- + -phobia]

trichorrhexis /trĭk′ə rĕk′sĭs/ a condition in which hairs split or break easily. [tricho- + -rrhexis]

trichotillomania /trĭk′ō tĭl′ō mā′nē ə/ the compulsion to pull out one's hair; considered to be a psychosomatic symptom.

trichuriasis /trĭk′yoo rī′ə sĭs/ intestinal infection caused by nematode worms.

tricuspid /trī kŭs′pĭd/ having three cusps, especially a molar tooth, or the tricuspid valve. [tri- + cuspid]

tricuspid stenosis /stĕ nō′sĭs/ abnormal narrowing of the orifice of the tricuspid valve. [tri- + cuspid]

tricuspid valve /vălv/ valve of the heart with three flaps or leaflets that opens to allow blood flow from the right atrium to the right ventricle and closes to prevent backflow. [tri- + cuspid]

tricyclic antidepressant (TCA) /trī sī′klĭk ăn′tē dĭ prĕs′ənt, -sĭk′lĭk/ antidepressant that inhibits reuptake of norepinephrine and serotonin, allowing more of these substances to act on receptors of the brain.

trifurcation /trī′fər kā′shən/ the point at which a three-rooted tooth divides; teeth with a trifurcation are the maxillary molars.

trigeminal /trī jĕm′ə nəl/ relating to the trigeminal nerve.

trigeminal nerve cranial nerve V; either one of a pair of main sensory and motor nerves of the face, mouth, and nasal cavity, having three major branches: mandibular nerve, maxillary nerve, ophthalmic nerve.

trigeminal neuralgia /noo răl′jə, -jē ə/ severe paroxysmal pain associated with the trigeminal nerve.

trigger /trĭg′ər/ **1.** *n.* an action or agent that sets off an event, especially something that sets off an allergic reaction. **2.** *v.* to set off.

trigger finger a finger that pops as it is straightened, because its swollen tendon passes through a normally narrow tendon sheath with difficulty, and suddenly slides through.

trigger point therapy a type of massage therapy which examines and treats muscles and muscle attachments in layers; can be self-administered; trigger points are similar to acupressure points.

triglycerides /trī glĭs′ə rīdz′/ lipoproteins found in the blood and adipose tissue.

trigone /trī′gōn/ triangular body part, especially the mucosa of the base of the bladder where the urethra exits.

trigonitis /trī′gō nī′tĭs/ inflammation of the trigone of the bladder.

triiodothyronine (T3, T₃) /trī ī′ə dō thī′rə nēn′/ a hormone secreted by the thyroid gland that regulates metabolism.

trimester /trī′mĕs tər, trī mĕs′-/ a period of three months, especially one of the three phases of pregnancy.

triplets /trĭp′lĭts/ group of three of the same kind, as in three offspring born at the same birth.

-tripsy *suffix.* crushing; pulverizing: *for example,* lithotripsy.

triptans /trĭp′tănz/ a class of drugs used to treat migraines.

trismus /trĭz′məs/ locking of the jaw, associated with tetanus (infection with *Calustridium tetani*), caused by muscle spasms in the motor branch of the trigeminal nerve. Informally called lockjaw.

trisomy /trī′sō mē/ condition of having three copies of a given chromosome in a cell instead of two, as in Down syndrome (trisomy 21).

trocar /trō′kär/ pointed surgical instrument used to insert a cannula (a small tube) into a body cavity for fluid drainage.

trochanter /trō kăn′tər/ one of two bony processes on the upper part of the femur, to which muscles are attached.

troche /trō′kē/ circular medicinal lozenge.

Trisomy (Down syndrome)

trochlear nerve /trŏ′klē ər nûrv′/ cranial nerve IV; one of two cranial nerves which innervate one of the extrocular muscles, the superior oblique.

-trophic *suffix.* relating to nutrition: *for example,* dystrophic.

trophoblast /trŏf′ə blăst′/ the outer cellular layer of a blastocyst which attaches the fertilized egg to the wall of the uterus and ultimately becomes part of the placenta. *Also called* trophoderm. [tropho- + blast]

trophocyte /trŏf′ə sīt′/ cell that provides nutrients.

trophoderm /trŏf′ə dûrm′/ trophoblast. [tropho- + derm]

-trophy *suffix.* nutrition; growth: *for example,* atrophy.

-tropia *suffix.* abnormal deviation of the eye from a normal line of vision: *for example,* hyperopia.

-tropic *suffix.* involuntary response of an organism to turn away from or toward a stimulus: *for example,* psychotropic.

-tropin *suffix.* Hormone: *for example,* thyrotropin.

troponin /trō′pə nĭn/ one of various muscle proteins involved in regulating actin and myosin in muscular contraction.

Trp *abbreviation.* tryptophan.

true ribs any of the seven pairs of ribs that attach directly to the sternum, as opposed to the false ribs which have a broad cartilaginous connection to the sternum or are free-floating (the last two pairs).

truncate /trŭng′kāt/ to shorten by cutting off.

truncation /trŭng kā′shən/ the act of cutting off.

trunk /trŭngk/ **1.** the torso, excluding the limbs and the head. **2.** the main portion of a vessel or nerve.

truss /trŭs/ a supportive bandage worn to hold a hernia in place or prevent its enlargement.

tryptophan (Trp) /trĭp′tə făn′/ an essential amino acid found in proteins, needed for normal metabolism and growth.

TSE *abbreviation.* **1.** transmissible spongiform encephalopathy, any of a group of brain diseases, such as kuru or Creutzfeldt-Jakob's disease, in which the brain matter deteriorates. *See also* spongiform encephalopathy. **2.** testicular self-examination.

TSH *abbreviation.* thyroid-stimulating hormone.

tsp. *abbreviation.* teaspoon; teaspoons.

TSS *abbreviation.* toxic shock syndrome.

T suppressor cell T cell that suppresses the immune response of other T cells, resulting in tolerance for a given antigen. *Also called* suppressor T cell.

tsutsugamushi disease /tso͞o′tsə gə mo͞o′shē/ acute infectious disease transmitted by mites, and widespread in Asia.

TTP *abbreviation.* thrombotic thrombocytopenic purpura.

tubal ligation /to͞o′bəl lī gā′shən/ surgical tying of the fallopian tubes, as a form of female sterilization.

tubal pregnancy /prĕg′nən sē/ ectopic pregnancy in the fallopian tube instead of in the uterus.

tube /to͞ob/ hollow cylinder that functions as a passage, especially for fluid.

tube feeding use of a nasogastric tube to introduce food directly into the gastrointestinal tract, for patients who cannot swallow.

tubehead /to͞ob′hĕd′/ or **tube housing** in dental radiography, a covering that incorporates the Coolidge vacuum tube, the filters, the collimator, and the cone.

tubercle /to͞o′bər kəl/ anatomical nodule, prominence or swelling.

tubercular /to͞o bûr′kyə lər/ **1.** relating to tuberculosis. **2.** resembling a tubercle.

tuberculin /too bûr′kyə lĭn/ liquid containing a protein of the tuberculosis bacterium, used as a diagnostic test for tuberculosis.

tuberculin skin test skin test to determine past or present tubercular infection.

tuberculin test test to determine sensitivity to tuberculin, used to diagnose past or present tubercular infection.

tuberculosis (TB) /too bûr′kyə lō′sĭs/ extremely contagious chronic lung disease caused by the inhalation of airborne bacterium, marked by fever, and hemoptysis (coughing up of bloody mucous). *See illustration* on page 366.

Tuberculosis (bacteria)

tuberculous /tōō bûr′kyə ləs/   having or relating to tuberculosis.

tuberosity /tōō′bə rŏs′ĭ tē/   rounded protuberance, especially at the end of a bone, where muscles or ligaments attach.

tubule /tōōb′yōōl/   small tube, especially in the body.

tularemia /tōō′lə rē′mē ə/   infectious disease of rodents and rabbits, transmissible to humans, and characterized by fever and swelling of the lymph nodes.

tumescent /tōō mĕs′ənt/   somewhat swollen.

tumor /tōō′mər/   **1.** non-inflammatory abnormal mass of tissue, benign or malignant, resulting from excessive cell division. **2.** swelling, as one of the four classic signs of inflammation. *See also* calor, dolor, rubor.

tumor marker   substance secreted by tumor tissue and found in blood serum that indicates the presence or continued presence (after treatment) of a particular type of tumor.

tumor necrosis factor (TNF) /nə krō′sĭs/   a protein produced by macrophages in response to an endotoxin, capable of destroying certain cancerous tumor cells in vitro and may ultimately be used in control of tumors, but also a cause of certain inflammations.

tumor stage   the degree to which a malignant tumor has spread from its original site.

tumor suppressor gene /jēn/   gene in normal cells that inhibits excessive cell division, and which when inactivated, increases a cell's risk for malignant growth.

tunica albuginea /tōō′nĭ kə ăl′byōō jĭn′ē ə/   layer of collagen surrounding a structure, especially the testis.

tunnel vision   narrow field of vision with a loss of peripheral vision.

TUR   *abbreviation.* transurethral resection.

turbid /tûr′bĭd/   cloudy with suspended particles.

turbinate /tûr′bə nĭt, -nāt′/   of or relating to one of the spongy, scroll-shaped bones of the nasal passages.

turbinectomy /tûr′bə nĕk′tə mē/   surgical removal of a turbinate bone.

turf toe   an injury involving the hyperextension of the hallux (big toe) resulting in the spraining or tearing of the ligament of the metatarsophalangeal joint; often associated with sports, such as football, played on turf.

turgor /tûr′gər/   normal, rigid state of a cell or vessel resulting from the internal pressure of its fluid content.

Turner('s) syndrome /tûr′nər(z)/   congenital condition of females lacking one X-chromosome, resulting in short stature, sexual underdevelopment, and other physical abnormalities.

TURP /tûrp/   *abbreviation.* transurethral resection of the prostate.

tussis   a cough.

tussive /tŭs′ĭv/   relating to a cough.

twenty-twenty/20/20 /twĕn′tē twĕn′tē/   normal visual acuity of the human eye.

twilight sleep /twī′līt′/   state produced by intravenous sedation, in which pain is dulled without a loss of consciousness.

twin /twĭn/   either of two offspring born at the same birth. *See also* monozygotic twins, dizygotic twins.

twisted ankle /twĭs′tĭd ăng′kəl/   minor injury to the ankle caused by a sudden twisting motion.

tylosis /tī lō′sĭs/   **1.** abnormal thickening and hardening of the skin. **2.** inflammation of the eyelids, characterized by thickening and hardening of the edges.

tympan-, tympano-   *combining form.* tympanum, eardrum: *for example,* tympanoplasty.

tympanectomy /tĭm′pə nĕk′tə mē/   surgical removal of the tympanic membrane. [tympan- + -ectomy]

tympanic /tĭm păn′ĭk/   relating to the eardrum. [tympan- + -ic]

tympanic cavity /kăv′ĭ tē/   the cavity between the eardrum and the inner ear. *Also called* middle ear. [tympan- + -ic]

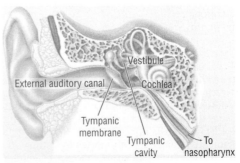

Tympanic Cavity

tympanic membrane /mĕm′brān/ the membrane that separates the external ear from the middle ear. *Also called* eardrum, tympanum.

tympanites /tĭm′pə nī′tēz/ distention of the abdomen resulting from gas in the intestine or peritoneal cavity causing a drumlike state of tension in the abdominal wall.

tympanitis /tĭm′pə nī′tĭs/ inflammation of the eardrum. [tympan- + -itis]

tympanometry /tĭm′pə nŏm′ĭ trē/ test for disorders of the middle ear by measuring the movement of the tympanic membrane. [tympano- + -metry]

tympanoplasty /tĭm′pə nō plăs′tē/ surgical repair of injuries to the middle ear or eardrum. [tympano- + -plasty]

tympanostomy /tĭm′pə nŏs′tə mē/ surgical incision of the eardrum to drain fluid from the middle ear space. Also called myringotomy, typmanotomy. [tympano- + -stomy]

tympanostomy tube tube inserted through the tympanic membrane to facilitate drainage from the middle ear space. [tympano- + -stomy]

tympanotomy /tĭm′pə nŏt′ə mē/ tympanostomy. Also called myringotomy. [tympano- + -tomy]

tympanum /tĭm′pə nəm/ the membrane that separates the external ear from the middle ear. Also called eardrum, tympanic membrane.

tympany /tĭm′pə ne/ distention of the abdomen resulting from gas in the intestine or peritoneal cavity.

type A or **type A personality** person having behavior patterns marked by aggression, impatience, and tension.

type A blood blood type whose red blood cells carry the A antigen.

type AB blood blood type whose red blood cells carry the A and B antigens; people with this type of blood are called "universal recipients."

type B blood blood type whose red blood cells carry the B antigen.

type O blood blood type whose red blood cells carry neither the A nor the B antigen; people with this type of blood are referred to as "universal donors."

type I/1 diabetes /dī′ə bē′tĭs, -tēz/ or **type I/1 diabetes mellitus** /mĕl′ĭ təs, mə lī′təs/ diabetes that develops primarily during childhood, characterized by insulin deficiency and high blood sugar. *Also called* insulin-dependent diabetes, juvenile diabetes.

type II/2 diabetes or type II/2 diabetes mellitus diabetes that develops primarily in obese adults and which is characterized by hyperglycemia because of the body's inability to utilize insulin and to compensate by increased insulin production. Also called adult-onset diabetes, non-insulin dependent diabetes.

typhoid /tī′foid/ or **typhoid fever** acute infectious disease caused by a bacterium (*Salmonella typhosa*), marked by fever and intestinal inflammation and ulceration.

typhus /tī′fəs/ or **typhus fever** rickettsial disease characterized by high fever and a skin rash, transmitted by mites, lice, or ticks.

tyrosine /tī′rə sēn′/ an amino acid found in most proteins; a precursor of epinephrine and melanin.

tyrosinemia /tī′rō sĭ nē′mē ə/ inherited disorder of tyrosine metabolism, resulting in abnormalities of the liver and kidneys.

tyrosinuria /tī′rō sĭ nŏŏr′ē ə/ excretion of tyrosine in the urine.

U

u *abbreviation.* atomic mass unit.

U *abbreviation.* **1.** uranium. **2.** unit; units. **3.** uracil. **4.** urine.

UA, U/A *abbreviation.* urinalysis.

ubiquinone /yoo′bĭ kwī′nōn, yoo bĭk′wə nōn′/ naturally occurring compound in the body that functions as an antioxidant and is often taken as a dietary supplement. *Also called* coenzyme Q₁₀.

ubiquitin /yoo bĭk′wĭ tĭn/ a chain of amino acids found in many plant and animal cells that is involved in the breakdown of protein within cells and in other cellular activities.

UBT *abbreviation.* urea breath test.

UGI *abbreviation.* upper gastrointestinal.

UGI series upper gastrointestinal series.

ulcer /ŭl′sər/ a small, open wound or sore in the skin, a mucous membrane, or an organ caused by infection, inflammation, or pressure.

ulcerating /ŭl′sə rā′tĭng/ **1.** forming an ulcer or ulcers. **2.** characterized by ulcers or ulceration.

ulceration /ŭl′sə rā′shən/ **1.** an ulcer. **2.** the formation of an ulcer or ulcers.

ulcerative /ŭl′sər ə tĭv/ characterized by or tending to form ulcers.

ulcerative colitis /kə lī′tĭs/ a serious inflammatory disease of the colon and rectum marked by ulcers of the intestinal lining and continual attacks of abdominal pain, diarrhea, and rectal bleeding. *See also* inflammatory bowel disease.

ulcerous /ŭl′sər əs/ **1.** characterized by ulcers or ulceration. **2.** affected by ulcers or ulceration.

-ule *suffix.* little; small (form of the thing specified): *for example,* tubule.

ulna /ŭl′nə/ (*pl.* **ulnas** or **ulnae** /ŭl′nē/) the larger of the two long bones of the forearm, extending from the elbow to the wrist on the side opposite the thumb and forming the olecranon (the outer point of the elbow) where it articulates with the humerus.

ulnar /ŭl′nər/ **1.** of or pertaining to the ulna. **2.** of or pertaining to the side of the forearm on which the ulna is located.

ulnar nerve a nerve that arises in the brachial plexus and branches into muscles and skin of the forearm and the hand. *See also* brachial plexus.

ultra- *prefix.* **1.** beyond or outside the limits of (the thing indicated): *for example,* ultrasonic. **2.** to an excessive or extreme degree of (the thing indicated): *for example,* ultrafast.

ultrafast CAT scan /ŭl′trə făst′ kăt′ skăn′/ a computerized x-ray that can detect very small deposits of calcium in the arteries, used to screen for early signs of heart disease.

ultrasonic /ŭl′trə sŏn′ĭk/ **1.** of or pertaining to sound waves of a frequency that is too high for humans to hear. **2.** of or pertaining to ultrasound. [ultra- + sonic]

ultrasonography /ŭl′trə sə nŏg′rə fē/ an imaging technique using sound waves to visualize the internal organs, especially the pregnant uterus and its developing fetus. [ultra- + sonography]

ultrasound /ŭl′trə sound′/ the very high frequency sound waves used in ultrasonography. [ultra- + sound]

ultraviolet (UV) /ŭl′trə vī′ə lĭt/ of, pertaining to, or indicating invisible light rays or radiation beyond the violet end of the spectrum.

ultraviolet radiation (UR) powerful, shortwave length radiation from sunlight that produces vitamin D₂ in the skin, causes tanning, sunburn, and other damage to the skin, and can be used, in artificial form, to treat some skin disorders.

umbilical /ŭm bĭl′ĭ kəl/ **1.** of, pertaining to, or associated with the umbilicus. **2.** pertaining to or associated with the umbilical region.

umbilical cord a long, flexible, rope-like structure connecting the circulatory system of a fetus to the placenta and containing two arteries and one vein through which oxygen and nourishment pass to the fetus and waste is carried away. *See illustration* on page 370.

umbilical hernia /hûr′nē ə/ an abdominal hernia of newborns in which a section of the intestine bulges up through an opening between the abdominal muscles beneath or near the umbilicus.

umbilical region the area of the abdomen surrounding the umbilicus.

umbilical vein vein through which blood is returned from the placenta to the fetus. *Also called* left umbilical vein.

umbilicus /ŭm bĭl′ĭ kəs/ (*pl.* **umbilici** /ŭm bĭl′ə sī′/) the scar in the center of the abdomen

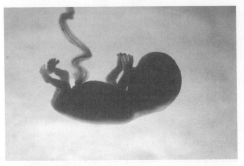

Umbilical Cord

showing where the umbilical cord was attached during fetal development. *Also called* belly button, navel.

un- *prefix.* not: *for example,* unconscious.

unconscious /ŭn kŏn′shəs/ *adj.* **1.** not in a normally conscious state; not mentally responsive. **2.** occurring or produced while not in a conscious state. **3.** occurring or done without thought or awareness. *n.* **4.** in psychology, the mental structure of the feelings of which one is not aware. [un- + conscious]

unconsciousness /ŭn kŏn′shəs nĭs/ the state of not being conscious; state of being mentally unresponsive.

undescended testicle /ŭn′dĭ sĕn′dĭd tĕs′tĭ kəl/ or **undescended testis** /tĕs′tĭs/ a condition in which one testicle has not completely migrated from the abdomen of the male fetus to its scrotum during development in the uterus; surgically corrected by orchidopexy. *Also called* cryptorchidism, cryptorchism.

undifferentiated /ŭn′dĭf ə rĕn′shē ā′tĭd/ (of cells) not having structure or function, as in the tissue of tumors; primitive in form.

undulant fever /ŭn′jə lənt/ a rare bacterial disease caused by exposure to infected milk or animal tissue. *Also called* brucellosis.

ung, ung. *abbreviation.* ointment.

ungual /ŭng′gwəl/ of or pertaining to a fingernail or toenail.

unguis /ŭng′gwĭs/ (*pl.* **ungues** /ŭng′gwēz/) a fingernail or toenail.

uni- *prefix.* one; single: *for example,* unicellular.

unicellular /yōō′nə sĕl′yə lər/ consisting of one cell. [uni- + cellular]

unilateral /yōō′nə lăt′ər əl/ on, at, or coming from one side only. [uni- + lateral]

uniocular /yōō′nē ŏk′yə lər/ pertaining to one eye only. [uni- + ocular]

uniparous /yōō nĭp′ər əs/ **1.** having given birth to only one child. *Also called* primiparous. **2.** producing only one egg or offspring at one time. [uni- + -parous]

unit /yōō′nĭt/ **1.** one piece, section, or set of the thing specified; a single, undivided item. **2.** (*also* **Unit**) a basic amount of something according to a standard measurement, as of blood (1 unit = 500 cc), a medication (in grams, milligrams, or micrograms), or a vitamin (in mg, international units, or percentage of minimum daily requirements).

United States Pharmacopeia (**USP**) /fär′mə kə pē′ə/ a publication of the United States Pharmacopeial Association containing the official, legally recognized standards for drugs and drug dosages, over-the-counter medications and preparations, dietary supplements, and related health care products. Full title: *United States Pharmacopeia—National Formulary.*

universal donor a person with type O in the ABO system of classification, so called because his or her blood can be transfused into persons with any blood type in that system.

universal recipient /rĭ sĭp′ē ənt/ a person with type AB in the ABO system of classification, so called because he or she can receive transfusions from persons of any blood type in that system.

UNOS /yōō′nŏs/ *abbreviation.* United Network for Organ Sharing.

unproductive cough /ŭn′prə dŭk′tĭv/ a cough in which no mucus is expelled from the bronchi or lungs; a dry cough.

unsanitary /ŭn săn′ĭ tĕr′ē/ not free from dirt or infection; unhealthful. [un- + sanitary]

unsaturated fat /ŭn săch′ə rā′tĭd/ a fat having chains of unsaturated fatty acids, generally considered a healthy form of edible fat; usually in liquid form at room temperature, such as canola oil and olive oil.

unstable diabetes /dī′ə bē′tĭs, -tēz/ a type of diabetes with Somogyi effect (quick swings of blood sugar from high to low). *Also called* brittle diabetes.

unwell /ŭn wĕl′/ not in good health; sick; ill. [un- + well]

upper extremities /ĭk strĕm′ĭ tēz/ the limbs of the body between the shoulders and the hands; the arms.

upper gastrointestinalseries /găs′trō ĭn tĕs′tə nəl/ or **upper GI series** or **UGI series** examination of the upper part of the digestive tract in which the patient drinks a liquid containing a contrast medium (barium sulfate) and images of the throat, esophagus, stomach, and duodenum are obtained by x-ray or fluoroscope. *Also called* barium swallow.

upper gastrointestinal (**GI**) **tract** the throat, esophagus, stomach, and duodenum.

upper respiratory condition /rĕs′pər ə tôr′ē/ any infection or disease of the upper respiratory tract.

Upper Respiratory Infection

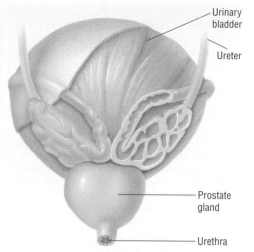

Urinary bladder
Ureter
Prostate gland
Urethra

Ureter

upper respiratory disorder   any of various conditions that affect the nasal cavity, sinuses, throat, and larynx, such as the common cold, sinusitis, allergic rhinitis, tonsillitis, and croup.

upper respiratory infection (URI) or **upper respiratory tract infection (URTI)**   the common cold.

upper respiratory tract   the nasal cavity, throat, and larynx.

uptake /ŭp′tāk′/   the absorption and retention of a substance by living tissue.

UR   *abbreviation.* ultraviolet radiation.

ur-, uro-   *combining form.* **1.** urine; urinary tract; urination: *for example,* uremia.

uranium (U) /yōō rā′nē əm/   a heavy, radioactive metallic element with numerous isotopes; found in the ores uraninite and pitchblende.

uranoschisis /yōōr′ə nŏs′kə sĭs/   a birth anomaly with a fissure in the roof of the mouth. *Also called* cleft palate.

urea /yōō rē′ə/   a nitrogenous compound resulting from the breakdown of protein that is excreted in the urine. *Also called* carbamide.

urea breath test (UBT)   a test to determine whether *Helicobacter pylori* bacteria (the cause of ulcers) is present in the stomach, in which the patient's breath is analyzed for the presence of radioactive carbon dioxide.

uremia /yōō rē′mē ə/   **1.** abnormally high levels of urea and other nitrogenous waste products in the blood. *Also called* azotemia. **2.** the pathological condition caused by this, generally regarded as chronic kidney failure and marked by such symptoms as nausea, vomiting, swelling, and disorders of the muscles and nerves. [ur- + -cmia]

uresis /yōō rē′sĭs/   urination.

-uresis   *suffix.* **1.** urination. **2.** excretion in the urine (of the substance indicated): *for example,* natriuresis, excretion of sodium in the urine.

ureter-, uretero-   *combining form.* ureter: *for example,* ureteritis.

ureter /yōō rē′tər/   a long (normally about 10 inches in length), thick tube that carries urine from each renal pelvis (kidney) to the urinary bladder.

ureteral /uōō rē′tər əl/   of or pertaining to the ureter.

ureteralgia /yōō rē′tə răl′jē ə, -jə/   pain in the ureter. [ureter- + -algia]

ureterectasis /yōō rē′tə rĕk′tə sĭs/   dilation of the ureter. [ureter + -ectasis]

ureterectomy /yōō rē′tə rĕk′tə mē/   surgical removal of all or part of the ureter, usually done as part of a nephrectomy (removal of a kidney). [ureter- + -ectomy]

ureteritis /yōō rē′tə rī′tĭs/   inflammation of a ureter. [ureter- + -itis]

ureterocele /yōō rē′tər ə sēl′/   a pouch-like formation of the ureter where it enters the urinary bladder. [uretero- + -cele]

ureterocolostomy /yōō rē′tə rō kə lŏs′tə mē/   surgical implantation of the ureter into the colon. [uretero- + colostomy]

ureterocystoneostomy /yōō rē′tə rō sĭs′tō nē ŏs′tə mē/   surgical reattachment of the ureter to a different position in the urinary bladder; this type of ureteral reimplantation is a cure for reflux from the bladder into the ureter and renal pelvis (kidney) above. *Also called* ureterocystostomy.

ureterocystostomy /yŏŏ rē′tə rō sĭ stŏs′tə mē/ ureterocystoneostomy. [uretero- + cyst + -ostomy]

ureterogram /yŏŏ rē′tər ə grăm′/ an x-ray image of the ureter. [uretero- + -gram]

ureteroileostomy /yŏŏ rē′tə rō ĭl′ē ŏs′tə mē/ surgical attachment of the ureters to a portion of the intestine, from which urine can drain through an opening made in the abdominal wall. [uretero- + ileostomy]

ureterolith /yŏŏ rē′tər ə lĭth/ a calculus (stone) formed or caught in the ureter. [uretero- + -lith]

ureterolithiasis /yŏŏ rē′tə rō lĭ thī′ə sĭs/ the development or presence of ureteroliths or calculi in the ureter. [uretero- + -lithiasis]

ureteropathy /yŏŏ rē′tə rŏp′ə thē/ any diseased condition of the ureter. [uretero- + -pathy]

ureteroplasty /yŏŏ rē′tər ə plăs′tē/ surgery to repair or improve the functioning of the ureter; plastic surgery of the ureter. [uretero- + -plasty]

ureteropyelitis /yŏŏ rē′tə rō pī′ə lī′tĭs/ inflammation of a ureter and its associated renal pelvis (kidney). *Also called* pyeloureteritis, ureteropylonephritis. [uretero- + pyelitis]

ureteropyelonephritis /yŏŏ rē′tə rō pī′ə lō nə frī′tĭs/ ureteropyelitis. [uretero- + pyelo- + nephritis]

ureteropyeloplasty /yŏŏ rē′tə rō pī′ə lə plăs′tē/ ureteropyelostomy. [uretero- + pyelo- + -plasty]

ureteropyelostomy /yŏŏ rē′tə rō pī′ə lŏs′tə mē/ surgery to create a wider junction for a ureter and the renal pelvis (kidney) to promote drainage of urine. *Also called* ureteropyeloplasty. [uretero- + pyel- + -ostomy]

ureteropyosis /yŏŏ rē′tə rō pī ō′sĭs/ the build-up of pus in a ureter. *Also called* pyoureter. [uretero- + -pyosis]

ureterorrhagia /yŏŏ rē′tər ə rā′jē ə, -jə/ bleeding from the ureter. [uretero- + -rrhagia]

ureterorrhaphy /yŏŏ rē′tə rôr′ə fē/ surgical suturing of a ureter. [uretero- + -rrhaphy]

ureterostenosis /yŏŏ rē′tə rō stĭ nō′sĭs/ abnormal narrowing of a ureter. [uretero- + stenosis]

ureterostomy /yŏŏ rē′tə rŏs′tə mē/ any of various surgically created openings or channels to allow drainage of urine from the ureter. [ureter- + -ostomy]

ureterotomy /yŏŏ rē′tə rŏt′ə mē/ surgical cutting of a ureter. [uretero- + -tomy]

ureterovesical /yŏŏ rē′tə rō vĕs′ĭ kəl/ of or pertaining to both a ureter and the urinary bladder or to their junction. *Also called* vesicoureteral. [uretero- + vesical]

urethr-, urethro- *combining form.* urethra: *for example,* urethralgia.

urethra /yŏŏ rē′thrə/ the narrow tube that carries urine from the bladder to be discharged outside the body.

urethralgia /yŏŏr′ĭ thrăl′jē ə, -jə/ pain in the urethra. [urethra- + -algia]

urethral meatus /yŏŏ rē′thrəl mē ā′təs/ the external opening in the body where urine is discharged from the urethra.

urethrism /yŏŏ rē′thrĭz əm/ spasmodic constriction of the urethra. *Also called* urethrospasm.

urethritis /yŏŏr′ĭ thrī′tĭs/ inflammation of the urethra. [urethr- + -itis]

urethrocystitis /yŏŏ rē′thrō sĭ stī′tĭs/ inflammation of both the urethra and the urinary bladder. [urethro- + cystitis]

urethrogram /yŏŏ rē′thrə grăm′/ an x-ray of the urethra. [urethro- + -gram]

urethropexy /yŏŏ rē′thrə pĕk′sē/ a surgical procedure to correct stress incontinence, in which the urethra is suspended from the back of the pubic symphysis. [urethro- + -pexy]

urethroplasty /yŏŏ rē′thrə plăs′tē/ surgical repair of the urethra. [urethro- + -plasty]

urethrorectal /yŏŏ rē′thrō rĕk′təl/ relating to or connecting the rectum and the urethra. *Also called* rectourethral. [urethro- + rectal]

urethrorrhaphy /yŏŏr′ĭ thrôr′ə fē/ surgical suturing of the urethra. [urethro- + -rrhaphy]

urethrorrhea /yŏŏ rē′thrə rē′ə/ abnormal discharge from the urethra. [urethro- + -rrhea]

urethroscope /yŏŏ rē′thrə skōp′/ a type of endoscope for internal examination of the urethra. [urethro- + -scope]

urethrospasm /yŏŏ rē′thrə spăz′əm/ spasmodic constriction of the urethra; sometimes causing urge incontinence. *Also called* urethrism. [urethro- + spasm]

urethrostomy /yŏŏr′ĭ thrŏs′tə mē/ **1.** surgical creation of an external opening for the urethra. **2.** the opening so created. [urethro- + -stomy]

urethrotomy /yŏŏr′ĭ thrŏt′ə mē/ surgical cutting of the urethra. [urethro- + -tomy]

urethrovaginal /yŏŏ rē′thrō văj′ə nəl/ of, pertaining to, or connecting to both the urethra and the vagina. [urethro- + vaginal]

urge incontinence or **urgency incontinence** /ĭn kŏn′tə nəns/ the inability to control the discharge of urine from the bladder or feces from the bowels after feeling a sudden, intense need to do so may result from an illness, an injury, or from the effects of aging.

urgency /ûr′jən sē/ a sudden, powerful, almost uncontrollable need to do or have something.

URI *abbreviation*. upper respiratory infection.

-uria *suffix*. urine: *for example,* dysuria.

uric /yo͞or′ĭk/ urinary.

uric acid a nitrogenous by-product of protein and purine metabolism that is excreted in the urine.

uric acid test any of various tests for the presence of uric acid in the blood or urine.

uricaciduria /yo͞or′ĭk ăs′ĭ do͞or′ē ə/ abnormally high levels of uric acid in the urine, often an indicator of gout. *Also called* hyperuricosuria. [uric + aciduria]

urin-, urino- *combining form*. urine: *for example,* urinalysis.

urinal /yo͞or′ə nəl/ **1.** a container into which urine can be discharged. **2.** a toilet or other fixture used for urination.

urinalysis (UA, U/A) /yo͞or′ə năl′ə sĭs/ examination of the urine, typically by chemical or microscopic means. [urin- + analysis]

urinary /yo͞or′ə nĕr′ē/ **1.** of, pertaining to, in, or coming from urine. **2.** of, pertaining to, or associated with the excretion of urine or the organs that excrete it.

urinary bladder the small, balloon-like organ at the front of the pelvis that collects and temporarily stores urine produced by the kidneys; often just called bladder.

urinary calculus /kăl′kyə ləs/ a stone or calcification in the urinary tract. *Also called* cystolith.

	Dr. Joel Chorzik 1420 Glen Road		
Run Date: 09/22/XX Run Time: 1507	Meadowvale, OK 44444 111-222-3333		Page 1 Specimen Report

Patient: James Delgado	Acct #: A994584732	Loc: ED	U #:
Reg Dr: S. Anders, M.D.	Age/Sx: 55/M	Room:	Reg: 09/22/XX
	Status: Reg ER	Bed:	Des:

Spec #: 0922 : U0009A	Coll: 09/22/XX	Status: Comp	Req #: 77744444
	Recd.: 09/22/XX	Subm Dr:	

Entered: 09/22/XX–0841   Other Dr:
Ordered: UA with micro
Comments: Urine Description: Clean catch urine

Test	Result	Flag	Reference
Urinalysis			
UA with micro			
COLOR	YELLOW		
APPEARANCE	HAZY	**	
SP GRAVITY	1.018		1.001-1.030
GLUCOSE	NORMAL		NORMAL mg/dl
BILIRUBIN	NEGATIVE		NEG
KETONE	NEGATIVE		NEG mg/dl
BLOOD	2+	**	NEG
PH	5.0		4.5-8.0
PROTEIN	TRACE	**	NEG mg/dl
UROBILINOGEN	NORMAL		NORMAL-1.0 mg/dl
NITRITES	NEGATIVE		NEG
LEUKOCYTES	2+	**	NEG
WBC	20-50	**	0-5 /HPF
RBC	2-5		0-5 /HPF
EPI CELLS	20-50		/HPF
BACTERIA	2+	**	
MUCUS			

Patient 1

Urinalysis

urinary catheterization /kăth′ĭ tər ə zā′shən/ insertion of a catheter through the urethra into the bladder to collect urine from the bladder for examination or to aid persons who are incontinent or unable to urinate on their own because of illness or injury.

urinary incontinence /ĭn kŏn′tə nəns/ the inability to voluntarily control the passage of urine from the bladder.

urinary infection /ĭn fĕk′shən/ a urinary tract infection.

urinary system the organs and passages of the body that function together to produce and excrete urine.

urinary tract the organs and passages of the urinary system: kidneys, ureters, bladder, urethra.

urinary tract infection (UTI) an infection in any of the parts of the urinary system.

urination /yo͞or′ə nā′shən/ the act or process of discharging urine from the urinary bladder to the outside of the body. *Also called* micturition.

urine /yo͞or′ĭn/ the normally wheat to pale yellowish fluid consisting mainly of waste produced by the kidneys, excreted through the ureter to the urinary bladder and from the bladder through the urethra, from which it is discharged from the body.

urinometer /yo͞or′ə nŏm′ĭ tər/ an instrument that measures the specific gravity of urine. [urino- + -meter]

uro- *See* ur-.

urobilinogen /yo͞or′ō bī lĭn′ə jən/ a by-product of the breakdown of bilirubin in the intestines.

urodynia /yo͞or′ō dĭn′ē ə/ pain during urination. [uro- + -dynia]

urogenital /yo͞or′ō jĕn′ĭ təl/ of or pertaining to both the urinary and reproductive systems. [uro- + genital]

urogenital system the organs and passages of the urinary system and the reproductive system taken together.

urogram /yo͞or′ə grăm′/ an x-ray of a portion of the urinary tract that has been treated with an opaque medium. [uro- + -gram]

urography /yo͞o rŏg′rə fē/ x-ray imaging of some portion of the urinary tract that has been treated with an opaque medium. [uro- + -graphy]

urolithiasis /yo͞or′ō lĭ thī′ə sĭs/ **1.** the formation of calculi in the urinary tract. **2.** a condition marked by the formation or presence of such calculi. [uro- + -lithiasis]

urologist /yo͞o rŏl′ə jĭst/ a physician who specializes in urology.

urology /yo͞o rŏl′ə jē/ the branch of medicine that studies, diagnoses, and treats diseases of the urinary tract in females and of the urogenital system in males.

uropathy /yo͞o rŏp′ə thē/ any disease or disorder of the urinary tract. [uro- + -pathy]

urostomy /yo͞o rŏs′tə mē/ a surgically created opening to the outside of the body from some part of the urinary tract. [uro- + -stomy]

URTI *abbreviation.* upper respiratory tract infection.

urticaria /ûr′tĭ kâr′ē ə/ an eruption of extremely itchy welts on the skin, sometimes accompanied by swelling and usually occurring as an allergic response, such as to a food or medication. *Also called* hives.

urticaria pigmentosa /pĭg mĕn tō′sə/ a form of mastocytosis (overproduction of mast cells, which are found in connective tissue and involved in allergic reactions) seen chiefly in children, marked by small, itchy, reddish brown eruptions on the trunk and sometimes the head, neck, and extremities.

USDA *abbreviation.* United States Department of Agriculture (www.usda.gov).

USFDA *abbreviation.* United States Food and Drug Administration (www.fda.gov).

Usher('s) syndrome /ŭsh′ər(z)/ an inherited condition marked by deafness and retinitis pigmentosa.

USP *abbreviation. United States Pharmacopeia.*

USP-NF *abbreviation. United States Pharmacopeia—National Formulary.*

uterine /yo͞o′tər ĭn/ **1.** of, pertaining to, or like the uterus. **2.** found in or associated with the uterus.

uterine cancer **1.** endometrial cancer; endometrial carcinoma. **2.** sarcoma of the uterus.

uterine contraction a muscle spasm of the uterus, especially one that occurs as part of the process of giving birth. *See also* labor pain.

uterine lining the lining of the uterus that is sloughed off during menstruation; the endometrium.

uterine tube a tube leading from each ovary to the uterus through which ova travel. *Also called* fallopian tube, oviduct.

utero- *combining form.* uterus: *for example,* uteroplasty.

uterofixation /yo͞o′tə rō fĭk sā′shən/ surgical fixing in place of a descended uterus. [utero- + fixation]

uteroglobin /yo͞o′tə rō glō′bĭn/ a protein found in the uterus, respiratory tract, and prostate of humans that has anti-inflammatory properties and is being studied as a possible inhibitor to the spread of prostate cancer in the body.

uteropexy /yo͞o′tər ə pĕk′sē/ surgical fixing in place of the uterus. [utero- + -pexy]

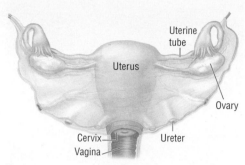

Uterus

uteroplasty /yoo′tər ə plăs′tē/ surgery to repair the uterus; plastic surgery of the uterus. *Also called* metroplasty. [utero- + -plasty]

uterus /yoo′tər əs/ (*pl.* **uteri** /yoo′tə rī′/) the hollow, pear-shaped organ in the lower abdomen of females that produces the menstrual flow and carries the developing fetus during pregnancy.

UTI *abbreviation.* urinary tract infection.

utricle /yoo′trĭ kəl/ the larger of two membranous, pouch-like organs in the inner ear; it helps maintain balance.

UV *abbreviation.* ultraviolet.

uve-, uveo- *combining form.* uvea: *for example,* uveoscleritis.

uvea /yoo′vē ə/ the middle layer of the eye, containing the choroid, the ciliary body, and the iris.

uveitis /yoo′vē ī′tĭs/ inflammation of the uvea. [uve- + -itis]

uveoscleritis /yoo′vē ō sklĭ rī′tĭs/ inflammation of the sclera that initially developed in the uvea. [uveo- + scleritis]

UV radiation *abbreviation.* ultraviolet radiation.

uvul-, uvulo- *combining form.* uvula: *for example,* uvulectomy.

uvula /yoo′vyə lə/ (*pl.* **uvuli** /yoo′vyə lī′/) a small, hanging fleshy mass, especially the clump of tissue that hangs from the soft palate near the opening to the throat.

uvulectomy /yoo′vyə lĕk′tə mē/ surgical removal of the uvula. [uvul- + -ectomy]

uvulitis /yoo′vyə lī′tĭs/ inflammation of the uvula. [uvul- + -itis]

uvulotomy /yoo′vyə lŏt′ə mē/ cutting of the uvula to remove all or part of it. [uvulo- + -tomy]

V

VA *abbreviation.* **1.** vertebral artery. **2.** Veterans Administration **3.** visual acuity.

vaccinate /văk′sə nāt′/ to administer a vaccine to (someone). *Also called* inoculate.

vaccination /văk′sə nā′shən/ **1.** the administration of vaccine. *Also called* inoculation. **2.** the mark or scar left where a dosage of vaccine has been injected.

vaccine /văk sēn′/ a preparation that provides immunity to a specific infectious disease by stimulating the body to produce antibodies, made from killed or attentuated (weakened) bacteria or viruses of that disease or from substances derived from them; usually given by injection.

vacuole /văk′yo͞o ōl′/ a small cavity within the cytoplasm of a cell containing water, secreted waste, and other material.

VAD *abbreviation.* **1.** vascular access device. **2.** vascular assist device; ventricular assist device.

vag-, vago- *combining form.* vagus nerve: *for example,* vagotomy.

vagal /vā′gəl/ of or pertaining to the vagus nerve. [vag- + -al]

vagin-, vagino- *combining form.* vagina: *for example,* vaginoplasty.

vagina /və jī′nə/ (*pl.* **vaginas** or **vaginae** /və jī′nē/) **1.** the female reproductive passage, extending from the cervix of the uterus to the vulva, from which the menstrual flow is discharged, into which the penis of the male is inserted during sexual intercourse, and through which the fetus is delivered in natural delivery. **2.** any type of enclosure in the body like a sheath or tube.

vaginal /văj′ə nəl/ of, pertaining to, or associated with a vagina or the female vagina. [vagin- + -al]

vaginal hysterectomy /hĭs′tə rĕk′tə mē/ surgical removal of the uterus through the vagina.

vaginectomy /văj′ə nĕk′tə mē/ surgical removal of the vagina. [vagin- + -ectomy]

vaginitis /văj′ə nī′tĭs/ inflammation of a vagina or of the female vagina. [vagin- + -itis]

vaginodynia /văj′ə nō dĭn′ē ə/ pain in the vagina. [vagino- + -dynia]

vaginolabial /văj′ə nō lā′bē əl/ of or pertaining to the vagina and labia. [vagino- + labial]

vaginomycosis /văj′ə nō mī kō′sĭs/ fungal infection of the vagina. [vagino- + mycosis]

vaginopathy /văj′ə nŏp′ə thē/ any diseased condition of a vagina or of the female vagina. [vagino- + -pathy]

vaginoplasty /văj′ə nə plăs′tē/ plastic surgery of the vagina. [vagino- + -plasty]

vagotomy /vā gŏt′ə mē/ surgical cutting of the vagus nerve or its branches, done to decrease the secretion of acid gastric juices in the presence of a stomach ulcer. [vago- + -tomy]

vagus /vā′gəs/ (*pl.* **vagi** /vā′jī/) the vagus nerve.

vagus nerve cranial nerve X; either of a pair of sensory and motor nerves involved in speech, swallowing heart muscles, smooth muscles, and certain glands. *Also called* vagus.

Val *abbreviation.* valine.

valgum /văl′gəm/ marked by an abnormal inward turning, as the knee. *See* genu valgum.

valgus /văl′gəs/ marked by an abnormal outward twist or bend of bone, as a deformity of the foot. *See* talipes valgus.

valine (Val) /vā′lēn, văl′ēn/ an essential amino acid, necessary for growth and development, found in most proteins.

vallecula /və lĕk′yə lə/ (*pl.* **valleculae** /və lĕk′yə lē′/) **1.** a groove or crevice on a surface, as of an organ. **2.** the space between the epiglottis and the anterior laryngeal wall

Valsalva maneuver /văl săl′və/ **1.** forcible exhalation of air while the nostrils and mouth are closed, increasing air pressure in the Eustachian tubes, middle ear, and eardrum. **2.** forcible exhalation of air while the glottis is closed, increasing pressure in the chest that impedes the return of venous blood to the heart.

valve /vălv/ **1.** a membranous flap or fold in an organ that opens and closes to prevent the fluid or solid matter moving through it from flowing backward, as in the heart, veins, and digestive tract. **2.** any artificial version of a natural valve used in valve replacement.

valvectomy /văl vĕk′tə mē/ surgical removal of a valve.

valve replacement **1.** surgery to remove a diseased or malfunctioning heart valve and replace it with an artificial or donor valve. **2.** the new valve itself.

valvotomy /văl vŏt′ə mē/ surgical cutting of a valve, especially to correct its functioning.

valvul-, valvulo- *combining form.* valve: *for example,* valvulitis.

valvulitis /văl′vyə lī′tĭs/ inflammation of a valve, especially a heart valve. [valvul- + -itis]

valvuloplasty /văl′vyə lə plăs′tē/ surgery to repair a valve in the heart or a vein. [valvulo- + -plasty]

vapor /vā′pər/ gaseous particles of a drug that can be inhaled as a therapeutic agent.

vaporize /vā′pə rīz′/ to change or cause to change into vapor.

vaporizer /vā′pə rī′zər/ a device for turning a liquid into a vapor, especially a medicinal liquid.

varicella /văr′ə sĕl′ə/ a highly infectious childhood disease with a blistering rash caused by the varicella-zoster virus. *Also called* chickenpox.

varicella-zoster virus /zŏs′tər/ the herpes virus that causes chickenpox in children and herpes zoster (shingles) in adults.

varices /văr′ə sēz′/ plural of varix.

varico- *combining form.* **1.** varix or varicosity. **2.** varicose. *For example,* varicocele.

varicocele /văr′ĭ kə sēl′/ distended or swollen veins in the spermatic cord or in the uterus or ovaries. [varico- + -cele]

varicocelectomy /văr′ĭ kō sē lĕk′tə mē/ surgical ligation of the veins of a varicocele.

varicophlebitis /văr′ĭ kō flə bī′tĭs/ inflammation of a varicose vein. [varico- + phlebitis]

varicose /văr′ĭ kōs′/ **1.** abnormally swollen and distended, as a vein. **2.** of or pertaining to a varix.

varicose veins a chronic, often painful condition marked by the presence of many dilated, misshapen veins in the legs caused by poorly functioning valves. *Also called* varices.

varicosity /văr′ĭ kŏs′ĭ tē/ **1.** the condition of being varicose. **2.** a varix.

variola /və rī′ə lə/ a highly contagious, severe viral disease with fever and pimples that blister and form pocks; has been globally eradicated by vaccine. *Also called* smallpox.

varix /văr′ĭks/ (*pl.* **varices** /văr′ə sēz′/) a distended, misshapen blood or lymph vessel.

varnish /vär′nĭsh/ any of various solutions of resins in solvent, applied to a cavity before placing a restoration in order to protect the tooth against the material making up the implant, crown, or other restoration.

varum /vâr′əm/ marked by an abnormal outward turning, as the knee. *See also* genu varum.

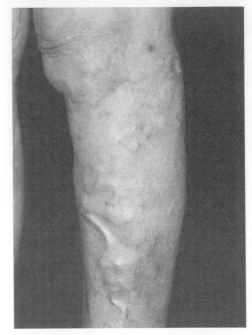
Varicose Veins

varus /vâr′əs/ marked by an abnormal inward twist or bend, as a deformity of the foot. *See also* talipes varus.

vas-, vaso- *combining form.* **1.** blood vessel. **2.** vessel. **3.** vas deferens. *For example,* vasodilation.

vasal /vā′zəl/ of or pertaining to a vessel, especially a blood vessel.

vascular /văs′kyə lər/ **1.** of or pertaining to a vessel, especially a blood vessel. **2.** well supplied with blood vessels. **3.** made up of vessels, especially blood vessels.

vascular access device (VAD) a catheter inserted into a large vein for long-term IV use. *Also called* central venous catheter.

vascular assist device (VAD) any of various small pumps implanted or attached to the central circulation to help pump blood after a heart attack or open-heart surgery. *Also called* ventricular assist device.

vascular disorder any disease or abnormality of the blood vessels.

vascular lesion /lē′zhən/ any abnormal tissue in a blood vessel.

vasculitis /văs′kyə lī′tĭs/ inflammation of a blood vessel. [vascul(ar) + -itis]

vas deferens /văs′ dĕf′ə rĕnz′/ (*pl.* **vasa deferentia** /vā′zə dĕf′ə rĕn′chə/) the duct that carries sperm from the testis up to the seminal vesicle, where it becomes the ejaculatory duct and ends at the prostatic urethra. *Also called* spermatic duct.

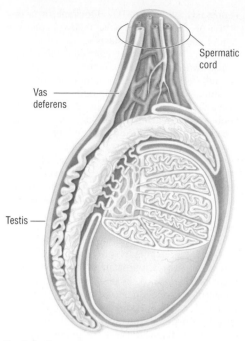

Spermatic cord

Vas deferens

Testis

Vas Deferens

vasectomy /vă sĕk′tə mē/   surgical severing or removal of the vas deferens to prevent sperm from being ejaculated, usually for purposes of birth control. [vas- + -ectomy]

vasoconstriction /vā′zō kən strĭk′shən/   the narrowing of a blood vessel caused by contraction of its muscle tissue, usually accompanied by a decrease in blood flow. [vaso- + constriction]

vasoconstrictor /vā′zō kən strĭk′tər/   **1.** *n.* something, such as ice or a medication, that causes vasoconstriction. **2.** *adj.* causing vasoconstriction. [vaso- + constrictor]

vasodepression /vā′zō dĭ prĕsh′ən/   lessening of resistance in blood vessels thereby lowering blood pressure.

vasodepressor /vā′zō dĭ prĕs′ər/   **1.** *n.* an agent that causes vasodepression and thereby lowers blood pressure. **2.** *adj.* causing vasodepression. [vaso- + depressor]

vasodilation /vā′zō dĭ lā′shən/ or **vasodilatation** /vā′zō dĭl′ə tā′shən/   dilation of a blood vessel. [vaso- + dilation *or* dilatation]

vasodilator /vā′zō dī′lā tər/ or **vasodilatator** /vā′zō dĭl′ĭ tā′tər/   **1.** *n.* something, such as a medication, that causes vasodilation and lowering of blood pressure. **2.** *adj.* causing vasodilation.

vasomotor /vā′zō mō′tər/   **1.** of, pertaining to, or affecting the diameter of a vessel, especially a blood vessel. **2.** of or pertaining to the muscles and nerves that control the diameter of a vessel. [vaso- + motor]

vasoneuropathy /vā′zō nŏŏ rŏp′ə thē/   disease of both the vascular and nervous systems. [vaso- + neuropathy]

vasopressin /vā′zō prĕs′ĭn/   a hormone secreted by the hypothalamus that stimulates or promotes contraction of various muscles, nerves, and organs and reduces the production of urine by the kidney. *Also called* antidiuretic hormone (ADH).

vasopressor /vā′zō prĕs′ər/   **1.** *n.* something that causes vasoconstriction, thereby raising blood pressure. **2.** *adj.* causing vasoconstriction, especially with a rise in blood pressure.

vasorrhaphy /vā zôr′ə fē/   suturing of the vas deferens. [vaso- + -rrhaphy]

vasospasm /vā′zō spăz′əm/   a sudden spasming of blood vessels that causes vasoconstriction. [vaso- + -spasm]

vasostomy /vā zŏs′tə mē/   surgery to create an opening into the vas deferens. [vas- + -ostomy]

vasotomy /vā zŏt′ə mē/   surgical cutting into the vas deferens. [vaso- + -tomy]

vasovagal /vā′zō vā′gəl/   of, pertaining to, affecting, or involving both the blood vessels and the vagus nerve. [vaso- + vagal]

vasovagal syncope /sĭng′kə pē/   fainting due to increased activity of the vagus nerve.

vasovasostomy /vā′zō vā zŏs′tə mē/   surgical reconnection of a vas deferens that has been severed in a vasectomy. [vaso- + vasostomy]

VATS *abbreviation.* video-assisted thoracoscopy.

VC *abbreviation.* **1.** vital capacity. **2.** vocal cord; vocal cords.

VCU *abbreviation.* voiding cystourethrography.

VCUG *abbreviation.* voiding cystourethrogram/cystourethrography.

VD *abbreviation.* venereal disease.

vector /vĕk′tər/   a person, animal, insect, or other organism that carries and transmits the agents of a disease to others without being affected by this disease; a host.

vegetation /vĕj′ĭ tā′shən/   **1.** any abnormal, fungus-like growth on or in tissue, especially in the cardiac valves. **2.** the process of plant growth.

vegetative state /vĕj′ĭ tā′tĭv/   a condition of deep and permanent unconsciousness, without voluntary movement or response, typically as a result of brain injury or disease; brain death.

veil /vāl/   a piece of the amniotic sac covering the head or face of an infant at birth. *Also called* caul.

vein /vān/   any blood vessel that carries blood to the heart.

V

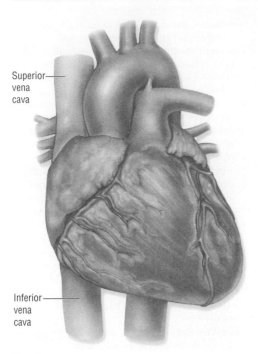

Superior
vena
cava

Inferior
vena
cava

Vena Cava

ven-, veni-, veno- *combining form.* vein: *for example,* venipuncture.

vena cava /vē′nə kā′və/ (*pl.* **venae cavae** /vē′nē kā′vē/)   one of the two large veins, superior and inferior vena cava, of the circulatory system that return deoxygenated blood to the right atrium of the heart.

venereal /və nêr′ē əl/   **1.** of, pertaining to, or caused by sexual intercourse. **2.** of or pertaining to sexually transmitted disease. **3.** of or pertaining to the genitals or genital area.

venereal disease (VD)   any of various contagious diseases contracted through sexual activity. *Also called* sexually transmitted disease, sexually transmitted infection.

venipuncture /vē′nə pŭngk′chər/   the insertion of a needle through the skin and into a vein, as to draw blood for examination or connect an intravenous line. [veni- + puncture]

venogram /vē′nə grăm′/   x-ray image of a vein. *Also called* phlebogram. [veno- + -gram]

venography /vē nŏg′rə fē/   x-ray imaging of a vein. *Also called* phlebography. [veno- + -graphy]

venom /vĕn′əm/   a poisonous fluid secreted by snakes, spiders, and some other creatures, usually transmitted by a bite or sting and ranging in effect from irritating to fatal.

venomous /vĕn′ə məs/   **1.** poisonous; toxic. **2.** secreting venom.

venostasis /vē nŏs′tə sĭs/   blockage or cessation of circulation in a vein. *Also called* venous stasis. [veno- + -stasis]

venotomy /vē nŏt′ə mē/   incision into a vein. *Also called* phlebotomy. [veno- + -tomy]

venous /vē′nəs/   **1.** of, pertaining to, or of the nature of a vein. **2.** belonging to or contained in a vein. **3.** made up of veins. [ven- + -ous]

venous claudication /klô′dĭ kā′shən/   claudication (limping due to insufficient blood flow) resulting from venous stasis.

venous stasis /stā′sĭs/   blockage or cessation of circulation in a vein. *Also called* venostasis.

vent /vĕnt/   an opening in a cavity or channel through which the contents of the cavity are discharged.

ventilation /vĕn′tə lā′shən/   **1.** the process of exchanging air in the lungs by inhaling and exhaling; breathing; respiration. **2.** the circulation or purification of air or gases within an enclosed space. **3.** in psychotherapy, an outpouring of one's pent-up thoughts and feelings.

ventilation-perfusion scan (V/Q) /pər fyōō′ zhən/   a diagnostic test for pulmonary embolism, in which images are taken of the distribution of inhaled and injected radionuclides.

ventilator /vĕn′tə lā′tər/   **1.** breathing device used in mechanical ventilation. *Also called* respirator. **2.** a device used to clear and freshen the air circulating in an enclosed space.

ventral /vĕn′trəl/   **1.** of, pertaining to, or indicating the side of the body opposite the back; anterior. **2.** of, pertaining to, on, or near the abdomen; abdominal.

ventricle /vĕn′trĭ kəl/   a naturally occurring chamber or cavity in an organ, as the bottom

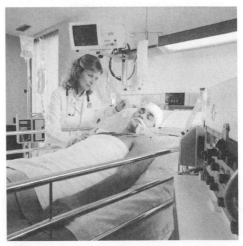

Ventilator

two chambers of the heart or any of the small cavities of the brain.

ventricul-, ventriculo-   *combining form.* ventricle: *for example,* ventriculostomy.

ventricular /věn trĭk′yə lər/   of, pertaining to, or occurring in a ventricle. [ventricul- + -ar]

ventricular assist device (VAD)   any of various small pumps implanted or attached to the central circulation to help pump blood after a heart attack or open-heart surgery. *Also called* vascular assist device.

ventricular fibrillation (VF) /fĭb′rə lā′shən/   rapid, irregular, or disorganized contraction of the ventricles of the heart such that no blood is pumped; fatal unless normal rhythm is immediately restored, as by electric shock.

ventricular septal defect (VSD) /sĕp′təl dē′fĕkt/   an abnormal opening in the ventricular septum, usually congenital and generally requiring surgical repair. *Also called* interventricular septal defect.

ventricular septum /sĕp′təm/   the membranous, muscular partition that separates the right and left ventricles of the heart. *Also called* interventricular septum.

ventricular tachycardia /tăk′ĭ kär′dē ə/   an abnormally fast heart rate initiated in the ventricles, sometimes leading to cardiac arrest.

ventriculitis /věn trĭk′yə lī′tĭs/   inflammation of the ventricles of the brain. [ventriculo- + -itis]

ventriculogram /věn trĭk′yə lə grăm′/   an x-ray image of the ventricles of the brain. [ventriculo- + -gram]

ventriculoperitoneal shunt /věn trĭk′yə lər pĕr′ĭ tə nē′əl shŭnt′/   a shunt of plastic tubing inserted between a cerebral ventricle and the peritoneum, used to treat hydrocephalus. [ventriculo- + peritoneal]

ventriculoscopy /věn trĭk′yə lös′kə pē/   visual examination of the ventricles using an endoscope. [ventriculo- + -scopy]

ventriculostomy /věn trĭk′yə lŏs′tə mē/   the surgical creation of an opening in a ventricle of the brain, used to treat hydrocephalus. [ventricul- + -ostomy]

venule /věn′yool/   a small vein, especially one that receives blood from the capillaries and merges into a larger vein.

vermiform appendix /vûr′mə fôrm ə pĕn′dĭx/   the worm-shaped structure attached to the beginning of the large intestine in the right lower abdomen, generally believed to have no special function but capable of becoming seriously infected. *Also called* appendix.

vernix caseosa /vûr′nĭks kăs′ē ō′sə/   a somewhat oily, cheese-like substance that forms a protective covering on the skin of a fetus or newborn.

verruca /və rōō′kə/ (*pl.* **verrucae** /və rōō′kē, -sē/)   a flesh-colored growth on the skin caused by intradermal viral infection. *Also called* verruga, wart.

verrucous /və rōō′kəs/   **1.** having warts; covered with warts. **2.** rough.

verruga /və rōō′gə/   verruca. *Also called* wart.

-version   *suffix.* turning (of the type specified): *for example,* dextroversion.

version /vûr′zhən/   **1.** the turning or tilting of an organ from its natural position. **2.** the turning of the fetus in the uterus, often done manually during labor to assist delivery. **3.** the rotation of both eyes together in the same direction.

vertebr-, vertebro-   *combining form.* vertebra or vertebrae: *for example,* vertebroplasty.

vertebra /vûr′tə brə/ (*pl.* **vertebrae** /vûr′tə brē′/)   any of the bony segments that make up the spinal column.

vertebral /vûr′tə brəl/   of or pertaining to a vertebra or the vertebrae.

vertebral arch   the bony structure on the dorsal side of a vertebrae, composed of two pedicles and two laminae.

vertebral artery (VA) /är′tə rē/   a branch of the subclavian artery, with four divisions that serve the neck, vertebrae, spinal cord, cerebellum, and cerebrum.

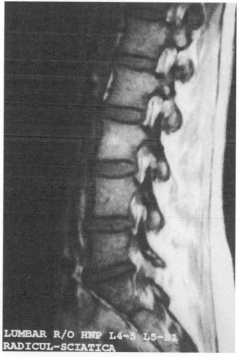

LUMBAR R/O HNP L4-5 L5-S1 RADICUL-SCIATICA

Vertebrae

vertebral body the thick, bony portion of a vertebra opposite the vertebral arch, one separated from the next by an intervertebral disk.

vertebral canal the canal through which the spinal cord, spinal meninges, and related structures pass. *Also called* spinal canal.

vertebral column the series of articulated vertebrae and intervertebral disks that encase the spinal cord. *Also called* spinal column.

vertebral foramen /fə rā′mən/ the opening in the center of a vertebra through which the spinal cord passes.

vertebral rib either of the bottom two ribs on each side of the body, which are not attached to the sternum at all. *Also called* floating rib. *See also* true rib, false rib.

vertebrocostal /vûr′tə brō kŏs′təl/ of or pertaining to both a vertebra and a rib. [vertebro- + costal]

vertebroplasty /vûr′tə brə plăs′tē/ surgical repair of a vertebra. [vertebro- + -plasty]

vertex /vûr′těks/ (*pl.* **vertexes** or **vertices** /vûr′tə sēz′/) the top of something, especially the crown of the head.

vertical /vûr′tĭ kəl/ **1.** located or occurring at right angles to the horizon; straight up and down; upright; perpendicular. **2.** of or pertaining to the vertex.

vertical transmission transmittal of something from one generation to another, as of genes.

vertices /vûr′tə sēz′/ a plural of vertex.

vertigo /vûr′tĭ gō′/ the sensation that oneself or one's surroundings are spinning.

very-high-density lipoprotein (VHDL) /lĭp′ə prō′tēn, -tē ĭn, lī′pə-/ a type of lipoprotein composed of proteins and free fatty acids.

very-low-density lipoprotein (VLDL) a type of lipoprotein that transports triglycerides to fat and muscles.

vesic-, vesico- *combining form.* **1.** bladder: *for example,* vesicoabdominal. **2.** blister: *for example,* vesicant.

vesica /və sī′kə/ (*pl.* **vesicae** /və sī′kē, -sē/) **1.** any membranous sac. **2.** the gallbladder or the urinary bladder.

vesical /věs′ĭ kəl/ of or pertaining to the urinary bladder. [vesic- + -al]

vesicant /věs′ĭ kənt/ **1.** *n.* something that causes a blister, as a drug. **2.** *adj.* causing or forming blisters.

vesicate /věs′ĭ kāt′/ to form a blister or blisters. [vesic- + -ate]

vesicle /věs′ĭ kəl/ **1.** a small, bladder-like structure. **2.** a small, raised, usually fluid-filled lesion on the skin.

vesicoabdominal /věs′ĭ kō ăb dŏm′ə nəl/ of or pertaining to both the abdomen and the urinary bladder or the gallbladder. [vesico- + abdominal]

vesicocele /věs′ĭ kə sēl′/ a herniation of the bladder into the vaginal canal. *Also called* cystocele. [vesico- + -cele]

vesicotomy /věs′ĭ kŏt′ə mē/ surgical incision into the bladder. *Also called* cystotomy. [vesico- + -tomy]

vesicoureteral /věs′ĭ kō yŏŏ rē′tər əl/ of or relating to the bladder and the ureters. *Also called* ureterovesical.

vesicovaginal /věs′ĭ kō văj′ə nəl/ of, pertaining to, or involving both the urinary bladder and the vagina. [vesico- + vaginal]

vesicul-, vesiculo- *combining form.* vesicle: *for example,* vesiculitis.

vesicular /və sĭk′yə lər/ **1.** of, pertaining to, or formed like a vesicle. **2.** formed or made up of vesicles. [vesicul- + -ar]

vesiculectomy /və sĭk′yə lěk′tə mē/ surgical removal of a vesicle, especially a seminal vesicle. [vesicul- + -ectomy]

vesiculitis /və sĭk′yə lī′tĭs/ inflammation of a vesicle, especially a seminal vesicle. [vesicul- + -itis]

vesiculography /və sĭk′yə lŏg′rə fē/ x-ray imaging of a seminal vesicle or vesicles. [vesiculo- + -graphy]

vessel /věs′əl/ a tube, canal, or channel that carries or conducts a fluid in the body, as blood.

vestibul-, vestibulo- *combining form.* vestibule: *for example,* vestibulocochlear.

vestibular /vě stĭb′yə lər/ of, pertaining to, or associated with a vestibule, as of the ear or the female genitals.

vestibular fold either of a pair of folded mucous membranes that stretch across the larynx, near the true vocal cords. Sometimes referred to as the "false vocal cord."

vestibular gland one of several mucus-secreting glands on either side of the vagina in the female or in the urethra of the male.

vestibular nerve either of two branches of a pair of sensory nerves, the vesitbulocochlear nerves (cranial nerve VIII) involved in balance and hearing; this branch carries information about balance from the vestibule of the inner ear to the brain. *See also* vestibulocochlear nerve.

vestibule /věs′tə byōōl′/ a space or chamber in the body leading to the entrance to a canal, as that of the ear, or to a channel, as the vagina.

vestibulocochlear /vě stĭb′yə lō kŏ′klē ər/ of, pertaining to, or involving both the vestibule and the cochlea of the ear. [vestibulo- + cochlear]

vestibulocochlear nerve cranial nerve VIII; either of a pair of sensory nerves which conduct impulses that control both balance and hearing.

Veterinarian

vestige /věs′tĭj/ the remains of a part that had a function in an early stage of development but has largely disappeared.

vestigial /vě stĭj′ē əl/ of, like, or occurring as a vestige; rudimentary; degenerate.

veterinarian /vĕt′ər ə nâr′ē ən/ someone who is licensed to practice veterinary medicine.

veterinary medicine /vĕt′ər ə nĕr′ē/ the branch of medicine concerned with the treatment of animals and their diseases and injuries.

veterinary technician a person who is trained to assist a veterinarian or other biological scientist in the care and management of animals and to perform basic laboratory procedures related to this.

VF *abbreviation.* 1. visual field. 2. ventricular fibrillation.

Vfib /vē′fĭb′/ *abbreviation.* ventricular fibrillation.

VHDL *abbreviation.* very-high-density lipoprotein.

viable /vī′ə bəl/ 1. able to live; able to sustain life. 2. (of a fetus or newborn infant) able to survive outside the uterus.

vial /vī′əl/ a small vessel for holding liquid; small bottle.

video-assisted thoracoscopy (VATS) /thôr′ə kŏs′kə pē/ a procedure for doing a biopsy or other surgery of lung tissue through incisions between two ribs, using surgical instruments and a videoscope.

videoscope /vĭd′ē ə skōp′/ the thin, lighted tube used in video-assisted thoracoscopy.

villus /vĭl′əs/ (*pl.* **villi** /vĭl′ī/) 1. a tiny projection from the surface of a membrane. 2. one of the many tiny vascular projections of the lining of the small intestine that aid in the absorption of nutrients.

Vincent('s) /vĭn′sənt(s)/ **angina** /ăn′jə nə, ăn jī′nə/ or **gingivitis** /jĭn′jə vī′tĭs/ or **infection** a painful pharyngitis marked by ulcerations and swelling, usually resulting from the spread of acute necrotizing ulcerative gingivitis. *Also called* furospirillary gingivitis, necrotizing gingivitis, trench mouth.

vir-, viro- *combining form.* virus: *for example,* virology.

viral /vī′rəl/ of, pertaining to, or caused by a virus. [vir- + -al]

viral hepatitis /hĕp′ə tī′tĭs/ hepatitis caused by a virus, as hepatitis A, hepatitis B, hepatitis C, and others.

viral infection any infection caused by a virus, such as chickenpox, mumps, and the common cold; viruses are not treatable by antibiotics, which work on bacterial infections.

viral load the amount of a virus in the blood, measured as the number of copies of virus RNA per milliliter of blood and used especially to determine the status of HIV disease in a patient.

viral meningitis /měn′ən jī′tĭs/ meningitis caused by a virus, usually of short duration.

viral pneumonia /nōō mōn′yə/ any pneumonia (inflammation of the lung) caused by a virus.

viremia /vī rē′mē ə/ the presence of viruses in the blood. [vir- + -emia]

virgin /vûr′jĭn/ a person who has not yet had sexual intercourse.

virginity /vər jĭn′ĭ tē/ the state or condition of being a virgin.

virile /vĭr′īl/ 1. of, pertaining to, or having the biological attributes and traits of a male; masculine. 2. having the power to procreate; sexually potent.

virilism /vĭr′ə lĭz′əm/ the development or presence of male secondary sexual characteristics in a female.

virilize /vĭr′ə līz′/ to cause (someone) to develop male characteristics; make masculine.

virology /vī rŏl′ə jē/ the branch of science that studies viruses and the diseases they cause and how to prevent and cure them. [viro- + -logy]

virulence /vĭr′yə ləns/ or **virulency** /vĭr′yə lən sē/ 1. the ability of a pathogen to cause a

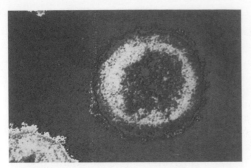

Virus (HIV)

disease. **2.** a severe degree of disease; malignancy; toxicity.

virulent /vĭr′yə lənt/ **1.** able to cause disease, especially severe disease. **2.** (of a disease or condition) marked by virulence; severely malignant or injurious; toxic; deadly.

virus /vī′rəs/ a submicroscopic, disease-causing particle that has some characteristics of a cell, such as RNA or DNA within a casing of protein, but is not considered a living organism and can only reproduce within the body of the host that it invades.

viscer-, viscero- *combining form.* viscera: *for example,* viscerogenic.

viscera /vĭs′ər ə/ (*sing.* **viscus** /vĭs′kəs/) the major internal organs of the body, especially those in the abdominal cavity.

visceral /vĭs′ər əl/ of, pertaining to, in, or involving a viscus or the viscera. [viscer- + -al]

visceralgia /vĭs′ə răl′jē ə, -jə/ pain in an organ or in the viscera. [viscer- + -algia]

visceral pleura /plŏor′ə/ the surface layer of cells on a lung.

viscerogenic /vĭs′ə rō jĕn′ĭk/ of, pertaining to, or indicating reflexes that originate in the viscera. [viscero- + -genic]

visceromotor /vĭs′ə rō mō′tər/ of, pertaining to, or involving movements of or impulses to the viscera. [viscero- + motor]

visceroptosis /vĭs′ə rŏp tō′sĭs/ a lowering or sagging of the viscera from their normal positions. [viscero- + -ptosis]

viscerosensory /vĭs′ə rō sĕn′sə rē/ of or involving sensation or the sensory nerves in the internal organs. [viscero- + sensory]

visceroskeletal /vĭs′ə rō skĕl′ĭ təl/ of or involving the parts of the skeleton that protect the internal organs, as the pelvis or the ribs. [viscero- + skeletal]

viscosity /vĭ skŏs′ĭ tē/ the state of being viscous.

viscous /vĭs′kəs/ thick and gummy; sticky; resistant to flow.

viscus /vĭs′kəs/ singular of viscera.

vision /vĭzh′ən/ the ability to see with the eyes; eyesight.

visual acuity (VA) /vĭzh′oo əl ə kyoo′ĭ tē/ sharpness of vision.

visual acuity test an examination to determine the state of the eyesight, especially one using the Snellen chart.

visual field (VF) the area that the eye can see without movement.

vital /vī′təl/ **1.** of, pertaining to, or characteristic of life or living beings. **2.** necessary for the maintenance of life.

vital capacity (VC) the maximum amount of air that can be exhaled from the lungs after inhaling the greatest possible amount of air.

vital signs (VS) the immediate indicators of a person's physical health, including blood pressure, body temperature, and pulse and respiration rates.

vitamin /vī′tə mĭn/ **1.** any of various fat-soluble or water-soluble organic compounds that occur naturally in foods and are crucial to health and functioning in small amounts but can be toxic in large amounts. **2.** a commercial preparation of such a compound, made to be taken as a dietary supplement.

vitamin A **1.** a fat-soluble compound occurring in several forms that protects the skin and eyesight and is obtained from fish-liver oils, egg yolks, dairy products, yellow fruits and vegetables, and leafy green vegetables. **2.** retinol. **3.** carotene.

vitamin B water-soluble compound (usually appearing as vitamin B complex since there are many compounds of vitamin B) occurring in a variety of forms that play an essential role in metabolism, growth, and the functioning of nerves and muscles and is obtained from a wide range of foods, especially whole-grain cereals, meat, fish, eggs, liver, milk, and yeast.

vitamin C a water-soluble compound that protects against scurvy and is obtained from vegetables and fruits, especially citrus fruits. *Also called* ascorbic acid.

vitamin D a fat-soluble compound occurring in several forms that is essential to the formation and maintenance of bone and is obtained from fish-liver oil, egg yolks, and butter and by exposure to sunlight.

vitamin E a fat-soluble compound occurring in a variety of forms that is essential in normal reproduction and muscle development and is obtained from cereals, wheat-germ oil, beef liver, vegetable oils, and egg yolks.

vitamin K a fat-soluble compound occurring in several forms that is essential to blood clotting and is obtained from spinach, cabbage, liver, and egg yolks through intermediary of certain required intestinal bacteria.

vitamin therapy the treatment of diseases and disorders with vitamins, especially in large dosages, generally used in some alternative medicine practices.

vitiligo /vĭt′ə lī′gō/ a benign, generally progressive skin disorder in which irregular, unpigmented white patches form on the exposed areas of the body.

vitrectomy /vĭ trĕk′tə mē/ surgical removal of the jelly-like matter in the vitreous chamber to clear a cloudy or opacified visual path to the retina of the eye. [vitr(eous) + -ectomy]

vitreous /vĭt′rē əs/ or **vitreous body** or **vitreous humor** the transparent, jelly-like substance that fills the inside of the eyeball between the lens and the retina.

vitreous chamber the interior space of the eyeball that contains the vitreous body.

VLDL *abbreviation.* very-low-density lipoprotein.

vocal /vō′kəl/ of, pertaining to, using, or associated with the voice.

vocal cord or **vocal fold** either of a pair of elastic, membranous folds of tissue that extend from the sides of the larynx and produce sound by vibrating when air from the lungs passes between them.

voice box the part of the respiratory tract between the pharynx and the trachea that contains the vocal cords; the larynx.

void /void/ **1.** *v.* to discharge urine from the body; empty the bladder. **2.** *n.* a discharge of all the urine in the bladder. **3.** *adj.* not effective or usable; not valid, legal, or acceptable.

voiding /voi′dĭng/ the act or process of discharging urine from the urinary bladder to the outside of the body. *Also called* micturition, urination.

voiding cystourethrogram (VCUG) /sĭs′tō yōō rē′thrə grăm′/ an x-ray image made during voiding cystourethrography.

voiding cystourethrography (VCU, VCUG) /sĭs′tō yōōr′ə thrŏg′rə fē/ x-ray imaging of the urethra and urinary bladder before, during, and after the subject urinates a radio-opaque liquid, which has been instilled in the bladder with a catheter.

volar /vō′lər/ of or pertaining to the palm of the hand or the sole of the foot. *See* palmar, plantar.

volume /vŏl′yōōm/ the amount of space that a substance or object occupies, measured in cubic units.

voluntary /vŏl′ən tĕr′ē/ done by choice; controlled by the will.

voluntary muscle any muscle that can be moved at will.

volvulus /vŏl′vyə ləs/ a knotting or twisting of the intestine that creates an obstruction; a surgical emergency because the compromise of blood supply causes the affected part of the bowel to die.

vomer /vō′mər/ or **vomer bone** a thin, flat bone forming the lower and back part of the nasal septum.

vomit /vŏm′ĭt/ **1.** *v.* to expel some or all of the contents of the stomach through the mouth in a forceful spasm, often several times in a row and usually without voluntary control. **2.** *n.* the matter that is expelled in this way; vomitus.

vomiting /vŏm′ĭ tĭng/ the act or action of forcefully expelling the stomach contents through the mouth; emesis; regurgitation.

vomitus /vŏm′ĭ təs/ vomit (def. 2).

Von Willebrand('s) disease /vŏn vĭl′ə brănd(z)/ a hereditary disorder marked by a tendency to bleed extensively, as after surgery or during menstruation, and by various clotting irregularities in the blood. *Also called* angiohemophilia.

voyeur /vwä yûr′, vô-/ a person who engages in voyeurism.

voyeurism /vwä yûr′ĭz əm, voi′ə rĭz′-/ a sexual disorder in which a person derives erotic satisfaction from imagining or secretly watching other people naked or involved in sexual activity. *See also* paraphilia.

V/Q *abbreviation.* ventilation-perfusion.

VS *abbreviation.* vital sign; vital signs.

VT *abbreviation.* ventricular tachycardia.

V-tach /vē′ tăk′/ short for ventricular tachycardia.

VSD *abbreviation.* ventricular septal defect.

vulv-, vulvo- *combining form.* vulva: *for example,* vulvectomy.

vulva vŭl′və/ (*pl.* **vulvae** /vŭl′vē/) the external genital organs of females, chiefly the labia majora, labia minora, clitoris, vestibule of the vagina, and vaginal opening.

vulval /vŭl′vəl/ vulvar. [vulv- + -al]

vulvar /vŭl′vər/ of or pertaining to the vulva. [vulv- + -ar]

vulvectomy /vŭl vĕk′tə mē/ surgical removal of the vulva. [vulv- + -ectomy]

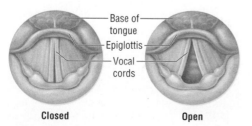

Base of tongue
Epiglottis
Vocal cords

Closed **Open**

Vocal Cords

vulvitis /vŭl vī′tĭs/   inflammation of the vulva. [vulv- + -itis]

vulvodynia /vŭl′vō dĭn′ē ə/   pain in the vulva. [vulvo- + -dynia]

vulvopathy /vŭl vŏp′ə thē/   any disease of the vulva. [vulvo- + -pathy]

vulvovaginal /vŭl′vō văj′ə nəl/   of, pertaining to, or associated with both the vulva and the vagina. [vulvo- + vaginal]

vulvovaginal   candidiasis   /kăn′dĭ dī′ə sĭs/ overgrowth in the vagina and on the vulva of the naturally occurring fungus *Candida*

albicans, usually found in women who have been taking antibiotics for other illnesses or who have immunosuppressive disease. *Also called* candidiasis, monilial vaginitis, moniliasis.

vulvovaginitis /vŭl′vō văj′ə nī′tĭs/   inflammation of both the vulva and the vagina or the vulvovaginal glands. [vulvo- + vagin- + -itis]

W

WAIS *abbreviation*. Wechsler Adult Intelligence Scale.

waist /wāst/ the narrowing part of the torso between the inferior surface of the ribs and the hips.

walker /wô′kər/ a lightweight, three-sided, frame (usually made of aluminum tubing) that is waist high and is used as a support and aid in walking; generally used by someone who has balance and support problems.

walleye /wôl′ī/ **1.** condition with one or both eyes deviating outward; exotropia. **2.** an eye that has no color in the iris. **3.** having a dense white opacity of the cornea. **4.** a large gazing eye.

walleyed /wôl′īd′/ the condition of having a walleye.

warfarin /wôr′fə rĭn/ an anticoagulant drug that is used to treat or prevent atrial fibrillation, blood clots, and overly thick blood; also used as rat poison as it causes the rats to bleed to death.

wart /wôrt/ a small, benign growth on the skin, often on the hands, face, and feet, that has a coarse surface and is caused by a virus. *Also called* verruca.

waste products organic residue produced by the body, such as excrement, urine, and dead cells.

wasting /wā′stĭng/ a process by which the body gradually deteriorates, as in a wasting disease, characterized by weight loss and diminished strength, appetite, and physical and mental vigor.

watchful waiting closely observing a patient's condition to look for changes that would determine the next step in treatment.

water /wô′tər/ a clear odorless fluid covering nearly three quarters of the earth's surface and essential to almost all animal and plant life; water freezes at 32 degrees and boils at 212 degrees (F); the most common solvent.

water-hammer pulse a jerky pulse marked by a strong beat followed by collapse, a sign of a malfunctioning aortic valve. *Also called* cannonball pulse, Corrigan's pulse.

wave /wāv/ a curved pattern of lines representing sound or electrical impulses on an imaging machine, such as an electroencephalogram.

wax /wăks/ **1.** any of various substances that are oily and insoluble in water but soluble in most other organic solvents, and which are solid at room temperature but become soft and melt when heated. **2.** cerumen (earwax). **3.** a substance derived from petroleum, such as paraffin, that can be used for medicinal purposes.

WBC *abbreviation*. **1.** white blood cell. **2.** white blood (cell) count.

WBC count *abbreviation*. white blood cell count.

WBC differential /dĭf′ə rĕn′shəl/ *abbreviation*. white blood cell differential.

WC *abbreviation*. wheelchair.

weakness /wēk′nĭs/ diminished physical strength and vigor.

Weber test /vā′bər, wĕb′ər/ a test for unilateral deafness using a tuning fork.

Wechsler Adult Intelligence Scale (WAIS) /wĕks′lər/ a standardized test for measuring general intelligence in adults (ages 17 and older).

Wechsler Intelligence Scale for Children (WISC) a standardized battery of tests for children ages 6 through 16 designed to evaluate intellectual abilities.

Wegener('s) granulomatosis /vā′gə nər(z) grăn′yə lō′mə tō′sĭs/ an uncommon but serious condition marked by vasculitis (inflammation of the small blood vessels, typically those supplying the lungs, sinuses, and kidneys, resulting in obstruction of the sinuses, bloody nasal discharge and sputum, fever, and weight loss. Thought to be due to an immune disorder, it usually occurs in young to middle-age adults and must be treated promptly or it can be fatal.

weight (wt, wt.) /wāt/ **1.** the force exerted on an object by the pull of gravity, calculated by multiplying the mass of the body by the force of gravity. **2.** a measurement of how heavy an object or the body is.

well-child visit a periodic medical checkup for infants and children aimed at checking a child's health and development; it includes routine immunizations, screening for early detection and treatment of diseases, and parental guidance in general health matters and child-rearing.

wellness /wĕl′nĭs/ the state of maintaining good physical and mental health with an awareness of proper hygiene, diet, exercise, and lifestyle choices.

welt /wĕlt/ a swelling on the skin produced by a blow or due to an allergic reaction. *Also called* wheal.

Wernicke('s) syndrome /vâr′nĭ kē(z)/ a nervous system disease most often seen in patients with long-term alcoholism and caused by a deficiency in thiamin; characterized by lesions in several parts of the brain, double vision, abnormal eye movements, lack of muscle coordination, and mental confusion. Avoiding this catastrophic syndrome is the reason that thiamine is administered to alcoholics who come to emergency rooms for a variety of other complaints.

West Nile virus a disease, transmitted by culex mosquitoes, that occurs in birds, humans, and other mammals and causes flu-like symptoms of varying degrees; in some cases, it causes encephalitis and meningitis.

West('s) syndrome an infantile seizure disorder marked by spasms, arrest of psychomotor development, and an abnormal, chaotic electroencephalogram.

Western blot a technique used in molecular biology to separate and identify protein antigens; used to detect whether antibodies are present for specific antigens.

Western medicine the practice of traditional or conventional medicine as contrasted with complementary or alternative therapies, many of which originated in the East, such as acupuncture and reiki.

wet lung /lŭng/ a rapid onset disorder in which the lungs fail to function as they should. *Also called* acute respiratory distress syndrome, adult respiratory distress syndrome.

wheal /hwēl/ a swelling on the skin produced by a blow or due to an allergic reaction. *Also called* welt.

wheelchair (WC) /hwēl′châr′/ a mobile chair with two large wheels and brakes used by sick or disabled people for transport.

wheeze /hwēz/ to breathe with difficulty due to a narrowed airway, producing a high-pitched or low-pitched whistling sound during both inspiration and expiration. On physical exam of an asthmatic patient, wheezing refers only to an *expiratory* sound of air whistling through tiny obstructed air passages.

whiplash injury /hwĭp′lăsh′/ nonmedical term for an injury to the vertebrae in the neck and the attached muscles and ligaments that is caused by a sudden back and forth motion of the neck and head, as occurs in a rear-end car collision.

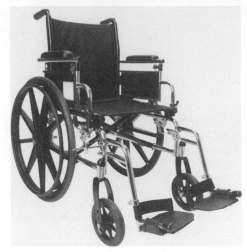

Wheelchair

Whipple('s) disease /hwĭp′əl(z)/ an uncommon intestinal disorder caused by a recently identified bacterium of the genus *Actinomyces*; it results in extreme intestinal malabsorption, arthritis, weight loss, diarrhea, and anemia.

white blood cell (WBC) any of various blood cells that separate into a thin white layer when whole blood is centrifuged, and help protect the body from infection and disease. White blood cells include neutrophils, eosinophils, basophils, lymphocytes, and monocytes. *Also called* leukocyte.

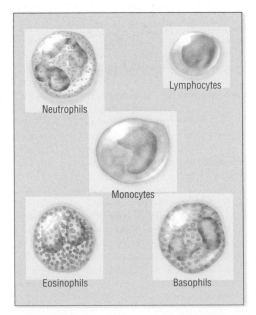

White Blood Cell

white blood cell count (WBC) a blood test that counts the number of white blood cells in a sample of blood; a routine measurement in a complete blood count.

white blood cell (WBC) differential /dĭf′ə rĕn′shəl/ a blood test that measures the percentage of each kind of leukocyte found in a sample of blood (lymphocytes, high in viral infection, eosinophils, high in allergic conditions, and so on; a routine measurement in a complete blood count.

white coat syndrome or **white-coat hypertension** /hī′pər tĕn′shən/ a temporary rise in a patient's blood pressure that occurs in the doctor's office—as it were, at the sight of medical personnel in white coats.

whitehead /hwīt′hĕd′/ a small white pimple or cyst on the skin that forms when a hair follicle is blocked by a combination of skin debris, oil, and bacteria, also known as a "closed comedo"; on exposure of this skin debris to air it becomes black with oxidation, becoming a blackhead.

white matter the areas of the spinal cord and brain that are composed primarily of whitish, myelinated nerve tissue, which contains few or no nerve cell bodies or dendrites; it surrounds and insulates the gray matter, which contains nerve cell bodies and their dendrites.

white of eye the visible white portion of the eye. *Also called* sclera.

WHO *abbreviation*. World Health Organization (www.who.int).

whooping cough /hōō′pĭng, hŏŏp′ĭng/ a highly infectious childhood respiratory disease, caused by the bacterium *Bordatella pertussis*, with spasmodic coughing and deep inhalations. *Also called* pertussis.

Williams(') **syndrome** /wĭl′yəmz(ĭz)/ a rare genetic disorder marked by mild mental retardation, cardiovascular abnormalities (usually supravalvular aortic stenosis—a narrowing of the aorta above the valve), unusual facial features, an overfriendly personality, and hypercalcemia in infancy; caused by the deletion of a small chromosome and a series of adjacent genes.

Wilms(') **tumor** /wĭlmz(ĭz)/ a malignant tumor of the kidney that occurs in young children—usually before age 5; one of the common malignancies of childhood.

Wilson('s) **disease** /wĭl′sən(z)/ a rare inherited disorder of copper metabolism in which excessive amounts of copper slowly accumulate in the liver and are then, over the years, released and taken up in other parts of the body, such as in the red blood cells, brain, and eyes, leading to liver disease and neurological and psychiatric problems; if treated early, recovery is possible.

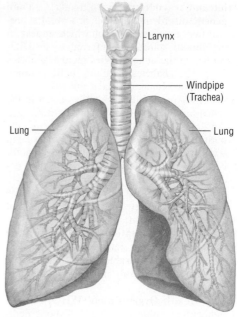

Windpipe

windpipe /wĭnd′pīp′/ membranous tube from the larynx to the bronchi through which inhaled air travels to and from the lungs. *Also called* trachea.

wink /wĭnk/ to close and then open the eyes in quick sequence, as happens involuntarily (blink), or to do so intentionally with one eye as a signal or message.

WISC /wĭsk/ *abbreviation*. Wechsler Intelligence Scale for Children.

wisdom tooth any of the four teeth that are last on either side of the upper and lower jaws; so named because they are the last teeth to emerge, usually when a person is fully grown. *Also called* third molar.

withdrawal /wĭth drô′əl/ **1.** the painful and potentially dangerous physiological changes that occur when a person who has been addicted to a substance over a long time is deprived of the substance. **2.** response to severe stress or danger by withdrawing into oneself, marked by depression, apathy, and lethargy; in extreme cases is associated with schizophrenia.

withdrawal symptoms a group of symptoms, for example, sweating, chills, insomnia, irritability, illness, and anxiety, that appear when a person suffering from addiction is deprived of the usual dose of the addictive substance.

Wolfram('s) syndrome /wŏŏl'frəm(z)/ a rare genetic disorder that results in several abnormalities, the first signs of which appear in childhood; sometimes referred to as DIDMOD, as the abnormalities include *d*iabetes *i*nsipidus, *d*iabetes *m*ellitus, *o*ptic atrophy (leading to blindness), and *d*eafness.

womb /wŏŏm/ hollow muscular organ in the female pelvic cavity in which a fertilized egg develops. *Also called* uterus.

Wood('s) lamp /wŏŏd(z)/ an ultraviolet lamp with a filter that holds back all light except for certain wavelengths that is widely used to examine the skin for infection with various species of fungus; if a fungus is present, the hairs will turn a greenish-yellow fluorescent color under the light.

worker's compensation payments made through a federal or state plan to an employee who is injured or disabled on the job, or who becomes ill as a result of the job, as required by law.

World Health Organization (WHO) an organization within the United Nations dedicated to international health issues, including coordinating global strategies to control and

Wound

prevent diseases and providing information and counseling in health matters (www. who.int).

wound /wŏŏnd/ injury that results in a breakdown in the skin, usually caused by physical force rather than by a disease.

wrist /rĭst/ the joint between the hand and the arm containing eight carpal bones. *Also called* carpus.

wt, wt. *abbreviation*. weight.

xanth-, xantho- *combining form.* yellow: *for example,* xanthoderma.

xanthelasma /zăn′thə lăz′mə/ a skin condition usually found in the elderly, with yellowish patches of plaque particularly on the eyelids.

xanthemia /zăn thē′mē ə/ yellow of the skin from too much carotene in the blood, seen in babies who have a lot of yellow vegetables in their diet. *Also called* carotenemia. [xanth- + (h)em- + -ia].

xanthine /zăn′thēn/ a by-product of the metabolism of nucleoproteins that is found in muscles, urine, and in many organs, and which yields uric acid on oxidation. [xanth- + -ine]

xanthinuria /zăn′thə nŏŏr′ē ə/ **1.** having an abnormally large amount of xanthine in the urine. **2.** a rare genetic disorder in which abnormally large amounts of xanthine are excreted in the urine because of the lack of a certain enzyme required in xanthine metabolism. The excess xanthine can lead to the formation of xanthine stones in the kidney.

xanthochromic /zăn′thə krō′mĭk/ yellowish in color.

xanthoderma /zän′thə dûr′mə/ skin having any kind of yellowish coloration. [xantho- + derma]

xanthoma /zăn thō′mə/ (*pl.* **xanthomas** or **xanthomata** /zăn thō′mə tə/) a nodule under the skin that is yellowish, fatty, and benign; usually caused by the accumulation of cholesterol and associated compounds. [xanth- + -oma]

xanthomatosis /zăn′thō mə tō′sĭs/ any of several disorders of lipid (fat) metabolism that result in the spread of xanthomas (yellowish, fatty deposits) under the skin and in internal organs. [xanthomat(a) + -osis]

xanthopsia /zăn thŏp′sē ə/ an abnormal condition affecting vision in which all objects have a yellow hue; it may occur in jaundice or some forms of drug toxicity. [xanth- + -opsia]

xanthosis /zăn thō′sĭs/ a yellowish discoloration; may be seen in the degenerating tissues of malignant tumors. [xanth- + -osis]

X chromosome /krō′mə sōm′/ the sex chromosome responsible for female characteristics in humans; it is present in both sexes but appears singly in males (XY) and in duplicate in females (XX).

xeno- *combining form.* strange; foreign matter: *for example,* xenophobia.

xenoantigen /zĕn′ō ăn′tĭ jən/ an antigen (something that causes an immune response as the body considers it foreign) that is found in more than a single species. [xeno- + antigen]

xenobiotic /zĕn′ō bī ŏt′ĭk/ of or related to a synthetic organic substance that is foreign to the body and potentially poisonous. [xeno- + -biotic]

xenograft /zĕn′ə grăft′/ tissue taken from an animal of one species and used as a graft, often temporarily, in an animal of another species. *Also called* heterograft. [xeno- + graft]

xenophobia /zĕn′ə fō′bē ə/ fear of strangers. [xeno- + -phobia]

xenophthalmia /zĕn′ŏf thăl′mē ə/ inflammation of the eye resulting from a foreign body in the eye.

xenotransplantation /zĕn′ō trăns′plăn tā′shən/ cross-species transplantation. [xeno- + transplantation]

xer-, xero- *combining form.* dryness: *for example,* xerophagia.

xeroderma /zĕr′ə dûr′mə/ having abnormally dry and rough skin. [xero- + derma]

xerogram /zĕr′ə grăm′/ xeroradiograph, which has the appearance of a negative with heightened contrast or "edge enhancement." [xero- + -gram]

xeromammography /zĕr′ō mă mŏg′rə fē/ the use of xeroradiography to produce x-ray images of the breasts. [xero- + mammography]

xerophagia /zĕr′ə fā′jə, -jē ə/ a dry diet. [xero- + -phagia]

xerophthalmia /zĕr′ŏf thăl′mē ə/ a condition in which the conjunctiva of the eye and the corneas are abnormally dry and without luster. [xer- + -ophthalm- + -ia]

xeroradiograph /zĕr′ō rā′dē ə grăf′/ an x-ray image created by xeroradiography. [xero- + radiograph]

xeroradiography /zĕr′ō rā′dē ŏg′rə fē/ an x-ray technique that uses a specially coated plate in place of film, and a powder toner in place of liquid chemicals, to create an image electrically rather than chemically; the resulting image, which has better edge contrast than a normal x-ray, is then transferred to paper as a permanent record. [xero- + radiography]

xerosis /zê rō′sĭs/ abnormal dryness in a body part or tissue; in particular, the skin, eyes, or mucous membranes. [xer- + -osis]

xerostomia /zêr′ə stō′mē ə/ dryness of the mouth. [xero- + stom- + -ia]

xiph-, xipho- *combining form.* sword-shaped; the xiphoid process: *for example,* xiphodynia.

xiphocostal /zĭf′ə kŏs′təl/ pertaining to the xiphoid process and the ribs. [xipho- + costal]

xiphodynia /zĭf′ə dĭn′ē ə/ pain in the xiphoid process. [xipho- + -dynia]

xiphoid process /zĭf′oid/ the lowest and smallest of the three parts of the sternum (breastbone); it comes to a point at the bottom and is made of cartilage early in life and may become bony in adulthood. [xiph- + -oid]

X-linked of or relating to a gene that is located on an X chromosome.

x-ray **1.** high-energy electromagnetic radiation that can penetrate most substances; the rays can be used in low doses to create radiographic images of the internal organs and structures of the body for diagnosing diseases and checking the integrity of the skeletal system; the rays can also be used in higher doses to destroy diseased tissues as a treatment for cancer. **2.** a radiographic image produced by projecting x-rays through the body onto film. **3.** to make a radiographic image.

XRT *abbreviation.* radiation therapy.

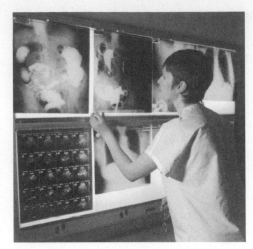

X-ray

Y

yawn /yôn/ **1.** *v.* to open the mouth fully while inhaling deeply and then gradually exhaling; usually done involuntarily, sometimes to balance the oxygen and carbon dioxide in the body or out of boredom, fatigue, or on seeing someone else yawn. **2.** *n.* the act of yawning.

yaws /yôz/ a common infectious disease of tropical areas caused by the spirochete *Treponema pertenue*, usually associated with overcrowding and poor hygiene; it is almost always found in children under age 15 and is marked by bumps on all the extremities, which later turn to ulcers and if left untreated, cause bone and joint deformities. It is easily treated with antibiotics, especially penicillin, when available.

Y chromosome /krō′mə sōm′/ the sex chromosome responsible for male characteristics; among humans, it is present only in males, and appears together with a single X chromosome.

yeast /yēst/ a group of single-celled fungi that are found in substances containing sugar, such as fruits, and in soil, the vegetative parts of plants, and many other places; they are sometimes the source of fungal infections in the body.

yeast infection an overgrowth of yeast, often from the *Candida* family, in various parts of the body, and usually in a moist area such as the mouth, digestive tract, or vagina; it is treated with antifungal medications.

yeast rash a slightly raised, reddish rash on the skin, often under the arms or in the groin, that results from the proliferation of yeast; it is most common in infants and can be treated with topical antifungal medications.

yellow bone marrow fat-laden bone marrow found at the end of long bones in adults.

yellow fever an infectious tropical disease caused by an arbovirus found most often in Africa and the Americas that is transmitted by mosquitoes, and in its most severe form is characterized by high fever, vomiting, gastrointestinal hemorrhaging, and degeneration of kidney and liver tissue leading to jaundice (hence the name "yellow" fever). Prevention with vaccination is best since treatment is purely supportive.

yersiniosis /yər sĭn′ē ō′sĭs/ a common infectious disease caused by bacteria of the genus *Yersinia*; it is most often transmitted by infected food and water, especially raw or undercooked pork products, and is characterized by diarrhea, enteritis, ileitis, and sometimes septicemia or acute arthritis.

Yoga

Y-linkage the state of being a gene located on a Y chromosome.

Y-linked of or relating to a gene that is located on a Y chromosome.

yoga /yō′gə/ a spiritual practice that combines ethical precepts, a prescribed diet, meditation, and specific physical exercises into a way of life aimed at attaining a healthy, balanced, and more transcendent state of mind and body.

yolk sac /yōk′ săk′/ a membranous sac that forms around the embryo in the earliest development as a source of nutrients and which, in humans, then disappears to be replaced by the appearance of the circulatory system.

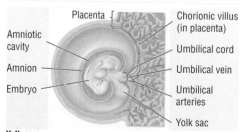

Yolk sac

393

ZIFT *abbreviation.* zygote intrafallopian transfer.

zinc /zĭngk/ a metallic element that is a cofactor in many proteins and essential for normal metabolism.

zinc oxide /ŏk′sīd/ a compound of zinc that is composed of a yellowish or white powder; often used as a pigment or as an astringent in pharmaceutical and cosmetic preparations, such as creams, powders, and ointments (used as an opaque sunscreen).

zona /zō′nə/ (*pl.* **zonae** /zō′nē/) in anatomy, zone.

zone /zōn/ **1.** a cylindrical, belt-like structure or area. **2.** an anatomical layer or band.

zonule /zōn′yōōl/ or **zonula** /zōn′yə lə/ (*pl.* **zonulae** /zōn′yə lē′/) a small belt-like area, as of a ligament.

zoo- *combining form.* animal: *for example,* zoograft.

zoograft /zō′ə′grăft′/ a graft taken from an animal. [zoo- + graft]

zoonosis /zō′ə nō′sĭs/ a disease infecting animals that can be transmitted to humans through its animal host, such as rabies.

zoonotic /zō′ə nŏt′ĭk/ of or pertaining to a zoonosis.

zooparasite /zō′ə păr′ə sīt′/ a parasite that is an animal, for example, a worm. [zoo- + parasite]

zoophilia /zō′ə fĭl′ē ə/ **1.** having a strong liking for animals, especially to an extreme degree. **2.** a sexual disorder of being sexually or erotically attracted to animals. [zoo- + -philia]

zoophobia /zō′ə fō′bē ə/ having an extreme, persistent, irrational fear of animals, especially a fear of dogs, snakes, insects, and mice. [zoo- + -phobia]

zyg-, zygo- *combining form.* a union; a pair or yoke: *for example,* zygoma.

zygoma /zī gō′mə/ (*pl.* **zygomas** or **zygomata** /zī gō′mə tə/) zygomatic bone. [zyg- + -oma]

zygomatic arch /zī′gə măt′ĭk/ zygomatic bone.

zygomatic bone the cheekbone—part of the temporal bone of the skull. *Also called* zygomatic arch.

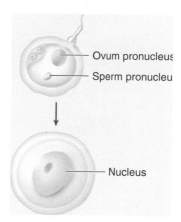

Ovum pronucleus

Sperm pronucleu

Nucleus

Zygote

zygomycosis /zī′gō mī kō′sĭs/ an acute fungal infection caused by a class of water molds that is usually transmitted by air; it is seen most often in patients whose immune systems are compromised. [zygo- + mycosis]

zygote /zī′gōt/ the fertilized egg or ovum; the cell resulting from the union of a sperm (male sex cell) and an ovum (female sex cell).

zygote intrafallopian transfer (ZIFT) /ĭn′trə fə lō′pē ən/ a fertilization technique in which a woman's eggs are retrieved from the body, fertilized and cultured in a laboratory, and then placed in one of her fallopian tubes for normal development (migration to the uterus and implantation in the endometrium).

-zygous *suffix.* of or relating to a zygote: *for example,* hemizygous.

zymo- *combining form.* fermentation; enzymes: *for example,* zymogenesis.

zymogenesis /zī′mō jĕn′ə sĭs/ the process by which a proenzyme (the precursor of an enzyme) is changed into an active enzyme. [zymo- + genesis]

zymosis /zī mō′sĭs/ **1.** an infectious disease caused by a fungus. **2.** fermentation.

zymotic /zī mŏt′ĭk/ of or relating to zymosis.

CONTENTS TO THE APPENDICES

Appendices

Appendix A:

Combining Forms, Prefixes, and Suffixes

Listed below are the combining forms, prefixes, and suffixes that appear in this dictionary. They are useful in building medical terms.

A

a-, an-   *prefix.* not, without, lacking.

ab-   *prefix.* from; away; off.

abdomin-, abdomino-   *combining form.* abdomen.

acanth-   *combining form.* thorny or having spines.

acet-, aceto-   *combining form.* two-carbon fragment of acetic acid.

- acousis, -acusis -   *suffix.* hearing.

acro-   *prefix.* **1.** end, tip, or peak. **2.** extremity.

acromi-, acromio-   *combining form.* the acromion.

actin-, actino-   *combining form.* ray, beam; having raylike structures.

ad-   *prefix.* to, toward, near the midline.

-ad   *suffix.* toward, in the direction of.

aden-, adeno-   *combining form.* gland or glandular.

adipo-   *combining form.* fat, fatty.

adren-, adreno-, adrenal-, adrenalo-   *combining form.* adrenal gland.

aero-   *combining form.* air.

agglutin-, agglutino-   *combining form.* adhere or combine.

-al   *suffix.* of or involving; process.

algesio-   *combining form.* pain.

-algesia   *suffix.* pain.

-algia   *suffix.* pain or a specific painful condition.

algo-   *combining form.* pain.

allo-   *prefix.* of the same species.

alveol-, alveolo-   *combining form.* alveolus.

ambi-   *combining form.* **1.** around, on all sides. **2.** both, double.

amnio-   *combining form.* amnion.

an-[1]   *prefix.* not.

an-[2]**, ana-**   *prefix.* up; upward; back; backward.

andr-, andro-   *combining form.* masculine.

angi-, angio-   *combining form.* blood or lymph vessel.

aniso-   *combining form.* not equal, disimilar.

ankyl-, anklyo-   *combining form.* fused; stiffened.

ant-, anti-   *prefix.* against, opposite.

ante-   *prefix.* **1.** before: *for example,* antepartum. **2.** in front of.

antero-   *prefix.* anterior.

anthrac-, anthraco-   *combining form.* coal; carbon; carbuncle.

-apheresis   *combining form.* removal, separation.

apic-, apico-   *combining form.* apex.

apo-   *prefix.* separated from; derived from.

aponeur-, aponeuro-   *combining form.* tendon-like.

append-   *combining form.* appendage, appendix.

appendic-, appendico-   *combining form.* appendix.

arteri-, arterio-   *combining form.* artery.

arteriol-, arteriolo-   *combining form.* arteriole.

arthr-, arthro-   *combining form.* joint.

astro-   *combining form.* star.

-ate   *suffix.* replaces "-ic" in acids after the acid has been neutralized, such as nitrate from nitric acid.

ather-, athero-   *combining form.* soft fatty deposit.

atri-, atrio-   *combining form.* atrium.

audio-   *combining form.* sound, hearing.

aut-, auto-   *combining form.* self, same.

B

bacteri-, bacterio-   *combining form.* bacteria.

balan-, balano-   *combining form.* glans penis.

bar-, baro-   *combining form.* weight, pressure.

bas-, baso-   *combining form.* base; foundation.

bi-   *prefix.* twice, double.

bio-   *combining form.* life, living.

blast-, blasto-   *combining form.* immature cell.

-blast   *suffix.* immature, forming.

blephar-, blepharo-   *combining form.* eyelid.

brachi-, brachio-   *combining form.* arm.

brachy-   *combining form.* short.

brady-   *combining form.* slow.

bronch-, bronchi-, broncho-   *combining form.* bronchus, bronchi.

bronchiol-   *combining form.* bronchiole.

bucc-, bucco-   *combining form.* cheek.

burs-, burso-   *combining form.* bursa, bursae.

C

calcaneo-   *combining form.* heel.

calic-, calico-, calio-   *combining form.* calyx.

capno-   *combining form.* carbon dioxide.

carcin-, carcino-   *combining form.* cancer.

card-, cardi-, cardio-   *combining form.* heart.

-cardia   *suffix.* the condition of having a specific kind of heart or heartbeat.

carp-, carpo-   *combining form.* wrist.

cata-   *prefix,* down.

cec-, ceco-   *combining form.* cecum.

-cele   *suffix.* **1.** tumor or swelling.. **2.** cavity.

celio-   *combining form.* abdomen.

-centesis   *suffix.* puncture.

centi-   *prefix.* one hundred.

cephal-, cephalo-   *combining form.* head.

-cephaly   *suffix.* head.

cerebr-, cerebro-   *combining form.* cerebrum.

cervic-, cervico-   *combining form.* neck.

cheil-, cheilo-   *combining form.* lips.

chemo-   *combining form.* chemical.

chlor-, chloro-   *combining form.* **1.** green. **2.** chlorine.

chol-, chole-, cholo-   *combining form.* bile.

cholang-, cholangi-, cholangio-   *combining form.* bile duct.

cholecyst-, cholecysto-   *combining form.* gallbladder.

choledoch-, choledocho-   *combining form.* the common bile duct.

chondr-, chondro-   *combining form.* cartilage.

chorio-   *combining form.* membrane, especially the chorion.

chrom-, chromat-, chromo-   *combining form.* color.

chron-, chrono-   *combining form.* time.

chyl-, chylo-   *combining form.* chyle.

-cidal   *suffix.* killing.

-cide   *suffix.* one that kills.

cine-   *combining form.* movement.

circum-   *prefix.* around.

-clasis   *suffix.* breaking.

-clast   *suffix.* breaking.

cleido-   *combining form.* clavicle.

clino-   *combining form.* sloping: curving.

co-, com-, con-   *prefix.* with, together.

-coccus   *suffix.* belonging to a group of bacteria having a spherical shape.

cochle-, cochleo-   *combining form.* of or relating to the inner ear.

col-, colo-   *combining form.* colon.

colp-, colpo-   *combining form.* vagina.

com-   *prefix.* with, together.

con-   *prefix.* with, together.

condyl-   *combining form.* rounded, knob-like, condyle.

contra-   *prefix.* opposed, against..

cor-, core-, coreo-   *combining form.* pupil.

corne-, corneo-   *combining form.* cornea.

cortic-, cortico-   *combining form.* cortex.

cost-, costo-   *combining form.* rib.

counter-   *prefix.* against.

crani-, cranio-   *combining form.* skull.

-crine   *suffix.* secreting.

cryo-   *combining form.* cold.

crypt-, crypto-   *combining form.* hidden or obscure.

culdo-   *combining form.* pouch.

-cusis   *suffix.* hearing.

cyan-   *combining form.* blue.

cycl-, cyclo-   *abbreviation.* circle; cycle; ciliary body.

cyst-, cysto-   *combining form.* **1.** the bladder. **2.** cyst.

cyt-, cyto-   *combining form.* a cell.

-cyte   *suffix.* a cell.

D

dacryo-   *combining form.* tear or tears; lacrymal sac or duct

dacryocyst-, dacryocysto-   *combining form.* of or involving the lacrimal sac.

dactyl-, dactylo-   *combining form.* fingers; toes.

-dactyly   *suffix.* the condition of have a specified kind or number of fingers or toes.

de-   *prefix.* away from.

dent-, denti-   *combining form.* teeth.

derm-, derma-, dermo-   *combining form.* skin.

-derma   *suffix.* skin.

dermat-, dermato-   *combining form.* skin.

-desis   *suffix.* binding.

desm-, desmo-   *combining form.* fibrous connection; ligament.

dextr-, dextro-   right.

dextro-   *combining form.* right; on the right side.

di-   *prefix.* two, twice.

dia-   *prefix.* through, throughout, completely.

dipl-, diplo-   *combining form.* double, two-fold.

dips-, dipso-   *combining form.* thirst.

dis-   *prefix.* in two, apart.

dors-, dorsi-, dorso-   *combining form.* back.

dynamo-   *combining form.* strength or force; energy.

-dynia   *suffix.* pain.

dys-   *prefix.* abnormal, difficult.

E

echo-   *combining form.* sound.

-ectasia, -ectasis   *suffix.* dilation, expansion.

ecto-   *combining form.* outer, on the outside.

-ectomy   *suffix.* excision, removal.

ectro-   *combining form.* missing (usually from birth).

-edema   *suffix.* swelling.

electro-   *combining form.* electrical.

embryo-   *combining form.* of or relating to an embryo.

-emesis   *suffix.* vomit.

-emia   *suffix.* blood.

encephal-, encephalo-   *combining form.* the brain.

end-, endo-   *combining form.* within, inner, absorbing, or containing.

enter-, entero-   *combining form.* intestines.

epi-   *prefix.* over.

epididym-, epididymo-   *combining form.* epididymis.

episo-   *combining form.* vulva.

erythro-   *combining form.* red, redness.

esophag-, esophago-   *combining form.* esophagus.

-esthesia   *suffix.* sensation, perception.

eu-   *prefix.* well, good, normal.

exo-   *prefix.* external, on the outside.

extra-   *prefix.* without, outside of.

F

fasci-, fascio-   *combining form.* a band of fibrous tissue.
femor-, femoro-   *combining form.* relating to the femur or thigh.
-ferous   *suffix.* carrying, yielding.
fet-, feti-, feto-   *combining form.* fetus
fibr-, fibro-   *combining form.* fiber.
fibrin-, fibrino-   *combining form.* fibrin.
fluor-, fluoro-   *combining form.* **1.** fluorine. **2.** fluorescence.
-form   *suffix.* having the form of.
fung-, fungi-, fungo-   *combining form.* fungus.

G

galact-, galacto-   *combining form.* milk.
gameto-   *combining form.* gamete.
gangli-, ganglio-   *combining form.* ganglion.
gastr-, gastro-   *combining form.* stomach.
-gen   *suffix.* precursor of.
-genesis   *suffix.* origin; production.
-genic   *suffix.* producing; generating.
geno-   *combining form.* gene, genetic.
geronto-   *combining form.* old age.
gingiv-, gingivo-   *combining form.* gum.
gli-, glia-, glio-   *combining form.* neuroglia.
-globin   *suffix.* protein.
-globulin   *suffix.* protein.
gloss-, glosso-   *combining form.* tongue.
gluc-, gluco-   *combining form.* glucose.
glyc-, glyco-   *combining form.* sugar, glycogen.
gnatho-   *combining form.* jaw.
gonio-   *combining form.* angle.
-gram   *suffix.* a written record.
granul-, granulo-   *combining form.* granule or granular.
-graph   *suffix.* instrument.
gyne-, gynec-, gyneco-   *combining form.* woman.

H

hem-, hemo-   *combining form.* blood.
hemangi-, hemangio-   *combining form.* blood vessel.
hemat-, hemato-   *combining form.* blood.
hemi-   *combining form.* half.
hepat-, hepato-   *combining form.* liver.
hernio-   *combining form.* hernia.
hetero-   *combining form.* other; different.
hidr-, hidro-   *combining for.* sweat; sweat glands.
hist-, histo-   *combining form.* body tissue.
histi-, histio-   *combining form.* body tissue, especially connective tissue.
homeo-, homo-   *combining form.* like; similar.
hyal-   *combining form.* glassy.

hydr-, hydro- *combining form.* water, liquid.
hymen-, hymeno- *combining form.* hymen.
hyper- *prefix.* excessive or above normal.
hypo- *prefix.* low, below normal.

I

-ia *suffix.* condition; disease.
-iasis *suffix.* pathological condition characterized or produced by.
-ic *suffix.* of, pertaining to, relating to, or characterized by.
ichthy-, ichthyo- *combining form.* fish or fishlike.
-ics *suffix.* the science or study of.
idio- *combining form.* unknown.
ile-, ileo- *combining form.* ileum.
immuno- *combining form.* immune; immunity.
in- *prefix.* into or not.
infra- *prefix.* inferior, below, or beneath.
inter- *prefix.* between; within.
intra- *prefix.* within.
irid-, irido- *combining form.* iris of the eye.
ischi-, ischio- *combining form.* ischium.
-ism *suffix.* state or condition of.
iso- *prefix.* equal; uniform.
-itis *suffix.* inflammation or disease of.

J

jejun-, jejuno- *combining form.* jejunum.

K

karyo- *combining form.* nucleus.
kerat-, kerato- *combining form.* **1.** the cornea. **2.** horny tissue or cells.
ket-, keto- *combining form.* ketone or ketone group.
-kinesia *suffix.* motion.
-kinesis *suffix.* movement or activation.
-kinetic *suffix.* of or relating to motion or movement.
kyph-, kypho- *combining form.* abnormal curvature of the spine; hunchback.

L

labi-, labio- *combining form.* lips.
lact-, lacti-, lacto- *combining form.* milk.
laparo- *combining form.* abdomen, abdominal wall.
laryng-, laryngo- *combining form.* the larynx.
later-, latero- *combining form.* side.
leiomy-, leiomyo- *combining form.* smooth muscle.
-lepsy *suffix.* seizure.
lept-, lepto- *combining form.* thin, narrow, weak, delicate.
-leptic *suffix.* a type of seizure.
leuk-, leuko- *combining form.* white.
levo- *combining form.* left.
lip-, lipo- *combining form.* fat.

lith-, litho-   *combining form.* stone, calculus, calcification.
-lith   *suffix.* stone, calculus, calcification.
-lithiasis   *suffix.* stone formation or condition.
lob-, lobo-   *combining form.* lobe.
-logy   *suffix.* the science or study of.
lumb-, lumbo-   *combining form.* loins.
lymph-, lympho-   *combining form.* lymph.
lymphaden-, lymphadeno-   *combining form.* lymph node.
-lytic   *suffix.* involving or pertaining to lysis (of the matter or type specified).

M

macro-   *prefix.* large; long.
mal-   *prefix.* bad, ill; abnormal.
-malacia   *suffix.* softening.
mamm-, mamma-, mammo-   *combining form.* breast.
-mania   *suffix.* having an extreme compulsion for something.
mast-, masto-   *combining form.* breast.
mastoid-, mastoido-   *combining form.* breast.
maxill-, maxillo-   *combining form.* maxilla.
meat-, meato-   *combining form.* meatus.
medi-, medio-   *combining form.* middle; central.
mediastin-, mediastino-   *combining form.* mediastinum.
megalo-   *prefix.* **1.** very large; huge. **2.** abnormally large; enlarged.
-megaly   *suffix.* abnormal enlargement or growth.
melan-, melano-   *combining form.* melanin.
-melia   *suffix.* limb.
mening-, meningi-, meningo-   *combining form.* meninges; membrane,
meno-   *combining form.* menses; menstruation.
mento-   *combining form.* chin.
mes-, meso-   *combining form.* **1.** middle; central. **2.** intermediate; in between. **3.** mesentery.
mesio-   *combining form.* mesial.
meta-   *prefix.* after, behind, altered.
-meter   *suffix.* instrument for or method of measuring.
metr-, metri-, metro-   *prefix.* uterus.
-metry   *suffix.* process or method of measuring something.
micro-   *prefix.* meaning small.
mid-   *prefix.* middle.
milli-   *prefix.* one thousand, especially in the metric system.
mon-, mono-   *combining form.* involving one element or part; single; alone.
-morph   *suffix.* having a specified form or shape.
morpho-   *combining form.* form, shape, or structure.
muc-, muci-, muco-   *combining form.* mucus; mucous.
multi-   *prefix.* many.
my-, myo-   *prefix.* muscle.
myc-, myco-   *combining form.* fungus.
myel-, myelo-   *combining form.* **1.** bone marrow. **2.** the spinal cord and medulla oblongata. **3.** the myelin sheath enclosing nerve fibers.
myo-   *combining form.* muscle.
myocardi, mycardio-   *combining form.* myocardium.
myx-, myxo-   *combining form.* mucus.

N

narc-, narco-   *combining form.* numbness or drowsiness.
nas-, naso-   *combining form.* nose.
necr-, necro-   *combining form.* death or corpse.
neo-   *prefix.* new, recent.
nephr-, nephro-   *combining form.* kidney.
neur-, neuri-, neuro-   *combining form.* nerve, nervous system.
noct-, nocti-, nocto-   *combining form.* night.
non-   *prefix.* the reverse or opposite of something; not.
norm-, normo-   *combining form.* normal,
nyct-, nycto-   *combining form.* night.

O

ocul-, oculo-   *combining form.* eye.
odont-, odonto-   *combining form.* tooth, teeth.
-odynia   *suffix.* pain.
-oid   *suffix.* like, resembling.
olig-, oligo-   *combining form.* too few, too little; scanty.
-oma (*pl.* **-omas** or **-omata**)   *suffix.* tumor, neoplasm.
oment-, omento-   *combining form.* omentum.
omphal-, omphalo-   *combining form.* navel; umbilicus.
onco-   *combining form.* tumor, mass, swelling.
onych-, onycho-   *combinng form.* nail.
oo-   *combining form.* egg.
oophor-, oophoro-   *combining form.* ovary.
ophthalm-, ophthalmo-   *combining form.* eye.
-opia   *suffix.* vision.
-opsia   *suffix.* defect in vision or eyesight.
-opsy   *suffix.* examination; viewing; process of viewing.
opt-, opto-   *combining form.* vision.
or-, oro-   *combining form.* mouth.
orch-, orchi-, orchid-, orchido-, orchio-   *combining form.* testicle.
organo-   *combining form.* organ.
orth-, ortho-   *combining form.* straight, correct.
-ose   *suffix.* **1.** full of. **2.** carbohydrate.
-osis   *suffix.* condition; disorder.
ost-, oste-, osteo-   *combining form.* bone.
ot-, oto-   *combining form.* ear.
-ous   *suffix.* full of, possessing.
ov-, ovi-, ovo-   *combining form.* egg.
ovari-, ovario-   *combining form.* ovary.
over-   *prefix.* excessive; above normal.
-oxia   *suffix.* oxygen.
oxy-   *combining form.* 1. oxygen. 2. pointed.

P

pachy-   *combining form.* thick.
palato-   *combining form.* palate.

pan- *prefix.* all; entire; the whole.

pancreat-, pancreato- *combining form.* pancreas.

par-, para- *prefix.* **1.** near; beside. **2.** beyond; outside. **3.** assistant; associate. **4.** abnormal.

-para *suffix.* woman who has borne the indicated number of children.

-parous *suffix.* giving birth to; bearing.

-partum *suffix.* labor and childbirth.

-pathic *suffix.* of or pertaining to disease.

patho- *combining form.* disease.

-pathy *suffix.* disease or diseased condition.

ped-, pedi-, pedo- *combining form.* **1.** child. **2.** foot or feet.

pelv-, pelvi- *combining form.* pelvis.

-penia *suffix.* lack, deficiency.

-pepsia *suffix.* digestion.

per- *prefix.* **1.** through. **2.** intensely.

peri- *prefix.* about, around, near.

pericardi-, pericardio- *combining form.* near the heart; pericardium.

perine-, perineo- *combining form.* perineum.

peritone-, peritoneo- *combining form.* peritoneum.

-pexy *suffix.* fixation; attachment.

phac-, phaco- *combining form.* shaped like a lens; birthmark.

-phag-, phago- *combining form.* consuming, eating.

-phage, -phagia, -phagy *suffix.* consuming, eating.

phalang-, phalango- *combining form.* finger, toe.

pharmaco- *combining form.* drugs.

-phasia *suffix.* speech disorder.

-phil, -phile, -philic, -philia *suffix.* love; desire for.

phleb-, phlebo- *combining form.* vein.

-phobia *suffix.* fear.

-phobic *suffix.* suffering from a phobia.

phon-, phono- *combining form.* sound, voice.

-phonia *suffix.* sound.

-phoresis *suffix.* carrying, transmission.

-phoria *suffix.* feeling.

phot-, photo- *combining form.* light.

phren-, phreno- *combining form.* diaphragm.

-phrenia *suffix.* mental disorder.

-phthisis *suffix.* wasting away, shriveling.

-phylaxis *suffix.* protection.

phyto- *combining form.* plant.

-plakia *suffix.* plaque (small patch on skin).

-plasia *suffix.* growth.

-plasm *suffix.* tissue.

-plastic *suffix.* forming.

-plasty *suffix.* shaping, forming, repairing.

-plegia *suffix.* paralysis.

-plegic *suffix.* a person who is paralyzed.

pleur-, pleuro- *combining form.* **1.** pleura. **2.** rib, side.

-pnea *suffix.* breath.

pneum-, pneuma-, pneumat-, pneumato-, pneumo- *combining form.* **1.** breath. **2.** air..

pneumon-, pneumono-   *combining form.* breath; lung.

-poiesis   *suffix.* formation, production.

-poietic   *suffix.* forming, producing.

poikilo-   *combining form.* varied, irregular.

poly-   *prefix.* many, much.

-porosis   *suffix.* lessening in density; thinning out.

post-   *prefix.* after, following.

pre-   *prefix.* before.

pro-   *prefix.* before, forward.

proct-, procto-   *combining form.* anus, rectum.

prostate-, prostat-, prostato-   *combining form,* prostate gland.

pseud-, pseudo-   *combining form.* false.

psych-, psycho-   *combining form.* mind.

-ptosis   *suffix.* falling down or sagging of an organ.

pub-, pubo-   *combining form.* pubic, pubis.

pulmon-, pulmono-   *combining form.* the lungs.

pupill-, pupillo-   *combining form.* pupil.

py-, pyo-   *combining form.* pus.

pyel-, pyelo-   *combining form.* pelvis.

pylor-, pyloro-   *combining form.* the pylorus (outlet of the stomach).

Q

quadri-   *prefix.* four.

R

rach-, rachi-, rachio-   *combining form.* spine.

radi-, radio-   *combining form.* radiation.

radicul-, radiculo-   *combining form.* relating to the root, as of a nerve or tooth.

re-   *prefix.* **1.** again. **2.** backward.

rect-, recto-   *combining form.* rectum.

ren-, reni-, reno-   *combining form.* kidney.

retic-, reticulo-   *combining form.* network.

retin-, retino-   *combining form.* retina.

retro-   *prefix.* **1.** backward. **2.** located behind.

rhabdomy-, rhabdomyo-   *combining form.* striated muscle.

rheumat-, rheumato-   *combining form.* joint.

rhin-, rhino-   *combining form.* the nose, nasal.

-rrhagia   *suffix.* an excessive flow.

-rrhaphy   *suffix.* suture.

-rrhea   *suffix.* flow or discharge.

-rrhexis   *suffix.* rupture.

S

sacr-, sacro-   *combining form.* sacrum

salping-, salpingi-, salpingo-   *combining form.* salpinx.

sarc-, sarco-   *combining form.* flesh.

-sarcoma   *suffix.* a malignant tumor formed in connective tissues.

-schisis   *suffix.* splitting.

schisto- *combining form.* split; cleft.

schiz-, schizo- *combining form.* **1.** split; cleft: schizonychia. **2.** schizophrenia.

scler-, sclero- *combining form.* **1.** hard. scleroderma. **2.** sclera.

-sclerosis *suffix.* sclerosis.

scoli-, scolio- *combining form.* twisted; curved.

-scope *suffix.* an instrument used for viewing or examining.

-scopy *suffix.* viewing; seeing; observing.

scot-, scoto- *combining form.* darkness.

semi- *prefix.* **1.** half; partial; similar to.

-sepsis *suffix.* sepsis.

septo- *combining form.* septum.

sero- *combining form.* serum.

sial-, sialo- *combining form.* saliva, salivary gland.

sidero- *combining form.* iron.

sigmoid-, sigmoido- *combining form.* sigmoid colon.

sinsitr-, sinistro- *combining form.* left.

sinus-, sinuso- *combining form.* sinus.

socio- *combining form.* social.

somat- somato- *combining form.* body.

-some *suffix.* body.

-somnia *suffix.* sleep

sono- *combining form.* sound.

-spasm *suffix.* spasm.

sperm-, spermat-, spermato- spermo- *combining form.* sperm.

sphen- spheno- *combining form.* wedge; wedge-shaped..

spher-, sphero- *combining form.* sphere.

sphygm-, sphygmo- *combining form.* pulse.

spin-, spino- *combining form.* spine, spinous.

spir-, spiro- *combining form.* respiration.

splen- spleno- *combining form.* spleen.

spondyl-, spondylo- *combining form.* vertebra, vertebrae.

staphyl-, staphylo- *combining form.* **1.** relating to staphylococci. **2.** relating to the uvula (of the soft palate of the mouth).

-stat *suffix.* implies something that prevents motion or change.

steat-, steato- *combining form.* fat.

-stenosis *suffix.* stenosis.

stereo- *combining form.* solid; three-dimensional.

stern-, sterno- *combining form.* sternum.

stomat-, stomato- *combining form.* mouth; stoma.

-stomy *suffix.* surgical opening in an organ or body part.

strepto- *combining form.* streptococcus.

styl-, stylo- *combining form.* styloid process.

sub- *prefix.* **1.** below. **2.** secondary. **3.** subdivision. **4.** not completely, almost.

super- *prefix.* **1.** above; upon. **2.** superior. **3.** exceeding. **4.** excessive. **5.** containing a large amount of a specific ingredient.

supra- *prefix.* above; over: supracostal.

syn- *prefix.* **1.** together; united. **2.** same; similar.

synov-, synovo- *combining form.* synovial membrane.

T

tachy-   *prefix*. speedy; fast; rapid.

tars-, tarso-   *combining form*. tarsus.

-taxy   *suffix*. order; arrangement.

tel-, tele-, telo-   *combining form*. **1.** distant. **2.** end.

ten-, teno-   *combining form*. tendon.

terat-, terato-   *combining form*. grossly deformed fetus or part.

tetr-, tetra-   *combining form*. four.

therm-, thermo-   *combining form*. heat.

thorac-, thoracico-, thoraco-   *combining form*. chest or thorax.

thromb-, thrombo-   *combining form*. blood clot.

thym-, thymo-   *combining form*. thymus.

thyr-, thyro-   *combining form*. thyroid.

thyroid-,   *combining form*. the thyroid gland.

tibi-, tibio-   *combining form*. of or relating to the tibia.

toco-   *combining form*. childbirth or labor.

-tome   *suffix*. **1.** cutting instrument. **2.** part, segment.

tomo-   *combining form*. cutting.

-tomy   *suffix*. incision.

-tonia   *suffix*. pressure; tension.

tono-   *combining form*. tone; pressure; tension.

tonsill-, tonsillo-   *combining form*. tonsil.

tox-, toxi-, toxic-, toxico-, toxo-   *combining form*. poison.

trache-, tracheo-   *combining form*. trachea.

trachel-, trachelo-   *combining form*. neck, usually of the uterus; uterine cervix.

trans-   *prefix*. across; through.

tri-   *prefix*. three.

trich-, tricho-   *combining form*. hair; thread.

-tripsy   *suffix*. crushing; pulverizing.

-trophic   *suffix*. relating to nutrition.

-trophy   *suffix*. nutrition; growth.

-tropia   *suffix*. abnormal deviation of the eye from a normal line of vision.

-tropic   *suffix*. involuntary response of an organism to turn away from or toward a stimulus.

-tropin   *suffix*. hormone.

tympan-, tympano-   *combining form*. tympanum, eardrum.

U

-ule   *suffix*. little; small (form of the thing specified).

ultra-   *prefix*. **1.** beyond or outside the limits of (the thing indicated). **2.** to an excessive or extreme degree of (the thing indicated).

un-   *prefix*. not.

uni-   *prefix*. one; single.

ur-, uro-   *combining form*. **1.** urine; urinary tract; urination.

-uresis   *suffix*. **1.** urination. **2.** excretion in the urine (of the substance indicated).

ureter-, uretero-   *combining form*. ureter.

urethr-, urethro-   *combining form*. urethra.

-uria   *suffix*. urine.

urin-, urino-   *combining form*. urine.

utero-   *combining form*. uterus.

uve-, uveo-   *combining form.* uvea.
uvul-, uvulo-   *combining form.* uvula.

V

vag-, vago-   *combining form.* vagus nerve.
vagin-, vagino-   *combining form.* vagina.
valvul-, valvulo-   *combining form.* valve.
varico-   *combining form.* **1.** varix or varicosity. **2.** varicose.
vas-, vaso-   *combining form.* **1.** blood vessel. **2.** vessel. **3.** vas deferens.
ven-, veni-, veno-   *combining form.* vein.
ventricul-, ventriculo-   *combining form.* ventricle.
-version   *suffix.* turning (of the type specified).
vertebr-, vertebro-   *combining form.* vertebra or vertebrae.
vesic-, vesico-   *combining form.* **1.** bladder. **2.** blister.
vir-, viro-   *combining form.* virus.
viscer-, viscero-   *combining form.* viscera.
vulv-, vulvo-   *combining form.* vulva.

X

xanth-, xantho-   *combining form.* yellow.
xeno-   *combining form.* strange; foreign matter.
xer-, xero-   *combining form.* dryness.
xiph-, xipho-   *combining form.* sword-shaped.

Z

zoo-   *combining form.* animal.
zyg-, zygo-   *combining form.* a union; a pair or yoke.
-zygous   *suffix.* of or relating to a zygote.
zymo-   *combining form.* fermentation; enzymes.

Appendices

Appendix B:

Medical Errors and Abbreviations

Recently, medical abbreviations have been linked to some of the worst medical errors, particularly those involving wrong doses of medication. As a result, the Joint Commission on Accreditation of Hospital Organizations (JCAHO) has come up with a list of nine prohibited abbreviations plus several as recommended for elimination in medical communication. For the prohibited abbreviations, it is suggested that the full words be substituted. In this dictionary, we use the symbol ⚠ to indicate such abbreviations. Table A-1 shows the prohibited abbreviations, what they can be confused with, and what should be substituted. Table A-2 shows suggested replacements for abbreviations that have the potential to cause medical errors. JCAHO has also suggested that each healthcare organization come up with its own list of frequently used and potentially misunderstood abbreviations.

Table A-1. Prohibited Abbreviations

Abbreviation	Potential Problem	Solution
1. U (for unit)	Mistaken as zero, four or cc.	Write or speak "unit"
2. IU (for international unit)	Mistaken as IV (intravenous) or 10 (ten).	Write or speak "international unit"
3. Q.D. (once daily) 4. Q.O.D. (every other day)	Mistaken for each other. The period after the Q can be mistaken for an "I" and the "O" can be mistaken for "I".	Write or speak "daily" and "every other day"
5. Trailing zero (X.0 mg) [Note: Prohibited only for medication-related notations]; 6. Lack of leading zero (.X mg)	Decimal point is missed and dosage is either too large or too small.	Never write a zero by itself after a decimal point (X mg), and always use a zero before a decimal point (0.X mg)
7. MS 8. MSO₄ 9. MgSO₄	Can mean morphine sulfate or magnesium sulfate. Potentially confused for one another.	Write or speak "morphine sulfate" or "magnesium sulfate"

Table A-2. Suggested Additional Abbreviations to Avoid.

Abbreviation	Potential Problem	Solution
µg (for microgram)	Mistaken for mg (milligrams) resulting in one thousand-fold dosing overdose.	Write "mcg" or speak microgram
H.S. (for half-strength or Latin abbreviation for bedtime)	Mistaken for either half-strength or hour of sleep (at bedtime). q.H.S. mistaken for every hour. All can result in a dosing error.	Write out or speak "half-strength" or "at bedtime"

Appendices

413

T.I.W. (for three times a week)	Mistaken for three times a day or twice weekly resulting in an overdose.	Write or speak "3 times weekly" or "three times weekly"
S.C. or S.Q. (for subcutaneous)	Mistaken as SL for sublingual, or "5 every".	Write or speak "Sub- Q", "subQ", or "subcutaneously"
D/C (for discharge)	Interpreted as discontinue whatever medications follow (typically discharge meds).	Write "discharge"
c.c. (for cubic centimeter)	Mistaken for U (units) when poorly written.	Write or speak "ml" for milliliters
A.S., A.D., A.U. (Latin abbreviation for left, right, or both ears)	Mistaken for OS, OD, and OU, etc.).	Write or speak "left ear," "right ear" or "both ears"

Listed below are the medical abbreviations

A

a   **1.** ante. **2.** area. **3.** asymmetric. **4.** artery.

A   **1.** adenine. **2.** alanine. **3.** as a subscript, used to refer to alveolar gas..

AA, aa   **1.** amino acid. **2. AA** Alcoholics Anonymous (www.alcoholics-anonymous.org).

AAA   abdominal aortic aneurysm.

AMA   American Medical Association. (www.ama-assn.org).

AAMA   American Association of Medical Assistants (www.aama-ntl.org).

AAMT   American Association for Medical Transcription (www.aamt.org).

A&P   **1.** auscultation and percussion. **2.** anterior and posterior.

ABC   airway, breathing, and circulation, used in cardiac life support.

ABCD   airway, breathing, circulation, and defibrillation, used in cardiac life support.

ABCDE   airway, breathing, circulation and cervical spine, disability, and exposure, used in advanced trauma life support.

ABG   arterial blood gas.

ABR   auditory brainstem response.

ABR test   auditory brainstem response test.

a.c.   Latin *ante cibum,* before meals.

AC   air conduction.

ACE   angiotensin-converting enzyme.

ACE2   angiotensin-converting enzyme 2.

AcG, ac-g   accelerator globulin.

Ach   acetylcholine.

ACL   anterior cruciate ligament.

ACR   American College of Radiology.

ACTH   adrenocorticotropic hormone.

AD   Alzheimer's disease.

A.D.   Latin *auris dextra,* right ear.

ADA   **1.** American Dental Association (www.ada.org). **2.** Americans With Disabilities Act.

ADAA   American Dental Assistants Association (www.dentalassistants.org).

ADD attention deficit disorder.

ADH antidiuretic hormone.

ADHD attention deficit hyperactivity disorder.

ADLs activities of daily living.

ad lib. Latin *ad libitum*, freely.

Adm admission.

ADR adverse drug reaction.

AF atrial fibrillation

AFB acid-fast bacillus.

AFO ankle-foot orthotic.

Ag Silver.

A/G albumin:globulin ratio.

AGN **1.** acute glomerulonephritis. **2.** acute necrotizing gingivitis.

AHD atherosclerotic heart disease.

AHIMA American Health Information Management Association (www.ahima.org).

AI aortic insufficiency.

AID artificial insemination by donor.

AIDS /ādz/ acquired immunodeficiency syndrome or acquired immunodeficiency disease.

AIH artificial insemination, homologous (using the husband's semen).

AK actinic keratosis.

A-K above-the-knee.

AKA above-the-knee amputation.

ALL acute lymphoblastic leukemia; acute lymphocytic leukemia.

ALS amyotrophic lateral sclerosis.

ALT alanine aminotransferase.

a.m., AM Latin *ante meridiem*, before noon.

AMA American Medical Association (www.ama-assn.org).

AMC arthrogryposis multiplex congenita.

AML acute myelogenous lymphocytic leukemia; acute myeloblastic leukemia; acute myelocytic leukemia; acute myeloid leukemia.

ANA antinuclear antibody titer, elevated in connective tissue disease.

ANUG acute necrotizing ulcerative gingivitis.

AP **1.** angina pectoris. **2.** arterial pressure. **3.** anterior pituitary. **4.** anteroposterior.

AP & LAT anteposterior and lateral.

APC **1.** acetylsalicylic acid, phenacetin, and caffeine, combined to make an analgesic. **2.** antigen-presenting cells.

APTT activated partial thromboplastin time.

AP view anteroposterior view.

aq. water.

ARB angiotensin II receptor blocker.

ARC AIDS-related complex.

ARDS adult respiratory distress syndrome or acute respiratory distress syndrome.

ARF **1.** acute renal failure. **2.** acute respiratory failure.

Arg arginine.

AROM active range of motion.

ART **1.** antiretroviral therapy. **2.** assisted reproductive technology.

A.S. Latin *auris sinister,* left ear.

ASA (drug caution code) abbreviation of acetylsalicylic acid (aspirin), placed on the label of a medication as a warning that it contains acytylsalysylic acid, which can cause complications for someone with specific medical conditions.

ASD   atrial septal defect.

ASL   American Sign Language.

ASP   aspartic acid.

AST   aspartate aminotransferase.

ATL   adult T-cell leukemia, adult T-cell leukemia/lymphoma, or adult T-cell lymphoma.

ATP   adenosine triphosphatase.

A.U.   Latin *auris unitas,* both ears.

AUL   acute undifferentiated leukemia.

AV   atrioventricular.

AVM   arteriovenous malformation.

AZT   azidothymadine, also known as zidovudine, a drug used in the treatment of HIV.

B

Ba   Barium.

BaE, Ba enema, BE   barium enema.

BAEP   brainstem auditory evoked potentials.

BAER   brainstem auditory evoked response.

BBB   blood-brain barrier.

BC   bone conduction.

BCG   bacillus of Calmette and Guerin (vaccination for tuberculosis).

BIA   biological impedance analysis.

b.i.d., bid, BID   Latin *bis in die*, two times a day (on prescriptions).

B-K   below the knee.

BKA   below-knee amputation.

BM   bowel movement.

BMD   bone mass density or bone mineral density.

BMI   body mass index.

BMR   basal metabolic rate.

BP, bp   blood pressure.

BPH   benign prostatic hyperplasia or benign prostatic hypertrophy.

BSA   body surface area.

BSE   bovine spongiform encephalopathy.

BUN   blood urea nitrogen.

bx, BX, Bx, Bx.   biopsy.

BZD   benzodiazepine.

C

C   1. calorie (kilocalorie). **2.** carbon. **3.** Celsius/centigrade. **4.** cervical vertebra/vertebrae. **5.** cytosine.

c   1. small calorie (gram calorie). **2.** centi-. **3.** curie.

Ca   calcium.

CA   1. (also **ca**) cancer/carcinoma. **2.** chronological age. **3.** coronary artery.

CA-125   cancer antigen 125.

CABG   coronary artery bypass graft.

CAD   coronary artery disease.

CAM   complementary and alternative medicine.

cap   capsule.

CAPD   continuous ambulatory peritoneal dialysis.

CAT   computerized axial tomography.

Cath, cath   catheter.

CBC   complete blood count.

CBT   cognitive behavioral therapy.

cc   cubic centimeter.

CCS   certified coding specialist (hospital).

CCS-P   certified coding specialist—physician.

CCU   coronary care unit.

CDA   certified dental assistant.

CDC   Centers for Disease Control and Prevention.

CEA   carcinoembryonic antigen.

CHF   congestive heart failure.

CIC   completely in the canal (said of hearing aids).

CIS   carcinoma in situ.

CJD   Creutzfeldt-Jakob's disease

CK   creatinine kinase.

Cl   chlorine.

CLL   chronic lymphocytic leukemia.

Cm   centimeter.

CMA   certified medical assistant.

CMI   cell-mediated immunity.

CML   chronic myelogenous leukemia.

CMS   Centers for Medicare and Medicaid Services (www.cms.gov).

CMT   certified medical transcriptionist.

CMV   cytomegalovirus.

CNS   central nervous system

CO   carbon monoxide.

CO$_2$ carbon dioxide.

CoA   coarctation of the aorta.

COBRA /kō′brə/   U.S. federal Consolidated Omnibus Budget Reconciliation Act.

COLD   chronic obstructive lung disease.

COPD   chronic obstructive pulmonary disease.

CP   cerebral palsy.

CPAP   continuous positive airway pressure.

CPC   certified professional coder.

CPC-H   certified profession coder hospital.

CPD   cephalopelvic disproportion.

CPK   creatine phosphokinase.

CPR   cardiopulmonary resuscitation.

CPT   Current Procedural Terminology.

CRF   corticotropin-releasing factor.

CRH   corticotropin-releasing horomone.

CRNA   Certified Registered Nurse Anesthetist.

CRP   cAMP receptor protein; C-reactive protein.

CSF   cerebrospinal fluid.

CSF   colony-stimulating factor.

CT   computed tomography.

CTS   carpal tunnel syndrome.

CVA   cerebrovascular attack; cerebrovascular accident.

CVC   central venous catheter.

CVD   cardiovascular disease.

CVP   central venous pressure.

CXR   chest x-ray.

D

D   (drug caution code) found on the label of some medication, indicating that it may cause drowsiness.

D & C, D and C   dilation and curettage.

D & E   dilation and evacuation.

dB   decibel.

DC   1. (also **d.c.**) direct current. 2. Doctor of Chiropractic.

DDS   1. Doctor of Dental Surgery. 2. Denver Developmental Screening Test.

def, DEF   decayed, extracted, and filled, said of teeth.

DES   diethylstilbestrol.

DEXA scan /dĕk′sə/   the image or data produced by a special x-ray machine, used to measure bone density. [*d*ual-*e*nergy *x*-ray *a*bsorptiometry].

DHEA   dehydroepiandrosterone.

DHF   dengue hemorrhagic fever.

DI   diabetes insipidus.

diff   differential

diff dx   differential diagnosis.

DLE   discoid lupus erythematosus.

DNA   deoxyribonucleic acid.

DNR   do not resuscitate.

D.O.   Doctor of Osteopathy.

DOA   dead on arrival.

Dr, Dr.   doctor.

DRE   digital rectal exam.

DRG   diagnosis-related group, payment categories used by hospitals to charge fees to insurers.

DRI   dietary reference intake.

DSA   digital subtraction angiography.

DSM   *Diagnostic and Statistical Manual.*

DT   1. duration tetany, the spasm of degenerated muscle upon application of electrical current. 2. diphtheria tetanus, a vaccine used for immunization of diphtheria and tetanus.

DTs   delirium tremens.

DV   daily value, as the recommended intake of a nutrient.

DVT   deep vein thrombosis.

dx, DX   diagnosis.

DXA   dual x-ray absorptiometry.

E

EBCT   electron beam computerized tomography.

EBV   Epstein-Barr virus.

ECG, EKG   electrocardiogram.

ECHO /ĕk′ō/   echocardiogram.

ECMO /ĕk′mō/   extracorporeal-membrane oxygenation, a complex therapeutic tool used in extreme ICU conditions where lung function has failed but is expected to recover within a few days.

ECT   electroconvulsive therapy; electroshock therapy.

ED   1. effective dose. 2. emergency department. 3. erectile dysfunction.

EDC   estimated date of confinement.

EEE　eastern equine encephalitis.

EEG　electroencephalogram.

EENT　eye, ear, nose, and throat. *See also* ENT.

EF　ejection fraction.

EGD　esophagogastroduodenoscopy.

EIA　enzyme immunoassay.

EKG, ECG　electrocardiogram.

ELISA /ĭ lī′zə, ĭ līs′ə/　enzyme-linked immunosorbent assay.

elix.　elixir.

EMG　electromyogram.

EMR　electronic medical record.

EMT　emergency medical technician.

ENT　ear, nose, throat. *See also* EENT.

EPO　erythropoietin.

ER　**1.** emergency room. **2.** estrogen receptor.

ERCP　endoscopic retrograde cholangiopancreatography.

ERT　estrogen replacement therapy.

ESP　extrasensory perception

ESR　erythrocyte sedimentation rate.

ESRD　end-stage renal disease.

ESWL　extracorporeal shock wave lithotripsy.

F

F　Fahrenheit.

FAE　fetal alcohol effects.

FAP　**1.** familial adenomatous polyposis. **2.** functional ambulation profile (analysis of a patient's ability to walk).

FAS　fetal alcohol syndrome.

FBS　fasting blood sugar.

FBG　fasting blood glucose.

FDA　Food and Drug Administration (www.fda.gov).

FEF　forced expiratory flow

FET　forced expiratory time.

FEV$_1$　forced expiratory volume measured during first second of expiration, useful in quantifying pulmonary disability.

FHR　fetal heart rate.

FHT　fetal heart tone.

fMRI　functional magnetic resonance imaging, a type of magnetic resonance imaging that demonstrates the correlation between physical changes and mental functioning.

FNA　fine needle aspiration biopsy.

FP　**1.** freezing point. **2.** family physician. **3.** family practice.

ft.　foot; feet.

FTT　failure to thrive.

FUO　fever of unknown origin.

FVC　forced vital capacity.

G

G　**1.** (drug caution code) abbreviation of glaucoma, placed on the label of a medication as a warning that it can cause complications for someone with the disease. **2.** gravida.

g　gram; grams.

Appendices

GB   gallbladder
GC   gas chromatography.
g-cal   gram calorie.
G-CSF   granulocyte colony-stimulating factor.
GDM   gestational diabetes mellitus
GERD /gûrd/   gastroesophageal reflux disease.
GH   growth hormone.
GHB   gamma hydroxybutyrate
GHz   gigahertz gigahertzes.
GI   gastrointestinal.
GI series   gastrointestinal series.
GI tract   gastrointestinal tract.
GIFT /gĭft/   *abbreviation.* gamete intrafallopian transfer.
GLC   gas-liquid chromatography
gm.   gram; grams.
GM-CSF   granulocyte-macrophage colony-stimulating factor.
GOT   glutamic-oxaloacetic transaminase.
gtt   Latin *guttae*, drops.
GSR   galvanic skin response.
GTT   glucose tolerance test.
GU   genitourinary.
Gy   gray.
GYN   gynecology; gynecologist.

H

H   **1.** hyperopia; hyperopic. **2.** hydrogen. **3.** (drug caution code) found on the label of medication indicating that it can be habit forming.
h   **1.** height. **2.** hour.
H&P   history and physical.
HAV   hepatitis A virus, the RNA virus that causes hepatitis A.
HB   hepatitis B vaccine.
Hb   hemoglobin.
HBIG   hepatitis B immune globulin.
HBV   hepatitis B virus, the DNA virus that causes hepatitis B.
HCFA   Health Care Finance Administration, now the Centers for Medicare and Medicaid Services.
HCG, HCG   human chorionic gonadotropin.
hct, HCT   hematocrit.
HCV   hepatitis C virus, the RNA virus that causes hepatitus C.
HD   Hodgkin's disease.
HDL   high-density lipoprotein.
HDN   hemolytic disease of the newborn.
HDV   hepatitis D virus, the RNA virus that causes hepatitis D.
HEV   hepatitis E virus, the RNA virus that causes hepatitis E.
Hg   mercury.
HGB, Hgb, HB   hemoglobin.
HGH   human growth hormone
HHS   U.S. Department of Health and Human Services (www.hhs.gov).

HIPAA   Health Insurance Portability and Accountability Act.

His   histidine.

HIV   human immunodeficiency virus.

HMD   hyaline membrane disease.

HMO   health maintenance organization.

H&P   history and physical.

HPV   human papillomavirus.

HRR   high-risk register

HRT   hormone replacement therapy.

HSG   hysterosalpingography.

HSV   herpes simplex virus.

HTLV   human T-cell leukemia virus.

HTN   hypertension.

Hz   hertz.

I

I   (drug caution code) a symbol placed on the label of a medication, indicating possible adverse interaction if taken with other drugs.

IBD   inflammatory bowel disease.

IBS   irritable bowel syndrome.

ICD-9-CM   title of *International Classification of Diseases, 9th Revision, Clinical Modification*; system for diagnosis classification now in use for medical coding. ICD-10 is under review and expected to be adopted by 2010.

ICF   **1.** intermediate care facility. **2.** intracellular acid

ICP   intracranial pressure.

ICU   intensive care unit.

IDDM   insulin-dependant diabetes mellitus.

Ig   immunoglobulin.

IgA   immunoglobulin A.

IgD   immunoglobulin D.

IgE   immunoglobulin E.

IGF   insulin-like growth factor(s).

IgG   immunoglobulin G.

IgM   immunoglobulin M.

IL   interleukin

IM   intramuscular.

IOL   intraocular lens.

IOP   intraocular pressure.

IPPB   intermittent positive pressure breathing

IPPV   intermittent positive pressure ventilation

IPV   inactivated polio vaccine.

IQ   intelligence quotient.

IU   international unit

IUD   intrauterine contraceptive device.

IUI   intrauterine insemination.

IV   *adj.* **1.** intravenous. *n.* **2.** intravenous injection. **3.** intravenous drip.

IVF   in vitro fertilization.

IVP   intravenous pyelogram.

J

JCAHO Joint Commission on Accreditation of Healthcare Organizations, an organization that inspects hospitals and reviews and gives accreditation to healthcare organizations (www.jcaho.org).

K

K potassium.

kg kilogram; kilograms.

KUB kidneys, ureter, and bladder.

L

l, L **1.** liter; liters. **2.** left.

LASIK /lā′sĭk/ laser-assisted in situ keratomileusis.

lb. pound; pounds.

LD lethal dose, often LD50 or LD95 to describe the dose at which 50% or 95% of the subjects (usually lab animals) die.

LDH lactate dehydrogenase.

LDL low-density lipoprotein.

LE **1.** left eye (usually abreviated OS or o.s.). **2.** lupus erythematosus (usually abbreviated SLE)

LEEP /lēp/ loop electrosurgical excision procedure.

LES lower esophageal sphincter.

LFT liver function test.

LI large intestine.

LLQ left lower quadrant

LP **1.** latency period. **2.** lipoprotein/low protein. **3.** lumbar puncture.

LPN licensed practical nurse.

LR **1.** labor room. **2.** lactated Ringer's (injection or solution). **3.** lateral rectus. **4.** light reaction or light reflex.

LRM left radical mastectomy.

LRT lower respiratory tract.

LS **1.** left side. **2.** liver and spleen. **3.** lumbosacral. **4.** lymphosarcoma.

LSH lutein-stimulating hormone.

LTC long-term care.

LUL **1.** left upper limb. **2.** left upper lobe (of lung).

LUQ left upper quadrant.

LV **1.** left ventricle. **2.** leukemia virus. **3.** live virus.

LVAD left ventricular assist device

LVN licensed vocational/visiting nurse.

LVRS lung volume reduction surgery.

Lys lysine.

M

Mb myoglobin.

MBC maximum breathing capacity.

mcg microgram; micrograms.

MCH **1.** mean corpuscular hemoglobin. **2.** maternal and child health (services).

MCHC mean corpuscular hemoglobin concentration.

MCP Metacarpophalangeal

MCS multiple chemical sensitivity.

MCV mean corpuscular volume.

MD   **1.** (*also* M.D.) Doctor of Medicine. **2.** muscular dystrophy.

MDI   metered-dose inhaler.

ME   medical examiner.

MEP   maximum expiratory pressure.

MET   **1.** metabolic equivalent. **2.** muscle energy technique.

mets   metastasis.

mg   milligram.

MG   myasthenia gravis.

Mg   magnesium

mGy   milligray.

mh   megahertz.

MHz   megahertz.

MI   **1.** myocardial infarction. **2.** mitral incompetence or inadequacy.

MIS   medical information system.

ml, mL   milliliter; milliliters.

mm   millimeter; millimeters.

MMPI   Minnesota Multiphasic Personality Inventory.

Mn   Manganese

MP   mentoposterior position.

MPD   **1.** multiple personality disorder. **2.** medical program director.

MR   mitral regurgitation.

MRA   magnetic resonance angiography.

MRI   magnetic resonance imaging.

MS   **1.** multiple sclerosis. **2.** mitral stenosis.

MUGA /mōō′gə/   multiple-gated acquisition scan.

MVP   mitral valve prolapse.

N

N   nitrogen.

Na   sodium.

NARP   neuropathy, ataxia, and retinitis pigmentosa, a genetic disease inherited from the mother, featuring weakness of the muscles near the trunk, ataxia (wobbliness), seizure, disease of the retina, and sometimes retardation or developmental delay.

ND   Doctor of Naturopathic Medicine.

NEC   not elsewhere classified (used in medical coding).

neg, neg.   negative.

NG   nasogastric.

NHL   non-Hodgkin lymphoma.

NICU   neonatal intensive care unit.

NIDDM   non-insulin-dependant diabetes mellitus.

NK cell   natural killer cell.

NMR   nuclear magnetic resonance.

noc.   Latin *nocte*, at night.

noc, n.o.c.   not otherwise classified.

NOS   not otherwise specified (used in medical coding).

NPC   Niemann-Pick's disease

NPO, n.p.o.   Latin *nil per os*, nothing by mouth.

NREM sleep /ĕn′rĕm′/ or **nonREM sleep** /nŏn′rĕm′/   non-rapid eye movement sleep.

NSAID   nonsteroidal anti-inflammatory drug.

NTD   neural tube defect.

O

O₂$_2$ oxygen.

OB obstetrics; obstetrician.

OB/GYN obstetrics and gynecology.

OBS organic brain syndrome.

OCD obsessive-compulsive disorder.

OD **1.** *n.* an overdose. **2.** *v.* to overdose.

o.d. Latin *oculus dexter,* the right eye (in optometry).

oint, oint. ointment.

OR operating room.

orth orthopedic surgeon.

OS, o.s. Latin *oculus sinister,* the left eye (in optometry).

OSA obstructive sleep apnea.

OSHA Occupation Safety and Health Administration (www.osha.gov).

OT occupational therapy; occupational therapist.

OTC over-the-counter (for sale without a prescription).

OU, o.u. Latin *oculus uterque,* each eye (in prescriptions)

oz, oz. ounce; ounces.

P

PA **1.** physician assistant. **2.** posteroanterior (as in a typical chest x-ray). **3.** pulmonary artery.

PAC premature atrial contraction.

PACU /păk′yo͞o′/ post-anesthesia care unit.

Pap /păp/ **1.** Papanicolaou('s). **2.** (*also* **pap**) Pap test. **3.** (*also* **pap**) Pap smear.

PAP **1.** positive airway pressure. **2.** pulmonary artery pressure.

Pb lead.

p.c. Latin *post cibum,* after meals.

PCA **1.** patient-controlled analgesia. **2.** posterior cerebral artery.

PCL posterior cruciate ligament.

PCP **1.** *Pneumocystis carinii* pneumonia. **2.** primary care physician; primary care provider.

PCR polymerase chain reaction, commonly used in medical testing to amplify particular sequences of DNA.

PCT patient care technician.

PCV packed cell volume.

PD peritoneal dialysis.

PDR **1.** *Physicians' Desk Reference.* **2.** primary drug resistance.

PDT photodynamic therapy.

PE **1.** physical examination. **2.** pleural effusion. **3.** pulmonary edema. **4.** pulmonary embolism.

PED pediatric emergency department.

peds pediatrics.

PEEP positive end-expiratory pressure.

PEFR peak expiratory flow rate.

PEG percutaneous endoscopic gastrostomy.

PERRL or **PERRLA** pupils equally round and reactive to light or pupils equally round and reactive to light and accommodation.

PET /pĕt/ positron emission tomography.

PFT pulmonary function test.

PICU pediatric intensive care unit.

PID pelvic inflammatory disease.

PIP   proximal interphalangeal joints.

PKD   polycystic kidney disease.

PKU   phenylketonuria.

PLT   platelet count.

PM, p.m.   Latin *post meridian*, at night.

PMS   premenstrual syndrome.

PN   parenteral nutrition.

PNS   peripheral nervous system.

p.o., PO   Latin *per os*, by mouth.

polio /pō′lē ō′/   poliomyelitis.

POS   point of service.

PPD   **1.** postpartum depression. **2.** purified protein derivative, used in a skin test for tuberculosis.

PPMA   postpolio muscular atrophy.

PPO   preferred provider organization.

PPS   postpolio syndrome.

PR   per rectum.

PRBC   packed red blood cells.

preop /prē′ŏp′/   preoperative.

primip /prī′mĭp, prī mĭp′/   primipara.

PRK   photorefractive keratectomy.

PRN, p.r.n.   Latin *pro re nata*, as needed (in prescriptions).

PROM   passive range of motion

PSA   prostate-specific antigen, a protein produced by the prostate gland that is used in the diagnosis of prostate cancer.

PSG   polysonmography

pt   patient.

PT   **1.** physical therapy. **2.** physical therapist. **3.** prothrombin time.

Pl   platinum.

PTA   percutaneous transluminal angioplasty.

PTCA   percutaneous transluminal coronary angioplasty.

PTSD   posttraumatic stress disorder.

PTT   partial thromboplastin time.

PUBS   percutaneous umbilical blood sampling, a technique used for diagnosing and treating a fetus in which a blood sample is taken from the umbilical vein by inserting a needle through the mother's abdominal and uterine walls.

PUD   peptic ulcer disease.

pulv.   powder (used in prescriptions).

PUVA   psoralen and UVA, a treatment for psoriasis that combines the medication psoralen with carefully timed UVA (ultraviolet light of A wavelength) exposure.

PV   **1.** polycythemia vera. **2.** peripheral vascular.

PVC   premature ventricular contraction.

PVD   peripheral vascular disease.

PVS   persistent vegetative state.

Q

q, q.   every.

qam, q.a.m.   every morning.

q.d., qd   Latin *quaque die*, every day.

q.h., qh   Latin *quaque hora*, every hour.

q.2h.   every 2 hours.

q.3h. every 3 hours.

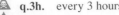 **q.i.d., qid** Latin *quatuor in die,* four times a day.

q.n.s., QNS quantity not sufficient; used by a laboratory when an insufficient amount of specimen is received to perform a requested test.

qod, q.o.d. every other day.

qoh, q.o.h. every other hour.

qpm, q.p.m. every evening.

q.s., QS quantity sufficient; quantity required.

qt 1. (*also* **qt.**) quart; quarts. 2. interval in QRS complex.

R

R, r roentgen.

Ra radium

RA rheumatoid arthritis.

rad /răd/ radiation absorbed dose.

RAST /răst/ radioallergosorbent test.

RBC 1. red blood cells. 2. red blood count.

RD registered dietitian.

RDA Recommended Daily Allowance; Recommended Dietary Allowance.

RDS respiratory distress syndrome.

rehab /rē′hăb/ rehabilitation.

REM /rĕm/ rapid eye movements.

RF rheumatoid factor.

RIA radioimmunoassay.

RLL right lower lobe.

RLQ right lower quadrant.

RMSF Rocky Mountain spotted fever.

Rn radon.

RN registered nurse.

RNA ribonucleic acid.

RP retinitis pigmentosa.

RT, rt 1. radiologic technologist. 2. reaction time. 3. recreational therapy. 4. respiratory therapist.

RUQ right upper quadrant.

RV 1. residual volume. 2. right ventricle

Rx, RX medical prescription.

S

S sulfur.

SA sinoatrial.

SAD seasonal affective disorder.

SA node sinoatrial node, the natural pacemaker of the heart.

SARS /särz/ severe acute respiratory syndrome.

SBC systolic blood pressure.

SBS shaken baby syndrome.

sc, SC subcutaneous.

Sc scandium.

Se selenium.

SERM selective estrogen receptor modulator.

SGOT serum glutamic oxaloacetic transaminase.

SGPT   serum glutamic pyruvic transaminase.

SIADH   syndrome of inappropriate ADH (antidiuretic hormone).

SIDS /sĭdz/   sudden infant death syndrome.

SL   sublingual.

SLE   systemic lupus erythematosus.

SLS   Sjogren-Larsson's syndrome.

SNOMED /snō′měd′/   abbreviation. Systematized Nomenclature of Medical Terms, an international standardized system of medical terminology gradually being instituted worldwide.

SOB   shortness of breath.

sol, sol.   solution.

SPECT   single photon emission computed tomography.

SPF   sun protection factor.

sq   subcutaneous.

Sr   strontium.

SR   **1.** sedimentation rate. **2.** sinus rhythm.

SSPE   subacute sclerosing panencephalitis.

SSRI   selective serotonin reuptake inhibitor.

STD   sexually transmitted disease.

STH   somatrophic hormone

STI   sexually transmitted infection.

STM   short-term memory.

strep /strĕp/   streptococcus.

supp.   supplement.

susp.   suspension.

syr.   syrup.

sz   seizure.

T

T   **1.** thymine. **2.** temperature. **3.** time. **4.** tablespoon; tablespoons.

t.   teaspoon; teaspoons.

T3, T$_3$ triiodothyronine.

T4, T$_4$ thyroxine.

tab.   tablet.

TB   tuberculosis.

TBI   **1.** traumatic brain injury. **2.** total body irradiation.

Tbsp, tbsp.   tablespoon; tablespoons.

TBV   total blood volume.

TCA   tricyclic antidepressant.

TCM   traditional Chinese medicine.

TDD   telecommunications device for the deaf.

TDM   therapeutic drug monitoring.

temp, temp. /tĕmp/   temperature.

TENS /tĕnz/   transcutaneous electrical nerve stimulation.

THC   tetrahydrocannabinol.

Thr   threonine.

THR   **1.** target heart rate. **2.** threshold heart rate. **3.** total hip replacement. **4.** thyroid hormone receptor.

Ti   titanium.

TIA   transient ischemic attack.

tid, t.i.d.   three times a day, used in writing prescriptions.

TL   thallium

TLC   total lung capacity.

TMJ   temporomandibular joint.

TNF   tumor necrosis factor.

TNM   tumor-node-metastasis.

tPA, TPA   tissue plasminogen activator.

TPN   total parenteral nutrition.

TPR   temperature, pulse, respiration.

Trp   tryptophan.

TSE   **1.** transmissible spongiform encephalopathy, any of a group of brain diseases, such as kuru or Creutzfeldt-Jakob's disease, in which the brain matter deteriorates. *See also* spongiform encephalopathy. **2.** testicular self-examination.

TSH   thyroid-stimulating hormone.

tsp.   teaspoon; teaspoons.

TSS   toxic shock syndrome.

TTP   thrombotic thrombocytopenic purpura.

TUR   transurethral resection.

TURP /tûrp/   transurethral resection of the prostate.

U

u   atomic mass unit.

U   **1.** uranium. **2.** unit; units. **3.** uracil. **4.** urine.

UA, U/A   urinalysis.

UBT   urea breath test.

UGI   upper gastrointestinal.

ung, ung.   ointment.

UNOS /yo͞o′nŏs/   United Network for Organ Sharing.

UR   ultraviolet radiation.

URI   upper respiratory infection.

URTI   upper respiratory tract infection.

USDA   United States Department of Agriculture (www.usda.gov).

USFDA   United States Food and Drug Administration (www.fda.gov).

USP   *United States Pharmacopeia.*

USP-NF   *United States Pharmacopeia—National Formulary.*

UTI   urinary tract infection.

UV   ultraviolet.

UV   radiation ultraviolet radiation.

V

VA   **1.** vertebral artery. **2.** Veterans Administration **3.** visual acuity. **4.** volt-ampere.

VAD   **1.** vascular access device. **2.** vascular assist device; ventricular assist device.

Val   valine.

VATS   video-assisted thoracoscopy.

VC   **1.** vital capacity. **2.** vocal cord; vocal cords.

VCU   voiding cystourethrography.

VCUG   voiding cystourethrogram/cystourethrography.

VD   venereal disease.

VF   **1.** visual field. **2.** ventricular fibrillation.

Vfib /vē′fĭb′/ · ventricular fibriilation.
VHDL · very-high-density lipoprotein.
VLDL · very-low-density lipoprotein.
V/Q · ventilation-perfusion.
VS · vital sign; vital signs.
VT · ventricular tachycardia.
V-tach /vē′ tăk′/ · ventricular tachycardia.
VSD · ventricular septal defect.

W

WAIS · Wechsler Adult Intelligence Scale.
WBC · **1.** white blood cell. **2.** white blood (cell) count.
WBC count · white blood cell count.
WBC differential /dĭf′ə rĕn′shəl/ · white blood cell differential.
WC · wheelchair.
WHO · World Health Organization (www.who.int).
WISC /wĭsk/ · Wechsler Intelligence Scale for Children.
wt, wt. · weight.

X

XRT · radiation therapy.

Z

ZIFT · zygote intrafallopian transfer.

Appendix C:

Laboratory Testing and Normal Reference Values

Health care professional order laboratory tests to diagnose diseases, conditions, and to assess the general health and functioning of various parts of the body. The basic types of tests are blood tests, urinalysis, stool tests, and spinal taps, which analyze spinal fluid to look for diseases, such as meningitis.

Blood Tests

The two most common blood tests are the complete blood count (CBC) and the blood culture. The CBC measures levels of substances in the blood as described in the following paragraphs. The blood culture is a test for bacteria or yeast. Blood is cultured in the laboratory and is bacteria or yeast is present, it is analyzed for what type it is and what infection it indicates.

The CBC

The CBC tests for electrolytes by measuring levels of sodium, potassium, chloride, and bicarbonate in the body. It also measures other substances, such as blood urea, nitrogen, glucose, and sugars. In addition, it measures the red blood cells, white blood cells, and platelets to look for signs of anemia or infection.

Sodium plays a major role in regulating the amount of water in the body. Also, sodium is necessary for many body functions, like transmitting electrical signals in the brain. The test determines whether there's the right balance of sodium and liquid in the blood to carry out important bodily functions. High levels of sodium can lead to certain conditions, such as high blood pressure.

Potassium is essential to regulate how the heart beats. When potassium levels are too high or too low, it can increase the risk of an abnormal heartbeat. Low potassium levels are also associated with muscle weakness.

Chloride also helps maintain a balance of fluids in the body.

Bicarbonate prevents the body's tissues from getting too much or too little acid. The kidney and lungs balance the levels of bicarbonate in the body. So if bicarbonate levels are abnormal, it might indicate that there is a problem with those organs.

Blood urea nitrogen (BUN) is a measure of how well the kidneys are working.

Creatinine levels in the blood that are too high can indicate that the kidneys aren't working properly. The kidneys filter and excrete creatinine. Both dehydration and muscle damage also can raise creatinine levels.

Glucose is the main type of sugar in the blood. Glucose levels that are too high or too low can cause problems and are often caused by diabetes.

Three tests that are part of a CBC measure red blood cell (RBC) count, hemoglobin, and mean (red) cell volume (MCV). These test anemia, a common condition that occurs when there aren't enough red blood cells.

- The red blood cell count is a measure of the number of RBCs in the body.
- Hemoglobin is the oxygen-carrying protein in red blood cells. RBCs carry oxygen to all parts of the body.
- MCV measures the average size of the red blood cells.

Other tests include the **hematocrit** (HCT), which is the percentage of red blood cells in the blood sample. This is also a test for anemia.

Also part of the CBC is the blood differential test that measures the relative numbers of white blood cells (WBCs) in the blood. WBCs (also called leukocytes) help the body fight infection. An abnormal white blood cell count may indicate that there is an infection, inflammation, or other stress in the body. There are five types of white blood cells: neutrophils, lymphocytes, eosinophils, basophils, and monocytes.

Platelets are the smallest blood cells and are important to blood clotting and the prevention of excessive bleeding. If the platelet count is too low, a person can be in danger of bleeding in any part of the body.

Blood Cultures

Blood is cultured when an infection or the condition of sepsis is suspected. Bacteria or yeast will show up in the blood culture if such conditions exist. Blood cultures are usually done twice if there is a positive result since false positives can lead to unnecessary treatment.

Urinalysis

The kidneys make urine as they filter wastes from the bloodstream while leaving substances in the blood that the body needs, like protein and glucose. Urinalysis checks for the presence of protein and glucose in the urine as well as other substances that can indicate infection, poor function of a body part, or the presence of illegal drugs. The urine is checked for blood as well as many other substances and is an important diagnostic tool.

Stool Test

The most common reason to collect stool is to determine whether a type of bacteria or parasite may be infecting the intestine. Stool is also checked for occult blood, possibly indicative of internal bleeding. Stool samples are also sometimes analyzed for the substances they contain. Some substances may indicated digestive disorders.

Spinal Tap

A spinal tap or lumbar puncture (LP) is a procedure in which a small amount of the fluid that surrounds the brain and spinal cord, called the cerebrospinal fluid (CSF), is removed and examined. The fluid is examined for meningitis and other diseases of the central nervous system.

Tests

The table that follows lists many of the laboratory tests that you will encounter in your allied health career. The table gives the normal ranges expected for each test.

Table of laboratory tests

The table below lists a number of common laboratory tests taken either in normal CBCs (complete blood counts) or a urinalysis or as separate diagnostic tools.

Abbreviations used in table:

W	women	mol	mole
M	men	l	liter
d	deci	m	milli
g	gram	m	micro
k	kilo	n	nano
kat	katal (unit of catalytic activity)	p	pico

Note that "normal" values can vary depending on a variety of factors, including the patient's age or gender, time of day test was taken, and so on. In addition, as new medical advances are made, the understanding of what is the best range for some readings has changed. For example, optimal blood pressure readings are now lower than they were ten years ago.

Laboratory Test	Normal Range in US Units	Normal Range in SI Units	To Convert US to SI Units
ALT (Alanine *aminotransferase)	W 7-30 units/liter M 10-55 units/liter	W 0.12-0.50 mkat/liter M 0.17-0.92 mkat/liter	x 0.01667
Albumin	3.1–4.3 g/dl	31–43 g/liter	x 10
Alkaline Phosphatase	W 30-100 units/liter M 45-115 units/liter	W 0.5-1.67 mkat/liter M 0.75-1.92 mkat/liter	x 0.01667
Aspartate aminotransferase	W 9-25 units/liter M 10-40 units/liter	W 0.15-0.42 mkat/liter M 0.17-0.67 mkat/liter	x 0.01667
Basophils	0-3% of lymphocytes	0.0-0.3 fraction of white blood cells	x 0.01
Bilirubin – Direct	0.0-0.4 mg/dl	0-7 mmol/liter	x 17.1
Bilirubin – Total	0.0-1.0 mg/dl	0-17 mmol/liter	x 17.1
Blood pressure	120/80 millimeters of mercury (mmHg). Top number is systolic pressure, when heart is pumping. Bottom number is diastolic pressure when heart is at rest. Blood pressure can be too low (hypotension) or too high (hypertension).		No conversion
Cholesterol, total Desirable Marginal High	<200 mg/dL 200–239 mg/dL >239 mg/dL	<5.17 mmol/liter 5.17–6.18 mmol/liter >6.18 mmol/liter	x 0.02586

*Variant of transaminase.

(*Continued*)

Laboratory Test	Normal Range in US Units	NormalRange in SI Units	To Convert US to SI Units
Cholesterol, LDL			
Desirable	<100 mg/dL	<2.59 mmol/liter	x 0.02586
Marginal	100–159 mg/dL	2.59–4.14 mmol/liter	
High	160–189 mg/dL	4.14–4.89 mmol/liter	
Very high	>190 mg/dL	>4.91 mmol/liter	
Cholesterol, HDL			
Desirable	>60 mg/dL	>1.55 mmol/liter	x 0.02586
Moderate	40-60 mg/dL	1.03–1.55 mmol/liter	
Low (heart risk)	<40 mg/dL	<1.03 mmol/liter	
Eosinophils	0-8% of white blood cells	0.0–0.8 fraction of white blood cells	x 0.01
Erythrocytes RBC	4.0–6.0 ml (females slightly lower than males)	4.0–6.0 10^{12}/liter	
Glucose, urine	<0.05 g/dl	<0.003 mmol/liter	x 0.05551
Glucose, plasma °fasting reading— often in self-test	70–110 mg/dl (nonfasting not to exceed 140 mg/dl)	3.9–6.1 mmol/liter	x 0.05551
Hematocrit	W 36.0%–46.0% of red blood cells M 37.0%–49.0% of red blood cells	W 0.36–0.46 fraction of red blood cells M 0.37–0.49 fraction of red blood cells	x 0.01
Hemoglobin	W 12.0–16.0 g/dl M 13.0–18.0 g/dl	W 7.4–9.9 mmol/liter M 8.1–11.2 mmol/liter	x 0.6206
Leukocytes (WBC)	4.5–11.0x10^3/mm^3	4.5–11.0x10^9/liter	x 10^6
Lymphocytes	16%–46% of white blood cells	0.16–0.46 fraction of white blood cells	x 0.01
Mean corpuscular hemoglobin (MCH)	25.0–35.0 pg/cell	25.0–35.0 pg/cell	No conversion
Mean corpuscular hemoglobin concentration (MCHC)	31.0–37.0 g/dl	310–370 g/liter	x 10
Mean corpuscular volume (MCV)	W 78–102 mm^3 M 78–100 mm^3 M 78–100 fl	W 78–102 fl	No conversion
Monocytes	4–11% of white blood cells	0.04–0.11 fraction of white blood cells	x 0.01
Neutrophils	45% –75% of white blood cells	0.45–0.75 fraction of white blood cells	x 0.01
Potassium	3.4–5.0 mmol/liter	3.4–5.0 mmol/liter	No conversion
Prostate specific antigen (PSA)	0–2.5 ng/ml		

Serum calcium	8.5–10.5 mg/dl	2.1–2.6 mmol/liter	x 0.25
Sodium	135–145 mmol/liter	135–145 mmol/liter	No conversion
Testosterone, total (morning sample)	W 6–86 ng/dl M 270-1070 ng/dl	W 0.21–2.98 nmol/liter M 9.36-37.10 nmol/liter	x 0.03467
Testosterone, unbound			
Age 20–40	W 0.6–3.1, M 15.0–40.0 pg/ml	W 20.8–107.5, M 520–1387 pmol/liter	
Age 41–60	W 0.4–2.5, M 13.0–35.0 pg/ml	W 13.9–86.7, M 451–1213 pmol/liter	x 34.67
Age 61–80	W 0.2–2.0, M 12.0–28.0 pg/ml	W 6.9–69.3, M 416–971 pmol/liter	
Triglycerides, fasting			
Normal	40–150 mg/dl	0.45–1.69 mmol/liter	
Borderline	150–200 mg/dl	1.69–2.26 mmol/liter	x 0.01129
High	200–500 mg/dl	2.26–-5.65 mmol/liter	
Very high	>500 mg/dl	>5.65 mmol/liter	
Urea, plasma (BUN)	8–25 mg/dl	2.9–8.9 mmol/liter	x 0.357
Urinalysis pH	5.0–9.0	5.0–9.0	No conversion
Specific gravity	1.001–1.035	1.001–1.035	
WBC (White blood cells, leukocytes)	$4.5–11.0 \times 10^3/mm^3$	$4.5–11.0 \times 10^9$ liter	$\times 10^6$

Table adapted from www.aidsinfonet.org

Appendix D:

Metric Conversions

The United States generally uses customary units of measure. The rest of the world uses the metric system. Below are useful tables for converting some common measurements from U.S. customary units to metric units.

U.S. Customary Units	Metric Units or Standard International (SI) Units
1 inch (in)	25.4 millimeters (mm)
.6 cubic inch	1 cubic centimeter (cc)
1 foot (ft)	30.5 centimeters (cm)
1 yard (yd)	91.4 centimeters (cm)
1 mile (mi)	1.6 kilometers (km)
1 fluid ounce (fl oz)	29.6 milliliters (mL)
1 dry ounce (oz)	28.3 grams (g)
1 dry pound (lb) or 16 oz	454 grams (g)
1 pint (pt)	551 milliliters (mL)
1 quart (qt)	1.1 liters (L)
1 gallon (gal)	4.4 liters (L)
1 teaspoon (tsp)	5 milliters (mL)
1 tablespoon (tbsp)	15 milliters (mL)
1 cup or 16 tbsp	240 milliters (mL)

Degrees Fahrenheit are used in the United States to measure temperatures in most non-scientific contexts.

- Pure water freezes at 32 °F and boils at 212 °F at 1 atm.
- Water saturated with common salt freezes at −6.02 °F.

$$F = \frac{9}{5}C + 32$$

- Conversion formula:

Appendix E:

Vitamins, Nutrition, and Dietary Reference Intake

The federal government has established various guidelines for the daily intake of vitamins as well as for nutrition. The Dietary Reference Intake (DRI) is a set of guidelines set up in 1997. It was formerly called the the Recommended Dietary Allowance (or RDA).

The free encyclopedia (wikipedia.com) has the following list of the DRI for an average 25-year-old male. The amounts may vary based on age, gender, size, and certain health conditions. The UL stands for upper limits of intake because those substances for which it is given are considered to be harmful in high doses.

Nutrient	RDA	UL	
Vitamin A	900	3,000	mcg/day
Vitamin C	90	2,000	mg/day
Vitamin D	5	50	mcg/day
Vitamin E	15	1,000	mg/day
Vitamin K	120		mcg/day
Folate	400	1,000	mcg/day
Vitamin B6	1.3	100	mg/day
Vitamin B12	2.4		mcg/day
Calcium	1000	2500	mg/day
Chloride	2300	3600	mg/day
Chromium	35		mcg/day
Copper	900	10,000	mcg/day
Fluoride	4	10	mg/day
Iodine	150	1100	mcg/day
Iron	8	45	mg/day
Magnesium	400		mg/day
Manganese	2.3	11	mg/day
Molybdenum	45	2000	mcg/day
Phosphorus	700	4000	mg/day
Potassium	4700		mg/day
Selenium	55	400	mcg/day
Sodium	1500	2300	mg/day
Zinc	11	40	mg/day

NUTRITIONAL INTAKE

The Food and Drug Administration (www.fda.gov) has set up daily value recommendations for key nutrients based on a 2,000 calorie daily diet. These are marked as % Daily Values on nutrition labels that are required on most packaged food sold in the United States. The % DV helps you determine if a serving of food is high or low in a nutrient. Note: a few nutrients, like *trans* fat, do not have a % DV because it is thought they should be severely limited or totally eliminated from most daily consumption. The chart that follows shows the % Daily Value as it appears on a typical nutrition label.

	% Daily Value*
Total Fat 12g	18%
Saturated Fat 3g	15%
Trans Fat 3g	
Cholesterol 30mg	10%
Sodium 470mg	20%
Total Carbohydrate 31g	10%
Dietary Fiber 0g	0%
Sugars 5g	
Protein 5g	
Vitamin A	4%
Vitamin C	2%
Calcium	20%
Iron	4%

The daily nutritional amounts that are recommended are shown in the following chart from the FDA. The goals shown indicate that a substance should be limited as much as possible or should be increased if possible.

Nutrient	**DV**	**%DV**	**Goal**
Total Fat	65g	= 100%DV	Less than
Sat Fat	20g	= 100%DV	Less than
Cholesterol	300mg	= 100%DV	Less than
Sodium	2400mg	= 100%DV	Less than
Total Carbohydrate	300g	= 100%DV	At least
Dietary Fiber	25g	= 100%DV	At least

The FDA website give examples of the difference in nutritional labeling between two types of milk shown on the next page. The label on the left is for whole milk and the label on the right is for skim milk.

Nutrition Facts

Serving Size 1 cup (236ml)
Servings Per Container 1

Amount Per Serving

Calories (120)   Calories from Fat 45

	% Daily Value*
Total Fat 5g	(8%)
Saturated Fat 3g	(15%)
Trans Fat 0g	
Cholesterol 20mg	7%
Sodium 120mg	5%
Total Carbohydrate 11g	4%
Dietary Fiber 0g	0%
Sugars 11g	
Protein 9g	17%

Vitamin A 10%   •   Vitamin C 4%
Calcium 30% • Iron 0% • Vitamin D 25%

*Percent Daily Values are based on a 2,000 calorie diet. Your daily values may be higher or lower depending on your calorie needs.

Nutrition Facts

Serving Size 1 cup (236ml)
Servings Per Container 1

Amount Per Serving

Calories (80)   Calories from Fat 0

	% Daily Value*
Total Fat 0g	(0%)
Saturated Fat 0g	(0%)
Trans Fat 0g	
Cholesterol Less than 5mg	0%
Sodium 120mg	5%
Total Carbohydrate 11g	4%
Dietary Fiber 0g	0%
Sugars 11g	
Protein 9g	17%

Vitamin A 10%   •   Vitamin C 4%
Calcium 30% • Iron 0% • Vitamin D 25%

*Percent Daily Values are based on a 2,000 calorie diet. Your daily values may be higher or lower depending on your calorie needs.

Appendices

Appendix F:

BMI

The National Institutes for Health (www.nih.gov) provides information about the BMI or (body mass index) on its website. For **adults,** a healthy weight is defined as the appropriate weight in relation to height. This ratio of weight to height is known as the body mass index (BMI). People who are overweight might have too much body weight for their height. People who are obese almost always have a large amount of body fat in relation to their height. To use the BMI chart below, find your height on the left of the chart. Go straight across from that point until you come to your weight in pounds. The number at the top is your BMI. This chart applies only to adults.

We Can! Watch Our Weight

	Healthy Weight						Overweight					Obese					
BMI	19	20	21	22	23	24	25	26	27	28	29	30	31	32	33	34	35
Height							Body Weight (pounds)										
4'10"	91	96	100	105	110	115	119	124	129	134	138	143	148	153	158	162	167
4'11"	94	99	104	109	114	119	124	128	133	138	143	148	153	158	163	168	173
5'0"	97	102	107	112	118	123	128	133	138	143	148	153	158	163	168	174	179
5'1"	100	106	111	116	122	127	132	137	143	148	153	158	164	169	174	180	185
5'2"	104	109	115	120	126	131	136	142	147	153	158	164	169	175	180	186	191
5'3"	107	113	118	124	130	135	141	146	152	158	163	169	175	180	186	191	197
5'4"	110	116	122	128	134	140	145	151	157	163	169	174	180	186	192	197	204
5'5"	114	120	126	132	138	144	150	156	162	168	174	180	186	192	198	204	210
5'6"	118	124	130	136	142	148	155	161	167	173	179	186	192	198	204	210	216
5'7"	121	127	134	140	146	153	159	166	172	178	185	191	198	204	211	217	223
5'8"	125	131	138	144	151	158	164	171	177	184	190	197	203	210	216	223	230
5'9"	128	135	142	149	155	162	169	176	182	189	196	203	209	216	223	230	236
5'10"	132	139	146	153	160	167	174	181	188	195	202	209	216	222	229	236	243
5'11"	136	143	150	157	165	172	179	186	193	200	208	215	222	229	236	243	250
6'0"	140	147	154	162	169	177	184	191	199	206	213	221	228	235	242	250	258
6'1"	144	151	159	166	174	182	189	197	204	212	219	227	235	242	250	257	265
6'2"	148	155	163	171	179	186	194	202	210	218	225	233	241	249	256	264	272
6'3"	152	160	168	176	184	192	200	208	216	224	232	240	248	256	264	272	279
6'4"	156	164	172	180	189	197	205	213	221	230	238	246	254	263	271	279	287

For **children and teens,** overweight is defined differently than it is for adults. Because children are still growing, and boys and girls develop at different rates, BMIs for children 2-20 years old are determined by comparing their weight and height against growth charts that take their age and gender into account. For more information about BMI-for-age and growth charts for children, visit www.cdc.gov/nccdphp/dnpa/bmi/bmi-for-age.htm.

Appendices

Appendix G:
Medical Terminology Style

Government agencies, national organizations, and educational institutions vary the rules set up for style of medical terminology. One area with great variation is the spelling of *eponyms,* terms derived from proper names. For example, Alzheimer's disease was named after Alois Alzheimer, a German neurologist. Several major organizations (especially the AMA—American Medical Association and AAMT—American Association for Medical Transcription) have decided to simplify eponyms by dropping the apostrophe S, so that Alzheimer's disease is known by some as Alzheimer disease. The national charitable organizations and the governmental health organizations currently retain the use of the possessive.

The list below shows examples of medical eponyms in the two different styles.

U.S. Government	AMA and AAMT
Alzheimer's disease	Alzheimer disease
Babinski's reflex	Babinski reflex
Bartholin's glands	Bartholin glands
Bell's palsy	Bell palsy
Cooley's anemia	Cooley anemia
Cushing's syndrome	Cushing syndrome
Fontan's operation	Fontan operation
Meniere's disease	Meniere disease
non-Hodgkin's lymphoma	non-Hodgkin lymphoma
Parkinson's disease	Parkinson disease
Raynaud's phenomemon	Raynaud phenomenon
Tinel's sign	Tinel sign
Wilms' tumor	Wilm tumor

For the name of the disease, structure, condition, and so on, the initial capital remains style. However, for words derived from eponyms, some organizations recommend the use of lowercase; for example, *parkinsonian symptom.*

Appendix H:

Bones of the Human Body

There are 206 bones in the adult human body. Infants start out with additional bones that fuse to form adult bones. The infant bones are as follows:

> sacral vertebrae (4 or 5), which fuse in adults to form the sacrum
> coccygeal vertebrae (3 to 5), which fuse in adults to form the coccyx
> ilium, ischium and pubis, which fuse in adults to form the pelvic girdle

Adult bones often come in pairs or in groups as indicated in parentheses.

Cranial bones:
> frontal bone
> parietal bone (2)
> temporal bone (2)
> occipital bone
> sphenoid bone
> ethmoid bone

Facial bones:
> zygomatic bone (2)
> superior and inferior maxilla
> nasal bone (2)
> mandible
> palatine bone (2)
> lacrimal bone (2)
> vomer bone
> inferior nasal conchae (2)

Middle ear bones:
> malleus (2)
> incus (2)
> stapes (2)

Throat bone:
> hyoid bone

Shoulder bones:
> clavicle or collarbone (2)
> scapula or shoulder blade (2)

Thorax bones:
> sternum
> ribs (2 sets of 12)

Pelvis bones:
> pelvis (2)

Bones of the neck and spinal column:

> cervical vertebrae (7) including the atlas and axis
> lumbar vertebrae (5)
> thoracic vertebrae (12)
> sacrum
> coccyx

Bones of the arm:

> humerus (2)
> ulna (2)
> radius (2)

Bones of the hands:

> Wrist (carpal) bones:
>> scaphoid bone (2)
>> lunate bone (2)
>> triquetrum bone (2)
>> pisiform bone (2)
>> trapezium (bone) (2)
>> trapezoid bone (2)
>> capitate bone (2)
>> hamate bone (2)

Palm or metacarpal bones:

> metacarpal bones (2 sets of 5 each)

Finger bones or phalanges:

> proximal phalanges (2 sets of 5 each)
> intermediate phalanges (2 sets of 4 each)
> distal phalanges (2 sets of 5 each)

Bones of the Leg:

> femur (2)
> patella (2)
> tibia (2)
> fibula (2)

Bones of the Feet:

> Ankle (tarsal) bones:
>> calcaneus (heel bone) (2)
>> talus (2)
>> navicular bone (2)
>> medial cuneiform bone (2)
>> intermediate cuneiform bone (2)
>> lateral cuneiform bone (2)
>> cuboidal bone (2)

Instep bones:

> metatarsal bone (2 sets of 5 each)

Toe bones:

> proximal phalanges (2 sets of 5 each)
> intermediate phalanges (2 sets of 4 each)
> distal phalanges (2 sets of 5 each)

Appendix I:
Nerves of the Human Body

The major nerves of the human body are grouped as cranial nerves, and spinal nerves. The spinal nerves are further divided into four groups discussed below. These nerves send and receive impulses from all parts of the body. The table gives the functions for which these nerves provide the controlling impulses.

Cranial Nerves (nerves of the brain)

Nerve	Name	Functions	Origin
Cranial Nerve I (CN I)	olfactory nerve	olfaction (sense of smell)	nasal cavity
Cranial Nerve II (CN II)	optic nerve	vision	retina
Cranial Nerve III	oculomotor nerve	eye muscles, eyelid muscles, contraction of pupil and shaping of eye lens	mesencephalon
Cranial Nerve IV (CN IV)	trochlear nerve	moves eyeball inferiorly and laterally	mesencephalon
Cranial Nerve V (CN V)	trigeminal nerve	conducts sensory impulses from cornea, nose, forehead, anterior scalp, nasal mucosa, palate, gums, cheek, from anterior part of tongue, skin of chin, lower jaw, lower teeth, and part of the ear	pons
Cranial Nerve VI (CN VI)	abducens or abducent nerve	abducts the eye	pons
Cranial Nerve VII (CN VII)	facial nerve	taste in the anterior section of the tongue; facial expression; salivary glands; lacrimal glands; and the submandibular and sublingual glands.	pons
Cranial Nerve VIII (CN VIII)	vestibulocochlear nerve	hearing and equilibrium	inner ear
Cranial Nerve IX (CN IX)	glossopharyngeal nerve	taste in the posterior section of the tongue; pharynx muscle; salivary gland	medulla oblongata; tongue
Cranial Nerve X (CN X)	vagus nerve	pharynx; larynx; trachea; heart; lungs; and abdominal organs	medulla oblongata
Cranial Nerve XI (CN XI)	accessory nerve	movement of head and neck; lifting of shoulder	medulla oblongata and spinal cord
Cranial Nerve XII (CN XII)	hypoglossal nerve	tongue muscles involved in swallowing and speech	medulla oblongata

Appendices

Spinal Nerves

The spinal nerves are divided into four groups.

1. Cervical spinal nerves (C1 to C8)

2. Thoracic spinal nerves (T1 to T12)

3. Lumbar spinal nerves (L1 to L5)

4. Sacral spinal nerves (S1 to S5)

The table below gives the major areas that the spinal nerves supply.

Nerve Group	Areas the Group Supplies
C1-C2	Head, face, upper neck, inner and middle ear, sympathetic nerve system, sinuses, eyes, auditory nerves
C3-C7	Neck, shoulders, thyroid, tonsils, teeth, outer ear, nose, mouth, vocal cords
T1-T12	Arms, hands, heart, coronary arteries, esophagus, trachea, lungs, bronchial tubes, gallbladder, liver, stomach, pancreas, spleen, kidneys, ureters, adrenal glands, small intestines
L1-L5	Large intestines, appendix, abdomen, bladder, reproductive organs, lower back, lower extremities, ankles, feet
S1-S5	Hip bones, tail bone, buttocks, rectum, anus, and more

Appendix J:

Muscles of the Human Body

There are three types of muscle in the human body.

1. Skeletal muscles are striated muscles attached to skeletal bones and usually contract voluntarily as in the movement of limbs.

2. Smooth muscles are nonstriated muscles that line hollow organs, such as the intestines, and are responsible for important functions, such as digestion, action of blood vessels, and amount of light reaching the retina.

3. Cardiac muscle is found only in the heart and is responsible for the pumping of blood.

The following lists separate groups of muscles by their location in the body. The body has hundreds of individual muscles and they are grouped according to their function within an area of the body.

Muscle Groups of the Head and Neck
Suboccipital
Prevertebral
Anterolateral Neck
Superficial Neck
Anterior Neck
Epicranial
Muscles of Facial Expression
Muscles of Mastication
Extraocular
Laryngeal

Muscle Groups of the Trunk
Superficial Back
Pectoral
Shoulder Girdle
Deep Back
    Splenius Muscles
    Erector Spinae Muscles
    Transversospinal Muscles
    Segmental Muscles

Muscle Groups of the Arms and Hands
Brachium
Antebrachial Flexors
Antebrachial Extensors
Hand & Wrist

Muscle Groups of the Legs and Feet
Gluteal
Posterior Thigh
Adductor Thigh
Anterior Thigh
Posterior Leg
Anterolateral Leg
Foot

Appendices

Appendix K:

Joints of the Human Body

Joints of the body are classified in two ways by their structure and by their function. There are three structural classifications:

1. **fibrous**—at bones connected by collagen. Fibrous joints are made of dense connective tissue and do not allow movement in adults. Cranial sutures are examples of fibrous joints.

2. **cartilaginous**—at bones connected by cartilage. Cartilaginous joints allow limited movement. An example are the joints between the ribs and between the vertebrae in the spinal colum.

3. **synovial**—where there is a space or synovial cavity between articulating bones. Synovial joints permit a lot of movement as the arm joints, hand joints, leg joints, and so on.

There are also three functional classifications:

1. **synarthrosis**—permit no movement. Fibrous joints are synarthroses.

2. **amphiarthrosis**—permit some but limited movement. Cartilaginous joints are amphiarthroses.

3. **diarthroses**—permit a lot of movement. Synovial joints are diarthroses.

The major joints of the human body (other than the cranial sutures and joints in the teeth) are:

Vertebral column:
    atlanto-axial
    atlanto-occipital
    temporomandibular
    sternocostal
    sacroiliac

Upper extremity:
    sternoclavicular
    acromioclavicular
    shoulder
    elbow/proximal radioulnar articulation
    wrist/distal radioulnar articulation
    carpometacarpal
    metacarpophalangeal
    interphalangeal

Lower extremity:
    hip
    knee
    ankle
    subtalar
    metatarsophalangeal

Appendix L:
English-Spanish Glossary

The following list of English words are followed by a translation into Spanish. The translations are a key to the Spanish words in Appendix M which are defined in Spanish. English definitions for the words in this list are available in the A-Z section of this dictionary.

A

abortifacient (abortifaciente)
abortion (aborto)
abscess (absceso)
absorption (absorción)
acetabulum (acetábulo)
acetone (acetona)
acetylcholine (acetilcolina)
achalasia (acalasia)
acidosis (acidosis)
acne (acne)
acne vulgaris (acné vulgar)
acromegaly (acromegalia)
acromion (acromion)
Adam's apple (manzana de adán)
adenoidectomy (adenoidectomía)
adenoiditis (adenoiditis)
adenoids (adenoides)
adipose (adiposo)
adrenal (adrenal)
adrenalectomy (adrenalectomía)
adrenaline (adrenalina)
afterbirth (secundina)
agglutination (aglutinación)
agglutinogen (aglutinógeno)
agnosia (agnosia)
agranulocyte (agranulocito)
albinism (albinismo)
albumin (albúmina)
albuminuria (albuminuria)
aldosterone (aldosterina)
allergen (alergeno)
allergy (alergia)
allograft (aloinjerto)
alopecia (alopecia)
alopecia areata (alopecia areata)
alveolus, pl. alveoli (alvéolo)
amenorrhea (amenorrea)

amino acid, AA (aminoácido(AA))
amnesia (amnesia)
amniocentesis (amniocentesis)
amnios (amnion)
amniotic (aminiótico)
amphiarthroses (anfiartroses)
amputation (amputación)
amylase (amilasa)
anacusis (anacusia)
analgesic (analgésico)
anaphylaxis (anafilaxia o anafilaxis)
anastomosis (anastomosis)
androgen (andrógeno)
anemia (anemia)
anesthetic (anestésico)
aneurysm (aneurisma)
angina (angina)
angina pectoris (angina de pecho)
angioplasty (angioplastia)
angioscopy (angioscopia)
anisocytosis (anisocitosis)
ankle (tobillo)
ankyloglossia (anquiloglosia)
ankylosis (anquilosis)
anorchism, anorchia (anorquia)
anthracosis (antracosis)
antibacterial (antibacteriano)
antibiotic (antibiótico)
antibody (anticuerpo)
antidiabetic (antidiabético)
antidote (antidoto)
antifungal (antifúngico)
antigen (antígeno)
antihistamines (antihistamines)
antitoxin (antitoxina)
anuria (anuria)
anus (ano)
aorta (aorta)
apex (apex)
aphagia (afagia)
aphakia (afaquia)
aphasia (afasia)
apnea (apnea)
appendix (apéndice)
apraxia (apraxia)
arachnoid (aracnoideo)
areola (aréola)
arrhythmia (arritmia)
arteriole (arteriola)

arteriosclerosis (arteriosclerosis)
arteritis (arteritis)
artery (arteria)
arthralgia (artralgia)
arthritis (artritis)
arthrocentesis (artrocentesis)
articulation (articulación)
asbestosis (asbestosis)
ascites (ascitis)
aspermia (aspermia)
aspiration (aspiración)
asthenopia (astenopía)
asthma (asma)
astigmatism (astimagtismo)
astrocyte, astroglia (astrocito, astroglia)
astrocytoma (astrocitoma)
asystole (asistolia)
ataxia (ataxia)
atelectasis (atelectasia)
atheroma (ateroma)
atherosclerosis (ateriosclerosis)
atlas (atlas)
atresia (atresia)
atrium, pl. atria (atrium, pl.atrio)
atrophy (atrofia)
audiogram (audiograma)
audiologist (audiólogo)
audiometry (audiometría)
aura (aura)
auricle (auricular)
auscultation (auscultatión)
autograft (autoinjerto)
axis(axis)
axon (axón)
Azoospermia (azoospermia)
azotemia (azoemia)

B

bacillus (bacillo)
balanitis (balanitis)
base (base)
basophil (basófilo)
basophilia (basofilia)
bile (bilis)
bilirubin (bilirrubina)
biopsy (biopsia)
blackhead (punto negro)
bladder (vejiga)
blepharitis (blefaritis)

blindness (ceguera)
blood (sangre)
body (cuerpo)
bone (hueso)
brachytherapy (braquiterapia)
bradycardia (bradicardia)
bradypnea (bradipnea)
brain (cerebro)
brainstem (tronco encefálico)
bronchiole (bronquiolo)
bronchitis (bronquitis)
bronchodilators (broncodilatador)
bronchography (broncografía)
bronchoplasty (broncoplastia)
bronchoscope (broncoscopio)
bronchus, pl. bronchi (bronquio)
bronchospasm (broncoespasmo)
bruit (ruido)
bulla (pl. bullae) (bulla)
bunion (bunio)
bunionectomy (bunionectomía)
burn (quemadura)
bursa pl. bursae(bursa)
bursa, pl. bursae (bolso)
bursectomy (bursectomía)
bursitis (bursitis)

C

calcaneus (calcáneo)
calcar (calcar)
calcitonin (calcitona)
calcium (calico)
callus (callo)
cancellous (canceloso)
candidiasis (candidiasis)
capillary (capilar)
carbon dioxide (dióxido de carbono)
carbuncle (carbunco)
cardiomyopathy (cardiomiopatía)
cartilage (cartílago)
casting (colado)
castration (castración)
cataract (catarata)
catecholamines (catecolaminas)
cauterization (cauterización)
cauterize (cauterizar)
cecum (ciego)
cellulitis (celulitis)
cerebellitis (cerebelitis)

cerebrum (cerebrum)

cervix (cervix)

chalazion (chalazión)

cheeks (carrillo)

cheilitis (queilitis)

chemotherapy (quimioterapia)

chlamydia (clamidia)

chloasma (cloasma)

cholangitis (colangitis)

cholecystectomy (colecistectomía)

cholecystitis (colecistitis)

cholecystography (colecistografía)

cholesterol (colesterol)

chondromalacia (condromalacia)

chorion (corion)

choroid (coroides)

chyme (quimo)

cicatrix, scar (cicatriz)

circumsicion (circumcisión)

cirrhosis (cirrosis)

claudication (claudicación)

clavicle (clavícula)

climacteric (climaterio)

clitoris (clítoris)

coagulation (coagulación)

coccyx (cóccix)

cochlea (caracol)

coitus (coito)

colectomy (colectomía)

colic (cólico)

colitis (colitis)

collagen (colágeno)

colon (colon)

colonoscopy (colonoscopia)

colostomy (colostomía)

coma (coma)

concussion (concusión)

condom (condón)

conductivity (conductividad)

condyloma (condiloma)

cones (conos)

conization (conización)

conjunctivitis (conjunctivitis)

conjuntiva, pl.conjunctivae (conjuntiva)

constipation (constipación)

constriction (constricción)

contraception (anticoncepción)

convolution (circunvolución)

copulation (copulación)

cordotomy (cordotomía)

corium (corium)

corn (callo)

cornea (cornea)

cortex (corteza)

corticosteroid (corticosteroide)

cortisol (cortisol)

craniectomy (cranietomía)

craniotomy (craneotomía)

creatine (creatina)

creatinine (creatinina)

crest (cresta)

croup (crup)

crust (costar)

cryosurgery (criocirugía)

cuticle (cutícula)

cyanosis (cianosis)

cystectomy (cistectomía)

cystitis (cistitis)

cystocele (cistocele)

cystolith (cistolito)

cystorrhaphy (cistorrafia)

cystoscopy (cistoscopia)

D

deafness (sordera)

decibel (decibel)

decubitus (decúbito)

defecation (defecación)

deglutition (deglución)

dementia (demencia)

dendrite (dentrita)

depolarization (despolarización)

dermabrasion (dermabrasión)

dermatitis (dermatitis)

dermatochalasis (dermatocalasia)

dermatology (dermatología)

dermis (dermis)

desmielinación (demyelination)

diabetes (diabetes)

diaphoresis (diaforesis)

diaphragm (diaphragma)

diaphysis (diáfisis)

diarrhea (diarrhea)

diastole (diástole)

diencephalon (diencéfalo)

digestion (digestion)

diphtheria (difteria)

diplopia (diplopía)

disk, disc (disco)
diskography (discografía)
dislocation (dislocación)
diverticulitis (diverticulitis)
diverticulosis (diverticulosis)
dopamine (dopamina)
drug (droga)
druggist (boticario)
duodenum (duodeno)
dwarfism (enanismo)
dyscrasia (discrasia)
dysentery (disentería)
dysmenorrhea (dismenorrea)
dyspareunia (dispareunia)
dyspepsia (dispepsia)
dysphagia (disfagia)
dysphasia (disfasia)
dysphonia (disfonía)
dyspnea (disnea)
dysrhythmia (disritmia)
dystonia (distonía)
dysuria (disuria)

E

ear (oreja, oído)
eardrum (tambor de oído)
ecchymosis (equimosis)
echocardiographya (ecocardiografía)
eczema (eccema)
edema (edema)
ejaculation (eyaculación)
elbow (codo)
electroencephalograph (electroencefalógrafo)
electrolyte (electrólito)
electromyogram (electromiógrafo)
electrophoresis (electroforesis)
embolectomy (embolectomía)
embolus (émbolo)
emesis (emesis)
emphysema (enfisema pulmonar)
empyema (empiema)
encephalitis (encefalitis)
encephalogram (encefalograma)
endocarditis (endocarditis)
endocardium (endocardio)
endocrine gland (glándula endocrina)
endolymph (endolinfa)
endometriosis (endometriosis)

endometrium (endometrio)
endoscope (endoscopio)
endosteum (endostio)
endothelium (endotelio)
enteritis (enteritis)
enucleation (enucleación)
enuresis (enuresis)
enzyme (enzima)
eosinophil (eosinófilo)
eosinophilia (eosinofilia)
epicardium (epicardio)
epidermis (epidermis)
epididymis (epidídimo)
epididymitis (epididimitis)
epiglottis (epiglotis)
epinephrine (epinefrina)
epiphora (epífora)
epiphysitis (epifisitis)
epispadias (epispadias)
epithalamus (epitálamo)
equilibrium (equilibrio)
erosion (erosion)
eructation (eructación)
erythrocyte (eritrocito)
erythropenia (eritropenia)
erythropoietin (eritropoyetina)
esophagitis (esofagitis)
esophagoplasty (esofagoplastia)
esophagoscopy (esofagoscopia)
esophagus (esófago)
esotropia (esotropía)
estrogen (estrógeno)
eupnea (eupnea)
euthanasia (euthanasia)
excitability (excitabilidad)
excoriation (excoriación)
exhalation (exahalación)
exocrine (exocrine)
exocrine gland (glándula ecrina)
exophthalmos, exophthalmus (exoftalmía)
exostosis (exostosis)
expiration (espiración)
exudate (exudado)
eye (ojo)
eyebrow (ceja)
eyelashes (pestaña)
eyelid (párpado)
eyestrain (vista fatigada)

F

fascia (fascia)
feces (heces)
femur (fémur)
fibrillation (fibrilación)
fibrinogen (fibrinógeno)
fibroid (fibroide)
fibula (peroné)
filtration (filtración)
fimbriae (fimbria)
fissure (fisura)
flaccid (flácido)
flagellum (flagelo)
flatulence (flatulencia)
flatus (flato)
flutter (aleteo)
fontanelle (fontanela)
foramen magnum (foramen magnum)
foramen (agujero)
foreskin (prepucio)
fossa (fosa)
phosphorus (fósforo)
fracture (fractura)
frenulum (frenillo)
fulguration (fulguración)
fundus (fondo)
furuncle (furúnculo)

G

gait (marcha)
gallbladder (vesícula biliar)
gallop (galope)
gallstone (cálculo biliar)
gamete (gameto)
gangliitis (ganglitis)
ganglion (ganglio)
gangrene (gangrena)
gastrectomy (gastrectomía)
gastritis (gastritis)
gastroenteritis (gastroenteritis)
gastroscopy (gastrocopia)
generic (genérico)
genetics (genética)
gestation (gestación)
gigantism (gigantismo)
gland (glándula)
glaucoma (glaucoma)
glioma (glioma)

globin (globina)
globulin (globulina)
glomerulus, pl. glomuleri (glomérulo)
glossitis (glositis)
glottis (glotis)
glucagon (glucagon)
glucose (glucosa)
glycogen (glucógeno)
goiter (bocio)
gonad (gónada)
goniometer (goniómetro)
gonorrhea (gonorrea)
granulocytosis (granulocitosis)
gravida (grávida)
gum (encía)
gynecologist (ginecólogo)

H

hair root (raíz de pelo)
halitosis (halitosis)
hearing (audición)
heart (corazón)
heel (talón)
hematemesis (hematemesis)
hematocrit (hematócrito)
hematocytoblast (hematocitoblasto)
hematuria (hematuria)
hemodialysis (hcmodiálisis)
hemoglobin (hemoglobina)
hemolysis (hemólisis)
hemophilia (hemofilia)
hemorrhoidectomy (hemorroidectomía)
hemorrhoids (hemorroides)
hemothorax (hemotórax)
heparin (heparina)
hepatitis (hepatitis)
hepatomegaly (hepatomegalia)
hepatopathy (hepatopatía)
hernia (hernia)
herniated disk (disco herniated)
herpes (herpes)
heterograft (heteroinjerto)
high blood pressure (presión arterial alta)
hilum, also hilus (hilio)
hirsutism (hirsutimo)
histamine (histamine)
histeroscopy (histeroscopia)
homograft (homoinjerto)
hordeolum (orzuelo)

hormone (hormona)
humerus (húmero)
hydrocephalus (hidrocefalia)
hymen (himen)
hyperopia (hiperopía)
hyperparathyroidism (hiperparatiroidismo)
hypersensitivity (hipersensibilidad)
hyperthyroidism (hipertiroidism)
hyperventilation (hiperventilación)
hypoadrenalism (hipoadrenalismo)
hypdermis (hipodermis)
hypoglycemia (hipoglucemia)
hypoglycemic (hipoglucémico)
hypoparathyroidism (hipoparatiroidismo)
hypopharynx (hipofaringe)
hypophysis (hipófisis)
hypospadias (hiposoadias)
hypotension (hipotensión)
hypothalamus (hipotálamo)
hypothyroidism (hipotiroidismo)
hypoventilation (hipoventilación)
hypoxemia (hipoxemia)
hypoxia (hipoxia)
hysterectomy (histerectomía)
hysterosalpingography (histerosalpingografía)

I

icterus (icterus)
ileitis (ileitis):
ileostomy (ileostomía)
ileum (íleon)
ileum (ilium)
ileus (íleo)
immunity (inmunidad)
immunoglobulin (inmunoglobina)
impetigo (impetigo)
impotence (impotencia)
incontinence (incontinecia)
incus (incus)
infarct, infarction (infarto)
infertility (infertilidad)
inhalation (inhalación)
insertion (inserción)
inspiration (inspiración)
insulin (insulina)
integument (integumento)
interleukin (interleucina)
interneuron (interneuronas)
intestine (intestino)

intradermal (intradérmico)
introitus (introito)
iridectomy (iridectomía)
iris (iris)
iritis (iritis)
ischemia (isquemia)
ischium (isquión)
isthmus (istmo)
IV (intavenoso)

J

jaundice (ictericia)
jejunum (yeyuno)
joint (empalme)

K

keloid (queloide)
keratin (queratina)
keratitis (queratitis)
keratoplasty (queratoplastia)
keratosis (queratosis)
ketoacidosis (cetoacidosis)
ketone (cetona)
ketonuria (cetonuria)
ketosis (cetosis)
kidney (riñón)
kyphosis (cifosis)

L

lacrimation (lagrimeo)
lactation (lactación)
lactiferous (lactífero)
lamina, pl. laminae (lamina)
laparoscopy (laparoscopia)
laryngitis (laringitis)
laryngoplasty (laringoplastia)
laryngoscopy (laringoscopia)
laryngostomy (laringostomía)
larynx (laringe)
lens (lens)
lesion (lesión)
leukoderma (leucodermia)
leukoplakia (leucoplaquia)
leukorrhea (leucorrea)
ligament (ligamento)
lip (labio)
liver (hígado)
lobectomy (lobectomía)

lobotomy (lobotomía)
lordosis (lordosis)
low blood pressure (presión de arterial baja)
lumen (lumen)
lung (pulmón)
lunula (lúnula)
lymph (linfa)
lymphadenectomy (linfadenectomía)
lymphadenopathy (linfadenopatía)
lymphocyte (linfocito)
lymphoma (linfoma)

M

macrocytosis (macrocitosis)
macrophage (macrófago)
macule, macula (mácula)
malleus (malleus)
mammography (mamografía)
mammoplasty (mamoplastia)
mandible (mandíbula)
mastectomy (mastectomía)
mastication (masticación)
mastitis (mastitis)
meatus (meato)
mediastinum (mediastino)
medication, medicine (medicación)
medulla (médula)
megakaryocyte (megacariocito)
melanin (melanina)
melanocyte (melanocito)
melena (melena)
menarche (menarca)
meninges, sing. meninx (nenunges, sing. meningis)
meningioma (meningioma)
meningitis (meningitis)
meningocele (meningocele)
meningomyelocele (meningomielocele)
menopause (menopausia)
menorrhagia (menorragia)
menstruation (menstruación)
mesentery (mesenterio)
mesothelioma (mesotelioma)
metacarpal (metacarpiano)
metaphysic (metáfisis)
metastasis (metastasis)
metrorrhagia (metrorragia)
microcytosis (microcitosis)
microglia (microglia)
microphage (micrófago)

midbrain (cerebro medio)

miscarriage (aborto espontáneo)

monocyte (monocito)

mouth (boca)

murmur (soplo)

muscle (músculo)

muscular dystrophy (distrofia muscular)

musculoskeletal (musculoesquelético)

myalgia (mialgia)

myeloblast (mieloblasto)

myelogram (mielograma)

myelography (mielografía)

myeloma (mieloma)

myocarditis (miocarditis)

myocardium (miocardio)

myodynia (miodinia)

myoma (mioma)

myomectomy (miomectomía)

myometrium (miometrio)

myopia, nearsightedness (miopía)

myositis (miositis)

myringitis (miringitis)

myxedema (mixedema)

N

nail (uña)

narcolepsy (narcolepsia)

nasopharynx (nasofaringe)

nausea (nausea)

necrosis (necrosis)

neoplasm (neoplasma)

nephrectomy (nefrectomía)

nephritis (nefritis)

nephroblastoma (nefroblastoma)

nerve (nervio)

neurectomy (neurectomía)

neurilemma (neurilema)

neuritis (neuritis)

neuron (neurona)

neurosurgeon (neurocirujano)

neurotransmitter (neurotramisor)

neutrophil (neutrófilo)

nevus (nevo)

nipple (pezón)

nocturia (nocturia)

lumpectomy (nodulectomía)

nodule (nódulo)

norepinephrine (norepinefrina)

nose (nariz)

nosebleed (epistaxis)
nostrils (naris)
NSAID (agents de antiiflamatorios, AINE)
nyctalopia (nictalopía)
nystagmus (nistagmo)

O

obesity (obesidad)
obstetrician (obstetra)
occlusion (oclusión)
olecranon (olecranon)
oligodendroglia (oligodendroglia)
oligodendroglioma (oligodendroglioma)
oligomenorrhea (oligomenorrea)
oligospermia (oligospermia)
oliguria (oliguria)
onychia, onychitis (oniquia)
onychopathy (onicopatía)
oocyte (oocito)
oophorectomy (ooforectomía)
ophthalmologist (oftalmología)
ophthalmoscopy (oftalmoscópia)
optometrist (optometrista)
orchidectomy (orquidectomía)
orchiectomy (orquietomía)
oropharynx (orofaringe)
orthopedist (ortopedista)
orthopnea (ortopnea)
orthosis, orthotics (ortósis, ortótica)
ossification (osificación)
ostealgia (ostealgia)
osteoarthritis (osteoartritis)
osteoblast (osteoblasto)
osteoclasis (osteoclasia)
osteoclast (osteoclasto)
osteocyte (osteocito)
osteodynia (osteodinia)
osteoma (osteoma)
osteomyelitis (osteomielitis)
osteopath (osteópata)
osteoplasty (osteoplastia)
osteoporosis (osteoporosis)
osteosarcoma (osteosarcoma)
osteotomy (osteotomía)
otalgia (otalgia)
otitis externa (otitis externa)
otitis media (otitis media)
otoliths (otolito)
otologist (otólogo)

otoplasty (otoplastia)
otorrhagia (otorragia)
otorrhea (otorrea)
otosclerosis (otosclerosis)
otoscopy (otoscopia)
ovary (ovario)
ovulation (ovulación)
ovum (óvulo)
oxytocin (ositocina)
oxytocin (oxitocina)

P

pacemaker (marcapaso)
palpitations (palpitaciones)
palsy (parálisis)
pancreas (páncreas)
pancreatectomy (pancreatectomía)
pancreatitis (pancreatitis)
pancytopenia (pancitopenia)
papilla (papila)
papule (pápula)
paracusis (paracusia)
paranychia (paroniquia)
parasiticide (parasiticida)
parathormone (parathormona)
parathyroid (paratiroide)
paroxysmal (paroxístico)
Parturition (parturición)
patella (rótula)
pathogen (patógeno)
pediculosis (pediculosis)
pelvis (pelvis)
pemphigus (pénfigo)
penis (pene)
pepsin (pepsina)
percussion (percusión)
pericarditis (pericarditis)
pericardium (pericardio)
perimetrium (perimetrio)
perineum (perineo)
periosteum (periostio)
peristalsis (peristaltismo)
peritoneoscopy (peritoneoscopia)
peritonitis (peritonitis)
pertussis (pertussis)
PET (TEP)
petechia (petequia)
phagocytosis (fagocitosis)
phalanges (falange)

pharmacology (farmacología)
pharyngitis (faringitis)
pharynx (faringe)
phimosis (fimosis)
phlebitis (flebitis)
phlebography (flebografía)
phlebotomy (flebotomía)
photophobia (fotobia)
pia mater (piamadre)
pinna (pinna)
placenta (placenta)
plaque, patch (placa)
plasma (plasma)
plasmapheresis (plasmaféresis)
platelet (plaqueta)
pleura, pl. pleurae (pleura)
pleuritis, pleurisy (pleuritis)
pneumoconiosis (neumoconiosis)
pneumonectomy (neumonectomía)
pneumonia (neumonía)
pneumonitis (neumonitis)
pneumothorax (neumotórax)
podagra (podagra):
podiatrist (podiatra)
poikilocytosis (poiquilolocitosis)
polarization (polarización)
polycythemia (policetemia)
polydipsia (polidipsa)
polyp (pólipo)
polypectomy (polipectomía)
polypoid (polipoide)
polyposis (poliposis)
polyuria (poliuria)
pons (pons)
pore (poro)
presbyacusis (presbiacusia)
presbyopia (presbiopía)
prescription (perscripción)
priapism (priapismo)
proctitis (proctitis)
proctoscopy (proctoscopia)
progesterone (progesterona)
prostate (próstata)
prostatectomy (prostatectomía)
prostatitis (prostatitis)
prothrombin (protrombina)
pruritus (prurito)
psoriasis (psoriasis)
puberty (pubertad)

pubes (pubis)
pulmonary artery (arteria pulmunar)
pulmonary valve (válvula pulmonar)
pulse (pulso)
pupil (pupila)
purpura (púrpura)
pustule (pustule)
pyelitis (pielitis)
pylorus (píloro)
pyoderma (pioderma)
pyuria (piuria)

R

radiculitis (radiculitis)
rales (rales)
receptor (receptor)
rectum (recto)
reduction (reducción)
reflejo (reflex)
reflux (reflujo)
refraction (refracción)
regurgitation (regurgitación)
renin (renina)
renogram (renograma)
repolarization (repolarización)
resectoscope (resectoscopio)
reticulocytosis (reticulocitosis)
retina (retina)
retinitis (retinitis)
retroflexion (retroflexión)
retroperitoneal (retroperitoneal)
retroversion (retroversión)
retrovirus (retrovirus)
rhabdomyoma (rabdomioma)
rhabdomyosarcoma (rabdomiosarcoma)
rheumatologist (reumatologo)
rhinitis (rinitis)
rhinoplasty (rinoplastia)
rhinorrhea (rinorrea)
rhonchi (ronquido)
rib (costilla)
rickets (raquitismo)
rigidity (rigidez)
rigor (rigor)
ringworm (tiña)
rods (bastoncillos)
roentgenology (roentgenología)
rosacea (rosácea)
rub (roce)

rubella, rubeola (rubéola)
rugae (rugae)

S

sacrum (sacro)
saliva (saliva)
salpingectomy (salpingectomía)
salpingitis (salpingitis)
sarcoidosis (sarcoidosis)
scabies (sarna)
scale (costar)
scale (escala)
scapula (escápula)
sciatica (ciática)
scirrhous (escirroso)
sclera (esclerótica)
scleritis (escleritis)
scleroderma (esclerodermia)
scoliosis (escolisis)
scotoma (escotoma)
scrotum (escroto)
seborrehea (seborrhea)
sebum (sebo)
sella turcica (silla turcica)
semen (semen)
septoplasty (septoplastia)
septostomy (septostomía)
pseudophakia (seudofaquia)
septum (tabique)
sequestrum (secuetro)
serum (suero)
shin (espinilla)
shingles (culebrilla)
sight (vista)
sigmoidoscopy (sigmoidoscopia)
singultus (singulto)
sinus (seno)
sinusitis (sinusitis)
skeleton (esqueleto)
skull (cráneo)
smell (olfacción, oler)
somnambulism (sonambulismo)
somnolence (somnolencia)
sonogram (sonograma)
sonography (sonografía)
spasm (espasmo)
sperm (esperma)
spermatozoon, pl.spermatozoa (espermatozoo)
spermicide (espermicida)

sphygmomanometer (esfigmomanómetro)
spina bifida (espina bífida)
spirometer (espirómetro)
spleen (bazo)
splenectomy (esplenectomía)
splinting (ferulización)
spondylolisthesis (espondilolistesis)
spondylolysis (espodilólisis)
spondylosyndesis (espodilosindesis)
sponge (esponja)
stapes, pl.stapes, stapedes (estribo)
steatorrhea (esteatorrea)
stenosis (estenosis)
sternum (esternón)
steroid (steroide)
stimulus (estimulo)
stomach (estómago)
strabismus (estrabismo)
stratum (estrato)
stratum corneum (estrato córne)
striae (estría)
stridor (estridor)
stroke (accidente cerebrovascular)
subluxation (sublaxación)
sulcus (surco)
suppository (supositorio)
suture (sutura)
sympathomimetic (simpatomimético)
symphysis (sínfisis)
synapse (sinapsis)
synarthrosis (sinartrosis)
syncope (síncope)
synovectomy (sinovectomía)
syphilis (sífilis)
syrine (jeringa)
labyrinthitis (laberintitis)
systole (sístole)

T

tachycardia (taquicardia)
tachypnea (taquipnea)
tears (lágrimas)
tendinitis, tendonitis (tendonitis)
tendon (tendon)
tenotomy (tenotomía)
testicle, testis (testículo)
testosterone (testosterona)
tetany (tetania)
thalamus (tálamo)

thalassemia (talasemia)
thoracocentesis (toracocentesis)
thoracostomy (torascostomía)
thorax (tórax)
throat (garganta)
throcotomy (toracotomía)
thrombectomy (trombectomía)
thrombin (trombina)
thrombocyte (trombocito)
thrombophlebitis (tromboflebitis)
thrombosis (trombosis)
thrombus (trombo)
thymectomy (timectomía)
thymoma (timoma)
thymosin (timosina)
thyroidectomy (tiroidectomía)
tibia (tibia)
tic (tic)
tinea (tiña)
tinnitus (tinnitus)
tongue (lengua)
tonometry (tonometría)
tonsillectomy (tonsilectomía)
tonsillitis (tonsilitis)
touch (tacto)
toxicology (toxicología)
trachea (tráquea)
tracheoplasty (traqueoplastia)
tracheostomy (traquestomía)
tracheotomy (traqueotomía)
traction (tracción)
transfusion (transfusion)
tremor (tremblor)
triglyceride (triglicérido)
trigone (trígono)
trochanter (trocánter)
trombolítico (thrombolytic)
tubercle (tubérculo)
tuberculosis (tuberculosis)
tuberosity (tuberosidad)
tumor (tumor)
tympanoplasty (timpanoplastia)

U

ulcer (úlcera)
ulna (ulna)
urea (urea)
uremia (uremia)
ureter (uréter)

urethra (uretra)
urinalysis (análisis de orina)
urine (orina)
urology (urología)
urticaria (urticaria)
uterus (útero)
uvea (úvea)
uvula (úvula)

V

vaccination (vacunación)
vaccine (vacuna)
vagina (vagina)
vaginitis (vaginitis)
valve (válvula)
valvulitis (valvulitis)
valvuloplasty (valvuloplastia)
varicella (varicela)
varicocele (varicocele)
vasectomy (vasectomía)
vasovasostomy (vasovasostomía)
vegetation (vegetación)
vein (vena)
venipuncture (venipuntura)
venography (venografía)
ventricle (ventrículo)
venule (vénula)
verruca, wart (verruga)
vertebra, pl. vertebrae (vertebra, pl. vertebras)
vertigo (vertigo)
vesicle (vesícula)
vestibule (vestíbule)
vial (vial)
villus (vellosidad)
virilism (virilismo)
vitamin (vitamina)
vitiligo (vitíligo)
volvulus (vólvulo)
vomer (vómer)
vulva (vulva)

W

wheal (roncha)
wheezes (sibilancia)

The glossary that follows is of selected medical terms commonly used in allied health. The definitions are in Spanish with the English translation in parentheses. The terms are pronounced on the Spanish audio CD which is available for purchase with this dictionary.

abortifaciente (abortifacient): 1. Abortivo; abortigénico; que produce aborto. 2. Se refiere al agente que provoca el aborto.

aborto espontáneo (miscarriage): Se dice de la expulsion espontánea de los productos de la gestación antes de la mitad del segundo trimestre.

aborto (abortion): 1. Se dice del nacimiento del embrión del estado de viabilidad de las 20 semanas de gestación (peso del feto menor de 500g). 2. Se refiere al producto de esto nacimiento no viable.

absceso (abscess): 1. Acumulación circunscripta de pus que se ubica en una infección ubicada, aguda, o crónica, y que se relaciona con destrucción hística y, usualmente, con tumefacción. 2. Cavidad formada por necrosis licuefactiva dentro de un tejido sólido.

absorción (absorption): Captación, incorporación o recepción de gases, líquidos, luz, calor, o nutrición. Se le conoce también en la radiología como la captación de energía de radiaciones por el medio a través del cual pasan.

acalasia (achalasia): La falta de relajación; refiriéndose especialmente a orificios viscerales, como el píloro, cardias u otros esfínteres musculares.

accidente cerebrovascular (stroke): Más conocido en inglés, es un término vulgar para referirse a una afección neurológica repentina, en general relacionada con la irrigación cerebral, como un ataque paralítico, afásico o amnésico.

acetábulo (acetabulum): Cavidad cotiloidea; cótilo.

acetilcolina (acetylcholine): Ion (2-acetoxietil) trimetilamonio; se refiere al es éster acético de la colina, aislado del cornezuelo de centeno.

acetona (acetone): Dimetilcetona.

acidosis (acidosis): El estado caracterizado por disminución relativa o real de los álcalis en los líquidos corporales en proporción al contenido ácido.

acné (acne): Erupción inflamatoria folicular, papular y pustulosa que implica al aparato sebáceo.

acne vulgar (acne vulgaris): Enfermedad inflamatoria de glándulas pilosebáceas.

acromegalia (acromegaly): El trastorno señalado por el crecimiento progresivo de las partes periféricas del cuerpo, en especial de la cabeza, la cara, las manos y los pies, ocasionado por la secreción excesiva de somatotropina.

acromion (acromion): Apófisis acromial; lado lateral de la cresta del omóplato.

adenoidectomía (adenoidectomy): Una cirugía para la extracción de los crecimientos adenoides de la nasofaringe.

adenoides (adenoids): Enfermedad adenoide; enfermedad de Meyer; hipertrofia de la amígdalas faríngeas como consecuencia de inflamación crónica.

adenoiditis (adenoiditis): Inflamación del tejido linfoide nasofaríngeo.

adiposo (adipose): Graso; con relación a la grasa.

adrenal (adrenal): 1. Se ubica cerca del riñón o sobre este; señala la glándula suprarrenal. 2. Una glándula suprarrenal o tejido separado de ésta.

adrenalectomía (adrenalectomy): Suprerrenalectomía; extracción de una o ambas suprarrenales.

adrenalina (adrenaline): Epinefrina.

afagia (aphagia): Disfagia.

afaquia (aphakia): Ausencia de cristalino.

afasia (aphasia): Alogia; anepia; logagnosia; logamnesia; logastenia.

agentes de antiiflamatorios no esteroideos, AINE (NSAID): Drogas antiiflamatorios sin esteroideos.

aglutinación (agglutination): 1. Proceso por el cual las bacterias, células u otras partículas con igual tamaño se adhieren y forman cúmulos o agregados. 2. Es la adherencia de las superficies de una herida.

aglutinógeno (agglutinogen): Se dice de la sustancia antigénetica que estimula la formación de aglutininas específicas.

agnosia (agnosia): Es la falta de la capacidad perceptivosensorial para identificar los objetos; agnea.

agranulocito (agranulocyte): Leucocito sin granulaciones.

agujero (foramen): Una abertura por un hueso.

albinismo (albinism): Leucodermia o leucopatía congenital.

albúmina (albumin): El tipo de proteína simple que es ampliamente distribuida entre tejidos y líquidos de plantas y animales.

albuminuria (albuminuria): Indica la presencia de proteína en la orina, principalmente albúmina, pero también globulina.

aldosterona (aldosterone): Hormona secretada por la corteza adrenal; aldocortina.

alergeno (allergen): Una sustancia que puede provocar una respuesta alergenica; antígeno.

alergia (allergy): 1. Se dice de la sensibilidad adquirida (inducida); estado inmunológico inducido en un individuo susceptible mediante un antígeno (alergeno), caracterizado por un cambio notable en la reactividad del sujeto. 2. Hipersensibilidad adquirida a ciertas drogas o materiales biológicos.

aleteo (flutter): Latido del corazón rapido, pero regular; agitación; temblor.

aloinjerto (allograft): Homoinjerto o injerto alogénico; homólogo; homoplástico.

alopecia (alopecia): Calvicie; pelada; pérdida de cabellos.

alvéolo (alveolus, pl. alveoli): 1. Célula o cavidad pequeña. 2. Célula aérea; dilatación secular terminal de las vías aéreas pulmonares.

amenorrea (amenorrhea): Es la no presencia o cese anormal de las menstruaciones.

amilasa (amylase): La enzima perteneciente al grupo de las enzimas que despliegan almidón, glucógeno, y polisacáridos relacionados, en el proceso de digestión.

aminoácido (amino acid): El ácido orgánico en el cual uno de los átomos de hidrógeno CH ha sido sustituido por NH2.

amnesia (amnesia): Se dice del trastorno de la memoria.

amniocentesis (amniocentesis): Se dice de la aspiración transabdominal de líquido del saco amniótico.

amnios (amnion): Bolsa o saco amniótico; indusium; una de las membranas más profundas que envuelven el embrión en el utero.

amniótico (amniotic): Amniótico; se relaciona con el amnios.

amputación (amputation): Retiro de un miembro, o parte de un miembro, por cirujía.

anacusia (anacusis): La pérdida completa o la ausencia de la capacidad de percibir un sonido como tal.

anafilaxia, anafilaxis (anaphylaxis): Se define como un tipo de reacción inmunológica (alérgica) transitorio, inmediato, caracterizado por contracción del músculo liso y dilatación capilar; se puede matar.

analgésico (analgesic): 1. Es el compuesto apto para producir analgesia. 2. Antálgico; está caracterizado por una respuesta disminuida a los estímulos dolorosos.

análisis de orina (urinalysis): Se refiere al análisis que se hace a la orina.

anastomosis (anastomosis): 1. Conexión natural, directa o indirecta, con dos vasos sanguíneos u otras estructuras tubulares. 2. Enlace quirúrgico de dos estructuras huecas o tubulares. 3. Cavidad creada por cirugía, traumatismo o una enfermedad entre dos o varias partes u órganos generalmente separados.

andrógeno (androgen): Testoide; el término genérico que se le da a un agente que estimula la actividad de los órganos sexuales accesorios del hombre y favorece el desarrollo de las características sexuales masculinas.

anemia (anemia): La condición por la cual el número y el volumen de glóbulos rojos son inferiores a lo normal.

anestésico (anesthetic): 1. Se refiere al compuesto que deprime en forma reversible la fusión neuronal, ocasionando la pérdida de la capacidad para sentir el dolor u otras sensaciones, o ambos. 2. Es el término colectivo para los agentes anestesiantes.

aneurisma (aneurysm): Dilatación circunscripta de una arteria, o de un tumor, que se compone de sangre conectada directamente con la luz de una arteria.

anfiartrosis (amphiarthrosis): Forma de articulación cartilaginosa en la que la union entre dos huesos se efectúa por medio de fibrocartílago.

angina (angina): Dolor agudo constrictivo; en este caso, se refiere normalmente a la angina pectoris, angina de pecho.

angina de pecho (angina pectoris): Se refiere al dolor en el pecho (estenocardia).

angioplastia (angioplasty): Restauramiento de un vaso sanguíneo.

angioscopia (angioscopy): Visualización con el microscopio del paso de sustancias (p.ej., formas de contraste, agentes radiopacos) por medio de capilares.

anisocitosis (anisocytosis): La variación en gran escala del tamaño de las células que son generalmente uniformes, especialmente con referencia a los glóbulos rojos.

ano (anus): El orificio anal.

anorquia (anorchism, anorchia): Ausencia congenital de testículos; anorquismo.

anquiloglosia (ankyloglossia): La fijación de la lengua.

anquilosis (ankylosis): Entumecimiento o fijación de una articulación como resultado de un proceso patológico, con unión fibrosa u ósea a través de la articulación.

antibacteriano (antibacterial): Que destruye o detiene el crecimiento de una bacteria.

antibiótico (antibiotic): 1. Referente a la antibiosis. 2. Componente soluble derivada de un moho o bacteria que inhibe el crecimiento de otros microorganismos.

anticoncepción (contraception): Se dice de la prevención de la concepción o fecundación.

anticuerpo (antibody): Antisustancia; sensibilizador.

antidiabético (antidiabetic): Sustancia que actúa contra la diabetes.

antidoto (antidote): Agente que se neutraliza una toxina.

antifúngico (antifungal): Antimicótico.

antígeno (antigen): Alergeno; inmunógeno; se refiere a toda sustancia que, como resultado de entrar en contacto con los tejidos apropiados de un organismo animal, induce un estado de sensibilidad y/o resitencia a la infección o a sustancias tóxicas.

antihistamina (antihistamine): Droga que tienen una acción antagónica a la de la histamina.

antitoxina (antitoxin): Se refiere al anticuerpo formado en respuesta a sustancias tóxicas antigénicas de origen biológico.

antracosis (anthracosis): Pulmón de Collier o de los mineros; melanedema.

anuria (anuria): Se dice de la ausencia de formación de la orina.

aorta (aorta): Arteria grande de forma elástica, que constituye el tronco principal del sistema arterial sistémico.

apéndice (appendix): Saco vermiforme adyacente al ciego; apéndice vermiforme.

apex (apex): Se dice del extremo de una estructura cónica o piramidal, como en el corazón o el pulmón.

apnea (apnea): Ausencia de respiración.

apraxia (apraxia): Se dice de la incapacidad parcial o completa para efectuar movimientos determinados, no obstante la preservación de la sensibilidad, fuerza y coordinación muscular en general; parectropia.

aracnoideo (arachnoid): Es el derivado ectodérmico similar a una telaraña.

aréola (areola): 1. Se dice de toda parte pequeña. 2. Es una de las áreas o intersticios del tejido areolar. 3. Aureola mamaria. 4. Halo; se dice de la área pigmentada, despigmentada o eritematosa que rodea a una pápula, pústula, roncha o neoplasia cutánea.

arritmia (arrhythmia): Pérdida del ritmo; denomina normalmente una irregularidad en los latidos cardíacos; disritmia.

arteria (artery): Vaso sanguíneo que transporta sangre de una dirección apartada del corazón.

arteria pulmunar (pulmonary artery): Arteria ubicada en el pulmón.

arteriola (arteriole): Arteria diminuta con una pared muscular; una arteria terminal que prosigue en la red capilar.

arteriosclerosis (arteriosclerosis): Esclerosis arterial o vascular; endurecimiento de las arterias.

arteritis (arteritis): Inflamación que involucra una o más arterias.

articulación (articulation): Artral; que se relaciona con una articulación.

artralgia (arthralgia): Dolor agudo en una articulación; artrodinia.

artritis (arthritis): Reumatismo articular; inflamación de varias articulaciones.

artrocentesis (arthrocentesis): Extirpación de líquido de una articulación mediante incisión de una aguja.

asbestosis (asbestosis): Neumoconiosis debida a la inhalación de las partículas de asbestos.

ascitis (ascites): Se define como hidroperitoneo; hidropesía abdominal.

asistolia (asystole): Paro cardíaco; carencia de contracciónes del corazón.

asma (asthma): Inicialmente, término usado con significado de "respiración dificultosa"; en la actualidad se usa para designar el asma bronquial.

aspermia (aspermia): Se refiere a la falta de secreción o expulsión del semen luego de la eyaculación; aspermatismo.

aspiración (aspiration): 1. Es la sustracción, mediante succión, de un gas o líquido. 2. Succión inspiratoria hacia las vías aéreas de líquidos o cuerpos extraños, como el vómito. 3. Es la técnica quirúrgica para las cataratas, que require una pequeña incisión corneal.

astenopía (asthenopia): Se refiere a los síntomas subjetivos de fatiga ocular, malestar, lagrimeo y cefaleas originadas en el uso de los ojos; vista fatigada.

astigmatismo (astigmatism): 1. Se dice del lente o sistema óptico que posee curvaturas diferentes en meridianos diferentes; astigmia. 2. Es la condición de curvaturas desiguales a lo largo de meridianos diferentes en una o más de las superficies de refracción del ojo.

astrocito, astroglia (astrocyte, astroglia): Célula de la astroglia o macroglia.

astrocitoma (astrocytoma): Se dice del glioma relativamente bien diferenciado, constituido de células neoplásicas que recuerdan a uno de los tipos de astrocitos, con cantidades variables de estroma fibrilar.

ataxia (ataxia): Disinergia; incoordinación; inhabilidad para organizar los músculos en la ejecución de un movimiento voluntario.

atelectasia (atelectasis): Ausencia de gas de una área o de todos los lóbulos pulmonares.

ateriosclerosis (atherosclerosis): Esclerosis nodular.

ateroma (atheroma): Depósito de lípidos en la capa íntima de las arterias que ocasionan una tumefacción amarillenta sobre la superficie endotelial; aterosis.

atlas (atlas): Primera vertebra cervical.

atresia (atresia): Se refiere a la ausencia de una abertura o rendija normal, o una luz generalmente potente; clausura.

atrium (atrium, pl. atria): 1. área de la cavidad timpánica que se ubica por debajo del tímpano. 2. En el pulmón, subdivisión del conducto alveolar, a partir de la cual se abre el saco alveolar.

atrofia (atrophy): Detereoro de tejidos, de órganos o de todo el cuerpo, como en la muerte y reabsorción celular, en la disminución de la proliferación celular, compresión, isquemia, desnutrición, disminución de la función o cambios hormonales.

audición (hearing): La capacidad de percibir sonidos.

audiograma (audiogram): Se define como el registro gráfico que se traza a partir de los resultados de las pruebas de audición con el audiómetro.

audiólogo (audiologist): Especialista en la evaluación, habilitación y rehabilitación de aquéllos cuyos trastornos de la comunicación se centran en toda o en parte de la función auditiva.

audiometría (audiometry): El uso del audiómetro para medir la agudeza auditiva.

aura (aura): Es la sensación típica que es percibida por el paciente y conduce imediatamente a un ataque epiléptico.

auricular (auricle): 1. Es el pabellón de la oreja. 2. Auricula atrialis.

auscultación (auscultation): Percepción de sonidos provocados por diversas estructuras del cuerpo como método de diagnóstico.

autoinjerto (autograft): Autoplastia; auto-trasplante.

axis (axis): Epístrofe, vertebra dentada u odontoide; segunda vértebra cervical.

axon (axon): El axon es el único, entre las prolongaciones de la célula nerviosa, que en situaciones normales conduce los impulsos nerviosos desde el cuerpo celular y sus restantes proyecciones (dendritas).

azoemia (azotemia): Exceso de urea y otros desechos nitrogenados en la sangre; uremia.

azoospermia (azoospermia): La ausencia de espermatozoides vivos en el semen.

bacillo (bacillus): 1. Palabra vernácula usada para referirse a cualquier miembro del género Bacillus. 2. Palabra utilizada anteriormente para referirse a toda bacteria en forma de bastoncillo.

balanitis (balanitis): La inflamación del glande del pene o del clítoris.

base (base): 1. Basamento; el área inferior o de abajo. 2. En farmacia, el ingreso principal de una mezcla. 3. Compuestos orgánicos que contienen nitrógeno.

basofilia (basophilia): Se refiere a la condición en la cual hay un número de leucocitos basófilos mayor de lo normal en la sangre circulante o un incremento en la propoción de células basófilas parenquimatosas en un órgano; basofilismo.

basófilo (basophil): 1. La célula con gránulos que se colorean propiamente con los colorantes básicos. 2. Referente a los componentes de tejidos que poseen semejanza por los colorantes básicos en condiciones de pH específicas. Un leucocito fagocítico de la sangre caracterizado por numerosos gránulos basófilos que contienen heparina e histamina.

bastoncillos (rods): 1. Formación cilíndrica fina y recta; 2. Célula de la retina.

bazo (spleen): Es el órgano linfático vascular grande, ubicado en la parte superior izquierda de la cavidad abdominal, compuesto por tejido linfático y sinusoides venosos.

bilirubinat (bilirubin): Pigmento biliar de color rojo encontrado en forma de bilirrubinato de sodio soluble o como sal calico insoluble en los cálculos biliares.

bilis (bile): Hiel; líquido de color pardo o verde secretado por el hígado y vertido hacia el duodeno.

biopsia (biopsy): Proceso de extracción de muestras de tejido en pacientes vivos para su examen diagnóstico. 2. Pieza o espécimen obtenido por biopsia.

blefaritis (blepharitis): Una inflamación de los párpados.

boca (mouth): Cavidad bucal.

bocio (goiter): Estruma; agrandamiento crónico del tiroides no debido a neoplasia, endémico en ciertos lugares.

bolso (bursa, pl. bursae): Bursa.

boticario (druggist): Farmacéutico.

bradicardia (bradycardia): Lentitud de los latidos cardíacos; braquicardia; bradirritmia; oligocardia.

bradipnea (bradypnea): Lentitud anormal de la respiración.

broncoespasmo (bronchospasm): Contracción del músculo liso de las paredes de bronquios y bronquiolos, que ocasiona estenosis de su luz.

broncografía (bronchography): Examen radiográfico del árbol traqueobronquial mediante la inyección de uno o varios materiales radiopacos.

broncoplastia (bronchoplasty): Alteración quirúrgica de la configuración de un bronquio.

broncoscopio (bronchoscope): Endoscopio para examinar el interior del árbol traqueobronquial.

bronquio (bronchus, pl. bronchi): Cada una de las subdivisiones de la tráquea que sirve para trasladar el aire hacia los pulmones y desde éstos.

bronquiolo (bronchiole): Una de las subdivisiones más delgadas de los tubos bronquiales.

bronquitis (bronchitis): Inflamación de la mucosa del árbol bronquial.

bulla (bulla, pl. bullae): Vesícula grande que se presenta como un área circunscripta de la separación de la epidermis de las estructuras subepidérmicas, o como un área circunscripta de separación de las células epidérmicas.

bunio (bunion): Tumefacción ubicada ya sea sobre la cara dorsal o medial de la primera articulación metatarsofalángica, causada por inflamación de la bolsa cerosa.

bunionectomía (bunionectomy): Escisión de un bunio.

bursa (bursa, pl. bursae): Se refiere a un saco lleno de líquido situado entre un hueso y un tendón o un músculo; bolsa.

bursectomía (bursectomy): Extirpación quirúrgica de una bolsa.

bursitis (bursitis): Inflamación de una bolsa; sinovitis bursal.

calcáneo (calcaneus): Hueso del talón.

calcar (calcar): 1. Espolón. 2. Espina o proyección chata o roma de un hueso. 3. Bulto córneo de la piel.

calcio (calcium): Es el mineral más abundante en el cuerpo; esencial para la formación y la reparación de los huesos y de dientes, pero también esencial para la transmisión del nervio, contracción del los músculos, coagulación de sangre y otras actividades metabólicas.

calcitonia (calcitonin): Hormona secretada por la glándua tiroide y otras glándulas endocrinas, que ayuda arreglar nivel de calcio en sangre; tirocalcitonina.

cálculo biliar (gallstone): Concreción en la vesícula biliar o en un conducto biliar; colelito; cololito.

cáliz, pl. calices (calix, pl. calyces): Estructra en forma de copa, de flor o de embudo; específicamente una de las ramas o recesos de la pelvis del riñón.

callo (callus): 1. Masa compuesta de tejido que se forma alrededor de una fractura para formar la continuidad entre ambos extremos del hueso. 2. Un espesamiento de la epidermis en un cierto punto, especialmente en los dedos del pie, por la fricción o la presión. 3. Callosidad.

canceloso (cancellous): Se refiere a la estructura abierta o enrejada o porosa de un hueso.

candidiasis (candidiasis): infección o enfermedad causada por Candida, principalmente C. albicans; candidosis; moniliasis.

capilar (capillary): 1. Relativo a un vaso, capilar sanguíneo o linfático. 2. Vaso capilar, sanguíneo o linfático.

caracol (cochlea): Cóclea.

carbunco (carbuncle): Infección profunda de la piel.

cardiomiopatía (cardiomyopathy): Enfermedad del miocardio; miocardiopatía.

carrillos (cheeks): Indica mejillas; bucca; mala; gena.

cartílago (cartilage) Tejido conectivo de consistencia firme, no vascular, elástico, que se encuentra principalmente en las articulaciones, las paredes del tórax y estructuras tubulares.

castración (castration): La remoción de los testículos u ovarios; esterilización.

catarata (cataract): La pérdida de transparencia del cristalino del ojo o de su cápsula.

catecolaminas (catecholamines): Pirocatecoles con una cadena lateral de alquilamina; son ejemplos de interés en bioquímica adrenalina, noradrenalina y dopa.

cauterización (cauterization): Se refiere a la acción de cauterizar.

cauterizar (cauterize): Aplicar un cauterio; quemar con un cauterio real o potencial.

ceguera (blindness): 1. La pérdida del sentido de la vista; tiflosis. 2. Pérdida de la apreciación visual de objetos aunque la agudeza visual sea normal. 3. Se refiere a la ausencia de la apreciación de una sensación.

ceja (eyebrow): 1. La línea semilunar de pelos que se ubica en el borde superior de la órbita. 2. Pelo individual de la ceja.

celulitis (cellulitis): Inflamación de el tejido celular o conjuntivo.

cerebelitis (cerebellitis): Se refiere a la inflamación del cerebelo.

cerebro (brain): Es el nombre original que se le da a la parte más grande del encéfalo, derivada del telencéfalo.

cerebro medio (midbrain): Mesencéfalo.

cerebrum (cerebrum): Cerebro; Es el nombre original que se le da a la parte más grande del encéfalo, incluyendo todo lo que queda dentro del cráneo menos el bulbo raquídeo, la protuberancia y el cerebelo; en la actualidad se refiere generalmente sólo a las partes derivadas del telencéfalo e incluye esencialmente los hemisferios cerebrales (corteza cerebral y ganglios basales).

cervix (cervix): 1. Cuello del útero. 2. Se refiere a cualquier estructura en forma de cuello.

cetoacidosis (ketoacidosis): Se refiere a los ácidos, como en la diabetes o la inanición, ocasionada por la mayor producción de cuerpos cetónicos.

cetona (ketone): Se dice de la sustancia con el grupo carbonilo que une a dos átomos de carbono.

cetonuria (ketonuria): Se refiere a la excreción urinaria incrementada de cuerpos cetónicos.

cetosis (ketosis): El estado caracterizado por una mayor producción de cuerpos cetónicos, como en la diabetes mellitus o la inanición.

chalazión (chalazion): Chalaza; el quiste de Meibomio o tarsiano; granuloma inflamatorio crónico de una glándula de Meibomio.

cianosis (cyanosis): Coloración azulada oscura o morada de la piel y las mucosas debida a deficiencia en la oxigenación de la sangre.

ciática (sciatica): 1. Dolor en la parte inferior de la pierna, proviene de la herniación de un disco u otra lesión o condición. 2. Se le conoce como la enfermedad de Cotunnius, isquialgia; neuralgia.

cicatriz (cicatrix; scar): Marca dejada (generalmente en la piel) por un tejido fino dañado o un tejido sanado.

ciego (cecum): Se refiere al Tiflón; intestine ciego; fondo de saco de unos 6cm de profundidad ubicado debajo del íleon terminal, que forma la primera parte del intestino grueso.

cifosis (kyphosis): Aumento postrero anormal en la curvatura de la espina dorsal torácica, también llamada joroba.

circuncisión (circumcision): Peritomía; postetomía; la operación de remover el prepucio o una parte de él.

circunvolución (convolution): 1. Es una de las elevaciones redondeadas prominentes que constituyen los hemisferios cerebrales, cada una de las cuales consisten en una área superficial expuesta y otra no visible en la pared y el piso del surco. 2. Es la área enroscada o arrollada de un órgano. 3. Específicamente, es una circunvolución de la corteza cerebral o cerebelosa.

cirrosis (cirrhosis): Una efermedad progresiva del hígado, se caracteriza por daños difusos de las células del parénquima hepático.

cistectomía (cystectomy): 1. Se dice de la escisión de la vejiga urinaria. 2. Es la escisión de la vesícula biliar (colecistectomía) 3. También se refiere a la extracción de un quiste.

cistitis (cystitis): Se refiere a la inflamación de una vejiga, normalmente la urinaria.

cistocele (cystocele): Colpocistocele; vesicocele; hernia de la vejiga.

cistolito (cystolith): Cálculo vesical.

cistorrafia (cystorrhaphy): La sutura de una herida o un defecto de la vejiga urinaria.

cistoscopia (cystoscopy): Examen del interior de la vejiga con un cistoscopio.

clamidia (chlamydia): Infección bacteriana transmitida por el acto sexual.

claudicación (claudication): Cojera (renquera) referida normalmente a c. Intermitente.

clavícula (clavicle): Un hueso largo y curvado y que forma parte de la cintura escapular; llamado a veces el collar-hueso.

climaterio (climacteric): Se refiere al período de la vida de la mujer que coincide con la terminación de la época de fecundidad.

clítoris (clitoris): Órgano primario de excitación sexual feminina.

cloasma (chloasma): Melanoderma o melasma identificada por la aparición de grandes placas parduscas de forma y tamaño irregular en la piel de la cara y otros sitios.

coagulación (coagulation): Se refiere al cambio de líquido a sólido, específicamente de la sangre.

cóccix (coccyx): Hueso coxal.

codo (elbow): Articulación localizada entre el brazo y antebrazo.

coito (coitus): El acto sexual; unión sexual entre dos personas, hombre y mujer; copulación; cópula.

colado (casting): Acción de crear un colado metálico formado en un molde o de yeso o plástico, para prevenir movimiento.

colágeno (collagen): Es el soporte primario de la piel, del tendón, del hueso, del cartílago y del tejido fino conectivo, el colágeno es una sustancia química de la proteína. Oseína; osteína; la principal proteína (que forma más de la mitad de la proteína de los mamíferos) de las fibras blancas del tejido conjuntivo, cartílago y hueso.

colangitis (cholangitis): Es la inflamación de un conducto biliar o de todo el árbol biliar; colangeítis; angiocolitis.

colecistitis (cholecystitis): La inflamación de la vesícula biliar.

colecistografía (cholecystography): La visualización de la vesícula biliar por rayos X después de administrar una sustancia radioopaca o un radiofármaco.

colectomía (colectomy): La escisión de una parte del colon, o de éste en su integridad.

colesterol (cholesterol): Colesterina; el esteroide más abundante en los tejidos animales.

cólico (colic): 1. Se define como el dolor espasmódico en el abdomen. 2. Paroxismo doloroso con llanto e irritabilidad en los niños pequeños.

colitis (colitis): La inflamación del colon.

colon (colon): La división del intestino grueso que se extiende desde el ciego hasta el recto.

colonoscopia (colonoscopy): Es el examen visual de la cara interna del colon a través de un colonoscopio; coloscopia.

colostomía (colostomy): Se dice del establecimiento de una abertura cutánea artificial que lleva al colon; coloproccia.

coma (coma): Se dice del estado de inconsciencia profunda del cual no es fácil o posible sacar al paciente.

concusión (concussion): Conmoción cerebral; lesión de alguna estructura blanda, como el cerebro, ocasionada por un golpe o por una sacudida violenta.

condiloma (condyloma): Es la verruga molusciforme; excrecencia verrugosa en el ano, la vulva o el glande.

condón (condom): Preservativo; es la vaina o cobertura para el pene utilizado como prevención de la concepción o la infección durante el coito.

condromalacia (chondromalacia): Ablandamiento de cartílagos.

conductividad (conductivity): 1. Es el poder de transmisión o transporte de ciertas formas de energía, como por ejemplo; calor, sonido y electricidad sin movimiento perceptible en el cuerpo conductor. 2. Se dice de la propiedad, inherente al portoplasma vivo, de transmitir un estado de excitación, como en un músculo o un nervio.

conización (conization): Se refiere a la escisión de un cono de tejido, como la mucosa del cuello uterino.

conjuntiva (conjunctiva, pl. conjunctivae): La mucosa que cubre la superficie anterior del globo ocular y tapiza los párpados.

conjuntivitis (conjunctivitis): La inflamación de la conjuntiva; blenoftalmía.

conos (cones): Células de la retina.

constipación (constipation): Estreñimiento.

constricción (constriction): 1. Contracción o encogimiento de una parte. 2. Sensación subjetiva de que el cuerpo, o una área de éste, se encuentra comprimido o firmemente apretado.

copulación (copulation): Coito.

corazón (heart): Órgano muscular hueco que recibe sangre de las venas y la suministra a las arterias.

cordotomía (cordotomy): 1. Es cualquier operación de la médula espinal. 2. Se refiere a la división de haces de la médula espinal que puede hacerse percutáneamente.

corion (chorion): Bolsa o saco coriónico.

corium (corium): Dermis; cutis verdadero; piel o cuero.

cornea (cornea): EL tejido transparente que forma la sexta parte anterior de la pared externa del ojo.

coroides (choroid): La túnica vascular media del ojo que se encuentra entre la retina y la esclerótica.

corteza (cortex): Es el área exterior de un órgano, como el riñón, diferente de su parte interna o medular.

corticosteroide (corticosteroids): Esteroide producido por la corteza suprarrenal; corticoide que contiene un esteroide.

cortisol (cortisol): Hidrocortisona.

costar (crust): Capa o cobertura exterior.

costilla (rib): Uno de los veinticuatro huesos que forman la pared del pecho.

costra (scale) Placa epithial fina y dura.

cráneo (skull): Calvaria.

craneotomía (craniotomy): Es la grieta producida en el cráneo.

cranietomía (craniectomy): Se refiere a la operación o escisión de una parte del cráneo.

creatina (creatine): Existe en la orina algunas veces como creatina pero normalmente como creatinina, y en el músculo por lo general en forma de fosfocreatina.

creatinina (creatinine): Se refiere al componete de la orina y producto final de catabolismo de la creatina.

cresta (crest): Línea elevada que se sobresale en una superficie plana o uniformemente redondeada.

criocirugía (cryosurgery): La operación en la que se emplea en forma local o general una temperatura disminuida por acción de nitrógeno líquido o anhídrido carbónico.

crup (croup): 1. Laringotraqueobronquitis ocasionada por los tipos 1 y 2 del virus parainfluenza. 2. Cualquier afectación de la laringe en los niños caracterizada por respiración difícil y ruidosa y tos ronca.

cuerpo (body): 1. El cuerpo humano, formado por la cabeza, el tronco, y las extremidades. 2. Es la masa principal de una órgano u otra estructura anatómica.

culebrilla (shingles): Enfermedad de los nervios del superficio exterior, causada por Herpes zoster.

cutícula (cuticle): 1. Capa delgada exterior, normalmente córnea. 2. Capa a veces quitinosa en los invertebrados, de la superficie de las células epiteliales. 3. Epidermis.

decibel (decibel): La décima parte de un bel; unidad que expresa el volumen relativo del sonido en escala logarítmica.

decúbito (decubitus): Posición horizontal del cuerpo; decubito dorsal o lateral que puede causar una úlcera en la piel.

defecación (defecation): El movimiento; evacuación de las heces del recto.

deglución (deglutition): Se refiere a la acción de tragar o deglutir del cuerpo.

demencia (dementia): Es el deterioro mental general debido a factores orgánicos o psicológicos; amencia.

dendrita (dendrite): Se refiere a uno de los dos tipos de prolongaciones protoplasmáticas de la célula nerviosa (el otro es el axón); endrón; prolongación dentrítica; neurodentrita; neurodendrón.

dermabrasión (dermabrasion): Procedimiento operatorio usado para extirpar cicatrices de acné, piel de agricultor-marinero y nevos dérmicos.

dermatitis (dermatitis): Inflamación de la piel.

dermatocalasia (dermatochalasis): Pérdida de elasticidad de la piel del párpado.

dermatología (dermatology): Es la rama de la medicina que se ocupa del estudio de la piel.

dermis (dermis): Corion.

desmielinación (demyelination): Es la destrucción o pérdida de mielina.

despolarización (depolarization): Destrucción, neutralización o cambio de dirección de la polaridad.

diabetes (diabetes): La diabetes insípida y diabetes mellitus o sacarina, enfermedades que tienen en común el síntoma de la poliuria. Solamente "diabctes" significa diabetes mellitus.

diáfisis (diaphysis): Configuración alargada cilindricamente, como parte de un hueso largo ubicado entre dos extremidades, las epífisis.

diaforesis (diaphoresis): Transpiración.

diafragma (diaphragm): 1. Tabique musculomembranoso que separa las cavidades abdominal y torácica. 2. Anillo flexible de metal cubierto por una lámina abovedada de material elástico, usado en la vagina para impedir el embarazo.

diarrea (diarrhea): La descarga anormalmente frecuente de material fecal más o menos líquida del intestino.

diástole (diastole): Dilatación de las cavidades cardíacas durante la cual se llenan de sangre.

diencéfalo (diencephalon): Área del prosencéfalo compuesta por el epitálamo, el tálamo, el subtálamo y el hipotálamo.

difteria (diphtheria): Se refiere a una enfermedad infecciosa específica debida a Corynebacterium diphtheriae y su toxina muy potente.

digestión (digestion): 1. El proceso de fomar una digesta. 2. Proceso por el cual el alimento que se ingiere es convertido en material apropiado para su asimilación.

dióxido de carbono (carbon dioxide): Un residuo de respiración y transportado en el sangre venoso.

diplopía (diplopia): Doble vision; percepción de un solo objeto como si fueran dos.

disco (disk, disc): Una superficie circular plana con una forma redonda del espacio intervertebral.

discografía (discography): Visualización radiográfica del espacio del disco intervertebral por inyección de medios de contraste.

discrasia (dyscrasia): El estado general morboso resultante de la presencia de material anormal en la sangre.

disentería (dysentery): La efermedad caracterizada por deposiciones acuosas frecuentes, a menudo con sangre y moco y clínicamente por dolor, tenesmo, fiebre y deshidratación.

disfagia (dysphagia): Dificultad para tragar; aglutición; afagia; odinofagia.

disfasia (dysphasia): Es la falta de coordinación del habla e incapacidad de disponer de las palabras en forma comprensible.

disfonía (dysphonia): Se dice de la dificultad o dolor al hablar.

dislocación (dislocation): Desplazamiento de un órgano o parte; luxación.

dismenorrea (dysmenorrhea): Menstruación difícil y con dolor; menorragia.

disnea (dyspnea): Se refiere a la carencia, dificultad o sufrimiento respiratorio, relacionado normalmente con enfermedad cardíaca o pulmonar graves.

dispareunia (dyspareunia): Dolor ocasionado durante el acto sexual.

dispepsia (dyspepsia): Indisgestión gástrica.

disritmia (dysrhythmia): Ritmo defectuoso.

distonía (dystonia): Tono anormal del músculo; carencia del tono del músculo.

distrofia muscular (muscular dystrophy): Debilidad progresiva y atrofia del músculo causada por una deficiencia de la proteína dystrophin.

disuria (dysuria): Se refiere a la dificultad o el dolor en la micción.

diverticulitis (diverticulitis): La inflamación de un divertículo.

diverticulosis (diverticulosis): La presencia de divertículos en el intestino, común en la edad madura.

dopamina (dopamine): intermediario del metabolismo de la tirosina y precursor de noradrenalina y adrenalina; 3-hidroxitiramina; dopa descarboxilada.

droga (drug): Agente terapéutico.

duodeno (duodenum): La primera división del intestino delgado.

eccema (eczema): Término genérico usado para referirse a estados inflamatorios agudos o crónicos de la piel.

ecocardiografía (echocardiographya): Cardiografía ultrasónica. Empleo de ultrasonido en el diagnóstico de lesiones cardiovasculares.

edema (edema): Se dice de la acumulación de grandes cantidades de líquido acuoso en las células, tejidos o cavidades serosas.

electroencefalógrafo (electroencephalograph): Instrumento formado por amplificadores y un sistema de escritura, que registra los fenómenos eléctricos del cerebro usando electrodos unidos al cuero cabelludo.

electroforesis (electrophoresis): El movimiento de partículas en un campo eléctrico hacia uno u otro polo eléctrico, ánodo o cátado; ionoforesis.

electrólito (electrolyte): Se dice de cualquier compuesto o solución que conduce una corriente eléctrica y es descompuesto por ella.

electromiógrafo (electromyograph): Aparato que registra corrientes eléctricas generadas en un músculo activo.

embolectomía (embolectomy): Remoción de un émbolo.

émbolo (embolus): Se refiere al tapón formado por un coágulo desprendido, una masa bacteriana u otro cuerpo extraño, que cierra un vaso sanguíneo.

emesis (emesis): Se refiere al vómito; regurgitación.

empalme (joint) 1. La forma o la manera en la cual las cosas se unen y juntan haciendo una conexión. 2. Articulación.

empiema (empyema): Pus en una cavidad corporal.

enanismo (dwarfism): La cualidad de una persona de tamaño marcadamente pequeño.

encefalitis (encephalitis): Se refiere a la inflamación del cerebro.

encefalograma (encephalogram): Es el registro obtenido por encefalografía.

encía (gum): El tejido fibroso denso cubierto por mucosa que envuelve los procesos alveolares de ambos maxilares y los cuellos de los dientes, a los que rodea.

endocardio (endocardium): La túnica más interna del corazón, que contiene endotelio y tejido conjuntivo subendotelial.

endocarditis (endocarditis): Inflamación del endocardio.

endolinfa (endolymph): el líquido contenido en el laberinto membranoso del oído interno; licor de Scarpa.

endometrio (endometrium): Se refiere a la túnica mucosa del útero.

endometriosis (endometriosis): Es la presencia ectópica de tejido endometrial que forma frecuentemente quistes que contienen sangre alterada.

endoscopio (endoscope): Instrumento utilizado para examinar el interior de un canal, un conducto o una víscera hueca.

endostio (endosteum): Membrana medular; perimielo; membrana delgada que cubre la superficie interior del hueso en la cavidad medular central.

endotelio (endothelium): Capa de células planas que tapiza en especial los vasos sanguíneos y linfáticos y el corazón.

enfisema pulmonar (emphysema): Crecimiento anormal del tamaño de los espacios aéreos distal al broquiolo terminal, con cambios destructivos en sus paredes y reducción de su número.

enteritis (enteritis): La inflamación del intestino, principalmente el delgado.

enucleación (enucleation): 1. La extirpación total de un tumor u otra estructura (como el globo del ojo), sin ruptura. 2. Remoción o destrucción del núcleo de una célula.

enuresis (enuresis): Se refiere a la evacuación involuntaria de orina.

enzima (enzyme): Proteína que causa cambios químicos en sustancias del sistema digestivo (y trambien en otros systemas del cuerpo); un catalizador orgánico; biocatalizador.

eosinofilia (eosinophilia): Leucocitosis eosinofílica.

eosinófilo (eosinophil): Leucocito eosinófilo.

epicardio (epicardium): Lamina visceralis.

epidermis (epidermis): Parte epitelial externa de la piel; cutícula; epidermo; epiderma.

epididimitis (epididymitis): La inflamación del epidídimo.

epidídimo (epididymis): La estructura en forma alargada que está unida a la cara posterior del testículo; parorquis.

epifisitis (epiphysitis): Inflamación de una epífisis.

epífora (epiphora): El lagrimeo; ojo acuoso; flujo de lágrimas sobre la mejilla debido a drenaje imperfecto por los conductos lagrimales.

epiglotis (epiglottis): Se refiere a la placa en forma de hoja de cartílago elástico cubierta de mucosa, ubicada en la raíz de la lengua, que sirve como válvula diversora sobre la abertura superior de la laringe durante la deglución.

epinefrina (epinephrine): Se refiere a una catecolamina, la principal neurohormona de la médula suprarrenal en casi todas las especies animales; adrenalina.

epispadias (epispadias): La malformación por la cual la uretra se abre en el dorso del pene.

epistaxis (epistaxis, nosebleed): Hemorragia nasal.

epitálamo (epithalamus): Es la pequeña parte dorsal interna del tálamo que corresponde a la habénula u sus estructuras asociadas.

equilibrio (equilibrium): El estado de balance uniforme; estado de reposo entre dos o más fuerzas anragonistas que se contrarrestran entre si.

equimosis (ecchymosis): Mancha violácea producida por estravasación de sangre a la piel; las equimoses se diferencian de las petequias sólo por su tamaño.

eritrocito (erythrocyte): El glóbulo o corpúsculo rojo; globulo rojo maduro.

eritropenia (erythropenia): Eritrocitopenia; la deficencia del número de glóbulos rojos.

eritropoyetina (erythropoietin): La hormona eritropyesis, o caracterizada por ella.

erosion (erosion): 1.Úlcera superficial. 2. Desgaste de un diente por acción química o abrasive; odontólisis.

eructación (eructation): Se refiere al ascenso de gas o de una pequeña cantidad de líquidos ácidos desde el estómago; regueldo.

escala (scale): Pieza de metal, vidrio u otra sustancia dividido en líneas utilizado para medir.

escápula (scapula): Hueso plano grande que forma la lámina del hombro.

escleritis (scleritis): La inflamación de la esclerótica; leucitis.

esclerodermia (scleroderma): Esclerosis cutánea o del crion; dermatosclerosis.

esclerótica (sclera): Membrana fibrosa y dura en el estrato externo del ojo.

escolisis (scoliosis): Curvatura lateral y posterior de la espina dorsal.

escotoma (scotoma): Se dice de la zona aislada de tamaño y forma variables dentro del campo visual, con visión ausente o deprimida.

escroto (scrotum): La bolsa testicular.

esfigmomanómetro (sphygmomanometer): Instrumento utilizado en la medición de la presión arterial; esfigmómetro.

esofagitis (esophagitis): La inflamación del esófago.

esófago (esophagus): La parte del aparato digestive entre la faringe y el estómago.

esofagoplastia (esophagoplasty): La reparación de un defecto en la pared del esófago por una operación plástica.

esofagoscopia (esophagoscopy): La inspección del interior del esófago por medio de un endoscopio.

esotropía (esotropia): El estrabismo cruzado; esodesviación.

espasmo (spasm): Una contracción involuntaria y anormal de un músculo.

esperma (sperm): 1. (plural collectiva) las células sexuales del hombre. 2. Semen.

espermatozoo (spermatozoon, pl. spermatozoa): El gameto o célula sexual masculine.

espermicida (spermicide): Agente que mata a los espermatozoides.

espinilla (shin): La parte delantera de la pierna humana entre la rodilla y el tobillo.

espiración (expiration): Exhalación.

espirómetro (spirometer): Se refiere a el gasómetro utilizado para medir los gases respiratorios.

esplenectomía (splenectomy): Se dice de la extripación del bazo.

espodilólisis (spondylolysis): Condición defectuosa de la parte interarticular de una vértebra.

espodilosindesis (spondylosyndesis): Fusión de dos o mas vértebras espinales.

espondilolistesis (spondylolisthesis): Condición degenerativa en la cual una vértebra se alinea mal con la que esta debajo de ella.

esponja (sponge): Es un material absorbente utilizado para absorber líquidos.

esqueleto (skeleton): El esqueleto esta compuesto por todos lo huesos del cuerpo considerados conjunto.

esteatorrea (steatorrhea): Se define como la evacuación de gran cantidad de grasa en las heces; estearrea.

estenosis (stenosis): Estrechez, de cualquier conduto, principalmente in estrechamiento de una de las válvulas cardíacas.

esternón (sternum): Hueso largo y plano que forma la parte media de la pared anterior del tórax.

estimulo (stimulus): Se refiere a cualquier factor interno o externo que es capaz de producir o evocar acción (respuesta).

estómago (stomach): Gran bolsa entre el esófago y el intestino delgado; gáster.

estrabismo (strabismus): Es la falta de manifiesta de paralelismo en los ejes visuales de los ojos; heterotropía.

estrato (stratum): Una de las capas de tejidos diferenciado, agregado forma indetermindad estrructura dada, como retina o piel.

estrato córne (stratum corneum): La capa exterior de la epidermis que consiste en las células muertas que mudan apagado.

espina bífida (spina bifida): Un defecto congénito de la espina dorsal.

estría (striae): Franja, banda, línea, tira, etc., que se caractereriza por su color, contexture, depresión, o elevación del tejido donde se ubica; estriación.

estribo (stapes, pl. stapes, stapedes): El mas pequeño de los tres huesecillos auditivos, así llamados por su forma.

estridor (stridor): Se refiere a la respiración ruidosa y de tono agudo, como el ruido del viento.

estrógeno (estrogen): Es el término genérico para cualquier sustancia natural o sintética que ejerce efectos biológicos caracterísacticos de hormonas estrogénicas, como el estradiol; estrina.

eupnea (eupnea): Respiración libre y fácil, del tipo observado en sujetos normales en reposo.

euthanasia (euthanasia): Es la muerte intencional por medios artificiales de personas con efermedades incurables y dolorosas.

exahalación (exhalation): Espiración.

excitabilidad (excitability): Se dice de la capacidad de ser excitable.

excoriación (excoriation): Seña de raspado o arañazo; ruptura lineal de la superficie de la piel, cubierta normalmente de sangre costras serosas.

exocrine (exocrine): 1. Muestra la secreción glandular descargada sobre una superficie; ecrino. 2. Muestra pertenencia a una glándula que secreta hacia afuera por conductos excretores.

exoftalmía (exophthalmos, exophthalmus): La protrusión de los globos oculars.

exostosis (exostosis): El crecimiento excesivo del un hueso normal.

exudado (exudate): Indeterminado líquido salido por exudación de un tejido o sus capilares, más específicamente por lesión o inflamación; exudación.

eyaculación (ejaculation): La emisión de líquidos seminal.

fagocitosis (phagocytosis): Es el proceso de ingestion y digestión por células de sustancias sólidas.

falange (phalanx): Se refiere a cada uno de los huesos largos de los dedos del pie y de las manos.

faringe (pharynx): La porción superior expandida del tubo digestivo, entre el esófago por debajo y la boca y las cavidades nasales por arriba y adelante.

furingitis (pharyngitis): Se dice de la inflamación de la mucosa y áreas subyacentes de la faringe.

farmacología (pharmacology): Ciencia que estudia las drogas, sus acciones y usos.

fascia (fascia): Vaina de tejido fibroso que cubre al cuerpo por debajo de la piel; también encierra músculos y grupos musculares, y separa sus diversas capas o grupos.

fémur (femur): El hueso situado entre la cadera y la rodilla; hueso del muslo.

ferulización (splinting): Aplicación de una tablilla para inmovilizar una parte del cuerpo.

fibrilación (fibrillation): Contracciones o torsiones excesivamente rápidas de las fibrillas musculares, pero no de todo el músculo.

fibrinógeno (fibrinogen): Globulina del plasma, la cual es convertida en fibrina, por acción de la trombina en presencia de calcio ionizado para producir la coagulación de la sangre; factor I (de la coagulación sanguínea).

fibroide (fibroid): 1. Tumor benigno de tejido conjuntivo, común en el útero; fibroma;

fibromioma; leiomioma; mioma. 2. Semejante a fibras o tejido fibroso, o compuesto de estos elementos.

filtración (filtration): Es el proceso de pasar un líquido atravéz de un filtro; percolación.

fimbria (fimbria): 1. Es la franja; se dice de cualquier estructura en forma de franja. 2. Pilus.

fimosis (phimosis): La estrechez de la abertura del prepucio que impide llevarlo hacia atrás sobre el glande.

fisura (fissure): 1. Cavidad profunda. 2. En odontología, se refiere a la ruptura o defecto del desarrollo en el esmalte de un diente.

fláccido (flaccid): Sin tono; relajado.

flagelo (flagellum): La organela locomotora en forma de látigo, de disposición estructural constante, se compone de nueve microtúbulos periféricos dobles y dos microtúbulos centrales simples (tal como se observa con microscopia electrónica).

flato (flatus): El gas o aire en el tubo gastrointestinal, que puede ser expelido a través del ano.

flatulencia (flatulence): La presencia de una cantidad excesiva de gas en el estómago e intestinos.

flebitis (phlebitis): Se refiere a la inflamación de una vena.

flebografía (phlebography): 1. Registro del pulso venoso. 2. Venografía.

flebotomía (phlebotomy): Venesección; venetomía; es la incisión en una vena para extraer sangre.

fondo (fundus): Es el área más inferior de un saco o víscera hueca; aquella área más alejada a la abertura.

fontanela (fontanelle): Abertura normal dentro del cráneo de infantes; el más grande de éstos es la fontanela anterior o el "punto suave" en el centro de la cabeza.

fosa (fossa): Cavidad normalmente de forma más o menos longitudinal, por debajo del nivel de la superficie de una parte o estructura; depresión, como en un hueso.

fósforo (phosphorus): Mineral importante para la formación del los huesos.

fotofobia (photophobia): 1. Se refiere a la sensibilidad anormal a la luz, principalmente en los ojos. 2. Temor morboso y evitación de la luz.

fractura (fracture): Una rotura en tejido fino rígido del cuerpo, tal como hueso, cartílago, o diente.

frenillo (frenulum): Se define con un pequeño freno o brida.

fulguración (fulguration): La destrucción de tejidos a través de una corriente eléctrica de alta frecuencia.

furúnculo (furuncle): Infección piógena ubicada originalmente en un folículo piloso.

galope (gallop): Triple cadencia de los sonidos cardíacos a frecuencia de 100 latidos por minuto o más, debida a un tercero o cuarto sonido cardíaco adicional al primero y segundo.

gameto (gamete): 1. Se refiere a una de dos células que experimenta cariogamia. 2. En herencia, cualquier célula germinal; óvulo, espermatozoide o célula de polen.

ganglio (ganglion): 1. (ganglio) Un agregado de cuerpos de células nerviosas ubicado en el sistema nervioso periférico; ganglio neural o nervioso. 2. (ganglion) Quiste que se compone de líquido rico en mucopolisacáridos dentro de tejido fibroso y en ocasiones, músculo o cartílago semilunar.

ganglitis (gangliitis): La inflamación de un ganglion; ganglionitis.

gangrena (gangrene): Necrosis debida a obstaculación, pérdida o disminución de la irrigación sanguínea; mortificación.

garganta (throat): 1. Fauces y faringe. 2. Cara anterior del cuello. 3. Cualquier entrada angosta a una parte hueca.

gastrectomía (gastrectomy): La enscisión de todo el estómago o de una parte.

gastritis (gastritis): La inflamación del estómago, principalmente de su mucosa.

gastrocopia (gastroscopy): La inspección de la superficie interna del estómago con un endoscopio.

gastroenteritis (gastroenteritis): La inflamación de la mucosa del estómago y el intestine; enterogastritis.

genérico (generic): Un género o que denota éste.

gestación (gestation): Se define como embarazo.

gigantismo (gigantism): Se dice del estado de tamaño anormal o crecimiento excesivo de todo el cuerpo o alguna de sus partes; gigantosoma; hipersomia; somatomegalia.

ginecólogo (gynecologist): Se refiere al médico especializado en ginecología.

glándula (gland): La agragación organizada de células que trabajan como un órgano secretorio o excretorio.

glándula ecrina (exocrine gland): Glándula que secreta hacia afuera por conductos excretorios.

glándula endocrina (endocrine gland): Glándula de secreción interna.

glaucoma (glaucoma): La enfermedad de ojo, que se caracteriza por el aumento de presión intraocular, excavación y atrofia del disco óptico; produce defectos en el campo de la visión.

glioma (glioma): Se dice de cualquier neoplasia derivada de uno de los diferentes tipos de células que componen el tejido intersticial de: el cerebro, la médula espinal, la glándula pineal, la posterohipófisis y la retina.

globina (globin): Proteína de la hemoglobina; hematohistona.

globulina (globulin): Se refiere al nombre de una familia de proteínas que precipitan del plasma o suero por semisaturación con sulfato de amonio.

glomérulo (glomerulus, pl. glomuleri): 1. Plexo de capilares. 2. Glomérulo o penacho de Malpighi. 3. Porción secretoria retocida de una glándula sudorípara. 4. Es el racimo de ramificaciones dendríticas y terminales axónicas en relación sináptica mutual compleja.

glositis (glossitis): La inflamación de la lengua.

glotis (glottis): Instrumento vocal de la laringe.

glucagon (glucagon): El factor hiperglucémico-glucogenolítico; factor HG; hormona hiperglucémica pancreática.

glucógeno (glycogen): Dextrano animal; se refiere al almidón animal o hepático; hepatina; zoamilina.

glucosa (glucose): Azúcar de la sangre; derivado del maíz, de la uva o del almidón; D-glucosa; celohexosa; dextrose; dextroglucose.

gónada (gonad): Órgano que produce células sexuales.

goniómetro (goniometer): Instrumento que se utiliza para medir el movimiento en los empalmes.

gonorrea (gonorrhea): Se refiere a la inflamación catarral contagiosa de la mucosa genital, trasmitida principalmente por el acto sexual o coito y debida a Neisseria gonorrhoeae; uretritis específica; uretritis venéreas.

granulocitosis (granulocytosis): El estado caracterizado por un número mayor que el normal de granulocitos en la sangre circulante en los tejidos.

grávida (gravida): Mujer embarazada.

halitosis (halitosis): Fetidez oral; indica el olor fétido de la boca; ozostomía; estomatodisodia.

heces (feces): Es la materia evacuada del intestino durante la defecación; excremento.

hematemesis (hematemesis): Vómito cruento; vómito de sangre.

hematocitoblasto (hematocytoblast): Hemocitoblasto.

hematócrito (hematocrit): 1. El porcentaje del volumen de una muestra de sangre ocupado por células, determinado por un hematócrito. 2. Centrífuga u otro aparato para separar las células y otros elementos particulados o figurados de la sangre del plasma.

hematuria (hematuria): Presencia de sangre o glóbulos rojos en la orina.

hemodiálisis (hemodialysis): Diálisis de sustancias solubles y agua de la sangre por difusión a través de una membrana semipermeable.

hemofilia (hemophilia): El trastorno hereditario de la sangre caracterizado por tendencia permanente a hemorragias espontáneas o traumáticas y debido a un defecto de la facultad de coagulación de la sangre.

hemoglobina (hemoglobin): La proteína respiratoria roja de los eritrocitos, esencial para transportar de oxígeno.

hemólisis (hemolysis): Disolución o destrucción de glóbulos rojos; eritrólisis; eritrocitólisis; hematólisis.

hemorroidectomía (hemorrhoidectomy): Exéresis quirúrgica de hemorroides.

hemorroides (hemorrhoids): Estado varicoso de las venas hemorroidales externas que produce tumefacciones dolorosas en el ano; almorrana.

hemotórax (hemothorax): Sangre en la cavidad pleural.

heparina (heparin): Ácido heparínico; un comienzo anticoagulante que es un componente de varios tejidos (especialmente el hígado y pulmón) y mastocitos en el hombre y varias especies de mamíferos.

hepatitis (hepatitis): La anflamación del hígado; generalmente por una infección viral, pero a veces por agentes tóxicos.

hepatomegalia (hepatomegaly): Se refiere al agrandamiento del hígado; megalohepatía.

hepatopatía (hepatopathy): La enfermedad del hígado.

hernia (hernia): La protrusion de una área o estructura a través de los tejidos que generalmente la contienen; ruptura.

herpes (herpes): Erupción de conjuntos de vesículas profundas sobre bases eritematosas.

heteroinjerto (heterograft): Xenoinjerto.

hidrocefalia (hydrocephalus): 1. Se dice del trastorno caracterizado por una acumulación excesiva de líquido que dilate los ventrículos cerebrales, adelgaza los tejidos encefálicos y produce separación de los huesos craneales. 2. En los lactantes, una acumulación de líquido en el espacio subaracnoideo o subdural.

hígado (liver): Se dice de la mayor glándula del organismo, que se localiza entre el diafragma en el hipocondrio derecho y la porción superior del epigastrio.

hilio (hilum, hilus): 1. Puerta; área de un órgano donde entran y salen los nervios y vasos. 2. Cavidad o hendidura que se asemeja al hilio del núcleo olivar del encéfalo.

himen (hymen): El pliegue membranoso semilunar o anular delgado que ocluye parcialmente el orificio vaginal externo en la virgen.

hiperopía (hyperopia): Vista larga o lejana; hipermetropía; presbicia.

hiperparatiroidismo (hyperparathyroidism): El trastorno ocasionado por un aumento en la secreción de las glándulas paratiroides.

hipersensibilidad (hypersensitivity): Se dice de la sensibilidad anormal; es el trastorno en el que existe una respuesta exagerada del organismo al estímulo de un agente extraño.

hipertiroidismo (hyperthyroidism): La anomalía de la glándula tiroides en la cual la secreción de hormona tiroidea suele estar aumentada y ya no está bajo control regulador de los centros hipotalamohipofisarios.

hiperventilación (hyperventilation): Es el aumento de la ventilación alveolar en relación con la producción metabólica de dióxido de carbono, de modo que la presión alveolar de dióxido de carbono disminuye por debajo de la normal; sobreventilación.

hipoadrenalismo (hypoadrenalism): La función adrenocortical reducida.

hipodermis (hypodermis): Tela subcutánea.

hipofaringe (hypopharynx): Se refiere a la porción laríngea de la faringe.

hipófisis (hypophysis): La glándula hipofisaria o basilar, hipófisis cerebral; glándula dominante; una glándula compuesta única, suspendida de la base del hipotálamo por una extensión corta del infundíbulo, el tallo infundibular o hipofisario.

hipoglucemia (hypoglycemia): Glucopenia; es la concentración anormalmente baja de glucosa en la sangre circulante.

hipoglucémico (hypoglycemic): Se relaciona con la hipoglucemia o se caracteriza por ella.

hipoparatiroidismo (hypoparathyroidism): un trastorno debido a disminución o ausencia de la secreción de hormonas paratiroideas; insuficiencia paratiroidea.

hipospadias (hypospadias): La anomalía del desarrollo que es caracterizada por un defecto sobre la cara ventral del pene.

hipotálamo (hypothalamus): El área ventrointerna del diencéfalo que forma las paredes de la mitad anterior del tercer ventrículo.

hipotensión (hypotension): Presión sanguínea arterial subnormal; hipopiesis.

hipotiroidismo (hypothyroidism): La producción disminuida de hormona tiroidea, que conduce a manifestaciones clínicas de insuficiencia tiroidea, incluyendo índice metabólico bajo, tendencia a la ganancia de peso y a veces, mixedema.

hipoventilación (hypoventilation): Ventilación alveolar disminuida en relación con la producción metabólica de dióxido de carbono, de manera que la presión alveolar de dióxido de carbono aumenta por encima de lo normal; subventilación.

hipoxemia (hypoxemia): Oxigenación subnormal de la sangre arterial, sin llegar a la anoxia.

hipoxia (hypoxia): Se refiere a la disminución de los niveles de oxígeno por debajo de lo normal en los gases inspirados, sangre arterial o tejido, sin llegar a la anoxia.

hirsutismo (hirsutism): Es la presencia de vello corporal y facial excesivos en un patrón masculino, principalmente en las mujeres; pilosis.

histamine (histamine): Una amina depresora derivada de la histidina por histidina descarboxilasa.

histerectomía (hysterectomy): Extracción del útero; uterectomía.

histerosalpingografía (hysterosalpingography): Radiografía del útero y las trompas uterinas después de la inyección de material radiopaco; ginecografía; histerotubografía; uterosalpingografía; uterotubografía.

histeroscopia (hysteroscopy): Se dice de la inspección instrumental visual de la cavidad uterina; uteroscopia.

homoinjerto (homograft): Aloinjerto.

hormona (hormone): Sustancia química, formada en un órgano o parte del organismo y llevada en la sangre hasta otro órgano o parte.

hueso (bone): Tejido óseo, tejido duro compuesto por células, incluidas en una matriz de sustancia fundamental mineralizada y fibras colagenosas.

húmero (humerus): El hueso del brazo, que se articula con la escápula por encima, y con el radio y el cúbito por debajo.

ictericia (jaundice): Se dice de la coloración amarillenta del integumento, la esclerótica y los tejidos profundos y excreciones, debida a pigmentos biliares que aumentan en el suero; icterus.

icterus (icterus): Ictericia.

ileítis (ileitis): La inflamación del íleon.

íleo (ileus): La obstrucción mecánica, dinámica o adinámica del intestino.

íleon (ileum): La tercera y última porción del intestino delgado, de unos tres metros y medio de largo, que se extiende desde la unión con el yeyuno hasta la abertura ileocecal.

ileostomía (ileostomy): Establecimiento de una fistula por la cual el íleon descarga directamente al exterior del cuerpo.

ilium (ileum): Hueso ilíaco.

impétigo (impetigo): Una infección piógena de la piel que manifesta un sarpullido costroso: impétigo contagioso o impétigo vulgar.

impotencia (impotence): La incapacidad del hombre para copular, o sea para lograr la erección del pene.

incontinencia (incontinence): Es la incapacidad de impedir la descarga de cualquier excreción, principalmente orina o heces.

incus (incus): El intermedio de los tres huesecillos del oído medio; yunque.

infarto (infarct o infarction): 1. (infarct) Área de necrosis ocasionada por insuficiencia repentina de irrigación sanguínea arterial o venosa. 2. (infarction) Insuficiencia repentina de irrigación sanguínea arterial o venosa debida a émbolos, trombos, torsión vacular o presión, que produce un área macroscópica de necrosis.

infertilidad (infertility): Esterilidad relativa; fertilidad disminuida o ausente.

inhalación (inhalation): 1. acto de aspirer el aliento; aspiración. 2. Acto de aspirar, junto con el aliento, un vapor medicado. 3. Solución de una droga o combinación de drogas que se administra como una nebulización que debe llegar al árbol respiratorio.

inmunidad (immunity): Insusceptibilidad; es el estado o cualidad de inmune.

inmunoglobina (immunoglobulin): Es una de una clase de proteínas estructuralmente afines formada por dos pares de cadenas de polipéptidos: un par de cadenas livianas (L) y un par de cadenas pesadas (H), las cuatro unidas por puentes disulfuro.

inserción (insertion): 1. Unión de un músculo a la parte más movible del esqueleto, al contrario de su origen. 2. En odontología, colocación intraoral de una prótesis dental.

inspiración (inspiration): Inhalación.

insulina (insulin): La hormona peptídica secretada por los islotes de Langerhans del páncreas.

integumento (integument): 1. La piel y sus partes; integumentum commune. 2. Cáscara, cápsula o cobertura de cualquier cuerpo o parte.

Interleucina (interleukin): Linfocina y hormona polipeptídica que es sintetizada por los monocitos.

interneuronas (interneurons): Combinaciones o grupos de neuronas entre neuronas sensitivas y motoras que rigen la actividad coordinada.

intestino (intestine): El tubo digestivo del estómago al ano.

intradérmico (intradermal): Intracutáneo.

intravenoso (IV) (intraveous IV): Dentro de uno vena.

introito (introitus): Se refiere a la entrada a un conducto u órgano hueco, como la vagina.

iridectomía (iridectomy): La excisión de una parte del iris.

iris (iris): La división anterior de la túnica vascular del ojo, un diafragma que tiene forma de disco perforado en el centro (la pupila), unido periféricamente al cuerpo ciliar.

iritis (iritis): La inflamación del iris.

isquemia (ischemia): Anemia local ocasionada por la obstrucción mecánica (especialmente estrechamiento arterial) de la irrigación sanguínea; hipoemia.

isquión (ischium): Hueso de la cadera.

istmo (isthmus): 1. Se dice de la constricción que une dos partes más grandes de un órgano u otra estructura anatómica. 2. Indica el pasaje estrecho que une dos cavidades más grandes. 3. La parte más angosta del tallo encefálico en la unión del mesencéfalo y el posencéfalo.

jeringa (syringe): Instrumento usada para inyectar or retirar líquidos.

laberintitis (labyrinthitis): inflamación del laberinto (oído interno) que a veces está acompañada por vértigo; otitis interna: íntima o laberíntica.

labio (lip): Cada uno de los dos pliegues musculares revestidos por una mucosa externa que tiene una capa superficial de epitelio escamoso estratificado y que limitan anteriormente la cavidad bucal. 2. Se dice de cualquier estructura en forma de labio que limite una cavidad o surco, como el de la vagina.

lactación (lactation): Se refiere a la producción de leche por la glándulas mamarias despues del parto.

lactífero (lactiferous): Lactígeno, que produce leche, galactóforo.

lágrimas (tears): El líquido secretado por las glándulas lagrimales que sirve para mantener húmeda a la conjuntiva y la córnea.

lagrimeo (lacrimation): La secreción de lágrimas, especialmente cuando es excesiva.

lámina (lamina, pl. laminae): Parte fina, plana de cualquier lado del arco de una vertebra.

laparoscopia (laparoscopy): Peritoneoscopia.

laringe (larynx): Órgano encargado de la producción de la voz; área del tracto respiratorio que se encuentra entre la faringe y la tráquea.

laringitis (laryngitis): Inflamación de la membrana mucosa de la laringe.

laringoplastia (laryngoplasty): Cirugía plástica o reparadora de la laringe.

laringoscopia (laryngoscopy): Inspección de la laringe por medio de un laringoscopio.

laringostomía (laryngostomy): Establecimiento de una abertura permanente en la laringe, desde el cuello.

lengua (tongue): Se define como cualquier estructura de forma semejante a la de la lengua.

lens (lens): El cuerpo celular biconvexo transparente que se encuentra entre el iris y el cuerpo vítreo y constituye uno de los medios de refracción del ojo.

lesión (lesion): 1. Cualquier herida o traumatismo. 2. Cambio patológico en un tejido. 3. Uno de los puntos individuales o placas de una enfermedad multifocal.

leucodermia (leukoderma): Falta de pigmento, total o parcial, de la piel; acromodermia; alfodermia; hipomelanosis; leucopatía.

leucoplaquia (leukoplakia): Manchas de color blanco localizadas en la mucosa oral que no pueden ser eliminadas y no se identifican clínicamente con ninguna entidad patológica específica.

leucorrea (leukorrhea): Se refiere al flujo blanco o líquido amarillento de la vagina, más o menos viscoso, que contiene moco y células de pus; leucorragia.

ligamento (ligament): Banda de tejido fibroso que conecta dos o más huesos, cartílagos u otras estructuras, o que sirve de sostén de las aponeurosis o músculos.

linfa (lymph): Es el líquido transparente, a veces un poco amarillento y opalescente, que se encuentra en los tejidos del cuerpo, pasa por los vasos linfáticos (a través de los ganglios linfáticos) y en ocasiones se incorpora a la circulación sanguínea venosa.

linfadenectomía (lymphadenectomy): Se refiere a la extirpación quirúrgica de los nódulos linfáticos.

linfadenopatía (lymphadenopathy): Se dice de cualquier proceso patológico que afecte a uno o a varios nódulos linfáticos.

linfocito (lymphocyte): Célula linfática; linfoleucocito.

linfoma (lymphoma): Linfoma maligno; término usado generalmente para las neoplasias, generalmente malignas, de los tejidos linfáticos y reticuloendoteliales que se presentan en forma de tumores sólidos aparentemente circunscriptos, compuestos por células que parecen primitivas o se asemejan a los linfocitos, células plasmásticas o histiocitos.

lobectomía (lobectomy): Es la extirpación de un lóbulo de un órgano o glándula.

lobotomía (lobotomy): 1. Incisión que se practica en un lóbulo. 2. División de uno o más tractos nerviosos en el lóbulo del cerebro.

lordosis (lordosis): Curvatura ventral convexa de la espina dorsal, poniendo en contraste con la condición normalmente cóncava.

lumen (lumen): Hueco dentro de una estructura tubular, igual a una arteria o el intestino.

lúnula (lunula): 1. Media luna o región blanca en la parte proximal de la lámina de la uña. 2. Estructura pequeña en forma de media luna.

macrocitosis (macrocytosis): Macrocitemia.

macrófago (macrophage): Cualquier célula mononucleada con actividad fagocítica que deriva de células troncales monocíticas de la médula ósea; clasmatocito; macrofagocito, célula ragiocrina.

mácula (macula o macule): 1. (macula) Estructura del oído interno que contiene pili que ayudan mantener equilibrio. 2. (macule) Área pequeña, de color diferente de la piel, que no se eleva ni se deprime con relación de la superficie de esta última.

malleus (malleus): Es el más grande de los tres huesecillos del oído; martillo.

mamografía (mammography): Es el examen de las mamas el cual se hace por medio de rayos X, ultrasonido, resonancia magnética nuclear etc.

mamoplastia (mammoplasty): Es la cirugía plástica de las mamas.

mandíbula (mandible): El hueso inferior de la quijada.

manzana de Adán (Adams apple): Prominencia laríngea; nuez de Adán, nuez de la garganta.

marcapaso (pacemaker): 1. El nodo sinoatrial. 2. Un aparato artificial insertado en el corazón para arreglar su latido.

marcha (gait): Se refiere a la forma característica de moverse a pie o caminar.

mastectomía (mastectomy): Escisión de una o ambas mamas.

masticación (mastication): El proceso de masticar alimentos como preparación para su deglución y digestión; se le dice también a la acción de moler, triturar y desmenuzar con los dientes.

mastitis (mastitis): Inflamación de las mamas; mamitis; mastadenitis.

meato (meatus): Pasaje o canal, especialmente la abertura externa de un conducto.

mediastino (mediastinum): Tabique entre dos partes de un órgano o una cavidad.

medicación, medecina (medication, medicine): Sustancia medicinal; sustancia que tiene propiedades curativas.

médula (medulla): Sustancia medular; se dice de cualquier estructura medulosa blanda, especialmente en el centro de una parte.

megacariocito (megakaryocyte): La célula grande de hasta 100 mm de diámetro con un núcleo casi siempre multilobulado, que produce las plaquetas; megalocariocito; tromboblasto.

melanina (melanin): Pigmento melanótico; cualquiera de los polímeros de color marrón oscuro a negro que existen generalmente en la piel, el pelo, la capa pigmentada de la retina, y en forma inconstante en la médula y zona reticular de la glándula suprarrenal.

melanocito (melanocyte): Célula pigmentaria de la piel; melanodendrocito.

melena (melena): La deposición de heces oscuras debido a la presencia de sangre alterada por los jugos intestinales; melanorrea; melanorragia.

menarca (menarche): Es el establecimiento de la función menstrual; se refiere al primer período o flujo menstrual.

meninges, sing. meningis (meninges, sing. meninx): Membranas, especialmente una de las envolturas membranosas del encéfalo.

meningioma (meningioma): Neoplasia benigna encapsulada de origen aracnoideo en los adultos.

meningitis (meningitis): Es la inflamación de las membranas del encéfalo o del raquis.

meningocele (meningocele): Se dice de la protrusión de las membranas del cerebro o del raquis a través de un defecto del cráneo o de la columna vertebral.

meningomielocele (meningomyelocele): Se dice de la protusión de las membranas y la médula espinal a través de un defecto de la columna vertebral; mielomeningocele; miclocistomeningocele.

menopausia (menopause): Es el período de cesación permanente de la menstruación; terminación de la vida menstrual.

menorragia (menorrhagia): Hipermenorrea.

menstruación (menstruation): Es el proceso de descarga endométrica cíclica de un líquido sanguinolento por el útero durante el período catamenial.

mesenterio (mesentery): 1. Se refiere a la doble capa de peritoneo unida a la pared abdominal y que encierra en sus pliegues parte o toda una víscera abdominal, a la que sirve sus vasos y nervios. 2. Se dice del pliegue de peritoneo en forma de abanico que rodea a la mayor parte del intestino delgado (yeyuno o íleon) y lo une a la pared abdominal posterior; mesenterio dorsal común; mesostenio.

mesotelioma (mesothelioma): Neoplasia rara derivada de las células que cubren la pleura y el peritoneo.

metacarpiano (metacarpal): Cualquier hueso de la mano entre la muñeca y los dedos.

metáfisis (metaphysis): Zona de crecimiento entre el epífisis y diáfisis durante el desarrollo de un hueso.

metastasis (metastasis): 1. Es el desplazamiento de una enfermedad o sus manifestaciones locales de una parte del cuerpo a otra. 2. En el cáncer, es la aparición de neoplasias en partes del cuerpo remotas del asiento del tumor primario.

metrorragia (metrorrhagia): Se refiere a cualquier sangrado acíclico irregular del útero entre períodos.

mialgia (myalgia): Dolor muscular.

microcitosis (microcytosis): Microcitemia.

micrófago (microphage): Leucocito fagocítico.

microglia (microglia): Células microgliales; células de del Río Hortega.

mieloblasto (myeloblast): Premielocito; es la célula inmadura de 10 a 18 mm de diámetro, perteneciente a la serie granulocítica y que existe generalmente en la médula ósea pero no en la sangre circulante, excepto en ciertas enfermedades.

mielografía (myelography): Visualización por rayos X de la médula espinal después de la inyección de una sustancia radioopaca en el espacio aracnoideo raquídeo.

mielograma (myelogram): Se refiere al estudio radiográfico de la médula espinal.

mieloma (myeloma): Un cáncer de las células del plasma en la médula. A veces se llama myeloma multiple.

miocardio (myocardium): Capa intermedia del corazón, que consiste en el músculo cardíaco.

miocarditis (myocarditis): Se dice de la inflamación de las paredes musculares del corazón.

miodinia (myodynia): Dolor en un músculo o un grupo de músculos mialgia.

mioma (myoma): Un tumor benigno integrado del tejido fino del músculo.

miomectomía (myomectomy): Es la remoción operatoria de un mioma, más específicamente de un mioma uterino.

miometrio (myometrium): Es el área muscular del útero.

miopía (myopia, nearsightedness): La vista corta, es el estado en el que por un error de refracción o elongación del globo del ojo los rayos paralelos se concentran por delante de la retina.

miositis (myositis): Inflamación de un músculo.

miringitis (myringitis): Inflamación de la membrana timpánica.

mixedema (myxedema): El hipotiroidismo caracterizado por un edema relativamente duro del tejido subcutáneo, temperatura subnormal, etc.

monocito (monocyte): El leucocito mononuclear relativamente grande, de 16 a 22 mm de diámetro, que generalmente constituye de 3 al 7% de los leucocitos de la sangre circulante y se encuentran en ganglios linfáticos, bazo, médula ósea y tejido conjuntivo no compacto.

músculo (muscle): Tejido fino contráctil que desempeña un papel importante en el movimiento del cuerpo.

musculoesquelético (musculoskeletal): Se refiere al sistema de músculos y de huesos.

narcolepsia (narcolepsy): Disposición del sueño repentino e incontrolable a intervalos irregulares, usualmente con causa predisponente o excitante visible.

naris (nostrils): Fosas nasales.

nariz (nose): Parte del aparato respiratorio situada por encima del paladar duro.

nasofaringe (nasopharynx): Parte nasal de la faringe; hueco faringonasal; epifaringe; rinofaringe; área de la faringe que se localiza por arriba del paladar blando; en su área anterior se abre en el hueco nasal.

náusea (nausea): Síntoma que tiene su origen en una propensión a vomitar.

necrosis (necrosis): Muerte patológica de una o más células o de cierta parte de un tejido u órgano, debido a daños irreversibles.

nefrectomía (nephrectomy): Extracción de un riñón.

nefritis (nephritis): Es la inflamación de los riñones.

nefroblastoma (nephroblastoma): Es el tumor de Wilms.

neoplasma (neoplasm): Neoplasia; nuevo crecimiento; tumor; tejido anormal que crece por proliferación celular más rápidamente que el tejido normal, y continúa creciendo aunque desaparezcan los estímulos que iniciaron el nuevo crecimiento.

nervio (nerve): Estructura parecida a un cordón compuesta por uno o varios fascículos de fibras nerviosas mielinizadas o no, o más frecuentemente una mezcla de ambas junto con tejido conectivo que los rodea.

neumoconiosis (pneumoconiosis): Neumonoconiosis; inflamación que induce comúnmente a fibrosis de los pulmones debida a la irritación causada por la inhalación de polvo que producen diferentes clases de trabajos.

neumonectomía (pneumonectomy): Remoción de todos los lóbulos pulmonares de un pulmón en una sola operación; neumectomía; pulmonectomía.

neumonía (pneumonia): Se refiere a la inflamación del parénquima pulmonar caracterizada por la consolidación de la parte afectada y porque los espacios alveolares están llenos de exudados, células inflamatorias y fibrina; pulmonía.

neumonitis (pneumonitis): Se dice de la inflamación de los pulmones; pulmonitis.

neumotórax (pneumothorax): Indica la presencia de aire o gas en la cavidad pleural; neumototórax;.

neurectomía (neurectomy): Escisión de un segmento de un nervio; neuroectomía.

neurilema (neurilemma): célula que envuelve a uno o más axones del sistema nervioso periférico; neurolema; vaina de Schwann.

neuritis (neuritis): Es la inflamación de un nervio, relacionada con neuralgia, hiperestesia, anestesia o parestesia, parálisis; atrofía muscular en el área inervada por el nervio afectado y por supresión de los reflejos.

neurocirujano (neurosurgeon): Cirujano especializado en las operaciones realizadas en el sistema nervioso.

neurona (neuron): Es la unidad morfológica y funcional del sistema nervioso, compuesto por el cuerpo de la célula nerviosa, las dendritas y el cilindroeje; célula nerviosa; neurocito.

neurotransmisor (neurotransmitter): Es cualquier agente químico específico liberado por una célula presináptica por excitación; que atraviesa la sinapsis para estimular o inhibir la célula postsináptica.

neutrófilo (neutrophil): 1. Glóbulo blanco maduro de la serie granulocítica, formado por tejido mielopoyético de la médula ósea, a veces también en sitios extramedulares, y liberado a la sangre circulante. 2. Se refiere a cualquier célula o tejido que no manifiesta afinidad especial por colorantes ácidos o básicos.

nevo (nevus): 1. Crecimiento pequeño, oscuro, a veces levantado en piel humana; espiloma; espilo; marca de nacimiento. 2. Exceso benigno localizado de células formadoras de melanina que surge en la piel a edad temprana.

nictalopía (nyctalopia): Es la menor capacidad para ver con iluminación reducida; ceguera nocturna; ambliopía nocturna; nictanopía.

nistagmo (nystagmus): Oscilación rítmica de los globos oculares, pendular o abrupta, sacudida; ataxia ocular.

nocturia (nocturia): Nicturia.

nodulectomía (lumpectomy): Se refiere especialmente a una lesión maligna de las mamas con conservación de la anatomía de estas últimas; tilectomía.

nódulo (nodule): 1. Pequeño nudo. 2. Región posterior del vermis inferior del cerebelo, que forma, junto con el velo nodular posterior, la porción central del lóbulo floculonodular.

norepinefrina (norepinephrine): La hormona carecolamina de forma natural D, si bien la forma L tiene cierta actividad. La base se considera como el mediador adrenérgico posganglgiona; norepinefrina arterenol; levarterenol.

obesidad (obesity): La corpulencia; adiposidad; aumento anormal de grasa en los tejidos conjutivos subcutáneos.

obstetra (obstetrician): Partero(a); es el médico especializado en la atención médica de las mujeres durante el embarazo y el parto.

oclusión (occlusion): 1. Cualquier contacto entre las caras incisales o masticatorias de los dientes superiores e inferiores. 2. Relación entre las caras oclusales de los dientes superiores e inferiores cuando entán en contacto.

oftalmología (opthalmology): Expecialidad médica que estudia el ojo.

oftalmoscopia (ophthalmoscopy): Examen del fondo del ojo por medio del oftalmoscopio.

ojo (eye): El órgano de la visión.

olécranon (olecranon): Extremo curvado del cúbito al cual los tendones de los músculos del brazo unen; prominencia huesuda del codo; apófisis olecraneana.

olfacción, oler (smell): 1. Olfato. 2. Percibir sensaciones por medio del aparato olfatorio.

oligodendroglia (oligodendroglia): Es uno de los tres tipos de células gliales (los otros dos son la macroglia o astrocitos, y la microglia) que junto con las células nerviosas pasan a formar el tejido del sistema nervioso central; oligodendria.

oligodendroglioma (oligodendroglioma): Glioma relativamente raro, moderadamente bien diferenciado y de crecimiento bastante lento, más frecuente en el cerebro de personas adultas.

oligomenorrea (oligomenorrhea): Menstruación escasa.

oligospermia (oligospermia): La concentración subnormal de espermatozoides en la eyaculación; oligozoospermia.

oliguria (oliguria): Micción escasa; oliguresis.

onicopatía (onychopathy): Iindeterminada enfermedad de las uñas; oniconosia.

oniquia (onychia, onychitis): Inflamación de la matriz de la uña; oniquitis; onixitis.

oocito (oocyte): Óvulo inmaduro; ovocito.

ooforectomía (oophorectomy): Ovariectomía.

optometrista (optometrist): El que practica la optometria.

oreja, oído (ear): 1. (oreja) Es la parte del órgano de la audición constituida por el pabellón de la oreja. 2. (oído) Es el órgano de la audición, formado por el oído externo, el oído medio y el oído interno o laberinto.

orina (urine): Es el líquido descchado por el riñón y que se compone por sustancias en solución.

orofaringe (oropharynx): Porción oral de la faringe.

orquidectomía (orchidectomy): Orquiectomía.

orquiectomía (orchiectomy): Extirpación de uno o ambos testículos; orquidectomía; orquectomía, testectomía.

ortopedista (orthopedist): Especialista en corregir deformidades del sistema esquelético.

ortopnea (orthopnea): Molestias al respirar, que se alivian en parte o por completo asumiendo la posición sentada o de pie erecta.

ortosis, ortótica (orthosis, orthotics): La aplicación externa usada para inmovilizar o amejorar el movimiento de la espina dorsal o de los miembros mediante el uso de aparatos ortopédicos.

orzuelo (hordeolum): La infección de una glándula marginal del párpado.

osificación (ossification): 1. Formación de hueso. 2. Conversión en hueso.

ostealgia (ostealgia): Dolor en el hueso.

osteoartritis (osteoarthritis): Enfermedad articular degenerativa; degeneración del cartílago articular que puede ser primaria o secundaria a traumatismo y otras causas; osteoartrosis; artritis degenerativa o hipertrófica.

osteoblasto (osteoblast): Célula formadora de hueso derivada del mesénquima; forma la matriz ósea, donde queda incluido como un osteocito.

osteocito (osteocyte): Célula o corpúsculo óseo.

osteoclasia (osteoclasis): La fractura intencional de un hueso a fin de corregir una deformidad.

osteoclasto (osteoclast): Célula grande que reabsorbe y elimna el tejido óseo.

osteodinia (osteodynia): Dolor de hueso.

osteoma (osteoma): Tumor benigno de crecimiento lento de hueso maduro que surge normalmente en el cráneo o la mandíbula.

osteomielitis (osteomyelitis): Inflamación de la médula ósea del hueso y el hueso adyacente.

osteópata (osteopath): Especialista en la osteopatía.

osteoplastia (osteoplasty): Reemplazo o reparación quirúrgico del hueso.

osteoporosis (osteoporosis): Una enfermedad caracterizada por la pérdida de calcio en huesos dando por resultado fragilidad.

osteosarcoma (osteosarcoma): Tumor maligno del hueso.

osteotomía (osteotomy): Procedimiento quirúrgico que implica el corte del hueso.

otalgia (otalgia): Dolor de oidos.

otitis externa (otitis externa): La inflamación del conducto auditivo externo.

otitis media (otitis media): La inflamación del oído medio, o tímpano.

otolito (otoliths): 1. Calcificaíones pequeñas en el oído interno.

otólogo (otologist): Especialista en otología.

otoplastia (otoplasty): La cirugía reparativa o plástica de la aurícula del oído.

otorragia (otorrhagia): La hemorragia del oído.

otorrea (otorrhea): La descarga del oído.

otosclerosis (otosclerosis): Capsulitis del laberinto; es la nueva formación de hueso esponjoso alrededor del estribo y la ventana vestibular (oval) que provoca una sordera progresiva.

otoscopia (otoscopy): La inspección del oído, principalmente la membrana timpánica.

ovario (ovary): Una de las glándulas reproductivas pares femeninas, que contiene los óvulos o células germinales.

ovulación (ovulation): Liberación de un óvulo del folículo ovárico.

óvulo (ovum): Se refiere a la célula sexual femenina.

oxitocina (oxytocin): Es la hormona nonapeptídica de la neurohipófisis que difiere de la vasopresina humana porque tiene leucocina en la posición 8 e isoleucina en la posición 3; ocitocina; a-hipofamina.

palpitaciones (palpitations): Pulsaciones fuertes del corazón que pueden ser perceptibles para el paciente; trepidaciones cardíaca.

pancitopenia (pancytopenia): La pronunciada reducción del número de eritrocitos, de todos los tipos de glóbulos blancos y de plaquetas en la sangre circulante.

páncreas (pancreas): La glándula salival del abdomen; glándula lobulada elongada desprovista de cápsula que se extiende desde la concavidad del duodeno hasta el bazo.

pancreatectomía (pancreatectomy): La escisión del páncreas.

pancreatitis (pancreatitis): La inflamación del páncreas.

papila (papilla): Cualquier prominencia pequeña en forma de pezón o similar.

pápula (papule): Pequeña elevación sólida y circunscripta de la piel que afecta en forma sobresaliente la epidermis o la dermis, y que depende del tipo de proceso patológico.

paracusia (paracusis): 1. Se define como las ilusiones o alucinaciones auditivas. 2. deterioro de la audición; paracusis.

parálisis (palsy): Frccuentcmente se refiere a la parálisis parcial o paresia.

parasiticida (parasiticide): Agente que elimina parásitos.

parathormona (parathormone): La hormona paratiroidea.

paratiroide (parathyroid): Glándula adyacente a la glándula tiroides.

paroniquia (paronychia): Oniquia lateral; oniquia periungular; inflamción del pliegue ungular con apartamiento de la piel de la porción proximal de la uña.

paroxístico (paroxysmal): Rclativo a los paroxismos o que ocurren ellos.

párpado (eyelid): Uno de los dos pliegues movibles de piel (párpado superior e inferior) cubiertos de conjuntiva frente al globo ocular; blefaron.

parturición (parturition): Parto; alumbramiento.

patógeno (pathogen): Cualquier virus, microorganismo o sustancia que ocasiona enfermedad.

pediculosis (pediculosis): Estado o condición que se le atribuye a infestación por piojos.

pelvis (pelvis): Anillo óseo en forma de taza, formado por ligamentos que se ubican en la parte inferior del tronco.

pene (penis): El miembro viril, falo, príapo, verga, órgano intromitente; el órgano de la copulación en el hombre.

pénfigo (pemphigus): Término normalmente utilizado para designar las enfermedades ampollares crónicas con acantólisis.

pepsina (pepsin): La enzima principal digestiva (proteasa) del jugo gástrico.

percusión (percussion): Método diagnóstico destinado a determinar la densidad de una parte por medio de los golpes dados en su superficie con un dedo o un plesor.

pericardio (pericardium): Cápsula, membrana o teca del corazón; bolsa cardíaca; membrana fibroserosa que consta de mesotelio y tejido conjuntivo submesotelial y cubre el corazón y el origen de los grandes vasos.

pericarditis (pericarditis): Inflamación del pericardio.

perimetrio (perimetrium): Túnica serosa del útero; capa serosa (peritoneal) del útero.

perineo (perineum): 1. Área ubicada entre los muslos, que se extiende desde el cóccix al pubis y queda por debajo del diafragma pélvico. 2. Superficie o cara externa del tendón central del perineo, ubicado entre la vulva y el ano en la mujer y entre el escroto y el ano en el hombre.

periostio (periosteum): Membrana fibrosa que cubre la superficie del hueso, excepto su cartílago articular.

peristaltismo (peristalsis): El movimiento vermicular; movimiento del intestino u otra estructura tubular; ondas de contracción y relajación circular alternada del tubo por las cuales su contenido es impelido hacia adelante.

peritoneoscopia (peritoneoscopy): Examen del contenido del peritoneo con un peritoneoscopio pasado a través de la pared abdominal; abdominoscopia; celioscopia; laparoscopia; ventroscopia.

peritonitis (peritonitis): La inflamación del peritoneo.

peroné (fibula): El hueso más pequeño y lateral de los dos huesos en la pierna, hueso de la pantorrilla; hueso peroneo.

pertussis (pertussis): Tos ferina o convulsa; enfermedad infecciosa aguda que es ocasionada por Bordetella pertussis.

pestaña (eyelash): Cilio.

petequia (petechia): Pequeña marca hemorrágica del tamaño de la cabeza de un alfiler, que brota en la piel y no se blanquea por diascopia.

pezón (nipple): Papila mamaria.

piamadre (pia mater): Pía: membrana delicada y fibrosa, vasculada, firmemente adherida a la cápsula glial del celebro [pia mater encephali] y a la médula espinal [pia mater spinalis] o membrana glial limitante, que sigue exactamente las marcas externas del cerebro y también la circunferencia tapizante ependimal, las membranas y el plexo coroides.

pielitis (pyelitis): Inflamación de la pelvis renal.

píloro (pylorus): El tejido muscular que rodea la abertura del estómago por la cuál pasan los alimentos hacia los intestinos.

pioderma (pyoderma): Indeterminada infección piógena de la piel; puede ser primario, como el impétigo contagioso, o secuandario a un estado preexistente; piodermatitis; piodermatosis.

piuria (pyuria): Es la presencia de pus en la orina excretada.

placa (plaque o patch): 1. (plaque) Zona de inhibición en un crecimiento confluente plano de bacterias o células tisulares por el efecto citopático de ciertos virus animales en una lámina de células tisulares cultivadas o por el efecto de un anticuerpo (hemolisina) producido por linfocitos 2. (plaque) Una zona bien definida de desmielinización característica de la esclerosis múltiple. 3. (patch): Área pequeña circunscripta de colo y/o estructura diferentes de la superficie que la rodea.

placenta (placenta): Órgano del intercambio metabólico entre el feto y la madre.

plaqueta (platelet): El fragmento citoplasmático de un megacariocito, de forma discoide, que es liberado en el seno medular y se ubica en la sangre periférica, donde actúa en la coagulación de la sangre.

plasma (plasma): 1. Plasma sanguíneo; porción líquida no celular de la sangre circulante, que se distingue del suero obtenido después de la coagulación. 2. Porción líquida de la linfa.

plasmaféresis (plasmapheresis): La extracción de sangre entera del organismo, separación de sus elementos celulares o figurados por centrifugación y reinfusión de éstos, suspendidos en solución fidiológica o algún otro sustituto del plasma, ocasionando así la depleción de la proteína plasmática del organismo pero no de sus células.

pleura (pleura, pl. pleurae): Membrana succingens; membrana serosa que envuelve los pulmones y tapiza las paredes de la cavidad pleural.

pleuritis (pleuritis, pleurisy): Inflamacíon de la pleura.

podagra (podagra): Dolor en el dedo gordo del pie, a menudo asociado con la gota.

podiatra (podiatrist): Podólogo; especialista en el tratamiento de las condiciones del pie humano.

poiquilolocitosis (poikilocytosis): Poiquilocitemia; presencia de poiquilocitos en la sangre periférica.

polarización (polarization): Aparición de diferencias de potencial entre dos puntos de tejido vivo.

policetemia (polycythemia): Eritrocitemia; hiperglobulia; hiperglobulismo; se define como el aumento que excede el número normal de glóbulos rojos de la sangre.

polidipsa (polydipsia): Acción de beber con frecuencia por sentir gran sed.

polipectomía (polypectomy): La escisión de un pólipo.

pólipo (polyp): Término descriptivo normal que indica cualquier masa de tejido que abulta o se proyecta hacia la superficie o arriba desde el nivel superficial normal.

poliposis (polyposis): La presencia de varios pólipos en alguna parte.

poliuria (polyuria): Hidruria; excreción extremada de orina, o micción profusa.

pons (pons): Protuberancia; en neuroanotomía, el puente del cerebelo o puente de Varolio; es el área del tronco encefálico entre el bulbo raquídep caudalmente y el mesencéfalo rostralmente, compuesta por la porción basilar y la calota de la protuberancia.

poro (pore): Agujero, perforación, orificio; una de las pequeñas aberturas de las glándulas sudoríparas de la piel.

prepucio (foreskin): Pliegue de piel que cubre más o menos completamente el glans del pene.

presbiacusia (presbyacusis): Presbiacusis; pérdida de la capacidad de percibir o discriminar sonidos, como parte del proceso de envejecimiento.

presbiopía (presbyopia): El cambio fisiológico del poder de acomodación de los ojos en las personas de edad madura.

prescripción (prescription): Fórmula escrita para la preparación y administración de un remedio.

presión arterial alta (high blood pressure): Tensión sanguínea alta; tensión alta.

presión arterial baja (low blood pressure): Tensión sanguínea baja; tensión baja.

priapismo (priapism): La erección persistente del pene; especialmente si se debe a enfermedad o cantidades excesivas de andrógenos, y no a deseo sexual.

proctitis (proctitis): Rectitis; inflamación de la mucosa del recto.

proctoscopia (proctoscopy): Rectoscopia; examen visual del recto y ano, como con un proctoscopio.

progesterona (progesterone): Hormona progestacional o del cuerpo amarillo; luteohormona; progestina; esteroide antiestrogénico considerado como el principio activo del cuerpo amarillo, aislado de éste y de la placenta o preparado sintéticamente.

próstata (prostate): Glándula que rodea a la uretra masculína.

prostatectomía (prostatectomy): Extirpación parcial o total de la próstata.

prostatitis (prostatitis): La inflamación de la próstata.

protrombina (prothrombin): El factor II de la coagulación de la sangre; trombinógeno; trombógeno; glucoproteína de PM aproximado 69.000, formada y almacenada en las células parenquimáticas del hígado.

prurito (pruritus): Comezón, picazón, escozor.

psoriasis (psoriasis): Alfos; psora; estado señalado por la erupción de maculopápulas escamosas plateado-rojizas, circunscriptas, discretas y confluyentes, sobre todo en los codos, las rodillas, el cuero cabelludo y el tronco.

pubertad (puberty): Serie de fenómenos por la cual los niños se transforman en jóvenes adultos.

pubis (pubes): 1. Hueso púbico. 2. Vello de la región púbica, inmediatamente por encima de los genitales externos.

pulmón (lung): Cada uno de los órganos de la respiración que ocupan la cavidad torácica, en los que se produce la oxigenación de la sangre.

pulso (pulse): Dilatación rítmica de una arteria producida por el mayor volumen de sangre expulsada al vaso por la contracción del corazón.

punto negro (blackhead): 1. Comedón abierto. 2. Histomoniasis.

pupila (pupil): El orificio circular en el centro del iris por el cual los rayos luminosos entran al ojo.

púrpura (purpura): Peliosis; el estado caracterizado por hemorragia en la piel.

pústula (pustule): Elevación pequeña y circunscripta de la piel que se compone por material purulento.

queilitis (cheilitis): Inflamación de los labios o de un labio.

queloide (keloid). Masa nodular, frecuentemente lobulada, firme, movible, no encapsulada, normalmente lineal, de tejido cicatrizal hiperplástico, formada por bandas paralelas relativamete anchas de tejido fibroso colágeno.

quemadura (burn): Lesión causada por el calor, or por algún agente cauterizante, inclusive fricción, electriciad y energía electromagnética.

queratina (keratin): Ceratina; escleroproteína o albuminoide presente en gran parte en estructuras cuticulares: pelo, uñas, astas, que contiene una cantidad relativamente grande de azufre.

queratitis (keratitis): La inflamación de la córnea.

queratoplastia (keratoplasty): La trepanación de la córnea; injerto corneal; remoción de una porción de la córnea que contiene una opacidad, y la inserción en su lugar de un trozo de igual forma y tamaño tomado de otra parte.

queratosis (keratosis): Queratiasis; cualquier lesión de la epidermis caracterizada por la presencia de neoformaciones circunscriptas de la capa córnea.

quimo (chyme): Pulpa; masa semilíquida de alimento parcialmente digerido que pasa del estómago al duodeno.

quiropráctico (keratoplasty): La trepanación de la córnea; injerto corneal; remoción de una porción de la córnea que contiene una opacidad, y la inserción en su lugar de un trozo de igual forma y tamaño tomado de otra parte.

queratosis (keratosis): Queratiasis; cualquier lesión de la epidermis caracterizada por la presencia de neoformaciones circunscriptas de la capa córnea.

quimioterapia (chemotherapy): Tratamiento de una enfermedad por medio de sustancias químicas o drogas.

quimo (chyme): Pulpa; masa semilíquida de alimento parcialmente digerido que pasa del estómago al duodeno.

rabdomioma (rhabdomyoma): Tumor benigno que deriva del músculo estriado, que se presenta en el corazón de los niños, probablemente como un proceso hamartomatoso.

rabdomiosarcoma (rhabdomyosarcoma): Tumor canceroso que se origina en los tejidos finos suaves del cuerpo tales como músculo, tendones, y tejido fino conectivo.

radiculitis (radiculitis): Inflamación del área intradural de una raíz nerviosa raquídea antes de su entrada en el agujero intervertebral, o del área ubicada entre éste ultimo y el plexo nervioso.

raiz de pelo (hair root): Se refiere a la raíz del cabello o pelo.

rales (rales): 1. Estertor. 2. Término ambiguo para un ruido adicional que se escucha al auscular el tórax.

raquitismo (rickets): Enfermedad del sistema esquelético, causada generalmente por deficiencia de la vitamina D.

receptor (receptor): 1. Molécula de proteína estructural en la superficie celular o en el citoplasma que se une a un factor específico, como una hormona, antígeno o neurotransmisor. 2. Término para cualquiera de las diferentes terminaciones nerviosas sensitivas de la piel, los tejidos profundos; las vísceras y los órganos especiales de los sentidos; ceptor.

recto (rectum): La porción terminal del tubo o aparato deigestivo que se extiende desde el colon sigmoide hasta el conducto anal.

reducción (reduction): La acción quirúrgica o manipulativa de volver una parte a sus relaciones anatómicas normales.

reflejo (reflex): Reacción involuntaria en respuesta a un estímulo aplicado a la periferia y transmitido a los centros nerviosos del cerebro o la médula espinal.

reflujo (reflux): El flujo retrograde; regurgitación.

refracción (refraction): Desviación de un rayo luminoso cuando pasa de un medio a otro de diferente densidad óptica; refringencia.

regurgitación (regurgitation): 1. Flujo retrogrado. 2. Retorno de gas o pequeñas cantidades de alimento desde el estómago.

renina (renin): Angiotensinogenasa que transforma angiotensinógeno en angiotensina.

renograma (renogram): Evaluación de la función renal a través de detectores de radiación externa después de la administración de un radiofármaco de caractcrísticas renotrópicas.

repolarización (repolarization): Proceso por el cual la membrana, la célula o la fibra vuelve a polarizarse después de su despolarización, con cargas positivas o en la superficie externa y negativas en la interna.

resectoscopio (resectoscope): Aparato utilizado como endoscopio especialmente para la extracción electroquirúgica transuretral de lesiones de la vejiga, la próstata o la uretra.

reticulocitosis (reticulocytosis): El aumento del número de reticulocitos circulantes más allá de lo normal, que es menos del 1% del total de glóbulos rojos.

retina (retina): La túnica interna del bulbo; optomeninge; túnica nerviosa del globo ocular.

retinitis (retinitis): La inflamación de la retina.

retroflexión (retroflexion): Inclinación hacia atrás, como la del útero cuando su cuerpo se dobla hacia atrás formando un ángulo con el cuello.

retroperitoneal (retroperitoneal): Externo o posterior al peritoneo.

retroversión (retroversion): Vuelta hacia atrás, p.ej., del útero.

retrovirus (retrovirus): Cualquier virus de la familia Retroviridae.

reumatólogo (rheumatologist): Médico que se especializa en el tratamiento de la artritis y de otras enfermedades reumáticas que pueden afectar empalmes, los músculos, los huesos, la piel, y otros tejidos finos.

rigidez (retroperitoneal): Externo o posterior al peritoneo.

rigor (rigor): Tiesura; rigidez.

rinitis (rhinitis): Catarro nasal; inflamación de la mucosa nasal.

riñón (kidney): Cada uno de dos órganos que excretan la orina.

rinoplastia (rhinoplasty): 1. Reparación de un defecto parcial o total de la nariz con tejido tomado de otra parte. 2. Operación plástica para cambiar la forma o el tamaño de la nariz.

rinorrea (rhinorrhea): Descarga de la mucosa nasal.

roce (rub): Sonido de friccíon que se oye entre latidas que puede indicar un soplo pericárdico.

roncha (wheal): Área evanescente circunscripta de edema de la piel que aparece como una lesión de urticaria ligeramente rojiza y que cambia a menudo de tamaño y forma y se extiende a áreas contiguas.

ronquido (rhonchi): Estertor. Sonido adicional ocasionado durante la aspiración oespiración, oído por auscultación del tórax y causado por aire que pasa a través de bronquios estrechados por inflamación, espasmo de músculo liso o por la presencia de moco en el lumen. [I'd say snore or snoring. Roncar means to snore.]

rosácea (rosacea): Acné rosácea o eritematosa; dilatación vascular y folicular que afecta la nariz y partes contiguas de las mejillas.

rótula (patella): El hueso movible triangular que protege el empalme de la rodilla.

rubéola (rubella,): Sarampión alemán o de los tres días; roséola epidérmica; tercera enfermedad; enfermedad exantematosa aguda provocada por el virus de la rubéola (Rubivirus) y caracterizado por agrandamiento de los ganglios linfáticos, pero normalmente con poca fiebre o reacción constitucional.

rubéola (rubeola) Palabra que se utiliza como sinónimo de dos patologías virósicas humanas diferentes, sarampión y rubéola.

ruga (rugae): Pliegue, reborde, doblez, arruga.

ruido (bruit): Sonido anormal en auscultación.

sacro (sacrum): La última vértebra espinal compuesta de cinco huesos fundidos; vértebra que formaparte de la pelvis; hueso sacro.

saliva (saliva): El líquido viscosa ligeramente ácido, inodoro, insípido y claro que consiste en la secreción de las glándulas salivales.

salpingectomía (salpingectomy): Tubectomía; ablación de la trompa de Falopio.

salpingitis (salpingitis): Inflamación de la trompa de Falopio o de Eustaquio.

sangre (blood): El "tejido circulante" del cuerpo; el líquido y sus elementos figurados suspendidos que circulan por el corazón, las arterias, los capilares y las venas.

sarcoidosis (sarcoidosis): Sarcoide; enfermedad granulomatosa sistémica, de causa desconocida, que ataca especialmente a los pulmones y causa fibrosis, pero también a los ganglios linfáticos, la piel, el hígado, el bazo, los ojos, los huesos de las falanges y la parótida.

sarna (scabies): Erupción debida a Sarcoptes scabiei hominis.

sebo (sebum): Esmegma; secreción de las glándulas sebáceas.

seborrea (seborrhea): Hiperactividad de las glándulas sebáceas con producción excesiva de sebo.

secuestro (sequestrum): Trozo de tejido necrosado, generalmente, hueso, que se ha separado del tejido sano que lo rodea.

secundina (afterbirth): La placenta y las membranas que se extruyen del útero después del parto.

semen (semen): Líquido seminal; esperma; eyaculación peniana; líquido viscoso, blanco amarillento, espeso que contiene espermatozoides.

seno (sinus): 1. canal o conducto para el paso de sangre o linfa sin las capas de revestimiento de un vaso común. 2. Hueco de un hueso u otro tejido. 3. Fístula o tracto que lleva a una cavidad supurante. 3. Cavidad hueca, especialmente cualquiera de dos cavidades en los lados de la nariz

septoplastia (septoplasty): Operación para corregir defectos o deformidades del tabique nasal, a menudo por alteración o extirpación parcial de las estructuras de sostén.

septostomía (septostomy): Creación quirúrgica de un defecto septal.

seudofaquia (pseudophakia): Lentículo.

sibilancia (wheeze): Sonido que hace que el aire que pasa por las fauces, la glotis o las vías aéreas traqueobronquiales estrechadas cuando la respiración es difícil.

sífilis (syphilis): Lúes venérea; mal venéreo; enfermedad infecciosa aguda y crónica ocasionada por Treponema pallidum, transmitida por contacto directo, normalmente mediante el acto sexual.

sigmoidoscopia (sigmoidoscopy): La inspección con un espéculo del interior del colon sigmoideo.

silla turcica (sella turcica): Estructura huesuda que contiene la glándula pituitaria.

simpatomimético (sympathomimetic): Señala algo que imita la acción del sistema simpático.

sinapsis (synapse): Contacto funcional de membrana a membrana de una célula efectora (músculo, glándula) o con una célula receptora sensitiva.

sinartrosis (synarthrosis): Es una articulación fibrosa o cartilaginosa sin movimiento. [Please check further. I think this is a broad definition of two types of joints, not one with two characteristics.]

síncope (syncope): Desmayo; caída repentina de la presión arterial o insuficiencia de la sístole cardíaca con la consiguiente anemia celebral y pérdida de la conciencia.

sinfisis (symphysis): Tipo de artículación cartilaginosa en la que la unión entre dos huesos se efectúa por medio de fibro cartílago.

singulto (singultus): Hipo.

sinovectomía (synovectomy): Procedimiento para quitar una parte de la membrana sinovial de una articulación, o la toda, como medio de reducir o de eliminar la inflamación común.

sinusitis (sinusitis): Inflamación de la membrana que cubre cualquier seno, principalmente uno de los senos paranasales.

sístole (systole): Contracción de corazón, especialmente de los ventrículos, por la cual la sangre atraviesa la aorta y la arteria pulmonar y después la circulación sistemática o general y lapulmonar, repectivamente.

somnolencia (somnolence): 1. Inclinación al sueño. 2. Es el estado de semiconciencia próximo al coma.

sonambulismo (somnambulism): Trastorno del sueño que incluye complejas acciones motoras; noctambulación; noctambulismo; orneirodinia activa, etc.

sonografía (sonography): Uso del ondas de sonido para producir imágenes del interior del cuerpo; ultrasonografía.

sonograma (sonogram): Imager producida por la sonografía; ultrasonograma.

soplo (murmur): 1. Ruido suave como el ocasionado por una espiración más o menos forzada con la boca abierta, que se percibe por auscultación del corazón, los pulmones o los vasos sanguíneos; susurro. 2. También se dice de otros ruidos no suaves que pueden ser fuertes, friccionales, ásperos, etc.

sordera (deafness): El término general para la pérdida de la capacidad de oír sin designar el grado de la pérdida ni su causa.

steroide (steroid): Nombre genérico de compuestos de estructura muy similar a los esteroides.

subluxación (subluxation): Dislocación parcial, como entre las superficies articulares comunes.

suero (serum): 1. El líquido acuoso claro, especialmente el que humedece la superficie de las membranas serosas o se exuda en la inflamación de éstas. 2. Parte líquida de la sangre obtenida por eliminación del coágulo de fibrina y los elementos celulares o figurados de la sangre.

surco (sulcus): 1. Hendidura, depresión, excavación, etc. en la superficie del cerebro, que limita las diferentes circunvoluciones. 2. Cualquier hendidura, depresión, excavación larga y angosta. 3. Hendidura o depresión en la cavidad oral o en la superficie de un diente.

sutura (suture) 1. (sutura) Material (hilo de seda, alambre, catgut, etc.) con el que dos superficies se mantienen en aposición. 2. (suturar) Unir dos superficies cosiéndolas mediante puntos o puntadas.

supositorio (suppository): Una sustancia medicada cuya forma permite su fácil introducción en uno de los orificios del cuerpo.

tabique (septum): 1. Una pared delgada que divide dos cavidades o masas de tejido más blando. 2. En los hongos, una pared transversal en una hifa.

tacto (touch): El sentido por el cual se aprecia o percibe el leve contacto con la piel o mucosas.

tálamo (thalamus): Voluminosa masa ovoide de sustancia gris que forma la mayor subdivisión dorsal del diencéfalo.

talasemia (thalassemia): Cualquiera de un grupo de trastornos hereditarios del metabolismo de la hemoglobina en el que se produce una reducción de la síntesis neta de una determinada cadena de globina sin cambios de la estructura de esa cadena.

talon (heel)· Porción trasera, redondeada del pie humano.

tambor de oído (eardrum): La membrana timpánica; tímpano.

taquicardia (tachycardia): Policardia, taquiarritmia; taquisistolia; latido rápido del corazón, se aplica normalmente a frecuencias superiores a 100 por minuto.

taquipnea (tachypnea): Polipnea; respiración rápida.

tendon (tendon): Una cuerda o banda fibrosa que conecta un músculo a un hueso u otra estructura.

tendonitis, (tendinitis, tendonitis): Inflamación del tendón.

tenotomía (tenotomy): La división quirúrgica de un tendón para aliviar una deformidad provocada por acortamiento congénito o adquirido de un músculo, como el pie bot o el estrabismo.

TEP (PET): Tomografía por Emisión de Positrones.

testículo (testicle, testis): Orquis; dídimo; cada una de las dos glándulas reproductoras masculinas ubicadas dentro de la cavidad del escroto.

testosterona (testosterone): El andrógeno natural más potente, formado en grandes cantidades por las células intersticiales de los testículos y posiblemente secretada también por el ovario y la corteza suprarrenal.

tetania (tetany): La calambre o tétano intermitente; tetanilla; tétanos apirético o benigno; trastorno caracterizado por contracciones musculares tónicas intermitentes acompañadas por temblores fibrilares, parestesias y dolores musculares.

tibia (tibia): Hueso medial y mayor de los dos de la pierna, que se articula con el fémur, el peroné y el astrágalo.

tic (tic): Contracción repetida más o menos involuntaria o contracción espasmódica habitual de músculos asociados; movimiento o contracción espasmódica habitual de una parte;

spasmo o corea habitual; enfermedad de Brissaud.

timectomía (thymectomy): La extirpación del timo.

timoma (thymoma): La neoplasia en el mediastino anterior, que se origina en el tejido tímico, por lo general benigno y con frecuencia capsulado.

timosina (thymosin): Factor linfopoyético tímico.

tiña (ringworm; tinea): Sérpigo; micosis (dermatofitosis) del pelo, piel y uñas.

tinnitus (tinnitus): Los ruidos (tintineo, silbidos, etc) en los oídos.

tiroidectomía (thyroidectomy): La extirpación del tiroides.

tobillo (ankle): El empalme formado por la articulación de los huesos más bajos de la pierna con el talus. El tobillo conecta el pie con la pierna. 2. Articulación astragalocrural.

tonometría (tonometry): Medición de la tensión o presión ocular.

tonsilectomía (tonsillectomy): Ablación de toda la amígdala; amigdalotomía.

tonsilitis (tonsillitis): Inflamación de una amígdala, principalmente de una palatina; amigdalitis.

toracocentesis (thoracocentesis): Punción quirúrgico de la cavidad pulmonar; toracentesis.

toracotomía (thorocotomy): Pleurotomía; incisión de la pared torácica.

toracostomía (thoracostomy): Establecimiento de una abertura en la cavidad torácica, como para el drenaje de un empiema.

tórax (thorax): Parte superior del tronco entre el cuello y el abdomen; pecho.

toxicología (toxicology): La ciencia que estudia los tóxicos.

tracción (traction): Fuerza de estiramiento o arrastre, usado para tirar una extremidad en dirección distal.

transfusión (transfusion): 1. Transferencia de sangre o de componentes de ésta de un individuo (donador) a otro (receptor). 2. Inyección intravascular de solución salina fisiológica.

tráquea (trachea): Conducto aéreo que se extiende desde la laringe hasta el tórax (a nivel de la quinta o sexta vertebra torácica) donde se bifurca para dar origen a los bronquios principales derecho e izquierdo.

traqueoplastia (tracheoplasty): Cirugía plástica de la tráquea.

traqueostomía (tracheostomy): La formación de una abertura en la tráquea o esa abertura.

traqueotomía (tracheotomy): La operación de realizar una abertura en la tráquea.

tremblor (tremor): Serie de movimientos musculares involuntarios.

triglicérido (triglyceride): Sustancia grasa en la sangre; triacilglicerol.

trígono (trigone): 1. cualquier área triangular, p. ej. el área al fundo de la vejigo por la cual entran los uréteres, sale la uretra.

trocánter (trochanter): Una de las prominencias óseas desarrolladas a partir de centros óseos independientes cerca de la extremidad superior del fémur.

trombectomía (thrombectomy): La escisión de un trombo.

trombina (thrombin): Enzima (proteinasa) formada en la sangre extravasada, que convierte el fibrinógeno en fibrina; trombosina; trombosa; fibrinogenasa.

trombo (thrombus): Un coágulo en el sistema cardiovascular formado durante la vida a partir de constituyentes de la sangre.

trombocito (thrombocyte): Plaqueta.

tromboflebitis (thrombophlebitis): Inflación venosa con formación de trombos.

trombosis (thrombosis): Formación o presencia de trombos; coagulación dentro de un vaso sanguíneo que causa infarto de los tejidos irritados por dicho vaso.

tronco encefálico (brainstem): tronco del encéfalo.

tubérculo (tubercle): 1. Nódulo, especialmente en sentido anatómico y no patológico. 2. Elevación sólida redondeada circunscripta a la piel, las mucosas o la superficie de un órgano. 3. Ligera elevación sobre la superficie de un hueso, que da inserción a un músculo o ligamento. 4. En odontología, pequeña elevación que sale de la superficie de un diente. 5. Lesión granulomatosa debida a infección por Mycobacterium tuberculosis.

tuberculosis (tuberculosis): Una enfermedad específica ocasionada por la presencia de Mycobacterium tuberculosis que puede afectar casi cualquier tejido u órgano del cuerpo, siendo los pulmones el asiento más común de la enfermedad.

tuberosidad (tuberosity): Una protuberancia en un hueso especialmente adherencia de un músculo o de un ligamento.

tumor (tumor): 1. Cualquier hinchazón o tumefacción. 2. Neoplasia.

úlcera (ulcer): Lesión de la superficie de la piel o las mucosas causada por pérdida superficial del tejido, en general con inflamación.

ulna (ulna): Hueso inferior del brazo; cúbito.

uña (nail): Cada una de las láminas córneas, delgadas y translúcidas que cubren la superficie dorsal del extremo distal de las falanges terminales de los dedos de las manos y de los pies.

urea (urea): Principal producto terminal del metabolismo formado en el hídago.

uremia (uremia): 1. Exceso de urea y otros desechos nitrogenados en la sangre. 2. El complejo de síntomas ocasionados por la insuficiencia renal persistente y grave, que pueden aliviarse con diálisis.

uréter (ureter): Tubo que conduce la orina del riñón a la vejiga.

uretra (urethra): El conducto urogenital; este conducto sale de la vejiga hasta el exterior y su función es descargar la orina.

urología (urology): Especialidad médica que se ocupa del estudio, diagnóstico y tratamiento de enfermedades del tracto genitourinario, principalmente del tracto urinario en ambos sexos y de los órganos genitales en el hombre.

urticaria (urticaria, hives): Erupción de ronchas pruriginosas de origen normalmente sistémico; cnidosis; uredo; urticación.

útero (uterus): Órgano muscular hueco donde el óvulo impregnado se desarrolla formando el feto; matriz; metra; seno materno.

úvea (uvea): Túnica vascular del bulbo.

úvula (uvula): Masa carnosa apendiente; estructura supuestamente semejante a la úvula palatina.

vacuna (vaccine): Originalmente, como vivo de vaccina, vaccina o viruela vacuna inoculado en la piel como profilaxis contra la viruela humana y obtenido de la piel de terneros inoculados con virus sembrado. Con el tiempo, su significado se ha extendido para incluir esencialmente cualquier preparación o profilaxis inmunológica activa.

vacunación (vaccination): Acto de administrar una vacuna. vagina conducto genital femenino que se extiende del útero hasta la vulva.

vaginitis (vaginitis): Inflamación de la vagina.

válvula (valve): 1. Cualquier reduplicación del tejido o estructura en forma de colgajo parecida a una valva. 2. Pliegue de la membrana que tapiza un conducto u otro órgano hueco y sirve para retardar o prevenir un reflujo de líquido.

válvula pulmonar (pulmonary valve): Válvula del tronco pulmonar.

valvulitis (valvulitis): Inflamación de una válvula, especialmente cardíaca.

valvuloplastia (valvuloplasty): La cirugía reparativa de una válvula cardíaca; valvoplastia.

varicela (varicella): Enfermedad contagiosa aguda que normalmente aparece sólo en los niños, causada por el virus de varicela-zoster y caracterizada por una erupción poco abundante de pápulas que se convierten en vesículas y pústulas, como en la viruela aunque menos grave; viruela de pollo; viruela de agua.

varicocele (varicocele): Afección que se manifiesta por dilatación anormal de las venas del cordón espermático, ocasionada por incompetencia de las válvulas de la vena espermática interna; pamponocele; cirsocele.

vasectomía (vasectomy): La deferentectomía; escisión de una área del vas deferens junto con prostatectomía o para producir esterilidad.

vasovasostomía (vasovasostomy): La conexión quirúrgica de los vasos deferentes para restaurar la fertilidad de un hombre previamente vasectomizado.

vegetación (vegetation): Un coágulo formado en gran parte por plaquetas fusionadas, fibrina y a veces bacterias que se adhiere a una válvula cardíaca enferma.

vejiga (bladder): 1. El órgano musculomembranoso distensible que sirve como receptáculo de líquido, como la vejiga urinaria. 2. Es cualquier estructura hueca o saco, normal o patológico, que contiene líquido seroso.

vellosidad (villus): 1. Proyección de una superficie, en especial mucosa. 2. Papila dérmica elongada que se proyecta en una vesícula o hendidura intraepidérmica.

vena (vein): Vaso sanguíneo que lleva la sangre hacia el corazón.

venipuntura (venipuncture): La punción de una vena, normalmente para sacar sangre o inyectar una solución.

venografía (venography): Visualización radiográfica o registro esquiagráfico de una vena después de inyectarle una sustancia radiopaca; flebografía.

ventrículo (ventricle): 1. El estómago. 2. Un hueco normal del cerebro o corazón. 3. Porción posterior agrandada del mesenterón del conducto alimentario de los insectos, donde tiene parte la digestion.

vénula (venule): Raicilla venosa que se continúa con un capilar; venita, venilla; vena capilar; vena diminuta.

verruga (verruca, wart): 1. Defecto elevado anormal firme en la piel, usualmente causado por un virus. 2. Bulto color carne identificado por hipertrofía circunscripta de las papilas del corion, con engrosamiento de las capas de Malpighi, granular y queratínica de la epidermis, y causado por papilomavirus.

vertebra pl., vertebras (vertebra, pl. vertebrae): Cada uno de los segmentos huesudos de la columna vertebral.

vértigo (vertigo): 1. Sensación de movimiento irregular o en torbellino. 2. También se usa en forma imprecisa como término general para describir el desvanecimiento.

vesícula biliar (gallbladder): Colecisto.

vesícula (vesicle): 1. Pequeña elevación circunscripta de la piel que contiene líquido seroso. 2. Pequeña bolsa o saco que contiene líquido o gas.

vestíbulo (vestibule): 1. Específicamente, la cavidad central más o menos ovoide del laberinto óseo, que comunica por delante con el carocol (cóclea) y por detrás con los conductos semicirculares. 2. Pequeña cavidad o espacio a la entrada de un canal o conducto.

vial (vial): Un receptáculo para contener medicinas.

virilismo (virilism): La posesión de características somáticas masculinas maduras en una joven, mujer o niña prepúber.

vista (sight): La capacidad o facultad de ver.

vista fatigada (eyestrain): Astenopía.

vitamina (vitamin): Un de grupo de substancias orgánicias que son essenciales para el metabolismo normal.

vitiligo (vitiligo): Piel manchada o multicolor; aparición en la piel normal de placas no pigmentadas, blancas, de diferentes tamaños y a menudo simétricas; leucasmo; leucoderma o leucopatía adquirida.

vólvulo (volvulus): El retorcimiento del intestino que causa obstrucción.

vómer (vomer): Hueso plano de forma trapezoidal que constituye la parte inferior y posterior del tabique nasal.

vulva (vulva): Pudendo femenino; órganos genitales externos de la mujer.

yeyuno (jejunum): El área del intestino delgado de unos 2,70 m de largo, entre el duodeno y el íleon.

Appendix N:

Internet Resources

The selected list of Internet resources for allied health that follows is divided into allied health career organizations; government sites and resources; billing and insurance information; professional associations; and charitable organizations.

Allied Health Careers

Anesthesiologist Assistant
American Academy of Anesthesiologists' Assistants (www.anesthestist.org)
Art Therapist
American Art Therapy Association (www.arttherapy.org)
Athletic Trainer
National Athletic Trainers' Association (www.nata.org)
Audiologist
American Speech-Language-Hearing Association (www.asha.org)
Blindness and Visual Impairment Professions
Association for Education and Rehilitation of the Blind and Visually Impaired (www.aerbvi.org)
Blood Bank Technology, Specialist in
American Society of Clinical Pathologists (www.ascp.org)
Cardiovascular Technologist
Society of Vascular Technologists (www.svtnet.org)
American Society of Echocardiography (www.asecho.org)
Alliance of Cardiovascular Professionals (www.acp-online.org)
Clinical Laboratory SciencëMedical Technology
American Society for Clinical Laboratory Science (www.alcls.org)
American Society for Clinical Pathology (www.ascp.org)
Association of Genetic Technologists (www.agt-info.org)
Counseling-related Occupations
American Counseling Association (www.counseling.org)
Cytotechnologist
American Society of Cytopathology (www.cytopathology.org)
Dental Assistant
American Dental Assistants Association (www.dentalassistant.org)
Dental Hygienist
American Dental Hygienists' Association (www.adha.org)
Dental Laboratory Technician
National Association of Dental Laboratories (www.nadl.org)
Diagnostic Medical Sonographer
Society of Diagnostic Medical Sonographers (www.sdms.org)
Dietetic Technician, Dietician
American Dietetic Association (www.eatright.org)
Electroneurodiagnostic Technology
American Society of Electroneurodiagnostic Technologists (www.aset.org)
Emergency Medical Technician-Paramedic
National Association of Emergency Medical Technicians (www.naemt.org)
Genetic Counselor
National Society of Genetic Counselors (www.nsgc.org)
Health Information Management
American Health Information Management Association (www.ahima.org)
Histologic Technician/Histotechnologist
National Society for Histotechnology (www.nsh.org)

Kinesiotherapist
American Kinesiotherapy Association (www.akta.org)
Medical Assistant
American Association of Medical Assistants (www.aama-ntl.org)
Music Therapist
American Music Therapy Association (www.musictherapy.org)
Nuclear Medicine Technologist
Society of Nuclear Medicine — Technologist Section (http://interactivesnm.org)
Occupational Therapy
American Occupational Therapy Association (www.aota.org)
Ophthalmic Dispensing Optician
Opticians Association of America (www.opticians.org)
Opthalmic Laboratory Technician
Optical Laboratories Association (www.ola-labs.org)
Opthalmic Medical Technician/Technologist
Joint Commission on Allied Health Personnel in Opthalmology (www.jcahpo.org)
Orthoptist
American Orthoptic Council (www.orthoptics.org)
Orthotist and Prosthetic
American Orthotic and Prosthetic Association (www.aopanet.org)
Pathologists' Assistant
American Association of Pathologists' Assistants (www.pathologistsassistants.org)
Perfusionist
American Society of Extra-Corporeal Technologists (www.amsect.org)
Pharmacy Technician
American Association of Pharmacy Technicians (www.pharmacytechnician.com)
Physical Therapist, Physical Therapist Assistant
American Physical Therapy Association (www.apta.org)
Physician Assistant
American Academy of Physician Assistants (www.aapa.org)
Radiation Therapist, Radiographer
American Society of Radiologic Technologists (www.asrt.org)
Rehabilitation Counselor
National Rehabilitation Counseling Association (http://nrca-net.org)
Respiratory Therapist, Respiratory Therapy Technician
American Association for Respiratory Care (www.aarc.org)
Speech-Language Pathologist
American Speech-Language-Hearing Association (www.asha.org)
Surgical Assistant
National Surgical Assistant Association (www.nsaa.net)
Surgical Technologist
Association of Surgical Technologists (www.ast.org)
Therapeutic Recreation Specialist
American Therapeutic Recreation Association (www.atra-tr.org)

Government Sites and Resources

CDC   Centers for Disease Control and Prevention (www.cdc.gov) links to many other sites set up by the CDC. For information, go to the main website and search for a specific subject or area and you will find the appropriate links.
CCI   The Medicare Correct Coding Initiative automated edits are online at cms.hhs.gov/physicians/cciedits/default.asp
CMS   Coverage of the Centers for Medicare and Medicaid Services: Medicare, Medicaid, SCHIP, HIPAA, CLIA topics
www.cms.hhs.gov
Medicare Learning Network: cms.hhs.gov/mlngeninfo
Online Medicare manuals: cms.hhs.gov/manuals/IOM

Medicare Physician Fee Schedule: cms.hhs.gov/PhysicianFeeSchedule

FDA   Food and Drug Administration (www.fda.gov) is the main website for this agency with links to its many other websites.

HCPCS   General information on HCPCS

www.cms.hhs.gov/MedHCPCSGenInfo

Annual alphanumeric Healthcare Common Procedure Coding System file

www.cms.hhs.gov/HCPCSReleaseCodeSets

SADMERC

www.palmettogba.com

HHS   Health and Human Services (www.hhs.gov) is the main website for this agency with links to its many other websites.

HIPAA

Home page

www.cms.hhs.gov/hipaa/hipaa2/

Questions and Answers on HIPAA Privacy Policies

answers.hhs.gov

HIPAA   Privacy Rule

"Standards for Privacy of Individually Identifiable Health Information; Final Rule." 45 CFR Parts 160 and 164. *Federal Register 65*, no. 250 (2000).

www.hss.gov/ocr/hipaa/finalreg.html

ICD-9-CM addenda

www.cms.hhs.gov/ICD9ProviderDiagnosticCodes

NCHS   (National Center for Health Statistics) posts the ICD-9-CM addenda and guidelines

www.cdc.gov/nchs/datawh/ftpserv/ftpicd9/ftpicd9.htm guidelines

NIH   National Institutes for Health (www.nih.gov) is the main website for this agency with links to its many websites.

NUBC   The National Uniform Billing Committee develops and maintains a standardized data set for use by institutional providers to transmit claim and encounter information. This group is in charge of the 837I and the CMS-1450 (UB 04) claim formats.

www.nubc.org

NUCC   The National Uniform Claim Committee develops and maintains a standardized data set for use by the non-institutional health care community to transmit claim and encounter information. This group is in charge of the 837P and the CMS-1500 claim formats.

www.nucc.org

OCR   The Office of Civil Rights of the HHS enforces the HIPAA Privacy Rule; Privacy Fact Sheets are online at

www.hhs.gov/ocr/hipaa

OIG   The Office of Inspector General of the HHA home page links to fraud and abuse, advisory opinions, exclusion list, and other topics

www.oig.hhs.gov

Model compliance programs are found at

oig.hhs.gov/fraud/complianceguidance.html

TRICARE and CHAMPVA

General TRICARE information

www.tricare.osd.mil

CHAMPVA Overview

www.military.com/benefits/veterans-health-care/champva-overview

WHO   The International Statistical Classification of Diseases and Related Health Problems, tenth revision. is posted on the World Health Organization site

www.who.int/whosis/icd10/

WPC   Washington Publishing Company is the link for HIPAA Transaction and Code Sets implementation guides. It also assists several organizations in the maintenance and distribution of HIPAA-related code lists that are external to the X12 family of standards:

- Provider Taxonomy Codes
- Claim Adjustment Reason Codes
- Claim Status Codes
- Claim Status Category Codes

Appendices

- Health Care Services Decision Reason Codes
- Insurance Business Process Application Error Codes
- Remittance Remark Codes

www.wpc-edi.com

Billing and Insurance Resources

BlueCross BlueShield Association
www.bluecares.com
The Kaiser Family Foundation Web site provides in-depth information on key health
policy issues such as Medicaid, Medicare, and prescription drugs.
www.kff.org
Various sites, such as www.benefitnews.com, www.erisaclaim.com and www.erisa.com, cover
EMTALA, ERISA regulations and updates concerning provider and patient appeals of managed care
organizations.
State insurance commissioners
www.oinc.state.ct.us
AHIMA   Coverage of Related Topics Located Under the Practice Brief tab on the AHIMA Home
Page www.ahima.org
Computer-based Patient Record Institute (CPRI)
www.cpri.org
Medical Record Institute
www.medrecinst.com

Professional Associations

AADA   American Dental Assistant Association (www.dentalassistants.org)
AAFP   American Academy of Family Physicians
www.aafp.org
AAHAM   American Association of Healthcare Administrative Management
www.aaham.org
AAMA   American Association of Medical Assistants
www.aama-ntl.org
AAMT   American Association for Medical Transcription (changing to Association for Integrity of
Healthcare Documentation)
www.aamt.org
AAPC   American Academy of Professional Coders
www.aapc.com
ACA   American Chiropractic Association (www.amerchiro.org)
ACA   International (formerly American Collectors Association)
www.acainternational.org
AHIP   America's Health Plans
Links to Member Health Plans
ww.ahip.org
ACHE   American College of Healthcare Executives
www.ache.org
ADA   American Dental Association (www.ada.org)
ADHA   American Dental Hygienists Association (www.adha.org)
AHIMA   American Health Information Management Association
www.ahima.org
AMB   Association of Medical Billers
www.billers.com
AHLA   American Health Lawyers Association
www.healthlawyers.org
AHA   American Hospital Association
www.aha.org
AMA   American Medical Association
www.ama-assn.org
AMT   American Medical Technologists
www.amt1.com

AMTA   American Massage Therapy Association (www.amtamassage.org)
ANA   American Nursing Association
www.ana.org
APA   American Psychiatric Association (www.psych.org)
APTA   American Physical Therapy Association (www.apta.org)
CAMA   Complementary Alternative Medicine Association (www.camaweb.org)
HBMA   Healthcare Billing and Management Association
www.hbma.com
HFMA   Healthcare Financial Management Association
www.hfma.org
JCAHO
MGMA   Medical Group Management Association
www.mgma.org
PAHCOM   Professional Association of Health Care Office Management
www.pahcom.com

Charitable Organizations

AIDS.ORG (www.aids.org)
Alzheimer's Foundation of America (www.alzfdn.org)
American Cancer Society (www.cancer.org)
American Diabetes Association (www.diabetes.org)
American Heart Association (www.americanheart.org)
American Lung Association (www.lungusa.org)
Arthritis Foundation (www.arthritis.org)
Asthma and Allergy Foundation of America (www.aafa.org)
Cystic Fibrosis Foundation (www.cff.org)
The Leukemia and Lymphoma Society (www.leukemia-lymphoma.org)
National Multiple Sclerosis Society (www.nationalmssociety.org)
National Parkinson Foundation (www.parkinson.org)
Skin Cancer Foundation (www.skincancer.org)
United Cerebral Palsy (www.ucp.org)

Appendix O:

List of Diagnosis Related Groups (DRGs)

Diagnosis Related Groups

The list that follows is a grouping of diagnoses used by hospitals in billing insurers and the governments. The list is from www.cms.gov, the governments' website for Medicare and Medicaid.

DRG	MDC	TYPE	DRG TITLE
001	1	SURG	CRANIOTOMY AGE >17 W CC
002	1	SURG	CRANIOTOMY AGE >17 W/O CC
003	1	SURG	CRANIOTOMY AGE 0–17
004	1	SURG	NO LONGER VALID
005	1	SURG	NO LONGER VALID
006	1	SURG	CARPAL TUNNEL RELEASE
007	1	SURG	PERIPH & CRANIAL NERVE & OTHER NERV SYST PROC W CC
008	1	SURG	PERIPH & CRANIAL NERVE & OTHER NERV SYST PROC W/O CC
009	1	MED	SPINAL DISORDERS & INJURIES
010	1	MED	NERVOUS SYSTEM NEOPLASMS W CC
011	1	MED	NERVOUS SYSTEM NEOPLASMS W/O CC
012	1	MED	DEGENERATIVE NERVOUS SYSTEM DISORDERS
013	1	MED	MULTIPLE SCLEROSIS & CEREBELLAR ATAXIA
014	1	MED	INTRACRANIAL HEMORRHAGE & STROKE W INFARCT
015	1	MED	NONSPECIFIC CVA & PRECEREBRAL OCCLUSION W/O INFARCT
016	1	MED	NONSPECIFIC CEREBROVASCULAR DISORDERS W CC
017	1	MED	NONSPECIFIC CEREBROVASCULAR DISORDERS W/O CC
018	1	MED	CRANIAL & PERIPHERAL NERVE DISORDERS W CC
019	1	MED	CRANIAL & PERIPHERAL NERVE DISORDERS W/O CC
020	1	MED	NERVOUS SYSTEM INFECTION EXCEPT VIRAL MENINGITIS
021	1	MED	VIRAL MENINGITIS
022	1	MED	HYPERTENSIVE ENCEPHALOPATHY
023	1	MED	NONTRAUMATIC STUPOR & COMA
024	1	MED	SEIZURE & HEADACHE AGE >17 W CC
025	1	MED	SEIZURE & HEADACHE AGE >17 W/O CC
026	1	MED	SEIZURE & HEADACHE AGE 0–17
027	1	MED	TRAUMATIC STUPOR & COMA, COMA >1 HR
028	1	MED	TRAUMATIC STUPOR & COMA, COMA <1 HR AGE >17 W CC
029	1	MED	TRAUMATIC STUPOR & COMA, COMA <1 HR AGE >17 W/O CC

030	1	MED	TRAUMATIC STUPOR & COMA, COMA <1 HR AGE 0-17
031	1	MED	CONCUSSION AGE >17 W CC
032	1	MED	CONCUSSION AGE >17 W/O CC
033	1	MED	CONCUSSION AGE 0–17
034	1	MED	OTHER DISORDERS OF NERVOUS SYSTEM W CC
035	1	MED	OTHER DISORDERS OF NERVOUS SYSTEM W/O CC
036	2	SURG	RETINAL PROCEDURES
037	2	SURG	ORBITAL PROCEDURES
038	2	SURG	PRIMARY IRIS PROCEDURES
039	2	SURG	LENS PROCEDURES WITH OR WITHOUT VITRECTOMY
040	2	SURG	EXTRAOCULAR PROCEDURES EXCEPT ORBIT AGE >17
041	2	SURG	EXTRAOCULAR PROCEDURES EXCEPT ORBIT AGE 0–17
042	2	SURG	INTRAOCULAR PROCEDURES EXCEPT RETINA, IRIS & LENS
043	2	MED	HYPHEMA
044	2	MED	ACUTE MAJOR EYE INFECTIONS
045	2	MED	NEUROLOGICAL EYE DISORDERS
046	2	MED	OTHER DISORDERS OF THE EYE AGE >17 W CC
047	2	MED	OTHER DISORDERS OF THE EYE AGE >17 W/O CC
048	2	MED	OTHER DISORDERS OF THE EYE AGE 0–17
049	3	SURG	MAJOR HEAD & NECK PROCEDURES
050	3	SURG	SIALOADENECTOMY
051	3	SURG	SALIVARY GLAND PROCEDURES EXCEPT SIALOADENECTOMY
052	3	SURG	CLEFT LIP & PALATE REPAIR
053	3	SURG	SINUS & MASTOID PROCEDURES AGE >17
054	3	SURG	SINUS & MASTOID PROCEDURES AGE 0–17
055	3	SURG	MISCELLANEOUS EAR, NOSE, MOUTH & THROAT PROCEDURES
056	3	SURG	RHINOPLASTY
057	3	SURG	T&A PROC, EXCEPT TONSILLECTOMY &/OR ADENOIDECTOMY ONLY, AGE >17
058	3	SURG	T&A PROC, EXCEPT TONSILLECTOMY &/OR ADENOIDECTOMY ONLY, AGE 0–17
059	3	SURG	TONSILLECTOMY &/OR ADENOIDECTOMY ONLY, AGE >17
060	3	SURG	TONSILLECTOMY &/OR ADENOIDECTOMY ONLY, AGE 0–17
061	3	SURG	MYRINGOTOMY W TUBE INSERTION AGE >17
062	3	SURG	MYRINGOTOMY W TUBE INSERTION AGE 0–17
063	3	SURG	OTHER EAR, NOSE, MOUTH & THROAT O.R. PROCEDURES
064	3	MED	EAR, NOSE, MOUTH & THROAT MALIGNANCY
065	3	MED	DYSEQUILIBRIUM
066	3	MED	EPISTAXIS
067	3	MED	EPIGLOTTITIS
068	3	MED	OTITIS MEDIA & URI AGE >17 W CC
069	3	MED	OTITIS MEDIA & URI AGE >17 W/O CC
070	3	MED	OTITIS MEDIA & URI AGE 0–17
071	3	MED	LARYNGOTRACHEITIS
072	3	MED	NASAL TRAUMA & DEFORMITY

073	3	MED	OTHER EAR, NOSE, MOUTH & THROAT DIAGNOSES AGE >17
074	3	MED	OTHER EAR, NOSE, MOUTH & THROAT DIAGNOSES AGE 0–17
075	4	SURG	MAJOR CHEST PROCEDURES
076	4	SURG	OTHER RESP SYSTEM O.R. PROCEDURES W CC
077	4	SURG	OTHER RESP SYSTEM O.R. PROCEDURES W/O CC
078	4	MED	PULMONARY EMBOLISM
079	4	MED	RESPIRATORY INFECTIONS & INFLAMMATIONS AGE >17 W CC
080	4	MED	RESPIRATORY INFECTIONS & INFLAMMATIONS AGE >17 W/O CC
081	4	MED	RESPIRATORY INFECTIONS & INFLAMMATIONS AGE 0–17
082	4	MED	RESPIRATORY NEOPLASMS
083	4	MED	MAJOR CHEST TRAUMA W CC
084	4	MED	MAJOR CHEST TRAUMA W/O CC
085	4	MED	PLEURAL EFFUSION W CC
086	4	MED	PLEURAL EFFUSION W/O CC
087	4	MED	PULMONARY EDEMA & RESPIRATORY FAILURE
088	4	MED	CHRONIC OBSTRUCTIVE PULMONARY DISEASE
089	4	MED	SIMPLE PNEUMONIA & PLEURISY AGE >17 W CC
090	4	MED	SIMPLE PNEUMONIA & PLEURISY AGE >17 W/O CC
091	4	MED	SIMPLE PNEUMONIA & PLEURISY AGE 0–17
092	4	MED	INTERSTITIAL LUNG DISEASE W CC
093	4	MED	INTERSTITIAL LUNG DISEASE W/O CC
094	4	MED	PNEUMOTHORAX W CC
095	4	MED	PNEUMOTHORAX W/O CC
096	4	MED	BRONCHITIS & ASTHMA AGE >17 W CC
097	4	MED	BRONCHITIS & ASTHMA AGE >17 W/O CC
098	4	MED	BRONCHITIS & ASTHMA AGE 0–17
099	4	MED	RESPIRATORY SIGNS & SYMPTOMS W CC
100	4	MED	RESPIRATORY SIGNS & SYMPTOMS W/O CC
101	4	MED	OTHER RESPIRATORY SYSTEM DIAGNOSES W CC
102	4	MED	OTHER RESPIRATORY SYSTEM DIAGNOSES W/O CC
103	PRE	SURG	HEART TRANSPLANT
104	5	SURG	CARDIAC VALVE & OTH MAJOR CARDIOTHORACIC PROC W CARD CATH
105	5	SURG	CARDIAC VALVE & OTH MAJOR CARDIOTHORACIC PROC W/O CARD CATH
106	5	SURG	CORONARY BYPASS W PTCA
107	5	SURG	CORONARY BYPASS W CARDIAC CATH
108	5	SURG	OTHER CARDIOTHORACIC PROCEDURES
109	5	SURG	CORONARY BYPASS W/O PTCA OR CARDIAC CATH
110	5	SURG	MAJOR CARDIOVASCULAR PROCEDURES W CC
111	5	SURG	MAJOR CARDIOVASCULAR PROCEDURES W/O CC
112	5	SURG	NO LONGER VALID
113	5	SURG	AMPUTATION FOR CIRC SYSTEM DISORDERS EXCEPT UPPER LIMB & TOE
114	5	SURG	UPPER LIMB & TOE AMPUTATION FOR CIRC SYSTEM DISORDERS

Appendices

115	5	SURG	PRM CARD PACEM IMPL W AMI/HR/SHOCK OR AICD LEAD OR GNRTR
116	5	SURG	OTHER PERMANENT CARDIAC PACEMAKER IMPLANT
117	5	SURG	CARDIAC PACEMAKER REVISION EXCEPT DEVICE REPLACEMENT
118	5	SURG	CARDIAC PACEMAKER DEVICE REPLACEMENT
119	5	SURG	VEIN LIGATION & STRIPPING
120	5	SURG	OTHER CIRCULATORY SYSTEM O.R. PROCEDURES
121	5	MED	CIRCULATORY DISORDERS W AMI & MAJOR COMP, DISCHARGED ALIVE
122	5	MED	CIRCULATORY DISORDERS W AMI W/O MAJOR COMP, DISCHARGED ALIVE
123	5	MED	CIRCULATORY DISORDERS W AMI, EXPIRED
124	5	MED	CIRCULATORY DISORDERS EXCEPT AMI, W CARD CATH & COMPLEX DIAG
125	5	MED	CIRCULATORY DISORDERS EXCEPT AMI, W CARD CATH W/O COMPLEX DIAG
126	5	MED	ACUTE & SUBACUTE ENDOCARDITIS
127	5	MED	HEART FAILURE & SHOCK
128	5	MED	DEEP VEIN THROMBOPHLEBITIS
129	5	MED	CARDIAC ARREST, UNEXPLAINED
130	5	MED	PERIPHERAL VASCULAR DISORDERS W CC
131	5	MED	PERIPHERAL VASCULAR DISORDERS W/O CC
132	5	MED	ATHEROSCLEROSIS W CC
133	5	MED	ATHEROSCLEROSIS W/O CC
134	5	MED	HYPERTENSION
135	5	MED	CARDIAC CONGENITAL & VALVULAR DISORDERS AGE >17 W CC
136	5	MED	CARDIAC CONGENITAL & VALVULAR DISORDERS AGE >17 W/O CC
137	5	MED	CARDIAC CONGENITAL & VALVULAR DISORDERS AGE 0–17
138	5	MED	CARDIAC ARRHYTHMIA & CONDUCTION DISORDERS W CC
139	5	MED	CARDIAC ARRHYTHMIA & CONDUCTION DISORDERS W/O CC
140	5	MED	ANGINA PECTORIS
141	5	MED	SYNCOPE & COLLAPSE W CC
142	5	MED	SYNCOPE & COLLAPSE W/O CC
143	5	MED	CHEST PAIN
144	5	MED	OTHER CIRCULATORY SYSTEM DIAGNOSES W CC
145	5	MED	OTHER CIRCULATORY SYSTEM DIAGNOSES W/O CC
146	6	SURG	RECTAL RESECTION W CC
147	6	SURG	RECTAL RESECTION W/O CC
148	6	SURG	MAJOR SMALL & LARGE BOWEL PROCEDURES W CC
149	6	SURG	MAJOR SMALL & LARGE BOWEL PROCEDURES W/O CC
150	6	SURG	PERITONEAL ADHESIOLYSIS W CC
151	6	SURG	PERITONEAL ADHESIOLYSIS W/O CC
152	6	SURG	MINOR SMALL & LARGE BOWEL PROCEDURES W CC
153	6	SURG	MINOR SMALL & LARGE BOWEL PROCEDURES W/O CC

154	6	SURG	STOMACH, ESOPHAGEAL & DUODENAL PROCEDURES AGE >17 W CC
155	6	SURG	STOMACH, ESOPHAGEAL & DUODENAL PROCEDURES AGE >17 W/O CC
156	6	SURG	STOMACH, ESOPHAGEAL & DUODENAL PROCEDURES AGE 0–17
157	6	SURG	ANAL & STOMAL PROCEDURES W CC
158	6	SURG	ANAL & STOMAL PROCEDURES W/O CC
159	6	SURG	HERNIA PROCEDURES EXCEPT INGUINAL & FEMORAL AGE >17 W CC
160	6	SURG	HERNIA PROCEDURES EXCEPT INGUINAL & FEMORAL AGE >17 W/O CC
161	6	SURG	INGUINAL & FEMORAL HERNIA PROCEDURES AGE >17 W CC
162	6	SURG	INGUINAL & FEMORAL HERNIA PROCEDURES AGE >17 W/O CC
163	6	SURG	HERNIA PROCEDURES AGE 0–17
164	6	SURG	APPENDECTOMY W COMPLICATED PRINCIPAL DIAG W CC
165	6	SURG	APPENDECTOMY W COMPLICATED PRINCIPAL DIAG W/O CC
166	6	SURG	APPENDECTOMY W/O COMPLICATED PRINCIPAL DIAG W CC
167	6	SURG	APPENDECTOMY W/O COMPLICATED PRINCIPAL DIAG W/O CC
168	6	SURG	MOUTH PROCEDURES W CC
169	6	SURG	MOUTH PROCEDURES W/O CC
170	6	SURG	OTHER DIGESTIVE SYSTEM O.R. PROCEDURES W CC
171	6	SURG	OTHER DIGESTIVE SYSTEM O.R. PROCEDURES W/O CC
172	6	MED	DIGESTIVE MALIGNANCY W CC
173	6	MED	DIGESTIVE MALIGNANCY W/O CC
174	6	MED	G.I. HEMORRHAGE W CC
175	6	MED	G.I. HEMORRHAGE W/O CC
176	6	MED	COMPLICATED PEPTIC ULCER
177	6	MED	UNCOMPLICATED PEPTIC ULCER W CC
178	6	MED	UNCOMPLICATED PEPTIC ULCER W/O CC
179	6	MED	INFLAMMATORY BOWEL DISEASE
180	6	MED	G.I. OBSTRUCTION W CC
181	6	MED	G.I. OBSTRUCTION W/O CC
182	6	MED	ESOPHAGITIS, GASTROENT & MISC DIGEST DISORDERS AGE >17 W CC
183	6	MED	ESOPHAGITIS, GASTROENT & MISC DIGEST DISORDERS AGE >17 W/O CC
184	6	MED	ESOPHAGITIS, GASTROENT & MISC DIGEST DISORDERS AGE 0–17
185	3	MED	DENTAL & ORAL DIS EXCEPT EXTRACTIONS & RESTORATIONS, AGE >17
186	3	MED	DENTAL & ORAL DIS EXCEPT EXTRACTIONS & RESTORATIONS, AGE 0–17
187	3	MED	DENTAL EXTRACTIONS & RESTORATIONS
188	6	MED	OTHER DIGESTIVE SYSTEM DIAGNOSES AGE >17 W CC

189	6	MED	OTHER DIGESTIVE SYSTEM DIAGNOSES AGE >17 W/O CC
190	6	MED	OTHER DIGESTIVE SYSTEM DIAGNOSES AGE 0–17
191	7	SURG	PANCREAS, LIVER & SHUNT PROCEDURES W CC
192	7	SURG	PANCREAS, LIVER & SHUNT PROCEDURES W/O CC
193	7	SURG	BILIARY TRACT PROC EXCEPT ONLY CHOLECYST W OR W/O C.D.E. W CC
194	7	SURG	BILIARY TRACT PROC EXCEPT ONLY CHOLECYST W OR W/O C.D.E. W/O CC
195	7	SURG	CHOLECYSTECTOMY W C.D.E. W CC
196	7	SURG	CHOLECYSTECTOMY W C.D.E. W/O CC
197	7	SURG	CHOLECYSTECTOMY EXCEPT BY LAPAROSCOPE W/O C.D.E. W CC
198	7	SURG	CHOLECYSTECTOMY EXCEPT BY LAPAROSCOPE W/O C.D.E. W/O CC
199	7	SURG	HEPATOBILIARY DIAGNOSTIC PROCEDURE FOR MALIGNANCY
200	7	SURG	HEPATOBILIARY DIAGNOSTIC PROCEDURE FOR NON-MALIGNANCY
201	7	SURG	OTHER HEPATOBILIARY OR PANCREAS O.R. PROCEDURES
202	7	MED	CIRRHOSIS & ALCOHOLIC HEPATITIS
203	7	MED	MALIGNANCY OF HEPATOBILIARY SYSTEM OR PANCREAS
204	7	MED	DISORDERS OF PANCREAS EXCEPT MALIGNANCY
205	7	MED	DISORDERS OF LIVER EXCEPT MALIG, CIRR, ALC HEPA W CC
206	7	MED	DISORDERS OF LIVER EXCEPT MALIG, CIRR, ALC HEPA W/O CC
207	7	MED	DISORDERS OF THE BILIARY TRACT W CC
208	7	MED	DISORDERS OF THE BILIARY TRACT W/O CC
209	8	SURG	MAJOR JOINT & LIMB REATTACHMENT PROCEDURES OF LOWER EXTREMITY
210	8	SURG	HIP & FEMUR PROCEDURES EXCEPT MAJOR JOINT AGE >17 W CC
211	8	SURG	HIP & FEMUR PROCEDURES EXCEPT MAJOR JOINT AGE >17 W/O CC
212	8	SURG	HIP & FEMUR PROCEDURES EXCEPT MAJOR JOINT AGE 0–17
213	8	SURG	AMPUTATION FOR MUSCULOSKELETAL SYSTEM & CONN TISSUE DISORDERS
214	8	SURG	NO LONGER VALID
215	8	SURG	NO LONGER VALID
216	8	SURG	BIOPSIES OF MUSCULOSKELETAL SYSTEM & CONNECTIVE TISSUE
217	8	SURG	WND DEBRID & SKN GRFT EXCEPT HAND, FOR MUSCSKELET & CONN TISS DIS
218	8	SURG	LOWER EXTREM & HUMER PROC EXCEPT HIP, FOOT, FEMUR AGE >17 W CC
219	8	SURG	LOWER EXTREM & HUMER PROC EXCEPT HIP, FOOT, FEMUR AGE >17 W/O CC
220	8	SURG	LOWER EXTREM & HUMER PROC EXCEPT HIP, FOOT, FEMUR AGE 0–17
221	8	SURG	NO LONGER VALID

222	8	SURG	NO LONGER VALID
223	8	SURG	MAJOR SHOULDER/ELBOW PROC, OR OTHER UPPER EXTREMITY PROC W CC
224	8	SURG	SHOULDER, ELBOW OR FOREARM PROC, EXC MAJOR JOINT PROC, W/O CC
225	8	SURG	FOOT PROCEDURES
226	8	SURG	SOFT TISSUE PROCEDURES W CC
227	8	SURG	SOFT TISSUE PROCEDURES W/O CC
228	8	SURG	MAJOR THUMB OR JOINT PROC,OR OTH HAND OR WRIST PROC W CC
229	8	SURG	HAND OR WRIST PROC, EXCEPT MAJOR JOINT PROC, W/O CC
230	8	SURG	LOCAL EXCISION & REMOVAL OF INT FIX DEVICES OF HIP & FEMUR
231	8	SURG	NO LONGER VALID
232	8	SURG	ARTHROSCOPY
233	8	SURG	OTHER MUSCULOSKELET SYS & CONN TISS O.R. PROC W CC
234	8	SURG	OTHER MUSCULOSKELET SYS & CONN TISS O.R. PROC W/O CC
235	8	MED	FRACTURES OF FEMUR
236	8	MED	FRACTURES OF HIP & PELVIS
237	8	MED	SPRAINS, STRAINS, & DISLOCATIONS OF HIP, PELVIS & THIGH
238	8	MED	OSTEOMYELITIS
239	8	MED	PATHOLOGICAL FRACTURES & MUSCULOSKELETAL & CONN TISS MALIGNANCY
240	8	MED	CONNECTIVE TISSUE DISORDERS W CC
241	8	MED	CONNECTIVE TISSUE DISORDERS W/O CC
242	8	MED	SEPTIC ARTHRITIS
243	8	MED	MEDICAL BACK PROBLEMS
244	8	MED	BONE DISEASES & SPECIFIC ARTHROPATHIES W CC
245	8	MED	BONE DISEASES & SPECIFIC ARTHROPATHIES W/O CC
246	8	MED	NON-SPECIFIC ARTHROPATHIES
247	8	MED	SIGNS & SYMPTOMS OF MUSCULOSKELETAL SYSTEM & CONN TISSUE
248	8	MED	TENDONITIS, MYOSITIS & BURSITIS
249	8	MED	AFTERCARE, MUSCULOSKELETAL SYSTEM & CONNECTIVE TISSUE
250	8	MED	FX, SPRN, STRN & DISL OF FOREARM, HAND, FOOT AGE >17 W CC
251	8	MED	FX, SPRN, STRN & DISL OF FOREARM, HAND, FOOT AGE >17 W/O CC
252	8	MED	FX, SPRN, STRN & DISL OF FOREARM, HAND, FOOT AGE 0–17
253	8	MED	FX, SPRN, STRN & DISL OF UPARM,LOWLEG EX FOOT AGE >17 W CC
254	8	MED	FX, SPRN, STRN & DISL OF UPARM,LOWLEG EX FOOT AGE >17 W/O CC
255	8	MED	FX, SPRN, STRN & DISL OF UPARM,LOWLEG EX FOOT AGE 0–17

256	8	MED	OTHER MUSCULOSKELETAL SYSTEM & CONNECTIVE TISSUE DIAGNOSES
257	9	SURG	TOTAL MASTECTOMY FOR MALIGNANCY W CC
258	9	SURG	TOTAL MASTECTOMY FOR MALIGNANCY W/O CC
259	9	SURG	SUBTOTAL MASTECTOMY FOR MALIGNANCY W CC
260	9	SURG	SUBTOTAL MASTECTOMY FOR MALIGNANCY W/O CC
261	9	SURG	BREAST PROC FOR NON-MALIGNANCY EXCEPT BIOPSY & LOCAL EXCISION
262	9	SURG	BREAST BIOPSY & LOCAL EXCISION FOR NON-MALIGNANCY
263	9	SURG	SKIN GRAFT &/OR DEBRID FOR SKN ULCER OR CELLULITIS W CC
264	9	SURG	SKIN GRAFT &/OR DEBRID FOR SKN ULCER OR CELLULITIS W/O CC
265	9	SURG	SKIN GRAFT &/OR DEBRID EXCEPT FOR SKIN ULCER OR CELLULITIS W CC
266	9	SURG	SKIN GRAFT &/OR DEBRID EXCEPT FOR SKIN ULCER OR CELLULITIS W/O CC
267	9	SURG	PERIANAL & PILONIDAL PROCEDURES
268	9	SURG	SKIN, SUBCUTANEOUS TISSUE & BREAST PLASTIC PROCEDURES
269	9	SURG	OTHER SKIN, SUBCUT TISS & BREAST PROC W CC
270	9	SURG	OTHER SKIN, SUBCUT TISS & BREAST PROC W/O CC
271	9	MED	SKIN ULCERS
272	9	MED	MAJOR SKIN DISORDERS W CC
273	9	MED	MAJOR SKIN DISORDERS W/O CC
274	9	MED	MALIGNANT BREAST DISORDERS W CC
275	9	MED	MALIGNANT BREAST DISORDERS W/O CC
276	9	MED	NON-MALIGANT BREAST DISORDERS
277	9	MED	CELLULITIS AGE >17 W CC
278	9	MED	CELLULITIS AGE >17 W/O CC
279	9	MED	CELLULITIS AGE 0–17
280	9	MED	TRAUMA TO THE SKIN, SUBCUT TISS & BREAST AGE >17 W CC
281	9	MED	TRAUMA TO THE SKIN, SUBCUT TISS & BREAST AGE >17 W/O CC
282	9	MED	TRAUMA TO THE SKIN, SUBCUT TISS & BREAST AGE 0–17
283	9	MED	MINOR SKIN DISORDERS W CC
284	9	MED	MINOR SKIN DISORDERS W/O CC
285	10	SURG	AMPUTAT OF LOWER LIMB FOR ENDOCRINE, NUTRIT, & METABOL DISORDERS
286	10	SURG	ADRENAL & PITUITARY PROCEDURES
287	10	SURG	SKIN GRAFTS & WOUND DEBRID FOR ENDOC, NUTRIT & METAB DISORDERS
288	10	SURG	O.R. PROCEDURES FOR OBESITY
289	10	SURG	PARATHYROID PROCEDURES
290	10	SURG	THYROID PROCEDURES
291	10	SURG	THYROGLOSSAL PROCEDURES
292	10	SURG	OTHER ENDOCRINE, NUTRIT & METAB O.R. PROC W CC
293	10	SURG	OTHER ENDOCRINE, NUTRIT & METAB O.R. PROC W/O CC

294	10	MED	DIABETES AGE >35
295	10	MED	DIABETES AGE 0–35
296	10	MED	NUTRITIONAL & MISC METABOLIC DISORDERS AGE >17 W CC
297	10	MED	NUTRITIONAL & MISC METABOLIC DISORDERS AGE >17 W/O CC
298	10	MED	NUTRITIONAL & MISC METABOLIC DISORDERS AGE 0–17
299	10	MED	INBORN ERRORS OF METABOLISM
300	10	MED	ENDOCRINE DISORDERS W CC
301	10	MED	ENDOCRINE DISORDERS W/O CC
302	11	SURG	KIDNEY TRANSPLANT
303	11	SURG	KIDNEY, URETER & MAJOR BLADDER PROCEDURES FOR NEOPLASM
304	11	SURG	KIDNEY, URETER & MAJOR BLADDER PROC FOR NON-NEOPL W CC
305	11	SURG	KIDNEY, URETER & MAJOR BLADDER PROC FOR NON-NEOPL W/O CC
306	11	SURG	PROSTATECTOMY W CC
307	11	SURG	PROSTATECTOMY W/O CC
308	11	SURG	MINOR BLADDER PROCEDURES W CC
309	11	SURG	MINOR BLADDER PROCEDURES W/O CC
310	11	SURG	TRANSURETHRAL PROCEDURES W CC
311	11	SURG	TRANSURETHRAL PROCEDURES W/O CC
312	11	SURG	URETHRAL PROCEDURES, AGE >17 W CC
313	11	SURG	URETHRAL PROCEDURES, AGE >17 W/O CC
314	11	SURG	URETHRAL PROCEDURES, AGE 0–17
315	11	SURG	OTHER KIDNEY & URINARY TRACT O.R. PROCEDURES
316	11	MED	RENAL FAILURE
317	11	MED	ADMIT FOR RENAL DIALYSIS
318	11	MED	KIDNEY & URINARY TRACT NEOPLASMS W CC
319	11	MED	KIDNEY & URINARY TRACT NEOPLASMS W/O CC
320	11	MED	KIDNEY & URINARY TRACT INFECTIONS AGE >17 W CC
321	11	MED	KIDNEY & URINARY TRACT INFECTIONS AGE >17 W/O CC
322	11	MED	KIDNEY & URINARY TRACT INFECTIONS AGE 0–17
323	11	MED	URINARY STONES W CC, &/OR ESW LITHOTRIPSY
324	11	MED	URINARY STONES W/O CC
325	11	MED	KIDNEY & URINARY TRACT SIGNS & SYMPTOMS AGE >17 W CC
326	11	MED	KIDNEY & URINARY TRACT SIGNS & SYMPTOMS AGE >17 W/O CC
327	11	MED	KIDNEY & URINARY TRACT SIGNS & SYMPTOMS AGE 0–17
328	11	MED	URETHRAL STRICTURE AGE >17 W CC
329	11	MED	URETHRAL STRICTURE AGE >17 W/O CC
330	11	MED	URETHRAL STRICTURE AGE 0–17
331	11	MED	OTHER KIDNEY & URINARY TRACT DIAGNOSES AGE >17 W CC
332	11	MED	OTHER KIDNEY & URINARY TRACT DIAGNOSES AGE >17 W/O CC

333	11	MED	OTHER KIDNEY & URINARY TRACT DIAGNOSES AGE 0–17
334	12	SURG	MAJOR MALE PELVIC PROCEDURES W CC
335	12	SURG	MAJOR MALE PELVIC PROCEDURES W/O CC
336	12	SURG	TRANSURETHRAL PROSTATECTOMY W CC
337	12	SURG	TRANSURETHRAL PROSTATECTOMY W/O CC
338	12	SURG	TESTES PROCEDURES, FOR MALIGNANCY
339	12	SURG	TESTES PROCEDURES, NON-MALIGNANCY AGE >17
340	12	SURG	TESTES PROCEDURES, NON-MALIGNANCY AGE 0–17
341	12	SURG	PENIS PROCEDURES
342	12	SURG	CIRCUMCISION AGE >17
343	12	SURG	CIRCUMCISION AGE 0–17
344	12	SURG	OTHER MALE REPRODUCTIVE SYSTEM O.R. PROCEDURES FOR MALIGNANCY
345	12	SURG	OTHER MALE REPRODUCTIVE SYSTEM O.R. PROC EXCEPT FOR MALIGNANCY
346	12	MED	MALIGNANCY, MALE REPRODUCTIVE SYSTEM, W CC
347	12	MED	MALIGNANCY, MALE REPRODUCTIVE SYSTEM, W/O CC
348	12	MED	BENIGN PROSTATIC HYPERTROPHY W CC
349	12	MED	BENIGN PROSTATIC HYPERTROPHY W/O CC
350	12	MED	INFLAMMATION OF THE MALE REPRODUCTIVE SYSTEM
351	12	MED	STERILIZATION, MALE
352	12	MED	OTHER MALE REPRODUCTIVE SYSTEM DIAGNOSES
353	13	SURG	PELVIC EVISCERATION, RADICAL HYSTERECTOMY & RADICAL VULVECTOMY
354	13	SURG	UTERINE,ADNEXA PROC FOR NON-OVARIAN/ADNEXAL MALIG W CC
355	13	SURG	UTERINE,ADNEXA PROC FOR NON-OVARIAN/ADNEXAL MALIG W/O CC
356	13	SURG	FEMALE REPRODUCTIVE SYSTEM RECONSTRUCTIVE PROCEDURES
357	13	SURG	UTERINE & ADNEXA PROC FOR OVARIAN OR ADNEXAL MALIGNANCY
358	13	SURG	UTERINE & ADNEXA PROC FOR NON-MALIGNANCY W CC
359	13	SURG	UTERINE & ADNEXA PROC FOR NON-MALIGNANCY W/O CC
360	13	SURG	VAGINA, CERVIX & VULVA PROCEDURES
361	13	SURG	LAPAROSCOPY & INCISIONAL TUBAL INTERRUPTION
362	13	SURG	ENDOSCOPIC TUBAL INTERRUPTION
363	13	SURG	D&C, CONIZATION & RADIO-IMPLANT, FOR MALIGNANCY
364	13	SURG	D&C, CONIZATION EXCEPT FOR MALIGNANCY
365	13	SURG	OTHER FEMALE REPRODUCTIVE SYSTEM O.R. PROCEDURES
366	13	MED	MALIGNANCY, FEMALE REPRODUCTIVE SYSTEM W CC
367	13	MED	MALIGNANCY, FEMALE REPRODUCTIVE SYSTEM W/O CC
368	13	MED	INFECTIONS, FEMALE REPRODUCTIVE SYSTEM
369	13	MED	MENSTRUAL & OTHER FEMALE REPRODUCTIVE SYSTEM DISORDERS

370	14	SURG	CESAREAN SECTION W CC
371	14	SURG	CESAREAN SECTION W/O CC
372	14	MED	VAGINAL DELIVERY W COMPLICATING DIAGNOSES
373	14	MED	VAGINAL DELIVERY W/O COMPLICATING DIAGNOSES
374	14	SURG	VAGINAL DELIVERY W STERILIZATION &/OR D&C
375	14	SURG	VAGINAL DELIVERY W O.R. PROC EXCEPT STERIL &/OR D&C
376	14	MED	POSTPARTUM & POST ABORTION DIAGNOSES W/O O.R. PROCEDURE
377	14	SURG	POSTPARTUM & POST ABORTION DIAGNOSES W O.R. PROCEDURE
378	14	MED	ECTOPIC PREGNANCY
379	14	MED	THREATENED ABORTION
380	14	MED	ABORTION W/O D&C
381	14	SURG	ABORTION W D&C, ASPIRATION CURETTAGE OR HYSTEROTOMY
382	14	MED	FALSE LABOR
383	14	MED	OTHER ANTEPARTUM DIAGNOSES W MEDICAL COMPLICATIONS
384	14	MED	OTHER ANTEPARTUM DIAGNOSES W/O MEDICAL COMPLICATIONS
385	15	MED	NEONATES, DIED OR TRANSFERRED TO ANOTHER ACUTE CARE FACILITY
386	15	MED	EXTREME IMMATURITY OR RESPIRATORY DISTRESS SYNDROME, NEONATE
387	15	MED	PREMATURITY W MAJOR PROBLEMS
388	15	MED	PREMATURITY W/O MAJOR PROBLEMS
389	15	MED	FULL TERM NEONATE W MAJOR PROBLEMS
390	15	MED	NEONATE W OTHER SIGNIFICANT PROBLEMS
391	15	MED	NORMAL NEWBORN
392	16	SURG	SPLENECTOMY AGE >17
393	16	SURG	SPLENECTOMY AGE 0–17
394	16	SURG	OTHER O.R. PROCEDURES OF THE BLOOD AND BLOOD FORMING ORGANS
395	16	MED	RED BLOOD CELL DISORDERS AGE >17
396	16	MED	RED BLOOD CELL DISORDERS AGE 0–17
397	16	MED	COAGULATION DISORDERS
398	16	MED	RETICULOENDOTHELIAL & IMMUNITY DISORDERS W CC
399	16	MED	RETICULOENDOTHELIAL & IMMUNITY DISORDERS W/O CC
400	17	SURG	NO LONGER VALID
401	17	SURG	LYMPHOMA & NON-ACUTE LEUKEMIA W OTHER O.R. PROC W CC
402	17	SURG	LYMPHOMA & NON-ACUTE LEUKEMIA W OTHER O.R. PROC W/O CC
403	17	MED	LYMPHOMA & NON-ACUTE LEUKEMIA W CC
404	17	MED	LYMPHOMA & NON-ACUTE LEUKEMIA W/O CC
405	17	MED	ACUTE LEUKEMIA W/O MAJOR O.R. PROCEDURE AGE 0–17

406	17	SURG	MYELOPROLIF DISORD OR POORLY DIFF NEOPL W MAJ O.R.PROC W CC
407	17	SURG	MYELOPROLIF DISORD OR POORLY DIFF NEOPL W MAJ O.R.PROC W/O CC
408	17	SURG	MYELOPROLIF DISORD OR POORLY DIFF NEOPL W OTHER O.R.PROC
409	17	MED	RADIOTHERAPY
410	17	MED	CHEMOTHERAPY W/O ACUTE LEUKEMIA AS SECONDARY DIAGNOSIS
411	17	MED	HISTORY OF MALIGNANCY W/O ENDOSCOPY
412	17	MED	HISTORY OF MALIGNANCY W ENDOSCOPY
413	17	MED	OTHER MYELOPROLIF DIS OR POORLY DIFF NEOPL DIAG W CC
414	17	MED	OTHER MYELOPROLIF DIS OR POORLY DIFF NEOPL DIAG W/O CC
415	18	SURG	O.R. PROCEDURE FOR INFECTIOUS & PARASITIC DISEASES
416	18	MED	SEPTICEMIA AGE >17
417	18	MED	SEPTICEMIA AGE 0–17
418	18	MED	POSTOPERATIVE & POST-TRAUMATIC INFECTIONS
419	18	MED	FEVER OF UNKNOWN ORIGIN AGE >17 W CC
420	18	MED	FEVER OF UNKNOWN ORIGIN AGE >17 W/O CC
421	18	MED	VIRAL ILLNESS AGE >17
422	18	MED	VIRAL ILLNESS & FEVER OF UNKNOWN ORIGIN AGE 0–17
423	18	MED	OTHER INFECTIOUS & PARASITIC DISEASES DIAGNOSES
424	19	SURG	O.R. PROCEDURE W PRINCIPAL DIAGNOSES OF MENTAL ILLNESS
425	19	MED	ACUTE ADJUSTMENT REACTION & PSYCHOSOCIAL DYSFUNCTION
426	19	MED	DEPRESSIVE NEUROSES
427	19	MED	NEUROSES EXCEPT DEPRESSIVE
428	19	MED	DISORDERS OF PERSONALITY & IMPULSE CONTROL
429	19	MED	ORGANIC DISTURBANCES & MENTAL RETARDATION
430	19	MED	PSYCHOSES
431	19	MED	CHILDHOOD MENTAL DISORDERS
432	19	MED	OTHER MENTAL DISORDER DIAGNOSES
433	20	MED	ALCOHOL/DRUG ABUSE OR DEPENDENCE, LEFT AMA
434	20	MED	NO LONGER VALID
435	20	MED	NO LONGER VALID
436	20	MED	NO LONGER VALID
437	20	MED	NO LONGER VALID
438	20		NO LONGER VALID
439	21	SURG	SKIN GRAFTS FOR INJURIES
440	21	SURG	WOUND DEBRIDEMENTS FOR INJURIES
441	21	SURG	HAND PROCEDURES FOR INJURIES
442	21	SURG	OTHER O.R. PROCEDURES FOR INJURIES W CC
443	21	SURG	OTHER O.R. PROCEDURES FOR INJURIES W/O CC
444	21	MED	TRAUMATIC INJURY AGE >17 W CC
445	21	MED	TRAUMATIC INJURY AGE >17 W/O CC

446	21	MED	TRAUMATIC INJURY AGE 0–17
447	21	MED	ALLERGIC REACTIONS AGE >17
448	21	MED	ALLERGIC REACTIONS AGE 0–17
449	21	MED	POISONING & TOXIC EFFECTS OF DRUGS AGE >17 W CC
450	21	MED	POISONING & TOXIC EFFECTS OF DRUGS AGE >17 W/O CC
451	21	MED	POISONING & TOXIC EFFECTS OF DRUGS AGE 0–17
452	21	MED	COMPLICATIONS OF TREATMENT W CC
453	21	MED	COMPLICATIONS OF TREATMENT W/O CC
454	21	MED	OTHER INJURY, POISONING & TOXIC EFFECT DIAG W CC
455	21	MED	OTHER INJURY, POISONING & TOXIC EFFECT DIAG W/O CC
456	22		NO LONGER VALID
457	22	MED	NO LONGER VALID
458	22	SURG	NO LONGER VALID
459	22	SURG	NO LONGER VALID
460	22	MED	NO LONGER VALID
461	23	SURG	O.R. PROC W DIAGNOSES OF OTHER CONTACT W HEALTH SERVICES
462	23	MED	REHABILITATION
463	23	MED	SIGNS & SYMPTOMS W CC
464	23	MED	SIGNS & SYMPTOMS W/O CC
465	23	MED	AFTERCARE W HISTORY OF MALIGNANCY AS SECONDARY DIAGNOSIS
466	23	MED	AFTERCARE W/O HISTORY OF MALIGNANCY AS SECONDARY DIAGNOSIS
467	23	MED	OTHER FACTORS INFLUENCING HEALTH STATUS
468			EXTENSIVE O.R. PROCEDURE UNRELATED TO PRINCIPAL DIAGNOSIS
469		**	PRINCIPAL DIAGNOSIS INVALID AS DISCHARGE DIAGNOSIS
470		**	UNGROUPABLE
471	8	SURG	BILATERAL OR MULTIPLE MAJOR JOINT PROCS OF LOWER EXTREMITY
472	22	SURG	NO LONGER VALID
473	17	MED	ACUTE LEUKEMIA W/O MAJOR O.R. PROCEDURE AGE >17
474	4	SURG	NO LONGER VALID
475	4	MED	RESPIRATORY SYSTEM DIAGNOSIS WITH VENTILATOR SUPPORT
476		SURG	PROSTATIC O.R. PROCEDURE UNRELATED TO PRINCIPAL DIAGNOSIS
477		SURG	NON-EXTENSIVE O.R. PROCEDURE UNRELATED TO PRINCIPAL DIAGNOSIS
478	5	SURG	OTHER VASCULAR PROCEDURES W CC
479	5	SURG	OTHER VASCULAR PROCEDURES W/O CC
480	PRE	SURG	LIVER TRANSPLANT
481	PRE	SURG	BONE MARROW TRANSPLANT
482	PRE	SURG	TRACHEOSTOMY FOR FACE, MOUTH & NECK DIAGNOSES

483	PRE	SURG	TRAC W MECH VENT 96+ HRS OR PDX EXCEPT FACE, MOUTH & NECK DX OSES
484	24	SURG	CRANIOTOMY FOR MULTIPLE SIGNIFICANT TRAUMA
485	24	SURG	LIMB REATTACHMENT, HIP AND FEMUR PROC FOR MULTIPLE SIGNIFICANT TRA
486	24	SURG	OTHER O.R. PROCEDURES FOR MULTIPLE SIGNIFICANT TRAUMA
487	24	MED	OTHER MULTIPLE SIGNIFICANT TRAUMA
488	25	SURG	HIV W EXTENSIVE O.R. PROCEDURE
489	25	MED	HIV W MAJOR RELATED CONDITION
490	25	MED	HIV W OR W/O OTHER RELATED CONDITION
491	8	SURG	MAJOR JOINT & LIMB REATTACHMENT PROCEDURES OF UPPER EXTREMITY
492	17	MED	CHEMOTHERAPY W ACUTE LEUKEMIA OR W USE OF HI DOSE CHEMOAGENT
493	7	SURG	LAPAROSCOPIC CHOLECYSTECTOMY W/O C.D.E. W CC
494	7	SURG	LAPAROSCOPIC CHOLECYSTECTOMY W/O C.D.E. W/O CC
495	PRE	SURG	LUNG TRANSPLANT
496	8	SURG	COMBINED ANTERIOR/POSTERIOR SPINAL FUSION
497	8	SURG	SPINAL FUSION EXCEPT CERVICAL W CC
498	8	SURG	SPINAL FUSION EXCEPT CERVICAL W/O CC
499	8	SURG	BACK & NECK PROCEDURES EXCEPT SPINAL FUSION W CC
500	8	SURG	BACK & NECK PROCEDURES EXCEPT SPINAL FUSION W/O CC
501	8	SURG	KNEE PROCEDURES W PDX OF INFECTION W CC
502	8	SURG	KNEE PROCEDURES W PDX OF INFECTION W/O CC
503	8	SURG	KNEE PROCEDURES W/O PDX OF INFECTION
504	22	SURG	EXTENSIVE 3RD DEGREE BURNS W SKIN GRAFT
505	22	MED	EXTENSIVE 3RD DEGREE BURNS W/O SKIN GRAFT
506	22	SURG	FULL THICKNESS BURN W SKIN GRAFT OR INHAL INJ W CC OR SIG TRAUMA
507	22	SURG	FULL THICKNESS BURN W SKIN GRFT OR INHAL INJ W/O CC OR SIG TRAUMA
508	22	MED	FULL THICKNESS BURN W/O SKIN GRFT OR INHAL INJ W CC OR SIG TRAUMA
509	22	MED	FULL THICKNESS BURN W/O SKIN GRFT OR INH INJ W/O CC OR SIG TRAUMA
510	22	MED	NON-EXTENSIVE BURNS W CC OR SIGNIFICANT TRAUMA
511	22	MED	NON-EXTENSIVE BURNS W/O CC OR SIGNIFICANT TRAUMA
512	PRE	SURG	SIMULTANEOUS PANCREAS/KIDNEY TRANSPLANT
513	PRE	SURG	PANCREAS TRANSPLANT
514	5	SURG	NO LONGER VALID
515	5	SURG	CARDIAC DEFIBRILLATOR IMPLANT W/O CARDIAC CATH
516	5	SURG	PERCUTANEOUS CARDIOVASC PROC W AMI
517	5	SURG	PERC CARDIO PROC W NON-DRUG ELUTING STENT W/O AMI

518	5	SURG	PERC CARDIO PROC W/O CORONARY ARTERY STENT OR AMI
519	8	SURG	CERVICAL SPINAL FUSION W CC
520	8	SURG	CERVICAL SPINAL FUSION W/O CC
521	20	MED	ALCOHOL/DRUG ABUSE OR DEPENDENCE W CC
522	20	MED	ALC/DRUG ABUSE OR DEPEND W REHABILITATION THERAPY W/O CC
523	20	MED	ALC/DRUG ABUSE OR DEPEND W/O REHABILITATION THERAPY W/O CC
524	1	MED	TRANSIENT ISCHEMIA
525	5	SURG	HEART ASSIST SYSTEM IMPLANT
526	5	SURG	PERCUTNEOUS CARDIOVASULAR PROC W DRUG ELUTING STENT W AMI
527	5	SURG	PERCUTNEOUS CARDIOVASULAR PROC W DRUG ELUTING STENT W/O AMI
528	1	SURG	INTRACRANIAL VASCULAR PROC W PDX HEMORRHAGE
529	1	SURG	VENTRICULAR SHUNT PROCEDURES W CC
530	1	SURG	VENTRICULAR SHUNT PROCEDURES W/O CC
531	1	SURG	SPINAL PROCEDURES W CC
532	1	SURG	SPINAL PROCEDURES W/O CC
533	1	SURG	EXTRACRANIAL PROCEDURES W CC
534	1	SURG	EXTRACRANIAL PROCEDURES W/O CC
535	5	SURG	CARDIAC DEFIB IMPLANT W CARDIAC CATH W AMI/HF/SHOCK
536	5	SURG	CARDIAC DEFIB IMPLANT W CARDIAC CATH W/O AMI/HF/SHOCK
537	8	SURG	LOCAL EXCIS & REMOV OF INT FIX DEV EXCEPT HIP & FEMUR W CC
538	8	SURG	LOCAL EXCIS & REMOV OF INT FIX DEV EXCEPT HIP & FEMUR W/O CC
539	17	SURG	LYMPHOMA & LEUKEMIA W MAJOR OR PROCEDURE W CC
540	17	SURG	LYMPHOMA & LEUKEMIA W MAJOR OR PROCEDURE W/O CC

Appendix P:

Standard, Droplet, and Airborne Precautions

The Centers Disease Control (www.cdc.gov) issues precautions to prevent the transmission of infection. Below are listed the standard, droplet, and airborne precautions. In addition, there are special precautions on the CDC website for transmission of diseases, such as tuberculosis.

Standard Precautions

Use Standard Precautions, or the equivalent, for the care of all patients.
- **a.** Handwashing
- **b.** Gloves
- **c.** Mask, Eye Protection, Face Shield
- **d.** Gown
- **e.** Patient Care Equipment
- **f.** Environmental Control
- **g.** Linen
- **h.** Occupational Health and Bloodborne Pathogens
- **i.** Patient Placement

A. Handwashing

1. Wash hands after touching blood, body fluids, secretions, excretions, and contaminated items, whether or not gloves are worn. Wash hands immediately after gloves are removed, between patient contacts, and when otherwise indicated to avoid transfer of microorganisms to other patients or environments. It may be necessary to wash hands between tasks and procedures on the same patient to prevent cross-contamination of different body sites.

2. Use a plain (nonantimicrobial) soap for routine handwashing. *Category IB*

3. Use an antimicrobial agent or a waterless antiseptic agent for specific circumstances (e.g., control of outbreaks or hyperendemic infections), as defined by the infection control program. (See Contact Precautions for additional recommendations on using antimicrobial and antiseptic agents.)

B. Gloves

Wear gloves (clean, nonsterile gloves are adequate) when touching blood, body fluids, secretions, excretions, and contaminated items. Put on clean gloves just before touching mucous membranes and nonintact skin. Change gloves between tasks and procedures on the same patient after contact with material that may contain a high concentration of microorganisms. Remove gloves promptly after use, before touching noncontaminated items and environmental surfaces, and before going to another patient, and wash hands immediately to avoid transfer of microorganisms to other patients or environments.

C. Mask, Eye Protection, Face Shield

Wear a mask and eye protection or a face shield to protect mucous membranes of the eyes, nose, and mouth during procedures and patient-care activities that are likely to generate splashes or sprays of blood, body fluids, secretions, and excretions.

D. Gown

Wear a gown (a clean, nonsterile gown is adequate) to protect skin and to prevent soiling of clothing during procedures and patient-care activities that are likely to generate splashes or sprays of blood, body fluids, secretions, or excretions. Select a gown that is appropriate for

Appendices

the activity and amount of fluid likely to be encountered. Remove a soiled gown as promptly as possible, and wash hands to avoid transfer of microorganisms to other patients or environments.

E. Patient-Care Equipment

Handle used patient-care equipment soiled with blood, body fluids, secretions, and excretions in a manner that prevents skin and mucous membrane exposures, contamination of clothing, and transfer of microorganisms to other patients and environments. Ensure that reusable equipment is not used for the care of another patient until it has been cleaned and reprocessed appropriately. Ensure that single-use items are discarded properly.

F. Environmental Control

Ensure that the hospital has adequate procedures for the routine care, cleaning, and disinfection of environmental surfaces, beds, bedrails, bedside equipment, and other frequently touched surfaces, and ensure that these procedures are being followed.

G. Linen

Handle, transport, and process used linen soiled with blood, body fluids, secretions, and excretions in a manner that prevents skin and mucous membrane exposures and contamination of clothing, and that avoids transfer of microorganisms to other patients and environments.

H. Occupational Health and Bloodborne Pathogens

1. Take care to prevent injuries when using needles, scalpels, and other sharp instruments or devices; when handling sharp instruments after procedures; when cleaning used instruments; and when disposing of used needles. Never recap used needles, or otherwise manipulate them using both hands, or use any other technique that involves directing the point of a needle toward any part of the body; rather, use either a one-handed "scoop" technique or a mechanical device designed for holding the needle sheath. Do not remove used needles from disposable syringes by hand, and do not bend, break, or otherwise manipulate used needles by hand. Place used disposable syringes and needles, scalpel blades, and other sharp items in appropriate puncture-resistant containers, which are located as close as practical to the area in which the items were used, and place reusable syringes and needles in a puncture-resistant container for transport to the reprocessing area.

2. Use mouthpieces, resuscitation bags, or other ventilation devices as an alternative to mouth-to-mouth resuscitation methods in areas where the need for resuscitation is predictable.

I. Patient Placement

Place a patient who contaminates the environment or who does not (or cannot be expected to) assist in maintaining appropriate hygiene or environmental control in a private room. If a private room is not available, consult with infection control professionals regarding patient placement or other alternatives.

Droplet Precautions

In addition to Standard Precautions, use Droplet Precautions, or the equivalent, for a patient known or suspected to be infected with microorganisms transmitted by droplets (large-particle droplets [larger than 5 μm in size] that can be generated by the patient during coughing, sneezing, talking, or the performance of procedures).

A. Patient Placement

Place the patient in a private room. When a private room is not available, place the patient in a room with a patient(s) who has active infection with the same microorganism but with no other infection (cohorting). When a private room is not available and cohorting is not achievable, maintain spatial separation of at least 3 ft between the infected patient and other patients and visitors. Special air handling and ventilation are not necessary, and the door may remain open.

B. Mask

In addition to wearing a mask as outlined under Standard Precautions, wear a mask when working within 3 ft of the patient. (Logistically, some hospitals may want to implement the wearing of a mask to enter the room.)

C. Patient Transport

Limit the movement and transport of the patient from the room to essential purposes only. If transport or movement is necessary, minimize patient dispersal of droplets by masking the patient, if possible.

Airborne Precautions

In addition to Standard Precautions, use Airborne Precautions, or the equivalent, for patients known or suspected to be infected with microorganisms transmitted by airborne droplet nuclei (small-particle residue [5 μm or smaller in size] of evaporated droplets containing microorganisms that remain suspended in the air and that can be dispersed widely by air currents within a room or over a long distance).

A. Patient Placement

Place the patient in a private room that has 1) monitored negative air pressure in relation to the surrounding areas, 2) 6 to 12 air changes per hour, and 3) appropriate discharge of air outdoors or monitored high-efficiency filtration of room air before the air is circulated to other areas in the hospital. Keep the room door closed and the patient in the room. When a private room is not available, place the patient in a room with a patient who has active infection with the same microorganism, unless otherwise recommended, but with no other infection. When a private room is not available and cohorting is not desirable, consultation with infection control professionals is advised before patient placement.

Respiratory Protection

Wear respiratory protection (N95 respirator) when entering the room of a patient with known or suspected infectious pulmonary tuberculosis. Susceptible persons should not enter the room of patients known or suspected to have measles (rubeola) or varicella (chickenpox) if other immune caregivers are available. If susceptible persons must enter the room of a patient known or suspected to have measles (rubeola) or varicella, they should wear respiratory protection (N95 respirator).(81) Persons immune to measles (rubeola) or varicella need not wear respiratory protection.

B. Patient Transport

Limit the movement and transport of the patient from the room to essential purposes only. If transport or movement is necessary, minimize patient dispersal of droplet nuclei by placing a surgical mask on the patient, if possible.

Appendix Q:

Complementary and Alternative Medicine (CAM)

The National Institutes of Health has established a department dealing with complementary and alternative medicine (NCCAM). The following information is from the NIH website (www.nih.gov) and gives an overview of complementary and alternative medicine practices that are currently being studied by NCCAM.

What is CAM?

- Complementary medicine is used **together with** conventional medicine. An example of a complementary therapy is using aromatherapy to help lessen a patient's discomfort following surgery.
- Alternative medicine is used **in place of** conventional medicine. An example of an alternative therapy is using a special diet to treat cancer instead of undergoing surgery, radiation, or chemotherapy that has been recommended by a conventional doctor.

Major types of complementary and alternative medicine?

NCCAM classifies CAM therapies into five categories, or domains:

1. Alternative Medical Systems

Alternative medical systems are built upon complete systems of theory and practice. Often, these systems have evolved apart from and earlier than the conventional medical approach used in the United States. Examples of alternative medical systems that have developed in Western cultures include homeopathic medicine and naturopathic medicine. Examples of systems that have developed in non-Western cultures include traditional Chinese medicine and Ayurveda. Some of the alternative systems are discussed in detail below.

Traditional Chinese Medicine

TCM is a complete system of healing that dates back to 200 B.C. in written form. Korea, Japan, and Vietnam have all developed their own unique versions of traditional medicine based on practices originating in China. In the TCM view, the body is a delicate balance of two opposing and inseparable forces: yin and yang. Yin represents the cold, slow, or passive principle, while yang represents the hot, excited, or active principle. Among the major assumptions in TCM are that health is achieved by maintaining the body in a "balanced state" and that disease is due to an internal imbalance of yin and yang. This imbalance leads to blockage in the flow of qi (or vital energy) and of blood along pathways known as meridians. TCM practitioners typically use herbs, acupuncture, and massage to help unblock qi and blood in patients in an attempt to bring the body back into harmony and wellness.

Treatments in TCM are typically tailored to the subtle patterns of disharmony in each patient and are based on an individualized diagnosis. The diagnostic tools differ from those of conventional medicine. There are three main therapeutic modalities:

1. Acupuncture and moxibustion (moxibustion is the application of heat from the burning of the herb moxa at the acupuncture point)
2. Chinese Materia Medica (the catalogue of natural products used in TCM)
3. Massage and manipulation

Although TCM proposes that natural products catalogued in Chinese Materia Medica or acupuncture can be used alone to treat virtually any illness, quite often they are used together and sometimes in combination with other modalities (e.g., massage, moxibustion, diet changes, or exercise).

Appendices

Ayurvedic Medicine

Ayurveda, which literally means "the science of life," is a natural healing system developed in India. Ayurvedic texts claim that the sages who developed India's original systems of meditation and yoga developed the foundations of this medical system. It is a comprehensive system of medicine that places equal emphasis on the body, mind, and spirit, and strives to restore the innate harmony of the individual. Some of the primary Ayurvedic treatments include diet, exercise, meditation, herbs, massage, exposure to sunlight, and controlled breathing. In India, Ayurvedic treatments have been developed for various diseases (e.g., diabetes, cardiovascular conditions, and neurological disorders). However, a survey of the Indian medical literature indicates that the quality of the published clinical trials generally falls short of contemporary methodological standards with regard to criteria for randomization, sample size, and adequate controls.

Naturopathy

Naturopathy is a system of healing, originating from Europe, that views disease as a manifestation of alterations in the processes by which the body naturally heals itself. It emphasizes health restoration as well as disease treatment. The term "naturopathy" literally translates as "nature disease." Today naturopathy, or naturopathic medicine, is practiced throughout Europe, Australia, New Zealand, Canada, and the United States. There are six principles that form the basis of naturopathic practice in North America (not all are unique to naturopathy):

1. The healing power of nature
2. Identification and treatment of the cause of disease
3. The concept of "first do no harm"
4. The doctor as teacher
5. Treatment of the whole person
6. Prevention

The core modalities supporting these principles include diet modification and nutritional supplements, herbal medicine, acupuncture and Chinese medicine, hydrotherapy, massage and joint manipulation, and lifestyle counseling. Treatment protocols combine what the practitioner deems to be the most suitable therapies for the individual patient.

Homeopathy

Homeopathy is a complete system of medical theory and practice. Its founder, German physician Samuel Christian Hahnemann (1755-1843), hypothesized that one can select therapies on the basis of how closely symptoms produced by a remedy match the symptoms of the patient's disease. He called this the "principle of similars." Hahnemann proceeded to give repeated doses of many common remedies to healthy volunteers and carefully record the symptoms they produced. This procedure is called a "proving" or, in modern homeopathy, a "human pathogenic trial." As a result of this experience, Hahnemann developed his treatments for sick patients by matching the symptoms produced by a drug to symptoms in sick patients. Hahnemann emphasized from the beginning that carefully examining all aspects of a person's health status, including emotional and mental states, and tiny idiosyncratic characteristics, was essential.

2.   Mind-Body Interventions

Mind-body medicine uses a variety of techniques designed to enhance the mind's capacity to affect bodily function and symptoms. Some techniques that were considered CAM in the past have become mainstream (for example, patient support groups and cognitive-behavioral therapy). Other mind-body techniques are still considered CAM, including meditation, prayer, mental healing, and therapies that use creative outlets such as art, music, or dance.

3.   Biologically Based Therapies

Biologically based therapies in CAM use substances found in nature, such as herbs, foods, and vitamins. Some examples include dietary supplements, herbal products, and the use of other so-called natural but as yet scientifically unproven therapies (for example, using shark cartilage to treat cancer).

NCCAM lists herbs and supplements and their uses on their website. Many of these herbs have been used for centuries but have not necessarily been scientifically tested. It is important to note that herbs can be powerful supplements and can have allergic and drug interactions that may be serious. On the other hand, many people have found herbal remedies very useful. The following table lists some of the herbs currently recognized by NCCAM and, in many cases, under study for effectiveness. This table does not include vitamin supplements which have current established guidelines for daily intake.

Herb	Where Found	Potential Uses
alfalfa	legume crop widely grown	lowering of blood cholesterol and glucose
aloe vera	gel found in leaves of aloe vera plants	topical use in dermatology for wounds, skin infections, burns, etc.
astragalus	Chinese herb	used to treat many major illnesses in Traditional Chinese Medicine, such as cancer, heart disease, infections, and so on
barley	widely grown grain crop	lowering cholesterol, high fiber
belladonna	widely available	long used for pain and inflammation, such as headache, menstrual symptoms, etc.
beta-carotene	found in colorful fruits, grains, and vegetables	important antioxidant, essential to sight, bone development, and other bodily functions
bilberry	a berry closely related to blueberry	used to treat various inflammations
black cohosh	herb	treatment of hormonal difficulties, such as menopausal symptoms
black tea	shrubs grown in China and other parts of Asia	antioxidant, contains caffeine, a stimulant, acts as a diuretic
bromelain	extracted from the stem of pineapple plants	used to enhance digestion and as an anti-inflammatory
burdock	plant with fruits	used for various ailments, such as arthritis; fruit is sometimes used in treating diabetes.
calendula (marigold)	plant	wound-healing
chamomile	plant	widely used for sleep disorders, digestion, and many other conditions
clove	cultivated in Africa, Asia, and South America	topical antiseptic; anesthetic, and other uses
cranberry	berry grown mainly in North America	prevention of urinary tract infections; may be useful in treating other infections

continued

continued

Herb	Where Found	Potential Uses
dandelion	plant found wild in pastures and cultivated in certain areas	widely used for a variety of ailments; respiratory diseases; liver ailments; hepatitis; digestive disorders; and others
devil's claw	southern African plant	used to treat fever and malaria plus other conditions
dong quai	plant found widely in Asia	used to treat the female reproductive system in Traditional Chinese Medicine
echinacea	flowering plant	widely believed to have immune-enhancing properties
elder	tree	flowers, berries, and leaves are used in analgesics, as a diuretic, a laxative, and an emetic; also, an antioxidant
eucalyptus oil	plant	used as an anti-inflammatory agent, particularly in upper respiratory infections
evening primrose oil	oil extracted from herb	believed to improve diseases affected by essential fatty acids
feverfew	herb	anti-pyretic
flaxseed/flaxseed oil	widely grown plant	essential fatty acid; thought to be helpful in coronary artery disease
garlic	widely cultivated bulb	used to lower blood pressure, aid in gastric problems, and thought to have some anti-cancer properties
ginger	underground stems of plant	used widely in Asian medicine as a digestive agent; antitussive, and other uses
gingko	leaves of a tree	used for centuries in Asian medicine for a various of mental conditions, reduction of fatigue, and many other uses
ginseng	plant	used widely in Asian medicine and now worldwide for many conditions, including mental conditions, heart disease, immune disorders, and so on

goldenseal	herb	used for upper respiratory ailments, eardrops, and as part of laxatives, cleansers, and so on
green tea	leaves of the tea plant	antioxidant, stimulant
gymnema	herb	lowers blood glucose
hops	crop plant	relaxation and sedative effects
horse chestnut	seed extract from tree	used in chronic venous insufficiency
horsetail	herb	used to treat edema
kava	roots of a shrub	used to treat anxiety
lavender	herb	relaxation effects
licorice	roots of a shrub	used for upper respiratory ailments
milk thistle	plant	treatment of liver and gallbladder disorders
passion flower	flowering plant	used as a sedative and in digestive disorders
peppermint	flowering plant	widely used for upper respiratory, indigestion, joint pain, nausea, and many other uses
propolis	natural resin created by bees	used as an antiviral; used to reduce dental caries and as an anti-infective agent
psyllium	cultivated crop	high fiber plant used as a laxative
pygeum	bark of an African evergreen	used in bladder and urinary disorders
red clover	legume	used to treat menopausal symptoms and for asthma and pertussis
red yeast rice	product of yeast grown on rice	cholesterol-lowering agent
saw palmetto	plant	used to treat prostate conditions
seaweed; kelp	grown in coastal waters	widely used as a food and medicine for tumors, ulcers, headaches, digestive disorders, and many others
soy	cultivated food crop	used in some estrogen disorders
St. John's wort	flowering plant	antidepressant
tea tree oil	distilled from the leaves of a plant	used as a topical antifungal
turmeric	root of a plant	anti-inflammatory; antioxidant; digestive disorders, and other uses

continued

continued

Herb	Where Found	Potential Uses
valerian	herb	widely used for heart disease, UTIs, insomnia, angina, and other uses
white horehound	herb	expectorant
wild yam	plant	used to treat menopausal symptoms
yohimbe	bark of a tree	male impotence

4. *Manipulative and Body-Based Methods*

Manipulative and body-based methods in CAM are based on manipulation and/or movement of one or more parts of the body. Some examples include chiropractic or osteopathic manipulation, and massage. The following is a list of some specific manipulative and body-based methods.

- **Alexander technique:** Patient education/guidance in ways to improve posture and movement, and to use muscles efficiently.
- **Bowen technique:** Gentle massage of muscles and tendons over acupuncture and reflex points.
- **Chiropractic manipulation:** Adjustments of the joints of the spine, as well as other joints and muscles.
- **Craniosacral therapy:** Form of massage using gentle pressure on the plates of the patient's skull.
- **Feldenkrais method:** Group classes and hands-on lessons designed to improve the coordination of the whole person in comfortable, effective, and intelligent movement.
- **Massage therapy:** Assortment of techniques involving manipulation of the soft tissues of the body through pressure and movement.
- **Osteopathic manipulation:** Manipulation of the joints combined with physical therapy and instruction in proper posture.
- **Reflexology:** Method of foot (and sometimes hand) massage in which pressure is applied to "reflex" zones mapped out on the feet (or hands).
- **Rolfing:** Deep tissue massage (also called structural integration).
- **Trager bodywork:** Slight rocking and shaking of the patient's trunk and limbs in a rhythmic fashion.
- **Tui Na:** Application of pressure with the fingers and thumb, and manipulation of specific points on the body (acupoints).

5. *Energy Therapies*

Energy therapies involve the use of energy fields. They are of two types:

- **Biofield therapies** are intended to affect energy fields that purportedly surround and penetrate the human body. The existence of such fields has not yet been scientifically proven. Some forms of energy therapy manipulate biofields by applying pressure and/or manipulating the body by placing the hands in, or through, these fields. Examples include qi gong, Reiki, and Therapeutic Touch.
- **Bioelectromagnetic-based therapies** involve the unconventional use of electromagnetic fields, such as pulsed fields, magnetic fields, or alternating-current or direct-current fields.

Appendix R:
American Sign Language

From Wikipedia.com

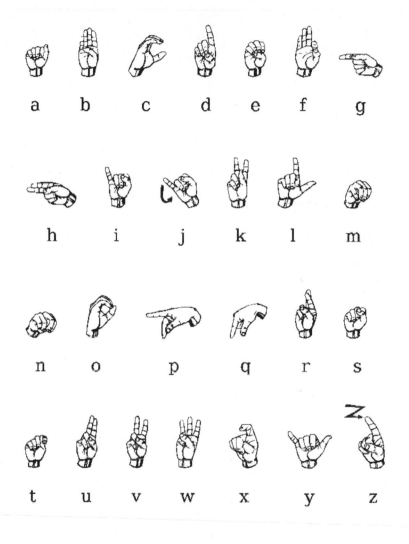

a　b　c　d　e　f　g

h　i　j　k　l　m

n　o　p　q　r　s

t　u　v　w　x　y　z

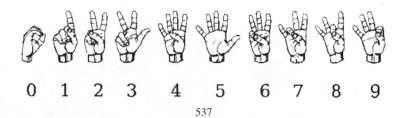

0　1　2　3　4　5　6　7　8　9

Appendix S:

HIPAA Overview

HIPAA (the Health Insurance Portability and Accountability Act of 1996) became Public Law 104-191 in 1996. A major provision of HIPAA, known as Administrative Simplification, affects medical practices as well as hospitals, health plans, and healthcare clearinghouses. Its rules have gradually been passed and then implemented in the healthcare industry.

Implementing HIPAA has changed administrative, financial, and case management policies and procedures. There are now strict requirements for the uniform transfer of electronic healthcare data such as for billing and payment; new patient rights regarding personal health information, including the right to access this information and to limit its disclosure; and broad new security rules that healthcare organizations must put in place to safeguard the confidentiality of patients' medical information.

There are four parts to HIPAA's Administrative Simplification provisions:

1. **HIPAA Electronic Transaction and Code Sets Standards requirements** National standards for electronic formats and data content are the foundation of this requirement. HIPAA requires every provider who does business electronically to use the same healthcare transactions, code sets, and identifiers.
2. **HIPAA Privacy requirements** The privacy requirements limit the release of patient protected health information without the patient's knowledge and consent beyond that required for patient care.
3. **HIPAA Security requirements** The security regulations outline the minimum administrative, technical, and physical safeguards required to prevent unauthorized access to protected healthcare information. The security standards help safeguard confidential health information during the electronic interchange of healthcare transactions.
4. **HIPAA National Identifier requirements** HIPAA will require healthcare providers, health plans, and employers to have standard national numbers that identify them on the standard transactions. Two of these standards are now law, and the others will be enacted in the future.

Who Must Comply?

Covered Entities

There are three categories of what is termed "covered entities"—health providers, health plans, and healthcare clearing houses—that must comply with HIPAA.

- Healthcare Providers. "Healthcare provider" includes any person or organization who furnishes, bills, or is paid for healthcare in the normal course of business. Providers include, among many others, physicians, hospitals, pharmacies, nursing homes, durable medical equipment suppliers, dentists, optometrists, and chiropractors. A healthcare provider is a covered entity under the HIPAA Privacy Rule only if it conducts any HIPAA standard transactions electronically or if another person or entity conducts the HIPAA standard transactions electronically on its behalf (such as a billing service company and a hospital billing department).

Appendices

- Health Plans. A health plan is an individual or group plan that provides or pays for the cost of medical care. Health plans include employee welfare benefit plans as defined under the Employee Retirement Income Security Act of 1974 (ERISA), including insured and self-insured plans, except plans with fewer than 50 participants that are self-administered by the employer.

- Healthcare Clearinghouses. Healthcare clearinghouses are companies that "translate" or "facilitate" translation of electronic transactions between the "standard" formats and code sets required under HIP AA and nonstandard formats and code sets.

Almost all physician practices are included under the HIPAA standards. A practice is *not* a covered entity only if it does not send any claims (or any other HIPAA transaction) electronically *and* does not employ someone else, such as a billing agency or clearinghouse, to send electronic claims or other electronic transactions to payers or health plans on its behalf. Since the Centers for Medicare and Medicaid Services (CMS) refuse to pay any Medicare claims that are not filed electronically from all but the smallest groups, noncompliance is not practical for physician practices.

Business Associates

HIPAA also indirectly affects many others in the healthcare field. For instance, software billing vendors and third- party billing services that are not clearinghouses are not required to comply with the law; however, they may need to make changes in order to be able to continue do business with someone who is a covered entity. Through business associate agreements, healthcare providers are responsible for making sure that the software they use or the third-party biller or clearinghouse they use to help process claims, is able to produce HIPAA-compliant transactions. Business associates must also provide the covered entity satisfactory assurances that it will appropriately guard information as required by HIPAA.

HIPAA Transaction and Code Set Standards

The HIPAA Transactions and Code Set Standards require standardization in healthcare e-commerce. These standards enable any provider to fill out a claim for a patient—regardless of the payer—and submit that claim electronically in the same format. Every payer must accept the standard format and standard codes and send electronic messages back to the provider, also in standard formats, advising the provider of claim status, remittance, and other key information necessary for payment to proceed.

Standard Transactions

The HIPAA transactions standards apply to exchanges for the most common provider-to-health plan messages between providers and payers, greatly expanding the amount of health information that is exchanged electronically as well as the types of patient information involved in electronic communications.

Technically described as X12, standards for eight electronic transactions have been adopted:

- Claims or encounters (equivalent to the paper CMS-1500, UB-92, and ADA Dental Claim forms)
- Claim status inquiry and response
- Eligibility inquiry and response
- Enrollment and disenrollment in a health plan

- Referral authorization inquiry and response
- Payment and remittance advice
- Health plan premium payments
- Coordination of Benefits (COB)

In the future, standards for First Report of Injury and claim attachments must be adopted, also due to HIPAA mandate.

Standard Code Sets

Under HIPAA, a code set is any group of codes used for encoding data elements, such as tables of terms, medical concepts, medical diagnosis codes, or medical procedure codes. Medical data code sets used in the healthcare industry include coding systems for diseases, impairments, other health related problems, and their manifestations; actions taken to diagnose, treat, or manage diseases, injuries, and impairments; and any substances, equipment, supplies, or other items used to perform these actions.

Code sets for medical data are required for data elements in the administrative and financial healthcare transaction standards adopted under HIPAA for diagnoses, procedures, and drugs. The HIPAA standard code sets are

- For diseases, injuries, impairments, and other health-related problems: International Classification of Diseases, 9th Edition, Clinical Modification (ICD-9-CM), Volumes 1 and 2
- For procedures or other actions taken to prevent, diagnose, treat, or manage diseases, injuries, and impairments:
  - ➤ Inpatient Hospital Services: International Classification of Diseases, 9th Edition, Clinical Modification, Volume 3: Procedures
  - ➤ Dental Services: Code on Dental Procedures and Nomenclature (CDT-4)
  - ➤ Physicians' Services: Current Procedural Terminology, 4th Edition (CPT)
- Other Hospital-related Services: Healthcare Common Procedures Coding System (HCPCS)

HIPAA Privacy Rule

The HIPAA Privacy Rule provides the first comprehensive federal protection for the privacy of health information. It is designed to provide strong privacy protections that do not interfere with patient access to, or the quality of, healthcare delivery. It creates for the first time creates national standards to protect individuals' medical records and other personal health information. The privacy rule is intended to

- Give patients more control over their health information.
- Set boundaries on the use and release of health records.
- Establish appropriate safeguards that healthcare providers and others must achieve to protect the privacy of health information.
- Hold violators accountable, with civil and criminal penalties that can be imposed if they violate patients' privacy rights.
- Strike a balance when public responsibility supports disclosure of some forms of data—for example, to protect public health.

Before the HIPAA Privacy Rule, the personal information that moves across hospitals, doctors' offices, insurers or third-party payers, and state lines, fell under a patchwork of

Appendices

federal and state laws. This information could be distributed—without either notice or authorization—for reasons that had nothing to do with a patient's medical treatment or healthcare reimbursement. For example, unless otherwise forbidden by state or local law, without the privacy rule patient information held by a health plan could, without the patient's permission, be passed on to a lender who could then deny the patient's application for a home mortgage or a credit card, or to an employer who could use it in personnel decisions. The privacy rule establishes a federal floor of safeguards to protect the confidentiality of medical information. State laws that provide stronger privacy protections will continue to apply over and above the federal privacy standards.

Protected Health Information (PHI)

The core of the HIPAA Privacy Rule is the protection, use, and disclosure of protected health information (PHI). Health information (HI) means any information, whether oral or recorded in any form or medium, that is created or received by a healthcare provider, health plan, public health authority, employer, life insurer, school or university, or healthcare clearinghouse; and which relates to the past, present, or future physical or mental health or condition of an individual; the provision of healthcare to an individual; or the past, present, or future payment for the provision of healthcare to an individual.

Protected health information (PHI) means individually identifiable health information that is transmitted or maintained by electronic (or other) media. The privacy rule protects all PHI held or transmitted by a covered entity, in any form or media, whether electronic, paper, or oral, including verbal communications among staff members, patients, and/or other providers. Under this definition, a report of the number of people treated by a physician who have diabetes is not PHI, but the names of the patients are protected. PHI includes many facts about people, such as names, addresses, birth dates, employers, telephone numbers, Social Security numbers, and health plan beneficiary numbers, any of which could be used to identify them.

Provider Responsibilities

The Privacy Rule recognizes that medical offices and payers must be able to exchange PHI in the normal course of business. The rule says that there are three everyday situations in which PHI can be released *without* the patient's permission: treatment, payment, and operations (TPO).

- *Treatment* means providing and coordinating the patient's medical care. Physicians and other medical staff members can discuss patients' cases in the office and with other physicians. Laboratory or X-ray technicians may call to clarify requests they cannot read because of the physician's handwriting. This information can be provided by the physician or another medical staff member.
- *Payment* refers to the exchange of information with health plans. Medical office staff members can take the required information from patients' records and prepare health care claims that are transmitted to health plans.
- *Operations* are the general business management functions needed to run the office.

For the average healthcare provider or health plan, the privacy rule requires activities such as:

1. Notifying patients about their privacy rights and how their information can be used.
2. Adopting and implementing privacy procedures for its practice, hospital, or plan.
3. Training employees so that they understand the privacy procedures.

4. Designating an individual to be responsible for seeing that the privacy procedures are adopted and followed.
5. Securing patient records containing individually identifiable health information so that they are not readily available to those who do not need them.

Medical office staff should be careful not to discuss patients' cases with anyone outside the office, including family and friends. Avoid talking about cases, too, in the practice's reception areas, where other patients might overhear comments. Close charts on desks when they are not being worked on. A computer screen displaying a patient's records should be positioned so that only the person working with the file can view it. Files should be closed when the computer is not in use.

A covered entity must disclose protected health information in only two situations: (a) to individuals (or their personal representatives) specifically when they request access to, or an accounting of disclosures of, their protected health information; and (b) to HHS when it is undertaking a compliance investigation or review or enforcement action.

The privacy rule must be followed by all covered entities—health plans, healthcare clearinghouses, and healthcare providers— even if they contract with others to perform some of their essential functions. These outside contractors are called business associates, defined as a person or organization that performs certain functions or activities for a covered entity that involve the use or disclosure of individually identifiable health information. When a covered entity uses a contractor or other non-workforce member to perform "*business associate*" services or activities, the rule requires that the covered entity include certain protections for the information in a business associate agreement. n the business associate contract, a covered entity must impose specified written safeguards on the individually identifiable health information used or disclosed by its business associates.

Notice of and Acknowledgment of Receipt of Notice of Privacy Practices

To comply with the Privacy Rule, medical offices, as well as other providers and health plans, must give each patient an explanation of privacy practices at the patient's first contact or encounter. To satisfy this requirement, medical offices give patients a copy of their Notice of Privacy Practices. The notice explains how patients' PHI may be used and describes their rights. The office must also ask patients to review this notice and sign an Acknowledgment of Receipt of Notice of Privacy Practices, showing that they have read and understand the document.

Minimum Necessary

When using or disclosing protected health information, a provider must make reasonable efforts to limit the use or disclosure to the minimum amount of PHI necessary to accomplish the intended purpose. Minimum necessary means taking reasonable safeguards to protect a person's health information from incidental disclosure. State laws may impose more stringent requirements regarding the protection of patient information.

These minimum necessary policies and procedures also reasonably must limit who within the entity has access to protected health information, and under what conditions, based on job responsibilities and the nature of the business. The minimum necessary standard does not apply to disclosures, including oral disclosures, among healthcare providers for treatment purposes. For example, a physician is not required to apply the minimum necessary standard when discussing a patient's medical chart information with a specialist at another hospital.

Appendices

Patient Rights

Under HIPAA, patients have an increased awareness of their health information privacy rights, including the following:

- The right to access, copy, and inspect their health information;
- The right to request an amendment to their healthcare information;
- The right to obtain an accounting of certain disclosures of their health information;
- The right to alternative means of receiving communications from providers;
- The right to complain about alleged violations of the regulations and the provider's own information policies.

For use or disclosure of PHI other than for treatment, payment, or operations (TPO), the patient must sign an authorization to release the information. For example, information about alcohol and drug abuse may not be released without a specific authorization from the patient. The authorization document must be in plain language and include the following:

- A description of the information to be used or disclosed.
- The name or other specific identification of the person(s) authorized to use or disclose the information.
- The name of the person(s) or group of people to whom the covered entity may make the disclosure.
- A description of the purpose of each requested use or disclosure.
- An expiration date.
- Signature of the individual (or authorized representative) and date.

Patients who observe privacy problems in their providers' offices can complain either to the medical office or to the Department of Health and Human Services (HHS). Complaints must be put in writing, on paper or electronically, and sent to the Office of Civil Rights (OCR), which is part of HHS, usually within 180 days. The office must cooperate with an HHS investigation and give HHS access to its facilities, books, records, and systems, including relevant protected health information.

Exceptions to the Privacy Rule

There are a number of exceptions to the privacy rule. All these types of disclosures must also be logged, and the release information must be available to the patient who requests it.

- ***Release Under Court Order***—If the patient's PHI is required as evidence by a court of law, the provider may release it without the patient's approval upon judicial order. In the case of a lawsuit, a court sometimes decides that a physician or medical practice staff member must provide testimony. The court issues a **subpoena,** an order of the court directing a party to appear and testify. If the court requires the witness to bring certain evidence, such as a patient's medical record, it issues a **subpoena *duces tecum,*** which directs the party to appear, to testify, and to bring specified documents or items.

- ***Workers' Compensation Cases***—State law may provide for release of records to employers in workers' compensation cases (see Chapter 12). The law may also authorize release to the state workers' compensation administration board and to the insurance company that handles these claims for the state.

- *Statutory Reports*—Some specific types of information are required by state law to be released to state health or social services departments. For example, physicians must make such statutory reports for patients' births and deaths and for cases of abuse. Because of the danger of harm to patients or others, communicable diseases such as tuberculosis, hepatitis, and rabies must usually be reported.

- *HIV and AIDS*—A special category of communicable disease control is applied to patients with diagnoses of human immunodeficiency virus (HIV) infection and acquired immunodeficiency syndrome (AIDS). Every state requires AIDS cases to be reported. Most states also require reporting of the HIV infection that causes the syndrome. However, state law varies concerning whether only the fact of a case is to be reported, or if the patient's name must also be reported. The medical office's guidelines will reflect the state laws and must be strictly observed, as all these regulations should be, to protect patients' privacy and to comply with the regulations.

- *Research Data*—PHI may be made available to researchers approved by the practice. For example, if a physician is conducting clinical research on a type of diabetes, the practice may share information from appropriate records for analysis. When the researcher issues reports or studies based on the information, specific patients' names may not be identified.

- *De-Identified Health Information*—There are no restrictions on the use or disclosure of "de-identified" health information that does not identify an individual.

HIPAA Security Rule

The regulations of the Security Rule work in concert with the final privacy standards and require that covered entities establish administrative, physical, and technical safeguards to protect the confidentiality, integrity and availability of health information covered by HIPAA. The security rule specifies how they must secure such protected health information (PHI) on computer networks, the Internet, disks and magnetic tape, and over extranets.

The security rule also mandates that

- A security official must be assigned the responsibility for the entity's security.
- All staff, including management, receive security awareness training.
- Organizations implement audit controls that record and examine workers who have logged into information systems that contain PHI.
- Organizations limit physical access to facilities that contain electronic PHI.
- Organizations must conduct risk analyses to determine information security risks and vulnerabilities.
- Organizations must establish policies and procedures that allow access to electronic PHI on a need-to-know basis.

HIPAA National Identifiers

The HIPAA aw requires identifiers for:

- Providers
- Employers
- Health plans
- Patients

CMS has only issued rules for two: the Employer and National Provider Identifiers.

Appendices

Employer Identifier

The HIPAA Employer identifier standard was needed because employers are frequently sponsors of health insurance for their employees. The identifier is used to identify the patient's employer on claims to the plan. In addition, employers must identify themselves in transactions when they enroll or disenroll employees in a health plan or make premium payments to plans on behalf of their employees. The final regulation establishes the Employer Identification Number (EIN) issued by the Internal Revenue Service as the HIPAA standard.

Healthcare Provider Identifier

The National Provider Identifier (NPI) rule provides a unique provider identifier for each provider. It is a 10- position numeric identifier with a check digit in the last position to help detect keying errors.

Patient and Health Plan Identifiers Not Issued

Due to the public concern over privacy, a patient identifier standard has not yet been adopted. Because of the central importance of health plans in the provision and administration of healthcare services, HIPAA requires the development of a Health Plan Identifier. CMS has not proposed such an identifier, and it is not certain when one will be issued.

Photo Credits

Researchers, Inc.; **page 159:** Courtesy of Fred Williams, U.S. Environmental Protection Agency; **page 163:** © Phanie/Photo Researchers, Inc.; **page 164:** © image100/PunchStock; **page 167:** © Gregory G. Dimijian/Photo Researchers, Inc.; **page 169:** © Francoise Sauze/Photo Researchers, Inc.; **page 170:** © Dynamic Graphics/JupiterImages.

I

Page 174: Royalty-Free/CORBIS; **page 176:** © Photodisc Collection/Getty Images; **page 178:** © image100/PunchStock; **page 179:** © Keith Brofsky/Getty Images; **page 180:** Royalty-Free/CORBIS; **page 181:** © Jim Wehtje/Getty Images; **page 183:** © Dynamic Graphics/JupiterImages; **page 186:** Dynamic Graphics/JupiterImages.

L

Page 196: © Royalty-Free/CORBIS; **page 201:** © Photodisc Collection/Getty Images; **page 205:** © Ryan McVay/Getty Images.

M

Page 210: Royalty-Free/CORBIS; **page 211 (left)** © Lawrence Lawry/Getty Images; **(right)** Centers for Disease Control; **page 212:** © Royalty-Free/CORBIS; **page 213 (top)** © Keith Brofsky/Getty Images, **(bottom)** CDC/Donald Kopanoff; **page 214 (top)** © Kim Steele/Getty Images; **(bottom)** © Keith Brofsky/Getty Images; **page 217:** © Dynamic Graphics/JupiterImages; **page 218** © Keith Brofsky/Getty Images; **page 227:** © Corbis Images/JupiterImages; **page 228 (top)** © Corbis/PictureQuest; **(bottom)** Royalty-Free/CORBIS; **page 230:** © Skip Nall/Getty Images; **page 231:** Royalty-Free/CORBIS; **page 232:** © Mauro Fermariello / Photo Researchers, Inc.; **p. 233:** © Biophoto Associates/Photo Researchers, Inc.; **page 236:** © Keith Brofsky/Getty Images.

N

Page 240: © Getty Images; **page** © Royalty-Free/Corbis; **page 242:** © Royalty-Free/Corbis; **page 244:** © Dynamic Graphics/JupiterImages; **page 246 (left)** © The McGraw-Hill Companies, Inc./Jill Braaten, photographer; **(right)** © Royalty-Free/CORBIS; **page 247:** © Royalty-Free/CORBIS; **page 249:** Getty Images / Mark Thornton.

O

Page 252: © Royalty-Free/CORBIS; **page 254:** © Royalty-Free/CORBIS; **page 255:** Photodisc Collection/Getty Images; **page 256:** © Royalty-Free/CORBIS; **page 257:** © Michael Evans/Life File/Getty Images; **page 258 (top)** © Keith Brofsky/Getty Images; **(bottom)** © Royalty-Free/CORBIS; **page 259:** © Skip Nall/Getty Images; **page 261:** © PhotoDisc/Getty Images.

P

Page 267: © Keith Brofsky/Getty Images; **page 268:** © Digital Vision; **page 270:** © Dynamic Graphics/JupiterImages; **page 271:** © Keith Brofsky/Getty Images; **page 272:** © Corbis/PictureQuest; **page 274:** © Scott Bodell/Getty Images; **page 276:** © Mel Curtis/Getty Images; **page 277:** © Stockbyte/PunchStock; **page 278:** © Stockbyte/PunchStock; **page 279:** page 280: © Keith Brofsky/Getty Images; **page 281:** © Dr. P. Marazzi / Photo Researchers, Inc.; **page 283:** © Keith Brofsky/Getty Images; **page 285 (left)** © Dr. P. Marazzi / Photo Researchers, Inc; **(right)** © Dr. P. Marazzi / Photo Researchers, Inc; **page 289:** © CMCD/Getty Images; **page 290 (top)** Royalty-Free/CORBIS; **(bottom)** © Don Farrall/Getty Images; **page 295 (top)** © PhotoLink/Getty Images; **(bottom)** © Comstock/PunchStock; **page 297:** © Phanie/Photo Researchers, Inc; **page 298:** © David Buffington/Getty Images.

Q

Page 306 (left) © Rita Nannini/Photo Researchers, Inc.; **(right)** Dr. Najeeb Layyous/Photo Researchers, Inc.

R

Page 308: © Photodisc Collection/Getty Images; **page 309:** © McGraw-Hill, photo by JW Ramsey; **page 311:** © Dynamic Graphics/JupiterImages; **page 312:** © Pascal Goetgheluck/Photo Researchers, Inc.; **page 314:** © Joshua Ets-Hokin/Getty Images; **page 318:** © Dr. P. Marazzi Photo Researchers, Inc.

S

Page 323: © Keith Brofsky/Getty Images; **page 325:** © PhotoLink/Photodisc/Getty Images; **page 327:** © Corbis Images/JupiterImages; **page 328:** © Corbis Images/JupiterImages; **page 329:** © Brand X/Corbis Images; **page 330:** © Will & Deni McIntyre/Photo Researchers, Inc.; **page 331 (left)** © Eye of Science/Photo Researchers, Inc.; **(right)** © The McGraw-Hill Companies, Inc./John Flournoy, photographer; **page 333:** Royalty-Free/CORBIS; **page 334:** © PhotoLink/Getty Images; **page 336:** © Keith Brofsky/Getty Images; **page 338:** © PhotoLink/Getty Images; **page 339:** © Dr. M.A. Ansary/Photo Researchers, Inc.; **page 340:** © Digital Vision/PunchStock; **page 341:** © Dynamic Graphics/JupiterImages; **page 343:** Royalty-Free/CORBIS; **page 345:** © The McGraw-Hill Companies, Inc./Elite Images; **page 346:** © Jack Star/PhotoLink/Getty Images; **page 348:** © Stockbyte/PunchStock.

T

Page 351: © Nancy R. Cohen/Getty Images; **page 360:** © Keith Brofsky/Getty Images; **page 361:** Royalty-Free/CORBIS; **page 362:** © PhotoLink/Getty Images; **page 363:** © Ryan McVay/Getty Images; **page 365:**

© Digital Vision/Punchstock/Punchstock; **page 366:** Centers for Disease Control and Prevention.

U

Page 370: © Dopamine/Photo Researchers, Inc.; **page 371:** © Getty Images.

V

Page 378: © Dr. P. Marazzi/Photo Researchers, Inc.; **page 380:** © Royalty-Free/Corbis; **page 381:** © Royalty-Free/Corbis; **page 383:** © Skip Nall/Getty Images; **page 384:** © Geostock/Getty Images.

W

Page 388: © TRBfoto/Getty Images; **page 390:** © Dynamic Graphics/JupiterImages.

X

Page 392: © Stockbyte/PunchStock.

Y

Page 393: © Ryan McVay/Getty Images.

INSERT

Plate 5 (upper left) CDC; **(upper right)** CDC/Dr. Thomas F. Sellers/Emory University; **(lower left)** CDC/Sherry Brinkman; **(lower right)** CDC/Dr. Lucille K. Georg.

Plate 13 (left) © PhotoLink/Getty Images; **(right)** © Jack Star/PhotoLink/Getty Images.

Plate 44 (left) © Keith Brofsky/Getty Images; **(right)** Keith Brofsky/Getty Images.

Plate 45 (upper left) © Stockbyte/PunchStock; **(upper right)** © Stockbyte/PunchStock; **(middle left)** © Royalty-Free/CORBIS; **(middle right)** © Keith Brofsky/Getty Images; **(lower left)** © Don Farrall/Getty Images **(lower right);** © PhotoLink/Getty Images.

Plate 46 (upper left) © Stockbyte/PunchStock; **(upper right)** Royalty-Free/CORBIS; **(middle left)** © Stockbyte/PunchStock; **(middle right)** © Reed Kaestner/PhotoLink/Getty Images; **(lower left)** © Keith Brofsky/Getty Images, **(lower right)** Royalty-Free/CORBIS.

Plate 47 (top) Royalty-Free/CORBIS; **(middle)** Royalty-Free/CORBIS; **(bottom)** Royalty-Free/CORBIS.

Plate 48 (top left) © Jack Star/PhotoLink/Getty Images; **(top right)** © Duncan Smith/Getty Images; **(middle left)** © Royalty-Free/Corbis; **(middle right)** © Royalty-Free/Corbis; **(lower left)** © image100/PunchStock; **(lower right)** © Royalty-Free/Corbis.